CLEMENT WOOD'S
UNABRIDGED
RHYMING
DICTIONARY

CLEMENT WOOD'S UNABRIDGED RHYMING DICTIONARY

by CLEMENT WOOD

Former Resident Poet and Instructor in Versification, College of William and Mary, Richmond Division. Author of *Poets' Handbook* and *The Craft of Poetry*

Introduction by TED ROBINSON

SIMON AND SCHUSTER

FOREWORD

THE DESIRE to write poetry and acceptable verse is practically universal. The rules for accurate versification are far simpler than the rules and procedure for playing contract bridge or solving crossword puzzles. They are incredibly easier than mathematics or any science. It is far simpler to be a master in versification than to learn to be a qualified mechanic, lawyer, doctor, pharmacist, trained nurse, stenographer, or cook. The rules for writing verse are as simple as the rules for writing prose. Writing good verse is as easy as writing good prose.

All these rules are contained in the three explanatory sections of this volume: The Vocabulary of Poetry; The Complete Formbook for Poets; and Versification Self-Taught. They are stated clearly and amply illustrated. When these three sections are absorbed, the versifier can fairly regard himself as a master.

As for the main portion of the book, let me quote from its summary:

"The UNABRIDGED RHYMING DICTIONARY is the most complete and modern rhyming dictionary ever written.

"It is strictly phonetic, and thus satisfies the first half—the repetition half—of the definition of rhyme.

"For the first time it eliminates the danger of using identity instead of rhyme, by grouping the words in each rhyme sound under the appropriate consonantal opening.

"For the first time it includes all types of mosaic rhymes, based upon rhymes constructed of two or more words.

"For the first time it gives the correct pronunciation of every syllable of every rhyming word included—to that extent eliminating the necessity for an ordinary dictionary.

"It has simplified the rules for accurate rhyming to one simple rule: *Choose and use only one word from each group.* By following that, your rhyming will be flawless."

The volume is thus indispensable to poets, versifiers, writers of song lyrics, advertising verses, and all other forms of verse, to instructors and students of poetics, libraries, librarians, and all interested in perfecting this more concentrated half of our verbal expression. It can make the technique of verse and rhyming as automatic as the technique of walking; and thus, as I have written elsewhere, "the poetic energy will be proportionately released for the more effective creation of poetry."

Acknowledgments

Among those who have contributed immensely to the making of this compendium, and have thereby earned my resultant gratitude, are Etta Josephean Murfey, Marcia Jones, Stephen Schlitzer, Diana Douglas, Alfred Turner, Amy Wheeler Morgan, Aimee Jackson Short, and John Thorntcn Wood. For earnest and painstaking collaboration throughout each stage of the work, thanks beyond my power of expression are due to the Assistant Editor, Gloria Goddard.

Bozenkill,   CLEMENT WOOD.
Delanson, N. Y.

INTRODUCTION

To A large portion of the laity (by which I mean the non-writing public) and, alas! to no small percentage of writers themselves, there is something humorous in the idea of a Rhyming Dictionary. Those practitioners of the lyric art who are so weak as to allow themselves to consult such texts find themselves the objects of scornful amusement; and so they come to conceal their reliance upon a lexicon of rhymes as if it were a shameful addiction.

The attitude of the critic who is responsible for this queer state of affairs might be thus expressed: "Jones, poor fellow, would like to be thought of as a fluent and original poet, but I happen to know that he makes constant use of a rhyming dictionary. You would think that a man who writes as much as he does would be able to think up his own rhymes. And how insincere and artificial must any composition be when its character is dictated by the forced use of words that rhyme, and when even these must be looked up in a book."

It should not be necessary to point out that this is an extremely unintelligent attitude. It is exactly the same as the attitude of the nearly illiterate person who is amazed and not a little shocked to note the frequency with which a scholar consults Webster. "I thought he was educated," says our naïve friend, "but he has to keep looking up words in the dictionary all the time. I guess he ain't so smart as he pretends to be."

For those poets, professional or amateur, who have added the present volume to their libraries, it is hardly necessary to write an apology for its existence or an explanation of its functions. But since versifiers are apt to be reticent concerning their own technique, it may be that a few hints here may be suggestive to members of the general public whose curiosity may lead them to glance at these pages. The rules of English rhyme are exceedingly simple; and yet, because of the eccentricity of English spelling, the inconsistency of English pronunciation, the differences in local accentuation and vowel quality, and a general ignorance of the science of phonetics, the practice of rhyming is full of pitfalls. There are those who endeavor to ape the British diction; and these are constantly in trouble on account of uncertainty as to which words have the broad *a* and which the flat. Professor J. S. Kenyon lists 150 words which commonly have the broad *a* in England (as in "father") and the flat *a* in America (as in "fat.")* Angels have been known to weep bitterly and Britons to

*American Pronunciation, p. 274. (Sixth Edition, Ann Arbor, Mich. 1935.)

exclaim "O, I say!" over the pathetic struggles of certain American broadcasters with this single phenomenon. Such a broadcaster, if he were writing verse, would rhyme *advance* with *finance*, confident that the broad *a* was used in both. The native American bard would rhyme those same words, because in his speech both are pronounced with the flat *a*• But the Englishman pronounces *advance* broad, and *finance* flat, and so would not consider these words correctly rhymed. The poet writing for international consumption will govern himself accordingly.

It is hardly necessary to list the hundreds of instances in which uncertainty as to the position of the accent in a word, or as to the quality or quantity of its rhyming syllable, may be instantly brought to an end by consulting such a work as this. It is unnecessary also to note that the poet may often save himself much embarrassment by having such an authority at his elbow. But I shall allow myself one more illustration, taken from my own experience.

With the conventional apologies for personal allusions, I may state that I have conducted newspaper columns for thirty-five years, and that it has been my invariable custom to lead this column every morning with some original verse. And during those years, I have contributed a great deal of verse to other publications. A quick exercise in mental arithmetic will convince the reader that the quantity output has been rather large. A certain facility is the inevitable result of this daily habit of versemaking; and since a large proportion of it has been of a light or humorous character, it is not difficult to gather that I must have done a great deal of experimenting with rhymes and with various metrical forms.

Now the writer of light verse is quite likely to be attracted by the possibilities of the so-called French forms—the ballade, the rondeau, etc. A line pops into his head; he thinks, "That would be a good ballade refrain," and he makes note of it. At his next working period, he gets busy on a ballade. Very well: a ballade (as you may see by consulting the division of this volume entitled "The Complete Formbook for Poets") is a fixed form with certain definite restrictions. There are 28 lines in such a composition, but the poet is allowed but three rhymes. For the first of these rhymes, he must have six rhyming words; for the third, he needs only five, since the refrain line is three times repeated. But for his middle rhyme, which binds the rest together, he must have fourteen rhyming words. And these dare not be *rimes parfaits* or identical rhymes (such as *wear* and *beware*) but must be fourteen different rhyming syllables, and none must be repeated. Is it not obvious that the poet would be foolish to set gaily forth upon the building of a ballade without considering the possibility of running out of rhymes before he was through?

The constructor of ballades knows all about this, and he usually sets down all the rhymes he can think of for his second line, before he begins writing. If there are not enough, he must discard his second line and think of another. This is the ordinary procedure. But the journeyman rhymester can save much time, and discover some words he must otherwise have missed, by consulting his Rhyming Dictionary. He may find that he has a wider choice than he thought, and that he is not so strictly bound by the list of words he must use; he may (and this is a frequent experience) discover a word that suggests a new and surprising turn or twist in his verses, and adds immensely to its humor or its aptness.

But this, says the non-professional critic, is artificial. Poetry is free, inspired, uplifted, unshackled. How can it be so, if it is carpentered by such mechanical means, drawing on the dry bones of rhyming dictionaries, and restricted in its sense by the fact that jingling words must be sought out? All these rules for versification, all this fussiness about some rhymes being correct and some wrong, all this dusty lore of anapaest, cesura, acatalectics, amphibrachs and sestinas—surely, these are chains and handicaps, shackling the Muse, and rendering poetry mechanical and unnatural!

All art, answers the practitioner, has its mechanics and its rules. Observe the finished actor on the stage. "He is not acting," declares the enthusiastic auditor, "he is just being natural!" That effect of "just being natural" is attained by constant rehearsal and re-rehearsal; by subjecting every move of the hand, every expression of the face, every tone of the voice, to the strict discipline imposed by technical rule and long experience. The amateur, going on the stage unrehearsed, "acts natural"—and the effect is of something highly mechanical and artificial. The painter, the musician, must learn the rules of their art so well and practice them so faithfully and long, that these rules become a part of their unconscious equipment, and they can forget them as they work. And only so can their inspiration have a fit instrument to work with. It takes a schoolboy a long time to discover the simple fact that, far from being a clog or a burden, a rule is a labor-saving device.

Many years ago, when I was a very young man, somebody presented me with Walker's Rhyming Dictionary. I used it, for it was the only one I had ever seen; but I found before long that it was inadequate for my need. It was a dictionary of terminations—but like terminations do not always rhyme. And Walker paid no attention to anything but spelling in his classification. I should never have known from his book that *beau* rhymed with *toe,* or either of them with *blow.* And I should have supposed that *blow* rhymed with *brow.* After that, I got Brewer; he was some improvement, but his words were few. Next came Barnum,

whose excellent volume was for many years the only rhyming dictionary that even approached adequacy. I shall not tell the names of later ones; I found them all faulty, and in one, which I have had on my desk for several years, I have marked more than 200 errors!

It appears to me that the compiler of the present volume has taken a step in advance of all his predecessors: that the latest item in the evolution of the Rhyming Dictionary is also the best. By devoting attention to the details of phonetic representation, he has for the first time guaranteed the user of the manual against errors arising from a misapprehension of the pronunciation of any given word. By dividing his rhymes into groups of identical syllables, so that one may be selected from each group, he keeps the student from blundering into *rimes parfaits*, so desirable in French poetry, and so reprehensible in English. And by adhering strictly to the phonetic values of the syllables and disregarding their spelling, he at once banishes the "eye-rhyme" from the picture and obviates a search under various sections to complete the list of available words.

There are other advantages which I see at my first examination of this book, and I doubt not that still more will appear as I become familiar with it by use. I do not proclaim it the Perfect Rhyming Dictionary—for perfection is an unattainable ideal, and I already see how I should set about to revise it. I should boldly discard all the diacritical marks that are necessary as long as we retain our traditional alphabet and spelling, and should adopt for the entire work the American adaptation of the International Phonetic Alphabet. But it is probable that by so doing I should frighten off many young and impatient poets, and so defeat my own purpose. And as long as the time is not yet ripe for such a revolutionary procedure, we may be thankful for such an accurate and scientific manual as this one of Mr. Clement Wood's.

As for that part of the volume which is a Formbook for Poets, I consider it admirable both as a work of scholarship and of common sense. It reconciles the procedure of English poets with the technical vocabulary of classic orthometry, and its practical advice is such as could come only from an experienced craftsman. For a number of years I have recommended to ambitious students a study of this author's "The Craft of Poetry." Since last November, I have been substituting his newer "Poet's Handbook." These two will remain standards in their field; but now I shall have a more comprehensive text to recommend. The addition of the technical rules to the new Rhyming Dictionary gives us a "Gradus ad Parnassum" which approaches the integration we have sought so long in vain.

TED ROBINSON.

Cleveland.

CONTENTS

THE VOCABULARY OF POETRY

THE VOCABULARY OF POETRY

Use a Living Vocabulary

The words, word order and idioms used by the poet and versifier should be precisely those that he uses in his living speech. Prose of all kinds uses these; or else it is stilted, affected, and repelling, instead of persuasive and convincing. Both prose and poetry have something to convey, to communicate; and, of the two, poetry is aimed more directly at the emotions. There has never been a time when the emotions were more moved by dead words, mutilated words, or words out of their natural order, than by live words, whole words, and words in their inevitable and logical order. Many versifiers use dead, mutilated and misplaced words, in imitation of the poetry of the past: overlooking the fact that the great poetry of any age always uses the living speech of that age, and only the second-raters imitatively enshrine the fossilized speech of interred poets.

In looking at accepted ancient poetry, words that are *different* from the living vocabulary stick out most prominently, like a pimple on a glamor girl's nose; the only fault is to regard the source of the glamor as the pimple, and not the living personality behind it. The fault has been partly that of the imitative poets, but quite as much that of their teachers. For these, seeking the secret of poetry, have come to the false conclusion that it lies in the archaic differentness; they have taught a dead and imitative style; and poetry is still paying the heavy price of public disinterest, distrust and disgust, because of its spurious vocabulary. The great poets of today, as of every age, rise above this public detestation, precisely because they use the living vocabulary.

Three and a half centuries ago, a major poet wrote these lines:

Macbeth.   Wherefore was that cry?

Seyton. The queen, my lord, is dead.

Macbeth.   She should have died hereafter;
There would have been a time for such a word,—
Tomorrow, and tomorrow, and tomorrow,
Creeps in this petty pace from day to day,
To the last syllable of recorded time;
And all our yesterdays have lighted fools
The way to dusty death. Out, out, brief candle!
Life's but a walking shadow; a poor player,

3

> That struts and frets his hour upon the stage,
> And then is heard no more; it is a tale
> Told by an idiot, full of sound and fury,
> Signifying nothing.

Let your vocabulary usage be as fresh and living as this still is, after three and a half centuries. For this is the lesson that all great poetry teaches.

Avoid Archaisms and Obsolescent Expressions

There is only one time when archaisms and obsolescent expressions are proper in your poetry. This is when you write of a previous age, and have the characters speak that language, as a sort of dialect. In that case, as in all uses of dialect, the important warning is, do not overdo the dialect, if you want to be understood. It is better to hint it, than to drown in it. And never forget that you, the author, who tell the story, are not of that antiquated period; hence do not have your own explanatory and connective remarks in the dialect.

Among the particular word groups to be avoided are:

1. All archaic and non-living pronouns.

This includes *thee, thou, thy, thine, ye,* etc. These are often used in the so-called "solemn style" in invoking the deity, a country, city, some abstractified personification, such as truth, peace, beauty, etc. If you wish to imply that the deity or the abstraction is dead, use this dead language; otherwise, avoid it entirely.

2. All non-living verb forms.

These naturally go with the dead pronouns, and include *didst, hast, hath, dost, art, wast, wert, wilt, wouldst, shalt,* and the whole tribe of *-est, -eth* verb forms, *adorest, adoreth,* etc. (including their contractions into *ador'st, ador'th,* etc.). Like all other archaic forms, these are asterisked in this rhyming dictionary, as a warning: Don't touch.

3. All non-living verbals beginning with *be-* or *a-*.

The sole test is, is the word at home in good living prose? Thus, for all that they have an old-fashioned sound, *bedecked, befell, beribboned,* might pass, as being suitable to second-rate prose; but not *bedight, bedimmed, bedewed, bespangled, bereft, beshrew, besprent, bethink, betide*—much less the following, approved by a modern unabridged dictionary: *beclasp, beshadow, berascal, bepretty, befop, betailor, beglue, bemercy, begabled.* Even if used in high ridicule, they are too bookish. The simpler forms, *clasp, clasped, shadow, shadowed,* are the proper ones to use. As for such forms as *a hunting* (also appearing as *a-hunting* or *ahunting*), and the thousands of similar forms, the dictionary says that

these are proper in "poetic, colloquial and dialectal use," but not in "standard literary speech." Since poetry has no other language than "standard literary speech," these forms must go, except where proper in prose.

4. All rhythm- or rhyme-induced emphatic verb phrases.

Where emphatic phrases are proper in prose, "*Do* hurry up!" "He *did* turn; I saw him," they are of course proper in poetry. But not when inserted as padding to fill out a rhythmic pattern, or to permit a rhyme: "When winking merry-buds do bloom," "when stars do shine," etc.

5. All rhythm- or rhyme-induced contractions.

All contractions acceptable in living conversation (it's, he's, who'd, we've, etc.) are of course proper, if of sufficient dignity for your poem or verse. But those consisting of words mutilated to fit the meter, or of an archaic pattern no longer admitted into living prose, must be rigorously excluded, including: 'tis (use *it's*), 'twas, 'gainst, 'neath, 'fore, 'tween, e'er, ne'er, e'en, 'gan, 'gins, 's we (for *thus we*), ta'en (for *taken*). This includes also such forms as *morn* for *morning*, *oft* for *often*, *yon* for *yonder*, *ope* for *open*, etc. An excess syllabification of a terminal *-ed* (weari-ed) is as bad.

6. All archaic words.

Including the following: *wroth, ruth, reft, bethinks, athwart, welkin, rathe, sooth, fardel, burthen, murther, con, burgeon,* etc. This also includes such poeticized words as *rue* (not, of course, the flower).

As far as possible, these words have been asterisked in this rhyming dictionary, as a reminder that they should be avoided.

Avoid Inversions

An inversion, in grammar, is any word out of its natural grammatical order in a sentence. "Came the dawn" is a typical example; horrendous in prose or verse. Wherever an inversion is acceptable in prose, it is acceptable in verse and poetry. Three powerful forces yank words out of their natural order, in poetry and verse:

1. To fit a rhyme pattern.

And, just across the way,
I saw a maiden gay. (For, "gay maiden.")

I turned on swift and frightened feet,
So that I might the villain greet. (For, "greet the villain.")

Then, straight through the limb,
Boldly struck he him. (For, "he struck him.")

2. To fit a metric pattern.

In Thomas Gray's *Elegy Written in a Country Churchyard*, such a line as:

Where heaves the turf in many a moldering heap

contains its inversion, to alter the natural rhythm of "where the turf heaves," to fit the preconceived iambic pattern. A more extreme example, from the same poem, is:

Now fades the glimmering landscape on the sight.

In its right order, this could be:

Now the glimmering landscape fades (from view),

and the "fades" was warped out of position to achieve the iambic pattern; while "on the sight" was substituted for "from view," to fit the rhyme scheme: that is, it is rhyme-induced. This particular poem, incidentally, is a classic museum of unnatural poeticized atrocities. Its persistence in some popularity is a tribute to the universality of its theme, and the evocative emotional words used.

3. Through the false idea that it is "poetical."

This applies to inversions dictated by neither rhyme nor meter. It is deplorable, but true, that some versifiers still think that this alters straightforward English from prose into poetry. No matter the motive, inversions are major blemishes in poetry and verse.

Avoid Ellipses and Word-Substitutions

A subtler and equally common fault is to omit needed words, in order to regularize your metric pattern; and, worst of all, to substitute a different, less appropriate, and often misleading word for the real one you mean, to fit either the rhyming or metric pattern. Articles are frequently omitted, where the meaning calls for them:

For them no more the blazing hearth shall burn,
Or (the) busy housewife ply her evening care.

This is from the same poem. Often analysis reveals that the product, including the ellipsis, does not make sense:

The applause of listening senates to command. . . .
Their lot forbade.

Not until we supply the omitted "them" (Their lot forbade *them* to command, etc.) does this emerge into intelligibility. Similarly, the adverbial ending *-ly* is constantly dropped for the sake of meter or rhyme, leaving an adjective ungrammatically used instead of an adverb:

> How jocund(ly) did they drive their team afield!

Again, an improper form of the verb is stuck in, to fit the pattern—as when Gray, in the same poem, arrives at "many a text . . . that *teach* the rustic moralist to die," instead of the proper singular form, "teaches."

Even commoner is exiling the perfect word, in favor of some inappropriate or inaccurate usurper, whose sole merit is that it fits the pattern. Thus, having used the terminal word *Muse*, Gray says that she *strews* many a holy text. But he makes clear twice that this *strewing* consists in engraving the texts on tombstones. You strew seeds in a field, or flowers before the feet of the loved one; but, while texts might conceivably be strewn around, the process of strewing would never consist of engraving on a stone. Thus *strews* is not only rhyme-induced by *Muse*, but is in every way inaccurate. This example could be multiplied by hundreds of thousands, when rhyme is involved; and by an equal number of cases, where meter is involved. Prose at its best uses the right, the perfect word, in each instance; no artificial convention is worth while, which forces poetry to use any other word than the perfect word.

Avoid Hackneyed Phrases, Clichés, Echoes

A fault not induced by the demands of the pattern is the use of clichés or hackneyed phrases, and echoes. When you fill your poetry with such overworked phrases as:

> red as a rose, white as snow, black as night, the boundless blue, the bounding main, the dewy earth, the purling brook, the golden sun, the sun-kist earth, the whispering breeze, teeth like pearls, eyes like stars or violets or woodland pools, cheeks like roses or sun-encarmined peaches, a throat like a swan, a voice like a lark or a nightingale,

and so on and on interminably, you are merely echoing the words of others, and not saying your own words. It is possible to make any of these your own, by altering or polishing it:

> red as a rambler rose, white as Himalayan snows, black as a starless midnight, the red-gold sun, the slily whispering breeze,

and all the rest.

The same thing applies to using stock saws and axioms, "a rolling stone gathers no moss," "a bird in the hand is worth two in the bush," "A miss is as good as a mile"—unless by some process of re-creation and altering you make these your own.

Direct echoes of the prose or poetry of others, "the forest primeval," "its pure serene," "the murmuring pines," "make our lives sublime"—

it is obvious that, since your poetry must be original, these must be eliminated. Unless you use them as a text to start with and alter with your own comment.

Avoid Plagiarism

Plagiarism, or adopting the words, idioms and phrases of other poets, clear up to appropriating their stanzas and complete poems, is literary theft, and of course to be avoided. The use of another's words as a text, to embroider, apply, or contradict, is of course entirely permissible.

Avoid Classical Tags and Allusions

Nothing so advertises the mediocrity of poetry and verse as a frequent use of the mythological and pastoral machinery of classical poetry. Reference to the sun as Sol, the moon as Diana, the more intimate Dian, or Luna, the dawn as Aurora, as well as talk of the Muse or the Muses, the Graces, or any of the Greek or Roman gods, demigods, or heroes, is wholly inappropriate; unless with specific reference to those ancient cultures, and even in this case always preferably requiring some fresh slant of your own. Few things are as ineffectual as likening Hitler to Mars, or an airplane to the wings of Daedalus or Icarus. Of course, a modern, scientific or psychoanalytic treatment of the old myths is a proper fresh slant on them.

Avoid Bookishness

The best prose uses the living vocabulary, taken from life, not a bookish speech distilled from books. As Walt Whitman says,

Rhymes and rhymers pass away, poems distill'd from poems pass
    away,
The swarms of reflectors and the polite pass, and leave ashes,
Admirers, importers, obedient persons, make but the soil of
    literature . . .

What is this you bring my America? . . .
Is it not something that has been better told or done before? . . .
Is it not a mere tale? a rhyme? a prettiness? . . .
Has it not dangled long at the heels of poets? . . .
Can your performance face the open fields and the seaside? . . .
Does it meet modern discoveries, calibres, facts, face to face?

Harsh talk, but true talk. "Can your performance face the open fields and the seaside?" Is it akin to reality, not a mere distillation of books? The choice is your own. But a distillate from books is doubly removed from the life whose essence books seek to catch. Let your vocabulary, at least, derive from life, and not from mechanical transcriptions of it.

A Horrible Example

The following verses, *The Tanager* (I borrow the title from the original poem they mimic) illustrate most of the faults we have discussed. The outstanding ones are italicized:

> *Ne'er* did I see a ray of light
> So strangely, *lovely*, warmly bright—
> A stream of red *as* flashing by
> *'Gainst fair Aurora's azure* sky.
> A scarlet tanager *so gay*
> Is carolling () sweet roundelay.
> His throat *a-bursting* with a song,
> As *fast* he flits and flies along;
> A *mem'ry* of gay brilliant thing*s*,
> A poppy bloom that *blows* on wings.

To indicate these faults: *Ne'er*, poetical contraction, unnatural in prose. *Lovely:* adjective used in place of an adverb, meter-induced; the proper adverb is *lovelily*. Also, too many *-ly* sounds together. *As*, padding, meter-induced. *'Gainst*, poetical contraction. *Fair*, cliché. *Aurora*, classical tag. *Azure*, bookish and cliché. *So*, padding, meter-induced. *Gay*, inversion, rhyme-induced. (), ellipsis of the needed *a*, or *his*. *A-bursting*, improper poeticized form. *Fast*, inversion, meter-induced. *Mem'ry*, improper contraction. Terminal *-s's*, too sibilant a sound, since they are unnecessary. *Blows*, bookish and poeticized; winds blow, flowers bloom.

But the poet, Amy Wheeler Morgan, did not commit any of these faults, when she wrote the lovely lyric *The Tanager*. I plead for forgiveness for committing them, and give the poem as she wrote it:

> I never saw a ray of light
> So strangely, passionately bright,—
> A streak of scarlet flashing by
> Against the bright blue summer sky.
> Whistling his merry roundelay,
> He makes the very landscape gay;
> And, as he darts and flits along,
> His throat seems bursting with his song,—
> A rondo in his carolling,
> A scarlet poppy on the wing!

Here every word, every word-usage, every idiom, is as natural as the best prose. Since it is far more helpful to remember the right way than the wrong, proceed to forget our Horrible Example, and memorize this notable lyric.

Use Emotion-Rousing Words

Poetry appeals more definitely to the emotions than prose. It is therefore all the more necessary to select words which are in their natures emotion-rousing. Short sharp native Anglo-Saxon words are almost invariably more effective than ponderous polysyllables derived from Latin or Greek. Precise specific words are as a rule far stronger than general, more abstract words. Thus *peony* is more effective than *flower;* but either is better than *Paeonia officinalis.* Windy talk about such abstractions as truth, beauty, justice, in prose or poetry, tends to be diluted, compared with the use of more specific words and instances. It is always valuable to use words with strong emotional overtones, of the type of:

home, mother, God, Heaven, love, moon, sun, earth, flag, England, father, France, hate, hell, wrong, enemy, death, traitor, war.

Use Figurative and Allusive Words

The highest power of the mind is the power of generalization—that is, finding the likenesses between objects, ideas, etc., no matter how remote. The figures of speech in the language are chiefly means of expressing such likenesses and unlikenesses. Allusive words and phrases—references to something, familiar to your reader, which evokes overtones far beyond the mere words you use—are also valuable. Consider all involved in such phrases as:

Cleopatra's asp, Napoleon's sword, the Pompadour's fan,
the Unknown Soldier, David's sling.

It is so that concentrated meaning can be expressed by an allusion.

Use Musical and Singable Words

Where there is any choice, let the very sounds of the words you use fit the mood you wish to arouse. For a song lyric, the words should be as singable as possible. A discussion of the important sounds, with regard to adaptability for songs, appears in the treatment of Writing Song Lyrics, in the concluding section of this book, Versification Self-Taught. To the extreme contrary, when you wish your words to convey something harsh or discordant, use appropriate word-sounds.

Summary

The vocabulary—word-choice, word-order and word-idiom—used by the poet or versifier should be the same as that used in the best living speech. In proportion as this idea is fully applied in your work, will be your individual excellence and acceptance as a poet. In proportion as it is fully applied by poets collectively, will be the re-emergence of poetry as a form of literary expression at least as important as prose.

THE COMPLETE FORMBOOK FOR POETS

PRELIMINARY DEFINITIONS

General

Poetry: verse which produces a deep emotional response.

Verse: words arranged according to some conventionalized repetition. In our Occidental culture, verse is words arranged with repetition in their accent rhythm, which tends toward uniformity or regularity, rather than toward variety.

Prose: words whose rhythm tends toward variety, rather than toward uniformity or regularity.

The Kinds of Poetry

Poems are classified, primarily according to the literary mechanism used in the poem, into lyric poetry, descriptive poetry, narrative poetry, dramatic poetry, didactic poetry, light verse, etc.

Lyric poetry: poetry in which the poet expresses the desire embodied in the poem directly. Lyric is also used loosely to describe any words set to music.

Song: a brief lyric, especially suitable to be set to music. Song has been broadened to include any words set to music.

> EXAMPLES: Ben Jonson's *To Celia* ("Drink to me only with thine eyes"); Clinton Scollard's *Sylvia;* popular songs.

Simple lyric: a brief lyric poem.

> EXAMPLES: Robert Browning's *Home Thoughts from Abroad;* Rose O'Neill's *Apollo Senex.*

Elegy: a formal expression of the poet's grief at death, whether of an individual, or in general.

> EXAMPLES: Thomas Gray's *Elegy Written in a Country Churchyard;* Alfred Tennyson's *In Memoriam;* Walt Whitman's *When Lilacs Last in the Dooryard Bloomed.*

Pastoral: a poem, primarily lyric, dealing with the lives of shepherds; in which the characters are pictured as idealized shepherds; or, by extension, dealing with outdoor and country life.

> EXAMPLE: John Milton's *Lycidas* (a pastoral elegy).

Ode: the longest and most dignified form of lyric verse.

EXAMPLES: Classic Pindaric ode: Thomas Gray's *The Bard.* The Horatian ode (in uniform stanzas): Percy Bysshe Shelley's *Ode to the West Wind.* Irregular ode: William Wordsworth's *Ode on the Intimations of Immortality from Recollections of Early Childhood.*

Chant: a poem to be chanted, rather than read or sung.

EXAMPLES: G. K. Chesterton's *Lepanto;* Vachel Lindsay's *The Congo, Simon Legree, etc.*

Descriptive poetry: poetry in which the poet expresses his desire by describing something, embodying his wish in picturing things as he would have them, or from which he would have them changed.

EXAMPLES: John Greenleaf Whittier's *Snowbound;* Robert Frost's *The Cow in Apple Time.*

Descriptive poetry is often loosely included under the lyric.

Narrative poetry: poetry telling a story of incidents and events, which involve, directly or indirectly, the poet's desire.

Ballad: a short narrative poem, usually using the versification devices found in the old popular ballads. (The term *ballad* is also loosely applied to any words to be sung.)

EXAMPLES: the ballads dealing with Robin Hood; Thomas Babington Macaulay's *Lays of Ancient Rome.* Longer ballads include Samuel Taylor Coleridge's *Rime of the Ancient Mariner.*

Metrical romance: a longer narrative poem, centered around some quest, usually dealing with war, love, or religion, or a combination of these.

EXAMPLES: Alfred Tennyson's *Idylls of the King.*

Story in verse: a brief short story or tale in verse.

EXAMPLES: John Keats's *The Eve of St. Agnes;* Henry Wadsworth Longfellow's *Paul Revere's Ride.*

Novel in verse: a book-length story in verse.

EXAMPLES: Sir Walter Scott's *Marmion;* Stephen Vincent Benet's *John Brown's Body.*

Epic: a long narrative poem, dealing with heroic events, usually with supernatural guidance and participation in the action. The earliest epics are anonymous, or are attributed to authors probably mythical or semi-mythical.

EXAMPLES: Homer's *Iliad* and *Odyssey;* John Milton's *Paradise Lost*.

Dramatic poetry: poetry in which a character or characters tell the story, by word and action. The poet's comments are restricted to stage directions.

Dramas in verse: dramatic poetry ranging from brief one-act verse dramas to full length plays, or trilogies or other groups of plays.

EXAMPLES: William Shakespeare's comedies, tragedies, and chronicle historical plays.

Short dramatic verse: short poems, in which the characters do all the talking.

EXAMPLES: the anonymous ballad *Edward, Edward;* George Macdonald's *Baby* ("Where did you come from, baby dear?").

Dramatic monolog, dramatic lyric: dramatic verse in which one character does all the speaking.

EXAMPLES: Robert Browning's *My Last Duchess, Caliban Upon Setebos,* etc.; Edgar Lee Masters' *Spoon River Anthology*.

Didactic poetry: poetry with its main emphasis upon the lesson taught. Many poems commonly classed as lyric, descriptive, narrative and dramatic properly come under this head.

EXAMPLES: Longfellow's *A Psalm of Life;* Edward Fitzgerald's *Rubaiyat of Omar Khayyam*.

Occasional verse: verse to signalize some especial occasion, as, a coronation, a victory, a birth, a wedding, a death, etc. It may be serious or light.

Light verse: verse written primarily to amuse.

Vers de société: smart sophisticated verse, "which glides smoothly between the Scylla of seriousness and the Charybdis of boisterous merriment. It never oversteps the bounds of etiquette, and welcomes sentiment, while exiling passion."

EXAMPLES: John Suckling's *Song* ("Why so pale and wan, fond lover?"); George Wither's *The Lover's Resolution;* Alexander Pope's *The Rape of the Lock*.

Satirical verse: verse ridiculing any customs, manners and beliefs of which the poet disapproves.

EXAMPLES: the famous satires by Juvenal and Horace; Pope's *The Dunciad*.

Humorous verse: humor expressed in verse.

EXAMPLES: Robert Burns's *Tam o' Shanter;* Ernest Lawrence Thayer's *Casey at the Bat.*

Witty verse: wit expressed in verse.

EXAMPLES: most Little Willies and limericks; Arthur Guiterman's *A Pure Mathematician.*

Punning verse: witty verse marked by puns.

EXAMPLE: Thomas Hood's *Faithless Nellie Gray.*

Newspaper chain verse: verse in which successive newspapers or wits each add, to some original stanza pattern, another stanza, in the same general mood.

> EXAMPLE: When many fiction writers try
> Their thoughts to give us hot,
> We get e-rot-ic novels, with
> The accent on the rot.
>> *Lippincott's Magazine.*

> When some hair-dressers seek to give
> Us hair to fit the hat,
> We get er-rat-ic coiffures, with
> The accent on the rat.
>> *Boston Traveler.*

> If I were a copy-reader, forced
> To suffer such attacks,
> Some poet would get the ax-sent, with
> The accent on the ax.
>> *Lippincott's Magazine.*

Nonsense verse: verse substituting nonsense for common sense.

EXAMPLES: Lewis Carroll's *Jabberwocky* (" 'Twas brillig, and the slithy toves"), from *Through the Looking-Glass;* Edward Lear's *The Pobble Who Has No Toes.*

Dialect verse: verse written in any dialect.

EXAMPLES: James Russell Lowell's *Bigelow Papers;* Clement Wood's *The Glory Road;* Will Christman's *Ballads of Jeremiah Saddlemire.*

Parody: in verse, an imitation of another example of verse, usually with intent to burlesque it.

Mosaic verse, composite verse: verse in which each line, group of

lines, or parts of a line, is selected from one or more poets or poems, and rearranged into a new pattern, serious or amusing.

Macaronic verse: verse in which two or more languages are intermingled.

Archaic verse: verse written in or parodying the speech of some earlier period.

> EXAMPLE: the limerick commencing, "When that Seinte George hadde sleyne ye draggon."

Shaped whimsies: verse whose typographical set-up represents the theme, or imitates any object. Here is an excellent example:

THE UMBRELLA MAN

One

day in May when Chamberlain

went out for exercise, he blithely strolled

down Oxford Street, beneath sun-brightened skies. But

suddenly he felt a qualm—what was it he forgot? Could he

have failed to tell the king about the Irish plot; or could he

have some conference set for this very hour; and did he warn the

royal guards to double guard the Tower? Now while he pondered

many things, a cloud shut out the sun, but Chamberlain kept wondering

what he had or hadn't done; until a downpour dashed all thoughts of

state and protocol. "By Jove! I recollect," he cried, "I left my parasol!"

"Ah"   "Ah"   "Ah"   "Ah"   "Ah"

!   !   !   !   !

"

C

h

e

w

!   !"

Ah   ew

!

Ch—

                                         Aimee Jackson Short.

Typographical oddities in verse: any unusual typography for your verse. Thus the terminal lines of your stanzas might represent, typographically, the way a person walks when sober, and when intoxicated; or when he falls down; or anything else that ingenuity can make the type represent. This famous anonymous limerick illustrates one method:

> There was a young lady of Diss,
> Who said, "Now I think skating bliss!"
>   This no more will she state,
>   For a wheel off her skate
> ¡sᴉɥʇ ǝʞᴉl ƃuᴉɥʇǝɯos dn ɥsᴉuɟ ɹǝɥ ǝpɐW

Another method would be printing the letters backward, so that they could only be read through a mirror, as Lewis Carroll did with *Jabberwocky*. Franklin P. Adams utilized in various verses all the variously named fonts of type; and even the signs on the railroad column, as in *Signal Service:*

> Time-table! Terrible and hard
>   To figure! At some station lonely
> We see this sign upon the card:
> *
>
> We read thee wrong; the untrained eye
>   Does not see always with precision.
> The train we thought to travel by
> †
>
> Again, undaunted, we look at
>   The hieroglyphs, and as a rule a
> Small double dagger shows us that
> ‡
>
> And when we take a certain line
>   On Tues., Wednes., Thurs., Fri., Sat., or Monday,
> We're certain to detect the sign:
> §

---

* Train 20: Stops on signal only.
† Runs only on North-west division.
‡ Train does not stop at Ashtabula.
§ $10 extra fare ex. Sunday.

And this is only half of what F. P. A. has to say, in this fascinating typographical oddity.

Acrostic verse: verse where some specified group of letters, as, the opening letters of each line; or the closing ones; or the first letter of the

first line, the second of the second, the third of the third, etc., or letters arranged by any preconceived plan—name a person, or convey a message. Many of the verses of Edgar A. Poe and his contemporaries contain this sort of cipher device. Believers in the Baconian theory use this as one of their major methods of establishing their thesis, that Francis Bacon wrote the plays commonly attributed to William Shakespeare. Acrostics are single, double, triple, etc., depending on how many groups of letters form the concealed messages. Here is an example of a double acrostic:

> *S*oftly let two words be hi*D*—
> *H*idden very deftly wher*E*
> *E*ach may search, yet stay at se*A*:
> *S*he is worth it all, I swea*R*!

In actual typography, the key letters would not be emphasized in any way.

Echo verse: verse with short lines echoing, often with a change of meaning, the sounds of the previous line's ending:

> What shall I do, when I behold her?
> —Hold her!
> She'd think that I'd make her a prey then.
> Pray, then.
> Yet she'll grow timid, and prate of honor.
> On her!
> I might grow bold. Do you think I should do so?
> Do so!

Rhythm Repetition

Rhythm: movement marked by recurrence of, or alternation in, features, elements, or phenomena used as a means of perceiving the rhythm. In our culture, rhythm, in verse or prose, means the movement of words marked by the recurrence of, or alternation in, accented and unaccented syllables and pauses.

Scansion, of verse or prose, is its division into its rhythmical units, called feet; with appropriate marks to distinguish accented from unaccented syllables, long from short syllables etc. Scansion is divided into natural scansion and pattern scansion.

Natural scansion: scansion based upon the normal division of words into foot-groups, such as is used in good conversation.

Pattern scansion: scansion dictated by a preconceived accent or metrical pattern.

In metric verse and poetry, the effect of naturalness is in proportion

to the difference between the natural and the pattern scansion of your lines.

Types of poetry, according to rhythm: There are three types of verse and poetry in English, from the standpoint of rhythm: free verse, accent verse, and metric verse.

Free verse: verse with no rhythmic requirement beyond the tendency toward regularity or uniformity in rhythm, as opposed to the tendency toward variety found in prose. It can be described negatively: words whose rhythm is more regular than prose, but lacking either an accent verse or a metric pattern. Examples:

Not a grave of the murder'd for freedom, but grows seed for
    freedom, in its turn to bear seed,
Which the winds carry afar and re-sow, and the rains and the
    snows nourish.
Not a disembodied spirit can the weapons of tyrants let loose,
But it stalks invisibly over the earth, whispering, counselling,
    cautioning.
    Europe: the 72nd and 73rd Years of These States, Walt Whitman.

Youth is the happy hour
When we are still young enough
To choose our own mistakes.
            Youth, Clement Wood.

Accent verse: verse whose rhythmic requirement is a definite number of accented syllables to the line, with the unaccented syllables ranging from none to as many as the poet desires, placed wherever he wishes. An example of 4-accent verse is:

Spring! Spring! Spring! Spring!
With the surge of sap and the fluttering of wing,
With buds mad to be blossoming
In honor of the Spring, the magnificent Spring!

Because of its greater naturalness, this is returning into increasing favor, especially in song lyrics.

Metric verse: in English, verse based upon accent meter.

Meter: that attribute of verse by which its rhythm consists of a repeated formalized arrangement of specific rhythmical feet; regular rhythm in poetry.

Metric feet in English (the commonest five are marked with asterisks):

Name of foot	Scansion	Accent pronunciation	Examples	Example scanned
		I. Two-syllabled Feet		
*Iamb	˘ ´	ta-TUM	delight, to go	de-líght
*Trochee	´ ˘	TUM-ta	going, bread and	gó-ing
Pyrrhic	˘ ˘	ta-ta	in a, and the	in a
Spondee	´ ´	TUM-TUM	dogwatch, huge sun	dóg-wátch
		II. Three-Syllabled Feet		
*Anapest	˘ ˘ ´	ta-ta-TUM	interfere, in a boat	in-ter-fére
*Amphibrach	˘ ´ ˘	ta-TUM-ta	dividing, at ending	di-víd-ing
*Dactyl	´ ˘ ˘	TUM-ta-ta	battlement, end of the	bát-tle-ment
Amphimacer	´ ˘ ´	TUM-ta-TUM	anti-war; end the man	án-ti-wár
Tribrach	˘ ˘ ˘	ta-ta-ta	and in the	and in the
Molossus	´ ´ ´	TUM-TUM-TUM	great white chief	gréat whíte chíef
Bacchius	˘ ´ ´	ta-TUM-TUM	a huge bear, adore food	a húge béar
Anti-bacchius	´ ´ ˘	TUM-TUM-ta	base-stealing	báse-stéal-ing

Metric lines or verses: described by naming number of feet and the type of foot. Thus, iambic monometer, or one-foot iambic, etc.

Common name	Classic name	Number of metric feet
One-foot	Monometer	one
Two-foot	Dimeter	two
Three-foot	Trimeter	three
Four-foot	Tetrameter	four
Five-foot	Pentameter	five
Six-foot	Hexameter	six
Seven-foot	Heptameter	seven
Eight-foot	Octometer	eight

Examples of flawless metric lines, divided into feet:

4-foot iambic: Ĭ thínk | thăt Í | shăll név- | ĕr sée.

4-foot trochaic: Thén thĕ | líttlĕ | Hía- | wăthă.

3-foot spondaic: Gréat mén | grów stróng; | áll díe.

3-foot anapestic: Ăt thĕ énd | ŏf thĕ lóft- | ĭest tráil.

3-foot amphibrachic: Ĭn góĭng | tŏ Bábў- | lŏn, chíldrĕn.

3-foot dactylic: Cáught ĭn thĕ | spéll ŏf thĕ | mélŏdў.

3-foot amphimacer: Mén ŏf Róme, | fíght ănd díe, | névĕr yíeld!

We have already seen that flawlessness is a fault in metric poetry; naturalness comes in proportion as the natural scansion differs from the pattern scansion. Many variations are commonly allowed in metric verse. Iambs and trochees are interchangeable; and a pyrrhic or a spondee may be used for either. Added unaccents are permitted, as grace-notes. Similarly the three commonest three-syllabled feet are interchangeable; a spondee may be substituted for any of the three; a two-syllabled foot may be used, a pause filling in the omitted unaccent; and additional grace-notes are permitted. Feet may be mingled formally or informally within the line; in alternate lines; etc. Any foot ending in an accent may have one or more unaccents added to its end. Any foot beginning with one or more unaccents may have one or more of these omitted. By a liberal use of these variations, metric verse in practice approaches accent verse. As a rule, the dominant foot should, of course, remain dominant, to justify the name given to the verse.

Other terms occasionally used in scansion:

Name of Foot	Scansion	Accent pronunciation	Example
Ditrochee	′ ⌣ ′ ⌣	TUM-ta-TUM-ta	sóftlў smílĭng
Paeon	′ ⌣ ⌣ ⌣	TUM-ta-ta-ta	shádŏwĭnĕss
Choriamb	′ ⌣ ⌣ ′	TUM-ta-ta-TUM	Kálămăzóo
Epitrite, 1st class	⌣ ′ ′ ′	ta-TUM-TUM-TUM	
" 2nd class	′ ⌣ ′ ′	TUM-ta-TUM-TUM	
" 3rd class	′ ′ ⌣ ′	TUM-TUM-ta-TUM	
" 4th class	′ ′ ′ ⌣	TUM-TUM-TUM-ta	

Acatalectic verse: verse not defective in the last foot; verse with the full number of syllables.

Anacrusis: addition of one or two unaccents to a foot properly be-
     ginning on an accent.
Cesura: a break in a verse caused by the ending of a word within a
     foot. A masculine cesura follows the accented part of a foot;
     a feminine cesura, an unaccented syllable within the foot.
     In classic prosody, cesuras were named for the precise
     foot inside which they occurred.
Catalectic verse: verse lacking a syllable at the beginning, or ter-
     minating in an imperfect foot.
Dieresis: the break caused by the coinciding of the end of a foot
     with the end of a word.
Enjambement: extending a sentence beyond the limitations of the
     couplet, or distich.

The Stanza

A stanza is one or more lines (sometimes called verses) of verse,
constituting a division of a poem or verse. A stanza in verse corresponds to a paragraph in prose. Stanzas may be in free, accent, or
metric verse, or any combination of these; with any number of feet to
each line; and any combination of feet within each line. They may be
unrhymed, rhymed, with or without any of the other devices of versification.

The one or more lines may, of course, constitute an entire poem;
in which case they cease to be a stanza.

STANZA FORMS

One Line Stanzas

A poem may have formal stanzas of only one line each. Some
rhymed alphabets follow this pattern. Informal stanzas of one line
may be inserted in any poem.

> This is the house that Jack built.
> > *Mother Goose.*
> Whoever you are, to you endless announcements!
> > *Starting from Paumanok*, Walt Whitman.
> fathandsbangrag.
> > *Portrait of a Pianist*, E. E. Cummings.

Stanzas of Two Lines; the Couplet

A stanza (or a poem) of two lines, unrhymed or rhymed, is called
a couplet.

Where the two lines of a couplet stanza rhyme together, this is called *couplet rhyming:*

> Poems are made by fools like me,   1
> But only God can make a tree.   1
>
> *Trees*, Joyce Kilmer.

The same numbers indicate the lines which rhyme together. Poems may have couplet rhyming, where the stanzas are longer than couplets:

> "Lights out!" the siren warnings roll.   1
> The cities silk, as black as coal.   1
> But that's no cause to cringe in fright: 2
> Earth has its blackout every night,   2
> Yet, every morning, sunbeams pour   3
> Freer, more glorious, than before!   3
>
> *World Situation: 1941*, Clement Wood.

Couplet rhyming may also be used in a poem not divided into stanzas. The poem is then said to be stichic.

Iambic pentameter couplets, couplet-rhymed, are called *heroic couplets:*

> A little learning is a dangerous thing;   1
> Drink deep, or taste not the Pierian spring.   1
>
> *Essay on Criticism*, Alexander Pope.

Couplets may have end rhyme, without couplet rhyming; as, when successive couplets are interlinked by rhyming:

> The craze to make new forms in verse   1
> Possesses poets everywhere.   2
>
> The theory breathes like a prayer;   2
> The practice often is a curse.   1

The interlinking may be far more elaborate; as, 1, 2; 3, 4; 3, 1; 4, 5; 5, 2, etc.

By far the most popular form is couplets or run-on lines with couplet rhyming. Here is an example which utilizes brilliantly the *surprise ending*, so popular in fiction since the time of Frank R. Stockton and O. Henry:

> When I get home at five o'clock,
> I pause outside my door, and knock.
> A gentle rap should let her know
> That now it's time for her to go
> And hide herself in some dark corner.
> I really do it just to warn her,
> And not because I'm scared. I'm blest
> With one small mouse as my house-guest.
>
> *Guest*, Marcia M. Jones.

Here is another example of the surprise ending—again with couplet rhyming, but effectively divided into quatrains:

> I love the way you gaze at me;
> Your admiration's plain to see;
> And this, I must confess, is true:
> I thrill as much when I see you.
>
> Aesthetic love like ours ascends
> To heights that no one comprehends.
> Your love for me cannot surpass
> My love for you, dear Looking Glass.
>
> *Enchantment*, Alfred Turner.

Stanzas of Three Lines: The Triplet or Tercet

A stanza or poem of three lines is called a triplet or tercet. Tercets have four possible end rhyme schemes within the stanza:

> They have all gone away   1
>   From the house on the hill;   2
> There is nothing more to say.   1
>
> *The House on the Hill*, Edwin Arlington Robinson.

The other possible patterns are 1, 1, 1; 1, 1, 2; 1, 2, 2. Triplets and other stanzas may be interlocked by rhyme from stanza to stanza, this being called chain rhyming; as, 1, 2, 1; 3, 2, 3; 4, 2, 4; or 1, 1, 2; 2, 2, 3; 4, 4, 2; or in any other desired fashion.

Terza Rima: an Italian pattern of rhymed triplets, interlocked by rhyme in this fashion: 1, 2, 1; 2, 3, 2; 3, 4, 3; 4, 5, 4; 5, 6, 5; with a final couplet, taking its rhyme sound from the termination of the middle line of the previous triplet. This can be of any length. In English, it is usually written in five-foot iambic lines. In *Ode to the West Wind*, Shelley used a terza rima pattern of four triplets followed by the usual couplet (1, 2, 1; 2, 3, 2; 3, 4, 3; 4, 5, 4; 5, 5), or 14 lines in all. This form is sometimes called a terza rima sonnet.

Stanzas of Four Lines: the Quatrain

A quatrain, or stanza (or poem) of four lines, is the most popular length of stanza in English versification. As in all cases, the stanzas may be unrhymed or rhymed; in free, accent, or metric verse; with any number of feet to each line; with any type of feet in each line. Famous quatrain patterns are:

Ballad Meter, Ballad Measure, or Service Stanza:

> It is an ancient Mariner,   1
>   And he stoppeth one of three.   2
> "By thy long gray beard and glittering eye,   3
>   Now wherefore stopp'st thou me?"   2
>
> *The Rime of the Ancient Mariner*, Samuel Taylor Coleridge.

This originated as accent verse, 4, 3, 4, 3 feet to the line; which in turn was derived from 4-accent couplets. It was later often used in iambic verse, the same number of feet, 4, 3, 4, 3, to the line. As used in the ballads, longer stanzas, slightly varied from this pattern, were occasionally employed. Coleridge's poem illustrates this as well.

Rubaiyat Stanza, in five-foot iambic lines:

> The Moving Finger writes; and, having writ, 1
> Moves on; nor all your Piety and Wit 1
>   Shall lure it back to cancel half a Line, 2
> Nor all your Tears wash out a Word of it. 1
>> *Rubaiyat of Omar Khayyam*, Edward Fitzgerald.

In Memoriam Stanza, in four-foot iambic lines:

> Ring out the shapes of foul disease; 1
>   Ring out the narrowing lust for gold; 2
>   Ring out the thousand wars of old, 2
> Ring in the thousand years of peace. 1
>
> Ring out false pride in place and blood, 3
>   The civic slander and the spite; 4
>   Ring in the love of truth and right, 4
> Ring in the common love of good. 3
>> *In Memoriam*, Alfred Tennyson.

Elegiac Stanza, in five-foot iambic lines:

> No puppet master pulls the strings on high, 1
>   Portioning our parts, the tinsel and the paint; 2
> A twisted nerve, a ganglion gone awry, 1
>   Predestinates the sinner and the saint. 2
>
> Each, held more firmly than by hempen band, 3
>   Slave of his entrails, struts across the scene; 4
> The malnutrition of some obscure gland 3
>   Makes him a Ripper or the Nazarene. 4
>> *Slaves*, George Sylvester Viereck.

The same rhyming pattern, in three-foot iambic lines, was formerly called *Gray's stanza*. Any of these quatrain rhyme-schemes, with different metric feet or line lengths, is acceptable; but then it ceases to be the named stanza. We would thus speak of a 4-foot iambic stanza with elegiac stanza rhyming, a 5-foot trochaic stanza with In Memoriam stanza rhyming, etc.

The possible quatrain rhyme schemes are as follows, with the ones already given in italics:

2 lines rhyming, 2 unrhymed: *1, 2, 3, 2;* 1, 1, 2, 3; 1, 2, 2, 3, 1, 2, 3, 3; 1, 2, 1, 3; 1, 2, 3, 1.
3 lines rhyming together, 1 unrhymed: 1, 1, 1, 2; *1, 1, 2, 1;* 1, 2, 1, 1; 1, 2, 2, 2.
All four lines rhymed: 1, 1, 1, 1; 1, 1, 2, 2 (couplet rhyming); *1, 2, 1, 2; 1, 2, 2, 1.*

The versifier can make for himself a similar analysis of the possible rhyme-schemes for stanzas of five and more lines.

Three common quatrains found in hymns—and any rhyming is permissible in all of them, although 1, 2, 3, 2 is common—are:

Long Meter: four 4-foot iambic lines.
Common Meter: four iambic lines of 4, 3, 4, 3 feet. This has the same number of feet as ballad measure.
Short Meter: four iambic lines, of 3, 3, 4, 3 feet. As a couplet of 6, 7 iambic feet, this was the popular 16th century Poulter's measure.

Sapphics: The most famous stanza of classic times is the Sapphic, written originally in quantity meter (long and short syllables), and more common in English versification in accent meter. It follows this quatrain pattern:

$$\prime \;\smile\; | \; \text{or} \; | \; \prime \; \smile \; \smile \; | \; \prime \; \smile \; | \; \text{or}$$
$$\prime \;\smile\; | \; \text{or} \; | \; \prime \; \smile \; \smile \; | \; \prime \; \smile \; | \; \text{or}$$
$$\prime \;\smile\; | \; \prime\; \smile \; | \; \prime \; \smile \; \smile \; | \; \prime \; \smile \; | \; \text{or}$$
$$\prime \;\smile\;\smile\; | \; \prime \; \smile$$

As written in English, this is usually unrhymed. It may have rhyme, consonance, or any other device of versification.

> I am part of night. In the silent darkness,
> When the moon brings balm and a silver rapture,
> Let me lift my soul to the starry heavens,
> One with their vastness.
>
> *Sapphics,* Ida Elaine James.

Stanzas of Five Lines: The Cinquain

A stanza (or poem) of five lines is called a cinquain. It was formerly called a quintain. We will reach the limerick, the tanka, and Adelaide Crapsey's form called the cinquain, under Fixed Forms. Besides these, popular cinquain rhyme schemes include 1, 2, 1, 2, 2; 1, 2, 3, 3, 2; 1, 2, 3, 2, 2.

Stanzas of Six Lines: the Sestet

A stanza (or poem) of six lines is called a sestet. A popular rhyme-scheme for narrative verse is the Venus and Adonis stanza, used by Shakespeare in the poem of that name: in iambic 5-foot lines, an alternately rhymed quatrain, followed by a terminal couplet, couplet-rhymed:

Torches are made to light, jewels to wear,	1
Dainties to taste, fresh beauty for the use,	2
Herbs for their smell, and sappy plants to bear;	1
Things growing to themselves are growth's abuse:	2
Seeds spring from seeds, and beauty breedeth beauty;	3
Thou wast begot—to get it is thy duty.	3

Another popular sestet rhyme-scheme is 1, 2, 1, 2, 1, 2. A favorite stanza with Robert Burns is this one, used here in his *Epistle to J. Lapraik:*

Gie me ae spark o' nature's fire,	1
That's a' the larning I desire;	1
Then tho' I drudge thro' dub an' mire	1
At pleugh or cart,	2
My muse, tho' hamely in attire,	1
May touch the heart.	2

The presence of two or more lines shorter than the others, serving as "tails" to the various parts of the stanza, causes this to be called *tail-rhyme*. Whittier's *The Last Leaf* is a tail-rhyme sestet, rhymed 1, 1, 2, 3, 3, 2. Longer examples of tail-rhyme stanzas include Michael Drayton's *Agincourt*, and Tennyson's *The Charge of the Light Brigade* and *The Lady of Shalott*.

Stanzas of Seven Lines: the Septet

A stanza (or poem) of seven lines is called a septet.

Rhyme Royal, the most famous septet rhyme-scheme, was first popularized by Chaucer. It is written in 5-foot iambic lines, and grew naturally out of the stanza now called the Venus and Adonis stanza, merely by adding a fifth line, rhyming on the (2) sound, between the alternately rhymed quatrain and the terminal couplet. The rhyme scheme appears from:

Why should the worm intrude the maiden bud?	1
Or hateful cuckoos hatch in sparrows' nests?	2
Or toads infect fair founts with venom mud?	1
Or tyrant folly lurk in gentle breasts?	2
Or kings be breakers of their own behests?	2
But no perfection is so absolute	3
That some impurity doth not pollute.	3

The Rape of Lucrece, William Shakespeare.

The Canopus stanza, first appearing in 1920, eliminated the two concluding couplets, and thus prevented any break in the flow of the narrative:

He sank into the stubble by her side,	1
Leaving a blankness in the upper night;	2
His lips leant in their urgency of pride	1
Toward her eyes, that made the blackness bright.	2
His lips spoke only to the reddened cheek,	3
And settled to a long-denied delight	2
Upon the goal they had not dared to seek.	3

Stanzas of Eight and More Lines

Ottava Rima is an Italian octave—that is, stanza of eight lines—made famous in English by Milton, Keats, Byron, and others. It consists of six 5-foot iambic lines rhyming alternately, followed by a terminal couplet, couplet-rhymed. An example is:

But never mind;—"God save the king!" and kings!	1
For if *he* don't, I doubt if *men* will longer—	2
I think I hear a little bird, who sings	1
The people by and by will be the stronger;	2
The veriest jade will wince when harness wrings	1
So much into the raw as quite to wrong her	2
Beyond the rules of posting,—and the mob	3
At last falls sick of imitating Job.	3

Don Juan, Lord Byron, VIII, 1.

The Spenserian Stanza, long a favorite in stately narrative verse, contains eight 5-foot iambic lines, terminated by a 6-foot iambic line, called an Alexandrine. The Alexandrine breaks the monotony of the terminal rhyming couplet. Example:

And still she slept an azure-lidded sleep,	1
In blanched linen, smooth, and lavender'd,	2
While he from forth the closet brought a heap	1
Of candied apple, quince, and plum, and gourd;	2
With jellies soother than the creamy curd,	2
And lucent syrops, tinct with cinnamon;	3
Manna and dates, in argosy transferr'd	2
From Fez; and spiced dainties, every one,	3
From silken Samarcand to cedar'd Lebanon.	3

The Eve of St. Agnes, John Keats.

Spenser sustained this stanza form for 3,848 stanzas in his *The Faerie Queene.* Thomas Chatterton's Chatterton Stanza grew out of it—nine

5-foot iambic lines terminated by an Alexandrine, and rhymed 1, 2, 1, 2, 2, 3, 2, 3, 4, 4.

Other Stanzas. The stanzas in Keats's four most famous odes are usually in 5-foot iambic lines, opening with a quatrain alternately rhymed, 1, 2, 1, 2; followed by a sestet, rhymed 3, 4, 5, then these three sounds repeated in various orders. *To a Nightingale* shortens the eighth line in each stanza to three feet.

Many poems vary the rhyme, metric and number-of-feet pattern from stanza to stanza. Poe's *To Helen, To One in Paradise, The Conqueror Worm* and *The Haunted Palace* show this, in masterly fashion. Stanzas in light verse tend to be regular, and rise to delightful complexity, especially in the verse of Guy Wetmore Carryl. The favorite stanza and chorus patterns in popular songs tend to vary from decade to decade, even from year to year. Writers of these would do well to become familiar with the more recent favorites.

THE FIXED FORMS

THE SONNET

THE SONNET is a poem or stanza of fourteen 5-foot iambic lines, with one of several rigidly prescribed rhyme-schemes.

The Italian or Petrarchan Sonnet

The Italian or Petrarchan sonnet has an octave rhymed 1, 2, 2, 1; 1, 2, 2, 1; followed by a sestet permitting certain variations in rhyming, but rigorously excluding a final couplet. The two permissible sestet rhyme-schemes are 3, 4, 5; 3, 4, 5 or 3, 4, 3; 4, 3, 4. This second should never be three couplets, rhymed 3, 4; 3, 4; 3, 4. The subject matter should consist of one idea, or one emotion elaborated throughout, and complete in itself. The octave, in turn, was divided into two quatrains; the sestet, into two tercets. The octave's first quatrain states the principal idea; the second quatrain illustrates and elaborates it; the first tercet of the sestet, after an intervening pause, treats it differently; and the final tercet treats it still differently, and requires at least the dignity of the opening, with some epigrammatic force.

Nothing is stable. Though the deeds we do	1
May bind the nations in a servile chain,	2
And give to cowering slaves their joy and pain,	2
The far result still frowns in open view.	1
A little wound will let great Caesar through,	1
An asp make Egypt's dusky charmer plain;	2
And all the power and beauty that remain	2
Go shivering naked up the mystic blue.	1
Earth smiles at tyrants, when the crown is laid	3
Upon the coffin, and their history	4
To after times with laughter is displayed.	3
Death and oblivion are the proudest fee	4
Of man's endeavor; and the delver's spade	3
Rounds all our hillocks fair and evenly.	4

On Profane Love, George Henry Boker.

In sonnet writing, the strict practice is to forbid internal rhymes; to have the rhyming sounds of the octave harmoniously at variance, with those of the sestet distinct in intonation from those of the octave. This distinct variance in rhyming sounds should as a rule be followed

in all uses of rhyme. As commonly written in English, the rule requiring complete breaks between the four sections of the Italian sonnet is ignored.

The Miltonic Sonnet

This is an Italian sonnet, with a complete break midway of the eighth line, its latter half being structurally a part of the ninth line. Five of Milton's nineteen sonnets follow this pattern. One makes a similar break in the ninth line.

When I consider how my light is spent,	1
Ere half my days in this dark world and wide,	2
And that one talent which is death to hide	2
Lodged with me useless, though my soul more bent	1
To serve therewith my Maker, and present	1
My true account, lest He returning chide,	2
"Doth God exact day-labor, light denied?"	2
I fondly ask.	
But Patience, to prevent	1
That murmur, soon replies, "God doth not need	3
Either man's work or his own gifts. Who best	4
Bear his mild yoke, they serve him best. His state	5
Is kingly: thousands at his bidding speed,	3
And post o'er land and ocean without rest;	4
They also serve who only stand and wait."	5

On His Blindness, John Milton.

It is not necessary to make the stanza break midway of the eighth line, as far as typography is concerned, as is done above. This, of course, emphasizes the structural difference of this sonnet from the strict Italian type.

The Wordsworthian Sonnet

The chief departure that Wordsworth made from the strict Italian sonnet was in the octave, which he repeatedly rhymed 1, 2, 2, 1: 1, 3, 3, 1; the sestet remaining regular. An example is:

It is not to be thought of that the flood	1
Of British freedom, which to the open sea	2
Of the world's praise, from dark antiquity	2
Hath flow'd, 'with pomp of waters, unwithstood,'—	1
Roused though it be full often to a mood	1
Which spurns the check of salutary bands,—	3
That this most famous stream in bogs and sands	3
Should perish; and to evil and to good	1
Be lost for ever. In our halls is hung	4
Armoury of all the invincible Knights of old:	5

We must be free or die, who speak the tongue   4
   That Shakespeare spake; the faith and morals hold   5
Which Milton held.—In everything we are sprung   4
   Of Earth's first blood, have titles manifold.   5

From England: 1802, William Wordsworth.

The liberal English use of the sonnet appears from this example. The first quatrain is not endstopped. The second quatrain is not endstopped, and introduces the Wordsworthian third rhyme of the octave. The first triplet of the sestet is not endstopped.

In acquiring this mood of liberality, do not be corrupted by the regrettable vocabulary which Wordsworth and so many more at times use: the occasional archaism, the poeticized ellipses and inversions, induced by meter and rhyme. However high the idea and the idealism here may be, the wording, sentence structure, etc., fall far below prose.

The Spenserian Sonnet

Edmund Spenser preferred a sonnet of three quatrains, interlocked in the following fashion, and with a terminal couplet: 1, 2, 1, 2; 2, 3, 2, 3; 3, 4, 3, 4; 5, 5. This interlocking is similar to that used by Spenser in the stanza named after him. As a sonnet, this form has never become popular.

The Wyattian Sonnet

Wyatt's departure from the familiar sonnet patterns followed this rhyme-scheme: an Italian octave, 1, 2, 2, 1; 1, 2, 2, 1; with a sestet in couplet rhyming, 3, 3, 4, 4, 5, 5. This pattern has been largely ignored.

The Shakespearean Sonnet

The Shakespearean sonnet, the most popular and natural of all in English versification, consists of three alternately rhymed quatrains, and a terminal couplet, rhymed 1, 2, 1, 2; 3, 4, 3, 4; 5, 6, 5, 6; 7, 7. Here is an example:

Let me not to the marriage of true minds   1
Admit impediments. Love is not love   2
Which alters when it alteration finds,   1
Or bends with the remover to remove: 2
O, no; it is an ever-fixed mark   3
That looks on tempests, and is never shaken;   4
It is the star to every wandering bark,   3
Whose worth's unknown, although his height be taken.   4
Love's not Time's fool, though rosy lips and cheeks   5
Within his bending sickle's compass come;   6
Love alters not with his brief hours and weeks,   5

But bears it out even to the edge of doom.   6
    If this be error, and upon me prov'd,   7
    I never writ, nor no man ever lov'd.   7

> *Sonnet cxvi*, William Shakespeare.

Shakespearean sonnets are usually indented in this fashion. He and later sonnetteers often varied from the strict iambic pattern, to give greater naturalness to the sonnet. He also used at times a double rhyme with great effectiveness, to break the monotonous flow of single rhymes. The Shakespearean sonnets, as written by Shakespeare, are at the same time stanzas in a sonnet sequence, and also independent poems, able to stand alone.

Sonnets as Stanzas

Sonnets may be used as stanzas, the complete poem being called a *sonnet sequence*. Formal sonnet sequences include:

The Crown of Sonnets: a sequence of seven Italian or other sonnets, in which the last line of the first six becomes successively the first line of the ensuing sonnet; while the last line of the seventh is the same as the first line of the first sonnet.

The Sonnet Redoublé consists of fifteen Italian or Shakespearean sonnets, in which the fourteen lines of the first sonnet are used successively as the final lines of the next fourteen sonnets. They may be used, instead, as the first lines of the next fourteen sonnets.

Miscellaneous Sonnets

Combined sonnets: sonnets with an octave from one type, and a sestet from another; or with any other mingling of patterns.

Irregular sonnets: fourteen-line poems in 5-foot iambic lines, with a rhyme-scheme differing from the foregoing. Shelley's *Ozymandias of Egypt* has as its rhyme-scheme 1, 2, 1, 2; 1, 3, 4, 3; 5, 4, 5; 6, 5, 6. This might be described as a Shakespearean sonnet opening, followed by terza rima units, without the concluding couplet of terza rima. My *Night Entrance* has as its pattern 1, 2, 2, 2; 3, 4, 4, 4; 5, 6, 6, 6; 7, 7. At times such irregularities are successful, whether regarded as irregular sonnets, or as fourteen-line poems. An occasional sonnet, especially in light verse, has less than five feet to the line, or a unit foot not iambic.

Terza rima sonnet: see under terza rima, in the discussion of tercets.

RULES FOR FORMAL VERSE

The rules for the fixed French and other forms, in English, are rigid, and allow no deviation:

1. No syllable or group of syllables, once used as a rhyme, can be used again as a rhyme in the same poem, even if spelled differently, nor if the whole word is altered by a prefix. Identities are strictly forbidden.

2. The refrain must not be a meaningless repetition of sounds, as in many ballads, songs, and jingles. It must aid in the progression of the thought; must come in naturally; and must be repeated in all its sounds, without any change of sound.

Unless otherwise stipulated, accent verse is as appropriate as metric; and in some forms is far commoner. The poet is safe in following the models given.

SYLLABLE-COUNT FORMS

The Hokku, or Haikai: a Japanese form, consisting of only three lines, having 5, 7, 5 syllables, or 17 in all. There is no requirement as to rhyme or rhythm.

> Two dark stars, fused by
> Sudden meeting into a
> Bright splendor: so love.
>
> *Nova,* Carroll Winters.

> I could reach your heart—
> Perhaps make you immortal—
> But not in three lines!
>
> *Love in a Hokku,* Stephen Schlitzer.

The Tanka: a Japanese form, usually of five lines, having 5, 7, 5, 7, 7 syliables, or 31 in all.

> On the jet brackish
> Pool, the gale whips the water
> Into white-arced foam,
> That lifts to soar out to sea:
> White gulls etched on a jet sky.
>
> *Inland of Cape May,* Carroll Winters.

Longer Japanese poems may be constructed on the tanka form, with an invariable alternation of 5 and 7 syllables to the line, terminating in an added terminal 7-syllable line.

The Cinquain: a variant from the tanka type, invented by Adelaide Crapsey. As she wrote it, its five iambic lines contain respectively 2, 4, 6, 8 and 2 syllables. In the hands of others, it is written without stipulation as to rhythm. It is usually unrhymed.

> Forget
> the glow of spring,
> the searing summer days,
> the gaudy autumn. Winter comes,
> and death.
>
> *Cinquain*, Beth Garner.

Hokku-Tanka Variations. Much ingenuity has been expended in varying these three syllable-count patterns. Among the chief variations are:

Name	Invented by	Syllable count	Remarks
Double Cinquain	Berta Hart Nance	4, 8, 12, 16, 4	Unless otherwise stated, no stipulation as to rhythm in any of these.
Lanterne	Lloyd Frank Merrell	1, 2, 3, 4, 1	Arranged in form like a Japanese lantern; a shaped whimsey.
Pensee	Alice Maude Spokes	2, 4, 7, 8, 6	A complete thought; strong end words.
Quintet	Mary Owen Lewis	3, 5, 7, 9, 3	Strong end words.
Vignette	Flozari Rockwood	2, 4, 4, 6, 7, 3	Strong end words.
Septet	Mary Owen Lewis	3, 5, 7, 9, 7, 5, 3	
Cameo	Alice Maude Spokes	2, 5, 8, 3, 8, 7, 2	Strong end words.
Sept	Etta Josephean Murfey	1, 2, 3, 4, 3, 2, 1	
Hexaduad	Gee Kaye	2, 2, 6, 6, 8, 8, 4, 4, 6, 6, 4, 4	Couplet rhymes.
Inverted Hexaduad	Same	2, 6, 8, 4, 6, 4, 4, 6, 4, 8, 6, 2	Couplet rhymes; first two lines transposed for last two.

Forms invented by James Neill Northe. [Where indicated, these may be Double (D), or pairs of lines of the same number of syllables; Twin (T), the whole pattern repeated; Inverted (I), the syllables

in the second half reversed; or several of these devices may be utilized in the same verses.]

Cinquo	1, 2, 3, 4, 1	Without Lanterne typography.
Shadorma	3, 5, 3, 3, 7, 5	
Hotan	5, 7, 5, 3, 5, 3, 5, 7, 5	Unless otherwise specified, all these forms hereafter may be D, T, I, ID, IT.
Cinquaino	2, 8, 6, 4, 2	
Quintine	1, 3, 5, 7, 9	
Quinquina	9, 7, 5, 3, 1	
Tri-Quin-Sep	3, 5, 7	
Tri-Sep-Quin	3, 7, 5	
Quin-Tri-Sep	5, 3, 7	
Quin-Sep-Tri	5, 7, 3	
Sep-Tri-Quin	7, 3, 5	
Sep-Quin-Tri	7, 5, 3	
Double Hokku	5, 5, 7, 7, 5, 5	Variations called T, D, DI.
Double Tanka	5, 5, 7, 7, 5, 5. 7 7, 7, 7	Variations called D, T, I, IT, ID.

Acknowledgment is gratefully given to Etta Josephean Murfey, for invaluable assistance in preparing this list, as well as the modern forms listed under Miscellaneous.

MISCELLANEOUS FORMS

The Limerick

The limerick is a five-line poem, following a rigid pattern. Its 1st, 2nd and 5th lines have three feet each, while its 3rd and 4th have two only. It is usually written in amphibrachs, sometimes with the addition of an extra unaccent at the beginning, which gives it an anapestic movement. Edward Lear ended his fifth lines on the same word that terminated his first; the preferred fashion is to let the line end differently. The first line often ends on a geographical or some other proper noun. The pattern is:

> There was a | young lady | of Lynn,
>
> Who was so | excessive- | ly thin,
>
> That when she | essayed
>
> To drink lem- | onade
>
> She slipped through | the straw and | fell in.

The latest edition of the *Encyclopedia Britannica* says of its choice, order and idiom of words, "A good limerick should have the con-

secutive fluency of conversational prose"—a stipulation which should control all verse and poetry. The limerick calls for every device of light verse, including tongue-twisters:

> "There's a train at 4:04," said Miss Jenny.
> "Four tickets I'll take; have you any?"
>   Said the man at the door,
>   "Not four for 4:04!
> For four for 4:04 is too many."

—as well as intricate trick and mosaic rhyming, punning, eccentric typography, stammering, intentional misspelling to emphasize a rhyme, and so on. All of the best limericks, says Arnold Bennett, are unquotable.

The Little Willie

A Little Willie is a quatrain, patterned after this version of Col. D. Streamer's (Harry Graham's) *Tender-Heartedness:*

> Little Willie, in bows and sashes,   1
> Fell in the fire and got burned to ashes. 1
> In the winter, when the weather is chilly, 2
> No one likes to poke up Willie.   2

This is in accent verse, with couplet rhyming; four accents to the line. A Little Willie deals preferably with some member of the family, and treats a family tragedy cynically and wittily. There is often definite sadism:

> Father heard his children scream,
> So he threw them in the stream;
> Saying, as he drowned the third,
> "Children should be seen, not heard."

This example is trochaic, instead of in accent verse. At times alternate rhyming replaces couplet rhyming:

> Baby in the caldron fell,—   1
> See the grief on Mother's brow;   2
> Mother loved her darling well,—   1
> Darling's quite hard-boiled by now. 2

Other Forms

The Sicilian Octave: eight 5-foot iambic lines, rhymed alternately on two sounds: 1, 2, 1, 2, 1, 2, 1, 2. It is used for a stanza, as well as for a fixed form.

> The wind of poetry blows high and strong,   1
> But not of its own choice in alien meter.   2
> Instead of miles of formalized ding-dong   1

Preferred by some super-involved frog-eater,   2
Exotic as Kamchatka or Hong-Kong,   1
Give us the homely strain of *Peter, Peter,*   2
Pumpkin-Eater to be our festive song: 1
The taste is homelier by far, and sweeter.   2
                              Home Cooking, Alan Dubois.

The Rispetto: a poem from six to ten lines, though usually eight.
The rhyming is 1, 2, 1, 2; 3, 3, 4, 4. At times it is divided into two
stanzas.

A multitude of formalized designs   1
Offends the very soul of poetry.   2
Why not have candid and spontaneous lines,   1
To picture what our souls would have life be?   2
Why fritter away the energy of the Muse   3
In lais and rondels and such trifling brews?   3
But I forget Light Verse, with trifling crowned;   4
These, lightsome queen, shall be *your* stamping-ground!   4
                              The Forgotten Muse, Aloysius Richardson.

The Sonnette: a form derived by Sherman Ripley from the Italian
sonnetto. It consists of seven 5-foot iambic lines, rhymed 1, 2, 2, 1;
3, 2, 3.

In the old days men at times went insane.   1
Frothing and frantic, they would rape and kill   2
And burn in wild destructiveness, until   2
Death ended the madness, amid their rotting slain.   1
Men go berserk still; the dictators   3
Bloodily seek to bend all men to their will,   2
And die, as ever, in the madness called wars.   3
                              Berserk, Charles Morgan Flood.

The Raccontino: a form invented by Etta Josephean Murfey. It is
in couplets, whose even-numbered lines end on the same rhyming
sound. The title, taken with the terminal words of the odd-numbered
lines, tells a brief story (or *raccontino*). An example is:

There is a little whispering that says,   1
Look up, forget the earth; the sky is glowing!   2

I have not scorned the insidious whisper; I   3
Have probed to where lost galaxies are growing   2

In passionate anguish. Yet I tell you, love,   4
Within my soul more tempestuous storms are blowing,   2

And all to drive me in the end to you.   5
This is all the wisdom my soul needs knowing.   2
                              The Song of My Heart, Ben Sterling.

The raccontino here is "The song of my heart says, 'I love you.' "

The Paean: a form invented by Evelyn M. Watson. It has thirteen lines: a 5-foot iambic quatrain rhymed 1, 2, 1, 2, followed by a briefer triply rhymed tercet, 3, 3, 3. A 5-foot couplet, rhymed 1, 2, repeats the theme, followed by a brief echo, 3; while a terminal triplet in 5-foot iambs, rhymed 4, 4, 4, completes the form. Iambic hexameter can be used instead of pentameter, if desired.

The Trine: a nine-line poem invented by Evelyn M. Watson. Three rhymed couplets of any length are followed by three single lines, using successively their rhyming sounds. The rhyme-scheme is 1, 1; 2, 2; 3, 3; 1, 2, 3.

The Quaternion: Miss Watson's similar 12-line poem, in units of four, not three. Rhyme-scheme, 1, 1; 2, 2; 3, 3; 4, 4; 1, 2, 3, 4.

The Donata, also by Miss Watson, uses the main accented words in the first line of each stanza as the rhyming sounds for the formal rhyme scheme of the stanza.

Muted Rhyme, by Miss Watson, inserts occasional rhyme in a blank verse pattern; frequently this being internal rhyme. Muted rhyme partakes of the nature of Amy Lowell's amorphous polyphonic prose.

Closed Rhyme, by Margaret Scott Copeland, has initial rhyme as well as terminal rhyme. Authorship of this form is said also to be claimed by her husband, James Neill Northe.

LINE-REPETITION FORMS

The Kyrielle: a poem in quatrains, with 8 syllables to each line, and with the last line of the first stanza used as a refrain to terminate each of the other stanzas.

It simply will not let me go—	1
A line of verse I stumbled on	2
While browsing, not so long ago:	1
"In Xanadu did Kubla Khan—"	2R
Where in the world is Xanadu?	3
Near the Niger, the Amazon,	2
Or beyond alien Timbuktu?	3
"In Xanadu did Kubla Khan. . . ."	2R
And who was Kubla Khan, and what	4
Was it that he achieved upon	2
That far and fascinating spot?	4
"In Xanadu did Kubla Khan. . . ."	2R

I've pondered till I'm wan and pale;   5
I've worried till I'm pale and wan.   2
Will *no* one finish the strange tale,   5
"In Xanadu did Kubla Khan—"   2R

Baffled, Clement Wood.

Many familiar hymns use this pattern, without recognizing it as a named form. Charlotte Elliott's *Just as I Am*, as commonly sung (with the terminal line "O Lamb of God, I come, I come") is a kyrielle. Notice that it satisfies the requirements of the form, although its rhyme scheme is 1, 1, 1, 2R; 3, 3, 3, 2R; 4, 4, 4, 2R, etc. 2R, of course, means a rhyme upon the *2* sound used as a refrain (R).

The Quatern: a variation of the kyrielle, in which the *first* line of the first quatrain, used as a refrain, reappears as the second line of stanza two, the third line of stanza three, and the final line of the final quatrain. The form was invented by Vivian Yeiser Laramore, who used lines of four feet each. An example is:

And we have reached the end, you say: 1R
There is a limit to all things,   2
And each can go his separate way,   1
Forgetting joint adventurings.   2

Life has become dull tiny stings,   2
And we have reached the end, you say,   1R
Each with sick soul that clings, and clings 2
As if to hamper till doomsday.   1

Too much "love, honor and obey,"   1
A role not fit for queens and kings. . . .   2
And we have reached the end, you say—   1R
(How dreadfully the cold word rings!)   2

Have you forgot that spring of springs, 2
And our high flights, that gathered gay 1
Stardust to glitter on our wings?   2
—And we have reached the end, you say!   1R

Against an Ultimatum, Carveth Wells.

The Retourné: a variation of the kyrielle, in which all the lines of the first quatrain are used to constitute a refrain. The 2nd line of the first quatrain opens the second quatrain; the 3rd line, the third quatrain; while the 4th opens the final quatrain, which consists of the lines of the first quatrain in the reverse order. The form was invented by Diana Douglas. When couplet rhyming is used in the first quatrain, the rhyme-scheme then becomes: 1R, 1R', 2R, 2R'; 1R', 1, 3. 3; 2R, 2, 4, 4; 2R', 2R, 1R', 1R. An example in this pattern is:

Love's the winner, after all.	1R
Hunger has an ancient call;	1R′
Death's a friend that all must seek;	2R
Love's word only hearts can speak.	2R′
Hunger has an ancient call,	1R′
Holding man and beast in thrall;	1
But the spirit's daily bread	3
Always comes from love instead.	3
Death's a friend that all must seek,	2R
Hand in hand and cheek to cheek;	2
But love's spell glows on and on	4
Long after gray death has gone.	4
Love's word only hearts can speak.	2R′
Death's a friend that all must seek,	2R
Hunger has an ancient call:	1R′
Love's the winner, after all!	1R

Eros, Lois Lodge.

If the pattern of the first quatrain is not couplet rhyming—and it may follow any of the possible quatrain rhyming patterns—the pattern of the rest will alter accordingly. Thus an alternately rhymed quatrain, 1, 2, 1, 2, would give us: 1R, 2R, 1R′, 2R′; 2R, 3, 2, 3; 1R′, 4, 1, 4; 2R′, 1R′, 2R, 1R. Other possible rhyme-schemes are obvious.

The Pantoum: a poem of Malay origin, written in quatrains, the 2nd and 4th lines of each stanza becoming successively the 1st and 3rd of the next stanza. In the last stanza, the 2nd and 4th lines are the 3rd and finally the 1st of the first quatrain; so that the opening line of the pantoum is used as its closing line. The rhyme scheme is: 1, 2, 1′, 2′; 2, 3, 2′, 3′; 3, 4, 3′, 4′; 4, 5, 4′, 5′; . . . n, 1′, n′, 1—with, of course, each line used twice in the poem, once in an odd-numbered line, once in an even-numbered one. The poem may be of any length, so long as the final stanza fits the pattern above.

"Gee, but that Hitler is a hound!"	1
"If you've seen Greta Garbo's latest,—"	2
"—Can you stand having *him* around?"	1′
"But Joe Di Maggio's the greatest!"	2′
"If you've seen Greta Garbo's latest,—"	2
"I think, instead, I'll have lamb chops."	3
"But Joe Di Maggio's the greatest!"	2′
"My dear, I've *tried* Park Avenue shops,—"	3′
"I think, instead, I'll have lamb chops."	3
"You think that Petain *wanted* peace?"	4
"My dear, I've *tried* Park Avenue shops,—"	3′
"—And face the girdle with cerise,—"	4′

"You think that Petain *wanted* peace?"   4
  "Can you stand having *him* around?"   1'
"—And face the girdle with cerise,—"   4'
  "Gee, but that Hitler is a hound!"   1

Any Cafe: Dinner, Aloysius Richardson.

CHAIN VERSE

Chain Rhyme and Chain Verse

In terza rima, the tercets are linked by rhyme thus: 1, 2, 1; 2, 3, 2;
3, 4, 3; 4, 5, 4; 5, 6, 5; ending with a couplet rhyming on the terminal
sound midway of the preceding stanza. Quatrains or other longer
stanzas could be similarly linked: as, 1, 1, 2, 1; 2, 2, 3, 2; 3, 3, 4, 3;
4, 4, 5, 4, and so on. This process could mount to a chain of sonnets,
with the final rhyme sound in each sonnet repeated as the opening
rhyme sound of the next, or any other chain rhyming device.

The link may be only of the rhyming *sound*, or it may include a
word, a phrase, a line, or even more, whether based on terminal
rhymes or not. The French chain rhyme requires that one word and
one only grow from each line into the next:

> Let us gaily carol Spring,
> Spring, that sets the world on fire
> With a fire that wakes the wing
> Of the forest's winged choir.
> When this choir is gaudiest,
> All the flowers are gaudy too,
> Flowers ending the bees' quest
> For the quested nectar dew.
>
> *Spring*, Lois Lodge.

Similarly, phrases may be interlocked:

> The rarer seen, the less in mind;
> The less in mind, the lesser pain;
> The lesser pain, less grief I find;
> The lesser grief, the greater gain.
>
> *Lines*, Barnaby Googe.

Another chain verse type, which we found in the Crown of Sonnets,
is to let each stanza's last line become the first line of the next:

> I have an easy chair,   1
> Cozy and sloping and deep.   2
> When I am seated there,   1
> I lull my cares to sleep.   2R

> I lull my cares to sleep,   2R
> And dreams of all I'd be
> Wake timidly, and creep
> Softly, to hearten me.   3R
>
> Softly, to hearten me,   3R
> Your lovely face appears,
> Bringing its ecstasy
> To brighten all my years.   4R
>
> To brighten all my years,   4R
> When other faces fade,

and so on. This is quoted from *Your Face*, by Lacey Beck.

The Lai Group

The Lai: a poem composed of couplets of 5-syllabled lines, all on the same rhyme, separated by single lines of 2 syllables, on a different rhyme. This is a type of tail rhyme. The number of lines per stanza is not fixed, nor the number of stanzas per poem. Each stanza has its own two rhyme sounds, without reference to the preceding stanzas. Typographically, all the lines are flush with the longer ones at the left margin—a French device called *Arbre fourchu* (a forked tree), from its supposed resemblance to a trunk with bare branches projecting from it. From this aspect, it partakes of the nature of a shaped whimsey.

> Sing, now, most of all!
> Wake the golden fall
> With glee,
> Till both great and small
> Share the bacchanal,
> Each tree
> Quivers to its tall
> Peak, in carnival
> With me!
>
> Sing, before the bright
> Autumn hues take flight
> And go,
> And eternal night
> Spreads its shroud of white
> Thick snow.
>
> *Song before Dusk*, J. K. Eden.

The Virelai Ancien: a lai interlocked by rhyme, in which the short lines of each stanza furnish the rhyming sound for the long lines of

the succeeding stanza; the last stanza having as the rhyming sound
of its short lines the terminal sound of the long lines of the first
stanza. The stanzas are uniform in length. The virelai ancien thus
becomes a type of chain rhyme, with the pattern, for a 12-line stanza,
of 1, 1, 2, 1, 1, 2, 1, 1, 2, 1, 1, 2; 2, 2, 3, 2, 2, 3, 2, 2, 3, 2, 2, 3; and so
on, until the last stanza rhymes n, n, 1, n, n, 1, n, n, 1, n, n, 1. Each
rhyming sound thus appears twice: once in the longer couplets, and
once in the short lines. Some users of the form depart from the French
model and make the couplet-rhymed lines longer than five syllables,
and even the single lines of the same length:

As I sat sorrowing,	1
Love came and bade me sing	1
A joyous song and meet,	2
For see (said he) each thing	1
Is merry for the Spring,	1
And every bird doth greet	2
The break of blossoming,	1
That all the woodlands ring	1
Unto the young hours' feet.	2
Wherefore put off defeat	2
And rouse thee to repeat	2
The chimes of merles that go,	3

and so to the ninth and last stanza:

So for the sad soul's ease	10
Remembrance treasures these	10
Against time's harvesting,	1
That so, when mild Death frees	10
The soul from Life's disease	10
Of strife and sorrowing,	1
In glass of memories	10
The new hope looks and sees	10
Through Death a brighter Spring.	1

Spring Sadness, John Payne.

The Virelai Nouveau: a formalized simplification of the lai, written
on two rhymes, and opening on a couplet used as a refrain. The lines
of this couplet alternately close each stanza until the last, when both
are used, in reverse order. There need be no uniformity of length of
stanza, or position of the two rhymes, except for the refrains:

Goodbye to the Town!—goodbye!	1R
Hurrah! for the sea and the sky!	1R'

In the street the flower-girls cry;	1
In the street the water-carts ply;	1
And a fluter, with features awry,	1
Plays fitfully, "Scots, who hae"—	2
And the throat of the fluter is dry;	1
Goodbye to the Town!—goodbye!	1R

And over the rooftops nigh	1
Comes a waft like a dream of the May;	2
And a lady-bird lit on my tie;	1
And a cockchafer came with the tray;	2
And a butterfly (no one knows why)	1
Mistook my Aunt's cap for a spray;	2
And "next door" and "over the way"	2
The neighbors take wings and fly:	1
Hurrah! for the sea and the sky!	1R'

Here 1R and 1R' are the two refrain lines. Succeeding stanzas proceed: 1, 1, 2, 1, 2, 1, 2, 1, 1R and 1, 2, 1, 2, 1, 2, 1, 2, 1, 1, 1, 1, 1, 1, 1R'. The conclusion is:

So Phyllis, the fawn-footed, hie	1
For a hansom. Ere close of the day,	2
Between us a "world" must lie,—	1
Hurrah! for the sea and the sky!	1R'
Goodbye to the Town!—GOODBYE!	1R

TEXT-EMBROIDERING GROUP

Tema con Variazioni

This poem form, in which the successive lines of a familiar stanza are used as the successive first lines of the various stanzas, and their meaning is embroidered to complete stanzas in the original stanza pattern, was invented by Lewis Carroll, in *Rhyme? and Reason?* The stanza used as a texte is not ordinarily first given as a whole, since its meaning is usually entirely altered; but there is no reason why it should not appear first as a whole, if desired. The spirit of this is the same as that of jazzing or swinging the classics, in music. Since the original texte may have any chosen rhyme or rhythm scheme, the possible variations are unlimited.

Out of the night that covers me	1R
I rise whene'er the doorbell rings,	3
To let in Mandy, Jane, Marie,	1
With all their frowsy bags and things.	3

Black as the pit, from Pole to Pole, 2R
 From Swede to Irish, Jap, Negro, 4
I greet the cooks, with quaking soul, 2
 Who sometimes come—and always go. 4

I thank whatever gods there be 1R'
 When one remains a week or more. 5
Yet they must toe the mark for me; 1
 To pert retorts I show the door. 5

For my unconquerable sole, 2R'
 Applied with vigor, makes it plain 6
I do not fear my bread to roll, 2R'
 Nor try "Help Wanted" ads again! 6

     Lament Culinaire, Margaret Thurston.

The resemblance of this to the retourné should be noted.

Rondeau Redoublé

This is a 25 line Theme with Variations, in which an opening quatrain is used as a texte, its four lines successively terminating the next four quatrains; while the concluding quatrain is tailed by the first half or some portion of the first line, as the concluding unrhymed refrain. It has no real kinship with the rondeau group, barring the 25th line. The rhyme scheme appears from:

Though I am not a bloated millionaire, 1R
 Though I'm no blooming Dupont or John D., 2R
Though I have scarce a jitney-piece to spare, 1R'
 Life as a whole goes very well with me. 2R'

 Imprimis, I am healthy as can be, 2
With appetite that is distinctly there. 1
 My meals? Each day I stow away my three, 2
Though I am not a bloated millionaire. 1R

Secundis, when it comes to what I wear, 1
 Blue Tux, slack suits—like any Christmas tree, 2
I cut a glittering figure everywhere, 2
 Though I'm no blooming Dupont or John D. 2R

 I write with pen unbought (so far) and free 2
Stuff that at times makes Proper People swear, 1
 And get it published rather frequently— 2
Though I have scarce a jitney-piece to spare. 1R'

 "A daughter of the gods, divinely fair" 1
Said "Yes, sir," to my heart's importunate plea. 2
 We make a torrid—and a handsome—pair; 1
Life as a whole goes very well with me. 2R'

I seem so needful to Society,	2
So high-removed from Plute and Proletaire,	1
That you might think a Superman you see,—	2
That I'm the Cosmic Kid, the Ages' Heir—	1
Though I am not.	R

Mainly About Me, J. K. Eden.

Villanelle

The villanelle is a poem in tercets, all rhymed 1, 2, 1; followed by a concluding quatrain, rhymed 1, 2, 1, 1. The first and third lines of the first stanza are used alternately as terminal refrains in the tercets; and both together comprise the refrain of the final quatrain. It is usual to restrict the villanelle to five tercets and a quatrain, although more stanzas may be used, providing the concluding quatrain comes as above, after some odd number of tercets (this permitting both refrain lines to appear an equal number of times).

Summer, with its awful heat,	1R
Comes upon us once again;	2
Don't we find it cool and sweet!	1R'
How the sun's hot arrows beat,	1
Bringing to poor city men	2
Summer with its awful heat!	1R
But, sequestered from the street,	1
With a breeze from some cool den,	2
Don't we find it cool and sweet!	1R'
Till the breeze, the spiteful cheat,	1
Shifts; and, hotter than cayenne,	2
Summer with its awful heat.	1R
At the end, dusk's chilly feet	1
Creep from some far icy glen—	2
Don't we find it cool and sweet!	1R'
Welcome, let me here repeat,	1
Charring now, and chilling then,	2
Summer with its awful heat—	1R
Don't we find it cool and sweet!	1R'

Midsummer, Claire Warfield.

Glose

A glose is a 44 line Theme with Variations, in which an opening quatrain, often a quotation, is used as a texte. Its four lines successively terminate the next four stanzas of 10 lines each. In each of these stanzas, the 6th, 9th and 10th (the refrain) lines rhyme on the same sound; the others are arranged in some rhyme-scheme, preferably uniform throughout the stanzas. No final refrain is used after the 10th line of the last stanza.

"If I'd as much money as I could tell,   1R
I never would cry old clothes to sell,   1R'
Old clothes to sell, old clothes to sell,   1R"
I never would cry old clothes to sell."   1R*

The flow of my dreams is at youth's high flood,   2
   A Spring flood, freighted with strange and new   3
Wonders of stars, and a touch of mud;   2
For all things are sweet to youth's wild blood.   2
   And fire-shod visions come to me too   3
Of a people hungry for stars as well,—   1
   Hungry for fare that the mangered few   3
   Grasp and hoard; there's a world to do— 3
Hunger and darkness I could dispel,   1
If I'd as much money as I could tell.   1R

But whether or no, it matters not;   4
   I am caught in the mire as well as they;   5
I am bound to squirm in a bitter spot
Where blindness grows, and high dreams rot;
   I coin my visions, to make them pay;
I traffic in things that decay and smell,   1
   Stopping my ears to the call of gay   5
   Life, and the words the visions say: 5
Ah, if I had the heart to rebel   1
I never would cry old clothes to sell!   1R'

But here I stay, and here I stay,
   And life is only a bitter jest
That a madman dreamed, and idiots play;
Tossing each precious thing away,
   Crowning the lowest, strangling the best:
And death will come ringing his peddler's bell,   1
   And gather the breath out of the breast,
   Calling our fairest and loveliest
Visions, but rags that shrink and swell,—   1
Old clothes to sell, old clothes to sell.   1R"

Well, I can call as well as he—
   And these dreams he despises so
I say will sooner or later be
Not dreams, but fair reality—
   In dreams and rags and mud will flow
The dreamer's passion, the will's hard spell;   1
   And very death will change, and glow
   With life; we will reap the dreams we sow;
And then, from earth or heaven or hell,   1
I never would cry old clothes to sell!   1R*

Rags and Dreams, Clement Wood.

After the texte, rhymed here 1, 1, 1, 1, the stanzaic rhyme-scheme is 2, 3, 2, 2, 3, 1, 3, 3, 1, 1R. Each stanza has only 3 rhyme sounds; but the only rhyming link, from stanza to stanza, is the refrain rhyme-sound. Since the texte may follow any quatrain rhyming (1, 2, 1, 2; 1, 2, 2, 1; 1, 2, 3, 2, etc.), the stanzaic rhyme-scheme may have to be built up differently. The sole stipulation is that the stanza's terminal refrain rhyme-sound appears also in the 6th and 9th lines; with the recommendation that the pattern from stanza to stanza be uniform.

The Glose on a Sonnet: a sonnet, followed by fourteen quatrains, each quatrain being terminated by the lines of the sonnet, used successively. The possibilities of other gloses are endless.

THE TRIOLET-RONDEAU FAMILY

The Triolet

The triolet, originally called a *simple rondeau,* is a poem of eight lines, the first two of which, not couplet rhymed, serve as a refrain. The first line of the refrain reappears as the fourth line of the triolet; while the complete refrain appears again, as the 7th and 8th lines of the rondeau.

I hear your call, To Arms!	1R
That will not let me wrest	2R
My soul from war's alarms.	1
I hear your call too, arms,	1R
And all the manifold charms,	1
Cool lips, and havening breast;	2
I hear your call, two arms,	1R
That will not let me rest!	2R

The Lover Speaks, Colin Westcott.

Note how the spelling of the refrain differs (*to arms; too, arms; two arms;* as well as *wrest, rest*). But the sounds remain identical. Such plays upon words are customary in light formal verse. Never forget that the refrain must aid in the progression of the thought, and come in naturally each time.

The Rondel

The rondel is a poem of fourteen lines, on two rhyme-sounds. The first two lines constitute a refrain, which reappear as the 7th and 8th lines, as well as forming the concluding couplet. The pattern appears from this example:

Kiss me, sweetheart; the Spring is here   1R
  And Love is Lord of you and me.   2R
  The bluebells beckon each passing bee;   2
The wild wood laughs to the flowered year.   1

There is no bird in brake or brere,   1
  But to his little mate sings he,   2
"Kiss me, sweetheart; the Spring is here,   1R
  And Love is Lord of you and me!"   2R

The blue sky laughs out sweet and clear,   1
  The missel-thrush upon the tree   2
  Pipes for sheer gladness loud and free;   2
And I go singing to my dear,   1
"Kiss me, sweetheart; the Spring is here,   1R
  And Love is Lord of you and me."   2R

Rondel, John Payne.

A pattern almost as common appears from:

Through the fresh fairness of the Spring to ride,   1R
  As in the old days when he rode with her,   2R
With joy of Love that had fond Hope to bride,   1
  One year ago had made her pulses stir.   2

Now shall no wish with any day recur   2
(For Love and Death part year and year full wide)   1
Through the fresh fairness of the Spring to ride,   1R
  As in the old days when he rode with her.   2R

No ghost there lingers of the smile that died   1
  On the sweet pale lip where his kisses were—   2
... Yet still she turns her delicate head aside,   1
  If she may hear him come with jingling spur—   2
Through the fresh fairness of the Spring to ride,   1R
  As in the old days when he rode with her.   2R

Ready for the Ride—1795, Henry Cuyler Bunner.

The Thirteen-Line Rondel

This is a rondel omitting one of the final refrain lines, either the
13th or the 14th.

Summer has seen decay   1R
  Of roses white and red,   2R
  And Love with wings outspread   2
Speeds after yesterday.   1

Blue skies have changed to grey, 1
  And love has sorrow wed;   2
Summer has seen decay   1R
  Of roses white and red.   2R

> May's flowers outlast not May;   1
> And when the hour has fled,
> Around the roses dead   2
> The mournful echoes say—   1
> Summer has seen decay.   1R

Rondel, George Moore.

The Rondelet

The rondelet is a seven-line poem, of which the 1st, 3rd and 7th are a 4-syllabled refrain, to which the 4th line rhymes; while this 4th, as well as the 2nd, 5th and 6th lines, all rhyming on a second rhyming sound, are eight syllables each. The pattern appears from this example:

> Say what you please,   1R
> But know, I shall not change my mind!   2
> Say what you please,   1R
> Even, if you wish it, on your knees—   1
> And, when you hear me next defined   2
> As something lighter than the wind,   2
> Say what you please!   1R

Rondelet, May Probyn.

The Chaucerian Roundel

The Chaucerian roundel is a ten-line form of the rondel, following this pattern:

> "Laugh while you may; for laughter will have ending!"   1R
> I heard it chuckled grossly from a low   2
> Valley, whose foul depths I hoped not to know.   2
>
> I swung instead up the high hill, ascending   1
> To greet the sun. But still a faint echo,   2
> "Laugh while you may; for laughter will have ending!"   1R
>
> Then, at the crest, I saw what was past mending,   1
> And climbed down, and lived on. And long ago   2
> I have warned others who strained upward so: 2
> "Laugh while you may; for laughter will have ending."   1R

Terminal, Alan Dubois.

The Rondeau

The rondeau, next to the triolet the most popular of the group, is a fifteen-line poem, of 8- or 10-syllabled lines. It is divided into three stanzas of unequal length, knit together by two rhymed sounds, and a refrain taken out of the first line. The pattern appears from this example:

A man must live. We justify   1
Low shift and trick to treason high,   1
   A little vote for a little gold   2
   To a whole senate bought and sold   2
By that self-evident reply.   1

But is it so? Pray tell me why   1
Life at such cost you have to buy?   1
   In what religion were you taught   2
    A man must live?   **R**

There are times when a man must die.   1
Imagine, for a battle-cry   1
   For soldiers, with a sword to hold,—   2
   For soldiers, with the flag unrolled, 2
This coward's whine, this liar's lie,—   1
    A man must live!   **R**

    A Man Must Live, Charlotte Perkins Gilman.

The Ten-Line Rondeau

This is a rondeau consisting of only ten lines, together with two additional refrain lines, consisting of the opening word of line one. Here is the pattern:

Death, of thy rigor I complain,   1
   Thou hast my lady torn from me,   2
   And yet wilt not contented be,   2
Till from me too all strength be ta'en   1
For languishment of heart and brain.   1
   What harm did she in life to thee,   2
    Death?   **R**

One heart we had between us twain;   1
   Which being dead, I too must dree   2
   Death, or, like carven saints, we see 2
In choir, sans life to live be fain,   1
    Death!   **R**

    Villon's *Rondeau;* translated by John Payne.

The Roundel

The roundel is a poem of eleven lines, two of which are the briefer refrain lines. The refrain consists of the opening word of the first line, or of half or some portion of this line; and, if it consists of more than one word, it is usually rhymed with the second rhyming sound (2), the terminal of the second line. Thus the pattern is either 1, 2, 1, R; 2, 1, 2; 1, 2, 1, R; or 1, 2, 1, 2R; 2, 1, 2; 1, 2, 1, 2R.

Far-fetched and dear bought, as the proverb rehearses,   1
   Is good, or was held so, for ladies; but nought   2
In a song can be good if the turn of the verse is   1
     Far-fetched and dear bought.   2R

As the turn of a wave should it sound, and the thought   2
Ring smooth, and as light as the spray that disperses   1
   By the gleam of the words for the garb thereof wrought.   2

Let the soul in it shine through the sound as it pierces   1
   Men's hearts with possession of music unsought;   2
For the bounties of song are no jealous god's mercies,   1
     Far-fetched and dear bought.   2R

     A Singing Lesson, Algernon Charles Swinburne.

In his *A Century of Roundels*, Swinburne's line-length ranges from four to sixteen syllables, usually metric. Accent verse is more common with most users of the form.

THE BALLADE FAMILY

The Ballade—Eight-Line Stanza

The ballade with eight-line stanza, the most popular form, is a poem of twenty-eight lines, consisting of three stanzas of eight lines each, with an envoy of four lines. Each stanza and the envoy close with a refrain line, identical as to sound, although spelling and meaning may be altered. The strict French rule, that an eight-line stanza requires lines of eight syllables throughout, and a ten-line stanza one of ten syllables, is not enforced, in English. The stanzas should not be broken up into two quatrains, or otherwise; but should carry an unbroken sense throughout. The rhyme scheme must be identical from stanza to stanza; and no identities are allowed anywhere in the poem, except in the repetition of the refrain line. The envoy always takes the rhyme-scheme of the last half of the preceding stanza. The sense of the refrain must be supreme throughout, and it must occur naturally to close each stanza and the envoy. This envoy should be addressed to some patron of the poet, or to some mythical or symbolic personification. The envoy is both a dedication and a climax, and should be richer in wording and more stately in imagery than the earlier stanzas.

An example, which furnishes the pattern, is:

"Shiver, Culture, and Cosmos, crack!   1
   Everything's wrong, from A to Z!   2
Up with Anarchy's dear old black!   1
   We are the Reds! Man *shall* be free.   2

Watch how we'll end the tyranny   2
Of shackles and shekels, and all that prey!"   3
    So they once squeaked . . . . interminably.   2
But where are the Reds of yesterday?   3R

Are they whimpering on the rack,   1
    Victims of ponderous cruelty?   2
Have they been banished to Sarawak   1
    And the bitter beaches of Waikiki?   2
    Men are in jail for bigamy   2
And women weep when it's time to pay,   3
    And federal judges have had to flee;   2
But where are the Reds of yesterday?   3R

One is the mayor of Hackensack,*   1
    Wearing the badge of the G. O. P.;   2
One has established a bivouac   1
    In a simple Park Avenue rectory;   2
    One, with an editorial "We,"   2
Spreads in a fourteen-point display: 3
    "Today's Reds jailed, by court decree;   2
But—where are the Reds of yesterday!"   3R

Envoy Extraordinary

They are scattered from Congress to Muscovy,   2
    And the crimson tinge has bleached away.   3
Hence this one queries conclusively,   2
    "But where are the Reds of yesterday?"   3R

A Ballade of the Dear Old Crimsons, Clement Wood.

Same—Ten-Line Stanza

This is a poem of thirty-five lines, consisting of three stanzas of ten lines each, with an envoy of five lines. The pattern appears from the opening stanza and the envoy of the following ballade—the envoy, as always, taking the rhyme scheme of the last half of the preceding stanza.

Men, brother men, that after us yet live,   1
    Let not your hearts too hard against us be;   2
For if some pity of us poor men ye give,   1
    The sooner God shall take of you pity.   2
    Here we are five or six strung up, you see,   2
And here the flesh that all too well we fed   3
Bit by bit eaten and rotten, rent and shred,   3
    And we the bones grow dust and ash withal;   4
Let no man laugh at us discomforted,   3
    But pray to God that he forgive us all.   4R

*Or, pick your burgh.

After two more stanzas following the same pattern, we have the envoy:

Prince Jesus, that of all art lord and head,   3
Keep us, that hell be not our bitter bed;   3
    We have nought to do in such a master's hall.   4
Be not ye therefore of our fellowhead,   3
    But pray to God that he forgive us all.   4R

The Epitaph in Form of a Ballad (after Villon),
Algernon Charles Swinburne.

The French required ten syllables per line to the 10-line stanza. The English usage varies, especially in Swinburne, where 10-line stanzas range from eight to twenty syllables per line.

Note that the ballade with eight-line stanzas requires 14 rhymes on the *2* sound; while the longer ballade with ten-line stanzas merely requires 9 rhymes on the *2* sound, and 12 rhymes on the *3* sound. It is obvious that the rhyme-check method (see Lesson X, Advanced Versification), by which the opening consonantal sounds of your rhymes are marked down as they are used, is essential for these two forms, as well as for the rondeau redoublé, villanelle, chant royal, etc.

Ballade with Double Refrain

Where the ballade with double refrain is used with the 8-line ballade stanza, the two refrains occur as the fourth and eighth lines of each stanza; and as lines 2 and 4 of the envoy, which is couplet-rhymed. In the 10-line stanza, the refrains occur as the fifth and tenth lines of each stanza, and as the 2nd or 3rd and the 5th lines of the envoy. It is effective to select antithetical refrains, and develop each stanza upon the contrasting refrains which end each half-stanza. The pattern appears in:

The car-signs lift their urgent lay   1
    For Industry's insistent sake: 2
"Buy Today—a Year to Pay!"   1
    "What a Whale of a Difference a Few Cents Make!"   2R
    "The Kind Your Mother Couldn't Bake—"   2
"The Latest Thing in Platinums."   3
    "Cash Registers Make No Mistake!"   2
"Run Your Finger Over Your Gums—'   3R

How can your purse resist them, pray?   1
    Their words would bugle the dead awake: 2
"The Best by Test!" "An Orange a Day—"   1
    "What a Whale of a Difference a Few Cents Make!"   2R

"Eventually, Why Not Now?" "Just Take	**2**
A Box Home." "Tasty, to the Crumbs!"	**3**
"You Get the Girl—We Bake the Cake!"	**2**
"Run Your Finger Over Your Gums—"	**3R**

"Just a Real Good Car." "The Pleasant Way	**1**
To Relieve a Cough." "They Stood the Quake!"	**2**
"Join the Regulars!" "This Paint Will Stay!"	**1**
"What a Whale of a Difference a Few Cents Make!"	**2R**
"The Fibre That Can Never Break—"	**2**
"Just Say It With—Chrysanthemums!"	**3**
"They Fit the Face—" "That Wheaty Flake—"	**2**
"Run Your Finger Over Your Gums—"	**3R**

Attentive Reader, "For Sprain and Ache"	**2**
"What a Whale of a Difference a Few Cents Make!"	**2R**
And through a hundred millenniums	**3**
"Run Your Finger Over Your Gums."	**3R**

"Four Out of Every Five," Alvin Winston.

The Double Ballade

The double ballade is a ballade of six stanzas, either of the eight-line or the ten-line pattern, and with the envoy omitted. Each stanza is rhymed as in the models already given; that is, either six stanzas of 1, 2, 1, 2, 2, *3*, 2, 3R; or six stanzas of 1, 2, 1, 2, 2, 3, 3, 4, 3, 4R. The former requires 24 separate rhymes on the *2* sound; the latter, 18 rhymes each on the *3* sound and the *4* sound.

W. E. Henley always used an envoy with his double ballades. Here is the opening stanza, and the envoy, of his *Double Ballade of Life and Fate:*

Fools may pine, and sots may swill,	**1**
Cynics jibe and prophets rail,	**2**
Moralists may scourge and drill,	**1**
Preachers prose, and faint hearts quail.	**2**
Let them whine, or threat, or wail!	**2**
'Tis the touch of Circumstance	**3**
Down to darkness sinks the scale—	**2**
Fate's a fiddler, Life's a dance.	**3R**

After five more similar stanzas,

Boys and girls, at slug and snail	**2**
And their compeers look askance.	**3**
Pay your footing on the nail:	**2**
Fate's a fiddler, Life's a dance.	**3R**

This double ballade required 12 rhymes on the *1* sound; 8, including the refrain rhyme, on the *3* sound; and a full 26 on the *2* sound. This calls for deft and accurate mastery of versification. As usual in Henley's work, this example is flawless throughout. Others of his double ballades are even more intricate. Thus his *Double Ballade of the Nothingness of Things* has 11 lines to each of its six stanzas, rhymed 1, 2, 1, 2, 2, 3, 3, 4, 5, 4, 5R; with an envoy rhymed 3, 3, 5, 4, 4, 5R (a variation from the requirement that the envoy must repeat the rhyme-scheme of the last half of the preceding stanza; but there is no full-line half to an 11-line stanza). Henley's *Ballade of Truisms* has only three stanzas; but each has 12 trochaic lines to the stanza, with the last unaccented syllable omitted. Each stanza has this metric pattern: 4, 2, 4 trochaic feet, repeated four times. The rhyming pattern is 1, 1, 2, 1, 1, 2, 2, 2, 1, 2, 2, 1R. The envoy repeats the pattern of the last half of the preceding stanza: 2, 2, 1, 2, 2, 1R:

Time the pedagogue his cane	2
Might retain,	2
But his charges all would stray	1
Truanting in every lane—	2
Jack with Jane!	2
If it could be always May.	1R

Thus even these rigid patterns crack and are reshaped successfully, in the hands of a master.

The Chant Royal

The chant royal is a poem similar to the ballade, with five stanzas of eleven lines each, and an envoy of five lines. It is written throughout on the five rhyming sounds used in the first stanza, which becomes the pattern for the rest. The envoy's pattern is that of the last five lines of the last preceding stanza. The pattern appears from this example:

The world is wide, and full of hopeful folk	1
Of varied races and of variant hue:	2
Suave Mongols, skinned as yellow as a yolk;	1 2
The copper worshippers of Manitou;	2
Negroes jet-cuticled, Malayans brown,	3
And the pink-whites, who keep the others down.	3
There is a sixth race, take it now from me,	4
The offspring of ouranial Poesie,	4
Quartered upon this too terrestrial ball;	5
As one of them, I warble lustily:	4
"Hail to the race of poets. one and all!"	5R

Leading the singers, let me first evoke
   The epickers. Homer, when bards were few,
Gurgled of bloody gore and battle-stroke;
   Virgil let Dido have her rendezvous
With cold Aeneas, near her Carthage town;
Milton had Lucifer achieve renown
   By settling Hell; Dante spoke his decree
   Of torrid fates for knave and debauchee;
And several others whom I can't recall
   Spun epics with enormous energy.
Hail to the race of poets, one and all!

And now the Muse of Tragedy awoke,
   With lordly Shakespeare captaining the crew,
And many a Grecian, towering like an oak,
   And Ibsen and the Problems of the New.
But man grew weary of the endless frown;
So gayer singers donned the rhyming gown,
   Bards who extolled a race, a fight, a spree;
   Poets who whispered love's hot-blooded plea,
Or gently sang sunrise and evenfall,
   Charming us with their sylvan melody;
Hail to the race of poets, one and all!

Gayer they grew—bards who could spoof and joke,
   And give the glooms a swift and sharp adieu,—
Yet who often carried, underneath the cloak,
   A whetted knife, to right things gone askew;
Bards who, if need arose, could act the clown,
Till, laughter-flooded, all man's sorrows drown:
   Keen Gilbert, Carroll's whimsicality,
   Ombliferous Lear, and many another he
Whose quick wits gallop while our snail ones crawl,—
   Who dealt in joy and merriment and glee—
Hail to the race of poets, one and all!

If I stopped here, I would that I might choke!
   For more Parnassians waddle into view;
And if I closed this list before I spoke
   Their name and fame, I should become taboo.
The cross-roads poets—let them go resoun-
Ding down through time: they earn the teazle crown—
   James Byron Elmore, Mary Ann O'B.,
   Who lifts in Watervliet her measures free;
All ruralites the Muses hold in thrall—
   Come join us in our lyric revelry—
Hail to the race of poets, one and all!

Envoy

Apollo, there are two of this company	4
Saved for the sniffers—namely, me and thee!	4
Hail then the Great, we who have hailed the Small.	5
Were ever such fair-minded bards as we?	4
Hail to the race of poets, one and all!	5R

Hail to the Bards, **Alan Dubois.**

There is a briefer form, with ten lines to each stanza, and six lines in the envoy. In this, the stanzaic rhyme-scheme is 1, 2, 1, 2, 2, 3, 3, 4, 3, 4R, with an envoy of 3, 3, 4, 3, 3, 4R.

THE SESTINA

The sestina is an unrhymed poem, consisting of six stanzas of six lines each of blank verse, followed by a tornado or envoy of three lines. Instead of rhyme, that late alien importation, the versification device is simple word-repetition. The six terminal words of the first stanza must also be the terminal words of the other five stanzas, and also the middle and terminal words of the envoy, in the following order—the numbers referring, not to rhyme-sounds, but to the positions of these six terminal words in stanza I: 1, 2, 3, 4, 5, 6; 6, 1, 5, 2, 4, 3; 3, 6, 4, 1, 2, 5; 5, 3, 2, 6, 1, 4; 4, 5, 1, 3, 6, 2; 2, 4, 6, 5, 3, 1; tornado, 2, 5; 4, 3; 6, 1. There has been no explanation of this original Provençal arrangement, except that there is an obvious symmetry in stanzas 1 and 6, and that each successive stanza begins with the terminal word of the preceding stanza. The numbers below refer, not to rhymes, but to terminal words, numbered from their order in stanza one. An example is:

When man first roamed upon this teeming earth,	1
He hid from red-fanged killers and their greed.	2
But as he learned the lore of a life for a life,	3
He tracked the helpless grazers to the death.	4
He was a child of jealous fear and hate,	5
Himself the only god he knew to love.	6
At length, moved by a more astute self-love,	6
He enslaved the furred and feathered ones of earth.	1
Only against the raiding hunters did hate	5
Move him to kill; until a slow-born greed	2
Led him to grow gross in wealth, though this meant death	4
To those who were less fortunate in life.	3
To ease the travail of this herding life,	3
He enslaved the plants. It was no sort of love	6
That drove him to this, but a dread of death.	4

The leisure that this bred on the lush earth   1
Taught him to enslave his fellows in his greed,   2
And lash and crucify them in his black hate.   5

There came a song that had no room for hate;   5
That said, I am the Way; I am the Life;   3
That lashed out of the temple the sons of Greed,   2
And whispered, "And the greatest of these is Love."   6
Yet while it spoke of a new heaven and a new earth,   1
Its song became a velvet croon of death.   4

Out of the ages dark as the spirit's death,   4
There grew a softer mood, remote from hate.   5
Romance and chivalry woke over the earth,   1
And art and beauty grew to statelier life.   3
The lords of ieisure rutted in pandering love,   6
As they held down their serfs in gross fat greed.   2

The machine woke in man a more terrible greed,   2
That bound the many to a fate bleaker than death: 4
Cogs in a vaster machine. No room for love,   6
Profit as god, with sudden hurricanes of hate   5
As dictators, like maggots, came to life,   3
And world war trod bloodily over the earth.   1

Men, let us end foul greed and shrivelling hate,   2, 5
And as red death yields to new freeborn life,   4, 3
Brotherly love will conquer the shining earth!   6, 1

The Upward Climb, J. K. Eden.

In writing a sestina, it is of course important to end your first
stanza with six strong words, to justify the constant repetition. Having
ended the first stanza, write down the number-scheme for all six stanzas and the tornado, as above. Next, fill in the six terminal words, in
their numbered places. Then proceed to write.

The essence of the sestina is that it alone, of the major forms, is
unrhymed. Versifiers who preferred rhyme proceeded to apply it to
the sestina. It became clear at once that, if the order of terminal
words given above was followed, there would be couplet rhyming every
so often. Swinburne avoided this ingeniously, in his sestina "I saw my
soul at rest upon a day," by using two rhyme sounds. The pattern
sounds simple:

> I saw my soul at rest upon a day
>   As a bird sleeping in the nest of night,
> Among soft leaves that gave the starlight way
>   To touch its wings but not its eyes with light;
> So that it knew as one in visions may,
>   And knew not as men waking, of delight.

The rhyming pattern here is simple: 1, 2, 1, 2, 1, 2. Swinburne alternates this, for the six stanzas, with 2, 1, 2, 1, 2, 1, used in the even-numbered stanzas, the second, fourth and sixth, while the pattern shown above is used in the first, third and fifth. The tornado is:

> Song, have thy day and take thy fill of light
> Before the night be fallen across thy way;
> Sing while he may, man hath no long delight—

the rhyme scheme here being 2, 1, 2; with the internal rhymes (day, night, may) being of course the reverse of this, 1, 2, 1. To achieve this simple rhyme scheme, which prohibits couplet rhyming, Swinburne arranged the six terminal words in stanza one as follows, throughout the entire sestina:

> 1, 2, 3, 4, 5, 6; 6, 1, 4, 3, 2, 5; 6, 5, 1, 4, 3, 2; 2, 5, 6, 1, 4, 3;
>   3, 2, 1, 6, 5, 4; 4, 3, 2, 6, 5, 1; envoy, 1, 4; 2, 3; 5, 6.

This pattern was imitated by several other poets. In his *Rizzio's Love-Song*, Swinburne used three rhymes, rhyming the first stanza 1, 2, 1, 3, 2, 3, and repeated this rhyme-scheme for his fourth stanza; for stanzas two and five, he used, 3, 1, 2, 3, 1, 2; for stanzas three and six, 2, 3, 2, 1, 3, 1; while the tornado is:

> Clothed as with power of pinions, O my heart,
> Fly like a dove, and seek one sovereign flower,
> Whose thrall thou art, and sing for love of love.

Here the end-rhyme scheme is 2, 3, 1; the internal rhyme scheme (power, dove, art) 3, 1, 2. To apply this rhyme-scheme, his terminal words came in the following order:

> 1, 2, 3, 4, 5, 6; 6, 1, 5, 4, 3, 2; 2, 6, 5, 1, 4, 3; 3, 2, 1, 6, 5, 4;
>   4, 3, 2, 1, 6, 5; 5, 4, 2, 3, 6, 1; envoy, 6, 2; 3, 4; 5, 1.

Swinburne wrote even a double sestina, 150 lines long altogether, writing his twelve terminal words 1, 2, 3, 1, 2, 4, 3, 5, 6, 5, 4, 6 in the first stanza, and thereafter proceeding with constant deftness. An analysis of it would be lengthier than the overlong poem.

THE MECHANICS OF RHYME

Rhyme Defined

In Lesson XI of The Foundations of Versification Course (the first half of Versification Self-Taught, at the end of this book), we have defined rhyme thus:

Rhyme is the repetition of an identical accented vowel sound, as well as of all the consonantal and vowel sounds following; with a difference in the consonantal sounds immediately preceding this accented vowel sound.

Rhyme is thus a matter of sound only; spelling is immaterial.

The accented vowel sound referred to is usually the last vowel sound receiving a major accent:

> *a*ce, f*a*ce; sp*o*ken, br*o*ken; w*ea*rily, dr*ea*rily.

It may, instead, be merely a minor accent, as in these two pairs of contiguous rhymes from Shakespeare's Sonnet cxxv:

> canop*y*, honour*ing*, eternit*y*, ruin*ing*.

It may be a major accent before the last one, in which case the last major accent is repeated without change. Examples are:

> we*á*ry s*ó*ng, ch*é*ery s*ó*ng; z*é*alous h*é*, j*é*alousy;
> b*ú*rn it, y*ó*u're, f*ú*rniture; l*ó*t o' n*é*ws, hyp*ó*tenuse;
> y*é*arning to h*ó*ld you f*á*st, b*ú*rning to h*ó*ld you f*á*st.

In every instance, the accented vowel which is the basis of the rhyme must rank, in end rhyme, as the chief accent in the last foot of your line —all subsequent sounds, no matter how many, being mere appendages to this last foot. Thus in sonnet meter, which requires five feet, the line "While Time's dull candle, slowly guttering," would be correct, if rhymed with *wing:*

> While Time's | dull can- | dle, slow- | ly gut- | te*ring*,

with the rhyme in the line consisting only of -*ring*. But if it were to be rhymed with *muttering*, it would be a defective line, containing only four feet:

> While Time's | dull can- | dle, slow- | ly *gutt*ering.

61

A foot would have to be inserted before the final word, to make this line complete, in triple rhyme.

The Two Elements of Rhyme

Rhyme thus has two elements:

(1) the identity of the accented vowel found in the two or more words, and of all subsequent sounds; and
(2) the preceding consonantal difference.

For the first time in the history of versification, we have here, in THE UNABRIDGED RHYMING DICTIONARY, a book which differentiates rhymes according to both of these elements.

(1) The identical rhyming sounds, constituting one-, two-, and three-syllabled rhymes, are collected under the phonetic symbol for each rhyme-sound.
(2) In each collection of rhyme-sounds, all of the words are grouped according to the differing consonantal opening sounds.

Naturally, any word rhymes *only* with the various words collected under the phonetic symbol of its rhyme-sound (barring those in its own group, which are prohibited, since they are identities, not rhymes), and not with any word in any other rhyme-sound. To rhyme accurately, only one rule is necessary, in using this rhyming dictionary:

In any given rhyme-sound, choose and use only one word from each group.

The groups referred to, of course, are the rhyming identities headed by the opening consonantal sounds.

The Accented Vowel Sounds

We have said that rhyme is a matter of sound only. Examples of certain of the variant spellings of the sounds included are found in the following lists.

In this phonetic arrangement, the accented vowel sounds are distinguished as follows:

A

ā as in fāte; also in lāid, gāol (jāl), gāuge (gāj); grĕat, ĕh, vĕil, prĕy.
ä as in fär, fä'ther; also in heärt, ser'geant (sär'), mem'oir ('wär).
à as in fàst, dànce.
ã as in cãre; also in ãir, prãyer (prãr), beãr, e'er (ãr), heir (ãr), where (hwãr).
a as in at; also in plaid (plad), bade (bad). In rhyming, the ă heard in tol'er-ănt is similar.

E

ē as in ēve; also in feed, sēam, bē-liēve′, rē-cēive′, pēo′ple, kēy, e-līte′ (-lēt′), Caē′sar (sē′), quay (kē), phoe′bē (fē′); also in mēre, drēar, wēird.

e as in ebb; also in hei′fer (he′fer), leo′pard (le′pard), friend (frend), Aet′na (et′), feath′er (feTH′), as-a-foet′i-da (-fet′), bur′y (ber′i), an′y (en′i), Thames (temz), said (sed), says (sez).

I

ī as in fīne; also in aīsle (īl), aȳe (ī) (meaning *yes*), heīght (hīt), eȳe (ī), līe, choīr (kwīr), buȳ (bī), bȳ, rȳe.

i as in it; also in pret′ty (prit′), breech′es (britch′ez), sieve (siv), wom′en (wim′), guild (gild), bur′y (ber′i), lack′ey (lak′i), lymph (limf).

O

ō as in bōld; also in tōne, ōh, fōam, tōe, bōul′der, glōw, ōwe, sew (sō), yeō′man (yō′), beau (bō), haut′boy (hō′), brōoch.

ǫ as in nǫr; also in bǫught (bǫt), brǫad, mem′ǫir (′wǫr), hạll, bạlk, wạrm, hạul, tạught, clạw.

o as in hot; also in wänt (wont), squäsh (skwosh), shone (shon).

oi as in boil; also in joy.

oo as in book; also in pụt, wolf (woolf), should (shood).

ou as in shout; also in brow, sauer′kraut (sour′krout).

U

ū as in mūse; also in beaū′ty, feūd, crew (krū), queūe (kū), lieū, re-view′ (-vū′), blūe, dūe, sūit, yoū; also in dö, mọọd, groụp, frụit, rheụm, ma-neụ′vre. The difference between such words as **dew** and **do** is that **dew** includes a consonantal y: **dyu,** while **do** is pronounced **dü**.

ụ̄ as in tūrn; also in fērn, ērr, hēard, sĭr, wŏrd, joūr′nal, myrrh (mūr), colo′nel (kēr′nl).

u as in cup; also in wŏn, dŏne, dŏes (duz), flood (flud), troub′le (trub′l).

The Consonantal Openings

This book has grouped together all the words with each different consonantal opening, for each one-, two-, or three-syllabled rhyme-sound in the language. The more usual of these are:

1. The vowel, not preceded by any consonantal sound. This includes any of the nineteen accented vowel sounds already listed.

Warning: be careful not to list as a vowel opening a consonant pronounced but not spelled: as, the *y* in *use* (yuz); the *w* in *one* (won).

Warning: be careful to include words opening with a silent consonant, one spelled but not pronounced: as, the *h* in *honor* (on'or).

2. **b,** as in bat.

3. **bl,** as in blow.

4. **br,** as in bright.

5. **ch,** as in church; heard also in catch, un-right'eous (-rī'chus), sug-ges'tion (-jes'chun).

Warning: *ch* is often pronounced *k*, as in Christian.

6. **d,** as in date.

Warning: in past tenses and other inflections, *d* after *ch, s, f, k,* and *p* is pronounced *t*.

7. **dr,** as in drag.

8. **dw,** as in Dwight.

9. **f,** as in foe; also in phan'tom (fan'), laugh (läf).

10. **fl,** as in flight; also in phlegm (flem).

11. **fr,** as in frog; also in phre-nol'o-gy (fre-).

12. **g,** as in go; also in guest, rogue, ghast'ly (gȧst').

Warning: *g* is often pronounced *j*, as in *gin.*

13. **gl,** as in glow.

14. **gr,** as in grow.

15. **gw,** as in Gwin.

16. **h,** as in hoe; also in whole (hōl).

17. **hw,** as in what.

18. **j,** as in jump; also in gem (jem), re-li'gion ('jun), pig'eon (pij'un), sol'dier ('jēr), dodge (doj).

19. **k,** as in keep; also in cat, cho'rus, rock, con'quer (kon'kēr), pique (pēk).

20. **kl,** as in Klon'dike; also in clean.

21. **kr,** as in Kris Krin'gle; also in cream.

22. **kw,** as in kwe'bird; also in queen.

23. **l,** as in late.

24. **m,** as in moon.

25. **n,** as in noon.

26. **p,** as in pat.

27. **pl,** as in ply.

28. **pr,** as in pray.

29. **r,** as in rose; also in rho-do-den'dron.

30. **s,** in son; also in race, scene, pass.

31. **sh,** as in shop.

32. **shr,** as in shriek.

33. **sk,** as in skoal; also in scalp, scheme.

34. **skr,** as in skrike; also in scream.

35. **skw,** as in square.
36. **sl,** as in slight (slīt).
37. **sm,** as in smite.
38. **sn,** as in sneer.
39. **sp,** as in spell.
40. **spl,** as in splint.
41. **spr,** as in spring.
42. **st,** as in stop.
43. **str,** as in strap.
44. **sv,** as in Sven-ga'li.
45. **sw,** as in swap.
46. **t,** as in top; also in walked.
47. **th,** as in thin.
48. **TH,** as in this.
49. **thr,** as in through.
50. **tr,** as in trap.
51. **tw,** as in twin.
52. **v,** as in vine.
53. **vl,** as in Vlach.
54. **w,** as in way; also in one.
55. **y,** as in yacht; also heard in use, muse.
56. **z,** as in zipper.
57. **zh,** as in azure, rouge.

Note that the letter *c* has no sound of its own, but appears under *k* or *s;* that *q*, rare in English, is pronounced *k*, and *qu*, far commoner, appears under *kw*. The letter *x* has no sound of its own; initially, it is *z;* otherwise, usually *gs* or *ks*. In words like *think*, *nk* is pronounced *ngk*. In plurals and other inflections, the *s* sound follows *f, k, p*, and *t;* the *z* sound, *b, chd, g, j, l, ks* (x), *m, n, r, s, v, z* and the unconsonanted vowel. The *ng* sound, not heard initially in English, is found also in *tongue, ink, sanction, linger, canker*.

Since rhyme is exclusively a matter of sound, identical spellings need not rhyme:

> plough, through, enough, dough, trough.

As we have seen above, differing spellings may rhyme perfectly:

> mate, freight, great, fete, straight, etc.

The Marks Used in This Dictionary

In order to conserve space, pronunciation in this dictionary is indicated directly on the word by a system of symbols, or diacritical marks. Thus, the symbol **c̟** is used to indicate the sound of the hard **c** in **cat,** and the word is entered in the vocabulary as **c̟at.** The Key

to Pronunciation on page 73 gives a complete description of the
symbols used, and the sounds they represent. The modified sounds are
unmarked, as the **e** in **cent,** the **a** in **apply,** the **i** in **pin,** the **u** in
tub, the **o** in **on,** and the **y** in **myth.**

When two vowels stand together, only the one which indicates the
sound of the word is marked, as in **strēak, brāin, mōat.**

In a few instances it is impossible to indicate the pronunciation of
a word on the word itself; in such cases the word, or part of it, is
respelled in parentheses immediately following the entry. The word
is respelled phonetically, that is, according to its sound, regardless of
the letters that compose it. Examples of respelling are **ę̄ight** (āt);
guīde (gīd); **heir** (ãr); and **här′le‑quin** (-kin *or* -kwin).

The accents are indicated thus: primary ′, secondary ″.

Hyphenation is indicated by the double hyphen ⹀.

Need for Differentiation by Consonantal Openings

We have learned that the ballade and other strict French forms forbid identities—the repetition of the same opening consonantal sound
in a rhyme. Identity, instead of rhyme, is as much of a blemish in all
rhymed poetry and verse. By selecting only one word from each group
in this rhyming dictionary, the use of identities instead of rhyme becomes impossible.

In his ballade, *On a Fan That Belonged to the Marquise de Pompadour,* Austin Dobson, usually a careful technician, makes these three
couplings:

> light, polite; through, overthrew; queue, cue.

All three are identities, and not rhymes; the otherwise exquisite ballade is thus triply defective. The use of such a volume as this rhyming
dictionary would have prevented the errors. The versifier is often
deceived by long lists of apparent rhymes in other rhyming dictionaries, and chooses from them blithely, unaware that he is using identities, and not rhymes. Thus, of the eighty-three words listed under
oj′i-kal, only one pair of rhymes is possible; for two have the *g* sound
(demagogical, synagogical); and the other eighty-one are all variations
on *logical,* each with the *l* sound. All the six words grouped under
u′di-nal (longitudinal, etc.), all nine under un′dan, all sixteen under
or′fizm, are identities; there are no rhymes (except mosaic ones) for
longitudinal, mundane, or *anthropomorphism.* Only such a rhyming
dictionary as this will permit the poet and versifier to steer safely
through the maze of identities.

The division into syllables, with hyphens, as given in most dictionaries, furnishes no safe guide. Hyphenization is for a printer's con-

venience; not for accurate pronunciation. If you followed usual hyphenization, you would list *exonerate, exaggerate, exasperate*, etc., under the *-ate* sounds, that is, the unconsonanted vowel. These are, however, all pronounced with the last syllable *-rate*. The same applies to the last syllable of such words as *fortunate, exorbitant, animate*, the syllable before the last in *exaggeration*, and so on.

In this volume, the words are grouped strictly according to pronunciation, not according to ordinary syllabification.

Composite or Mosaic Rhymes

Rhyme may involve more than two or more single words. We have accurate rhyme in these pairs:

> heel, feel
> satin, matin
> happily, snappily

We have rhymes as accurate in:

> he'll, she'll
> sat in, that inn; wholesale, soul sail
> end of it, blend of it; heartbroken, part broken;
> finding her, blinding her; Pocono, smoke? O, no.

When using these mosaic or composite rhymes, be sure to have the accents correspond. At times, this may require the use of italics, to indicate where you wish the accent to fall.

This book for the first time includes types of mosaic rhymes for all the rhyme-sounds which have these. In using mosaic rhymes, make sure that the opening consonantal sounds are different; otherwise you have no rhyme, but only identity. Thus *satin* rhymes with *that inn;* but not with its identity, *sat in.*

Mosaic rhymes may be used, often effectively, in light verse, by using merely parts of words, instead of complete ones. Examples are:

> Peers shall teem in Christendom,
> And a duke's exalted station
> Be attainable by com-
> Petitive examination.
> Finale to Act I, *Iolanthe*, W. S. Gilbert.

> Who would not give all else for two p-
> Enny worth of beautiful soup?
> *Soup of the Evening*, from *Alice in Wonderland*, Lewis Carroll.

Sun, moon, and thou vain world, adieu,
    That kings and priests are plotting in;
Here doomed to starve on water gru-
El, never shall I see the U-
    Niversity of Gottingen,
    Niversity of Gottingen.
                    Song of Rogero, George Canning.

Vodvil houses flame intrigue a-
Bove the glittering of Vega. . . .

By '45, Canton and Kalamazoo,
Boise City and Baton Rou-
Ge, Indianapolis, clear to the coast
Will lift the ululated boast. . . .

Flee Scylla's pains, and then *ad lib* dis-
Card your fear, and wed Charybdis.
            The Greenwich Village Blues, Clement Wood.

        Mama throw a nickel,
        And the man will pick a l-
            Ittle tune you love.
        The Man with the Mandolin (Popular song.)

            Sang out with gusto,
            And just o-
                Verlorded the place.
            Johnny One Note, Lorenz Hart.

The countless mosaic rhymes involving split words are not included
in this volume. They can easily be created, following these examples.
Both types of mosaic rhymes are valuable, to increase the limited
rhyming facilities of the language.

Finding Consonance in a Rhyming Dictionary

Another device for increasing the rhyming facilities of the language
is consonance (also called sour rhyme, off rhyme, and analyzed rhyme),
explained in detail in Lesson VII of Advanced Versification, at the end
of this book. It is defined:

Consonance is the repetition of all the consonantal and vowel sounds
following an accented vowel sound in a word, with a difference in the
accented vowel sound preceding the repeated sound elements.

There are thus eighteen possible groups of words in consonance with
any given word: the eighteen other vowel sounds, followed by the
identical subsequent sounds. As the lesson referred to indicates, the

method is of necessity slower than locating rhymes; yet the result often justifies the effort.

Thus, for words in consonance with *feel*, we would look up these sounds:

al, āl, äl, a̤l, a̍l; el, ēl; il, īl; ōl, ol, o̤l, oil, o̤o̤l, oul; ul, ūl, ūl.

For accurate consonance, three of these must be eliminated—äl, ēl, ūl, because they appear only with an *r* before them: ärl, ērl, ūrl. Yet these are often coupled successfully with a word lacking the *r*. We might then have:

fāil, Sal, mo-rȧle', fell, vīle, will, sōul,
doll, bawl, toil, fṳll, foul, rȕle, dull; as well as snärl, and cūrl—

there being no ērl word. Note that several of these have the same opening consonantal sound: fāil, fell, foul. This is permissible, in consonance; since the difference is in the accented vowel sounds, hence the preceding consonants may be identical. Thus all of these are in consonance:

feel, fāil, fell, fīle, fill, fōal, fa̤ll, foil, foul, fo̤o̤l, fṳll, and fūrl.

Similarly, seeking two-syllabled words in consonance with *winter*, we might select:

painter, scanter, enchanter, dissenter, saunter,
anointer, counter, hunter.

The same process may be applied to three-syllabled rhymes.

Additional Rhymes

To avoid needless duplication of lists, possessives, plurals and other accurate rhymes are often grouped together by a *Plus*, followed by a typical example, at the end of a list. Thus, after the list under ĀTZ, we might have:

Plus Kate's, etc.
Plus ĀT+s.

To include words so close to a ryhme that they may be so used, the additional word or group of words is introduced by a *Cf.* (the Latin *confer*, meaning "compare"). Thus, after the list under OUR, we might find:

Cf. OU'ūr.

Similarly, after the list under ŌN'ŭr, we might find:

Cf. donor.

Archaic Words

Since this rhyming dictionary is relatively complete, it is necessary that it include archaic words and word forms: *welkin, abhorreth, dost,* etc. As a continuing warning against using these, except in period verse calling for them, each of these words is marked with an asterisk (*).

Opening u Sounds

The presence of an initial *y* sound before many long *u* syllables adds certain rhymes expressed phonetically in this volume, although the words are still grouped together. Just as you learn to differentiate between *ūse* (yūz) and *ooze* (u̇z), which are perfect rhymes, there are many other examples in the *u* sections where words grouped together form perfect rhymes. Examples are:

> tūne, spit-to͏̤on'
> bo͏̤o'ty, beaū'ty
> dö'a-ble, re-view'a-ble (-vū')

By careful examination of the long *u* rhymes, you can often locate perfect rhymes even in the same groups. This is the one outstanding exception to the general rule for the use of this book, that one should select and use only one word out of each group.

Summary

WOOD'S UNABRIDGED RHYMING DICTIONARY is the most complete and modern rhyming dictionary ever written.

It is strictly phonetic, and thus satisfies the first half—the repetition half—of the definition of rhyme.

For the first time it eliminates the danger of using identity instead of rhyme, by grouping the words in each rhyme sound under the appropriate consonantal opening.

For the first time it includes all types of mosaic rhymes, based upon rhymes constructed of two or more words.

For the first time it gives the correct pronunciation of every syllable of every rhyming word included, to that extent eliminating the necessity for an ordinary dictionary.

Barring the use of the type mosaic rhymes included so frequently, and the additional long *u* rhymes in certain groups, it has simplified the rules for accurate rhyming to one simple rule:

How to Use This Rhyming Dictionary

Choose and use only one word from each group. By following that, your rhyming will be flawless.

DICTIONARY OF RHYMES

KEY TO PRONUNCIATION

ā....as in fāte, āle, ā'corn, be-rāte', nat"u-ral-i-zā'tion.
ä.... " " fär, fä'ther, ärch, mär'shal, cär-toon'; also as in whät, wänt.
ȧ.... " " fȧst, glȧss, a-lȧs'; also as in so'dȧ, ȧ-dapt'ȧ-ble.
a̤.... " " fa̤ll, pa̤w, a̤w'ful, ap-pla̤ud'.
ă.... " " fĭ'năl, sea'măn, tŏl'er-ănt, men'ăce.
ã.... " " cãre, ãir, mil'ĭ-tãr-y, de-clãre'.
a.... " " at, ac-claim', com-par'ĭ-son, car'ry.

ē.... " " ēve, mēte, hē, Ē'den, in-ter-vēne'; also as in hēre, drēar'y.
e̠.... " " pre̠y, e̠ight, o-be̠y'.
ê.... " " hêr, vêrse, sêr'vice, in-têr'.
e.... " " met, ebb, en-dorse', mon'e-tar-y, dis-tend'.
ee.... " " feed, pro-ceed', lee'way.

ī.... " " pīne, ī-de'a, īce'berg, de-cīde', al-lī'ance.
ï.... " " clïque, ma-rïne', La-lïque'; also as in Mar-tï'ni.
ĩ.... " " bĩrd, stĩr, ex'tĩr-pate, fĩrm'a-ment.
i.... " " it, hit, re-mit', cit'y; also as in pos'si-ble, grav'ĭ-ty, pu'pil.

ō.... " " nōte, ōat, sō, ō'pen, hel-lō'; also as in ren'ō-vate, prō-pel'.
ö.... " " möve, pröve, tömb.
o̠.... " " lo̠ng, cro̠ss, o̠ff, o̠rb, fo̠r-bid', do̠r'mer.
ŏ.... " " at'ŏm, plŏv'er; also as in ac'tŏr, wŏrd, wŏrk; also as in but'tŏn.
o.... " " not, for'est, non'sense; also as in dog, broth, cost; also as in con-fess', con-cur'.
o̤o̤.... " " mo̤o̤n, co̤o̤, fo̤o̤d, bro̤o̤d'er.
oo.... " " book, hood, foot, look, cook'y.

ū.... " " ūse, fūse, ū-til'ĭ-ty, fū'tile, im-mūne'; also as in fu'tūre, | pic'tūre.
u̠.... " " bu̠ll, pu̠t, fu̠l-fil', boun'ti-fu̠l.
u̇.... " " brüte, jü'ry; also used for the German ü.
ū.... " " tūrn, fūr, būr-lesque', de-mūr'
u.... " " up, rub, sun'set, in-sult'.

73

ȳ.... " " crȳ, eȳe.
y.... " " myth, cit'y.

c̟.... " " c̟at, to-bac̟'c̟o.
c̟.... " " ma-c̟hine'.
c.... " " ace, ce'dar.

ch.... " " church.
c̱h.... " " c̱hord, loc̱h.

ġ.... " " ġem.

n̄.... " " an̄'ger, sphin̄x.
ṅ.... " " boṅ [Fr.].
ng.... " " ring.
ṣ.... " " mi'ṣer, aṣ.

TH.... " " THis.
th.... " " thin.
z̟.... " " as in az̟ure.

au.... " " umlaut.
aw.... " " straw.

ou.... " " out.
oi.... " " oil.
oy.... " " boy.

ew.... " " new.

ow.... " " now.

-ṣion..as -zhun (in vision).

-ġeous...as -jus (in courageous, advantageous).

-tiăl...⎫
       ⎬as -shul (in confidential, impartial, artificial, special).
-ciăl...⎭

-tion..⎫
     ⎬as -shun (in nation, tension).
-sion..⎭

-tiăn .. ⎱
-siăn .. ⎰ as -shun (in Martian, Melanesian).

-liŏn .... as -lyun *or* -yun (in million).

-ceous .. ⎫
-(s)cious ⎬ as -shus (in cretaceous, deliciously, conscious, contentious,
-tious ... ⎭   propitious).

-ous ..... as -us (in porous).

ph- ...... as f- (in phone, etc.).

-le .... as -l (at end of syllable, as in able, cycle, etc.).

-iă .... as -yà (in pharmacopœia).

wh- ..... as hw- in whale, etc.

(Choose only one word out of each group)

SINGLE RHYMES (MASCULINE RHYMES)

(Monosyllables and Words Accented on the Last Syllable)

A

Words including the following accented vowel sounds:

ā as in fāte; also in lāid, gāol (jāl), gāuge (gāj); grĕat, ĕh, vĕil, prĕy.

ä as in fär, fä'ther; also in heärt, ser'geant (sär'), mem'oir ('wär).

ȧ as in fȧst, dȧnce.

ã as in cãre; also in ãir, prãyer (prãr), beãr, e'er (ãr), heir (ãr), where (hwãr).

a as in at; also in plaid (plad), bade. In rhyming, the ă heard in tol'er-ănt is similar.

For the vowel sound ạ heard in fạll, pạw, tạlk (tạk), swạrm, hạul, and cạught, see under ọ.

For the vowel sound ä heard in wänt and wäsh, see under o.

Ā

Vowel: āye, cöu-tu̧'ri-ȩr ('ri-ā), ȩh, hab-it"ū-ȩ', rō-tu̧'ri-ȩr (-ri-ā').

b: bāy, bȩy, Bom-bāy', dap'ple bāy, dis-ō-bȩy', ō-bȩy'.

br: brāe, brāy.

d: ȧ-lack'ȧ-dāy'*, As-cen'sion-dāy ('shun-), bĭrth'dāy, Christ'măs-dāy (kris'), dāy, dȩy, dọọms'dāy, Ēas'tẽr-dāy, fĭrst'dāy, hā'lȧ-dāy, good⸗dāy', hȩy'dāy, hĭgh'⸗dāy*, hol'i-dāy, judġ'ment-dāy, lack'ȧ-dāy, Lā'dy-dāy, Lọrd's'⸗dāy, mär'ket-dāy, mid'dāy, noọn'dāy, Ŏ'-Dāy', pāy'dāy, plāy'dāy, quȧr'tẽr-dāy, Sat'ūr-dāy, sett'ling-dāy, sev'enth-dāy, tö-dāy', tryst'ing-dāy, wed'ding-dāy, week'dāy, well'ȧ-dāy,

wŏrk'ȧ-dāy, wŏrk'ing-dāy, yes'tẽr-dāy.

dr: drāy.

f: au fāit' (ō fā'), au"tō⸗dȧ⸗fȩ', cọr-y-phȩe' (-fā'), fāy, fȩy, San'tȧ Fȩ'.

fl: flāy, söu-fflȩ'.

fr: af-frāy', dē-frāy', frāy.

g: as-sȧ-gāi', dis-tin-gué' (-tang-gā'), gāy, nōṣe'gāy.

gl: ȧ-glȩy'*.

gr: dap"ple⸗grāy', ȩm"i-gré', grāy, grȩy, hod'den⸗grāy, ĭ'ron⸗grāy (ĭ'ẽrn-), lead'en⸗grāy (led'), sil'vẽr-grāy.

h: Hāigh (hā), hāy, hȩy.

hw: whȩy.

j: J, jāy, pop'in-jāy.

k(c): K, Bis-cāy', böu-quȩt' (-kā'), com-mū"ni-qué', crō-quȩt', Kāy, Kāye, ō'kāy', ris-qué,

(Choose only one word out of each group)

rō-que̱t', sō'bri-que̱t, Tō-kāy',
toŭr'ni-que̱t.
kl: çlāy, fīre çlāy.
kw(qu): quā.
l: al-lāy', bē-lāy',
Bo̱r-de-lāis' (-lā'),
ça̱b″ri-ō-le̱t', Ça-lāis',
Çhev-rō-le̱t', dē-lāy', fōre-lāy',
fo̱r-lāy', in-lāy', in″tēr-lāy',
lāi, lāy, Le̱igh (lā), Mȧ-lāy',
Man″dȧ-lāy', mis-lāy',
out-lāy', ō″vēr-lāy', rē-lāy',
rē-veil-le̱' (-vel-), roun'de-lāy,
un″dēr-lāy, un-lāy', up-lāy',
vïr-e-lāi', vir'e-lāy, wāy-lāy'.
m: dis-māy',
en'trē-me̱ts (än'trē-mā),
goŭr-me̱t' (-mā'), māy,
re̱″su̱-me̱', Sal″ō-me̱'.
n: Çlois̱-on-ne̱',
de̱-je̱u-ne̱r' (-nā'), drȧ-go̱n-ne̱',
hog'mȧ-nāy', mat″i-ne̱e', nāy,
ne̱, ne̱e (nā), ne̱igh,
rai-ṣo̱n-ne̱' (re-zō-nā').
p: çöu-pe̱', dead pāy,
ō″vēr-pāy', pāy, prē-pāy',
rē-pāy', töu-pe̱e', töu-pe̱t',
un″dēr-pāy'.
pl: dis-plāy', fāir plāy, ho̱rse
plāy, in″tēr-plāy',
Pas'sion plāy (pash'un), plāy,
stȧġe plāy, un″dēr-plāy'.
pr: bē-prāy', Dū-pre̱', prāy,
pre̱y, un-prāy'.
r: ar-rāy', bē-wrāy'*,
dis″ar-rāy', Dō-re̱', fo̱-rāy',
Hon-ō-re̱' (on-), hoo-rāy',
Mon″te-re̱y', Mon″tēr-re̱y, rāy,
soi-re̱e' (swä-), Wrāy (rā).
s: as-sāy', es'sāy, fōre-sāy',
gāin″sāy', hēar'sāy, mis-sāy',

pas-se̱', sāy, soo̱th'sāy″,
un″dēr-sāy', un-sāy'.
sh: çrō-çhe̱t' (-shā'), Ō'-Shāy',
pap'i-ēr=mȧ-çhe̱' (pā'pēr-ma-shā'
or pa-pyā'mȧ-shā'), ri-çō-çhe̱t',
sa-çhe̱t', shāy.
skr(sçr): sçrāy.
sl: bob sle̱igh (slā), slāy,
sleigh, sle̱y.
sp: spāy, strath-spe̱y'.
spl: splāy.
spr: fea'THēr sprāy (fe'), sprāy.
st: ȧ-stāy', bob'stāy, fōre-stāy',
māin'stāy, out-stāy',
ō″vēr-stāy', stāy, up-stāy'.
str: ȧ-strāy', strāy.
sw: swāy.
t: tāy, the̱ (tā).
TH: THe̱y.
tr: bē-trāy', dis-trāit' (-trā'),
es-trāy', öu-tre̱', po̱r-trāy',
trāy, tre̱y.
tw: twāy*.
v: çon-ve̱y', ço̱r-ve̱e',
in-ve̱igh', pūr-ve̱y', su̱r-ve̱y'.
w: ȧ-wāy', ȧ-we̱igh' (-wā'),
brī'dle-wāy, bȳ'wāy,
ça̱r'ȧ-wāy, ça̱st'ȧ-wāy,
ça̱use'wāy, çross'wāy,
fāir'wāy, foot'wāy, gal'lō-wāy,
gang'wāy, get'=ȧ-wāy,
hȧlf'wāy', hīgh'wāy (hī'),
lee'wāy, mid'wāy,
Mil'ky=Wāy',
out-we̱igh' (-wā'), pȧth'wāy,
rāil'wāy, run'ȧ-wāy,
steer'ȧġe-wāy, stōw'ȧ-wāy,
sub'wāy, THere'ȧ-wāy,
tram'wāy, wa̱'tēr-wāy, wāy,
we̱igh (wā), well'ȧ-wāy*, we̱y.

(Choose only one word out of each group)

y: Chev″al-ier′ (-yā′),
em-plō′yé, em-plō′yée, yea.

z: ex″pō-sé′, San Jō-se′ (hō-zā′)
vï-sé′.

zh: ne-gli-ġée′ (-zhā′),
prō-té-ġé′, prō-té-ġée′, Rō-ġet′.

Ä

a: Ä′ ä, a″gōr-à-phō′bi-à, äh,
am-phib′i-à, añ-glō-phō′bi-à.
bac-tē′ri-à, cà-mēl′li-à,
claus-trō-phō′bi-à,
cȳ-clō-pē′di-à, däh′li-à,
dys-pep′si-à, ef-flù′vi-à,
Ē-ġē′ri-à, eū-thăn-ā′si-à,
fan-tä′si-à, hȳ-drō-phō′bi-à,
hȳ-pō-chon′dri-à, hys-ter′i-à,
in-ēr′ti-à (′shi-), in-som′ni-à,
mel-ăn-chō′li-à, mȳ-ō′pi-à,
neū-ral′ġi-à, par″à-phêr-nā′li-à,
pà-rī′äh, phan-tas′mà-gō′ri-à,
phō′bi-à, rē-gā′li-à,
Sat-ūr-nā′li-à, schiz-ō-phren′i-à,
sē′pi-à, Ū-tō′pi-à.

b: bäa, bäh.

bl: bläh.

br: al′ġe-brà,
chà-peau′ bräs′ (shà-pō′ brä′),
vēr′te-brà.

d: An-drom′e-dä, dä.

dr: clep-sȳ′drà.

f: à-po′cry-phä (-fä), fä,
ton′ic sōl-fä′.

h: ä-hä′, hä, hä″-hä′.

j: Jäh.

k(c): bas-il′i-cà, Käa,
mà-jol′i-cä, re′pli-cà,
scī-at′i-cà, sil′i-cà.

kl: é-clät′ (-klä′).

kw(qu): quä.

l: an″i-mal′cū-là,
A′qui-là (′kwi-), cū′pō-là,
for′mū-là, gon′dō-là, hol-lä′,
lä, neb′ū-là, pà-rab′ō-là,
pen-in′sū-là, spat′ū-lä,
tar-an′tū-lä, ū′vū-là,
vï′ō-là (or vï′).

m: A-cel′dà-mà, an-ath′e-mà,
cin′e-mà, grand′mäm-mä″,
mä, mä-mä′, mäm′mä,
quäd″ri-ġes′i-mà,
quin″quà-ġes′i-mà,
sep″tū-à-ġes′i-mà,
sex″ū-à-ġes′i-mà.

n: à-lū′mi-nà,
phē-nom′e-nà (fē-),
prō-le-gom′e-nà,
quäd-rū′mà-nà, ret′i-nà.

p: faux-päs (fō-pä′), pä, päh,
pä-pä′, päs.

r: bac-cà-rät′ (-rä′), cam′e-rà,
cär-niv′ō-rä, chol′e-rà,
e-phem′e-rà (-fem′),
et cet′e-rà, ġen′e-rà, Hē-ġï′rà,
hūr-räh′, man-drag′ō-rà,
op′e-rà, pleth′ō-rà, Rä.

s: säh, yes′säh.

sh: päd′i-shäh, pä-shä′, shäh.

sp: spä.

t: au-tom′à-tà, in-cog′ni-tà,
taf′fe-tà.

th: Gol-gō′thà, Ptäh.

tr: or′ches-trà.

y: jä (yä), Jäh (yä), yäh.

z: huz-zä′.

zhw: böur-ġeois′ (-zhwä′).

ĀB

Vowel: Ābe.

b: bābe, fos′tēr-bābe.

l: as′trō-lābe, cos′mō-lābe.

(Choose only one word out of each group)

AB

Vowel: abb.
b: bab, Babb, bā'ō-bab.
bl: blab.
d: bē-dab', dab.
dr: drab.
f: çon'fab.
fr: frab.
g: gab.
gr: grab.
j: jab.
k(c̣): c̣ab, tax'i-c̣ab.
kr: c̣rab.
l: lab.
m: mab*, Mab.
n: knab*, Mc̣-Nabb', nab.
r: rab.
sk(sc̣): sc̣ab.
sl: slab.
st: stab.
sh: shab.
t: Çan-tab', tab.

ÄB

skw(squ): squäb.
sw: swäb.
Cf. ob, blob, etc.

ĀCH

Vowel: aitch, H.

ACH

b: batch.
bl: Blatch.
br: brach.*
h: hatch.
k(c̣): c̣atch.
kl: käf'fee klatsch.
kr: c̣ratch.
l: latch, un-latch'.

m: match, ō"vēr-match',
pēr-c̣us'sion, match.
p: dis-patch', patch.
r: ratch.*
sk(sc̣): sc̣atch.*
skr(sc̣r): sc̣ratch.
sl: slatch.
sm: smatch.*
sn: snatch.
t: at-tach', dē-tach', tach.*
th: thatch.

ÄCH

sw: swätch.
w: wätch.
Cf. och, blotch, etc.

ACHT

h: hatched.
t: at-tached', sem"i-dē-tached'.
Also ach + ed.

ĀD

Vowel: āid, c̣ō'=āid,
lem"ŏn-āde', or"äṅge-āde',
un"dēr-āid'.
b: bāde, gam-bāde'.
bl: blāde, Dȧ-mas'c̣us blāde,
grȧss blāde.
br: ȧ-brāde', ȧ-brāid'*, brāid,
un-brāid', up-brāid'.
d: dāde*, Mc̣Dāde'.
f: fāde.
fl: flāyed.
fr: ȧ-frāid', un-ȧ-frāid'.
g: bri-gāde', fīre bri-gāde',
ren'ē-gāde.
gl: glāde.
gr: Bel-grāde', cen'ti-grāde,
dē-grāde', grāde, māke the
grāde, plan'ti-grāde
re'trō-grāde.

(Choose only one word out of each group)

h: hāde.

j: bē-jāde'*, jāde.

k(c): al-cāide', am-bus-cāde', är-cāde', bar-ri-cāde', blo-ckāde', brō-cāde', cāde, cas-cāde', cav-ăl-cāde', co-ckāde', de'cāde, es-tȧ-cāde', fal-cāde', sac-cāde', sto-ckāde'.

kw(qu): Mc-Quāde'.

l: ac-cō-lāde', Ad'e-lāide, deep'⸗lāid', dē-fĭ-lāde', dē-lāyed', en-fi-lāde', es'cȧ-lāde, fū-sil-lāde', gril-lāde', in-lāid', in"tẽr-lāid', lāde, lāid, mär-mȧ-lāde', ō"vẽr-lāid', pis-tō-lāde'*, scȧ-lād'*, un-dẽr-lāid', un-lāde', un-lāid'.

m: dāi'ry māid, hand'māid, māde, māid, mẽr'māid, milk'māid, new māde, ōld māid, po-māde', rea'dy⸗māde', sēa māid, self'⸗māde', sẽrv'ing māid, un-dis-māyed', un-māid', un-māde'.

n: bas-ti-nāde', can-no-nāde', car-ro-nāde', cas-so-nāde', col-ŏn-nāde', drag-ŏn-nāde', es-plȧ-nāde', fan"far-o-nāde', flañ-cŏn-nāde', gā"bi-ŏn-nāde', gas-co-nāde', gre-nāde', här"le-qui-nāde' (-ki- or -kwi-), le-mo-nāde', mar-i-nāde', pȧ-nāde'*, pas-qui-nāde', pro-me-nāde', ser-e-nāde'.

p: crŏu-pāde', es-cȧ-pāde', es-trȧ-pāde', gal-lō-pāde', ō"vẽr-pāid', pāid, pōst'pāid", prē-pāid', uṇ-pāid', un"rē-pāid'.

pl: dis-plāyed', plāid, plāyed, ō"vẽr-plāyed', un"dẽr-plāyed', un"dis-plāyed', un-plāyed'.

pr: prāyed, prẹyed, un-prāyed', un-prẹyed'.

r: ar-rāyed', bē-wrâyed'*, cam-e-rāde'*, chȧ-rāde', cor-rāde'*, mas-quē-rāde' (-kē-), pȧ-rāde', rāid, rāyed, tī-rāde', un-ar-rāyed', un-rāyed'.

s: am-bas-sāde'*, as-sāyed', cam-i-sāde'*, crū-sāde', es-sāyed', glis-sāde', här"quē-bu-sāde', lan"ce-pe-sāde'*, pal-i-sāde', pas-sāde', pe-sāde', un-as-sāyed', un-es-sāyed'.

sh: nīght'shāde (nīt'), ō-vẽr-shāde', shāde.

sl: slāde.

sp: spāde, spāyed.

spl: splāyed.

spr: sprāyed.

st: ō"vẽr-stāyed', stāde*, stāid, storm stāyed, un-stāid'.

str: strāyed.

sw: dis-suāde' (-swād'), ō"vẽr-pẽr-suāde', pẽr-suāde', suāde*, suède (swād).

t: rod"ō-mon-tāde'.

tr: bal-us-trāde', free trāde, trāde.

v: ē-vāde', in-vāde', pẽr-vāde'.

w: un-wẹighed', wāde, wẹighed.

Also ā+ed.

Also they'd, etc.

AD

Vowel: add, chil'i-ad, Il'i-ad, Lū'si-ad, myr'i-ad, Ō-lym'pi-ad, sū"pẽr-add'.

b: bad, bade, fọr-bade', un"fọr-bade'.

(Choose only one word out of each group)

br: brad.
ch: Chad, Tchad.
d: bē-dad', dad, Trin'i-dad.
f: fad.
g: bē-gad'*, ē-gad'*, gad.
gl: en-glad', glad.
gr: grad, Len'in-grad,
Pet'rō-grad, un″dēr-grad'.
h: had.
k(ç): çad.
kl: çlad, hēath'=çlad,
ī'ron=çlad (ī'ērn-), ī'vy=çlad,
moss'=çlad, pīne'=çlad, un-çlad',
win'tēr=çlad', y-çlad'* (i-).
l: lad.
m: heb'dō-mad, mad.
p: foot'pad, pad,
tŏngue pad (tung).
pl: plaid (plad).
r: rad*.
s: sad, un-sad'.
sk(sç): sçad.
sh: shad.
t: tad.

ÄD

b: bäa'd.
h: hä'd, hä'hä'd'.
l: bal-läde', röu-läde'.
m: çhà-mäde'*, pō-mäde'.
n: pro-me-näde'.
r: çhà-räde', hur-rähed' (-räd').
s: fa-çäde', glis-säde',
lànce-pē-säde'.
sh: pshä'd (shäd).
tr: es-träde'.
v: çoù-väde'.
w: wäd.
y: noy-äde' (nwä-yäd').
z: huz-zähed' (-zäd').
Also ah+ed or ah'd.
Cf. od, cod, etc.

ADZ

Vowel: adṣ, adze.
sk(sç): sçadṣ.
Also ad+s.

ĀF

ch: chāfe, en-chāfe'.
s: sāfe, un-sāfe', vouch-sāfe'.
str: strāfe.
w: wāif.

AF

ch: chaff.
dr: draff.
g: gaff, pen'ny gaff,
shan'dy-gaff.
gr: aç-tin'ō-graph, à-graffe',
an'à-graph, au'tō-graph,
çal'li-graph, çär'di-ō-graph.
çhron'ō-graph,
çin″ē-mat'ō-graph,
çryp'tō-graph, dī'à-graph,
diç'tō-graph, eī'dō-graph,
ep'i-graph, graff*, graf,
haġ'i-ō-graph, hē'li-ō-graph,
hō'lō-graph, ī'dē-ō-graph,
id'i-ō-graph, lith'ō-graph,
mon'ō-graph, pal'ē-ō-graph,
pan'tō-graph, par'à-graph,
phōn'ō-graph (fōn'),
phō'tō-graph (fō'), pol'y-graph,
sten'ō-graph, stēr'ē-ō-graph,
tel'ē-graph, tel″ē-phō'tō-graph.
h: bē-half', bet'tēr half, half,
half'=and=half'.
k(ç): çalf, moọn çalf.
kw(qu): quaff.
l: bel'ly laugh, laugh.
r: çà-rafe', ġi-raffe', raff,
riff'raff.
s: Saph.
st: çross'=staff, flȳ staff,
half'=staff, quar'tēr=staff, staff,
tip'staff, whip'staff (hwip').

(Choose only one word out of each group)

str: strafe.
t: cen'ō-taph, dis'taff,
ep'i-taph.

ÄF

gr: gräf.
h: bē-hälf', bet'tēr hälf, häaf,
hälf, hälf'=and=hälf'.
k(c̣): cȧlf, mͻͻn c̣älf.
l: bel'ly läugh, läugh.
str: sträfe.

ȦFT

Vowel: ȧft.
b: ȧ-bȧft'.
ch: chȧffed.
d: dȧft.
dr: drȧft, drȧught (drȧft),
ō'vēr-drȧft.
gr: en-grȧft', grȧft, in-grȧft'.
h: hȧft.
kr(c̣r): c̣rȧft, fel'lōw c̣rȧft,
han'di-c̣rȧft, priēst'c̣rȧft,
riv'ēr c̣rȧft, sēa'c̣rȧft,
witch'c̣rȧft.
kw(qu): quȧffed.
l: lȧughed.
r: rȧft.
str: strȧfed.
sh: shȧft.
t: Tȧft.
w: wȧft.
Also af+ed.

ĀG

h: Hāgue.
pl: plāgue.
pr: Prāgue.
v: vāgue.

AG

ag: Ag.
b: bag, sad'dle bag.
br: brag, Bragg.
dr: drag

f: fag, fish fag.
fl: bat'tle flag, flag.
g: gag.
h: hag, nīght hag (nīt).
j: jag.
k(c̣): c̣ag.
kr: c̣rag.
kw(qu): quag.
l: lag.
m: mag.
n: Brob'ding-nag, knag (nag),
nag.
r: bul'ly-rag, chew the rag,
rag, Wragg.
s: sag.
sh: shag.
shr: shrag*.
skr(sc̣r): sc̣rag.
sl: slag.
sn: snag.
spr: sprag.
st: stag.
sw: swag.
t: rag'tag, tag.
w: sc̣al'lȧ-wag, wag.
z: zig'zag.

ÄG

bl: blägue.
pr: Prägue.

ĀGD

pl: un-plāgued'.

AGD

t: bē-tagged'.
Also ag+ed.

ĀJ

Vowel: ā'c̣re-āġe, āġe,
ā'lien-āġe, an'c̣hŏr-āġe,
ap'păn-āġe, är'mit-āġe,
av'ēr-āġe, bar'ŏn-āġe,
bev'ēr-āġe, brig'and-āġe,

(Choose only one word out of each group)

AJ

brō'kẽr-āġe, c̢hap'ẽr-ōn-āġe,
c̢on-c̢ū'bin-āġe, c̢o̤o̤p'ẽr-āġe,
e'quip-āġe, flow'ẽr-āġe,
fō'li-āġe, här'bŏr-ăġe,
her'it-āġe, hẽr'mit-āġe,
hos'pit-āġe, lev'ẽr-āġe,
lin'ē-āġe, mā'trŏn-āġe,
mid'āge, pär'ent-āġe,
pär'sŏn-āġe, pȧs'tŏr-āġe,
pȧs'tūr-āġe, pā'trŏn-āġe,
pē'ŏn-āġe, pẽr's̾n-āġe,
pil'grim-āġe, pī'lŏt-āġe,
plun'dẽr-āġe, pōr'tẽr-āġe,
pū'pil-āġe, qua̧r'tẽr-āġe,
sēign'iŏr-āġe (sēn'yẽr-āj),
sũr'plus-āġe, tū'tŏr-āġe,
vas'săl-āġe, vẽr'bi-āġe,
vic̢'ăr-āġe, vic̢'in-āġe,
vil'lăn-āġe*, vil'lein-āġe.

f: an'thrō-pō-phāġe,
thē'ō-phāġe.

fr: sax'i-frāġe.

g: dis″en-gāġe', en-gāġe',
gāġe, gāuġe, prē″en-gāġe',
ram gāuġe, rē″en-gāġe',
weaTH'ẽr gāuġe.

k(c̢): c̢āġe, dis-c̢āġe', en-c̢āġe',
un-c̢āġe'.

l: c̢är'ti-lāġe, fōr'ti-lāġe*,
mū'ci-lāġe, tū'tē-lāġe.

m: māġe.

n: es'pi-ō-nāġe.

p: c̢om-pāġe'*, foot pāġe,
pāġe, ram'pāġe.

r: en-rāġe', hem'or-rhāġe (-rāj),
out-rāġe', rāġe.

s: prē-sāġe', sāġe, un-sāġe'.

st: stāġe.

sw: as-suāġe' (-swāj'), swāġe.

tr: är'bi-trāġe.

w: wāġe.

Cf. for polysyllables, ij.

b: badġe.
f: fadġe.
h: hadj.
k(c̢): c̢adġe.
m: Madġe.

ÄJ

r: räj.
Cf. aj, badge, etc.

ĀK

Vowel: āc̢he (āk), back'āc̢he,
bel'ly-āc̢he, ēar'āc̢he,
heärt'āc̢he, stŏm'ăc̢h꞊āc̢he,
to̤o̤th'āc̢he.

b: bāke, härd'bāke.
bl: Blāke.
br: bär'ley brāke, brāke,
breāk, dāy'break, heärt'break,
out'break, up'break,
wa̧'tẽr-break.
dr: drāke, man'drāke,
shel'drāke.
f: fāke.
fl: flāke, c̢orn'flāke, snōw'flāke.
h: hāke.
j: jāke.
k(c̢): c̢āke, hōe c̢āke,
john'ny-c̢āke (jon'), seed c̢āke,
short'c̢āke, tēa c̢āke,
wed'ding c̢āke.
kr: c̢rāke, wa̧'tẽr c̢rāke.
kw(qu): ēarth'quāke ('kwāk),
quāke (kwāk).
l: lāke.
m: māke, on the māke,
un-māke'.
p: ō-pāque' (-pāk'), Pāke.
r: åf'tẽr-rāke, rāke.
s: for-sāke', nāme'sāke, sāke.
sh: shāke, she̤ik.
sl: ȧ-slāke'*, slāke.

AK
AKS

fāte, fär, fåst, fạll, finăl, cãre, at; mēte. prĕy, hẽr, met; pīne,
marĭne, bĭrd, pĭn; nōte, mŏve, fọr, atŏm, nọt; mọọn, book;

84

(Choose only one word out of each group)

sn: black'snāke, cọr'ăl snāke,
gär'tẽr snāke, milk snāke,
rat'tle-snāke, rib'bŏn snāke,
snāke, wạ'tẽr snāke.

sp: fōre-spāke'*, spāke*.

st: stāke, steāk, sweep'stāke.

str: strāke.

t: bē-tāke', mis-tāke',
ō"vẽr-tāke', pär-tāke', tāke,
un"dẽr-tāke', up'tāke,
wäp'en-tāke.

w: à-wāke', rob'in-wāke, wāke.

AK

Vowel: am-mō'ni-ạc, bi'vöu-ạc,
cär'di-ạc, dē-mō'ni-ạc,
dip-sō-mā'ni-ạc, Dȳ'ak,
ē"gō-mā'ni-ạc, el-e-ġī'ạc,
hȳ-pō-chon'dri-ạc, kaȳ'ak,
klep"tō-mā'ni-ạc, mā'ni-ạc,
mon"ō-mā'ni-ạc, Pon'ti-ạc,
pȳ"rō-mā'ni-ạc, sal am-mō'ni-ạc,
sym-pō'si-ạc, ū'mi-ak,
zō'di-ạc.

b: à-back', baç, back,
bāre'back, họrse'back,
huck'à-back, hump'back,
pick'à-back, stick'le-back,
zweī'back.

bl: black.

br: brach*, bric'à-braç,
lā'dy-brach*.

ch: chack.

d: dak, kō'dak.

h: hack.

hw: whack (hwak).

j: black'jack, bọọt'jack, jack,
leaTH'ẽr jack, nat'tẽr-jack,
skip'jack, slap'jack,
Ūn'iŏn jack, yel'lōw-jack.

k(ç): mà-caque' (-kak'),
ip'e-cac.

kl: clack, claque (klak).

kr: crack, jim'crack,
thun'dẽr-crack.

kw(qu): quack.

l: à-lack'*, Fond dù Laç,
good lack*, laç, lack,
lakh (lak).

m: yash'mak.

n: ạl'mà-naç, knack,
knick'nack (nik').

p: pack, un-pack', wool pack.

pl: plack.

r: rack, sēa wrack,
tam'à-rack, wrack.

s: çul"=dē=saç', grip'sack,
Hack'en-sack, hav'ẽr-sack,
ran'sack, ruck'sack, saç,
sack, sacque, wool sack.

sh: shack

sl: slack.

sm: smack.

sn: snack.

st: hāy'stack, stack.

t: at-tack', hack'mà-tack,
tack, tick'tack.

thr: thrack.

thw: thwack.

tr: track.

v: Slō'vak.

w: Sar'à-wak, Wack.

y: yack.

ÄK

p: pläque.

w: Sar'a-wäk.

ĀKS

j: jākes.
Also āk+s.

AKS

Vowel: ax, bat'tle=ax.

f: Hal'i-fax.

fl: flax.

85 ūse, bu̇ll, brůte, tůrn, up; crȳ, myth; c̦at, ma̧chine, ace.
    church, c̦hord; ġem, aṅger, (Fr.) boṅ, a̧ș; THis, thin; aẓure

ĀKT
ĀL

(Choose only one word out of each group)

l: An′a̧-lax, lax, par′al-lax, rē-lax′.
m: an″ti-c̦lī′max.
n: As-tȳ′a̧-nax.
p: pax.
s: Sa̧chs, Saxe
sl: slacks.
t: in′c̦o̧me tax, tax.
w: wax.
z: zax.
Also ak+s.

ĀKT

b: bāked, hälf′₌bāked′.
Also āk+d.

AKT

Vowel: ac̦t, c̦oun″tēr-ac̦t′, en-ac̦t′, e̊ntr′ac̦te′ (oṅ-trakt′), ō″vēr-ac̦t′, rē-ac̦t′, rē″en-ac̦t′, re″trō-ac̦t′, un″dēr-ac̦t′.
b: sad′dle₌backed, backed, hump′backed.
br: brac̦t.
d: rē-dac̦t′.
f: fac̦t, mat″tēr₌of₌fac̦t′.
fr: dif-frac̦t′, in-frac̦t′, rē-frac̦t′.
h: hacked.
p: c̦om-pac̦t′, im-pac̦t′, pac̦t.
r: c̦at′a̧-rac̦t.
s: sacked.
str: ab-strac̦t′.
t: at-tacked′, in-tac̦t′, tac̦t,
tr: at-trac̦t′, c̦on-trac̦t′, dē-trac̦t′, dis-trac̦t′, ex-trac̦t′, prō-trac̦t′, rē-trac̦t′, sub-trac̦t′, trac̦t, un-tracked′.
z: ex-ac̦t′ (egz-), tran-sac̦t′.
Also ak+ed.

ĀL

Vowel: āil, āle, ġin″ġēr-āle′.
b: bāil, bāle.

br: brāil, Brāille (brāl).
d: Bloo̧m′ing-dāle, dāle.
dw: dwāle.
f: fāil.
fl: flāil.
fr: frāil.
g: Ab′i-gāil, fär″THin-gāle, Gāel, Gāil, gāle, mär′tin-gāle, nīght′in-gāle (nīt′), rē-gāle′.
gr: en-grāil′, grāil.
h: a̧ll hāil, ex-hāle′ (eks-), hāil, hāle, in-hāle′.
hw: whāle.
j: en-ġāol′ (-jāl′), en-jāil′, ġāol (jāl), jāil.
k: kāil, kāle.
kw(qu): quāil.
m: black′māil, c̦a̧-māil′, māil, māle.
n: c̦a̧-nāille′, hob′nāil, nāil, te-nāille′.
p: bē-pāle′, dead pāle, death′pāle (deth′), em-pāle′, im-pāle′, in″tēr-pāle′*, pāil, pāle.
r: dē-rāil′, hand′rāil, mon′ō-rāil, rāil.
s: as-sāil′, fōre′sāil, grĭ-sāille′, māin′sāil, out′sāil, sāil, sāle, top′sāil, whōle′sāle (hōl′).
sh: shāle.
sk(sc̦): en-sc̦āle′, sc̦āle, slīd′ing sc̦āle.
sn: snāil.
sp: spāle.
st: stāle.
sw: swāle.
t: av′en-tāil, bē-tāil′, bob′tāil, c̦ock′tāil, c̦ūr-tāil′, dē-tāil′,

(Choose only one word out of each group)

dis″en-tāil′, dŏve′tāil,
drag′gle-tāil, en-tăil′,
fãir′y-tāle, pig′tāil, rē′tāil,
tāel, tāil, tāle, trun′dle-tāil*.
TH: THẹy′ll.
thr: thrāle.
tr: en-trāil′*, trāil.
v: ȧ-vāil′, çoun″tẽr-vāil′,
in-vẹil′, ō″vẽr-vāil′, par′ȧ-vāil,
prē-vāil′, tra-vāil′, un-vẹil′,
vāil, vāle, vẹil.
w: bē-wāil′, wāil, wāle.
y: Yāle.
Also Mav′ll. etc.

AL, ĂL

Vowel: aç-cen′tū-ăl,
ā-ē′ri-ăl, Al, al-lō′di-ăl,
al-lū′vi-ăl, am-ȧ-tō′ri-ăl,
an′nū-ăl, an″tē-di-lū′vi-ăl,
är-bō′rē-ăl, bȧ-rō′ni-ăl,
bō′rē-ăl, çaṣ′ū-ăl (kazh′),
çol-lō′qui-ăl, çon-nū′bi-ăl,
çon-san-guin′ē-ăl,
çon-sis-tō′ri-ăl, çŏn-tin′ū-ăl,
çŏn-ven′tū-ăl, diç-tȧ-tō′ri-ăl,
di-lū′vi-ăl, ef-feç′tū-ăl,
em-pyr′ē-ăl, ē-thē′rē-ăl,
ē-ven′tū-ăl, ex-pūr-gȧ-tō′ri-ăl,
fū-nē′rē-ăl, ġēn′i-ăl, grad′ū-ăl,
hab-it′ū-ăl, hӯ-me-nē′ăl,
im-mȧ-tē′ri-ăl, im-mem-ō′ri-ăl,
im-pē′ri-ăl, in-çor-pō′rē-ăl,
in-di-vid′ū-ăl, in-dus′tri-ăl,
in-ef-feç′tū-ăl, in-fū-sō′ri-ăl,
in-i′ti-ăl (′shi-ăl),
in-quiṣ-i-tō′ri-ăl,
in-tel-leç′tū-ăl, jō′vi-ăl,
mem-ō′ri-ăl, mẽr-çū′ri-ăl,
min-is-tē′ri-ăl, mū′tū-ăl,
neç-tā′rē-ăl, pa-tri-mō′ni-ăl,
pē-des′tri-ăl, pẽr-en′ni-ăl.

pẽr-pet′ū-ăl,
phan-taṣ-mȧ-gō′ri-ăl (fan-),
piç-tō′ri-ăl, pōst-pran′di-ăl,
prī-mọr′di-ăl, prō-fes-sō′ri-ăl,
prō-vẽr′bi-ăl, punç′tū-ăl,
pūr-pūr′ē-ăl, quäd-ren′ni-ăl,
rē-mē′di-ăl, rē-ṣid′ū-ăl,
rit′ū-ăl, sär-tō′ri-ăl,
sēign-eū′ri-ăl (sēn-ū′),
sī-dē′rē-ăl, ter-res′tri-ăl,
ter-ri-tō′ri-ăl, tes-ti-mō′ni-ăl,
triv′i-ăl, ū′ṣụ-ăl (′zhụ-),
ux-ō′ri-ăl, ven-tri-lō′qui-ăl,
vī-çãr′i-ăl, viç-tō′ri-ăl,
vĭr′tū-ăl, viṣ′ū-ăl (vizh′).
b: bal, çȧ-bal′, çan′ni-băl,
hẽr′băl (ẽr′).
br: vẽr′tē-brăl.
d: an-ti′pō-dăl, dal, i′ri-dăl,
py-ram′i-dăl, quäd-rụ′pē-dăl.
f: ȧ-poç′ry-phăl.
g: çon′jụ-găl, gal, mad′ri-găl.
Pọr′tū-găl, Sen′ē-găl.
h: Hal.
k(ç): aç-ȧ-dem′i-çăl,
aes-the′ti-çăl, al-chem′i-çăl,
am″chem-is′ti-çăl,
ȧ-lex″i-phär′mi-çăl (fär′),
ȧ-lex″i-ter′i-çăl, al-ġē-brā′i-çăl,
al″kȧ-li-met′riç-ăl,
al-lē-gōr′i-çăl,
al-phȧ-bet′i-çăl (-fȧ-),
an-ȧ-loġ′i-çăl, an-ȧ-lyt′i-çăl,
ȧ-när′chi-çăl, an″ȧ-tom′i-çăl,
an-ġel′i-çăl, an″thō-loġ′i-çăl,
an″ti-thet′i-çăl,
ȧ-pol″ō-ġet′i-çăl,
ap″os-tol′i-çăl,
är″chē-ō-loġ′i-çăl,
ar″ith-met′i-çăl, är-sen′i-çăl,
as-cet′i-çăl,
aṣth-mat′i-çăl (az-),

87

ūse, bu̯ll, brúte, tûrn, up; crȳ, myth; c̣at, maç̇hine, ace,
church, c̣hord; ġem, añger, (Fr.) boṅ, aṣ; THis, thin; aẕure **AL**

(Choose only one word out of each group)

as″trō-loġ′i-c̣ăl,
at″mŏs-pher′i-c̣al (-fer′),
Bab″y-lon′i-c̣ăl, baç′c̣hi-c̣al,
baç-tē″ri-ō-loġ′i-c̣ăl,
bạl-sam′i-c̣ăl, bar″ō-met′ri-c̣ăl,
bas-il′i-c̣ăl, bē-à-tif′i-c̣ăl,
bib′li-c̣ăl,
bib″li-ō-graph′i-c̣ăl (-graf′),
bib″li-ō-mā-nī′à-c̣ăl,
bib″li-ō-phil′i-c̣ăl (-fil′),
bī-ō-graph′i-c̣ăl (-graf′),
bi″ō-loġ′i-c̣ăl, bot-an′i-c̣ăl,
Bräh-min′i-c̣ăl,
bū″reau-c̣rat′i-c̣ăl (″rō-),
c̣ac̣-ō-phon′i-c̣ăl (-fon′), C̣al,
C̣al-vin-is′ti-c̣ăl, c̣an-on′i-c̣ăl,
c̣ar′à-c̣ăl,
c̣är-tō-graph′i-c̣ăl (-graf′),
c̣aṣ-ū-is′ti-c̣ăl, c̣at-ē-gọr′i-c̣al,
c̣ath-ol′i-c̣ăl, cēr′vi-c̣ăl,
char″ac̣-tēr-is′ti-c̣ăl,
c̣hem′i-c̣ăl, che-rú′bi-c̣al,
c̣hī-mer′i-c̣ăl,
c̣hron-ō-loġ′i-c̣ăl, c̣las′si-c̣ăl,
c̣ler′i-c̣ăl, c̣lī-maç′ti-c̣ăl,
c̣lī-mat′i-c̣ăl, c̣lin′i-c̣ăl,
c̣om′i-c̣ăl, c̣on′i-c̣ăl,
c̣on-ven′ti-c̣ăl, c̣ọr′ti-c̣ăl,
c̣oṣ-met′i-c̣ăl, c̣oṣ′mi-c̣ăl,
c̣ox-c̣omb′i-c̣ăl, c̣rit′i-c̣ăl,
c̣ryp′ti-c̣ăl, c̣ū′bi-c̣ăl,
cȳ′c̣li-c̣ăl, cy-lin′dri-c̣ăl,
cyn′i-c̣ăl, dē-is′ti-c̣ăl,
dem-ō-c̣rat′i-c̣ăl,
dē-mō-nī′à-c̣ăl,
dē″mŏn-ō-loġ′i-c̣ăl,
dī-à-bol′i-c̣ăl, dī-à-c̣rit′i-c̣ăl,
dī-à-graph′i-c̣ăl (-graf′),
dī-à-lec̣t′i-c̣ăl, dī-à-loġ′i-c̣ăl,
dī″à-loġ-is′ti-c̣ăl,
dī-à-met′ri-c̣ăl,
dī-à-phon′i-c̣ăl (-fon′),

dī-dac̣′ti-c̣ăl, dī-e-tet′i-c̣ăl,
dip-lō-mat′i-c̣ăl,
dip″sō-man-ī′à-c̣ăl,
dog-mat′i-c̣ăl, dol-ŏr-if′i-c̣ăl,
dō-min′i-c̣ăl, dram-at′i-c̣ăl,
drop′si-c̣ăl, Drú-id′i-c̣ăl,
dȳ-nam′i-c̣ăl, eç-cen′tri-c̣ăl,
eç-c̣lē″ṣi-as′ti-c̣ăl,
ē-c̣ō-nom′i-c̣ăl, eç-stat′i-c̣ăl,
eç-ū-men′i-c̣ăl, ē-gō-is′ti-c̣ăl,
ē-gō-tis′ti-c̣ăl, ē-leç′tri-c̣ăl,
el″e-ġī′à-c̣ăl, el-lip′ti-c̣ăl,
em-blem-at′i-c̣ăl,
em-phat′i-c̣ăl (-fat′),
em-pir′i-c̣ăl,
en-c̣ō″mi-as′ti-c̣ăl,
en-cȳ′c̣li-c̣ăl,
en-cȳ-c̣lō-pē′di-c̣ăl,
en-dem′i-c̣ăl, en″ēr-ġet′i-c̣ăl,
ē-nig-mat′i-c̣ăl,
en-thū-si-as′ti-c̣ăl, ep′i-c̣ăl,
ep-i-dem′i-c̣ăl,
ep″i-gram-mat′i-c̣ăl,
ep-i-sod′i-c̣ăl, ep-i-thet′i-c̣ăl,
ē-quiv′ō-c̣ăl, e-rot′i-c̣ăl,
es-ō-ter′i-c̣ăl, eth′i-c̣ăl,
eth′ni-c̣ăl, eth-nō-loġ′i-c̣ăl,
et″y-mō-loġ′i-c̣ăl,
Eū-c̣hà-ris′ti-c̣ăl,
eū-lō-ġis′ti-c̣ăl,
eū-phem-is′ti-c̣ăl (-fem-),
eū-phon′i-c̣ăl (-fon′),
ē-van-ġel′i-c̣ăl, ex-ē-ġet′i-c̣ăl,
ex-ō-ter′i-c̣ăl, ex-ot′i-c̣ăl,
ex-trin′si-c̣ăl, fan-at′i-c̣ăl,
fan-tas′ti-c̣ăl fär′ci-c̣ăl,
fin′i-c̣ăl, fọr-en′si-c̣ăl,
gal-van′i-c̣ăl, ġen″ē-à-loġ′i-c̣ăl,
ġē-ner′i-c̣ăl,
ġē-ō-graph′i-c̣ăl (-graf′),
ġē-ō-loġ′i-c̣ăl, ġē-ō-met′ri-c̣ăl,
gram-mat′i-c̣ăl,

(Choose only one word out of each group)

graph'i-cȧl (graf'),
här-mon'i-cȧl, Hē-brā'i-cȧl,
hē-lī'ȧ-cȧl, hem-is-phēr'i-cȧl,
hē-ret'i-cȧl, hē-rō'i-cȧl,
hī-ēr-ärch'i-cȧl, his-tọr'i-cȧl,
hȳ-ġi-en'i-cȧl, hȳ-pēr-bol'i-cȧl,
hȳ-pēr-crit'i-cȧl,
hȳ"pō-chon-drī'ȧ-cȧl,
hyp-ō-crit'i-cȧl, hys-ter'i-cȧl,
ī-den'ti-cȧl, id-i-ot'i-cȧl,
il-loġ'i-cȧl, im"mech-an'i-cȧl,
in-im'i-cȧl, ī-ron'i-cȧl,
jes-ū-it'i-cȧl, jů-rid'i-cȧl,
lack-ȧ-dāi'si-cȧl, lā'i-cȧl,
lē-thär'ġi-cȧl, Lē-vit'i-cȧl,
lit-ūr'ġi-cȧl, loġ'i-cȧl, lyr'i-cȧl,
maġ'i-cȧl, mag-nif'i-cȧl,
maj-es'ti-cȧl, mȧ-nī'ȧ-cȧl,
math-ē-mat'i-cȧl, mē-chan'i-cȧl,
med'i-cȧl,
met-ȧ-phọr'i-cȧl (-fọr'),
met-ȧ-phys'i-cȧl (-fiz'),
meth-od'i-cȧl,
Meth-ŏd-is'ti-cȧl, met'ri-cȧl,
mī-crō-scop'i-cȧl,
mis-an-throp'i-cȧl,
mon-ärch'i-cȧl, mūs'i-cȧl,
mys'ti-cȧl, myth'i-cȧl,
myth-ō-loġ'i-cȧl, nȧut'i-cȧl,
non-sen'si-cȧl, nū-mer'i-cȧl,
op'ti-cȧl, ọr-ȧ-tōr'i-cȧl,
par"ȧ-dī'sā'i-cȧl, par-ȧ-bol'i-cȧl,
par-en-thet'i-cȧl, path-et'i-cȧl,
path-ō-loġ'i-cȧl,
pat-rō-nym'i-cȧl,
ped-ȧ-goġ'i-cȧl, ped-an'ti-cȧl,
pēn-ō-loġ'i-cȧl, pē-ri-od'i-cȧl,
per-i-phras'ti-cȧl (-fras'),
phan-tas-mȧ-gọr'i-cȧl (fan-),
Phar-i-sā'i-cȧl (far-),
phär-mȧ-ceūt'i-cȧl,

phil-an-throp'i-cȧl,
phil-ō-loġ'i-cȧl,
phil-ō-soph'i-cȧl,
phō-tō-graph'i-cȧl,
phren-ō-loġ'i-cȧl,
phthis'i-cȧl (tiz'),
phys'i-cȧl (fiz'),
phys"i-ō-loġ'i-cȧl,
pī"e-tis'ti-cȧl, pī-rat'i-cȧl,
plȧ-ton'i-cȧl,
pneū"mȧ-tō-loġ'i-cȧl (nū),
pō-et'i-cȧl, pol-em'i-cȧl,
pol-it'i-cȧl, pon-tif'i-cȧl,
prac'ti-cȧl, prag-mat'i-cȧl,
prob-lem-at'i-cȧl,
pro-phet'i-cȧl (-fet'),
psȳ-chi-at'ri-cȧl (sī-),
psȳ'chi-cȧl (sī'),
psȳ-chō-loġ'i-cȧl,
pū-ri-tan'i-cȧl, pyr-ȧ-mid'i-cȧl,
pȳ-rō-tech'ni-cȧl,
quiz'zi-cȧl (kwiz'), rad'i-cȧl,
rē-cip'rō-cȧl,
rhap-sod'i-cȧl (rap-),
rhē-tōr'i-cȧl (rē),
rheū-mat'i-cȧl (rū-),
rhyth'mi-cȧl, sab-bat'i-cȧl,
sā-tan'i-cȧl, sȧ-tir'i-cȧl,
scēn'i-cȧl (sēn'), scep'ti-cȧl,
schis-mat'i-cȧl (skiz-),
schō-las'ti-cȧl (skō-),
sē-raph'i-cȧl (-raf'),
sō"ci-ō-loġ'i-cȧl, Soc-rat'i-cȧl,
sō-phis'ti-cȧl (-fis'),
spas-mod'i-cȧl,
spher'i-cȧl (sfer'),
spō-rad'i-cȧl, stō'i-cȧl,
strat-ēġ'i-cȧl, syb-ȧ-rit'i-cȧl,
sym-bol'i-cȧl, sym-met'ri-cȧl,
syn-chron'i-cȧl, syn-od'i-cȧl,
syn-ō-nym'i-cȧl, syn-op'ti-cȧl,

(Choose only one word out of each group)

syn-thet′i-çăl, sys-tem-at′i-çăl,
taç′ti-çăl, tech′ni-çăl,
tech″ni-çō-loġ′i-çăl,
thē-at′ri-çăl, thē″ō-loġ′i-çăl,
thē-ō-ret′i-çăl,
thē-ō-soph′i-çăl (-sof′),
top′i-çăl, top-ō-graph′i-çăl,
traġ′i-çăl, trop′i-çăl,
typ′i-çăl,
tȳ-pō-graph′i-çăl (-graf′),
tȳ-ran′ni-çăl, um-bil′i-çăl,
un-çan-on′i-çăl, vat′i-çăl,
vēr′ti-çăl, vo̧r′ti-çăl,
whim′ṣi-çăl (hwim′),
zō-dī′a̧-çăl, zō-ō-loġ′i-çăl.

l: Lal.

m: an′i-măl, deç′i-măl,
in″fin-i-tes′i-măl, lach′ry-măl,
mall, quäd-riġ-es′i-măl (kwäd-),
syn-on′y-măl.

n: ab-ō-riġ′i-năl,
af-feç′tiŏ-năl (′shu-),
an-tiph′ō-năl (-tif′),   är′se-năl,
baç′cha̧-năl, bā′năl, ça̧-nal′,
ça̧r′di-năl,
cir″çum-lō-çū′tio-năl (′shu-),
çom′mū-năl,
çom-plex′io-năl,
çŏn-çlu′ṣio-năl (-shu-),
çŏn-di′tio-năl,
çŏn-fes′sio-năl (-fesh′),
çŏn-gres′sio-năl,
con-sti-tū′tio-năl,
çon-trà-diç′tio-năl,
cŏn-ven′tio-năl (′shu-),
con-vēr-sā′tio-năl (′shu-),
crim′i-năl,
deç′a̧-năl,
dē-nom-i-nā′tio-năl (′shu-),
dē-scen′sio-năl, des′ti-năl,
dē-vō′tio-năl, dī-aç′ō-năl,

dī-ag′ō-năl,
dī-gres′siŏ-năl (-gresh′u-),
dis-çre′tiŏ-năl (-kresh′u-),
di-vi′ṣiŏ-năl (vizh′u-),
doç′tri-năl,
ed′ū-çā′tiŏ-năl (′shu-),
ē-mō′tiŏ-năl (′shu-),
ev-ō-lū′tiŏ-năl (′shu-),
ex-cep′tiŏ-năl (-sep′shu-),
fiç′tiŏ-năl (′shu-),
fraç′tiŏ-năl (′shu-),
funç′tiŏ-năl (′shu-),
ġem′i-năl, ġērm′i-năl,
hep-tag′ō-năl, hex-ag′ō-năl,
im-aġ′i-năl,
im-i-tā′tiŏ-năl (′shu-),
im-pēr′sŏ-năl,
in-spi-rā′tiŏ-năl (′shu-),
in-sti-tū′tiŏ-năl (′shu-),
in-struç′tiŏ-năl (′shu-),
in-sūr-reç′tiŏ-năl (′shu-),
in-ten′tiŏ-năl (′shu-),
in-tēr-ces′siŏ-năl (sesh′u-),
in-tēr-jeç′tiŏ-năl (′shu-),
in-tēr-na′tiŏ-năl (′shu-),
lon-ġi-tū′di-năl, mär′ġi-năl,
mat′i-năl, mā′trō-năl,
med-i′ci-năl, mē-rid′i-ō-năl,
na′tiŏ-năl (′shu-),
nom′i-năl, nō′tiŏ-năl (′shu-),
oç-çā′ṣiŏ-năl (′zhu-),
oç-tag′ō-năl, op′tiŏ-năl (′shu-),
ō-ri′ġi-năl, pas′siŏ-năl (pash′u-),
pa′trŏ-năl, pen-tag′ō-năl,
pēr′sŏ-năl, phē-nom′ē-năl,
prē-ça̧u′tiŏ-năl (′shu-),
prō-bā′tiŏ-năl (′shu-),
prō-ces′siŏ-năl (-sesh′u-),
prō-fes′siŏ-năl (-fesh′u-·),
prō-gres′siŏ-năl (-gresh′u-),
prō-po̧r′tiŏ-năl (′shu-),

ÄL
ALT

fāte, fär, fȧst, fᶏll, fĭnăl, cãre, at; mēte, prey, hēr, met; pīne,
marīne, bīrd, pin; nōte, möve, fǫr, atŏm, not; mǫǫn, book;

90

(Choose only one word out of each group)

prō-vi'șĭŏ-năl ('zhu-),
ra'tiŏ-năl ('shu-),
rē-ces'sĭŏ-năl (-sesh'u-),
ret'i-năl, sen-sā'tiŏ-năl ('shu-),
syn'çhrō-năl, tēr'mi-năl,
trȧ-di'tiŏ-năl ('shu-), ū'ri-năl,
vim'i-năl, vīr'ġi-năl,
vi'șĭŏ-năl ('zhu-),
vō-li'tiŏ-năl ('shu-).

p: Ē-pis'çŏ-ᴗăl, mū-ni'ci-păl,
pal, prin'ci-păl.

r: ad'mi-răl, ag-ri-çul'tū-răl,
är"bō-ri-çul'tū-răl,
är-chi-teç'tū-răl, chap-ăr-ral',
çol-lat'e-răl, çŏn-jeç'tū-ᴗăl,
çǫr'pō-răl , çǫr-ral',
eph-em'e-răl (ef-),
ex-tem'pō-răl (eks-),
fal'de-ral", fed'e-răl,
fū'ne-răl, ġen'e-răl,
hǫr"ti-çul'tū-răl, in-au'gū-răl,
lib'e-răl, lit'e-răl, lit'tō-răl,
min'e-răl, nat'ū-răl, pas'tō-răl,
pē-riph'e-răl (-rif'), piç'tū-răl,
prē-tēr-nat'ū-răl,
quäd-ri-lat'e-răl, sçrip'tū-răl,
sçulp'tū-răl, sev'e-răl,
sid'e-răl, sū-pēr-nat'ū-răl,
tem'pō-răl, ves'pe-răl.

s: sal.

sh: mar-e-çhal',
sen-e-sçhal' (-shal'), shall.

t: çap'i-tăl, diġ'i-tăl,
hos'pi-tăl, mar'i-tăl,
ped'es-tăl, piv'ō-tăl, veġ'e-tăl.

v: çär'ni-văl, fes'ti-văl,
in'tēr-văl, Val.

ÄL

kr: kräal.
r: mō-räle'.

s: Lä Sälle.

ALB

Vowel: alb.
k: Dē Kalb.

ĀLD

Vowel: āiled.
h: hāled, un-hāled'.
s: as-sāiled', sāiled,
un"as-sāiled'.
t: bob'tāiled, short'⹀tāiled,
tāiled.
w: bē-wāiled', un"bē-wāiled',
wāiled.
Also āl+ed.

ALD

b: çȧ-balled'.
p: palled.
r: çǫr-ralled', em'e-răld.
Also al+ed.
Also Hal'd, etc.

ALF

Vowel: Alf, Alph.
r: Ralph.

ALK

f: çat'ȧ-falque.
t: talç.

ALKS

k(ç): çalx.
Also alk+s.

ALP

Vowel: alp.
p: palp.
sk(sç): sçalp.

ALPS

Vowel: Alps.
Also alp+s.

ALT

sh: shalt*

(Choose only one word out of each group)

ALV

s: salve.
v: bĭ′valve, prīm′ing valve,
  sāfe′ty valve, ū′ni-valve,
  valve.

ĀLZ

s: Mär-seilleṣ′.
tr: Trāilṣ.
w: Wāleṣ.
Also āl+s.

ĀM

Vowel: āim.
bl: blāme.
çh: Çhāim.
d: dāme.
dr: mel′ō-drāme.
f: dē-fāme′, dis-fāme′, fāme.
fl: à-flāme′, flāme, in-flāme′.
fr: frāme.
g: gāme.
gr: Grāeme.
h: hāme.
k(ç): bē-çāme′, çāme,
  ō-vēr-çāme′.
kl: aç-çlāim′, çlāim,
  çoun′tēr-clāim″, dē-çlāim′,
  dis-çlāim′, ex-clāim′ (eks-),
  prō-clāim′, rē-çlāim′.
kr: çrème dē lä çrème.
l: lāme.
m: māim, Māme.
n: mis-nāme′, nāme,
  nick′nāme, sūr′nāme.
s: sāme, self′sāme.
sh: à-shāme′, shāme.
t: en-tāme′, tāme.

AM

Vowel: ad nau′sē-am, am,
  THē Greāt Ī Am.

b: Al″à-bam′.
ch: cham.
d: Am′stēr-dam, çof′fēr-dam,
  dam, damn, mà-dame′,
  Mç-Ad′am, Rot′tēr-dam,
  Scheï′dam (shī′).
dr: drachm (dram), dram.
fl: flim′flam, ọr′i-flamme.
fr: dī′à-phragm.
g: çryp′tō-gam (krip′), gam.
gr: an′à-gram, çā′ble-gram,
  çryp′tō-gram (krip′),
  dī′à-gram, ep′i-gram, gram,
  mon′ō-gram, par-al-lel′ō-gram,
  rā′di-ō-gram, ster′ē-ō-gram,
  tel′e-gram.
h: Ā′brà-ham, Bĭr′ming-ham,
  Çun′ning-ham, ham,
  Not′ting-ham.
hw: wham (hwam),
  whim′wham (hwim′hwam).
j: jam, jamb, Ram′à-jam.
k(ç): çam.
kl: çlam.
kr: çram.
l: lam, lamb, sà-laam′.
m: ma′am, Mam.
p: Pam.
pr: pram.
r: bat′tēr-ing ram, dith′y-ramb,
  mär′jō-ram, ram.
s: Sam, Uñ′çle Sam.
sh: Pē′tēr-sham, sham.
shr: shram.
skr: sçram.
sl: slam.
sw: swam.
t: tam.
tr: tram.
y: yam.
z: Nĭ′zam.

ÄM
ÄN

fāte, fär, fȧst, fạll, finăl, cãre, at; mēte, prẹy, hĕr, met; pīne,
marīne, bĭrd, pin; nōte, mŏve, fọr, atŏm, not; mọọn, book;

92

(Choose only one word out of each group)

ÄM

b: bälm, em-bälm'.
gw: Guäm (gwäm).
k(c̣): be-c̣älm', cälm.
kw(qu): quälm.
l: Is'läm, sȧ-läam'.
m: i-mäm', mä'am (mäm),
  mälm.
p: im-pälm', pälm.
s: psälm (säm).

AMB

Vowel: c̣hō'ri-amb.
g: gamb.
r: dith'y-ramb.

ĀMD

bl: blāmed, un-blāmed'.
fr: frāmed, un-frāmed'.
kl: c̣lāimed, un-c̣laimed',
  un"rē-c̣lāimed'.
n: nāmed, un-nāmed'.
sh: ȧ-shāmed', shāmed,
  un"ȧ-shāmed'.
t: tāmed, un-tāmed'.
Also ām+ed.

AMP

Vowel: amp.
ch: champ.
d: af'tẽr-damp, damp,
  death'damp (deth'),
  fīre'damp, mīne damp.
g: gamp, guimpe (gamp).
k(c̣): c̣amp, dē-c̣amp',
  en-c̣amp'.
kl: c̣lamp.
kr: c̣ramp.
l: Dā'vy lamp, lamp,
  sāfe'ty lamp, sig'năl lamp.
r: ramp.
s: samp.

sk(sc̣): sc̣amp.
st: en-stamp', stamp.
t: tamp.
tr: tramp.
v: rē-vamp', vamp.

ÄMP

sw: swämp.
Cf. omp.

AMPT

d: damped, un-damped'.
k(c̣): c̣amped.
Also amp+ed.

ĀMZ

Vowel: Āmeṣ.
j: Jāmeṣ.
Also ām+s.

ÄMZ

Vowel: älmṣ.
Also äm+s.

ĀN

Vowel: Āisne (ān), āne,
  C̣ock-āigne', Dū-āne', in-āne'.
b: bāne, Bāyne, flēa'bāne,
  hen'bāne, in"ūr-bāne',
  ūr-bāne'.
bl: blāin, Blāine, chil'blāin.
br: brāin, sc̣at'tẽr-brāin.
ch: chāin, en-chāin',
  in"tẽr-chāin', un-chāin'.
d: c̣ō"ọr-dāin', Dāne, dẹign,
  dis-dāin', fōre-ọr-dāin',
  ọr-dāin', prē"ọr-dāin'.
dr: drāin.
f: ā'rē-ō-phāne, al'lō-phāne,
  cel'lō-phāne, dī'ȧ-phāne, fāin,
  fāne, fẹign, hȳ'drō-phāne,
  lith'ō-phāne, mis-fẹign',
  prō-fāne'.
fr: rē-frāin'.

93

ūse, bᴜll, brúte, tᴜ̃rn, up; crȳ, myth; c̜at, mac̜hine, ace,
church, c̜hord; ġem, anger, (Fr.) boṅ, aṣ; THis, thin; aᴣure

AN

(Choose only one word out of each group)

g: à-gāin'*, gāin, rē-gāin'.
gr: en-grāin', grāin, in-grāin'.
j: jāin, Jāne, Jāyne, jeān.
k(c̜): C̜āin, C̜āine, c̜āne,
chi-c̜āne', c̜ō-c̜āine',
Dū-que̱sne' (-kān'),
hūr'ri-c̜āne,
su̱g'ăr c̜āne (shu̱g'ēr).
kr: c̜rāne, wạ'tēr c̜rāne.
l: chām'bēr-lāin, c̜hat'e-lāine,
Ē-lāine', dē-lāine', lāin, lāne,
Mc̜-Lāin', Mc̜-Leān',
po̱r'ce-lāin.
m: à-māin', chow-me̱in',
dē-me̱sne', dō-māin',
ġēr-māne', hū-māne',
im-māne', leġ"ēr-de-māin',
māin, Māine, māne, Māyne,
mo̱rt'māin, rē-māin'.
p: c̜am-pāign', c̜am-pāne',
c̜ham-pāgne', c̜ham-pāign',
c̜oun'tēr-pāne, el-ē-c̜am-pāne',
fran'ġi-pāne, pāin, Pāine,
pāne, Pāyne.
pl: ā'ēr-ō-plāne, a'quà-plāne,
C̜ham-plāin', c̜ŏm-plāin',
ex-plāin' (eks-), hȳ'drō-plāne,
plāin, plāne, pūr-sūit' plāne.
r: ăr-rāign', beār'ing re̱in,
brī'dle re̱in, dē-rāign',
in"tēr-re̱ign', Lo̱r-rāine',
med-i-tēr-rāne', mō-rāine',
quät'rāin (kwät'rān), rāin,
re̱ign, re̱in, sub'tēr-rāne,
sū'ze-rāin, tēr-rāin', un-re̱in'.
s: in-sāne', sāne, Se̱ine.
sh: Dū-c̜he̱sne' (shān'), Shāne.
sk(sc̜): ske̱in.
sl: slāin.
sp: Spāin.
spr: sprāin.

st: ab-stāin', bē-stāin', stāin.
str: c̜ŏn-strāin', rē-strāin',
strāin.
sw: bōat'swāin,
c̜ox'swāin (koks'), swāin.
t: ap-pēr-tāin', as-cēr-tāin',
at-tāin', c̜ŏn-tāin', dē-tāin',
en-tēr-tāin', māin-tāin',
ob-tāin', pēr-tāin', rē-tāin',
sex-tāin' (seks-), söu-tāne',
sus-tāin', tā'en* (tān), tāin.
th: bow'ēr thāne, thāne,
the̱gn (thān).
tr: bat'tēr-iñg trāin, dē-trāin',
dis-trāin', en-trāin',
pleaṣ'ūre trāin (plezh'), trāin,
up-trāin'.
tw: à-twāin'*, twāin.
v: vāin, vāne, ve̱in, vēr'vāin,
weaTH'ēr-vāne.
w: Chärle̱ṣ'ṣ Wāin, Gà-wāin',
wāin, wāne.
z: Zāne.

AN, ĂN

Vowel: Å-c̜ā'di-ăn,
Al-à-bam'i-ăn, al-à-bas'tri-ăn,
Al-ex-an'dri-ăn (-eks-),
Al-ġē'ri-ăn, a-mà-tō'ri-ăn,
am-à-zon'i-ăn,
am-phib'i-ăn (-fib'), an, Ann,
Anne, an"tē-di-lū'vi-ăn,
Är-c̜ā'di-ăn, A̱us'tri-ăn,
Bā-c̜ō'ni-ăn, Bär-bā'di-ăn,
bär-bā'ri-ăn, Bà-tā'vi-ăn,
Bà-vā'ri-ăn, Bē-zō'ni-ăn,
Bō-hē'mi-ăn, Brī-ā'rē-ăn,
Bul-gā'ri-ăn, C̜à-dū'cē-ăn,
C̜al-ē-dō'ni-ăn, C̜am'bri-ăn.
C̜an-ā'di-ăn, Cim-mē'ri-ăn
C̜ō-lum'bi-ăn, c̜om-ē'di-ăn,
C̜o̱r-in'thi-ăn, c̜us-tō'di-ăn,

(Choose only one word out of each group)

Cyp'ri-ăn, Del'phi-ăn ('fĭ-),
di-lū'vi-ăn,
ē-ques'tri-ăn (kwes'),
Ē-thi-ō'pi-ăn, gär-gan'tū-ăn,
Hes-pē'ri-ăn, his-tō'ri-ăn,
In'di-ăn, lat"i-tū"di-nā'ri-ăn,
lī-brā'ri-ăn, Mãr-i-ănne',
mēr-id'i-ăn, Mex'i-căn (meks'),
nec-tā'rē-ăn, oc̩"tō-ġen-ā'ri-ăn,
Ō-lym'pi-ăn, ped-es'tri-ăn,
Pē-rù'vi-ăn,
plat"i-tū"di-nā'ri-ăn,
pōst"mēr-id'i-ăn, praē-tō'ri-ăn,
prē-tō'ri-ăn,
prē-des"ti-nā'ri-ăn,
Pres-by-tē'ri-ăn,
prō-crus'tē-ăn,
prō-le-tā'ri-ăn, Prō-mē'thē-ăn
quō-tid'i-ăn (kwō-),
Sab-băt-ā'ri-ăn,
Sac̩"rà-men-tā'ri-ăn,
Styġ'i-ăn, sub-tēr-rā'nē-ăn,
Thes'pi-ăn, trá-ġē'di-ăn,
ū-til"i-tā'ri-ăn, Ū-tō'pi-ăn,
val-ē'ri-ăn,
val"e-tū"di-nā'ri-ăn,
Val-kyr'i-ăn, veġ-ē-tā'ri-ăn,
Vē-sū'vi-ăn, vet"ẽr-i-nā'ri-ăn,
vul-gā'ri-ăn,
Zō"rō-as'tri-ăn.
b: ban, cọr'băn.
br: bran.
ch: chan.
d: Dan, e-chin'-i-dăn,
foọ yŏung dan (yung),
hãr'ri-dăn, Mō-ham mē-dăn,
op'pi-dăn, Ram-à-dhan' (-dan')
rē-dan', Sē-dan',
shan'dry-dan.
f: fan.
fl: flan.

fr: Fran.
b: bē-gan', Mich'i-găn,
suf'frà-găn, tzi-gane'.
gr: Gran.
h: Han, Is'fȧ-han.
j: Jan.
k(c̩): Af'ri-căn, Ȧ-mer'i-căn,
Añ'gli-căn, bär'bi-căn,
bar'rȧ-can, bȧ-sil'i-căn,
can, Cō-pēr'ni-căn,
Dō-min'i-căn, Gal'li-căn,
khan, pē-can', pel'i-căn,
pem'mi-căn, pub'li-căn,
rē-pub'li-căn, Vat'i-căn.
kl: clan, Klan.
kr: cran.
l: cas'tel-lăn, Cat'ȧ-lăn,
Mĭ-lan', ọr'tō-lăn.
m: ạl'dẽr-măn, clẽr'ġy-măn,
Cọr'nish-măn, cŏuṃ'try-măn,
Ēñg'lish-măn, fīre'măn,
fish'ẽr-măn, fōre'màst-măn,
fū'gle-măn, ġen'tle-man,
huṣ'bănd-măn,
Isle of Man (īl ov),
joŭr'ney-măn, jù'ry-măn,
līght'ẽr-măn (līt'),
liv'ẽr-y-măn, man
med'i-cine man,
mēr'chănt-măn, mēr'man,
mid'ship-măn,
min'ute-man ('it-),
Mus'sul-măn, nō'ble-măn,
ot'tō-măn, ō'vẽr-man,
quär'ry-măn, sẽrv'ing man,
sig'năl-măn, sū'pẽr-man,
tal'is-măn, tal'ly-ṃăn,
un-man', wạt'ẽr-măn,
wher'ry-măn (hwer').
n: Nan.

95 ūse, bu̜ll, brûte, tũrn, up; crȳ, myth; ça̤t, maçhine, ·ace, church, çhord; ġem, añger, (Fr.) boṅ, a̤ṣ; THis, thin; a̤z̧ure

ÂN AND

(Choose only one word out of each group)

p: frȳ'ing pan, härd'pan, Ja̤-pan', Mat'a̤-pan, pan, trē-pan', wa̤rm'ing pan.

pl: plan.

r: Al-ço̅-ran', Al-deb'a̤-ran, a̤l'so̅꞊ran, ça̤t"ȧ-mȧ-ran', fo̅re-ran', out-ran', o̅-vēr-ran', ran, vet'e-rǎn.

s: Pär-mē-san', pär'ti-sǎn.

sk(sç): sça̤n.

sp: in-span', out-span', span, spick'꞊and꞊span'.

t: çhär'la̤-tǎn, ços-mo̅-pol'i-tǎn, met-ro̅-pol'i-tǎn, Nē-ȧ-pol'i-tǎn, o̅-rang"u-tan', pū'ri-tǎn, rat-tan', sa̤ç'ris꞊tǎn, Sȧ-mar'i-tǎn, tan.

TH: THan.

v: ça̤r'ȧ-van, di-van', lug'gȧġe van, pȧ-van', pris̨'ön van, van.

z: är'ti-ṣǎn, bär'ti-zǎn ço̅ŭr'te-ṣǎn.

ÄN

b: çor-bän'.

sw: swän.

w: wän.

Cf. on.

ȦNCH

bl: blȧnch, cärte blȧnche

br: brȧnch.

fl: flȧnch.

g: gȧnch.

l: av'ȧ-lȧnche.

r: rȧnch.

skr(sçr): sçrȧnch.

st: stȧnch.

A̤NCH

bl: Bla̤nche.

h: ha̤unch.

l: launch.

m: ma̤nche.

p: pa̤unch.

st: sta̤nch, staunch.

A̤NCHT

st: sta̤nched, un-sta̤nched'. Also a̤nch+ed.

ĀND

br: brāined, feaTH'ēr꞊brāined (feTH'), hāre'꞊brāined, hot'꞊brained, mud'dy꞊brāined, rat'tle꞊brāined, sça̤t'tēr꞊brāined, shal'lo̅w꞊brāined, shat'tēr꞊brāined.

ch: chāined, un-chāined'.

d: dis-dāined'.

dr: drāined, un-drāined'.

f: dī-ȧ-phāned', fei̯gned, pro̅-fāned', un-fei̯gned', un"pro̅-fāned'.

m: māned.

pl: plāned, un-plāined'*, un-plāned'.

r: rei̯ned, un-rei̯ned'.

st: blood'꞊stāined, stāined, trav'el꞊stāined, un-stāined'.

str: ço̅n-strāined', rē-strāined' self꞊rē-strāined', strāined, un"ço̅n-strāined', un"rē-strāined', un-strāined'.

t: as-cēr-tāined', sus-tāined', un"as-cēr-tāined', un"sus-tāined'.

tr: trāined, un-trāined'.

v: in-tēr-vei̯ned', vei̯ned. Also ān+ed.

AND

Vowel: and.

b: ȧ-band'*, band,

ÄND
ANGK
fāte, fär, fȧst, fạll, finăl, cãre, at; mēte, prẹy, hēr, met; pīne,
marīne, bĭrd, pĭn; nōte, mŏve, fọr, atŏm, not; mọọn, book;
96

(Choose only one word out of each group)

cọn'trȧ-band, dis-band',
im-band', sär'ȧ-band.
bl: bland.
br: brand, fīre'brand.
d: dē'ō-dand.
f: fanned.
gl: gland, gōat gland,
mŏn'key gland.
gr: grand, Rï'ō Grande.
h: brī'dle hand, fĭrst'=hand,
fōur'=in=hand, hand,
mas'tēr hand, min'ute hand,
ō'vēr-hand, seç"ŏnd-hand',
seç'ŏnd hand, un'dēr-hand,
un-hand', up'pēr-hand.
k(ç): mul"ti-pli-çand',
Sam'ăr-çand.
l: ab'bẹy-land, fāir'y-land,
färm'land, fäTH'ēr-land,
Hō'ly Land, land, lō'tus land,
ō'vēr-land.
m: çŏm-mand',
çoun"tēr-mand', dē-mand',
fụll'=manned, ill'=manned,
manned, rē-mand',
rep'ri-mand, self=çŏm-mand',
un-manned'.
p: ex-pand' (eks-).
r: rand.
s: am'pēr-sand, sand.
sk(sç): sçanned, un-sçanned'.
st: stand, un-dēr-stand',
wạsh'stand, with-stand'.
str: strand.
Also an+ed.
Also man'd, etc.

ÄND

w: wänd.
cf. ond.

ANG

b: bang, gō-bang', shē-bang',
slap'=bang'.
ch: Chang.
d: dang.
f: fang.
g: gang.
h: hang, ō-vēr-hang', up-hang'.
hw: whang.
kl: çlang.
l: Lang.
n: Pē-nang'.
p: pang, trē-pang'.
r: bọọm"e-rang, hȧ-rangue',
mē-ringue' (-rang'), rang,
sē-rang'.
s: sang.
sl: slang.
sp: spang.
spr: sprang.
st: stang.
sw: swang.
t: mus'tang, ō-rang'öu-tang',
sēa tang, taṅg.
tw: twang.
v: vang.
w: Wang.

ANGD

b: banged.
l: langued.
p: un-panged'.
Also ang+ed.

ANGK

b: bañk, em-bañk',
moun'te-bañk, sāv'ingṣ bañk.
bl: Blañç, blañk,
point'=blañk'.
br: brañk.
ch: chañk.
d: dañk.

97
ūse, bụll, brůte, tůrn, up; crȳ, myth; çat. maçhine, ace,
church, çhord; ġem, aṅger, (Fr.) boṅ, aṣ; THis, thin; aẓure

ANGKS
ANS

(Choose only one word out of each group)

dr: draṅk.
fl: flaṅk, out-flaṅk'.
fr: fraṅç, fraṅk.
h: haṅk.
kl: çlaṅk.
kr: çraṅk.
l: láṅk.
pl: plaṅk.
pr: praṅk.
r: en-raṅk', out-raṅk', raṅk.
s: saṅk.
sh: shaṅk.
shr: shraṅk.
sl: slaṅk.
sp: spaṅk.
st: staṅk, out-staṅk'.
t: taṅk, wạt'ẽr taṅk.
th: thaṅk.
tw: twaṅk.
y: yaṅk.

ANGKS

m: Maṅx.
Also angk+s.

ANGKT

s: saç'rō-saṅçt.
sh: spin'dle=shaṅked.
sp: spaṅked, un-spaṅked'.
Also angk+ed.

ĀNJ

ch: chāṅġe,
coun'tẽr-chāṅġe,
ex-chāṅġe' (eks-),
in"tẽr-chāṅġe', sẽa chāṅġe.
gr: grāṅġe.
m: māṅġe.
r: ar-rāṅġe', dē-rāṅġe',
dis"ar-rāṅġe', en-rāṅġe', rāṅġe,
rē"ar-rāṅġe'.
str: strāṅġe.
tr: es-trāṅġe'.

ANJ

fl: flaṅġe.
l: phá-laṅġe' (fá-).

ANS, ÁNS

Vowel: çŏn-tin'ū-ance,
lux-ūr'i-ance, rā'di-ance,
sup'pli-ance, vā'ri-ance.
ch: bē-chánce', chánce,
mis-chánce', pēr-chánce'.
d: bärn dánce,
coun'try dánce, dánce,
death dánce (deth),
fōlk dánce (fōk), squāre dánce.
fr: Fránce.
g: ar'rō-gance, el'ē-gance,
ex-trav'á-gance (eks-),
gl: glánce.
h: en-hánce'.
k(ç): in"sig-nif'i-çance,
sig-nif'i-çance.
l: am'bū-lance, de'mi-lance,
ē-lánce'*, fer"=dē-lánce',
lánce, pet'ū-lance, sib'i-lance,
viġ'i-lance.
m: mánce, rō-mánce'.
n: ap-pūr'te-nance,
çon'sō-nance, çoun'te-nance,
dis-çoun'te-nance,
dis'sō-nance, dom'i-nance,
fi-nánce', in-çon'sō-nance,
Nánce, or'di-nance,
prē-dom'i-nance, reṣ'ō-nance.
p: ex-pánse' (eks-).
pr: pránce.
r: dē-liv'ē-rance,
ex-ūb'ē-rance (egz-),
fūr"THē-rance, iġ'nō-rance,
in-tem'pē-rance,
in-tol'ē-rance,
prē-pon'dē-rance,

(Choose only one word out of each group)

prō-tū′bē-rance, suf′fē-rance,
tol′ē-rance, ut′tē-rance.

s: ҫom-plāi′sance,
ҫon′vẽr-sance, im-pū′is-sance,
pū′is-sance, rē-ҫon′nāis-sance.

sk: ȧ-skȧnce′.

st: cĩr′ҫum-stance, stȧnce.

t: ҫon-ҫom′i-tance,
her′i-tance, in-ҫog′i-tance,
in-hab′i-tance, in-her′i-tance,
prē-cip′i-tance.

tr: en-trȧnce′, pen′e-trance,
trȧnce.

v: ad-vȧnce′, ir-rel′ē-vȧnce,
rel′e-vance, Vȧnce.

z: ҫog′ni-zance,
in-ҫog′ni-zance,
rē-ҫog′ni-zance.

Cf. ant+s.

ÄNS

Vowel: in-söu″ci-änce′.

l: fer′=dē=länce′.

ĀNT

Vowel: āin't.

d: dāint*.

f: fāint, feint.

h: hāin't.

kw(qu): aҫ-quāint′, quāint.

m: māyn't.

p: bē-pāint′, dē-pāint′, pȧint,

pl: ҫom-plāint′,
liv′ẽr ҫom-plāint′, plāint.

r: Gē-rāint′.

s: bē-sāint′, sāint, un-sāint′.

str: ҫon-strāint′, dis-trāint′,
rē-strāint′, self′=rē-strāint′,
strāint, un-ҫŏn-strāint′.

t: at-tāint′, tāint, 'tāint,
'tāin't, teint.

ANT, ȦNT

Vowel: ant, ȧunt,
ir-rād′i-ant, lux-ū′ri-ant,
mis′ҫrē-ant, prō′ҫrē-ant,
reҫ′rē-ant, sup′pli-ant,
vā′ri-ant.

b: bȧnt, Cọr′y-bant.

br: brȧnt.

ch: chȧnt, dis-en-chȧnt′,
en-chȧnt′.

d: ҫom″măn-dȧnt′, ҫon-fi-dȧnt′,
ҫon-fi-dȧnte′.

f: el′ē-phant, hiēr′ō-phant,
syҫ′ō-phant.

g: ar′rō-gant, el′ē-gant,
ex-trav′ȧ-gant (eks-), Gant,
lit′i-gant, suf′frȧ-gant,
tẽr′mȧ-gant.

gr: em′i-grant, grant,
im′mi-grant.

h: hȧ′nt.

k(ҫ): ab′di-ҫant, ap′pli-ҫant,
ҫȧnt, ҫȧn't, ҫom-mū′ni-ҫant,
dē-ҫant′, des-ҫant′,
ex″ҫom-mū′ni-ҫant,
fab′ri-ҫant, in″sig-nif′i-ҫant,
in-tox′i-ҫant (-toks′), Kant,
men′di-ҫant, rē-ҫȧnt,
sȧ-ҫri′fi-ҫant, sig-nif′i-ҫant,
sup′pli-ҫant, tox′i-ҫant.

kw(qu): quant.

l: al-tiv′ō-lant*, am′bū-lant,
ҫon-grat′ū-lant, flag′el-lant,
gal-lȧnt′, grat′ū-lant,
jū′bi-lant, non-chȧ-lant′,
pet′ū-lant, pos′tū-lant,
scin′til-lant (sin′),
sib′i-lant, stim′ū-lant,
tin″tin-nab′ū-lant, un′dū-lant,
vig′i-lant.

m: ad′ȧ-mant.

(Choose only one word out of each group)

n: ag-glū'ti-nant,
al-tis'ō-nant*, ap-pūr'te-nant,
con'sō-nant, cŏv'e-nant,
dē-tēr'mi-nant, dis'sō-nant,
dom'i-nant, ful'mi-nant,
ġēr'mi-nant, il-lū'mi-nant,
im-aġ'i-nant*, in-con'sō-nant,
lū'mi-nant, prē-dom'i-nant,
reṣ'ō-nant, rùm'i-nant.

p: an-ti'ci-pant, oc'cū-pant,
pȧnt.

pl: dē-plant', im-plȧnt, plȧnt,
sen'si-tive plȧnt, sup-plȧnt',
trans-plȧnt'.

r: à-dul'tē-rant, cor'mō-rant,
cŏr-rō'bō-rant, cöu-rȧnt',
ex-ū'bē-rant, fig'ū-rant,
fig-ū-rȧnte', iġ'nō-rant,
in-tol'ē-rant, i-tin'ē-rant,
ō'dŏ-rant, prē-pon'dē-rant,
prō-tū'bē-rant, rȧnt,
rē-friġ'ē-rant, rē-it'ē-rant,
rē-vēr'bē-rant, tol'ē-rant,
vō-ci'fē-rant.

s: com-plāi'sant, con-vēr'sant,
cor'pō-sant, im-pū'is-sant,
in-coġ'ni-sant, pū'is-sant,
rec'ū-sant.

sh: shȧn't.

sk(sc): à-skȧnt', scȧnt.

sl: à-slȧnt', slȧnt.

t: ad'jū-tant, an-nū'i-tant,
com'bà-tant, cŏn-com'i-tant,
dil″et-tȧnt', dis'pū-tant,
ex-ec'ū-tant (egz-),
ex-or'bi-tant (egz-),
ex-tȧnt' (eks-), hab'i-tant,
heṣ'i-tant, in-coġ'ni-tant,
in-hab'i-tant, ir'ri-tant,
mil'i-tant, prē-cip'i-tant,

Prot'es-tant, rē-sus'ci-tant,
tȧnt*, viṣ'i-tant.

tr: pen'e-trant, rē-cal'ci-trant.

v: gal'li-vant, ir-rel'ē-vant,
Le-vȧnt', pūr'sui-vant (-swi-),
rel'ē-vant.

ÄNT

Vowel: äunt.

k: cän't.

sh: shän't.

t: deb-ū-tänte'.

ANTH

Vowel: a'mi-anth.

k: trag'à-canth.

r: am'à-ranth.

ANTS

h: Hants.

p: pants.

Also ant+s.

Cf. ans.

ĀNZ

h: Hāineṣ (Hānz).

r: Rāineṣ, Rāyneṣ.

Also ān+s.

Also Cain's, etc.

ANZ

b: bannṣ.

Also an+s.

Also Dan's, etc.

ÄNZH

mé-läṅge' (mä-loṅzh').

ĀP

Vowel: āpe.

ch: chāpe.

dr: drāpe.

g: à-gāpe', gāpe.

gr: grāpe.

AP
APT

fāte, fär. fàst, fạll, finăl, cãre, at; mēte, prẹy, hĕr, met; pīne, marĭne, bĭrd, pĭn; nōte, mŏve, fọr, atŏm, not; mọọn, book;

100

(Choose only one word out of each group)

j: jāpe.
k(c̣): c̣āpe, es-c̣āpe', fīre es-c̣āpe', un-c̣āpe'.
kr: c̣rāpe, c̣rèpe (krāp).
l: Lāpe.
n: nāpe.
p: pāpe.
r: rāpe.
sh: shāpe, ship'shāpe, trans-shāpe', un-shāpe'.
sk(sc̣): land'sc̣āpe, sc̣āpe, sēa'sc̣āpe.
skr(sc̣r): sc̣rāpe.
t: red"≠tāpe', tāpe.
tr: trāpe.

AP

Vowel: lagn'i-appe (lan').
ch: chap.
d: dap.
dr: drap.
f: Fap.
fl: flap, flip'flap.
fr: frap.
g: à-gape', gap, gape, stop gap.
h: hap, māy-hap', mis-hap'.
j: Jap.
k(c̣): c̣ap, fọolsc̣ap, fọr'ăge c̣ap, han'di-c̣ap, nīght'c̣ap (nīt'), pĕr-c̣us'sion c̣ap (-kush'), wish'ing c̣ap.
kl: àf'tĕr-c̣lap, c̣lap, thun'dĕr-c̣lap.
kr: c̣rap.
l: lap, Lapp, ō-vĕr-lap', un-lap'.
m: map.
n: g̣e-napp', g̣e-nappe', knap (nap), nap.

p: pap.
r: en-wrap', rap, un-wrap', wrap.
s: sap.
skr(sc̣r): sc̣rap.
sl: slap.
sn: snap.
str: bē-strap', shōul'dĕr strap, strap.
t: heel tap, tap, wạt'ĕr tap.
tr: c̣lap'trap, en-trap', rat'tle-trap, trap.
w: wapp.
y: lagn-iappe' (lan-yap'), yap.

ÄP

g: gäpe.
sw: swäp.
Cf. op.

ĀPS

m: Māpes.
n: jack'à-nāpes.
tr: trāipse.
Also āp+s.
Also ape's, etc.

APS

aps: apse.
h: pĕr-haps'.
kr: c̣raps.
l: c̣ŏl-lapse', ē-lapse', il-lapse', in"tĕr-lapse', lapse, rē-lapse'.
shn: sc̣hnapps (shnaps).
Also ap+s.
Also Jap's, etc.

ĀPT

Vowel: āped (āpt).
Also āp+d.

APT

Vowel: apt, in-apt'.
d: à-dapt'.

(Choose only one word out of each group)

k: c̦apped, moss′=c̦apped″,
snōw′=c̦apped″.

r: en-rapt′, rapt, wrapt.

str: bē-strapped′.

Also ap+ed.

ĀR

Vowel: ãir, ãire,
ar′ri-ère (ar′ri-ãr), Āyr,
ãyre*, e′er (ãr), ere (ãr) eyre (ãr),
heir (ãr), how-e̯′er′, mid″=ãir′,
Pi-erre′, pōr-ti-ère′ (-ti-ãr′),
vï-väṅ-di-ère′ (-di-ãr′),
whät-e′er′, whät-sō-e′er′,
when-e′er′, wher-e′er′,
where-sō-e′er′.

b: bãre, beãr,
C̦am-em-bert′ (-bãr′),
fōr-beãr′, thread′bãre (thred′),
un-dĕr-beãr′, up-beãr′.

bl: blãre.

ch: ärm′chãir, chãir, chãre,
sē-dan′chãir.

d: Ȧ-dãir′, bē-dãre′, dãre,
out-dãre′.

f: af-fãir′, af-fãire′,
c̦härġe̦s′ d′áf-fãires′
                (shär-zhā′dȧf-fãr′),
fãir, fãre,
lãis-sez′ fãire (les-sā′fãr′),
mis-fãre′, thŏr-ōugh-fãre (′ō-),
un-fãir′.

fl: flãir, flãre.

fr: frère (frãr).

g: gãre.

gl: bē-glãre′, glãir, glãre.

h: hãir, hãre, mãid′en-hãir,
mō′hãir.

hw: an′y-where (en′i-hwãr),
else′where, ev′e-ry-where,
ŏTH′ẽr-where,

sŏme′where,
where.

j: ē′tȧ-ġère.

k(c̦): c̦ãre, dev″il=mãy=c̦ãre′.

kl: c̦lãire, c̦lãre*, dē-c̦lãre′,
ē-c̦lãir′, Sin-c̦lãir′.

kw(qu): quãir*.

l: c̦ap-il-lãire′, lãir.

m: bêche dē mer (besh),
mal dē mer, mãre.

n: bil-liŏ-nãire′,
c̦ŏm-mis″sio-nãire′,
c̦ŏn-ces″sio-nãire′,
deb″ō-nãir′, doc̦″tri-nãire′,
jär-di-nière′ (-nyãr′), Mc̦-Nãir′,
Mc̦-Nãre′, mil-liŏ-nãire′,
ne′er (nãr), tril-liŏ-nãire′,
viṅ or-di-nãire′ (vaṅ).

p: c̦om-pãre′, des-pãir,
dis″rē-pãir, im-pãir′, pãir,
pãre, peãr, prē-pãre′,
prick′ly peãr, rē-pãir′.

pr: prãyer.

r: rãre.

s: Sãyre.

sh: c̦rop′shãre, shãre.

sk(sc̦): sc̦ãre.

skw(squ): squãre, T squãre.

sn: en-snãre′, snãre.

sp: spãre.

st: back·stãir, c̦ock′le-stãir*,
out-stãre′, stãir, stãre, stere,
up-stãre′.

sw: for-sweãr′, out-sweãr′,
swãre*, sweãr, un-sweãr′.

t: pär-terre′, prō-lē-tãire′,
sol′i-tãire, tãre, teãr, up-teãr′.

TH: THeir, THere.

ty: pōr-tière′.

v: tröu-vère′, vãir, vãre.

ÄR
ÄRCH

fāte, fär, fȧst,♦fạll, finăl, cãre, at; mēte, prey, hẽr, met; pīne,
marïne, bĭrd, pin; nōte, mŏve, fọr, atŏm, not; mọọn, book;

102

(Choose only one word out of each group)

w: ȧ-wãre, bē-wãre',
Del'ȧ-wãre, earth'en-wãre,
out-weãr', un-ȧ-wãre',
un"bē-wãre'*, un'dẽr-weãr,
wãre, weãr.

y: Grü-yère', tú-yère', yãre.

ÄR

Vowel: äre, cav-i-är', jag-ū-är'.

b: ax'le-bär (aks'), bär,
cin'nȧ-bär, dē-bär', dis-bär',
em-bär', Ex-cal'i-bär (eks-),
Mal'ȧ-bär, sad'dle-bär,
shack'le-bär, un-bär', up-bär',
Zan'zi-bär.

ch: chär.

d: cal'en-där, där, dē'ō-där,
hos'pō-där, jem'ȧ-där,
sub-äh-där', zä-min-där'.

f: ȧ-fär', fär, Färr.

g: ci-gär', gär, vin'e-gär.

j: ȧ-jär', jär, nīght'jär (nīt').

k(c): cär, jaunt'ing cär,
Las'cär.

l: añ'gū-lär, an-i-mal'cū-lär,
an'nū-lär, bi-noc'ū-lär,
cīr'cū-lär, con'sū-lär,
cre-pus'cū-lär, dis-sim'i-lär,
fu-ni'cū-lär, glob'ū-lär,
in'sū-lär, ir-reg'ū-lär,
joc'ū-lär, jug'ū-lär, lär,
mod'ū-lär, mol-ec'ū-lär,
oc'ū-lär, pär-tic'ū-lär,
pẽr-pen-dic'ū-lär, pop'ū-lär,
quäd-rañ'gū-lär (kwäd-),
reg'ū-lär, scap'ū-lär, sec'ū-lär,
sim'i-lär, siñ'gū-lär,
som-nam'bū-lär,
spec-tac'ū-lär, stel'lū-lär,
tab"ēr-nac'ū-lär, tab'ū-lär,
tin"tin-nab'ū-lär, tit'ū-lär,

trī-añ'gū-lär, tū'te-lär,
ū'vū'lär, val'vū-lär,
vē-hic'ū-lär, vẽr-mic'ū-lar,
vẽr-nac'ū-lär, vẽr-sic'ū-lär.

lw: Loire (lwär).

m: cy-mär', mär,
tin'tȧ-märre*.

n: cȧ-närd', gnär (när),
knär (när).

p: pär, pärr.

sk(sc): scär.

sp: feld'spär, spär, un-spär'.

st: dāy'stär, ēve'ning stär,
fạl'ling stär, in-stär',
lōde'stär, mọr'ning stär,
north stär, pī'lŏt stär,
sēa stär, shoọt'ing stär, stär.

str: reg-is-trär'.

t: av'ȧ-tär, cȧ-tärrh',
gui-tär' (gi-), scim'i-tär (sim'),
tär.

ts: tsär.

tr: re-gis-trär'.

v: böul'e-värd (boọl'e-vär).

w: jag'ūär (wär).

z: bȧ-zäar', czär (zär), hus-sär'.

ÄRB

b: bärb.

g: gärb.

y: yärb.

ÄRCH

Vowel: ärch, in-ärch',
ō"vẽr-ärch'.

l: lärch.

m: coun'tẽr-märch,
dead märch (ded), marcn,
out-märch', ō"vẽr-märch'.

p: pärch.

st: stärch.

103 ūse, bṳll, brûte, tûrn, up; crȳ, myth; çat, maçhine. ace, church, çhord; ġem, aṅger, (Fr.) boṅ, aş; THis, thin; azure

ÃRD
ÄRK

(Choose only one word out of each group)

ÃRD

Vowel: un-heired′ (-ãrd′).
b: Bãird.
h: black′=hãired′, gōl′den=hãired′, red′=hãired′, sil′vēr=hãired′.
k(c̨): un-c̨āred′.
l: lãird, lãired.
p: im-pãired′, un″im-pãired′, pãired, un-pãired′, prē-pãred′, un″prē-pãred′.
sh: shãred, un-shãred′.
sp: spãred, un-spãred′.
Also ãr+ed.

ÄRD

Vowel: mil-li-ärd′.
b: bärd, bom-bärd′, c̨lōse′=bärred′.
ch: chärd.
f: färd*.
g: áf′tēr′guärd, à-vänt′=gärde′, black′guärd (blag′), bod′y-guärd, dis″rē-gärd′, en-guärd′, guärd, līfe′guärd, rē-gärd′, un-guärd′.
h: härd.
k(c̨): c̨all′ing c̨ärd, c̨ärd, dis-c̨ärd′, pla′c̨ärd, wed′ding c̨ärd.
l: föu-lärd′, in″tēr-lärd′, lärd.
m: märred, un-märred′.
n: Bēr-närd′, c̨à-närd′, närd, spīke′närd.
p: c̨am-el′ō-pärd, pärd.
r: Ġe-rärd′, Ġi-rärd′.
s: särd.
sk(sc̨): sc̨ärred, un-sc̨ärred′.
sp: spärred, un-dēr-spärred′.
st: ē′vil=stärrēd′, stärred.
sh: shärd.

t: dȳ-nam′i-tärd, pē-tärd′, rē-tärd′, tärred.
v: boù-lē-värd′.
y: back-yärd′, frŏnt yärd, chick′en-yärd, pōul′try yärd, yärd.
Also är+ed.
Also stär′d.

ÄRF

Vowel: ′ärf′=and=′ärf′.
l: lärf.
sk: sc̨ärf.

ÄRJ

b: bärġe, em-bärġe′*.
ch: chärġe, dis-chärġe′, en-chärġe′*, ō-vēr-chärġe′, sūr′charġe, un-chärġe′, un-dēr-chärġe′.
f: Färġe, La Färġe.
l: en-lärġe′, lärġe.
m: märġe, sēa′märġe′
s: särġe.
sp: spärġe.
t: tärġe.
th: li-thärġe′.

ÄRJD

b: bärged.
ch: chärged, dis-chärged′, un″dis-chärged′.
Also ärj+ed.

ÄRK

Vowel: ärc̨, ärk, Ā′si-ärc̨h(′shi-), ec̨-c̨lē′si-ärc̨h, her-ē′si-ärc̨h, hī′ēr-ärc̨h, mā′tri-ärc̨h, pā′tri-ärc̨h.
b: bärk, bärque, dē-bärk′, dis″em-bärk′, em-bärk′.
d: bē-därk′, därk, en-därk′'*.
g: ol′i-gärc̨h.

(Choose only one word out of each group)

h: härk.
k(c̣): c̣ärk.
kl: C̣lärke, c̣lerk (klärk).
l: lärk, mead′ōw‗lärk (med′),
  sēa lark, skȳ′lärk.
m: ēaṣ′y-märk, flood′märk,
  foot′märk, märc̣, märk,
  märque (märk), rē-märk′,
  wạ′tẽr-märk.
n: ï′re-närc̣h, knärk (närk).
p: dis-pärk′, im-pärk′, pärk.
s: särk.
sh: shärk.
sn: snärk.
sp: spärk.
st: stärk, Stärke.
v: äard′värk.

ÄRKS
m: Märx.
Also ärk+s.

ÄRKT
b: bärked.
m: märked, un-märked′.
Also ärk+ed.

ÄRL
h: härl.
j: järl.
k(c̣): c̣ärl, Kärl.
m: Al′bẽr-märle, märl.
n: gnärl (närl).
p: im-pärl′, pärle*.
sn: snärl.

ÄRLZ
ch: Chärleṣ.
Also ärl+s.

ÄRM
Vowel: ärm, ax′le ärm (aks′l),
  dis-ärm′, fïre′ärm, fōre′ärm,
  un-ärm′.
b: bärm.

ch: bē-chärm′, chärm,
  c̣oun′tẽr-chärm, dē-chärm′,
  dis″en-chärm′, lŏve chärm,
  un-chärm′.
d: ġen-därme′ (zhän-).
f: c̣oun′ty färm, färm.
  pọọr färm.
h: härm, un-härm′.
l: ȧ-lärm′, fạlse ȧ-lärm′.
m: märm, sc̣họọl′märm.

ÄRMD
Vowel: ärmed, fōre-ärmed′.
l: ȧ-lärmed′, un″ȧ-lärmed′.
Also ärm+ed.
Also arm′d, etc.

ÄRMZ
Vowel: Ärmeṣ,
  as-sạult′‗at‗ärmṣ′,
  ġen′tle-măn‗at‗ärmṣ′,
  king′‗at‗ärmṣ′, man′‗at‗ärmṣ′.
Also ärm+s.
Also harm′s, etc.

ÃRN
b: bãirn.
k(c̣): c̣ãirn.
t: tãirn.

ÄRN
b: bärn, im-bärn′*.
d: därn.
k(c̣): in c̣ärn.
m: Märne.
s: c̣on-särn′.
t: tärn.
y: yärn.

ÄRNZ
b: Bärneṣ.
Also ärn+s.
Also yarn′s, etc.

105 ūse, bu̯ll, brúte, tŭrn, **up;** crȳ, myth; c̦at, machine, ace,
church, c̦hord; ġem, añger, (Fr.) boṅ, aṣ; THis, thin; aẓure

ÄRP
ĀS

(Choose only one word out of each group)

ÄRP

h: härp.
k(c̦): c̦ärp, ep"i-c̦ärp', es-c̦ärp',
mon'ō-c̦ärp, per'i-c̦ärp.
sh: shärp.
sk(sc̦) sc̦ärp.

ÃRS

sk(sc̦): sc̦ãrce.

ÄRS

f: färce.
p: pärse.
s: särse.
sp: spärse.

ÄRSH

h: härsh.
m: märsh.

ÄRT

Vowel: ärt.
b: bärt., Bärt.
ch: chärt.
d: därt, in-därt'.
h: flint'heärt, härt, heärt,
lī'ŏn-heärt, sweet'heärt,
un-heärt'.
k(c̦): c̦ärt, quärte (kärt),
un-c̦ärt', wa̱t'ēr-c̦ärt.
m: märt.
p: à-pärt', coun'tēr-pärt,
dē-pärt', dis-pärt', im-pärt',
pärt.
s: särt.
sm: smärt.
st: stärt, up'stärt.
t: tärt.

ÄRTH

g: Ap'ple-gärth, gärth.
h: heärth.
sw: swärth.

ÄRV

k(c̦): c̦ärve.
l: lärve.
st: stärve.

ÄRTS

h: Härz.
Also ärt+s.
Also art's, etc.

ÃRZ

pr: prãyerṣ (prãrz).
st: back-stãirṣ', stãirṣ.
TH: THeirṣ (THãrz).
m: un-à-wãreṣ', un-bē-wãreṣ',
un-wãreṣ'.
Also ãr+s.
Also chair's, etc.

ÄRZ

l: Lärṣ.
m: Märṣ.
Also är+ṣ.
Also tar's, etc.

ĀS

Vowel: āce.
b: à-bāse', bāse, bāss, dē-bāse',
thŏr'ōugh bāss (thēr'ō-).
br: brāce, em-brāce',
un-brāce', un"dēr-brāce'.
ch: chāse, en-chāse',
stee'ple-chāse.
d: dāce.
f: à-fāce', bon'i-fāce, dē-fāce',
ef-fāce', fāce, out-fāce'.
gr: bē-grāce', dis-grāce', grāce,
scāpe'grāce.
k(c̦): c̦āse, en-c̦āse', ū-kāse',
un-c̦āse'.
kr: id'i-ō-c̦rāse.
l: an'ē-lāce, bē-lāce', en-lāce',
in"tēr-lāce', lāce, pop'ū-lāce,
un-lāce'.

(Choose only one word out of each group)

m: gri-māce′, māce.
p: à-pāce′, car′à-pāce, foot′pāce, out-pāce′, pāce.
pl: bĩrth′plāce, com′mŏn-plāce, dis-plāce′, hīd′ing plāce, mis-plāce′, plāce, plāice, rē-plāce′, rest′ing plāce, tryst′ing plāce.
r: chăr′i-ŏt rāce, ē-rāse′, foot rāce, horse rāce, rāce.
sp: brēaTH′ing spāce, in″tẽr-spāce′, spāce.
thr: Thrāce.
tr: rē-trāce′, trāce.
v: vāse.

AS, ÁS

Vowel: ā′li-as, ȧss, hā′bē-as, pā′tẽr-fȧ-mil′i-as.
b: bȧss, rụ-bȧsse′.
br: brȧss.
fr: sas′sȧ-fras.
g: gas.
gl: flint glȧss, gal′lō glȧss, glȧss, hour′glȧss (our′), ī′șin-glȧss, look′ing glȧss, min′ute glȧss (′it), ob′ject glȧss wat′ẽr-glȧss, weaTH′ẽr glȧss.
gr: af′tẽr-grȧss, eel grȧss, grȧss, spar′rōw-grȧss″.
kl(cl): clȧss, dē-clȧss′, fĩrst′-clȧss′, mid′dle-clȧss″, wŏrk′ing clȧss.
kr: crȧss, hip′pō-crȧs.
kv: kvȧss.
l: ȧ-lȧs′, bon′ni-lȧss*, lȧss, pail-lȧsse′ (pȧl-yȧs′).
m: All″hal′lōw-mas, ȧ-mȧss′, Can′dle-mas, en mȧsse (äṅ), Hal′lōw-mas, mȧss. Mich-ael-mas (mik′el-).
p: Khȳ′bẽr Pȧss (kī′), ō′vẽr-pȧss, pȧss, sũr-pȧss′, un′dẽr-pȧss.
r: cuï-rȧss′ (kwē-), mō-rȧss′.
s: gär′den sass, sass.
str: strȧss.
t: dem-i-tȧsse′, tar″an-tȧss′, tȧss.
v: cre-vȧsse′, kȧ-vȧss′.
y: yas.

ÄS

m: en mässe (äṅ).

ĀSH

kr(cr): crèche.

ASH

Vowel: ash, moun′tain ash (′tin), weep′ing ash.
b: ȧ-bash′, bash, cal′ȧ-bash. squȧ-bash′.
br: brache*, brash.
d: bal′dẽr-dash, bē-dash′, dash, in″tẽr-dash′, slap′dash′, splat′tẽr-dash.
f: fash.
fl: flash.
g: gash.
h: hash, rē-hash′.
k(c): cache, cash.
kl: clash.
kr: crash.
l: cȧ-lash′, lache, lash, un-lash′.
m: mash.
n: gnash (nash), Nash.
p: cal′i-pash, pash.
pl: plash.

(Choose only one word out of each group)

r: rash.
s: sash.
sl: slash.
sm: smash.
spl: splash.
t: mŏus-tac̗he' (mus-),
pȧ-tac̗he',
sā'bre-tac̗he (sā'bēr-).
thr: thrash.
tr: trash.

ÄSH

kw: quäsh.
skw: squäsh.
w: wäsh.
Cf. osh.

ASHT

b: ȧ-bashed'.
d: dashed, un-dashed'.
l: lashed, un-lashed'.
thr: thrashed, un-thrashed'.
Also ash+ed.
Also lash'd, etc.

ȦSK

Vowel: ȧsk.
b: bȧsk, bȧsque.
fl: flȧsk, hip flȧsk,
pow'dēr flȧsk.
k(c̗): c̗ȧsk, c̗ȧsque,
wȧt'ēr-c̗ȧsk.
m: an'ti-mȧsk, bē-mȧsk',
Bēr'gȧ-mȧsk, im-mȧsk'*,
mȧsk, mȧsque, un-mȧsk'.
p: Pȧsc̗h.
t: ō"vēr-tȧsk', tȧsk.

ȦSKT

Vowel: ȧsked, un-ȧsked'.
b: bȧsked.
m: mȧsked, un-mȧsked'.
Also ȧsk+ed.

ASP

Vowel: asp.
g: gasp.
gr: en-grasp', grasp.
h: hasp.
kl: c̗lasp, en-c̗lasp', un-c̗lasp'.
r: rasp.

ÄSP

w: wäsp.

AST

b: bāste, lam-bāste' ȧ-bāsed',
self'₌ȧ-bāsed'.
br: brāced, un-brāced'.
ch: chāsed, chāste, un-chāste'.
f: ap'ple₌fāced, bȧre'₌fāced,
brā'zen₌fāced, dē-fāced',
dŏu'ble₌fāced (dub'l),
dōugh'fāced (dō'), fȧir'₌fāced,
freck'le₌fāced, fũr'rōw₌fāced,
hard'₌fāced, hatch'et₌fāced,
horse'₌fāced, Jā'nus₌fāced,
lēan'fāced, li'ly₌fāced,
mot'tle₌fāced, pāle'₌fāced,
pā'pēr₌fāced, pīe'₌fāced,
pick'le₌fāced, pim'ple₌fāced,
pip'pin₌fāced, plat'tēr₌fāced,
plump'₌fāced, pṵd'ding₌fāced,
pug'₌fāced, sad'₌fāced,
shāme'₌fāced, sheep'₌fāced,
smock'₌fāced, smooTH'₌fāced,
smug'₌fāced, tal'lōw₌faced,
twö'₌fāced (too'), tri'ple₌fāced,
un"dē-fāced', un-shāme'fāced",
vin'e-gȧr₌fāced, wēa'șel₌fāced,
whey'₌fāced (hwā'),
wiz'en₌fāced.
gr: grāced, un"dis-grāced',
un-grāced', well'₌grāced'.
h: hāste, pōst'hāste'.
k(c̗): c̗āsed, un-c̗āsed'.

AST
ĀT
fāte, fär, fàst, fạll, finăl, cãre, **at**; mēte, prẹy, hêr, met; pīne
marïne, bîrd, pin; nōte, mŏve, fọr, atŏm, not; mọọn, book;   **108**

(Choose only one word out of each group)

l: lāced, strāight'=lāced (strāt'),
un-lāced'.

p: im-pāste',
lead'en=pāced (led'), pāste,
slōw'=pāced, snāil'=pāced,
thŏr'ough=pāced ('ō-).

r: rāced, ē-rāsed'.

sp: spāced.

t: ăf'tēr=tāste, dis-tāste',
fōre'tāste, tāste.

tr: rē-trāced', trāced
un-trāced'.

w: wāist, wāste.
Also ās+d.

AST, ÀST

Vowel: eç-çlē'şi-ast, el-ē'ġi-ast,
en-çōm'i-ast, en-thū'şi-ast,
ọr'ġi-ast, sçhōl'i-ast,
sym-pō'şi-ast.

b: bàst, bom'bàst.

bl: blàst, çoun'tēr-blàst,
storm'blàst.

d: dàst.

f: em'bēr-fàst, fàst, hand'=fàst,
hōld'fàst, stead'fàst (sted'),
un-fàst'.

fr: met'à-phràst (-fràst).
par'à-phràst.

g: à-ghàst', flab'bēr-gàst,
ghàst*.

h: hàst*.

k(ç): çàst, çàste, down'çàst,
fōre'çàst, hīgh'=çàste' (hī'),
lōw'=çàste', ō-vēr-çàst',
rē-çàst'.

kl: ī-çon'ō-çlàst, ī-dol'ō-çlàst,
thē'ō-çlàst.

l: làst, out-làst'.

m: à-màssed', fōre'màst,
hälf'=màst' (häf'), jù'ry màst,

māin'màst, màssed, màst,
miz'zen màst.

p: pàssed, pàst, rē-pàst',
sūr-pàssed', un-pàssed',
un″sūr-pàssed'.

pl: met'à-plàst, prō'tō-plàst.

s: sàssed.

tr: çon'tràst.

v: à-vàst', dē-vàst', vàst.

w: wàst.
Also as+ed.

ÄST

w: wäst.
Cf. ost.

ĀT

Vowel: ab-brē'vi-āte,
ab-sin'thi-āte, aç-cen'tū-āte,
aç'tū-āte, af-fil'i-āte,
al-lē'vi-āte, am'pli-āte,
an-nun'ci-āte,
ap-prē'ci-āte ('shi-),
ap-prō'pri-āte,
as-phyx'i-āte (-fiks'),
as-sō'ci-āte ('shi-), āte,
at-ten'ū-āte, ạu'rē-āte,
ā'vi-āte, baç-çà-lạu'rē-āte,
çal-um'ni-āte, çhal-yb'ē-āte,
cîr-çum-stan'ti-āte ('shi-),
çol-lē'ġi-āte, çon-cil'i-āte,
çrē-āte', dē-lin'ē-āte,
dē-nun'ci-āte,
dē-prē'ci-āte ('shi-), dē'vi-āte,
dif″fēr-en'ti-āte ('shi-),
dis-sō'ci-āte ('shi-), ef-feç'tū-āte,
ēight (āt), ē-mā'ci-āte ('shi-),
ē-mol'li-āte, ē-nun'ci-āte,
ē-vaç'ū-āte, ē-val'ū-āte,
ē-ven'tū-āte, ex-çọr'i-āte (eks-),
ex-çrū'ci-āte ('shi-),
ex-pā″ti-āte ('shi-),

(Choose only one word out of each group)

ex-pā'tri-āte (eks-), ex'pi-āte,
ex-ten'ū-āte, fluc̨'tū-āte,
fruc̨'tū-āte, glā'ci-āte ('shi-),
grad'ū-āte, hab-it'ū-āte,
hū-mil'i-āte, im-mȧ-tē'ri-āte*,
im-mē'di-āte, im-prō'pri-āte,
in″ap-prō'pri-āte, in-c̨hō'āte,
in-c̨rē-āte', in-di-vid'ū-āte,
in-ē'bri-āte, in-fat'ū-āte,
in-fū'ri-āte, in-grā'ti-āte ('shi-),
in-i'ti-āte ('shi-),
in-sā'ti-āte ('shi-), in-sin'ū-āte,
in″tēr-mē'di-āte, ir-rā'di-āte,
lau̧'rē-āte, lī-cen'ti-āte ('shi-),
lix-iv'i-āte, lux-ū'ri-āte,
mēd'i-āte, nē-gō'ti-āte ('shi-),
nō-vit'i-āte (-vish'), ob'vi-āte.
of-fi'ci-āte ('shi-), ōp'i-āte,
pal'li-āte, pēr'mē-āte,
pēr-pet'ū-āte, pō'et lau̧'rē-āte,
prō'c̨rē-āte, prō-fes-sōr'i-āte,
prō-pi'ti-āte ('shi-),
prō-vin'ci-āte ('shi-),
puñc̨'tū-āte, rā'di-āte,
rē″c̨rē-āte', rē-mē'di-āte,
rē-pā'tri-āte, rē-pū'di-āte,
rē-tal'i-āte, rō'ṣē-āte,
sā'ti-āte ('shi-), sec̨-rē-tā'ri-āte,
sit'ū-āte, spō'li-āte,
sub-stan'ti-āte ('shi-),
sū″pēr-an'nū-āte,
tran″sub-stan'ti-āte ('shi-),
un-c̨rē-āte', vā'ri-āte,
vī-c̨ār'i-āte, vit'i-āte (vish').

b: ȧ-bāte', ap'prō-bāte, bāit,
bāte, cel'i-bāte, dē-bāte',
ex-ac'ēr-bāte, in'c̨ū-bāte,
rē'bāte, rep'rō-bāte,
stȳ'lō-bāte.

br: cel'ē-brāte, in-vēr'tē-brāte,
lū'c̨ū-brāte, vēr'tē-brāte.

d: ab'nō-dāte*, ac̨-c̨om'mō-dāte,
an'tē-dāte, c̨an'di-dāte,
con-sol'i-dāte, dāte, dē'ō-dāte*,
dep'rē-dāte, di-lap'i-dāte,
ē-lū'ci-dāte, in-tim'i-dāte,
in'un-dāte, in-val'i-dāte,
li'qui-dāte, prē-dāte', sē-dāte',
val'i-dāte.

f: c̨al'i-phāte, fāte, fȩte.

fl: con-flāte', ef-flāte', in-flāte',
suf-flāte'.

fr: af-frei̧ght' (-frāt'),
frei̧ght (frāt).

g: ab'nē-gāte, ab'rō-gāte,
ag'grē-gāte, ar'rō-gāte,
Bil'lings-gāte, c̨as'ti-gāte,
con'grē-gāte, con'ju̇-gāte,
cor'ru̇-gāte, del'ē-gāte,
der'ō-gāte, ex-trav'ȧ-gāte,
flood'gāte, fū'mi-gāte, gāit,
gāte, in'sti-gāte, in-ter'rō-gāte,
in-ves'ti-gāte, ir'ri-gāte,
lev'i-gāte, lit'i-gāte, mit'i-gāte,
nav'i-gāte, ob'li-gāte,
prof'li-gāte, prō-mul'gāte,
prop'ō-gāte, rel'ē-gāte,
run'ȧ-gāte, Sēa Gāte,
seg'rē-gāte, sub'ju̇-gāte,
sub'rō-gāte, sū₌pēr-er'ō-gate,
vār'i-e-gāte.

br: dis-in'tē-grāte, em'i-grāte,
grāte, greāt, im'mi-grāte,
in-grāte'*, in'tē-grāte,
mī'grāte, rē-grāte'.

h: hāte, Hāi̧ght (hāt).

k(c̨): ab'di-c̨āte, ab'lō-c̨āte*,
ad-ju̇'di-c̨āte, ad'vō-c̨āte,
al'lō-c̨āte, aļ'tēr-c̨āte,
ap'pli-c̨āte, au̧s'pi-c̨āte,
au̧-then'ti-c̨āte, c̨āte,
cēr-tif'i-c̨āte, c̨ol'lō-c̨āte,

(Choose only one word out of each group)

com-mū′ni-çāte, com′pli-çāte,
con′fis-çāte, ded′i-çāte,
del′i-çāte, dep′rē-çāte,
dī″ag-nos′ti-çāte, dis′lō-çāte,
dō-mes′ti-çāte, dū′pli-çāte,
ed′ū-çāte, ē-quiv′ō-çāte,
ē-rad′i-çāte, ex″çom-mū′ni-çāte,
ex′tri-çāte, fab′ri-çāte,
hȳ-poth′ē-çāte, im′pli-çāte,
im′prē-çāte, in-çul′çāte,
in-del′i-çāte, in′di-çāte,
in-tox′i-çāte, in′tri-çāte,
in′vō-çāte, Kāte, lō′çāte,
lū′bri-çāte, mas′ti-çāte,
plā′çāte, pon-tif′i-çāte,
pred′i-çāte, prē-vār′i-çāte,
prog-nos′ti-çāte,
quäd-rú′pli-çāte, rē-cip′rō-çāte,
rus′ti-çāte, sil′i-çāte,
sō-phis′ti-çāte (-fis′),
spif′fli-çāte, suf′fō-çāte,
sup′pli-çāte, syn′di-çāte,
vȧ-çāte′, vin′di-çāte.

kr: con′sē-çrāte, çrāte,
des′ē-çrāte, ex′ē-çrāte, krāit.

kw(qu): ad′ē-quāte,
an′ti-quāte, ē-quāte′,
in-ad′ē-quāte.

l: ab-squat′ū-lāte,
aç-çū′mū-lāte, a-cid′ū-lāte,
ad′ū-lāte, al-vē′ō-lāte,
am′bū-lāte, añ′gū-lāte,
an-nī′hi-lāte, an′nū-lāte,
ȧ-pos′tō-lāte, är-tiç′ū-lāte,
as-sim′i-lāte, as-sim′ū-lāte*,
bē-lāte′, bī-maç′ū-lāte,
bī-noç′ū-lāte, çal′çū-lāte,
cam-pan′ū-lāte, can′cel-lāte,
cap-it′ū-lāte, cär′di-nȧ-lāte,
choç′ō-lāte, cir′çū-lāte,
çō-ag′ū-lāte, col-lāte′,

cŏn-fab′ū-lāte, con-grat′ū-lāte,
con′sū-lāte, cop′ū-lāte,
cor′rē-lāte, cren′el-lāte,
dē-lāte′, dē-pop′ū-lāte,
dē-pū′ce-lāte*, des′ō-lāte,
dī-lāte′, dis-con′sō-lāte,
dis-sim′ū-lāte, ē-jaç′ū-lāte,
ē-lāte, ē-mas′çū-lāte, em′ū-lāte,
et-ī′ō-lāte, ex-pos′tū-lāte,
flaġ′el-lāte, fō′li-ō-lāte,
for′mū-lāte, fū-nam′bū-lāte,
ġes-tiç′ū-lāte, gran′ū-lāte,
grat′ū-lāte*, im-maç′ū-lāte,
im′mō-lāte, in″är-tiç′ū-lāte
in-ças′tel-lāte*, in-oç′ū-lāte,
in′sū-lāte, in-tēr′pō-lāte,
in-vī′ō-lāte, is′ō-lāte,
lan′cē-ō-lāte, lāte, leġ′is-lāte,
man-ip′ū-lāte, mȧ-triç′ū-lāte,
mod′ū-lāte, mū′ti-lāte,
os′cil-lāte, os′çū-lāte,
peç′ū-lāte, pe-nin′sū-lāte,
pēr-am′bū-lāte, pēr′çō-lāte,
pop′ū-lāte, pos′tū-lāte,
rē″cap-it′ū-lāte, reg′ū-lāte,
rē-lāte′, re-tiç′ū-lāte,
scin′til-lāte (sin′), sib′i-lāte,
sim′ū-lāte, som-nam′bū-lāte,
speç′ū-lāte, stel′lū-lāte,
stim′ū-lāte, stip′ū-late,
strid′ū-lāte, tab′ū-lāte,
tit′il-lāte, trans-lāte′,
trī-añ′gū-lāte, ūl′ū-lāte,
un′dū-lāte, vȧ′cil-lāte,
vas′sȧ-lāte, ven′ti-lāte,
vēr-miç′ū-lāte, vī′ō-lāte.

m: aç′clȧ-māte*, aç′cli-māte,
ȧ-mal′gȧ-māte, an′i-māte,
an″tē-pē-nul′ti-māte,
ap-prox′i-māte, çāse′māte,
check′māte, çlȧss′māte,

(Choose only one word out of each group)

con'sum-māte, crē'māte,
dec'i-māte, es'ti-māte,
fïrst māte, help'māte,
in-an'i-māte, in'ti-māte,
leġ-it-'i-māte, māte, mess'māte
plāy'māte, prox'i-māte,
school'māte, ship'māte,
stāle'māte, sub'li-māte,
ul'ti-māte.

n: ab-ā'li-e-nāte, a-ba'ci-nāte,
ab-om'i-nāte, a-cū'mi-nāte,
af-fec'tio-nāte,
ag-glu'ti-nāte, ā'li-e-nāte,
al'tēr-nāte, as-sas'si-nāte,
cach'in-nāte, cär'bō-nāte,
com'mi-nāte,
com-pas'sio-nāte,
con-cat'ē-nāte,
con-di'tio-nāte,
con-tam'i-nāte, cō=or'di-nāte,
cor'ō-nāte, crim'i-nāte,
cul'mi-nāte, dē-nom'i-nāte,
deş'iġ-nāte, dē-tēr'mi-nāte,
det'ō-nāte, dē-vĭr'ġi-nāte,
dī-ac'ō-nāte, dis-crim'i-nāte,
dis-sem'i-nāte, dom'i-nāte,
dō-nāte', ef-fem'i-nāte,
ē-lim'i-nāte, em'a-nāte,
ex-tēr'mi-nāte,
ex-tor'tio-nāte,
fas'ci-nāte, fōre-or'di-nāte,
for'tū-nāte, ful'mi-nāte,
ġe-lat'i-nāte, ġēr'mi-nāte,
hī'bēr-nāte, il-lū'mi-nāte,
ĭm-mär'ġi-nāte,
im-pas'sio-nāte,
im-pēr'sō-nāte, im-por'tū-nāte,
in"com-pas'sio-nāte,
in-crim'i-nāte, in"dē-tēr'mi-nāte,
in"dis-crim'i-nāte,
in-doc'tri-nāte, in-ġēr'mi-nāte,

in-nāte', in-or'di-nāte,
in-sem'i-nāte, in"sub-or'di-nāte,
in"tēr-ces'sio-nāte*,
in-tēr'mi-nāte, in'tō-nāte,
mach'i-nāte, maġ'nāte,
mar'i-nāte, Nāte, nom'i-nāte,
ob'sti-nāte, or-iġ'i-nāte,
or-nāte', ox-yġ'ē-nāte,
pas'sio-nāte,
pā'trō-nāte, per'ē-gri-nāte,
pēr'sō-nāte, prē-des'ti-nāte,
prē-dom'i-nāte, prō-cras'ti-nāte,
prō-por'tio-nāte,
rat-i-ō'ci-nāte (rash-),
rē-crim'i-nāte, rē-jū've-nāte,
rùm'i-nāte, sub-or'di-nāte,
tēr'mi-nāte, un-for'tū-nāte,
vac'ci-nāte, vat-i'ci-nāte,
vēr-ti'ġi-nāte.

p: an-ti'ci-pāte, con'sti-pāte,
dis'si-pāte, dun'dēr-pāte,
ē-man'ci-pāte, ē-pis'cō-pāte,
ex'cul-pāte, ex'tĭr-pāte,
pär-tic'i-pāte, pāte,
rat'tle-pāte, syñ'cō-pāte.

pl: är'mŏr plāte, con'tem-plāte,
cop'pēr-plāte, dī'al plāte,
el-ec'trō-plāte, nick'el-plāte,
plāit, plāte, sil'vēr plāte.

pr: prāte.

r: ac-cel'ē-rāte, ac'cū-rāte,
ad-ul'tē-rāte, ā'ē-rāte,
ag-glom'ē-rāte, a-mē'li-ō-rāte,
an-nūm'ē-rāte*, as'pi-rāte,
as-sev'ē-rāte, aug'ū-rāte*,
bē-rāte, bĭrth rāte,
cam'phō-rāte ('fō-),
col-lab'ō-rāte, com-mem'ō-rāte,
com-men'sū-rāte,
com-miş'ē-rāte, con-fed'ē-rāte,
con-glom'ē-rāte, con-sid'ē-rāte,

ĀT

fāte, fär, fȧst, fạll, finăl, cãre, at; mēte, prĕy, hẽr, met; pīne,
marïne, bĭrd, pin; nōte, mȯve, fȯr, atŏm, nǫt; mōǫn, book;

112

(Choose only one word out of each group)

cō⸗op′ē-rāte, cǫr′pō-rāte,
cǫr-ro′bō-rāte,
death rāte (deth), dē-cǫl′ō-rāte,
dec̣′ō-rāte, dē-g̣en′ē-rāte,
dē-lib′ē-rāte, dē-sid′ē-rāte,
des′pē-rāte, dē-tē′ri-ō-rāte,
dī-rec̣′tō-rāte, doc̣′tō-rāte,
ē-lab′ō-rāte, e-lec̣′tō-rāte,
ē-nū′mē-rāte, ē-vap′ō-rāte,
ex-ag̣′g̣ē-rāte, ex-as′pē-rāte,
ex-hil′ȧ-rāte (eg-zil′),
ex-on′e-rāte (eg-zon′),
ex-pec̣′tō-rāte, fed′e-rāte,
first′rāte′, g̣en′ē-rāte,
il-lit′ē-rāte, in-men′sū-rāte*,
im-mod′ē-rāte, in-ac̣′c̣ū-rāte,
in-au′gū-rāte, in-c̣är′cē-rāte,
in-cin′ē-rāte,
in″cǫm-men′sū-rāte,
in″con-sid′ē-rāte, in-cǫr′pō-rāte,
in′dū-rāte, in-ten′ē-rāte,
in-tem′pē-rāte, in-vet′ē-rāte,
in-vig̣′ō-rāte, ī′rāte, it′ē-rāte,
ī-tin′ē-rāte, lac̣′ē-rāte,
lev′i-rāte, lib′ē-rāte, lit′ē-rāte,
mac̣′ē-rāte, mod′ē-rāte,
nar-rāte′, ob′dū-rāte,
ob-lit′ē-rāte, ȯp′ē-rāte, ō-rāte′,
ō″vẽr-rāte′, pas′tō-rāte,
pẽr′fō-rāte, per′ō-rāte,
prē-pon′dē-rāte, prō-rāte′,
prō-tec̣′tō-rāte, prō-tū′bē-rāte,
rāte, rec̣′tō-rāte, rē-c̣ū′pē-rāte,
rō-frig̣′ē-rāte, rē-g̣en′ē-rāte,
rē-it′ē-rāte, rē-mū′nē-rāte,
rē-vẽr′bē-rāte, sat′ū-rāte,
sec̣′ŏnd⸗rāte′, sep′ȧ-rāte,
stē-ȧ-rāte, sup′pū-rāte,
tem′pē-rāte, thĭrd′⸗rāte′,
tol′ē-rāte, trans-lit′ē-rāte,
trit′ū-rāte, trī-um′vi-rāte,

ul′cē-rāte, un″dẽr-rāte′,
ven′ē-rāte, vẽr′bē-rāte,
vī-tū′pē-rāte, viz-iē′rāte,
vō-ci′fē-rāte, wạt′ẽr rāte.

s: cǫm′pen-sāte, im-prov′i-sāte,
mär′qui-sāte (′kwi-), pul′sāte,
sāte, tẽr′g̣iv-ẽr-sāte″.

sk(sc̣): chēap′skāte,
rōl′lẽr skāte, skāte,

sl: slāte.

sp: spāte.

st: in-stāte′, ō-vẽr-stāte′,
rē-in-stāte′, rē-stāte′, stāte,
un-dẽr-stāte′, un-stāte′.

str: dem′ŏn-strāte,
rē-mon′strāte, strāight (strāt),
strāit (strāt).

t: ag̣′i-tāte, am′pū-tāte,
an′nō-tāte, c̣ap-ac̣′i-tāte,
c̣ap′i-tāte, cǫg̣′i-tāte,
crep′i-tāte, dē-bil′i-tāte,
dē-c̣ap′i-tāte, de′văs-tāte,
dic̣′tāte, dig̣′i-tāte, es-tāte′,
ex-cǫg̣′i-tāte, ex-ōr′bi-tāte,
fac̣-il′i-tāte, fe-lic̣′i-tāte,
grav′i-tāte, hab-il′i-tāte,
heṣ′i-tāte, im′i-tāte,
in-cap-ac̣′i-tāte, in-gūr′g̣i-tāte,
ir′ri-tāte, med′i-tāte,
ne-ces′si-tāte, pal′pi-tāte,
pō′ten-tāte, prē-cip′i-tāte,
prē-med′i-tāte, rē-gūr′g̣i-tāte,
rē-hab-il′i-tāte, rē-sus′ci-tāte,
rō′tāte, san′i-tāte, Tāit, Tāte,
tête′⸗à⸗tête′ (tāt′⸗à⸗tāt′),
veg̣′ē-tāte.

tr: är′bi-trāte, cǫn′cen-trāte,
frus′trāte, il′lus-trāte,
im′pē-trāte, mag̣′is-trāte,
ǫr′ches-trāte, pen′ē-trāte,

113 ūse, bụll, brúte, tûrn, **up**; crȳ, myth; c̩at, mac̩hine, ace,
church, c̩hord; ġem, añger, (Fr.) boṅ, aṣ; THis, thin; aᴢure

AT
ĀTH

(Choose only one word out of each group)

pēr′pē-trāte, trāit, pros′trāte,
rē-c̩al′ci-trāte.

v: ag′grȧ-vāte, c̩ap′ti-vāte,
c̩ul′ti-vāte, der′i-vāte,
el′ē-vāte, en′ēr-vāte, es′ti-vāte,
ex′c̩ȧ-vāte, in′nō-vāte,
mō′ti-vāte, ren′ō-vāte,
sal′i-vāte, tit′i-vāte.

w: ȧ-wāit′,
dead weight (ded wāt),
feaTH′ēr-weight (feTH′),
heav′y-weight (hev′),
līght′weight (līt′),
mid′dle-weight, ō′vēr-weight,
pā′pēr-weight, pen′ny⸗weight,
un″dēr-weight′, wāit, weight.

AT

Vowel: at, c̩av′ē-at,
c̩om-mis-sā′ri-at, hēre-at′,
lār′i-at, prō-lē-tār′i-at,
sec̩-rē-tār′i-at, THere-at′,
where-at′.

b: ac̩′rō-bat, bat, brick′bat,
frúit bat, vam′pīre bat.

bl: blat.

br: Bradt, brat.

ch: chat, fal′lōw chat.

d: dis and dat.

dr: drat.

f: fat, mar′rōw fat.

fl: ā flat, flat.

fr: frat.

g: for-gat′*, gat.

h: hat, hīgh′⸗hat′ (hī′),
top hat, un-hat′.

k(c̩): c̩at, civ′et c̩at, hell′c̩at,
kit′ty⸗c̩at, Mag-nif′-i-c̩at,
pōle′c̩at, pus′sy⸗c̩at,
re-qui-es′c̩at (-kwi-),
tab′by c̩at, tom′c̩at.

kr: ar-is′tō-c̩rat, au̩′tō-c̩rat,
bū′reau-c̩rat (′rō-), dem′ō-c̩rat,
mon′ō-c̩rat, plú′tō-c̩rat,
thē′ō-c̩rat.

m: au̩′tō-mat, dip′lō-mat,
mat, Matt, matte.

n: as′sig-nat, gnat, Nat.

p: bē-pat′, pat, pit′⸗ȧ⸗pat.

pl: plait, plat, Platt, Platte.

pr: dan′di-prat, Pratt.

r: Ar′ȧ-rat, rat, Sú′rat,
wa̩t′ēr-rat.

s: sat.

sk(sc̩): sc̩at.

sl: slat.

sp: spat.

spr: sprat, Spratt.

st: hē′li-ō-stat, hȳ′drō-stat,
rhē′ō-stat (rē′), thēr′mō-stat.

t: hab′i-tat, tit′⸗for⸗tat′, tat.

TH: THat.

v: c̩rȧ-vat′, vat.

ÄT

hw: whät.

kw(qu): c̩ŏm′quät, kum′quät.

l: Kȧ-lät′, Khē-lät′.

skw(squ): squät.

sw: swät.

w: wätt.

y: yächt.

Cf. ot.

ĀTH

b: bāTHe.

l: lāTHe.

sk(sc̩): sc̩āTHe.

sn: snāTHe.

sp: spāTHe.

sw: swāTHe, un-swāTHe′.

ĀTH
ĀZ

fāte, fär, fàst, fạll, finăl, cãre, at; mēte, prey, hẽr, met; pīne, marïne, bïrd, pin; nōte, mŏve, fọr, atŏm, not; mọọn, book;

114

(Choose only one word out of each group)

ĀTH

f: fāith, i'-fāith'*, mis-fāith', un-fāith'.

r: rāthe*, wạt'ẽr-wrāith, wrāith.

sn: Snāith.

ĀTTH

Vowel: eighth.
Also hate'th*, etc.

ATH

g: Gath.

h: hath*.

m: àf'tẽr-math, math, phil'ō-math (fil').

p: al'lō-path, hō'mē-ō-path, os'tē-ō-path, phyṣ'i-ō-path (fiz') psȳ'chō-path (sī').

sn: snath.

ȦTH

b: bȧth.

l: làth.

p: brī'dle pȧth, foot'pȧth, pȧth.

r: rȧth, wrȧth (rȧth).

ĀTS

b: Bātes.

k: Cātes.

st: Stātes, Ū-nīt'ed Stātes.

y: Yātes, Yeāts.

Also āt+s.

ĀV

br: brāve, out-brāve'.

d: Dāve.

dr: drāve*.

g: fọr-gāve', gāve, mis-gāve'.

gl: glāive.

gr: en-grāve', grāve, un-grāve'.

h: bē-hāve', mis"bē-hāve'.

k(c): cāve, con-cāve', en-cāve'.

kl: an-gus'ti-clāve, en-clāve'.

kr: crāve.

l: bē-lāve', é-lève' (ā-lāv'), lāve.

n: knāve (nāv), nāve.

p: im-pāve', pāve.

pr: dē-prāve'.

r: rāve.

s: sāve.

sh: shāve.

sl: bē-slāve', en-slāve', gal'ley slāve (gal'i), slāve, wāge slāve.

st: stāve.

sw: suāve (swāv).

thr: thrāve.

TH: THey've (THāv).

tr: är'chi-trāve, trāve.

w: wāive, wāve.

AV

h: have.

sl: Slav.

ÄV

av: zöu-äve'.

h: hälve.

k: cälve.

kl: en-cläve'.

s: sälve.

sl: Släv.

sw: suäve (swäv).

ĀZ

Vowel: ā'ṣ.

b: bāize, bāyṣ.

bl: à-blāze', bēa'çŏn blāze, Blāiṣe, blāze, em-blāze', out-blāze', up-blāze'.

br: brāiṣe, brāze.

d: à-dāze', dāyṣ, dāze, now'à-dāyṣ, THen'à-dāyṣ.

(Choose only one word out of each group)

dr: drāyṣ.
f: fāze, feāṣe, phāṣe (fāz).
fl: flāyṣ.
fr: frāiṣe, met′à-phrāṣe,
par′à-phrāṣe, phrāṣe.
g: gāze, in-gāze′, out-gāze′,
up-gāze′.
gl: glāze.
gr: Grāyṣ, grāze.
h: Hāaṣ (hāz), Hāyeṣ, Hāyṣ,
hāze.
j: jāyṣ.
k(c̣): ′c̣āze.
kl: c̣lāyṣ.
kr: c̣rāze.
l: lāyṣ, lāze, mà-lāiṣe′ (-lāz′),
Mär-seil-lāiṣe′ (-se-lāz′).
m: à-māze′, māize, Māyṣ,
Māyeṣ, Māze, wŏn′dēr-māze*.
n: māy″ŏn-nāiṣe′, nāze,
pol′ō-nāiṣe.
pr: ap-prāiṣe′, bē-prāiṣe′,
c̣hrys′ō-prāṣe (kris′),
dis-prāiṣe′, prāiṣe, self′=prāiṣe′,
un″dēr-prāiṣe′, un-prāiṣe′.
r: rāiṣe, rāṣe, rāyṣ, rāze,
up-rāiṣe′.
sh: c̣hāiṣe (shāz).
v: vāṣe.
Also ā+s.
Also c̣lāy′s, etc.

AZ

Vowel: aṣ, where-aṣ′ (hwãr-az′)
h: haṣ.
j: jazz.
r: razz.

ÄZ

r: Shī-räz′.
v: väṣe (väz).

Also ä+ṣ.
Also Shah′s, etc.

ĀZD

d: à-dāzed′.
m: à-māzed′, bē-māzed′,
un″à-māzed′.
pr: un-prāiṣed′.
Also āz+d.

AZD

j: jazzed.
r: razzed.

ĀZH

t: c̣or-tège′ (kor-tāzh).

ÄZH

fl: c̣am′öu-fläġe, pēr′si-fläġe.
n: bad-i-näġe′, mé-näġe′ (mā-).
r: bar-räġe′,
eñ-töu-räġe′ (àñ-too-räzh′),
gà-räġe′, mi-räġe′.

AZM

Vowel: dē-mōn′i-aṣm,
en-thū′ṣi-aṣm, mī′aṣm,
or′gi-aṣm.
f: phaṣm*.
g: or′gaṣm.
k(c̣): c̣haṣm, sär′c̣aṣm.
kl: ī-c̣on′ō-c̣laṣm.
n: plē′ō-naṣm.
pl: bī′ō-plaṣm, c̣at′à-plaṣm,
plaṣm, ec̣′tō-plaṣm,
met′à-plaṣm, prō′tō-plaṣm.
sp: spaṣm.
t: phan′taṣm (fan′).

(Choose only one word out of each group)

E

Words including the following accented vowel sounds:

ē: as in ēve; also in feed, sēam, bē-liēve', rē-cēive', pēo'ple, kēy,
e-līte' (-lēt'), Caē'sar (sē'), quay (kē), phoē'bē (fē'); also as in mēre,
drēar, wēird.

e: as in ebb; also in hei'fer (he'fer), leo'pard (le'pard), friend (frend),
Aet'na (et'), feath'er (feTH'), as-a-foet'i-da (-fet'), bur'y (ber'i),
an'y (en'i), Thames (temz), said (sed), says (sez).

Ē

Vowel: ad-vow-ee', ar'rōw-y,
ȧ-vow-ee', bil'lōw-y, draw-ee',
fȧ-cē'ti-aē ('shi-),
mi-nū'ti-aē ('shi-), pil'lōw-y,
shad'ōw-y, sin'ew-y ('ū-),
wil'lōw-y.

b: A.B., B, baw-bee', bē, bee,
bum'ble-bee, hŏn'ey-bee,
Nī'ō-bē, scar'ȧ-bee.

bl: blēa.

br: de-brĭs' (-brē'), vẽr'te-braē.

ch: li'tchĭ, vouch-ee'.

d: B.V.D., C.O.D., Chald-ee',
chick'ȧ-dee, D, D.D., Dee,
fid'dle=dē=dee, gran-dee',
kill'dee, M.D., ọṅ dĭt' (dē'),
Ph.D., Twee'dle=dee', ven-dee',
bas'tărd-y, com'e-dy, cus'tō-dy,
jeop'ȧrd-y (jep'), Lom'bărd-y,
mal'ȧ-dy, mel'ō-dy, mon'ō-dy,
Nor'măn-dy, par'ō-dy,
pẽr'fid-y, Piç'ȧr-dy,
psälm'ō-dy (säm'), rem'e-dy,
rhap'sō-dy (rap'), sub'si-dy,
thren'ō-dy, traġ'e-dy.

dr: dree, her'ăld-dry.

dw: läṅge d'ouï' (dwē').

f: an-tis'trō-phē, ȧ-pos'trō-phē,
at'rō-phy, bī-og"rȧ-phee',
bī-og'rȧ-phy, cȧ-tas'trō-phe,
cō-ry-phee', fee, ġē-oġ'rȧ-phy,
Mc-Fee', phi-los'ō-phy (fi-),
pọr-nog'rȧ-phy, te-leg'rȧ-phy,
thē-os'ō-phy, tō-pog'rȧ-phy.

fl: flēa, flee.

fr: fan'cy=free, en-free', free,
heärt'=free, un-free'.

g: ghee, Mc-Gee'.

gl: glee.

gr: ȧ-gree', dē-gree',
dis"ȧ-gree', fil'i-gree, ped'i-gree,
thĭrd dē-gree'.

h: bō-hēa', hē, tē-hee'.

hw: whee.

j: ȧ-nal'ō-ġy, ap'ō-ġee,
ȧ-pol'ō-ġy, as-trol'ō-ġy,
bär-ġee', bī-ol'ō-ġy, būr'ġee,
chrō-nol'ō-ġy, dox-ol'ō-ġy,
ef'fi-ġy, el'e-ġy, en'ẽr-ġy,
eū'lō-ġy, G, ġee, ġee'ġee',
ġen-ē-al'ō-ġy, ġē-ol'ō-ġy,
leth'ăr-ġy, lit'ūr-ġy,
mọrt-gȧ-ġee' (mọr-),
my-thol'ō-ġy, N.G., O.G.,
ob-li-ġee', ō-ġee', per'i-ġee,
pledġ-ee', pon-ġee', prod'i-ġy,
ref-ū-ġee', sal-văġ-ee',
strat'e-ġy, thē-ol'ō-ġy,
tril'ō-ġy, zō-ol'ō-ġy.

k(ç): an'är-çhy, Cher'ō-kee',
kēy, Man'i-çhee, mär-quee',

(Choose only one word out of each group)

mas′tēr kēy, Mc̦-Kēy′,
mon′ärc̦h-y, quay (kē), rä-kï′,
sy-nec̦′dō-c̦hē.
kr: dē-c̦ree′, C̦ree.
kw(qu): c̦ol′lō-quy, ob′lō-quy,
sō-lil′ō-quy.
l: ab-so̯rb′ing-ly, à-bū′sive-ly,
ac̦-c̦o̯rd′ing-ly, ac̦′c̦ū-rāte-ly,
ac′id-ly, af-fec̦t′ed-ly,
āim′less-ly, āir′i-ly, à-lee′,
al-lūr′ing-ly, al-lū′sive-ly,
am-bi′tious-ly, à-mūs′ing-ly,
ān′cient-ly (′shent-),
à-nom′à-ly, ap-pēal′ling-ly,
ap″pel-lee′, är′dent-ly,
as-sēr′tive-ly,
à-trō′cious-ly, aus-pi′cious-ly,
aw′fu̯l-ly, bāil-ee′, bāne′fu̯l-ly,
bē-c̦ŏm′ing-ly, bē-lee′,
bē-fit′ting-ly, beg′găr-ly,
bē-sot′ted-ly, bē-spot′ted-ly,
bē-wāil′ing-ly, bit′tēr-ly,
blood′less-ly (blud′),
blo̯o̯m′ing-ly, blo̯o̯m′less-ly,
blush′ing-ly, blush′less-ly,
bod′i-ly, bo̯o̯t′less-ly,
böuil′lï (bo̯o̯l′yē),
bound′less-ly, boy′ish-ly,
brāin′less-ly,
breath′less-ly (breth′),
bro̯o̯d′ing-ly, brŏTH′ēr-ly,
brú′tăl-ly, bump′tious-ly,
c̦āre′fu̯l-ly, c̦āre′less-ly,
chānġe′less-ly, chȋrp′ing-ly,
chōk′ing-ly, chûrl′ish-ly,
civ′il-ly, c̦lown′ish-ly
c̦ŏm-plāin′ing-ly,
con-c̦lúd′ing-ly, con-c̦lù′sive-ly,
con-dē-scend′ing-ly (-send′),
con-dū′cive-ly, con-found′ed-ly
con-fūș′ed-ly, con-fūse′ly,

con-sum′măte-ly,
con-viv′i-ăl-ly, count′less-ly,
c̦ŏuș′in-ly (kuz′), c̦ow′ărd-ly,
c̦rāv′ing-ly, c̦rouch′ing-ly,
c̦rown′less-ly, c̦rù′el-ly,
c̦rush′ing-ly,
c̦um′brous-ly, Cyb′e-lē,
das′tărd-ly, da̯ugh′tēr-ly (da̯u′),
de-c̦ō′rous-ly (′rus),
dē-duc̦′tive-ly, dē-fence′less-ly,
dē-li′cious-ly, dē-lū′sive-ly,
dē-vōt′ed-ly, dis-ap-pröv′ing-ly,
dis-cērn′i-bly, dis-cērn-ing-ly,
dis-o̯r′dēr-ly, dis-tāște′fu̯l-ly,
dis-trust′fu̯l-ly, di-vēr′ġent-ly,
di-vēr′ting-ly, dog′ged-ly,
dōle′fu̯l-ly, doubt′fu̯l-ly (dout′),
doubt′ing-ly, drēam′fu̯l-ly,
drēam′i-ly, drēam′ing-ly,
drēam′less-ly, drip′ping-ly,
dro̯o̯p′ing-ly, dust′i-ly,
dust′less-ly, ēast′ēr-ly,
ē-lū′sive-ly, en-dūr′à-bly,
en-dūr′ing-ly, en′gāġ-ing-ly,
en-grōss′ing-ly, ē-tēr′năl-ly,
Eù′là-liē″ (ù′), ex-c̦lū′sive-ly,
ex-pan′sive-ly, ex-ten′sive-ly,
ex-tē′ri-o̯r-ly, ex-tor′tion-āte-ly,
ex-trao̯r″di-nā-ri-ly,
ex-trav′àġănt-ly, ex-trēme′ly,
ex′tri-c̦à-bly, ex-trin′si-c̦ăl-ly,
ex-ū′bēr-ănt-ly, ex-ul′tănt-ly,
ex-ult′ing-ly, fac̦-sim′i-lē,
fāde′less-ly, fāir′i-ly,
fāith′fu̯l-ly, fāith′less-ly,
fà-mil′iăr-ly (′yēr), fam′i-ly,
fā′mous-ly, fan′ci-fu̯l-ly,
fan-tas′ti-c̦ăl-ly, fär′ci-c̦ăl-ly,
fas′ci-nāt-ing-ly, fā′tăl-ly,
fā″tăl-is′ti-c̦ăl-ly, fä″THēr-ly,
fa̯ult′i-ly, fa̯ult′less-ly,

(Choose only one word out of each group)

fā'vŏr-à-bly,   fēar'fụl-ly,
fēa'ṣi-bly,   feel'ing-ly,
fe-lic'i-tous-ly,   fē-rō'cious-ly,
fẽr'vid-ly,   feū'dăl-ly,
fē'vẽr-ish-ly,
fic̣-ti'tious-ly,   fiērce'ly,
fīer'i-ly,   fig'ūr-à-tive-ly,
fil'i-ăl-ly,   filth'i-ly,   fish'i-ly,
flā'grảnt-ly,   flash'i-ly,
fleūr'꞊dē꞊līs (-lē'),   flex'i-bly,
flīght'i-ly (flīt'),   flip'pănt-ly,
flọr'id-ly,   floss'i-ly,
floūr'ish-ing-ly,   flour'ing-ly,
flow'ẽr-i-ly,   flū'ent-ly,
flũr'ri-ed-ly,   flush'ing-ly,
flut'tẽr-iñg-ly,   fọọl'här-di-ly,
fọọl'ish-ly,   fop'pish-ly,
fōre-bōd'ing-ly,   fọrce'fụl-ly,
fōre-knōw'ing-ly (-nō'),
fọr-get'fụl-ly,   fọr-giv'ing-ly,
fọr'măl-ly,   fọr'mẽr-ly,
fọr'mi-då-bly,   fọr-sāk'en-ly,
fọr'tu-nāte-ly,   fox'i-ly,
frag'il-ly,   frag-men-tā'ri-ly,
frā'grănt-ly,   fran'ti-c̣ăl-ly,
frå-tẽr'năl-ly,   frạud'ū-lent-ly,
frēak'ish-ly,   fren'zied-ly ('zid-),
frē'quent-ly,   fret'fụl-ly,
frīght'fụl-ly (frīt'),   frig'id-ly,
friv'ō-lous-ly,   frost'i-ly,
froth'i-ly,   frū'găl-ly,
frūit'fụl-ly,   frūit'i-ly,
frūit'less-ly,   fụl'sŏme-ly,
func̣'tion-ăl-ly,   fun'ni-ly,
fū'ri-ous-ly,   fũr'tive-ly,
fuss'i-ly,   fū'tile-ly,   gāin'fụl-ly,
Gal'i-lee,   gal'lănt-ly,
gar'rū-lous-ly,   gawk'i-ly,
ġen'ẽr-ăl-ly,   ġē-ner'i-căl-ly,
ġen'ẽr-ous-ly,   ġē'ni-ăl-ly,
ġen-teel'ly,   ġen'ū-ine-ly,

gid'di-ly,   ġin'ġẽr-ly,   gīrl'ish-ly,
glā'ciăl-ly,   glad'sŏme-ly,
glam'ŏr-ous-ly ('ẽr-),   giass'i-ly,
glee'fụl-ly,   glọọm'i-ly,
glō'ri-ous-ly,   gloss'i-ly,
glut'tŏn-ous-ly,   god'li-ly,
gōld'en-ly,   gọr'ġeous-ly,
grāce'fụl-ly,   grā'cioụs-ly,
grad'ū-ăl-ly,   gran'di-ōse-ly,
graph'i-c̣ăl-ly,   grāte'fụl-ly,
grav'el-ly,   grēas'i-ly,   greed'i-ly,
grim'i-ly,   grit'ti-ly,   grōp'ing-ly,
grouch'i-ly,   ground'less-ly,
grudġ'ing-ly,   grūe'sŏme-ly,
grum'bling-ly,   grump'i-ly,
guīle'fụl-ly (gīl'),   guīle'less-ly,
guilt'i-ly (gilt'),   guilt'less-ly,
gush'ing-ly,   gust'i-ly,
gut'tūr-ăl-ly,   hab'it-à-bly,
ha-bit'ū-ăl-ly,   hag'gărd-ly,
hand'i-ly,   hand'sŏme-ly,
hap'less-ly,   hap'pi-ly,   här·di-ly,
härm'fụl-ly,   härm'less-ly,
här-mon'i-c̣ăl-ly,
här-mō'ni-ous-ly,   hāst'i-ly,
hāte'fụl-ly,   hạugh'ti-ly (hạu'),
haz'ărd-ous-ly,   hāz'i-ly,
health'fụl-ly (helth'),
health'i-ly,   heärt'brō"ken-ly,
heärt'i-ly,   heärt'less-ly,
heärt'rend-ing-ly,
heav'en-ly (hev'),
heav'i-ly (hev'),   heed'less-ly,
help'fụl-ly,   help'less-ly,
hē-red"i-tā'ri-ly,   hē-ret'i-c̣ăl-ly,
hex-ag'ō-năl-ly,   hid'ē-ous-ly,
his-tōr'i-c̣ăl-ly,   hōme'less-ly,
hom'i-ly,   hon'est-ly (on'),
hon'ōr-à-bly (on'),   hōpe'fụl-ly,
hōpe'less-ly,   hor-i-zon'tăl-ly,
hor'rid-ly,   hū-māne'ly,

(Choose only one word out of each group)

hū'măn-ly, huñ'gri-ly,
hŭr'ried-ly ('rid-), hŭrt'fŭl-ly,
hȳ-pĕr'bō-lē, hyp″o-çrit'i-çăl-ly,
hys-ter'i-çăl-ly, ī-dē'ăl-ly,
ī-den'ti-çăl-ly, id″i-ot'i-çăl-ly,
iġ'nō-rănt-ly, il-leġ'i-bly,
il-loġ'i-çăl-ly, il-lū'sive-ly,
im-aġ'i-nȧ-bly,
im-mea'ṣūr-ȧ-bly (-me'zhēr-),
im-mē'di-ăte-ly, im'mi-nent-ly,
im-mod'ēr-ăte-ly,
im-mod'est-ly, im-mor'ăl-ly,
im-mor'tăl-ly, im-möv'ȧ-bly,
im-pär'tiăl-ly,
im-pā'tient-ly ('shent-),
im-peç'çȧ-bly, im-pen'ē-trȧ-bly,
im-per'ȧ-tive-ly, im-pē'ri-ăl-ly,
im-pēr'sŏn-ăl-ly,
im-pet'ū-ous-ly, im-pī'ous-ly,
im'pish-ly, im-plic'it-ly,
im-plōr'ing-ly, im″pō-līte'ly,
im-por'tănt-ly, im-pos'si-bly,
im'pō-tent-ly, im-prob'ȧ-bly,
im-prop'ēr-ly, im-prü'dent-ly,
im'pū-dent-ly, in-ces'sănt-ly,
in-ci-den'tăl-ly, in-ᴄlū'sive-ly,
in-ᴄō-hēr'ent-ly,
in-ᴄom'pē-tent-ly,
in″ᴄom-plēte'ly, in-ᴄrēas'ing-ly,
in-ᴄred'ū-lous-ly, in-dē'cent-ly,
in-dē-pen'dent-ly,
in-diġ'nănt-ly, in-dī-reᴄt'ly,
in″di-vid'ū-ăl-ly, in-dul'ġent-ly,
in-dus'tri-ăl-ly, in-dus'tri-ously,
in'fȧ-mous-ly,
in-fēr'năl-ly, in'fi-nite-ly,
in-ġē'nious-ly ('nyus-),
in-hēr'ent-ly, in-hū'măn-ly,
in-jù'ri-ous-ly, in'nō-cent-ly,
in-sāne'ly, in-sen'sāte-ly,
in-sip'id-ly, in'stănt-ly,

in-stiñç'tive-ly, in-struç'tive-ly,
in-sult'ing-ly, in-tel'li-ġent-ly,
in″tēr-mit'tent-ly, in-trep'id-ly,
in-trin'si-çăl-ly, in'wărd-ly,
ĭrk'sŏme-ly, ī-ron'i-çăl-ly,
It'ȧ-ly, jȧunt'i-ly,
jeal'ous-ly, jōk'ing-ly,
joy'fŭl-ly, joy'ous-ly, jù'bi-lee,
jū-di'ciăl-ly,
ju-di'cious-ly, jùic'i-ly,
knōw'ing-ly (nō'),
lȧ-bō'ri-ous-ly, lag'gărd-ly,
last'ing-ly, läugh'ing-ly (läf'),
lav'ish-ly, lēa, lee, lē'găl-ly,
leġ″end-ā'ri-ly,
lēi'ṣūre-ly ('zhēr-), lev'el-ly,
lēy, lï, lib'ēr-ăl-ly, līfe'less-ly,
līght″≠foot'ed-ly (līt″),
lim'pid-ly, lit'ēr-ăl-ly,
lōaTH'ing-ly, lōaTH'sŏme-ly,,
lō'çal-ly, loġ'i-çal-ly,
lōne'sŏme-ly, lounġ'ing-ly,
lŏve'less-ly, lŏv'ēr-ly,
lŏv'ing-ly, loy'ăl-ly, lū'cid-ly,
luck'i-ly, luck'less-ly,
lū'di-ᴄrous-ly, lū'rid-ly,
lūr'ing-ly, lust'i-ly,
lus'trous-ly, lux-ū'ri-ous-ly,
lȳ'ing-ly, lyr'i-çāl-ly,
maġ'i-çăl-ly, māid'en-ly,
mȧ-lev'ō-lent-ly, mȧ-li'cious-ly,
man'fŭl-ly, man'i-fest-ly,
man'nēr-ly, mas'tēr-fŭl-ly,
mas'tēr-ly, mȧ-tē'ri-ăl-ly,
mȧ-tēr'năl-ly, mā'trŏn-ly,
mēa'ġēr-ly, mēan'ing-ly,
melt'ing-ly, mē'ni-ăl-ly,
mēr'ci-fŭl-ly, mer'ri-ly,
mind'fŭl-ly, mis-giv'ing-ly,
mis-tāk'en-ly, mis-trust'fŭl-ly,
mis-trust'ing-ly, mock'ing-ly,

E

fāte, fär, fȧst, fạll, finȧl, cãre, ȧt; mēte, prẹy, hẽr, met; pīne,
marĭne, bĭrd, pin; nōte, mŏve, fọr, atŏm, not; mọọn, book;

120

(Choose only one word out of each group)

mod′ẽr-āte-ly, mod′est-ly,
mō-nop′ō-ly, mọr′ăl-ly,
mọr′bid-ly, mọr′tăl-ly,
mŏTH′ẽr-ly, mōurn′fụl-ly,
mōurn′sŏme-ly,
mū-nif′i-cent-ly, mūr′dẽr-ous-ly,
mūṣ′ing-ly, mū′tū-ăl-ly,
mys-tē′ri-ous-ly, mys′ti-çăl-ly,
myth′i-çăl-ly, nā′ked-ly,
nāme′less-ly, nar′rōw-ly,
na-tion-ăl-ly, nā′tive-ly,
nat′ū-răl-ly, neb′ū-laē,
nec-es-sā′ri-ly, need′i-ly,
need′less-ly, nẹigh′bŏr-ly (nā′),
nẽrv′i-ly, nẽrve′less-ly,
neū′trăl-ly, nig′gărd-ly,
noiṣ′i-ly, noiṣe′less-ly,
noi′sŏme-ly, nọr′măl-ly,
nọrTH′ẽr-ly, nọrTH′wărd-ly,
nū′mẽr-ăl-ly, ō-bē′di-ent-ly,
ob-jeç′tive-ly, ō-blīġ′ing-ly,
ob-nox′ious-ly, ob-sē′qui-ous-ly,
ob-strep′ẽr-ous-ly,
ob-struç′tive-ly, ob-strú′sive-ly,
ob-trū′sive-ly, ob′vi-ous-ly,
of-fen′sive-ly, of-fi′cious-ly,
om-niv′ō-rous-ly, on′ẽr-ous-ly,
ō′pen-ly, op-pōṣ′ing-ly,
op-pres′sive-ly, op′ū-lent-ly,
ọr′dẽr-ly, ọr-di-nā′ri-ly,
out-land′ish-ly,
out-rā′ġeous-ly,
out′wărd-ly, ō′vẽr-ly,
ō″vẽr-top′ping-ly,
ō″vẽr-ween′ing-ly, owl′ish-ly,
pāin′fụl-ly, pāin′less-ly,
pal′lid-ly, pap′ū-laē,
par′ȧ-mount-ly, pãr′ent-ly,
pär′tiăl-ly, pas′sive-ly,
pȧ-thet′i-çal-ly,
pā′tient-ly (′shent-),

pēace′fụl-ly,
pē-çū′liăr-ly (′lyẽr-),
peer′less-ly, pee′vish-ly,
pel-lū′cid-ly, pẽr-emp′tō-ri-ly,
pẽr′feçt-ly, per′il-ous-ly,
pẽr-vẽrt′ed-ly, pet′ū-lănt-ly,
pī′quănt-ly (pē′kănt-),
pit′i-fụl-ly, plāint′fụl-ly*
plāint′less-ly*, plas′ti-çăl-ly,
plāy′fụl-ly, plēad′ing-ly,
pleaṣ′ănt-ly (plez′),
plēaṣ′ing-ly, plen′ti-fụl-ly,
plī′ănt-ly, pluck′i-ly,
pō-et′i-çăl-ly, point′less-ly,
pop′ū-lăr-ly, pọr-ten′tous-ly,
poṣ′i-tive-ly, pō′tent-ly,
pow′ẽr-fụl-ly,
prāyer′fụl-ly (prãr′),
prē-çō′cious-ly,
prē″pos-ṣess′ing-ly,
prē-tend′ing-ly, prē′vi-ous-ly,
prī-mā′ri-ly, prī′văte-ly,
prō-duç′tive-ly, prop′ẽr-ly,
pro-pi′tious-ly,
prō-vōk′ing-ly, prú′dent-ly,
pub′liç-ly, pū′is-sănt-ly,
pun′ġent-ly, pūr-sū′ănt-ly,
quạr′tẽr-ly, quer′ū-lous-ly,
quī-es′cent-ly, rab′id-ly,
rad′i-çăl-ly, rap′id-ly,
ra′tion-ăl-ly, read′i-ly (red′),
read′y⹀wit′ted-ly, rē′ăl-ly,
reck′less-ly, rē-çūr′rent-ly,
rē-ful′ġent-ly, rē-joiç′ing-ly,
rē-lent′less-ly, rē-luç′tănt-ly,
rē-mọrse′fụl-ly, rē-mọrse′less-ly,
rē-ṣẽrv′ed-ly, reṣ′ō-lūte-ly,
rē-spon′sive-ly, res′tive-ly,
rē-venġe′fụl-ly,
rīght′eously (rī′chus-), riġ′id-ly,
rip′ping-ly, rip′pling-ly,

121

ūse, bu̧ll, brúte, tūrn, up; crȳ, myth; c̟at, mac̟hine, ace,
church, c̟hord; ġem, añger, (Fr.) boṅ, aṣ; THis, thin; azure

Ē

(Choose only one word out of each group)

rōar'ing-ly, Rōṣ'a̤-liē,
rot'ten-ly, rōv'ing-ly, roy'ăl-ly,
rúe'fu̧l-ly, ruf'fi-ăn-ly,
rug'ged-ly, rus'ti-c̟ăl-ly,
sat-is-fac̟'tō-ri-ly, sav'ăge-ly,
sc̟an'dăl-ous-ly,
scēn'i-c̟ăl-ly (sēn'), sc̟hol'ăr-ly,
sc̟orn'fu̧l-ly, sc̟owl'ing-ly,
sē'c̟re-tive-ly, sē'c̟ret-ly,
sec̟'ū-lăr-ly, sē-dū'cive-ly,
sē-duc̟'tive-ly, seem'ing-ly,
self'=ac̟-c̟ūṣ'ing-ly,
self'=c̟on'scious-ly, self'ish-ly,
sen'si-tive-ly, sep'a̤-răte-ly,
sē'ri-ous-ly, sev'ēr-ăl-ly,
shād'i-ly, shāk'i-ly, shal'lōw-ly,
shāme'fu̧l-ly, shāme'less-ly,
shāpe'less-ly, shärp'=wit'ted-ly,
sheep'ish-ly, shift'less-ly,
shock'ing-ly, shrew'ish-ly,
Sic'i-ly, sig'năl-ly, sī'lent-ly,
sim'i-lăr-ly, sim'i-lē, sin'fu̧l-ly,
siñ'gū-lăr-ly, sis'tēr-ly,
skil'fu̧l-ly, skil"li-ga̤-lee',
slan'dēr-ous-ly, sleep'i-ly,
sleep'less-ly, slouch'i-ly,
slǒv'en-ly, slug'gish-ly,
smī'ling-ly, smōk'i-ly,
sneer'ing-ly, snob'bish-ly,
sōak'ing-ly, sō'bēr-ly,
sō'ciăl-ly,
sōl'diēr-ly ('jēr-),
sol'emn-ly ('em-), sol'id-ly,
som'bēr-ly, sor'did-ly, sor'ri-ly,
sor'rōw-fu̧l-ly, sōul'fu̧l-ly,
sound'less-ly, south'wărd-ly,
spe'ciăl-ly, spē'cious-ly,
speed'i-ly, spher'i-c̟ăl-ly (sfer'),
spī'răl-ly, spir'i-tū-ăl-ly,
splen'did-ly, spoo̧n'i-ly,
spōrt'fu̧l-ly, spōrt'i-ly,

spōr'tive-ly, spot'less-ly,
spring'i-ly, spū'ri-ous-ly,
squän'dēr-ing-ly, squēam'ish-ly,
stärt'ling-ly, stat'i-c̟ăl-ly,
stead'fàst-ly (sted'),
stead'i-ly, stick'i-ly,
stir'ring-ly, stock'i-ly,
stō'lid-ly, stōn'i-ly,
storm'fu̧l-ly, storm'i-ly,
storm'less-ly,
strāight"for'wărd-ly (strāt"),
stren'ū-ous-ly, strī'dent-ly,
strīk'ing-ly, string'i-ly,
strin'ġent-ly, stub'bòrn-ly,
stud'ied-ly ('id-), stuff'i-ly
stū-pen'dous-ly, stū'pid-ly,
stūr'di-ly, stȳl'ish-ly,
sud'den-ly, sulk'i-ly, sul'tri-ly,
sun'ni-ly,
sū"pēr-fi'ciăl-ly,
sū"pēr-hū'măn-ly,
sū"pēr-sti'tious-ly,
sure"=foot'ed-ly (shoor"),
sus-pi'cious-ly, swa̤rth'i-ly,
swim'ming-ly, swīn'ish-ly,
swōl'len-ly, syl'van-ly,
sys"tem-at'i-c̟ăl-ly, sys'tō-lē,
tac̟'tū-ăl-ly, tär'di-ly,
tāste'fu̧l-ly, ta̧unt'ing-ly,
tēar'fu̧l-ly, tē'di-ous-ly,
ter̠'dēr-ly, tes'ti-ly,
thañk'fu̧l-ly,
thañk'less-ly, Thēr-mop'y-laē,
thorn'i-ly, thōr'ōugh-ly ('ō-),
thought'fu̧l-ly (tho̧t'),
thought'less-ly,
threat'en-ing-ly (thret'),
thump'ing-ly, thun'dēr-ous-ly,
tī'di-ly, tīme'less-ly, tim'id-ly,
tīre'less-ly, tol'ēr-ănt-ly,
tōne'less-ly, top'i-c̟ăl-ly,

(Choose only one word out of each group)

tọr'pid-ly, tō'tăl-ly, touch'i-ly,
tran'quil-ly,
treach'ẽr-ous-ly (trech'),
trē-men'dous-ly, trench'ănt-ly,
trip'ping-ly, tri-um'phănt-ly,
troub'le-sŏme-ly (trub'l-),
troub'lous-ly,
trust'fụl-ly, trust'i-ly,
trust'ing-ly, trȧth'fụl-ly,
trȧth'less-ly, tūne'fụl-ly,
tūne'less-ly, tūr'bid-ly,
typ'i-çăl-ly, ul'ti-măte-ly,
un″bē-çŏm'ing-ly,
un-bend'ing-ly, un-bid'den-ly,
un-blush'ing-ly, un-bound'ed-ly,
un-cēas'ing-ly, un-cẽr'tăin-ly,
un-chănġ'ing-ly, un-çloud'ed-ly,
un-çom'mŏn-ly,
un-çon'scious-ly, un-ē'quăl-ly,
un-ẽr'ring-ly, un-ē'ven-ly,
un-fāil'ing-ly, un-fāith-fụl-ly,
un-feel'ing-ly,
un-fẹign'ed-ly (-fān'),
un-flag'ging-ly,
un-guärd'ed-ly (-gärd'),
un-knōw'ing-ly (-nō'),
un-lŏv'ing-ly, un-luck'i-ly,
un-māid'en-ly, un-man'nẽr-ly,
un-mĩnd'fụl-ly, un-mŏTH'ẽr-ly,
un-nat'ū-răl-ly,
un-nẹigh'bŏr-ly (-nā'),
un″rē-ṣist'ing-ly,
un-swẽrv'ing-ly,
un-wēar'ied-ly ('id-),
un-wit'ting-ly, un-wŏnt'ed-ly,
un-yiēld'ing-ly, ũr'ġent-ly,
ū-ṣũrp'ing-ly, ut'tẽr-ly,
vē'ni-ăl-ly, vẽr-băl-ly, ver'i-ly,
vẽr'năl-ly, vi'cious-ly,
viġ'i-lănt-ly, vig'ŏr-ous-ly,
vī'ō-lent-ly, vĩr'tū-ăl-ly,

viṣ'ū-ăl-ly, viv'id-ly, vō'çăl-ly,
vol″un-tā'ri-ly, vul'găr-ly,
wän'tŏn-ly, wā'ri-ly,
wạrn'ing-ly, wāste'fụl-ly,
wätch'ful-ly, wāy'wărd-ly,
wealth'i-ly (welth'), wēa'ri-ly,
whōle'sŏme-ly (hōl'), will'fụl-ly,
wind'i-ly, win'sŏme-ly,
wish'fụl-ly, wit'ting-ly,
wŏnt'ed-ly, wŏrd'i-ly,
wŏrTH'i-ly, wŏrth'less-ly,
wöund'i-ly*,
wrȧth'fụl-ly (rȧth'),
wrong'ful-ly (rọng'),
yẽarn'ing-ly, yeō'măn-ly,
yiēld'ing-ly, youth'fụl-ly,
zeal'ous-ly (zel'), zest'fụl-ly.

m: ȧ-çad'em-y, ag-ron'ō-my,
al'çhe-my, an'ti-mō-ny,
ap-pen-deç'tō-my, as-tron'ō-my,
at'ō-my, ạu-ton'ō-my,
big'ȧ-my, blas'phe-my,
blos'sŏm-y,
bon″hō-miē' (″ō-mē'),
deū-tẽr-og'ȧ-my,
Deū-tẽr-on'ō-my, ē-çon'ō-my,
en-dog'ȧ-my, en'e-my,
e-pit'ō-mē, in'fȧ-my,
neū-rot'ō-my, phlē-bot'ō-my,
phyṣ-i-og'nō-my, pō-lyg'ȧ-my,
Ptol'e-my (tol'), tax-on'ō-my,
trī-çhot'ō-my, zō-ot'ō-my.

n: ȧ-ban-dŏn-nē' aç-çŏm'pȧ-ny,
Ag-ȧ-pem'ō-nē, ag'ō-ny,
ȧ-knee' (-nē'), Ạl'bȧ-ny,
ȧ-nem'ō-nē, as-sĩgn-ee' (-sīn-),
bal'ço-ny, bar'ō-ny, Bim'i-ni,
bot'ȧ-ny, brȳ'ō-ny, çal'um-ny,
Chī-nee', çol'ō-ny, çŏm'pȧ-ny,
çon-sĩgn-ee' (-sīn-), des'ti-ny,
dom'i-nē, dō-nee', eb'ō-ny,

(Choose only one word out of each group)

e-piph′a̧-ny,
Eū′ġē-niē (ū′zhē-nē), eū′phō-ny,
Eū-phros′y-nē, ex-am″in-ee′,
fel′ō-ny, Ġēr′ma̧-ny,
Geth-sem′a̧-nē, glut′tŏn-ẏ,
här′mō-ny, hē-ġem′ō-ny,
ig′no-mi-ny, ī′rō-ny,
Jap″a̧-nee′, jin-nee′,
kid′nēy, knee (nē), la-drō-nē′,
lär′ce-ny, lit′a̧-ny, mac̣-a̧-rō′ni,
ma̧-hog′a̧-ny, Mel-pom′e-nē,
mō-not′ō-ny, mū′ti-ny,
nom″i-nee′, pat′ri-mō-ny,
Paw-nee′, pe-ti″tion-ee′,
proġ′e-ny, rä′nï, Rom′a̧-ny,
sc̣rū′ti-ny, sim′ō-ny,
sym′phō-ny, tyr′ăn-ny,
vil′lăin-y.

p: ag′a̧-pē, al-lot′rō-py,
c̣al′i-pee, C̣al-lī′ō-pē, c̣al′li-pee,
c̣an′ō-py, c̣ap″₌a̧₌piē′, en′trō-py,
ep′ō-pee, hȳ″drō-ther′a̧-py,
ja̧-lo′py, mis-an′thrō-py, P,
pēa, Pe-nel′ō-pē,
phi-lan′thrō-py, rap-pee′,
rec̣′i-pē, rú-pee′, ther′a̧-py,
tō-pee′, töu-pee′.

pl: pan′ō-ply, plēa.

pr: dū-pree′.

pw: point d'ap-puï′
(pwaṅ′da-pwē′).

r: a̧-dul′tē-ry, an″ni-vēr′sa̧-ry,
ärch′ē-ry, är′mŏ-ry, är′tē-ry,
är-til′lē-ry, a̧u′gū-ry,
bain″₌ma̧-riē′ (baṅ″), bāk′ē-ry,
bat′tē-ry, beg′gă-ry, brāv′ē-ry,
brīb′ē-ry, būr′glă-ry, c̣al′ō-ry,
C̣al′va̧-ry, c̣är′tū-lă-ry,
c̣a̧u′tē-ry, c̣av′ăl-ry, cen′tū-ry,
chan′cē-ry, chick″a̧-ree′,
c̣hiv′ăl-ry, c̣om″pli-men′ta̧-ry,

c̣om-pul′sō-ry, c̣on-trá-dic̣′to-rȳ,
c̣or-rob″ō-ree′, dē-ba̧uch′ē-ry,
dē-liv′ē-ry, dē′mŏn-ry,
dev′il-ry, di-ä′ble-riē, dī′a̧-ry,
dī-rec̣′tō-ry, dis-c̣ŏv′ē-ry,
dis-sat″is-fac̣′tō-ry,
dis-suā′sō-ry (-swā′), drāp′ē-ry,
drudġ′ē-ry, duñ″ga̧-ree′,
ef-frŏnt′ē-ry, el-ē-men′ta̧-ry,
ē-lū′sō-ry, en′ġine-ry (′jin-),
e′quēr-ry, ex-tem′pō-rē,
fac̣′tō-ry, fā′ē-riē,
feaTH′ē-ry (feTH′), fērn′ē-ry,
fī′ē-ry, fīn′ē-ry, flat′tē-ry,
flum′mē-ry, flow′ē-ry,
fop′pē-ry, for′est-ry, for′ġēr-y,
gal′lē-ry, heaTH′ē-ry (heTH′),
hick′ō-ry, his′tō-ry, hos′tel-ry,
hu̧s′bănd-ry, il-lū′sō-ry,
im′ăġe-ry, in-fīr′mā-ry,
in′jù-ry, ī′vō-ry, jam-bō-ree′,
jew′el-ry (jo̧o′), jug′glē-ry,
knāv′ē-ry (nāv′), liv′ē-ry,
lot′tē-ry, lux′ū-ry,
ma̧-c̣hïn′ēr-y, Má-riē,′
mā′sŏn-ry, mas′tē-ry,
mem′ō-ry, mēr′c̣u-ry,
mim′ic̣-ry, mi̧s′ēr-y,
mock′ē-ry, mum′mē-ry,
mys′tē-ry, nō′tá-ry, nûrs′ē-ry,
pal′ma̧-ry,
pär″lia-men′ta̧-ry (″li-),
pas′sē-riē*, passe-men′te-riē,
pen′ū-ry, pep′pē-ry,
pēr-fūm′ē-ry, pēr-func̣′tō-ry,
pēr′jù-ry, phȳ-lac̣′tē-ry,
pil′lō-ry, pōp′ē-ry,
pōt″pöur-rï′ (pō″po̧o-rē′),
prē-c̣ūr′sō-ry, prī′ō-ry,
prō-fes′sō-ry, prū′dē-ry,
pug-a̧-ree′, quack′ē-ry,

E

fāte, fär, fȧst, fąll, fĭnăl, cāre, at; mēte, prey, hẽr, met; pīne,
marīne, bĭrd, pin; nōte, mŏve, fǫr, atŏm, not; mǫǫn, book; 124

(Choose only one word out of each group)

quän'dȧ-ry, rāil'lē-ry,
rap"pȧ-ree', rē-cǫv'ē-ry,
reç'tō-ry, ref-ẽr-ee',
rē-fraç'tō-ry, rev'el-ry
rev'ẽr-iē, rib'ăld-ry, rī'văl-ry,
rob'bẽr-y, rock'ē-ry, rō'guē-ry,
rook'ē-ry, rō'ṣȧ-ry, rōṣe'mā-ry,
rú"di-men'tȧ-ry, sal'ȧ-ry,
sañ-gȧ-ree', sat-is-faç'tō-ry,
Saulte St. Mȧ-riē
      (sǫǫ sānt mȧ-rē')
sav'ăge-ry, scēn'ē-ry (sēn'),
sēi'gniŏr-y (sē'nyŏr-ē),
shiv'ē-ry, sil'vē-ry, slāv'ē-ry,
slip'pē-ry, snug'gē-ry, sǫr'cē-ry,
sting-ȧ-ree', sug'ăr-y (shųg'),
sum'mȧ-ry, Tẽrp-sich'ō-rē,
tes-tȧ-men'tȧ-ry, thē'ō-ry,
thiēv'ē-ry, thun'dē-ry,
trăc'ē-ry, trans-fẽr-ee',
treach'ē-ry (trech'),
trea'ṣu-ry (tre'zhū-), trick'ē-ry,
trump'ē-ry, un-sā'vō-ry,
ū'ṣū-ry, val-ē-diç'tō-ry,
vā'pō-ry, viç'tō-ry, vō'tȧ-ry,
wag'gẽr-y, wȧ'tē-ry, win'tē-ry,
witch'ē-ry, yeō'măn-ry,
zeph'yr-y.

s: ab'bȧ-cy, ad-dres-see',
ā'gen-cy, Añ'gli-cē, ȧ-pos'tȧ-sy,
är'gŏ-sy, ar-is-toç'rȧ-cy,
as-cen'den-cy,
bril'liȧn-cy ('lyăn-), C,
çā'den-cy, çlem'en-cy,
ço'gen-cy, çŏm-plā'cen-cy,
çon-sis'ten-cy, çon-spir'ȧ-cy,
çon'stăn-cy, çon-tin'gen-cy,
çon-tū'mȧ-cy,
çō-rē-spon'den-cy, çoûr'te-sy,
çū'rȧ-cy, dē'cen-cy,

dē-moç'rȧ-cy, dē-pen'den-cy,
di-plō'mȧ-cy, dis-çǫr'dăn-cy,
dis-çoûr'te-sy, dis-çrep'ăn-cy,
di"vǫr-cee', eç'stȧ-sy,
ef-fi'cien-cy ('shen-), em'băs-sy,
ē-mẽr'gen-cy, en"dǫr-see',
ex-peç'tăn-cy, ex-pē'di-en-cy,
fal'lȧ-cy, fan'tȧ-sy, fē'lō=dē=sē',
fẽr'ven-cy, flā'grăn-cy,
flip'pān-cy, flū'en-cy, fōre-see',
frā'grăn-cy, frē'quen-cy,
friç"ăs-see', gal'ăx-y, her'e-sy,
hy-poç'ri-sy, id'i-ō-cy,
id"i-ō-syn'çrȧ-sy, il-lit'ẽr-ȧ-cy,
im-pen'den-cy, im-pǫr'tū-nȧ-cy,
in"ăd-vẽr'ten-cy, in-çlem'en-cy,
in"çŏn-sis'ten-cy, in-çon'stăn-cy,
in-dē'cen-cy, in-del'i-çȧ-cy,
in-dē-pen'den-cy, in'făn-cy,
in"suf-fi'cien-cy ('shen-),
in-sūr'gen-cy, in-tes'tȧ-cy,
jeal'ous-y (jel'), leg'ȧ-cy,
lē'ni-en-cy, les-see', lī"cen-see',
lū'nȧ-cy, lux-ū'ri-ăn-cy,
mal-ig'năn-cy, Märsh'ăl-sēa,
nǫrm'ăl-cy, o-bēi'săn-cy,
Od'ys-sey, ō"vẽr-sēa',
ō"vẽr-see', pā'pȧ-cy, Pär-see',
Phar'i-see, pī'rȧ-cy, plī'ăn-cy,
pō'e-sy, poign'ăn-cy (poin'yăn-),
pol'i-cy, pō'ten-cy, pre'lȧ-cy,
prī'vȧ-cy, prō-fi'cien-cy ('shen-),
prom-is-ee', proph'e-cy,
pun'gen-cy, quī-es'cen-cy,
rē-çum'ben-cy, rē'gen-cy,
rē-gen'ẽr-ȧ-cy, rē-lēas-ee',
rē-nās'cen-cy, rē-pel'len-cy,
rē-splen'den-cy, Sad-dū-cee',
sēa, see, sē'çre-cy, sol'ven-cy,
stag'năn-cy, sub-sis'ten-cy,
suf-fi'cien-cy ('shen-),

(Choose only one word out of each group)

sū-prem'ȧ-cy, sy-cee',
syc'ō-phan-cy, ten'an-cy,
ten'den-cy, Ten-nes-see',
thē-oc'rȧ-cy, tru'ăn-cy,
un"fōre-see', ũr'ġen-cy,
vā'căn-cy, vā'grăn-cy,
va'liăn-cy ('lyăn-), vẽr'dăn-cy.
sh: ban'shee, deb"au-chee',
gär-nish-ee', shē, skï (shē).
sk(sç): skï (skē).
skr(sçr): sçree.
sn: snee, snick'ẽr-snee.
spr: bel es-prït' (-prē'),
es-prït' (-prē'),
joie d'es-prït' (zhwȧ des-prē'),
spree.
st: me-stee', mu-stee'.
t: ȧ-bil'i-ty, ab-sen-tee',
ab-ṣũrd'i-ty, aç-çliv'i-ty,
ȧ-cẽr'bi-ty, ȧ-cid'i-ty,
aç-rid'i-ty, aç-tiv'i-ty,
aç-tū-al'i-ty, ȧ-dapt"ȧ-bil'i-ty,
ad-vẽr'si-ty, ad-vīṣ"ȧ-bil'i-ty,
af-fȧ-bil'i-ty, af-fin'i-ty,
ȧ-ġil'i-ty, ȧ-laç'ri-ty, al-lot-tee',
am-bi-gū'i-ty, ȧ-mē-nȧ-bil'i-ty,
ȧ-men'i-ty, am"i-çȧ-bil'i-ty,
am'i-ty, am'nes-ty,
an-i-mos'i-ty, an-nū'i-ty,
an-ō-nym'i-ty,
an-tiq'ui-ty (-tik'wi-),
añx-ī'e-ty (angz-),
ap"pli-çȧ-bil'i-ty, ap-point-ee',
ȧ-rid'i-ty, as-per'i-ty,
as-si-dū'i-ty, ȧ-troc'i-ty,
au-dac'i-ty, au-ster'i-ty,
au-then-tic'i-ty, au-thor'i-ty,
ȧ-vid'i-ty, bär-bar'i-ty,
Ben"e-dic'i-tē, bo̤ot'ee,
bē-nig'ni-ty (-nī'), brev'i-ty,
bru-tal'i-ty, çal-am'i-ty,
çā-pȧ-bil'i-ty, çȧ-pac'i-ty,
çap-tiv'i-ty, çaṣ'ū-ăl-ty,
çath-ō-lic'i-ty, çaus-tic'i-ty,
çav'i-ty, ce-leb'ri-ty, ce-ler'i-ty,
cẽr'tăin-ty, chānge-ȧ-bil'i-ty,
chãr-i-ot-ee', chãr'i-ty,
chas'ti-ty,
Çhris-ti-an'i-ty (-chi-),
ci-vil'i-ty, çoat-ee',
çom-bus-ti-bil'i-ty, çom'i-ty,
çom-mod'i-ty, çom-mūn'i-ty,
çom-pat-i-bil'i-ty, çom-plex'i-ty,
çom-plic'i-ty,
çom"pre-hen'si-bil'i-ty,
çon-form'i-ty, çon-nū-bi-al'i-ty,
çon-san-guīn'i-ty (-gwīn'),
çon-ti-gū'i-ty, çon-trȧ-rī'e-ty,
çon-ven-tion-al'i-ty,
çon-vex'i-ty, çrē-dū'li-ty,
çrim-i-nal'i-ty, çrotch'et-y,
çru'di-ty, çru'el-ty, çū-pid'i-ty,
çū-ri-os'i-ty, dē-bil'i-ty,
dē-çliv'i-ty, ded-i-çȧ-tee',
dē-form'i-ty, dē'i-ty, den'si-ty,
dē-prav'i-ty, dep'ū-ty,
dev-ō-tee', dex-ter'i-ty,
dig'ni-ty, dim'i-ty,
dis-hon'es-ty (-on'), dis-par'i-ty,
dis-sim-i-lãr'i-ty, di-vẽr'si-ty,
di-vin'i-ty, dō-cil'i-ty,
dō-mes-tic'i-ty, dū-bī'e-ty,
dū-plic'i-ty, dȳ'năs-ty,
ē-las-tic'i-ty, ē-leç-tric'i-ty,
en'mi-ty, ē-nor'mi-ty, en'ti-ty,
ē-quäl'i-ty (-kwäl'),
e-quȧ-nim'i-ty, eq'ui-ty (ek'wi-),
ē-tẽr'ni-ty, ex-trem'i-ty,
fȧ-cil'i-ty, faç'ul-ty, fal'si-ty,
fȧ-mil-i-ar'i-ty, fā-tal'i-ty,
fȧ-tū'i-ty, fē-çun'di-ty,
fē-lic'i-ty, fē-roc'i-ty,

(Choose only one word out of each group)

fĕr-til′i-ty, fes-tiv′i-ty,
fī-del′i-ty, fidġ′et-y, fix′i-ty,
fọr-mal′i-ty, fọr-tū′i-ty,
frȧ-ġil′i-ty, frȧ-tēr′ni-ty,
fri-ġid′i-ty, fri-vol′i-ty,
frů-gal′i-ty, fū-til′i-ty,
fū-tū′ri-ty, gāi′e-ty,
gar-rů′li-ty, ġen-ēr-os′i-ty,
ġē-ni-al′i-ty, ġen-til′i-ty,
gōa-tee′, grant-ee′, grȧ-tū′i-ty,
grav′i-ty, guar-an-tee′,
hē-red′i-ty, hī-lår′i-ty,
hon′es-ty (on′), hos-pi-tal′i-ty,
hos-til′i-ty, hū-man′i-ty,
hū-mil′i-ty, ī-den′ti-ty,
im-bē-cil′i-ty, im-mȧ-tūr′i-ty,
im-men′si-ty, im-mod′es-ty,
im-mō-ral′i-ty, im-mọr-tal′i-ty,
im-mū′ni-ty, im-par′i-ty,
im-pas-siv′i-ty,
im″pē-çu-ni-os′i-ty,
im-pet″ū-os′i-ty, im-pī′e-ty,
im″pọr-tū′ni-ty, im-prō-prī′e-ty,
im-pū′ni-ty, im-pū′ri-ty,
in-ȧ-bil′i-ty, in-çȧ-pac′i-ty,
in″çom-pȧ″rȧ-bil′i-ty,
in″çom-pat″i-bil′i-ty,
in-çom″prē-hen″si-bil′i-ty,
in″çoñ-grů′i-ty, in″çre-dū′li-ty,
in-diġ′ni-ty, in″di-vid″ū-al′i-ty,
in-ē-brī′e-ty, in-fal″li-bil′i-ty,
in-fē-lic′ĭ-ty, in-fē-ri-ōr′i-ty,
in-fĕr-til′i-ty, in-fī-del′i-ty,
in-fin′i-ty, in-fīr′mi-ty,
in-ġe-nū′i-ty, in-hū-man′i-ty,
in-iq′ui-ty (ik′wi-), in-san′i-ty,
in-sin-cer′i-ty, in-si-pid′i-ty,
in-sū-lar′i-ty, in-teg′ri-ty,
in-ten′si-ty, in-ter-rō″gȧ-tee′,
in-tre-pid′i-ty, jō-çun′di-ty,
jol′li-ty, jō″vi-al′i-ty,

jů-ve-nil′i-ty, lā′i-ty, lax′i-ty,
lē-gal′i-ty, leg-ȧ-tee′, len′i-ty,
lev′i-ty, lib-ēr-al′i-ty, lib′ēr-ty,
lim-pid′i-ty, lū-bric′i-ty,
lū-cid′i-ty, lū-min-os′i-ty,
maj′es-ty, mȧ-jọr′i-ty,
man-ȧ-tee′, mod′es-ty,
moi′e-ty, mō-ral′i-ty,
mọr-tal′i-ty, mū-tū-al′i-ty,
nā-tiv′i-ty, neb-ū-los′i-ty,
neū-tral′i-ty, non-en′ti-ty,
nọr-mal′i-ty, nū′di-ty,
ob″jeç-tiv′i-ty, par′i-ty,
pas-siv′i-ty, pat-en-tee′,
pēr-mit-tee′, pi-çō-tee′, pī′e-ty,
pon-tee′, prē-şen-tee′, priv′i-ty,
prō-çliv′i-ty, prō-lix′i-ty,
prō-pen′si-ty, prō-pin′qui-ty,
prō-prī′e-ty, pū′ri-ty, quäl′i-ty,
quän′ti-ty, Q T, rē″cep-tiv′i-ty,
rē-mit-tee′, rep-är-tee′,
san′i-ty, set-tee′, sin-cer′i-ty,
sut-tee′, T, tēa, tee,
tem-er′i-ty, ten′si-ty,
tọr-pid′i-ty, trē-pid′i-ty,
trin′i-ty, triv-i-al′i-ty, trus-tee′,
u-til′i-ty, wạr-ran-tee′.

th: al-lop′ȧ-thy, an-tip′ȧ-thy,
ap′ȧ-thy, hō-mē-op′ȧ-thy,
sym′pȧ-thy.
TH: THē, THee.
thr: three.
tr: an′ces-try, är′tis-try,
ax′le-tree, bar′rȧ-try,
bar′re-try, big′ŏ-try,
bĭ′jöu-try (bē′zhọọ-),
Çhrist′măs tree (kris′),
çō′que-try (′ket-), çŏv′en-try,
dev′il-try, er′răn-try,
gal′lăn-try, gal′lōwş tree,
ġē-om′e-try, här′veş-try.

(Choose only one word out of each group)

ī-dol′a̓-try, in′dus-try,
in′făn-try,
knight′=er′răn-try (nīt),
mēr′chăn-try, min′is-try,
paġ′eant-ry (′ent-),
pälm′is-try (päm′),
peaṣ′ant-ry (pez′), ped′ănt-ry,
pleaṣ′ănt-ry (plez′), pō′e-try,
psȳ-c̣hī′a̓-try (sī-),
soph′is-try (sof′), sym′me-try,
tap′es-try, ten′ăn-try, tree,
weep′ing tree whif′fle-tree,
whip′ple-tree.

tw: t̓-tuï′ (ā-tᵗwē′).
v: joie de vïe (zhwȧ de vē),
lev-ee′, vïṣ′=a̓=vïs′ (vēz′=a̓=vē′).
w: en-nuï′ (on-wē′), wē, wee.
y: em-ploy-ee′, pāy-ee′, yē.
z: böur-ġeoi-ṣïe (bọor-zhwä-zē′),
chim-pan-zee′, dev-i-ṣee′,
fū-ṣee′, Zuȳ′dēr Zee (zī′).

ĒB

gl: glēbe (glēb).
gr: grēbe.

EB

Vowel: ebb.
d: deb.
k(c̣): keb.
n: neb.
s: Seb.
w: c̣ob′web, web, Webb.

EBD

Vowel: ebbed.
w: c̣ob′webbed, webbed.

ĒBZ

th: Thēbeṣ.
Plus glēbe′ṣ, etc.
Plus ēb+s.

EBZ

Vowel: ebbṣ.
d: Debṣ.
pl: plebṣ.
Plus eb+s.
Plus deb′ṣ, etc.

ĒCH

Vowel: ēach.
b: bēach, beech.
bl: blēach.
br: brēach, breech, un-breech′.
fl: fleech.
k(c̣): keech.
Kw(qu): quēach.
l: lēach, leech.
p: im-pēach′, pēach.
pl: plēach.
pr: prēach, un-prēach′.
r: fōre-rēach′, ō″vēr-rēach′,
rēach, sēa′rēach.
s: bē-seech′.
skr(sc̣r): sc̣reech.
sl: sleech.
sp: fōre-speech′*, speech.
t: fōre-tēach′*, tēach.

ECH

Vowel: etch.
f: fetch.
fl: fletch.
k(c̣): Jack Ketch, ketch.
l: letch.
r: retch.
sk(sc̣): sketch.
str: out-stretch′, stretch.
t: tetch.
v: vetch.
w: wetch.

ÉCHD
ED
fāte, fär, fȧst, fạll, finăl, cãre, at; mēte, prey, hẽr, met; pīne,
marīne, bĩrd, pin; nōte, mŏve, fọr, atŏm, not; mọọn, book;
128

(Choose only one word out of each group)

ÉCHD·

bl: un-blēached'.
p: un-im-pēached'.
Plus ēch+ed.

ECHD

f: fär'₌fetched'.
Plus ech+ed.

ĒD

Vowel: Ēad.
b: bēad, Bēde.
bl: bleed.
br: brēde*, breed,
crọss'breed, hälf'breed (häf'),
in-breed', in″tẽr-breed',
up-breed'.
d: deed, in-deed', mis-deed'.
f: feed, ọff hiṣ feed, ō″vẽr-feed',
un″dẽr-feed', un-feed'.
fr: freed.
gl: glēde, gleed.
gr: greed, ped'i-greed,
un-ped'i-greed.
h: hē'd, heed.
kr: creed, dē-creed',
un″dē-creed'.
kw(qu): Queed.
l: in″văl-ĭd', lēad, mis-lēad',
up-lēad'.
m: Gan'y-mēde, mēad, Mēde,
meed, Run'ny-mēde.
n: knēad (nēd),
knock'₌kneed' (nok'₌nēd'), need.
p: cen'ti-pēde, im-pēde',
mil'li-pēde, stam-pēde',
vē-loc'i-pēde.
pl: im-plēad', in″tẽr-plēad',
plēad.
r: jer-eed', mis-rēad', rēad,
Rēade, rēde*, reed, Rēid,
rē-rēad'.

s: ac-cēde', an'i-seed,
an-tē-cēde', con-cēde', ex-ceed',
in-tẽr-cēde', prē-cēde',
prō-ceed', rē-cēde', re'trō-cēde,
sē-cēde', seed, suc-ceed',
sū-pẽr-sēde'.
sh: shē'd.
skr(scr): screed.
sp: di-speed'*, god-speed',
out-speed', speed.
spr: spreed.
st: steed.
sw: Swēde.
t: teed.
tr: treed.
tw: Tweed.
w: sēa'weed, weed, wē'd.
y: yē'd.
Plus ē+d.
Plus sēa'd, etc.

ED

Vowel: co-ed', Ed,
con-tin″ū-ed*, sor'rōw-ed*,
wēar″i-ed'*, win'nōw-ed*.
b: a-bed', bed,
death'bed (deth'), em-bed',
sũr'bed, truck'le bed,
trun'dle bed.
bl: bled.
br: bread, bred, ġin'ġẽr-bread″,
hīgh'bred″ (hī'), hōme'bred″,
in-bred', pī'lŏt bread,
shew'bread (shō'),
thŏr'ōugh-bred ('ō-),
trūe'₌bred', un″dẽr-bred',
well'₌bred'.
d: dead, bē-dī-a-mŏn-ded',
dī'a-mŏn-ded, gär'lăn-ded,
her'ăl-ded, jeop'ăr-ded (jep'),
shep'hẽr-ded ('ẽr-).

(Choose only one word out of each group)

dr: à-dread′*, dread.

f: fed, fṳll′=fed′, ō″vēr-fed′,
un″dēr-fed′, well′=fed′.

fl: fled.

fr: à-frāid′, Fred, Win′i-fred.

h: à-head′, ar′rōw-head,
bē-head′, bil′let-head,
black′head, blun′dēr-head,
bul′let-head, check′le-head,
çop′pēr-head, dead′head,
death′s′=head′ (deths′),
dun′dēr-head,
feaTH′ēr-head (feTH),
fig′ūre-head, foun′tăin-head,
gō′=à-head′, head, jol′lēr-head,
log′gēr-head, lōw′li-head*,
māid′en-head, mas′tēr-head,
nē′grō-head, nig′gēr-head,
ō″vēr-head′, pop′py head,
thun′dēr-head, tim′bēr-head,
trun′dle head, un-head′,
wool′ly head.

j: rav′à-ġed*.

k(ç): ked.

l: lead (led), led, mis-led′,
mär′vel-led*, rī′văl-led′*.

m: aç-çus′tŏ-med*, mead.

n: Ned, em-blā′zŏn-ed*,
glis′ten-ed* (″n-), här′ken-ed′*,
im-priṣ′ŏn-ed*, pär′dŏn-ed*,
sañç′tion-ed*.

p: brev′i-ped, fiss′i-ped,
quäd′rú-ped, wŏr′ship-ped*.

pl: plead, pled.

r: añ-çhō-red*,
an′swēr-ed* (′sēr-),
bē-wil′dēr-ed*, blis′tēr-ed*,
çlus′tēr-ed′*,
coñ′quēr-ed* (′kēr-), çŏv′ēr-ed*,
dis-çŏv′ēr-ed, dow′ēr-ed′*,
en-am′ŏr-ed*, flow′ēr-ed*,

gaTH′ēr-ed*, glim′mēr-ed*,
huñ′gēr-ed*, liñ′gēr-ed*,
mea′ṣūr-ed* (′zhēr-),
mūr′mūr-ed*,
ō″vēr-pow′ēr-ed*,
ō″vēr-tow′ēr-ed*, pēr′jūr-ed*,
read, rē-çŏv′ēr-ed*, red, redd,
rē-mem′bēr-ed*, shim′mēr-ed*,
show′ēr-ed*, shud′dēr-ed*,
slum′bēr-ed*, suf′fēr-ed*,
tem′pēr-ed*, thun′dēr-ed*,
un-read′, wän′dēr-ed*,
wŏn′dēr-ed*.

s: à-fōre′said, bal′ăn-ced*,
em-bar′răs-sed*,
fōre-said′*, said, un-said′,
wit′nes-sed*.

sh: à-ston′ish-ed*, ban′ish-ed*,
blem′ish-ed*, bran′dish-ed*,
būr′nish-ed*, di-min′ish-ed*,
fam′ish-ed*, fūr′nish-ed*,
lañ′guish-ed*, pun′ish-ed*,
rē-liñ′quish-ed*, shed,
wạ′tēr-shed.

shr: shred.

sl: sled.

sp: sped, un-sped′, well′=sped′.

spr: bed′spread, bē-spread′,
out-spread′, ō-vēr-spread′,
spread.

st: bed′stead, bē-stead′,
in-stead′, stead.

t: at-trib′ūt-ed, bal′las-ted,
bar′ren=spir′it-ed,
bāse′=spir′it-ed, big′ŏt-ed,
bōld′=spir′it-ed, bon′net-ed,
break′făst-ed (brek′),
çär′pet-ed, çon-trib′ūt-ed,
çŏv′et-ed, çres′cent-ed,
dis-çom′fit-ed, dis-çom′fort-ed,
dis-çred′it-ed, dis″in-her′i-ted,

EDST
EFT

fāte, fär, fȧst, fạll, fĭnăl, cãre, at; mēte, prey, hẽr, met; pīne,
marĭne, bĭrd, pin; nōte, mŏve, fọr, atŏm, not; mọọn, book; **130**

(Choose only one word out of each group)

dis-pir'it-ed, dis-quī'et-ed,
dis-trib'ūt-ed, ex-hib'it-ed (-ib'),
fac'et-ed, fīne'=spir'it-ed,
for'feit-ed ('fit-),
gāy'=spir'it-ed, hel'met-ed,
hīgh'=spir'it-ed (hī'),
in-hab'it-ed, in-her'it-ed,
in-spir'it-ed,
līght'=spir'it-ed (līt'), lim'it-ed,
lōw'=spir'it-ed, mēan'=spir'it-ed,
mer'it-ed, pat'ent-ed, pī'răt-ed,
poọr'=spir'it-ed, prof'i-ted,
prō-hib'it-ed, pub'lic=spir'it-ed,
quī'et-ed, ring'let-ed,
sig'net-ed, soft=spir'it-ed,
spir'it-ed, tal'ent-ed, ted,
ten'ănt-ed, tũr'ret-ed,
un-bal'lăs-ted, un-bon'net-ed,
un-in-hab'it-ed, un-in-hib'it-ed,
un-lim'it-ed, un-mer'it-ed,
un-prof'it-ed, un-res'pit-ed,
un-ten'ănt-ed, viṣ'it-ed,
wēak'=spir'it-ed.

tr: tread.
thr: thread, rē-thread',
un-thread'.
w: rē-wed', 'un-wed', wed.
z: zed.

EDST

dr: dread'st*.
f: fed'st*.
fl: fled'st*.
l: led'st*.
s: said'st*.
spr: bē-spread'st'*,
o"vẽr-spread'st'*.
tr: tread'st*.
thr: thread'st*.
w: wed'st*.

EDTH

br: breadth, hãir'breadth.
Plus bē-spread'th'*, etc.

ĒDZ

Vowel: Ēadeṣ.
l: Leedṣ.
Plus Mede's, etc.

ĒF

b: beef.
br: brief.
ch: chief.
f: fief.
gr: grief.
l: bȧs rē-lief' (bȧ), bē-lief',
dis"bē-lief', in"tẽr-lēaf',
lēaf, lief, rē-lief', un"bē-lief'.
r: reef, shē-reef', Ten-ẽr-ĭffe'.
sh: shēaf.
th: thief.

EF

Vowel: f.
d: deaf.
f: en-feoff', feoff.
j: Jeff.
kl: clef.
n: nef.
sh: chef.

EFT

Vowel: eft.
d: deft.
f: en-feoffed'.
h: heft.
kl: cleft.
l: ȧ-left', left.
r: bē-reft', reft, un"bē-reft'.
th: theft.
w: weft, wheft.

(Choose only one word out of each group)

ĒG

gr: Griēg.
kl: kliēg.
l: c̲ol′lēague, en-lēague′, lēague.
n: rē-nēge′.
t: fà-tïgue′, Mc̲-Tēague′.
tr: in-trïgue′.

EG

Vowel: egg, go̲o̲se egg.
b: beg, beg′lĕr-beg, phil′i-beg.
dr: dreg.
k: keg.
l: leg.
m: Meg.
p: peg, un-peg′, Win′ni-peg.
sk: skeg.
t: teg.
y: yegg.

ĒGD

t: fà-tïgued′, ō″vĕr-fà-tïgued′.
Plus ēg+d.

EGD

l: spin′dle-legged.
Plus eg+d.

EGZ

l: sēa legṣ.
m: Meggṣ.
Plus eg+s.
Plus Meg's, etc.

ĒJ

l: liēġe.
s: bē-siēġe′, siēġe.

EJ

Vowel: edġe, rē-edġe′, un-edġe′.
dr: dredġe.
fl: fledġe.
h: en-hedġe′, hedġe.

j: "jedġe".
k: kedġe.
kl: c̲ledġe.
l: al-leġe′, ledġe, priv′i-leġe, sac̲′ri-leġe.
pl: im-pledġe′, in-tĕr-pledġe′, pledġe.
s: sedġe.
sl: sledġe.
t: tedġe.
w: wedġe.

EJD

Vowel: dŏub′le⸗edġed (dub′), twö′⸗edġed′ (to̲o̲′).
h: un-hedġed′.
s: sedġed.
Plus ej+d.

ĒK

Vowel: ēke, c̲ä-ïque′.
b: bēak.
bl: blēak, ob-lïque′.
ch: cheek, chïc̲.
d: Dēke.
fr: frēak.
gl: gleek.
gr: Greek.
k(c̲): c̲ä-c̲ïque′.
kl: c̲leek, c̲lïque.
kr: c̲rēak, c̲reek.
l: à-lēak′, lēak, leek, re-lïque′.
m: c̲o-mïque′, Mär-ti-nïque′, mēak, meek, Mō-zam-bïque′.
n: c̲li-nïque′, ū-nïque′.
p: àf′ter-pēak, à-pēak′, Ches′à-pēake, pēak, pïque.
r: à-reek′, reek, wrēak.
s: hïde′⸗and⸗seek′, seek, Sïkh (sēk), up-seek′.
sh: shēik.
shr: shriēk.

EK
EKT

fāte, fär, fȧst, fa̧ll, finăl, cãre, ȧt; mēte, pre̦y, hẽr, mĕt; pīne,
marĭne, bĭrd, pin; nōte, mȯve, fo̧r, atŏm, not; mo̧o̧n, book;

132

(Choose only one word out of each group)

skw(squ): bub'ble=and=squēak',
squēak.
sl: sleek.
sn: snēak.
sp: bē-spēak', fōre-spēak',
spēak, un-spēak'.
str: strēak.
t: an-tīque', c̦ri-tīque', tēak.
tw: twēak.
w: Hō'ly week,
Pas'sion week, wēak, week.
z: phy-șïque', be-zïque'.

EK

b: beck, Ken'ne-bec̦, Quē-bec̦'.
ch: check, cheque,
Czec̦h (chek).
d: bē-deck', deck,
quȧr'tẽr-deck, un-deck'.
fl: fleck.
h: by heck, heck.
k(c̦): keck.
n: breāk=neck,
leaTH'ẽr-neck (leTH'), neck,
neck'=and=neck', rub'bẽr-neck.
p: hen'peck, peck.
r: bē-wreck', reck, ship'wreck,
wreck.
sp: spec̦, speck.
t: Tec̦h, Teck.
tr: trek.

ĒKS

br: breeks.
sn: snēaks.
Plus ēk+s.
Plus creek's, etc.

EKS

Vowel: ex, Exe.
b: becks.
d: bē=decks'.

fl: cīr'c̦um-flex, flex, in'flex,
rē'flex.
h: hex.
k(c̦): kex.
l: lex.
m: Mex.
n: an-nex'.
pl: c̦om-plex', m̊ul'ti-plex,
pẽr-plex'.
pr: prex.
r: re̊x.
s: Mi̊d'dle-sex, sex, un-sex'.
t: Cel'ō-tex.
v: c̦on-vex', vex.
Cf. ek+s.
Plus deck's, etc.

EKST

n: next.
pl: pẽr-plexed', un''pẽr-plexed'.
s: sexed, sext, un-sexed':
t: prē'text, text.
v: un-vexed'.
Plus eks+d.
Plus deck'st*, etc.

ĒKT

ch: cher'ry=cheeked',
rōș'y=cheeked.
p: pēaked.
r: un-wrēaked'.
Plus ēk+d.
Plus beak'd, etc.

EKT

ch: ·checked, rē-checked',
un-checked'.
d: bē-decked', decked,
un-decked'.
f: af-fec̦t', c̦on-fec̦t', dē-fec̦t',
dis-af-fec̦t', dis-in-fec̦t', ef-fec̦t',

(Choose only one word out of each group)

in-fec̨t', pĕr-fec̨t', prē'fec̨t, rē-fec̨t'*.

fl: dē-flec̨t', g̈en'ū-flec̨t, in-flec̨t', rē-flec̨t'.

gl: neg-lec̨t'.

j: ab-jec̨t', ad-jec̨t', c̨on-jec̨t', dē-jec̨t', ē-jec̨t', in-jec̨t', in″tĕr-ject', ob-jec̨t', prō-jec̨t', rē-jec̨t', sub-jec̨t', trà-jec̨t'.

l: an'à-lec̨t, c̨ol-lec̨t', dī'à-lec̨t, ē-lec̨t', in'tel-lec̨t, non'ē-lec̨t, prē-lec̨t', re-c̨ol'lec̨t', sē-lec̨t'.

n: an-nec̨t'*, c̨on-nec̨t', dis-c̨on-nec̨t'.

p: ex-pec̨t', prō-spec̨t', sus-pec̨t'.

r: ar-rec̨t'*, c̨or-rec̨t', dī-rec̨t', ē-rec̨t', in″c̨or-rec̨t', in″di-rec̨t', mis″dī-rec̨t', por-rec̨t', re-şūr-rec̨t'.

s: bī-sec̨t', dis-sec̨t', ex-sec̨t', in″tĕr-sec̨t', sec̨t, trī-sec̨t'.

sp: cīr'c̨um-spec̨t, dis″rē-spec̨t', in-spec̨t', in-trō-spec̨t', rē-spec̨t', re'trō-spec̨t, self'₌rē-spec̨t'.

t: är'c̨hi-tec̨t, dē-tec̨t', prō-tec̨t'.

tr: trekked.

Plus ek+d.

ĒL

Vowel: eel.

b: au̲″tō-mō-bïle', Bēale, deş-hà-bïlle' (dez″à-bēl'), Mō-bïle'.

ch: chiēl.

d: dēal, dēil, in-tĕr-dēal'*, rē-dēal', mis-dēal'.

f: fēal, feel, fōre-feel'.

h: a̲ll″hēal', hēal, heel, hē'll.

hw: bal'ănce wheel, dī'ăl wheel, drī'ving wheel, flȳ'wheel, pad'dle wheel, whēal, wheel.

j: c̨on-g̈ēal', un″c̨on-g̈ēal'.

k(c̨): keel, Kiēl, và-kïl'.

kr: c̨reel.

l: lēal, Lïlle.

m: bär'ley mēal, C̨à-mïlle', É-mïle', mēal, c̨am-ō-mïle.

n: an-nēal', c̨he-nïlle', c̨och'i-nēal, kneel, Nēal, Nēil, Nēill, Ō'-Nēal', Ō'-Nēill'.

p: ap-pēal', pēal, peel, rē-pēal', thun'dĕr-pēal.

r: rēal.

s: c̨on-cēal', dif-fi-cïle', en-sēal', im-be-cïle', Lū-cïlle', priv'y sēal, sēal, seel, un-sēal', un-seel'*.

sh: Ō'-Sheel', shēal, shē'll.

skw(squ): squēal.

sp: speel, spiēl.

st: bas-tïlle', C̨as-tïlle', pas-tïlle', stēal, steel.

sw: swēal.

t: g̈en-teel', in'făn-tïle, shab'by g̈en-teel', tēal.

tw: tweel.

TH: THee'll*.

v: rē-vēal', vēal.

w: c̨om'mŏn-wēal, ne'er'₌dö₌weel″ (när'), wēa̲l̲, weel, wē'll.

z: al-guà-zïl' (-gà-), zēal.

Plus sea'll, etc.

EL

Vowel: A. W. O. L., El, ell, Em-man'ū-el, Im-man'u̲-el, L (el), vï-elle'.

b: bel, bell, belle, bon'ni-bel*, C̨an'tĕr-būr″y bell, c̨lar'i-bel,

ELCH
ELD

fāte, fär, fàst, fạll, finăl, cãre, at; mēte, prey, hẽr, met; pīne,
marīne, bĭrd, pin; nōte, mŏve, fọr, atŏm, nọt; mọọn, book; **134**

(Choose only one word out of each group)

death′bell (deth′), din′nẽr bell,
dīv′ing bell, gà-belle′, hãre′bell,
heaTH′ẽr bell (heTH′), Iṣ′à-bel,
Jez′e-bel, min′ute bell (′it),
pas′sing bell, re′bel,
sā′c̣ring bell, sañc̣′tus bell,
ves′pẽr bell.

d: as′phō-del, cit′à-del,
c̣or-delle′, dell, fri-c̣an-del′,
in′fi-del, ron-delle′.

dr: quäd-relle′*.

dw: dwell.

f: As′trō-phel, be-fell′, fell,
rē-fel′*.

h: hell.

j: jeĺ, g̣el.

k(c̣): kell.

kw(qu): quell.

l: par′al-lel.

m: bé̱-c̣hà-mel′ (bā-), c̣ar′à-mel,
hȳ′drō-mel, in″tẽr-mell′*,
pall′=mall′ (pel′=mel′),
pell′=mell′, phil′ō-mel.

n: À-bär′bà-nel, c̣ō′rō-nel*,
C̣ran-nell′, c̣re-nelle′,
fon-tà-nel′, jär-gō-nelle′, knell,
Lī′ōn-el′, man′gō-nel, Nell,
Pär-nell′, pẽr-sŏn-nel′,
pet′rō-nel, pim′pẽr-nel,
Pūr-nell′, sen′ti-nel, vil′là-nelle.

p: c̣om-pel′, dis-pel′, ex-pel′,
im-pel′, là-pel′, pell, prō-pel′,
rē-pel′.

r: c̣hant-ẽr-elle′, c̣ock′ẽr-el,
dog′g̣ẽr-el, mack′ẽr-el,
non-pà-reil′ (-rel′), toūr-elle′*.

s: cell, ex-cel′, pen-non-celle′,
pū-celle′, sell, rē-sell′,
un″dẽr-sell′.

sh: c̣ock′le-shell, in-shell′,
sēa′shell, shell, un-shell′.

sm: smell.

sn: snell.

sp: lŏve spell, spell, un-spell′.

sw: ground swell, swell,
up-swell′.

t: bag-à-telle′, broc̣-à-tel′,
C̣hau-mon-tel′ (shō-),
c̣lī-en-tele′, den-telle′, fōre-tell′,
hō-tel′, im-mọr-telle′,
mus-c̣à-tel′, tell.

v: c̣a′rà-vel.

w: fãre-well′, well.

y: yell.

z: c̣ar-roù-sel′,
da-moi-ṣelle′* (-mwà-),
da-mō-ṣelle′*,
de-moi-ṣelle′ (-mwà-), gà-zelle′,
mà-de-moi-ṣelle′ (-mwà-),
Mō-ṣelle′, zel, Zell.

Cf. miracle, etc.

ELCH

b: belch.

skw(squ): squelch.

w: welch, Welsh.

ĒLD

f: à-fiēld′, bat′tle-fiēld,
Ches′tẽr-fiēld, Dān′g̣ẽr-fiēld,
Del′à-fiēld′, fiēld, här′vest fiēld,
whēat fiēld.

n: an-nēaled′, un-à-nēled′*.

p: un-rē-pēaled′.

sh: en-shiēld′, shiēld.

w: wēald, wiēld.

y: yiēld.

Plus ēl+d.

Plus squeal′d, etc.

ELD

Vowel: eld*.

b: belled (beld).

(Choose only one word out of each group)

g: geld.
h: bē-held′, held, un-bē-held′, up-held′, with-held′.
j: jelled.
kw(qu): un-quelled′.
l: un-par′ăl-lelled.
m: meld.
n: un-knelled′ (-neld′).
s: seld*.
w: weld.
Plus el+d.
Plus yell'd, etc.

ELF
Vowel: elf.
d: delf.
gw: Guelph.
p: pelf.
s: hĕr-self′, him-self′, it-self′, mine-self′*, mȳ-self′, ŏne-self′ (wun-), our-self′, self, THȳ-self′*, yoūr-self′ (ūr-).
sh: man′tel shelf, shelf.

ELFT
d: delft.

ELFTH
tw: twelfth.

ELK
Vowel: elk.
hw: whelk.
y: yelk.

ELM
Vowel: elm.
h: dis-helm′, helm, un-helm′, weaTH′ĕr-helm (weTH′).
hw: ō″vĕr-whelm′, whelm*.
r: realm.

ELP
h: help, self′⸗help′.
hw: whelp.
k: kelp.

sk(sc̣): skelp.
sw: swelp.
y: yelp.

ELPS
f: Phelps.
Plus elp+s.
Plus help's, etc.

ELS
Vowel: else.
Cf. elt+s.

ELSH
w: Welsh.
Cf. elch.

ELT
b: belt, un-belt′.
d: dealt.
dw: dwelt.
f: felt, heärt′felt, un-felt′, veldt (felt).
g: gelt.
k(c̣): C̣elt, Kelt.
m: melt.
n: knelt.
p: pelt.
s: Celt.
sm: smelt.
sp: mis-spelt′, spelt.
sv: svelte.
sw: swelt*.
v: veldt.
w: welt.

ELTH
h: health.
st: stealth.
w: c̣om′mŏn-wealth, wealth.
Plus dwell'th*, etc.

ELV
d: delve.
h: helve.

(Choose only one word out of each group)

sh: shelve.
tw: twelve.

ELVZ

Vowel: elveṣ.
s: our-selveṣ', selveṣ,
THem-selveṣ',
yoūr-selveṣ' (ūr-).
Plus elv+ṣ.
Plus helve'ṣ, etc.

ELZ

Vowel: Elleṣ.
n: Där-dȧ-nelleṣ'.
s: Lȧs-celleṣ'.
sh: Sey-cͅhelleṣ' (sā-).
w: Welleṣ, Wellṣ.
Plus el+ṣ.
Plus spell'ṣ, etc.

ĒM

b: ȧ-bēam', bēam, em-bēam'*,
mọọn'bēam.
br: brēam.
d: acͅ-ȧ-dēme', deem,
mis-deem', rē-deem'.
dr: dāy'drēam, drēam.
f: blas'phēme.
fl: flēam.
gl: glēam,
weaTH'ẽr-glēam (weTH').
j: ré-g̣īme' (rā-zhēm').
kr: cͅrēam, ice-cͅrēam'.
l: lēam.
pr: sū-prēme'.
r: rēam, reem, riēm.
s: bē-seem', en-sēam', sēam,
seem, un-bē-seem', un-sēam'.
sk(sͅcͅ): scͅhēme.
skr(sͅcͅr): scͅrēam.
st: stēam.
str: strēam.

t: ceṅ-tīme' (sȧṅ-tēm'),
dis⹀es-teem', es-teem',
self'⹀es-teem', tēam, teem.
th: an'ȧ-thēme, thēme.
tr: dis-trēam', ex-trēme'.

EM

Vowel: em, 'em,
rē'qui-em ('kwi-).
d: an'ȧ-dem, bē-dī'ȧ-dem,
cͅon-demn', dī'ȧ-dem.
f: femme.
fl: phlegm.
h: ȧ-hem', Beth'le-hem,
hem.
j: bē-g̣em', Brum'mȧ-g̣em,
g̣em, strat'ȧ-g̣em.
kl: cͅlem.
kr: cͅrème de lȧ cͅrème.
m: mem.
n: ad hō'mi-nem.
r: thē'ō-rem.
sh: Shem.
st: stem.
t: cͅon-temn', prō tem.
th: ap'ō-thegm.
TH: THem.

ĒMD

d: un-rē-deemed'.
dr: un-drēamed'.
Plus ēm+d.
Plus cream'd, etc.

EMD

d: un-dī'ȧ-demed,
un-cͅon-demned'.
Plus em+d.
Plus gem'd, etc.

(Choose only one word out of each group)

EMP
h: hemp.
k: Kemp.

EMS
t: temṣe.

EMT
Vowel: ex-empt', prē-empt'.
dr: a̦-dreamt', dreamt, un-dreamt'.
k(c̦): kempt, un-kempt'.
t: at-tempt', c̦on-tempt', self'=c̦on-tempt', tempt.

ĒMZ
s: mē-seemṣ'.
Plus ēm+s.
Plus dream's, etc.

EMZ
t: temṣe, Thameṣ (temz).
Plus em+ṣ.
Plus hem's, etc.

ĒN
Vowel: ēan, e'en*, good-e'en'*, Hal"lōw-e'en'.
b: bēan, been, shē-been'.
br: Breen.
ch: C̦ap-ū-chïn'.
d: al-măn-dïne', c̦ō'dēine, dēan, dēne, dū-deen', gab-ăr-dïne', Ġer-ăl-dïne', gra̦-dïne', Guñ'ga̦ Dïn, in-c̦är'na̦-dïne, sär-dïne'.
f: c̦af-fēine, Jō'ṣe-phïne, tre-phïne'.
fr: Peek Frēan.
g: Bē-guïne', c̦ar-ra̦-geen'.
gl: glēan, gleen*.
gr: bōw'ling green, c̦ha̦-grïn', e'vĕr-green, gra̦ss green,

green, lo̦ng green, per'e-grïne, put'ting green, sēa green, sha̦-green', win'tēr-green.
h: fel'la̦-hïn.
j: al'pi-ġēne, Eū-ġēne', gaz'ō-ġēne, ġēne, het-ēr'ō-ġēne, in'di-ġēne, Jēan, po̦r-phy'rō-ġēne, quäd'ra̦-ġēne*, selt'zō-ġēne.
k(c̦): keen, nan-keen'.
kl: c̦lēan, c̦ŏme c̦lēan, un-c̦lēan'.
kw(qu): fāir'y queen, här'vest queen, Māy queen, mead'ōw queen (med'), pal'ăn-quïn, quēan, queen, un-queen'.
l: an'i-lïne, ba̦-leen', ban-dō-lïne', c̦ol'leen, c̦rin'ō-lïne, liēn, E-van'ġe-lïne, gas-ō-lïne', Ghib'el-lïne (gib'), lēan, lēne*, Mag'da̦-lēne, naph'tha̦-lēne (naf'), ō'pal-ïne, Paṵl-ïne', sc̦ā-lēne', toūr'ma̦-lïne, up-lēan', vas'ō-lïne.
m: dē-mēan', dē-mēsne', mēan, mēsne, miēn, mis-dē-mēan'.
n: mez-za̦-nïne', quï-nïne'.
p: at'rō-pïne, fil-li-peen', pēan, peen, Phil-ip-pïne', spal-peen'.
pr: im-prēgn'*, preen.
r: Al-ġe-rïne', an-sēr-ïne', a-qua̦-ma̦-rïne', c̦a̦-reen', c̦hō-rïne', Ī-rēne', mär'ga̦-rïne', ma̦-rïne', maz-a̦-rïne', mō-reen', Naz-a̦-rēne', nec̦-tăr-ïne', ō"lē-ō-mär'ga̦-rïne', Pal'my-rēne, pis-ta̦-reen', se-rēne', sub'ma̦-rïne', sub-tēr-rēne', sū"pēr-ter-rēne',

EN
ENCH

fāte, fär, fȧst, fąll, finăl, cãre, at; mēte, prey, hẽr, met; pīne,
marïne, bïrd, pin; nōte, mŏve, fǫr, atŏm, not; mǫǫn, book;

138

(Choose only one word out of each group)

tam-boū-rïne', ter-rēne',
tū-reen', ul"trȧ-mȧ-rïne',
wŏl-vẽr-ïne'.

s: dam'ȧ-scēne, Ē'ō-cēne,
ep'i-cēne, fas-cïne', fōre-seen',
ker'ō-sēne, Mï'ō-cēne,
Nï-cēne', ob'scēne, ō-vẽr-seen',
Pleis'tō-cēne (plis'), Plï'ō-cēne,
scēne, seen, sēine,
un-fōre-seen', un-seen'.

skr(scr): bē-screen', screen.

spl: spleen.

st: Ẽr-nest-ïne', stēin.

sh: mȧ-chïne',
prāy'ing mȧ-chïne', Shēan,
sheen, vō'ting mȧ-chïne.

t: Är'ġen-tïne, Au'gus-tïne,
bärk'en-tïne, bot-tïne',
brig-ăn-tïne', can-teen',
cȧ-rŏt-ēne', Cǫn'stăn-tïne,
dū-ve-tyn' (-tēn'),
eight'een (āt'), fif'teen,
Flǫr'en-tïne, fōur'teen,
gal'ăn-tïne, ġel'ȧ-tïne,
guil'lō-tïne (gil'), lȧ-teen',
lib'ẽr-tïne, nic'ō-tïne,
nïne'teen, pō-teen',
quȧr-ăn-tïne', roù-tïne',
St. Au'gus-tïne, sa-teen',
sẽr'pen-tïne, sev'en-teen,
six'teen, teen, thïr'teen,
umf'teen, vel-vet-ēen'.

tr: yes-treen'*.

tw: ȧ-tween', bē-tween',
gō'=bē-tween', tween.

v: ad-vēne', cǫn-trȧ-vēne',
cǫn-vēne', in-tẽr-vēne',
mär'grȧ-vïne, rȧ-vïne',
sub-vēne', sū-pẽr-vene', vïsne.

w: ō-vẽr-ween', wēan, ween*.

y: yēan.

z: ben-zēne', ben'zïne,
bom-bȧ-zïne', cuī-sïne' (kwē-),
mag-ȧ-zïne'.

EN

Vowel: caȳ-enne' (kī-en'),
Cheȳ-enne' (shī-en'), Dăr'i-en,
ē-ques"tri-enne', Pȧ-rï"si-enne',
trȧ-ġē"di-enne', Vȧ-len"ci-ennes',
vär-sō"vi-enne'.

b: ben.

d: den.

f: fen.

g: ȧ-gain' (-gen').

gl: glen.

h: hen, prāi'riē hen, sāġe hen,
tūrk'hen, wą'tẽr hen.

hw: when.

j: hal'ō-ġen, hȳ'drō-ġen,
nï'trō-ġen, ox'y-ġen.

k(c): ken.

l: Len, Mag'dȧ-len.

m: ąl'dẽr-men, ā-men',
cȳc'lȧ-men, men, reġ'i-men,
spec'i-men.

p: brev'i-pen, foun'tăin pen,
im-pen', pen, un-pen'.

r: wren.

s: Sar'ȧ-cen, sen, sen'sen,

t: ten.

TH: THen.

w: wen.

y: yen.

z: cit'i-zen, den'i-zen.

ENCH

b: bench.

bl: blench.

dr: bē-drench', drench,
rē-drench'.

fl: flench.

fr: French.

139 ūse, bu̯ll, brúte, tū̆rn, up; crȳ, myth; c̣at, mac̣hine, ace, church, c̣hord; g̣em, añger, (Fr.) boṅ, aṣ; THis, thin; aẓure

ENCHD
ENJ

(Choose only one word out of each group)

kl: c̣lench, un-c̣lench′.
kw(qu): quench.
r: mŏñ′key wrench, wrench.
skw(squ): squench.
st: stench.
t: tench.
tr: in-trench′, rē-trench′, trench.
w: wench.

ENCHD

bl: un-blenched′.
Plus ench+d.
Plus stench'd, etc.

ĒND

f: ärch′⹀fiēnd′, fiēnd.
p: piēnd.
t: tiēnd.
Plus ēn+d.
Plus scēne'd, etc.

END

Vowel: an-end′*, end, gā′ble end, min′ū-end, tag end, up⹀end′.
b: bend, South Bend, un-bend′.
bl: blend, ho̯rn′blende, in-tēr-blend′, pitch′blend.
d: div′i-dend.
f: dē-fend′, fend, fōre-fend′*, of-fend′, weaTH′ēr fend (weTH′).
fr: bē-friend′, friend, im-friend′.
h: ap-prē-hend′, c̣om-prē-hend′, mis″ap-prē-hend′, re-prē-hend′, sub′trȧ-hend.
k(c̣): kenned, un-kenned′.
l: lend.
m: ȧ-mend′, c̣om-mend′, ē-mend′, mend, re-c̣ŏm-mend′.

p: ap-pend′, dē-pend′, ex-pend′, im-pend′, penned, pēr-pend′, prē-pend′*, sti′pend, un-penned′, vil′i-pend.
r: rend, rev′ēr-end.
s: as-cend′, c̣on-dē-scend′, dē-scend′, God′send, send, tran-scend′, up-send′.
sp: mis-spend′, spend, sus-pend′.
t: at-tend′, c̣on-tend′, dis-tend′, ex-tend′, in-tend′, ob-tend′, Os-tend′, po̯r-tend′, prē-tend′, rep′e-tend, sub-tend′, sū″pēr-in-tend′, tend.
tr: trend.
v: vend.
w: wend.
z: Zend.
Plus en+d.
Plus hen'd, etc.

ENDZ

m: ȧ-mendṣ′.
plus end+s.
Plus end's, etc.

ENGK

sh: Sc̣heñck (shengk).

ENGKS

j: Jeñkes, Jeñks.
sh: Sc̣heñck's (shengks).

ENGTH

l: fu̯ll′⹀length′, length.
str: strength.

ENJ

h: Stōne′heṅge.
v: ȧ-venṅge′, rē-venṅge′.

ENJD
ENS

fāte, fär, fȧst, fạll, finăl, cãre, at; mēte, prey, hẽr, met; pīne,
marĭne, bĭrd, pin; nōte, mōve, fọr, atŏm, not; mọọn, book;

140

(Choose only one word out of each group)

ENJD

v: ȧ-venġed', rē-venġed',
un-ȧ-venġed'.
Plus stonehenge'd, etc.

ENS

Vowel: af'flū-ence, cọn'flu-ence,
cọn-vē'ni-ence, dis-ō-bē'di-ence,
ex-pē'di-ence, ex-pē'ri-ence,
in-ci'pi-ence, in-cọn'gru-ence,
in″cọn-vē'ni-ence,
in″ex-pē'di-ence,
in-ex-pē'ri-ence, in'flū-ence,
in-si'pi-ence, mel-li'flū-ence,
nes'ci-ence, ō-bē'di-ence,
om-nis'ci-ence, prē-ci'pi-ence,
prēs'ci-ence ('shi-), prù'ri-ence,
rē-ṣil'i-ence, sā'li-ence,
sā'pi-ence, sub-sẽr'vi-ence.

d: ac'ci-dence, cō-in'ci-dence,
cọn-dense', cọn'fi-dence, dense,
dif'fi-dence, dis'si-dence,
ev'i-dence, im'pū-dence,
in'ci-dence, cō-in'ci-dence,
non-reṣ'i-dence, prov'i-dence,
reṣ'i-dence, self'⸗cọn'fi-dence,
sub'si-dence.

f: dē-fence', fence, of-fence',
self⸗'dē-fence'.

h: hence.

hw: whence.

j: dil'i-ġence, ex'i-ġence,
in'di-ġence, in-tel'li-ġence,
neg'li-ġence.

kw(qu): blan-dil'ō-quence,
brev-il'ō-quence, cọn'sē-quence,
el'ō-quence, gran-dil'ō-quence,
in-cọn'sē-quence,
mag-nil'ō-quence.

l: bē-nev'ō-lence, cọr'pū-lence,

ē-quiv'ȧ-lence, ex'cel-lence,
flat'ū-lence, floc̣'c̣ū-lence,
frạud'ū-lence, im-prev'ȧ-lence,
in'dō-lence, in'sō-lence,
mȧ-lev'ō-lence, op'ū-lence,
pes'ti-lence, prev'ȧ-lence,
quän-ti-vā'lence, red'ō-lence,
som'nō-lence, suc̣'c̣ū-lence,
truc̣'ū-lence, tũr'bū-lence,
vī'ō-lence, vir'ū-lence.

m: cọm-mence', im-mense',
vē'hē-mence.

n: ab'sti-nence, cọn'ti-nence,
em'i-nence, im'mȧ-nence,
im'mi-nence, im-pẽr'ti-nence,
in-cọn'ti-nence, pẽr'mȧ-nence,
pẽr'ti-nence, prē-em'i-nence,
pro'mi-nence,
sū″pẽr-em'i-nence.

p: dis-pense', ex-pense', pence,
prē-pense', prō-pense'*,
rec̣'ŏm-pense, sus-pense'.

r: cĩr-c̣um'fẽr-ence, cọn'fẽr-ence,
def'ẽr-ence, dif'fẽr-ence,
in-dif'fẽr-ence, in'fẽr-ence,
ir-rev'ẽr-ence, pref'ẽr-ence,
ref'ẽr-ence, rev'ẽr-ence.

s: bē-nef'i-cence, cọm'mŏn sense,
cọn-c̣ū'pi-scence, frañk'in-cense,
in-cense', in'nō-cence,
mag-ni'fi-cence, mū-ni'fi-cence,
ret'i-cence, sense.

sp: spence.

t: cọm'pē-tence, im-pen'i-tence,
im'pō-tence, in-cọm'pē-tence,
in-tense', om-ni'pō-tence,
pen'i-tence, ple-nip'ō-tence,
prē-tence', sub-tense', tense.

TH: THence.

Cf. ents.

Plus Lent's, etc.

(Choose only one word out of each group)

ENST

Vowel: ex-pē′ri-enced,
in-ex-pē′ri-enced, in′flū-enced.
d: <u>c</u>on-densed′, ev′i-denced.
f: fenced.
g: à-gainst (-genst′),
'gainst (genst).
m: <u>c</u>om-menced′.
n: à-nenst′, fōre-nenst′.
p: dis-pensed′.
r: rev′ēr-enced.
s: in-censed′, sensed.
Plus ens+d.
Plus fenc'd, etc.

ENT

Vowel: a<u>c</u>-ci′pi-ent, af′flū-ent,
am′bi-ent, à-pē′ri-ent,
cĭr-<u>c</u>um-am′bi-ent,
cĭr-<u>c</u>um′flū-ent, <u>c</u>on′flū-ent,
<u>c</u>on′grù-ent, <u>c</u>on-stit′ū-ent,
<u>c</u>on-vē′ni-ent, dif′flū-ent,
dis-ō-bē′di-ent, ē-mol′li-ent,
ē-sū′ri-ent, ex-pē′di-ent,
grā′di-ent, in-ci′pi-ent,
in-<u>c</u>on′grù-ent, in-<u>c</u>on-vē′ni-ent,
in″ex-pē′di-ent, in′flū-ent,
in-grē′di-ent,
in-sen′ti-ent ('shi-), in-si′pi-ent,
lē′ni-ent, mel-li′flū-ent,
ō-bē′di-ent, ō′ri-ent,
pĕr-cip′i-ent, pres′ci-ent,
prū′ri-ent, rē-cip′i-ent,
ref′lū-ent, rē-<u>s</u>il′i-ent,
sā′li-ent, sā′pi-ent,
<u>s</u>en′ti-ent ('shi-), sub-sēr′vi-ent.
b: bent, un-bent′.
bl: blent.
br: brent.
d: a<u>c</u>′ci-dent, <u>c</u>ō-in′ci-dent,
<u>c</u>on′fi-dent, dent, dif-fi′dent,

dis′si-dent, ev′i-dent,
im-prov′i-dent, im′pū-dent,
in′ci-dent, in″<u>c</u>ō-in′ci-dent,
in-<u>c</u>om′pē-tent, in-dent′,
o<u>c</u>′ci-dent, prec′ē-dent,
pre<u>s</u>′i-dent, prov′i-dent,
re<u>s</u>′i-dent.
f: fent.
g: Ghent (gent).
j: dil′i-ġent, ex′i-ġent, ġent,
in′di-ġent, in-tel′li-ġent,
neg′li-ġent.
k(c): a<u>c</u>′cent, Kent, un-kent′*.
kw(qu): a<u>c</u>-quent′, <u>c</u>on′sē-quent,
el′ō-quent, frē-quent′,
gran-dil′ō-quent,
in-<u>c</u>on′sē-quent,
mag-nil′ō-quent, sub′sē-quent.
l: bē-nev′ō-lent, <u>c</u>or′pū-lent,
ē-qui′và-lent, es′<u>c</u>ū-lent,
ex′cel-lent, flo<u>c</u>′<u>c</u>ū-lent,
fraud′ū-lent, grā′ci-lent*,
in′dō-lent, in′sō-lent, leant,
lent, lū′<u>c</u>ū-lent, mà-lev′ō-lent,
op′ū-lent, pes′ti-lent,
prev′à-lent, red′ō-lent, rē-lent′,
som′nō-lent, su<u>c</u>′<u>c</u>ū-lent,
tru<u>c</u>′ū-lent, tūr′bū-lent,
vin′ō-lent, vī′ō-lent, vir′ū-lent.
m: à-ban′dŏn-ment,
à-bol′ish-ment,
a<u>c</u>-<u>c</u>ŏm′păn-i-ment,
a<u>c</u>-<u>c</u>om′plish-ment,
a<u>c</u>-<u>c</u>où′tēr-ment,
a<u>c</u>-knowl′edġe-ment (-nol′ej-),
ad-mea′<u>s</u>ūre-ment ('zho<u>o</u>r-),
ad-mon′ish-ment,
ad-vēr′ti<u>s</u>e-ment,
af-fam′ish-ment*,
af-fran′chi<u>s</u>e-ment,
ag-gran′di<u>s</u>e-ment, al′i-ment,

ENT

fāte, fär, fȧst, fạll, finăl, cāre, at; mēte, prẹy, hẽr, met; pīne,
marïne, bĭrd, pin; nōte, mŏve, fọr, atŏm, not; mọọn, book;

142

(Choose only one word out of each group)

ap-pọr'tion-ment,
är-bit'rȧ-ment, är'gū-ment,
ärm'ȧ-ment, ȧ-ston'ish-ment,
ạug-ment', bab'ble-ment,
ban'ish-ment, bat'tle-ment,
bē-dev'il-ment, bē-diz'en-ment,
bet'tẽr-ment, bē-wil'dẽr-ment,
blan'dish-ment, blā'zŏn-ment,
blem'ish-ment, boTH'ẽr-ment,
brab'ble-ment, cē-ment',
chas'tiṣe-ment, cher'ish-ment,
com'ment, com'plē-ment,
com'pli-ment, con'di-ment,
daz'zle-ment, dē-cī'phẽr-ment,
dec'rē-ment, dē-ment',
dē-mol'ish-ment,
det'ri-ment, dē-vel'ŏp-ment,
dev'il-ment, di-min'ish-ment,
dim'ple-ment, dis-ā'ble-ment,
dis-ärm'ȧ-ment,
dis-ҫoūr'ȧġe-ment,
dis-fig'ūre-ment,
dis-fran'chiṣe-ment,
dis-pär'ăġe-ment,
dis-pir'it-ment,
dis-tiñ'guish-ment ('gwish-),
di-vẽr'tiṣe-ment, doҫ'ū-ment,
el'e-ment, em-bar'rass-ment,
em-bat'tle-ment,
em-bel'lish-ment,
em-bez'zle-ment,
em-bit'tẽr-ment,
em-blā'zŏn-ment,
em-bod'i-ment, ē-mol'ū-ment,
em-pan'el-ment, en-ā'ble-ment,
en-ҫŏm'păss-ment,
en-coūr'ăġe-ment,
en-dān'ġer-ment,
en-deav'ŏr-ment (-dev')*,
en-fee'ble-ment,
en-fran'chiṣe-ment,

en-līght'en-ment (-līt'),
en-nō'ble-ment, en-rav'ish-ment,
en-tān'gle-ment, en-vel'ŏp-ment,
en-vī'rŏn-ment, en-viṣ'ăġe-ment,
es-tab'lish-ment, ex'ҫre-ment,
ex-per'i-ment,
ex-tiñ'guish-ment ('gwish-),
fam'ish-ment, fẽr-ment',
fil'ȧ-ment, fĭrm'ȧ-ment,
fō-ment', fōre-meant',
fos'tẽr-ment, fran'chiṣe-ment,
gär'nish-ment, gŏv'ẽrn-ment,
hȧ-bil'i-ment, har'ăss-ment,
her-e-dit'ȧ-ment, im-ped'i-ment,
im-per'il-ment, im'plē-ment,
im-pov'ẽr-ish-ment,
im-priṣ'ŏn-ment, in'ҫrē-ment,
in'strù-ment, in-teg'ū-ment,
in-vēi'gle-ment, lȧ-ment',
lañ'guish-ment ('gwish-),
lav'ish-ment, lig'ȧ-ment,
lin'ē-ȧ-ment, lin'i-ment,
man'ăġe-ment,
mea'ṣūre-ment (me'zhọọr-),
med'i-ҫȧ-ment, mer'ri-ment,
mon'ū-ment, mū'ni-ment,
noūr'ish-ment, nū'tri-ment,
ọr'nȧ-ment, pär'liȧ-ment ('lȧ-),
ped'i-ment, pes'tẽr-ment*,
prat'tle-ment, prē-dic'ȧ-ment,
prē-mon'ish-ment,
prē-ṣen'ti-ment, pun'ish-ment,
rav'ish-ment, reġ'i-ment,
rē-liñ'quish-ment ('kwish-),
rē-plen'ish-ment, rù'di-ment,
sac'rȧ-ment, sed'i-ment,
sen'ti-ment, set'tle-ment,
sup'plē-ment, tem'pẽr-ȧ-ment,
ten'ē-ment, tes'tȧ-ment,
tọr-ment', toūr'nȧ-ment,
trem'ble-ment,

143 ūse, bṳll, brūte, tûrn, up; crȳ, myth; çat, maçhine, ace, church, çhord; ġem, añger, (Fr.) boṅ, aṣ; THis, thin; aẓure

ĒNTH
ĒP

(Choose only one word out of each group)

un-meant' (-ment'),
van'ish-ment,
vañ'quish-ment ('kwish-),
vē'he-ment, wän'dẽr-ment*,
well'=meant', wil'dẽr-ment*,
wŏn'dẽr-ment, wŏr'ri-ment.

n: ab'sti-nent, à-nent',
çon'ti-nent, em'i-nent,
fọr-nent', im'mà-nent,
im'mi-nent, im-pẽr'ti-nent,
in-çon'ti-nent, pẽr'mà-nent,
pẽr'ti-nent, prē=em'i-nent,
prom'i-nent, su"pẽr-em'i-nent,
THere'=à-nent' (THãr').

p: pent, rē-pent'.

r: bel-liġ'ẽr-ent, def'ẽr-ent,
dif-fẽr'ent, in-dif'fẽr-ent,
ir-rev'ẽr-ent, rent, rev'ẽr-ent.

s: ab-sent', as-cent', as-sent',
bē-nef'i-cent, cent, çon-sent',
dēs-cent', dis-sent', in'nō-cent,
mag-ni'fi-cent, mà-lef'i-cent,
mū-nif'i-cent, ret'i-cent, scent,
sent, un-sent'.

sp: fōre-spent'*, mis-spent',
ō"vẽr-spent', spent, un-spent',
well'=spent'.

spr: bē-sprent'*, sprent.

st: stent.

t: at-tent'*, çom'pē-tent,
çon-tent', dē-tent',
dis"çon-tent', ex-tent',
ill'=çon-tent', im-pen'i-tent,
im'pō-tent, ig-ni'pō-tent,
in-tent', mal"çon-tent',
mis-çon-tent', om-ni'pō-tent,
os-tent', pen'i-tent,
ple-nip'ō-tent, pọr'tent, tent,
un-tent', well'=çon-tent'.

tr: Trent.

v: cĩr"çum-vent', ē-vent',
in-vent', prē-vent', vent.

w: un-dẽr-went', went.

z: mis"rep-rē-ṣent', prē-ṣent',
rep-rē-ṣent', rē-ṣent'.

ĒNTH

gr: greenth.
t: fōur-teenth', thĩr-teenth',
etc.
Plus lean'th*, etc.

ENTH

t: tenth.
Plus pen'th*, etc.

ENTS

m: aç-çoù'tẽr-ments.
t: çon'tents.
Plus cents, etc.
Plus cent's, etc.
Cf. ens.

ĒNZ

gr: greenṣ.
r: smiTH-ẽr-eenṣ'.
s: Es-sēneṣ'.
t: teenṣ.
Plus ēn+s.

ENZ

Vowel: enṣ, Val-en"ci-enneṣ'.
fl: flenṣe.
g: ġenṣ.
l: lenṣ.
s: Vin-cenneṣ'.
Plus en+s.
Plus den's, etc.

ĒP

ch: chēap, cheep, chēpe*.
.d: à-deep', deep.
h: à-hēap', hēap.

EP
ĒR

fāte. fär. fàst, f**ạ**ll, finăl, cāre, **at**; mēte, pr**ẹ**y, hēr. met; pīne,
marīne, bĭrd, pĭn; nōte, mŏve, f**ọ**r, atŏm, not; m**ọọ**n, book;

144

(Choose only one word out of each group)

k(c̣): keep, up'keep.
kl: c̣lēpe*.
kr: c̣reep.
l: lēap, out-lēap', ō"vēr-lēap'.
n: nēap.
p: bō'peep', peep, un-dēr-peep'.
r: rēap.
s: seep.
sh: sheep.
sl: à-sleep', beaū'ty sleep (bū'),
    out-sleep', ō"vēr-sleep', sleep.
st: steep.
sw: chim'nēy-sweep,
    en-sweep', sweep, swēpe*.
thr: thrēap.
tr: es-trēpe'.
w: bē-weep', f**ọ**r-weep'*,
    out-weep', weep.

EP

h: hep.
p: pep.
pr: prep.
r: dem'i-rep, rep.
sk(sc̣): skep.
st: foot'step, mis-step',
    ō"vēr-step', step, steppe.

ĒPS

kr: c̣reeps.
Plus ēp+s.
Plus sleep's, etc.

EPS

ep+s.
Plus step's, etc.

ĒPT

h: up-hēaped'.
n: bē-nēaped', nēaped.
st: un-steeped'.

Plus ēp+d.
Plus sleep'd, etc.

EPT

Vowel: in-ept'.
d: à-dept'.
k(c̣): kept, un-kept'.
kl: y-c̣lept' (i-)*.
kr: c̣rept.
l: leapt.
p: pepped.
s: ac̣-cept', ex-cept',
    in-tēr-cept', sept.
sl: out-slept', ō"vēr-slept', slept.
st: mis-stepped', ō"vēr-stepped',
    stepped.
sw: swept, un-swept'.
w: un-wept', wept.

EPTH

d: depth.
Plus stepp'th*, etc.

ĒR

Vowel: ēar, mad'ri-ēr.
b: beer, biēr, g̣in'g̣ēr beer.
bl: blēar.
ch: cheer, up-cheer'.
d: bāy-ăd-ēre', bel-vē-dēre',
    bom-băr-diēr', brig-à-diēr',
    c̣om-man-deer', dēar, deer,
    en-dēar', fal'lōw deer,
    gren-à-diēr', hal-bēr-diēr',
    in-dēar'*, kill'deer,
    pe'tär deer, re̤in'deer.
dr: drēar.
f: ā-ē'rō-sphēre (-sfēr), af-feer'*,
    at'mos-phēre, en-sphere', fēar,
    hem'i-sphēre, in-sphēre',
    in-tēr-fēre', per'i-sphēre,

145 ūse, bṳll, brúte, tŭrn, up; crȳ, myth; çat, maçhine, ace,
church, çhord; g̣em, añger, (Fr.) boṅ, aş; THis, thin; aᶎure   **ĒRD
ĒRT**

(Choose only one word out of each group)

plan′i-sphēre, sphēre,
un′dĕr-sphēre, un-sphēre′.

fl: fleer.

g: bev′el gēar, friç′tion gēar,
gēar, rē-gēar′, un-gēar′.

h: ad-hēre′, çō-hēre′, in-hēre′.

hy: hēar, Heer, hēre,
ō-vĕr-hēar′.

j: jeer.

k(ç): fȧ′kïr.

kl: çhan′ti-çleer, çlēar.

kw(qu): queer.

l: ban-dō-leer′, çan-ce-leer′,
çav-ȧ-liēr′, çhan-de-liēr′
çhev-ȧ-liēr′,
çoṅ-g̣é′ d′é-lïre′ (-zhā′dā-lēr′),
fū-si-leer′, gas-e-liēr′,
gon-dō-liēr′, lēar, leer,
pis-tō-leer′.

m: ȧ-mïr′, çhi-mēre′*, e-meer′,
e-mïr′, meer, mēre, mïr.

n: ȧ-nēar′, a̤uç-tion-eer′,
buç-çȧ-neer′, çan-nŏn-eer′,
çar-ȧ-van-eer′, çär-ȧ-bin-eer′,
çär-bi-neer′, çhif-fō-nïer′,
dom-i-neer′, ē-leç″tion-eer′,
en′g̣i-neer″, fi-neer′*,
gon-fȧ-lŏn-ïer′, In-di-ăn-eer′,
moun″tăin-eer′, muf-fin-eer′,
mū″ti-neer′, nēar, pī″ō-neer′,
sçrù-ti-neer′, sĕr″mŏn-eer′,
soù-ve-nïr′, speck-sion-eer′,
ti-mŏn-eer′, un-nēar′*, ve-neer′.

p: ap-pēar′, çom-peer′,
dis-ap-pēar′, peer, piēr,
rē″ap-pēar′.

r: ar-rēar′, çȧ-reer′, rēar,
up-rēar′.

s: cēre, çuī-răs-siēr′ (kwē-),
en-sēar′*, fin-an-ciēr′,

in-sin-cēre′, ō′vĕr-seer, sēar,
seer, sēre, sin-cēre′.

sh: çash-iēr′, shēar, sheer,
tab-ȧ-sheer′.

sk(sç): skeer.

sm: ȧ-smēar′, bē-smēar′,
smēar.

sn: sneer.

sp: spēar.

st: steer, stēre, tim′bĕr stēre*.

t: a̤us-tēre′, char-i-ŏt-eer′,
cīr-çū-i-teer′, çrō-çhe-teer′,
frŏn-tïer′, gar-ret-eer′,
gaz-et-teer′, mū′le-teer′,
mus-ket-eer′, pam-phlet-eer′,
prī-vȧ-teer′, pṳl-pit-eer′,
rack-et-teer′, son-net-eer′,
tär-get-eer′, tēar, teer, tïer,
Tyr (tēr), vol-un-teer′.

v: bre-viēr′, pĕr-se-vēre′,
rē-vēre′, se-vēre′, veer.

w: wēir.

y: Good′yēar, yēar.

z: grand vi-ziēr′, vi-ziēr′.

ĒRD

Vowel: flap′ēared, lop′ēared,
un-ēared′*.

b: bēard.

f: un-fēared′.

p: un-peered′.

w: wēird.

Plus ēr + d.

Plus beer′d, etc.

ĒRS

b: Biērce.

f: fiērce.

p: piērce, trans-piērce′.

t: tiērce.

ĒRT

p: pēart.

ĒRZ
ES

fāte, fär, fȧst, fᶐll, fīnᵃl, cãre, at; mēte, prᴇy, hᵉr, met; pīne,
marῐne, bῐrd, pin; nōte, mŏve, fᴏr, atŏm, not; mᴏᴏn, book;   **146**

(Choose only one word out of each group)

ĒRZ

j: Al-ġiērṣ'.
sh: shēarṣ, sheerṣ
Plus ēr+s.
Plus year's, etc.

ĒS

b: ō-bēse'.
fl: fleece.
g: geese.
gr: am'bēr-grïs, grēase, grēce,
Greece, vēr'di-grïs.
kr: ᴄrēase, ᴄreese, de-ᴄrēase',
in-ᴄrēase', Lū-ᴄrēce',
pop'ping ᴄrēase.
kw(qu): ēs-quïsse'.
l: ᴄoú-lïsse', Fe-lïce', lēase,
pe-lïsse', pō-lïce', rē-lēase',
vȧ-lïse'.
m: se-mēse'.
n: Bĕr-e-nïce', Bĕr-nïce',
Nïce, nïece.
p: ȧf'tēr-pïēce, ȧ-pïēce',
bat'tle-pïēce, chim'nēy-pïēce,
fow'ling pïēce, frŏn'tis-pïēce,
man'tel-pïēce, mȧs'tēr-pïēce,
pēace, pïēce, pock'et-pïēce.
pr: ᴄȧ-prïce'.
r: ce-rïse', ᴄlȧ-rïce', Mᴀu-rïce',
Reese, The-rïse' (te-rēs').
s: cēase, dē-cēase', prē"dē-cēase'
sūr-cēase'.
tr: ᴄan'tȧ-trïce.

ES

Vowel: aᴄ-qui-esce', S, S.O.S.
b: Bess.
bl: bless, nō-blesse' (-bles'),
un-bless'.
ch: chess.
d: fron-desce',

shep'hērd-ess ('ĕrd-),
stew'ărd-ess.
dr: ad-dress', am-bas'sȧ-dress,
dïv'ing dress, dress,
fᴜll dress, gȧ'lȧ dress,
head'dress (hed'), rē-dress',
un'dēr-dress, un-dress'.
f: ᴄon-fess', fess.
g: fōre-guess', guess.
gr: ag-gress', dī-gress', ē'gress,
in'gress, trans-gress'.
h: Hess.
j: jess, tūr-ġesce'.
kr: aᴄ-ᴄresce', ᴄress, Kress,
mus'tărd ᴄress, wᴀ'tēr=ᴄress.
kw(qu): del-i-quesce'.
l: blem'ish-less, bod'i-less,
bot'tŏm-less, ᴄō-ȧ-lesce',
ᴄŏl'ŏr-less, ᴄŏm'fŏrt-less,
ᴄon'science-less ('shens-),
ᴄon-vȧ-lesce', ᴄul'tūre-less,
ᴄum'bēr-less, din'nēr-less,
ef'fŏrt-less, fan'ci-less,
fä"THēr-less, faTH'ŏm-less,
fā'vŏr-less, fēa'tūre-less,
fet'tēr-less, flā'vŏr-less,
flow'ēr-less, fᴏr'tūne-less,
ġen"ti-lesse'*, här'bŏr-less,
less, lim'it-less, mȧs'tēr-less,
mēan'ing-less,
mea'sūre-less (me'zhᴏᴏr-),
mēr'ci-less, mŏn'ēy-less,
mŏTH'ēr-less, mō'tion-less,
mō'tive-less, shāde'less,
shel'tēr-less, sil'vēr-less,
slum'bēr-less, spir'it-less,
temp-tā'tion-less, un-less',
val'ūe-less, vīr'tūe-less,
weap'ŏn-less (wep'), etc.
m: in-tū-mesce', mess.
n: ab-jeᴄt'ed-ness, ab-jeᴄt'ness,

147

ūse, bu̧ll, brûte, tŭrn, up; crȳ, myth; c̣at, ma̧chine, ace,
church, c̣hord; ġem, aṅger, (Fr.) boṅ, a̧ş; THis, thin; aᴢure **ES**

(Choose only one word out of each group)

ab-strac̣t'ed-ness,
ab-strac̣t'ness, a-bū'sive-ness,
ac̣-ci-den'tăl-ness,
à-dap'tive-ness, ad-dic̣t'ed-ness,
ad-hē'sive-ness,
ad-van-tā'geous-ness,
af-fec̣t'ed-ness, af-frŏn'tive-ness,
āġ'ed-ness, ag-gres'sive-ness,
aġ'ile-ness, à-gree'à-ble-ness,
āir'i-ness, al-i-men'tive-ness,
al-lit'ēr-à-tive-ness,
al-lū'sive-ness,
a̧l-mĭght'i-ness (-mīt'),
à-māz'ed-ness, am-bi'tious-ness,
ā'mi-à-ble'ness, am'i-c̣à-ble-ness,
am'ple-ness,
ān'cient-ness ('shent-),
an-ġel'i-c̣ăl-ness, añ'gri-ness,
à-non'y-mous-ness, an'tic̣-ness,
añ'xious-ness (angk'shus-),
āp'ish-ness, ap-par'ent-ness,
ap-pēa̧ş'à-ble-ness,
ap'pō-ṣite-ness,
ap''prē-hen'sive-ness,
ap-prōach'à-ble-ness,
är'bi-trär''i-ness, är'dent-ness,
är'dū-ous-ness, ār'id-ness,
ärt'fu̧l-ness, är-tic̣'ū-lăte-ness,
är-ti-fi'ciăl-ness, ärt'less-ness,
as-sid'ū-ous-ness,
à-trō'cious-ness, at-ten'tive-ness,
at-trac̣'tive-ness,
a̧us-pi'cious-ness,
av-à-ri'cious-ness, aw'fu̧l-ness,
awk'wărd-ness,
back-hand'ed-ness,
back'wărd-ness, bāle'fu̧l-ness,
bāne'fu̧l-ness,
bāre'head''ed-ness ('hed''),
bar'ŏn-ess, bār'ren-ness,
bash'fu̧l-ness, bēast'li-ness,

beer'i-ness, bē-seech'ing-ness,
bē-sot'ted-ness, bit'tēr-ness,
blāme'less-ness, bless'ed-ness,
bliss'fu̧l-ness,
blīTHe'sŏme-ness,
blōat'ed-ness, block'ish-ness,
blood'guilt-i-ness ('gilt-),
blood'i-ness (blud'),
blood'less-ness,
blood-thĭrst'i-ness,
blo̧om'ing-ness, blo̧om'less-ness,
blunt'ish-ness, bōast'fu̧l-ness,
bois'tēr-ous-ness, bon'ni-ness,
book'ish-ness, bo̧or'ish-ness,
bo̧ot'less-ness, bound'less-ness,
boun'tē-ous-ness, boy'ish-ness,
brack'ish-ness, brass'i-ness,
brawn'i-ness, brā'zen-ness,
breath'less-ness (breth'),
bril'liănt-ness ('lyănt-),
brit'tle-ness, brōk'en-ness,
brŏTH'ēr-li-ness, brush'i-ness,
brút'ish-ness, bulk'i-ness,
bump'tious-ness, bunch'i-ness,
bûrl'i-ness, bu̧sh'i-ness,
bux'ŏm-ness, c̣an'did-ness,
c̣an'ŏn-ess, c̣à-pā'cious-ness,
c̣à-pri'cious-ness, c̣ap'tious-ness,
c̣āre'fu̧l-ness, c̣āre'less-ness,
c̣au'tious-ness, cēase'less-ness,
cha̧lk'i-ness (cha̧k'),
chānge'fu̧l-ness, chār'i-ness,
chärm'ing-ness, chat'ti-ness,
cheer'fu̧l-ness, cheer'i-ness,
cheer'less-ness, chĭld'ish-ness,
chĭld'less-ness, chil'li-ness,
chub'bi-ness, chûrl'ish-ness,
c̣lan-des'tine-ness,
c̣lan'nish-ness,
c̣lean'li-ness (klen'),
c̣lēar'sĭght'ed-ness (-sīt'),

ES

fāte, fär, fȧst, fạll, finăl, cãre, at; mēte, prẹy, hẽr, met; pīne,
marïne, bĭrd, pin; nōte, mŏve, fọr, atŏm, not; mọọn, book;

148

(Choose only one word out of each group)

clev'ẽr-ness,
clïqu'ish-ness (klēk')
clod'dish-ness, cloud'i-ness,
cloud'less-ness, clown'ish-ness,
clum'ṣi-ness, cōld'heärt'ed-ness,
col-lect'ed-ness, col-lū'sive-ness,
cŏme'li-ness, com'mŏn-ness,
com-pōṣ'ed-ness,
com-prē-hen'sive-ness,
com-pul'sive-ness,
con-cēit'ed-ness,
con-clū'sive-ness,
con-dū'cive-ness,
con-fūṣ'ed-ness,
con-junc'tive-ness,
con-sci-en'tious-ness (-shi-),
con'scious-ness,
con-sec'ū-tive-ness,
con-spic'ū-ous-ness,
con-struc'tive-ness,
con-tent'ed-ness,
con-ten'tious-ness,
con-trȧ-dic'tious-ness,
con-trȧ-dic'tō-ri-ness,
con-trā'ri-ness,
con-tū-mā'cious-ness,
cō'pi-ous-ness,
cor'diăl-ness ('dyăl-),
cor-rō'sive-ness, cost'li-ness,
coŭ-rā'ġeous-ness, court'li-ness,
cŏv'ẽrt-ness, cŏv'et-ous-ness,
crab'bed-ness, craft'i-ness,
crag'ged-ness, crag'gi-ness,
crāv'ing-ness, crāz'i-ness,
crēam'i-ness, cred'ū-lous-ness,
crook'ed-ness, crú'el-ness,
crust'i-ness, cum'brous-ness,
cū'ri-ous-ness, cūrl'i-ness,
cus'tŏm-ā'ri-ness, dāin'ti-ness,
damp'ish-ness, där'ing-ness,
daunt'less-ness, dau'phin-ess,

dēa'cŏn-ess, dead'li-ness (ded'),
death'ful-ness (deth'),
death'i-ness, death'less-ness,
dē-bauch'ed-ness,
dē-cēit'ful-ness, dē-cep'tive-ness,
dē-cī'sive-ness,
dec'ō-rȧ-tive-ness,
dē-fec'tive-ness,
dē-fence'less-ness,
dē-fī'ȧnt-ness, def'i-nite-ness,
dē-form'ed-ness,
dē-ġen'ẽr-ăte-ness,
dē-ject'ed-ness, dē-li'cious-ness,
dē-līght'ful-ness (-līt'),
dē-līght'sŏme-ness,
dē-lir'i-ous-ness, dē-lū'sive-ness,
dē-ment'ed-ness, dē'mŏn-ess,
dē-pres'sive-ness, dē-rī'sive-ness,
dē-ṣīr'ous-ness, dē-spīte'ful-ness,
de-struc'tive-ness,
des'ul-tō-ri-ness,
dē-tẽr'sive-ness,
dē-trac'tive-ness, dē-vōt'ed-ness,
dew'i-ness (dū'), dif-fūṣ'ed-ness,
dif-fūṣ'ive-ness, dil-ȧ-tō'ri-ness,
dī-lūt'ed-ness, din'ġi-ness,
dīre'ful-ness, diṣ-as'trous-ness,
dis-con-tent'ed-ness,
dis-cūr'sive-ness,
dis-dāin'ful-ness,
dis-in'tẽr-est-ed-ness,
diṣ'măl-ness, dis-pōṣ'ed-ness,
dis-pū-tā'tious-ness,
dis-tāste'ful-ness,
dis-tinc'tive-ness, diz'zi-ness,
dog'ged-ness, dōle'ful-ness,
doubt'ful-ness (dout'),
dought'i-ness (dout'),
down'i-ness,
dread'ful-ness (dred'),
drēam'i-ness, drēar'i-ness,

(Choose only one word out of each group)

drought'i-ness (drout'),
drows̱'i-ness, druñk'en-ness,
dump'ish-ness, dusk'i-ness,
dust'i-ness, dwạrf'ish-ness,
ēa'g̣ēr-ness, ĕar'li-ness,
ĕar'nest-ness, ĕarth'i-ness,
ĕarth'li-ness,
ĕarth'ly⸗mīnd'ed-ness,
ēaṣe'fṵl-ness, ēaṣ'i-ness,
eer'i-ness, ef-feç'tive-ness,
ef-fi-çā'cious-ness,
ef-fū'sive-ness,
ē-grē'g̣ious-ness ('jus-),
ē-lāt'ed-ness, ē-mō'tive-ness,
emp'ti-ness, en-dēar'ed-ness,
end'less-ness, en-dūr'ing-ness,
en-gāg̣'ing-ness,
ē-nọr'mous-ness,
en-tēr-tāin'ing-ness, ē'quăl-ness,
es-sen'tial-ness, es-träng̣'ed-ness,
ev-à-nesce', ē-vā'sive-ness,
ev″ēr-last'ing-ness,
ex-ạlt'ed-ness, ex-cep'tious-ness,
ex-ces'sive-ness, ex-çlū'sive-ness,
ex-çūr'sive-ness,
ex-pan'sive-ness,
ex-pē-di'tious-ness,
ex-pen'sive-ness, ex-plic'it-ness,
ex-pres'sive-ness,
ex'qui-ṣite-ness, ex-ten'sive-ness,
fà-cē'tious-ness, faç'tious-ness,
fāith'fṵl-ness, fāith'less-ness,
fal-lā'cious-ness,
fạlse'⸗heärt'ed-ness,
fär'sīght-ed-ness ('sīt-),
fas-tid'i-ous-ness, fāte'fṵl-ness,
fä″THer-li-ness, fạult'i-ness,
fạult'less-ness, fā'vŏr-ed-ness,
fēar'fṵl-ness, fēar'less-ness,
fee″ble⸗mīnd'ed-ness,
fee'ble-ness, fẹign'ed-ness (fān'),

fē-rō'cious-ness, fēr'vid-ness,
fick'le-ness, fiç'tious-ness,
fiç-ti'tious-ness, fiēnd'ish-ness,
fī'ēr-i-ness, film'i-ness,
fi-nesse', fish'i-ness,
fit'fṵl-ness, fix'ed-ness,
flab'bi-ness, flaç'cid-ness,
flāk'i-ness, flash'i-ness,
flesh'i-ness, flesh'less-ness,
flesh'li-ness, flex'i-ble-ness,
flīght'i-ness (flīt'-), flim'ṣi-ness,
flip'pănt-ness, flọr'id-ness,
flow'ēr-i-ness, flū'ent-ness,
fog'gi-ness, fọọl'härd-i-ness,
fọọl'ish-ness, fop'pish-ness,
fọrc'ed-ness, fọr'eign-ness ('in-),
for-get'fṵl-nesṣ, fọrm'less-ness,
fọr'wărd-ness, fraç'tious-ness,
frag̣'ile-ness,
frank'⸗heärt″ed-ness,
fran'tiç-ness, frạud'less-ness,
frēak'ish-ness,
freck'led-ness ('l'd-),
free'⸗heärt″ed-ness, fret'fṵl-ness,
friend'less-ness (frend'),
friend'li-ness,
frīght'fṵl-ness (frīt'),
frīg̣'id-ness, frisk'i-ness,
friv'ō-lous-ness, frost'i-ness,
froth'i-ness, frō'wărd-ness,
frōz'en-ness, frù'găl-ness,
frúit'fṵl-ness, frúit'less-ness,
frump'ish-ness, fū-gā'cious-ness,
fṵl'sŏme-ness, fūm'ish-ness,
fun-dà-men'tăl-ness,
fū'ri-ous-ness, fus'si-ness,
fust'i-ness, gad'dish-ness,
gal'lănt-ness, gāme'sŏme-ness,
gar'ish-ness, gar'rù-lous-ness,
gash'li-ness, gast'ness,
gạud'i-ness, g̣en'ēr-ous-ness,

ES

fāte, fär, fàst, fạll, finăl, cãre, at; mēte, prey, hẽr, met; pīne,
marïne, bĩrd, pin; nōte, mŏve, fọr, atŏm, not; mọọn, book;

150

(Choose only one word out of each group)

ġē'ni-ăl-ness, ġen'tle-ness,
ghàst'li-ness (gàst'),
ghōst'li-ness (gōst'),
gid'di-ness, gift'ed-ness,
gĩrl'ish-ness, glad'fụl-ness,
glad'sŏme-ness, glär'i-ness,
glass'i-ness, glọọm'i-ness,
glō'ri-ous-ness, gloss'i-ness,
god'less-ness, god'li-ness,
good'li-ness, gọr'ġeous-ness,
gŏv'ẽrn-ess, grāce'fụl-ness,
grāce'less-ness, grā'cious-ness,
graph'iç-ness, grass'i-ness,
grāte'fụl-ness, grēas'i-ness,
greed'i-ness, green'ish-ness,
griēv'ous-ness, grīm'i-ness,
grit'ti-ness, grog'gi-ness,
ground'less-ness,
guärd'ed-ness (gärd'),
guīde'less-ness (gīd'),
guīle'fụl-ness (gīl'),
guīle'less-ness,
guilt'i-ness (gilt'),
guilt'less-ness, gust'fụl-ness,
hāir'i-ness, hand'i-ness,
hand'sŏme-ness, hap'less-ness,
hap'pi-ness,
härd'=heärt″ed-ness, härd'i-ness,
härm'fụl-ness, härm'less-ness,
här-mō'ni-ous-ness, hāst'i-ness,
hāte'fụl-ness,
hạught'i-ness (hawt'),
hāz'i-ness, head'i-ness (hed'),
health'fụl-ness (helth'),
health'i-ness, health'less-ness,
heärt'ed-ness, heärt'i-ness,
heärt'less-ness, hēa″THen-ness,
heav'en-li-ness (hev'),
heav'en-ly=mīnd'ed-ness,
heav'i-ness (hev'),
heed'fụl-ness, heed'less-ness,

heed'less-ness,
hei'nous-ness (hā'),
hel'lish-ness, help'fụl-ness,
help'less-ness,
het″ẽr-ō-ġē'nē-ous-ness,
hid'den-ness, hid'ē-ous-ness,
hīgh″=mīnd'ed-ness (hī'),
hil'li-ness, hōar'i-ness,
hog'gish-ness, hōl'i-ness,
hol'lōw-ness, hōme'less-ness,
hōme'li-ness, hōpe'fụl-ness,
hōpe'less-ness, hor'rid-ness,
huf'fish-ness, hum'ble-ness,
hū'mid-ness, hū'mŏr-ous-ness,
hũrt'fụl-ness, husk'i-ness,
īc'i-ness, ī'dle-ness,
ig-nō'ble-ness, il-lic'it-ness,
il-lit'ẽr-ăte-ness,
ill=nā'tūred-ness, il-lū'sive-ness,
il-lus'tri-ous-ness,
im-aġ'i-nà-tive-ness,
im'i-tā-tive-ness,
im-maç'ū-lăte-ness (-lit-),
im-pär'tial-ness,
im-pas'sive-ness,
im-pẽr'feçt-ness,
im-pē'ri-ous-ness,
im-pẽr'vi-ous-ness,
im-pet'ū-ous-ness,
im-pī'ous-ness,
im-plic'it-ness,
im-pon'dẽr-ous-ness,
im-pōṣ'ing-ness,
im-pres'sive-ness,
im-pul'sive-ness,
in″at-ten'tive-ness,
in-ạus-pi'cious-ness,
in-cà-pā'cious-ness,
in-cạu'tious-ness,
in-ci-den'tăl-ness,
in-cō-hẽr'ent-ness,

(Choose only one word out of each group)

in-çom-prē-hen′sive-ness,
in-çon-çlū′sive-ness,
in-çon′grù-ous-ness,
in-çon-sis′tent-ness,
in-çon-spiç′ū-ous-ness,
in-debt′ed-ness,
in-dē-cī′sive-ness,
in-de′çō-rous-ness,
in″ef-fi-çā′cious-ness,
in-feç′tious-ness,
in-ġē′ni-ous-ness,
in-ġen′ū-ous-ness,
in-jū′ri-ous-ness, **ink′i-ness,**
in-nox′ious-ness,
in-ob-trú′sive-ness,
in-of-fen′sive-ness,
in-sid′i-ous-ness, in-sip′id-ness,
in-struç′tive-ness,
in-ten′sive-ness, in-trú′sive-ness,
in-ven′tive-ness,
in-vid′i-ous-ness,
in-vin′ci-ble-ness,
in-vol′un-tār-i-ness,
in′wărd-ness, īre′fųl-ness,
īrk′sŏme-ness, jag′ged-ness,
jąunt′i-ness, jeal′ous-ness (jel′),
jet′ti-ness, Jew′ish-ness,
jol′li-ness, jō′vi-ăl-ness,
joy′fųl-ness, joy′less-ness,
joy′ous-ness, jù-di′cious-ness,
jùic′i-ness (jùs′), jump′i-ness,
kīnd′꞊heärt″ed-ness,
kīnd′li-ness, king′li-ness,
knāv′ish-ness (nāv′),
knīght′li-ness (nīt′),
knot′ti-ness (not′),
lañ′guid-ness (′gwid-),
lärġe′꞊heärt″ed-ness,
las-civ′i-ous-ness, law′fųl-ness,
law′less-ness, lāz′i-ness,
lēaf′i-ness, lēaf′less-ness,

lēav′i-ness*, length′i-ness,
lī-cen′tious-ness, līfe′less-ness,
līght′꞊heärt″ed-ness (līt′),
līght′sŏme-ness, līke′à-ble-ness,
līke′li-ness, lim′bĕr-ness,
lim′pid-ness,
liq′uid-ness (lik′wid-),
lis′sŏme-ness, list′less-ness,
lit′ĕr-ăl-ness, li-tiġ′ious-ness,
lit′tle-ness, līve′li-ness,
liv′id-ness, liv′ing-ness,
lōaTH′li-ness, lōaTH′sŏme-ness,
loft′i-ness, lōne′li-ness,
lōne′sŏme-ness, long′sŏme-ness,
lō-quā′cious-ness, lọrd′li-ness,
lout′ish-ness, lŏve꞊in꞊ī′dle-ness,
lŏve′li-ness, lŏv′ing-ness,
lōw′li-ness, loy′ăl-ness,
lū′cid-ness, luck′i-ness,
lū-gù′bri-ous-ness,
lū′mi-nous-ness, lump′ish-ness,
lus′cious-ness (lush′us-),
lust′fųl-ness, lust′i-ness,
māid′en-li-ness, mà-li′cious-ness,
man′fųl-ness, man′li-ness,
man′nĕr-li-ness, man′nish-ness,
man′y꞊sīd′ed-ness (men′),
mär′chion-ess (′shun-),
märsh′i-ness, mas′si-ness*,
mas′sive-ness, match′less-ness,
mawk′ish-ness, māz′i-ness,
mēa′gre-ness (′gĕr-),
mēal′i-ness, mēan′ness,
mēat′i-ness, med′i-tā″tive-ness,
mel′lōw-ness, melt′ing-ness,
mer-ē-tri′cious-ness, mer′ri-ness,
mīght′i-ness (mīt′),
milk′i-ness, mīnd′fųl-ness,
mi-raç′ū-lous-ness, mīr′i-ness,
mĭrth′fųl-ness, mĭrth′less-ness,
mis-cel-lā′nē-ous-ness,

ES
fāte, fär, fȧst, fạll, finăl, căre, ạt; mēte, prey, hẽr, met; pīne,
marïne, bĭrd, pin; nōte, mŏve, fọr, atŏm, nŏt; mọọn, book;
152

(Choose only one word out of each group)

mis′chie-vous-ness (′chi-),
mis-shāpe′en-ness, miss′ish-ness,
mist′i-ness, mod′ērn-ness,
mōd′ish-ness, mō-men′tous-ness,
mŏnk′ish-ness,
mō-not′ō-nous-ness,
mon′strous-ness, mọọd′i-ness,
mōp′ish-ness, mọr′bid-ness,
mor′tăl-ness, mọss′i-ness,
mŏTH′ēr-li-ness, mōuld′i-ness,
mōurn′fụl-ness, mūl′ish-ness,
mul″ti-fā′ri-ous-ness,
mump′ish-ness, mūrk′i-ness,
musk′i-ness, must′i-ness,
mū′ti-nous-ness,
mys-tē′ri-ous-ness,
mys′ti-căl-ness, nāk′ed-ness,
nāme′less-ness,
nar′rōw⹀mīnd′ed-ness,
nar′rōw-ness, nast′i-ness,
na′tion-ăl-ness, nā′tive-ness,
nat′ti-ness, nat′ū-răl-ness,
nạught′i-ness (nạut′),
nēar′⹀sīght″ed-ness (-sīt″),
neb′ū-lous-ness,
nec′es-sā-ri-ness,
nē-ces′si-tous-ness,
nec-tā′ri-ous-ness, need′fụl-ness,
need′i-ness, need′less-ness,
nē-fā′ri-ous-ness,
neg-lect′ed-ness,
neg-lect′fụl-ness,
neigh′bŏr-li-ness (nā′),
nēr′vous-ness, nig′gărd-li-ness,
nim′ble-ness, nō′ble-ness,
noise′less-ness, noiṣ′i-ness,
noi′sŏme-ness, nōt′ȧ-ble-ness,
nōt′ed-ness, nōte′less-ness,
nŏth′ing-ness, nō-tō′ri-ous-ness,
nox′ious-ness, nū′mēr-ous-ness,
nū-tri′tious-ness.

ob-jec′tive-ness,
ob′li-gȧ-tō″ri-ness,
ō-blīg′ing-ness, ob-liv′i-ous-ness,
ob-sē′qui-ous-ness,
ob-ṣērv′ȧ-ble-ness,
ob-strep′ēr-ous-ness,
ob-trú′sive-ness, ob′vi-ous-ness,
ō′di-ous-ness,
ō″dŏr-if′ēr-ous-ness,
ō′dŏr-ous-ness, of-fen′sive-ness,
of-fi′cious-ness, oil′i-ness,
ō″lē-aġ′i-nous-ness,
ō″pen⹀hand′ed-ness,
ō″pen-heärt′ed-ness, ō′pen-ness,
op-pres′sive-ness,
op-prō′bri-ous-ness,
ọr′dēr-li-ness,
os″ten-tā′tious-ness,
out-land′ish-ness,
out-rā′ġeous-ness,
out′wărd-ness, pāin′fụl-ness,
pāin′less-ness, pal′lid-ness,
pạl′tri-ness, pär′lous-ness,
pär-si-mō′ni-ous-ness,
pas′sive-ness, pawk′i-ness,
pēace′ȧ-ble-ness, pēace′fụl-ness,
pēarl′i-ness, peer′less-ness,
peev′ish-ness, pel-lū′cid-ness,
pen-ē-trā′tive-ness,
pen′ni-less-ness, pen′sile-ness,
pen′sive-ness, pē-nū′ri-ous-ness,
pēr-emp′tō-ri-ness, pēr′fect-ness,
pēr-fid′i-ous-ness,
pēr-func′tō-ri-ness,
per′il-ous-ness, pēr-ni′cious-ness,
pēr-plex′ed-ness,
pēr-plex′ive-ness,
pēr-spi-cā′cious-ness,
pēr-spic′ū-ous-ness,
pēr-suā′sive-ness,
pēr-ti-nā′cious-ness,

(Choose only one word out of each group)

pĕr-vĕrse′ness,
pĕr-vi-çā′cious-ness,
pĕr′vi-ous-ness,
pes-ti-len′tiăl-ness,
pet′ti-ness, pet′tish-ness,
piērc′ing-ness,
pig′=head″ed-ness (-hed″),
pitch′i-ness, pit′ē-ous-ness,
pith′i-ness, pit′i-à-ble-ness,
pit′i-fu̯l-ness, pit′i-less-ness,
plā′çà-ble-ness, plac′id-ness,
plāin′tive-ness, plāy′fu̯l-ness,
plāy′sŏme-ness,
pleaṣ′ănt-ness (plez′),
plēaṣ′ing-ness, plen′tē-ous-ness,
plī′ănt-ness, pōach′i-ness,
point′ed-ness, pom′pous-ness,
pon′dĕr-ous-ness, po̯o̯r′li-ness,
pō′rous-ness, po̯rt′li-ness,
poṣ′i-tive-ness, pow′ĕr-fu̯l-ness,
pow′ĕr-less-ness,
praç′ti-căl-ness,
prāiṣe′wŏr″THi-ness,
prāyer′fu̯l-ness (prăr′),
prāyer′less-ness,
prē-çăr′i-ous-ness,
pre′cious-ness,
prē-cip′i-tous-ness,
prē-çō′cious-ness,
prej-ū-di′cial-ness,
prē-pos′tĕr-ous-ness,
prē-şump′tū-ous-ness,
prē-ten′tious-ness,
pret′ti-ness (prit′),
prē′vi-ous-ness, prick′li-ness,
prīde′fu̯l-ness, priēst′li-ness,
prig′gish-ness, prim′i-tive-ness,
prince′li-ness, prō-diġ′ious-ness,
prō-duç′tive-ness,
prō-gres′sive-ness, prop′ĕr-ness,
prō-pi′tious-ness, prōṣ′i-ness,

pros-peç′tive-ness,
prō-teç′tive-ness, prúd′ish-ness,
pub′liç=mīnd′ed-ness,
puf′fi-ness, pug-nā′cious-ness,
pulp′i-ness, pulp′ous-ness,
pulse′less-ness,
punç-til′i-ous-ness, pū′ni-ness,
pūrs′i-ness,
pū-sil-lan′i-mous-ness,
pū′trid-ness, quāk′i-ness,
quälm′ish-ness (kwäm′),
quēa′ṣi-ness,
queen′li-ness, quench′less-ness,
quer′ū-lous′ness,
quick′=sīght″ed-ness (-sīt″),
quick′=wit″ted-ness, quī′et-ness,
rab′id-ness, rāc′i-ness,
rag′ged-ness, rāin′i-ness,
rāk′ish-ness, ran′cid-ness,
rà-pā′cious-ness, rap′id-ness,
rav′en-ous-ness,
read′i-ness (red′),
rē-bel′lious-ness, rē′cent-ness,
rē-cep′tive-ness, reck′less-ness,
red′dish-ness, rē-fleç′tive-ness,
rē-fraç′tive-ness,
rē-fraç′tō-ri-ness,
rē-gärd′less-ness, rel′à-tive-ness,
rē-lent′less-ness,
rē-mo̯rse′fu̯l-ness,
rē-mo̯rse′less-ness,
rē-prōach′fu̯l-ness,
rē-pul′sive-ness,
rē-ṣist′less-ness, reṣ′ō-lūte-ness,
rē-speç′tfu̯l-ness,
rē-spon′sive-ness, rest′fu̯l-ness,
res′tive-ness, rest′less-ness,
rē-striç′tive-ness,
rē-ten′tive-ness,
rē-venġe′fu̯l-ness,
rīght′fu̯l-ness (rīt′),

(Choose only one word out of each group)

rīght′=hand″ed-ness,
rīght′=mind″ed-ness, rig′id-ness,
rig′ŏr-ous-ness, rī′ŏt-ous-ness,
rō-bus′tious-ness, rock′i-ness,
rōgu′ish-ness (rōg′),
romp′ish-ness, rọọm′i-ness,
rōp′i-ness, rōṣ′i-ness,
rot′ten-ness, rud′di-ness,
rùe′fụl-ness, rug′ged-ness,
rùth′less-ness, sā′c̣red-ness,
sac̣-ri-lē′ġious-ness (′jus-),
sȧ-gā′cious-ness, sāint′li-ness,
sȧ-lā′cious-ness, sal′lōw-ness,
sal′ū-tãr″i-ness,
sanc̣″ti-mō′ni-ous-ness,
sand′i-ness,
sañ′guine-ness (′gwin-),
sap′pi-ness, sat-is-fac̣′tō-ri-ness,
sauc̣′i-ness, sav′ăġe-ness,
sāv′ing-ness, sā-vŏr′i-ness,
sc̣al′i-ness, sc̣ọrch′ing-ness,
sc̣ọrn′fụl-ness, sc̣rag′gi-ness,
sc̣ûr′vi-ness, sēa′wŏr″THi-ness,
sec̣′ŏn-dā-ri-ness,
sē′c̣re-tive-ness, sē′c̣ret-ness,
sed′en-tā″ri-ness,
se-di′tious-ness, seed′i-ness,
seem′ing-ness, seem′li-ness,
sel′dŏm-ness,
self′=c̣on-cēit′ed-ness,
self′=c̣on′scious-ness,
self′ish-ness,
self′=rīght′eous-ness (-rīt′chus-),
sense′less-ness, sen′si-tive-ness,
sen′sū-ous-ness (′shọọ-),
sen-ten′tious-ness,
sē′ri-ous-ness, shab′bi-ness,
shād′i-ness, shad′ow-i-ness,
shag′gi-ness, shāk′i-ness,
shal′lōw-ness, shāme′fụl-ness,
shāme′less-ness, shāpe′less-ness,

shāpe′li-ness, sheep′ish-ness,
shīēld′less-ness, shift′i-ness,
shift′less-ness, shīn′ing-ness,
shōal′li-ness,
shọrt′=sīght″ed-ness (-sĭt″),
show′ẽr-i-ness, shōw′i-ness,
shrew′ish-ness, shrub′bi-ness,
sick′li-ness, sīght′less-ness (sĭt′),
sī′lent-ness, sulk′i-ness,
sil′li-ness, sim′ple=mīnd′ed-ness,
sim′ple-ness,
sī″mul-tā′nē-ous-ness,
sin′fụl-ness, siñ′gle-ness,
sin′less-ness, sketch′i-ness,
skil′fụl-ness, skit′tish-ness,
slab′bi-ness, slāt′i-ness,
slāv′ish-ness, slēa′zi-ness,
sleep′i-ness, sleep′less-ness,
sleet′i-ness, slen′dẽr-ness,
slīm′i-ness, slip′pẽr-i-ness,
slōth′fụl-ness, slug′gish-ness,
smīl′ing-ness, smōk′i-ness,
snap′pish-ness, snēak′i-ness,
snob′bish-ness,
sō″bẽr=mīnd′ed-ness,
sō′bẽr-ness,
sō′ciȧ-ble-ness (′shȧ-),
sọft′=heärt″ed-ness, sol′id-ness,
sol′i-tãr-i-ness, sol′ū-ble-ness,
som′bẽr-ness, som′brous-ness,
sō-nō′rous-ness, sọr′did-ness,
sor′ri-ness, sor′rōw-fụl-ness,
sot′tish-ness, spā′cious-ness,
spärk′ling-ness, spē′cious-ness,
speck′led-ness (′l′d-),
spec̣′ū-lā-tive-ness,
speech′less-ness, speed′i-ness,
spīc̣′i-ness, spīte′fụl-ness,
splen′did-ness, spŏnġ′i-ness,
spon-tā′nē-ous-ness,
spọr′tive-ness, spot′less-ness,

(Choose only one word out of each group)

spot'ted-ness, spot'ti-ness,
spring'i-ness, sprīte'li-ness,
spūm'i-ness, spū'ri-ous-ness,
squēam'ish-ness, stärch'i-ness,
stär'ri-ness, stāte'li-ness,
stead'fàst-ness (sted'),
stead'i-ness,
stealth'fụl-ness (stelth'),
stealth'i-ness, steel'i-ness,
steep'i-ness*, stick'i-ness,
sting'i-ness, stint'ed-ness,
stol'id-ness, stōn'i-ness,
storm'i-ness,
strāight'₌for'wǎrd-ness (strāt'),
stren'ū-ous-ness, strin'ġent-ness,
string'i-ness, stub'bi-ness,
stub'bǒrn-ness, stū'di-ous-ness,
stuf'fi-ness, stunt'ed-ness,
stū-pen'dous-ness, stū'pid-ness,
stūrd'i-ness, stȳl'ish-ness,
sub-jeç'tive-ness,
sub-mis'sive-ness,
sub-or'di-nāte-ness,
sub-stan'tiǎl-ness,
sub'tle-ness (sut'l-),
suç-cess'fụl-ness, sud'den-ness,
sụġ'ǎr-i-ness (shoog'),
sug-ġes'tive-ness,
sùit'à-ble-ness, sulk'i-ness,
sul'len-ness, sul'tri-ness,
sump'tū-ous-ness, sun'ni-ness,
sū-pēr-cil'i-ous-ness,
sū-pēr-sti'tious-ness,
sup'ple-ness, sup'pli-ǎnt-ness,
sūr'li-ness, sūr-priṣ'ing-ness,
sus-cep'tive-ness,
sus-peçt'ed-ness,
sus-pi'cious-ness,
swạr'THi-ness,
sweat'i-ness (swet'),
sweet'ish-ness.

tạlk'à-tive-ness (tạk'),
tāme'less-ness, tär'di-ness,
tāste'fụl-ness, tāst'i-ness,
taw'dri-ness, taw'ni-ness,
tē'di-ous-ness,
tem-pes'tū-ous-ness,
tem'pō-rā"ri-ness,
tempt'ing-ness, tē-nā'cious-ness,
ten"dĕr₌heärt'ed-ness,
tep'id-ness, tes'ti-ness,
thañk'fụl-ness, thiēv'ish-ness,
thïrst'i-ness,
thǒr'ōugh-ness ('ō-),
thọught'fụl-ness (thọt'),
thọught'less-ness,
thread'i-ness (thred'),
thrift'i-ness, thrift'less-ness,
thrīv'ing-ness, tick'lish-ness
tī'di-ness, tīme'less-ness,
tīme'li-ness, tim'id-ness,
tim'ǒr-ous-ness, tip'si-ness,
tīre'sǒme-ness, toil'sǒme-ness,
tooth'sǒme-ness, tor'pid-ness,
tor'rid-ness, tor'tū-ous-ness,
tō'tǎl-ness, touch'i-ness (tuch'),
toy'ish-ness, track'less-ness,
trāi'tǒr-ous-ness, tran'quil-ness,
tran-scen-den'tǎl-ness,
tran'sient-ness ('shent-),
tran'si-tive-ness,
tran'si-tō"ri-ness,
trans-pär'ent-ness, trash'i-ness.
treach'ēr-ous-ness (trech'),
trē-men'dous-ness,
trem'ū-lous-ness,
trib'ū-tā"ri-ness, trick'i-ness,
trick'ish-ness, trick'si-ness,
trùe"heärt'ed-ness,
trust'fụl-ness, trust'i-ness,
trust'less-ness,
trust'wǒr-THi-ness,

ES

fāte, fär, fást, fạll, finăl, cãre, at; mēte, prey, hẽr, met; pīne,
marĭne, bĭrd, pin; nōte, mŏve, fọr, atŏm, not; mọọn, book;

156

(Choose only one word out of each group)

trúth'fụl-ness, trúth'less-ness,
tūne'fụl-ness, tūne'less-ness,
tũrf'i-ness, tũr'ġid-ness,
ug'li-ness, um-brā'ġeous-ness,
ū-nan'i-mous-ness,
un-bend'ing-ness,
un-bless'ed-ness,
un-bound'ed-ness,
un-çlean'li-ness (-klen'),
un-çloud'ed-ness,
un-çõurt'li-ness,
un-dạunt'ed-ness, un-ēas'i-ness,
un-ex-peçt'ed-ness,
un-fẹign'ed-ness (-fān'),
un-friend'li-ness (-frend'),
un-gāin'li-ness, un-ġen'tle-ness,
un-god'li-ness,
un-ground'ed-ness,
un-hō'li-ness, ū-ni-vẽr'săl-ness,
un-kĭnd'li-ness, un-līke'li-ness,
un-lŏve'li-ness, un-man'li-ness,
un-prē-pãr'ed-ness,
un-quī'et-ness,
un-read'i-ness (-red'),
un-rīght'eous-ness (-rīt'chus-),
un-rù'li-ness,
un-sēa'wŏr'''THi-ness,
un-seem'li-ness, .
un-sīght'li-ness (-sīt'),
un-stā'ble-ness,
un-tō'wård-ness,
un-trust'i-ness, un-wiēld'i-ness,
un-wil'ling-ness,
un-wŏnt'ed-ness,
un-wŏrld'li-ness,
un-wŏr''THi-ness, up'pish-ness,
ūse'fụl-ness, ūse'less-ness,
ux-ō'ri-ous-ness, vaç'ū-ous-ness,
vā'grănt-ness,
val-ē-tū''di-nā'ri-ness,
val'iănt-ness, val'id-ness,

vap'id-ness, vex-ā'tious-ness,
vi'cious-ness, viç-tō'ri-ous-ness,
vig'ŏr-ous-ness,
vin-diç'tive-ness, vir'id-ness,
vir'ile-ness, vĩr'tū-ous-ness,
vis'çous-ness, vi'şion-ā-ri-ness,
vit'rē-ous-ness, vi-vā'cious-ness,
viv'id-ness, vō-cif'ẽr-ous-ness,
vō-lū'mi-nous-ness,
vol'un-tā''ri-ness,
vō-lup'tū-ous-ness,
vō-rā'cious-ness, vul'găr-ness,
wag'gish-ness, wāke'fụl-ness,
wän'tŏn-ness, wãre'fụl-ness*,
wãr'i-ness, wạrm''heärt'ed-ness,
wäsh'i-ness, wäsp'ish-ness,
wāste'fụl-ness, wätch'fụl-ness,
wā'vẽr-ing-ness, wāv'i-ness,
wax'i-ness, wāy'wård-ness,
wealth'i-ness (welth'),
wēa'ri-ness, wēa'ri-sŏme-ness,
weight'i-ness (wāt'),
wel'çõme-ness,
whim'şi-çăl-ness (hwim'),
whīt'ish-ness,
whōle'sŏme-ness (hōl'),
wick'ed-ness, wil'dẽr-ness,
wil'fụl-ness, wī'li-ness,
wil'ling-ness, win'sŏme-ness,
wĩr'i-ness, wish'fụl-ness,
wist'fụl-ness, wiTH'ẽr-ed-ness,
wit'less-ness, wit'ti-ness,
wōe'fụl-ness,
wo'măn-li-ness (woo'),
wŏn'drous-ness, wŏnt'ed-ness,
wood'i-ness, wool'li-ness,
wŏrd'i-ness, wŏrd'ish-ness,
wŏrld'li-ness,
wŏrld''ly-mīnd'ed-ness,
wŏr'ship-fụl-ness,
wŏr''THi-ness, wŏrth'less-ness,

(Choose only one word out of each group)

wrath'fu̱l-ness (rath'),
wretch'ed-ness (rech'),
wretch'less-ness,
wro̱ng'fu̱l-ness (ro̱ng'),
wro̱ng″⸗head'ed-ness (ro̱ng″hed'),
yēast'i-ness, yel'lōw-ish-ness,
yel'lōw-ness, yiēld'ing-ness,
yoūth'fu̱l-ness,
zeal'ous-ness (zel'), etc.

pr: co̱m-press', dē-press',
ex-press', im-press', sup-press'.

r: ärch'ēr-ess, ça̱-ress',
co̱ñ'quĕr-ess ('kēr-), dū-ress',
ef″flō-resce', mȧy'ŏr-ess,
so̱r'cĕr-ess, tāi'lŏr-ess,
vō'tȧ-ress.

s: as-sess', cess, ex-cess',
su̱c-cess'.

str: stress.

t: ġī'ăn-tess, Tess.

tr: an'ces-tress, co̱m'fŏrt-ress,
dis-tress', ed'i-tress,
ex-eç'ū-tress, ī-dol'ȧ-tress,
in-her'i-tress, min'is-tress,
mon'i-tress, vō'tress, tress.

v: ef-fĕr-vesce' (-ves').

y: yes.

z: dis″pōş-şess', pōş-şess',
rē″pōş-şess'.

ÊSH

f: af-fĭçhe' (-fēsh').

l: lēash, Mc̠Lēish (-lēsh'),
un-lēash'.

n: Mc̠Nēish (-nēsh').

t: sc̠hot-tĭsche' (shot-ēsh').

ESH

b: tête'⸗bêçhe' (tet'besh').

fl: flesh.

fr: ȧ-fresh', fresh, rē-fresh'.

kr: c̠rêçhe.

m: en-mesh', mesh.

n: nesh.

s: sē-ceçh'.

t: Baȳ'öu Têçhe (bī'o̱o̱ tesh).

thr: thresh.

ESK

Vowel: stat″ū-esque˙.

b: ar″à-besque'.

d: desk, rēad'ing desk.

l: būr-lesque', nat″ū-răl-esque'.

n: gär″den-esque',
Rō″măn-esque'.

r: bär″bä-resque',
c̠hiv″ăl-resque', Mō-resque',
pic̠″à-resque', pic̠″tūr-esque',
plat″ēr-esque', sc̠ulp″tūr-esque'.

t: Dȧn-tesque', ġī″gan-tesque',
grō-tesque', sol″dȧ-tesque'.

ĒST

Vowel: ēast, no̱rth-ēast',
south-ēast'.

b: bēast, här'te-beest,
wĭl'de-beest.

d: mō-dĭste'.

f: fēast, här'vest fēast,
wed'ding fēast.

fl: fleeced.

kw(qu): queest.

l: lēast, pō-lĭced',
un″dĕr-pō-lĭced'.

pr: ärch'prĭēst″, prĭēst,
un-prĭēst'.

t: är-tĭste', ba-tĭste'.

tr: trĭste.

y: yēast.

Plus ēs + d.

EST

fāte, fär, fȧst, fạll, finăl, cãre, at; mēte, prey, hẽr, met; pīne,
marïne, bĩrd, pin; nōte, mȯve, fọr, atŏm, not; mọọn, book; **158**

(Choose only one word out of each group)

EST

Vowel: bēam'i-est,
bē-guīl'ing-est (-gīl'),
blēar'i-est, breez'i-est,
brīn'i-est, būr'li-est, cheer'i-est,
cheer'li-est, chil'li-est,
chōk'i-est, clean'li-est (klen'),
cō'zi-est, cost'li-est,
cōurt'li-est, crēam'i-est,
creep'i-est,
crust'i-est, cūrl'i-est,
dāin'ti-est, din'ġi-est,
diz'zi-est, dough'ti-est (dou'),
dow'di-est, drēam'i-est,
drēar'i-est, drow'si-est,
dust'i-est, ēar'li-est, ēas'i-est,
ee'ri-est, emp'ti-est, en'vi-est*,
ēv'en-est, film'i-est, filth'i-est,
fleec'i-est, flīght'i-est (flīt'),
flim'si-est, flint'i-est, fōam'i-est,
friend'li-est (frend'), fun'ni-est,
fus'si-est, gid'di-est, glōom'i-est,
glos'si-est, gout'i-est, grīm'i-est,
guilt'i-est (gilt'), gust'i-est,
hap'pi-est, haugh'ti-est (hau'),
health'i-est (helth'), heärt'i-est,
heav'i-est, hō'li-est, hōme'li-est,
huf'fi-est, huñ'gri-est,
husk'i-est, īc'i-est, ink'i-est,
in'li-est, jol'li-est, jùic'i-est,
kīnd'li-est, king'li-est,
knīght'li-nest (nīt'), līke'li-est,
līve'li-est, loft'i-est, lōne'li-est,
lŏve'li-est, lōw'li-est, mer'ri-est,
mīght'i-est (mīt'), moist'i-est,
mos'si-est, mōuld'i-est
musk'i-est, must'i-est,
nois'i-est, pēarl'i-est, pōrt'li-est,
prince'li-est, prōs'i-est,
read'i-est (red'), res'cū-est*,

rōs'i-est, row'di-est, rust'i-est,
sedġ'i-est, seem'li-est,
shīn'i-est, shod'di-est,
shōw'i-est, sīght'li-est (sīt'),
sil'li-est, sketch'i-est,
skin'ni-est, sleep'i-est,
slīm'i-est, smōk'i-est, snuf'fi-est,
sōap'i-est, spīc'i-est, spīk'i-est,
spŏnġ'i-est, spọọn'i-est,
spring'i-est, sprīte'li-est,
stead'i-est (sted'),
stealth'i-est (stelth'),
stil'li-est, stin'ġi-est, stọrm'i-est,
stuf'fi-est, stūr'di-est, sun'ni-est,
sūr'li-est, thĩrst'i-est,
thrift'i-est, Trï-este', trust'i-est,
ug'li-est, un-hō'li-est,
un-read'i-est (-red'), ver'i-est,
wealth'i-est (welth'), wēa'ri-est.
wheez'i-est (hwēz'), wind'i-est,
win'tri-est, wŏr'ri-est*,
yēast'i-est, etc.

b: best, sec'ŏnd best.

bl: blest, un-blest'.

br: a-breast', breast, Brest,
un-breast'.

ch: chest.

d: af-fect'ed-est, ef-fect'ed-est,
hor'rid-est, mor'bid-est,
rug'ged-est, sā'cred-est,
sol'id-est, splen'did-est,
stū'pid-est, tim'id-est.

dr: dressed, ō''vẽr-dressed',
rē-dressed', un''dẽr-dressed',
un-dressed', un''rē-dressed'.

f: in-fest', man'i-fest.

g: Gest, guest (gest),
un-guessed'.

h: al'kȧ-hest, bē-hest', hest.

j: con-ġest', di-ġest', ġest.

159
ūse, bṳll, brûte, tûrn, up; crȳ, myth; çat, maçhine, ace.
church, çhord; ġem, aṅger, (Fr.) boṅ, aṣ; THis, thin; aᴣure **EST**

(Choose only one word out of each group)

ġeste, in-ġest′, jessed, jest,
prē″di-ġest′, sug-ġest′.
kr: çrest, in-çrest′.
un′dẽr-çrest″.
kw(qu): aç-quest′*, bē-quest′,
quest, rē-quest′.
l: blest′fṳl-est, bliss′fṳl-est,
blīTHe′fṳl-est, cheer′fṳl-est,
crṳ′el-lest, fōrce′fṳl-est,
ġē′ni-ăl-est, guīle′fṳl-est (gīl′),
hōpe′fṳl-est, lī′bel-est*,
loy′ăl-est, mär′vel-est*,
mōurn′fṳl-est, quar′rel-est*,
rest′fṳl-est, rīght′fṳl-est (rīt′),
rī′văl-est*, roy′ăl-est,
skil′fṳl-est, tēar′fṳl-est,
wil′fṳl-est.
m: blīTHe′sŏm-est,
lis′sŏm-est, līTHe′sŏm-est,
win′sŏm-est.
n: dē-tẽr′min-est*,
em-blā′zŏn-est*, fresh′en-est*,
fṳ′nest, glis′ten-est (″n-)*,
heärk′en-est*, lis′ten-est (″n-)*,
līv′en-est*, nest, pär′dŏn-est*,
prē-des′tin-est*,
ques′tiŏn-est (′chun-)*.
p: an′à-pest, Bṳ′dà-pest, pest.
pr: dē-pressed′, härd″ₔpressed′,
im-prest′, pressed,
un″ex-pressed, un-pressed′
r: an′swẽr-est* (′sẽr-), ar-rest′,
blis′tẽr-est*, blun′dẽr-est*,
Bṳ′chà-rest, çlus′tẽr-est*,
coñ′quẽr-est* (′kẽr-), çŏv′ẽr-est*,
dow′ẽr-est*, Ev′ẽr-est,
flow′ẽr-est*, gaTH′ẽr-est*,
glim′mẽr-est*, glow′ẽr-est*,
huñ′gẽr-est*, in-çum′bẽr-est*,
in′tẽr-est, lā′bŏr-est*,

liñ′gẽr-est*, low′ẽr-est*,
mṳr′mur-est*, of′fẽr-est*,
plea′ṣūr-est* (′zhǫǫr-),
rē-çŏv′ẽr-est*, rē-mem′bẽr-est*,
rest, sev′ẽr-est*, se-vẽr′est,
shim′mẽr-est*, shud′dẽr-est*,
slum′bẽr-est*, suf′fẽr-est*,
sun′dẽr-est*, tem′pẽr-est*,
thun′dẽr-est*, un-rest′,
vul′găr-est (′gẽr-),
wän′dẽr-est*, wŏn′dẽr-est*,
wrest (rest).
s: cest, ob-sessed′, pal′imp-sest,
pre′cious-est, rē-cessed′,
wit′nes-sest*.
sh: à-ston′ish-est*, ban′ish-est*,
lañ′guish-est* (′gwish-),
noūr′ish-est*, pun′ish-est*,
rē-liñ′quish-est*.
str: stressed, un-stressed′.
t: at-test′, at-trib′ūt-est*,
bril′liănt-est (′lyănt-),
çon-test′, dē-test′,
ex-hib′it-est*, fŏr′feit-est* (′fit-),
in-her′it-est*, in-spir′it-est*,
mer′it-est*, ob-test′, pat′ent-est,
pleaṣ′ănt-est (plez′), prō-test′,
quī′et-est, sī′lent-est,
spir′it-est*, test.
tr: dis-tressed′, gōl′den=tressed,
tressed, un-tressed′.
v: at-ten′tiv-est, dē-cī′siv-est,
dē-rī′siv-est, dē-vest′, di-vest′,
in-vest′, pen′siv-est, vest,
vin-diç′tiv-est.
w: Kēy West, mel′lōw-est,
nar′rōw-est, nŏrth-west′,
sŏr′rōw-est*, west,
win′nōw-est*.
y: yessed (yest).

(Choose only one word out of each group)

z: self′=pōṣ-ṣessed′,
un-prē″pōṣ-ṣessed′, zest.
Plus es+d.

ĒT

Vowel: ēat (ēt), ō″vẽr-ēat′.
b: bēat, beet, dead-beat′ (ded-),
sēa bēat, sụ′găr beet (shoo′).
bl: blēat.
ch: chēat, cheet, es-chēat′.
f: dē-fēat′, ef-fēte′, fēat, feet,
Lä-fĭtte′.
fl: fleet.
fr: ȧ-freet′.
g: gēat.
gl: gleet.
gr: greet.
h: dead hēat (ded), hēat,
ō-vẽr-heat′.
hw: whēat.
j: veġ-ēte′.
k(c̣): lọr′i-keet, par′rȧ-keet.
kl: c̣lēat, c̣leet.
kr: ac̣-c̣rēte′, c̣on-c̣rēte′,
C̣rēte, dis-c̣reet′, in″dis-c̣reet′,
sē-c̣rēte′.
l: ath′lēte, dē-lēte′, é-lĭte′ (e-lēt′),
lēat, leet, ob″sō-lēte′.
m: dead mēat (ded), help′meet,
mēat, meet, mēte, un-meet′.
n: nēat.
p: c̣om-pēte′, pēat, Pēte,
rē-pēat′.
pl: c̣om-plēte′, dē-plēte′,
in″c̣om-plēte′, plēat, rē-plēte′.
r: mär-guē-rīte′ (-gē-), te-rēte′.
s: c̣on-cēit′, c̣ǒun′try sēat (kun′),
c̣ǒun′ty sēat, dē-cēit′, fȧ-cēte′*,
judġe′ment sēat (juj′),
mẽr′cy seat, prē″c̣on-ceit′*,

rē-cēipt′, sēat, self′=c̣on′cēit′,
self′=dē-cēit′, un-sēat′.
sh: bal′ănce sheet, sheet,
wĭnd′ing sheet.
sk(sc̣): skeet.
sl: sleet.
str: street.
sw: bit′tẽr-sweet, hǒ′nēy=sweet,
mead′ōw-sweet (med′),
suïte (swēt), sun′ny-sweet,
sweet, un-sweet′.
t: tēat.
tr: Dutch trēat (duch),
en-trēat′, es-trēat′, ill″=trēat′,
mal-trēat′, rē-trēat′, trēat.
tw: tweet tweet.
w: weet.
z: c̣ärte dē viṣ-ïte′.

ET

Vowel: dū-et′, Har′ri-et,
his-tō′ri-ette, Jō′li-et, Jù′li-et,
Jù″li-ette′, min-ū-et′,
öu-bli-ette′, pir-öu-ette′,
sẽr-vi-ette′, sil-höu-ette′ (-ọọ-),
stat-ū-ette′.
b: ȧ-bet′, al′phȧ-bet′, bär-bette′,
bet, Thi-bet′ (ti-), Tĭ·bet′.
bl: blet.
br: Brett, söu-brette′.
ch: Chet.
d: c̣ȧ-det′, debt (det),
judġ′ment debt (juj′),
vē-dette′.
f: es-tȧ-fet′, es-tȧ-fette′.
fl: flet.
fr: fret, frett, un-fret′*.
g: ba-guette′ (-get′), bē-get′,
fọr-get′, get, mis″bē-get′,
un-get′.

(Choose only one word out of each group)

gr: āi-grette′, rē-gret′,
vin″āi-grette′.
h: het.
hw: whet.
j: jet, suf-frȧ-ġette′.
k(c̣): bañ-quette′, blan-quette′,
c̣ō-quette′, c̣rō-quette′;
et′i-quette, par″rō-ket′,
pär-quet′, pi-quet′, pi-quette′;
toūr′ni-quet.
l: āi-lette′, ā-lette′, am′ū-let,
ān′jel-et, c̣as-sō-lette′,
c̣ŏv′ēr-let, ep″ạu-let′, eȳe′let,
flaġe-ō-let′, Ġil-lette′,
glob′ū-let, lan′dau-let (′dō-),
let, Lett, märt′let, med′ăl-et,
nov″el-ette′, om′e-let, riv′ū-let,
röu-lette′, toi-lette′, vī′ō-let,
zon′ū-let.
m: al-lū-mette′, C̣al-ū-met′,
fū-mette′, met, well′=met′.
n: An-nette′,
An-toi-nette′ (-twȧ-), Bär-nett′,
bar-ŏn-et′, bas-si-net′,
bāy-ō-net′, be′net, bob′i-net,
brü-nette′, Bŭr-nett′, c̣ab′i-net,
c̣an′zō-net, c̣är′cȧ-net,
c̣ast′ȧ-net, c̣ast′net,
c̣han-sōṅ-ette′, c̣lar-i-net′,
c̣or-ō-net′, fal-c̣ŏn-et′, ġe′net,
Jean-nette′ (jen-),
lor-gnette′ (-nyet′),
lunch-eŏn-ette′, lū-nette′,
mar″i-ō-nette′, mär-ti-net′,
mï-gnoṅ-ette′ (mē-nyoṅ-),
min-iŏn-ette′ (-yun-)*,
Nȧ-nette′, net, pi-ȧ-nette′,
sär′ce-net, tab′i-net, töur-nette′,
vi-gnette′ (-nyet′), vil-lȧ-nette′,
wag′ŏn-ette.
p: pȧr′ȧ-pet, pet, pī-pette′.

r: am-öu-rette, añ-c̣hō-ret′,
ban″nēr-et′, cel-lăr-et′,
cig-ȧ-rette′, fär″mēr-ette′,
flow′ēr-et, fọrm′ēr-et,
kead-ēr-ette′ (ked-), lev′ēr-et,
Mär′gȧ-ret, min′ȧ-ret,
pil′lăr-et, ret, Rhett, tab′ȧ-ret,
tab-ō-ret′.
s: an-i-sette′, back′set, bē-set′,
c̣hem-i-sette′, c̣ros-sette′,
c̣rys′tăl set, danc-ette′,
dead′=set′ (ded′), fa-cette′,
fos-sette′, ill′=set′, in′set,
in-tēr-set′, Lū-cette′,
mär′mō-set, mū-set′, ọff-set′,
ō-vēr-set′, pöus-sette, set, sett,
shärp′=set′, smärt set,
sŏm′ēr-set, sun′set, thick′=set′,
un-dēr-set′, up-set′.
sh: brō-c̣hette′, föur-c̣hette′,
plaṅ-c̣hette′, ri-c̣ō-c̣het′.
st: stet.
sw: sweat.
t: mō-tet′, oc̣-tet′, quạr-tet′,
quin-tet′, sep-tet′, ses-tet′,
sex-tet′.
th: ep′i-teth.
thr: threat.
tr: tret.
v: bre-vet′, c̣or-vette′, c̣ūr-vet′,
Ol-i-vet′, rē-vet′, vet.
w: ạll wet, bē-wet′, wet.
y: yet.
z: an-i-ṣette′, c̣hem-i-ṣette′,
gȧ-zette′, gri-ṣette′,
mär-mō-ṣet′, mū-ṣet′, rō-ṣette′.

ĒTH

br: brēaTHe, in′brēaTHe,
up-brēaTHe′.
kw(qu): bē-quēaTH′.

ĒTH
ĿTH

fāte, fär, fȧst, fạll, finăl, cãre, at; mēte, prey, hẽr, met; pīne,
marïne, bĩrd, pin; nōte, mȯve, fọr, atŏm, not; mọọn, book;

162

(Choose only one word out of each group)

r: en-wrēaTHe',
in-tẽr-wrēaTHe'', in-wrēaTHe',
un-wrēaTHe', wrēaTHe.
s: seeTHe.
sh: en-shēaTHe', in-shēaTHe'
shēaTHe, un-shēaTHe'.
sn: snēaTHe.
t: teeTHe.

ĒTH

h: hēath.
k(c): Kēith.
l: Lēith.
n: bē-nēath', 'nēath,
un-dẽr-nēath'.
r: wrēath (rēth).
sh: shēath.
sn: snēath.
t: teeth.

ETH

Vowel: buṣ'i-eth (biz')*,
con-tin'ū-eth*, eight'i-eth (āt'),
en'vi-eth*, fif'ti-eth, fọr'ti-eth,
nīne'ti-eth, res'cū-eth*,
sev'en-ti-eth, six'ti-eth,
sor'rōw-eth*, thĩr'ti-eth,
twen'ti-eth, wēa'ri-eth*,
win'nōw-eth*, wŏr'ri-eth*.
b: Ē-liz'ȧ-beth, Mac-beth'.
br: breath.
d: death, 'ṣdeath*.
kr: Creath.
l: lī'bel-leth*, mär'vel-leth*,
quar'rel-leth*, rī'văl-leth*,
shib'bō-leth.
n: dē-tẽr'min-eth*,
em-blā'zŏn-eth*,
glis'ten-eth (''n-)*,
heärk'en-eth*, lis'ten-eth (''n-)*,

līv'en-eth*, pär'dŏn-eth*,
prē-des'tin-eth*,
ques'tiŏn-eth ('chun-)*.
p: wŏr'ship-peth*.
r: an'swẽr-eth ('sẽr-)*,
As'tō-reth, blis'tẽr-eth*,
blun'dẽr-eth*, clus'tẽr-eth*,
con'quẽr-eth ('kẽr-)*,
cŏv'ẽr-eth*, dow'ẽr-eth*,
flow'ẽr-eth*, gaTH'ẽr-eth*,
glow'ẽr-eth*, huñ'gẽr-eth*,
in-cum'bẽr-eth*, lā'bŏr-eth*,
liñ'gẽr-eth*, low'ẽr-eth*,
mea'ṣũr-eth* ('zhọọr-),
mũr'mũr-eth*, of'fẽr-eth*,
ō''vẽr-pow'ẽr-eth*,
ō''vẽr-tow'ẽr-eth*,
plea'ṣũr-eth* ('zhọọr-),
rē-cŏv'ẽr-eth*, rē-mem'bẽr-eth*,
sev'ẽr-eth*, shim'mẽr-eth*,
show'ẽr-eth*, shud'dẽr-eth*,
sli'vẽr-eth*, slum'bẽr-eth*,
suf'fẽr-eth*, sun'dẽr-eth*,
tem'pẽr-eth*, thun'dẽr-eth*,
ven'tũr-eth*, wän'dẽr-eth*,
whis'pẽr-eth (hwis')*,
wŏn'dẽr-eth*.
s: saith (seth)*, Seth,
wit'ness-eth*.
sh: ȧ-ston'ish-eth*, ban'ish-eth*,
blem'ish-eth*,
lañ'guish-eth ('gwish-)*,
noūr'ish-eth*, pun'ish-eth*,
re-liñ'quish-eth ('qwish-)*.
t: at-tri'būt-eth*,
en-spir'it-eth*,
ex-hib'it-eth (-ib')*,
fọr'feit-eth ('fit-)*,
in-her'it-eth*, in-spir'it-eth*,
mer'it-eth*, quī'et-eth*,
spir'it-eth*.

163 ūse, bull, brúte, tŭrn, up; crȳ, myth; cat, machine, ace,
church, chord; gem, anger, (Fr.) bon, as; THis, thin; azure

ĒTHD
ĒZ

(Choose only one word out of each group)

ĒTHD

b: un-brēaTHed′.
kw(qu): bē-quēaTHed′.
Plus ēTH+d.

ĒTZ

d: Diētz.
k: Kēats.
Plus ēt+s.
Plus meat's, etc.

ETZ

m: Metz.
Plus et+s.
Plus bet's, etc.

ĒV

Vowel: Christ′măs ēve (kris′),
ēave, ēve, nä-ïve′,
New Yēar's Ēve, yes′tēr-ēve*.
b: beeve.
br: brēve.
ch: à-chiēve′.
d: deev, Khē-dïve′ (kē-).
gr: ag-griēve′, en-griēve′*,
grēave, griēve.
h: hēave, up-hēave′.
k(c): keeve.
kl: clēave.
l: bē-liēve′, dis″bē-liēve′,
in″tēr-lēave′, lēave, liēve,
māke′=bē-liēve′, rē-liēve′.
p: peeve.
pr: rē-priēve′.
r: bē-rēave′, rēave, reeve,
shïre reeve*, un-rēave′,
un-reeve′.
s: con-cēive′, dē-cēive′,
mis-con-cēive′, pēr-cēive′,
prē-con-cēive′, rē-cēive′,
sēave, un-dē-cēive′.

sh: shēave.
shr: Shrēve, shriēve*.
sl: slēave, sleeve.
st: steeve, Stēve.
t: rec″i-tà-tïve′.
th: thiēve.
tr: rē-triēve′.
v: quï vïve (kē vēv), vïve (vēv).
w: in″tēr-wēave′, in-wēave′,
un-wēave′, wēave, wē've.

ĒVD

l: un-bē-liēved′, un-rē-liēved′.
s: self′=dē-cēived′,
un-pēr-cēived′.
Plus ev+d.
Plus sleeve'd, etc.

ĒVZ

Vowel: ēves (ēvz).
Plus ēv+s.
Plus eve's, etc.

ĒZ

Vowel: Cär-lȳl-ese′, ēase,
heärt's′ēase, Löu-ïse′,
rā′bi-ēs, un-ēase′.
b: bïse.
br: breeze, sēa breeze.
ch: cheese.
d: an-tip′ō-dēs, B. V. D.'s,
Car-y-a′ti-dēs, Eū-men′i-dēs,
Hes-per′i-dēs, Maï-mon′i-dēs,
Pï-ēr′i-dēs, Plēi′à-dēs.
f: fēaze.
fl: flēas.
fr: che-val′ de frïse, en-freeze′*,
freeze, friēze, un-freeze′.
g: Pōrt′ū-guēse.
gr: grēase.
h: heeze, hē's.

(Choose only one word out of each group)

hw: wheeze.
j: Jeez.
k(c): kēyş.
kw(qu): ob′sē-quieş.
l: Be-lïze′, Ben-gȧ-lēşe′,
Her′ȧ-klēş, Hĕr′cū-lēş,
ï-sos′ce-lēş, joŭr-nᶏl-ēşe′, leeş,
Nē-pa̤ul-ēşe′,
Siñ-ghȧ-lēşe′ (-gȧ-),
Tyr-ō-lēşe′, vȧ-lïşe′.
m: An-nȧ-mēşe′, As-sᶏm-ēşe′,
Bŭr-mēşe′, che-mïşe′, mēa̤şe,
rē-mïşe′, Sï-ȧ-mēşe′.
n: ab-ō-rig′i-nēşe, Ar-ak″ȧ-nēşe′,
Ar″ȧ-gŏn-ēşe′, bee′ş kneeş,
Bō″lō-gnēşe′ (-nēz′),
Cēy″lŏn-ēşe′ (sē-),
chĕr′sō-nēşe, Chï-nēşe′,
Dï-og̣′e-nēş, Hȧ-van-ēşe′,
Jap″ȧ-nēşe′, Jav″ȧ-nēşe′,
John-sŏn-eşe′ (jon-), Lē-ō-nēşe′,
Mil″ȧ-nēşe′, Pol″ō-nēşe′*,
Pyr″e-neeş′, Ve″rō-nēş′,
Vi″en-nēşe′.
p: ap-pēa̤şe′, pēa̤şe, trȧ-pēze′.
pl: plēa̤şe.
pr: im-prēşe′.
r: cē-rişe′, con-ge-rieş′,
Na″vȧr-rēşe′.

s: ȧ-nal′y-sēş, an-tith′ē-sēş,
hȳ-poth′ē-sēş, in′di-cēş,
pȧ-ren′thē-sēş, sēize,
syn′thē-sēş, vᶍr′ti-cēş.
sh: shē′ş.
skw(squ): squeeze.
sn: sneeze.
spl: dis-plēa̤şe′.
st: steeş.
t: D. T.′ş, Ma̤l-tēşe′, tēa̤şe
tw: tweeze.
TH: THēşe.
v: G̣en-e-vēşe′.
z: diş-ēa̤şe′, pe-riph′rȧ-sēş (-rif′).
Plus ē+s.
Plus sea′s, etc.

EZ

f: fez.
s: sayş.
t: Cᶍr-tez′.

ĒZH

pr: pres-tïge′.
t: tïge.

EZH

n: mȧ-nège′.
r: bȧ-rège′.
t: cᶍr-tege′.

(Choose only one word out of each group)

I

Words including the following accented vowel sounds:

ī: as in fīne; also in aisle (īl), aȳe (ī) (meaning *yes*), heīght (hīt), eȳe (ī), līe, choīr (kwīr), buȳ (bī), bȳ, rȳe.

i: as in it; heard also in pretty (prit′i), breech′es (britch′ez), sieve (siv), wom′en (wim′en), guild (gild), bur′y (ber′i), lack′ey (lak′i), lymph (limf).

Ī

Vowel: aȳ (ī), aȳe (ī),
black eȳe, eȳe, ġe′ni-ī, Ī,
in-eȳe′*, mȳ eȳe, sheep's eȳe,
weaTH′ẽr eȳe (weTH′), Y.

b: al′i-bī, buȳ, bȳ, bȳe,
bȳe′⁼bȳe′, bȳ′⁼and⁼bȳ′,
bȳ′⁼THẽ⁼bȳ′, for-bȳ′, gō′⁼bȳ,
good-bȳe′, hēre⁼bȳ′, hush′⁼à⁼bȳ,
in′c̨ū-bī, lul′là-by, pas-sẽr-bȳ′,
stānd′bȳ, stand′ẽr-bȳ,
THere-bȳ′ (THãr-),
un″dẽr-buȳ′, where-bȳ′ (hwãr-).

d: bē-dȳe′, dīe, dȳe.

dr: à-drȳ′, drȳ,
hīgh′⁼and⁼drȳ′ (hī′).

f: ac-id′i-fȳ, à-lac̨′ri-fȳ
al′kà-li-fȳ, amp′li-fȳ,
an-ġel′i-fȳ, Aṅg′li-fȳ,
bē-at′i-fȳ, beaū′ti-fy (bū′),
brùt′i-fy, c̨an′di-fȳ, cẽr′ti-fȳ,
c̨la′ri-fȳ, c̨las′si-fȳ, c̨ock′ney-fȳ,
c̨od′i-fȳ, c̨ŏun′tri-fȳ, c̨rū′ci-fȳ,
dam′ni-fȳ, dan′di-fȳ, dē-fȳ′,
dē′i-fȳ, dig′ni-fȳ, dis-quäl′i-fȳ,
dis-sat′is-fȳ, di-vẽr′si-fȳ,
ɛd′i-fȳ, ē-lec̨′tri-fȳ, ē-mul′si-fȳ,
ē-tẽr′ni-fȳ*, ex-emp′li-fȳ,
fal′si-fȳ, fīe, for′ti-fȳ,
fos-sil′i-fȳ, French′i-fȳ,
fruc̨′ti-fȳ, gas′i-fȳ, glō′ri-fȳ,
grat′i-fȳ, hor′ri-fȳ, hū-man′i-fȳ,

ī-den′ti-fȳ, in-dem′ni-fȳ,
in-ten′si-fȳ, jus′ti-fȳ, lab′ē-fy,
len′i-fȳ, lig′ni-fȳ,
liq′ue-fȳ (lik′wē-), mag′ni-fȳ,
mod′i-fȳ, mol′li-fȳ, mor′ti-fȳ,
mys′ti-fȳ, nōt′i-fȳ, nul′li-fȳ,
os′si-fȳ, pac′i-fȳ, pẽr-son′i-fȳ,
pet′ri-fȳ, phī (fī), prēach′i-fȳ,
pū′ri-fȳ, pūt′re-fȳ, quäl′i-fȳ,
quän′ti-fȳ, ram′i-fȳ, rãr′ē-fȳ,
rat′i-fȳ, rec̨′ti-fȳ, rē-viv′i-fȳ,
sac̨-cha′ri-fȳ, sanc̨′ti-fȳ,
sat′is-fȳ, scar′i-fȳ, scō′ri-fȳ,
sig′ni-fȳ, simp′li-fȳ, sol-id′i-fȳ.
spec′i-fȳ, stel′li-fȳ, stil′ti-fȳ,
stul′ti-fȳ, stū′pē-fȳ, tab′ē-fȳ,
ter′ri-fȳ, tes′ti-fȳ, tor′pi-fȳ,
tor′rē-fȳ, trans-mog′ri-fy,
typ′i-fȳ, ū′ni-fy, vẽrb′i-fȳ,
ver′i-fȳ, vẽr′si-fȳ, vil′i-fȳ,
vit′ri-fȳ, viv′i-fȳ.

fl: but′tẽr-flȳ, drag′ŏn-flȳ,
fīre′flȳ, flȳ, gad′flȳ, horse′flȳ,
shoo′flȳ, out-flȳ′.

fr: frȳ, small frȳ.

g: fall guȳ (gī), guȳ,
wīse guȳ.

gr: grī.

h: heīgh (hī), hīe (hī),
hīgh (hī),
skȳ′⁼hīgh′.

hw: whȳ.

k(c̨): c̨hī.

ĬB
ICH

fāte, fär, fàst, fall, finăl, cāre, at; mēte, prey, hẽr, met; pīne,
marĭne, bĭrd, pĭn; nōte, mŏve, fŏr, atŏm, not; mọọn, book;

166

(Choose only one word out of each group)

kr: crȳ, dē-crȳ', des-crȳ',
out-crȳ'.

l: al'kà-lĭ, al-lȳ', bē-lĭe', Jù-lȳ',
laz'ū-lĭ, lĭe, lȳe, rē-lȳ',
Thẽr-mop'y-lae (-lĭ), un"dẽr-lĭe'.

m: dem'ĭ*, dē-mȳ', mȳ.

n: dē-nȳ', nĭgh (nī), nȳe,
tẽr'mi-nĭ, well'₌nĭgh' (-nĭ').

p: ap'ple pĭe, es-pȳ',
hum'ble pĭe, mag'pĭe,
mince pĭe, oc'cū-pȳ, pī, pĭe,
prē-oc'cū-pȳ, sēa pĭe,
um'ble pĭe*.

pl: ap-plȳ', com-plȳ', im-plȳ',
mul'ti-plȳ, plȳ, rē-plȳ',
sup-plȳ'.

pr: prȳ.

r: à-wrȳ' (-rī'), rȳe, wrȳ (rī).

s: proph'ē-sȳ, psī (sī), scȳe (sī),
sĭgh (sī).

sh: shȳ, un-shȳ'.

sk(sc): en-skȳ', skȳ, Skȳe.

sl: slȳ.

sn: snȳ.

sp: bē-spȳ', spȳ,
weaTH'ẽr-spȳ (weTH').

spr: sprȳ.

st: stȳ.

t: tĭe, un-tĭe'.

th: Thaī (thī), thĭgh (thī).

TH: THȳ*.

tr: trȳ.

v: out-vĭe', vĭe.

w: wȳe, Y.

ĪB

b: im-bībe'.

br: brībe.

j: gībe, jībe.

k(c): kībe.

skr(scr): à-scrībe',
cir'cum-scrībe, dē-scrībe',

in-scrībe', in"tẽr-scrībe',
prē-scrībe', prō-scrībe', scrībe,
sub-scrībe', sū-pẽr-scrībe',
tran-scrībe'.

tr: dī'à-trībe, trībe.

ĬB

b: bib, Bibb.

d: dib.

dr: drib.

f: fib.

g: gib, Gibb.

gl: glib.

j: jib.

kr: crib.

kw(qu): quib*.

l: ad lib.

n: nib.

r: rib.

s: sib.

skw(squ): squib.

ĪBD

skr(scr): in-scrībed',
un"in-scrībed'.

Plus īb+d.

ĬBD

r: ribbed, rock ribbed.

Plus ib+d.

ĬBZ

d: dibs.

g: Gibbs.

n: his nibs.

Plus ib+s.

Plus Bibb's, etc.

ICH

Vowel: itch.

b: bitch.

ch: chich*.

d: ditch.

(Choose only one word out of each group)

f: fitch.
fl: flitch.
h: hitch, un-hitch′.
hw: which.
kw(qu): quitch.
l: lich*.
m: miche.
n: niche.
p: pitch.
r: en-rich′, rich.
s: sich.
skr(sçr): sçritch.
sn: snitch.
st: chāin stitch,
  feaTH′ĕr stitch (feTH′), stitch.
sw: switch.
tw: twitch.
v: czär′ē-vitch (zär′).
w: bē-witch′, Ca͡e-ṣär′ē-witch,
  czär′ē-witch (zär′),
  Ga̤-bril′ō-witch, witch.

ICHT

h: hitched, un-hitched′.
w: un″bē-witched′, un-witched′.
Plus ich+d.

ĪD

Vowel: äl′mŏnd″eȳed
    (ä′mund″ĭd),
  Är′gus″eȳed, çälf′꞊eȳed (käf′),
  çock′꞊eȳed, çross′꞊eȳed,
  dī-ox′ĭde, dŏve′꞊eȳed,
  dull′꞊eȳed, ēa′gle꞊eȳed,
  ē′vil꞊eȳed, eȳed, fu̧ll′꞊eȳed,
  gog′gle꞊eȳed′, green′꞊eȳed,
  hawk′꞊eȳed, Ī′d, ĭd, ĭde,
  lynx′꞊eȳed (links′꞊),
  meek′꞊eȳed (′ĭd), mon-ox′ĭde,
  ō′pen꞊eȳed, owl′꞊eȳed,
  ox′꞊eȳed′, ox′ĭde, pāle′꞊eȳed,
  pĕr-ox′ĭde, pīe′꞊eȳed, pop′꞊eȳed,

slōe′꞊eȳed, snāke′꞊eȳed,
so̧ft′꞊eȳed, squint′꞊eȳed,
wa̧ll′꞊eȳed.
b: a̤-bīde′, bīde, çär′-bīde.
br: brīde, chĭld brīde.
ch: chīde.
d: dŏu′ble꞊dȳed′, dīed, dȳed,
  ī′ō-dīde, tīe′꞊dȳed′.
dr: drīed, rē-drīed′, un-drīed′.
f: bō-na̤ fīde, çon-fīde′,
  çǒun′tri-fīed, dē-fīed′,
  dig′ni-fīed, dis-sat′is-fīed,
  di-vĕr′si-fīed, fo̧r′ti-fīed,
  jus′ti-fīed, pū′ri-fīed,
  quäl′i-fīed, sañç′ti-fīed,
  sat′is-fīed, self′꞊sat′is-fīed,
  sul′phīde, un-dig′ni-fīed,
  un-grat′i-fīed, un-pū′ri-fīed,
  un-quäl′i-fīed, un-sañç′ti-fīed,
  un-sat′is-fīed, vit′ri-fīed.
fr: frīed.
g: guīde (gīd), mis-guīde′.
gl: glīde.
gr: grīde.
h: fo̧r-mal′dē-hȳde, hīde,
  hīed, Hȳde.
kl: Çlȳde.
kr: çried.
l: çol-līde′, ē-līde′, līed,
  tīde, mis″al-līed′.
m: brō′mīde.
n: nīde.
p: pīed, un″es-pīed′.
pl: un″ap-plīed′.
pr: prīde, Prȳde, self′꞊prīde′.
r: dē-rīde′, out-rīde′,
  ō″vĕr-rīde′, rīde.
s: a̤-lo̧ng-sīde′, a̤-sīde′,
  Bär′mē-cīde, bed′sīde, bē-sīde′,
  broad′sīde, çō-in-cīde′,

(Choose only one word out of each group)

cŏun′try-sīde, dē-cīde′,
dē′i-cīde, ex-cīde′, fīre′sīde,
fōre′sīde, frat′ri-cīde,
hẽr′pi-cīde, hill′sīde, hōm′i-cīde,
in-fan′ti-cīde, in-sec′ti-cīde,
in-sīde′, lāke′sīde, lap′i-cīde,
lib-ẽr′ti-cīde, mat′ri-cīde,
moun′tăin sīde, out-sīde′,
par-en′ti-cīde, par′ri-cīde,
pat′ri-cīde, reg′i-cīde,
ri′vẽr-sīde, sēa′sīde, sīde,
sō-rọr′i-cīde, stil′li-cīde,
sub-sīde′, sū′i-cīde,
ty-ran′ni-cide, un′dẽr-sīde,
ūx-ọr′i-cīde, vat′i-cīde,
vẽrm′i-cīde, vul′pi-cīde,
wạ′tẽr-sīde, wāy′sīde,
weaTH′ẽr-sīde (weTH′).

sk(sc): skīed.

skr(scr): un-dē-scrīed′.

sl: back′slīde, land′slīde, slīde.

sn: snīde.

sp: spīed, un-spīed′.

str: à-strīde′, bē-strīde′,
out-strīde′, strīde.

t: Ạll-hal′lōw-tīde,
Bär-thol′ō-mew-tīde, bē-tīde′,
Christ′măs-tīde (kris′),
Ēast′ẽr-tīde, Em′bẽr-tīde,
ebb′tīde, ē′ven-tīde, flood tīde,
Hal′lōw-tīde, hīgh tīde (hī),
Lam′măs-tīde, lee tīde,
mọrn′ing tīde, nēap tīde,
nọọn tīde, Pas′sion-tīde,
Shrōve′tīde, Spriñg′tīde, tīde,
un″bē-tīde′, un′dẽr-tīde,
weaTH′ẽr-tīde (weTH′),
Whit′sun-tīde, Yūle′tīde.

tr: trīed, un-trīed′.

v: di-vīde′, prō-vīde′,
sub′di-vīde.

w: nā′tion=wīde, stāte′wīde,
wīde, wŏrld′=wīde′.

z: prē-sīde′, rē-sīde′.

Plus ī+d.

Plus I′d, guy′d, etc.

ID

Vowel: id.

b: bid, fọr-bid′, out-bid′,
ō″vẽr-bid′, rē-bid′, un-bid′,
un″dẽr-bid′, un-fọr-bid′.

ch: chid*.

d: did, fọr-did′*, kā′ty-did,
out-did′, ō″vẽr-did′, un-did′.

dr: Mà-drid′.

f: fid.

g: gid.

gr: grid.

h: hid.

k(c): kid.

kw(qu): quid.

l: in′và-lid, eȳe′lid, lid.

m: à-mid′, mid, pyr′à-mid.

r: rid.

s: Cid.

sk(sc): skid.

skw(squ): squid.

sl: slid.

str: bē-strid′*, strid*.

thr: thrid*.

IDST

b: bid′st*, fọr-bid′st′*.

ch: chid′st*.

d: did′st*.

h: hid′st*.

k(c): kid′st*.

m: à-midst′, midst.

r: rid′st*.

sl: slid′st*.

(Choose only one word out of each group)

IDTH

w: width.
Plus id+'th*.

ĪDZ

Vowel: īdeṣ.
s: bē-sīdeṣ'.
Plus īd+s.
Plus bride's, etc.

ĪF

f: fīfe.
l: af'tẽr-līfe, līfe, still līfe.
n: bōw'ie knīfe, çlasp'knīfe.
jack'knīfe, knīfe.
r: rīfe.
str: strīfe.
w: fish'wīfe, good'wīfe,
house'wīfe, mid'wīfe, wīfe.

IF

Vowel: if.
b: biff.
ch: hand'kẽr-chief (hang'),
neck'ẽr-chief.
d: diff.
gl: glyph (glif), hī'ẽr-ō-glyph.
gr: griff, hip'pō-griff.
hw: whiff.
j: jiff.
kl: çliff, un'dẽr-çliff.
kw(qu): quiff.
m: miff.
r: Ten'ẽr-ife (-if), Ten'ẽr-iffe.
sk(sç): skiff.
sn: sniff.
st: stiff.
t: tiff.
w: wiff.

IFT

b: biffed.
dr: a-drift', drift, snōw'drift.
spin'drift.

g: gift.
hw: whiffed.
kl: çliffed.
l: fōre-lift'*, lift, top'ping lift,
up-lift'.
m: miffed.
r: rift.
s: sift.
sh: shift.
shr: shrift.
skw(squ): squiffed.
sn: sniffed.
sp: spiffed.
sw: chim'ney swift, swift.
t: tift.
thr: spend'thrift, thrift,
un-thrift'.
Plus if+d.

IFTH

f: fifth.
Plus biff''th*, etc.

IG

b: big.
br: brig.
d: dig, in'fra dig.
f: fig, hŏn'ey fig.
fr: frig.
g: gig, whĩrl'i-gig.
gr: grig.
hw: whig.
j: jig, thing'a-ma-jig.
n: nig, rē-nege' (-nig').
p: guin'ēa pig (gin'ē), pig.
pr: prig.
r: thim'ble-rig, un-rig', rig.
s: cig.
sn: snig.
spr: sprig.
sw: swig.
tr: trig.

(Choose only one word out of each group)

tw: twig.
w: wig, per'i-wig.

IGD

r: fu̱ll'⸗rigged', jù'ry⸗rigged',
 squãre'⸗rigged'.
w: bē-wigged'.
Plus ig+d.

IGZ

b: Biggṣ.
br: Briggṣ.
d: Diggeṣ.
h: Higgṣ.
j: Jigṣ.
r: Riggṣ.
w: Wiggṣ.
Plus ig+s.
Plus prig's, etc.

ĪJ

bl: ō-blīġe'.
l: Līje.

IJ

br: ȧ-bridġe', bridġe.
m: midġe.
n: nidġe.
r: en-ridġe'*, ridġe, up-ridġe'.
Plus polysyllables ending in āj.

IJD

br: ȧ-bridġed', un"ȧ-bridġed',
 un-bridġed'.
Plus ij+d.

ĪK

Vowel: Al'i-bī Īke, Īke.
b: bīke.
bl: ō-blīque'.
d: dīke, dȳke, Van-ȧȳke',
 Van-dȳck'.
f: fȳke.

h: hīke, hitch'hīke.
k(c̠): kīke.
l: ȧ-līke', as-sas'sin-like,
 bē-līke'*, brŏTH'ẽr-līke,
 dis-līke', fãir'y-līke,
 ghōst'līke (gōst'), līke,
 māid'en-līke, man'līke,
 mis-līke', peaṣ'ănt-līke (pez'),
 stär'līke, un-līke', wŏ'măn-līke,
 wŏrk'măn-līke.
m: mīke.
p: bōard'ing-pīke, pīke,
 tũrn'pīke.
s: cȳc̠, psȳc̠h (sīk).
shr: shrīke.
sp: mär'lin-spīke, spīke.
str: strīke, ten strīke.
t: tȳke.
w: Van Wȳck, Wȳke.

IK

br: brick.
ch: chick.
d: Ben'ē-dick, dick.
fl: flick.
fr: Fricke.
h: hick.
k(c̠): kick.
kl: c̠lick.
kr: c̠rick.
kw(qu): dŏub'le⸗quick, quick.
l: C̠ath'ō-lic̠, lick.
m: mick.
n: är'se-nic̠, kin"ni-kin-nick',
 nick.
p: pick.
pr: prick.
r: bish'ŏp-ric̠, c̠hiv'ăl-ric̠,
 c̠hol'ẽr-ic̠, lim'ẽr-ick,
 mav'ẽr-ick, plē-thọr'ic̠,
 rhet'ō-ric̠ (ret'), rick, tū'mẽr-ic̠.

(Choose only one word out of each group)

s: heärt'sick, lŏve'sick.
siç, sick.
sh: çhiç.
sl: slick.
sn: snick.
sp: spick.
st: bē-stick', çan'dle-stick, fid'dle-stick, pō'gō-stick, siñ'gle-stick, stiçh, stick, wạlk'ing stick (wạk'), yärd'stick.
t: à-rith'mē-tiç, her'ē-tiç, im-pol'i-tiç, lū'nà-tiç, pol'i-tiç, tiç, tick, trip'tyçh.
th: thick.
tr: trick.
v: Viç.
w: bāi'li-wick, çan'dle-wick, wick

ĪKS

d: Dȳkes.
r: Rīkes.
s: Sȳkes.
Plus īk+s.
Plus bike's, etc.

IKS

d: Dix.
f: à-fix', çrū'ci-fix, fix, prē'fix, suf'fix, trans-fix'.
h: Hicks, Hix.
l: prō-lix'.
m: ad-mix', çom-mix', im-mix', in″tēr-mix', mix.
n: nix, Pnyx (nix).
p: pyx.
r: Ricks, Rix.
s: six.
st: fid'dle-sticks, Styx.
t: pol'i-tiçs.

tr: Bē'à-trix, ciç'à-trix, ex-e'çū-trix, in-her'i-trix, Trix.
Plus ik+s.
Plus Dick's, etc.

IKST

f: fixed, rē-fixed', trans-fixed', un-fixed'.
k(ç): kick'st*.
kl: çlick'st*.
l: lick'st*.
m: ad-mixed', in″tēr-mixed', mixed, rē-mixed', un-mixed'.
p: pick'st*.
pr: prick'st*.
st: stick'st*.
tr: ciç'à-trixed, trick'st*.
tw: à-twixt', bē-twixt', 'twixt.

IKSTH

s: sixth.
Plus iks+'th*.

IKT

br: bricked, rē-bricked'.
d: ad'diçt, ben'ē-diçt, çon-trà-diçt', in″tēr-diçt', prē-diçt'.
fl: af-fliçt', çon-fliçt', in-fliçt', flicked.
kl: çlicked.
l: dē-liçt', der'ē-liçt, licked, re'liçt, ụn-licked'.
p: dē-piçt', Piçt, un-picked'.
s: siçced.
str: à-striçt', çon-striçt', rē-striçt', striçt.
v: çon-viçt', ē-viçt'.
Plus ik+d.

ĪL

Vowel: aīsle (īl), Ī'll, īsle (īl).
b: bīle, Kà-bȳle'

IL

fāte, fär, fȧst, fạll, finăl, cãre, at; mēte, prey, hẽr, met; pīne,
marïne, bĩrd, pin; nōte, mŏve, fọr, atŏm, not; mọọn, book;

172

(Choose only one word out of each group)

d: croc̣'ō-dīle.

f: Añg'lō-phīle, bib'li-ō-phīle,
dē-fīle', fīle, Frañc̣'ō-phīle,
Ġẽr-man'ō-phīle, pā'pẽr fīle,
rē-fīle', siñ'gle fīle, Sīn'ō-phīle,
Slav'ō-phīle, Tũrk'ō-phīle,
Zī'ŏn-ō-phīle, etc.

g: bē-guīle', guīle.

hw: à-whīle', ere-whīle' (ãr-)*,
ẽrst'whīle*, mēan'whīle,
ŏTH'ẽr-whīle, sŏme'whīle,
THere'whīle (THãr'), whīle.

k(c̣): chīle, chȳle, Kȳle.

l: līsle (īl), Lȳle.

m: cam'ō-mīle, mīle.

n: cam'pȧ-nīle, en-īsle' (-īl')*,
jū've̅-nīle, Nīle, sē'nīle.

p: cŏm-pīle', pīle, Pȳle,
up-pīle', vol-tā'ic̣ pīle.

r: pū'ẽr-īle, rīle.

s: en-sīle', rec̣'ŏn-cīle, rē-sīle'.

sm: smīle.

sp: spīle.

st: dī'ȧ-stȳle, pen'tȧ-stȳle,
per'i-stȳle, stīle, stȳle.

t: in'făn-tīle, mẽr'căn-tīle, tīle,
vẽr'sȧ-tīle, vī'brȧ-tīle.

v: rē-vīle', vīle.

w: wīle.

Plus pie'll, etc.

IL

Vowel: ill.

b: bill, crāne'ṣ bill,
spọọn'bill.

br: brill.

ch: chill.

d: daf'fō-dil, dill, spȧ-dille'.

dr: drill, es-pȧ-drille',
quä-drille'.

f: Añg'lō-phile, bib'li-ō-phile,
chlō'rō-phyl, chry'sō-phyl, fill,

Frañc̣'ō-phile, fụl-fil',
Ġẽr-man'ō-phile, Phil,
rē-fill', Sīn'ō-phile,
Slav'ō-phile, Tũrk'ō-phile,
Zī'ŏn-ō-phile, etc.

fr: bē-frill', frill.

g: gill.

gr: grill, grille.

h: ant'hill, down-hill', hill,
up-hill'.

j: ġill, jill.

k(c̣): Bōz'en-kill,
Cō'bleṣ-kill ('b'lz-), kill,
kiln (kil), Nọr'mănṣ kill.

kw(qu): quill.

l: Lil.

m: grist'mill, mill,
· pow'dẽr-mill, wạ'tẽr-mill.

n: jú've̅-nile, nil.

p: pill.

pr: prill.

r: pū'ẽr-ile, rill.

s: cod'i-cil, dom'i-cile,
im'bē-cile, sill.

sk(sc̣): skill.

skw(squ): squill.

sp: spill.

st: bē still, in-stil', still,
stock'=still'.

sw: swill.

shr: shrill.

t: dis-til', in'făn-tile,
mẽr'căn-tile, till, 'till, un-til',
vẽr'sȧ-tile, vī'brȧ-tile,
vol'ȧ-tile.

th: thill.

thr: en-thrill', thrill.

tr: trill.

tw: twill, 'twill.

(Choose only one word out of each group)

v: Am'i-ty-ville, Ev'ăns̩-ville, Löu'ĭs-ville (lo̧o̧'ē-), Se-ville', vill.

w: free will, good will, ill will, self=will', un-will', whip'po̧o̧r-will, will.

z: Brá-zil'.

ILCH

f: filch.
m: milch.
p: pilch.
z: Zilch.

ĪLD

Vowel: aĭsled (īld).
ch: chīld, chīlde, fos'tẽr chīld, lŏve chīld, un-chīld'.
f: dē-fīled', en-fīled', fīled.
g: un"bē-guīled'.
m: mīld, un-mīld'.
s: un-reҫ'ŏn-cīled.
st: self'=stȳled'.
w: un-wīld', wīld, Wīlde.
Plus īl+d.

ILD

b: build (bild), rē-build', un-build', up-build'.
ch: un-chilled'.
f: un"fu̧l-filled'.
g: bē-gild', gild, guild (gild).
sk(sҫ): un-skilled'.
t: un-tilled'.
w: self'=willed', un-willed'.
Plus il+d.

ILF

s: sylph.

ILJ

b: bilġe.

ILK

Vowel: ilk.
b: bilk.
m: milk.
s: silk, spun silk.

ILKS

w: Wilkes.
Plus ilk+s.
Plus milk's, etc.

ILM

f: film.

ILN

k(ҫ): kiln.
m: Milne.

ILS

gr: grilse.
Cf. ilts.

ĪLST

hw: whīlst.
Plus beguil'st*, etc.

ILT

b: built, çliñk'ẽr=built, çlip'pẽr=built, frig'ăte=built, rē-built', un-built', Van'dẽr-bilt'.
g: bē-gilt', gilt, guilt, rē-gilt', un-gilt'.
h: bas'ket hilt, hı̧lt.
j: jilt.
k(ҫ): kilt.
kw(qu): quilt.
l: lilt.
m: milt.
s: silt.
sp: spilt, un-spilt'.
st: stilt.
t: à-tilt', tilt, up-tilt'.
w: wilt.

ILTH
ĪMD
fāte, fär, fȧst, fạll, finăl, cāre, ȧt; mēte, prẹy, hẽr, met; pīne,
marĭne, bĭrd, pin; nōte, mŏve, fọr, atŏm, not; mọọn, book;
174

(Choose only one word out of each group)

ILTH

f: filth.
sp: spilth.
t: tilth.
Plus befrill'th*, etc.

ILTS

k: kilts.
Plus ilt+s.
Cf. grilse.

ĪLZ

hw: ŏTH'ẽr-whīleṣ, whīleṣ.
j: Ġīleṣ.
m: Mīleṣ.
n: Nīleṣ.
w: wīleṣ.
Plus īl+s.
Plus aisle's, etc.

ĪM

ch: chīme.
d: dīme.
gr: bē-grīme', grīme.
h: Gug'gen-heīm, Rōṣ'en-heīm.
k: c̗hȳme.
kl: c̗līmb, c̗līme, up-c̗līmb'.
kr: c̗rīme.
l: bē-līme', bĭrd'līme,
brook'līme, līme, Lȳme,
quick'līme, sub-līme'.
m: mīme, pan'tō-mīme.
pr: prīme.
r: bē-rhȳme', rhȳme, rīme.
s: cȳme.
sl: bē-slīme', slīme.
t: ȧf'tẽr-tīme, bed'tīme,
brēaTH'ing tīme, dāy'tīme,
ēan'ing tīme, ēat'ing tīme,
här'vest tīme, hāy'ing tīme,
life'tīme, mar'i-tīme,
mēan'tīme, ō'vẽr-tīme,

pāir'ing tīme, seed'tīme,
sŏme'tīme, spring'tīme,
sum'mēr-tīme, thȳme (tīm),
tīme, win'tẽr-tīme.
Plus I'm.

IM

b: cher'u-bim.
br: brim.
d: bē-dim', dim.
dr: San'hē-drim.
f: ser'ȧ-phim.
g: gim*.
gl: glim.
gr: grim.
h: him, hymn.
hw: whim.
j: ġym, Jim.
k(c̗): Kim.
kl: Klim.
l: en-limn', limb, limn,
prē-lim'.
n: an'tō-nym, Nym,
pseū'dō-nym, syn'ō-nym.
p: Pym.
r: in'tẽr-im.
pr: prim.
r: rim.
s: Sim.
sh: shim.
sk(sc̗): skim.
skr(sc̗r): sc̗rim.
sl: slim.
sw: swim.
t: mar'i-time, Tim.
tr: bē-trim', rē-trim', trim.
v: vim.
z: Zim, zimb.

ĪMD

r: fạlse⹀rhȳmed' (-rīmd'),
rhȳmed, un-rhȳmed'.

175 ūse, bṳll, brúte, tũrn, up; crȳ, myth; çat, maçhine, ace,
church, çhord; ġem, añger, (Fr.) boṅ, aṣ; THis, thin; aᶎure

IMD
ĪN

(Choose only one word out of each group)

t: well′₌tīmed′.
Plus īm+d.

IMD

tr: un-trimmed′.
Plus im+d.

IMF

l: lymph.
n: nymph, sēa nymph,
wood nymph.

IMP

Vowel: imp.
bl: blimp.
ch: chimp.
g: gimp, guimpe (gimp).
j: jimp.
kr: çrimp.
l: limp.
p: pimp.
pr: primp.
s: simp.
shr: shrimp.
sk(sç): skimp.
skr(sçr): sçrimp.
t: tymp.

IMPS

gl: glimpse.
Plus imp+s.
Plus imp's, etc.

ĪMZ

t: bē-tīmeṣ′, oft′en-tīmeṣ (of″n-),
oft-tīmeṣ′, sŏme′tīmeṣ.
Plus īm+ṣ.
Plus chime's, etc.

IMZ

s: Simmṣ.
Plus im+s.
Plus limb's, etc.

ĪN

Vowel: eȳne (īn)*.
b: bīne, çar′à-bīne, çol′um-bīne,
çom-bīne′, çon′çū-bīne,
wood′bīne.
br: brīne.
ch: chīne.
d: an′ō-dȳne, cel′ăn-dīne,
çon-dīgn′ (-dīn′), dīne, dȳne,
in-çär′nà-dīne, mus′çà-dīne.
f: çaf′feīne (′fīn), çon-fīne′,
dē-fīne′, fīne, rē-fīne′,
sū′pēr-fīne, trē′phīne.
gr: per′ē-grīne.
hw: whīne.
j: jīne.
k(ç): kīne.
kl: Çlȳne, dē-çlīne′,
dis-in-çlīne′, in-çlīne′, Kleīn,
Klīne, rē-çlīne′.
l: A′dà-līne, A′dē-līne,
à-līgn′ (-līn′), al′kà-līne,
an′i-līne, aq′ui-līne (ak′wi-),
ça′băl-līne, Çap′i-tō-līne,
Çar′ō-līne, çor′ăl-līne,
çrys′tăl-līne, Es′qui-līne,
Ev′à-līne, E-van′ġē-līne,
Ghib′el-līne (gib′), hȳ′à-līne,
in′tēr-līne, Jaç′que-līne (′ke-),
līfe′līne, līne, lōad′līne,
Ma′dē-līne, mà-līgn′ (-līn′),
ō′păl-īne, pet′à-līne, sā′līne,
sib′yl-līne, sīde′līne, snōw′līne,
tim′bēr-līne, un′dēr-līne,
un-līne′, Ūr′sū-līne, wạ′tēr-līne
m: çoun′tēr-mīne, in-tēr-mīne′,
mīne, pow′dēr-mīne,
sy′çà-mīne, un′dēr-mīne.
n: Ap′en-nīne, as′i-nīne,
bē-nīgn′, Fes′cen-nīne,

IN

fāte. fär. fást, fạll, finăl, cãre, at; mēte, prey, hẽr, met; pīne.
marīne, bĭrd, pĭn; nōte, mŏve, fọr, atŏm, not; mọọn, book; **176**

(Choose only one word out of each group)

lē'ō-nīne, nīne, pa'vō-nīne,
sa'tūr-nīne, un"bē-nĭgn' (-nĭn').

p: ō-pīne', pīne, pọr'çū-pīne,
Pro'sēr-pīne, rē-pīne',
rē"sū-pīne', sū-pīne',
un"sū-pīne'.

r: à-dul'tēr-īne, an'sēr-īne,
Rhīne (rīn),
sap'phi-rīne (sa'fi-rīn),
Tūrn've-reīn ('fe-), vī'pēr-īne,
vul'tūr-īne, wŏl'vēr-īne,
zōll'vēr-eīn (tsōl'fēr-).

s: as-sīgn' (-sīn'), çal'cīne,
çon-sīgn', çoun'tēr-sīgn,
en'sīgn, sīgn, sīne, sub-sīgn'*.
sȳne, un'dēr-sīgn.

sh: à-shīne', bē-shīne',
mọọn'shīne, out-shīne', shīne,
stär'shīne, sun'shīne.

shr: en-shrīne', shrīne.

sp: spīne.

spl: splīne.

st: Beck'steīn, Ep'steīn,
Gōld'steīn, Hof'fen-steīn,
Hōl'steīn, Lieçh'ten-steīn (lik'),
Rù'ben-steīn, steīn,
Weīn'steīn.

sw: swīne.

t: ag'à-tīne, är'gen-tīne,
brig'ăn-tīne, Byz'ăn-tīne,
Ce-les'tīne, Clem'en-tīne,
Con'stăn-tīne, eg'lăn-tīne,
Flọr'en-tīne, in'făn-tīne,
lib'ēr-tīne, ma'tū-tīne,
pal'à-tīne, Phi'lis-tīne,
sēr'pen-tīne, tīne, Tūr'pen-tīne,
Tȳne (tīn), val'en-tīne,
ves'pēr-tīne.

TH: THīne*.

tr: trīne.

tw: en-twīne', in"tēr-twīne',
ō"vēr-twīne', twīne, un-twīne'.

v: di-vīne', sub"di-vīne', vīne.

w: ap'ple wīne, Es'en-weīn,
wīne.

z: dē-sīgn' (-zīn'), lang sȳne*,
rē-sīgn', sȳne*.

IN

Vowel: ạll in, ġen'ū-ine,
her'ō-ine, hēre-in', in, inn,
tāke in, THere-in' (THär-),
where-in' (hwär-),
whip"pēr-in' (hwip"), wiTH-in'.

b: been, bin, çar'à-bine,
haş'been, Jaç'ō-bin.

ch: chin.

d: al'măn-dine, çō'deine ('din),
din, in-çär'nà-dine, pal'à-din.

f: çaf'feine ('fin), fin, Finn,
Mick'ēy Finn.

fl: Flynn.

g: bē-gin', gyn.

gl: Glyn, Glynn.

gr: à-grin', çhà-grin', grin,
per'ē-grine.

hw: whin.

j: djinn (jin), ġin, ġyn, jinn,
ọr'i-ġin.

k(ç): à-kin', bal'dà-çhin,
çan'ni-kin, fin'i-kin, kil'dēr-kin,
kin, man'i-kin, min'i-kin,
tī'gēr-kin.

kw(qu): här'lē-quin.
Quinn (kwin).

l: al'kà-line, an'i-line,
aq'ui-line (ak'wi-), ban'dō-line,
Bēr-lin', Bō-leyn' (-lin'),
ça'băl-line, çọr'ăl-line,
çrin'ō-line, çrys'tăl-line,
Ē-van'ġē-line, frañ'çō-lin.

177 ūse, bu̲ll, brúte, tũrn, up; crȳ, myth; c̢at, maçhine, ace, church, c̢hord; ġem, añger, (Fr.) boṅ, as̢; THis, thin; azure

INCH IND

(Choose only one word out of each group)

Ghib'el-line (gib'), hȳ'a̲-line, jave'lin, lin, Lynn, man'dō-lin, mas'c̢ū-line, ō'păl-ine, pet'ăl-ine, sib'yl-line, töur'ma̲-line, Ũr'sū-line, Va'se-line, vī'ō-lin, Zep'pe-lin.

m: jes'sa̲-mine, Min, syc̢'a̲-mine.

n: fem'i-nine, Fes'cen-nine, mez'za̲-nine, pa'vō-nine.

p: a'trō-pine, bē-lāy'ing pin, chiñ'ka̲-pin, chiñ'qua̲-pin ('ka̲-), pin, rē-pin', un″dĕr-pin', un-pin'.

pl: dis'ci-pline.

r: a̲-dul'tēr-ine, a̲-liz'a̲-rin, an'sēr-ine, as'pēr-in, C̢ath'ē-rine, c̢ul'vēr-in, glyc̢'ēr-ine, Kath'ē-rine, man'da̲-rin, nec̢'ta̲-rine, sac̢'cha̲-rine, sap'phi-rine (sa'fi-rin), tam'böu-rin, vī'pēr-ine, vul'tūr-ine.

s: c̢lav'e-cin, moc̢'ca̲-sin, sin, un-sin'.

sh: C̢ap'ū-c̢hin, shin.

sk(sc̢): beār'skin, buck'skin, sēal'skin, skin, tī'gēr skin.

sp: sīde'spin, spin, tāil'spin.

t: ag'a̲-tine, är'ġen-tine, bu̲l'le-tin, Byz'ăn-tine, car'ō-tin, Ce'les-tine, Flor'en-tine, ġel'a̲-tin, in'făn-tine, lib'ēr-tine, nic̢'ō-tine, Phi'lis-tine, tin, ves'pēr-tine.

th: thick'⹀and⹀thin', thin.

tw: twin.

w: win.

INCH

Vowel: inch.
ch: chinch.
f: fal'lōw finch, finch, gōld'finch, gràss'finch.
fl: flinch.
kl: c̢linch, un-c̢linch'.
l: linch, lynch.
p: be-pinch', pinch.
s: cinch.
w: winch.

IND

b: bīnd, in-bīnd', re-bīnd', un-bīnd', un″dĕr-bīnd', up-bīnd'.
bl: blīnd, c̢ŏl'ŏr-blīnd, hälf blīnd (häf), pūr'blīnd, sand blīnd, snōw'blīnd, un-blīnd'.
f: fīnd, un″c̢on-fīned' (fīnd'), un-dē-fīned', un-rē-fīned'.
gr: grīnd.
h: bē-hīnd', hīnd.
k(c̢): gav'el-kīnd, hū'man-kīnd, kīnd, man-kīnd', un-kīnd', wo'măn-kīnd (woo').
kl: dis-in-c̢līned'.
kr: crīned.
m: màs'tēr mīnd, mīnd, rē-mīnd'.
r: rīnd, rȳnd.
s: un'dēr-sīgned.
shr: un-shrīned'.
tw: in″tēr-twīned' ō″vēr-twīned'.
w: in″tēr-wīnd', rē-wīnd', storm'wīnd*, un-wīnd', up-wīnd', wīnd*, wīnd.

IND
ING

fāte, fär, fȧst, fạll, fĭnȧl, cãre, at; mēte, prĕy, hẽr, met; pīne,
marīne, bĭrd, pĭn; nōte, mŏve, fọr, atŏm, not; mọọn, book;

178

(Choose only one word out of each group)

z: un″dē-sīgned′, un″rē-sīgned′.
Plus ĭn+d.
Plus vine′d, etc.

IND

Vowel: Ind.
l: lind, Lynd, Ros̩′ȧ-lind.
pl: un-dis′ci-plined.
r: tam′ȧ-rind.
s: ab-scind′ (-sind′), ex-scind′,
rē-scind′.
sk(sc̩): thick′=skinned′ (-skind′),
thin′=skinned′.
w: storm′wind, wind.
Plus in+d.
Plus skin′d, etc.

ING

Vowel: är′gū-ing, ban′dy-ing,
bel′lōw-ing, blär′ney-ing (′ni-),
bụl′ly-ing, bur′y-ing (ber′),
bus̩′y-ing (biz′), c̩an′dy-ing,
c̩ar′ry-ing, c̩on-tin′ū-ing,
dal′ly-ing, dis-hal′lōw-ing,
em-bod′y-ing, em-pit′y-ing,
emp′ty-ing, en′vy-ing,
fan′cy-ing, far′rōw-ing,
flūr′ry-ing, fol′lōw-ing,
fōre-shad′ōw-ing, hal′lōw-ing,
har′rōw-ing, har′ry-ing,
is′sū-ing (ish′ū-), jol′ly-ing,
lā′zy-ing, lob′by-ing,
mar′ry-ing, mŏn̄′key-ing,
nar′rōw-ing, ō-vẽr-shad′ōw-ing,
par′ry-ing, quạr′ry-ing,
quē′ry-ing (kwē′), ral′ly-ing,
res′c̩ū-ing, sal′ly-ing,
shad′ōw-ing, sor′rōw-ing,
tal′ly-ing, tar′ry-ing,
tōad′y-ing, un″dẽr-val′ū-ing,
un-pit′y-ing, val′ū-ing,

vol′ley-ing, wēa′ry-ing,
whin′ny-ing (hwin′),
win′nōw-ing, wŏr′ry-ing.
b: bing, Byng.
br: bring.
ch: Ching.
d: ding, fọr′wård-ing,
gär′länd-ing, haz′ård-ing,
her′åld-ing, jeop′ård-ing (jep′),
plac̩′ård-ing, sc̩af′fōld-ing,
shep′hẽrd-ing (′ẽrd-).
fl: fling.
j: chal′leng-ing, dam′ȧg-ing,
dis-c̩oūr′ȧg-ing, dis-par′ȧg-ing,
en-c̩oūr′ȧg-ing, en-vis̩′ȧg-ing,
Man′ȧg-ing, pil′lȧg-ing,
rav′ȧg-ing, sav′ȧg-ing,
sc̩av′en-ġing, voy′ȧg-ing.
k(c̩): fãir′y king, king,
sēa king, un-king′,
bar′răck-ing, fin′ick-ing,
maf′ē-king, traf′fick-ing.
kl: c̩ling.
l: ap-par′el-ling, ath′el-ing,
bar′rel-ling, bē-dev′il-ing,
bē-pum′mel-ling, bev′el-ling,
c̩an′cel-ling, c̩ar′ŏl-ling,
c̩a′vil-ling, chan′nel-ling,
chis̩′el-ling, chit′tẽr-ling,
c̩udg′el-ling,
dạugh′tẽr-ling (dạu),
dev′il-ling, driv′el-ling,
dū′el-ling, ēast′ẽr-ling,
ē-nam′el-ling, en-tram′mel-ling,
gam′bŏl-ling, grav′el-ling,
grov′el-ling, lā′bel-ling,
lev′el-ling, lī′bel-ling, ling,
mär′shăl-ling, mär′vel-ling,
mod′el-ling, out-rī′văl-ling,
pŏm′mel-ling, quạr′rel-ling,
pan′el-ling, ped′ăl-ling,

(Choose only one word out of each group)

pen'cil-ling, nā'vel-ling,
rev'el-ling, rī'văl-ling,
sniv'el-ling, spī'răl-ling,
sten'cil-ling, tas'sel-ling,
tin'sel-ling, tow'el-ling,
trav'el-ling, tun'nel-ling,
un'dēr-ling, un-ra'vel-ling,
un-rī'văl-ling, wäs'săil-ling.

m: ac̨-c̨us'tŏm-ing, blos'sŏm-ing,
em-boş'ŏm-ing (-booz'),
faTH'ŏm-ing, Ming,
ran'sŏm-ing.

n: ēve'ning, à-ban'dŏn-ing,
ac̨'tion-ing, auc̨'tion-ing,
à-wāk'en-ing, bär'găin-ing,
bē-tō'ken-ing, black'en-ing,
blā'zŏn-ing, broa̧d'en-ing,
bûr'den-ing, c̨an'ŏn-ing,
c̨au'tion-ing,
chāst'en-ing (chās'),
c̨hris'ten-ing (kris'n-),
c̨ŏm-pas'siŏn-ing, därk'en-ing,
dead'en-ing (ded'), des'tin-ing,
dē'tēr'min-ing,
em-blā'zŏn-ing, em-bōl'den-ing,
en-heärt'en-ing, ex-am'in-ing,
fash'ion-ing, fo̧r-tō'ken-ing,
fresh'en-ing, gam'mŏn-ing,
gär'den-ing, glad'den-ing,
hap'pen-ing, här'den-ing,
hās'ten-ing ('n-), heärk'en-ing,
heärt'en-ing, im-aġ'in-ing,
im-priş'ŏn-ing, les'sen-ing,
lis'ten-ing ('n-), līv'en-ing,
mad'den-ing, men'tion-ing,
ō'men-ing, ō'pen-ing,
ō"vēr-bûr'den-ing,
prē-des'tin-ing,
ques'tion-ing ('chun-),
pär'dŏn-ing, pas'sion-ing,
pen'sion-ing, rav'en-ing,

rēa'şŏn-ing, reck'ŏn-ing,
sad'den-ing, sañc̨'tion-ing,
sēa'şŏn-ing, sick'en-ing,
slack'en-ing, smärt'en-ing,
stā'tion-ing, sweet'en-ing,
un-rēa'şŏn-ing, vi'şion-ing,
wän'tŏn-ing, wāk'en-ing,
wēak'en-ing.

p: ping, gal'lŏp-ing,
wäl'lŏp-ing, wŏr'ship-ping.

r: äl'tēr-ing, añ'gēr-ing,
ans'wēr-ing (an'sēr-),
är'mŏur-ing, au'gūr-ing,
badġ'ēr-ing, ban'tēr-ing,
bär'bēr-ing, bär'tēr-ing,
bat'tēr-ing, bē-flat'tēr-ing,
beg'găr-ing, bē-lā'bŏr-ing,
bē-lēa'guēr-ing ('gēr-)
bē-lec̨'tūr-ing, bē-pat'tēr-ing,
bē-pow'dēr-ing, bē-sc̨at'tēr-ing,
bē-slab'bēr-ing, bē-smēar'ing,
bē-spat'tēr-ing, bē-wil'dēr-ing,
bick'ēr-ing, blaTH'ēr-ing,
blis'tēr-ing, blub'bēr-ing,
blun'dēr-ing, blus'tēr-ing,
bōl'stēr-ing, bu̧tch'ēr-ing,
c̨añ'kēr-ing, c̨an'tēr-ing,
c̨ā'pēr-ing, c̨ap'tūr-ing,
chär'tēr-ing, chat'tēr-ing,
cī'phēr-ing, c̨lam'bēr-ing,
c̨lam'ŏr-ing, c̨lat'tēr-ing,
c̨lus'tēr-ing, c̨ock'ēr-ing,
c̨ŏl'ŏr-ing, c̨on'jec̨'tūr-ing,
c̨oñ'quēr-ing ('kēr),
c̨on-sid'ēr-ing, c̨ŏv'er-ing,
c̨ow'ēr-ing, c̨um'bēr-ing,
dē-cī'phēr-ing, dick'ēr-ing,
dis-fā'vŏr-ing,
dis-hon'ŏr-ing (-on'),
dis-pleaş'ūr-ing (-plezh'),
dis-sev'ēr-ing, dow'ēr-ing,

ING

fāte, fär, fåst, fạll, finăl, cãre, at; mēte, prẹy, hẽr, met; pīne,
marïne, bĩrd, pin; nōte, mŏve, fọr, atŏm, not; mọọn, book;

180

(Choose only one word out of each group)

en-am'ŏr-ing, en-çum'bẽr-ing,
en-här'bŏr-ing, en-ring',
en'tẽr-ing, fạl'tẽr-ing,
fā'vŏr-ing,
feaTH'ẽr-ing (feTH'),
fes'tẽr-ing, fil'tẽr-ing,
fiñ'gẽr-ing, flat'tẽr-ing,
flā'vŏr-ing, flick'ẽr-ing,
flit'tẽr-ing, flow'ẽr-ing,
flus'tẽr-ing, flut'tẽr-ing,
fōre-gaTH'ẽr-ing, fũr"THẽr-ing,
gaTH'ẽr-ing, ġes'tūr-ing,
glim'mẽr-ing, glit'tẽr-ing,
glow'ẽr-ing, ham'mẽr-ing,
ham'pẽr-ing, hañ'kẽr-ing,
här'bŏr-ing, hŏv'ẽr-ing,
hū'mŏr-ing, huñ'gẽr-ing,
in-çum'bẽr-ing, in-den'tūr-ing,
jab'bẽr-ing, lā'bŏr-ing,
lac'quẽr-ing ('kẽr-), laTH'ẽr-ing,
leç'tūr-ing, liñ'gẽr-ing,
lit'tẽr-ing, lọng'⸗suf'fẽr-ing,
low'ẽr-ing, lōw'ẽr-ing,
lum'bẽr-ing, man-ū-faç'tūr-ing,
mär'tyr-ing ('tẽr-),
mē-an'dẽr-ing,
meaṣ'ūr-ing (mezh'),
mir'rŏr-ing, mŏTH'ẽr-ing,
mō'tŏr-ing, mūr'dẽr-ing,
mūr'mūr-ing, mus'tẽr-ing,
mut'tẽr-ing, nẹigh'bŏr-ing (nā'),
num'bẽr-ing, of'fẽr-ing,
ọr'dẽr-ing, out-num'bẽr-ing,
ō"vẽr-mȧst'ẽr-ing,
ō"vẽr-pow'ẽr-ing,
ō"vẽr-tow'ẽr-ing, pạl'tẽr-ing,
pam'pẽr-ing, pan'dẽr-ing,
pat'tẽr-ing, pep'pẽr-ing,
pẽr'jūr-ing, pes'tẽr-ing,
pil'fẽr-ing, plȧs'tẽr-ing,
pleaṣ'ūr-ing (plezh'),

plun'dẽr-ing, pon'dẽr-ing,
pot'tẽr-ing, pow'dẽr-ing,
pros'pẽr-ing, put'tẽr-ing,
quar'tẽr-ing, quā'vẽr-ing,
qui'vẽr-ing, rap'tūr-ing,
rē-çŏv'ẽr-ing, rē-mem'bẽr-ing,
ren'dẽr-ing, ring, roys'tẽr-ing,
rub'bẽr-ing, rup'tūr-ing,
sạun'tẽr-ing, sā'vŏr-ing,
sçam'pẽr-ing, sçat'tẽr-ing,
sēal ring, sev'ẽr-ing,
shat'tẽr-ing, shim'mẽr-ing,
shiv'ẽr-ing, shōul'dẽr-ing,
show'ẽr-ing, shud'dẽr-ing,
sig'net ring, sil'vẽr-ing,
sim'mẽr-ing, sim'pẽr-ing,
sis'tẽr-ing, slan'dẽr-ing,
slạugh'tẽr-ing (slạu'),
slob'bẽr-ing, slum'bẽr-ing,
smat'tẽr-ing, smōl'dẽr-ing,
spat'tẽr-ing, splut'tẽr-ing,
stam'mẽr-ing, stut'tẽr-ing,
suf'fẽr-ing, sụg'ăr-ing (shụg'),
sum'mẽr-ing, sun'dẽr-ing,
tam'pẽr-ing, tā'pẽr-ing,
tem'pẽr-ing, thun'dẽr-ing,
tit'tẽr-ing, tot'tẽr-ing,
tow'ẽr-ing, un-fạl'tẽr-ing,
un-flat'tẽr-ing, un-mūr'mūr-ing,
un-rē-mem'bẽr-ing,
un-slum'bẽr-ing,
un-wän'dẽr-ing, un-wā'vẽr-ing,
up-hōl'stẽr-ing, ut'tẽr-ing,
vā'pŏr-ing, ven'tūr-ing,
wän'dẽr-ing, wạ'tẽr-ing,
wā'vẽr-ing,
weaTH'ẽr-ing (weTH'),
wes'tẽr-ing,
whim'pẽr-ing (hwim'),
whis'pẽr-ing (hwis'),
win'tẽr-ing, wŏn'dẽr-ing.

(Choose only one word out of each group)

s: bal'ănc-ing, bē-sing', but'tress-ing, c̱an'văs-sing, C̱hrist'măs-ing (kris'), c̱on-vey'ănc-ing, em-bar'răss-ing, fō'c̱us-sing, har'ăss-ing, men'ăc-ing, out-bal'ănc-ing, ō"vĕr-bal'ănc-ing, prac̱'tis-ing, pro'mis-ing, pūr'pŏs-ing, sing, Synge (sing), un-pro'mis-ing, wit'ness-ing.

sh: ac̱-c̱ŏm'plish-ing, ad-mon'ish-ing, à-ston'ish-ing, ban'ish-ing, blan'dish-ing, blem'ish-ing, bran'dish-ing, būr'nish-ing, di-min'ish-ing, dis"es-tab'lish-ing, dis-tin̄'guish-ing ('gwish-) em-bel'lish-ing, en-ra'vish-ing, es-tab'lish-ing, fam'ish-ing, fin'ish-ing, floūr'ish-ing, fūr'nish-ing, gär'nish-ing, lan̄'guish-ing ('gwish-), lav'ish-ing, noūr'ish-ing, per'ish-ing, pol'ish-ing, pub'lish-ing, pun'ish-ing, ra'vish-ing, rub'bish-ing, tär'nish-ing, un-per'ish-ing, van'ish-ing, van̄'quish-ing ('kwish-), vär'nish-ing.

sl: sling, un-sling'.

spr: dāy spring, drīv'ing spring, līfe spring, māin'spring, spring, wätch spring, weep'ing sprīng.

st: af-fo̱r'est-ing, bal'lăst-ing, break'făst-ing (brek'), här'vest-ing, sting.

str: heärt'string, string, un-string'.

sw: fu̱ll swing, swing.

t: ac̱-c̱red'it-ing, at-trib'ūt-ing, au̱'dit-ing, blan̄'ket-ing, bon'net-ing, buf'fet-ing, c̱är'pet-ing, c̱on-trib'ūt-ing, c̱ŏv'et-ing, c̱red'it-ing, dī'et-ing, dis-c̱red'it-ing, dis-pir'it-ing, dis-quī'et-ing, dis-trib'ūt-ing, ex-hib'it-ing (-ib'), fo̱r'feit-ing ('fit-), in-hab'it-ing, in-her'it-ing, in-spir'it-ing, jun̄'ket-ing, lim'it-ing, mär'ket-ing, mer'it-ing, pat'ent-ing, prō-hib'it-ing, quī'et-ing, rack'et-ing, riv'et-ing, spir'it-ing, ting, un-mer'it-ing, vel'vet-ing, vis̱'it-ing.

th: an'y-thing (en'), eve'ry-thing (ev'), thing.

w: bē-wing', out-wing', sēa wing, shuf'fle-wing, un'dēr-wing, wing.

INGD

d: dinged.
w: ēa'gle winged, un-winged', winged.
Plus ing+d.

INGK

Vowel: in̄k.
bl: blin̄k, snōw blin̄k.
br: brin̄k.
ch: chin̄k.
d: Din̄k, Hum'pēr-din̄ck, rin̄k'y=din̄k.
dr: drin̄k.
f: Fin̄ck, Fin̄k, fin̄k.
g: gin̄k.
j: jin̄k.
k(c̱): kin̄k.

(Choose only one word out of each group)

kl: çlink.

l: bob'ō-liñk, en-liñk',
in-tẽr-liñk', liñk, un-liñk'.

m: miñk.

p: Dept'fŏrd piñk,
mead'ōw piñk (med'), piñk,
sēa piñk.

pl: pliñk.

pr: priñk.

r: riñk.

s: ciñque (siñk), çoun'tẽr-siñk,
siñk.

shr: shriñk.

sk(sç): skiñk.

sl: sliñk.

sp: spiñk.

st: stiñk.

t: tiñk.

th: be-thiñk', fōre-thiñk'*,
thiñk, un-thiñk'.

tr: triñk.

tw: twiñk.

w: hood'wiñk, tid'dly-wiñk,
wiñk.

z: ziñç.

INGKS

j: Çap'tăin Jiñks,
hīgh jiñks (hī), jiñx.

l: lyñx.

m: miñx.

sf: sphiñx.

th: mē-thiñks'.

w: tid'dle-dy-wiñks.

Plus ingk+s.

Plus drink's, etc.

INGKT

s: prō-ciñçt'*, suç-ciñçt'.

st: in'stiñçt.

t: dis-tiñçt', ex-tiñçt',

in"dis-tiñçt', tiñçt.

Plus ingk+d

INGZ

n: a-wāk'en-ings.

st: lēad'ing strings.

Plus ing+s.

Plus king's, etc.

INJ

Vowel: Inġe.

b: binġe.

d: dinġe.

fr: bē-fringe', fringe,
in-fringe'.

h: hinġe, un-hinġe'.

kr: çrinġe.

p: im-pinġe'.

r: syr-inġe'.

s: sinġe.

skr(sçr): sçrinġe.

spr: sprinġe.

str: çon-stringe', pẽr-stringe'.

sw: swinġe.

t: tinġe.

tw: twinġe.

INJD

s: sinġed, un-sinġed'.

Plus inj+d.

INS

Vowel: Ince.

bl: blintz.

ch: chintz.

kw(qu): quince.

m: mince.

pr: mẽr'chănt prince, prince,
un-prince'.

r: rinse.

s: since.

(Choose only one word out of each group)

v: çon-vince', ē-vince', Vince.
w: wince.
Cf. int+s.

INSK

m: Minsk.
p: Pinsk.
v: Dvinsk.

ĪNT

h: à-hīnt', bē-hīnt'.
p: çùck'ọọ pīnt, pīnt.

INT

Vowel: in't.
d: dint.
fl: flint.
gl: glint.
h: hint.
j: sep-tū'à-ġint.
kw(qu): quint.
l: lint.
m: çal'à-mint, họrse'mint, mint, pep'pẽr-mint, sō'dà-mint, spēar'mint.
pr: foot'print, im'print, mis'print, print, rē'print.
skw(squ): à-squint', squint.
spl: splint.
spr: sprint.
st: stint.
t: a'quà-tint, mez'zō-tint (medz'), tint.
v: vint.

ĪNTH

n: nīnth.
Plus pine'th*, etc.

INTH

b: ter'ē-binth.
pl: plinth.
r: la'by-rinth.

s: çol'ō-cynth, hȳ'à-cinth.
Plus win'th*, etc.

ĪNTZ

h: Heīntz.
p: pīntș.
Plus pint's, etc.

INTS

See int+s.
Cf. ins.
Plus stint's, etc.

ĪNZ

n: Ap'en-nīneș, bāse'bạll nīneș, nīneș.
t: Tȳneș.
Plus īn+s.
Plus wine's, etc.

INZ

k(ç): odș bod'i-kinș.
sh: wiTH'ẽr-shins.
w: winze.
Plus in+s.
Plus shin's, etc.

ĪP

gr: grīpe.
h: hȳpe.
k(ç): kīpe.
p: bag'pīpe, blōw'pīpe. họrn'pīpe, In'di-ăn pīpe, pīpe, pitch'pīpe. wind'pīpe.
r: dead rīpe (ded), ō″vẽr-rīpe', rīpe, un-rīpe'.
sn: gut'tẽr-snīpe, snīpe.
st: stīpe.
str: strīpe.
sw: swīpe.
t: an'ti-tȳpe, är'çhē-tȳpe, ạu'tō-type,

(Choose only one word out of each group)

då-guerre'ō-tȳpe (-ger'),
ē-leç'trō-tȳpe, gråph'ō-tȳpe,
hē'li-ō-tȳpe, līn'ō-tȳpe,
log'ō-tȳpe, mon'ō-tȳpe,
prō'tō-tȳpe, stē'rē-ō-tȳpe,
tel'ē-tȳpe, tin'tȳpe, tȳpe.
tr: trīpe.
w: wīpe.

IP

b: bip.
ch: chip.
d: dip.
dr: drip.
fl: flip, sher'ry flip.
gr: grip, grippe.
h: hip, hyp.
hw: họrse'whip, whip.
j: ġyp.
k(ç): kip.
kl: çlip.
kw(qu): ē-quip', quip.
l: håre'lip, lip, un'dẽr-lip.
n: nip.
p: ap'ple pip, pĩp.
r: rip, un-rip'.
s: sip.
sh: aç-quāin'tănce-ship,
ad-min'is-trā″tŏr-ship,
ā'ġent-ship, ạl'dẽr-măn-ship,
ap-pren'tice-ship, är'çhŏn-ship,
bā'by-ship, bach'ē-lŏr-ship,
bat'tle-ship, çär'di-năl-ship,
cen'sŏr-ship, chāir'măn-ship,
cham'pi-ŏn-ship,
chan'cel-lŏr-ship,
chap'lain-ship ('lin-),
chiēf'tăin-ship,
chũrch'măn-ship,
chũrch mem'bẽr-ship,
cit'i-zen-ship, çŏl-leç'tŏr-ship,

çŏm-man'dẽr-ship,
çŏm-pan'ion-ship, çon'sọrt-ship,
çon'sul-ship, çon-trōl'lẽr-ship,
çō-pärt'nẽr-ship, çōurt'ship,
çŏuş'in-ship, çrafts'măn-ship,
çrē-ā'tŏr-ship, dēa'çŏn-ship,
dē'mŏn-ship,
draughts'măn-ship (dråfts'),
el'dẽr-ship, ē-leç'tŏr-ship,
em'pẽr-ŏr-ship,
en'sīgn-ship ('sīn),
fär'mẽr-ship, fạ″THẽr-ship,
fel'lōw-ship, fīre'ship,
ġen'ẽr-ăl-ship,
good'₌fel'lōw-ship,
gŏv'ẽrn-ŏr-ship,
guärd'i-ăn-ship (gärd'),
họrse'măn-ship,
hunts'măn-ship,
im-pos'tẽr-ship, in-speç'tŏr-ship,
jock'ey-ship, jus'tice-ship,
lā'dy-ship, lēad'ẽr-ship,
leç'tūre-ship, leġ″is-lā'tŏr-ship,
lĭ-brā'ri-ăn-ship,
līght'ship (līt'), lọrd'ship,
märks'măn-ship, märsh'ăl-ship,
måst'ẽr-ship, mem'bẽr-ship,
Mes-sī'ăh-ship,
neigh'bŏr-ship (nā'),
nov'ice-ship, ōwn'ẽr-ship,
pāint'ẽr-ship, pärt'nẽr-ship,
pas'tŏr-ship, pen'măn-ship,
praē'tŏr-ship, prēach'ẽr-ship,
prel'ăte-ship, prō-bā'tion-ship,
prō-fes'sŏr-ship,
prō-prī'e-tŏr-ship, ques'tŏr-ship,
rä'jăh-ship, rānġ'ẽr-ship,
rēad'ẽr-ship, rē-çọrd'ẽr-ship,
reç'tŏr-ship, rē'ġent-ship,
rē-lā'tion-ship, rē-ship',
sçhol'ăr-ship, sēa'măn-ship,

(Choose only one word out of each group)

sec̲'rē-tā-ry-ship, sen'a̲-tŏr-ship,
sex'tŏn-ship, sher'iff-ship, ship,
sīz'ăr-ship, spēak'ĕr-ship,
spon'sŏr-ship, stātes'măn-ship,
stew'ărd-ship, stū'dent-ship,
sul'tăn-ship,
sūre'ty-ship (shūr'),
sūr-vīv'ŏr-ship,
swōrds̲'măn-ship (sōrdz'),
trāin'ing ship, trans-ship',
treas̲'ūre ship (trezh'),
um'pīre-ship, un-ship',
vīce'roy-ship, vīr-tū-ō'sō-ship,
wa̲r'den-ship, wa̲r'ship,
wŏrk'măn-ship,
wrañ'glĕr-ship (rang').
sk(sc̲): skip.
skr(sc̲r): sc̲rip.
sl: land'slip, slip, un'dĕr-slip.
sn: snip.
str: out-strip', strip,
weaTH'ĕr-strip (weTH').
t: tip.
tr: a̲-trip', ō-vĕr-trip'*,
pleas̲'ūre trip (plezh'), trip.
y: yip.
z: zip.

ĪPS

See īp+s.
Plus pipe's, etc.

IPS

f: Phipps.
kl: ē-c̲lipse'.
l: A̲-poc̲'a̲-lypse, el-lipse'.
Plus ip+s.
Plus hip's, etc.

IPST

ch: chip'st*.
d: dip'st*.
gr: grip'st*.

hw: whip'st*.
kl: c̲lip'st*, ē-c̲lipsed',
un"ē-c̲lipsed'.
kw(qu): ē-quip'st'*.
r: rip'st*.
s: sip'st*.
sh: ship'st*.
sk(sc̲): skip'st*.
sl: slip'st*.
str: strip'st*.
t: tip'st*.
tr: trip'st*.

ĪPT

gr: grīped, huñ'gĕr=grīped.
str: pri's̲ŏn=strīped, strīped.
Plus īp+d.

IPT

kr: c̲rypt.
l: a̲-poc̲'a̲-lypt.
n: frost'=nipped.
skr(sc̲r): man'ū-sc̲ript, sc̲ript,
sub'sc̲ript, sū'pĕr-sc̲ript.
t: tipt.
Plus ip+d.

ĪR

Vowel: Eīre (īr), īre.
b: bȳre.
br: brīar (brīr), brīer (brīr).
d: dīre.
f: a̲-fīre', bēa'c̲ŏn fīre,
death fīre (deth), fīre,
gal'ley fīre ('li), hell'=fīre,
St. John's̲ fīre, sig'năl fīre,
spit'fīre, swämp fīre, wīld'fīre.
fl: flȳer (flīr).
fr: frīar (frīr).
gw: Mc̲-Guīre' (-gwīr'),
Mol'ly Ma̲-guīre'.
h: hīre.
j: ġȳre.

ĪRD
IS

fāte, fär, fȧst, fạll, finăl, cāre, at; mēte, prẹy, hẽr, met; pīne,
marïne, bĩrd, pin; nōte, mŏve, fọr, atŏm, not; mọọn, book;

186

(Choose only one word out of each group)

kw(qu): aç-quīre', choïr (kwĩr),
en-quīre', in-quīre', quīre,
rē-quīre'.

l: līar (lĩr), lȳre.

m: ad-mīre', bē-mīre',
Meȳer (mĩr), mīre, Mȳer,
Un'tẽr-mȳẽr.

p: pȳre.

pl: plīer (plĩr).

pr: prīor (prĩr).

s: grand'sīre, sīre.

sh: shīre.

skw(squ): es'quīre, squīre,
un-squīre'.

sp: as-pīre', çon-spīre', ex-pīre',
in-spīre', pẽr-spīre', rē-spīre',
spīre, sus-pīre', trans-pīre'.

sw: swīre*.

t: at-tīre', en-tīre', flat tīre,
Mç'In-tȳre (mak'), ō-vẽr-tīre',
rē-tīre', tīre, Tȳr, tȳre.

v: vīre.

w: wīre.

z: dē-ṣīre'.

Cf. ī'ũr.

m: mīce.

n: gneïss (nīs), nīce, ō"vẽr-nīce'.

pr: prīce.

r: rīce.

s: çon-cīse', prē-cīse', sīce, sȳce.

sl: slīce.

sp: ạll'spīce, bē-spīce', spīce.

spl: splīce.

t: en-tīce', tīce.

thr: thrīce.

tr: trīce.

tw: twīce.

v: ad-vīce', de-vīce', ẹ'del-weïss,
vīce.

w: Weïss.

z: Zeïss.

ĪRD

kw(qu): un"aç-quīred'.

sp: un"ex-pīred', un"in-spīred'.

z: un"dē-sīred'.

Plus īr+d.

Plus fire'd, etc.

ĪS

Vowel: çam'phŏr īce, īce.

b: bīce.

br: Brīce, Brȳce.

d: dīce, par'ȧ-dīse.

f: fīce, saç'ri-fīce, suf'fīce'.

gr: grīce.

l: beg'găr'ṣ līce, līce.

IS

b: a-byss', bis.

bl: bliss.

d: çow'ãrd-ice, Dis,
pre'jù-dice.

f: är'ti-fice, ben'e-fice,
ed'i-fice, ọr'i-fice.

fr: den'ti-frice.

gr: am'bẽr-gris, vẽr'di-gris.

h: dē-hisce' (-his'), hiss.

k(ç): kiss.

kw(qu): çuisse (kwis).

l: ȧ-çrop'ō-lis, chrys'ȧ-lis,
fọrt'ȧ-lice, Liss, mē-trop'ō-lis,
M'liss', nē-çrop'ō-lis.

m: ȧ-miss', dis-miss', miss,
rē-miss', Sal'ȧ-mis.

p: piss, prec'i-pice.

r: av'ȧ-rice, liq'uō-rice (lik'ō-),
sū'ĭ ġen'ẽr-is.

s: ab"i-ō-ġen'e-sis,
ad"i-pō-ġen'e-sis, ȧ-nab'ȧ-sis,
ȧ-nal'y-sis, an-tith'e-sis,
ȧ-pher'e-sis, aph'e-sis,
bī-ō-ġen'e-sis, dī-aēr'e-sis,

(Choose only one word out of each group)

dī-al′y-sis, dī-ath′e-sis,
eç″tō-ġen′e-sis,
el″e-phan-tī′a̱-sis, em′pha̱-sis,
ġen′e-sis, hȳ-pos′ta̱-sis,
hȳ-poth′e-sis, mē-tab′a̱-sis,
met-a̱-mo̱r′phō-sis, me-tast′a̱-sis,
me-tath′e-sis, nem′e-sis,
pa̱-ral′y-sis, pa̱-ren′the-sis,
par-ē′sis, pe-riph′ra̱-sis, sis,
siss, syn′the-sis.
st: är′mi-stice.
sw: Swiss.
t: çlem′a̱-tis.
TH: THis.
tr: Bē′a̱-trice, ci′ça̱-trice,
çock′a̱-trice.
v: vis.
w: wis*, y-wis′*.

ISH

Vowel: bā′by-ish,
Çock′ney-ish (′ni-), dow′dy-ish.
b: Bysshe.
d: chāf′ing dish, dish.
f: ān′ġel-fish, çut′tle-fish,
dev′il-fish, fish, flȳ′ing fish,
pī′lŏt fish.
g: Gish.
l: dev′il-ish.
n: cnish (nish), Mç-Nish′,
hēa″THen-ish, kit′ten-ish,
mam′mŏn-ish, vix′en-ish,
wo′mă̱n-ish (woo′).
p: pish.
r: bit′tēr-ish, çle′vēr-ish,
fē′vēr-ish, ġib′bēr-ish,
im-pov′ēr-ish, lick′ēr-ish,
ō′gre-ish (′ġer-), quāk′ēr-ish,
tī′ġer-ish, vā′pŏr-ish,
vī′pēr-ish, vul′tūr-ish,
wa̱′tēr-ish.

sh: shish.
skw(squ): squish.
sl: slish.
sw: swish.
t: tish.
w: wish, un-wish′, wil′lōw-ish,
yel′lōw-ish, etc.

ISK

b: bisque.
br: brisk.
d: disç, disk.
f: fisç, Fiske.
fr: frisk.
hw: whisk.
l: bas′i-lisk, ob′e-lisk,
od′a̱-lisque.
r: as′tēr-isk, risk, tam′a̱-risk.
t: tisk.

ISP

hw: whisp.
kr: çrisp, en-çrisp′*.
l: lisp.
w: wisp.

ĪST

d: em-pa̱′ra̱-dīsed.
kr: an′ti-çhrīst, Çhrīst.
l: bē-līced′, līced.
t: en-tīced′.
tr: trȳst.
Plus īs+d.

IST

Vowel: ā′thē-ist, ça̱s′ū-ist,
ē′gō-ist, es′sāy-ist, eū′phū-ist,
Hē′bra̱-ist, Ju̱′da̱-ist, lob′by-ist,
sō′lō-ist, va′çū-ist.
b: Ar′a̱-bist.
br: ē-quil′i-brist.
d: bal′lă̱d-ist, çhī-rop′ō-dist,
mel′ō-dist, meth′ō-dist,

IST

fāte, fär, fȧst, fạll, fĭnăl, cāre, at; mēte, prĕy, hẽr, met; pīne,
marïne, bĭrd, pĭn; nōte, mŏve, fọr, atŏm, not; mọọn, book;

188

(Choose only one word out of each group)

prej'ū-diced,
psälm'ō-dist (säm'),
rhap'sō-dist (rap'), syn'ŏd-ist,
thren'ō-dist.

f: ben'e-ficed, çhī-rog'rȧ-phist,
fist, ġym-nos'ō-phist, pa'ci-fist,
phil-os'ō-phist, phō-tog'rȧ-phist,
steg-an-og'rȧ-phist,
sten-og'rȧ-phist, tel-eg'rȧ-phist,
thē-os'ō-phist, top-og'rȧ-phist,
tȳ-pog'rȧ-phist.

fr: frist*.

gl: glist*.

gr: grist.

h: hissed, hist.

hw: whist.

j: ā-ẽr-ol'ō-ġist, ȧ-ġist',
an-al'ō-ġist, an-thrō-pol'ō-ġist,
ȧ-pol'ō-ġist, är-çhaē-ol'ō-ġist,
bī-ol'ō-ġist, çam-păn-ol'ō-ġist,
çhrō-nol'ō-ġist, çon-chol'ō-ġist,
dē-mŏn-ol'ō-ġist, dī-al'ō-ġist,
eç-çlē"ṣi-ol'ō-ġist,
ē-leç"trō-bī-ol'ō-ġist, el'e-ġist,
en-tō-mol'ō-ġist, et-y-mol'ō-ġist,
eū'lō-ġist, fos-sil'ō-ġist,
ġen-ē-al'ō-ġist, ġē-ol'ō-ġist,
ġist, ġyn-e-çol'ō-ġist,
lith-ol'ō-ġist, mär-tyr-ol'ō-ġist,
mē"tē-ŏr-ol'ō-ġist,
min-ẽr-al'ō-ġist, my-thol'ō-ġist,
ne-çrol'ō-ġist, nē-ol'ō-ġist,
on-tol'ō-ġist, ọr-ni-thol'ō-ġist,
pȧ-thol'ō-ġist, pē-nol'ō-ġist,
pe-trol'ō-ġist,
phär-mȧ-çol'ō-ġist,
phi-lol'ō-ġist, phrē-nol'ō-ġist,
phyṣ-i-ol'ō-ġist,
pneū-mȧ-tol'ō-ġist (nū-),
psȳ-çhol'ō-ġist (sī-),
seïs-mol'ō-ġist, sō-ci-ol'ō-ġist,

stra'te-ġist, suf'frȧ-ġist,
tạu-tol'ō-ġist, teçh-nol'ō-ġist,
tel-ē-ol'ō-ġist, thē-ol'ō-ġist,
tox-i-çol'ō-ġist, zō-ol'ō-ġist.

k(ç): an'är-çhist, bē-kissed',
çat'e-çhrist, kissed, un-kissed'.

kw(qu): çol'lō-quist,
ven-tril'ō-quist.

l: ag-ri'çō-list,
ag-ri-çul'tūr-ăl-ist, an'ȧ-lyst,
an-i-mal'çū-list, an'nȧ-list,
an'nū-ăl-ist, bib-li-o'phil-ist,
bib-li-op'ō-list, bī'cyç-list,
bī-met'ăl-list, çab'ȧ-list,
çap'i-tăl-ist, cen'trăl-ist,
çhō'răl-ist, çlas'si-çăl-ist,
çon-grē-gā'tion-ăl-ist,
çon-sti-tū'tion-ăl-ist,
çon-trō-vẽr'si-ăl-ist, daç'tyl-ist,
dē-vō'tion-ăl-ist, dī'ăl-ist,
dū'ăl-ist, dū'el-list,
ed-ū-çā'tion-ăl-ist, ē-nam'el-ist,
en-list', ē-tẽr'năl-ist,
ē-van'ġel-ist,
ex-per-i-men'tăl-ist,
ex-tẽr'năl-ist, fab'ū-list,
fā'tăl-ist, fed'ẽr-ăl-ist,
feū'dăl-ist, fī-nan'ciăl-ist,
fọrm'ăl-ist, fos'sil-ist,
fū-nam'bū-list, fū'til-ist,
glā'ciăl-ist, hẽrb'ăl-ist,
hȳ-pẽr'bō-list, ī-dē'ăl-ist,
im-mȧ-tē'ri-ăl-ist,
im-mọr'tăl-ist, im-pē'ri-ăl-ist,
in-strủ-men'tăl-ist,
in-tel-leç'tū-ăl-ist,
in-tẽr-na'tion-ăl-ist, joūr-năl-ist,
lib'ẽr-ăl-ist, list, lit'ẽr-ăl-ist,
loy'ăl-ist, mȧ-tē'ri-ăl-ist,
med'ăl-list, me-mō'ri-ăl-ist,
met'ăl-ist, min-is-tē'ri-ăl-ist,

(Choose only one word out of each group)

mō-nop′ō-list,　mo̯r′ăl-ist,
na′tion-ăl-ist,　na′tūr-ăl-ist,
nī′hil-ist,　nom′i-năl-ist,
nov′el-ist,　oᴄ′ū-list,
ō-ri-en′tăl-ist,　phi-lat′e-list,
plu̇′răl-ist,　prō-vēr′bi-ăl-ist,
prō-vin′ciăl-ist,
psȳ-ᴄhō-an′à-lyst (sī-),
pū′ġi-list,　ra′tion-ăl-ist,
rē′ăl-ist,　rē-vī′văl-ist,
rit′ū-ăl-ist,　roy′ăl-ist,
rū′răl-ist,　scī′ō-list (sī′),
sᴄrip′tūr-ăl-ist,　sen-sā′tion-ăl-ist,
sen′sū-ăl-ist,　sen-ti-men′tăl-ist,
sex′ū-ăl-ist,　sib′yl-list,
sō′ciăl-ist,　som-nam′bū-list,
spe′ciăl-ist,　spir′i-tū-ăl-ist,
sym′bō-list,　tex′tū-ăl-ist,
trà-di′tion-ăl-ist,
trans-cen-den′tăl-ist,
ū-ni-vēr′săl-ist,　vēr′băl-ist,
vī′ō-list,　vī′tăl-ist,
vō-ᴄab′ū-list,　vō′ᴄăl-ist,
zō-oph′i-list.

m: à-ᴄad′e-mist,　a′ġà-mist*,
al′ᴄhe-mist,　an-at′ō-mist,
an′i-mist,　an-tin′ō-mist,
at′ŏm-ist,　bē-mist′,　big′à-mist,
deū-tēr-og′à-mist,　dis-missed′.
ē-ᴄon′ō-mist,　e-pit′ō-mist,
lē-ġit′i-mist,　mis-og′à-mist,
missed,　mist,　mon-og′à-mist,
op′ti-mist,　pes′si-mist,
phlē-bot′ō-mist,
phyṣ-i-og′nō-mist,　pō-lyg′à-mist,
sy-non′y-mist,　un-missed′,
vol′ūm-ist,　zō-ot′ō-mist.

n: ab-ō-li′tion-ist,
aᴄ-ᴄŏm′pà-nist,　ag′ō-nist,
ā′lien-ist (′lyen-),　an-tag′ō-nist,
bot′à-nist,　Boŭr′bŏn-ist,

Bräh′măn-ist,　Ċal′vin-ist,
ᴄan′ŏn-ist,　cīr-ᴄum-lō-ᴄū′tion-ist,
ᴄō-à-li′tion-ist,　ᴄol′ō-nist,
Ċom′mū-nist,
Ċon-fū′ciŏn-ist (′shun-).
ᴄon-sti-tū′tion-ist,
ᴄŏn-struᴄ′tion-ist,
ᴄon-to̯r′tion-ist,
ᴄon-vēr-sā′tion-ist,
ᴄo̯r-rup′tion-ist,　ᴄrē-mā′tion-ist,
Där′win-ist,　dē-ġen-ēr-ā′tion-ist,
dē′mŏn-ist,　des′tin-ist,
dē-struᴄ′tion-ist,　dē-vō′tion-ist,
ed-ū-ᴄā′tion-ist,　el-ō-ᴄū′tion-ist,
eū-dē′mŏn-ist,　ev-ō-lū′tion-ist,
ex-ᴄūr′ṣion-ist,　fiᴄ′tion-ist,
gal′văn-ist,　här′mō-nist,
hēd′ŏn-ist,　Hel′len-ist,
hū′măn-ist,　il-lū′ṣion-ist,
im-i-tā′tion-ist,　im-mēr′ṣion-ist,
in-spi-rā′tion-ist,
in-sūr′reᴄ-tion-ist,　Lat′in-ist,
Mal-thū′ṣian-ist (′zhun-),
mam′mŏn-ist,　meᴄh′à-nist,
mis-cel′là-nist,　mis-o′ġy-nist,
mod′ērn-ist,　Nà-pō′lē-ŏn-ist,
Nē-ō-plā′tō-nist,
ob-struᴄ′tion-ist,
ō-pin′iŏn-ist (′yun-),
op-po̯r-tū′nist,　op-pō-ṣi′tion-ist,
o̯r′găn-ist,　pan-Hel′len-ist,
pas′sion-ist,
pēr-feᴄ′tion-ist,　phē-nom′ē-nist,
Phil-hel′len-ist,　pi-an′ist,
plā′tō-nist,
prē-ci′ṣion-ist,　prō-gres′sion-ist,
prō-hib-i′tion-ist,　prō-tag′ō-nist,
prō-teᴄ′tion-ist,　pȳ′thŏn-ist,
rab′bin-ist,　rē-liġ′iŏn-ist,
rē-pū-di-ā′tion-ist,
reṣ-ūr-reᴄ′tion-ist,

(Choose only one word out of each group)

rev-ō-lū′tion-ist, Rō′măn-ist,
sā′tăn-ist,
sē-ces′sion-ist, So̠r′bŏn-nist,
tel′e-phōn-ist, tō-ba̠c̠′c̠ō-nist,
trādes̠-ū′niŏn-ist (′nyun-),
trȧ-di′tion-ist,
ū′niŏn-ist (′nyun-), va̠c̠′cin-ist,
Vat′ĭ-c̠ăn-ist, vi′s̠ion-ist.

p: mis-an′thrō-pist,
phil-an′thrō-pist, syn′c̠ō-pist,
thē″ō-phil-an′thrō-pist.

r: ag-ri-c̠ul′tūr-ist, al′lē-gō-rist,
am′ō-rist, aph′ŏ-rist,
ā′pi-ȧ-rist, är-bŏr-c̠ul′tūr-ist,
är′bŏr-ist, är-til′lē-rist,
a̠u′gū-rist, c̠ŏl′ŏr-ist,
c̠ul′tūr-ist, Eū′chȧ-rist,
flō-ri-c̠ul′tūr-ist,
ho̠r-ti-c̠ul′tūr-ist, hū′mŏr-ist,
man′nēr-ist, mes̠′mēr-ist,
mō′tŏr-ist, plā′gi-ȧ-rist,
pleas̠′ūr-ist (plezh′), pos′tūr-ist,
rap′tūr-ist, rig′ŏr-ist, sat′ĭ-rist,
sc̠rip′tūr-ist, sec̠′ū-lȧr-ist,
ter′rŏr-ist, thē′ō-rist,
vō′tȧ-rist, wrist (rist).

s: as-sist′, bib′li-cist, cist,
c̠las′si-cist, c̠on-sist′, cyst,
em-pir′ĭ-cist, eth′ĭ-cist,
ex′o̠r-cist, in-sist′, pēr-sist′,
pub′li-cist, phär′mȧ-cist,
phy′s̠i-cist, rō-man′ti-cist,
sissed (sist), sist, sub-sist′,
syn′thē-sist, tech′ni-cist.

sh: sc̠hist (shist).

t: ab-sō-lū′tist,
an-ȧ-gram′mȧ-tist, des′pŏ-tist,
di-plō′mȧ-tist, dog′mȧ-tist,
drä′mȧ-tist, ē′gō-tist,
ē-nig′mȧ-tist, ep-i-gram′mȧ-tist,
hyp′nō-tist, mag′ne-tist,

mel-ō-drä′mȧ-tist, nep′ō-tist,
nū-mis̠′mȧ-tist, pī′e-tist,
prag′mȧ-tist, prel′ȧ-tist,
quī′e-tist, sc̠hē′mȧ-tist,
scī′en-tist (sī′), syñ′c̠rē-tist,
zeal′ŏt-ist (zel′).

th: am′ē-thyst, al-lop′ȧ-thist,
an-ti′pȧ-thist, ap′ȧ-thist,
sym′pȧ-thist.

tr: trist*, tryst.

tw: ȧ-twist′, en-twist′,
in″tēr-twist′, twist, un-twist′.

v: Bol′shē-vist, Men′shē-vist,
po̠s̠′i-tiv-ist, sub-jec̠′tiv-ist.

w: un-wist′*, wist*.

z: cō″ex-ist′, dē-s̠ist′, ex-ist′,
prē″ex-ist′, rē-s̠ist′, xyst (zist).

Plus is + d.

ĪT

Vowel: Pū′sey-īte, Trot′sky-īte.

b: bīght (bīt), bīte, Jac̠′ō-bīte,
Mō′ăb-īte, Rech′ȧ-bīte.

bl: blīght.

br: brīght.

d: bē-dīght′*, dīght*, er′u-dīte,
ex′pē-dīte, in-dīct′ (-dīt′),
in-dīte′, ō-vēr-dīght′*,
rec̠′ŏn-dīte, trog′lō-dy̆te,
un-dīght′*.

dw: Dwīght.

f: fīght, Fīte, nē′ō-phy̆te,
sēa fīght, zō′ō-phy̆te.

fl: flīght.

fr: af-frīght′, frīght,
stāge frīght.

h: bē-hīght′*, Fär′en-heĭt,
heĭght (hīt), hīght*.

hw: snōw′-whīte′, whīte.

k(c̠): box kīte, kīte,
mal′ȧ-c̠hīte.

191

ūse, ḅull, brúte, tŭrn, up; crȳ, myth; ̣cat, ma̧chine, **ace,**
church, ̧chord; ḡem, aḥger, (Fr.) boṅ, ạ̧; THis, thin; ạure

IT

(Choose only one word out of each group)

kl: het′ēr-ō-̧clīte.
kw(qu): quīte, rē-quīte′.
l: a̧c′ō-lȳte, a̧c-tin′ō-lȳte,
    ā-ēr′ō-līte, ȧ-līght′, Bā′ăl-īte,
    ̧Cär′mē-līte, ̧chrys′ō-līte,
    ̧cọs-mop′ō-līte, ̧crys′tăl-līte,
    dāy′līght, dead līght (ded),
    dē-līght′, ē-lȩc′trō-lȳte,
    en-tom′ō-līte, graph′ō-līte,
    här′bŏr līght, head′līght (hed′),
    i̧ch′nō-līte, im″pō-līte′,
    Ish′mā-el-īte, Is′lăm-īte,
    Is′rā-el-īte, līght, moọn′līght,
    pō-līte′, prē=Raph′ā-el-īte,
    pros′ē-lȳte, sat′el-līte,
    sēa līght, sid′ēr-ō-līte,
    sig′năl līght, stär′līght,
    stop′līght, sun′līght,
    thē-od′ō-līte, tox-oph′i-līte,
    traf′fi̧c līght, twī′līght,
    zō′ō-līte.
m: Ad′ăm-īte, Ad-ul′lȧ-mīte,
    bed′lăm-īte, Beth′lē-hem-īte,
    dō′lō-mīte, dȳn′ȧ-mīte,
    El′ȧ-mīte, er′ē-mīte,
    Goth′ăm-īte, mid′ship-mīte,
    mīght, mīte, prē=Ad′am-īte.
n: Aār′ŏn-īte, a̧c′ō-nīte,
    ȧ-lū′mi-nīte, Am′mŏn-īte,
    ȧ-nīght′*, Bab′y-lŏn-īte,
    bē-knīght′, be′lem-nīte,
    bē-nīght′, ̧Cā′năan-īte,
    dis″ū-nīte′, Eb-ī′ō-nīte,
    eb′ŏn-īte, good-nīght′, ig-nīte′,
    knīght (nīt), mam′mŏn-īte,
    Mar′ō-nīte, M̧c-Knīght′ (-nīt′),
    mid′nīght, Mọr′mŏn-īte,
    nīght (nīt), ō″vēr-nīght′,
    rē″ū-nīte′, tö-nīght′, ū-nīte′,
    vul′̧căn-īte, yes′tēr-nīght*.
pl: plīght, troth plīght.

r: añ′̧chō-rīte, ȧ-rīght′,
    ̧cop′y-rīght, down′rīght,
    en-wrīte′ (-rīt′), fọrth′rīght,
    mē′tē-ŏr-ite, Naz′ȧ-rīte,
    out′rīght, rē-wrīte′, rīght,
    rīte, sid′ēr-īte, Syb′ȧ-rīte,
    un-dēr-wrīte′, un-rīght′*,
    un-wrīte′, up′rīght,
    wheel′wrīght (hwēl′), wrīght,
    wrīte.
s: an′thrȧ-cīte, cīte, ex-cīte′,
    fōre′sīght, in-cīte′, in′sīght,
    ō′vēr-sīght, par′ȧ-sīte,
    pleb′i-scīte (-sīt), rē-cīte′,
    sȩc′ŏnd sīght, sīght, sīte,
    un-sīght′.
sk(şc): blaTH′ēr-skīte.
sl: sleīght (slīt), slīght.
sm: smīte.
sp: dē-spīte′, spīte.
spr: sprīte, wạ′tēr-sprīte.
t: āir′tīght, ap′pē-tīte,
    bī-pär′tīte, hem′ȧ-tīte, tīght,
    trī-pär′tīte, wạ′tēr-tīght.
tr: ̧con-trīte′, trīte.
v: in-vīte′, Mus′̧cō-vīte.
w: wīght.

IT

Vowel: it, Jẹs′ū-it (jezh′).
b: bit, bitt, tid′bit, un-bit′.
ch: chit.
f: bē-fit′, ben′ē-fit, ̧cŏm′fit,
    ̧coun′tēr-feit, fit, mis′fit,
    out′fit, rē-fit′, un-fit′
fl: flit.
fr: frit.
g: git.
gr: grit.
h: hit.
hw: whit.
k(̧c): kit.

ĪTH
ĪV
fāte, fär, fȧst, fạll, finăl, cãre, at; mēte, prey, hẽr, met; pīne,
marīne, bĭrd, pin; nōte, mōve, fọr, atŏm, not; mọọn, book;
192

(Choose only one word out of each group)

kr: hyp'ō-crite.
kw(qu): ac-quit', quit.
l: lit, mọọn'lit, stär'lit.
m: ad-mit', cŏm-mit', dē-mit',
ē-mit', im-mit', in-tẽr-mit',
in-trō-mit', man'ū-mit, mitt,
ō-mit', pẽr-mit', prē'tẽr-mit,
rē"com-mit', rē-mit', sub-mit',
trans-mit'.
n: bē-knit' (-nit'), def'i-nite,
in-def'i-nite, in'fi-nite,
in-knit' (-nit')*, in-tẽr-knit',
knit, Mc-Nitt', nit, un-knit'.
p: pit, Pitt, rī'fle pit.
r: fā'vŏr-ite, pret'ẽr-ite,
writ (rit).
s: cit, out-sit', pleb'ē-scite (-sit),
sit.
shm: Schmidt.
sk(sc): skit.
sl: slit.
sm: smit.
sp: spit.
spl: split.
spr: bow'sprit, sprit.
t: tit, tom'tit.
tw: twit.
w: ȧf'tẽr-wit, Dē-Witt',
mŏTH'ẽr wit, out-wit',
tö wit, un-wit'*, wit, Witt.
z: ap'pō-site, ex'qui-site,
op'pō-site, pẽr'qui-site,
prē-re'qui-site, re'qui-site.

ĪTH

bl: blīTHe.
l: līTHe.
r: wrīTHe.
s: scȳTHe'(sīTH).
sm: SmȳTHe.
st: stȳTHe.

t: tīTHe.
w: wīTHe.

ĪTH

m: mȳth.
st: stȳthe.

ITH

w: fôrth-wiTH', hēre-wiTH',
THere-wiTH' (THăr-),
where-wiTH' (hwăr-), wiTH,
wiTHe.

ITH

fr: frith.
k(c): kith.
l: ac'rō-lith, ā-ẽr'ō-lith, lith,
mon'ō-lith, pā'laē-ō-lith.
m: myth.
p: pith.
s: sith*.
sm: Ar'rōw-smith,
Lā'dy-smith, smith.
w: fọrth-with', hēre-with',
THere-with' (THăr-),
where-with' (hwăr-), with,
withe.

ĪTS

l: foot'līghts ('līts).
n: ȧ-nīghts'.
t: tīghts.
Plus īt.+s.
Plus night's, etc.

ITS

fr: Fritz.
kw(qu): quits.
shl: Schlitz.
Plus it+s.
Plus pit's, etc.

ĪV

ch: chīve.
d: dīve, nōse'dīve,
pow'ẽr-dīve.

193   ūse, bu̱ll, brûte, tûrn, up; crȳ, myth; ça̱t, ma̱chine, ace,
church, c̱hord; ġem, añger, (Fr.) boṅ, a̱ş; THis, thin; azure   **IV**
IVD

(Choose only one word out of each group)

dr: chāin drīve, drīve.
f: fīve.
h: hīve, un-hīve′.
j: ġȳve.
kl: C̱līve.
l: a̱-līve′, līve.
n: c̱on-nīve′.
pr: dē-prīve′.
r: ăr-rīve′, dē-rīve′, rīve.
sh: shīve.
shr: shrīve.
sk(sc̱): skīve′.
st: stīve.
str: strīve.
thr: thrīve.
tr: c̱on-trīve′.
v: rē-vīve′, sûr-vīve′.
w: wīve.
Plus I've.

IV

fl: fliv.
g: fo̱r-give′, give, mis-give′.
l: live, out-live′, ō-vēr-live′.
s: sieve (siv).
t: ab′la̱-tive, ac̱-c̱ū′sa̱-tive,
ac̱-qui′şi-tive, ad-mon′i-tive,
af-fīr′ma̱-tive, a̱l-tēr′na̱-tive,
a′ma̱-tive, är-gū-men′ta̱-tive,
c̱au̱ş′a̱-tive, c̱ō-ēr′ci-tive,
c̱om′ba̱-tive, c̱om-par′a̱-tive,
c̱om-pel′la̱-tive, c̱om-pen′sa̱-tive,
c̱om-pe′ti-tive,
c̱om-pli-men′ta̱-tive,
c̱om-pul′sa̱-tive, c̱on-fīr′ma̱-tive,
c̱on-sec̱′ū-tive, c̱on-sēr′va̱-tive,
c̱on-tem′pla̱-tive,
c̱on-tri′bū-tive, c̱o̱r-re′la̱-tive,
c̱ūr′a̱-tive, dē-c̱lär′a̱-tive,
dē-fin′i-tive, dē-mon′stra̱-tive,
dē-riv′a̱-tive, dē-rog′a̱-tive,
des-ic̱′c̱a̱-tive, di-mi′nū-tive,

dis-pen′sa̱-tive, dis-pū′ta̱-tive,
dis-tri′bū-tive, ē-vo′c̱a̱-tive,
ex-cla′ma̱-tive, ex-e′c̱ū-tive,
ex′plē-tive, fig′ūr-a̱-tive,
fo̱r′ma̱-tive, fū′ġi-tive,
ġe′ni-tive, il-lu′stra̱-tive,
im-pe′di-tive, im-per′a̱-tive,
im-pū′ta̱-tive, in-c̱är′na̱-tive,
in-c̱hō′a̱-tive, in-c̱ras′sa̱-tive,
in-di′c̱a̱-tive, in-fin′i-tive,
in-fo̱r′ma̱-tive, in-qui′şi-tive,
in-sen′si-tive, in-ten′sa̱-tive,
in-tēr-rog′a̱-tive, in-tū′i-tive,
la̱u̱′da̱-tive, len′i-tive,
lū′c̱ra̱-tive, neg′a̱-tive,
no′mi-na̱-tive, nū′tri-tive,
prē-mo′ni-tive, prē-pär′a̱-tive,
prē-ro′ga̱-tive, prē-şēr′va̱-tive,
pri′mi-tive, prō-hi′bi-tive,
prō-vo′c̱a̱-tive, pul′sa̱-tive,
pū′ni-tive, pū′ta̱-tive,
quän′ti-tive, rē-ci′ta̱-tive,
rē-fo̱r′ma̱-tive, rē-pär′a̱-tive,
rep-rē-şen′ta̱-tive, rē-stōr′a̱-tive,
rē-trib′ū-tive, san′a̱-tive,
se′da̱-tive, sem′bla̱-tive,
sen′si-tive, sic̱′c̱a̱-tive,
sub′stăn-tive, sū-pēr′la̱-tive,
ta̱lk′a̱-tive (ta̱k′), ten′ta̱-tive,
tran′si-tive, vī′bra̱-tive,
vo′c̱a̱-tive.

ĪVD

l: lo̱ng′=līved′, sho̱rt′=līved′.
shr: un-shrīved′.
w: un-wīved′.
Plus īv+d.

IVD

l: lo̱ng′=lived′, neg′a̱-tived,
out-lived′, sho̱rt′=lived′,
un-lived′.

ĬVZ
Ĭz

fāte, fär, fȧst, fạll, finăl, cãre, at; mēte, prẹy, hêr, met; pīne,
marīne, bĭrd, pin; nōte, mŏve, fọr, atŏm, not; mọọn, book; **194**

(Choose only one word out of each group)

ĪVZ

Vowel: St. Īveṣ.

f: fīveṣ.

l: līveṣ.

n: knīveṣ (nīvz).

Plus īv + s.

Plus hive's, etc.

ĪZ

Vowel: ā'thē-īze, dan'dy-īze,
eū'phū-īze, Hē'brȧ-īze,
Jú-dȧ'īze.

d: ag-gran'dīze, bal'lăd-īze,
bas'tärd-īze, das'tärd-īze,
flū'id-īze, gọr'măn-dīze,
jeop'ärd-īze (jep'), li'quid-īze,
mêr'chăn-dīze, meth'ŏd-īze,
ox'i-dīze, psälm'ō-dīze (säm'),
rhap'sō-dīze (rap'), sub'si-dīze,
vag'ȧ-bond-īze.

f: ȧ-pos'trō-phize,
phi-los'ō-phīze, saẹ'ri-fīce (-fīz),
thē-os'ō-phīze.

g: dis-guīṣe' (-gīz'), guīṣe,
ŏTH'ẽr-guīṣe*.

j: ȧ-pol'ō-ġīze, as-trol'ō-ġīze,
bat-tol'ō-ġīze,
dī-al'ō-ġīze, dox-ol'ō-ġīze,
en'ẽr-ġīze, et-y-mol'ō-ġīze,
eū'lō-ġize, ġen-ē-ăl'ō-ġīze,
ġē-ol'ō-ġīze, leth'ăr-ġīze,
myth-ol'ō-ġīze, phi-los'ō-ġīze,
syl'lō-ġīze, tạu-tol'ō-ġīze,
thē-ol'ō-ġīze.

k(ẹ): ẹat'ē-ẹhīze.

kw(qu): sō-lil'ō-quīze,
ven-tril'ō-quīze.

l: aẹ'tū-ăl-īze, al'ẹō-hol-īze,
al'kȧ-līze, am-brō'ṣiăl-īze ('zhăl-)
an'ȧ-lȳze, ān'ġel-īze,
an'i-măl-īze, an'nȧ-līze,

är-ti-fi'ciăl-īze,
brú'tăl-īze, ẹap'i-tăl-īze,
cen'trăl-īze, civ'i-līze,
ẹon-sti-tū'tion-ăl-īze,
ẹon-ven'tion-ăl-īze, ẹrys'tăl-līze,
dec'i-măl-īze, dē-mor'ăl-īze,
dē-na'tion-ăl-īze,
dē-nat'ū-răl-īze, dev'il-īze,
dē-vī'tăl-īze, dī-a'bŏl-īze,
dī'ȧ-lȳze, ē-leẹ'trō-līze,
ē'quăl-īze, ē-têr'năl-īze,
ē-thē'rē-ăl-īze, ē-van'ġel-īze,
ex-per-i-men'tăl-īze, fab'ū-līze,
fed'ẽr-ăl-īze, fêr'ti-līze,
feū'dăl-īze, fō'ẹăl-īze,
for'măl-īze, fọr'mū-līze,
fos'sil-īze, ġen'ẽr-ăl-īze,
ġen'til-īze, gos'pel-īze,
gut'tūr-ăl-īze, hȳ-pêr'bō-līze,
ī-dē'ăl-īze, ī'dō-līze,
im-mọr'tăl-īze, im-pē'ri-ăl-īze,
in-di-vid'ū-ăl-īze,
in-têr-na'tion-ăl-īze,
joūr'năl-īze, lē'găl-īze,
lib'ẽr-ăl-īze, lit'ẽr-ăl-īze, Līze,
lō'ẹăl-īze, mär'tiăl-īze,
mȧ-tē'ri-ăl-īze, me-mō'ri-ăl-ize,
min'ẽr-ăl-īze, mō'bil-īze,
mod'el-īze, mō-nop'ō-līze,
mor'ăl-īze, nā'ṣăl-īze,
na'tion-ăl-īze, nat'ū-răl-īze,
neū'trăl-īze, nov'el-īze,
par'al-lel-īze, par'ȧ-lȳze,
pē'năl-īze, pêr'sŏn-ăl-īze,
plú'răl-īze, prō-vêr'bi-ăl-īze,
prō-vin'ciăl-īze,
ra'tion-ăl-īze, rē'ăl-īze,
roy'ăl-īze, rū'răl-īze,
sẹan'dăl-īze, sẹrú'pū-līze,
sen'sū-ăl-īze, sen-ti-men'tăl-īze,
sē-pul'ẹhrăl-īze, sex'ū-ăl-īze,

(Choose only one word out of each group)

sig'năl-īze, sō'ciăl-īze,
spe'ciăl-īze,
spir'i-tū-ăl-īze, ster'il-īze,
sub'til-īze', sym'bŏl-īze,
tan'tà-līze, tō'tăl-īze,
tran'quil-līze, ū-ni-vēr'săl-īze,
ū'til-īze, vēr'băl-īze,
viṣ'ū-ăl-ize (vizh'), vī'tăl-īze,
vō'çăl-īze, vol'à-til-īze.

m: al'çhē-mīze, à-mal'gà-mīze,
à-nat'ō-mīze, as-tro'nō-mīze,
a'tŏm-īze, çom'prō-mīṣe,
dē-mīṣe', ē-çon'ō-mīze,
em'blem-īze, ē-pit'ō-mīze,
eū'phē-mīze, măç-ad'ăm-īze,
man'ū-mīze, mi'ni-mīze,
pes'si-mīze, phy-ṣi-og'nō-mīze,
pil'grim-īze, pō-lyg'à-mīze,
rē-mīṣe', sūr-mīṣe',
sy-non'y-mīze, sys'tem-īze,
viç'tim-īze.

n: à-dō'nīze, Af'ri-çà-nīze,
ag'ō-nīze, ag-rā'ri-ăn-īze,
al-bū'men-īze, À-mer'i-căn-īze,
an-tag'ō-nīze, at-ti-tū'di-nīze,
bot'à-nīze, çan'ŏn-īze,
Çhris'tiăn-īze (kris'chun-),
çog'nīze, çol'ō-nīze,
dē-hū'măn-īze, det'ō-nīze,
dis-il-lū'ṣiŏn-īze,
dis-ọr'găn-īze, e'bō-nīze,
Ē'den-īze, ef-fem'i-nīze,
eū'phō-nīze, Eū-rō-pē'ăn-īze,
ex-çūr'ṣiŏn-īze,
fra'tēr-nīze, gal'và-nīze,
ġē-lat'i-nīze, glut'tŏn-īze,
gọr'gŏn-īze, här'mō-nīze,
hēa''THen'īze, Hel'len-īze,
his'tri-ŏn-īze, hū'măn-īze,
im-pat'rō-nīze,
I-tal'iăn-īze ('yăn-), Lat'in-īze,

lī'ŏn-īze, Lŏn'dŏn-īze,
Mà-hom'ed-ăn-īze,
mam'mŏn-īze, māt'rŏn-īze,
mech'ăn-īze, mod'ērn-īze,
Mō-ham'mē-dăn-īze, ọr'găn-īze,
ox'y-ġen-īze, pā'găn-īze,
pat'rŏn-īze, pav'ŏn-īze,
pē-des'tri-ăn-īze, pēr'sŏn-īze,
plat-i-tūd'i-nīze, Plā'tō-nīze,
plē-bē'iăn-īze ('yăn-),
pol'len-īze, Pū'ri-tăn-īze,
reç'og-nīze, rē-jù'ven-īze,
rē-pub'li-çăn-īze,
reṣ-ūr-reç'tion-īze,
rev-ō-lū'tion-īze, Rō'măn-īze,
scrù'ti-nīze, seç-tā'ri-ăn-īze,
sēr'mŏn-īze, Sī'mŏn-īze,
Sō-cin'i-ăn-īze, sol'em-nīze,
sym'phō-nīze, syñ'çhrō-nīze,
Teū'tŏn-īze, Ti'mŏn-īze,
tyr'ăn-nīze, vil'lăin-īze,
vul'çăn-īze, wän'tŏn-īze.

p: mis-an'thrō-pīze, syñ'çō-pīze.

pr: ap-prīṣe', çom-prīṣe',
em-prīze', en'tēr-prīṣe,
mis-prīze', prīze, rē-prīṣe',
sūr-prīṣe', un''dēr-prīze'.

r: al'lē-gō-rīze, a'phō-rīze,
à-rīṣe', au'gū-rīze, au'thŏr-īze,
bär'bàr-īze, bowd'lēr-īze,
çau'tēr-īze, char'aç-tēr-īze,
chī'mē-rīze, cīr'çū-lăr-ꞩīze,
dē-çŏl'ŏr-īze, dē-ō'dŏr-īze,
ē'thēr-īze, ex-tem'pō-rīze,
fà-mil'iàr-īze ('yēr-),
mär'tyr-īze, mem'ō-rīze,
mēr'çēr-īze, meṣ'mēr-īze,
mọọn'rīṣe, pan'ē-ġy-rīze,
pär-tiç'ū-lăr-īze, pau'pēr-īze,
pē-çū'liàr-īze ('yēr-),
plā'ġi-à-rīze, pō'lăr-īze,

(Choose only one word out of each group)

pop'ū-lăr-īze, pul'vẽr-īze,
rap'tūr-īze, rhe'tŏr-īze (re'),
rīṣe, saç'çhȧ-rīze, sat'i-rīze,
seç'ū-lăr-īze,
sēi'gniŏr-īze ('nyẽr-),
sē'niŏr-īze ('nyẽr-), sil'vẽr-īze,
siñ'gū-lăr-īze, sō'bẽr-īze,
sō'lăr-īze, sum'mă-rīze,
sun'rīṣe, tab'ū-lăr-īze,
tem'pō-rīze, ter'rŏr-īze,
thē'ō-rīze, up'rīṣe, vā'pŏr-īze,
vul'găr-īze.

s: Añ'gli-cīze, ap-ō-thē'ō-sīze,
as-sīze', at'ti-cīze, çap-sīze',
çri'ti-cīze, eç'stȧ-cīze,
em-blem-at'i-cīze, em'phȧ-sīze,
ex-cīze', ex'ẽr-cīse, ex'ọr-cīṣe,
fȧ-nat'i-cīze, Hē-brā'i-cīze,
Hī-bẽrn'i-cīze, hȳ-poth'ē-sīze,
in-cīṣe', i-tal'i-cīze, os'trȧ-cīze,
sçep'ti-cīze, Sçot'ti-cīze,
sīce (sīz), sīze, syn'thē-sīze.

sp: dē-spīṣe'.

t: aç-çlī'mȧ-tīze, ȧ-çhrō'mȧ-tīze,
ad'vẽr-tīze, ag'ȧ-tīze,
al'phȧ-bet-īze, ȧ-nath'ē-mȧ-tīze,
ȧ-pos'tȧ-tīze, ap'pē-tīze,
a-rō'mȧ-tīze, bap'tīze,
chas-tīṣe', çlī'mȧ-tīze,
dē-mag'net-īze, dē-moç'rȧ-tīze,
dē-mon'ē-tīze, dē-när'çō-tīze,
dep'ū-tīze, dog'mȧ-tīze,
drȧ'mȧ-tīze, em'blem-ȧ-tīze,
ē-nig'mȧ-tīze, ep-i-gram'mȧ-tīze,
hyp'nō-tīze, id'i-ō-tīze,
lē-ġit'i-mȧ-tīze, mag'net-īze,
mē'di-ȧ-tīze, mon'e-tīze,
när'çō-tīze, pō'et-īze,
prel'ȧ-tīze, pros'ē-ly-tīze,
Prot'es-tănt-īze, re-mon'ē-tīze,
sçhiṣ'mȧ-tīze, son'net-īze,

stig'mȧ-tīze, syn'thē-tīze,
sys'tem-ȧ-tīze.

th: sym'pȧ-thīze.

tr: ġē-om'ē-trīze, ī-dol'ȧ-trīze.

v: ad-vīṣe', dē-vīṣe',
im'prō-vīṣe, rē-vīṣe',
sū'pẽr-vīṣe.

w: ȧf'tẽr-wīṣe, an'y-wīse (en'i-),
çon'trā-ri-wīṣe, çọr'nẽr-wīṣe,
çre'scent-wīse, līke'wīṣe,
ŏTH'ẽr-wīṣe, ō"vẽr-wīṣe'.
pen'ny-wīṣe', un-wīṣe',
weaTH'ẽr-wīṣe' (weTH'), wīṣe.

Plus ī+s.
Plus sky's, etc.

IZ

Vowel: iṣ.
b: biz.
d: Çȧ-diz'.
f: fizz, ġin fizz, gōl'den fizz,
phiz, rum fizz, sil'vẽr fizz.
fr: bē-friz', friz.
h: hiṣ.
hw: ġee whizz, whizz.
kw(qu): quiz.
l: Liz.
r: A'riz, riz.
s: sizz.
t: 'tiṣ, Tiz.
v: viṣ.
w: wiz.

ĪZD

g: dis-guīsed', un-dis-guīṣed'.
l: civ'i-līzed, un-civ'i-līzed.
m: sūr-mīṣed', un-sūr-mīṣed'.
n: çan'ŏn-īzed, un-çan'ŏn-īzed.
pr: ap-prīṣed', sūr-prīṣed',
un-ap-prīṣed', un-prīzed',
un-sūr-prīṣed'.

(Choose only one word out of each group)

r: au̯'thŏr-īzed, un-au̯'thŏr-īzed.
s: un-dēr-sīzed'.
sp: dē-spīṣed', un-dē-spīṣed'.
t: bap'tīzed, un-bap'tīzed.
v: ad-vīṣed', ill'=ad-vīṣed',
un-ad-vīṣed'.
Plus īz+d.

IZM

Vowel: al'trú-iṣm, är'c̣hä-iṣm,
as'tē-iṣm, ā'thē-iṣm, bā'by-iṣm,
blūe"=stock'ing-iṣm,
bō'gey-iṣm ('gi-), boo̯'by-iṣm,
C̣ock'ney-iṣm ('ni-), dan̯'dy-iṣm,
ē'gō-iṣm, eū'phū-iṣm,
fāir'y-iṣm, fluñ'key-iṣm ('ki-),
fō'gey-iṣm ('gi-),
Ghän'di-iṣm (gän'), Hē'brȧ-iṣm,
hē'rō-iṣm, Hin'dú-iṣm, iṣm,
Ī'rish-iṣm, jock'ey-iṣm ('i-),
Jū'dȧ-iṣm, lā'dy-iṣm,
mŏn'key-iṣm ('ki-),
ō'gre-iṣm ('gēr-), pan'thē-iṣm,
par'ox-yṣm, pup'py-iṣm,
Pū'sey-iṣm ('si-), Shin'tō-iṣm,
Tō'ry-iṣm, Yañ'kee-iṣm,
zā'ny-iṣm.
b: ȧ-byṣm'.
ch: Chiṣhŏlm (chiz''m).
d: brag'gȧrd-iṣm, Lol'lȧrd-iṣm,
meth'ŏd-iṣm.
f: pa'ci-fiṣm, phi-los'ō-phiṣm,
thē-os'ō-phiṣm.
g: dī'ȧ-log-iṣm.
j: nē-ol'ō-g̣iṣm, sav'åg̣-iṣm,
syl'lō-g̣iṣm.
k(c̣): an'är-c̣hiṣm, c̣at ē-c̣hiṣm,
mon'ärc̣h-iṣm.
kl: c̣at'ȧ-c̣lyṣm.
kr: c̣hriṣm.
kw(qu): ven-tril'ō-quiṣm.

l: ac̣-ci-den'tăl-iṣm,
al'c̣ō-hol-iṣm, an'i-măl-iṣm,
ȧ-nom'ȧ-liṣm, Bā'ăl-iṣm,
bib-li-oph'i-liṣm,
bib-li-op'ō-liṣm, bī-met'ăl-liṣm,
brú'tăl-iṣm, c̣ab'ȧ-liṣm,
cen'trăl-iṣm, c̣hlō'răl-iṣm,
c̣las'si-c̣ăl-iṣm, c̣ler'i-c̣ăl-iṣm,
c̣ol-lō'qui-ăl-iṣm, c̣ō-lō'ni-ăl-iṣm,
c̣om-mū'năl-ism,
c̣on-grē-gā'tion-ăl-iṣm,
c̣on-sti-tū'tion-ăl-iṣm,
de-nom-i-nā'tion-ăl-iṣm,
dev'il-iṣm, dī-ab'ō-liṣm,
dū'ăl-iṣm, em'bō-liṣm,
ē-mō'tion-ăl-iṣm, ē-thē're-ăl-iṣm,
ē-van'g̣el-iṣm, fā'tăl-iṣm,
fed'ēr-ăl-iṣm, feū'dăl-iṣm,
for'măl-iṣm, fos'sil-iṣm,
friv'ō-liṣm, g̣en'tīl-iṣm,
hȳ-pēr'bō-liṣm, ī-dē'ăl-iṣm,
im-mȧ-tē'ri-ăl-iṣm,
im-pē'ri-ăl-iṣm,
in-di-vid'ū-ăl-iṣm,
in-dus'tri-ăl-iṣm,
in-tel-lec̣'tū-ăl-iṣm,
in-tēr-na'tion-ăl-iṣm,
joūr'năl-iṣm, lib'ēr-ăl-iṣm,
lit'ēr-ăl-iṣm, lō'c̣ăl-iṣm,
loy'ăl-iṣm, mȧ-tē'ri-ăl-iṣm,
mē-di-ē'văl-iṣm, mor'ăl-iṣm,
nat'ū-răl-iṣm, nī'hil-iṣm,
nom'i-năl-iṣm, ō-ri-en'tăl-iṣm,
par'al-lel-iṣm, pēr'sŏn-ăl-iṣm,
phē-nom'ē-năl-iṣm, plú'răl-iṣm,
prē=Raph'ā-el-iṣm,
prō-vēr'bi-ăl-iṣm,
prō-vin'ciăl-iṣm,
pū'g̣i-liṣm, rad-i-c̣ăl-iṣm,
rē'ăl-iṣm, ra'tion-ăl-iṣm,
rē-vīv'ăl-iṣm, rıt'u-ăl-iṣm,

IZM

fāte, fär, fåst, fạll, finăl, cãre, at; mēte, prey, hẽr, met; pine, marïne, bïrd, pin; nōte, mŏve, fọr, atŏm, not; mọọn, book; **198**

(Choose only one word out of each group)

roy'ăl-işm, rū'răl-işm,
sac-ẽr-dō'tăl-işm, scī'ō-lişm (sī'),
scoun'drel-işm, scrip'tūr-ăl-işm,
sen-sā'tion-ăl-işm, sen'sū-ăl-işm,
sen-ti-men'tăl-işm, sō'ciăl-işm,
som-nam'bū-lişm, som'nō-lişm,
sub'til-işm* (sut'l-),
sū-pẽr-nat'ū-răl-işm,
sym'bō-lişm, trȧ-di'tion-ăl-işm,
trans-cen-den'tăl-ism,
trīb'ăl-işm, ū-ni-vẽr'săl-işm,
van'dăl-işm, vẽr'băl-işm,
vī'tăl-işm, vō'căl-işm.

m: ac-a'dem-işm, ȧ-nat'ō-mişm,
an'i-mişm, at'ŏm-işm,
eū'phē-mişm, Is'lăm-işm,
lē-ġit'i-mişm, op'ti-mişm,
pes'si-mişm, tō'tem-işm.

n: ab-ō-li'tion-işm, ac'tin-işm,
Af'ri-căn-işm, ag'ō-nişm,
ȧ-grā'ri-ăn-işm,
ā'lien-ism ('lyen-).

Ȧ-mer'i-căn-işm,
ȧ-nach'rō-nişm, Añ'gli-căn-işm,
Añ'glō⹀Sax'ŏn-işm,
an-tag'ō-nişm,
an-ti-quā'ri-ăn-işm,
bac-chȧ-nā'li-ăn-işm,
Bō-hē'mi-ăn-işm, Boūr'bŏn-işm,
Bräh'măn-işm, Buck'măn-işm,
Cal'vin-işm, chau'vin-işm (shō'),
Com'mū-nişm,
Con-fū'ciăn-işm ('shăn-),
cos-mō-pol'i-tăn-işm,
crē'tin-işm, Där'win-işm,
dē-mō-nī'ăn-işm, dē'mŏn-işm,
dē-tẽr'min-işm,
ep-i-cū'rē-ăn-işm,
ē-ques'tri-ăn-işm,
Ē-ras'ti-ăn-işm, eū-dē'mŏn-işm,
eū'phō-nişm, Fē'ni-ăn-işm,

fọr'eign-işm ('in-), gal'văn-işm,
Ğẽr'măn-işm, hēa'THen-işm,
hē'dŏn-işm, Hel'len-işm,
Hī-bẽr'ni-ăn-işm, his'tri-ō-nişm,
hū'măn-işm, Ib'sen-işm,
I-tal'i-ăn-işm, lac̣'ō-nişm,
Lat'in-işm,
lat-i-tū"di-nā'ri-ăn-işm,
Le'nin-işm, lib'ẽr-tin-işm,
Lŏn'dŏn-işm,
Mȧ-hom'et-ăn-işm,
mam'mŏn-işm, mech'ȧ-nişm,
mod'ẽrn-işm,
Mō-ham'mē-dăn-işm,
Mon'tăn-işm, Mọr'mŏn-işm,
nec-es-sā'ri-ăn-ism,
ne-ces"si-tā'ri-ăn-ism,
Nē-ō-plā'tō-nişm, ọr'găn-işm,
pā'găn-işm, pa-tri'ciăn-işm,
pē'ăn-işm, pe-des'tri-ăn-işm,
pē'ŏn-işm, phē-nom'ō-nişm,
Phil-hel'len-işm, Phi-lis'tin-işm,
Plā'tō-nişm,
plē-bē'iăn-işm ('yăn-),
prē-ci'şiŏn-işm,
prē-des-ti-nā'ri-ăn-işm,
Pres-by-tē'ri-ăn-işm,
prō-lē-tā'ri-ăn-işm,
prō-tec'tion-işm, Pū'ri-tăn-işm,
pȳ'thŏn-işm, rab'bin-işm,
rē-li'ġiŏn-işm,
Rē-pub'li-căn-işm, Rō'măn-işm,
ruf'fi-ăn-işm,
sab-bȧ-tā'ri-ăn-işm, sā'tăn-işm,
Sax'ŏn-işm, sē-ces'sion-işm,
sec-tār'i-ăn-işm, shā'măn-işm,
Shā'vi-ăn-işm, Sō-cin'i-ăn-işm,
Stä'lin-işm, syñ'chrō-nişm,
Syr'i-ăn-işm,
trādeş'⹀ū'niŏn-işm ('nyun-),
ū'niŏn-işm ('nyun-),

(Choose only one word out of each group)

Ū-ni-tā′ri-ăn-iṣm,
ū-til-i-tā′ri-ăn-iṣm,
Ū-tō′pi-ăn-iṣm,
val-ē-tū-di-nā′ri-ăn-iṣm,
Vat′i-çăn-iṣm,
veġ-ē-tā′ri-ăn-iṣm, vul′pin-iṣm,
Wes′ley-ăn-iṣm (′li-).

pr: priṣm.

r: ag-ri-çul′tūr-iṣm, an′eū-riṣm,
a′phō-riṣm, as′tēr-iṣm,
bach′ē-lŏr-iṣm, bär′băr-iṣm,
bē-hāv′iŏr-iṣm (′yēr-),
blọọm′ēr-iṣm, çhar′aç-tēr-iṣm,
ē′thēr-iṣm, Föu′ri-ēr-iṣm,
Hit′lēr-iṣm, man′nēr-iṣm,
meṣ′mēr-iṣm, pạu′pēr-iṣm,
phal-an′stēr-iṣm, plā′ġi-ă-riṣm,
Quāk′ēr-iṣm, rig′ŏr-iṣm,
seç′ū-lăr-iṣm, ter′rŏr-iṣm,
tī′gēr-iṣm, vam′pīr-iṣm,
vul′găr-iṣm, vul′tūr-iṣm.

s: aes-the′ti-ciṣm (es-),
ag-nos′ti-ciṣm, Añ′gli-ciṣm,
as-cet′i-ciṣm,
Ā-ṣi-at′i-ciṣm (-zhi-),
bib′li-ciṣm, Ça-thol′i-ciṣm,
çlas′si-ciṣm, çri′ti-ciṣm,
cyn′i-ciṣm, dē-mō-nī′á-ciṣm,
eç-çlē′ṣi-as′ti-ciṣm,
eç-leç′ti-ciṣm, ē-leç′ti-ciṣm,
em-pi′ri-ciṣm, es-ō-ter′i-ciṣm,
ex′ŏr-ciṣm, ex-ot′i-ciṣm,
fá-nat′i-ciṣm, fan-tas′ti-ciṣm,
Gal′li-ciṣm, Hī-bēr′ni-ciṣm,

his-tri-o′ni-ciṣm,
hȳ″pēr-çrit′i-ciṣm,
hȳp-ō-çhon′dri-á-ciṣm,
I-tal′i-ciṣm, lā-çon′i-ciṣm,
lyr′i-ciṣm, met′á-ciṣm,
mō-nas′ti-ciṣm, mys′ti-ciṣm,
os′trá-ciṣm, per-i-pá-tet′i-ciṣm,
phil-an-throp′i-ciṣm,
phyṣ′i-ciṣm, rō-man′ti-ciṣm,
sçep′ti-ciṣm, schiṣm (sizm),
schō-las′ti-ciṣm, Sçot′ti-ciṣm,
sol′ē-ciṣm, stō′i-ciṣm,
Teū-ton′i-ciṣm, wit′ti-ciṣm.

sh: fe′tish-iṣm.

t: ab′sō-lū-tiṣm, á-çhrō′má-tiṣm,
á-nath′ē-má-tiṣm,
an-ti-Sem′i-tiṣm, as-tig′má-tiṣm,
çon-sēr′vá-tiṣm, des′pō-tiṣm,
dī-á-mag′net-iṣm,
di-plō′má-tiṣm, dog′má-tiṣm,
ē′gō-tiṣm, ex′qui-ṣit-iṣm,
hyp′nō-tiṣm, id′i-ŏt-iṣm,
Jeṣ′ū-it-iṣm (jezh′),
mag′net-iṣm, nep′ō-tiṣm,
oç′çul-tiṣm, pā′tri-ŏt-iṣm,
pe′dăn-tiṣm, pī′e-tiṣm,
prag′má-tiṣm, prel′á-tiṣm,
Prot′es-tănt-iṣm, quī′et-iṣm,
quix′ot-iṣm, rheú′má-tiṣm (rů′),
Sem′i-tiṣm, So′viet-iṣm (′vyet-),
syñ′çrē-tiṣm.

v: at′á-viṣm, Bol′shē-viṣm,
Men′shē-viṣm, nā′tiv-iṣm,
poṣ′i-tiv-iṣm, sub′jeç-tiv-iṣm.

(Choose only one word out of each group)

O

ō: as in bōld; also in tōne, ōh, fōam, tōe, bōul'dẽr, glōw, ōwe,
sew (sō), yeō'man, beau (bō), haut'boy (hō'), brōoch.

ọ: as in nọr; also in bọught (bọt), brọad, mem'ọir ('wọr), hạll,
bạlk (bạk), wạrm, hạul, tạught (tọt), clạw.

o: as in hot; also in wänt, squäsh, shone (shon).

oi: as in boil; also in joy.

oo: as in book; also in pụt, wolf (woolf), should (shood).

ou: as in shout; also in brow, sauer'kraut (sour'krout).

(For the vowel sound in do, see under ụ.)

(For the vowel sound in none, blood, see under u.)

Ō

Vowel: ȧ-dä'ġi-ō,
brag-gȧ-dō'ci-ō ('shi-), ça'mē-ō,
çä-rȧ-bā'ō, Çủ-rä-çä'ō, ēau (ō),
em-brō'gli-ō ('li-ō), em'bry-ō,
ex of-fi'çi-ō ('shi-), fō'li-ō,
im-brō'gli-ō ('li-ō),
im-pre-sä'ri-ō, in-tä'gli-ō ('li-ō),
mus-tach'i-ō, nun'ci-ō ('shi-),
Ō, Ōh, ō'li-ō, ọr-ȧ-tō'ri-ō,
ōwe, Pä-pi'li-ō, pis-tach'i-ō,
pọrt-fō'li-ō, puñç-ti'li-ō,
rä'ti-ō ('shi-), Rō'mē-ō,
sē-ra'gli-ō ('li-ō), stū'di-ō,
Tō'ki-ō, vir'ē-ō.

b: beau (bō), bō, bōw,
em-bōw'*, gȧ-zā'bō,
jȧ-bōt' (zhȧ-bō'), lọng bōw,
ō'bōe, rāin'bōw, sȧ-bōt' (-bō'),
sad'dle bōw.

bl: blōw, death blōw (deth).

d: Bọr-deaux' (-dō'), dō, dōe,
dōugh (dō), ron'deau ('dō).

f: cŏmme ïl faut (fō), fōe.

fl: Flō, flōe, flōw, īce flōe,
īce flōw, in'flōw, out'flōw,
ō'ver-flōw.

fr: frō, tö'=and=frō'.

g: ȧ-gō', är-c̣hi-pel'ȧ-gō,
fōre-gō', gō, in'di-gō,
lit'tle gō, lọng ȧ-gō', out'gō,
tŏuch'=and=gō' (tuch'),
un-dẽr-gō', vẽr'ti-gō.

gl: ȧ-glōw', glōw, mọọn'glōw.

gr: grōw, out-grōw',
ō-vẽr-grōw', up'grōw.

h: heīgh'=hō" (hī'), hō, hōe,
Sō'hō, tal-ly-hō',
West'wȧrd hō.

hw: whōa.

j: ȧ-dä'ġi-ō, ban'jō, Jō, Jōe.

k: çal'i-c̣ō, har'i-c̣ōt (-kō),
mag-ni'fi-c̣ō, Mex'i-c̣ō,
pōrt'i-ço.

kr: c̣rōw, es'c̣rōw, ō-vẽr-c̣rōw'.

kw: in sta'tū quō', quid prō quō.

l: ȧ-lōw', bē-lōw', buf'fȧ-lō,
bum'mȧ-lō, buñ'gȧ-lōw,
cach'ȧ-lōt (-lō), fūr'bē-lōw,
ġig'ō-lō, hel-lō', hul-lō', lō,
lōw, Lōwe (lō), röu-leau' (-lō'),
tab-leau' (-lō'), trem'ō-lō.

m: bọn̄ mōt' (mō'),
bräv-is'si-mō, dū-ō-de'ci-mō,
Es'ki-mō, fọr-tis'si-mō,
ġen-ẽr-ăl-is'si-mō,

(Choose only one word out of each group)

hälf á mō (häf), mōt (mō),
mōw, pĭ-á-nis′si-mō, prox′i-mō,
ul′ti-mō.

n: dom′i-nō, fōre-knōw′ (-nō′),
knōw, nō, un-knōw′.

p: á-prō-pōs′ (-pō′),
çhá-peau′ (-pō′), dē′pōt (′pō),
en″trē-pōt′ (än′trē-pō′),
mal″ap-rō-pōs′ (-pō′), Pō, Pōe.

pr: prō.

r: á-rōw′, bú-reau′ (-rō′),
Dï″de-rōt′ (-rō′), rhō (rō),
rōw, R̥ōwe.

s: Çū-rá-çaō′ (-sō′), çū-răs-sōw′,
how sō, mor-ceau′ (-sō′),
Röus-seau′ (-sō′), sew (sō), sō,
sō′‗and‗sō′, sō′‗sō′, sōw,
tröus-seau′ (-sō′).

sh: fōre-shōw′, rā′ree shōw,
shew (shō)*, shōw.

sl: slōe, slōw.

sn: bē-snōw′, snōw.

st: bē-stōw′, stōw, Stōwe.

t: ba-teau′ (-tō′), çha-teau′.
in-çog′ni-tō, ma′ni-tō,
mis′tle-tōe (″l-), pla-teau′,
pōrt-man′teau, tim′bĕr-tōe,
tip′tōe, tōe, tōw, un′dĕr-tōw.

TH: a̱l-THōugh′ (-THō′),
THōugh (THō).

thr: death thrōw (deth),
ō-vēr-thrōw′, thrōe, thrōw.

tr: dē trōp′ (trō′), trōw*.

w: wōe, whōa (wō).

Q

Vowel: a̱we, ō-vēr-a̱we′.

b: Ba̱ugh (bo̱),
us′quē-ba̱ugh (-bo̱).

br: bra̱w.

ch: çha̱w.

d: da̱u̯w (do̱), da̱w, da̱we*,
jack′da̱w, lan′da̱u.

dr: dra̱w, ō-vēr-dra̱w′,
rē-dra̱w′, un-dra̱w′, with-dra̱w′.

f: fa̱ugh (fo̱), guf-fa̱w′.

fl: fla̱w.

gr: Mc̱-Gra̱w′.

h: ha̱ugh (ho̱), ha̱w, hee′ha̱w.

j: ja̱w, un′dēr-ja̱w.

k(c̱): ca̱w, má-ca̱w′.

kl: c̱law.

kr: c̱raw.

l: brŏTH′ēr‗in‗la̱w,
daugh′tēr‗in‗la̱w″, in′‗la̱w,
la̱w, mŏTH′ēr‗in‗la̱w, pi-la̱u′,
sis′tēr‗in‗la̱w″ sŏn′‗in‗la̱w″,
un-la̱w′.

m: ma̱w.

n: bē-gna̱w′ (-no̱′), gna̱w, na̱w.

p: A̱uch′im-pa̱ugh (-po̱),
pá-pa̱w′, Peck′in-pa̱ugh (-po̱),
pa̱w.

r: ra̱w.

s: Är′kăn-sa̱s (-so̱), fōre-sa̱w′,
ō-vēr-sa̱w′, sa̱w, see′‗sa̱w′.

sh: psha̱w (sho̱), Sha̱w.

sk(sc̱): sc̱a̱w.

skw: squa̱w.

sl: c̱ōle sla̱w, sla̱w.

sm: sma̱′.

sp: spa̱.

str: stra̱w.

t: ta̱u, ta̱w.

th: tha̱w.

thr: thra̱w.

y: ya̱w.

ŌB

gl: c̱ŏn-glōbe′, glōbe.

j: Jōb.

l: lōbe, Lōeb.

ŎB
ŌD
fāte, fär, fȧst, fạll, finăl, cãre, at; mēte, prey, hẽr, met; pīne,
marïne, bĭrd, pin; nōte, mŏve, fọr, atŏm, not; mọọn, book;
202

(Choose only one word out of each group)

pr: prōbe.
r: dis-rōbe', en-rōbe', rē-rōbe',
rōbe, un-rōbe'.

ŎB

d: bē-dạub', dạub.
w: nȧ-wạb'.

OB

b: bob, cạ-bob', nā'bob,
thing'um-bob.
bl: blob.
f: fob.
g: gob.
h: hob.
j: job.
k(c): cob, Cobb, cọrn'cob.
kw: quäb.
l: lob.
m: mob.
n: hob'=and=nob', hob'nob,
knob (nob), nob.
r: rob.
s: sob.
skw: squäb.
sl: slob.
sn: snob.
st: stob.
sw: swäb.
thr: ȧ-throb', heärt'throb,
throb.

OBZ

b: ods bobs.
d: Dobbs.
h: Hobbes, Hobbs.
k(c): Cobbs.
sk: scobs.
Plus ob+s.

ŌCH

br: ȧ-brōach', brōach, brōoch.
k: cōach, en-cōach', slōw cōach.

kr: crōche, en-crōach'.
l: lōach.
p: pōach.
pr: ap-prōach', rē-prōach',
self'=rē-prōach'.
r: cock'rōach, rōach.

ŎCH

b: dē-bạuch'.
n: nạutch.

OCH

b: botch.
bl: blotch.
g: gotch.
h: hotch.
kr: crotch.
n: notch, top'notch.
p: hotch'=potch'.
sk(sc): hop'scotch, Scotch.
spl: splotch.
sw: swätch.
w: añ'chŏr wätch,
death'wätch (deth'),
dog'wätch, här'bŏr wätch,
lär'boȧrd wätch, out-wätch',
stär'boȧrd wätch, wätch.

ŌCHD

br: un-brōached'.
pr: un-ap-prōached'.
Plus ōch+d.
Plus rōach'd, etc.

ŌD

Vowel: ōde, ōwed, un-ōwed'.
b: ȧ-bōde', bōde, fōre-bōde'.
bl: blōwed.
g: gōad.
k(c): cōde.
kl: Clōde.
l: lōad, lōde, ō"vẽr-lōad',
rē-lōad', un-lōad'.

203 ūse, bŭll, brûte, tûrn, up; crȳ, myth; çat, maçhine, ace, church, çhord; ġem, aṅger, (Fr.) boṅ, aş; THis, thin; aẓure

QD
ŌF

(Choose only one word out of each group)

m: ä-là-mōde', çom-mōde', dis"çom-mōde', in"çom-mōde', mōde.
n: nōde.
p: an'ti-pōde, lȳ'çō-pōde.
pl: ex-plōde'.
r: ar-rōde'*, brī'dle rōad, çor-rōde', rāil'rōad, ē-rōde', rōad, rōde.
s: ep'i-sōde.
sp: spōde.
st: un"bē-stōwed'.
str: bē-strōde', strōde.
t: pig'eŏn=tōed', tōad.
w: wōad.
Plus ō+d.
Plus bow'd, etc.

QD
Vowel: ō"vĕr-awed', un-awed'.
b: bawd.
br: à-broad, broad.
fr: dē-fraud', fraud.
g: gaud.
j: lan'tērn=jawed", whop'pēr=jawed (hwop').
kl: Claud, Claude.
l: bē-laud', laud.
m: maud, Maude.
pl: ap-plaud'.
r: mà-raud'.
Plus o+d.
Plus jaw'd, etc.

OD
Vowel: od, odd.
d: Dodd.
f: Eïs'tedd-fod ('teth-).
g: bē-god'*, dem'i-god, god, ri'vēr god, sēa god, un-god'.

h: hod.
k(c): çod, Çodd.
kl(cl): çlod.
kw: quäd, quod.
n: nod.
p: lȳ'çō-pod, plat'y-pod, pod.
pl: plod.
pr: prod.
r: Ãar'ŏn'ş rod, di-vīn'ing rod, em'ēr-od, gōl'den-rod, pis'tŏn rod, rod.
s: sod.
sh: drȳ'=shod', rē-shod', rough'=shod' (ruf'), shod, slip'shod, un-shod'.
skr(scr): sçrod.
t: tod.
tr: trod, un-trod'.
v: Eïs-tedd'fod (īs-teth'vod).
w: wäd.
Cf. wa'd, etc.

ŌDZ
r: Rhōadeş (rōdz), Rhōdeş (rōdz).
Plus ōd+ş.
Plus load'ş, etc.

ODZ
Vowel: oddş.
r: em'ēr-odş.
Plus od+s.
Plus rod's, etc.

ŌF
Vowel: ōaf.
g: gōaf.
l: lōaf, quär'tērn lōaf, su'gär lōaf (shug').
sh: çhauf (shōf).

OF
OI

fāte, fär, fȧst, fạll, fĭnal, cãre, at; mēte, prey, hẽr, met; pĭne,
marïne, bĭrd, pin; nōte, mŏve, fọr, atŏm, not; mọọn, book;
204

(Choose only one word out of each group)

OF

Vowel: long fĭēld off, off,
pãir'ing off, sīgn off, tāke'off.
d: doff.
g: golf (gof).
h: Hoff.
k(c̣): c̣ough (kof), c̣off.
kl: c̣loff.
pr: prof.
s: phi-lō-sophe' (-sof'), soph.
sk(sc̣): sc̣off.
shr: shroff.
t: toff, toph.
tr: trough (trof).

OFT

Vowel: oft.
kr(c̣r): c̣roft, un'dẽr-c̣roft.
l: ȧ-loft', hāy'loft, loft.
s: soft.
t: toft.
Plus of+d.

ŌG

b: bōgue, em-bōgue'*.
br: brōgue.
h: Hōag, Hōgue.
l: ap'ō-lōgue, as'trō-lōgue,
c̣ol-lōgue', họr'ō-lōgue.
r: pĭ-rōgue', prō-rōgue', rōgue.
t: tōgue.
tr: trōgue.
v: vōgue.

OG

Vowel: Og.
b: bog, bogue, em-bog'.
br: Dan'nē-brog.
ch: Pat-chogue'.
d: bụll'dog, dog, hot dog,
prãi'rie dog, sun dog.
f: bē-fog', fog, pet'ti-fog.
fl: flog.

fr: frog.
g: ȧ-gog', dem'ȧ-gogue (-gog),
Gog, myst'ȧ-gogue,
ped'ȧ-gogue,
syn'ȧ-gogue.
gr: grog.
h: ground'hog, hedġe'hog (hej'),
hog, quȧ-hog'.
j: jog.
k(c̣): c̣og, in-c̣og', Pō-kogue'.
kl(c̣l): c̣log, rē-c̣log', un-c̣log'.
kw(qu): Quogue.
l: an'ȧ-logue, ap'ō-logue,
c̣at'ȧ-logue, dec̣'ȧ-logue,
dī'ȧ-logue, ep'i-logue, log,
mọn'ō-logue, phil'ō-logue,
thē'ō-logue, trav'el-og.
n: egg'nog, nog.
pr: prog.
sh: shog.
skr(sc̣r): sc̣rog.
sl: slog.
t: tog.
w: gol'li-wog, pọ.'li-wog.
z: Hẽr'zog (hẽrt'), Zog.

OGD

fr: frogged.
l: wạ'tẽr-logged.
Plus og+d.
Plus dog'd, etc.

OGZ

t: togṣ.
Plus og+s.
Plug grog's, etc.

OI

Vowel: oi, oy.
b: ạl'tȧr boy, boy, buoy (boi),
breech'eṣ buoy (brich'ez),

(Choose only one word out of each group)

char'i-ty boy, lob'lol-ly boy,
yel'lōw boy.
f: foy.
g: goy.
h: à-hoy', hob'ble⸗de⸗hoy', hoy.
j: en-joy', joy, ō''vēr-jōy'.
k(ç): çoy, dē-çoy'.
kl: çloy.
l: al-loy', Loy, sav'e-loy.
n: an-noy', Il-li-nois' (-noi').
p: poi, sē'poy, tēa'poy.
pl: dē-ploy', em-ploy'.
r: çor'dù-roy, Pom'e-roy,
vīce'roy.
s: pad'ū-à-soy, soy.
str: dē-stroy'.
t: toy.
tr: Troy.
v: çon'voy, Sà-voy'.

OID

b: "boid", un-buoyed' (-boid').
d: pyr-à'mid-oid.
dr: den'droid.
fl: Floyd.
fr: Freud (froid).
gr: nē'groid.
j: ō-vēr-joyed'.
k(ç): hel'e-çoid.
l: al'kà-loid, cel'lū-loid,
çor'ăl-loid, çrys'tăl-loid,
hȳ'à-loid, Lloyd (loid),
met'ăl-loid, moñ'gō-loid,
pà-rab'ō-loid, pet'à-loid,
tab'loid, un-ăl-loyed',
vā'ri-ō-loid.
n: aç'ti-noid, al-bū'mi-noid,
ga'noid.
p: an'thrō-poid.
pl: un-em-ployed'.
r: an'ē-roid, as'tēr-oid.

t: del'toid, paçh-y-dērm'à-toid.
v: à-void', dē-void', ō'void,
void.
z: trap'ē-zoid.
Plus oi+d.
Plus joy'd, etc.

OIDZ

l: Lloydṣ.
Plus oid+s.
Plus Freud's, etc.

OIF

k(ç): çoif.

OIL

Vowel: oil.
b: à-boil', boil, Boyle,
pär'boil.
br: broil, dis-em-broil',
em-broil'.
d: Doyle, läṅgue d'oil (läṅg doil).
f: ciṅque'foil (saṅk'),
çoun'tēr-foil, foil,
quä'tre-foil (kä'tr-), trē'foil,
tin'foil.
g: "goil".
h: Hoyle.
k(ç): çoil, Çoyle, rē-çoil',
un-çoil', up-çoil'.
m: moil, tūr'moil.
n: noil.
r: roil.
s: as-soil'*, soil.
sp: dē-spoil', spoil.
t: en-toil', es-toile', ō-vēr-toil',
toil.
Plus boy'll, etc.

OILD

b: härd'⸗boiled'.
s: soiled, un-soiled'.

OILT
OJ
fāte, fär, fȧst, fạll, finăl, cãre, at; mēte, prḙy, hẽr, met; pīne,
marǐne, bĩrd, pǐn; nōte, mŏve, fǫr, atŏm, not; mọọn, book;
206

(Choose only one word out of each group)

sp: spoiled, un-spoiled'.
Plus oil+d.
Plus boil'd, etc.

OILT

sp: spoilt.

OILZ

See oil+s.
Plus Boyle's, etc.

OIN

b: Boyne.
f: foin*.
g: Būr-goyne'.
gr: groin.
j: ad-join', ҫon-join', dis-join',
en-join', in-tẽr-join', join,
rē-join', sē-join', sub-join'.
k(ҫ): ҫoigne (koin), ҫoin.
kw(qu): quoin.
l: ē-loign' (-loin'), loin,
pūr-loin', sĩr'loin, ten'dẽr-loin.
m: al-moign' (-moin'),
Dēs-Moines' (dē-moin'),
frañk'ăl-moigne (-moin).

OIND

k(ҫ): un-ҫoined' (-koind').
p: dead poind, poind.
Plus oin+d.
Plus coin'd, etc.

OINT

j: ad-joint', ҫon-joint',
dis-joint', dow'el joint, joint.
n: ȧ-noint'.
p: ap-point', ҫoun'tẽr-point,
ҫö'vẽr-point, dis-ap-point',
drȳ point, point, rē-ap-point',
rē-point', steel point,
West Point.
r: ȧ-roint'*

OIS

b: Boyce.
ch: choice.
j: Joyce, rē-joice'.
r: Royce.
v: in'voice, out-voice', voice.

OIST

f: foist.
h: hoist.
j: joist, un-rē-joiced'.
m: moist.
v: loud'=voiced',
shrill'=voiced'', un-voiced'.
Plus ois+d.

OIT

d: doit.
dr: ȧ-droit', droit, mal-ȧ-droit'.
k(ҫ): dȧ-ҫoit'.
kw(qu): quoit.
pl: ex-ploit'.
tr: Dē-troit'.
v: Voight (voit).

OIZ

fr: froise (froiz).
n: ẽr'min-ois, noise, Noyes.
p: av''ŏir-dū-pois',
ҫoun'tẽr-poise, e'qui-poise,
poise.
Plus oi+s.
Plus boy's, etc.

ŌJ

b: gam-bōġe'.
d: dōġe.
l: hǫr'ō-lōġe.

OJ

d: dodġe.
h: hodġe.
l: dis-lodġe', hǫr'ō-loġe, lodġe,
un-lodġe'.

(Choose only one word out of each group)

p: hodġe′podġe″.
spl: splodġe.
st: stodġe.

ŌK

Vowel: hōlm ōak (hōm),
līve ōak, ōak, ōke, sc̣rub ōak.
bl: blōke.
br: brōke, dead brōke (ded),
out-brōke′, un-brōke′,
up-brōke′.
ch: är′ti-chōke, chōke.
d: dōke.
f: fōlk (fōk), ġen′tle-fōlk.
j: jōke.
k(c̣): c̣ōak, c̣ōke.
kl: c̣lōak, mōurn′ing c̣lōak,
un-c̣lōak′.
kr: c̣rōak.
l: lōke.
m: mōke.
p: pōke.
r: bȧ-rōque′, Lȧ-rōc̣que′.
s: ȧ-sōak′, sōak.
sl: slōke.
sm: bē-smōke′, smōke.
sp: bē-spōke′, fōre-spōke′,
fȯr-spōke′, spōke.
st: stōke.
str: c̣oun′tēr-strōke,
death strōke (deth),
mȧs′tēr strōke, strōke,
thun′dēr-strōke, un′dēr-strōke.
t: tōke, tōque.
v: c̣on-vōke′, e′qui-vōke′,
ē-vōke′, in-vōke′, prō-vōke′,
rē-vōke′.
w: ȧ-wōke′, wōke.
y: rē-yōke′, un-yōke′, yōke,
yōlk (yōk).

ǪK

Vowel: ạuk, ạwk*.
b: bạlk.
ch: chạlk.
d: dạwk.
f: Fạlk.
g: gạwk.
h: chick′en hạwk, hạwk,
Mō′hạwk, spar′rōw hạwk,
tom′ȧ-hạwk.
k(c̣): c̣ạlk, rē-c̣ạlk′, un-c̣ạlk′.
l: Lạwk.
m: mạwk.
p: pạwk.
skw(squ): squạwk.
st: stạlk.
t: tạlk.
w: c̣āke′wạlk, c̣at′wạlk,
out-wạlk′, sīde′wạlk, wạlk.

OK

Vowel: An′ti-oc̣h.
b: Bäc̣h, bock.
bl: ạuc̣′tion block, Bloc̣h,
block, chock′⸗ȧ⸗block′,
stumb′ling block.
br: brock.
ch: chock.
d: doc̣, dock, läṅgue d′oc̣ (läṅg),
Mẹ-doc̣′, un-dock′.
fl: flock.
fr: frock, un-frock′.
h: hoc̣*, hock, hol′ly-hock,
Mō′hock.
j: jock.
k(c̣): ȧ-c̣ock′, Bab′c̣ock,
Baṅ′kok, bil′ly c̣ock,
hälf′⸗c̣ock′ (häf′), Hitch′c̣ock,
pēa′c̣ock, pet′c̣ock,
pop′py-c̣ock, shut′tle-c̣ock,
spatch′c̣ock, tūr′key-c̣ock,

ŌKS
ŌL

fāte, fär, fåst, fạll, finăl, cãre, at; mēte, prẹy, hẽr, met; pīne,
marïne, bïrd, pin; nōte, mŏve, fọr, atŏm, not; mọọn, book;   208

(Choose only one word out of each group)

tŭrn'cock,
weaTH'ẽr-cock (weTH'),
wood'cock.
kl: clock.
kr: crock.
l: bē-lock', dead'lock (ded'),
fet'lock, fīre'lock, flint'lock,
fōre'lock, have'lock,
in-tẽr-lock', loch, lock,
lŏve'lock, pad'lock,
pẽr-cus'siŏn lock, rē-lock',
un-lock'.
m: à-mok', bē-mock', mock.
n: knock (nok).
p: pock.
pl: plock.
r: bà-roque' (-rok'), bed'rock,
Lit'tle Rock, Pāint'ed Rock,
Rag'nà-rock, roç, rock,
weep'ing rock.
s: soç, sock.
sh: shock.
sm: lā'dy's smock, smock.
st: al'pen-stock,
läugh'ing-stock (läf'),
pen'stock, rē-stock', stock,
un'dẽr-stock.
t: tick'=tock".

ŌKS

Vowel: Ōakes.
h: hōax.
k(ç): çōax.
n: Nōkes.
st: stōkes.
v: Vōkes.
Plus ōk+s.
Plus coke's, etc.

OKS

Vowel: ox.
b: bal'lŏt box, band'box, box,

Çhrist'măs box (kris'), hat'box,
māil'box, pad'dle box,
pil'lăr box, pow'dẽr box,
sig'năl box.
d: het'ẽr-ō-dox, ọr'thō-dox,
par'à-dox.
f: fox, Foxx.
fl: phlox.
k(ç): Çox.
n: ē'qui-nox.
p: chick'en-pox, pox,
small'pox.
s: sox.
v: vox.
Plus ok+s.
Plus lock's, etc.

ŌKT

s: wạ'tẽr=sōaked".
v: un"prō-vōked'.
Plus ōk+d.
Plus choke'd, etc.

OKT

k(ç): çon-çoçt', dē-çoçt',
rē-çoçt'.
Plus ok+d.

ŌL

Vowel: ạu'rē-ōle, çap'ri-ōle,
ça'ri-ōle, fō'li-ōle, glō'ri-ōle,
ōle, ō'ri-ōle, pet'i-ōle,
vaç'ū-ōle, vã'ri-ōle.
b: bōle, bōll, bōwl,
çär'ăm-bōle, em-bōwl',
wäs'săil bōwl.
d: çon-dōle', dhōle (dōl), dōle,
ġir'ăn-dōle.
dr: drōll.
f: fōal.
g: gōal, sē'gōl.

(Choose only one word out of each group)

h: a̱u'gûr hōle, blōw'hōle, buñg'hōle, but'tŏn-hōle, glō'ry hōle, heärt'=whōle', hōle, lo̱o̱p'hōle, peep'hōle, piġ'eŏn-hōle, pin'hōle, pōrt'hōle, so̱up'pẽr-hōle, top hōle, un-whōle'*, whōle (hōl).

j: ça̱-jōle', jōwl.

k(c̱): bō'rē-c̱ōle, ça̱r'a̱-c̱ōle, c̱ōal, c̱ōle, kōhl (kōl).

m: mōle.

n: ça̱r'ma̱-gnōle (-nōl), knōll (nōl), pi-nōle', Se'mi-nōle.

p: bib'li-ō-pōle, c̱ûr'tăin pōle, flag'pōle, Māy'pōle, pōle, pōll. ran'ti-pōle, tad'pōle.

r: ban'dē-rōle, bär'ça̱-rōlle, ças'sē-rōle, en-rōll', fū'ma̱-rōle, fū'rōle, fū'sa̱-rōle, jel'ly-rōll, log'rōll, pa̱-rōle', pāy'rōll, rē-rōll', rig'ma̱-rōle, rōle, rōll, un-rōll', up-rōll', vi-rōle'.

s: ça̱m'i-sōle, ço̱n-sōle', feme sōle' (fem), ġir'a̱-sōle, hälf'=sōle" (häf'), rē-sōle', sōle, sōul, un-sōle', un-sōul'.

sh: shōal, shōle.

sk(sc̱): skōal.

skr(sc̱r): en-sc̱rōll', in-sc̱rōll', sc̱rōll.

st: stōle.

str: strōll.

t: ex-tōll', pis-tōle', tōll.

th: thōle.

tr: c̱omp-trōl' (kon-), c̱on-trōl', pa̱-trōl', self'=ço̱n-trōl', trōll.

v: vōle.

Plus bōw'll, etc.

ǪL

Vowel: a̱ll, a̱ll'=in=a̱ll', a̱wl, free'=fo̱r=a̱ll', THere'wiTH-a̱l" (THär"), where'wiTH-a̱l" (hwär'), wiTH-a̱l'.

b: ba̱ll, bāse'ba̱ll, bas'ket-ba̱ll, ba̱wl, black'ba̱ll, fīre'ba̱ll, foot'ba̱ll, snōw'ba̱ll.

br: bra̱wl.

dr: dra̱wl.

dw: dwa̱l.

f: bē-fa̱ll', ē'ven-fa̱ll, fa̱ll, foot'fa̱ll, land'fa̱ll, nīght'fa̱ll (nīt'), ō-vẽr-fa̱ll', pit'fa̱ll, rāin'fa̱ll, wa̱'tẽr-fa̱ll, wind'fa̱ll.

g: Beñ'gal, ga̱ll, Ga̱ul, spûr ga̱ll.

h: bañ'quet ha̱ll, dánce ha̱ll, ha̱ll, ha̱ul, judġ'ment ha̱ll, ō-vẽr-ha̱ul'.

k(c̱): ça̱ll, ça̱ul, Mc̱-Ça̱ll', mis-ça̱ll', rē-ça̱ll', trum'pet ça̱ll.

kr: cra̱wl, kra̱al.

m: bē-ma̱wl', ma̱ll, ma̱ul.

p: ap-pa̱l', pa̱ll, Paul, pa̱wl, St. Pa̱ul.

s: Sa̱ul.

sh: sha̱wl.

sk(sc̱): sca̱ll.

skr(sc̱r): sc̱ra̱wl.

skw(squ): squa̱ll.

sm: sma̱ll.

sp: spa̱ll, spa̱wl.

spr: spra̱wl.

st: box'sta̱ll, fōre-sta̱ll', in-sta̱ll', sta̱ll.

t: ta̱ll.

OL
ŌLT

fāte, fär, fȧst, fạll, finăl, cãre, at; mēte, prĕy, hẽr, met; pīne,
marïne, bĭrd, pĭn; nōte, mŏve, fọr, atŏm, not; mọọn, book;

210

(Choose only one word out of each group)

thr: bē-thrạll′, dis-en-thrạll′,
en-thrạll′, thrạll.
tr: trạwl.
w: ȧt′ẽr-wạul, sēa wạll, wạll.
y: yạwl.
Plus jaw′ll, etc.

OL

Vowel: vit′ri-ol.
d: bā′by doll, doll.
h: al′cō-hol.
k(c): prō′tō-col.
l: loll.
m: gun moll, moll.
p: poll.
r: fol′=dē=rol′.
s: con′sol, en′tre-sol (′tẽr-),
ġir′ȧ-sol, par′ȧ-sol, Sol.
t: ā′toll, ȧp′i-tol, ex-tol′.

ỌLCH

b: Bạlch.
w: Wạlch.

ŌLD

Vowel: ōld.
b: bōld, ō″vẽr-bōld′.
f: blīnd′fōld, en-fōld′, fōld,
fōur′fōld, in-fōld′, in-tẽr-fōld′,
man′i-fōld, mul′ti-fōld, rē-fōld′,
thou′sănd-fōld,
twö′fōld (tọọ′), etc.,
un-fōld′.
g: gōld, mar′i-gōld,
spun gōld.
h: ȧf′tẽr-hōld, ȧ-hōld′,
añ′chŏr hōld, bē-hōld′,
cọ′py-hōld, foot′hōld,
free′hōld, hōld, house′hōld,
lēase′hōld, strọng′hōld,
up-hōld′, with-hōld′.

k(c): ȧ-cōld′, clay cōld, cōld,
īce cōld, stōne cōld.
m: bụl′let mōuld (mōld),
lēaf mōld, mōld, mōuld.
p: Lē′ŏ-pōld.
s: hälf′=sōled′ (häf′),
hīgh′=sōuled′ (hī′),
sōld, un-sōled′.
sk(sc): scōld.
st: sā′ble=stōled′.
t: fōre-tōld′, rē-tōld′, tōld,
twīce′=tōld′, un-tōld′.
tr: un-con-trōlled′.
w: wōld.
Plus ōl+d.
Plus soul′d, etc.

ỌLD

Vowel: ạuld.
b: Är′chi-bạld, bạld,
black′bạlled.
g: un-gạlled′.
k(c): sō′=cạlled′, un-cạlled′,
un″rē-cạlled′.
p: un″ap-pạlled′.
sk(sc): scạld.
thr: un″en-thrạlled′.
Plus ạl+d.
Plus call′d, etc.

ŌLN

sw: swōln.

ỌLSH

w: Wạlsh.
Cf. ọlch.

ŌLT

b: bōlt, rē-bōlt′, shack′le-bōlt,
thun′dẽr-bōlt, un-bōlt′.
d: dōlt.
h: hōlt.
j: jōlt.

(Choose only one word out of each group)

k(c̦): C̦ōlt, wood c̦ōlt.
m: mōlt.
p: pōult.
sm: smōlt.
v: dem'i-vōlt, là-vōlt',
rē-vōlt', vōlt.

ǪLT

b: c̦ō'bạlt.
f: dē-fạult', fạult.
g: Gạlt, gạult.
h: hạlt.
m: mạlt.
s: as-sạult', bà-sạlt', sạlt,
sēa sạlt, sŏm'ēr-sạult.
sm: smạlt.
sp: spạlt.
v: en-vạult', vạult.
z: ex-ạlt'.

ǪLTS

f: fạlse.
v: vạlse.
w: wạltz.
Plus ọlt+s.
Plus fault's, etc.

OLV

s: ab-solve' (-solv'), solve.
v: cĭr'c̦um-volve, c̦on-volve',
dē-volve', ē-volve',
in"tēr-volve', in-volve',
rē-volve'.
z: diṣ-ṣolve', ex-olve'*,
rē-ṣolve'.

OLVD

s: un-solved'.
z: un"diṣ-ṣolved', un"rē-ṣolved'.
Plus olv+d.

ŌM

Vowel: ōhm (ōm).
b: Bōhm.

br: brōme.
d: dōme, en-dōme',
Tēa'pot Dōme.
dr: āe'rō-drōme, a'quà-drōme,
hip'pō-drōme, pa'lin-drōme.
f: à-fōam', bē-fōam', fōam,
sēa'fōam.
fr: Frōme.
gl: glōam*.
h: at hōme, här'vest hōme,
hōlm (hōm), hōme,
nō'bod-y hōme, sēa hōlm (hōm).
k(c̦): c̦at'à-c̦ōmb (-kōm), c̦ōmb,
c̦ocks'c̦ōmb,
c̦ūr'ry-c̦ōmb (-kōm),
hŏn'ey-c̦ōmb (hun'i-).
kl: c̦lōmb (klōm)*.
kr: c̦hrōme (krōm),
hē'li-ō-c̦hrōme,
me-tal'lō-c̦hrōme,
mon'ō-c̦hrōme, po'ly-c̦hrōme.
l: lōam (lōm), Sà-lōme'.
n: gas'trō-nōme, gnōme (nōm),
me'trō-nōme, nō'm, Nōme.
p: pōme.
r: Je-rōme', rōam, Rōme.
s: c̦hrō'mō-sōme, mī'c̦rō-sōme.
sl: slōam.
t: tōme.

ǪM

h: hạum.
m: i-mạum', mạum.
sh: shạwm.

OM

Vowel: ax'i-om, om.
b: bomb (bom), gas bomb.
d: dom.
fr: from, THere-from' (THär-).
gr: pō-grom'.
p: pom'pom.

(Choose only one word out of each group)

pl: a-plomb'.
pr: prom.
r: rhomb (rom).
sw: swom.
t: hec̣'a-tomb.

OMP

k(c̣): c̣omp.
p: pomp.
r: romp.
sw: swämp.
tr: trompe.

OMPT

k: ac̣-c̣ompt'*.
pr: im-prompt'*, prompt.
Plus omp+d.

OMZ

h: Hōlmes̩ (hōmz).
s: Sōames̩ (sōmz).
Plus ōm+s.
Plus loam's, etc.

ŌN

Vowel: dis-ōwn', ōwn.
b: back'bōne, bōne,
knuck'le-bōne (nuk'l-),
mar'rōw-bōne, trom'bōne,
whāle'bōne (hwāl').
bl: blōwn, flȳ'blōwn,
fresh'⸗blōwn', fụll'⸗blōwn',
out-blōwn', un-blōwn',
weaTH'ẽr-blōwn (weTH').
d: c̣on-dōne', Dōane,
Dọr-dōgne' (-dōn').
dr: drōne, là-drōne', pà-drōne'.
f: an'ti-phōne, au'di-phōne,
dic̣'ta-phōne, ē-lec̣'trō-phōne,
gram'a-phōne, graph'ō-phōne,
meg'a-phōne, mī'c̣rō-phōne,

phōne, rā'di-ō-phōne,
sax'ō-phōne, tel'ē-phōne,
vīt'a-phōne, xyl'ō-phōne (zil').
fl: flōwn, hīgh'⸗flōwn' (hī').
g: bē-grōan', fụll'⸗grōwn',
grȧss'⸗grōwn'', grōan, grōwn,
hälf'⸗grōwn' (häf'),
mọss'⸗grown'', ō''vẽr-grōwn',
un-grōwn'.
h: hōne.
j: Jōan.
k(c̣): C̣ōhn, c̣one, ō-c̣hōne'.
kr: c̣rōne.
l: a-lōne', Ath-lōne',
Böu-lōgne' (-lōn'),
C̣ō-lōgne' (-lōn'),
eau dē C̣ō-lōgne' (ō dē), lōan,
lōne, mà-lōne'.
m: bē-mōan', mōan, mōwn,
rē-mōwn', un-mōwn'.
n: fōre-knōwn' (nōn'), knōwn,
un''bē-knōwn', un''fōre-knōwn',
un-knōwn'.
p: c̣ọrn pōne, dē-pōne',
dis-pōne', im-pōne'*,
in-tẽr-pōne', pōne, pōst-pōne',
prō-pōne'.
pr: prōne.
r: c̣ha'pẽr-ōne, ci'ce-rōne,
Rhōne (rōn), rōan.
s: rē-sewn' (-sōn'), rē-sōwn',
sewn (sōn), sōwn, un-sewn',
un-sōwn'.
sh: fōre-shōwn',
shewn (shōn)*, shōne, shōwn.
sk(sc̣): sc̣ōne.
sl: Slōan.
st: brim'stōne, c̣ling'stōne,
c̣ọr'nẽr-stōne, c̣ûrb'stōne,
flag'stōne, foun-dā'tion stōne,
grīnd'le-stōne*, grīnd'stōne,

(Choose only one word out of each group)

hāil'stōne, head'stōne (hed'),
heärth'stōne, hō'ly-stōne,
im-pōṣ'ing stōne, kēy'stōne,
līme'stōne, lōad'stōne,
lōde'stōne, mīle'stōne,
mill'stōne, mo̱on'stōne,
sōap'stōne, stōne,
whet'stōne (hwet').

t: à-tōne', bār'i-tōne, in-tōne',
mac̣'rō-tōne, mon'ō-tōne,
sem'i-tōne, tōne, un'dĕr-tōne.

thr: dē-thrōne', en-thrōne',
ō-vĕr-thrōwn', thrōne,
thrōwn, un-thrōne'.

z: en'zōne, zōne.

O̱N

Vowel: a̱wn.
b: ba̱wn.
br: bra̱wn.
d: da̱wn.
dr: dra̱wn, in-dra̱wn',
rē-dra̱wn', un-dra̱wn',
with-dra̱wn'.
f: fa̱un, fa̱wn.
k(c̣): c̣a̱wn.
l: la̱wn.
p: im-pa̱wn', pa̱wn.
pr: pra̱wn.
s: sa̱wn.
sh: De̱'ni-sha̱wn, Sha̱wn.
sp: spa̱wn.
y: ya̱wn.

ON

Vowel: en″c̣hī-rid'i-on,
en-c̣ō'mi-on*, En-dym'i-on,
hañg'ĕr꞊on', hēre-on',
Hȳ-pē'ri-on, Lā-oc̣'ō-on,
lo̱ng fiēld on, on,
THere-on' (THär-),
where-on' (hwär-).

b: bon'bon, bonne.
d: cel'à-don, don, Donne,
Eū-rō'c̣ly-don, glyp'tō-don,
i-guän'ō-don, mȧst'ō-don,
myr'mi-don.
f: an'ti-phon, Bel-ler'ō-phon,
c̣hif-fon', c̣ol'ō-phon.
g: à-gone'*, be-gone',
dec̣'à-gon, gone, hep'tà-gon,
hex'à-gon, oc̣'tà-gon,
Ō'rē-gon, par'à-gon,
pent'à-gon, po'ly-gon,
tar'rà-gon, un-dĕr-gone',
wōe'꞊bē-gone″.
j: dem'i-john (-jon),
Jeanne (zhon), John (jon),
Lit'tle-john, Mick'le-john.
k(c̣): c̣on, Hel'i-c̣on,
ī-ren'i-c̣on, lex'i-c̣on,
pan-tec̣h'ni-c̣on, Rú'bi-c̣on,
sil'i-c̣on, ster-ē-op'ti-c̣on.
l: Ba'by-lon, Cēy-lon',
ec̣h'ē-lon, en-ceph'à-lon (-cef'),
gon'fà-lon.
m: ho̱ot mon.
n: à-non', dī'ēṣ non,
Pär″thē-non, phē-nom'ē-non,
prō″lē-gom'ē-non, sī'nē quā non.
p: hēre″up-on', pu̱t up-on',
THere″up-on' (THär″), up-on',
where'up-on″ (hwär').
r: Ō'bē-ron.
s: ben'i-son, ven'i-son.
sh: out-shone', shone.
sw: swän.
t: a̱u-tom'à-ton, c̣rē-tonne',
phā'e-ton.
v: von, Y-vonne'.
w: Sas-katch'ē-wän (-won), wän.
y: yon.

(Choose only one word out of each group)

z: am'ȧ-zon, Lū-zon'.
Cf. accordion, etc., under un.

ǪNCH

h: haunch.
kr: craunch.
l: launch.
p: paunch.

ŌND

Vowel: un-ōwned'.
m: un-mōaned'.
t: hīgh"=tōned' (hī"),.
un-ȧ-tōned'.
z: un-zōned', zōned.
Plus ōn+d.
Plus zone'd, etc.

ǪND

fr: Frǫnde.
m: beau mǫnde (bō),
dem'i-mǫnde, mǫnde.
r: Ǧi-rǫnde'.
Plus yawn'd, etc.

OND

b: bond, vag'ȧ-bond.
bl: blond, blonde.
d: donned.
f: fond, ō"vẽr-fond', plȧ-fond'.
fr: frond.
g: un-par'ȧ-goned.
m: beau monde (bō),
dem'i-monde, monde.
p: pond.
sk(sc): ab-scond'.
sp: cǫr-rē-spond', dē-spond',
rē-spond'.
w: wänd.
y: bē-yond', yond*.
Plus on+d.
Plus don'd, etc.

ONG

d: ding'dong.
fl: flong.
g: dū'gong, gong.
j: mäh'jongg'.
k(c): Hong Kong, King Kong.
l: all-ȧ-long', ȧ-long', bē-long',
dāy'=long', ere long (ãr),
head'long (hed'), līfe'long,
līve'long, long,
nīght'long (nīt'), ō"vẽr-long'.
n: scup'pẽr-nong.
p: ping'pong.
pr: prong.
r: wrong.
s: bat'tle song, drink'ing song,
ē'ven-song, sing'song, song,
un'dẽr-song.
sh: söu-chong'.
st: Stong.
str: head'strong (hed'), strong.
t: tong.
th: thong.
thr: throng.
w: wong.

ONGD

r: un-wronged'.
Plus ong+d.
Plus song'd, etc.

ONGK

h: honk.
k(c): conch, conk.
t: honk'y=tonk.

ONGKS

br: Bronx.
Plus ongk+s.
Plus honk'y=tonk's, etc.

(Choose only one word out of each group)

ONGST

l: à-longst', bē-long'st'*, long'st*, prō-long'st'*.
r: wrong'st*.
thr: throng'st*.

ONGZ

See ong+ṣ.
Plus gong's, etc.

ONS

n: nonce.
sk(sç): en-sçonce', sçonce.
sp: rē-sponse'.
Plus ont+s.
Plus font's, etc.

ŌNT

d: dōn't.
w: wōn't.

ǪNT

d: daunt.
fl: à-flaunt', flaunt.
g: gaunt.
h: haunt.
j: jaunt.
m: rō-maunt'.
t: à-taunt', taunt.
v: à-vaunt'*, vaunt.
w: want.

ONT

f: font.
p: Dū-pont', Hel'les-pont, pont.
w: wänt.

ONTS

See ont+s.
Cf. ons.

ŌNZ

b: lā'zy-bōneṣ, rōll'ing the bōneṣ.

j: Dā'vy Jōneṣ, Jōneṣ.
n: nōneṣ.
Plus ōn+s.
Plus bone's, etc.

ONZ

b: bonze.
br: bronze.
g: bȳ'goneṣ.
j: Johnṣ (jonz), St. John'ṣ.
p: ponṣ.
Plus on+ṣ.
Plus John's, etc.

OOD

g: good.
h: ān'ġel-hood, bā'by-hood, brŏTH'ẽr-hood, dēa'çŏn-hood, fäTH'ẽr-hood, fool'här-di-hood, ġen'tle-măn-hood, här'di-hood, hood, king'li-hood, kit'ten-hood, lā'dy-hood, līke'li-hood, līve'li-hood, lus'ti-hood*, māid'en-hood, man'hood, māt'rŏn-hood, mŏnk's'hood, mŏTH'ẽr-hood, neigh'bŏr-hood (nā'), ǫr'phăn-hood, par'ent-hood, Rob'in Hood, sis'tẽr-hood, spin'stẽr-hood, un-līke'li-hood, wid'ōw-ẽr-hood, wid'ōw-hood, wo'măn-hood (woo').
k(ç): çould (kood).
p: Pud (pood).
sh: should (shood).
st: mis"un-dẽr-stood', stood, un-dẽr-stood', with-stood'.
w: dead wood (ded), fīre'wood, plas'tiç wood, pūr'ple-wood, san'dăl-wood, Un'dẽr-wood, wīld'wood, wood, would (wood).

OOK
OOL

fāte, fär, fȧst, fᶏll, finᶏl, cãre, at; mēte, prĕy, hēr,ˑmet; pīne,
marīne, bîrd, pin; nōte, mŏve, fọr, atŏm, not; mọọn, book;

216

(Choose only one word out of each group)

OOK

b: book, min'ute book ('it),
pock'et-book.
br: brook.
h: hook, rē-hook', un-hook'.
k(c̨): c̨ook, pās'try c̨ook.
l: look, out'look, ō"vēr-look',
up'look.
n: Chi-nook', iñ'gle-nook,
nook.
r: rook.
s: fọr-sook'.
sh: shook.
t: bē-took', mis-took',
ō"vēr-took', pär-took', took,
un-dēr-took'.

OOKS

h: ten'tēr-hooks.
kr: C̨rookes.
sn: snooks.
Plus ook+s.
Plus book's, etc.

OOL

b: ac̨-cep'tȧ-ble, ac̨-ces'si-ble,
ac̨-c̨ount'ȧ-ble, ad-mis'sȧ-ble,
ȧ-dọr'ȧ-ble, af'fȧ-ble,
ȧ-men'ȧ-ble, ā-mi'ȧ-ble,
at-tāin'ȧ-ble, au'di-ble,
ȧ-vāil'ȧ-ble, ȧ-void'ȧ-ble,
bē-liēv'ȧ-ble, bᶙll, c̨āp'ȧ-ble,
chānġe'ȧ-ble, c̨ock"=and=bᶙll',
c̨om-bus'ti-ble,
c̨om-men'dȧ-ble,
c̨om-pat'i-ble,
c̨om-prē-hen'si-ble, c̨on'stȧ-ble,
c̨on-temp'ti-ble, c̨ọr-rup'ti-ble,
c̨red'i-ble,
c̨rü'ci-ble, c̨ulp'ȧ-ble,

c̨ūr'ȧ-ble, dam'nȧ-ble,
dē-lec̨'tȧ-ble, dē-plō'rȧ-ble,
dē-sīr'ȧ-ble, dē-tes'tȧ-ble,
flex'i-ble, fọr'ci-ble, họr'ri-ble,
il-le'ġi-ble, im-möv'ȧ-ble,
im-mū'tȧ-ble, im-pal'pȧ-ble,
im-pas'sȧ-ble, im-pec̨'c̨ȧ-ble,
im-pēr-tūr'bȧ-ble, im-pla'c̨ȧ-ble,
im-pos'si-ble, im-preg'nȧ-ble,
im-pro'bȧ-ble, im-pröv'ȧ-ble,
in-ac̨-ces'si-ble, in-ad-mis'si-ble,
in-au'di-ble, in-c̨āp'ȧ-ble,
in-c̨om'pȧ-rȧ-ble,
in-c̨om-pat'i-ble,
in-c̨om-prē-hen'si-ble,
in-c̨ŏn-cēiv'ȧ-ble,
in-c̨ŏn-tes'tȧ-ble,
in-c̨on-trō-vēr'ti-ble,
in-c̨ọr-rup'ti-ble, in-c̨re'di-ble,
in-c̨ūr'ȧ-ble, in-del'i-ble,
in-dē-sc̨rīb'ȧ-ble,
in-dē-struc̨'ti-ble,
in-di-spen'sȧ-ble, in-ef'fȧ-ble,
in-ef-fāce'ȧ-ble, in-ex-c̨ūs'ȧ-ble,
in-ex-haust'i-ble (-aust'),
in-ex-pres'si-ble, in-fal'li-ble,
in-flam'mȧ-ble, in-flex'i-ble,
in-fran'ġi-ble, in-sc̨rü'tȧ-ble,
in-sen'si-ble, in-sol'ū-ble,
in-sup-pọrt'ȧ-ble,
in-sup-pōs'ȧ-ble,
in-sup-pres'si-ble,
in-sūr-mount'ȧ-ble,
in-tanġ'i-ble, in-tel'li-ġi-ble,
in-tēr-chānġe'ȧ-ble,
in-trac̨'ti-ble, in-val'ū-ȧ-ble,
in-vin'ci-ble, i-ras'ci-ble,
ir-rē-pres'si-ble,
ir-rē-prōach'ȧ-ble,
ir-rē-sis'ti-ble,
ir-rē-spon'si-ble,

217 ūse, bull, brúte, tũrn, up; crȳ, myth; çat, maçhine, ace, church, çhord; ġem, añger, (Fr.) boñ, aṣ; THis, thin; aẓure

OOLF
ŌP

(Choose only one word out of each group)

ir-rē-triēv'à-ble,
jus"ti-fī'à-ble, laud'à-ble,
le'ġi-ble, Mē-hit'à-ble,
mū'tà-ble, nōt'à-ble,
os-ten'si-ble, pal'pà-ble,
pas'sà-ble, pẽr-cep'ti-ble,
pẽr-mis'si-ble, pla'çà-ble,
plau'ṣi-ble, pōrt'à-ble,
pos'si-ble, prāiṣ'à-ble,
prē-ṣent'à-ble, pro'bà-ble,
prō-çūr'à-ble, prō-dū'ci-ble,
prō-nounce'à-ble, rāt'à-ble,
rē-deem'à-ble, rē-lī'à-ble,
rep-rē-hen'si-ble,
rē-speç'tà-ble,
rē-spon'si-ble, sen'si-ble,
Sit'ting Bull, sus-cep'ti-ble,
syl'là-ble, tanġ'i-ble, ten'à-ble,
ter'ri-ble, traç'tà-ble,
un-im-pēach'à-ble,
un-match'à-ble,
un-quench'à-ble, vi'ṣi-ble,
vol'ū-ble.

f: full, beaū'ti-ful,
boun'ti-ful, dū'ti-ful,
fan'ci-ful, màs'tẽr-ful,
mẽr'ci-ful, pi'ti-ful, plen'ti-ful,
pow'ẽr-ful, sor'rōw-ful,
thim'ble-ful, un-mẽr'ci-ful,
wēar'i-ful, wŏn'dẽr-ful,
wŏr'ship-ful.

p: pull, prin'ci-ple.
w: abb wool, çot'tŏn wool,
lamb'ṣ wool, wool.
Cf. prin'ci-păl.

OOLF
w: wolf.

OOLVZ
w: wolveṣ.

OOM
r: rootm.

OOS
p: puss.

OOSH
b: bram'ble-bush, bush.
p: push.

OOSK
br: brusque.

OOT
f: à-foot', foot, fōre'foot,
pus'sy-foot, un"dẽr-foot'.
p: put.

ŌP
Vowel: ōpe.
d: dōpe.
gr: à-grōpe', grōpe.
h: Çape of Good Hōpe, hōpe.
k(ç): çōpe.
l: an'tē-lōpe, çan'tà-lōupe,
ē-lōpe', en've-lōpe,
in"tẽr-lōpe', lōpe.
m: mōpe.
n: nōpe.
p: an'ti-pōpe, dis-pōpe', pōpe,
un-pōpe'.
r: foot'rōpe, rōpe.
s: sōap.
sk(sç): as'trō-sçōpe,
bar'ō-sçōpe, bī'ō-sçōpe,
ē-leç'trō-sçōpe, gal-van'ō-sçōpe,
ġȳ'rō-sçōpe, hē'li-ō-sçōpe,
hor'ō-sçōpe, hȳ'drō-sçōpe,
kà-leī'dō-sçōpe, mī'çrō-sçōpe,
pō-lar'i-sçōpe, sçōpe,
seīs'mō-sçōpe, speç'trō-sçōpe,
ster'ē-ō-sçōpe, steth'ō-sçōpe,
tel'ē-sçōpe, thẽrm'ō-sçōpe.
sl: à-slōpe', slōpe.
st: stōpe.

OP
OR

fāte, fär, fåst, fạll, finăl, cãre, at; mēte, prey, hẽr, met; pīne,
marīne, bĩrd, pin; nōte, mŏve, fọr, atŏm, not; mọọn, book;

218

(Choose only one word out of each group)

sw: swōpe.
t: taupe (tŏp), tōpe.
thr: mis'ăn-thrōpe.
tr: hē'li-ō-trōpe, trōpe.

OP

g: gạup.
hw: whạup.
sk(sc): scạup.
y: yạwp.

OP

Vowel: cō꞊op'.
bl: blop.
ch: chop.
dr: bē-drop', dew'drop, drop,
ēaves'drop (ēvz'), snōw'drop.
f: fop.
fl: flip'flop, flip'pi-ty꞊flop, flop.
h: hop.
hw: whop.
k(c): cop.
kl: klop'꞊klop'.
kr: åf'tẽr-crop, crop,
rīd'ing crop.
l: gạ'lop, lop.
m: mop.
n: knop (nop).
p: g̣in'g̣ẽr pop, lol'li-pop, pop,
sō'då pop.
pl: plop.
pr: prop, un-dẽr-prop'.
s: sop, sour'sop, sweet'sop.
sh: shop, wŏrk'shop.
sl: slop.
st: stop, un-stop'.
str: strop.
sw: swäp.
t: å-top', es-top', fōre'top,
miz'zen-top, ō-vẽr-top',
tip'top, top.
w: wop.

OPS

k: c̣opse.
Plus op+s.
Plus chop's, etc.

ŌPT

h: un-hōped'.
s: un-sōaped'.
Plus ōp+d.
Plus slope'd, etc.

OPT

Vowel: opt, co꞊opt'.
d: å-dopt'.
k(c): c̣opped, C̣opt.
kr: out-c̣ropped', un-c̣ropped'.
st: un-stopped'.
Plus op+d.
Plus crop'd, etc.

ŌR

Vowel: ōar, ō'er, ōre.
b: bōar, Bōer, bōre,
fōre-bōre', hel'lē-bōre.
ch: chōre.
d: å-dōre', back-dōor',
bat'tle-dōre, com'mō-dōre,
death's dōor (deths),
dōor, mat'å-dōr,
mir'å-dōr, pic̣'å-dōr,
stēv'e-dōre, Thē'ō-dōre,
trŏu'bå-dōur.
f: å-fōre', bē-fōre', fōre, fōur,
hẽre'tö-fōre, pin'å-fōre,
sem'å-phōre.
fl: fĩrst flōor (flōr), flōor.
fr: frōre*.
g: gōre.
h: hōar, Lå-hōre',
whōre (hōr).

(Choose only one word out of each group)

k(ç): al'bȧ-çōre, çōre, çōrps (kōr), eṅ-çōre' (äṅ-).

kr: crōre.

l: fōlk'lōre (fōk'), gȧ-lōre', lōre.

m: Bạl'ti-mōre, ev-ēr-mōre', fŭr''THēr-mōre, mōre, nev'ēr-mōre, sag'ȧ-mōre, soph'ō-mōre, sy'çȧ-mōre.

n: ig-nōre', Nōre.

p: out-pōur', pōre, pōur, Sing'ȧ-pōre.

pl: dē-plōre', ex-plōre', im-plōre'.

r: out-rōar', rōar, up'rōar.

s: foot'sōre, heärt'sōre, out-sōar', sōar, sōre, up-sōre'.

sh: ȧ-shōre', fōre-shōre', in-shōre', off'shōre'', sēa'shōre, shōre, weaTH'ēr shōre (weTH').

sk(sç): fōur sçōre, sçōre, un'dēr-sçōre.

sn: snōre.

sp: spōre.

st: rē-stōre', stōre.

sw: fōre-swōre', swōre.

t: tōre.

w: out-wōre', wōre.

y: yōre.

QR

Vowel: an-tē'ri-ọr, ex-cel'si-ọr, ex-tē'ri-ọr, in-fē'ri-ọr, in-tē'ri-ọr, mē'tē-ọr, ọr, Ọrr, pos-tē'ri-ọr, sū-pē'ri-ọr, ul-tē'ri-ọr.

b: Dūk'hō-bọr.

d: am-bas'sȧ-dọr, çọr'ri-dọr, dọr, E'çuȧ-dōr ('kwȧ-), La'brȧ-dọr, löu'is d'ọr (lọọ'i), mat'ȧ-dọr, mir'ȧ-dōr,

Sal'vȧ-dọr, tō'rē-ȧ-dọr, tröu'bȧ-dọur.

f: fọr, met'ȧ-phọr, THere'fọr (THãr').

h: ab-họr'.

j: mọrt'gȧġ-ọr (mọr').

l: bach'ē-lọr, chan'cel-lọr, çoun'cil-lọr, çoun'sel-lọr, lọr, vīce chan'cel-lọr.

n: as-sīgn'ọr (-sīn'), gŏv'ēr-nọr, nō'mi-nọr, nọr.

r: çoñ'quẽr-ọr ('kẽr-), em'pẽr-ọr, vẽr'dẽr-ọr.

s: di'nō-sạur, ich-thȳ'ō-sạur, les'sọr, pleīs'ō-sạur.

sk(sç): sçạur.

t: an'ces-tọr, ap-par'i-tọr, ạu'di-tọr, çom-pet'i-tọr, çom-pos'i-tọr, çon-spi'rȧ-tọr, çon-tri'bū-tọr, çre'di-tọr, dē-poş'i-tọr, e'di-tọr, ex-e'çū-tọr, ex-poş'i-tọr, guar''ăn-tọr, in-her'i-tọr, in-qui'şi-tọr (-kwi'), in-tēr-loç'ū-tọr, jan'i-tọr, leg'ȧ-tọr, mi'nō-tạur, mo'ni-tọr, ọr'ȧ-tọr, prī-mō-ġen'i-tọr, prō-ġen'i-tọr, prō-prī'ē-tọr, sen'ȧ-tọr, sẽr'vi-tọr, sō-li'ci-tọr, tọr, vi'şi-tọr.

th: Thọr.

w: man''=of=wạr' (=ov=), tug''=of=wạr', wạr.

y: sē'niọr ('nyọr), se-ñọr' (sā-nyọr').

QRB

Vowel: ọrb.

k(ç): çọrb.

ǪRBD
ǪRKD
fāte, fär, fȧst, fạll, fĭnăl, cãre, at; mēte, prey, hẽr, met; pīne,
marïne, bĭrd, pin; nōte, mŏve, fọr, atŏm, not; mọọn, book;
220

(Choose only one word out of each group)

s: ab-sọrb', rē-ăb-sọrb',
rē-sọrb'.

ǪRBD

Vowel: fụll'=ọrbed'.
Plus ọrb+d.

ǪRBZ

f: Fọrbeṣ.
Plus ọrb+s.
Plus orb's, etc.

ŌRCH

p: pōrch.

ǪRCH

b: bọrtsch.
sk(sc̣): sc̣ọrch.
t: tọrch.

ŌRD

Vowel: ōared.
b: ȧ-bōard', bēa'vẽr-bōard,
bōard, ī'rŏn-ing bōard ('ẽrn-),
mōuld bōard, sēa'bōard,
shuf'fle-bōard, sũrf'bōard,
weaTH'ẽr bōard (weTH').
d: ȧ-dōred'.
f: af-fōrd', fōrd.
g: gōurd, un-gōred'.
h: hōard, hōrde, un-hōard',
whōred (hōrd).
pl: un"dē-plōred', un"ex-plōred',
un"im-plōred'.
s: brọad'swọrd ('sọrd), swọrd.
st: un"rē-stōred'.
Plus ōr+d.
Plus store'd, etc.

ǪRD

Vowel: fĭ-ọrd', Ǫrd, Ǫrde.
b: bọrd.
fy: fyọrd.
h: ab-họrred'.
k(c̣): ac̣-c̣ọrd', c̣họrd,

c̣on'c̣ọrd*, c̣ọrd, dis"ac̣-c̣ọrd',
härp'si-c̣họrd, lyr'i-c̣họrd,
mȧs'tẽr-c̣họrd, Mc̣-C̣ọrd',
miṣ'ẽr-i-c̣ọrd, po'ly-c̣họrd,
rē-c̣ọrd'.
l: bē-lọrd', land'lọrd, lọrd,
ō'vẽr-lọrd, un-lọrd'.
n: Nọrd.
sw: swạrd.
w: ȧ-wạrd', rē-wạrd', wạrd.
Plus ọr+d.
Plus war'd, etc.

ǪRF

d: Dĭēf'en-dọrf.
dw: dwạrf.
hw: whạrf.
k(c̣): c̣ọrf.

ǪRG

m: mọrgue.

ŌRJ

f: fōrġe.

ǪRJ

g: dis-gọrġe', en-gọrġe', gọrġe,
rē-gọrġe'.
j: Ġeọrġe, St. Ġeọrġe.

ŌRK

p: pōrk.

ǪRK

Vowel: ọrk.
f: fọrk, pitch'fọrk,
weed'ing fọrk.
k(c̣): c̣ọrk, un-c̣ọrk'.
st: stọrk.
t: tọrque.
y: New Yọrk, Yọrk.

ǪRKD

st: stọrked.
Plus ọrk+d.
Plus fork'd, etc.

221 ūse, bu̧ll, brute, tūrn, up; crȳ, myth; çat, ma̧chine, ace, church, çhord; ġem, an̄ger, (Fr.) bon̄, a̧s̯; THis, thin; aᵶure

ORL
ORN

(Choose only one word out of each group)

ORL

Vowel: oŗle.
hw: who̧rl.
sh: sçho̧rl.

ORM

Vowel: Oŗme.
d: do̧rm.
f: ā'ĕr-i-fo̧rm, a'qui-fo̧rm, çhlō'rō-fo̧rm, çon-fo̧rm', cru̇'ci-fo̧rm, çū'nē-i-fo̧rm, dē-fo̧rm', dē'i-fo̧rm, den'dri-fo̧rm, di-vĕr'si-fo̧rm, flō'ri-fo̧rm, fo̧rm, in-fo̧rm', mis-fo̧rm', mis-in-fo̧rm', mul'ti-fo̧rm, pĕr-fo̧rm', rē-fo̧rm', stel'li-fo̧rm, trans-fo̧rm', ū'ni-fo̧rm, vĕr'mi-fo̧rm.
k(ç): ço̧rm.
n: no̧rm.
st: bē-sto̧rm', snōw'sto̧rm", sto̧rm, thun'dĕr-sto̧rm.
sw: swa̧rm, up-swa̧rm'.
w: sun'ny wa̧rm, un-wa̧rm', wa̧rm.

ORMD

f: un-fo̧rmed', un-in-fo̧rmed', un"pĕr-fo̧rmed', un"rē-fo̧rmed', well'=in-fo̧rmed'.
st: un-sto̧rmed'.
Plus o̧rm+d.
Plus storm'd, etc.

ORMTH

w: wa̧rmth.
Plus storm'th*, etc.

ŌRN

b: bōrne, bōurn, fo̧r-bōrne', ō"vĕr-bōrne'.
m: bē-mōurn'. mōurn.

sh: shōrn, un-shōrn'.
sw: fo̧r-swōrn', swōrn, un-swōrn'.
t: bē-tōrn', tōrn.
w: foot'wōrn, out-wōrn', sēa'wōrn, toil'wōrn, wa̧'tĕr-wōrn, wāve'wōrn, wāy'wōrn, weaTH'ĕr-wōrn (weTH'), wōrn. Cf. o̧rn.

ORN

Vowel: Oŗne.
b: bo̧rn, çloud'=bo̧rn", first'=bo̧rn", hea'ven=bo̧rn', hīgh'=bo̧rn" (hī'), in-bo̧rn', nīght'=bo̧rn" (nīt'), rē-bo̧rn', sēa'=bo̧rn", skȳ'=bo̧rn", still'=bo̧rn", su-bo̧rn', trūe'=bo̧rn", un-bo̧rn', vir'ġin=bo̧rn".
d: a̧-do̧rn', dis-a̧-do̧rn', rē-a̧-do̧rn'.
h: al'pen-ho̧rn, Çāpe Ho̧rn, çow ho̧rn, dis-ho̧rn', drin̄k'ing ho̧rn, fog'ho̧rn, French ho̧rn, green'ho̧rn, ho̧rn, Ho̧rne, hunt'ing ho̧rn, Lang'ho̧rne, Mat'tĕr-ho̧rn, pow'dĕr-ho̧rn, prīm'ing ho̧rn.
k(ç): bär'ley-ço̧rn ('li-), Çap'ri-ço̧rn, ço̧rn, lo̧n'ġi-ço̧rn, pep'pĕr-ço̧rn, pop'ço̧rn, trī'ço̧rn, ū'ni-ço̧rn.
l: fo̧r-lo̧rn', lo̧rn, lŏve'lo̧rn.
m: mo̧rn, yes'tĕr-mo̧rn*.
n: No̧rn.
sk(sç): bē-sço̧rn', sço̧rn, self'=sço̧rn'.
th: black'tho̧rn, buck'tho̧rn, ha̧w'tho̧rn, tho̧rn.
w: fōre-wa̧rn', wa̧rn.

ŌRND
ǪRT

fāte, fär, fȧst, fạll, finăl, cãre, at; mēte, prey, hẽr, met; pīne,
marïne, bĭrd, pin; nōte, mȯve, fǫr, atŏm, not; mọọn, book;

222

(Choose only one word out of each group)

ŌRND

m: bē-mōurned', mōurned,
un-mōurned'.

ǪRND

d: un-à-dǫrned'.
w: un"fōre-wạrned'.
Plus ǫrn+d.
Plus morn'd, etc.

ǪRP

d: dǫrp.
th: Ō'gle-thǫrpe, thǫrp.
w: wạrp.

ǪRPS

k(ç): cǫrpse.
Plus ǫrp+s.
Plus dǫrp's, etc.

ŌRS

f: en-fōrce', fōrce, pẽr-fōrce',
rē"in-fōrce'.
h: hōarse.
k(ç): çōarse, çōurse,
dis-çōurse', in'tẽr-çōurse,
rē-çōurse', wạ'tẽr-çōurse.
s: rē-sōurce', sōurce.
v: di-vōrce'.

ǪRS

d: dǫrse*, en-dǫrse'.
g: gǫrse.
h: Çrā'zy Hǫrse,
dead hǫrse (ded),
hob'by-hǫrse, hǫrse,
rock'ing hǫrse, sēa'hǫrse,
stạlk'ing-hǫrse (stạk'),
un-hǫrse'.
k(ç): cǫrse.
m: Mǫrse, rē-mǫrse'.

n: Nǫrse.
t: tǫrse.
tr: dex-trǫrse', rē-trǫrse',
sin'is-trǫrse.

ǪRSK

t: tǫrsk.

ǪRST

d: ad-dǫrsed', en-dǫrsed'.
h: hǫrsed, Hǫrst, un-hǫrsed'.

ŌRT

f: fōrt, fōrte.
k(ç): çoun'ty çōurt, çōurt,
dē-çōurt'*.
p: çom'pōrt, da'ven-pōrt,
dē-pōrt', dis-pōrt', ex-pōrt',
im-pōrt', mis"rē-pōrt',
pàss'pōrt, pōrt, Pōrte,
rap-pōrt', rē-pōrt', sal'ly-pōrt,
sēa'pōrt, trans-pōrt'.
sp: spōrt.
Cf. ǫrt.

ǪRT

Vowel: ǫrt*.
b: à-bǫrt', bǫrt.
h: ex-hǫrt'.
k(ç): es-cǫrt'.
kw(qu): quạrt.
m: à-mǫrt', mǫrt.
s: as-sǫrt', çon-sǫrt', rē=sǫrt'.
sh: shǫrt.
sn: snǫrt.
sw: swạrt*.
t: çon-tǫrt', dē-tǫrt'*,
dis-tǫrt', ex-tǫrt', rē-tǫrt',
tǫrt.
thw: à-thwạrt', thwạrt.
v: cà-vǫrt'.
w: wạrt.

(Choose only one word out of each group)

z: rē-ṣọrt′.
Cf. ōrt.

ŌRTH

f: fōrth, fōurth, hence-fōrth′,
set′tēr=fōrth′, thence-fōrth′.
Plus pour′th*, etc.

ỌRTH

Vowel: Ọrth.
n: nọrth.
sw: swạrth.
Plus abhorr′th*, etc.

ỌRTS

kw(qu): quạrtz.
sh: shọrts.
sw: Schwạrtz (swọrts),
Swạrz (swọrts).
Plus ọrt+s.
Plus short′s, etc.

ỌRVZ

hw: whạrves.

ŌRZ

d: in-dōorṣ′, out-dōorṣ′.
f: all′=fōurṣ′, plus′=fōurṣ′.
z: Ā′zōreṣ.
Plus ōr+s.
Plus floor′s, etc.

ỌRZ

kw(qu): Löu′is Quȧ-tọrze′
　　　　(lö′i kȧ-tọrz′),
quȧ-tọrze′.
Plus ọr+s.
Plus war′s, etc.

ŌS

Vowel: aç-tū-ōse′*, fō′li-ōse,
gran′di-ōse, ō′ti-ōse.
b: ġib′bōse, glō′bōse, vēr-bōse′.

d: dōse, nō′dōse, ō′vēr-dōse,
un′dēr-dōse.
gr: en-grōss′, grōss.
k(ç): bel′li-çōse, çōse, floç′çōse,
glū′çōse, jō′çōse,
mē-temp′sy-çhōse (′si-).
kl: çlōse.
l: an′nū-lōse, cel′lū-lōse.
m: a′ni-mōse*.
n: al-bū′mi-nōse, dĭ′ag-nōse.
p: a′di-pōse.
r: ag′ġē-rōse, mō-rōse′.
t: çom′ȧ-tōse.

ỌS

s: ap′ple-sạuce, sạuce.

OS

Vowel: os.
b: Bos, boss, em-boss′,
Set′ē-bos.
d: doss.
dr: dross.
f: fosse.
fl: sloss.
g: Gosse.
gl: gloss.
j: joss.
k(ç): ços.
kr: ȧ-çross′, çross,
dŏu′ble=çross, fīe′ry çross,
lȧ-çrosse′, rē-çross′,
rō′ṣy çross, weep′ing çross.
l: çō-loss′*, loss.
m: moss, sēa moss.
r: rhĭ-noc′ē-ros (rĭ-).
t: toss.
tr: al′bȧ-tross.

ŌSH

f: Fōçh.
g: gauçhe (gōsh).
l: guil-lōçhe′ (gil-lōsh′).

OSH
ŌT

fāte, fär, fàst, fạll, finăl, cãre, at; mēte, prey, hẽr, met; pīne, marïne, bĩrd, pĭn; nōte, mŏve, fọr, atŏm, not; mọọn, book;

224

(Choose only one word out of each group)

OSH

b: bosçh, bosh, dē-bosh', kĭ-bosh'.
fr: frosh.
g: gosh.
j: josh.
kw(qu): mus'quäsh, quäsh.
l: gà-losh'.
skw(squ): squäsh.
sl: slosh.
spl: splosh.
sw: swäsh.
t: mack'in-tosh, Mç'In-tosh, tosh.
w: à-wäsh', bel'ly-wäsh, bē-wäsh', hog'wäsh, wäsh.

OSHT

b: çà-boshed'.
w: greāt un-wäshed', un-wäshed'.
Plus osh+d.

OSK

Vowel: kĭ-osk'.
b: bosk, im-bosk'*.
m: mosque.

OSP

w: wäsp.

ŌST

Vowel: ōast.
b: bōast.
d: dōsed.
g: ghōst (gōst).
gr: en-grōssed'.
h: hōst.
k(ç): çōast, sēa'çōast.
m: àf'tẽr-mōst, bet'tẽr-mōst, bot'tŏm-mōst, fōre'mōst, fũr''THẽr-mōst, hĭn'dẽr-mōst, hiTH'ẽr-mōst, in'nẽr-mōst, lō'wẽr-mōst, mōst, neTH'ẽr-mōst, nọrTH'ẽr-mōst, out'ẽr-mōst, sŏuTH'ẽr-mōst, un'dẽr-mōst, up'pẽr-mōst, ut'tẽr-mōst, west'ẽr-mōst.
p: fiñ'gẽr-pōst, hitch'ing-pōst, pōst, ri-pōste', sĩgn'pōst (sĭn'), sound'pōst, whip'ping-pōst'' (hwip').
r: rōast.
t: tōast.
v: Van-Vōst'.
y: Yōst.
Plus ōs+d.

ỌST

h: ex-hạust'.
k(ç): hō'lō-çạust.
Plus ọs+d.

OST

b: çà-bossed', em-bossed'.
d: à-dossed'.
fr: frost, hōar frost.
k(ç): aç-çost', çost, Là-çoste', Pen'tē-çost.
kr: dŏu'ble-çrossed', un-çrossed'.
l: lost, un-lost'.
m: en-mossed'.
n: ġē-og-nost'.
t: bē-tossed', sēa'-tossed', tem'pest-tossed'.
w: wäst*.
Plus ọs+d.

ŌT

Vowel: ōat.
b: bōat, lĭfe'bōat, pī'lŏt bōat, ri'vẽr bōat, sēa bōat, stēam'bōat.
b: blōat.
ch: Chōate.

225

ūse, bu̱ll, brůte, tữrn, up; crȳ, myth; ça̱t, ma̱chine, ace,
church, çhord; g̱em, an̊ger, (Fr.) bon̊, a̱ṣ; THis, thin; aẕure

Q̱T
OT

(Choose only one word out of each group)

d: an'eç-dōte, an'ti-dōte,
bē-dōte'*, dōte,
tā'ble d'hôte (tāb'l dōt).

f: tel'ē-phōte.

fl: à-flōat', flōat.

g: bil'ly gōat, gōat,
nan'ny gōat, re'din̊-gōte.

gl: glōat.

gr: grōat.

k(ç): çōat, çōte, ō'vēr-çōat,
pet'ti-çōat.

kw(qu): bē-quōte', mis-quōte',
quōte, rē-quōte', un-quōte'.

l: lōte*.

m: ço̱m-mōte',
dē-mōte', ē-mote',
fōlk mōte (fōk), mōat, mōte,
prō-mōte', rē-mōte',
Wit'e-nà-ge-mōt".

n: ço̱n-nōte', dē-nōte',
foot'nōte, nōte.

p: çà-pōte'.

r: gar-rōte', rōte, rē-wrōte',
un'dēr-wrōte', wrōte.

s: çrē'ō-sōte.

sh: shōat, shōte.

sk(sç): sçōte.

sl: slōte.

sm: smōte, un-smōte'.

st: stōat.

t: as'ymp-tōte, tōte.

thr: thrōat.

tr: trōat.

v: dē-vōte', out-vōte',
rē"dē-vōte', vōte.

Q̱T

Vowel: a̱ught, o̱ught (o̱t).

b: bo̱ught, dēar'=bo̱ught',
rē-bo̱ught', un-bo̱ught'.

br: bro̱ught, up-bro̱ught'.

f: fo̱ught, ha̱rd'=fo̱ught',
un-fo̱ught'.

fr: fra̱ught, un-fra̱ught'.

g: gha̱t.

k(ç): ça̱ught, rē-ça̱ught',
un-ça̱ught', up-ça̱ught'.

m: ma̱ut.

n: ā'ēr-ō-na̱ut, är'gō-na̱ut,
dread'no̱ught (dred'),
Jug'gēr-na̱ut, na̱ught, no̱ught.

r: bē-wro̱ught'*, in-wro̱ught',
ō"vēr-wro̱ught', rē-wro̱ught',
un-wro̱ught', up-wro̱ught',
wro̱ught.

s: bē-so̱ught', so̱ught,
un"bē-so̱ught', un-so̱ught'.

sl: on'sla̱ught.

str: à-stra̱ught'*, bē-stra̱ught'*.

t: rē-ta̱ught', self'=ta̱ught',
ta̱ught, ta̱ut, un-ta̱ught'.

th: àf'tēr-tho̱ught, bē-tho̱ught'
fōre'tho̱ught, free tho̱ught,
mer'ry tho̱ught, mē-tho̱ught'*,
rē-tho̱ught', tho̱ught,
un-tho̱ught'.

tr: dis-tra̱ught'.

OT

Vowel: ço̱m-pā'tri-ot, pā'tri-ot.

b: bott.

bl: blot.

br: Brädt.

d: dot.

g: bē-got', fīrst'=bē-got',
fo̱r-got', got, Gott, härd'=got',
ill'=got', mis"bē-got',
un"bē-got'*, un"fo̱r-got',
un-got'.

gl: po̱'ly-glot̊.

gr: grot.

h: fīe'ry hot, hot.

fāte, fär, fåst, fạll, finăl, cāre, at; mēte, prey, hẽr, met; pīne,
marïne, bĩrd, pin; nōte, möve, fọr, atŏm, not; mọọn, book;

(Choose only one word out of each group)

hw: sŏme-whät′, whät.

j: jot.

k(c̦): ā′pri-c̦ot, c̦ō-c̦otte′, c̦ot.

kl: c̦lot.

kw(qu): al′i-quot, kum′quät,
lō-quät′, quot.

l: al-lot′, c̦ach′å-lot, c̦å-lotte′,
C̦am′ē-lot, esc̦h′å-lot (esh′),
Lanc̦′ē-lot, lot,
säṅs c̦ù-lotte′ (säṅ), shal-lot′,
Shå-lotte′.

m: bẽr′gå-mot,
wit′e-nå-ge-mot″.

n: fọr-get′=mē=not′,
Hū′gue-not (′ge-), knot (not),
lŏve′knot (′not), not, re-knot′,
shōul′dẽr-knot, un-knot′.

p: C̦å-pot′, gal′li-pot, iñk′pot.
pot.

pl: c̦oun′tẽr-plot, gråss′plot,
plot, un′dẽr-plot.

r: drȳ rot, gar-rote′, rot,
tom′my-rot.

s: bē-sot′, sot.

sh: grāpe′shot, ō-vẽr-shot′,
shot, sīght′ing shot (sīt′),
un′dẽr-shot.

sk(sc̦): Sc̦ot, Sc̦ott.

skw(squ): å-squät′, squät.

sl: slot.

sn: snot.

sp: beaū′ty spot,
plāgue spot (plăg), spot.

st: Stott.

sw: swät.

t: Hot′ten-tot, tot.

tr: dog′trot, jog′trot, trot.

v: gå-votte′.

w: wät*, wätt, wot*.

y: yächt (yot).

ŌTH

kl: c̦lōTHe, rē-c̦lōTHe′,
un-c̦lōTHe′.

l: lōaTHe.

ŌTH

Vowel: ōath.

b: bōth

gr: åf′tẽr-grōwth, grōwth,
ō′vẽr-grōwth, rē-grōwth′,
un′dẽr-grōwth.

kw(qu): quōth*.

l: lōath.

m: bē-hē′mōth.

sl: slōth.

th: Thōth.

tr: bē-trōth′, trōth.

ỌTH

r: wrạth, wrọth.

sw: swạth.

OTH

br: bär′lēy broth, broth.

fr: froth.

g: Goth, Ọs′trō-goth,
Vi′și-goth.

k(c̦): C̦oth.

kl: broạd′c̦loth, c̦loth,
pī′lŏt c̦loth, sad′dle c̦loth.

m: bē-hē′moth, moth.

r: Ash′tå-roth, wroth (roth).

th: Thoth.

tr: troth.

ŌTS

Vowel: Ōates.

k(c̦): C̦ōates.

Plus ōt+s.

Plus float′s, etc.

(Choose only one word out of each group)

OTS

p: Potts.
Plus ot+s.
Plus cot's, etc.

OU

Vowel: ou.
b: bough (bou), bow, gōl'den bough.
br: brow, hīgh'brow (hī'), ō'vĕr-brow.
ch: chow, chow'chow", Foo'chow", Kwang'chow", Soo'chow", Wen'chow".
d: dhow (dou), en-dow', lan'dau ('dou).
fr: frau (frou), frow.
g: hoose'gow.
h: an'y-how (en'i-), how, Howe, sŏme'how.
k(ç): çow, Hañ'kow".
l: al-low', dis'al-low.
m: mow.
n: ē-now'*, now.
pl: plough (plou), plow, snōw'plough, up-plow'.
pr: prow.
r: row.
s: sough, sow.
sk(sç): sçow.
sl: slough.
t: kow'tow', Swä'tow'.
TH: THou*.
v: à-vow', dis'à-vow, vow.
w: bow'⁼wow', pow'⁼wow', wow.

OUCH

Vowel: ouch.
gr: grouch.
k(ç): çouch.
kr: çrouch.

m: sçar'à-mouch.
p: pouch.
sl: slouch.
v: à-vouch', vouch.

OUD

b: un-bowed'.
br: bee'tle⁼browed'.
d: dis"en-dowed'.
kl: be-çloud', çloud, en-çloud', in"tĕr-çloud', ō-vĕr-çloud', rē-çloud', thun'dĕr-çloud, un-çloud'.
kr: çrowd, ō"vĕr-çrowd'.
l: à-loud', loud, al-lowed'.
pr: proud.
shr: bē-shroud', dis"en-shroud', en-shroud', rē-shroud', un-shroud'.
Plus ou+d.
Plus bow'd, etc.

OUJ

g: gouġe.
skr(sçr): sçrouġe.

OUL

Vowel: owl, sçreech owl.
d: dowl.
f: à-foul', bē-foul', foul, fowl, gui'nēa fowl (gi'nē), pēa'fowl, sēa'fowl, wạ'tĕr-fowl.
gr: growl.
h: bē-howl', howl.
j: jowl.
k(ç): çowl.
pr: prowl.
sk(sç): sçowl.

OULD

k(ç): un-çowled'.
Plus oul+d.
Plus foul'd, etc.

OUN
OUNT

fāte, fär, fȧst, fall, finăl, cāre, at; mēte, prey, hĕr, met; pīne,
marīne, bĭrd, pin; nōte, mȯve, fǫr, atŏm, not; mǫǫn, book;

228

(Choose only one word out of each group)

OUN

b: Bowne.

br: brown, Browne,
em-brown', nut'=brown'.

d: a-down', down, eī'dĕr-down,
gō down, hand'=mē=down",
rēach'=mē=down",
swän's'=down", tum'ble=down",
up"sīde=down'.

dr: drown.

fr: frown.

g: gown, nīght' gown (nīt'),
rē-gown', town and gown,
un-gown'.

k: McKown'.

kl: clown.

kr: crown, dē-crown',
dis-crown', rē-crown',
un-crown'.

l: lown*.

n: noun, rē-nown'.

t: down"town', town,
up'town".

OUND

b: a-bound', bound,
hell'bound, hīde'bound,
hōme'bound, īce'bound,
in'bound, ī'ron-bound ('ĕrn-),
out'bound, out'wărd=bound',
rē-bound', spell'bound,
sū'pĕr=a=bound', un-bound'.

br: browned.

d: downed, rē-dound'.

f: con-found',
dumb-found' (dum-), found,
prō-found'.

gr: a-ground', back'ground,
ground, mid'dle ground,
pleas'ūre ground (plezh'),
un-dĕr-ground', un-ground',
vant'ăge ground.

h: blood'hound (blud'),
bǫǫze'hound, hōar'hound,
hound, Má-hound',
smut hound.

kr: flow'ĕr=crowned,
pīne'=crowned',
tri'ple=crowned', etc.

m: mound.

n: rē-nowned'.

p: com'pound, ex-pound',
im-pound', pound, prō-pound'.

r: a-round', mer'ry=gō=round',
round, sŭr-round'.

s: rē-sound', sound, un-sound'.

t: as-tound'.

w: wound.

z: rē-sound'.

Plus oun+d.

Plus frown'd, etc.

OUNDZ

z: zounds*.

Plus ound+s.

Plus sound's, etc.

OUNJ

l: lounge.

OUNS

Vowel: ounce.

b: bounce.

fl: flounce.

fr: frounce.

n: an-nounce', dē-nounce',
ē-nounce', prō-nounce',
rē-nounce'.

p: pounce.

r: rounce.

tr: trounce.

Cf. ount+s.

OUNT

f: fount.

k(c): ac-count', count,

(Choose only one word out of each group)

dis-çount', mis-çount', rē-çount', un-çount'.

m: à-mount', çat'à-mount dis-mount', mount, par'à-mount, rē-mount', sŭr-mount', tan'tà-mount, un-mount'.

OUNTS

See ount+s.
Cf. ouns.

OUR

Vowel: hour (our), our, sus-tāin'ing hour.
fl: dē-flower' (-flour'), flour.
s: bē-sour', sour
sk(sç): bē-sçour', rē-sçour', sçour.
v: dē-vour'.
Cf. ou'ŭr.

OURD

s: un-soured'.
Plus our+d.
Plus flour'd, etc.

OUS

bl: blouse.
ch: chouse.
d: douse.
gr: grouse.
h: back'house, bȋrd'house, bōat'house, bug'house, çat house, chap'tēr house, chär'nel house, chär'tēr-house, çlub'house, çus'tŏm house, dog'house, frat house, hot'house, house, mad'house, out'house, pent'house, pleaṣ'ūre house (plezh'), pōōr'house, pri'ṣŏn house, pub'liç house, round'house,

slaught'ẽr-house (slau'), spor'ting house, stōre'house, wãre'house, whōre'house (hōr'), wŏrk'house.
kr: Kraus.
l: louse, wood louse.
m: Fliė'dẽr-maus (-mous), flin'dẽr-mouse, flit'tẽr-mouse, Mick'ey Mouse (mik'i), mouse.
n: Gnauss (nous), nous.
r: Rouse.
s: souse.

OUST

Vowel: oust.
br: browst.
h: un-housed'.
r: roust.
Plus ous+d.

OUT

Vowel: dīn'ẽr⸗out', hēre-out'*, hōl'ing⸗out', knock'out (nok'), look'out, out, out'⸗and⸗out', THere-out' (THãr-), thröugh-out' (thrû-), where-out' (hwãr), wiTH-out'.
b: à-bout', bout, driṅk'ing bout, gad'à-bout, hēre'à-bout, knock'à-bout (nok'), rīght'à-bout (rīt'), round'à-bout, roust'à-bout, stȋr'à-bout, THere'à-bout (THãr'), where'à-bout (hwãr').
d: doubt, rē-doubt'.
dr: drought.
fl: flout.
g: gout.

(Choose only one word out of each group)

gr: grout.

h: mà-hout'.

kl: ҫlout.

kr: kraut,
sauer'kraut (sour'krout).

l: lout.

n: knout.

p: pout.

r: rout.

sh: bē-shout', shout.

sk(sҫ): boy'sҫout", gĭrl'sҫout",
sҫout.

sn: snout.

sp: bē-spout', spout,
wạ'tēr-spout.

spr: sprout.

st: stout, stȳl'ish stout.

t: tout.

tr: trout.

v: dē-vout'.

OUTH

m: mouTHe.

OUTH

dr: drouth.

m: bē-mouth', mouth.

s: south.

Plus allow'th*, etc.

OUTS

Vowel: outs.

b: hēre"à-bouts' (hēr"),
THere'à-bouts (THär'),
where'à-bouts (hwär').

Plus out+s.

Plus snout's, etc.

OUZ

b: bouṣe.

bl: blouṣe.

br: browṣe.

dr: drowṣe.

h: houṣe, rē-houṣe', un-houṣe'.

p: es-pouṣe'.

r: à-rouṣe', ҫà-rouṣe', rouṣe,
up-rouṣe'.

s: souṣe.

sp: spouṣe.

t: touṣe.

Plus ou+s.

Plus vow's, etc.

ŌV

d: dōve.

dr: drōve.

gr: grōve.

h: hōve.

j: Jōve.

k(ҫ): ҫōve.

kl: ҫlōve.

m: mauve (mōv).

r: rōve.

shr: shrōve.

st: stōve.

str: strōve.

thr: thrōve.

tr: treaṣ'ūre trōve (trezh').

w: in-tēr-wōve', in-wōve', wōve.

ŎV

Vowel: hēre-ŏf' (-uv'), ŏf (uv),
THere-ŏf' (THär-uv'),
where-ŏf' (hwär-uv').

ŌZ

b: Dū-bōṣe'.

br: brōṣe.

ch: chōṣe.

d: dōze.

fr: frōze, rē-frōze', un-frōze'.

gl: glōze.

h: hälf'-hōṣe" (häf'), hōṣe.

(Choose only one word out of each group)

kl: c̣lōṣe, c̣lōtheṣ (klōz), dis-c̣lōṣe', en-c̣lōṣe', fōre-c̣lōṣe', in-c̣lōṣe', in"tẽr-c̣lōṣe', rē-c̣lōṣe', un-c̣loṣe'.

m: Mōṣe.

n: nōṣe.

p: c̣om-pōṣe', dē"c̣om-pōṣe', dē-pōṣe', dis"c̣om-pōṣe', dis-pōṣe', ex-pōṣe', im-pōṣe', in"dis-pōṣe', in"tẽr-pōṣe', op-pōṣe', pōṣe, prē-dis-pōṣe', prē"sup-pōṣe', prō-pōṣe', rē"c̣om-pōṣe', rē-pōṣe', sū-pẽr-pōṣe', sup-pōṣe', trans-pōṣe'.

pr: prōṣe.

r: à-rōṣe', bram'ble rōṣe, c̣öu-leŭr' dē rōṣe, dam'ăsk rōṣe, moss rōṣe, rōṣe, tūbe'rōṣe.

TH: THōṣe.

Plus ō+s.

Plus blow's, etc.

OZ

d: Dạweṣ.

g: gạuze.

h: Hạweṣ, hạwṣe.

l: lan'tẽrn jạwṣ.

k(c̣): bē-c̣auṣe', c̣auṣe.

kl: c̣lauṣe, San'tạ Klạuṣ.

p: me'nō-pạuṣe, pạuṣe.

pl: ap-plạuṣe'.

t: tạwṣ.

v: vạṣe.

y: yạwṣ.

Plus ọ+s.

Plus jaw's, etc.

OZ

Vowel: Oz.

b: Boz.

w: wäṣ.

ŌZD

d: dōzed.

p: ill'=dis-pōṣed', in"dis-pōṣed', jux'tạ-pōṣed', prē"dis-pōṣed'. un"op-pōṣed', well'=dis-pōṣed'.

Plus ōz+d.

Plus roṣe'd, etc.

ŌZH

l: ē-lōġe' (-lōzh'), lōġe (lōzh).

OZM

k(c̣): mac̣'rō-c̣oṣm, mīc̣'rō-c̣oṣm.

(Choose only one word out of each group)

U

ū: as in mūse; also in beaū'ty, feūd, crew, queue (kū), lieu (lū), re-view' (vū'), dūe, sūit, blūe, yoū; also in dö, mọọd, groūp, frūit, rheūm, ma-neū'ver.

Such words as **dew** include a consonantal y: **dyū,** while **do** is pronounced **du̇.** These properly rhyme; although for convenience they are not separated here.

ũ: as in tũrn; also in fẽrn, ẽrr, hẽard, sĩr, wŏrd, joũr'nal myrrh (mūr), colo'nel (kẽr'nl).

u: as in cup; also in wŏn, dŏne, dŏes (duz), flood (flud), troub'le (trub'l).

For the vowel sound in full, see under oo.

Ū

Vowel: tọọ'dle-dē-ọọ'.

b: bȧ-bọọ', bam-bọọ', bọọ, bug'ȧ-bọọ, çar'i-boù, dē-būt' (-bū'), im-būe', jig'ȧ-bọọ, peek'ȧ-bọọ, ta-bọọ', zē'bū.

bl: blew, blūe, skȳ'blūe, trúe'⁼blūe'.

br: bär'ley brọọ (bär'li), brew, im-brúe'.

ch: çat'ē-choū, chew, es-chew' (-chū').

d: ȧ-dieū (-dū'), ȧ-dö', bē-dew', bil″let⁼doùx' (bil″e-dù'), chan-dọọ', der'ring⁼dö', dew, dö, dūe, en-dew', en-dūe', fọr-dö'*, Hin'dù. hŏn'ey-dew (hun'i-), họọ'dọọ, in-dūe', mis-dö', moun'tăin dew, nĩght dew (nīt), out-dö', ō-vẽr-dö', ō-vẽr-dūe', pẽr-dū', priē″dieū', Pūr-dūe', reṣ'i-dūe, ski-dọọ', sub-dūe', sun'dew, tö'⁼dö', un-dẽr-dö', un-dö', un-dūe', vọọ'dọọ, well'⁼tö⁼dö'.

dr: drew, wiTH-drew'.

f: feū, fē've̅r-few, few, phew.

fl: flew, flū, flūe.

g: gọọ, gọọ'⁼gọọ', haut goùt (hō gù), ra-goùt' (-gù').

gl: glūe, i'glọọ, rē-glūe', un-glūe'.

gr: grew, out-grew'.

h: bal'ly-họọ, bọọ'⁼họọ', E'li-hū, Fitz-hūgh' (-hū'), hew, hūe, Hūgh (hū), rŏugh⁼hew' (ruf-), wä-họọ', yä-họọ', yọọ'⁼họọ'.

hw: tö whit tö whọọ, whew, whö.

j: aç'ȧ-joù, Jew, kiñk'ȧ-joù.

k(ç): bär'bē-çūe, çọọ, çoùp (kù), çùck'ọọ, çūe, Dāi-kō-kū', kew.

kl: çlew, çlūe, un-çlūe'.

kr: aç-çrūe', çrew.

kw(qu): queūe (kū).

l: çûr'lew, hal-lọọ', hul″là-bȧ-lọọ', lieū (lū), lọọ, view hal-lọọ' (vū), Zú'lù.

m: ē'mū, im-mew', mew, mọọ, mū, sēa mew, un-mew'.

233   ūse, bu̯ll, brúte, tŭrn, up; crȳ, myth; c̣at, mac̣hine, ace,
church, c̣hord; ġem, añger, (Fr.) boṅ, aṣ; THis, thin; aᴢure

ŪB
UB

(Choose only one word out of each group)

n: á-new′, av′e-nūe, c̣à-nöe′,
eṅ′trē noús (än′trē nú),
fīre new, fōre-knew′ (-nū′),
gnū (nū), in-ġe-nūe′,
knew (nū), new, nū,
pär′ve-nūe, rē-new′, ret′i-nūe,
rev′e-nūe.

p: Dē-pew′, nȧ-po̱o̱′, pew,
po̱o̱h (po̱o̱), Pūgh (pū),
sham-po̱o̱′.

r: gil′la-ro̱o̱, kañ-gȧ-ro̱o̱′,
kar-ro̱o̱′, mead′ōw rùe (med′),
Pē-rù′, roúx (rù), rúe,
wal′lȧ-ro̱o̱, wän′dēr-o̱o̱

s: á-pēr-c̣ū′ (-sū′), Daï′bu̯t-sù,
en-sūe′, pūr-sūe′, Sioúx (sù),
soù, sūe.

sh: c̣ȧ-c̣hoú′, c̣a′shew, fi′c̣hù,
shoe (shù), sho̱o̱.

shr: bē-shrew′*, shrew.

sk(sc̣): á-skew′, skew.

skr(sc̣r): c̣ork′sc̣rew, sc̣rew,
un-sc̣rew′.

sl: slew, slo̱o̱, sloúgh (slú), slūe.

sm: smew.

sp: spew.

spr: sprùe.

st: stew.

str: bē-strew′, c̣on-strùe′,
mis″c̣on-strùe′, ō-vēr-strew′,
strew.

t: bat-tùe′, c̣ock′ȧ-to̱o̱,
Ġen-to̱o̱′, hēre-in-tö′, hēre-tö′,
hēre-un-tö′, hiTH′ēr-tö,
im-promp′tū, in-tran′si-tū,
man′i-toù, pȧsse pär-toùt,
set′=tö′, sūr-toùt′, tat-to̱o̱′,
tew, THere-in′tö (THär-),
THere-tö′, THere-un-tö′,
thiTH′ēr-tö, Tim″buck-tù′, tö,
to̱o̱, twö (to̱o̱), vĭr-tù′,

where-in-tö′ (hwär-),
where-tö′ (hwär-), where-un-tö′.

th: thew.

thr: ō-vēr-threw′, threw,
throùgh.

tr: trūe, un-trūe′.

v: in′tēr-view (-vū), prē′view,
reṅ′dē-voùs (räṅ′dē-vù),
rē-view′, sūr-view′*, view.

w: wo̱o̱.

y: bä-yoū′, ewe (ū), I. O. U.,
yew, yoù.

z: Ka-la-mȧ-zo̱o̱′, zo̱o̱.

ŪB

b: bo̱o̱b.

k(c̣): c̣ūbe.

r: Reúb, rúbe.

t: tūbe.

UB

b: Bē-el′zē-bub, bub,
hub′bub, sil′lȧ-bub.

bl: blub.

ch: chub, Chubb.

d: dub, rub′=ȧ=dub′.

dr: drub.

f: fub.

fl: flub.

gr: grub.

h: hub.

k(c̣): c̣ub.

kl: bat′tle c̣lub, c̣lub, C̣lubb.

n: nub.

p: pub.

r: rub.

s: sub.

shr: shrub.

skr(sc̣r): sc̣rub.

sl: slub.

sn: snub.

ŪCH
ŪD

fāte, fär, fàst, fạll, finăl, cãre, at; mēte, prĕy, hēr, met; pīne,
marīne, bîrd, pin; nōte, mŏve, fọr, atŏm, not; mọọn, book;

234

(Choose only one word out of each group)

st: stub.
t: tub.

ŪCH

br: brọọch.
h: họọch.
k(c̣): c̣ọọch, họọch'=y=c̣ọọch'.
m: mọọch.
p: pọọch, pùtsch (pùch).
sp: "spọọch."

UCH

d: Dutch.
h: hutch.
k(c̣): c̣utch.
kl: c̣lutch.
kr: c̣rutch.
m: fọr-as-much', in-aṣ-much',
in-sō-much', much, mutch,
ō-vēr-much'.
s: such.
sk(sc̣): sc̣utch.
sm: smutch.
t: màs'tēr tŏuch, rē-tŏuch',
tŏuch.

UCHD

t: un-tŏuched'.
Plus uch+d.
Plus Dutch'd, etc.

ŪD

br: à-brọọd', brewed, brọọd,
hōme=brewed', un-brewed'.
d: dūde, sub-dūed',
un-sub-dūed'.
f: feūd, fọọd.
gl: un-glūed'.
h: rāin'bōw=hūed".
j: Jūde.
kl: c̣on-c̣lūde', ex-c̣lūde',
in-c̣lūde', in-tēr-c̣lūde'*,

oc̣-c̣lūde', prē-c̣lūde',
rē-c̣lūde'*, sē-c̣lūde'.
kr: c̣rùde.
l: al-lūde', c̣ol-lūde', dē-lūde',
ē-lūde', il-lūde', in'tēr-lūde,
lewd, pre'lūde.
m: mọọd.
n: dē-nūde', nūde, sub-nūde',
un-rē-newed'.
p: pọọd.
pr: prūde.
r: rọọd, rùde, un-rùde'*,
un-rùed'.
s: tran-sūde', un-pūr-sūed'.
shr: shrewd.
sl: slewed.
sn: snọọd.
st: stewed, stūde.
str: ab-strùde'*, un-strùde'.
t: à-cēr'bi-tūde*, ac̣'ri-tūde*,
al'ti-tūde, am-är'i-tūde*,
amp'li-tūde, ap'ti-tūde,
as-sū'ē-tūde, at'ti-tūde,
bē-a'ti-tūde, cēr'ti-tūde,
c̣lā'ri-tūde*, c̣on-sū'ē-tūde,
c̣ras'si-tūde, dē-c̣rep'i-tūde,
de-fin'i-tūde, dē-sū'ē-tūde,
dis-quī'et-ūde, ex-ac̣t'i-tūde,
fi'ni-tūde, fọr'ti-tūde,
gra'ti-tūde, ha'bi-tūde,
he'bē-tūde, in-ap'ti-tūde,
in-cēr'ti-tūde, in-ep'ti-tūde,
in-fi'ni-tūde, in-gra'ti-tūde,
in-quī'et-ūde, in-sū'ē-tūde,
las'si-tūde, la'ti-tūde,
le'ni-tūde, lon'ġi-tūde,
mag'ni-tūde, man-sū'ē-tūde,
mol'li-tūde, mul'ti-tūde,
ne-ces'si-tūde, pär'vi-tūde,
pla'ti-tūde, ple'ni-tūde,
promp'ti-tūde, pul'c̣hri-tūde,

(Choose only one word out of each group)

quī′et-ūde, rec̨′ti-tūde,
sē-nec̨′ti-tūde, sē-ren′i-tūde*,
sĕr′vi-tūde, si-mil′i-tūde,
sō-lic′i-tūde, to̱r′pi-tūde,
tûr′pi-tūde, va̱st′i-tūde,
ve″ri-si-mil′i-tūde, vi-cis′si-t̲ūde.
th: thewed.
tr: dē-trúde′, ex-trúde′,
in-trúde′, ob-trúde′, prō-trúde′,
rē-trúde′, sub-trúde′.
w: un-wo̤o̤ed′.
y: ex-ūde′.
Plus ū+d.
Plus you'd, etc.

g: go̤o̤f.
h: bē-ho̤o̤f′, ho̤o̤f.
l: à-lo̤o̤f′, lo̤o̤f.
pr: bu̱l′let=pro̤o̤f″, dis-pro̤o̤f′,
fīre′pro̤o̤f, fo̤o̤l′pro̤o̤f, pro̤o̤f,
rē-pro̤o̤f′, vîr′tūe=pro̤o̤f″,
wa̱′tĕr-pro̤o̤f,
weaTH′ĕr-pro̤o̤f (weTH′).
r: gā′ble ro̤o̤f, rē-ro̤o̤f′, ro̤o̤f,
un-ro̤o̤f′.
sp: spo̤o̤f.
t: Tär-túffe′.
tr: trúfe.
w: wo̤o̤f.

UD

b: bud, Budd.
bl: blood, līfe′blood, ′s̱blood*.
d: dud.
f: fud.
fl: flood.
j: Judd.
k(c̨): c̨ud.
l: lud.
m: mud.
r: rud.
s: sud.
sk(sc̨): sc̨ud.
sp: spud.
st: bē-stud′, stud.
th: thud.

UDZ

d: dud̠s̱.
s: sud̠s̱.
Plus ud+s.
Plus mud's, etc.

ŪF

Vowel: o̤o̤f.
b: o′pĕ-rȧ boùffe.
d: shȧ-do̤o̤f′.

UF

b: blīnd′man's̱=buff′, buff,
coun′tĕr-buff, rē-buff′.
bl: bluff, C̨oun′cil Bluff.
ch: chough (chuf), chuff.
d: duff, Măc̠-duff′,
plum duff.
fl: Fluff.
g: guff.
h: Hough (huf), huff.
k(c̨): c̨uff.
kl: c̨lough (kluf).
l: luff.
m: muff.
n: ē-nough′ (-nuf′).
p: bē-puff′, pow′dĕr puff, puff.
r: rough (ruf), ruff.
s: sough (suf).
sk(sc̨): sc̨uff.
skr(sc̨r): sc̨ruff.
sl: slough (sluf).
sn: bē-snuff′, snuff.
st: bread′stuff (bred′),
gär′den stuff, stuff.
t: tough (tuf), tuff.

(Choose only one word out of each group)

UFS

k(c̱): fist′i-c̱uffs.
Plus uf+s.
Plus snuff's, etc.

ŪFT

h: c̱lōv′en=ho̤o̤fed′, ho̤o̤fed.
Plus ūf+d.

UFT

sc̱: sc̱uft.
t: c̱an′dy-tuft, tuft.
Plus uf+d.
Plus ruff'd, etc.

ŪG

f: fūgue.

UG

b: bug, do̤o̤′dle-bug.
ch: chug.
d: dug.
dr: drug.
f: fug.
gl: glug.
h: bun′ny hug, hug.
j: jug.
l: lug.
m: mug.
p: pug.
pl: plug.
r: rug.
shr: shrug.
sl: slug.
sm: smug.
sn: snug.
t: tug.
th: thug.
tr: trug.

UGZ

b: gō bugs̱.
Plus ug+s.
Plus bug's, etc.

ŪJ

b: gam-böġe′.
f: dē-mon′i-fūġe, feb′ri-fūġe, in-sec̱′ti-fūġe, sub′tẽr-fūġe, vẽr′mi-fūġe.
h: hūġe.
skr(sc̱r): Sc̱ro̤o̤ġe, sc̱rouġe.
st: sto̤o̤ġe.

UJ

b: budġe.
dr: drudġe.
f: fudġe.
gr: bē-grudġe′, grudġe.
j: ad-judġe′, fo̤r-judġe′, judġe, mis-judġe′, prē-judġe′, rē-judġe′.
n: nudġe.
r: Rudġe.
sl: sludġe.
sm: smudġe.
tr: trudġe.

UJD

j: ill′=judġed′, un-judġed′.
Plus uj+d.

ŪK

b: c̱hi-bouk′, rē-būke′.
d: ärch′dūke, bē-dūke′, dūke, Mär′mȧ-dūke.
fl: flūke.
j: jūke.
l: Lūke, Ma′mē-lūke.
n: Chi-no̤o̤k′.
p: pūke.
r: pē-rūke′, sē-rūke′.
sn: sno̤o̤k.
sp: spo̤o̤k.
st: sto̤o̤k.
t: Hep′tȧ-teūc̱h, Hex′ȧ-teūc̱h, Pen′tȧ-teūc̱h.
y: ūke.
z: bash″i-bȧ-zo̤o̤k′.

(Choose only one word out of each group)

UK

b: buck, rōe'buck, wạ'tẽr-buck.
ch: chuck, wood'chuck.
d: bē-duck', Don'ăld Duck,
  duck, lāme duck.
h: huck.
kl: çluck.
l: chuck'⸗ȧ⸗luck″, ill'⸗luck',
  luck, mis-luck', pot'luck.
m: ȧ-muck',
  hīgh muck'⸗ȧ⸗muck″ (hī),
  Kal'muck, muck.
n: Çȧ-nuck'.
p: puck.
pl: pluck.
r: lav'ẽr-ŏck, ruck, rukh (ruk).
s: suck.
sh: shuck.
st: stuck.
str: ạwe'⸗struck″,
  họr'rŏr⸗struck″, struck,
  ter'rŏr⸗struck, thun'dẽr-struck,
  wŏn'dẽr-struck.
t: tuck.
tr: truck.

UKS

d: dux.
fl: flux.
kr: çrux.
l: lux.
sh: shucks.
t: tux.
Plus uk+s.
Plus luck's, etc.

UKT

d: ab-duçt', a'quē-duçt,
  çon-duçt', dē-duçt', duçt,
  ē-duçt', in-duçt',
  mis-çon'duçt, ō'vi-duçt,

pro'duçt*, rē-duçt'*, sub-duçt',
  vī'ȧ-duçt.
fr: ū'sū-fruçt.
l: rē-luçt'.
pl: good⸗plucked', plucked,
  un-plucked'.
r: ē-ruçt'.
str: çon-struçt', in-struçt',
  mis-çon-struçt', ob-struçt',
  sub-struçt', sū-pẽr-struçt'.
Plus uk+d.
Plus luck'd, etc.

ŪL

b: būhl, I-stam-búl', ves'ti-būle.
dr: drọol.
f: Āp'ril fọol, bē-fọol', fọol.
g: ghoùl.
h: whö'll (húl).
k(ç): çọol, mo'lē-çūle,
  re'ti-çūle, ri'di-çūle,
  vẽr'mi-çūle.
m: mewl, mūle.
p: Li'vẽr-pọol, pọol, pūle,
  whĩrl'pọol (hwĩrl').
r: mis-rùle', ō″vẽr-rùle', rùle,
  slīde'rùle.
sk(sç): cha'ri-ty⸗sçhọol',
  sçhọol, Sun'dāy sçhọol.
sp: spọol.
st: duck'ing stọol, foot'stọol,
  stọol, tōad'stọol.
t: Ō'-Tọole', tọol, Tọole,
  tùlle.
th: Thūle, Ul'ti-mȧ Thūle.
y: Yūle, yoū'll (yūl).
Plus few'll, etc.

UL

d: dull.
g: gull, Mō-gul' (also Mō'gul),
  ṣēa'gull.

ULB
ŪM

fāte, fär, fȧst, fạll, finăl, cāre, at; mēte, prey, hẽr, met; pīne,
marīne, bĭrd, pin; nōte, mŏve, fọr, atŏm, not; mọọn, book;

238

(Choose only one word out of each group)

h: ȧ-hull', hull.

k(c): bär'nȧ-cle, can'ti-cle,
chro'ni-cle, cọr'ȧ-cle, cull,
mi'rȧ-cle, mon'ō-cle,
ob'stȧ-cle, or'ȧ-cle, pin'nȧ-cle,
spec'tȧ-cle, vē'hi-cle, vẽr'si-cle.

l: lull.

m: mull.

n: an-nul', dis-an-nul', null.

sk(sc): num'skull, scull, skull.

st: stull.

tr: trull.

ULB

b: bulb.

ULCH

g: gulch.

m: mulch.

ŪLD

r: un-rūled'.

sk(sc): un-schọọled'.

Plus ūl+d.

Plus fool'd, etc.

ULD

sk(sc): thick'=skulled'.

Plus ul+d.

Plus lull'd, etc.

ULF

g: en-gulf', gulf.

ULJ

b: bulġe.

d: in-dulġe', ō"vẽr=in-dulġe'.

f: ef-fulġe'.

m: prō-mulġe'.

v: di-vulġe'.

ULK

b: bulk.

h: hulk.

s: sulk.

sk(sc): skulk.

ULKT

m: mulct.

Plus ulk+d.

Plus bulk'd, etc.

ULM

k(c): culm.

ŪLP

p: poùlp.

ULP

g: gulp.

p: pulp.

sk(sc): sculp.

ULS

b: bulse.

d: dulse.

m: mulse.

p: ap-pulse', ex-pulse',
im'pulse, pulse, rē-pulse'.

v: con-vulse'.

Cf. ult+s.

ULT

d: ȧ-dult', un'dult.

k(c): cult, dif'fi-cult, in-cult',
oc-cult'.

p: cat'ȧ-pult.

s: con-sult', in-sult'.

z: ex-ult', rē-ṣult'.

ŪLZ

g: gūleṣ.

j: Júleṣ.

Plus ūl+s.

Plus rule's, etc.

ŪM

Vowel: Ọọm.

b: bọọm, jib bọọm.

bl: ȧ-blọọm', blọọm,
em-blọọm', rē-blọọm'.

(Choose only one word out of each group)

br: broo̧m, broúgham (brúm), brúme.

d: ad-doo̧m′*, doo̧m, fōre-doo̧m′. prē-doo̧m′, rē-doo̧m′.

f: fūme, pēr-fūme′.

fl: flūme.

g: le-gūme′.

gl: bē-gloo̧m′, en-gloo̧m′, gloo̧m.

gr: brīde′groo̧m, groo̧m, grúme.

h: ex-hūme′, in-hūme′, whöm (hùm).

k(c̩): coo̧m, coo̧mb.

l: heir′loo̧m (är′lúm), il-lūme′, loo̧m, pow′ēr-loo̧m, rē-loo̧m′, rē-lūme′.

m: si-moo̧m′.

pl: bē-plūme′, dis-plūme′, plūme, un-plūme′.

r: an′tē-roo̧m, dīn′ing-roo̧m, dra̧w′ing roo̧m′, dress′ing roo̧m, el′bōw roo̧m, liv′ing roo̧m, lum′bēr roo̧m, rēad′ing roo̧m, rheúm (rùm), roo̧m, sēa′roo̧m, sun′roo̧m.

s: as-sūme′, c̩on-sūme′, rē″as-sūme′, sub-sūme′.

sp: spoo̧m, spūme.

t: c̩os′tūme, dis″en-tömb′, en-tömb′, Khär-toùm′ (kär-), tömb, un-tömb′.

w: en-wömb′, wömb.

y: Fi-ūme′.

z: prē-ṣūme′, rē-ṣūme′.

UM

Vowel: à-quä′ri-um, a̧u-di-tō′ri-um, c̩om-pen′di-um,

c̩rā′ni-um, c̩rē-mà-tō′ri-um, dē-li′ri-um, em-pō′ri-um, en-c̩ō′mi-um, ep-i-thà-lā′mi-um, ē-qui-li′bri-um, ex-o̧r′di-um, g̣e-rā′ni-um, g̣ym-nā′si-um, mē′di-um, mil-len′i-um, mo̧r-à-tō′ri-um, na-tā-tō′ri-um, ō′di-um, ō′pi-um, op-prō′bri-um, pal-la′di-um, pan-dē-mō′ni-um, pel-är-gō′ni-um, per-i-c̩är′di-um, pe-trō′lē-um, prē′mi-um, rā′di-um, rē-ṣid′ū-um, sa-ni-tō′ri-um, sen-sō′ri-um, sym-pō′ṣi-um, tē′di-um, va′c̩ū-um.

b: bum.

ch: chum.

d: Bum′ble-dŏm, C̩hrist′en-dŏm (kris′), C̩ock′nēy-dŏm (kok′ni-), dumb, fluñ′key-dŏm (′ki-), ha′li-dŏm*, hēaTH′en-dŏm, mär′tyr-dŏm, prú-d′hŏmme′ (-dum′), ras′c̩ăl-dŏm, re′bel-dŏm, Sax′ŏn-dŏm, Twee′dle-dum.

dr: drum, hum′=drum′, ket′tle-drum.

f: fä fē fī fō fum, fē fī fō fum.

g: gum.

gl: glum.

gr: grum.

h: hum.

k(c̩): bē-c̩ome′, c̩ome, mis″bē-c̩ome′, mō′di-c̩um, ō″vēr-c̩ome′, rē-c̩umb′*, suc̩-c̩umb′, vī-a′ti-c̩um.

kl: "c̩lumb".

kr: c̩rum, c̩rumb.

(Choose only one word out of each group)

l: cŭr-ri'cū-lum, Lum,
pa'bū-lum, pen'dū-lum,
poúr l'hŏmme (lum),
spec'ū-lum.

m: cär'då-mŏm,
chry-san'thē-mum, max'i-mum,
mi'ni-mum, mum.

n: bē-numb', laud'å-num,
numb, pla'ti-num,
tym'på-num.

pl: plum, plumb,
su'găr plum (shug'),
un-plumb'.

r: rhumb (rum), rum.

s: ad-ven'tūre-sŏme,
būr'den-sŏme, cum'bēr-sŏme,
drēar'i-sŏme, fro'lic-sŏme,
hūm'ŏr-sŏme,
in-ter-med'dle-sŏme,
med'dle-sŏme, met'tle-sŏme,
quar'rel-sŏme, quī'et-sŏme,
sŏme, sum, trŏu'ble-sŏme,
ven'tūre-sŏme, wēa'ri-sŏme,
wŏr'ri-sŏme,
wrañ'gle-sŏme (rang'gl-).

sk(sc): scum.

skr(scr): scrum.

sl: slum.

st: stum.

str: strum.

sw: swum.

t: ad li'bi-tum, a'dy-tum,
tum, tum'≠tum'.

th: thumb.

thr: thrum.

ŪMD

b: full'≠bloomed'.

f: un-fūmed'.

gl: un-gloomed'.

l: un-il-lūmed'.

pl: im-plūmed'.

Plus ūm+d.

Plus bloom'd, etc.

UMD

g: bē-gummed'.

pl: un-plumbed'.

th: bē-thumbed'.

Plus um+d.

Plus some'd, etc.

ŪMF

Vowel: oomph.

UMP

Vowel: ump.

b: bump.

ch: chump.

d: dump.

fr: frump.

g: An'dy Gump.

gr: grump.

h: hump.

j: jump.

kl: clump.

kr: crump.

l: lump.

m: mump.

p: pump.

pl: plump.

r: rump.

s: sump.

sl: slump.

st: stump.

t: tump.

th: bē-thump', thump.

tr: trump.

w: mug'wump.

(Choose only one word out of each group)

UMPS

Vowel: umps.

m: mumps.

Plus ump+s.

Plus chump's, etc.

ŪN

b: ba-boon', boon.

bl: dŏu-bloon'.

br: Broun, gam-broon'.

d: bri-doon', cär-doon', Doon, dune, ri-gà-doon'.

dr: gà-droon', quä-droon', spà-droon'.

f: buf-foon', tȳ-phoon'.

g: drà-goon', goon, là-goon', Rañ-goon'.

h: Cal-houn', hewn, Mà-houn', rē-hewn', rough'=hewn' (ruf'), un-hewn'.

j: je-jeune', Jūne.

k(c): bar-rà-coon', cō-coon', Col-quoun' (-kùn'), coon, là-cūne', rac-coon', Tȳ-coon'.

kr: croon.

l: băl-loon', găl-loon', loon, lūne, pan-tà-loon', sà-loon', shăl-loon', Wäl-loon'.

m: com-mūne', ex-com-mūne'*, här'vest moon, hŏn'ey-moon (hun'i-), im-mūne', in"tēr-com-mūne', moon, si-moon'.

n: àf-tēr-noon', fōre'noon, mid'noon, noon.

p: ex-pūgn' (-pūn')*, här-poon', im-pūgn', lam-poon', op-pūgn'.

pr: prune.

r: ma-cà-roon', mà-roon', oc-tō-roon', pi-cà-roon', rune, sē-roon'.

s: băs-soon', eft-soon'*, gos-soon', mon-soon', ō-vēr-soon', soon.

sh: shoon*.

skr(scr): Schroon.

sp: spoon.

str: bē-strewn'*, ō-vēr-strewn', strewn.

sw: à-swoon', swoon.

t: at-tūne', bà-toon'*, cär-toon', en-tūne', fes-toon', frig-à-toon', in-op-pŏr-tūne', im"pŏr-tūne', musk-ē-toon'. op-pŏr-tūne', plà-toon', pon-toon', rà-toon', rē-tūne', spit-toon', spon-toon', tūne, un-tūne'.

tr: pà-troon', pol-troon', quin-troon.'

y: pi-cà-yūne'.

z: ga-zön'*.

UN

Vowel: ac-cor'di-ŏn, Al'bi-ŏn, gal'lē-ŏn, gañ'gli-ŏn, hal'cy-ŏn, ō-bli'vi-ŏn, quä-tēr'ni-ŏn.

b: bun, Bunn.

d: dŏne, dun, Dunn, fōre-dŏne', myr'mi-dŏn, out-dŏne', ō-vēr-dŏne', rē-dŏne', un-dŏne'.

f: co'lō-phŏn, fun.

g: bē-gun', gun, Gunn, hep'tà-gŏn, hex'à-gŏn, min'ute gun ('it), oc'tà-gŏn par'à-gŏn, pent'à-gŏn, pēr-cus'siŏn gun (-kush'un) po'ly-gŏn, un"bē-gun'.

(Choose only one word out of each group)

h: hŏn, Hun.

k(c̣): He′li-c̣ŏn,
pan-tech′ni-c̣ŏn.

l: gon′fȧ-lŏn, Sal′ly Lunn.

m: c̣är′dȧ-mŏn, cin′nȧ-mŏn,
"mŏn".

n: nŏne, nun, Pär′thē-nŏn,
phē-no′mē-nŏn,
prō″lē-gom′ē-nŏn, un-nun′.

p: pun.

r: fōre-run′, härd′-run′,
Ō′bē-rŏn, out-run′, ō-vẽr-run′,
run, un-dẽr-run′.

s: c̣ȧ-par′i-sŏn, c̣om-par′i-sŏn,
fos′tẽr sŏn, gar′ri-sŏn,
jet′ti-sŏn, ō′ri-sŏn, sŏn,
step′sŏn, sun, sunn, ū′ni-sŏn,
ven′i-sŏn, Whit′sun.

sh: shun.

sp: hōme′spun, spun.

st: stun.

t: Ches′tẽr-tŏn, Gal′ves-tŏn,
Mid′dle-tŏn, simp′le-tŏn,
siñ′gle-tŏn, skel′ē-tŏn, tŏn,
tun.

w: A1, härd′-wŏn′,
num′bẽr one (wun), one (wun),
wŏn.

z: a′mȧ-zŏn, ben′i-ṣŏn.

Cf. Hyperion, etc., under *on*.

UNCH

b: bunch.

br: brunch.

h: hunch.

kl: c̣lunch.

kr: c̣runch.

l: lunch.

m: munch.

p: punch.

skr(sc̣r): sc̣runch.

ŪND

kr: c̣rọọned.

t: at-tūned′, dis-at-tūned′,
tūned′, un-tūned′.

w: wöund.

Plus ūn+ed.

UND

b: bund, c̣um′mẽr-bund,
mọr′i-bund.

d: dunned.

f: fund, rē-fund′.

g: un-par′ȧ-gŏned.

k(c̣): rub′i-c̣und, ver′ē-c̣und.

m: im-mund′, Rōṣ′ȧ-mŏnd,
Rōṣ′ȧ-mund.

p: punned.

s: sunned, un-sunned′.

sh: shunned.

st: stunned.

t: ob′rō-tund, ọr′ō-tund,
rē-tund′*, rō-tund′.

Plus un+ed.

Plus fun′d, etc.

UNG

Vowel: Ung.

b: bung.

br: "brung".

d: dung.

fl: flung.

h: bē-hung′*, hung,
ō-vẽr-hung′, un-dẽr-hung′,
un-hung′.

kl: c̣lung.

l: lung, one lung (wun).

m: ȧ-mŏng′.

p: pung, un-rung′.

r: rung, un-wrung′,
wiTH′ẽr-wrung′, wrung.

s: sung.

(Choose only one word out of each group)

sl: slung, un-slung'.
spr: sprung, up-sprung'.
st: stung.
str: hīgh'-strung', strung, un-strung'.
sw: swung, up-swung'.
t: bē-tŏngue', mŏTH'ēr tŏngue, tŏngue.
y: yŏung (yung).

UNGD

b: bunged.
l: leaTH'ēr=lunged' (leTH'), loud'=lunged'.
t: dŏu'ble=tŏngued', hŏn'ey=tŏngued' (hun'i-), pleaṣ'ănt=tŏngued' (plez'), shrill'=tŏngued', sil'vēr=tŏngued', sǫft'=tŏngued', tŏngued, trum'pet=tŏngued'.
Plus ung+ed.
Plus dung'd, etc.

UNGK

Vowel: uñk.
b: buñk.
ch: chuñk.
d: duñk.
dr: druñk.
f: fuñk.
fl: fluñk.
h: huñk.
j: juñk.
m: mŏñk.
n: quid nuñç.
p: puñk.
pl: kēr-pluñk', pluñk.
s: suñk.
shr: shruñk.
sk: skuñk.

sl: sluñk.
sp: spuñk.
st: stuñk.
t: Tuñk.
tr: truñk.
w: "wuñk".

UNGKT

b: buñked.
f: dē-fuñçt', fuñked.
j: çon-juñct', dis-juñçt'.
p: çom-puñçt'*.
tr: truñked.
Plus unk+ed.
Plus spunk'd, etc.

UNGST

m: à-mŏngst'.
Plus ung'st*.

UNJ

bl: blunġe.
l: al-lŏnġe'*, lunġe, mus'kel-lunġe.
pl: plunġe.
sp: dis-punġe'*, ex-punġe', spŏnġe.

UNS

d: dunce.
w: ŏnce (wuns).
Plus unt+s.
Plus hunt's, etc.

UNT

Vowel: ex'ē-unt.
b: bunt.
bl: Blount (blunt), blunt.
br: brunt.
fr: af-frŏnt', à-frŏnt', çon-frŏnt', fōre'frŏnt, frŏnt.
gr: grunt.
h: hunt.

(Choose only one word out of each group)

l: Lunt.
p: punt.
r: runt.
sh: shunt.
spr: sprunt.
st: stunt.
w: wŏnt.
Plus done't*, etc.

UNTH

m: mŏnth.
Plus run'th*, etc.

ŪNZ

r: Çam-ē-rọọnṣ'.
s: eft-sọọnṣ'*.
Plus ūn+s.
Plus tūne's, etc.

ŪP

b: Bet'ty Bọọp.
d: bọọp'⸗bọọp'⸗ȧ⸗dọọp', dūpe.
dr: ȧ-drọọp', drọọp, drūpe.
g: gọọp.
gr: ag-groúp', groúp.
h: çock'⸗ȧ⸗họọp', họọp,
un-họọp'.
hw: whọọp.
j: jūpe.
k(ç): çọọp, rē-çoúp'.
kr: çroúp, Krúpp.
l: çan'tȧ-loúpe, Guäd'e-loúpe,
lọọp, lọọp'⸗THĕ⸗lọọp',
un-lọọp'.
p: lir'i-pọọp", nin'çom-pọọp,
pọọp.
r: roúp.
s: soúp, sūpe.
sk(sç): ap'ple sçọọp, sçọọp.
skr(sçr): sçrọọp.
sl: slọọp.
st: stọọp, stoúp.

sw: swọọp.
tr: trọọp, troúpe.

UP

Vowel: blōw'ing up, fed'⸗up',
härd'⸗up', kēyed'⸗up' (kēd'),
māke'up, set'up, set'tẽr⸗up',
slap up, up, up'⸗and⸗up'.
d: dup*.
g: gup.
k(ç): but'tẽr-çup, çup,
grāce çup, grēase çup,
lŏv'ing⸗çup, stir'rup çup,
tēa'çup, was'săil çup.
kr: çrup*, Krupp.
p: pup.
s: sup.
sk(sç): sçup.
t: tup.

ŪPS

Vowel: ọọps.
hw: whọọps.
Plus ūp+s.
Plus group's, etc.

UPS

See up+s.
Plus cup's, etc.

UPT

k(ç): çupped.
r: ab-rupt', çor-rupt',
dis-rupt', ē-rupt',
in"çor-rupt', in"tẽr-rupt'.
s: supped.
t: tupped.
Plus pup'd, etc.

ŪR

b: bọọr.
bl: Blọọr.
d: dūre*, en-dūre', pẽr-dūre',
pẽr"en-dūre', troú'bȧ-doúr.

(Choose only one word out of each group)

h: hewer.

j: ab-jùre', ad-jūre', con-jūre'.

k(ç): çūre, ep'i-çūre,
in"sē-çūre', li-queúr' (-kùr'),
man'i-çūre, ped'i-çūre,
prō-çūre', sē-çure', sīn'ē-çūre,
waṭ'ēr-çūre.

l: al-lūre', çŏ-lūre', lūre.

m: à-moùr', black'à-moọr,
dē-mūre', im-mūre',
in-tēr-mūre'*, moọr, Moọre,
Os'tēr-moọr, par'à-moùr,
un-moọr'.

n: Kōh'i-noọr (kō'), man-ūre'.

p: gui-pūre' (gi-), im-pūre',
poọr, pūre.

r: Rùhr.

s: con-nois-seùr' (kon-i-sūr').

sh: as-sūre' (-shūr'),
brō-çhūre' (-shūr'), çock-sūre',
cȳ'nō-sūre, en-sūre', in-sūre,
rē"as-sūre', rē-in-sūre', sūre,
un-sūre'.

sk: on-sçūre'.

sm: smoọr.

sp: spoọr.

t: ab'à-tūre, ab-brē'vi-à-tūre*,
am'à-teūr (-tūr), ap'ēr-tūre,
är'mà-tūre, brev'i-à-tūre,
çal'en-tūre, çan'di-dā-tūre,
çar'i-çà-tūre, çŏm'fi-tūre,
con'toùr, çŏ'vēr-tūre,
çūr'và-tūre, dē-toùr',
dis-çŏm'fi-tūre, di-ves'ti-tūre,
en-tab'là-tūre, ex-pen'di-tūre,
fọr'fei-tūre ('fi-), fūr'ni-tūre,
gär'men-tūre, gär'ni-tūre,
im-mà-tūre', in-ves'ti-tūre,
jù'di-çà-tūre, lig'à-tūre,
lit'ē-rà-tūre, mà-tūre',
min'i-à-tūre, ō'vēr-tūre,

pọr'trăi-tūre, prē"mà-tūre',
prī-mō-ġen'i-tūre, quäd'rà-tūre,
se'pul-tūre, sig'nà-tūre,
tab'là-tūre, tem'pēr-à-tūre,
toùr, ves'ti-tūre.

y: Eūer (yūr), ewer (yūr),
in-ūre', yoūr, yoū're (yūr),
Cf. ū'ēr, ū'ûr.
Plus crew're, etc.

ŪR

Vowel: blēar'i-ēr, bor'rōw-ēr,
breez'i-ēr, brīn'i-ēr, būr'li-ēr,
cheer'i-ēr, chil'li-ēr,
çlean'li-ēr (klen'), çōş'i-ēr,
çost'li-ēr, çrēam'i-ēr, çreep'i-ēr,
çūr'li-ēr, din'ġi-ēr, diz'zi-ēr,
dọugh'ti-ēr (dọ'), dow'di-ēr,
drēar'i-ēr, drow'şi-ēr,
dus'ti-ēr, ēar'li-ēr, ēaş'i-ēr,
eer'i-ēr, emp'ti-ēr, ērr,
fil'mi-ēr, fil'thi-ēr, fleec'i-ēr,
flīght'i-ēr (flīt'), flim'şi-ēr,
fōam'i-ēr, friend'li-ēr (frend'),
fun'ni-ēr, fus'si-ēr, gid'di-ēr,
glọom'i-ēr, glos'si-ēr, gout'i-ēr,
grīm'i-ēr, guilt'i-ēr (gilt'),
hap'pi-ēr, heal'thi-ēr (hel'),
heav'i-ēr (hev'), hil'li-ēr,
hōl'i-ēr, hōme'li-ēr, huf'fi-ēr,
huñ'gri-ēr, hus'ki-ēr, īc'i-ēr,
iñk'i-ēr, jol'li-ēr, jùic'i-ēr,
kīnd'li-ēr, king'li-ēr,
knīght'li-ēr (nīt'),
līke'li-ēr (līk'), līve'li-ēr,
lof'ti-ēr, lōne'li-ēr (lōn'),
lŏve'li-ēr, lōw'li-ēr (lō'),
mer'ri-ēr, mīght'i-ēr (mīt'),
mōl'di-ēr, mos'si-ēr, mus'ki-ēr,
mus'ti-ēr, nar'rōw-ēr,
noi'şi-ēr, pēar'li-ēr, pit'i-ēr,

(Choose only one word out of each group)

pōrt'li-ēr, prince'li-ēr,
prō'şi-ēr, rō'şi-ēr, row'di-ēr,
seem'li-ēr, shĭ'ni-ēr,
shod'di-ēr, shōw'i-ēr,
sīght'li-ēr (sīt'), sil'li-ēr,
skin'ni-ēr, sleep'i-ēr, slīm'i-ēr,
sōap'i-ēr, spīc'i-ēr, spīk'i-ēr,
spŏn'ġi-ēr, spọọn'i-ēr,
spring'i-ēr, sprīte'li-ēr,
stead'i-ēr (sted'),
stealth'i-ēr (stelth'), sting'i-ēr,
storm'i-ēr, stuf'fi-ēr,
stŭr'di-ēr, sun'ni-ēr, sŭr'li-ēr,
ter'ri-ēr, thĭr'sti-ēr, thrif'ti-ēr,
trus'ti-ēr, val'ū-ēr,
weal'thi-ēr (wel'),
wēar'i-ēr (wēr'),
wheez'i-ēr (hwēz'), wid'ōw-ēr,
win'di-ēr, win'tri-ēr.

b: ȧ-bērr'*, bŭrr, Ex-çal'i-bŭr.
bl: blŭr.
br: "brēr".
ch: chĭrr.
d: çal'en-dēr, cyl'in-dēr,
   Fron-deūr' (-dūr'), họr'ri-dēr,
   ĭs'lăn-dēr (ī'), la'ven-dēr,
   Lōw'lăn-dēr, prov'en-dēr,
   rug'ged-ēr, sol'id-ēr,
   stū'pid-ēr, tim'id-ēr, viv'id-ēr.
f: au″tō-bī-og'rȧ-phēr, bē-fūr',
   bib-li-og'rȧ-phēr, bī-og'rȧ-phēr,
   çhauf-feūr' (shō-fūr'), çon-fēr',
   dē-fēr', fĭr, fūr, in-fēr',
   Jen'ni-fēr, li-thog'rȧ-phēr,
   lū'ci-fēr, phil-os'ō-phēr,
   phō-nog'rȧ-phēr,
   phō-tog'rȧ-phēr, prē-fēr',
   rē-fēr', ste-nog'rȧ-phēr,
   tō-pog'rȧ-phēr, trans-fēr',
   tȳ-pog'rȧ-phēr.
fl: fleūr, per″sĭ-fleūr'.

h: Ben Hūr, hēr.
hw: whĭrr.
j: är'mi-ġer, as-trol'ō-ġer,
   chal'len-ġer, çot'tȧ-ġer,
   dis-par'ȧ-ġer, dow'ȧ-ġer,
   en-çoūr'ȧ-ġer, for'ă-ġer,
   här'bin-ġer, man'ă-ġer,
   mes'sen-ġer, pas'sen-ġer,
   phil-ol'ō-ġer, pil'lă-ġer,
   por'rin-ġer, rav'ă-ġer,
   sçav'en-ġer, vil'lă-ġer,
   vin'tă-ġer, vol-ti-ġeur',
   voy'ă-ġer,
   voy-ä-ġeūr' (vwä-yä-).
k(ç): çoeur (kŭr), çon-çūr',
   çūr, in-çūr', Kērr,
   lī-queūr' (-kūr'),
   mas'sȧ-çre (-kŭr), oç-çūr',
   rē-çūr', se'pul-çhre (-kŭr).
kl: çhron'i-çlēr.
l: cheer'fụl-lēr, çrü'el-lēr,
   driv'el-lēr, en-am'el-lēr,
   lev'el-lēr, lī'bel-lēr, loy'ăl-lēr,
   märsh'mel-lēr, mĭt-răil-leūr',
   mod'el-lēr, mōurn'fụl-lēr,
   quạr'rel-ēr, rev'el-lēr,
   skil'fụl-lēr, trav'el-lēr,
   vic'tuăl-lēr (vit'l-lūr),
   was'săil-ēr.
m: as-tron'ō-mēr, çus'tŏ-mēr,
   dē-mūr', gọs'săm-ēr, lis'sŏm-ēr,
   līTHe'sŏm-ēr, lōne'sŏm-ēr,
   myrrh (mūr), ran'sŏm-ēr,
   win'sŏm-ēr.
n: al'mŏn-ēr, bär'găin-ēr,
   blāz'ŏn-ēr, bŭr'den-ēr,
   çom-mis'siŏn-ēr (-mish'un),
   çom'mŏn-ēr, çon-feç'tion-ēr,
   çor'ō-nēr, dē-tēr'min-ēr,
   em-blāz'ŏ-nēr,
   en-līght'en-ēr (-līt'), en-līv'en-ēr,

(Choose only one word out of each group)

ēv'en-ēr, ex-am'in-ēr,
ex-e-cū'tion-ēr, fash'iŏn-ēr,
for'eign-ēr ('in-), gär'den-ēr,
im-priṣ'ŏn-ēr, knŭr (nŭr),
Lŏn'dŏn-ēr, mar'i-nēr,
mil'li-nēr, par-ish'iŏn-ēr,
pe-ti'tiŏn-ēr, prac̣-ti'tion-ēr,
priṣ'ŏn-ēr, prō-bā'tion-ēr,
ques'tiŏn-ēr (kwes'chun-),
rēa'ṣŏn-ēr,
rē-vēr'ṣion-ēr ('zhun-),
wag'ŏn-ēr.

p: c̣al'i-pēr, dī'à-pēr,
gal'lŏp-ēr, gọs'sip-ēr, jṳn'i-pēr,
pēr, pūrr, wŏr'ship-pēr.

r: ad-ul'tēr-ēr, ad-ven'tūr-ēr,
an'swēr-ēr ('sēr-), är'mŏr-ēr,
är'moūr-ēr, ban'tēr-ēr,
bär'tēr-ēr, bat'tēr-ēr,
bick'ēr-ēr, blun'dēr-ēr,
blus'tēr-ēr, boTH'ēr-ēr,
broid'ēr-ēr, c̣ät'ēr-ēr, cel'lăr-ēr,
chaf'fēr-ēr, chat'tēr-ēr,
c̣of'fēr-ēr, c̣on'jūr-ēr,
c̣ŏv'ēr-ēr, dē-cī'phēr-ēr,
dē-liv'ēr-ēr, dis-c̣ŏv'ēr-ēr,
em-broid'ēr-ēr,
en-deav'ŏr-ēr (-dev'),
en-ġen'dēr-ēr, fāv'ŏr-ēr,
flat'tēr-ēr, flut'tēr-ēr,
franc̣'-tï-reūr', fūr'thēr-ēr,
gaTH'ēr-ēr, här'bŏr-ēr,
jab'bēr-ēr, lec̣'tūr-ēr,
liñ'gēr-ēr, loi'tēr-ēr,
mà-liñ'gēr-ēr, man-ū-fac̣'tūr-ēr,
meaṣ'ūr-ēr (mezh'),
mūr'dēr-ēr, mūr'mūr-ēr,
mūr''THēr-ēr*, mut'tēr-ēr,
of'fēr-ēr, pal-a'vēr-ēr,
pan'dēr-ēr, pas'tūr-ēr,
pat'tēr-ēr, pep'pēr-ēr,

pēr'jūr-ēr, pes'tēr-ēr,
pew'tēr-ēr, pil'fēr-ēr,
plàs'tēr-ēr, plun'dēr-ēr,
pos'tūr-ēr, pōul'tēr-ēr,
prof'fēr-ēr, quāv'ēr-ēr,
rois'tēr-ēr, sạun'tēr-ēr,
slan'dēr-ēr, slạught'ēr-ēr (slạut'),
slum'bēr-ēr, smat'tēr-ēr,
sọr'cēr-ēr, splut'tēr-ēr,
squän'dēr-ēr, stut'tēr-ēr,
suc̣'c̣ŏr-ēr, suf'fēr-ēr,
swag'gēr-ēr, tam'pēr-ēr,
thun'dēr-ēr, tọr'tūr-ēr,
tot'tēr-ēr, treaṣ'ūr-ēr (trezh'),
up-hōl'stēr-ēr, ū'ṣūr-ēr ('zhūr-),
ut'tēr-ēr, vāp'ŏr-ēr, ven'tūr-ēr,
vēr'dēr-ēr, wāġ'ēr-ēr,
wän'dēr-ēr, wāv'ēr-ēr,
whim'pēr-ēr (hwim'),
whis'pēr-ēr, wŏn'dēr-ēr.

s: af-fī'ăn-cēr, är'ti-fi-cēr,
c̣hàs-seūr', c̣on-nois-seūr' (-nis-),
of'fi-cēr, pūr'chăs-ēr, sîr,
tres'păs-sēr.

sh: ac̣''c̣où-cheūr', ad-mon'ish-ēr,
ban'ish-ēr, blan'dish-ēr,
būr'nish-ēr, cher'ish-ēr,
dē-mol'ish-ēr, em-bel'lish-ēr,
es-tab'lish-ēr, lañ'guish-ēr,
lav'ish-ēr, noūr'ish-ēr,
pol'ish-ēr, pub'lish-ēr,
pun'ish-ēr, rav'ish-ēr,
rē-liñ'quish-ēr, shĭrr,
skĭr'mish-ēr, vañ'quish-ēr.

sl: slūr.

sp: spūr.

st: ad-min'is-tēr, à-stĭr',
bal'us-tēr, ban'nis-tēr, bē-stĭr',
c̣an'is-tēr, for'es-tēr,
här'ves-tēr, mal-ad-min'is-tēr,
min'is-tēr.

ŪRB
ŪRD

fāte, fär, fȧst, fąll, finăl, cāre, at; mēte, prẹy, hēr, met; pīne,
marīne, bĭrd, pin; nōte, möve, fọr, atŏm, not; mọọn, book;

248

(Choose only one word out of each group)

t: am'ȧ-teūr,
am'phi-thē"ȧ-tre (-tūr),
är'bi-tēr, är"chi-ā'tēr,
bañ'quet-ēr, bar-om'ē-tēr,
bar'ris-tēr, çär'pen-tēr,
char'aç-tēr, chōr'is-tēr,
çol"pōr-teūr', çŏm'fŏr-tēr,
crick'e-tēr, dē-tēr', dī-am'ē-tēr,
dis-in-tēr', dis-trib'ū-tēr,
for'feit-ēr ('fit), hau-teūr' (hō-),
hex-am'ē-tēr, ī-dol'ā-tēr,
in-tēr', in-tēr'pre-tēr, Jú'pi-tēr,
lit"tēr-ȧ-teūr', pen-tam'ē-tēr,
pleaṣ'ăn-tēr (plez'), pres'by-tēr,
reġ'is-tēr,
res"tau-rä-teūr' (-tō-), rī'ŏ-tēr,
riv'e-tēr, scim'i-tēr (sim'),
sī'len-tēr, sin'is-tēr,
so'phis-tēr, tet-ram'ē-tēr,
thē'ȧ-tēr, thē'ȧ-tre (-tūr),
thēr-mom'ē-tēr, trum'pe-tēr,
viṣ'i-tēr.
v: ȧ-vēr', min'i-vēr, troŭ-vēre'.
w: wēre.
z: frĭṣ-ṣeūr'.
Cf. **ambassador,** and other or
words.

ŪRB

Vowel: hērb.
b: su'būrb.
bl: blūrb.
h: hērb.
k(ç): çūrb.
p: sù-pērb'.
s: ȧ-cērb', Sērb.
t: dis-tūrb', pēr-tūrb'.
v: vērb.

ŪRBD

k(ç): çūrbed, un-çūrbed.
t: im"pēr-tūrbed',
un"dis-tūrbed'. un"pēr-tūrbed'.

Plus ūrb+ed.
Plus Serb'd, etc.

ŪRCH

b: bĭrch, weep'ing bĭrch.
ch: chūrch, un-chūrch'.
l: lūrch.
p: pērch.
s: rē-sēarch', sēarch.
sm: bē-smĭrch', smĭrch.

ŪRCHT

b: bĭrched, un-bĭrched'.
sm: smĭrched, un-smĭrched'.
Plus ūrch+ed.
Plus search'd, etc.

ŪRD

g: goŭrd.
sh: as-sūred' (-shūrd'),
in-sūred', rē"as-sūred' (-shūrd'),
self'=as-sūred', un"ăs-sūred',
un"in-sūred'.
t: mȧ-tūred', un"mȧ-tūred'.
Plus ūr+d.
Plus cure'd, etc.

ŪRD

b: bĭrd, frig'ăte bĭrd,
gal'lōwṣ bĭrd, hedġe'bĭrd,
hum'ming-bĭrd, lā'dy-bĭrd,
lŏve'bĭrd, mock'ing-bĭrd,
nĭght'bĭrd (nīt'), pī'lŏt-bĭrd,
sēa'bĭrd, snōw'bĭrd, sọng'bĭrd,
storm'bĭrd.
f: Fērd.
g: bē-gĭrd', en-gĭrd', gĭrd,
un-dēr-gĭrd', un-gĭrd'.
h: hēard', hērd, ō"vēr-hēard'.
k(ç): çūrd, Kūrd,
un-sep'ul-çhred (-kūrd).
s: ab-sūrd', sūrd.

(Choose only one word out of each group)

sh: shĕrd, shĭrred.

sn: Mo̦r'ti-mēr Snĕrd.

t: dē-tĕrred', un″dē-tĕrred'.

v: C̣āpe Vērde, vĕrd.

w: wŏrd.

Plus ūr+ed.

Plus fur'd, etc.

ŪRF

s: sērf, sūrf.

sk(sc̣): sc̣ūrf.

t: tūrf.

ŪRG

Vowel: ērg.

b: bērg, būrg, bŭrgh,
Gōld'bĕrg, Green'bĕrg,
Heï'del-bĕrg, Hel'dēr-bĕrg,
Hel'lē-būrg, īce'bĕrg,
Rōș'en-bĕrg.

s: ex-ērgue'.

ŪRJ

Vowel: dem'i-ūrġe, ūrġe.

d: dīrġe.

g: gūrġe, rē-gūrġe'.

m: ē-mērġe', im-mērġe',
mērġe, sub-mērġe'.

p: pūrġe.

s: sērġe, sūrġe.

sk(sc̣): sc̣oūrġe.

sp: spūrġe.

spl: splūrġe.

t: dē-tērġe', dram'à-tūrġe,
tha̦u'mà-tūrge.

v: c̦ŏn-vērġe', dī-vērġe', vērge.

ŪRJD

Vowel: ūrġed, un-ūrġed'.

sk: sc̣oūrġed, un-sc̣oūrġed'.

Plus ūrj+d.

ŪRK

b: Boůrke.

r: Ō'-Roůrke'.

ŪRK

Vowel: ĭrk.

b: Bŭrk, Bŭrke.

d: dĭrk.

f: fĭrk.

j: jērk, jērque.

k(c̣): kĭrk.

kl(c̦l): c̦lērk.

kw: quĭrk.

l: lūrk.

m: mūrk.

p: pērk.

s: cĭrque.

sh: shĭrk.

sm: smĭrk.

st: stĭrk.

t: Tūrk.

w: dĭr'ty wŏrk, fan'cy-wŏrk,
frost'wŏrk, han'di-wŏrk,
mȧs'tēr-wŏrk, ō″vēr-wŏrk',
un″dēr-wŏrk', wa̦t'ēr-wŏrk,
wŏn'dēr-wŏrk, wŏrk.

y: yĕrk.

ŪRKZ

d: Dŭrkeṣ.

y: Yērkeṣ.

Plus ūrk+s.

Plus murk's, etc.

ŪRKT

w: ō″vēr-wŏrked',
un″dēr-wŏrked'.

Plus ūrk+ed.

Plus Turke'd, etc.

ŪRL

Vowel: ĕarl.

b: bŭrl.

ch: chŭrl.

f: fŭrl, un-fŭrl'.

g: char'i-ty gĭrl, gĭrl.

(Choose only one word out of each group)

h: hūrl.

hw: up-whĭrl', whĭrl, whŏrl.

k: bē-c̜ūrl', c̜ūrl', un-c̜ūrl',
up-c̜ūrl'.

kw: quẽrl.

m: mẽrle.

n: knūrl.

p: bē-pẽarl', im-pẽarl',
mŏTH'ẽr-ŏf-pẽarl' (-uv-),
pẽarl, pĭrl, pūrl, seed'pẽarl.

sk: skĭrl.

sw: swĭrl, up-swĭrl'.

t: tĭrl.

th: thūrl.

tw: twĭrl.

ŪRLZ

s: Sēarleș.
Plus ūrl+s.
Plus girl's, etc.

ŪRLD

k(c̜): bē-c̜urled', c̜urled,
un-c̜urled'.

p: im-pẽarled', pẽarled.

w: new'-wŏrld', ōld'-wŏrld',
un'dẽr-wŏrld, wŏrld.
Plus ūrl+ed.
Plus girl'd, etc.

ŪRM

b: bẽrm.

d: dẽrm, pac̜h'y-dẽrm.

f: af-fĭrm', c̜on-fĭrm',
dis"af-fĭrm', fĭrm, in-fĭrm',
rē"af-fĭrm'.

j: ġẽrm.

skw: squĭrm.

sp: spẽrm.

t: mis-tc̜rm', tẽrm.

th: ĭ'sō-thẽrm.

w: grub'wŏrm, wŏrm.

ŪRMZ

See ūrm+s.
Plus germ's, etc.

ŪRMD

f: af-fĭrmed', c̜on-fĭrmed',
dis"af-fĭrmed', rē"af-fĭrmed'.
Plus ūrm+ed.
Plus worm'd, etc.

ŪRN

b: boủrn.

y: "yoủrn".

ŪRN

Vowel: ēarn, ẽrne, in-ūrn',
ūrn.

b: Bẽrne, būrn, Byrne,
Ēast Bẽrne, West Bẽrne,
Ō'-Byrne'.

ch: chūrn.

d: dẽrn, dūrn.

f: fẽrn.

h: Hẽarn, Hẽarne, hẽrn.

j: ad-joủrn', sō-joủrn'.

k: kẽrn.

kw: quẽrn (kwūrn).

l: lẽarn, un-lẽarn'.

p: ē-pẽrgne' (-pẽrn'), pĭrn.

s: c̜ọn-cẽrn', dis-cẽrn',
lū-cẽrn', lū-cẽrne', sē-cẽrn',
un"c̜on-cẽrn'.

sp: spūrn.

st: stẽrn.

t: at-tŏrn', ē-tẽrne'*,
ex-tẽrne', in'tẽrn, in-tẽrne',
ō"vẽr-tūrn', rē-tūrn',
sub-ạl'tẽrn, tac̜'i-tūrn', tẽrn,
tūrn, up-tūrn'.

y: yẽarn.

z: diș-cẽrn' (di-zẽrn').

251 ūse, bᴜll, brúte, tŭrn, **up**; crȳ, myth; çat, maçhine, ace,
church, çhord; ġem, añger, (Fr.) boṅ, aş; THis, thin; aʒure

ŪRND
ŪRST

(Choose only one word out of each group)

ŪRND

Vowel: ēarned′, härd′=ēarned′,
ill′=ēarned′, well′=ēarned′.
l: lēarned′, un-lēarned′.
s: çon-cērned′, un″çon-cērned′.
t: tŭrned, un-tŭrned′.
z: diṣ-cērned′.
Plus ūrn+ed.
Plus fern′d, etc.

ŪRNT

Vowel: ēarnt.
b: bŭrnt, un-bŭrnt′.
l: lēarnt, un-lēarnt′.
w: wēren′t.

ŪRNZ

b: Bŭrnṣ.
h: Hēarn′ṣ.
k: Kēarnṣ.
Plus ūrn+s.
Plus fern′s, etc.

ŪRP

b: bŭrp.
bl: blŭrp.
ch: chĭrp.
s: dis-cērp′.
t: ex-tĭrp′*.
tw: twĭrp.
z: ū-ṣŭrp′.

ŪRPS

See ūrp+s.
Plus chirp′s, etc.

ŪRPT

ch: chĭrped.
s: ex=cērpt′.
z: ū-ṣŭrped′ (-zŭrpt′).
Plus ūrp+ed.
Plus twirp′d, etc.

ŪRS

b: boúrse.

ŪRS

Vowel: çō-ērce′, Ērse.
b: bĭrse, bŭrse, dis-bŭrse′,
im-bŭrse′, rē″im-bŭrse′.
h: hēarse, hērse, in-hēarse′,
rē-hēarse′.
k(ç): aç-çŭrse′, bī-çŭrse′,
çŭrse′, ex-çŭrse′, prē-çŭrse″.
m: à-mērce′, im-mērse′,
sub-mērse′.
n: foṣ′tēr nŭrse, nŭrse,
wet′=nŭrse″.
p: as-pērse′, çut′pŭrse,
dis-pērse′, pŭrse.
sp: in″tēr-spērse′.
t: ses-tērce′, tērce, tērse.
v: ad-vērse′, à-vērse′,
çon-vērse′, di-vērse′, in-vērse′,
pēr-vērse′, rē-vērse′, sub-vērse′,
trans-vērse′, trà-vērse′,
ūn′i-vērse′, vērse.
w: wŏrse.

ŪRST

Vowel: ērst*.
b: bŭrst, out′bŭrst,
stär′bŭrst, sun′bŭrst.
d: dŭrst.
f: dŏu′ble fĭrst, fĭrst.
h: hēarsed (hŭrst), Hēarst,
Hŭrst.
k(ç): aç-çŭrsed′, aç-çŭrst′,
bē-çŭrst′, çŭrst, un-çŭrsed′.
th: à-thĭrst′, thĭrst.
v: un-vērsed′, vērsed, vērst.
w: blūt′wŭrst, brät′wŭrst,
knäck′wŭrst (näk′),
li′vēr-wŭrst, wiē′nēr-wŭrst,
wŏrst, wŭrst.
Plus ūrs+d.
Plus curse′d, etc.

ŨRT
ŨRZ

fāte, fär, fàst, fạll, finăl, cãre, at; mēte, prey, hër, met; pīne,
marïne, bĩrd, pin; nōte, mŏve, fọr, atŏm, not; mọọn, book;

252

(Choose only one word out of each group)

ŨRT

Vowel: in-ẽrt'.

b: Ad'el-bẽrt, Bẽrt,
Eñ'gle-bẽrt, E'thel-bẽrt.

bl: blũrt.

ch: chẽrt.

d: dĩrt.

fl: flĩrt.

g: bē-gĩrt', en-gĩrt', gĩrt, gũrt,
sēa'gĩrt, un-gĩrt'.

h: hũrt, un-hũrt'.

k(c̣): c̣ũrt, Kũrt.

kw: quĩrt.

l: à-lẽrt'.

p: ex-pẽrt', in"ex-pẽrt',
al'à-pẽrt, pẽart, pẽrt.

s: as-sẽrt', cẽrt, c̣on'cẽrt,
dis"c̣on-cẽrt', ex-sẽrt', in-sẽrt',
in"tẽr-sẽrt', prē"c̣on-cẽrt',
syrt (sũrt).

sh: shĩrt.

sk: skĩrt.

skw: squĩrt.

sp: spũrt, spũrt.

v: ad-vẽrt', an-i-mad-vẽrt',
à-vẽrt', c̣on-trō-vẽrt', c̣on-vẽrt',
dī-vẽrt', ē-vẽrt', ex'trō-vẽrt,
in'tẽr-vẽrt, in'trō-vẽrt, in-vẽrt',
ob-vẽrt', pẽr-vẽrt', re'trō-vẽrt,
rē-vẽrt', sub-vẽrt',
trans-vẽrt', vẽrt.

w: liv'ẽr-wŏrt, louse'wŏrt,
mŏ'THẽr-wŏrt,
thŏr'ōugh-wŏrt ('ō-), wẽrt*,
Wĩrt, wŏrt.

z: dē-sẹrt', deṣ-sẹrt', ex-ẽrt',
in"dē-sẹrt'.

ŨRTH

Vowel: ẽarth, fụl'lẽr'ṣ ẽarth,
in-ẽarth', nīght'ẽarth (nīt'),
un-ẽarth'.

b: bẽrth, bĩrth, still'bĩrth.

d: dẽarth.

f: fĩrth.

g: gĩrth, Gũrth.

m: mĩrth.

p: Pẽrth.

w: pen'ny-wŏrth, un-wŏrth',
wŏrth.

Plus furr'th*, etc.

ŨRTZ

n: "nẽrtṣ".

w: Wũrtz.

Plus ũrt+s.

Plus hurt's, etc.

ŨRV

Vowel: Ĩrv.

d: họrs d'oeũvre (ọr dũrv).

h: Hẽrve.

k(c̣): c̣ũrve, in-c̣ũrve',
out-c̣ũrve'.

n: nẽrve, un-nẽrve'.

s: c̣on-sẽrve', dis-sẽrve',
sẽrve, sub-sẽrve'.

sw: swẽrve.

v: vẽrve.

z: dē-ṣẽrve', ob-ṣẽrve',
prē-ṣẽrve', rē-ṣẽrve'.

ŨRVD

z: ill'⸗dē-ṣẽrved', un"dē-ṣẽrved',
well'⸗prē-ṣẽrved'.

Plus ũrv+d.

Plus curve'd, etc.

ŨRVZ

t: tũrveṣ.

Plus ũrv+s.

Plus curve's, etc.

ŨRZ

t: Toừrṣ.

y: yoừrṣ.

253 ūse, bụll, brúte, tũrn, up; crȳ, myth; c̦at, mac̦hine, ace,
church, c̦hord; ġem, aṅger, (Fr.) boṅ, aṣ; THis, thin; aẓure

ŪRZ
US

(Choose only one word out of each group)

Plus ūr+s.
Plus cure's, etc.

y: dis-ūse′, mis-ūse′, ūse.
z: Zeūs.

ŪRZ

US

f: fũrze.
Plus ūr+s.
Plus fir's, etc.

ŪS

b: ȧ-būse′, c̦ȧ-boọse′,
c̦al-ȧ-boọse′.
br: Brúce.
d: ad-dūce′, c̦on-dūce′,
dē-dūce′, deúce, doúce,
ē-dūce′, in-dūce′,
in″trō-dūce′, prō-dūce′,
rē-dūce′, rē″prō-dūce′,
sē-dūce′, sū″pēr-in-dūce′,
trȧ-dūce′.
f: dif-fūse′, prō-fūse′.
g: goọse.
h: Van Hoọse.
j: júice.
k(c̦): Syr′ȧ-c̦úse.
kl: oc̦-c̦lūse′, rē′c̦lūse.
kr: crúse.
l: flow′ēr≠dē≠lúce′, loọse, lūce,
Toú-loúse′, trans-lūce′*,
un-loọse′.
m: moọse, moússe, vȧ-moọse′.
n: būr-noọse′, hȳ-pot′ē-nūse,
noọse, noús.
p: pap-poọse′, pūce.
r: c̦här′lŏtte rússe, Roọs,
Rúss.
sk(sc̦): ex-c̦úse′.
sl: slūice, un-slūice′.
spr: sprúce.
str: ab-strúse′.
t: ob-tūse′, pēr-tūse′, rē-tūse′.
tr: trúce.

Vowel: ab-stē′mi-ous,
al-i-mō′ni-ous, al-lū′vi-ous,
a-mȧ-tō′ri-us, am-big′ū-ous,
am-phib′i-ous, an-frac̦′tū-ous,
ā′quē-ous, är′dū-ous,
as-sid′ū-ous, beaū′tē-ous (bū′),
boun′tē-ous, būr-glā′ri-ous,
c̦ȧ-dū′cē-us, c̦al-c̦ā′rē-ous,
c̦al-um′ni-ous, cen-sō′ri-ous,
cer-ē-mō′ni-ous, cin-ēr′ē-ous,
c̦om-mō′di-ous, c̦oñ′grū-ous,
c̦om-pen′di-ous,
c̦on-sañ-guin′ē-ous,
c̦on-spic̦′ū-ous,
c̦on-tem-pō-rā′nē-ous,
c̦on-temp′tū-ous, c̦on-tig′ū-ous,
c̦on-tin′ū-ous, c̦on-trā′ri-ous,
c̦on-tū-mē′li-ous, c̦ō′pi-ous,
c̦oúr′tē-ous, C̦rē-tā′cē-ous,
c̦úr′i-ous, de-cid′ū-ous,
de-lē-tēr′i-ous, dē-li′ri-ous,
dē-nā′ri-us, dē′vi-ous,
dis-c̦oúr′tē-ous, dis-in-ġen′ū-ous,
dū′bi-ous, dul-ci′flū-ous,
dū′tē-ous, en′vi-ous,
ē-qui-li′bri-ous, er-rō′nē-ous,
ē-thē′rē-ous, ex-id′ū-ous,
ex-pūr-gȧ-tō′ri-ous,
ex-tem-pō-rā′nē-ous,
ex-trā′nē-ous, far-i-nā′ce-ous,
fas-tid′i-ous, fat′ū-ous,
fē-lō′ni-ous, fūr′i-ous,
glō′ri-ous, grē-gā′ri-ous,
här-mō′ni-ous, hēr-bā′ce-ous,
het-ēr-ō-ġēn′ē-ous, hid′ē-ous,
hi-lā′ri-ous, hō-mō-ġē′nē-ous,
ig′nē-ous, ig′nis fat′ū-us,

US

fāte, fär, fåst, fạll, finăl, cãre, at; mēte, prey, hẽr, met; pīne,
marïne, bïrd, pin; nōte, mŏve, fọr, atŏm, not; mọọn, book;

254

(Choose only one word out of each group)

ig-nō-min'i-ous, il-lus'tri-ous,
im-pē-çū-ni'ous, im-pēr'i-ous,
im-pēr'vi-ous, im-pet'ū-ous,
im'pi-ous, in-cen'di-ous,
in-ces'tū-ous, in-çom-mō'di-ous,
in-çoñ'grú-ous,
in-çon-spiç'ū-ous, in-çū'ri-ous,
in-dū'bi-ous, in-dus'tri-ous,
in-ē'bri-ous, in-ġē'ni-ous,
in-ġen'ū-ous, in-glō'ri-ous,
in-här-mō'ni-ous, in-jú'ri-ous,
in-noç'ū-ous, in-quiṣ-i-tō'ri-ous,
in-sen'sū-ous, in-sid'i-ous,
in-stan-tā'nē-ous, in-vid'i-ous,
là-bō'ri-ous, las-civ'i-ous,
lig'nē-ous, li-ti'ġi-ous,
lū-gū'bri-ous, lux-ūr'i-ous,
mel-li'flū-ous, mel-ō'di-ous,
mer-i-tō'ri-ous,
mis-cel-lā'nē-ous,
mul-ti-fā'ri-ous, mul-ti'vi-ous,
mys-tē'ri-ous, nạu'se-ous,
neç-tā'rē-ous, nē-fā'ri-ous,
nō-tō'ri-ous, nū'çlē-us,
ob-li'vi-ous, ob-sē'qui-ous,
ob'vi-ous, ō'di-ous,
op-prō'bri-ous,
pär-si-mō'ni-ous, pē-nū'ri-ous,
pēr-fid'i-ous, pēr-spiç'ū-ous,
pēr'vi-ous, pit'ē-ous,
plen'tē-ous, prē-çā'ri-ous,
prē-dā'cē-ous ('shē-),
prē-ṣump'tū-ous, prē'vi-ous,
prō-mis'çū-ous, puñç-til'i-ous,
rād'i-us, rē-bel'li-ous,
sal-ā'ci-ous ('shi-),
sal-ū'bri-ous, sañç-ti-mō'ni-ous,
sañ-guin'ē-ous,
sa-pō-nā'cē-ous ('shē-),
sen'sū-ous ('shū-), sēr'i-ous,
sē-tā'cē-ous ('shē-),

sīm-ul-tā'nē-ous, sin'ū-ous,
spon-tā'nē-ous, spūr'i-ous,
sten-tō'ri-ous, stren'ū-ous,
stū'di-ous, sub-tēr-rā'nē-ous,
sump'tū-ous, sū-pēr-cil'i-ous,
sū-pēr'flū-ous, Syr'i-us,
tē'di-ous, te-mēr-ā'ri-ous,
tem-pes'tū-ous, ten'ū-ous,
tọr'tū-ous, tū-mul'tū-ous,
up-rōar'i-ous, us,
ū-ṣū'ri-ous (-zhū'), ux-ōr'i-ous,
vaç'ū-ous, vȧ-gā'ri-ous,
vāin-glō'ri-ous,
val-ē-tū-di-nā'ri-ous, vãr'i-ous,
vī-çā'ri-ous, viç-tō'ri-ous,
vïr'tū-ous, vi'trē-ous,
vol-up'tū-ous.

b: är'quē-bus ('kwē-),
blun'dēr-buss, bus, buss,
Er'ē-bus, här'quē-bus,
in'çū-bus, om'ni-bus,
suç'çū-bus, syl'lȧ-bus.

br: ten'ē-brous.

d: ha'zȧr-dous,
jeo'pär-dous (je'), tim'i-dous*.

f: fuss.

g: an-al'ȧ-gous,
an-dro'phȧ-gous, ē-so'phȧ-gus,
ġym-noph'ȧ-gous,
hō-mol'ō-gous,
sär-çoph'ȧ-gus, tạu-tol'ō-gous,
thē-oph'ȧ-gous, zō-oph'ȧ-gous.

h: Huss.

k(ç): ab'ȧ-çus, Ȧ-mer'i-çus,
çuss, dis-çuss', ex-çuss',
in-çuss'*, Le-vit'i-çus,
pēr-çuss', rē-pēr-çuss'.

kr: lū'di-crous.

l: ȧ-baç'ū-lus, ȧ-ceph'ȧ-lous,
ac-id'ū-lous, ag-riç'ū-lous,
al'kȧ-lous, am-phib'ō-lous,

(Choose only one word out of each group)

an-ēm-o'phil-ous, an'ġē-lus,
añ'gū-lous, à-nom'à-lous,
bib'ū-lous, bī-ceph'à-lous,
bī-pet'à-lous, çau'te-lous,
çon-vol'vū-lous, çŏn-vol'vū-lus,
çrap'ū-lous, çred'ū-lous,
çrē-pus'çū-lous, çū'mū-lus,
em'ū-lous, fab'ū-lous,
friv'ō-lous, gar'rū-lous,
glob'ū-lous, hȳ-drō-ceph'à-lous,
in-çred'ū-lous, lī'bel-lous,
mär've-lous, mē-tiç'ū-lous,
mir-aç'ū-lous, nau'ti-lus,
neb'ū-lous, pen'dū-lous,
pēr-iç'ū-lous, per'i-lous,
pet'à-lous, pop'ū-lous,
quär'rel-ous*, quer'ū-lous,
rà-nuñ'çū-lous, rid-i'çū-lous,
sçan'dà-lous, scin'til-lous (sin'),
sçroph'ū-lous, sçūr'ri-lous,
sçrū'pū-lous, se'dū-lous,
si'bi-lous, stim'ū-lus,
strid'ū-lous, tan'tà-lus,
tin-tin-nab'ū-lous, trem'ū-lous,
tū-bēr'çū-lous, un'dū-lous,
un-sçrú'pū-lous, ven-triç'ū-lous,
ver-i-sim'i-lous, vēr-naç'ū-lous.

m: an'i-mus, à-non'y-mous,
big'à-mous, blas'phē-mous,
dī-at'ō-mous, ep-on'y-mous,
hip-pō-pot'à-mous, in'fà-mous,
mag-nan'i-mous, min'i-mus,
mō-nog'à-mous, muss,
pol-yg'à-mous,
pos'thū-mous ('tū-),
pseū-don'y-mous (sū-),
pūs-il-lan'i-mous,
sū-non'y-mous, ū-nan'i-mous,
ven'ŏm-ous.

n: al-bū'mi-nous, à-lū'mi-nous,
an-dro'ġē-nous, an-dro'ġy-nous,

bī-tū'mi-nous, būr'de-nous*,
ça'vēr-nous, çon-tēr'mi-nous,
çrim'i-nous, dī-aph'à-nous,
en-do'ġē-nous, fer-rú'ġi-nous,
flū'mi-nous, for-ti-tū'di-nous,
fū-liġ'i-nous, ġē-lat'i-nous,
glū'tē-nous, glū'ti-nous,
glut'tŏn-ous, mem'brà-nous,
mō-not'ō-nous, moun'tăin-ous,
mū-ci-laġ'i-nous,
mul-ti-tū'di-nous, mū'ti-nous,
ō-lē-aġ'i-nous, om'i-nous,
pla'ti-nous, pla-ti-tū'di-nous,
poi'ṣŏn-ous, rav'ē-nous,
reṣ'in-ous, rú'i-nous,
sçrù'ti-nous, syn'çhrō-nous,
trēa'ṣŏn-ous, tēr'min-us,
tyr'ăn-nous, val-ē-tū'di-nous,
vē-lū'ti-nous, vēr'mi-nous,
vēr-tiġ'i-nous,
vi-cis-si-tū'di-nous,
vil'lăin-ous, vol-ū'mi-nous,
vor-à'ġi-nous, vor-tiġ'i-nous.

p: oç'tō-pus, plat'y-pus,
pol'y-pus, pus.

pl: non'plus", ō'vēr-plus', plus.

r: à-dul'tē-rous, ad-ven'tū-rous,
al-i'fē-rous, à-liġ'ē-rous,
a'mō-rous, an'sē-rous,
är'bō-rous, är-mi'ġē-rous,
au'gū-rous, bal-sà-mi'fē-rous,
bär'bà-rous, blus'tē-rous,
bois'tē-rous, bul-bi'fē-rous,
çà-da'vē-rous, çan'çē-rous,
çañ'kē-rous, çan-tañ'kē-rous,
çär-bō-ni'fē-rous,
çär-ni'vō-rous, Çēr'bē-rus,
çhi'văl-rous, çlam'ō-rous,
dān'ġē-rous, dex'te-rous,
dō-lō-ri'fē-rous, dō'lō-rous,
fos-ṣi-li'fē-rous, ġen'ēr-ous,

ŪSH
USK

fāte, fär, fast, fall, finăl, cāre, at; mēte, prey, hēr, met; pīne,
marīne, bīrd, pin; nōte, mŏve, fŏr, atŏm, not; mọọn, book;

256

(Choose only one word out of each group)

gram-i-ni'vō-rous, Hes'pē-rus,
hū'mŏr-ous, hū'mē-rus,
im-pon'dē-rous, im-pos'tū-rous,
in-de'çō-rous, in-ō'dŏ-rous,
lañ'guŏr-ous, le'chēr-ous,
me-tăl-li'fē-rous, mūr'dēr-ous,
mūr'mūr-ous, nū'mēr-ous,
ob-strep'ē-rous, ō-dō-rif'ē-rous,
ō'dŏ-rous, om-ni'vŏr-ous,
o'nē-rous, ō-vi'pȧ-rous,
pēr'jū-rous, pes'tē-rous,
pes-ti'fē-rous, phos'phō-rus,
pon'dē-rous, prē-pos'tē-rous,
pros'pē-rous, rañ'çŏr-ous,
rap'tūr-ous, rhus (rus),
ri'gŏr-ous, rois'tēr-ous, Russ,
saç-chăr-i'fē-rous, sā'vŏr-ous,
slan'dēr-ous, slum'bēr-ous,
som-ni'fē-rous, sul'phū-rous,
Tär'tȧ-rus, thun'dēr-ous,
tim'ŏ-rous, tọr'tūr-ous,
trāit'ŏ-rous,
treach'ē-rous (trech'),
un-çhiv'ăl-rous, un-ġen'ē-rous,
val'ŏr-ous, vā'pŏr-ous,
ven'tū-rous, vēr'dūr-ous,
vi'gŏr-ous, vī'pēr-ous,
vi-vi'pȧ-rous, vō-ci'fē-rous,
vul'tū-rous.

s: Peg'ȧ-sus.

st: stuss.

t: aç-çliv'i-tous, çȧ-lam'i-tous,
cīr-çū'i-tous, çŏv-e-tous,
fȧ-tū'i-tous, fē-lic'i-tous,
fọr-tū'i-tous, grȧ-tū'i-tous,
im-mer'i-tous*, im'pē-tus,
in-fē-li'ci-tous, in-i'qui-tous,
nē-ces'si-tous,
paçh-y-dēr'mȧ-tous,
prē-cip'i-tous, rī'ŏ-tous,

sō-lic'i-tous, ū-bi'qui-tous,
veġ'ē-tous*.

th: an-ti'pȧ-thous.

TH: THus.

tr: truss, un-truss',
ī-dol'ȧ-trous.

v: mis'chiev-ous ('chiv-).

ŪSH

b: bŏnne böuçhe (bun būsh),
boùçhe, dē-boùçh'.

d: doùçhe.

j: "Jọọsh".

k: Hin'dù Kùsh.

m: gōbe-moùçhe', moùçhe,
Sçar'ȧ-moùçh.

r: bȧ-roùçhe', rùçhe.

t: çär-toùçhe'.

USH

bl: blush, out-blush',
un-blush'.

br: brush,
clōTHes'brush,
un'dēr-brush.

fl: flush, out-flush', un-flush'.

g: gush, Lā'dy Gush.

h: hush.

kr: crush.

l: lush.

m: mush.

pl: plush.

r: out-rush', rush, up-rush'.

sl: slush.

t: tush.

thr: hēr'mit thrush,
mis'săl thrush, thrush.

USK

b: busk.

br: brusque.

257　ūse, bull, brúte, tŭrn, up; crȳ, myth; çat, machine, ace,
church, çhord; ġem, añger, (Fr.) boṅ, aş; THis, thin; azure

USP
ŪT

(Choose only one word out of each group)

d: à-dusk′, dusk.
f: fusç, sub-fusk′.
h: dē-husk′, husk.
l: Lusk.
m: musk.
r: rusk.
t: tusk.

USP

k(ç): çusp.

ŪST

b: boost.
br: bröwst.
d: ad-dūced′, dē-dūced′,
in″trō-dūced′, prō-dūced′,
rē-dūced′, rē″prō-dūced′,
un″prō-dūced′,
un-rē-prō-dūced′.
j: joost.
l: loosed, un-loosed′.
m: và-moosed′.
r: roost, roùst.
spr: sprúced.
Plus ūs+d.
Plus juice′d, etc.

UST

b: bust, çom-bust′, rō-bust′.
d: à-dust′, bē-dust′, dŏst,*
dust, stär′dust.
f: fussed, fust.
g: an-gust′*, au-gust′,
dis-gust′, gust.
j: ad-just′, çō″ad-just′, **just,**
un-just′.
k(ç): dis-çussed′.
kr: çrust, en-çrust′.
l: lust.
m: must.
pl: non-plussed′.
r: rust.

tr: bē-trust′, dis-trust′,
en-trust′, mis-trust′,
self′=dis-trust′, trust, un-trust′.
thr: thrust.
Plus us+ed.
Plus fuss′d, etc.

ŪT

b: at′tri-būte, beaūt, boot,
Būtte, mar′à-böut, un-boot′.
br: brùit, brùte, im-brùte′.
f: çon-fūte′, rē-fūte′.
fl: flūte.
fr: fïrst frùit, for-bid′den frùit,
frùit, gal′lōwṣ frùit.
g: är-gūte′.
h: çà-hoot′, hoot.
j: jūte.
k(ç): à-çūte′, bal′di-çoot,
ban′di-çoot, çoot, çūte,
el-eç′trō-çūte, ex′ē-çūte (eks′),
pēr′sē-çūte, pros′ē-çūte,
sub″à-çūte′.
kr: rē-çrùit′.
l: ab-sō-lūte′, dī-lūte′,
dis′sō-lūte′, gà-loot′, in″vō-lūte′,
ir·reṣ′ō-lūte′, loot, lūte,
pol-lūte′, re′vō-lūte′, sà-lūte′,
sō-lūte′, vol-ūte′.
m: çŏm-mūte′, deaf′mūte,
ē-meūte′*, im-mūte′*, meūte,
moot, mūte, pēr-mūte′,
trans-mūte′.
n: çom′mi-nūte′, çor-nūte′,
mī-nūte′, newt.
p: çom-pūte′, dē-pūte′,
dis-pūte′, dis″rē-pūte′,
im-pūte′, Räj′pūt, rē-pūte′,
sup-pūte′.
r: ar′rōw-root, çhē-root′,

UT
ŪV

fāte, fär, fȧst, fạll, fĭnăl, cãre, at; mēte, prĕy, hẽr, met; pīne,
marïne, bĭrd, pin; nōte, mŏve, fọr, atŏm, not; mọọn, book;

258

(Choose only one word out of each group)

en-rọọt', eṅ roùte' (äṅ), rọọt,
roùte, un-rọọt'.
s: bĭrth'dāy sūit, hĭr-sūte',
pŭr-sūit', sọọt, sūit, vẽr-sūte'*.
sh: bum'bẽr-shọọt, çhūte,
out-shọọt', ō-vẽr-shọọt',
Shūte, up'shọọt.
sk(sç): sçọọt, sçūte.
sn: snọọt.
t: as-tūte', çon'sti-tūte,
des'ti-tūte, in'sti-tūte,
pros'ti-tūte, sub'sti-tūte, tọọt.
y: Pī-ūte', Ūte.

UT

b: ȧ-but', but, butt, hal'i-but,
rē-but', sçut'tle butt,
sūr'rē-but, wạt'ẽr butt.
g: çat'gut, gut.
gl: glut.
h: hut.
j: jut.
k(ç): çlẽar'-çut', çut, un-çut',
wood'çut.
kr: çrut.
m: Mutt.
n: beech'nut, bē'tel-nut,
Brȧ-zil'nut, çash'ew nut,
chest'nut, çō'çō-nut,
hā'zel-nut, hick'ō-ry nut,
Mç-Nutt', nut, pēa'nut,
wạl'nut.
p: Lil'li-put, oç'ci-put, putt.
r: rut.
sh: out-shut', shut.
sk(sç): sçut.
sl: slut.
sm: bē-smut', smut.
str: ȧ-strut', strut.
t: tut, Tutt.
Cf. so what.

ŪTH

b: bọọTH, pōl'ling bọọTH,
vōt'ing bọọTH.
s: sọọTHe.
sm: bē-smọọTH', smọọTH.

ŪTH

b: bọọth, pōl'ling bọọth,
vōt'ing bọọth.
k(ç): çoùth, un-çoùth'.
l: Dū-lūth'.
r: rūth.
s: fọr-sọọth', in-sọọth'*, sọọth.
sl: sleùth.
t: tọọth, un-tọọth'.
tr: trùth, un-trùth'.
y: youth.

UTH

d: dŏth*.

ŪTHD

s: un-sọọTHed'.
Plus ūTH+ed.
Plus booth'd, etc.

ŪTS

h: çȧ-họọts'.
Plus ūt+s.
Plus suit's, etc.

UTS

sm: smuts.
st: Stutz.
Plus ut+s.
Plus cut's, etc.

ŪV

gr: grọọve, in-grọọve'.
h: bē-họọve'.
hw: whō've.
m: ȧ-mọọve', mọọve, rē-mọọve'.
pr: ap-prŏve', dis"ap-prŏve',

(Choose only one word out of each group)

dis-pröve′, im-pröve′, pröve, rē-pröve′.

y: you̇′ve.

UV

b: ȧ-bŏve′, 'bŏve.

d: dŏve, mōurn′ing dŏve, tŭr′tle dŏve.

gl: fox′glŏve, glŏve, un-glŏve′.

l: bē-lŏve′*, lā′dy-lŏve, li̇ght′⸗ō′⸗lŏve′ (li̇t), lŏve, self′⸗lŏve′, trūe′⸗lŏve′.

sh: shŏve.

ŪVD

m: mōved, rē-mōved′, un-mōved′, un″rē-mōved′.

pr: ap-pröved′, im-pröved′, pröved, rē-pröved′, un″ap-pröved′, un″im-pröved′, un-pröved′, un″rē-pröved′.

Plus ūv+d.

Plus groove′d, etc.

UVD

l: bē-lŏved′, lŏved, un″bē-lŏved′, un-lŏved′.

Plus uv+d.

Plus dove′d, etc.

ŪZ

Vowel: o̜o̜ze.

b: ȧ-būṣe′, do̜o̜ze, dis-ȧ-būṣe′.

bl: blūeṣ, the blūeṣ.

br: brúiṣe.

ch: cho̜o̜ṣe.

f: ci̇r-c̣um-fūṣe′, c̣on-fūṣe′, dif-fūṣe′, ef-fūṣe′, fūṣe, in-fūṣe′, in″tēr-fūṣe′, pēr-cus′siŏn fūṣe, pēr-fūṣe′, rē-fūṣe′, suf-fūṣe′, sū″pēr-in-fūṣe′, trans-fūṣe′.

g: Bet′el-geūṣe, gūze.

h: Heweṣ, Hūgheṣ (hūz).

hw: who′ṣ, whōṣe (hwūz).

k(c̣): ac̣-c̣ūṣe′, in-c̣ūṣe′.

kr: c̣rewṣ, c̣rúiṣe, c̣rúṣe, San′tȧ C̣rúz, Vēr′ȧ C̣rúz.

l: lōṣe.

m: ȧ-mūṣe′, bē-mūṣe′, mewṣ, mūṣe.

n: newṣ, no̜o̜ṣe.

r: pē-rúṣe′, rúṣe.

s: sūeṣ.

sh: shöeṣ.

sk(sc̣): ex-c̣ūṣe′.

sn: sno̜o̜ze.

t: c̣on-tūṣe′.

th: en-thūṣe′, thūṣe.

tr: trewṣ, trúeṣ.

y: dis-ūṣe′, mis-ūṣe′, ūṣe, "yo̜uṣe."

Plus ū+ṣ.

Plus blue's, etc.

ŪZ

tr: C̣här-trēuṣe′.

UZ

Vowel: Uz.

b: ȧ-buzz′, buzz.

d: dŏes, dŏz.

f: fuzz.

k(c̣): c̣ŏz.

l: Luz.

ŪZD

b: ȧ-būṣed′, dis″ȧ-būṣed′.

f: fūṣed′, trans-fūṣed′.

k(c̣): ac̣-c̣ūṣed′, self′⸗ac̣-c̣ūsed′.

y: ill′⸗ūṣed′, ūṣed.

Plus ūz+d.

Plus bruise′d, etc.

ŪZH

br: Brūġes.

r: rou̇ġe.

Ā'ĂD
AB'ẼR

fāte, fär, fȧst, fạll, finăl, cãre, at; mēte, prey, hẽr, met; pīne,
marïne, bĩrd, pin; nōte, mŏve, fọr, atŏm, not; mọọn, book;

260

(Choose only one word out of each group)

DOUBLE RHYMES

(Words Accented on the Syllable before the Last, the Penult; also Called Feminine Rhymes)

A

The accented vowel sounds included are listed under **A** in Single Rhymes.

Ā'ĂD
n: nāi'ăd.
Plus display ad, etc.
Plus may add, etc.

Ā'ĂL
b: Bā'ăl.
fr: dē-frāy'ăl.
tr: bē-trāy'ăl, pọr-trāy'ăl.
v: sũr-vey'ăl.
Plus say, Al, etc.

Ā'ĂN
k(ç): Bis-çāy'ăn.
m: Māy'ăn.
Plus play an, etc.

Ā'ĂNS
b: ȧ-bey'ănce.
v: çŏn-vey'ănce, pũr-vey'ănce, sũr-vey'ănce.
Cf. stray ants, etc.

Ā'ĂNT
b: ȧ-bey'ănt.
Plus stray ant, etc.

Ā'BȦ
f: Fā'bȧ.
p: çō-pāi'bȧ.
Plus give Abe a, etc.

Ä'BȦ
b: Ad'dis Ä-bä'bȧ, Ăl'ï Bä'bȧ.
k: Käa'bȧ.
t: mas-tä'bȧ.
Plus squab, a, etc.

Ā'BĂN
l: Lā'băn.
Plus play ban, etc.
Plus babe, Ann *or* an, etc.

ĂB'ĂRD
sk(sç): sçab'bărd.
t: tab'bărd.
Cf. also ab'ũrd.
Plus jab hard, etc.

AB'ĂS
r: Bȧ-rab'băs.

AB'ĂTH
s: Sab'băth.
Cf. grab bath, etc.
Cf. ab'eth*.

Ā'BĒ
r: Rā'bē.
Cf. ā'bi.

AB'ẼR
Cf. ab'ũr, etc.

(Choose only one word out of each group)

AB′ES

Vowel: ab′bess.
Cf. grab Bess, etc.

AB′EST

bl: blab′best*.
d: dab′best*.
dr: drab′best.
g: gab′best*.
gr: grab′best*.
j: jab′best*.
st: stab′best*.
Cf. jab best, etc.

AB′ETH

bl: blab′beth*.
d: dab′beth*.
g: gab′beth*.
gr: grab′beth*.
j: jab′beth*.
st: stab′beth*.
Cf. stab Beth, etc.

Ā′BĒZ

j: Jā′bēz.
t: tā′bēṣ.
Plus stray bees, etc.

Ā′BI

Vowel: Ā′bey, Ā′bie.
b: bā′by.
m: māy′bē.
Plus stray bee, etc.

AB′I

Vowel: ab′bey, Ab′bie.
b: bab′by.
bl: blab′by.
d: dab′by.
dr: drab′by.
fl: flab′by.

g: gab′by.
gr: grab′by.
k(c): cab′by.
kr: crab′by.
r: rab′bi.
s: no sab′ē, sab′ē.
sh: shab′by.
sk(sc): scab′by.
sl: slab′by.
t: tab′by, tāme tab′by.
Plus grab, he, etc.

Ä′BI

h: Wä-hä′bi.
r: kōhl-rä′bi, Rä′bē.
t: tä′bi.
Plus squab, he, etc.

AB′ID

r: rab′id.
t: tab′id.
Cf. jab hid, etc.

AB′IJ

k(c): cab′băġe.
Cf. crab age, etc.

AB′IK

l: de″cà-syl-lab′ic, dis″syl-lab′ic,
hen″de-cà-syl-lab′ic,
im-par″i-syl-lab′ic,
mon″ō-syl-lab′ic,
mul″ti-syl-lab′ic, oc″tō-syl-lab′ic,
par″i-syl-lab′ic, pol″y-syl-lab′ic,
quäd″ri-syl-lab′ic, syl-lab′ic,
trī″syl-lab′ic.

ĀB′IL

l: lā′bile.
Cf. āb′l.

Ā′BĪN

s: Sā′bīne.

AB'IN
AB'LET

fāte, fär, fàst, fạll, finăl, cāre, at; mēte, prey, hẽr, met; pīne,
marïne, bĩrd, pin; nōte, mŏve, fọr, atŏm, not; mọọn, book;

262

(Choose only one word out of each group)

AB'IN

k(c): ̣cab'in, log ̣cab'in.
Plus grab in, etc.
Plus drab inn, etc.

AB'ING

bl: blab'bing.
d: dab'bing.
f: ̣con-fab'bing.
g: gab'bing.
gr: grab'bing.
j: jab'bing.
k(c): ̣cab'bing, tax'i-̣cab"bing.
kr: ̣crab'bing.
n: nab'bing.
sk(sc): ̣scab'bing.
sl: slab'bing.
st: stab'bing.
t: tab'bing.

AB'IT

h: ̣cō-hab'it, hab'it, in-hab'it,
rīd'ing hab'it.
r: rab'bet, rab'bit.
Plus grab it, etc.
Cf. crab bit, etc.

AB'JEKT

Vowel: ab'ject.

Ā'BL

Vowel: Ā'bel, ā'ble, dis-ā'ble,
en-ā'ble, un-ā'ble.
b: Bā'bel.
f: fā'ble.
fl: flā'ble*.
g: gā'ble.
k(c): ̣cā'ble.
l: lā'bel.
m: Mā'bel.
s: sā'ble.

st: stā'ble, un-stā'ble.
t: tā'ble.
Plus Abe'll, etc.
Plus gay bull, etc.

AB'L

b: bab'ble.
br: brab'ble.
d: bē-dab'ble, dab'ble.
dr: bē-drab'ble, drab'ble.
g: gab'ble, gib'ble=gab'ble.
gr: grab'ble.
k(c): ̣cab'ble.
r: rab'ble, rib'ble=rab'ble.
sk(sc): ̣scab'ble.
skr(scr): ̣scrab'ble.
Plus taxicab'll, etc.

Ā'BLEST

Vowel: ā'blest.
k(c): ̣cā'blest*.
l: lāb'lest*.
st: stā'blest*.
t: tā'blest*.
Plus play blest, etc.
Plus Abe, lest, etc.

AB'LEST

b: bab'blest*.
br: brab'blest*.
d: bē-dab'blest*, dab'blest*.
dr: drab'blest*.
g: gab'blest*.
skr(scr): ̣scrab'blest*.
Plus crab, lest, etc.

AB'LET

t: tab'let.
Plus crab let, etc.

263 ūse, bu̧ll, brûte, tûrn, **up**; crȳ, myth; çat, ma̧chine, ace,
church, çhord; g̈em, aṅger, (Fr.) boṅ, a̧s; THis, thin; aẓure

ĀB'LETH
AB'ŎT

(Choose only one word out of each group)

ĀB'LETH

k(ç): çā'bleth*.
l: lā'b'leth*.
n: e-nā'bleth*.
st: stā'bleth*.
t: tā'bleth*.

AB'LETH

b: bab'bleth*.
br: brab'bleth*.
d: bē-dab'bleth*, dab'bleth*.
dr: drab'bleth*.
g: gab'bleth*.
gr: grab'bleth*.
skr(sçr): sçrab'bleth*.

AB'LI

b: bab'bly.
d: dab'bly.
dr: drab'ly.
Cf. Chab'lis ('li).
Plus crab, Lee *or* lea, etc.

ĀB'LING

Vowel: dis-āb'ling.
f: fā'bling.
k(ç): çā'bling.
l: lā'b'ling.
n: e-nā'bling.
st: stā'bling, un-stā'bling.
t: tā'bling.

AB'LING

b: bab'bling.
br: brab'bling.
d: bē-dab'bling, dab'bling.
dr: drab'bling.
g: gab'bling.
gr: grab'bling.
k(ç): çab'bling.
skr(sçr): sçrab'bling.

AB'LISH

st: stab'lish*.
t: dis-es-tab'lish, es-tab'lish,
rē-es-tab'lish.

AB'LOID

t: tab'loid.
Plus grab Lloyd, etc.

Ā'BLŨR

Vowel: ā'blẽr, dis-ā'blẽr,
en-ā'blẽr.
f: fā'blẽr.
st: stā'blẽr.
t: tā'blẽr.
Plus gray blur, etc.

AB'LŨR

b: bab'blẽr.
br: brab'blẽr.
d: bē-dab'blẽr, dab'blẽr.
dr: bē-drab'blẽr, drab'blẽr.
g: gab'blẽr.
gr: grab'blẽr.
k(ç): çab'blẽr.
sk(sç): sçab'blẽr.
skr(sçr): sçrab'blẽr.
Plus cab blur, etc.

Ā'BOB

n: nā'bob.
Plus stray bob, etc.

AB'ŎT

Vowel: ab'bŏt, Ab'bŏtt.
k(ç): Ça'bŏt.
s: sab'ŏt.
Cf. grab at, *or* it, etc

(Choose only one word out of each group)

AB′RÅ

d: ab″rȧ-cȧ-dab′rȧ.
Cf. can-de-la′brȧ.
Plus nab Ra, etc.
Cf. swab Ra, etc.

Ā′BRĀK

d: dāy′breāk.
Plus play break, etc.
Plus Abe, rake, etc.

AB′SENS

Vowel: ab′sence.
Plus crab sense, etc.

AB′SENT

Vowel: ab′sent.
Plus cab sent *or* scent, **etc.**

Ā′BŨR

g: Ghe′bẽr.
k(c): Cā′bẽr.
l: bē-lā′bŏr, lā′bŏr.
n: beg′găr⸗mȳ⸗neigh′bŏr (nā′),
neigh′bŏr (nā′).
s: sā′bẽr.
t: tā′bẽr.
v: von We′bẽr (vā′),
We′bẽr (vā′).
Plus gay burr, etc.

AB′ŨR

bl: blab′bẽr.
d: dab′bẽr.
g: gab′bẽr.
gr: grab′bẽr.
j: jab′bẽr, ġib′bẽr⸗ġab′bẽr.
kl: bon″ny⸗clab′bẽr, clab′bẽr.
kr: crab′bẽr.
n: knab′bẽr, nab′bẽr.
sk(sc): scab′bẽr.

sl: bē-slab′bẽr, slab′bẽr.
st: stab′bẽr.
Plus jab her, etc.

Ä′BŨR

f: Fä′bre.
Cf. ob′ūr.
Plus swab her, etc.

ĀB′ŨRD

l: bē-lāb′ŏred, lā′bŏred,
un-lā′bŏred.
n: neigh′bŏred (nā′).
s: sā′bẽred.
Cf. gray beard.
Plus gray burred, etc.
Plus Abe erred, etc.

AB′ŨRD

j: jab′bẽred.
sk(sc): scab′bărd.
sl: bē-slab′bẽred, slab′bẽred.
t: tab′ărd.
Cf. grab hard, etc.

Ā′CHEL

r: Rā′chel.
v: Vā′chel.
Plus H′ll, etc.

ACH′EL

h: hatch′el.
s: satch′el.
Plus batch ′ll, etc.
Cf. batch ill, etc.
Plus scratch L, etc.

ACH′EST

h: hatch′est*.
k(c): catch′est*.
l: latch′est*, un-latch′est*.
m: match′est*.

(Choose only one word out of each group)

p: dis-patch'est*, patch'est*.
skr(sꞔr): sꞔratch'est*.
sn: snatch'est*.
t: at-tach'est*, dē-tach'est*.
th: thatch'est*.

ACH'ET

h: hatch'et.
kr: Bob Ꞔratch'et.
l: latch'et.
r: ratch'et.
Plus batch it, etc.
Cf. scratch it, etc.

ACH'ETH

b: batch'eth*.
h: hatch'eth*.
k(ꞔ): ꞔatch'eth*.
l: latch'eth*, un-latch'eth*.
m: match'eth*.
p: dis-patch'eth*, patch'eth*.
skr(sꞔr): sꞔratch'eth*.
sn: snatch'eth*.
t: at-tach'eth*, dē-tach'eth*.
th: thatch'eth*.

ACH'EZ

b: batch'eṣ.
h: hatch'eṣ.
k(ꞔ): ꞔatch'eṣ.
kl: Käf'fee Klatch'eṣ.
l: lach'eṣ, latch'eṣ, un-latch'eṣ.
m: match'eṣ.
n: Nat'chez.
p: dis-patch'eṣ, patch'eṣ.
skr(sꞔr): sꞔratch'eṣ.
sn: snatch'eṣ.
t: at-tach'eṣ, dē-tach'eṣ.
th: thatch'eṣ.
Plus latch is, etc.

ACH'Ī

k(ꞔ): ꞔatch'y.
p: patch'y.
sn: snatch'y.
Plus latch, he, etc.

ACH'ING

b: batch'ing.
h: hatch'ing.
k(ꞔ): ꞔatch'ing.
kl: käf'fee‌klatch'ing.
l: latch'ing, un-latch'ing.
m: match'ing.
p: dis-patch'ing, patch'ing.
skr(sꞔr): sꞔratch'ing.
sn: snatch'ing.
t: at-tach'ing, dē-tach'ing.
th: thatch'ing.

ACH'LES

m: match'less.
p: patch'less.
skr(sꞔr): sꞔratch'less.
th: thatch'less.
Plus catch less, *or* Les, etc.

ACH'MENT

h: hatch'ment.
k(ꞔ): ꞔatch'ment.
p: dis-patch'ment.
r: ratch'ment*.
t: at-tach'ment, dē-tach'ment.
Plus hatch meant, etc.

ACH'UP

k(ꞔ): ꞔatch'up.
Plus snatch up, etc.

(Choose only one word out of each group)

ACH'ŪR

h: hatch'ẽr.
k(c̣): c̣atch'ẽr, c̣ō'ny=c̣atch-ẽr, flȳ'c̣atch-ẽr.
l: latch'ẽr, un-latch'ẽr.
m: match'ẽr.
p: dis-patch'ẽr, patch'ẽr.
skr(sc̣r): back'=sc̣ratch'ẽr, sc̣ratch'ẽr.
sn: bo'dy snatch'ẽr, snatch'ẽr.
t: at-tach'ẽr, dē-tach'ẽr.
th: Thach'ẽr, thatch'ẽr.
Plus catch her, err *or* er, etc.

ACH'WĀ

h: hatch'wāy.
Plus catch way *or* weigh, etc.

ACH'WŪRK

k(c̣): c̣atch'wŏrk.
p: patch'wŏrk.
Plus match work, etc.

Ā'DĀ

h: hey'dāy.
l: lāy dāy.
m: Māy dāy.
p: pāy'dāy.
pl: plāy'dāy.
Plus play day, etc.
Plus grade A, etc.

Ā'DȦ

Vowel: Ā'dȧ.
k(c̣): ci-c̣ā'dȧ.
m: är-mā'dȧ, Māid'ȧ.
n: Grē-nä'dȧ.
v: Ve'dȧ.
z: Zāi'dȧ, Zāy'dȧ.

AD'Ȧ

d: da'dȧ.
Plus glad a, etc.

ÄD'Ȧ

d: Dä'dȧ.
g: hag-gä'dȧ.
k(c̣): ci-c̣ä'dȧ.
m: är-mä'dȧ.
n: Grȧ-nä'dȧ, Grē-nä'dȧ, Nä'dȧ.
s: pȧ-sä'dȧ.
v: Nē-vä'dȧ, Si-er'rá Nē-vä'dȧ.
Plus wad a, etc.

AD'ĂM

Vowel: Ad'ăm, Mc̣-Ad'ăm.
b: Bad'hăm.
k(c̣): mȧ-c̣ad'ăm.
m: mad'ăm.
Plus had 'em, etc.
Cf. sad damn, etc.

ĀD'ĂNS, ĀD'ENS

Vowel: āid'ănce.
k(c̣): c̣ā'dence, dē-c̣ā'dence.
Plus gay dance, etc.
Plus grayed ants *or* aunts, etc.
Plus play dents *or* dense, etc.

ĀD'ĂNT, ĀD'ENT

Vowel: āid'ănt.
k(c̣): c̣ā'dent, dē-c̣ā'dent.
r: ab-rād'ănt.
Plus gay dent, etc.
Plus old maid aunt *or* ant, etc.

ĀD'ED

Vowel: āid'ed, un-āid'ed.
bl: blād'ed.
br: ȧ-brād'ed, brāid'ed, un-brāid'ed, up-brāid'ed.
f: fād'ed, un-fād'ed.

(Choose only one word out of each group)

gl: glād'ed.
gr: dē-grād'ed, grād'ed.
j: bē-jād'ed, jād'ed.
k(ç): am-bus-çād'ed,
  bar-ri-çād'ed, block-ād'ed,
  brō-çād'ed.
n: çan-nŏn-ād'ed, ser-ē-nād'ed.
r: mas-quẽr-ād'ed (-kẽr-),
  pà-rād'ed, rāid'ed.
s: çrū-sād'ed.
sh: shād'ed, un-shād'ed.
sp: spād'ed.
sw: dis-suād'ed (-swād'),
  pẽr-suād'ed (-swād').
tr: trād'ed.
v: ē-vād'ed, in-vād'ed,
  pẽr-vād'ed.
w: wād'ed.
Plus play dead, etc.
Cf. May did, etc.

AD'ED

Vowel: ad'ded, sū-pẽr-ad'ded.
p: pad'ded.
pl: plaid'ed (plad').
Plus lad dead, etc.
Plus lad did, etc.

Ā'DEN

Vowel: Ā'den, Āi'denn.
h: men-hā'den.
l: hea'vy=lā'den (he'), lā'den,
  ō-vẽr-lā'den, un-dẽr-lā'den,
  un-lā'den.
m: bow'ẽr=māi'den,
  dāi'ry-māi-den, hand'māi-den,
  māi'den, mẽr'māi-den,
  milk'māi-den, sēa'=māi"den,
  sẽrv'ing=māi"den.
Plus play den, etc.
Cf. grade hen, etc.

AD'EN

f: Maç-fad'den, Mç-Fad'den.
gl: en-glad'den, glad'den.
m: mad'den.
s: sad'den.
Plus bad den, etc.
Cf. bad hen, etc.

ÄD'EN

Vowel: Ä'den.
b: Bä'den, Bä'den Bä'den.
Cf. quad hen, etc.

ĀD'ENS

k(ç): çā'dence.
Cf. ād'ăns.

ĀD'ENT

k(ç): çā'dent.
Cf. ād'ănt.

ĀD'EST

Vowel: āid'est*.
br: à-brād'est*, brāid'est*,
  up-brāid'est*.
f: fād'est*.
gr: dē-grād'est*.
j: bē-jād'est*.
m: mād'est*.
st: stāid'est.
sw: dis-suād'est (-swād')*,
  ō"vẽr-pẽr-suād'est*,
  pẽr-suād'est*.
tr: trād'est*.
v: ē-vād'est*, in-vād'est*,
  pẽr-vād'est*.
w: wād'est*.

AD'EST

Vowel: ad'dest*.
b: bad'dest.
g: gad'dest*.

(Choose only one word out of each group)

gl: glad'dest.
m: mad'dest.
p: pad'dest*.
s: sad'dest.

ĀD'ETH

Vowel: āid'eth*.
br: brāid'eth*, up-brāid'eth*.
f: fād'eth*.
j: bē-jād'eth*.
m: mād'eth*.
n: ser-ē-nād'eth*.
r: rāid'eth*.
sp: spād'eth*.
sw: dis-suād'eth (-swād')*,
ō"vēr-pēr-suād'eth (-swād')*,
pēr-suād'eth (-swād')*.
tr: trād'eth*.
v: ē-vād'eth*, in-vād'eth*,
pēr-vād'eth*.
w: wād'eth*.
Plus play death, etc.

AD'ETH

Vowel: add'eth*.
gl: glad'deth*.
p: pad'deth*.
Plus sad death, etc.

ĀD'ĒZ

h: Hā'dēṣ.
l: lā'dieṣ.
Plus made ease, or E's, etc.

AD'FỤL

gl: glad'fụl.
m: mad'fụl.
s: sad'fụl.
Plus dad full, etc.

Ā'DI

br: Brā'dy, brāid'y.
f: fā'dy.
fr: 'frāid'y.
gl: glā'dy.
gr: Grā'dy, Ō'-Grā'dy.
k(c̨): c̨ā'di, c̨as-c̨ā'dy.
l: bē-lā'dy, lā'dy, land'lā-dy.
m: Māi'die ('di).
sh: shā'dy.
Plus made, he, etc.
Plus say Dee, or D, etc.

AD'I

d: dad'dy, sụg'ăr dad'dy (shụg').
f: fad'dy.
h: had'die.
k(c̨): c̨ad'die, c̨ad'dy.
l: lad'die.
p: pad'dy.
pl: plaid'ie (plad').
Plus had he, etc.

Ä'DI

k(c̨): c̨ä'di.
m: Mäh'dĭ.
r: ĭ-rä'dē.
w: wä'di.
Plus wad he, etc.

AD'IJ

Vowel: ăd'ăge.
Plus sad age, etc.

AD'IK

Vowel: dȳ-ad'ic̨, trī-ad'ic̨.
g: hag-gad'ic̨.
k(c̨): dē-c̨ad'ic̨.
m: nō-mad'ic̨.
n: mō-nad'ic̨, vȧ-nad'ic̨.

(Choose only one word out of each group)

r: fȧ-rad'iç, spō-rad'iç.
t: Sō-tad'iç.
tr: te-trad'iç.
Plus mad Dick, etc.

ĀD'ING

Vowel: āid'ing, çō-āid'ing.
br: ȧ-brād'ing, brāid'ing, un-brāid'ing, up-brāid'ing.
f: fād'ing.
gr: dē-grād'ing, grād'ing, re-trō-grād'ing.
j: bē-jād'ing, jād'ing.
k(ç): am-bus-çād'ing, bar-ri-çād'ing, block-ād'ing, brō-çād'ing, ças-çā'ding.
l: en-fi-lād'ing, lād'ing, ō-vēr-lād'ing, un-lād'ing.
n: gas-çō-nād'ing, ser-ē-nād'ing.
r: mas-que-rād'ing (-ke-), pȧ-rād'ing, rāid'ing.
s: çrù-sād'ing.
sh: shād'ing.
sp: spād'ing.
sw: dis-suād'ing (-swād'), ō"vēr-pēr-suād'ing, pēr-suād'ing.
tr: free'=trād'ing, trād'ing.
v: ē-vād'ing, in-vād'ing, pēr-vād'ing.
w: wād'ing.

AD'ING

Vowel: ad'ding, sū-pēr-ad'ding.
g: gad'ding.
gl: glad'ding.
m: mad'ding.
p: pad'ding.

AD'IS

Vowel: Ad'dis.
k(ç): çad'dis.
Cf. bad is, etc.

ĀD'ISH

m: māid'ish, mēr-māid'ish, ōld"=māid'ish.
st: stāid'ish.
Plus gay dish, etc.

AD'ISH

b: bad'dish.
f: fad'dish.
gl: glad'dish.
k(ç): çad'dish.
m: mad'dish.
r: rad'ish.
s: sad'dish.
Cf. bad dish, etc.

AD'IT

Vowel: ad'it.
Plus had it, etc.

ĀD'IZ

l: lā'dieş.
Cf. ᵃd'ēz.

AD'IZ

d: dad'dieş.
 sug'ăr dad'dieş (shug').
h: fin'năn had'dieş.
k(ç): çad'dieş.
l: lad'dieş.
pl: plaid'ieş.
Plus had ease, etc.

AD'KAP

m: mad'çap.
Plus plaid cap, etc.

ĀD'L
AD'MĂN   fāte, fär, fȧst, fạll, fĭnăl, cãre, at; mēte, prey, hẽr, met; pīne,
         marĭne, bĭrd, pĭn; nōte, mŏve, fọr, atŏm, nŏt; mọọn, book;   **270**

(Choose only one word out of each group)

ĀD'L

kr: c̲rā'dle, en-c̲rā'dle.
l: lā'dle.
Plus maid 'll, etc.
Plus stay dull, etc.

AD'L

Vowel: ad'dle.
d: dad'dle, skē-dad'dle.
f: fad'dle, fid'dle≠fad"dle.
p: pad'dle.
r: rad'dle.
s: sad'dle, un-sad'dle.
spr: sprad'dle.
st: stad'dle.
str: ȧ-strad'dle, bē-strad'dle,
  strad'dle.
Plus lad 'll, etc.
Cf. mad dull, etc.

ĀD'LES

Vowel: āid'less.
bl: blāde'less.
br: brāid'less.
f: fāde'less.
g: bri-gāde'less.
gr: grāde'less.
k(c̲): bar-ri-c̲āde'less,
  brō-c̲āde'less.
m: māid'less.
n: ser-ē-nāde'less.
r: pȧ-rāde'less.
sh: shāde'less.
sp: spāde'less.
tr: trāde'less.
Plus played less, etc.

ĀD'LI

gr: grāde'ly, re-trō-grāde'ly.
st: stāid'ly.
Plus grayed lea *or* Lee, etc.

AD'LY

b: bad'ly.
br: Brad'ley.
gl: glad'ly.
h: Had'ley.
m: mad'ly.
s: sad'ly.
Plus had Lee *or* lea, etc.

ĀD'LING

kr: c̲rād'ling, en-c̲rād'ling.
l: lād'ling.

AD'LING

Vowel: ad'dling.
d: dad'dling, skē-dad'dling.
f: fad'dling, fid'dle≠fad"dling.
p: pad'dling.
r: rad'dling.
s: sad'dling, un-sad'dling.
spr: sprad'dling.
str: bē-strad'dling, strad'dling.

AD'LOK

p: pad'lock.
Plus bad lock, etc.

AD'LŨR

Vowel: ad'dlẽr, Ad'lẽr.
d: dad'dlẽr, skē-dad'dlẽr.
f: fad'dlẽr, fid'dle≠fad"dlẽr.
p: pad'dlẽr.
r: rad'dlẽr.
s: sad'dlẽr.
str: strad'dlẽr.

AD'MĂN

k(c̲): C̲ad'măn.
Plus bad man, etc.

(Choose only one word out of each group)

AD′MUS

k: Çad′mus.
Plus sad muss, etc.

AD′NĒ

Vowel: A-ri-ad′nē.
Plus bad knee, etc.

ĀD′NES

st: stāid′ness, un-stāid′ness.

AD′NES

b: bad′ness.
gl: glad′ness.
m: mad′ness.
pl: plaid′ness (plad′).
s: sad′ness.

Ā′DŌ

b: gam-bā′dō.
d: dā′dō.
g: re-nē-gā′dō.
k(ç): am-bus-çā′dō*,
  bar-ri-çā′dō, stoҫ-çā′dō.
kr: ҫre′dō.
l: sçà-lā′dō*.
m: fū-mā′dō.
n: bas-ti-nā′dō, çär-bō-nā′dō,
  grē-nā′dō*, tọr-nā′dō.
p: strap-pā′dō.
r: des-pe-rā′dō, Là-re′dō.
s: çam-i-sā′dō, çrù-sā′dō*.
v: mus-çō-vā′dō.
Plus weigh dough, etc.
Plus play do, etc.
Plus wade O, etc.
Plus maid owe, etc.

AD′Ō

sh: fōre-shad′ōw, shad′ōw,
  ō-vēr-shad′ōw.

Plus cad owe, etc.
Cf. sad dough, doe, *or* do, etc.

Ä′DŌ

d: dä′dō.
k(ç): a-vō-çä′dō, im-brō-çä′dō*,
  Mi-kä′dō, stoҫ-çä′dō*.
ly: À-mon-til-lä′dō (-lyä′).
p: strap-pä′dō.
pr: Prä′dō.
r: ä-mō-rä′dō*, Çol-ō-rä′dō,
  des-pe-rä′dō, El Dō-rä′dō.
s: pas-sä′dō.
t: pin-tä′dō.
v: brà-vä′dō, trà-vä′dō.
Plus shah dough, doe *or* do, etc.

AD′ŌD

sh: fōre-shad′ōwed,
  ō-vēr-shad′ōwed, shad′ōwed,
  un-shad′ōwed.
Plus sad ode, etc.

AD′ŎK

h: had′dŏck.
p: pad′dŏck.
r: rad′dŏcke*.
sh: shad′dŏck.
Cf. sad dock, etc.

AD′ŎN

b: À-bad′dŏn.
Plus had on, etc.
Cf. lad don, etc.

ĀD′ŌS

tr: ex-trā′dōs, in-trā′dōs.

AD′PÔL

t: tad′pôle.
Plus glad pole *or* Pole, etc.

(Choose only one word out of each group)

AD'SŎM

gl: glad'sŏme.
m: mad'sŏme.
Plus had some, bad sum, etc.

ĀD'ÛR

Vowel: āid'ẽr.
br: brāid'ẽr, un-brāid'ẽr,
up-brāid'ẽr.
gr: dē-grād'ẽr, grād'ẽr.
k(c̲): bar-ri-c̲ād'ẽr, block-ād'ẽr.
n: gas-c̲ō-nād'ẽr, prom-ē-nād'ẽr,
ser-ē-nā'dẽr.
r: pȧ-rā'dẽr, rāid'ẽr.
s: c̲rü-sād'ẽr, här"quē-bu-sā'dẽr.
st: stāid'ẽr.
sw: dis-suād'ẽr (-swād'),
ō"vẽr-pẽr-suād'ẽr (-swād'),
pẽr-suād'ẽr (-swād').
tr: free trād'ẽr, trād'ẽr.
v: ē-vād'ẽr, in-vād'ẽr.
w: wād'ẽr.
Plus degrade her, etc.
Plus made err, etc.

AD'ÛR

Vowel: ad'dẽr.
bl: blad'dẽr.
g: gad'dẽr.
gl: glad'dẽr.
l: lad'dẽr, step'lad-dẽr.
m: mad'dẽr.
p: pad'dẽr.
s: sad'dẽr.
Plus had her, etc.
Plus lad err, etc.

ÄD'ÛR

k(c̲): c̲ä'dre.
Plus wad her, etc.
Plus squad err, etc.

ĀD'US

gr: grād'us.
Plus made us, etc.

AD'VENT

Vowel: ad'vent.
Plus bad vent, etc.

AD'VÛRB

Vowel: ad'vẽrb.
Plus sad verb, etc.

Ā'EST

b: bāy'est*, dis"ō-bẹy'est*,
ō-bẹy'est*.
br: brāy'est*.
fl: flāy'est*.
fr: dē-frāy'est*, frāy'est*.
g: gāy'est.
gr: grāy'est, grẹy'est.
l: al-lāy'est*, dē-lāy'est*,
in-lāy'est*, lāy'est*,
mis-lāy'est*, up-lāy'est*,
wāy-lāy'est*.
m: dis-māy'est*.
p: ō"vẽr-pāy'est*, pāy'est*,
rē-pāy'est*, un-dẽr-pāy'est*.
pl: dis-plāy'est*, plāy'est*.
pr: prāy'est*, prẹy'est*.
r: ar-rāy'est*, bē-wrāy'est*.
s: as-sāy'est*, as-sāy'ist,
es-sāy'est*, es'sāy-ist,
gāin-sāy'est*, mis-sāy'est*,
sāy'est*.
sl: slāy'est*.
sp: spāy'est*.
spr: sprāy'est*.
st: ō-vẽr-stāy'est*, stāy'est*.
sw: swāy'est*.
tr: bē-trāy'est*, pōr-trāy'est*.

(Choose only one word out of each group)

v: çon-vey′est*,
in-veigh′est (-vā′)*,
pŭr-vey′est*, sŭr-vey′est*.
w: weigh′est (wā′)*.

Ā′ETH

b: dis″ō-bey′eth*, ō-bey′eth*.
br: brāy′eth*.
fr: dē-frāy′eth*, frāy′eth*.
k(ç): dē-çāy′eth*.
l: al-lāy′eth*, dē-lāy′eth*,
in-lāy′eth*, lāy′eth*,
mis-lāy′eth*, up-lāy′eth*,
wāy-lāy′eth*.
m: dis-māy′eth*.
p: ō-vēr-pāy′eth*, pāy′eth*,
rē-pāy′eth*, un-dēr-pāy′eth*.
pl: plāy′eth*.
pr: prāy′eth*, prey′eth*.
r: ar-rāy′eth*, bē-wrāy′eth*.
s: as-sāy′eth*, es-sāy′eth*,
gāin-sāy′eth*, mis-sāy′eth*,
sāy′eth*.
sl: slāy′eth*.
sp: spāy′eth*.
st: ō-vēr-stāy′eth*, stāy′eth*.
str: strāy′eth*.
sw: swāy′eth*.
tr: bē-trāy′eth*, pōr-trāy′eth*.
v: çŏn-vey′eth*,
in-veigh′eth (-vā′)*,
pŭr-vey′eth*, sŭr-vey′eth*.
w: weigh′eth (wā′)*.

AF-Ā′

k(ç): ça-fe′.
Cf. laugh, Fay, etc.

Ā′FÄR

m: Māy′fäir.
pl: Plāy′fäir.
Plus weigh fair, etc.

Ā′FĒLD

m: Māy′fiēld.
r: Rāy′fiēld.
Plus play field, etc.

ĀF′EST

ch: chāf′est*.
s: sāf′est, vouch-sāf′est*.
Plus May fest, etc.

ĀF′ETH

ch: chāf′eth*.
j: Jā′pheth.
s: vouch-sāf′eth*.

AF′GAN

Vowel: Af′ghan.

AF′I

b: baf′fy.
ch: chaf′fy.
d: daf′fy.
dr: draf′fy.
t: taf′fy.
Plus laugh, he, etc.

AF′IK

gr: an″à-glyp-tō-graph′iç,
au″tō-bī-ō-graph′iç,
au-tō-graph′iç, bib″li-ō-graph′iç,
bī-ō-graph′iç, çaç-ō-graph′iç,
çal-li-graph′iç, çär-tō-graph′iç,
çin″ē-mat-ō-graph′iç,
çhī-rō-graph′iç,
çhō-rē-ō-graph′iç,
çhō-rō-graph′iç, çlī-nō-graph′iç,
çoṣ-mō-graph′iç,
çryp-tō-graph′iç,
çrys″tăl-lō-graph′iç,
dī-à-graph′iç, ep-i-graph′iç,
eth-nō-graph′iç,

ĀF'ING
ĀF'LI

fāte, fär, fàst, fᾳll, fĭnăl, cãre, at; mēte, prᶒy, hēr, met; pīne,
marĭne, bĭrd, pin; nōte, mŏve, fᶎr, atŏm, not; mᶎᶎn, book;

274

(Choose only one word out of each group)

gal-van″ō-graph′iᶜ,
ġē-ō-graph′iᶜ, glyp-tō-graph′iᶜ,
graph′iᶜ, hē″li-ō-graph′iᶜ,
he″tēr-ō-graph′iᶜ,
hĭ″ēr-ō-graph′iᶜ,
his-tō″ri-ō-graph′iᶜ,
hō-lō-graph′iᶜ,
ho″mō-lō-graph′iᶜ,
hor-ō-lō″ġi-ō-graph′iᶜ,
hȳ-drō-graph′iᶜ,
hȳ-ē″tō-graph′iᶜ,
iᶜh-nō-graph′iᶜ, id″ē-ō-graph′iᶜ,
id″i-ō-graph′iᶜ,
lex″i-ᶜō-graph′iᶜ, lex-i-graph′iᶜ,
līᶜh″en-ō-graph′iᶜ,
lith-ō-graph′iᶜ, log-ō-graph′iᶜ,
mon-ō-graph′iᶜ, or-ō-graph′iᶜ,
ᶎr-thō-graph′iᶜ, pāl″ē-ō-graph′iᶜ,
pan-tō-graph′iᶜ, par-ᶏ-graph′iᶜ,
pas-i-graph′iᶜ, pe-trō-graph′iᶜ,
phō-tō-graph′iᶜ, pol-y-graph′iᶜ,
pᶎr-nō-graph′iᶜ,
scēn-ō-graph′iᶜ (sēn′),
scī-ᶏ-graph′iᶜ, seĭṣ-mō-graph′iᶜ,
sēl″ē-nō-graph′iᶜ,
sid″ēr-ō-graph′iᶜ,
sphēn-ō-graph′iᶜ,
sten-ō-graph′iᶜ,
ster″ē-ō-graph′iᶜ,
strat-i-graph′iᶜ,
strat-ō-graph′iᶜ, stȳ-lō-graph′iᶜ,
taᶜh-y-graph′iᶜ, tel-ē-graph′iᶜ,
top-ō-graph′iᶜ, ū-rān-ō-graph′iᶜ,
xȳ-lō-graph′iᶜ, ziñ-ᶜō-graph′iᶜ,
zō-ō-graph′iᶜ.
m: maf′fick.
r: sē-raph′iᶜ.
s: Sap′phiᶜ (sa′).
t: ep-i-taph′iᶜ.
tr: traf′fiᶜ.

ĀF'ING

ch: chāf′ing, en-chāf′ing.
s: vouch-sāf′ing.
str: strāf′ing.

AF'ING

ch: chaf′fing.
g: gaf′fing.
gr: graf′fing, hē′li-ō-graph-ing,
lith′ō-graph-ing,
par′ᶏ-graph-ing,
phō′tō-graph-ing,
sten′ō-graph-ing,
tel′ē-graph-ing.

ÄF'ING

kw(qu): quäf′fing
l: läugh′ing.
str: sträf′ing.

AF'FĪR

s: sap′phīre (sa′).
Plus chaff fire, etc.

AF'ISH

r: raf′fish.
Plus half fish, etc.

AF'L

b: baf′fle.
g: gaf′fle.
h: haf′fle.
r: raf′fle.
skr(sᶜr): sᶜraf′fle.
sn: snaf′fle.
y: yaf′fle.
Plus laugh 'll, etc.

ĀF'LI

s: sāfe′ly, un-sāfe′ly.
Plus chafe, Lee, etc.

275 üse, bull, brúte, tûrn, up; crȳ, myth; çat, machine, ace, church, çhord; ġem, añger, (Fr.) boṅ, aṣ; THis, thin; aᵹure

AF'LING
ÅF'TI

(Choose only one word out of each group)

AF'LING

b: baf'fling.
h: haf'fling.
k(ç): çalf'ling (kaf').
r: raf'fling.
skr(sçr): sçraf'fling.
sn: snaf'fling.

AF'LŬR

b: baf'flēr.
h: haf'flēr.
r: raf'flēr.
skr(sçr): sçraf'flēr.

AF'NĒ

d: Daph'nē.
Plus half knee, etc.

AF'ŌLD

s: Saf'fōld.
sk(sç): sçaf'fōld.
Plus half fold, *or* foaled, **etc.**
Plus half old, etc.
Cf. af'l+d, as baffled, etc.

AF'RĀL

t: taf'frāil.
Plus half rail, etc.

AF'RIK

Vowel: Af'riç.
Plus half rick, etc.
Cf. calf Frick, etc.

AF'RŎN

s: saf'frŏn.
Plus calf run, etc.

ÅF'SŎM

l: làugh'sŏme.
Plus half some *or* sum, etc.

ÄF'TED

w: up-wäf'ted, wäf'ted.
Plus laugh, Ted, etc.
Plus laughed, Ed, etc.
Cf. åf'ted.

AF'TED

dr: dráf'ted.
gr: en-gráf'ted, gráf'ted, in-gráf'ted.
r: ráf'ted.
sh: sháf'ted.
w: un-wáf'ted, wáf'ted.
Plus laugh, Ted; laughed, Ed, etc.

ÅF'TEST

d: dåf'test.
dr: dráught'est (dráft')*.
gr: gráft'est*.
w: wáft'est*.
Plus half test, etc.

ÅF'TETH

dr: dráught'eth (dráft')*.
gr: gráft'eth*.
w: wáft'eth*.

ÅFT'HORS

dr: dráft horse.
sh: sháft horse.
Plus daft horse, etc.

ĀF'TI

s: sāfe'ty.
Plus vouchsafe tea, **etc.**

ÅF'TI

dr: dráf'ty.
gr: gráf'ty.
kr: cráf'ty.
Plus half tea, etc.

(Choose only one word out of each group)

ÂF'TIJ

w: wȧf'tăge.
Plus daft age, etc.

ÂF'TING

dr: drȧft'ing.
gr: en-grȧft'ing, grȧft'ing.
h: hȧft'ing.
r: rȧft'ing.
sh: shȧft'ing.
w: wȧft'ing.

ÂFT'LES

dr: drȧft'less.
gr: grȧft'less.
kr: crȧft'less.
r: rȧft'less.
sh: shȧft'less.
Plus laughed less, etc.

AF'TŎN

Vowel: Af'tŏn.
gr: Graf'tŏn.
Plus laughed on, etc.

ÂFTS'MĂN

dr: drȧfts'măn.
kr: crȧfts'măn,
han'di-crȧfts-măn.
r: rȧfts'măn.
Plus draughts, man, etc.

ÂF'TŪR

w: wȧf'tūre.
Plus laughed your, etc.

ÂF'TŪR

Vowel: ȧf'tẽr, hēre-ȧf'tẽr,
hēre-in-ȧf'tẽr. THere-ȧf'tẽr.

d: dȧf'tẽr.
dr: drȧf'tẽr.
gr: grȧf'tẽr.
h: hȧf'tẽr.
l: lȧugh'tẽr (lȧf').
r: rȧf'tẽr.
w: wȧf'tẽr.
Plus laughed her, etc.

Ā'FU̧L

pl: plāy'fu̧l.
tr: trāy'fu̧l.
Plus stay full, etc.
Plus Rafe 'll, etc.

Ā'FŨR

ch: chāf'ẽr, cock'chāf-ẽr.
s: sāf'ẽr.
w: wā'fẽr.
Plus strafe her, etc.

AF'ŨR

k: Kaf'fĩr.
z: zaf'fẽr.
Cf. ȧf'ũr.

ÂF'ŨR

ch: chȧf'fẽr.
g: gȧf'fẽr.
gr: grȧf'fẽr*.
l: lȧugh'ẽr (lȧf').
kw: quȧf'fẽr.
Plus chaff her, etc.
Plus half fur *or* fir, etc.

AF'ŪRD

s: Saf'fŏrd.
st: Staf'fŏrd.
tr: Traf'fŏrd.
Plus calf ford, etc.

277 ūse, bull, brúte, tŭrn, up; crȳ, myth; çat, machine, ace, church, chord; ġem, añger, (Fr.) boń, aş; THis, thin; aȥure

ĀG'Å
AG'ETH

(Choose only one word out of each group)

ĀG'Å

b: rū-tȧ-bā'gȧ.
pl: plā'gȧ.
s: sā'gȧ.
Plus vague a, etc.

AG'Å

Vowel: ag'ȧ.
kw: quag'gȧ.
Plus bag a, etc.

Ä'GÅ

Vowel: ä'gȧ.
s: sä'gȧ.

ĀG'AL

pl: plāg'al.
v: vāg'al.
Plus play gal, etc.
Plus vague, Al, etc.

ĀG'ĂN

h: Hā'găn, Hā'gen, Ō'-Hā'găn.
p: pā'găn.
r: Re'găn.
Plus plague Ann, *or* an, etc.
Cf. Dā'gon.

AG'ĂRD

h: hag'gărd.
l: lag'gărd.
st: stag'gărd, stag'gēred.
sw: swag'gēred.
Plus drag hard, etc.
Plus Mag guard, etc.

AG'ĂRT

br: brag'gărt.
t: Tag'gărt.
Plus flag art, etc.

AG'ĂT

Vowel: ag'ăte, moss ag'ăte.
f: fag'ŏt.
m: mag'gŏt, ma'gŏt.
Plus drag it, etc.

AG'ED

j: jag'ged.
kr: crag'ged.
r: rag'ged.
skr(scr): scrag'ged.
Cf. bag head, etc.
Plus hag, Ed, etc.

AG'END

f: fag end.
l: lag end.
Plus Mag end, etc.

ĀG'EST

pl: plā'guest*.
v: vā'guest.
Plus stay, guest, etc.

AG'EST

br: brag'gest*.
dr: drag'gest*.
f: fag'gest*.
fl: flag'gest*.
g: gag'gest*.
l: lag'gest*.
n: nag'gest*.
w: wag'gest*.
Plus hag guest, etc.

AG'ETH

br: brag'geth*.
dr: drag'geth*.
f: fag'geth*.
fl: flag'geth*.
g: gag'geth*.

AG'I
AG'LING

fāte, fär, fȧst, fạll, finăl, cãre, at; mēte, prey, hẽr, met; pīne,
marïne, bĩrd, pin; nōte, mŏve, fǫr, atŏm, not; mọọn, book;

278

(Choose only one word out of each group)

l: lag'geth*.
n: nag'geth*.
r: rag'geth*.
w: wag'geth*.

AG'I

Vowel: Ag'gie.
b: bag'gy.
br: brag'gy.
dr: drag'gy.
f: fag'gy.
fl: flag'gy.
g: gag'gy.
kr: crag'gy.
kw(qu): quag'gy.
l: lag'gy.
m: Mag'gie.
n: knag'gy (nag'), nag'gy.
r: rag'gy.
s: sag'gy.
sh: shag'gy.
skr(scr): scrag'gy.
sl: slag'gy.
sn: snag'gy.
sw: swag'gy.
t: tag'gy.
w: wag'gy.
Plus rag he, etc.

AG'IJ

b: bag'găġe.
Plus hag age, etc.

AG'ING

b: bag'ging.
br: brag'ging.
dr: drag'ging.
f: fag'ging.
fl: flag'ging, un-flag'ging.
g: gag'ging.
j: jag'ging.

l: lag'ging.
m: mag'ging.
n: nag'ging.
r: rag'ging.
s: sag'ging.
sh: shag'ging.
sl: slag'ging.
sn: snag'ging.
t: tag'ging.
w: wag'ging.

AG'IS

h: hag'gis.
Cf. bag is, etc.

AG'ISH

h: hag'gish.
l: lag'gish.
n: nag'gish.
w: wag'gish.

AG'L

d: bē-dag'gle*, bọọn'dag-gle,
   dag'gle.
dr: bē-drag'gle, drag'gle.
g: gag'gle.
h: hag'gle.
r: rag'gle.
str: strag'gle.
t: rag'gle=tag''gle.
w: wag'gel, wag'gle.
Plus flag 'll, etc.
Cf. drag hell, etc.

AG'LING

d: bē-dag'gling*, bọọn'dag-gling,
   dag'gling.
dr: bē-drag'gling, drag'gling.
g: gag'gling.
h: hag'gling.
r: rag'gling.
str: strag'gling.
w: wag'gling.

279 ūse, bu̯ll, brûte, tûrn, up; crȳ, myth; c̣at, ma̧chine, ace, church, c̩hord; g̣em, añger, (Fr.) boṅ, aṣ; THis, thin; aẓure

AG′LŪR
AG′ŎN

(Choose only one word out of each group)

AG′LŪR

d: bo̧o̧n′dag-glēr, dag′glēr.
dr: bē-drag′glēr, drag′glēr.
h: hag′glēr.
str: strag′glēr.
w: wag′glēr.

AG′MAG

k(c̣): c̣ag′mag.
Plus tag Mag, etc.

AG′MĂN

b: bag′măn.
dr: drag′măn.
fl: flag′măn.
r: rag′măn.
Plus drag man, etc.

AG′MENT

fr: frag′ment.
Plus flag meant, etc.

AG′MĪR

kw: quag′mīre.
Plus drag mire, etc.

AG′MĪT

l: stȧ-lag′mīte.
Plus flag might or mite, etc.

AG′NĂNT

st: stag′nănt.

AG′NĀT

Vowel: ag′nāte.
m: mag′nāte.
st: stag′nāte.
Plus flag, Nate, etc.

AG′NES

Vowel: Ag′nes.

AG′NET

m: mag′net.
Plus Mag met, etc.

AG′NUM

m: mag′num.

Ā′GŌ

Vowel: ⁓San Di-e̱′gō,
Ti-er′rȧ del Fủ-e̱′gō.
b: lum-bā′gō, plum-bā′gō,
Tō-bā′gō.
d: Dā′gō.
m: i-mā′gō.
r: far-rā′gō, vi-rā′gō, vŏ-rā′gō.
s: sā′gō.
Plus may⁀go, etc.

Ä′GŌ

Vowel: San-ti-ä′gō.
k(c̣): C̣hi-c̣ä′gō.
r: far-rä′gō.
Cf. Fär′gō.
Plus shah go, etc.
Cf. dog owe or O, etc.

Ā′GON

d: Dā′gon.
Cf. āg′ăn.

AG′ŎN

dr: drag′ŏn, pen-drag′ŏn,
snap-drag′ŏn.
fl: flag′ŏn.
w: wag′ŏn.
Plus flag on, etc.

AG'ŎT
Ä-HOO'
fāte, fär, fȧst, fa̧ll, finǎl, cãre, at; mēte, prȩy, hẽr, met; pīne,
marǐne, bȋrd, pin; nōte, mȯve, fo̧r, ȧtŏm, not; mo̧o̧n, book;
280

(Choose only one word out of each group)

AG'ŎT

Vowel: ag'ăte.
f: fag'ŏt.
m: mag'gŏt, mag'ŏt.
Cf. flag it, etc.

AG'PĪ

m: mag'pīe.
Plus stag pie, etc.

AG'PĪP

b: bag'pīpe.
Plus drag pipe, etc.

ĀG'RĂNS

fl: flā'grănce.
fr: frā'grănce.
v: vā'grănts.
Plus Hague rants, etc.

ĀG'RĂNT

fl: flā'grănt.
fr: frā'grănt, in-frā'grănt.
v: vā'grănt.
Plus Hague rant, etc.

AG'RIK

d: pō-dag'ri̧c.
r: ȩhī-rag'ri̧c.
Plus drag rick, etc.

Ā'GŪ

Vowel: ā'gūe.
Plus Hague, you, etc.

ĀG'ŪR

m: māi'gre.
pl: plā'guẽr.
v: vā'guẽr.
Plus plague her, etc.

AG'ŪR

Vowel: ag'ăr=ag'ăr.
b: bag'gẽr, ȩär'pet-bag"gẽr,
ŏne'=bag'gẽr (wun'),
fōur'=bag'gẽr, three'=bag'gẽr,
twö'=bag'gẽr (to̧o̧').
br: brag'gẽr.
d: dag'gẽr.
dr: drag'gẽr.
f: Fag'gẽr.
fl: flag'gẽr.
g: gag'gẽr.
j: jag'gẽr.
l: lag'gẽr.
m: mag'gẽr.
n: nag'gẽr.
r: rag'gẽr.
s: sag'gẽr.
sh: shag'gẽr.
st: stag'gẽr.
sw: swag'gẽr.
t: tag'gẽr.
w: wag'gẽr, wig'wag-gẽr.
Plus drag her, etc.

Ā'GUS

m: är-ȩhi-mā'gus, mā'gus.
r: ȩhō-rā'gus.
Plus plague us, etc.

AGZ'MĂN

dr: dragş'măn.
kr: ȩragş'măn.
Plus drags man, etc.

Ä-HOO'

w: wä-ho̧o̧'.
y: yä-ho̧o̧'.
Plus shah, who, etc.

(Choose only one word out of each group)

Ā′Ī

hw: whey′ey.
kl: çlāy′ey.
spr: sprāy′ey.
Plus say he, etc.

Ä′Ĭ

t: Hä-tä′y (-tä′i).
Cf. Hawaii.

Ä′ĬB

s: sä′hib.

Ā′ĪJ

dr: drāy′ăġe.
w: weigh′ăġe (wā′).
Plus play age, etc.

Ā′ĪK

br: al-ġē-brā′iç, Al-ham-brā′iç, Hē-brā′iç.
d: Çhal-dā′iç, Ed-dā′iç, Jú-dā′iç, sō-dā′iç, spon-dā′iç.
k(ç): Al-çā′iç, är-çhā′iç, trō-çhā′iç.
l: lā′iç.
m: Ar-à-mā′iç, Bräh-mā′iç, Ptol-ē-mā′iç (tol-), Rō-mā′iç.
n: Cȳ-rē-nā′iç, Sī-nā′iç.
t: tes-sē-rā′iç.
s: phar-i-sā′iç, Pas-sā′iç, sad-dū-sā′iç.
t: al-tā′iç, del-tā′iç, Jag-à-tā′iç, vol-tā′iç.
z: an″ti-Mō-ṣā′iç, mō-ṣā′iç, par″à-di-ṣā′iç, prō-ṣā′iç, stan-zā′iç.

Ā′ĬNG

b: bāy′ing, dis-ō-bey′ing, ō-bey′ing.
br: brāy′ing.

fl: flāy′ing.
fr: dē-frāy′ing, frāy′ing.
gr: grāy′ing.
h: hāy′ing.
k(ç): dē-çāy′ing, un″dē-çay′ing.
kl: çlāy′ing.
l: al-lāy′ing, bē-lāy′ing, dē-lāy′ing, in-lāy′ing, in-tēr-lāy′ing, lāy′ing, mis-lāy′ing, out-lāy′ing, ō-vēr-lāy′ing, rē-lāy′ing, wāy-lāy′ing.
m: à-māy′ing, dis-māy′ing, māy′ing.
n: neigh′ing (nā′).
p: ō-vēr-pāy′ing, pāy′ing, prē-pāy′ing, rē-pāy′ing, un-dēr-pāy′ing.
pl: dis-plāy′ing, horse′plāy-ing, in-tēr-plāy′ing, plāy′ing, un-dēr-plāy′ing.
pr: prāy′ing, prey′ing.
r: ar-rāy′ing, bē-wrāy′ing, dis-ar-rāy′ing, hūr-rāy′ing.
s: as-sāy′ing, es-sāy′ing, fōre-sāy′ing, gāin-sāy′ing, mis-sāy′ing, sāy′ing, sooTH′sāy-ing, un-sāy′ing.
sl: slāy′ing.
sp: spāy′ing.
spr: sprāy′ing.
st: out-stāy′ing, ō-vēr-stāy′ing, stāy′ing.
sw: swāy′ing.
tr: bē-trāy′ing, pōr-trāy′ing.
v: çon-vey′ing, in-veigh′ing (vā′), pūr-vey′ing, sūr-vey′ing.
w: out-weigh′ing (-wā′), un-weigh′ing, weigh′ing.

Ā′IS
ĀJ′EZ

fāte, fär, fȧst, fạll, finăl, cãre, at; mēte, prẹy, hẽr, met; pīne,
marīne, bĭrd, pin; nōte, mŏve, fọr, atŏm, not; mọọn, book;

282

(Choose only one word out of each group)

Ā′IS

d: dā′is.
l: Lā′is.
Cf. May is, etc.

Ā′ISH

g: gāy′ish.
gr: grāy′ish, grẹy′ish,
sil′vẽr=grāy′ish.
kl: c̱lāy′ish.

Ā′IST

br: al-g̱ē-brā′ist.
k(c̱): är-c̱hā′ist.
m: Ptol-ē-mā′ist (tol-).
z: prō-sā′ist.

Ā′IZM

d: C̱hal-dā′ism.
l: Lā′ism.
z: Mō-sa′ism, prō-sā′ism.

Ä′JȦ

r: mȧ-hä′rä′jȧh, rä′jȧh.

AJ′ĂNT

p: pag̱e′ănt (paj′).
Plus badge aunt *or* ant, etc.

ĀJ′ED

Vowel: āg̱′ed.
Plus enrage Ed, etc.
Plus say, Jed, etc.

Ā′JENT

Vowel: ā′g̱ent, rē-ā′g̱ent.
Plus play gent, etc.

ĀJ′EST

Vowel: āg̱′est*.
g: en-gāg̱′est*, gāg̱′est*,
gāug̱′est*.
r: en-rāg̱′est*, out-rāg̱′est*,
rāg̱′est*.
s: prē-sāg̱′est*, sāg̱′est.
st: stāg̱′est*.
sw: as-suāg̱′est (-swāj′)*,
swāg̱′est*.
w: wāg̱′est*.
Plus May jest, etc.

AJ′ET

g: gad′g̱et.
p: Pad′g̱ett, Pag̱′et.
Plus cadge it, etc.
Plus sad jet, etc.
Plus Madge et, etc.

ĀJ′ETH

Vowel: āg̱′eth*.
g: en-gāg̱′eth*, gāg̱′eth*,
gāug̱′eth*.
r: en-rāg̱′eth*, out-rāg̱′eth*,
rāg̱′eth*.
s: prē-sāg̱′eth*.
sw: as-suāg̱′eth (-swāj′)*.
w: wāg̱′eth.

ĀJ′EZ

Vowel: āg̱′es̱.
g: dis-en-gāg̱′es̱, en-gāg̱′es̱,
gāg̱′es̱, gāug̱′es̱, green′gāg-es̱,
prē=en-gāg̱′es̱,
weaTH′ẽr-gāug̱-es̱ (weTH′).
k(c̱): c̱āg̱′es̱, en-c̱āg̱′es̱.
m: māg̱′es̱.
p: pāg̱′es̱.

(Choose only one word out of each group)

r: en-rāġ'eṣ, out'rāg-eṣ, rāġ'eṣ.
s: prē-sāġ'eṣ, sāġ'eṣ.
st: stāġ'eṣ.
sw: as-suāġ'eṣ (-swāj').
w: wāġ'eṣ.
Plus rage is, etc.

ĀJ'I

k(ç): çāġ'ey.
r: rāġ'y.
s: sāġ'y.
st: stāġ'ey, stāġ'y.
Plus wage he, etc.

AJ'I

h: had'ji.
k(ç): çad'ġy.
w: hō-wad'ji.
Plus Madge, he, etc.

AJ'IK

f: an-drō-phaġ'iç, lō-tō-phaġ'iç,
  om-ō-phaġ'iç, sär-çō-phaġ'iç,
  thē-ō-phaġ'iç.
l: är-çhi-pel-aġ'iç, el-laġ'iç,
  pē-laġ'iç.
m: maġ'iç.
r: hem-ŏr-rhaġ'iç (-raj').
tr: traġ'iç.

AJ'IL

Vowel: aġ'ile.
fr: fraġ'ile.
Plus Madge ill, etc.

AJ'IN

m: i-maġ'ine.
Plus Madge in, etc.

AJ'IND

m: im-aġ'ined, un-im-aġ'ined.

ĀJ'ING

Vowel: āġ'ing.
g: en-gāġ'ing, gāġ'ing,
  gāuġ'ing, dis-en-gāġ'ing.
k(ç): çāġ'ing, en-çāġ'ing.
p: pāġ'ing.
r: en-rāġ'ing, out-rāġ'ing,
  rāġ'ing.
s: prē-sāġ'ing.
st: stāġ'ing.

AJ'ING

b: badġ'ing.
k(ç): çadġ'ing.

ĀJ'LES

Vowel: āġe'less.
g: gāġe'less, gāuġe'less.
k(ç): çāġe'less.
p: pāġe'less.
r: rāġe'less.
s: sāġe'less.
st: stāġe'less.
w: wāġe'less.
Plus page less, etc.

ĀJ'LI

s: sāġe'ly.
Plus enrage Lee or lea, etc.

ĀJ'LING

k(ç): çāġe'ling.

ĀJ'MENT

g: en-gāġe'ment,
  prē-en-gāġe'ment.
k(ç): en-çāġe'ment.
r: en-rāġe'ment.
s: prē-sāġe'ment.
sw: as-suāġe'ment (-swāj'ʹ
Plus page meant, etc.

ĀJ'NES
ĀK'DOUN

fāte, fär, fȧst, fạll, finăl, cãre, at; mēte, prey, hẽr, met; pīne,
marïne, bĭrd, pin; nōte, mŏve, fọr, atŏm, not; mọọn, book; **284**

(Choose only one word out of each group)

ĀJ'NES

s: sāge'ness.

ĀJ'ŪR

g: dis-en-gāg'ẽr, en-gāg'ẽr,
gāg'ẽr, gāuġ'ẽr.
k(c): cāġ'ẽr.
m: māj'ŏr, trum'pet māj'ŏr.
p: pāġ'ẽr.
r: en-rāġ'ẽr.
s: prē-sāġ'ẽr, sāġ'ẽr.
st: ōld'=stāg"ẽr, stāġ'ẽr.
sw: as-suāġ'ẽr (-swāj').
w: wāġ'ẽr.
Plus enrage her, etc.

AJ'ŪR

Vowel: aġ'ġẽr.
b: bad'ġẽr.
k(c): cad'ġẽr.
Plus badge her, err *or* er, etc.

ĀJ'US

b: am-bāġ'ious.
br: um-brāg'eous.
p: ram-pāg'eous.
r: coū-rā'ġeous, ō-rā'ġious,
out-rā'ġeous.
t: ad-van-tāġ-eous, con-tāġ'ious,
dis"ad-van-tāġ'eous.
Plus enrage us, etc.

Ā'KȦ

m: Jȧ-māi'cȧ.
r: rā'cȧ.
Plus flake a, etc.

AK'Ȧ

l: Mȧ-lac'cȧ, pō-lac'cȧ.
p: al-pac'ȧ.
Plus pack a, etc.

Å'KÅ

r: jä-rȧ-rȧc'ȧ (zhä-).
Plus plaque a, etc.

AK'ẠL

j: jack'ạl.
p: pack ạll.
Plus smack all, etc.

AK'ÄRD

p: Pack'ărd.
pl: plac'ărd.
Cf. smack hard, etc.
Cf. stack card, etc.

AK'ĀT

b: bac'cāte.
pl: pla'cāte.
s: sac'cāte.
Plus smack eight *or* ate, etc.

AK'BRĀND

kr: crack'brāined.
sl: slack'=brāined'.
Plus Jack brained, etc.

AK'BUT

h: hack'but.
s: sack'but.
Plus Jack, but *or* butt, etc.

AK'DAW

j: jack'daw.
Plus sack daw, etc.

ĀK'DOUN

br: breāk'down.
sh: shāke'down.
Plus make down, etc.

(Choose only one word out of each group)

ĀK′ED

n: nāk′ed.
Plus wāk′ed*, etc.
Plus stray ked, etc.

ĀK′EN

Vowel: Āik′en.
b: bā′c̟ŏn.
kr: krā′ken.
m: Jȧ-māi′c̟ăn.
s: for̟-sāk′en.
sh: shāk′en, wind′᷃-shāk″en.
t: mis-tāk′en, ō-ver-tāk′en,
tāk′en, un-dĕr-tāk′en,
up-tāk′en.
w: ȧ-wāk′en, wāk′en.
Cf. wake hen, etc.

AK′EN

bl: black′en.
br: brack′en.
sl: slack′en.
Cf. black hen, etc.

Ä′KEN

kr: krä′ken.
Cf. mock hen, etc.

ĀK′END

b: bā′c̟ŏnned.
w: ȧ-wāk′ened, un-ȧ-wāk′ened,
wāk′ened.
Plus make end, etc.

ĀK′EST

Vowel: ac̟h′est*.
b: bāk′est*.
br: breāk′est*.
f: fāk′est*.
kw: quāk′est*.

m: māk′est*.
p: ō-pā′quest.
r: rāk′est*.
s: for̟-sāk′est*.
sh: shāk′est*.
sp: spāk′est*.
st: stāk′est*.
t: bē-tāk′est*, mis-tāk′est*,
ō-vēr-tāk′est*, pär-tāk′est*,
tāk′est*, un-dēr-tāk′est*.
w: ȧ-wāk′est*, wāk′est*.

AK′EST

b: back′est*.
bl: black′est.
h: hack′est*.
hw: whack′est*.
kl: c̟lack′est*.
kr: c̟rack′est*.
kw: quack′est*.
l: lack′est*.
p: pack′est*, un-pack′est*.
r: rack′est*.
s: ran-sack′est*, sack′est*.
sl: slack′est.
sm: smack′est*.
t: at-tack′est*, tack′est*.
tr: track′est*.

AK′ET

br: brack′et.
fl: flack′et.
h: Hack′ett.
j: jack′et.
p: pack′et.
pl: plack′et.
r: rack′et, rac̟′quet (′ket).
t: tack′et.
Plus attack it, etc.
Plus Jack et, etc.

(Choose only one word out of each group)

ĀK′ETH

Vowel: āch′eth*.
b: bāk′eth*.
br: breāk′eth*.
f: fāk′eth*.
k(c): cāk′eth*.
kw: quāk′eth*.
m: māk′eth*.
r: rāk′eth*.
s: fọr-sāk′eth*.
sh: shāk′eth*.
st: stāk′eth*.
t: bē-tāk′eth*, mis-tāk′eth*,
ō-vẽr-tāk′eth*, pär-tāk′eth*,
tāk′eth*, un-dẽr-tāk′eth*.
w: ȧ-wāk′eth*, wāk′eth*.

AK′ETH

b: back′eth*.
bl: black′eth*.
h: hack′eth*.
hw: whack′eth*.
kl: clack′eth*.
kr: crack′eth.
kw: quack′eth*.
l: lack′eth*.
p: pack′eth*, un-pack′eth*.
r: rack′eth*.
s: ran-sack′eth*, sack′eth*.
sl: slack′eth*.
sm: smack′eth*.
t: at-tack′eth*, tack′eth*.
tr: track′eth*.

ĀK′FỤL

w: wāke′fụl.
Plus make full, etc.

ĀK′I

Vowel: āch′ey.
br: brāk′y.

f: fāk′y.
fl: flāk′y.
k(c): cāk′y.
kw: quāk′y.
sh: shāk′y.
sn: snāk′y.
Plus snake, he, etc.
Plus take key, etc.

AK′I

bl: black′y.
kr: crack′y.
l: lack′ey.
n: knack′y (nak′).
s: Nag-à-sak′i, sak′i.
w: wack′y.
Plus track, he, etc.
Plus pack key, etc.

Ä′KI

k: khä′ki (kä′).
s: sä′kē, sä′ki.

ĀK′IJ

br: breāk′ăge.
Cf. snake age, etc.

AK′IJ

p: pack′ăge.
r: wrack′ăge.
s: sack′ăge.
st: stack′ăge.
tr: track′ăge.
Plus black age, etc.

AK′ĪK

b: bac′chic.
m: stō-mach′ic.
Cf. back kick, etc.

287   ūse, bṳll, brûte, tûrn, up; crȳ, myth; c̱at, ma̱chine, ace, church, c̱hord; ġem, añger, (Fr.) boṅ, a̱ş; THis, thin; a̱zure

AK'SĒN
AK'L

(Choose only one word out of each group)

AK'SĒN

v: vac̱'cīne.
Plus track seen *or* scene, etc.

ĀK'ING

Vowel: ac̱h'ing.
b: bāk'ing.
br: brāk'ing, breāk'ing,
  heärt'breāk-ing, up-breāk'ing.
f: fāk'ing.
fl: flāk'ing.
k(c̱): c̱āk'ing.
kw: quāk'ing.
m: māk'ing, un-māk'ing.
r: rāk'ing.
s: fo̱r-sāk'ing.
sh: shāk'ing.
sl: slāk'ing.
sp: spāk'ing.
st: stāk'ing.
t: bē-tāk'ing, mis-tāk'ing,
  ō-vẽr-tāk'ing, pär-tāk'ing,
  tāk'ing, un-dẽr-tāk'ing,
  up-tāk'ing.
w: à-wāk'ing, wāk'ing.
Plus play king, etc.

AK'ING

Vowel: bi-vöu-ac̱'ing.
b: back'ing.
bl: black'ing.
h: hack'ing.
hw: whack'ing.
j: jack'ing.
kl: c̱lack'ing.
kr: c̱rack'ing.
kw: quack'ing.
l: lack'ing.
n: knack'ing (nak').

p: pack'ing, un-pack'ing.
r: rack'ing.
s: ran'sack-ing, sack'ing.
sl: slack'ing.
sm: smack'ing.
sn: snack'ing.
st: stack'ing.
t: at-tack'ing, tack'ing.
tr: track'ing.
thw: thwack'ing.
Cf. black king, etc.

ĀK'ISH

r: rāk'ish.
sn: snāk'ish.

AK'ISH

bl: black'ish.
br: brack'ish.
kw: quack'ish.
n: knack'ish (nak').

AK'KLO̱TH

p: pack'c̱lo̱th.
s: sack'c̱lo̱th.
Plus black cloth, etc.

AK'L

gr: grack'le.
h: hack'le.
k(c̱): c̱ack'le.
kr: c̱rack'le.
kw: quack'le.
m: ma'c̱le.
sh: ram-shack'le, shack'le.
t: tack'le.
Plus black 'll, etc.

AK′LD
Ä′KŌ

fāte, fär, fȧst, fₐll, finăl, cāre, at; mēte, prᵉy, hẽr, met; pīne,
marïne, bĭrd, pĭn; nōte, möve, fₒr, atŏm, not; mๅๅn, book;

288

(Choose only one word out of each group)

AK′LD

sh: un-shack′led.
Plus ak′l+ed.
Plus stack culled, etc.

AK′LES

n: knack′less.
s: sack′less.
tr: track′less.
Plus black less, etc.

ĀK′LET

l: lāke′let.
Plus snake let, etc.

AK′LI

bl: black′ly.
k(c̨): c̨ack′ly.
kr: c̨rack′ly.
sh: ram-shack′ly, shack′ly.
t: tack′ly.
Plus track Lee or lea, etc.

AK′LING

h: hack′ling.
k(c̨): c̨ack′ling.
kw: c̨rack′ling.
sh: shack′ling.
t: tack′ling.

AK′LOG

b: back′log.
h: hack′log.
Plus stack log, etc.

AK′LŨR

h: hack′lẽr.
k(c̨): c̨ack′lẽr.
kr: c̨rack′lẽr.
sh: shack′lẽr.
t: tack′lẽr.

AK′MĂN

bl: black′măn.
j: jack′măn.
p: pack′măn.
Plus attack man, etc.

AK′MĒ

Vowel: ac̨′mē.
l: Lac̨′mē.
Plus thwack me, etc.

AK′NES

bl: black′ness.
sl: slack′ness.

AK′NĒ

Vowel: ac̨′nē.
h: hack′ney (′ni).
Plus black knee, or nee, etc.

ĀK′NING

w: à-wāke′ning, wāke′ning.

Ā′KŌ

m: Mā′kō.
s: Sā′c̨ō.
w: Wā′c̨ō.
Plus stake owe or O, etc.

AK′Ō

b: tō-bac̨′c̨ō.
r: gō-rac̨′c̨ō.
s: Sac̨′c̨ō.
sh: shak′ō.
Plus black owe or O, etc

Ä′KŌ

ch: Grän Chä′c̨ō.
gw: guä′c̨ō.
n: guä-nä′c̨ō.
Cf. lock owe, etc.

289 ūse, bụll, brūte, tŭrn, up; crȳ, myth; çat, maçhine, ace, church, çhord; ġem, añger, (Fr.) boṅ, aṣ; THis, thin; aᴢure

ĀK'ǪF
AK'SHUN

(Choose only one word out of each group)

ĀK'ǪF

r: rāke'ǫff.
t: tāke'ǫff.
Plus snake off, etc.

Ā'KŎB

j: Jā'çŏb.
Plus stray cob or Cobb, etc.
Cf. make cob, etc.

ĀK'ŎN

b: bā'çŏn.
l: Lā'çŏn.
m: Mā'çŏn.
Cf. āk'en.
Plus bake on or an, etc.

Ā'KǪRN

Vowel: ā'çǫrn.
Plus shake horn, etc.
Plus May corn, etc.
Cf. make corn, etc.

AK'POT

j: jack'pot.
kr: çrack'pot.
Plus stack pot, etc.

ĀK'RED

s: sā'çred.
Plus stake red, etc.

AK'RID

Vowel: aç'rid.
Plus Jack rid, etc.

ĀK'RING

s: sā'çring.
Plus make ring, etc.

ĀK'RIST

s: sā'çrist.
Plus shake wrist, etc.

AK'RUM

l: sim-ū-laç'rum.
s: saç'rum.
Plus black rum, etc.

AK'SENT

Vowel: aç'cent.
Plus black cent or scent, etc.

AK'SES

Vowel: aç'cess.

AK'SHUN

Vowel: aç'tion, çō-aç'tion,
coun″tēr-aç'tion, ex-aç'tion,
in-aç'tion, in-tēr-aç'tion,
rē-aç'tion, re-trō-aç'tion,
sub-aç'tion.
d: rē-daç'tion.
f: ā-rē-faç'tion,
as-suē-faç'tion (-swē-)*,
ben-ē-faç'tion, çal-ē-faç'tion,
dis-sat-is-faç'tion, faç'tion,
lab-ē-faç'tion, li-quē-faç'tion,
lū-bri-faç'tion, mad-ē-faç'tion,
mal-ē-faç'tion, pe-tri-faç'tion,
pū-trē-faç'tion, rār-ē-faç'tion,
rùb-ē-faç'tion, sat-is-faç'tion,
stū-pē-faç'tion, tab-ē-faç'tion,
tep-ē-faç'tion, tor-rē-faç'tion,
tū-mē-faç'tion.
fr: dif-fraç'tion, fraç'tion,
in-fraç'tion, rē-fraç'tion.
p: çom-paç'tion, paç'tion.

AK′SHUS
AK′STŎN

fāte, fär, fȧst, fạll, finăl, cãre, at; mēte, prey, hẽr, met; pīne,
marïne, bĭrd, pin; nōte, mŏve, fọr, atŏm, not; mọọn, book;

290

(Choose only one word out of each group)

str: ab-strac′tion.

t: con-tac′tion, tac′tion.

tr: at-trac′tion, con-trac′tion,
coun″tẽr-at-trac′tion,
dē-trac′tion, dis-trac′tion,
ex-trac′tion, prō-trac′tion,
rē-trac′tion, sub-trac′tion,
trac′tion.

z: tran-sac′tion.

Plus black shun, etc.

AK′SHUS

f: fac′tious.

fr: frac′tious.

AK′SEZ

Vowel: ax′eṣ, bat′tle=ax″eṣ,
hand ax′eṣ.

l: rē-lax′eṣ.

m: Max′ie′ṣ.

t: tax′eṣ.

w: wax′eṣ.

Plus Jack sees *or* seize, etc.

AK′SI

br: brax′y.

fl: flax′y.

p: Cō-tō-pax′i.

t: bī′ō-tax-y, het′ẽr-ō-tax-y,
hō′mō-tax-y, tax′i.

w: wax′y.

Plus Jack see, etc.

AK′SID

fl: flac′cid.

Plus back, Sid, etc.

AK′SIM

m: max′im.

Plus black Sim, etc.

Plus cracks him, etc.

AK′SIS

Vowel: ax′is.

n: sy-nax′is.

pr: prax′is.

t: tax′is.

Cf. taxes, etc.

AK′SL

Vowel: ax′le.

Plus cracks ′ll, etc.

AKS′MĂN

kr: cracks′măn.

t: tacks′măn.

Plus backs man, etc.

AK′SŎN

fl: flax′en.

j: Jack′sŏn.

k(c): cax′ŏn*.

kl: Klax′ŏn.

s: Añ″glō=Sax′ŏn, Sax′ŏn.

w: wax′en.

Cf. wax hen, etc.

Plus tacks on, etc.

Plus black sun *or* son, etc.

AK′STĀ

b: back′stāy.

j: jack′stāy.

Plus black stay, etc.

AK′STŌN

bl: Black′stōne.

Plus crack stone, etc.

Plus cracks tone, etc.

AK′STŎN

br: Brax′tŏn.

k(c): Cax′tŏn.

(Choose only one word out of each group)

kl: Klax'tŏn.
Plus cracks ton *or* tun, etc.
Plus black stun, etc.

AKS'WELL

m: Max'well.
Plus smacks well, etc.
Plus tack swell, etc.

AK'TĀT

l: ab-lac̹'tāte, lac̹'tāte.
tr: trac̹'tāte.
Plus bract eight *or* ate, etc.
Plus tracked eight, etc.

AK'TED

Vowel: ac̹'ted, c̹oun-tĕr-ac̹'ted,
en-ac̹'ted, ō-vĕr-ac̹'ted,
rē-ac̹'ted, un-ac̹'ted,
un-dĕr-ac̹'ted.
fr: dif-frac̹'ted, rē-frac̹'ted.
p: c̹om-pac̹'ted.
str: ab-strac̹'ted.
t: at-trac̹'ted, c̹on-trac̹'ted,
dē-trac̹'ted, dis-trac̹'ted,
ex-trac̹'ted, prō-trac̹'ted,
rē-trac̹'ted, sub-trac̹'ted.
z: ex-ac̹'ted, tran-ṣac̹'ted.
Cf. cracked head, etc.
Plus crack Ted, etc.
Plus smacked Ed, etc.

AK'TEST

Vowel: ac̹'test*,
c̹oun-tĕr-act'est*, en-ac̹'test*,
rē-ac̹'test*.
str: ab-strac̹'test*.
tr: at-trac̹'test*, c̹on-trac̹'test*,
dē-trac̹'test*, ex-trac̹'test*,
rē-trac̹'test*, sub-trac̹'test*.

z: ex-ac̹'test, tran-ṣac̹'test*.
Plus track test, etc.

AK'TETH

Vowel: ac̹'teth*,
c̹oun-tĕr-ac̹'teth*, en-ac̹'teth*,
rē-ac̹'teth*.
str: ab-strac̹'teth*.
tr: at-trac̹'teth*, c̹on-trac̹'teth*,
dē-trac̹'teth*, ex-trac̹'teth*,
prō-trac̹'teth*, rē-trac̹'teth*,
sub-trac̹'teth*.
z: ex-ac̹'teth*, tran-ṣac̹'teth*.

AKT'FUL

t: tact'ful.
Plus packed full, etc.

AK'TIK

d: dī-dac̹'tic̹.
fr: em-phrac̹'tic̹.
l: c̹at-al-lac̹'tic̹, gȧ-lac̹'tic̹,
lac̹'tic̹, par-al-lac̹'tic̹,
prō-phy-lac̹'tic̹, stȧ-lac̹'tic̹.
pr: eū-prac̹'tic̹.
t: prō-tac̹'tic̹, syn-tac̹'tic̹,
tac̹'tic̹.
Plus black tick, etc.

AK'TIKS

l: c̹at-al-lac̹'tic̹s.
t: tac̹'tic̹s.
Plus ak'tik+s.

AK'TIL

d: dac̹'tyl, dī-dac̹'tyl,
het″ĕr-ō-dac̹'tyl, lep-tō-dac̹'tyl,
pac̹h-y-dac̹'tyl,
pter-ō-dac̹'tyl (ter-).

AK'TING
AK'TŌ

fāte, fär, fȧst, fạll, finăl, cãre, **at;** mēte, prĕy, hẽr, met; pīne,
marīne, bĭrd, pin; nōte, mŏve, fọr, atŏm, not; mọọn, book; **292**

(Choose only one word out of each group)

t: tac'tile.
tr: at-trac'tile, con-trac'tile,
prō-trac'tile, rē-trac'tile.
trac'tile.
Plus crack till, etc.
Plus lacked ill, etc.

AK'TING

Vowel: ac'ting,
coun-tēr-ac'ting,
dŏu'ble=ac'ting, en-ac'ting,
ō-vēr-ac'ting, rē-ac'ting,
re-trō-ac'ting, self'=ac'ting,
un-dēr-ac'ting.
fr: dif-frac'ting, in-frac'ting,
rē-frac'ting.
str: ab-strac'ting.
tr: at-trac'ting, con-trac'ting,
dē-trac'ting, dis-trac'ting,
prō-trac'ting, rē-trac'ting,
sub-trac'ting.
z: ex-ac'ting, tran-sac'ting.

AK'TIS

pr: prac'tise.
Cf. fact is, etc.

AK'TĪT

l: stȧ-lac'tīte.
Plus black tight, etc.

AK'TIV

Vowel: ac'tive, cō-ac'tive,
coun-tēr-ac'tive, en-ac'tive,
in-ac'tive, rā"di-ō-ac'tive,
rē-ac'tive, re-trō-ac'tive.
f: cal-ē-fac'tive, li-quē-fac'tive,
ol-fac'tive, pe-tri-fac'tive,
pū-trē-fac'tive, rȧr-ē-fac'tive,
sat-is-fac'tive, stū-pē-fac'tive.

fr: dif-frac'tive, rē-frac'tive.
str: ab-strac'tive.
tr: at-trac'tive, con-trac'tive,
coun"tēr-at-trac'tive,
dē-trac'tive, dis-trac'tive,
ex-trac'tive, prō-trac'tive,
rē-trac'tive, sub-trac'tive,
trac'tive.

AKT'LES

Vowel: act'less.
br: bract'less.
f: fact'less.
t: tact'less.
tr: tract'less.
Plus stacked less, etc.

AKT'LI

f: mat'tēr=ŏf=fact'ly (-ŏv-).
p: com-pact'ly.
z: ex-act'ly.
Plus tracked Lee or lea, etc.

AKT'MENT

n: en-act'ment, rē"=en-act'ment.
tr: ex-tract'ment.
Plus bract meant, etc.

AKT'NES

p: com-pact'ness.
t: in-tact'ness.
z: ex-act'ness.

AK'TŌ

f: dē fac'tō, ex pōst fac'tō.
Plus black toe, etc.
Plus tract owe or O, etc.

293 ūse, bu̲ll, brúte, tū̃rn, up; crȳ, myth; c̲at, ma̲chine, ace, church, c̲hord; g̲em, an̊ger, (Fr.) bon̊, as̲; THis, thin; azure

AK′TRES
AK′ŪR

(Choose only one word out of each group)

AK′TRES

Vowel: ac̲′tress.
f: ben-ē-fac̲′tress, fac̲′tress, mal-ē-fac̲′tress.
tr: c̲on-trac̲′tress, dē-trac̲′tress.
z: ex-ac̲′tress.
Plus black tress, etc.

AK′TŪR

f: fac̲′tūre, man-ū-fac̲′tūre, bī-tri-fac̲′tūre.
fr: frac̲′tūre.
Plus lacked your, etc.

AK′TŬR

Vowel: ac̲′tĕr, ac̲′tŏr, en-ac̲′tŏr.
f: ben-ē-fac̲′tŏr, fac̲′tŏr, mal-ē-fac̲′tŏr, ol-fac̲′tŏr.
fr: dif-frac̲′tŏr, in-frac̲′tŏr, rē-frac̲′tŏr.
l: phy-lac̲′tĕr.
m: c̲lī-mac̲′tĕr*.
p: c̲om-pac̲′tĕr.
str: ab-strac̲′tĕr.
tr: at-trac̲′tĕr, c̲on-trac̲′tĕr, c̲on-trac̲′tŏr, dē-trac̲′tŏr, dis-trac̲t′ĕr, ex-trac̲′tĕr, prō-trac̲′tŏr, rē-trac̲′tŏr, sub-trac̲′tĕr, trac̲′tŏr.
z: ex-ac̲′tĕr, tran-s̲ac̲′tŏr.
Plus backed her, etc.

AK′TUS

k: c̲ac̲′tus.
Plus lacked us, etc.

ĀK′UP

br: breāk′up″.
m: māke′⸗up″.
w: wāke′⸗up″.
Plus shake up, etc.

Plus stray cup, etc.
Cf. take cup, etc.

ĀK′ŪR

Vowel: ā′c̲re, God′s̲ ā′c̲re.
b: bāk′ēr.
br: breāk′ēr, heärt′breāk-ēr, im′ág̲e breāk′ēr, la̲w′breāk-ēr, Sab′băth-breāk-ēr, trûce′breāk-ēr.
f: fāk′ēr, fā′kĭr.
fl: flāk′ēr.
kw: Quāk′ēr.
m: bal′lăd māk′ēr, book′māk⸗ēr, dress′māk-ēr, māk′ēr, match′māk-ēr, mis′chief⸗māk′ēr (′chif), pāce′māk-ēr, pēace′māk-ēr, wätch′māk-ēr.
n: nā′c̲re.
r: rāk′ēr.
s: for-sāk′ēr.
sh: shāk′ēr.
st: grub′stāk-ēr.
t: pāins̲′tāk-ēr, pär-tāk′ēr, mis-tāk′ēr, tāk′ēr, un-dēr-tāk′ēr.
w: a̲-wāk′ēr.
Plus shake her, etc.
Plus stray cur *or* Kerr, etc.

AK′ŬR

Vowel: Ack′ēr.
b: back′ēr.
bl: black′ēr.
h: hack′ēr.
hw: bu̲sh′whack-ēr, whack′ēr.
j: hī′jack-ēr.
kl: c̲lack′ēr.
kr: c̲rack′ēr, nut′c̲rack-ēr, sō′dà c̲rack′ēr.

(Choose only one word out of each group)

kw: quack'ẽr.
l: lack'ẽr, laç'quẽr ('kẽr).
n: knack'ẽr (nak').
p: pack'ẽr, un-pack'ẽr.
r: rack'ẽr.
s: ran-sack'ẽr, sack'ẽr.
sl: slack'ẽr.
sm: smack'ẽr.
sn: snack'ẽr.
st: stack'ẽr.
t: at-tack'ẽr, tack'ẽr.
tr: track'ẽr.
Plus pack her, *or* err, etc.

ĀK'ŨRZ

br: breāk'ẽrṣ.
Plus āk'er+s.

AK'US

b: Baç'çhus.
fl: Flaç'çus.
j: jaç'çhus.
Plus back us, etc.
Cf. jack'ass.

AK'WĀ

b: back'wāy.
p: pack'wāy.
tr: track'wāy.
Plus black way, etc.
Plus crack weigh, etc.

Ā'KWĒN

f: fāy queen.
m: Māy queen.
Plus play queen, etc.

AK'WOODZ

b: back'woodṣ.
Plus track woods, etc.
Plus smack Wood's, etc.

Ā'LÅ

g: gā'lå.
l: shil-lā'låh.
Plus sail a, etc.

AL'Å

Vowel: Al'låh.
g: gal'lå.
h: Val-hal'lå.
k(ç): çal'lå.
sh: må-shal'lå.
t: At-tal'å.
Plus shall a, etc.

Ä'LÅ

g: gä'lå.

AL'ĂD

b: bal'lăd.
s: sal'ăd.
Cf. in-val'id, val'id, etc.

AL'ĂNS

b: bal'ănce, çoun-tẽr-bal'ănce,
out-bal'ănce, ō-vẽr-bal'ănce.
v: val'ănce.
Cf. gallants, talents, etc.

AL'ĂNST

b: bal'ănced, out-bal'ănced,
ō-vẽr-bal'ănced, un-bal'ănced.
v: val'ănced.
Cf. pal lanced, etc.

ĀL'ĂNT

h: ex-hāl'ent, in-hāl'ent.
s: as-sāil'ănt.

(Choose only one word out of each group)

sk(sç): in-tran-sçāl'ent,
tran-sçāl'ent.
Plus May lent *or* leant, etc.

Ā'LANGKS

f: phā'lañx.

AL'ĂRD

Vowel: Al'lărd.
b: Bal'lărd.
k(ç): Çal'lărd.
m: mal'lărd.
Cf. val'ŏred.

AL'ĂS

b: bal'ăs.
d: Dal'lăs.
p: pal'ăce, Pal'lăs.
Also al'us.
Cf. al'is.
Plus pal us, etc.

AL'ĂST

b: bal'lăst.
Plus pal last, etc.

AL'BUM

Vowel: al'bum.
Plus pal bum, etc.

ĀL'BŪRD

j: jāil'bĭrd.
Plus rail bird, etc.

AL'BŪRT

Vowel: Al'bērt.
Plus pal, Bert, etc.

AL'DIK

r: he-ral'diç.
Plus shall Dick, etc.

AL'DĪN

Vowel: Al'dīne.
Plus shall dine.

Ä'LĒ

k: Kä'lï.
m: tä-mä'lē.
n: baç-çhä-nä'lē, fi-nä'lē.
r: pas-tō-rä'lē.
Cf. ol'i.
Plus ma Lee, etc.

Ā'LEB

k(ç): Ça'leb.
Plus sail ebb, etc.

AL'EK

Vowel: Al'eck, smärt al'eck.
h: Hal'leck.
t: Tal'leck.

AL'ĂN, AL'EN

Vowel: Al'ăn, Al'len.
Cf. al'ŏn.
Plus pal, Ann *or* an, etc.

AL'ENJ

ch: chal'lenge.

AL'ENJD

ch: chal'lenged, un-chal'lenged.

ĀL'ENS

v: am-bi-vāl'ence, vāl'ence.
Cf. sail hence, etc.

Ā'LES

d: dāy'less.
h: hāy'less.

(Choose only one word out of each group)

kl(cl): clāy'less.
p: pāy'less.
pl: plāy'less.
pr: prey'less.
r: rāy'less.
spr: sprāy'less.
w: wāy'less.
Plus play less, *or* Les, etc.

ĀL'EST

Vowel: āil'est*.
b: bāil'est*, bāl'est*.
f: fāil'est*.
fr: frāil'est.
g: rē-gāl'est*.
h: hāil'est*, hāl'est, in-hāl'est*.
j: en-ġāol'est*, en-jāil'est*.
kw: quāil'est*.
m: māil'est*.
n: nāil'est*.
p: im-pāl'est*, pāl'est.
r: dē-rāil'est*, rāil'est*.
s: as-sāil'est*, out-sāil'est*,
    sāil'est*.
sk(sc): scāl'est*.
t: cūr-tāil'est*, dē-tāil'est*,
    en-tāil'est*, rē-tāil'est*.
tr: trāil'est*.
v: ȧ-vāil'est*, prē-vāil'est*,
    un-veil'est*.
w: bē-wāil'est*, wāil'est*.
Cf. jail, lest, etc.

AL'ET

g: gal'let.
m: mal'let.
p: pal'ăte, pal'ette, pal'let.
s: sal'let.
v: val'et.
Plus Sal et, etc.
Cf. pal it, etc.

ĀL'ETH, ĀIL'ETH

b: bāil'eth*, bāl'eth*.
g: rē-gāl'eth*.
h: ex-hāl'eth*, hāil'eth*,
    in-hāl'eth*.
j: en-ġāol'eth*, en-jāil'eth*,
    jāil'eth*.
kw: quāil'eth*.
n: nāil'eth*.
p: im-pāl'eth*, pāl'eth*.
r: dē-rāil'eth*, rāil'eth*.
s: as-sāil'eth*, out-sāil'eth*,
    sāil'eth*.
sk(sc): scāl'eth*.
t: cūr-tāil'eth*, dē-tāil'eth*,
    en-tāil'eth*, rē-tāil'eth*.
tr: trāil'eth*.
v: ȧ-vāil'eth*, prē-vāil'eth*,
    un-veil'eth*, veil'eth*.
w: bē-wāil'eth*, wāil'eth*.

Ä'LĒZ, Ā'LĒZ, A'LĒZ

z: Gon-zä'lēṣ.
Plus gray lees, etc.

AL'FȦ

Vowel: al'phȧ.
f: al-fal'fȧ.
Plus Ralph a, etc.

AL'FRED

Vowel: Al'fred.
Plus pal Fred, etc.

ĀL'FŲL

b: bāle'fŲl.
p: pāil'fŲl.
w: wāil'fŲl.
Plus ale full, etc.

(Choose only one word out of each group)

AL'GĂM

m: à-mal'găm.

Ā'LI

Vowel: Ā'ley, Eil'i Eil'i.
b: Bāi'ley, bāil'ie.
br: Brā'ley.
d: dāi'ly, Dā'ly.
g: gāi'ly.
h: Hā'ley.
k(ç): çap-ér-çāil'lie, kā'li.
l: shil-lā'ly, ū-ke-lė'lē.
m: Māil'ly, Mā'ley.
n: ra-tiō-nā'lē (-shō-).
p: Pā'ley ('li).
sh: shāl'y.
v: vā'lē.
Plus male, he, etc.
Plus may Lee *or* lea, etc.

AL'I

Vowel: al'ley, Al'lie.
b: bal'ly.
d: dal'ly, dil'ly=dal'ly.
g: gal'ley.
h: Hal'lie.
k: ka'li.
l: Lal'lie ('li).
m: Ō'-Mal'ley, tà-ma'lē.
p: pal'ly.
r: ral'ly.
s: Aunt Sal'ly, sal'ly.
sh: çhal'lis, shil'ly=shal'ly.
t: Tal'ley, tal'ly.
v: val'ley, Val'li Val'li.
Plus shall he, etc.

AL'ID

d: dal'lied, dil'ly=dal'lied.
p: im-pal'lid, pal'lid.
r: ral'lied.

s: sal'lied.
sh: shil'ly=shal'lied.
t: tal'lied.
v: val'id, ral'lied ('lid).

ĀL'IF

b: bāil'iff.
k(ç): Çā'liph.
Plus jail, if, etc.

ĀL'IJ

b: bāil'ăġe.
t: çúr-tāil'ăġe, rē'tāil-ăġe.
Plus jail age, etc.

ĀL'IK

g: Gāel'iç.
m: māl'iç.
s: Sāl'iç.
Plus play lick, etc.

AL'IK

d: mē-dal'liç, Van-dal'iç.
f: aç"rō-çē-phal'iç,
   braçh"is-tō-çē-phal'iç,
   çē-phal'iç, do"li-çhō-çe-phal'iç,
   en-çē-phal'iç, eū"ry-çē-phal'iç,
   maç"ren-çē-phal'iç,
   maç"rō-çē-phal'iç,
   me"so-çē-phal'iç,
   mïç"rō-çē-phal'iç, phal'liç,
   plat"y-çē-phal'iç.
g: Gal'liç.
gr: gral'liç.
k(ç): vō-çal'iç.
m: mal'iç.
r: Ū-ral'iç.
s: ox-al'iç, sal'iç.
t: bī-me-tal'liç, i-tal'iç,
   mē-tal'liç, mon-ō-mē-tal'liç.
th: thal'liç.
Plus shall lick, etc.

AL'IK
AL'KĂT

fāte, fär, fåst, fall, finăl, cāre, at; mēte, prey, hēr, met; pīne,
marïne, bĭrd, pin; nōte, mŏve, fọr, atŏm, not; mọọn, book;

298

(Choose only one word out of each group)

AL'IK

sh: på-shal'ik.

ĀL'IKS

k(c̦): c̦ā'lyx.
s: Sā'lix.
Plus play licks, etc.

ÄL'IN, AL'IN

st: Stäl'in.
Plus pal in, etc.

ĀL'ING

Vowel: āil'ing.
b: bāil'ing, bāl'ing.
f: fāil'ing.
fl: flāil'ing.
gr: grāy'ling, Grey'ling.
h: ex-hāl'ing, hāil'ing, hāl'ing, in-hāl'ing.
hw: whāl'ing.
j: jāil'ing.
kw: quāil'ing.
m: black'māil"ing, māil'ing.
n: nāil'ing.
p: em-pāl'ing, im-pāl'ing, pāl'ing.
r: dē-rāil'ing, rāil'ing.
s: as-sāil'ing, out-sāil'ing, sāil'ing, whōle'sāl-ing.
shm: Sc̦hmel'ing.
sk(sc̦): sc̦āl'ing.
sn: snāil'ing.
t: c̦ūr-tāil'ing, dē-tāil'ing, en-tāil'ing, rē-tāil'ing, tāil'ing.
tr: trāil'ing.
v: å-vāil'ing, c̦oun-tēr-vāil'ing, prē-vāil'ing, un-veil'ing, veil'ing.
w: bē-wāil'ing, wāil'ing.

AL'ING

b: c̦å-bal'ling.
p: pal'ling.

AL'IS

Vowel: Al'ice, al'lice.
ch: chal'ice, Chal'lis.
m: mal'ice.
Cf. al'ăs, al'us.

ÄL'IS

w: C̦orn-wäl'lis.
Cf. pōrt-col'lis, etc.

ĀL'ISH

p: pāl'ish.
sh: shāl'ish.
st: stāl'ish.

AL'JI

Vowel: Al'ġiē, Al'ġy.
l: ce-phå-lal'ġy.
r: neū-ral'ġy.
t: nos-tal'ġy, ō-don-tal'ġy.
Cf. al'ġaē.
Plus pal, Gee, etc.

AL'JIK

f: ce-phal'ġic̦.
r: neū-ral'ġic̦.
t: an-tal'ġic̦, nos-tal'ġic̦, ō-don-tal'ġic̦.

ĀL'KÄR

m: māil c̦är.
r: rāil c̦är.
Plus trail car, etc.

AL'KĀT

f: dē-fal'c̦āte, fal'c̦āte.
Plus pal Kate, etc.

299 ūse, bụll, brúte, tŭrn, up; crȳ, myth; çat, machine, ace,
church, çhord; ġem, añger, (Fr.) boṅ, aṣ; THis, thin; aẓure

AL′KIN
AL-ON′

(Choose only one word out of each group)

AL′KIN

m: gri-mal′kin.
Plus shall kin, etc.

AL′KĒR

v: Val′kyr.

ĀL′LI

fr: frāil′ly.
h: hāle′ly.
p: pāle′ly.
st: stāle′ly.
Cf. āl′i.
Plus frail Lee *or* lea, etc.

AL′MẢ

Vowel: Al′mȧ.
th: Thal′mȧ.
Plus shall ma, etc.

AL′MĀT

p: pal′māte.
Plus shall mate, etc.

ĀL′MENT

Vowel: āil′ment.
b: bāil′ment.
g: rē-gāle′ment.
h: in-hāle′ment.
p: im-pāle′ment.
r: dē-rāil′ment.
s: as-sāil′ment.
t: çūr-tāil′ment, en-tāil′ment,
rē-tāil′ment.
v: ȧ-vāil′ment, prē-vāil′ment.
w: bē-wāil′ment.
Plus sale meant, etc.

AL′MUD

t: Tal′mud.
Plus shall mud, etc.

AL′MUK

k: Kal′muck.
Plus shall muck, etc.

ĀL′NES

fr: frāil′ness.
h: hāle′ness.
m: māle′ness.
p: pāle′ness.
st: stāle′ness.

Ā′LŌ

h: hā′lō.
Plus whale owe *or* O, etc.
Plus play low, etc.

AL′Ō

Vowel: al′ōe.
f: fal′lōw, sum′mēr fal′lōw.
h: Ạll-hal′lōw, dis-hal′lōw,
hal′lōw, un-hal′lōw.
k(ç): çal′lōw.
m: mal′lōw, märsh′mal-lōw.
s: sal′lōw.
sh: shal′lōw.
t: tal′lōw.
Plus shall low, etc.
Plus shall owe *or* O, etc.

ÄL′Ō

sw: swäl′lōw.
w: wäl′lōw.
Cf. ol′ō.

AL′ŎN

g: gal′lŏn.
t: tal′ŏn.
Plus pal on, etc.
Plus shall an, etc.

AL-ON′

s: sal-on′.
Cf. doll on, etc.

AL'ŎP
AL'ŪR

fāte, fär, fȧst, fạll, finăl, cãre, at; mēte, prey, hẽr, met; pīne,
marǐne, bǐrd, pin; nōte, mŏve, fọr, atŏm, not; mọọn, book;

300

(Choose only one word out of each group)

AL'ŎP

g: gal'lŏp.
j: jal'ăp.
sh: shal'lŏp.
sk(sç): sçal'lŏp.
Cf. pal up, etc.

AL'ŎT

b: bal'lŏt.
Cf. shall it, etc.

AL'ŌZ

g: gal'lōwṣ.
Also al'ō+s.

AL'PĪN

Vowel: Al'pīne, cis-al'pīne.
z: tranṣ-al'pīne.
Plus shall pine, etc.

AL'PING

sk(sç): sçalp'ing.

ĀL'SPIN

t: tāil'spin.
Plus frail spin, etc.

ĀL'TI

fr: frāil'ty.
Plus pale tea, etc.

AL'TŌ

Vowel: al'tō.
tr: çon-tral'tō.
Plus shall toe, etc.

AL'TŌ

Vowel: ri-al'tō.

AL'Ū

v: un-dẽr-val'ūe, val'ūe.
Plus shall you, etc.

AL'UM

Vowel: al'um.
Plus pal 'em, etc.

ĀL'ŪR

f: fāil'ūre.
Plus whale your *or* you're, etc.

ĀL'ŪR

b: bāil'ẽr, bāl'ẽr.
f: fāil'ẽr.
fl: flāil'ẽr.
fr: frāil'ẽr.
g: rē-gāl'ẽr.
h: hāl'ẽr, in-hāl'ẽr.
hw: whāl'ẽr.
j: ḡāol'ẽr, jāil'ẽr.
kw: quāil'ẽr.
m: māil'ẽr.
n: nāil'ẽr.
p: im-pāl'ẽr, pāl'ẽr.
r: dē-rāil'ẽr, rāil'ẽr.
s: as-sāil'ẽr, sāil'ẽr, sāil'ŏr,
   Sāy'lẽr.
sk(sç): sçāl'ẽr.
skw: squāl'ŏr.
st: stāl'ẽr.
t: çūr-tāil'ẽr, dē-tāil'ẽr,
   en-tāil'ẽr, rē-tāil'ẽr, tāil'ŏr,
   Tāy'lŏr.
tr: trāil'ẽr.
v: prē-vāil'ẽr, un-veil'ẽr.
w: bē-wāil'ẽr, wāil'ẽr.
Plus assail her, etc·

AL'ŪR

b: çȧ-bal'lẽr.
p: pal'lŏr.
v: val'ŏr.
Plus shall err, er *or* her, etc.

(Choose only one word out of each group)

AL′US

g: gal′lus.
k(c̣): ça̧l′lous.
Cf. also al′ăs, al′is.
Plus pal us, etc.

AL′VÅ

Vowel: Al′vå, Al′våh.
h: Hal′veh.
Plus valve a, etc.

AL′VIJ

s: sal′văg̊e.
Plus valve age, etc.

AL′VIN

Vowel: Al′vin.
k(c̣): Ça̧l′vin.
Plus valve in, etc.

AL′VŌ

s: sal′vō.

AL′VUR

s: quack′sal-vĕr, sal′vĕr,
sal′vŏr.
Plus valve or, etc.

AL′VŨRT

k(c̣): Ça̧l′vĕrt.

AL′WIN

Vowel: Al′win.
Plus pal win, etc.

ĀL′YÅ

d: dāh′liå.
g: rē-gā′liå.
m: mam-mā′liå.
n: Bac̣-chan-āl′iå, mär-g̊i-nāl′iå,
par-å-phĕr-nāl′iå, sat-ūr-nāl′iå,
tĕr-mi-nāl′iå.

t: c̣as-tāl′iå.
tr: Cen-trāl′iå, pen-ē-trāl′iå.
z: å-zāl′eå (′yå).
Cf. fail you (yuh), etc.

ÄL′YÅ, AL′YÅ

d: dähl′iå.
Cf. pal you (yuh), doll you, etc.

ĀL′YĂN

Vowel: āl′ien (′yen).
d: Daē-dāl′iăn, Ī-dāl′iăn,
ses″quip-ē-dāl′iăn.
g: rē-gāl′iăn.
j: Phi-gāl′iăn.
m: mam-māl′iăn,
phan-taș-māl′iăn, Pyg-māl′iŏn.
n: bac̣-chå-nāl′iăn,
sat-ūr-nāl′iăn, te-nāil′lŏn (′yun),
tō-bac̣″c̣ō-nāl′iăn.
p: ē-pis″c̣ō-pāl′iăn,
mär-sū-pi-āl′iăn.
r: på-rāl′iăn*.
s: Mes-sāl′iăn, ūn″i-vĕr-sāl′iăn.
tr: A̧us-trāl′iăn.
Plus trail yon, etc.
Cf. ā′li-ăn.

AL′YĂNT

v: val′iănt.

ĀL′YÄRD

j: g̊āol′yärd, jäil′yärd.
k: käil′yärd.
Plus sail yard, etc.

AL′YŌ

r: sē-rag′liō (-ral′yō).
t: in-tag′liō (-tal′yō).

AL′YŎN
Ā′MĂT

fāte, fär, fȧst, fạll, finăl, cāre, at; mēte, prẹy, hêr, met; pīne,
marīne, bĭrd, pĭn; nōte, mŏve, fọr, atŏm, not; mọọn, book;   **302**

(Choose only one word out of each group)

AL′YŎN

d: mē-dal′liŏn.
sk(sc̣): rap-sc̣al′liŏn, ras-c̣al′liŏn,
   sc̣al′liŏn.
st: stal′liŏn.
t: bat-tal′iŏn, I-tal′iăn.
Plus shall yon, etc.

AL′YŪRD

h: hal′yȧrd, hal′liărd.

ĀLZ′MĂN

d: dāleṣ′măn.
hw: whāleṣ′măn.
s: sāleṣ′măn.
t: tāleṣ′măn.
Plus fails man, etc.

ĀM′Ȧ

h: Bȧ-hä′mȧ.
kr: krä′mȧ.
Plus stray, ma, etc.

AM′Ȧ

b: Al-ȧ-bam′ȧ.
g: dĭ-gam′mȧ.
m: mam′mȧ.
Plus damn a, etc.

Ä′MȦ

b: Al-ȧ-bä′mȧ.
br: Bräh′mȧ.
dr: drä′mȧ, mel′ō-drä-mȧ.
g: gäm′mȧ.
h: Bȧ-hä′mȧ, Yōk-ȧ-hä′mȧ.
j: pȧ-jä′mȧ, py-jä′mȧ.
k: Käa′mȧ, Kä′mȧ.
l: Dä′laī Lä′mȧ, lä′mȧ,
   llä′mȧ, Tẹ′shù Lä′mȧ.
m: mäm′mȧ.

r: c̣oṣ-mō-rä′mȧ, cȳ-c̣lō-rä′mȧ,
   dī-ō-rä′mȧ, ġe-ō-rä′mȧ,
   nē-ō-rä′mȧ, pan-ō-rä′mȧ,
   Rä′mȧ.
y: Fù-jĭ-yä′mȧ, Yä′mȧ.
Plus salaam a, etc.

Ā′MĂN

d: dāy′măn.
dr: drāy′măn.
k(c̣): c̣āi′măn, c̣āy′măn.
l: lāy′măn.
w: hīgh′wāy-măn (hī′),
   Wẹy′măn.
Plus wẹigh′man, etc.
Plus also a′men.

ĀM′ĂNT

kl: c̣lāim′ănt.
Also ā′ment.

AM′ĂNT

kl: c̣lam′ănt.
Plus scram ant *or* aunt, etc.

Ā′MĂR

t: Tā′măr.
Cf. ām′ēr.

AM′AS

l: Lam′măs.
t: Tam′măs.

AM′ȦSK

d: dam′ȧsk.
Plus ham, ask, etc.

Ā′MĀT

d: dāy′māte.
h: hā′māte.

(Choose only one word out of each group)

kw: des-quā′māte.
pl: plāy′māte.
Plus say, mate, etc.
Plus game ate or eight, etc.

ÄM′ĂZ

h: Bȧ-hä′mȧṣ.
j: çat's pȧ-jä′mȧṣ.
Also äm′a+s.

AM′BȦ

g: gam′bȧ.
Plus lamb, bah!, etc.

AM′BENT

l: lam′bent.
Plus ram bent, etc.

AM′BI

p: nam′by⸗pam′by.
Plus damn bee or be, etc.

AM′BIK

Vowel: çhōl-i-am′biç,
çhōr-i-am′biç, el-ē-ġī-am′biç,
gal-li-am′biç, ī-am′biç.
r: di-thy-ram′biç.

AM′BIST

g: gam′bist.
k(ç): çam′bist.

AM′BIT

Vowel: am′bit.
g: gam′bit.
Plus lamb bit, etc.
Plus dithyramb it, etc.

AM′KIN

l: lamb′kin (lam′).
Plus am kin, etc.

AM′BL

Vowel: am′ble, prē-am′ble.
br: bram′ble.
g: gam′ble, gam′bŏl.
r: ram′ble.
sh: sham′ble.
sk(sç): sçam′ble,
skim′ble⸗skam″ble.
skr(sçr): sçram′ble,
sçrim′ble⸗sçram″ble.
Plus damn bull, etc.

AM′BLEST

Vowel: am′blest*.
g: gam′blest*.
r: ram′blest*.
sh: sham′blest.
skr(sçr): sçram′blest*.
Plus lamb blest or blessed, etc.
Plus dithyramb, lest, etc.

AM′BLETH

Vowel: am′bleth*.
g: gam′bleth*.
r: ram′bleth*.
sh: sham′bleth*.
skr(sçr): sçram′bleth*.

AM′BLING

Vowel: am′bling.
br: bram′bling.
g: gam′bling.
r: ram′bling.
sh: sham′bling.
sk(sç): sçam′bling.
skr(sçr): sçram′bling.

AM′BLŪR

Vowel: am′blẽr.
g: gam′blẽr.
r: ram′blẽr.

(Choose only one word out of each group)

sh: sham'blẽr.
sk(sc): scam'blẽr.
skr(scr): scram'blẽr.

AM'BLZ

Vowel: am'bleṣ.
g: gam'bleṣ.
r: ram'bleṣ.
sh: sham'bleṣ.
skr(scr): scram'bleṣ.
Plus ram bulls, etc.

AM'BŌ

Vowel: am'bō.
fl: flam'beau ('bō).
kr: cram'bō.
s: Sam'bō.
z: zam'bō.
Plus yam, bo *or* beau, etc.

AM'BŎL

g: gam'bŏl.
Cf. am'bl.

ĀM'BRIK

k(c): cām'bric.
Plus claim brick, etc.

ĀM'BŪR

ch: an'tē-chām-bẽr, chām'bẽr.
Plus same burr, etc.

AM'BŪR

t: tam'boūr.
Plus damn boor, etc.

AM'BẼR

Vowel: am'bẽr.
k(c): cam'bẽr.
kl: clam'bẽr.
Plus ram burr, etc.

AM'BUS

Vowel: ī-am'bus.
r: dith-y-ram'bus.
Plus jam bus *or* buss, etc.

AM'BUSH

Vowel: am'bush.
Plus jam bush, etc.

AM'DÅ

l: lamb'då (lam').
Plus slammed a, etc.
Plus slam da, etc.

AM'EL

h: Ham'ăl.
k(c): cam'el, Camp'bell (kam').
m: mam'măl.
n: ē-nam'el.
tr: en-tram'mel, tram'mel.
Plus ram 'll, etc.

AM'ELD

n: ē-nam'elled.
tr: un-tram'melled.

Ā'MEN

Vowel: ā'men.
br: Bre'men.
fl: flā'men.
h: Hā'măn.
l: Leh'mănn.
r: fō-rā'men.
st: stā'men.
v: grà-vā'men.
z: ex-ā'men.
Plus also a man.
Plus weigh men, etc.
Cf. shame in, etc.

(Choose only one word out of each group)

Ä'MEN

Vowel: ä'men.

Ā'MENT

Vowel: ā'ment.
fr: dē-frāy'ment.
kl: çlāim'ănt.
l: al-lāy'ment.
p: pāy'ment, rē-pāy'ment.
r: rāi'ment.
tr: bē-trāy'ment.
Plus trey meant, etc.
Cf. claim ant *or* aunt, etc.

ĀM'EST

Vowel: āim'est*.
bl: blām'est*.
f: dē-fām'est*.
fl: flām'est*, in-flām'est*.
fr: frām'est*.
g: gām'est.
kl: aç-çlāim'est*, çlāim'est*,
   dē-çlāim'est*, dis-çlāim'est*,
   ex-çlāim'est*, prō-çlāim'est*,
   rē-çlāim'est*.
l: lām'est, lām'est*.
m: māim'est*.
n: nām'est*.
sh: shām'est*.
t: tām'est.
Plus May messed, etc.

AM'EST

d: dam'mest*, damn'est (dam')*.
kr: çram'mest*.
r: ram'mest*.
sh: sham'mest*.
sl: slam'mest*.
Plus Ham messed, etc.

ÄM'EST

b: em-bälm'est (-bäm')*.
k: çälm'est (käm').
l: sà-läam'est*.
Cf. calm messed, etc.

ĀM'ETH

Vowel: āim'eth*.
bl: blām'eth*.
f: dē-fām'eth*.
fl: flām'eth*, in-flām'eth*.
fr: frām'eth*.
k(ç): ō-vēr-çām'eth*.
kl: aç-çlāim'eth*, çlāim'eth*,
   dē-çlāim'eth*, dis-çlāim'eth*,
   ex-çlāim'eth*, prō-çlāim'eth*,
   rē-çlāim'eth*.
l: lām'eth*.
m: māim'eth*.
n: nām'eth*.
sh: fōr-shām'eth*, shām'eth*.
t: tām'eth*.

AM'ETH

d: dam'meth*,
   damn'eth (dam')*.
kr: çram'meth*.
r: ram'meth*.
sh: sham'meth*.
sl: slam'meth*.

ÄM'ETH

b: em-bälm'eth (-bäm')*.
k(ç): çälm'eth (käm')*.
l: sà-läam'eth*.

AM'FĪR

s: sam'phīre.
Plus sham fire. etc.

(Choose only one word out of each group)

AM'FLET

p: pam'phlet.

AM'FŎR

k(ç): çam'phŏr.
Plus slam for, etc.

ĀM'FỤL

bl: blāme'fụl.
fl: flāme'fụl.
sh: shāme'fụl.
Plus name full, etc.

Ā'MI

Vowel: Ā'my.
fl: flām'y.
g: gām'y.
m: Mā'mie.
Plus pray me, etc.
Plus game, he, etc.

AM'I

d: dam'mē.
g: gam'my.
kl: çlam'my.
m: mam'my.
r: ram'my.
sh: çham'ois ('i), sham'my.
t: tam'my.
Plus slam me, etc.
Plus slam, he, etc.

ÄM'I

Vowel: Mĭ-äm'i.
b: bäl'my (bä').
k(ç): çäl'my (kä').
kw: quäl'my (kwä').
p: päl'my (pä').
s: säl'mi.
sw: swä'mi.

tr: pas-träm'i.

Plus calm me, etc.
Plus calm, he, etc.

AM'IJ

d: dam'ȧge.
Plus sham age, etc.

AM'IK

d: Ȧ-dam'iç, prē"ad-am'iç.
g: ȧ-gam'iç, çryp-tō-gam'iç,
 gam'iç, mon-ō-gam'iç,
 phan"ẽr-ō-gam'iç, pol-y-gam'iç
gr: mon-ō-gram'miç,
 par"al-lel-ō-gram'miç,
 tel-ē-gram'miç, trī-gram'miç.
h: Ā-brȧ-ham'iç.
l: ep"i-thȧ-lam'iç, Is-lam'iç.
n: ā"dȳ-nam'iç,
 aṵ"tō-dȳ-nam'iç,
 bī"ō-dȳ-nam'iç, cin-nam'iç,
 dȳ-nam'iç, ēl-eç"trō-dȳ-nam'iç,
 hȳ"drō-dȳ-nam'iç,
 hȳ"pẽr-dȳ-nam'iç,
 ī"sō-dȳ-nam'iç.
r: cē-ram'iç, çoṣ-mō-ram'iç,
 cȳ-çlō-ram'iç, dī-ō-ram'iç,
 kē-ram'iç, pan-ō-ram'iç.
s: bạl-sam'iç.
t: pō-tam'iç.
Cf. slam Mick, etc.

AM'IL

Vowel: am'yl.
h: Ham'mill.
t: tam'il.
Plus am ill, etc.

AM'IN

f: fam'ine.
g: gam'in.

(Choose only one word out of each group)

z: ex-am'ine.
Plus ram in, etc.

ĀM'ING

Vowel: āim'ing.
bl: blām'ing.
f: dē-fām'ing.
fl: flām'ing, in-flām'ing.
fr: frām'ing.
g: gām'ing.
kl: ac-clāim'ing, clāim'ing,
dē-clāim'ing, dis-clāim'ing,
ex-clāim'ing, prō-clāim'ing,
rē-clāim'ing.
l: lām'ing.
m: māim'ing.
n: mis-nām'ing, nām'ing,
nick-nām'ing, sũr-nām'ing.
sh: shām'ing.
t: tām'ing.

AM'ING

d: dam'ming, damn'ing (dam').
kr: cram'ming.
l: lamb'ing (lam'), lam'ming.
r: ram'ming.
sh: sham'ming.
sl: slam'ming.
tr: tram'ming.

ÄM'ING

b: em-bälm'ing (-bäm').
k(c): bē-cälm'ing (-käm'),
cälm'ing (käm').
kw: quälm'ing (kwäm').
l: sà-läam'ing.

AM'IS

Vowel: am'ice.
kl: chlam'vs.

t: tam'is.
Cf. slam miss, etc.

ĀM'ISH

l: lām'ish.
t: tām'ish.

AM'ISH

Vowel: Am'ish.
f: af-fam'ish, en-fam'ish,
fam'ish.
h: Ham'ish.
r: ram'mish.

ÄM'ISH

k(c): cälm'ish (käm').
kw: quälm'ish (kwäm').

ÄM'IST

b: em-bälm'ist (-bäm').
p: pälm'ist (päm').
s: psälm'ist (säm').
Plus shah missed or mist, etc.
Cf. calm mist or missed, etc.

AM'ĪT

s: sam'īte.
Cf. slam might or mite, etc.

ĀM'LES

Vowel: āim'less.
bl: blāme'less.
f: fāme'less.
fl: flāme'less.
fr: frāme'less.
g: gāme'less.
kl: clāim'less.
n: nāme'less.
sh: shāme'less.
t: tāme'less.
Plus same less, etc.

(Choose only one word out of each group)

ÄM'LES

b: bälm'less (bäm').
kw: quälm'less (kwäm').
p: pälm'less (päm').
s: psälm'less (säm').
Plus calm less, etc.

AM'LET

h: ham'let.
k(c): çam'let.
s: sam'let.
Plus jam let, etc.

ĀM'LI

g: gāme'ly.
l: lāme'ly.
n: nāme'ly.
t: tāme'ly.
Plus shame, Lee, *or* lea, etc.

ÄM'LI

k(c): çälm'ly (käm').
Plus balm Lee *or* lea, etc.

AM'LING

l: lamb'ling (lam').

ÄM'MENT

b: em-bälm'ment (-bäm').
k(c): bē-çälm'ment (-käm').
Plus psalm meant, etc.

ĀM'NES

g: gāme'ness.
l: lāme'ness.
s: sāme'ness.
t: tāme'ness.

ÄM'NES

k(c): çälm'ness (käm').

AM'OK

h: ham'mock.
m: mam'mock.
Plus slam mock, etc.

AM'ŎN

Vowel: Am'mŏṇ.
d: dam'ăn.
g: back-gam'mŏn, gam'mŏn.
m: mam'mŏn.
s: sal'mŏn (sa').
sh: sham'ăn.
Plus ham on, etc.
Plus slam an, etc.

Ā'MŎND

r: Rāy'mŏnd.

AM'ŎND

h: Ham'mŏnd.

Ā'MŎS

Vowel: Ā'mŏs.
s: Sā'mŏs.
sh: Shāe'măs.
Plus lame us, etc.

AM'ŎTH

m: mam'mŏth.
Plus sham moth, etc.

AM'PĂN

j: jam'păn.
s: sam'păn.
t: tam'păn.
Plus sham pan, etc.

309

ūse, bu̧ll, brúte, tũrn, up; crȳ, myth; c̦at, ·mac̦hine, ace,
church, c̦hord; ġem, añger, (Fr.) boñ, a̧ș; THis, thin; azure

AM′PÄRT
AM′PL

(Choose only one word out of each group)

AM′PÄRT

r: ram′pärt.
Plus slam part, etc.
Plus vamp art, etc.

AM′PĂZ

p: pam′pă̧s.
Plus Tampa's, grampa's, etc.

AM′PEN

d: dam′pen.
Plus damn pen, etc.
Cf. damp hen, etc.

AM′PĒR

Vowel: am′pēre.
Plus sham peer, etc.
Cf. camp here, etc.

AM′PEST

d: damp′est.
k(ç): çamp′est*, dē-çamp′est*,
  en-çamp′est*.
kr: çramp′est*.
r: ramp′est*.
sk(sç): sçamp′est*.
st: stamp′est*.
tr: tramp′est*.
v: vamp′est*.
Plus sham pest, etc.

AM′PETH

d: damp′eth*.
k(ç): çamp′eth*, dē-çamp′eth*,
  en-çamp′eth*.
kr: çramp′eth*.
r: ramp′eth*.
sk(sç): sçamp′eth*.
st: stamp′eth*.
tr: tramp′eth*.
v: vamp′eth*.

AM′PI

kr: çram′py.
v: vamp′y.
Plus damp, he, etc.
Plus sham pea, etc.

AM′PING

ch: champ′ing.
d: damp′ing.
k(ç): çamp′ing, dē-çamp′ing,
  en-çamp′ing.
kl: çlamp′ing.
kr: çramp′ing.
l: lamp′ing.
r: ramp′ing.
sk(sç): sçamp′ing.
st: stamp′ing.
t: tamp′ing.
tr: tramp′ing.
v: vamp′ing.

AM′PĪR

v: vam′pīre.
Plus sham pyre, etc.
Plus damp ire, etc.
Cf. camp hire *or* higher, etc.

AM′PISH

d: damp′ish.
sk(sç): sçamp′ish.

AM′PL

Vowel: am′ple.
s: en-sam′ple*, sam′ple.
tr: tram′ple.
z: ex-am′ple.
Plus ram pull, etc.
Plus scamp 'll, etc.

(Choose only one word out of each group)

AM'PLD

tr: un-tramp'led.
Plus am'pl+d.
Plus example'd, etc.

AMP'LI

d: damp'ly.
Plus camp lea *or* Lee, etc.
Plus sham plea, etc.

AMP'LING

s: en-samp'ling, samp'ling.
tr: tramp'ling.

AMP'LŪR

Vowel: amp'lẽr.
s: samp'lẽr.
tr: tramp'lẽr.
z: ex-amp'lẽr.

AMP'MENT

k(c̱): dē-c̱amp'ment,
en-c̱amp'ment.
Plus scamp meant, etc.

AMP'NES

d: damp'ness.

AM'PRI

l: lam'prey.

AMP'SŎN

l: Lamp'sŏn.
s: Samp'sŏn.
Cf. Sam'sŏn.
Cf. sham sun *or* son, etc.
Plus damp sun *or* son, etc.

AMP'TŎN

h: Hamp'tŏn.
kr: C̱ramp'tŏn.

Plus scamp ton *or* tun, etc.
Plus camped on, etc.

AM'PŪR

ch: champ'ẽr.
d: dam'pẽr.
h: ham'pẽr.
k(c̱): c̱am'pẽr.
kl: c̱lam'pẽr.
kr: c̱ram'pẽr.
p: pam'pẽr.
sk(sc̱): sc̱am'pẽr.
st: stam'pẽr.
t: tam'pẽr.
tr: tram'pẽr.
v: vam'pẽr.
Plus vamp her, err *or* er, etc.

AM'PŪRD

h: ham'pẽred, un-ham'pẽred.
p: pam'pẽred.
t: tam'pẽred.
Plus camp heard, etc.
Plus Sam purred, etc.

AM'PUS

gr: gram'pus.
k(c̱): c̱am'pus.
Plus lamp us, etc.
Cf. sham puss, etc.

AM'ROD

r: ram'rod.
Plus sham rod, etc.

AM'ROK

sh: sham'rock.
Plus slam rock, etc.

(Choose only one word out of each group)

ĀM′STŪR

g: gāme′stẽr.
Plus fame stir, etc.

ÄM′ŎND

Vowel: äl′mŏnd (ä′),
 bit′tẽr äl′mŏnd,
 Jọr′dăn äl′mŏnd.
Cf. Ham′mond.

ĀM′ŪR

Vowel: āim′ẽr.
bl: blām′ẽr.
f: dē-fām′ẽr, dis-fām′ẽr.
fl: in-flām′ẽr.
fr: frām′ẽr.
g: gām′ẽr.
kl: aç-çlāim′ẽr, çlāim′ẽr,
 dē-çlāim′ẽr, dis-çlāim′ẽr,
 ex-çlāim′ẽr, prō-çlāim′ẽr,
 rē-çlāim′ẽr.
kr: Krām′ẽr.
l: lām′ẽr.
m: māim′ẽr.
n: mis-nām′ẽr, nām′ẽr,
 nick′nām-ẽr.
sh: shām′ẽr.
t: Tā′măr, tām′ẽr, tes-tā′mũr.
Plus shame her, err, or er, etc.
Plus spray myrrh, etc.

AM′ŪR

d: dam′mẽr, damn′ẽr (dam′).
dr: mel′lōw-dram-mẽr.
g: gam′mẽr.
gl: glam′ŏr.
gr: gram′măr, gram′mẽr.
h: ham′mẽr, nin′ny-ham-mẽr,
 sledǧe ham′mẽr,
 yel′lōw-ham-mẽr.

j: jam′mẽr, Ram′mẽr Jam′mẽr,
 wind′jam-mẽr.
kl: çlam′ŏr.
kr: çram′mẽr.
l: lamb′ẽr (lam′).
n: ē-nam′ŏr.
r: ram′mẽr.
sh: sham′mẽr.
skr(sçr): sçram′mẽr.
sl: slam′mẽr.
st: stam′mẽr.
y: yam′mẽr.
Plus slam her, err or er, etc.

ÄM′ŪR

b: Bälm′ẽr (bäm′),
 em-bälm′ẽr (-bäm′).
k(ç): çälm′ẽr (käm′).
p: pälm′ẽr (päm′).
Plus calm her, err or er, etc.

AM′WĀ

tr: tram′wāy.
Plus sham weigh or way, etc.

ĀM′US

d: man-dā′mus.
f: fā′mous.
h: hā′mous.
r: bī-rām′ous, ig-nō-ɹᴀ́m′ous.
skw: squā′mous.
Plus reclaim us, etc.
Plus may muss, etc.

AM′UT

g: gam′ut.
Cf. damn mutt, etc.

AM′ZEL

Vowel: am′ṣel.
d: dam′ṣel.

(Choose only one word out of each group)

Plus clam sell, etc.
Cf. clams, hell!, etc.

ÄM'ZI

m: Mälm'ṣey (mäm'zi).
Plus calms, he, etc.

AM'ZŎN

d: dam'ṣŏn.

Ā'NȦ

Vowel: ā'nȧ, fis-ti-ā'nȧ,
Ni-co͟o"ti-ā'nȧ, poin-ci-ā'nȧ;
also Jef"fẽr-sō"ni-ā'nȧ,
John-sōn"i-ā'nȧ,
Shākes-pēar"i-ā'nȧ, etc.
j: C̦är-tȧ-ġĕ'nȧ.
k(c̦): A-mer-i-c̦ā'nȧ, etc.;
är-c̦ā'nȧ.
p: c̦am-pā'nȧ.
m: vōx hū-mā'nȧ.
n: ȧ-nā'nȧ.
sh: sc̦ĕ'nȧ (shā').
t: C̦ūr-tā'nȧ.
Plus explain a, etc.

AN'Ȧ

Vowel: an'ᵾȧ, C̦hris-ti-an'ȧ,
Dī-an'ȧ, fis-ti-an'ȧ,
Ġeo͟org̣-i-an'ȧ, In-di-an'ȧ,
i"pē-c̦ac̦"ū-an'hȧ, Jō-an'nȧ,
Jū-li-an'ȧ, Löu-ĭṣ"i-an'ȧ,
Pol-ly-an'nȧ; also
Jef"fẽr-sō"ni-an'ȧ,
John-sōn"i-an'ȧ,
Shākes-pēar"i-an'ȧ, etc.
b: Ŭr-ban'ȧ.
d: ban-dan'ȧ.
f: Stⲅ̄-phan'ȧ.
h: Han'nȧ, Han'nȧh,
Sus-quē-han'nȧ.

k(c̦): A-mer-i-c̦an'ȧ, etc.;
c̦an'nȧ, Tex"är-kan'ȧ.
m: man'nȧ.
s: Rox-an'ȧ.
t: Mon-tan'ȧ, sul-tan'ȧ.
v: Hȧ-van'ȧ, sȧ-van'nȧ,
Sȧ-van'nȧh.
w: Tī'ȧ Jua'nȧ (wa').
z: ho-ṣan'nȧ, Sū-ṣan'nȧ.
Plus plan a, etc.

ÄN'Ȧ

Vowel: fis-ti-än'ȧ,
Guĭ-än'ȧ (gē-), ig-uän'ȧ (-wä'),
lĭ-ä'nȧ; also Jef"fẽr-sō"ni-än'ȧ,
John-sōn"i-än'ȧ,
Shākes-pēar"i-än'ȧ, etc.
f: äq'uä tō-fän'ȧ.
g: Fä'tä Mo͟or-gän'a.
hw: mar-i-juä'nȧ (-hwä').
k(c̦): A-mer"i-c̦än'ȧ, etc.;
ġym-khä'nȧ.
n: ȧ-nä'nȧ, bȧ-nä'nȧ, zē-nä'nȧ.
r: ker-än'ȧ, pū-rä'nȧ.
s: Mes-sä'nȧ.
t: C̦ūr-tä'nȧ, sul-tän'ȧ.
th: thä'nȧ.
v: Nĭr-vä'nȧ.
Plus wan a, etc.

Ā'NĂL

Vowel: ā'năl.
b: bā'năl.
Plus Blaine 'll, etc.
Cf. brain all, etc.
Plus brain, Al, etc.

AN'ĂL, AN'EL

Vowel: an'năl.
ch: chan'nel.

(Choose only one word out of each group)

d: Dan"l.
fl: flan'nel.
k(c̱): c̱an'nel.
p: em-pan'el, im-pan'el,
pan'el, un-pan'el.
skr(sc̱r): sc̱ran'nel.
st: stan'nel.
Cf. plan 'll, etc.

AN'ĂLZ

Vowel: an'năl̤ṣ.
Plus an'ăl+s.

ĀN'ĂNT

pl: c̱om-plāin'ănt.
Plus plain aunt or ant, etc.

ĀN'ĀT

l: lān'āte.
p: im-pān'āte.
Plus reign eight, plain ate, etc.

AN'ĀT

gr: pome'gran-āte.
kh: khan'āte.
t: tan'nāte.
Plus Fan ate or eight, etc.

ÄN'ĀT

k: khän'āte.
Plus wan eight or ate, etc.

ĀN'BŌ

r: rāin'bōw.
Plus gain beau, bow, or bo, etc.

ÄN'CHEST

l: läunch'est*.
st: stänch'est.
Plus wan chest, etc.

AN'CHEST

bl: blanch'est*.
skr(sc̱r): sc̱ranch'est*.

AN'CHET

m: man'chet.
pl: plan'chet.
Plus can Chet, etc.

ÄN'CHETH

l: läunch'eth*.
st: stänch'eth*.

AN'CHETH

bl: blanch'eth*.
skr(sc̱r): sc̱ranch'eth*.

ÄN'CHEZ

l: läun'che̱ṣ.
p: päun'che̱ṣ.
st: stän'che̱ṣ.
Cf. paunch is, etc.

AN'CHEZ

bl: blan'che̱ṣ.
br: bran'che̱ṣ.
l: à-và-lan'che̱ṣ.
r: ran'che̱ṣ.
Cf. ranch is, etc.

ÄN'CHI

p: päun'chy.
Plus launch, he, etc.

AN'CHI

br: bran'chy.
Plus ranch, he, etc.

(Choose only one word out of each group)

ÄN'CHING

l: läun'ching.
st: stän'ching.

AN'CHING

bl: blan'ching.
br: bran'ching.
l: ȧ-vȧ-lan'ching.
r: ran'ching.

AN'CHĪZ

fr: af-fran'chīṣe, dis-fran'chīṣe,
en-fran'chīṣe, fran'chīṣe.
Plus ranch eyes, etc.

ÄNCH'LES

l: läunch'less.
p: päunch'less.
Plus launch less, etc.

ANCH'LES

br: branch'less.
l: av-ȧ-lanch'less.
r: ranch'less.
st: stanch'less.
Plus blanch less, etc.

ÄN'CHŬR

l: läun'chẽr.
st: stän'chẽr.
Plus launch her, etc.

AN'CHŬR

br: bran'chẽr.
r: ran'chẽr.
Plus blanch her *or* err, etc.

AN'DȦ

g: prō-pȧ-gan'dȧ.
m: Ȧ-man'dȧ.

r: jȧc-ȧ-ran'dȧ, Mi-ran'dȧ,
mem-ō-ran'dȧ, ve-ran'dȧ.
Plus land a, etc.

AN'DĂL

r: Ran'dăll.
See also an'dl.

AN'DĂNT

m: cọm-man'dănt,
dē-man'dănt, man'dănt.
Plus banned ant *or* aunt, etc.

AN'DĀT

m: man'dāte.
Plus plan date, etc.
Plus planned eight *or* ate, etc.

AND'BAG

h: hand'bag.
s: sand'bag.
Plus grand bag, etc.

AND'BẠL

h: hand'bạll.
s: sand'bạll.
Plus grand ball, etc.

AND'BOI

b: band'boy.
s: sand'boy.
Plus grand boy, etc.

AND'BOKS

b: band'box.
s: sand'box.
Plus planned box, etc.

AND'CHĪLD

gr: grand'chĭld.
Plus banned child, etc.

315   ūse, bu̧ll, brúte, tũrn, up; crȳ, myth; çat, maçhine, ace,
church, c̠hord; ġem, añger, (Fr.) boṅ, aş; THis, thin; aẓure   ÄN′DÊ
AN′DĒZ

(Choose only one word out of each group)

ÄN′DĒ

gr: Rĭ′ō Grän′dē.
Cf. an′di.

AN′DED, ÅN′DED

b: ban′ded, çon-trȧ-ban′ded,
dis-ban′ded.
br: bran′ded, un-bran′ded.
d: dē-ō-dan′ded.
gl: glan′ded, gōat′=glan′ded,
mŏñ′key=glan′ded.
h: back′han-ded, black′=han-ded,
çlēan′han-ded, çlōse′han-ded,
emp′ty=han-ded, ē′ven-han-ded,
fîrst′han-ded, fōre′han-ded,
fôur′=han-ded, free′han-ded,
fu̧ll′=han-ded, han′ded,
härd′han-ded,
heav′y-han-ded (hev′),
hīgh′han-ded (hī′),
left′han-ded,
līght′=han-ded (līt′),
li′ly-han-ded, nēat′=han-ded,
ō′pen-han-ded, ō′vēr-han-ded,
red′=han-ded,
rīght′=han-ded (rīt′),
shōrt′han-ded, sin′gle=han-ded,
swift′=han-ded,
twö′=han-ded (tö),
un′dēr-han-ded, un-han′ded.
k(ç): çan′did.
l: lan′ded, un-lan′ded.
m: çom-man′ded,
çoun′tēr-man-ded, dē-man′ded,
rē-man′ded, rep-ri-man′ded.
p: ex-pan′ded.
s: san′ded.
str: stran′ded.
Plus man dead, etc.
Cf. Klan did. etc.

AN′DENT

k(ç): çan′dent.
sk(sç): sçan′dent.
Plus man dent, etc.

ĀN′DĒR

r: rein′deer.
Plus plain dear *or* deer, etc.
Plus obtained ear, etc.

AN′DEST

b: ban′dest*, dis-ban′dest*.
br: bran′dest*.
gr: gran′dest.
h: han′dest*.
l: lan′dest*.
m: çom-man′dest*,
dē-man′dest*, rē-man′dest*,
re-pri-man′dest*.
p: ex-pan′dest*.
st: stan′dest*, with-stan′dest*.

AN′DETH

b: ban′deth*, dis-ban′deth*.
br: bran′deth*.
h: han′deth*.
l: lan′deth*.
m: çom-man′deth*,
dē-man′deth*, rē-man′deth*,
re-pri-man′deth*.
p: ex-pan′deth*.
st: stan′deth*, with-stan′deth*.
Plus plan death, etc.

AN′DĒZ

Vowel: An′dēṣ.
n: Hĕr-nan′dēṣ.
Plus planned ease, etc.

(Choose only one word out of each group)

AND'FÅST

h: hand'fȧst.
Plus stand fast, etc.

AN'DI

Vowel: An'dy.
b: ban'dy.
br: bran'dy.
d: dan'dy, jack꞊à꞊dan'dy,
Jim꞊Dan'dy,
Yañ'kee꞊Dọọ'dle Dan'dy.
g: Ghan'di.
gl: glan'dy.
gr: Rï'ō Gran'dē.
h: han'dy, un-han'dy.
k(c̣): c̣an'dy,
sụg'ăr꞊c̣an'dy (shoog').
m: Man'dy.
p: pan'dy.
r: jab-ō-ran'di, ran'dy.
s: san'dy.
t: Tan'dy.
Plus and he, etc.
Plus Ann D., etc.

AN'DID

b: ban'did.
br: bran'died.
k(c̣): c̣an'did, c̣an'died,
un-c̣an'did.
Plus an'ded.
Plus Ann did, etc.

AN'DIJ

b: ban'dăge.
gl: glan'dăge.
st: stan'dăge.
Cf. grand age, etc.

AN'DING, ÅN'DING

b: band'ing, dis-band'ing.
br: brand'ing.
h: hand'ing, un-hand'ing.
l: land'ing.
m: c̣om-mand'ing,
c̣oun-tẽr-mand'ing,
dē-mand'ing, rē-mand'ing,
rep-ri-mand'ing.
p: ex-pand'ing.
s: am-pẽr-sand'ing, sand'ing.
st: not"with-stand'ing,
out-stand'ing, stand'ing,
un-dẽr-stand'ing,
with-stand'ing.
str: strand'ing.

AN'DISH

bl: blan'dish.
br: bran'dish.
gr: gran'dish.
l: out-lan'dish.
Plus plan dish, etc.

AN'DIST

b: c̣on-trȧ-ban'dist.
g: prō-pȧ-gan'dist.

AN'DIT

b: ban'dit.
Plus hand it, etc.

AN'DL

d: dan'dle.
h: han'dle, man'han-dle,
mis-han'dle.
k(c̣): c̣an'dle.
r: Ran'dăll, Ran'dle.
s: san'dăl.
sk(sc̣): sc̣an'dăl.

(Choose only one word out of each group)

v: van'dăl.
Plus brand'll, etc.
Cf. man dull, etc.

AND'LES, ÅND'LES

b: band'less.
br: brand'less.
gl: gland'less.
h: hand'less.
l: land'less.
m: com-mand'less.
s: sand'less.
str: strand'less.
Plus stand less, *or* Les, etc.

AN'DLING

br: bran'dling.
h: han'dling, man-han'dling,
mis-han'dling.
k(c): can'dling.

AND'LŨR

Ch: chand'lẽr,
tal'lōw chand'lẽr.
d: dan'dlẽr.
h: hand'lẽr.
k(c): can'dlẽr.

AND'LORD

l: land'lord.
Plus sand lord, etc.

AND'LI

bl: bland'ly.
gr: grand'ly.
Plus manned, Lee *or* lea, etc.

AND'MĀD

h: hand'māde, hand'māid.
Plus sand made, etc.

AND'MÄRK

l: land'märk.
Plus sand mark, etc.

AND'MENT, ÅND'MENT

b: dis-band'ment.
m: com-mand'ment,
rē-mand'ment.
Plus land meant, etc.

AND'NES

bl: bland'ness.
gr: grand'ness.

AN'DŌ, ÄN'DŌ

gr: gran'dō*.
l: Or-lan'dō.
m: com-man'dō.
n: Fẽr-di-nan'dō, Fẽr-nan'dō,
Hẽr-nan'dō.
t: len-tan'dō.
Plus plan dough *or* doe, etc.

AN'DŎN

b: à-ban'dŏn.
l: Lan'dŏn.
sh: Shan'dŏn.
Plus land on, etc.
Plus man don, etc.

AND'OUT

h: hand'out.
Plus planned out, etc.
Plus man doubt, etc.

AN'DRÅ, ÅN'DRÅ

s: Al-es-san'drå, Al-ex-an'drå,
Cas-san'drå.

AN'DREL
AN'DŪR

fāte, fär, fȧst, fạll, finăl, cãre, at; mēte, prey, hêr, met; pīne,
marïne, bïrd, pin; nōte, mōve, fǫr, atŏm, not; mọọn, book;   318

(Choose only one word out of each group)

AN'DREL

sp: span'drel.
Cf. hand rail.

AN'DRES

p: pan'dress.
Plus can dress, etc.

ẠN'DRES

l: lạun'dress.
Plus faun dress, etc.

AN'DRIK

Vowel: pol-y-an'driç,
  thē-an'driç.
Plus grand rick, etc.

AN'DRIL

m: man'dril.
Plus can drill, etc.
Plus planned rill, etc.

AN'DRIN

m: sal-ȧ-man'drine.
s: Al-ex-an'drine.

AN'DRI, ȦN'DRI

Vowel: mē-an'dry, pol-y-an'dry.
ch: chan'dry*.
m: çom-man'dry.
sh: shan'dry.

ẠN'DRI

l: lạun'dry.

AN'DRUS

Vowel: mē-an'drous,
pol-y-an'drous.

AND'SĪR

gr: grand'sīre.
Plus fanned sire, etc.
Cf. band's ire, etc.

AND'SKĀP

l: land'sçāpe.
Cf. band's cape, etc.

AND'SŎN

gr: grand'sŏn.
Plus planned sun, *or* son, etc.

AND'STAND

b: band'stand.
gr: grand'stand.
Plus land stand, etc.

AN'DUM

m: man'dŏm.
r: mem-ō-ran'dum, ran'dŏm.
t: ad çap-tan'dum, tan'dem.
z: av-i-zan'dum.
Plus land 'em, etc.
Plus man dumb, etc.

ĀN'DŨR

m: rē-māin'dẽr.
t: at-tāin'dẽr.
Plus obtained her *or* err, etc.

AN'DŪR

gr: gran'deūr.
Plus land your *or* you're, etc.

AN'DŨR, ȦN'DŨR

Vowel: çŏr-i-an'dẽr, Lē-an'dẽr,
  mē-an'dẽr, ō-lē-an'dẽr.
b: dis-ban'dẽr.
bl: blan'dẽr.

(Choose only one word out of each group)

br: bran′dĕr.

d: dan′dĕr.

g: gan′dĕr, gǫǫs′ey=gan′dĕr.

gl: glan′dĕr.

gr: gran′dĕr.

h: back′han-dĕr, han′dĕr, left′=han″dĕr, right′=han″dĕr (rīt′).

k(ç): Af-ri-çan′dĕr, çan′dŏr.

l: Green′lan-dĕr, Ice′lan-dĕr, lan′dĕr, New-found′lan-dĕr, phi-lan′dĕr, Uit′lan-dĕr (oit′).

m: ço̧m-man′dĕr, dē-man′dĕr, ger-ry-man′dĕr, Pō-man′dĕr, rē-man′dĕr, rep-ri-man′dĕr, sal-à-man′dĕr.

n: Mē-nan′dĕr.

p: ex-pan′dĕr, pan′dăr, pan′dĕr.

s: Al-ex-an′dĕr, san′dĕr.

sl: slan′dĕr.

st: bȳ′stan-dĕr, stan′dĕr, un-dĕr-stan′dĕr, with-stan′dĕr.

str: stran′dĕr.

t: dit-tan′dĕr.

Plus command her *or* err, etc.

ÄN′DĔR

l: läun′dĕr.

Plus pawned her *or* err, etc.

AN′DŪRD, ÀN′DŪRD

Vowel: mē-an′dĕred.

l: phi-lan′dĕred.

p: pan′dĕred.

sl: slan′dĕred.

st: stan′dărd.

ÄN′DŪRZ

s: Sän′dĕrṣ, Säun′dĕrṣ.

Cf. on′dūrz.

Cf. glan′dĕrs.

ANDZ′MĂN

b: bandṣ′măn.

l: landṣ′măn.

Plus commands man, etc.

Ā′NES

g: gāy′ness.

gr: grāy′ness, grey′ness.

Plus plain S, etc.

ĀN′EST

Vowel: in-ān′est.

b: ūr-bān′est.

ch: chāin′est*, en-chāin′est*, un-chāin′est*.

d: deign′est (dān′)*, dis-dāin′est*, fōre″ǫr-dāin′est*, ǫr-dāin′est*.

dr: drāin′est*.

f: feign′est (fān′)*, prō-fān′est.

fr: rē-frāin′est*.

g: gāin′est*, rē-gāin′est*.

gr: grāin′est*.

k(ç): çān′est*.

kr: çrān′est*.

m: hū-mān′est, rē-māin′est*.

p: ça̧m-pāign′est (-pān′)*, pāin′est*.

pl: ço̧m-plāin′est*, ex-plāin′est*, plāin′est.

r: ar-rāign′est (-rān′)*, rāin′est*, reign′est (rān′)*, rein′est*.

s: sān′est.

spr: sprāin′est*.

st: ab-stāin′est*, stāin′est*.

str: ço̧n-strāin′est*, rē-strāin′est*, strāin′est*.

t: ap-pēr-tāin′est*, as-çēr-tāin′est*, at-tāin′est*, ço̧n-tāin′est*, dē-tāin′est*, en-tēr-tāin′est*, māin-tāin′est*,

AN'EST
ĀN'GANG

fāte, fär, fȧst, fall, finăl, cāre, at; mēte, prey, hêr, met; pīne,
marïne, bïrd, pin; nōte, mŏve, fŏr, atŏm, not; mŏŏn, book;

320

(Choose only one word out of each group)

ob-tāin'est*, rē-tāin'est*,
sus-tāin'est*.
tr: trāin'est*.
v: vāin'est.
w: wān'est*.
Plus play nest, etc.

AN'EST

b: ban'nest*.
f: fan'nest*.
m: man'nest*, un-man'nest*.
pl: plan'nest*.
sk(sc): scan'nest*.
sp: span'nest*.
t: tan'nest.

AN'ET

g: gan'net.
gr: gran'ite, pome-gran'ăte.
j: Jan'et.
kw: quan'net.
pl: plan'et.
Cf. plan it, etc.

ĀN'ETH

ch: chāin'eth*, en-chāin'eth*,
un-chāin'eth*.
d: deign'eth (dān')*,
dis-dāin'eth*, fōre″ŏr-dāin'eth*,
ŏr-dāin'eth*, prē″ŏr-dāin'eth*.
dr: drāin'eth*.
f: feign'eth (fān')*, prō-fān'eth*.
fr: rē-frāin'eth*.
g: gāin'eth*, rē-gāin'eth*.
gr: grāin'eth*.
k(c): cān'eth*.
kr: crān'eth*.
m: rē-māin'eth*.
p: pāin'eth*.
pl: com-plāin'eth*, ex-plāin'eth*.
r: ar-rāign'eth (-rān')*,
rāin'eth*, reign'eth (rān')*,
rein'eth*.

spr: sprāin'eth*.
st: ab-stāin'eth*, stāin'eth*.
str: con-strāin'eth*,
rē-strāin'eth*, strāin'eth*.
t: ap-pēr-tāin'eth*,
as-cēr-tāin'eth*, at tāin'eth*,
con-tāin'eth*, dē-tāin'eth*,
en-tēr-tāin'eth*, māin-tāin'eth*,
ob-tāin'eth*, rē-tāin'eth*,
sus-tāin'eth*.
tr: trāin'eth*.
w: wān'eth*.

AN'ETH

b: ban'neth*.
f: fan'neth*.
m: man'neth*, un-man'neth*.
pl: plan'neth*.
sk(sc): scan'neth*.
sp: span'neth*.
t: tan'neth*.

AN'FĀR

f: fan'fāre.
Plus plan fair or fare, etc.
Plus Banff air, etc.

AN'FĒLD

k(c): Can'fiēld.
Plus plan field, etc.

ĀN'FUL

b: bāne'ful.
d: dis-dāin'ful.
p: pāin'ful.
pl: com-plāin'ful.
Plus skein full, etc.

ĀN'GANG

ch: chāin gang.
tr: trāin gang.
Plus restrain gang, etc.

(Choose only one word out of each group)

ANG'GĂR

h: hang'ăr.
Plus sprang gar, etc.

ANG'GŎR

l: langu'ŏr.

ANG'GRI

Vowel: añ'gry.

ANG'GŬR

Vowel: añ'gĕr, añ'gŏr.
kl: çlañ'gŏr.

ANG'GWID

l: lañ'guid.

ANG'GWIJ

l: lan'guăġe.

ANG'GWIN

Vowel: añ'guine.
s: en-sañ'guine, sañ'guine.
Cf. gang win, etc.

ANG'GWISH

Vowel: añ'guish.
l: lañ'guish.
Cf. gang wish, etc.

ANG'I

f: fang'y.
kl: çlang'y.
sl: slang'y.

ANG'ING

b: bang'ing.
h: hang'ing, ō-vẽr-hang'ing,
pā'per hang'ing.
hw: slang'-whang'ing,
whang'ing.

kl: çlang'ing.
r: hȧ-rangu'ing.
sl: slang'ing.
tw: twang'ing.

ANG'KEST

b: em-bañk'est*.
bl: blañk'est.
d: dañk'est.
fl: flañk'est*, out-flañk'est*.
fr: frañk'est.
kl: çlañk'est*.
l: lañk'est.
r: rañk'est.
s: sañk'est*.
sp: spañk'est*.
th: thañk'est*.

ANG'KET

b: bañk'et.
bl: blañk'et.
Cf. spank it, etc.

ANG'KETH

b: em-bañk'eth*.
bl: blañk'eth*.
fl: flañk'eth*, out-flañk'eth*.
kl: çlañk'eth*.
r: rañk'eth*.
s: sañk'eth*.
sp: spañk'eth*.
th: thañk'eth*.

ANGK'FṶL

pr: prañk'fṳl.
th: thañk'fṳl.
Plus sank full, etc.

ANG'KI

h: hañk'y.
kr: çrañk'y.
l: lañk'y.

ANG'KING
ANGK'NES

fāte, fär, fȧst, fạll, finăl, cãre, at; mēte, prey, hẽr, met; pīne,
marïne, bĭrd, pin; nōte, mŏve, fọr, atŏm, not; mọọn, book;

322

(Choose only one word out of each group)

p: hañk'y=pañk'y.
pl: plañk'y.
pr: prañk'y.
t: tañk'y.
y: Yañ'kee.
Plus rang key, etc.

ANG'KING

b: bañk'ing, em-bañk'ing.
bl: blañk'ing.
fl: flañk'ing, out-flañk'ing.
fr: frañk'ing.
kl: clañk'ing.
pl: plañk'ing.
r: out-rañk'ing, rañk'ing.
sp: spañk'ing.
t: tañk'ing.
th: thañk'ing.
y: yañk'ing.
Plus hang king, etc.

ANG'KISH

d: dañk'ish.
fr: frañk'ish.
l: lañk'ish.
pr: prañk'ish.
Plus hang Kish, etc.

ANG'KL

Vowel: añk'le.
h: hañk'le.
kr: crañk'le.
r: rañk'le.
Plus spank'll, etc.
Cf. gang cull or kill, etc.

ANGK'LES

b: bañk'less.
bl: blañk'less.
fl: flañk'less.

kl: clañk'less.
kr: crañk'less.
pl: plañk'less.
pr: prañk'less.
r: rañk'less.
sh: shañk'less.
sp: spañk'less.
th: thañk'less.
Plus hank less, etc.

ANGK'LET

Vowel: añk'let.
Plus spank let or Lett, etc.

ANGK'LI

bl: blañk'ly.
d: dañk'ly.
fr: frañk'ly.
l: lañk'ly.
r: rañk'ly.
Plus thank Lee or lea, etc.

ANGK'LIN

fr: Frañk'lin.
Plus ranklin', etc.
Plus spank Lynn, etc.

ANGK'LING

h: hañk'ling.
r: rañk'ling.
Plus gang cling, etc.

ANGK'MENT

b: bañk'ment, em-bañk'ment.
fl: out-flañk'ment.
Plus rank meant, etc.

ANGK'NES

bl: blañk'ness.
d: dañk'ness.

ūse, bull, brūte, tūrn, up; crȳ, myth; çat, machine, ace,
church, çhord; ġem, añger, (Fr.) boṅ, aṣ; THis, thin; aẓure
323
ANG'KŌ
ANG'L

(Choose only one word out of each group)

fr: frañk'ness.
kr: çrañk'ness.
l: lañk'ness.
r: rañk'ness.

ANG'KŌ

b: bañ'çō.
m: çal-à-mañ'çō.
Plus spank owe, *or* O, etc.

ANGK'SHUN

s: sañç'tion.
Plus bank shun, etc.

ANGK'SHUS

Vowel: añx'ious.

ANGK'TUM

s: sañç'tum.
Plus ranked 'em, etc.

ANGK'WET

b: bañ'quet.
Plus hank wet, etc.

ANGK'WIL

tr: trañ'quil.
Plus bank will, etc.

ANGK'WISH

v: vañ'quish.
Plus frank, wish, etc.

ANG'KŬR

Vowel: añ'çhŏr,
sheet añ'çhŏr, un-añ'çhŏr,
up=añ'çhŏr.
b: bañ'kĕr.
bl: blañ'kĕr.
çh: çhañ'çre ('kĕr).

d: dañ'kĕr.
fl: flañ'kĕr, out-flañ'kĕr.
fr: frañ'kĕr.
h: hañ'kĕr.
k(ç): çañ'kĕr, en-çañ'kĕr.
kl: çlañ'kĕr.
kr: çrañ'kĕr.
l: lañ'kĕr.
pl: plañ'kĕr.
pr: prañ'kĕr.
r: rañ'çŏr, rañ'kĕr.
sh: shañ'kĕr.
sp: spañ'kĕr.
t: tañ'kĕr.
th: thañ'kĕr.
y: yañ'kĕr.
Plus yank her *or* err, etc.

ANG'KŬRD

Vowel: añ'çhŏred, un-añ'çhŏred.
br: brañ'çărd.
k(ç): çañ'kĕred.
t: tañ'kărd.
Plus ang'kŭr+ed.

ANG'L

Vowel: añ'gle, trī'añ-gle.
b: bañ'gle.
br: brañ'gle, em-brañ'gle.
d: dañ'gle.
j: in-tēr-jañ'gle, jañ'gle.
l: phā-lañ'găl.
m: bē-mañ'gle, mañ'gle,
miñ'gle=mañ″gle.
r: quäd-rañ'gle, Wrañ'gel,
wrañ'gle.
sp: bē-spañ'gle, spañ'gle.
str: strañ'gle.
t: dis-en-tañ'gle, en-tañ'gle,
in-tēr-tañ'gle, sea tañ'gle,
tañ'gle, un-tañ'gle.

(Choose only one word out of each group)

tw: twañ'gle.
w: wañ'gle.
Cf. rang gull, etc.
Cf. Wang'll, etc.

ANG'LD

f: new'=fañ'gled.
sp: spañ'gled, stär'=spañ-gled.
Plus ang'l+d.

ANG'LES

f: fang'less.
p: pang'less.
Plus hang less, etc.

ANG'LI

sp: spañ'gly.
t: tañ'gly.
Plus rang, Lee *or* lea, etc.

ANG'LING

Vowel: ang'ling.
Plus ang''l+ing.

ANG'LŪR

Vowel: ang'lẽr.
Plus ang''l+ẽr.

ANG'MĂN

h: hang'măn.
Plus sang, man, etc.

ANG'Ō

d: fan-dang'ō.
m: mang'ō.
p: Pag'ō Pag'ō (pang'),
  Pang'ō Pang'ō.
t: con-tang'ō, tang'ō.
Plus gang go, etc.

ANG'RŌV

m: mañ'grōve.
Plus plan grove, etc.

ANG'STŨR

g: gang'stẽr.
Plus sang, stir, etc.

ANG'ŨR

b: bang'ẽr.
g: gang'ẽr.
h: hang'ăr, hang'ẽr,
  pā'pẽr hang'ẽr, strap'hang-ẽr.
hw: slang'=whang-ẽr.
kl: çlang'ŏr.
r: hȧ-rangu'ẽr.
Plus hang her *or* err, etc.

ANG'WILL

z: Zang'will.
Plus gang will, etc.

AN'HOOD

m: man'hood.
Plus scan hood, etc.

Ā'NI, ĀN'I

br: brāin'y.
ch: Chey'ney.
g: Al-lē-ghẹ'ny.
gr: grāin'y.
l: Dē-lān'ey.
r: Rāin'ey, rāin'y.
v: veịn'y.
z: zā'ny.
zh: Eū-ġen'iē.
Plus main, he, etc.
Plus play knee, etc.

(Choose only one word out of each group)

AN'I

Vowel: An'nie.
br: bran'ny.
f: Fan'nie, Fan'ny.
gr: gran'ny.
k(ç): çan'ny, un-çan'ny.
kr: çran'ny.
l: Lan'nie.
m: man'nie.
n: Nan'nie.
Plus plan, he, etc.

ÄN'I

p: fran-ġi-pä'ni.
pr: sō-prä'ni.
r: rä'ni.
st: Hin-dú-stä'ni.
v: Gal-vä'ni.
Cf. don, he, etc.

AN'ID

kr: çran'nied.
Cf. plan, hid, etc.

ĀN'IJ

dr: drāin'ăġe.
kr: çrān'ăġe.
Cf. main age, etc.

AN'IJ

m: man'ăġe.
p: pan'năġe.
t: tan'năġe.
Cf. scan age, etc.

AN'IK

Vowel: cȳ-an'iç, fer″ri-cȳ-an'iç,
hȳ″drō-cȳ-an'iç,
in″tĕr-ō-cē-an'iç (-shē-),
Mes-si-an'iç, ō-cē-an'iç (-shē-),
Os-si-an'iç, val-er-i-an'iç.
d: rhō-dan'iç.
f: Ar-is-tō-phan'iç, dī-à-phan'iç,
lex-i-phan'iç, thē-ō-phan'iç.
g: ọr-gan'iç, pā-gan'iç.
k(ç): mē-çhan'iç, vol-çan'iç,
vul-çan'iç.
l: Mà-ġel-lan'iç.
m: ạl-dĕr-man'iç, Al-ē-man'niç,
Bräh-man'iç, Ġĕr-man'iç,
In'dō⸗Ġĕr-man'iç,
Mus-sul-man'iç, Rō-man'iç,
tal-is-man'iç.
p: pan'iç, tym-pan'iç.
st: stan'niç.
t: bō-tan'iç, Brit-an'niç,
çhär-là-tan'iç, mon-tan'iç,
Pūr-i-tan'iç, quer-ci-tan'niç,
sà-tan'iç, sul-tan'iç, tan'niç,
tē-tan'iç, tī-tan'iç.
v: gal-van'iç.
Cf. man nick *or* Nick, etc.

AN'IKS

k(ç): mē-çhan'içs.
m: hū-man'içs.
p: pan'içs.
Plus an'ik+s.
Cf. plan nix *or* nicks, etc.

AN'IL

Vowel: an'il.
Plus man ill, etc.
Cf. plan nil, etc.

AN'ĪL

Vowel: an'īle.
Cf. man, Nile, etc.

Ā'NIM
AN'ISH

fāte, fär, fàst, fąll, finăl, căre, at; mēte, prĕy, hẽr, met; pīne,
marïne, bĭrd, pin; nōte, mŏve, fọr, atŏm, not; mọọn, book;

326

(Choose only one word out of each group)

Ā'NIM

p: pāy'nim.
Plus gay Nym, etc.
Plus pain him, etc.

AN'IN

t: tan'nin.
Plus plan in *or* inn, etc.

ĀN'ING

br: brāin'ing.
ch: chāin'ing, en-chāin'ing,
un-chāin'ing.
d: dĕign'ing (dān'),
dis-dāin'ing, fōre-ọr-dāin'ing,
ọr-dāin'ing, prĕ"ọr-dāin'ing.
dr: drāin'ing.
f: fĕign'ing (fān'), prō-fān'ing,
un-fĕign'ing (-fān').
fr: rē-frāin'ing.
g: gāin'ing, rē-gāin'ing.
gr: grāin'ing, in-grāin'ing.
k(c): cān'ing.
kr: crān'ing.
m: rē-māin'ing.
p: cam-pāign'ing (-pān'),
cham-pāgn'ing (-pān'),
pāin'ing.
pl: āir-plān'ing, com-plāin'ing,
ex-plāin'ing, hȳ'drō-plān"ing,
plāin'ing*, plān'ing,
un-com-plāin'ing.
r: ar-rāign'ing (-rān'),
dē-rāign'ing (-rān'), rāin'ing,
rĕign'ing (rān'), rĕin'ing.
spr: sprāin'ing.
st: ab-stāin'ing, bē-stāin'ing,
stāin'ing.
str: con-strāin'ing,
rē-strāin'ing, strāin'ing.

t: ap-pẽr-tāin'ing,
as-cẽr-tāin'ing, at-tāin'ing,
con-tāin'ing, dē-tāin'ing,
en-tẽr-tāin'ing, māin-tāin'ing,
ob-tāin'ing, pẽr-tāin'ing,
rē-tāin'ing, sus-tāin'ing.
tr: en-trāin'ing, trāin'ing,
up-trāin'ing.
v: vĕin'ing.
w: wān'ing.

AN'ING

Vowel: An'ning.
b: ban'ning.
f: fan'ning.
fl: flan'ning.
k(c): can'ning.
m: man'ning, rē-man'ning,
un-man'ning.
p: jà-pan'ning, pan'ning,
trē-pan'ning.
pl: plan'ning.
sk(sc): scan'ning.
sp: in-span'ning, out-span'ning,
span'ning.
t: tan'ning.

AN'IS

Vowel: an'ise.
Cf. man is, etc.

ĀN'ISH

b: ûr-bān'ish.
d: Dān'ish.
s: sān'ish.
v: vāin'ish.

AN'ISH

b: ban'ish.
f: fan'nish.
kl: clan'nish.

327 ūse, bụll, brúte, tŭrn, up; crȳ, myth; cat, machine, ace,
church; chord; ġem, añger, (Fr.) boñ, as; THis, thin; azure
AN'IST
ĀNJ'LI

(Choose only one word out of each group)

m: man'nish, Mus-sul-man'ish.
pl: plan'ish.
r: Al-cō-ran'ish.
sp: Span'ish.
v: ē-van'ish, van'ish.

AN'IST

Vowel: pi-an'ist.
r: Al-cō-ran'ist.
t: tan'ist.

ĀN'JEL

Vowel: ān'ġel.
Plus range'll, etc.
Plus reign jell, etc.

AN'JEL

v: ē-van'gel.
Plus plan jell, etc.

AN'JENT

fr: fran'ġent.
pl: plan'ġent.
t: cō-tan'ġent, tan'ġent.
Plus fan gent, etc.

ĀN'JEST

ch: chān'ġest*, ex-chāng'est*,
in-tēr-chān'ġest*.
r: ar-rān'ġest*, dē-rān'ġest*,
dis-ar-rān'ġest*, rān'ġest*.
str: strān'ġest.
tr: es-trān'ġest*.
Plus main jest, etc.

ĀN'JETH

ch: chān'ġeth*, ex-chān'ġeth*,
in-tēr-chān'ġeth*.
r: ar-rān'ġeth*, dē-rān'ġeth*,
dis-ar-rān'ġeth*, rān'ġeth*.
tr: es-trān'ġeth*.

ĀN'JEZ

ch: chān'ġes, ex-chān'ġes,
in-tēr-chān'ġes.
gr: grān'ġes.
r: ar-rān'ġes, dē-rān'ġes,
dis-ar-rān'ġes, en-rān'ġes,
rān'ġes.
tr: es-trān'ġes.
Cf. mange is, etc.
Cf. main jizz, etc.

AN'JEZ

fl: flan'ġes.
g: Gan'ġes.
l: phā-lan'ġes.
Cf. flange is, etc.

ĀN'JI

m: mān'ġy.
r: rān'ġy.
Plus strange, he, etc.
Plus plain gee, or G, etc.

ĀN'JING

ch: chān'ġing,
coun-tēr-chān'ġing,
ex-chān'ġing, in-tēr-chān'ġing,
un-chān'ġing.
r: ar-rān'ġing, dē-rān'ġing,
dis-ar-rān'ġing, rān'ġing.
tr: es-trān'ġing.

ĀNJ'LES

ch: chānġe'less.
r: rānġe'less.
Plus mange less or Les, etc.

ĀNJ'LI

str: strānġe'ly.
Plus mange, Lee or lea, etc.

ĀNJ'LING
ĀN'LES

fāte, fär, fȧst, fall, finăl, cãre, at; mēte, prey, hẽr, met; pīne,
marïne, bĭrd, pin; nōte, mȯve, fȯr, atŏm, not; mọọn, book;
328

(Choose only one word out of each group)

ĀNJ'LING

ch: chānge'ling.

ĀNJ'MENT

ch: ex-chānge'ment,
in-tẽr-chānge'ment.
r: ar-rānge'ment, dē-rānge'ment,
dis-ar-rānge'ment.
tr: es-trānge'ment.
Plus mange meant, etc.

ĀNJ'NESS

str: strānge'ness.

ĀN'JŨR

ch: chān'gẽr, ex-chān'gẽr,
in-tẽr-chān'gẽr,
mŏn'ey=chān'gẽr.
d: dān'gẽr, en-dān'gẽr.
gr: grān'gẽr.
m: mān'gẽr.
r: ar-rān'gẽr, bụsh'rān-gẽr,
dē-rān'gẽr, dis-ar-rān'gẽr,
rān'gẽr.
str: strān'gẽr.
tr: trān'gẽr.
Plus change her *or* err, etc.

AN'KȦ, ȦN'KȦ

Vowel: Bi-añ'cȧ.
s: Sañ'kȧ.
t: tañ'kȧ.
Plus spank a, etc.

AN'KIN

h: Han'kin.
r: Ran'kin.
Plus plan kin, etc.
Plus thank in *or* inn, etc.

AN'KING

n: Nan'king.
Cf. ang'king.
Plus plan king, etc.

AN'KINZ

h: Han'kinṣ.
r: Ran'kinṣ.
Plus thank inns *or* ins, etc.
Plus plan kin's, etc.

AN'KOK

h: Han'cock.
Plus ran cock, etc.

ĀN'LAND

m: māin'land.
Plus Seine land, etc.

ĀN'LES

b: bāne'less, dog'bāne-less, etc.
br: brāin'less.
ch: chāin'less.
dr: drāin'less.
g: gāin'less.
gr: grāin'less.
k(c): cāne'less.
kr: crāne'less.
m: dō-māin'less, māne'less.
p: pāin'less.
r: rāin'less.
sk: skẹin'less.
spr: sprāin'less.
st: stāin'less.
str: strāin'less.
sw: swāin'less.
th: thāne'less.
tr: trāin'less.
v: vāne'less.
Plus insane, Les *or* less.

üse, bull, brúte, tũrn, up; crÿ, myth; çat, maçhine, ace,
church, çhord; ġem, aṅger, (Fr.) boṅ, aṣ; THis, thin; aʒure

(Choose only one word out of each group)

AN'LES

b: ban'less.
f: fan'less.
kl: çlan'less.
m: man'less.
pl: plan'less.
sp: span'less.
t: tan'less.
Plus ran less, *or* Les, etc.

ĀN'LI

Vowel: in-āne'ly.
f: prō-fāne'ly.
g: gāin'ly.
m: hū-māne'ly, māin'ly.
pl: plāin'ly.
s: in-sāne'ly, sāne'ly.
v: vāin'ly.
Plus gain, Lee, *or* lea, etc.

AN'LI

d: Dan'ley.
m: Man'ley, man'ly,
    un-man'ly.
sp: spick'=and=span'ly.
st: Stan'ley.
Plus plan Lee *or* lea, etc.

AN'LING

m: man'ling.
t: tan'ling.

ĀN'MENT

d: or-dāin'ment.
r: ar-rāign'ment (-rān').
t: as-cẽr-tāin'ment,
    at-tāin'ment, ob-tāin'ment.
Plus reign meant, etc.

ĀN'NES

Vowel: in-āne'ness.
f: prō-fāne'ness.
m: hū-māne'ness.
pl: plāin'ness.
s: in-sāne'ness, sāne'ness.

Ā'NŌ

k(ç): vol-çā'nō.
Plus say no *or* know, etc.
Plus main owe *or* O, etc.

AN'Ō

Vowel: pi-an'ō.
·h: Han'nō.
pr: sō-pran'ō.
Plus plan owe *or* O, etc.
Cf. plan no *or* know, etc.

Ä'NŌ

Vowel: gū-ä'nō, pi-än'ō.
pr: sō-prä'nō.
s: Mon-tē-sä'nō.
Cf. on no *or* know, etc.

AN'ŎK

b: ban'nŏck.
j: jan'nŏck.
Plus can knock, etc.

AN'ŎN

f: fan'ŏn.
·k(ç): çan'nŏn, çan'ŏn.
sh: Bal'ley-shan'nŏn,
    Shan'nŏn.
Plus ran on, etc.

ĀN'SĀ

g: gāin'sāy.
Plus plain say, etc.

ĂN'SĂL
AN'SHENT
fāte, fär, fást, fạll, finăl, cāre, at; mēte, prẹy, hẽr, met; pīne,
marïne, bïrd, pin; nōte, mōve, fǫr, atŏm, not; mǫǫn, book;
330

(Choose only one word out of each group)

ĀN'SĀL

m: māin'sāil.
Cf. plain sail, etc.

AN'SEL

ch: chan'cel.
h: hand'sel (han').
k(ç): çan'cel.
Plus man sell, etc.
Plus pants'll, etc.

AN'SEST

ch: chan'cest*.
d: dan'cest*.
gl: glan'cest*.
h: en-han'cest*.
m: rō-man'cest*.
pr: pran'cest.
tr: en-tran'cest*.
v: ad-van'cest*.

AN'SET

l: lan'cet.
Plus man set, etc.
Plus Vance et, etc.

AN'SETH

ch: chan'ceth*.
d: dan'ceth*.
gl: glan'ceth*.
h: en-han'ceth*.
m: rō-man'ceth*.
pr: pran'ceth*.
tr: en-tran'ceth*.
v: ad-van'ceth*.
Plus ran, Seth, etc.

AN'SEZ

ch: chan'cẹs, mis-chan'cẹs.
d: dan'cẹs.
gl: glan'cẹs.
h: en-han'cẹs.
l: lan'cẹs.
m: rō-man'cẹs.
n: fi-nan'cẹs.
p: ex-pan'sẹs.
pr: pran'cẹs.
tr: en-tran'cẹs, tran'cẹs.
v: ad-van'cẹs.
Cf. manse is, etc.
Plus man says, etc.
Plus dance, Ez, etc.

ANS'FŪR

tr: trans'fẽr.
Plus manse fir or fur, etc.

AN'SHĂL

n: fi-nan'ciăl.
st: cīr-çum-stan'tiăl,
  sub-stan'tiăl,
  sū"pẽr-sub-stan'tiăl.
Plus man shall, etc.
Plus ranch, Al, etc.

AN'SHĒ

b: ban'shee.
Plus can she, etc.

ĀN'SHENT

Vowel: ān'cient.

AN'SHENT

tr: tran'sient ('shent).

(Choose only one word out of each group)

AN′SHUN

m: man′sion.
p: ex-pan′sion.
sk(sç): sçan′sion.
st: stan′çhion.
Plus man shun, etc.

AN′SI

Vowel: An′sey.
ch: chan′cy, mis-chan′cy,
un-chan′cy.
d: dan′cy.
f: fan′cy, syç′ō-phan-cy.
g: ex-trav′à-gan-cy,
tēr′mà-gan-cy.
k(ç): men′di-çan-cy,
sig-nif′i-çan-cy,
sup′pli-çan-cy.
kl: C̩lan′cey.
l: Dē-lan′cey, pet′ū-lan-cy,
sib′i-lan-cy.
m: ā′ēr-ō-man-cy, a̧l′dēr-man-cy,
à-leç′tō-rō-man-cy,
à-leç′try-ō-man-cy,
à-leū′rō-man-cy,
al-phit′ō-man-cy*,
an′thrō-pō-man-cy,
as-tra′găl-ō-man-cy,
a̧us′trō-man-cy,
ax-in′ō-man-cy, bel′ō-man-cy,
bib′li-ō-man-cy,
bot′an-ō-man-cy,
çap′tō-man-cy,
çà-top′trō-man-cy,
cēr′ō-man-cy, çhīr′ō-man′cy,
çler′ō-man-cy,
ço-scin′ō-man-cy (-sin′),
crith′ō-man-cy,
crys′tăl-lō-man-cy,
daç-tyl′i-ō-man-cy,

ē-nop′trō-man-cy,
gas′trō-man-cy, ġē′ō-man-cy,
ḡȳr′ō-man-cy, hal′ō-man-cy,
hī′ēr-ō-man-cy, hȳ′drō-man-cy,
içh′thy-ō-man-cy,
le′çan-ō-man-cy, lith′ō-man-cy,
mēt′ē-ŏr-ō-man″cy,
mȳ′ō-man-cy, ne′crō-man-cy,
ōen′ō-man-cy, ō′nō-man-cy,
ō′ny-çhō-man-cy,
ō′phi-ō-man-cy,
or′nith-ō-man-cy,
ped′ō-man-cy, pȳr′ō-man-cy,
psē′phō-man-cy (sē′),
psȳ′çhō-man-cy, scī′ō-man-cy,
sid′ēr-ō-man-cy, spō′dō-man-cy,
stiçh′ō-man-cy,
teph′rà-man-cy.
n: çon′sō-nan-cy, Miss Nan′cy,
Nan′cy.
p: oç′cū-pan-cy.
r: ex-ū′bēr-an-cy.
t: ex-or̩′bi-tan-cy, hes̩′i-tan-cy,
mil′i-tan-cy, prē-cip′i-tan-cy.
Plus man see, etc.
Plus manse, he, etc.

AN′SID

f: fan′cied.
r: ran′cid.
Plus span, Sid, etc.
Plus manse hid, etc.

AN′SING

Vowel: af″fī-an′cing, fī-an′cing.
ch: chan′cing.
d: dan′cing.
gl: glan′cing.
h: en-han′cing.
l: lan′sing, Lan′sing.

(Choose only one word out of each group)

m: c̱hī'rō-man-cing,
ne'c̱rō-man-cing, etc.,
rō-man'cing.
pr: pran'cing.
tr: en-tran'cing.
v: ad-van'cing.
Plus man sing, etc.

AN'SIS

fr: Fran'ces, Fran'cis.
Plus plan, sis, etc.

AN'SIST

m: rō-man'cist.
Plus span cyst, etc.

AN'SIV

p: ex-pan'sive.
v: ad-van'cive.
Plus plan sieve, etc.

ANS'MENT

h: en-hance'ment.
tr: en-trance'ment.
v: ad-vance'ment.
Plus glance meant, etc.

AN'SŎM

h: hand'sŏme, han'sŏm,
un-hand'sŏme.
r: ran'sŏm.
tr: tran'sŏm.
Plus plan some or sum, etc.

AN'SŎN

Vowel: An'sŏn.
h: Han'sŏn.
Plus plan, son or sun, etc.

AN'STĀ

m: māin'stāy.
Plus plain stay, etc.

AN'SŨR

Vowel: An'sẽr, an'swẽr ('sẽr).
ch: chan'cẽr.
d: bel'ly=dan'cẽr,
bub'ble=dan'cẽr, dan'cẽr,
fan'=dan-cẽr, hú'lȧ=dan'cẽr, etc.
g: mẽr-gan'sẽr.
gl: glan'cẽr.
k(c̱): c̱an'cẽr.
l: lan'cẽr.
m: c̱hīr'ō-man-cẽr,
g̱ē'ō-man-cẽr, nec̱'rō-man-cẽr,
etc., rō-man'cẽr.
pr: pran'cẽr.
tr: en-tran'cẽr.
v: ad-van'cẽr.
Plus advance her or err, etc.

AN'TĀ

f: in-fan'te̱.
Plus plant a, etc.

AN'TÀ

Vowel: an'tȧ.
d: Vē-dan'tȧ.
f: in-fan'tȧ.
l: At-ȧ-lan'tȧ, At-lan'tȧ.
s: San'tȧ.
Cf. plan "tuh", etc.
Plus plant a, etc.

ÄN'TÀ

d: Ve̱-dän'tȧ.
Cf. want a, etc.

(Choose only one word out of each group)

AN′TĂL

dr: quä-dran′tăl.
g: ġī-gan′tăl*.
n: çon-sō-nan′tăl.
Plus plant, Al, etc.

AN′TĂM

b: ban′tăm.
f: phan′tŏm.
Plus scant 'em, etc.

ĀN′TĂNS

kw: aç-quāin′tănce.
Plus paint aunts *or* ants, etc.

AN′TAZM

f: phan′taṣm.
Cf. aunt has 'em, etc.

AN′TĒ

Vowel: an′tē.
d: Dan′tē.
r: Dū-ran′ty, pō-çō-çū-ran′tē.
t: dil-et-tan′tē.
z: zan′tē.
Plus plant, he, etc.
Plus plan tea *or* T, etc.

ÄN′TĒ

Vowel: çhi-än′ti.
d: än-dän′tē, Dän′tē.
Plus aunt, he, etc.

ĀN′TED

f: fāin′ted, fẹin′ted.
kw: aç-quāin′ted,
  un-aç-quāin′ted.
p: bē-pāin′ted, dē-pāin′ted*,
  pāin′ted.

s: bē-sāin′ted, sāin′ted,
  un-sāin′ted.
t: at-tāin′ted, tāin′ted,
  un-at-tāin′ted, un-tāin′ted.
Plus paint, Ed, etc.
Plus pain, Ted, etc.

AN′TED, ĂN′TED

ch: chan′ted, en-chan′ted.
gr: gran′ted.
h: "han′ted".
k(ç): çan′ted, dē-çan′ted,
  rē-çan′ted.
p: pan′ted.
pl: im-plan′ted, plan′ted,
  sup-plan′ted.
r: ran′ted.
sl: slan′ted.
Plus plan, Ted, etc.
Plus scant, Ed, etc.

ĀN′TEST

f: fāin′test*, fẹin′test*.
kw: aç-quāin′test*, quāin′test.
p: pāin′test*.
t: tāin′test*.
Plus main test, etc.

AN′TEST, ĂN′TEST

ch: chan′test*, en-chan′test*.
gr: gran′test*.
k(ç): çan′test*, dē-çan′test*,
  rē-çan′test*.
p: pan′test*.
pl: im-plan′test*, plan′test*,
  sup-plan′test*.
r: ran′test*.
sk(sç): sçan′test.
sl: slan′test*.
Plus plan test, etc.

(Choose only one word out of each group)

ĀN'TETH

f: fāin'teth*, fein'teth*.
kw: ac-quāin'teth*.
p: pāin'teth*.
t: tāin'teth*.

AN'TETH, ȦN'TETH

ch: chan'teth*, en-chan'teth*.
gr: gran'teth*.
k(c): can'teth*, dē-can'teth*,
 rē-can'teth*.
p: pan'teth*.
pl: im-plan'teth*, plan'teth*,
 sup-plan'teth*.
r: ran'teth*.
sk(sc): scan'teth*.
sl: slan'teth*.

AN'TĒZ

b: cor-y-ban'tēs.
d: Dan'tē's, Dan'tēs.
l: at-lan'tēs.
Cf. an'ti+s.
Plus can tease *or* T's, etc.
Plus plant ease *or* E's, etc.

AN'THEM

Vowel: an'them.
Plus amaranth 'em, etc.

AN'THIK

n: oē-nan'thic.
z: xan'thic.
Plus plan thick, etc.

AN'THIN

Vowel: an'thine.
m: Rhad-ȧ-man'thine.

k: ȧ-can'thine, trag-ȧ-can'thin.
r: am-ȧ-ran'thine.
z: xan'thin.
Plus ran thin, etc.
Plus amaranth in *or* inn, etc.

ĀNT'HOOD

s: sāint'hood.
Plus paint hood.

AN'THŪR

Vowel: an'thẽr.
p: pan'thẽr.
Plus amaranth her *or* err, etc.

AN'THUS

Vowel: a-mi-an'thus,
 an-an'thous, dī-an'thus,
 pol-y-an'thous, syn-an'thous.
k(c): ȧ-can'thous, ȧ-can'thus,
 an-ȧ-can'thous, can'thus.
l: aī-lan'thus, Gȧ-lan'thus.
m: Haē-man'thus.
n: Chī-mō-nan'thus.
p: Ag-ȧ-pan'thus, ē-pan'thous.
r: hys-tẽr-an'thous.
Plus amaranth us, etc.

ĀN'TI

d: dāin'ty.
f: fāin'ty, fein'ty.
Plus plain tea *or* T, etc.
Plus ain't he, etc.

AN'TI

k(c): bac-chan'tē, can'ty.
p: pan'ty.
sh: shan'ty.
sk(sc): scan'ty.
Plus ant he, etc.
Plus span tea *or* T, etc.

335 ūse, bull, brúte, tûrn, up; crȳ, myth; çat, maçhine, ace, church, çhord; ġem, añger, (Fr.) boṅ, aṣ; THiṣ, thin; aᴢure

ÄN′TI
ĀN′TIV

(Choose only one word out of each group)

ÄN′TI

Vowel: äun′ty.
Cf. can't he, etc.

ĀN′TIF

pl: plāin′tiff.
Plus main tiff, etc.
Plus paint, if, etc.

AN′TIJ

pl: plan′tăġe*.
v: ad-van′tăġe, dis″ad-van′tăġe, van′tăġe.
Cf. scant age, etc.

AN′TIK

Vowel: an′tiç.
b: çor-y-ban′tiç.
d: pē-dan′tiç.
f: hī″ēr-ō-phan′tiç, syç-ō-phan′tiç.
fr: fran′tiç.
g: ġī-gan′tiç.
l: At-lan′tiç, trans-at-lan′tiç.
m: çhīr-ō-man′tiç, ġē-ō-man′tiç, hȳ-drō-man′tiç, man′tiç, neç-rō-man′tiç, o-nō-man′tiç, pȳr-ō-man′tiç, spod-ō-man′tiç, etc.; rō-man′tiç.
n: çon-sō-nan′tiç.
Plus plan tick, etc.

AN′TIK

d: Vē-dan′tiç.

AN′TIN, AN′TĪN

b: Brà-ban′tine.
f: çhrys-el-ē-phan′tine, Dī-ō-phan′tine, el-ē-phan′tine.
g: ġī-gan′tine*.

m: ad-à-man′tine.
v: Lē-van′tine.
z: By-zan′tine.
Plus plan tin, etc.
Plus plant in or inn, etc.
Plus plan tine, etc.

ĀN′TING

f: fāin′ting, fein′ting.
kw: aç-quāin′ting.
p: pāin′ting, wŏrd pāin′ting.
t: at-tāin′ting, tāin′ting.

AN′TING, ÁN′TING

b: ban′ting.
ch: chan′ting, dis-en-chan′ting, en-chan′ting.
gr: gran′ting.
h: "han′ting".
k(ç): çan′ting, dē-çan′ting, des-çan′ting, rē-çan′ting.
p: pan′ting.
pl: im-plan′ting, plan′ting, sup-plan′ting, trans-plan′ting.
r: ran′ting.
sk(sç): sçan′ting.
sl: slan′ting.

AN′TIST

k: Kan′tist.
r: ig-nō-ran′tist.

ÄN′TIST

d: Vē-dän′tist.

ĀN′TIV

pl: plāin′tive.
str: çon-strāin′tive.

(Choose only one word out of each group)

AN'TIZM

k: Kan'tiṣm.
r: ig-nō-ran'tiṣm,
ob-sc̣ū-ran'tiṣm,
pō-c̣ō-c̣ū-ran'tiṣm, ran'tiṣm.
t: dil-et-tan'tiṣm.
Plus plant ism, etc.

AN'TL

k(c̣): c̣an'tle.
m: dis-man'tle, im-man'tle,
man'tel, man'tle.
sk(sc̣): sc̣an'tle.
Plus plant'll, etc.

AN'TLD

m: dis-man'tled,
i'vy=man'tled, man'tled.
Plus cantle'd, etc.

ANT'LET

k(c̣): c̣ant'let.
m: mant'let.
pl: plant'let.
Plus ant let *or* Lett, etc.

ANT'LET

g: g̣aunt'let.
Plus want Lett *or* let, etc.

ĀNT'LI

kw: quãint'ly.
s: sãint'ly, un-sãint'ly.
Plus paint Lee *or* lea, etc.

ANT'LI

sk(sc̣): sc̣ant'ly.
sl: à-slant'ly.
Plus plant lea *or* Lee, etc.

ĀNT'LĬK

s: sãint'līke.
Plus paint like, etc.

ANT'LING

b: bant'ling.
m: man'tling.
sk(sc̣): sc̣ant'ling.

ANT'LŨR

Vowel: ant'lẽr.
m: dis-man'tlẽr, man'tlẽr.
p: pant'lẽr*.

ANT'MENT

ch: dis-en-chant'ment,
en-chant'ment.
Plus plant meant, etc.

ĀNT'NES

f: fãint'ness.
kw: quãint'ness.

ANT'NES

sk(sc̣): sc̣ant'ness.

AN'TŌ, ȦN'TŌ

k(c̣): c̣an'tō.
m: pōrt-man'teau ('tō).
r: c̣ō-ran'tō, quō wạr-ran'tō.
t: prō-tan'tō.
Plus plan toe, etc.
Plus plant owe *or* O, etc.

AN'TŎM

See an'tăm.

AN'TŎN

d: Dan'tŏn.
k(c̣): C̣an'tŏn.

(Choose only one word out of each group)

kl: Çlan'tŏn.
skr(sçr): Sçran'tŏn.
st: Stan'tŏn.
Plus plant on, etc.
Plus plan tun *or* ton, etc.

AN'TŎR

gr: gran'tŏr.
k(ç): çan'tŏr.
Cf. an'tūr.
Plus plant, or, etc.
Plus plan tor, etc.

AN'TRES

ch: chan'tress, en-chan'tress.
Plus plan tress, etc.

AN'TRI

p: pan'try.
Plus scan tree, etc.

AN'TRI

ch: chan'try.
Cf. plant tree, etc.

AN'TRUM

t: tan'trum
Plus scant rum, etc.

AN'TŮ

b: Ban'tů.
Plus can two, to *or* too, etc.

ĀN'TŪR

f: fāin'tẽr, feïn'tẽr.
kw: aç-quāin'tẽr, quāin'tẽr.
p: pāin'tẽr, wŏrd pāin'tẽr.
t: tāin'tẽr.
Plus taint her *or* err, etc.

AN'TŪR

b: ban'tẽr.
ch: chan'tẽr, dis-en-chan'tẽr,
en-chan'tẽr.
gr: gran'tẽr.
k(ç): çan'tẽr, dē-çan'tẽr,
des-çan'tẽr, rē-çan'tẽr,
trō-chan'tẽr.
p: pan'tẽr.
pl: im-plan'tẽr, plan'tẽr,
sup-plan'tẽr, trans-plan'tẽr.
r: ran'tẽr.
st: in-stan'tẽr.
v: Lē-van'tẽr.
Plus plant her *or* err, etc.

AN'TŪRN

l: lan'tẽrn.
Plus can turn, etc.
Plus can't erne, urn *or* earn, etc.

ĀN'ŪR

Vowel: in-ān'ẽr.
ch: chāin'ẽr, en-chāin'ẽr,
un-chāin'ẽr.
d: dis-dāin'ẽr, ọr-dāin'ẽr.
dr: drāin'ẽr.
f: feïgn'ẽr (fān'), prō-fān'ẽr.
fr: rē-frāin'ẽr.
g: gāin'ẽr, Gāy'nŏr, rē-gāin'ẽr.
gr: grāin'ẽr.
p: çam-pāign'ẽr (-pān'),
çham-pāgn'ẽr (-pān').
pl: çom-plāin'ẽr, ex-plāin'ẽr,
plāin'ẽr.
r: ar-rāign'ẽr (-rān').
s: in-sān'ẽr, sān'ẽr.
st: ab-stāin'ẽr, bē-stāin'ẽr,
non-ab-stāin'ẽr, stāin'ẽr.

AN'ŪR
AN'ZÅ   fāte, fär, fåst, fạll, finăl, cãre, at; mēte, prẹy, hẽr, met; pīne,
marĭne, bĭrd, pin; nōte, mŏve, fọr, atŏm, not; mọọn, book;   **338**

(Choose only one word out of each group)

str: cọn-strāin'ẽr, rē-strāin'ẽr,
strāin'ẽr.

t: ap-pẽr-tāin'ẽr, as-cẽr-tāin'ẽr,
at-tāin'ẽr, cọn-tāin'ẽr,
dē-tāin'ẽr, en-tẽr-tāin'ẽr,
māin-tāin'ẽr, ob-tāin'ẽr,
rē-tāin'ẽr, sus-tāin'ẽr.

tr: trāin'ẽr, up-trāin'ẽr.

v: vāin'ẽr.

w: cọrd'wāin-ẽr.

Plus gain her *or* err, etc.

AN'ŪR

b: ban'nẽr.

f: fan'nẽr.

k(c): cạn'nẽr.

l: lan'nẽr.

m: man'nẽr, man'ŏr.

p: jạ-pan'nẽr, trē-pan'nẽr.

pl: plan'nẽr.

sk(sc): scạn'nẽr.

sp: span'nẽr.

t: tan'nẽr.

v: van'nẽr.

Plus ran her *or* err, etc.

AN'ŪRD

b: ban'nẽred, un-ban'nẽred.

m: ill'=man'nẽred, man'nẽred,
un-man'nẽred, well'=man'nẽred.

Plus tanner'd, etc.

ĀN'US

Vowel: ān'us.

h: hẹin'ous.

j: Jā'nus.

k(c): in-cān'ous.

v: Sil-vān'us, vẹin'ous.

Plus ordain us, etc.

AN'VĂS

k(c): cạn'văs, cạn'văss.

AN'VIL

Vowel: an'vil.

d: Dan'ville.

gr: Gran'ville.

m: Man'ville.

ĀN'WŪRK

br: brāin'wŏrk.

ch: chāin'wŏrk.

pl: plāin wŏrk.

Plus explain work, etc.

AN'YĂN, AN'YUN

b: ban'yăn.

k(c): cạn'yŏn.

p: cọm-pan'iŏn ('yun).

AN'YĂRD

l: lan'yărd.

sp: Span'iărd.

Plus man yard, etc.

AN'YEL

d: Dan'iel.

sp: span'iel, wạt'ẽr span'iel.

th: Nạ-than'iel.

Plus can yell, etc.

AN'YŪR

p: pan'niẽr.

Cf. can your *or* you're, etc.

AN'ZÅ

g: ex-trav-ạ-gan'zȧ, gan'zȧ.

gr: gran'zȧ.

n: bō-nan'zȧ.

p: Pan'zȧ.

r: Cär-ran'zȧ.

st: stan'zȧ.

Plus plans a, etc.

(Choose only one word out of each group)

ANZ'FĒLD

m: Manṣ'fiēld.
Plus plans field, etc.

AN'ZI

p: chim-pan'zee, pan'ṣy.
t: tan'ṣy.
Plus plans, he, etc.

ĀNZ'VIL

j: Jāneṣ'ville.
z: Zāneṣ'ville.

Ā'Ō

k(ç): çȧ-çā'ō.
tr: te-trā'ō.

Ā'ON

f: Phā'on.
kr: çrāy'on.
r: rāy'on.
Plus stay on, etc.

Ä'ŌN

g: Gä'ōn.
Plus spa on, etc.

Ā'OS

k(ç): çhā'os.
t: Tā'os.

Ā'OTH

b: Sa-bā'oth.

AP'Ȧ

k: ƙap'pȧ.
Plus strap a, etc.

AP'EN

h: hap'pen.
Cf. slappin', etc.
Cf. gap in, etc.
Cf. tap pen, etc.

ĀP'EST

Vowel: āp'est*.
dr: drāp'est*.
g: gāp'est*.
k(ç): es-çāp'est*.
r: rāp'est*.
sh: shāp'est*.
skr(sçr): sçrāp'est*.
Plus gay pest, etc.

AP'EST

fl: flap'pest*.
kl: çlap'pest*.
l: lap'pest*.
m: map'pest*.
n: nap'pest*.
r: en-wrap'pest*, rap'pest*, wrap'pest*.
s: sap'pest*.
sl: slap'pest*.
sn: snap'pest*.
tr: trap'pest*.

AP'ET

l: lap'pet.
t: tap'pet.
Cf. trap, pet, etc.
Cf. trap it, etc.

ĀP'ETH

Vowel: āp'eth*.
dr: drāp'eth*.
g: gāp'eth*.
k(ç): es-çāp'eth*.

AP'ETH
AP'ING

fāte, fär, fȧst, fȧll, fĭnȧl, cãre, at; mēte, prey, hēr, met; pīne,
marĭne, bĭrd, pin; nōte, mȯve, fȯr, atŏm, not; mōon, book;

340

(Choose only one word out of each group)

r: rāp'eth*.
sh: shăp'eth*.
skr(scr): scrāp'eth*.

AP'ETH

fl: flap'peth*.
kl: clap'peth*.
l: lap'peth*.
m: map'peth*.
n: nap'peth*.
r: en-wrap'peth*, rap'peth*,
wrap'peth*.
s: sap'peth*.
sl: slap'peth*.
sn: snap'peth*.
tr: trap'peth*.

ĀP'GŌT

sk(sc): scāpe'gōat.
Plus drape goat, etc.

ĀP'GRĀS

sk(sc): scāpe'grāce.
Plus drape Grace, etc.

ĀP'I

g: gāp'y.
kr: crāp'y.
skr(scr): scrāp'y.
t: red'=tāpe'y.
Plus drape, he, etc.

AP'I

ch: chap'py.
g: gap'py, gap'y.
h: hap'py.
n: knap'py (nap'), nap'py.
p: pap'py.
s: sap'py.
skr(scr): scrap'py.
sn: snap'py.
Plus clap, he, etc.

AP'ID

r: rap'id.
s: sap'id.
v: vap'id.
Cf. map hid, etc.

AP'IK

l: jȧ-lap'ic, Lap'pic.
Cf. trap pick, etc.

ĀP'IN

r: rāp'ine.
Plus play pin, etc.

ĀP'ING

Vowel: āp'ing.
dr: drāp'ing.
g: gāp'ing.
k(c): es-cāp'ing.
r: rāp'ing.
sh: shāp'ing.
skr(scr): scrāp'ing.
t: tāp'ing.

AP'ING

ch: chap'ping.
d: dap'ping.
fl: flap'ping.
g: gap'ing, gap'ping.
k(c): cap'ping, han'di-cap-ping.
kl: clap'ping.
l: lap'ping, ō-vēr-lap'ping.
m: map'ping.
n: nap'ping.
r: en-wrap'ping, rap'ping,
un-wrap'ping, wrap'ping.
s: sap'ping.
skr(scr): scrap'ping.
sl: slap'ping.

(Choose only one word out of each group)

sn: snap'ping.
str: strap'ping,
un'dĕr-strap-ping,
un-strap'ping.
t: tap'ping.
tr: en-trap'ping, trap'ping.
y: yap'ping.

ĀP'IS

Vowel: āp'is.
l: lāp'is.
r: Sē-rāp'is.
t: tāp'is.

AP'IS

l: lap'is.
t: tap'is.

ĀP'ISH

Vowel: āp'ish.
p: pāp'ish.
Plus say pish, etc.

AP'ISH

n: knap'pish (nap').
sn: snap'pish.

ĀP'IST

p: pāp'ist.
r: rāp'ist.
sk(sċ): land'sċāp-ist.
t: red'⸗tāp'ist.

ĀP'IZM

p: pāp'iṣm.
t: red'⸗tāp'iṣm.

ĀP'L

k(ċ): ċāp'el.
m: mā'ple.

p: an-ti-pāp'ăl, pāp'ăl.
st: stā'ple, wool stā'ple.
Plus crape'll, etc.
Cf. play pull, etc.

AP'L

Vowel: ap'ple, lŏve ap'ple,
pīne'ap-ple.
ch: an'tē-chap-el, chap'el,
Chap'pell.
d: dap'ple.
gr: grap'ple.
n: knap'ple (nap')*.
r: rap'pel.
sk(sċ): sċap'ple.
skr(sċr): sċrap'ple.
thr: thrap'ple.
Plus map'll, etc.

ĀP'LES

Vowel: āpe'less.
gr: grāpe'less.
k(ċ): ċāpe'less, es-ċāpe'less.
kr: ċrāpe'less.
n: nāpe'less.
r: rāpe'less.
sh: shāpe'less.
skr(sċr): sċrāpe'less.
t: tāpe'less.
Plus drape less *or* Les, etc.

AP'LES

h: hap'less.
k(ċ): cap'less.
n: nap'less.
s: sap'less.
sl: slap'less.
Plus slap less, etc.

(Choose only one word out of each group)

AP'LET

ch: chap'let.
Plus slap Lett or let, etc.

ĀP'LI

sh: shāpe'ly.
Plus drape Lee, or lea, etc.
Plus stay plea, etc.

AP'LI

h: hap'ly.
Plus map lea, or Lee, etc.

AP'LIN

ch: chap'lain, Chap'lin.
Plus map Lynn, etc.

AP'LING

d: dap'pling.
gr: grap'pling.
l: lap'ling*.
s: sap'ling.

ĀP'LZ

n: Nā'pleş.
st: stā'pleş.
Plus āp'l+s.
Cf. dray pulls, etc.

AP'MĂN

ch: Chap'măn.
k(ç): Çap'măn.
n: Knap'măn (nap').
Plus trap man, etc.

AP'NEL

gr: grap'nel.
shr: shrap'nel.
Plus trap Nell, or knell, etc.

ĀP'ŎN, ĀP'UN

k(ç): çāp'ŏn.
sh: mis-shāp'en, un-shāp'en.
t: tāp'en.
Plus scrape on, etc.
Cf. say pun, etc.

ĀP'RIL

Vowel: Āp'ril.
Plus drape rill, etc.

AP'SHUN

k(ç): çap'tion, rē-çap'tion.
l: çol-lap'sion*, ē-lap'sion*.
tr: çon-trap'tion.
Plus slap shun, etc.

AP'SHUS

k(ç): çap'tious.

AP'SING

l: çol-lap'sing, lap'sing,
rē-lap'sing.
Plus trap sing, etc.

AP'STĂN

k(ç): çap'stăn.
Plus wraps tan, etc.
Cf. slap stun, etc.

AP'STŨR

t: tap'stũr.
Plus clap stir, etc.
Plus elapsed, her, or err, etc.

AP'TED

d: å-dap'ted.
Plus slap Ted, etc.
Plus wrapped Ed, etc.

(Choose only one word out of each group)

AP′TEST

Vowel: ap′test, in-ap′test.
d: a-dap′test*.
r: rap′test.
Plus map test.

AP′TIN

k(ç): çap′tain.
Plus wrap tin, etc.
Plus wrapped in, or inn, etc.

AP′TIV

d: a-dap′tive.
k(ç): çap′tive.

AP′TIZM

b: an-a-bap′tiṣm, bap′tiṣm.

APT′LI

Vowel: apt′ly, in-apt′ly.
r: rapt′ly.
Plus scrapped, Lee, or lea, etc.

APT′NES

Vowel: apt′ness, in-apt′ness,
  un-apt′ness.
r: rapt′ness.

AP′TRAP

kl: çlap′trap.
Plus slap trap, etc.
Plus snapped wrap, or rap, etc.

AP′TŪR

k(ç): çap′tūre, rē-çap′tūre.
r: en-rap′tūre, rap′tūre.
Plus strapped your or you′re, etc.

AP′TŨR

Vowel: ap′tẽr.
ch: chap′tẽr.
d: a-dap′tẽr.
k(ç): çap′tŏr, rē-çap′tŏr.
r: rap′tẽr.
Plus wrapped her or err, etc.

ĀP′ŨR

Vowel: āp′ẽr.
dr: drāp′ẽr, un-drāp′ẽr.
g: gāp′ẽr.
k(ç): çāp′ẽr, es-çāp′ẽr.
p: flȳ′pā-pẽr, newṣ′pā-pẽr,
  pā′pẽr, sand′pā-pẽr.
r: rāp′ẽr.
s: sā′pŏr.
sh: shāp′ẽr, un-shāp′ẽr.
sk(sç): land′sçāp-ẽr.
skr(sçr): sçrāp′ẽr, skȳ′sçrāp-ẽr.
t: tāp′ẽr, tāp′ĩr.
v: vā′pŏr.
Plus say purr or per, etc.
Plus scrape her or err, etc.

AP′ŨR

d: dap′pẽr.
fl: flap′pẽr, flȳ′flap-pẽr.
g: gap′ẽr.
k(ç): çap′pẽr, han′di-çap-pẽr.
kl: çlap′pẽr.
l: lap′pẽr, ō-vẽr-lap′pẽr.
m: map′pẽr.
n: nap′pẽr.
r: en-wrap′pẽr, rap′pẽr,
  un-wrap′pẽr, rap′pẽr.
s: sap′pẽr.
skr(sçr): sçrap′pẽr.
sl: slap′pẽr.

(Choose only one word out of each group)

sn: red snap'pēr, snap'pēr,
  snip'pēr-snap-pēr,
  whip'pēr-snap-pēr.
str: strap'pēr, un'dẽr-strap-pēr,
  un-strap'pēr.
t: tap'pēr, wīre tap'pēr.
tr: en-trap'pēr, trap'pēr.
y: yap'pēr.
Plus slap her, *or* err, etc.

Ā'PŨRZ

p: pā'pērₛ,
  wₐlk'ing pā'pērₛ (wₐk').
Plus āp'ũr+s.

AP'US

p: pap'pus.
tr: trap'pous.
Plus slap us, etc.

AP'WING

l: lap'wing.
Plus flap wing, etc.

Ā'RÅ

l: cọr-dil-le'rå (-lyā').
m: dul-cå-mā'rå, Mā'råh.
s: Sā'rå, Sā'råh.
Plus play Ra, etc.

ÃR'Å

Vowel: tǐ-ãr'å.
h: Så-hãr'å.
Plus where a, etc.

A'RÅ

b: Ba'rå.
kl: Cla'rå, San'tå Cla'rå.

Ä'RÅ

Vowel: tǐ-är'å.
h: Så-hä'rå.
k(c): cär-å-cär'å, cas-cär'å.
m: Ge-mä'rå.
r: Fer-rä'rå.
t: sōl-fä-tär'å.
Plus far a, etc.
Cf. or'å.

Ä'RĀ

m: moi-ré' (mwä-).
p: Poi-ret' (pwä-rā').
sw: soi-rée' (swä-).
Plus star A, etc.
Plus ma ray, etc.

AR'AB

Vowel: Ar'ab.
sk(sc): scar'ab.

AR'ĂK

Vowel: ar'răck.
b: bar'răck.
k(c): car'răck.

Ã'RĂNS

b: å-beãr'ănce, fōr-beãr'ănce.
Cf. ap-pãr'ence.
Cf. ãr'ent+s.

Ã'RĂNT

b: fōr-beãr'ănt.
kl: dē-clãr'ănt.
Cf. ãr'ent.
Plus scare ant *or* aunt, etc.

AR'ANT

Vowel: ar'rant.

(Choose only one word out of each group)

ÄR′ĂNT

w: wär′rănt.
Cf. or′ent.
Cf. for rent, etc.
Plus far ant *or* aunt, etc.

AR′ĂS

Vowel: ar′răs.
b: dē-bar′răss,
dis-em-bar′răss, em-bar′răss.
h: har′ăss.

ÃR′BEL

h: hãre′bell.
pr: prãyer′bell.
Plus care bell *or* Belle, etc.

ÄR′BEL

b: bär′bel.
k(ç): cär bell.
t: Tär′bell.
Plus scar bell *or* Belle, etc.

ÄR′BI

d: Där′by, Der′by (där′).
Plus scar bee *or* be, etc.
Plus garb he, etc.

ÄR′BIJ

g: gär′băġe.
Cf. barb age, etc.

ÄR′BL

b: bär′bel.
g: gär′bel, gär′ble.
m: em-mär′ble, mär′ble.
Cf. är′bel.
Plus garb′ll, etc.
Cf. far bull, etc.

ÄR′BLŬR

g: gär′blĕr.
m: mär′blĕr.

ÄR′BLING

g: gär′bling.
m: mär′bling.

ÄR′BOIL

p: pär′boil.
Plus gar boil, etc.
Plus barb oil, etc.

ÄR′BŎN

k(ç): çär′bŏn.
sh: çhär′bŏn.
Plus garb on, etc.

ÄR′BŌRD

k(ç): çär′bōard.
l: lär′bōard.
st: stär′bōard.
Plus jar board, etc.
Cf. garb hoard, etc.

ÄR′BŬR

Vowel: är′bŏr.
b: bär′bĕr, Bär′bour.
h: en-här′bŏr, här′bŏr,
un-här′bŏr.
Cf. garb, or etc.
Plus garb her *or* err, etc.

ÄR′CHEST

Vowel: är′chest*, en-är′chest*.
m: mär′chest*.
p: pär′chest*.
st: stär′chest*.
Plus scar chest, etc.

(Choose only one word out of each group)

ÄR'CHETH

Vowel: är'cheth*, en-är'cheth*.
m: mär'cheth*.
p: pär'cheth*.
st: stär'cheth*.

ÄR'CHEZ

Vowel: är'cheṣ, ō-vēr-är'cheṣ.
l: lär'cheṣ.
m: çoun"tẽr-mär'cheṣ,
mär'cheṣ, out-mär'cheṣ.
p: pär'cheṣ.
st: stär'cheṣ.
Cf. starch is, etc.

ÄR'CHI

Vowel: Är'chie, är'chy.
l: lär'chy.
st: stär'chy.
Plus march, he, etc.

ÄR'CHING

Vowel: är'ching, ō-vēr-är'ching.
m: çoun"tẽr-mär'ching,
mär'ching, out-mär'ching,
ō-vēr-mär'ching.
p: pär'ching.
st: stär'ching.

ÄRCH'MENT

Vowel: ärch'ment.
p: em-pärch'ment, pärch'ment.
Plus march meant, etc.

ÄRCH'NES

Vowel: ärch'ness.

ÄR'CHŬR

Vowel: är'chẽr.
l: Lär'chẽr.

m: mär'chẽr.
p: pärch'ẽr, pop'çọrn pärch'ẽr.
st: stärch'ẽr.
Plus starch her or err, etc.

ÄRCH'WĀY

Vowel: ärch'wāy.
Plus march way, etc.

ÄR'DĂNT

g: gär'dănt, rē-gär'dănt.
Cf. är'dent.
Plus hard aunt or ant, etc.

ÄRD'ÄRM

y: yärd'ärm.
Plus guard arm, etc.

ÄR'DED

b: bom-bär'ded.
g: dis-rē-gär'ded, guär'ded,
rē-gär'ded, un-guär'ded,
un-rē-gär'ded.
k(ç): çär'ded, dis-çär'ded.
l: lär'ded.
sh: shär'ded.
t: rē-tär'ded, un-rē-tär'ded.
Plus hard, Ed, etc.
Plus tsar dead, etc.

ÄR'DEL

f: fär'del.
Plus hard L or el, etc.
Plus scar, Dell, etc.

ÄR'DEN, ÄR'DŎN

b: bom-bär'dŏn.
g: beer gär'den, gär'den,
rock gär'den, sēa gär'den.

347　ūse, bṳll, brúte, tŭrn, up; crȳ, myth; çat, maçhine, aċe,
church, çhord; ġem, aṅger, (Fr.) boṅ, aş; THis, thin; aẓure

ÄR′DEND
ÄRD′LES

(Choose only one word out of each group)

h: çāse′här-den, en-här′den,
här′den.
p: pär′dŏn.
Plus guard on, etc.
Plus mar den, etc.
Plus scar, Don, etc.

ÄR′DEND, ÄR′DŎND

h: çāse′här-dened, här′dened,
weaTH′ẽr=här′dened (weTH′).
p: pär′dŏned, un-pär′dŏned.
Plus czar donned, etc.

ÄR′DENT

Vowel: är′dent.
Cf. är′dănt.
Plus tsar dent, etc.

ÄR′DEST

b: bom-bär′dest*.
g: dis-rē-gär′dest*, guär′dest*,
rē-gär′dest*.
h: här′dest.
k(ç): dis-çär′dest*,
false′=çär′dest*.
l: lär′dest*.
t: rē-tär′dest*.

ÄR′DETH

b: bom-bär′deth*.
g: dis-rē-gär′deth*, guär′deth*,
rē-gär′deth*.
k(ç): dis-çär′deth*,
false′=çär′deth*.
l: lär′deth*.
t: rē-tär′deth*.
Plus mar death, etc.

ÄRD′FṲL

g: dis-rē-gärd′fṳl, guärd′fṳl,
rē-gärd′fṳl.
Plus nard full, etc.

ÄR′DI

h: fọọl′här-dy, här′dy.
t: tär′dy.
Plus scarred, he, etc.
Plus mar Dee or D, etc.

ÄR′DIK

Vowel: be-zō-är′diç.
b: bär′diç, Lom-bär′diç.
k(ç): an-à-çär′diç, per-i-çär′diç.
Plus bar Dick, etc.

ÄR′DÏN

n: när′dïne.
s: sär′dïne.
Plus czar dean, etc.

ÄR′DING

b: bom-bär′ding.
g: dis-rē-gär′ding, guär′ding,
rē-gär′ding, un-guär′ding.
h: Här′ding.
k(ç): çär′ding, dis-çär′ding,
false′=çär′ding, pla-çär′ding,
wool çär′ding.
l: lär′ding.
t: rē-tär′ding.

ÄR′DL

Vowel: Mç-Är′dle.
b: Bär′dle.
Plus card′ll, etc.
Cf. scar dull, etc.

ÄRD′LES

g: guärd′less, rē-guärd′less.
k(ç): çärd′less.
Plus hard, Les or less, etc.

ÄRD'LI
AR'ELD
fāte, fär, fȧst, fạll, finăl, cãre, at; mēte, prẹy, hẽr, met; pīne,
marĭne, bĭrd, pin; nōte, mŏve, fọr, atŏm, not; mọọn, book;
348

(Choose only one word out of each group)

ÄRD'LI

h: härd'ly.
Plus bard, Lee *or* lea, etc.

ÄRD'MENT

b: bom-bärd'ment.
t: rē-tärd'ment.
Plus card meant, etc.

ÄRD'NES

h: härd'ness.

ÄRD'NING

g: gär'dening.
h: här'dening.
p: pär'doning.

ÄRD'NŪR

g: gär'denēr.
h: här'denēr.
p: pärd'nēr, pär'donēr.

ÄR'DŌ

b: bom-bär'dō, Lom-bär'dō.
k(ͽ): bō-ͽär'dō.
n: Lē-ō-när'dō.
Plus card owe *or* O, etc.
Plus scar dough *or* doe, etc.

ÄR'DŎM

Vowel: heir'dŏm (är').
st: back-stäir'dŏm.
Plus where dumb, etc.

ÄRD'SHIP

g: guärd'ship.
h: härd'ship.
Plus starred ship, etc.

ÄRDZ'MĂN

g: guärdṣ'măn.
Plus retards man, etc.

ÄR'DŪR

Vowel: är'dŏr.
b: bom-bär'dēr.
g: dis-rē-gär'dēr, guär'dēr,
rē-gär'dēr.
h: här'dēr.
k(ͽ): ͽär'dēr, dis-ͽär'dēr,
fạlse'=ͽär'dēr, wool ͽär'dēr.
l: lär'dēr.
t: rē-tär'dēr.
Plus marred her *or* err, etc.

ÄR'Ē

k: shi-kär'ee.
Cf. är'i.
Plus far, he, etc.

AR'EL

b: bar'rel, beer bar'rel,
pōrk bar'rel.
f: Far'rell.
h: Har'rell.
k(ͽ): ͽar'ŏl, Ͽar'rel, Ͽar'rŏll.
p: ap-par'el, dis-ap-par'el,
par'rel.

AR'ELD

b: dŏu'ble=bar'relled,
siñ'gle=bar'relled.
k(ͽ): ͽar'ŏlled.
p: ap-par'relled,
dis-ap-par'relled.

(Choose only one word out of each group)

ĀR´EM

h: hãr´em.
Cf. ãr´um.
Plus scare 'em, etc.

ÄR´EN

k: Kär´en.
l: Mc̲-Lär´en (mak-).
Cf. far in, etc.

ĀR´ENS

kl: C̲lãr´ence.
p: ap-pãr´ence, trans-pãr´ence.
Cf. ãr´ăns.
Cf. bear hence, etc.

ĀR´ENT

l: C̲e-lãr´ent.
p: ap-pãr´ent, pãr´ent, trans-pãr´ent.
Cf. dē-c̲lãr´ănt.

ĀR´ES

Vowel: heir´ess (ãr´).

ĀR´EST

Vowel: ãir´est*.
b: bãr´est, beãr´est*, for-beãr´est*.
d: dãr´est*, out-dãr´est*.
f: fãir´est, fãr´est*, un-fãir´est.
fl: flãr´est*.
gl: glãr´est*.
k(c̲): c̲ãr´est*.
kl: dē-c̲lãr´est*.
p: c̲om-pãr´est*, des-pãir´est*, im-pãir´est*, pãir´est*, pãr´est*, prē-pãr´est*, rē-pãir´est*.
r: rãr´est.
sh: shãr´est*.

skw: squãr´est.
sn: en-snãr´est*, snãr´est*.
sp: spãr´est.
st: stãr´est*.
sw: for-sweãr´est*, sweãr´est*
t: teãr´est*.
w: weãr´est*.
Cf. there rest, etc.

ÄR´EST

b: bär´rest*, dē-bär´rest*, un-bär´rest*.
j: jär´rest*.
m: mär´rest*.
sk(sc̲): sc̲är´rest*.
sp: spär´rest*.
st: stär´rest*.
t: tär´rest*.
Cf. far rest, etc.

AR´ET

g: gar´ret, Gar´rett.
k(c̲): c̲ar´ăt, c̲ar´rŏt.
kl: c̲lar´et.
p: par´rŏt.

ĀR´ETH

Vowel: ãir´eth*.
b: bãr´eth*, beãr´eth*, for-beãr´eth*.
d: dãr´eth*, out-dãr´eth*.
f: fãr´eth*.
fl: flãr´eth*.
gl: glãr´eth*.
k(c̲): c̲ãr´eth*.
kl: dē-c̲lãr´eth*.
p: c̲om-pãr´eth*, dēs-pãir´eth*, im-pãir´eth*, pãir´eth*, pãr´eth*, prē-pãr´eth*, rē-pãir´eth*.

ÄR′ETH
ÄR′GŪ

fāte, fär, fàst, fạll, finăl, cãre, at; mēte, prẹy, hẽr, met; pīne, marïne, bïrd, pin; nōte, mŏve, fọr, atŏm, not; mọọn, book;

350

(Choose only one word out of each group)

sh: shãr′eth*.
skw: squãr′eth*.
sn: en-snãr′eth*, snãr′eth*.
sp: spãr′eth*.
st: stãr′eth*.
sw: fọr-sweãr′eth*, sweãr′eth*.
t: teãr′eth*.
w: weãr′eth*.

ÄR′ETH

b: bär′reth*, dē-bär′reth*, un-bär′reth*.
j: jär′reth*.
m: mär′reth*.
sk(sc̣): sc̣är′reth*.
sp: spär′reth*.
st: stär′reth*.
t: tär′reth*.

ÃR′ĒZ

Vowel: Buẹ′nōs Ãy′rẹ̄s.
n: Bē-när′ẹ̄s.
Cf. ãr′i+s.
Plus there ease *or* E's, etc.

ÃR′FĀST

b: bāre′fāced″.
f: fãir′=fāced″.
Plus square faced, etc.

ÄR′FISH

g: gär′fish.
st: stär′fish.
Plus tar fish, etc.

ÃR′FŌR

hw: where′fōre.
TH: THere′fōre.
Plus swear four *or* fore, etc.

ÄR′FỤL

k(c̣): c̣āre′fụl, un-c̣āre′fụl.
pr: prāyer′fụl.
Plus mare full, etc.

ÄR′GĂN

d: Där′găn.
g: Gär′găn.

ÄR′GET

t: tär′get.
Plus spar get, etc.

ÄR′GIN

b: bär′gain.

ÄR′GL

b: är′gle=bär′gle.
g: gär′gle.

ÄR′GŌ

Vowel: Är′gō, är′gōt (′gō).
b: em-bär′gō.
d: Där′gō.
f: Fär′gō, Wellṣ Fär′gō.
k(c̣): c̣är′gō, sū-pẽr-c̣är′gō.
l: lär′gō.
m: Mär′gōt (′gō).
sp: Spär′gō.
t: bō-tär′gō.
Plus scar go, etc.

ÄR′GŎN

Vowel: är′gŏn.
j: jär′gŏn.
Plus scar gone, etc.

ÄR′GŪ

Vowel: är′gūe.

(Choose only one word out of each group)

ÃR'HWĬL

Vowel: ere'whīle (ãr').
Plus care, while, etc.

ÃR'I

Vowel: aç-ci-den'ti-ãr-y,
aç'tū-ãr"y, ãir'y,
ben-e-fic'i-ãr-y (-fish'),
es'tū-ãr-y, Feb'rū-ãr-y,
fi-dū'ci-ãr-y ('shi-),
in-cen'di-ãr-y, in-tēr-mēd'i-ãr-y,
Jan'ū-ãr-y, mor'tū-ãr-y,
ŏ-bit'ū-ãr-y, pē-çū'ni-ãr-y,
ques'tū-ãr-y, rē-ṣid'ū-ãr-y,
sanç'tū-ãr-y, stat'ū-ãr-y,
stī-pen'di-ãr-y, sub-sid'i-ãr-y,
sump'tū-ãr-y, tēr'ti-ãr-y ('shi-),
tū-mul'tū-ãr-y, vŏl-up'tū-ãr-y.
bl: blãr'y.
ch: chãr'y, un-chãr'y.
d: dãir'y, drom'ē-dãr-y,
heb-dom'a̱-dãr-y, leġ'en-dãr-y,
p̍re'ben-dãr-y, quän'dãr-y,
seç'ŏn-dãr-y.
f: fãir'y.
g: Gãr'y, va̱-gã'ry.
gl: glãir'y.
h: hãir'y.
k(ç): ap-o'thē-çãr-y, Çãr'ey,
Çãr'y.
kw: an'ti-quãr-y, rel'i-quãr-y.
l: ad'min-i"çū-lãr-y, an'cil-lãr-y,
cap'il-lãr-y, çon-stab'ū-lãr-y,
çor'ŏl-lãr-y, ē-pis'tō-lãr-y,
for'mū-lãr-y, max'il-lãr-y,
sçap'ū-lãr-y, tit'ū-lãr-y,
tū'mū-lãr-y, tūt'ē-lãr-y,
vō-çab'ū-lãr-y.

m: aç-çus'tō-mãr-y,
Ã've Mãr'y, çus'tō-mãr-y,
Mãr'y, rōṣe'mãr-y.
n: ab-lū'tio-nãr-y,
ad-di'tio-nãr-y, bī-cen'tē-nãr-y,
ça̱-nãr'y, ça̱u'tio-nãr-y,
cen'tē-nãr-y, çon-feç'tio-nãr-y,
çū'li-nãr-y, diç'tio-nãr-y,
dis'ci-pli-nãr-y, dis-çre'tio-nãr-y,
el-ee-mos'y-nãr-y,
el-ō-çū'tio-nãr-y,
ev-ō-lū'tio-nãr-y,
ex-trä-or'di-nãr-y,
funç'tio-nãr-y, gan'gli-ō-nãr-y,
im-aġ'i-nãr-y,
in-sūr-reç'tio-nãr-y,
lē'ġiŏ-nãr-y, lū'mi-nãr-y,
mēr'cē-nãr-y, mil'lē-nãr-y,
mis'sio-nãr-y, nãr'y,
or'di-nãr-y,
pas'sio-nãr-y (pash'),
pen'sio-nãr-y, pē-ti'tio-nãr-y,
prō-ces'sio-nãr-y,
prō-leg-om'ē-nãr-y,
prō-viṣ'io-nãr-y, pul'mō-nãr-y,
ques'tio-nãr-y, rē-aç'tio-nãr-y,
rē-vēr'ṣio-nãr-y ('zhun-),
re-vō-lū'tio-nãr-y,
sañ'gui-nãr-y ('gwi-),
sē-di'tio-nãr-y, sem'i-nãr-y,
stā'tio-nãr-y, sub'lū-nãr-y,
trä-di'tio-nãr-y, tū-i'tio-nãr-y,
val-ē-tū'di-nãr-y, vet'ēr-i-nãr-y,
vi-cis"si-tū'di-nãr-y,
viṣ'io-nãr-y (vizh'un-).
pr: prãi'rie.
r: çon-tem'pō-rãr-y,
hon'ō-rãr-y (on'), lit'ē-rãr-y,
sū-pēr-nū'mē-rãr-y,
tem'pō-rãr-y, Tip'pē-rãr-y,
vul'nē-rãr-y.

AR'I
AR'IK

fāte, fär, fàst, fạll, finǎl, cāre, at; mēte, prey, hẽr, met; pīne,
marïne, bîrd, pin; nōte, mŏve, fọr, atŏm, not; mọọn, book;

352

(Choose only one word out of each group)

s: ac̣-ces'sãr-y, ad'vẽr-sãr-y,
com'mis-sãr-y, jan'is-sãr-y,
nec'es-sãr-y, un-nec'es-sãr-y.
sk(sc̣): sc̣ãr'y.
sn: snãr'y.
st: stãr'y.
t: com'men-tãr-y,
con-trib'ū-tãr-y, dē-poṣ'i-tãr-y,
dī'e-tãr-y, dig'ni-tãr-y,
frag'men-tãr-y, hẽr-ed'i-tãr-y,
mil'i-tãr-y, mō'men-tãr-y,
mon'ē-tãr-y, plan'ē-tãr-y,
prō-prī'e-tãr-y, prō-tho'nō-tãr-y,
sal'ū-tãr-y, san'i-tãr-y,
sec̣'rē-tãr-y, se'den-tãr-y,
sol'i-tãr-y, trib'ū-tãr-y,
ūb-i'qui-tãr-y, vol'un-tãr-y.
v: sal'i-vãr-y, vãir'y, vãr'y.
w: c̣as'sō-wãr-y, un-wãr'y,
wãr'y.
Plus where he, etc.

AR'I

b: Bar'rie, Bar'ry, Dū Bar'ry.
h: har'ry.
k(c̣): C̣ar'rie, c̣ar'ry,
har'i-kar'i, mis-c̣ar'ry.
l: Lar'ry.
m: in-tẽr-mar'ry, mar'ry,
rē-mar'ry.
p: par'ry.
t: tar'ry.
v: c̣har-i-var'i.

ÄR'I

b: bär'ry.
ch: chär'ry.
n: C̣är-bō-när'ï.
s: är-à-c̣är'ï.
sk(sc̣): sc̣är'ry.
sp: spär'ry.

st: stär'ry.
t: tär'ry.
Cf. shi-kär'ee.
Plus far he, etc.

ÃR'ID

v: vãr'ied.
Cf. fair hid, etc.

AR'ID

Vowel: ar'id.
h: har'ried.
k(c̣): c̣ar'ried, mis-c̣ar'ried.
m: in-tẽr-mar'ried, rē-mar'ried,
un-mar'ried.
p: par'ried.
t: tar'ried.

ÃR'IF, AR'IF

h: hãir'if.
Plus scare, if, etc.
Plus far, if, etc.

AR'IF

h: har'if.
t: tar'iff.

AR'IJ

k(c̣): c̣ar'riǎge, mis-c̣ar'riǎge,
rãil'wāy c̣ar'riǎge,
wa'tẽr c̣ar'riǎge.
m: in-tẽr-mar'riǎge, mar'riǎge,
rē-mar'riǎge.
p: dis-par'ǎge.

AR'IK

Vowel: Bal-ē-ar'ic̣, stē-ar'ic̣.
b: bär-bar'ic̣, bar'ic̣,
cin-nà-bar'ic̣, īs-ō-bar'ic̣.
d: Pin-dar'ic̣.

(Choose only one word out of each group)

g: a̯-gar′i̯c, Bul-gar′i̯c, Gar′rick, Mē-gar′i̯c.
h: Am-har′i̯c.
k(c̯): sac̯-c̯har′i̯c.
l: pō-lar′i̯c.
m: pim-ar′i̯c.
t: tär-tar′i̯c.
v: Var′ick.

ÄR′IK

h: Äm-här′i̯c.
Cf. far rick, etc.

ÃR′ING

Vowel: ãir′ing, heir′ing (ãr′).
b: bãr′ing, beãr′ing, chīld′beãr-ing, fo̯r-beãr′ing, ō-vēr-beãr′ing, tāle′beãr-ing, un-beãr′ing, un-dēr-beãr′ing, up′beãr-ing.
ch: chãir′ing, chãr′ing.
d: dãr′ing, out-dãr′ing.
f: fãir′ing, fãr′ing, sēa′fãr-ing, wāy′fãr-ing.
fl: flãr′ing.
gl: glãr′ing.
k(c̯): c̯ãr′ing, un-c̯ãr′ing.
kl: dē-clãr′ing.
p: cheeṣe′pãr-ing, c̯om-pãr′ing, im-pãir′ing, pãir′ing, pãr′ing, prē-pãr′ing, rē-pãir′ing.
r: "rãr′ing".
sh: shãr′ing.
sk(sc̯): sc̯ãr′ing.
skw: squãr′ing.
sn: en-snãr′ing, snãr′ing.
sp: dē-spãir′ing, spãr′ing, un-spãr′ing.
st: out-stãr′ing, stãr′ing, up′stãr-ing.

sw: fo̯r-sweãr′ing, out-sweãr′ing, sweãr′ing.
t: teãr′ing, up′teãr-ing.
w: out-weãr′ing, weãr′ing.
Cf. wear ring, etc.

ÄR′ING

b: bär′ring, dē-bär′ring, dis-bär′ring, un-bär′ring.
ch: chär′ring.
j: jär′ring.
m: mär′ring.
sk(sc̯): sc̯är′ring.
sp: spär′ring.
st: stär′ring.
t: tär′ring.
Cf. scar ring, etc.

AR′INGKS

f: phar′yñx.
l: lar′yñx.

AR′IS

f: Far′ris.
h: Har′ris.
l: pha̯-lar′is, pō-lar′is.
p: Par′is.
Cf. ar′ăs.

ÃR′ISH

b: beãr′ish.
f: fãir′ish.
g: gãir′ish, gãr′ish.
m: mãr′ish.
n: de-bōn-ãir′ish.
skw: squãr′ish.
t: tãr′ish.

AR′ISH

m: mar′ish.
p: par′ish.

(Choose only one word out of each group)

ÃR′IZM

t: prō-lē-tãir′iṣm, Vōl-tãir′iṣm.

ÄR′JENT

Vowel: är′ġent.
s: ser′ġeant (sär′jent).
Plus star gent, etc.

ÄR′JEST

ch: chär′ġest*, dis-chär′ġest*,
ō-vēr-chär′ġest*.
l: en-lär′ġest*, lär′ġest.
Plus far jest, etc.

ÄR′JET

g: gär′ġet.
p: pär′ġet.
Plus scar jet, etc.

ÄR′JETH

ch: chär′ġeth*, dis-chär′ġeth*,
ō-vēr-chär′ġeth*.
l: en-lär′ġeth*.

ÄR′JEZ

b: bär′ġeṣ.
ch: chär′ġeṣ, dis-chär′ġeṣ,
ō-vēr-chär′ġeṣ.
l: en-lär′ġeṣ.
m: mär′ġeṣ.
t: tär′ġeṣ.

ÄR′JIK

th: lē-thär′ġịc.

ÄR′JIN

m: mär′ġin.
Plus bar gin, etc.

ÄR′JING

b: bär′ġing.
ch: chär′ġing, dis-chär′ġing,
ō-vēr-chär′ġing.
l: en-lär′ġing.

ÄRJ′LI

l: lärġe′ly.
Plus barge, Lee *or* lea, etc.

ÄRJ′MENT

l: en-lärġe′ment.

ÄR′JŨR

b: bär′ġẽr.
ch: chär′ġẽr, dis-chär′ġẽr,
ō-vēr-chär′ġẽr, sũr-chär′ġẽr,
un″dēr-chär′ġẽr.
l: en-lär′ġẽr, lär′ġẽr.
sp: spär′ġẽr.
Plus charge her *or* eɪr, etc.

ÄR′KĂL

Vowel: mā-tri-är′çhăl,
pā-tri-är′çhăl.
g: ol-i-gär′çhăl.
n: a-när′çhăl, mō-när′çhăl.
r: hī-ēr-är′çhăl, squïre-är′çhăl.
Plus far, Cal, etc.
Plus ark, Al, etc.

ÄR′KAZM

s: sär′çaṣm.
Cf. park has ′em, etc.
Plus far chasm, etc.

ÄR′KEN

d: bē-där′ken, där′ken,
en-där′ken.

(Choose only one word out of each group)

h: heär′ken.
Plus far ken, etc.

ÄR′KEST

b: bär′kest*, em-bär′kest*.
d: där′kest.
m: mär′kest*, rē-mär′kest*.
st: stär′kest.

ÄR′KET

m: mär′ket.
Cf. spark it, etc.
Plus lark et, etc.

ÄR′KETH

b: bär′keth*, em-bär′keth*.
m: mär′keth*, rē-mär′keth*.

ÄR′KI

Vowel: mä′tri-är-çhy,
pä′tri-är-çhy.
b: bär′ky.
d: där′ky.
g: ol′i-gär-çhy.
l: lär′ky.
r: het′ër-är-çhy, hī′ër-är-çhy.
t: hep-tär′çhy.
Plus spark, he, etc.
Plus far key, etc.

ÄR′KIK

Vowel: mä-tri-är′çhiç,
pä-tri-är′çhiç.
g: ol-i-gär′çhiç.
n: a-när′çhiç, an″ti-a-när′çhiç,
mō-när′çhiç.
r: hī-ër-är′çhiç.
t: çlī-má-tär′çhiç, hep-tär′çhiç.
Plus far kick, etc.

ÄR′KIN

l: Lär′kin.
Plus far kin, etc.
Plus dark inn *or* in, etc.

ÄR′KING

b: bär′king, dis-em-bär′king,
em-bär′king.
h: här′king.
k(ç): çär′king.
l: lär′king, skȳ′lär-king.
m: mär′king, rē-mär′king.
p: pär′king.
Plus far king, etc.

ÄR′KISH

d: där′kish.
l: lär′kish.
sp: spär′kish.

ÄR′KIST

g: ol′i-gär-çhist.
r: hī′ër-är-çhist.
t: hep-tär′çhist.

ÄR′KĪVZ

Vowel: är′chīveş.
Cf. dark hives, etc.
Plus mark Ives, etc.

ÄR′KL

d: där′kle.
sp: spär′kle.
Plus mark′ll, etc.
Cf. far cull, etc.

ÄRK′LET

p: pärk′let.
sp: spärk′let.
Plus mark, let *or* Lett, etc.

(Choose only one word out of each group)

ÄRK′LI

d: därk′ly.
kl: çlärk′ly, çlerk′ly (klärk′).
st: stärk′ly.
Plus spark, Lee *or* lea, etc.

ÄRK′LING

d: därk′ling.
sp: spärk′ling.

ÄRK′NES

d: därk′ness.

ÄRK′NŪR

dɕ därk′enẽr.
h: heärk′enẽr.

ÄR′KŌL

ch: chär′çōal.
Cf. dark hole, etc.
Plus far coal *or* Cole, etc.

ÄRK′SŎM

d: därk′sŏme.
Plus spark some *or* sum, etc.
Cf. sparks hum, etc.

ÄRK′SPŪR

l: lärk′spūr.
Plus spark spur, etc.
Plus marks purr *or* per, etc.

ÄRK′TIK

Vowel: Ärç′tiç.
t: Ant-ärç′tiç.
Plus mark tick, etc.

ÄR′KŪR

b: bär′kẽr, em-bär′kẽr.
d: där′kẽr.
h: här′kẽr.
l: lär′kẽr.
m: mär′çŏr, mär′kẽr.
p: pär′kẽr.
sh: shär′kẽr.
sp: spär′kẽr.
st: stär′kẽr.
Plus mark her *or* err, etc.

ÄRK′WIS

m: mär′quis.
Plus dark wis*, etc.

ÄR′LĂND

f: Fär′lănd, Mç-Fär′lănd.
g: en-gär′lănd, gär′lănd.
p: Mç-Pär′lănd.
Plus scar land, etc.
Plus snarl and, etc.

ÄR′LES

Vowel: ãir′less, heir′less (ãr′).
h: hãir′less.
k(ç): çãre′less.
p: pãir′less.
pr: prãyer′less.
sn: snãre′less.
t: tãre′less.
Plus wear less, etc.

ÄR′LES

g: çi-gär′less, gär′less.
k(ç): çär′less.
sk(sç): sçär′less.
st: stär′less.
t: çȧ-tärrh′less.

(Choose only one word out of each group)

z: czär'less (zär'), etc.
Plus far less, etc.

ÄR'LET

k(ç): çär'let.
sk(sç): sçär'let.
st: stär'let.
v: vär'let.
Cf. här'lŏt.
Plus jar let *or* Lett, etc.

ÃR'LI

b: bãre'ly.
f: fãir'ly, un-fãir'ly.
r: rãre'ly.
y: yãre'ly*.
Plus swear, Lee *or* lea, etc.

ÄR'LI

Vowel: Är'leigh.
b: bär'ley.
ch: Chär'ley, Chär'lie.
f: Fär'ley.
h: Här'ley.
k(ç): Mç-Çär'ley.
m: mär'li.
n: gnär'ly (när').
p: pär'ley.
Plus scar, Lee *or* lea, etc.
Plus snarl, he, etc.

ÄR'LĪK

st: stär'līke.
z: czär'līke (zär'), etc.

ÄR'LIK

g: gär'liç, pil-gär'lick.
s: sär'lyk.
Plus scar lick, etc.

ÃR'LĪN

Vowel: âir'līne.
h: hãir'līne.
Plus swear line, etc.

ÃR'LĪND

h: hãir'⸗līned".
k(ç): çãre'⸗līned".
Plus fare lined, etc.

ÄR'LING

d: där'ling.
h: Här'ling.
sn: snär'ling.
sp: spär'ling.
st: stär'ling.

ÄR'LĪT

st: stär'līght.
Plus far light, etc.

ÄR'LIT

f: fär'lit.
st: stär'lit.
Plus scar lit, etc.
Plus snarl it, etc.

ÄR'LOK

ch: chär'lock.
h: här'lock.
Cf. Här'leçh.
Plus mar lock, etc.

ÄR'LŎT

h: här'lŏt.
sh: Çhär'lŏtte.
Plus mar lot, etc.
Cf. är'let.

(Choose only one word out of each group)

ĂR'LŪM

Vowel: heir'lọọm (ār').
Plus snare loom, etc.

ĂR'LŨR

n: gnär'lẽr (när').
p: pär'lŏr.
sn: snär'lẽr.
Plus snarl her *or* err, etc.

ĂR'LUS

p: pär'lous.
Plus snarl us, etc.

ĂR'MĀD

b: bär'māid.
Plus far maid *or* made, etc.

ĂR'MĂN

ch: chāir'măn.
Plus swear, man, etc.

ĂR'MEN

k(c): çär'men.
Plus bar men, etc.

ĂR'MENT

b: dē-bär'ment, dis-bär'ment.
g: gär'ment.
s: sär'ment.
Plus scar meant, etc.

ĂR'MEST

Vowel: är'mest*, dis-är'mest*.
ch: chär'mest*.
f: fär'mest*.
h: här'mest*.
l: à-lär'mest*.
Plus gar messed, etc.

ĂR'MET

Vowel: är'met.
Plus car met, etc.
Cf. harm it, etc.

ĂR'METH

Vowel: är'meth*, dis-är'meth*.
ch: chär'meth*.
f: fär'meth*.
h: här'meth*.
l: à-lär'meth*.

ĂRM'FỤL

Vowel: ärm'fụl.
ch: chärm'fụl.
h: härm'fụl, un-härm'fụl.
Plus charm full, etc.

ĂR'MI

Vowel: är'my.
b: bär'my.
Plus scar me, etc.
Plus harm, he, etc.

ĂR'MIK

f: al-ex"i-phär'miç,
   lex-i-phär'miç.
t: ptär'miç (tär').
Plus far Mick, etc.

ĂR'MIN

h: här'mine.
k(c): çär'mine, en-çär'mine.
Plus harm in *or* inn, etc.
Plus scar, Min, etc.

ĂR'MING

Vowel: är'ming, dis-är'ming,
fōre-är'ming, un-är'ming.

(Choose only one word out of each group)

ch: chärm′ing, un-chär′ming.
f: bā′by fär′ming,
dāi′ry fär′ming,
dĭrt fär′ming, fär′ming.
h: här′ming, un-här′ming.
l: à-lär′ming, un-à-lär′ming.
Plus far Ming, etc.

ÄRM′LES

Vowel: ärm′less.
ch: chärm′less.
h: härm′less.
Plus alarm less *or* Les, etc.

ÄRM′LET

Vowel: ärm′let.
ch: chärm′let.
Plus farm, let *or* Lett, etc.

ÄR′MOT

k(ç): çär′mot.
m: mär′mot.

ÄR′MŨR

Vowel: är′mŏr, chāin är′mŏr,
plāte är′mŏr.
ch: chär′mēr, sēr′pent chär′mēr,
snāke chär′mēr.
f: bā′by fär′mēr,
dāi′ry fär′mēr,
dĭrt fär′mēr, fär′mēr.
h: här′mēr.
l: à-lär′mēr.
Plus harm her, etc.
Plus far myrrh, etc.

ÄR′NĂL

ch: chär′nel, un-chär′nel.
k(ç): çär′năl, çär′nel*.
Plus barn, Al, etc.

ÄR′NĂRD

b: Bär′nărd.
Cf. gär′nĕred.
Plus mär′nărd, etc.

ÄR′NĀT

k(ç): çär′nāte*, in-çär′nāte.
Plus far, Nate, etc.
Plus barn ate *or* eight, etc.

ÃR′NES

b: bãre′ness,
thread′bãre-ness (thred′).
f: fãir′ness, un-fãir′ness.
hw: where′ness.
n: de-bō-nãir′ness.
r: rãre′ness.
skw: squãre′ness.
sp: spãre′ness.

ÄR′NES

f: fär′ness.
h: här′ness.

ÄRN′HĂM

f: Färn′hăm.
Cf. Fär′num, Bär′num.
Plus barn ham, etc.

ÄR′NI

b̄l: blär′ney.
k(ç): çär′ney.
l: Kil-lär′ney.
Plus far knee, etc.
Plus yarn, he, etc.

ÄR′NIJ

k(ç): çär′năġe.
Cf. barn age, etc.

(Choose only one word out of each group)

ÄR'NING

d: där'ning.
y: yär'ning.

ÄR'NISH

g: gär'nish.
t: tär'nish.
v: vär'nish.

ÄR'NISHT

g: gär'nished, un-gär'nished.
t: tär'nished, un-tär'nished.
v: un-vär'nished, vär'nished.

ÄR'NŎLD

Vowel: Är'nŏld.
Plus darn old, etc.

ÄRN'LI

d: Därn'ley.
Plus barn, Lee or lea, etc.

ÄR'NŨR

d: där'nẽr.
g: gär'nẽr.
y: yär'nẽr.
Plus darn her or err, etc.

Ā'RŌ

br: som-bre'rō.
f: fā'rō, phā'raōh.
k: Kā'rō.
l: bō-le'rō.
n: Rï'ō de Jà-nei'rō.
t: tā'rō.
Plus play row or roe, etc.

ÃR'Ō

br: som-brer'ō (-brär').
f: fãr'ō.

k: và-quer'ō (-kär').
l: bō-ler'ō (-lär'),
    çä-bäl-ler'ō (-lär').
n: llä-ner'ō (lyä-när').
Plus scare owe or O, etc.

AR'Ō

Vowel: ar'rōw.
b: bar'rōw.
f: far'rōw.
h: har'rōw.
m: mar'rōw.
n: nar'rōw.
sp: spar'rōw.
y: yar'rōw.

ÄR'Ō

kl: çlär'ō.
n: Çär-bōn-är'ō.
t: tär'ō.
Plus scar owe or O, etc.
Plus shah row or roe, etc.

AR'ŎLD

h: Har'ŏld.
k(ç): çar'ŏlled.

ÃR'ŎN

Vowel: Ãa'rŏn.
ch: Chã'rŏn.
sh: Shã'rŏn.
Cf. where'on.
Cf. square on or an, etc.

AR'ŎN

b: bar'ŏn, bar'ren.
k(ç): Mc-Çar'ren.

ÄR'PEST

h: här'pest*.
k(ç): çär'pest*.

(Choose only one word out of each group)

sh: shär´pest.
Plus mar pest, etc.

ÄR´PET

k(c̲): c̲är´pet.
Cf. sharp it, etc.
Plus scar pet, etc.

ÄR´PETH

h: här´peth*.
k(c̲): c̲är´peth*.

ÄR´PI

h: här´py.
k(c̲): c̲är´py.
Plus sharp, he, etc.

ÄR´PING

h: här´ping.
k(c̲): c̲är´ping.
sh: shär´ping.
Plus czar ping, etc.

ÄR´PIST

h: här´pist.

ÄRP´NES

sh: shärp´ness.

ÄR´PŪR

h: här´pēr.
k(c̲): c̲är´pēr.
sh: shär´pēr.
Plus sharp her or err, etc.
Plus far purr or per, etc.

ÄR´SĂL

t: met-á-tär´săl, tär´săl.
v: vär´săl.
Plus car, Sal, etc.

ÄR´SEL

p: pär´cel.
s: sär´cel*.
Plus scar sell, etc.

ÄR´SEZ

f: fär´ces̱.
p: pär´ses̱.
s: sär´ses̱.
Plus Carr says, etc.

ÄR´SHĂL

m: ēarl mär´shăl,
fiēld mär´shăl, im-mär´tiăl,
mär´shăl, Mär´shăll,
un-mär´tiăl.
p: im-pär´tiăl, pär´tiăl.
Plus scar shall, etc.

ÃRS´LI

sk(sc̲): sc̲ãrce´ly.

ÃRS´LI

p: pärs´ley.
Plus farce, Lee, etc.

ÃRS´NES

sk(sc̲): sc̲ãrce´ness.

ÄR´SŎN

Vowel: är´sŏn.
k(c̲): C̲är´sŏn.
l: Lär´sen, Lär´sŏn.
p: pär´sŏn.
Plus mar son or sun, etc.

ÄR´SŪR

p: pär´sēr.
sp: spär´sēr.
Plus far, sir, etc.
Plus farce her or err, etc.

(Choose only one word out of each group)

ÄR'TĂN

sp: Spär'tăn.
t: tär'tăn.
Cf. är'ten, är'tŏn.
Plus scar tan, etc.
Plus start an *or* Ann, etc.

ÄR'TED

Vowel: är'ted.
ch: chär'ted, un-chär'ted.
d: där'ted.
h: brōk"en-heär'ted,
chick'en-heär"ted,
cōld'heär"ted,
dŏu'ble=heär"ted,
down'heär"ted,
fāint'heär"ted,
fạlse'heär"ted,
flint'heär"ted, frank'heär"ted,
free'heär"ted, fụll'heär"ted,
ġen'tle=heär"ted, greāt'heär"ted,
hälf'heär"ted (häf'),
härd'heär"ted, hãre'heär"ted,
heär'ted, hen'heär"ted,
hīgh'heär"ted (hī'),
ī'rŏn-heär"ted ('ẽrn-),
kīnd'heär"ted, lärġe'heär"ted,
lead'en-heär"ted (led'),
līght'heär"ted (līt'),
lĭ'ŏn-heär"ted,
mär'ble-heär"ted,
ō'pen-heär"ted, pāle'heär"ted,
piġ'eŏn-heär"ted,
proud'heär"ted,
pub'lic-heär"ted,
rīght'heär"ted (rīt'),
sad'heär"ted, shal'lōw-heär"ted,
sim'ple-heär"ted,
siñ'gle-heär"ted, sọft'heär"ted,
stō'ny-heär"ted, stout'heär"ted,
ten'dẽr-heär"ted,
trāi'tŏr-heär"ted,
trúe'heär"ted, un-heär"ted,
wạrm'heär"ted, wēak'heär"ted,
wīse'heär"ted.
k(c): cär'ted.
p: dē-pär'ted, im-pär'ted,
pär'ted, trī-pär'ted,
un-im-pär'ted.
sm: smär'ted.
st: stär'ted, up-stär'ted.
Plus car, Ted, etc.
Plus start, Ed, etc.

ÄR'TEN, ÄR'TŎN

b: bär'tŏn.
g: kin'dẽr-gär-ten.
h: dis-heär'ten, en-heär'ten,
heär'ten.
k(c): cär'tŏn.
m: mär'ten.
sm: smär'ten.
sp: Spär'tăn.
t: tär'tăn.
Cf. scar ten, etc.
Plus mar ton *or* tun, etc.

ÄR'TEST

d: där'test*.
k(c): cär'test*.
p: dē-pär'test*, im-pär'test*,
pär'test*.
sm: smär'test.
st: stär'test*, up-stär'test*.
Plus far test, etc.

ÄR'TETH

d: där'teth*.
k(c): cär'teth*.
p: dē-pär'teth*, im-pär'teth*,
pär'teth*.
sm: smär'teth*.
st: stär'teth*, up-stär'teth*.

(Choose only one word out of each group)

ÄRT′FṴL

Vowel: ärt′fṳl.
Plus heart full, etc.

ÄR′THÅ

m: Mär′thȧ.
Plus hearth a, etc.

ÄR′THEST

f: fär′THest.

ÄR′THI

k(ç): Mç-Çär′thy.

ÄR′THING

f: fär′THing.

ÄR′THŨR

f: fär′THẽr.

ÄR′THŨR

Vowel: Är′thũr.
Plus hearth err *or* her, etc.

ÄR′TI

h: heär′ty.
k(ç): Mç-Çär′ty.
p: chär′tẽr pär′ty, ex pär′tē,
    pär′ty.
t: As-tär′tē.
Plus mar tea *or* T, etc.
Plus start, he, etc.

ÄR′TIN

m: mär′tin.
Cf. är′tăn, är′ten, är′tŏn.
Plus scar tin, etc.
Plus start inn *or* in, etc.

ÄR′TING

d: där′ting.
h: heär′ting, sweet′heär-ting.
k(ç): çär′ting, un-çär′ting.
p: dē-pär′ting, im-pär′ting,
    pär′ting.
sm: smär′ting.
st: stär′ting, up-stär′ting.

ÄR′TIST

Vowel: är′tist.
ch: Chär′tist.

ÄR′TĪT

p: bī-pär′tīte.
Plus scar tight, etc.

ÄR′TL

d: där′tle.
st: stär′tle.
Plus cart′ll, etc.

ÄRT′LES

Vowel: ärt′less.
ch: chärt′less.
h: heärt′less.
Plus start less *or* Les, etc.

ÄRT′LET

h: heärt′let.
m: märt′let.
t: tärt′let.
Plus start let *or* Lett, etc.

ÄRT′LI

p: pärt′ly.
sm: smärt′ly.
t: tärt′ly.
Plus start Lee *or* lea, etc.

(Choose only one word out of each group)

ÄRT′LING

st: stärt′ling.

ÄRT′MENT

p: à-pärt′ment, com-pärt′ment,
dē-pärt′ment, im-pärt′ment.
Plus start meant, etc.

ÄRT′NES

sm: smärt′ness.
t: tärt′ness.

ÄR′TRIJ

k(c): cär′tridge.
p: pär′tridge.
Plus start ridge, etc.

ÄRT′WĀ

k(c): cärt′wāy.
p: pärt′=wāy′.
Plus smart way or weigh, etc.

ÄR′TŪR

b: bär′tẽr.
ch: chär′tẽr.
d: där′tẽr.
g: gär′tẽr.
k(c): cär′tẽr.
m: bē-mär′tyr (′tẽr), mär′tyr,
prō-tō-mär′tyr, un-mär′tyr.
p: dē-pär′tẽr, im-pär′tẽr,
pär′tẽr.
sm: smär′tẽr.
st: self′=stär′tẽr, stär′tẽr,
up-stär′tẽr.
t: tär′tȧr.
Plus cart her or err, etc.

AR′UM

Vowel: ar′um.
k(c): car′rŏm.
l: lar′um*.
m: mar′um.
sk(sc): har′um=scar′um.
Cf. hår′em.

ÄR′UM

l: à-lär′um.
Plus scar ′em, etc.

ÃR′ŪR

Vowel: ãir′ẽr.
b: ärms′=beãr′ẽr, bãr′ẽr,
beãr′ẽr, cup′beãr-ẽr,
fọr-beãr′ẽr, māce′=beãr′ẽr,
ō-vẽr-beãr′ẽr,
stan′dãrd=beãr′ẽr,
swōrd′=beãr′ẽr (sōrd′),
tāle′beãr-ẽr, tañ′kãrd beãr′ẽr,
train′beãr″ẽr, up′beãr-ẽr.
bl: blãr′ẽr.
d: dãr′ẽr, out-dãr′ẽr.
f: fãir′ẽr, fãr′ẽr, sēa′fãr-ẽr,
wāy′fãr-ẽr.
fl: flãr′ẽr.
gl: glãr′ẽr.
kl: dē-clãr′ẽr.
p: com-pãr′ẽr, im-pãir′ẽr,
pãr′ẽr, prē-pãr′ẽr, rē-pãir′ẽr.
sh: shãr′ẽr.
skw: squãr′ẽr.
sn: en-snãr′ẽr, snãr′ẽr.
sp: dē-spãir′ẽr, spãr′ẽr.
st: out-stãr′ẽr, stãr′ẽr.
sw: fọr-sweãr′ẽr, sweãr′ẽr.
t: teãr′ẽr.
w: weãr′ẽr.
Plus spare her or err, etc.

(Choose only one word out of each group)

ÄR′ŪR

b: bär′rēr, dē-bär′rēr,
  dis-bär′rēr.
m: mär′rēr.
sp: spär′rēr.
t: tär′rēr.
z: bi-zär′rēr.
Plus scar her or err, etc.

ÄR′VĂL

!: lär′văl.
Plus carve, Al, etc.

ÄR′VEL

k(ç): çär′vel.
m: mär′vel.
Plus starve el or L, etc.

ÄR′VELD

m: mär′velled.

ÄR′VEN

k(ç): çär′ven.

ÄR′VEST

h: här′vest.
st: stär′vest*.
Plus mar vest, etc.

ÄR′VI

g: Gär′vey.
h: Här′vey.
Plus starve, he, etc.
Plus far, Vee, etc.

ÄR′VING

k(ç): çär′ving.
st: stär′ving.

ÄRV′LING

m: mär′velling.
st: stärve′ling.

ÄR′VŪR

k(ç): çär′vēr.
m: mär′vēr.
st: stär′vēr.
Plus starve her or err, etc.

ÃR′WĀVZ

Vowel: āir wāveṣ.
Plus share waves, etc.

ÃR′WEL

f: fãre′well.
Plus scare well, etc.

ÃR′WŌRN

k(ç): çāre′wōrn.
pr: prãyer′⸗wōrn″.
Plus scare worn, etc.

Ā′SȦ

Vowel: Ā′sȧ.
m: Ȧ-mā′sȧ.
Plus face a, etc.

AS′Ȧ

d: Hȧ-das′sah.
n: Mȧ-nas′seh.
Cf. "yas suh".
Plus class a, etc.

ĀS′ĂL

b: bās′ăl.
k(ç): çās′ăl.
Plus race, Al, etc.
Plus play, Sal, etc.

(Choose only one word out of each group)

AS′ĀT

k(c̣): c̣as′sāte*.
kr: in-c̣ras′sāte.
Plus class ate *or* eight, etc.

Ā′SENS, Ā′SĂNS

b: ȧ-bāi′săn̈ce*, ō-bei′săn̈ce.
j: ad-jā′cence, in-tẽr-jā′cence.
n: c̣on-nās′cence, rē-nās′cence.
pl: c̣om-plā′cence.
Plus say sense, scents *or* cents, etc.
Cf. chase hence, etc.

Ā′SENT

b: ō-bei′sănt.
d: "dāy′cent".
j: ad-jā′cent, cĭr-c̣um-jā′cent,
  in-tẽr-jā′cent, jā′cent,
  sub-jā′cent, sū-pẽr-jā′cent.
n: c̣on-nās′cent, ē-nās′cent*,
  nāis′sănt, nās′cent,
  rē-nāis′sănt, rē-nās′cent.
pl: c̣om-plā′cent,
  un″c̣om-plā′cent.
r: in-dū-rās′cent, "rāy sent".
Plus play sent, scent *or* cent, etc.

ĀS′EST

b: ȧ-bās′est*, bās′est,
  dē-bās′est*.
br: brāc′est*, em-brāc′est*.
ch: chās′est*.
f: dē-fāc′est*, ef-fāc′est*,
  fāc′est*.
gr: bē-grāc′est*, dis-grāc′est*,
  grāc′est*.
l: bē-lāc′est*, en-lāc′est*,
  in-tẽr-lāc′est*, lāc′est*,
  un-lāc′est*.
p: out-pāc′est*, pāc′est*.

pl: dis-plāc′est*, plāc′est*,
  rē-plāc′est*.
r: ē-rās′est*, rāc′est*.
sp: spāc′est*.
tr: rē-trāc′est*, trāc′est*.

AS′EST

kl: c̣las′sest*.
kr: c̣ras′sest.
m: ȧ-mas′sest*, mas′sest*.
p: pas′sest*, sūr-pas′sest*.

AS′ET

Vowel: as′set.
b: bas′set, Bas′sett.
br: bras′set.
f: 'fas′cet.
pl: plac′et.
Cf. tac′it.
Cf. pass it, etc.
Plus class et, etc.
Cf. class set, etc.

ĀS′ETH

b: ȧ-bās′eth*, bās′eth*,
  dē-bās′eth*.
br: brāc′eth*, em-brāc′eth*.
ch: chās′eth*.
f: dē-fāc′eth*, ef-fāc′eth*,
  fāc′eth*.
gr: bē-grāc′eth*, dis-grāc′eth*,
  grāc′eth*.
l: bē-lāc′eth*, en-lāc′eth*,
  in-tẽr-lāc′eth*, lāc′eth*,
  un-lāc′eth*.
p: out-pāc′eth*, pāc′eth*.
pl: dis-plāc′eth*, plāc′eth*,
  rē-plāc′eth*.
r: ē-rās′eth*, rāc′eth*.
sp: spāc′eth*.

(Choose only one word out of each group)

tr: rē-trāc′eth*, trāc′eth*.
Plus Say, Seth, etc.

AS′ETH

kl: çlas′seth*.
m: à-mas′seth*, mas′seth*.
p: pas′seth*, sûr-pas′seth*.

ĀS′EZ

Vowel: āc′eṣ.
b: bās′eṣ, bāss′eṣ,
coun′tēr-bās-seṣ, dē-bās′eṣ.
br: brāc′eṣ, em-brāc′eṣ.
ch: chās′eṣ, stee′ple-chās-eṣ.
f: dē-fāc′eṣ, ef-fāc′eṣ, fāc′eṣ,
out-fāc′eṣ.
gr: bē-grāc′eṣ, dis-grāc′eṣ,
grāc′eṣ.
k(ç): çās′eṣ, ū-kās′eṣ,
un-çās′eṣ.
l: bē-lāc′eṣ, en-lāc′eṣ,
in-tēr-lāc′eṣ, lāc′eṣ, un-lāc′eṣ.
m: gri-māc′eṣ, māc′eṣ.
p: foot′pāc-eṣ, out-pāc′eṣ,
pāc′eṣ.
pl: çom′mŏn-plāc-eṣ,
dis-plāc′eṣ, hĭd′ing plāc′eṣ,
mis-plāc′eṣ, plāc′eṣ,
rē-plāc′eṣ, res′ting plāc′eṣ,
trys′ting plāc′eṣ.
r: char′i-ŏt rāc′eṣ, foot rāc′eṣ,
horse rāc′eṣ, rāc′eṣ.
sp: brēaTH′ing spāc′eṣ,
in-tēr-spāc′eṣ, spāc′eṣ.
tr: rē-trāc′eṣ, trāc′eṣ.
v: vās′eṣ.
Plus ace, Ez, etc.
Cf. ace is, etc.
Plus May says, etc.

AS′EZ

Vowel: as′seṣ, jack′as-seṣ.
br: bras′seṣ.
g: gas′eṣ.
gl: fiēld glas′seṣ, glas′seṣ,
look′ing glas′seṣ,
win′dōw glas′seṣ, etc.
gr: gras′seṣ.
kl: çlas′seṣ.
l: las′seṣ, "′las′seṣ",
mō-las′seṣ.
m: à-mas′seṣ, mas′seṣ.
p: pas′seṣ, sûr-pas′seṣ.
r: mō-ras′seṣ.
s: sas′seṣ.
t: dem′i-tas-seṣ.
v: çre-vas′seṣ.
Plus pass, Ez, etc.
Cf. pass is, etc.

ĀS′FṲL

gr: dis-grāce′fṳl, grāce′fṳl,
un-grāce′fṳl.
Plus space full, etc.

ASH-Ā′

k(ç): çach-et′.
s: sach-et′.
t: at-tach-é′.
Plus smash a, etc.

Ā′SHĂL

b: ab-bā′tiăl.
f: çrā″ni-ō-fā′ciăl, fā′ciăl,
ūn-i-fā′ciăl.
gl: glā′ciăl.
l: pà-lā′tiăl, rē-lā′tiăl.
r: rā′ciăl.
sp: spā′tiăl.
Cf. ba′siăl.
Plus May shall, etc.

(Choose only one word out of each group)

Ā′SHĂN

See ā′shun.

ASH′BŌRD

d: dash′bōard.
spl: splash′bōard.
Plus crash board *or* bored, etc.

Ā′SHENS

p: pā′tience.

Ā′SHENT

p: im-pā′tient, pā′tient.

ASH′EST

d: dash′est*.
fl: flash′est*.
g: gash′est*.
k(c): cash′est*.
kl: clash′est*.
kr: crash′est*.
l: lash′est*.
m: mash′est*.
n: gnash′est (nash′)*.
sl: slash′est*.
sm: smash′est*.
spl: splash′est*.
thr: thrash′est*.

ASH′ETH

d: dash′eth*.
fl: flash′eth*.
g: gash′eth*.
k(c): cash′eth*.
kl: clash′eth*.
kr: crash′eth*.
l: lash′eth*.
m: mash′eth*.
n: gnash′eth (nash′)*.
sl: slash′eth*.

sm: smash′eth*.
spl: splash′eth*.
thr: thrash′eth*.

ASH′EZ

Vowel: ash′es.
b: à-bash′es, bash′es.
d: dash′es.
f: fash′es.
fl: flash′es, hot flash′es.
g: gash′es.
h: hash′es, rē-hash′es.
k(c): cach′es, cash′es.
kl: clash′es.
kr: crash′es.
l: lash′es, un-lash′es.
m: mash′es.
n: gnash′es (nash′).
pl: plash′es.
r: rash′es.
s: sash′es.
sl: slash′es.
sm: smash′es.
spl: splash′es.
t: mŏus-tach′es, mus-tach′es.
thr: thrash′es.
Plus hash, Ez, etc.
Cf. hash is, etc.

ASH′FỤL

b: bash′fụl, un-bash′fụl.
g: gash′fụl.
r: rash′fụl.
Plus sash full, etc.

ASH′Ĭ

Vowel: ash′y.
fl: flash′y.
h: hash′y.
m: mash′ie, mash′y.
pl: plash′y.

(Choose only one word out of each group)

sl: slash'y.
spl: splash'y.
tr: trash'y.
Plus thrash, he, etc.
Cf. thrash, she, etc.

ASH'ING

b: à-bash'ing, bash'ing.
d: bal'dēr-dash-ing, dash'ing.
f: fash'ing.
fl: flash'ing.
g: gash'ing.
h: hash'ing.
k(ç): çash'ing.
kl: çlash'ing.
kr: çrash'ing.
l: lash'ing, un-lash'ing.
m: mash'ing.
n: gnash'ing (nash').
pl: plash'ing.
sl: slash'ing.
sm: smash'ing.
spl: splash'ing.
thr: thrash'ing.

ASH'LI

Vowel: Ash'leigh ('li),
Ash'ley ('li).
fl: flash'ly.
g: gash'ly.
Plus thrash Lee or lea, etc.

ASH'MĂN

Vowel: ash'măn.
fl: "flash man".
Plus crash man, etc.

Ā'SHŌ

r: Hō-rā'tiō ('shō).
Plus play show, etc.

Ā'SHUN

Vowel: ab-brē-vi-ā'tion,
aç-tū-ā'tion,
aç"ū-puñç-tū-ā'tion,
af-fil-i-ā'tion, al-lē-vi-ā'tion,
am-pli-ā'tion, an-nun-ci-ā'tion,
ap-prē-ci-ā'tion (-shi-),
ap-prō-pri-ā'tion, är-çu-ā'tion,
Ā'siăn, as-phyx-i-ā'tion,
as-sō-ci-ā'tion, at-ten-ū-ā'tion,
ā-vi-ā'tion, çal-um-ni-ā'tion,
çol-um-ni-ā'tion, çon-cil-i-ā'tion,
çon"sub-stan"ti-ā'tion (-shi-),
çon-tin-ū-ā'tion, çrē-ā'tion,
dē-lin-ē-ā'tion, dē-nun-ci-ā'tion,
dē-prē-ci-ā'tion (-shi-),
des-pō-li-ā'tion, dē-vi-ā'tion,
dif-far-rē-ā'tion,
dif"fēr-en"ti-ā'tion (-shi-),
di-mid-i-ā'tion,
dis"çon-tin"ū-ā'tion,
dis-sō-ci-ā'tion,
do"mi-cil"i-ā'tion,
ef-feç-tū-ā'tion, ef-fō-li-ā'tion,
ē-mā-ci-ā'tion (-shi-),
ē-nū-çlē-ā'tion, ē-nun-ci-ā'tion,
ē-vaç-ū-ā'tion, ē-ven-tū-ā'tion,
ex-çōr-i-ā'tion,
ex-çrū-ci-ā'tion (-shi-),
ex-fō-li-ā'tion,
ex-pā-ti-ā'tion (-shi-),
ex-pā-tri-ā'tion, ex-pi-ā'tion,
ex-pō-li-ā'tion*,
ex-prō-pri-ā'tion,
ex-ten-ū-ā'tion,
fas-ci-ā'tion (fash-i-),
fil-i-ā'tion, fluç-tū-ā'tion,
fōl-i-ā'tion, frī-ā'tion*,
glā-ci-ā'tion (-shi-),
glō-ri-ā'tion*, grad-ū-ā'tion,
hab-it-ū-ā'tion, hū-mil-i-ā'tion,

(Choose only one word out of each group)

ī-dē-ā′tion, il-la-quē-ā′tion,
in″ap-prē″ci-ā′tion (-shi-),
in-chō-ā′tion, in″di-vid″ū-ā′tion,
in-ē-bri-ā′tion, in-fat-ū-ā′tion,
in-grā-ti-ā′tion (-shi-),
in-i-ti-ā′tion (-shi-),
in-sin-ū-ā′tion,
in″tẽr-col-um″ni-ā′tion,
in″tẽr-lin″ē-ā′tion,
in″tẽr-mēd″i-ā′tion,
ir-rā-di-ā′tion, lan-i-ā′tion,
lau-rē-ā′tion,
lī-cen-ti-ā′tion (-shi-),
lin-ē-ā′tion, lix-iv-i-ā′tion,
lux-ūr-i-ā′tion,
mal-ē-fic-i-ā′tion (-fish-),
mal-lē-ā′tion, mà-tēr-i-ā′tion,
mēd-i-ā′tion, mūt-ū-ā′tion*,
nē-gō-ti-ā′tion (-shi-),
ob-vi-ā′tion, ōt-i-ā′tion (ōsh-)*,
pal-li-ā′tion, pẽr-mē-ā′tion,
pẽr-pet-ū-ā′tion, prō-crē-ā′tion,
prō-nun-ci-ā′tion,
prō-pi-ti-ā′tion (-shi-),
punc-tū-ā′tion, rād-i-ā′tion,
rē″cŏn-cil″i-ā′tion, re-crē-ā′tion,
rē-nun-ci-ā′tion, rē-pā-tri-ā′tion,
rē-pū-di-ā′tion, rē-tal-i-ā′tion,
sāt-i-ā′tion (sāsh-),
self′=rē-nun-ci-ā′tion,
sin-ū-ā′tion, sit-ū-ā′tion,
spōl-i-ā′tion, strī-ā′tion,
sub-lin-ē-ā′tion,
sub-stan-ti-ā′tion (-shi-),
sū-pēr-an-nū-ā′tion,
trab-ē-ā′tion,
tran″sub-stan″ti-ā′tion (-shi-),
trī-pū-di-ā′tion,
tū-mul-tū-ā′tion, val-ū-ā′tion,
vär-i-ā′tion, vin-dē-mi-ā′tion,
vit-i-ā′tion (vish-).

b: ac-cu-bā′tion,
ap-prō-bā′tion, cū-bā′tion*,
dē-cū-bā′tion,
dis-ap-prō-bā′tion,
ex-ac-ẽr-bā′tion, in-cū-bā′tion,
jōb-ā′tion, lī-bā′tion,
pẽr-tūr-bā′tion, prō-bā′tion,
rē-cū-bā′tion*, re-prō-bā′tion,
tit-ū-bā′tion.

bl: à-blā′tion, ō-blā′tion,
su-blā′tion.

br: ad-um-brā′tion,
an″ti-lī-brā′tion, cel-ē-brā′tion,
cer-ē-brā′tion, ē″qui-lī-brā′tion,
lī-brā′tion, lū-cū-brā′tion,
rē-vī-brā′tion, ten-ē-brā′tion,
vī-brā′tion.

d: ac-com-mō-dā′tion,
back-wăr-dā′tion,
com-men-dā′tion,
cŏn-sol-i-dā′tion,
dē-frau-dā′tion, de-grà-dā′tion,
dē-nū-dā′tion, dē-ox-i-dā′tion,
de-prē-dā′tion, di-lap-i-dā′tion,
ē-lu-ci-dā′tion, ē-men-dā′tion,
ex-ū-dā′tion, fē-cun-dā′tion,
foun-dā′tion, fron-dā′tion*,
grā-dā′tion, grav-i-dā′tion,
in-com-mō-dā′tion,
in-feū-dā′tion, in-grav-i-dā′tion,
in-tim-i-dā′tion, in-un-dā′tion,
in-val-i-dā′tion, lap-i-dā′tion,
lau-dā′tion, li-qui-dā′tion,
nō-dā′tion, nū-dā′tion,
ox-i-dā′tion,
prē-dā′ceăn (′shăn),
prē-dā′tion, re-cŏm-men-dā′tion,
re-cŏr-dā′tion, rē-tär-dā′tion,
re-trō-grā-dā′tion,
se-cun-dā′tion, sū-dā′tion,
tran-sū-dā′tion, trep-i-dā′tion,

(Choose only one word out of each group)

trū-ci-dā´tion,
val-i-dā´tion.
dr: hȳ-drā´tion.
f: phil-os-ō-phā´tion*.
fl: af-flā´tion, ef-flā´tion,
ex-suf-flā´tion, in-flā´tion,
in-suf-flā´tion, suf-flā´tion.
g: ab-nē-gā´tion, ab-rō-gā´tion,
ag-grē-gā´tion, al-lē-gā´tion,
al-li-gā´tion, ar-rō-gā´tion,
ças-ti-gā´tion,
cir″çum-nav-i-gā´tion,
çol-li-gā´tion, çom-pūr-gā´tion,
çon-grē-gā´tion, çon-jū-gā´tion,
çor-rū-gā´tion, de-le-gā´tion,
de-rō-gā´tion, dī-vȧ-gā´tion,
di-vul-gā´tion, ex-pūr-gā´tion,
fū-mi-gā´tion, hō-mol-ō-gā´tion,
in-sti-gā´tion, in-ter-rō-gā´tion,
ir-ri-gā´tion, lē-gā´tion,
lev-i-gā´tion, lit-i-gā´tion,
mit-i-gā´tion, nav-i-gā´tion,
nē-gā´tion, noç-tiv-i-gā´tion,
nū-gā´tion*, ob-jūr-gā´tion,
ob-li-gā´tion, prof-li-gā´tion,
prō-lọn-gā´tion, prō-mul-gā´tion,
prop-ō-gā´tion, prō-rō-gā´tion,
pūr-gā´tion, re-lē-gā´tion,
re-nē-gā´tion, rō-gā´tion,
se-grē-gā´tion, sub-jū-gā´tion,
sub-li-gā´tion, sub-rō-gā´tion,
su″pēr-rō-gā´tion, sūr-rō-gā´tion,
vār-i-e-gā´tion.
gr: çon-flȧ-grā´tion,
dē-flȧ-grā´tion,
dis-in-tē-grā´tion, em-i-grā´tion,
im-mi-grā´tion, in-tē-grā´tion,
in″tēr-mī-grā´tion, mī-grā´tion,
red-in-tē-grā´tion,
trans-mī-grā´tion.
h: Hāi´tiȧn, Hāy´tiȧn.

k(ç): ab-di-çā´tion,
ab-jū-di-çā´tion,
ac-id-i-fi-çā´tion,
ad-jū-di-çā´tion, ad-vō-çā´tion,
al-lō-çā´tion, ạl-tēr-çā´tion,
am″pli-fi-çā´tion,
An″gli-fi-çā´tion, ap-pli-çā´tion,
ạu-then-ti-çā´tion,
a-ver-run-çā´tion, a-vō-çā´tion,
bās-i-fi-çā´tion, bē-at″if-i-çā´tion,
beaū″ti-fi-çā´tion, bī-fūr-çā´tion,
brūt″i-fi-çā´tion, çal″ci-fi-çā´tion,
çȧl-or″if-i-çā´tion,
çap″rif-i-çā´tion, çēr″tif-i-çā´tion,
çlar″i-fi-çā´tion, çlas″si-fi-çā´tion,
çōd″i-fi-çā´tion, çol-lō-çā´tion,
çŏm-mū-ni-çā´tion,
çom-pli-çā´tion, çon-fis-çā´tion,
çon-vō-çā´tion,
çọr″nif-i-çā´tion, çor-us-çā´tion,
dam″nif-i-çā´tion,
dē-bär-kā´tion,
dē-çal″ci-fi-çā´tion,
dē-çor-ti-çā´tion, ded-i-çā´tion
dē-fal-çā´tion, de-fē-çā´tion,
dē″i-fi-çā´tion, del″tȧ-fi-çā´tion,
dē-mär-çā´tion, de-prē-çā´tion,
des-si-çā´tion, dē-trun-çā´tion,
dis-lō-çā´tion,
dis-quäl″i-fi-çā´tion,
dī-var-i-çā´tion,
di-vēr″si-fi-çā´tion,
dō-mes-ti-çā´tion,
dul″ci-fi-çā´tion, dū-pli-çā´tion,
ed″i-fi-çā´tion, ed-ū-çā´tion,
ēl-eç″tri-fi-çā´tion,
em-brō-çā´tion, ē-qui-vō-çā´tion,
ē-rad-i-çā´tion, ē-vō-çā´tion,
ex-çŏm-mu-ni-çā´tion,
ex-em″pli-fi-çā´tion,
ex-pli-çā´tion, ex-siç-çā´tion,

(Choose only one word out of each group)

ex-tri-çā′tion, fab-ri-çā′tion,
fal-çā′tion, fąl″si-fi-çā′tion,
flōr″i-fi-çā′tion, flos″si-fi-çā′tion,
fŏr″ti-fi-çā′tion,
fos-sil″if-i-çā′tion, fri-çā′tion*,
fruç″ti-fi-çā′tion, fūr-çā′tion,
gas″i-fi-çā′tion,
ġēn-er″if-i-çā′tion,
glōr″if-i-çā′tion,
gran″it-i-fi-çā′tion,
grat″i-fi-çā′tion, hor″ri-fi-çā′tion,
hȳ-poth-ē-çā′tion,
ī-den″ti-fi-çā′tion,
im-bri-çā′tion, im-pli-çā′tion,
im-prē-çā′tion, in-ap-pli-çā′tion,
in-çär″nif-i-çā′tion,
in-çul-çā′tion,
in-dem″ni-fi-çā′tion,
in-di-çā′tion, in-ten″si-fi-çā′tion,
in″tēr-çŏm-mū-ni-çā′tion,
in″tēr-lō-çā′tion,
in″tēr-strat-i-fi-çā′tion,
in-tox-i-çā′tion, in-tri-çā′tion,
in-vō-çā′tion, jol″li-fi-çā′tion,
jus″ti-fi-çā′tion,
lap″id-i-fi-çā′tion,
li″qui-fi-çā′tion, lō-çā′tion,
lū-bri-çā′tion, mag″nif-i-çā′tion,
mas-ti-çā′tion, med-i-çā′tion,
mel″lif-i-çā′tion*,
men-di-çā′tion, mod″i-fi-çā′tion,
mōd″i-fi-çā′tion,
mŏr″ti-fi-çā′tion,
mul″ti-pli-çā′tion,
mum″mi-fi-çā′tion,
mun″di-fi-çā′tion,
mys″tif-i-çā′tion, nid″i-fi-çā′tion,
ni″gri-fi-çā′tion, nī″tri-fi-çā′tion,
nŏt″i-fi-çā′tion, nūd″i-fi-çā′tion,
nul″li-fi-çā′tion, ob-fus-çā′tion,
os″si-fi-çā′tion, ō-zō″ni-fi-çā′tion,

pā-çā′tion, pac″i-fi-çā′tion,
pal″i-fi-çā′tion, pan-if-i-çā′tion,
pēr-son″if-i-çā′tion,
pe″tri-fi-çā′tion, pis-çā′tion,
plā-çā′tion, ple″bi-fi-çā′tion,
plī-çā′tion, pre-di-çā′tion,
prē-var-i-çā′tion,
prog-nos-ti-çā′tion,
prō-lif-i-çā′tion, pro-vō-çā′tion,
pub-li-çā′tion, pūr-i-fi-çā′tion,
quäd-rū-pli-çā′tion,
quän″ti-fi-çā′tion, rad-i-çā′tion*,
ram″i-fi-çā′tion, rat″i-fi-çā′tion,
rē-cip-rō-çā′tion,
reç″tif-i-çā′tion, rē-lō-çā′tion,
re-pli-çā′tion, rēş″in-if-i-çā′tion,
rē-viv″i-fi-çā′tion, re-vō-çā′tion,
rhē-tor-i-çā′tion*,
rū″bi-fi-çā′tion, rus-ti-çā′tion,
saç″ri-fi-çā′tion, sal″i-fi-çā′tion,
sañç″ti-fi-çā′tion,
sañ″gui-fi-çā′tion,
sà-pon″i-fi-çā′tion,
sçar″i-fi-çā′tion, sçōr″i-fi-çā′tion,
siç-çā′tion, sig″nif-i-çā′tion,
sil-i″ci-fi-çā′tion,
sim″pli-fi-çā′tion,
sol-id″i-fi-çā′tion,
sō-phis-ti-çā′tion,
spec″i-fi-çā′tion,
speech″i-fi-çā′tion,
spif-li-çā′tion, strat″i-fi-çā′tion,
stul″ti-fi-çā′tion,
sub-lim″if-i-çā′tion,
suf-fō-çā′tion, sul-çā′tion,
sup-pli-çā′tion, syl-lab-i-çā′tion,
syl-lab″i-fi-çā′tion,
tes″ti-fi-çā′tion,
thū″ri-fi-çā′tion, trans-lō-çā′tion,
trans-mog″ri-fi-çā′tion,
tri-pli-çā′tion, truñ-çā′tion,

(Choose only one word out of each group)

typ″i-fi-ça′tion, ūn″i-fi-çā′tion,
vā-çā′tion, vel-li-çā′tion,
ver″i-fi-çā′tion, vēr″si-fi-çā′tion,
ves-i-çā′tion, vil″i-fi-çā′tion,
vin-di-çā′tion, vi″tri-fi-çā′tion,
viv″i-fi-çā′tion, vō-çā′tion.

kr: çon-sē-çrā′tion,
dē-çon-sē-çrā′tion,
des-ē-çrā′tïon, ex-ē-çrā′tion,
ob-sē-çrā′tion.

kw: ad-ē-quā′tion, ē-quā′tion,
in-ad-ē-quā′tion, in-ē-quā′tion,
lī-quā′tion.

l: aç-çū-mū-lā′tion, ad-ū-lā′tion,
am-bū-lā′tion, añ-gū-lā′tion,
an-nī-hi-lā′tion, an-nū-lā′tion,
ap-pel-lā′tion, är-tiç-ū-lā′tion,
as-sim-i-lā′tion, as-sim-ū-lā′tion,
blood rē-lā′tion (blud),
bom-bi-lā′tion, çal-çū-lā′tion,
çan-cel-lā′tion, çan-til-lā′tion,
çap-it″ū-lā′tion,
çär-buñ-çū-lā′tion,
ças-tel-lā′tion, cīr-çū-lā′tion,
cīr″çum-val-lā′tion,
çō-ag-ū-lā′tion, çŏl-lā′tion,
çom-pel-lā′tion, çom-pi-lā′tioʀ,
çŏn-fab-ū-lā′tion, çon-ġe-lā′tion,
çŏn-grat-ū-lā′tion,
çon-sō-lā′tion, çon-stel-lā′tion,
çon″trá-val-lā′tion,
çop-ū-lā′tion, çor-re-lā′tion,
çren-el-lā′tion, çū-pel-lā′tion,
dē-çŏl-lā′tion, dē-lā′tion,
den-tiç″ū-lā′tion, den-ti-lā′tion,
dē-op-pi-lā′tion, dē-os-çū-lā′tion,
de-pi-lā′tion, dē-pop-ū-lā′tion,
des-ō-lā′tion, dī-lā′tion,
dis-sim-ū-lā′tion, dis-til-lā′tion,
ē-jaç-ū-lā′tion, e-jū-lā′tion*,
ē-lā′tion, ē-mas-çū-lā′tion,

em-ū-lā′tion, ēt-i-ō-lā′tion,
ev-ō-lā′tion*, ex-há-lā′tion,
ex-pos-tū-lā′tion, flaġ-el-lā′tion,
floç-cil-lā′tion, ġen-iç″ū-lā′tion,
ġes-tiç″ū-lā′tion, glan-dū-lā′tion,
gran-ū-lā′tion, grat-iç-ū-lā′tion,
grat-ū-lā′tion, har″i-ō-lā′tion,
il-lā′tion, im-maç-ū-lā′tion,
im-mō-lā′tion,
in-är-tiç-ū-lā′tion, in-há-lā′tion,
in-oç-ū-lā′tion, in-os-çū-lā′tion,
in-sta̟l-lā′tion, in-stil-lā′tion,
in-sū-lā′tion, in″tēr-çá-lā′tion,
in″tēr-pel-lā′tion,
in-tēr-pō-lā′tion,
in″tēr-rē-lā′tion, īs-ō-lā′tion,
jaç-ū-lā′tion, jūb-i-lā′tion,
lal-lā′tion, leġ-is-lā′tion,
má-chi-çō-lā′tion, ma-çū-lā′tion,
man-ip-ū-lā′tion,
mat-riç-ū-lā′tion,
mod-ū-lā′tion, mūt-i-lā′tion,
nid-ū-lā′tion,
noç-tam″bū-lā′tion,
ob-nū-bi-lā′tion,
o̟r-biç-ū-lā′tion, os-cil-lā′tion,
os-çū-lā′tion, pan-diç-ū-lā′tion,
peç-ū-lā′tion, pēr-am-bū-lā′tion,
pēr-çō-lā′tion, pes-til-lā′tion,
pop-ū-lā′tion, pos-til-lā′tion,
pos-tū-lā′tion, prō-lā′tion,
pul-lū-lā′tion, rē-çap-it-ū-lā′tion,
rē-ġe-lā′tion, re-gū-lā′tion,
rē-lā′tion, rē-tiç-ū-lā′tion,
rev-e-lā′tion, scin-til-lā′tion,
ser-rū-lā′tion, sib-i-lā′tion,
sim-ū-lā′tion,
som-nam-bū-lā′tion,
speç-ū-lā′tion, stel-lā′tion,
stim-ū-lā′tion, stip-ū-lā′tion,
strañ-gū-lā′tion, strid-ū-lā′tion,

(Choose only one word out of each group)

sug-ġi-lā′tion,   tab-ū-lā′tion,
tes-sel-lā′tion,
tin″tin-nab-ū-lā′tion,
tit-il-lā′tion,   trȧ-lā′tion*,
trans-ō-lā′tion*,   trans-lā′tion,
trem-ū-lā′tion,   trī-añ-gū-lā′tion,
trib-ū-lā′tion,   tū-bū-lā′tion,
ū-lū-lā′tion,   un-dū-lā′tion,
us-tū-lā′tion,   vac-il-lā′tion,
vac″ū-ō-lā′tion,   vap-ū-lā′tion,
ven-ti-lā′tion,   vẽr-miç-ū-lā′tion,
vex-il-lā′tion,   vī-ō-lā′tion,
vit″ri-ō-lā′tion.

m: aç-çlȧ-mā′tion,
aç-çli-mā′tion,   af-fīr-mā′tion,
ȧ-mal-gȧ-mā′tion,   an-i-mā′tion,
ap-prox-i-mā′tion,
çhriṣ-mā′tion,   çon-fīr-mā′tion,
çon-fọr-mā′tion,
çon-sum-mā′tion,   çrē-mā′tion,
Dal-mā′tiăn,   dec-i-mā′tion,
de-çlȧ-mā′tion,   de-fȧ-mā′tion,
dē-fọr-mā′tion,   des-quȧ-mā′tion,
es-ti-mā′tion,   ex-çlȧ-mā′tion,
ex-hū-mā′tion,   fọr-mā′tion,
in-an-i-mā′tion,   in-çrē-mā′tion,
in-flam-mā′tion,   in-fọr-mā′tion,
in-hū-mā′tion,   in-ti-mā′tion,
laçh-ry-mā′tion,
lēġ-it-i-mā′tion,   mal-fọr-mā′tion,
proç-lȧ-mā′tion,   ra-cē-mā′tion,
re-çlȧ-mā′tion,   re-fŏr-mā′tion,
sub-li-mā′tion,   sum-mā′tion,
trans-an-i-mā′tion,
trans-fọr-mā′tion,   ul-ti-mā′tion,
vīġ-es-i-mā′tion.

n: ab-ac-i-nā′tion,
ab-āl″i-e-nā′tion,
ȧ-bom-i-nā′tion,
aç-çrim-i-nā′tion,
aç-ū-mi-nā′tion,   ad-ọr-nā′tion,

ag-glū-ti-nā′tion,   ag-nā′tion,
ag-nom-i-nā′tion,
ā″li-e-nā′tion,   ạl-tẽr-nā′tion,
an-nom-i-nā′tion,
as-sas-si-nā′tion,   as-sig-nā′tion,
ça-çhin-nā′tion,   çal-ci-nā′tion,
çär-nā′tion,   çog-nā′tion,
çom-bi-nā′tion,   çom-mi-nā′tion,
çon-dem-nā′tion,
çon-dō-nā′tion,
çon-stẽr-nā′tion,
çon-tam-i-nā′tion,
çō꞊ọr-di-nā′tion,   çor-ō-nā′tion,
çrim-i-nā′tion,   çul-mi-nā′tion,
dam-nā′tion,   de-çli-nā′tion,
dē-nom-i-nā′tion,
dē-ox″y-ġe-nā′tion,
deṣ-ig-nā′tion,   des-ti-nā′tion,
dē-tẽr-mi-nā′tion,
dē-vīr-ġi-nā′tion,
dis-çrim-i-nā′tion,
dis-in-çli-nā′tion,
dis-sem-i-nā′tion,   di-vi-nā′tion,
doç-tri-nā′tion,   dom-i-nā′tion,
dō-nā′tion,   ef-fem-i-nā′tion,
ē-lim-i-nā′tion,   e-mȧ-nā′tion,
ex-am-i-nā′tion,   ex-plȧ-nā′tion,
ex-pug-nā′tion,
ex-tẽr-mi-nā′tion,   fas-ci-nā′tion,
fer-rù-mi-nā′tion,   fī-bri-nā′tion,
fōre-ọr-di-nā′tion,
fra-tẽr-nā′tion,   ful-mi-nā′tion,
ġē-lat″i-nā′tion,   ġem-i-nā′tion,
ġẽr-mi-nā′tion,   glù-ti-nā′tion,
gụ-nā′tion,   hal-lū-ci-nā′tion,
hī-bẽr-nā′tion,   im-aġ-i-nā′tion,
im-mȧ-nā′tion,   im-pȧ-nā′tion,
im-pẽr-sŏ-nā′tion,
im-preg-nā′tion,
im-pug-nā′tion,   in-çär-nā′tion,
in-çli-nā′tion,

ūse, bṵll, brûte, tûrn, up; crȳ, myth; c̣at, mac̣hine, ace,
church, c̣hord; g̣em, ang̣er, (Fr.) boṅ, as̱; THis, thin; azure   Ā′SHUN

(Choose only one word out of each group)

in-dē-tēr-mi-nā′tion,
in-dig-nā′tion,
in-dis-c̣rim-i-nā′tion,
in-doc̣-tri-nā′tion,
in-g̣em-i-nā′tion,
in-ọr-di-nā′tion,
in-sub-ọr-di-nā′tion,
in-tō-nā′tion, lam-i-nā′tion,
lan-ci-nā′tion, lū-nā′tion,
ma-c̣hi-nā′tion,
mis-cē-g̣ē-nā′tion, nā′tion,
nom-i-nā′tion, ob-sti-nā′tion,
op-pug-nā′tion, ọr-di-nā′tion,
ōr-ig̣-i-nā′tion, ox″y-g̣e-nā′tion,
ō-zō-nā′tion, pag̣-i-nā′tion,
pec̣-ti-nā′tion, per″ē-gri-nā′tion,
pēr-fec̣-tio-nā′tion,
pēr-sō-nā′tion, phō-nā′tion,
pol-li-na′tion, prē-des-ti-nā′tion,
prē-dom-i-nā′tion,
prō-c̣ras-ti-nā′tion,
pro-fà-nā′tion, prō-nā′tion,
pro-pi-nā′tion*,
prō-pug-nā′tion,
rat″i-o-ci-nā′tion (rash″),
rē-c̣rim-i-nā′tion,
rē-jụ-vē-nā′tion, re-mà-nā′tion,
re-s̱ig-nā′tion, rē-sū-pi-nā′tion,
rōs̱e c̣är-nā′tion, rù-i-nā′tion,
rūm-i-nā′tion, sal-i-nā′tion,
sem-i-nā′tion, sig-nā′tion,
stag-nā′tion, sub-ọr-di-nā′tion,
sub-ọr-nā′tion, sū-pi-nā′tion,
′tär-nā′tion, tēr-mi-nā′tion,
tūr-bi-nā′tion, vac̣-ci-nā′tion,
vat″i-ci-nā′tion, vē-nā′tion,
ve-nē-nā′tion, vēr-nā′tion*.
p: an-ti-ci-pā′tion,
dis-c̣ul-pā′tion, dis-s̱i-pā′tion,
ē-man-ci-pā′tion, ex-c̣ul-pā′tion,
ex-tîr-pā′tion, fọr-ci-pā′tion,

in-c̣ul-pā′tion, oc̣-cū-pā′tion,
pal-pā′tion, pär-ti-ci-pā′tion,
prē-oc̣-c̣ū-pā′tion,
syñ-c̣ō-pā′tion, ūs̱-ûr-pā′tion.
pl: c̣on-tem-plā′tion.
pr: stū-prā′tion.
r: ab-ēr-rā′tion, ab-jụ-rā′tion,
ac̣-cel-ē-rā′tion, ad-jụ-rā′tion,
ad-mi-rā′tion, ad-ō-rā′tion,
ad-ul-tē-rā′tion, ā-ē-rā′tion,
ag̣-g̣ē-rā′tion, ag-glom-ē-rā′tion,
al-lit-ē-rā′tion, ạl-tē-rā′tion,
à-mē″li-ō-rā′tion,
an-nū-mē-rā′tion, à-rā′tion,
as-pi-rā′tion, as-sev-ē-rā′tion,
ạu-gū-rā′tion, blus-tē-rā′tion,
boTH-ē-rā′tion, c̣am-ē-rā′tion,
cin-ē-rā′tion,
cîr″c̣um-g̣ȳ-rā′tion,
c̣ŏl-ŏ-rā′tion,
c̣ŏm-mem-ō-rā′tion,
c̣ŏm-men-sụ-rā′tion (-shoo-),
c̣ŏm-mis̱-ē-rā′tion,
c̣ŏn-fed-ē-rā′tion,
c̣ŏn-fig-ū-rā′tion,
c̣ŏn-glom-ē-rā′tion,
c̣on-jụ-rā′tion,
c̣ŏn-sid-ē-rā′tion,
c̣ō-op-ē-rā′tion, c̣ọr-pō-rā′tion,
c̣ŏr-ro-bō-rā′tion,
de-c̣là-rā′tion, de-c̣ō-rā′tion,
de-flō-rā′tion, dē-g̣en-ē-rā′tion,
dē-lib-ē-rā′tion,
de-li-rā′tion, de-plō-rā′tion,
de-pū-rā′tion, dē-sid-ē-rā′tion,
des-pē-rā′tion,
dē-tēr″i-ō-rā′tion,
dē-ter-rā′tion, dis-c̣ŏl-ŏ-rā′tion,
dis-fig-ū-rā′tion,
dis-sev-ē-rā′tion, dū-rā′tion,
ē-dul-c̣ō-rā′tion.

(Choose only one word out of each group)

ē-lab-ō-rā'tion,

ē-nū-mē-rā'tion,

ē-vap-ō-rā'tion, ē-vis-cē-rā'tion,

ex-aġ-ġē-rā'tion,

ex-as-pē-rā'tion,

ex-hil-ȧ-rā'tion, ex-on-ē-rā'tion,

ex-peç-tō-rā'tion, ex-pi-rā'tion,

ex-plō-rā'tion, fed-ē-rā'tion,

fen-ē-rā'tion*, fig-ū-rā'tion,

fis-si-pȧ-rā'tion, flus-tē-rā'tion,

ful-gū-rā'tion, fŭr-fū-rā'tion,

ġen-ē-rā'tion, glom-e-rā'tion,

ġȳ-rā'tion, im-mod-ē-rā'tion,

im-plō-rā'tion, in-ạu-gū-rā'tion,

in-ạu-rā'tion*,

in-çam-ē-rā'tion,

in-çär-cē-rā'tion,

in-cin-ē-rā'tion,

in-cŏn-sid-ē-rā'tion,

in-cọr-pō-rā'tion, in-dū-rā'tion,

in-spi-rā'tion, in-stạu-rā'tion,

in-ten-ē-rā'tion, in-tol-ē-rā'tion,

in-vig-ō-rā'tion, i-tē-rā'tion,

lac-ē-rā'tion, lib-ē-rā'tion,

mac-ē-rā'tion, mär-mō-rā'tion,

mat-ū-rā'tion, mēl″i-ō-rā'tion,

men-sụ-rā'tion (-shoo-),

mod-ē-rā'tion, mūr-mū-rā'tion,

nar-rā'tion, nŭm-ē-rā'tion,

ob-lit-ē-rā'tion, ob-sçū-rā'tion,

o-nē-rā'tion, op-ē-rā'tion,

ō-rā'tion, pēr-fō-rā'tion,

per-ō-rā'tion, pếr-spi-rā'tion,

pre-pȧ-rā'tion,

prē-pon-dē-rā'tion,

prō-çū-rā'tion,

prō-tū-bē-rā'tion, rā'tion,

rē-çū-pē-rā'tion,

rē-friġ-ē-rā'tion,

rē-ġen-ē-rā'tion, rē-i-tē-rā'tion,

rē-mū-nē-rā'tion, re-pȧ-rā'tion,

res-pi-rā'tion, res-tō-rā'tion,

re-vếr-bē-rā'tion, ro-bō-rā'tion,

sa-bŭr-rā'tion, sat-ū-rā'tion,

sep-ȧ-rā'tion, ser-rā'tion,

sid-ē-rā'tion, sub-ar-rhā'tion,

sul-phū-rā'tion, sup-pū-rā'tion,

sus-pi-rā'tion, sū-sŭr-rā'tion,

tem-ē-rā'tion*, tīt-rā'tion,

tit-tē-rā'tion, tol-ē-rā'tion,

traç-tō-rā'tion,

trans-fig-ū-rā'tion,

trans-lit-ē-rā'tion,

tran-spi-rā'tion, tri-tū-rā'tion,

ul-cē-rā'tion, vāp-ō-rā'tion,

ven-ē-rā'tion, vếr-bē-rā'tion,

vī-tū-pē-rā'tion,

vō-cif-ē-rā'tion.

s: ad-vếr-sā'tion, Al-sā'tiăn,

an-nex-ā'tion, ças-sā'tion,

ces-sā'tion, çō-ax-ā'tion,

çom-pen-sā'tion,

çon-vếr-sā'tion, dē-çus-sā'tion,

dis-pen-sā'tion, e-lix-ā'tion*,

fix-ā'tion, flux-ā'tion,

in-spis-sā'tion, in-ten-sā'tion,

lax-ā'tion, lux-ā'tion,

mal-vếr-sā'tion, prē-sen-sā'tion,

pul-sā'tion, quas-sā'tion,

rē-lax-ā'tion, sā'tion*,

sen-sā'tion, suç-çus-sā'tion,

sus-pen-sā'tion, tax-ā'tion,

tếr-ġiv-ếr-sā'tion, vex-ā'tion.

st: ãer-ō-stā'tion,

af-for-e-stā'tion, bus stā'tion,

chāin stā'tion,

pōl-īce' stā'tion,

pōl'ling stā'tion,

rāil'rōad stā'tion, stā'tion.

str: ad-min-is-trā'tion,

de-mŏn-strā'tion,

fen-es-trā'tion, frus-trā'tion,

(Choose only one word out of each group)

mal-ad-min-is-trā'tion,
min-is-trā'tion, mon-strā'tion*,
re-ġis-trā'tion,
rē-mon-strā'tion.

t: ab-laç-tā'tion, ab-sen-tā'tion,
aç-cep-tā'tion, aç-çlī-mȧ-tā'tion,
aç-çred-i-tā'tion,
a-dap-tā'tion, ad-hor-tā'tion,
af-feç-tā'tion, aġ-i-tā'tion,
al-i-men-tā'tion, am-pū-tā'tion,
an-nō-tā'tion, är-ġen-tā'tion,
är-gū-men-tā'tion,
ar-res-tā'tion, as-sen-tā'tion,
at-tes-tā'tion, at-treç-tā'tion*,
ạug-men-tā'tion,
ạus-çul-tā'tion, çap-i-tā'tion,
ças"trȧ-mē-tā'tion,
cē-men-tā'tion,
cē-tā'ceăn ('shăn),
cīr"çum-nū-tā'tion, cī-tā'tion,
çoġ-i-tā'tion, çō-hab-i-tā'tion,
çom-mū-tā'tion, çom-pō-tā'tion,
çom-pū-tā'tion, çon-cēr-tā'tion,
çon-frŏn-tā'tion, çon-fū-tā'tion,
çon-nō-tā'tion, çon-sul-tā'tion,
çō-op-tā'tion, çrep-i-tā'tion,
çrus-tā'ceăn ('shăn),
çrus-tā'tion, dē-bil-i-tā'tion,
dē-çan-tā'tion, dē-çap-i-tā'tion,
dē-çrep-i-tā'tion, dē-gus-tā'tion,
de-hor-tā'tion, dē-leç-tā'tion,
dē-lim-i-tā'tion, dē-men-tā'tion,
dē-nō-tā'tion, den-tā'tion,
dē-por-tā'tion, dē-poṣ-i-tā'tion,
dep-ū-tā'tion, dē-tes-tā'tion,
de-vas-tā'tion, diç-tā'tion,
diġ-i-tā'tion, di-lȧ-tā'tion,
dis-pū-tā'tion, dis-sen-tā'tion,
dis-sēr-tā'tion,
doç-ū-men-tā'tion, dō-tā'tion,
e-qui-tā'tion, ē-ruç-tā'tion,

ex-ạl-tā'tion, ex-cī-tā'tion,
ex-çoġ-i-tā'tion, ex-ēr-cī-tā'tion,
ex-hor-tā'tion, ex-peç-tā'tion,
ex-per"i-men-tā'tion,
ex-ploi-tā'tion, ex-pōr-tā'tion,
ex-ul-tā'tion, fȧ-cil-i-tā'tion,
fĕr-men-tā'tion, flaġ-i-tā'tion,
flĭr-tā'tion, flō-tā'tion,
fō-men-tā'tion, frē-quen-tā'tion,
frú-men-tā'tion, ġes-tā'tion,
grav-i-tā'tion, gus-tā'tion,
hȧ-bil-i-tā'tion, hab-i-tā'tion,
heb-ē-tā'tion, heṣ-i-tā'tion,
hor-tā'tion, hū-meç-tā'tion,
im-i-tā'tion, im-pōr-tā'tion,
im-pū-tā'tion, in-af-feç-tā'tion,
in-çan-tā'tion, in-fes-tā'tion,
in-gūr"ġi-tā'tion,
in-hab-i-tā'tion,
in"stṛu-men-tā'tion,
in-sul-tā'tion*,
in-teg"ū-men-tā'tion,
in'tēr-diġ-i-tā'tion,
in"tēr-mū-tā'tion,
in-tēr"prē-tā'tion, in-vi-tā'tion,
ir-ri-tā'tion, jaç-ti-tā'tion,
laç-tā'tion, la-men-tā'tion,
lev-i-tā'tion, lim-i-tā'tion,
man"i-fes-tā'tion,
med-i-tā'tion, mō-les-tā'tion,
mū-tā'tion, nā-tā'tion,
nē-ces-si-tā'tion, niç-tā'tion,
niç-ti-tā'tion, nō-bil"i-tā'tion,
nō-tā'tion, oç-çul-tā'tion,
ō"ri-en-tā'tion,
ọr"nȧ-men-tā'tion,
os-ci-tā'tion, os-ten-tā'tion,
pal-pi-tā'tion, pēr-feç-tā'tion,
pēr-mū-tā'tion, pēr-noç-tā'tion,
pēr-sçrū-tā'tion, plan-tā'tion,
pŏl-li-ci-tā'tion, pō-tā'tion,

(Choose only one word out of each group)

pre-cip″i-tā′tion,
prē″med-i-tā′tion,
pre-ṣen-tā′tion,
pres″ti-dig-i-tā′tion,
prō-tes-tā′tion, quar-tā′tion,
quō-tā′tion, rē-çan-tā′tion,
rec-i-tā′tion, re-fū-tā′tion,
rē″hȧ-bil″i-tā′tion,
re″prē-ṣen-tā′tion, rep-tā′tion,
rep-ū-tā′tion, rē-sus-ci-tā′tion,
rē-traç-tā′tion, rō-tā′tion,
sal-tā′tion, sal-ū-tā′tion,
san-i-tā′tion, scis-ci-tā′tion*,
sçrȧ-tā′tion, sed-i-men-tā′tion,
seg-men-tā′tion, sōl-ic-i-tā′tion,
spū-tā′tion*, stēr-nū-tā′tion,
sub-lim-i-tā′tion,
sup-plan-tā′tion,
sup″plē-men-tā′tion,
sup-pōr-tā′tion, sus-ten-tā′tion,
temp-tā′tion,
tes-tā′ceăn ('shăn),
tes″tȧ-men-tā′tion, tes-tā′tion,
traç-tá′tıon, trans-mū-tā′tion,
trans-plan-tā′tion,
trans-pōr-tā′tion, veġ-ē-tā′tion,
viṣ-i-tā′tion.
thr: Thrā′ciăn.
tr: är-bi-trā′tion,
çon-cen-trā′tion, fil-trā′tion,
il-lus-trā′tion, in-fil-trā′tion,
in″tēr-pen-ē-trā′tion,
lus-trā′tion, ob-lȧ-trā′tion,
ọr-çhes-trā′tion, pen-ē-trā′tion,
pēr-lus-trā′tion, pēr-pē-trā′tion,
pros-trā′tion, rē-çal-ci-trā′tion,
self″≈çon-cen-trā′tion,
sē-ques-trā′tion.
v: a-cēr-vā′tion, aç-ti-vā′tion,
ag-grȧ-vā′tion, çap-ti-vā′tion,
çon-sēr-vā′tion, çul-ti-vā′tion,

çọr-vā′tion, de-prȧ-vā′tion,
de-pri-vā′tion, de-ri-vā′tion,
el-ē-vā′tion, e-nēr-vā′tion,
es-ti-vā′tion, ex″çȧ-vȧ′tion,
in-nēr-vā′tion, in-nō-vā′tion,
lā-vā′tion, lē-vā′tion*,
nēr-vā′tion, Nō-vā′tiăn,
nō-vā′tion, ob-ṣēr-vā′tion,
ō-vā′tion, pre-ṣēr-vā′tion,
re-ṣēr-vā′tion, sal-i-vā′tion,
sal-vā′tion, self′≈pre-ṣēr-vā′tion,
stär-vā′tion.
z: aç-clī″mȧ-ti-zā′tion,
aç-çū-ṣā′tion, aç″tū-ăl-i-zā′tion,
ag-gran-di-zā′tion,
al″çō-họl-i-zā′tion,
al″kȧ-li-zā′tion,
al″lē-gor-i-zā′tion,
Ȧ-mer″i-çăn-i-zā′tion,
an″ăl-y-ṣā′tion,
an-ath″ē-mat-i-zā′tion,
añ″gli-ci-zā′tion,
an″i-măl-i-zā′tion,
ȧ-rō″mat-i-zā′tion,
a″tŏ-mi-zā′tion,
ạu″thŏr-i-zā′tion,
brȧ″tăl-i-zā′tion,
çan-al-i-zā′tion,
çan″ŏn-i-zā′tion,
çap″i-tăl-i-zā′tion,
çär″bŏn-i-zā′tion,
çat″ē-çhi-zā′tion, çạu-ṣā′tion,
çạu″tēr-i-zā′tion,
cen″trăl-i-zā′tion,
char″ăç-tēr-i-zā′tion,
Çhris″tiăn-i-zā′tion (″chăn-),
civ″i-li-zā′tion, çol″ō-ni-zā′tion,
crys″tăl-li-zā′tion,
dē-cen″trăl-i-zā′tion,
dē-mon″ē-ti-zā′tion,
dē-mor″ăl-i-zā′tion,

(Choose only one word out of each group)

dē-nat″ion-ăl-i-zā′tion,
de-ni-zā′tion, dē-ō″dŏr-i-zā′tion,
de″tōn-i-zā′tion*,
ē-c̣on″ōm-i-zā′tion,
ef-fem″i-ni-zā′tion,
ē-lec̣-tri-zā′tion,
ēl-ec̣″trōl-y-zā′tion,
en-den″i-zā′tion*,
en-thrōn″i-zā′tion,
ē″quăl-i-zā′tion, ē-tẽr″ni-zā′tion,
ē-thẽr″ē-ăl-i-zā′tion,
ē-van″ġe-li-zā′tion,
ex-tem″pōr-i-zā′tion,
ex-tẽr″năl-i-zā′tion,
ex-tra″và-ṣā′tion,
fam-il″i-ăr-i-zā′tion,
fẽr″til-i-zā′tion,
feū″dăl-i-zā′tion,
fọr″mū-li-zā′tion,
fos″sil-i-zā′tion,
fra″tẽr-ni-zā′tion,
gal″văn-i-zā′tion,
gē-la″tin-i-zā′tion,
ġen″ẽr-ăl-i-zā′tion,
här″mōn-i-zā′tion,
Hel″len-i-zā′tion,
he″pat-i-zā′tion,
Hī″bẽr-ni-zā′tion,
hū″măn-i-zā′tion,
hȳ″brid-i-zā′tion,
ī-dēal-i-zā′tion,
im-mọr″tăl-i-zā′tion,
im-prō-vi-ṣā′tion,
in-di-vid″ū-ăl-i-zā′tion,
Jṵ″dā-i-zā′tion, Lat″in-i-zā′tion,
lē″găl-i-zā′tion,
lit″ẽr-ăl-i-zā′tion,
lō″căl-i-zā′tion,
mac̣-ad″a-mi-zā′tion,
mag′ne-ti-zā′tion,
mär′tyr-i-zā′tion (″tẽr-),

mat-ēr″i-ăl-i-zā′tion,
max″im-i-zā′tion,
mēd″i-at-i-zā′tion,
meṣ″mẽr-i-zā′tion,
me″tăl-li-zā′tion,
me″thŏd-i-zā′tion,
mō″bil-i-zā′tion,
mod″ēr-ni-zā′tion,
mon″ē-ti-zā′tion,
mor″ăl-i-zā′tion,
nāṣ″ăl-i-zā′tion,
nat″ūr-ăl-i-zā′tion,
nē-o″lō-ġi-zā′tion,
neū″trăl-i-zā′tion,
nọr″măl-i-zā′tion,
ọr″găn-i-zā′tion,
ō″zōn-i-zā′tion,
par″ăl-y-zā′tion,
pā″trōn-i-zā′tion,
pạu″pẽr-i-zā′tion, **pạu-ṣā′tion,**
phō-net-i-zā′tion,
plū″răl-i-zā′tion,
pō″lăr-i-zā′tion,
pọr″phy-ri-zā′tion,
pul″vẽr-i-zā′tion,
rē″ăl-i-zā′tion, **rē-c̣og-ni-zā′tion,**
re-c̣ū-ṣā′tion,
rē-mon″ē-ti-zā′tion,
se″c̣ū-lăr-i-zā′tion,
sen″sṵ-ăl-i-zā′tion (″shoo-),
sō″lăr-i-zā′tion,
sol″em-ni-zā′tion,
spec″iăl-i-zā′tion (**spesh″**),
spir″it-ū-ăl-i-zā′tion,
stig″mà-ti-zā′tion,
sub″til-i-zā′tion,
syl″lō-ġi-zā′tion,
sym″bol-i-zā′tion,
syñ″c̣hrōn-i-zā′tion,
sys″tem-at-i-zā′tion,
tab″ū-lăr-i-zā′tion,

(Choose only one word out of each group)

tan″tȧ-li-zā′tion,
tär′tăr-i-zā′tion,
tem″pō-ri-zā′tion,
thē″ō-ri-zā′tion,
tran″quil-li-zā′tion,
trul-li-zā′tion, ū″til-i-zā′tion,
vā″pŏr-i-zā′tion,
vẽr″băl-i-zā′tion,
vī″tăl-i-zā′tion,
vi″tri-ŏl-i-zā′tion,
vō″çăl-i-zā′tion,
vol″ȧ-til-i-zā′tion,
vol″çăn-i-zā′tion,
vul″çăn-i-zā′tion.
Plus may shun, etc.

ASH'EN, ASH'UN

Vowel: ash′en.
f: fash′ion.
p: çom-pas′sion, im-pas′sion,
  mȧs′tẽr pas′sion, pas′sion.
Cf. Cïr-ças′sian.
Cf. ash′i+ăn.
Cf. crash shun.
Plus smash Hun.
Plus rash ′un, etc.

ASH'UND

f: fash′ioned, ōld′=fash′ioned,
  un-fash′ioned.
p: dis-pas′sioned
  im-pas′sioned, pas′sioned,
  un-im-pas′sioned,
  un-pas′sioned.

ASH'ŪR

Vowel: Ash′ẽr.
b: bash′ẽr.
br: brash′ẽr.
d: dash′ẽr, hab′ẽr-dash-ẽr.
fl: flash′ẽr.
g: gash′ẽr.

k(ç): çash′ẽr, check çash′ẽr.
kl: çlash′ẽr.
kr: çrash′ẽr.
l: lash′ẽr, un-lash′ẽr.
m: mash′ẽr.
n: gnash′ẽr (nash′).
p: pash′ẽr.
r: rash′ẽr.
sl: slash′ẽr.
sm: bag′găġe=smash-ẽr,
  smash′ẽr.
spl: splash′ẽr.
thr: thrash′ẽr.
Plus smash her or err, etc.

Ā'SHUS

Vowel: al-li-ā′ceous,
  çōr-i-ā′ceous, fōl-i-ā′ceous,
  lil-i-ā′ceous, sçōr-i-ā′ceous.
b: bi-bā′cious, bul-bā′ceous,
  fȧ-bā′ceous, hẽr-bā′ceous,
  sa-bā′ceous, sē-bā′ceous.
d: ạu-dā′cious, ē-dā′cious,
  lär-dā′ceous, men-dā′cious,
  mọr-dā′cious, ọr-çhi-dā′ceous,
  pẽr-dā′ceous.
dr: cyl-in-drā′ceous.
f: tō-phā′ceous, tọr-fā′ceous.
g: fū-gā′cious, fuñ-gā′ceous,
  sȧ-gā′cious, sax″i-frȧ-gā′ceous.
gr: dis-grā′cious, grā′cious,
  mis-grā′cious, un-grā′cious.
gw: liñ-guā′cious*.
k(ç): ef-fi-çā′cious,
  in-ef-fi-çā′cious, mīç-ā′ceous,
  pẽr-spi-çā′cious, pẽr-vi-çā′cious,
  prō-çā′cious, sal-i-çā′ceous.
kr: ex-ē-çrā′tious*.
kw: lō-quā′cious, sē-quā′cious.
l: am-y-lā′ceous, çap-il-lā′ceous,
  çọr-ăl-lā′ceous, fal-lā′cious,

381 ūse, bṳll, brúte, tŭrn, up; crȳ, myth; çat, maçhine, ace,
church, çhord; ġem, aṅger, (Fr.) boṅ, aṣ; THis, 'thin; aẓure

ASH'VIL
ĀS'IK

(Choose only one word out of each group)

fer-ṳ-lā'ceous, fil-ā'ceous,
mär-lā'ceous, pȧ-lā'cious*,
pēr-lā'ceous, rȧ-nuñ-çū-lā'ceous,
sȧ-lā'cious, sçhọr-lā'ceous,
vī-ō-lā'ceous.

m: çon-tū-mā'cious,
fū-mā'cious, ġem-mā'ceous,
pal-mā'ceous, pō-mā'ceous.

n: a-çȧ-nā'ceous, a-rē-nā'ceous,
çär-bō-nā'ceous, er-i-nā'ceous,
far-i-nā'ceous, gal-li-nā'ceous,
min-ā'cious, peç-ti-nā'ceous,
pēr-ti-nā'cious, pug-nā'cious,
reṣ-i-nā'ceous, sa-pō-nā'ceous,
tē-nā'cious, tŭr-bi-nā'ceous,
vī-nā'ceous.

p: çȧ-pā'cious, in-çȧ-pā'cious,
lap-pā'ceous, ram-pā'cious,
rȧ-pā'cious.

r: çam-phō-rā'ceous, fē-rā'cious,
fūr-fū-rā'ceous, pip-ē-rā'ceous,
pọr-rā'ceous, pul-vē-rā'ceous,
stēr-ço-rā'ceous, ve-rā'cious,
vō-rā'cious.

s: vex-a'tious.

sp: spā'cious.

t: çaç-tā'ceous, cē-tā'ceous,
çrē-tā'ceous, çrus-tā'ceous,
dis-pū-tā'tious, flĭr-tā'tious,
frṳ-men-tā'ceous,
os-ten-tā'tious,
psit-tā'ceous (sit-), rṳ-tā'ceous,
sär-men-tā'ceous, sē-tā'ceous,
tes-tā'ceous, trṳt-tā'ceous.

th: a-çăn-thā'ceous.

v: ol-i-vā'ceous, vī-vā'cious.

z: rō-ṣā'ceous.

ASH'VIL

Vowel: Ash'ville.
n: Nash'ville.

ĀS'I

gr: Grā'cie.
l: Lāc'ey, lāc'y.
pr: prę́'cïs ('sē).
r: rāc'y.
Plus face, he, etc.
Plus may see, etc.

AS'I

br: bras'sie ('i), bras'sy.
g: gas'sy, Mal-ȧ-gas'y.
gl: glas'sy.
gr: gras'sy.
h: Tal-lȧ-has'see.
kl: çlas'sy.
l: las'sie.
m: mas'sy.
r: mō-ras'sy.
s: sas'sy.
Plus pass, he, etc.

Ā'SĪD

b: bāy'sīde.
br: brāe'sīde.
w: wāy'sīde.
Plus May sighed *or* side, etc.
Plus face, I'd *or* eyed, etc.

AS'ID

Vowel: ac'id.
pl: plac'id.
Cf. pass hid, etc.

AS'IJ

br: bras'sȧge.
p: pas'sȧge.
Cf. class age, etc.

ĀS'IK

b: bās'iç, bī-bās'iç, dī-bās'iç,
quäd-ri-bās'iç, trī-bās'iç.

AS'IK
AS'IT
fāte, fär, fàst, fạll, finăl, cãre, at; mēte, prey, hẽr, met; pīne,
marĭne, bĭrd, pin; nōte, mŏve, fọr, atŏm, not; mọọn, book; **382**

(Choose only one word out of each group)

f: à-phās'iç.
Plus stay sick, etc.

AS'IK

Vowel: Lī-as'siç, Trī-as'siç.
b: sē-bac'iç.
kl: çlas'siç.
r: bō-rac'iç, Jù-ras'siç,
thō-rac'iç.
t: pō-tas'siç.
Cf. class sick, etc.

AS'IL

f: fac'ile.
gr: grac'ile.
Plus class ill, etc.

ĀS'IN

b: bās'in.
Cf. ās'n, ās'ŏn.
Plus face in *or* inn, etc.

AS'IN

s: as-sas'sin.
Plus class in *or* inn, etc.
Cf. mass sin, etc.

ÄS'IN

d: spà-däs'sin.
Plus en masse in *or* inn, etc.
Plus ma sin, etc.

ĀS'ING

b: à-bās'ing, bās'ing, bās'sing,
dē-bās'ing, self'-à-bās'ing.
br: brāc'ing, em-brāc'ing,
un″dẽr-brāc'ing.
ch: chās'ing, gĭrl chās'ing,
skĭrt chās'ing, etc.,
stee'ple-chās-ing.
f: dē-fāc'ing, ef-fāc'ing,
fāc'ing, out-fāc'ing.

gr: bē-grāc'ing, dis-grāc'ing,
grāc'ing.
k(ç): çās'ing, un-çās'ing.
l: bē-lāc'ing, en-lāc'ing,
in″tẽr-lāc'ing, lāc'ing,
rē-lāc'ing, tĭght lāc'ing (tĭt),
un-lāc'ing.
p: out'pāc-ing, pāc'ing.
pl: dis-plāc'ing, mis-plāc'ing,
plāc'ing, rē-plāc'ing.
r: ē-rās'ing, bōat rāc'ing,
foot rāc'ing, họrse rāc'ing,
rāc'ing, yächt rāc'ing (yät).
sp: in-tẽr-spāc'ing, spāc'ing.
tr: rē-trāc'ing, trāc'ing.
Plus may sing, etc.

AS'ING

g: gas'sing.
kl: çlas'sing, un'dẽr-çlas-sing.
m: à-mas'sing, mas'sing.
p: ō-vẽr-pas'sing, pas'sing,
sũr-pas'sing.
Cf. class sing, etc.

ĀS'IS

Vowel: ō-ās'is.
b: bās'is.
f: phās'is.
gl: glāc'is.
kr: crās'is.
Cf. face is, face's, faces, etc.
Plus say, sis, etc.

AS'IS

ch: chas'sis.
Cf. as'ez.
Cf. class is, etc.

AS'IT

t: tac'it.
Cf. as'et.
Plus class it, etc.

383　üse, bᴜll, brúte, tŭrn, up; crȳ, myth; c̦at, mac̦hine, ace,
church, c̦hord; ġem, añger, (Fr.) boṅ, aṣ; THis, thin; aẓure

ĀS′IV
AS′KŪR

(Choose only one word out of each group)

ĀS′IV

sw: as-suās′ive (-swās′),
dis-suās′ive, pĕr-suās′ive,
suās′ive.
v: ē-vās′ive, in-vās′ive,
pĕr-vās′ive.
Plus stray sieve, etc.

AS′IV

m: mas′sive.
p: im-pas′sive, pas′sive.
Cf. class sieve, etc.

AS′KÅ

b: Ath-å-bas′kå.
br: Nē-bras′kå.
l: Å-las′kå.
Plus ask a, etc.

AS′KĂL, AS′KEL

h: Has′kell.
m: mas′c̦le.
p: pas′c̦hăl.
r: ras′c̦ăl.
Plus task′ll, etc.
Plus class cull, etc.

AS′KĂR

g: Mad-å-gas′c̦ăr.
l: Las′c̦ăr.
Cf. ask′ūr.
Plus class car, etc.

ÅS′KEST

Vowel: ås′kest*.
b: bås′kest*.
m: bē-mås′kest*, mås′kest*,
un-mås′kest*.
t: tås′kest*.

ÅS′KET

b: bås′ket,
bread′bås-ket (bred′),
flow′ĕr bås′ket.
fl: flås′ket.
g: gås′ket.
k(c̦): c̦ås′ket.
l: lås′ket.
t: tås′ket.
Cf. ask it, etc.

ÅS′KETH

Vowel: ås′keth*.
b: bås′keth*.
m: bē-mås′keth*, mås′keth*,
un-mås′keth*.
t: tås′keth*.

ÅS′KING

Vowel: ås′king.
b: bås′king.
m: bē-mås′king, mås′king,
un-mås′king.
t: ō-vĕr-tås′king, tås′king.
Plus class king, etc.

AS′KŌ

Vowel: fĭ-as′c̦ō.
b: tá-bas′c̦ō.
l: Be-las′c̦ō.
t: tas′c̦ō.
Plus task owe *or* O, etc.

AS′KŪR

Vowel: ask′ĕr.
b: bas′kĕr.
g: Mad-å-gas′c̦ăr.
k(c̦): c̦as′kĕr, c̦as′quĕr ('kĕr).
l: Las′c̦ăr.

(Choose only one word out of each group)

m: mas'kẽr, un-mas'kẽr.
Plus ask her *or* err, etc.
Plus class cur, etc.

AS'KUS

m: Dȧ-mas'̣cus.
Plus ask us, etc.
Plus class cuss, etc.

ASK'WITH

Vowel: As'quith.
Plus bask with, etc.

AS'L

k(c̣): c̣as'tle.
r: wras'tle.
t: en-tas'sel, tas'sel.
v: en-vas'săl, vas'săl.
Plus class'll, etc.

ĀS'LES

Vowel: āce'less.
b: bāse'less.
f: fāce'less.
gr: grāce'less.
k(c̣): c̣āse'less.
l: lāce'less.
m: māce'less.
p: pāce'less.
pl: plāce'less.
r: rāce'less.
sp: spāce'less.
tr: trāce'less.
Plus lace less, etc.

ĀS'LET

br: brāce'let.
Plus face let *or* Lett, etc.

AS'LET

h: has'let.
t: tas'let.
Plus class let *or* Lett, etc.

ĀS'LI

b: bāse'ly.
pl: c̣om'mŏn-plāce'ly.
Plus trace, Lee *or* lea, etc.

ĀS'MĂN

b: bāse'măn, fĭrst bāse'măn,
sec̣'ŏnd bāse'măn,
thĭrd bāse'măn.
l: lāce'măn.
p: pāce'măn.
pl: plāce'măn.
r: rāce'măn.
Plus face man, etc.

AS'MAN

g: gas'man.
gl: glass'man.
kl: c̣lass'măn, un-dẽr-c̣lass'măn,
up-pẽr-c̣lass'măn.
Plus surpass man, etc.

ĀS'MENT

b: ȧ-bāse'ment, bāse'ment,
dē-bāse'ment.
self'-ȧ-bāse'ment,
sub'bāse-ment.
br: em-brāce'ment.
f: dē-fāce'ment, ef-fāce'ment.
gr: bē-grāce'ment.
k(c̣): c̣āse'ment, en-c̣āse'ment.
l: bē-lāce'ment, en-lāce'ment,
in-tẽr-lāce'ment.
pl: dis-plāce'ment,
mis-plāce'ment, plāce'ment,
rē-plāce'ment.

(Choose only one word out of each group)

r: ē-rāse'ment.
tr: rē-trāce'ment.
Plus space meant, etc.

AS'MENT

m: à-mass'ment.
r: hà-rass'ment.
Plus class meant, etc.

AS'MIN, AZ'MIN

j: jas'mine.
Plus class, Min *or* razz, Min, etc.

ĀS'N

ch: chās'ten, en-chās'ten.
h: hās'ten.
Cf. ās'in, ās'ŏn.
Cf. face in, etc.

AS'N

f: fas'ten ('en).
Cf. cas'sŏn.
Cf. class in, etc.

ĀS'NÛR

ch: chās'tenēr ('nēr).
h: hās'tenēr ('nēr).

AS'NES

kr: crass'ness.

Ā'SŌ

s: sāy'sō.
Plus play so, sow *or* sew, etc.
Plus place owe *or* O, etc.

AS'Ō, ÄS'Ō

b: bas'sō.
g: Sär-gas'sō.
l: las'sō.

t: Tas'sō.
Plus class owe *or* O, etc.

AS'ŎK

h: has'sŏck.
k(c): cas'sŏck.

ĀS'ŎN

gr: Grāy'sŏn.
j: Jā'sŏn.
k(c): cāis'sŏn.
m: mās'ŏn.
Plus place on *or* an, etc.
Plus play, sun *or* son, etc.

AS'ŎN

k(c): cas'sŏn.
Cf. fas'ten.
Plus class on, *or* an, etc.

AS'PEN

Vowel: as'pen.
Cf. clas'pin', etc.
Plus mass pen, etc.

AS'PEST

g: gas'pest*.
gr: gras'pest*.
kl: clas'pest*, en-clas'pest*,
un-clas'pest*.
r: ras'pest*.
Plus mass pest, etc.

AS'PETH

g: gas'peth*.
gr: gras'peth*.
kl: clas'peth*, en-clas'peth*
un-clas'peth*.
r: ras'peth*.

AS'PIK
ĀS'TETH

fāte, fär, fȧst, fᶏll, finăl, cāre, at; mēte, prᶒy, hĕr, met; pīne,
marĭne, bĭrd, pin; nōte, mŏve, fᶲr, atŏm, not; mᶨᶨn, book; **386**

(Choose only one word out of each group)

AS'PIK

Vowel: as'piç.
Plus class pick, etc.

AS'PING

g: gas'ping.
gr: en-gras'ping, gras'ping.
kl: çlas'ping, en-çlas'ping,
un-çlas'ping.
r: ras'ping.
Plus class ping, etc.

AS'PŪR

Vowel: as'pĕr.
g: gas'pĕr.
gr: gras'pĕr.
j: jas'pĕr.
k(ç): Ças'păr, Ças'pĕr.
kl: çlas'pĕr, en-çlas'pĕr,
un-çlas'pĕr.
r: ras'pĕr.
Plus grasp her *or* err, etc.
Plus mass purr *or* per, etc.

AS'TÅ

sh: Shas'tȧ.
Plus past a, etc.

Ā'STÄR

d: dāy'⸗stär'.
Plus play star, etc.
Plus face tar, etc.
Plus waist, are, etc.

ĀS'TED

b: bās'ted, un-bās'ted.
h: hās'ted.
p: pās'ted, un-pās'ted.
t: tās'ted, un-tās'ted.

w: lᶲng⸗wāis'ted,
shᶲrt'⸗wāis'ted, un-wās'ted,
wᶏr'⸗wās'ted, wāis'ted,
wās'ted.
Plus face, Ted, etc.
Plus disgraced, Ed., etc.

AS'TED

bl: blas'ted, un-blas'ted.
f: fas'ted.
g: flab'bĕr-gas-ted.
l: las'ted, out-las'ted.
m: mas'ted, un″dĕr-mas'ted.
tr: çon-tras'ted.
Plus mass, Ted, etc.
Plus past, Ed, etc.

AS'TEL

p: pas'tel.
Plus class tell, etc.

ĀS'TEST

b: bās'test*.
ch: chās'test.
h: hās'test*.
p: pās'test*.
t: fōre-tās'test*, tās'test*.
w: wās'test*.
Plus face test, etc.

AS'TEST

f: fas'test.
k(ç): ças'test*.
l: las'test*, out-las'test*.
tr: çon-tras'test*.
v: vas'test.
Plus mass test, etc.

ĀS'TETH

b: bās'teth*.
h: hās'teth*.
p: pās'teth*.

387 ūse, bųll, brûte, tūrn, up; crȳ, myth; ç̣at, maç̣hine, ace, church, ç̣hord; ġem, añger, (Fr.) boṅ, aṣ; THis, thin; aẓure

AS'TETH
AS'TIKS

(Choose only one word out of each group)

t: fōre-tās'teth*, tās'teth*.
w: wās'teth*.

AS'TETH

f: fas'teth*.
k(ç̣): ç̣as'teth*.
l: las'teth*, out-las'teth*.
tr: ç̣on-tras'teth*.

ĀST'FŲL

t: dis-tāste'fųl, tāste'fųl.
w: wāste'fųl.
Plus placed full, etc.

ĀS'TI

h: hās'ty.
p: pās'ty.
t: tās'ty.
Plus face tea, tee *or* T, etc.
Plus displaced, he, etc.

AS'TI

bl: blas'ty.
m: mas'ty.
n: ep-i-nas'ty, nas'ty.
pl: ġēn-ī'ō-plas-ty, plas'ty.
v: vas'ty.
Plus class tea, tee *or* T, etc.
Plus outclassed, he, etc.

AS'TIF

m: mas'tiff.
Plus class tiff, etc.
Plus past, if, etc.

ĀS'TIJ

w: wās'tăġe.
Cf. faced age, etc.

AS'TIK

Vowel: ç̣hil-i-as'tiç̣,
eç̣-ç̣lē-ṣi-as'tiç̣, en-ç̣ō-mi-as'tiç̣,

en-thū-ṣi-as'tiç̣, ọr-ġi-as'tiç̣,
par″à-sceū-as'tiç̣,
sç̣hōl-i-as'tiç̣.
b: bom-bas'tiç̣.
bl: am-phi-blas'tiç̣.
br: Hū-di-bras'tiç̣.
dr: dras'tiç̣.
fr: an-ti-phras'tiç̣,
met-à-phras'tiç̣,
par-à-phras'tiç̣,
per-i-phras'tiç̣.
k(ç̣): dī-ç̣has'tiç̣, sär-ç̣as'tiç̣.
kl: an-à-ç̣las'tiç̣, ç̣las'tiç̣,
ī-ç̣on-ō-ç̣las'tiç̣, plāg″i-ō-ç̣las'tiç̣.
l: ē-las'tiç̣, ġē-las'tiç̣,
in-ē-las'tiç̣, sç̣hō-las'tiç̣.
m: an″tō-nō-mas'tiç̣,
doc-i-mas'tiç̣, mas'tiç̣,
on-ō-mas'tiç̣, par″ōn-ō-mas'tiç̣.
n: dȳ-nas'tiç̣, ġym-nas'tiç̣,
mō-nas'tiç̣, plē-ō-nas'tiç̣.
pl: bī-ō-plas'tiç̣, cēr-ō-plas'tiç̣,
den-tō-plas'tiç̣, em-plas'tiç̣,
es-em-plas'tiç̣,
gal″van-ō-plas'tiç̣, nē-ō-plas'tiç̣,
phel-lō-plas'tiç̣, plas'tiç̣,
prō-plas'tiç̣, prō-tō-plas'tiç̣.
r: ped-ē-ras'tiç̣, peī-ras'tiç̣.
sp: spas'tiç̣.
t: fan-tas'tiç̣.
tr: te'tras-tiç̣h.
Plus class tick, etc.
Cf. mass stick, etc.

AS'TIKS

Vowel: eç̣-ç̣lē-ṣi-as'tiç̣s.
l: ē-las'tiç̣s.
n: ġym-nas'tiç̣s
pl: phel-lō-plas'tiç̣s.
t: fan-tas'tiç̣s.
Plus as'tik+s.

AS'TĪM
AS'TRUS

fāte, fär, fåst, fąll, fĭnăl, cāre, at; mēte, prey, hẽr, met; pīne,
marĭne, bĭrd, pin; nōte, mŏve, fọr, atŏm, not; mọọn, book;

388

(Choose only one word out of each group)

AS'TĪM

p: pas'tīme.
Plus fast, I'm, etc.
Plus class time, etc.

ĀS'TING

b: bās'ting.
h: hās'ting.
p: pās'ting.
t: fōre-tās'ting, tās'ting.
w: un-wās'ting, wās'ting.
Plus play sting, etc.

AS'TING

bl: blas'ting.
f: fas'ting.
g: flab'bẽr-gas-ting.
k(c): cas'ting, fōre-cas'ting,
  rē-cas'ting.
l: ev-ẽr-las'ting, las'ting.
tr: con-tras'ting.
Plus mass sting, etc.

ĀS'TINGZ

h: Hās'tings.
Plus ās'ting+s.

ĀST'LES

b: bāste'less.
h: hāste'less.
p: pāste'less.
t: tāste'less.
w: wāist'less, wāste'less.
Plus placed less, etc.

AST'LI

f: stead'fast-ly (sted').
g: ghast'ly (gast').
l: last'ly.
v: vast'ly.
Plus massed, Lee or lea, etc.

AST'MENT

bl: blast'ment.
tr: con-trast'ment.
Plus fast meant, etc.

AST'NES

f: fast'ness.
v: vast'ness.

AST'NING

f: fas'tening.

AS'TŎN

Vowel: As'tŏn.
g: Gas'tŏn.
Plus mass ton or tun, etc.
Plus fast 'un, etc.

AS'TRĂL

Vowel: as'trăl, sub-as'trăl.
d: cà-das'trăl.

ĀS'TRI

p: pās'try.
Plus place tree, etc.

AS'TRIK

g: cac-ō-gas'tric, dī-gas'tric,
  gas'tric, hȳ-pō-gas'tric,
  per-i-gas'tric.
Plus mass trick, etc.
Plus outclassed rick, etc.

AS'TRON

Vowel: ap-as'tron.
pl: plas'tron.
Cf. fast run, etc.

AS'TRUS

Vowel: dis-as'trous.

(Choose only one word out of each group)

ĀS′TŪR

b: bās′tēr.
ch: chās′tēr.
p: pās′tēr.
t: fōre-tās′tēr, tās′tēr.
w: wās′tēr.
Plus waste her *or* err, etc.

AS′TŪR

p: pas′tūre.
Plus classed your *or* you're, etc.

AS′TŪR, ȦS′TŪR

Vowel: as′tēr, As′tŏr,
Chī′nȧ as′tēr, ġē-as′tēr,
Gōn-i-as′tēr, ōl-ē-as′tēr,
pī-as′tēr, Zōr-ō-as′tēr.
b: al-ȧ-bas′tēr.
bl: blas′tēr.
d: çȧ-das′tre ('tēr).
f: fas′tēr.
g: flab′bēr-gas-tēr.
k(ç): ças′tēr, ças′tŏr,
crit′i-ças-tēr, fōre′ças-tēr,
gram-mat-i-ças′tēr,
med-i-ças′tēr.
l: in″tēr-pī-las′tēr, pī-las′tēr.
m: band′mas-tēr,
bar′răck mas′tēr,
bŭr′gō-mas-tēr, bush′mas-tēr,
grand mas′tēr, mas′tēr,
ō-vēr-mas′tēr, pōst′mas-tēr,
quȧr′tēr-mas-tēr,
sçhọol′mas-tēr, task′mas-tēr.
n: çȧ-nas′tēr.
p: pas′tŏr.
pl: bē-plas′tēr,
çōurt plas′tēr, plas′tēr,
shin plas′tēr,
stick′ing plas′tēr.
s: dis-as′tēr.

t: Lȧ-tin′i-tas-tēr, pō′e-tas-tēr.
tr: çon-tras′tēr.
v: vas′tēr.
z: di-şas′tēr.
Plus cast her *or* err, etc.

ÄS′TŪR

sh: shäs′tēr.
Plus en massed her, etc.
Plus shah stir, etc.

AS′TŪRD, ȦS′TŪRD

b: bas′tărd.
d: das′tărd.
l: pī-las′tēred.
m: mas′tēred, ō-vēr-mas′tēred,
un-mas′tēred.
pl: bē-plas′tēred, plas′tēred.

AS′TUS

r: Ē-ras′tus, Ras′tus.
Plus cast us, etc.

AS′TYUN

b: bas′tion.
Cf. Ē-ras′tian.

ĀS′ŬR

b: ȧ-bās′ēr, bās′ēr, dē-bās′ēr.
br: brāc′ēr, em-brāc′ēr.
ch: am′bū-lănce chās′ēr,
chās′ēr, ġĭrl chās′ēr,
skĭrt chās′ēr, stee′ple-chās-ēr.
f: dē-fāc′ēr, ef-fāc′ēr, fāc′ēr.
gr: bē-grāc′ēr, dis-grāc′ēr,
grāc′ēr.
k(ç): en-çās′ēr.
l: bē-lāc′ēr, in-tēr-lāc′ēr,
lāc′ēr, un-lāc′ēr.
m: gri-māc′ēr, māc′ēr.
p: out-pāc′ēr, pȧc′ēr.

AS'ŪR
ĀT'ED

fāte, fär, fȧst, fᶏll, finăl, cãre, at; mēte, prᶒy, hêr, met; pīne,
marïne, bïrd, pin; nōte, mŏve, fᶁr, atŏm, not; mᶁᶁn, book;

390

(Choose only one word out of each group)

pl: dis-plāc'ẽr, mis-plāc'ẽr,
plāc'ẽr, rē-plāc'ẽr.
r: ē-rās'ẽr, foot rāc'ẽr,
hᶁrse rāc'ẽr, rāc'ẽr.
sp: spāc'ẽr.
tr: rē-trāc'ẽr, trāc'ẽr.
Plus chase her *or* err, etc.
Plus play, sir, etc.

AS'ŪR

k(c̲): an″ti-mȧ-c̲as'săr.
m: ȧ-mas'sẽr, mas'sẽr.
p: pas'sẽr, sŭr-pas'sẽr.
pl: plac'ẽr.
Plus pass her *or* err, etc.

ÄS'ŪR

v: kïrsc̲h'wäs-sẽr (kïrsh'väs-).
Plus en masse her.

Ā'Tȧ

Vowel: e̲'tȧ.
b: al-bā'tȧ, be̲'tȧ.
br: In-vẽr-tē-brā'tȧ,
Vẽr-tē-brā'tȧ.
d: dā'tȧ.
l: pos-tū-lā'tȧ.
m: ul-ti-mā'tȧ.
r: er-rā'tȧ, prō rā'tȧ.
str: strā'tȧ.
t: den-tā'tȧ.
th: the̲'tȧ.
z: ze̲'tȧ.
Plus state a, etc.

AT'Ȧ

g: rē-gat'tȧ.
m: mat-ȧ-mat'ȧ, yẽr'bȧ mat'ȧ.
str: strat'ȧ.
Plus sat a, etc.

Ä'TȦ

Vowel: rē-ä'tȧ.
d: dä'tȧ.
k(c̲): im-brō-c̲ä'tȧ.
l: ä bäl-lä'tȧ.
m: yẽr'bȧ mä'tȧ.
n: ser-e-nä'tȧ, sō-nä'tȧ.
r: in-am-ō-rä'tȧ, Mäh-rät'tȧ,
prō rä'tȧ.
t: bȧ-tä'tȧ c̲an-tä'tȧ.
Plus what a, etc.

ĀT'ĂL

f: fāt'ăl.
n: nāt'ăl, pōst-nāt'ăl,
prē-nāt'ăl.
st: Stāt'ăl.
Plus plate, Al, etc.

ĀT'ĂN

s: Sāt'ăn.
Cf. āt'n.
Plus mate an, etc.

ĀT'ĂNT

bl: blāt'ănt.
l: lāt'ent.
n: nāt'ănt.
p: pāt'ent.
st: stāt'ănt.
Plus rate aunt *or* ant, etc.

ĀT'ED

Vowel: ab-brē'vi-āt-ed,
ac̲-cen'tū-āt-ed, ac̲'tū-āt-ed,
af-fil'i-āt-ed, al-lē'vi-āt-ed,
am'pli-āt-ed, an-nun'ci-āt-ed,
ap-prē'ci-āt-ed ('shi-),
ap-prō'pri-āt-ed,
as-phyx'i-āt-ed,
as-so'ci-āt-ed ('shi-),

(Choose only one word out of each group)

as-tēr′i-āt-ed, at-ten′ū-āt-ed,
çal-um′ni-āt-ed,
cîr-çum-stan′ti-āt-ed (′shi-),
çŏn-cil′i-āt-ed, çrē-āt′ed,
dē-lin′ē-āt-ed,
dē-prē′ci-āt-ed (′shi-),
dē′vi-āt-ed,
dif-fēr-en′ti-āt-ed (′shi-),
dis-sō′ci-āt-ed (′shi-),
ef-feç′tū-āt-ed,
ē-mā′ci-āt-ed (′shi-),
ē-nun′ci-āt-ed (′shi-),
ē-ven′tū-āt-ed, ex-çōr′i-āt-ed,
ex-pā′ti-āt-ed (′shi-),
ex-pā′tri-āt-ed, ex′pi-āt-ed,
ex-ten′ū-āt-ed, fluç′tū-āt-ed,
grad′ū-āt-ed, hab-it′ū-āt-ed,
hūm-il′i-āt-ed, im-prō′pri-āt-ed,
in-ē′bri-āt-ed, in-fat′ū-āt-ed,
in-fū′ri-āt-ed,
in-grā′ti-āt-ed (′shi-),
in-i′ti-āt-ed (′shi-),
in-sin′ū-āt-ed, ir-rā′di-āt-ed,
lux-ūr′i-āt-ed,
nē-gō′ti-āt-ed (′shi-),
ob′vi-āt-ed, of-fi′ci-āt-ed (′shi-),
pal′li-āt-ed, pēr′mē-āt-ed,
pēr-pet′ū-āt-ed,
prō-pit′i-āt-ed (-pish′),
puñç′tū-āt-ed, rād′i-āt-ed,
re′çrē-āt-ed, rē-pāt′ri-āt-ed,
rē-pū′di-āt-ed, rē-tal′i-āt-ed,
sāt′i-āt-ed (sāsh′), sit′ū-āt-ed,
sub-stan′ti-āt-ed (′shi-),
sū-pēr-an′nū-āt-ed,
un-ap-prō′pri-āt-ed,
un-çrē-āt′ed, vār′i-āt-ed,
vit′i-āt-ed (vish′).

b: à-bāt′ed, ap′prō-bāt-ed,
bāit′ed, bāt′ed, dē-bāt′ed,
in′çū-bāt-ed, un-à-bāt′ed.

br: cel′ē-brāt-ed.
d: aç-çom′mō-dāt-ed,
an-tē-dāt′ed, çŏn-sol′i-dāt-ed,
dāt′ed, di-lap′i-dāt-ed,
ē-lū′ci-dāt-ed, in-tim′i-dāt-ed,
in′un-dāt-ed, in-val′i-dāt-ed,
li′qui-dāt-ed, val′i-dāt-ed.
f: fāt′ed, fet′ed, ill′⸗fāt′ed.
fl: ef-flāt′ed, in-flāt′ed.
fr: freight′ed (frāt′).
g: ab′nē-gāt-ed, ab′rō-gāt-ed,
ag′grē-gāt-ed, ar′rō-gāt-ed,
ças′ti-gāt-ed, çon′grē-gāt-ed,
çon′jū-gāt-ed, çor′rū-gāt-ed,
del′ē-gāt-ed, der′ō-gāt-ed,
fūm′i-gāt-ed, gāit′ed, gāt′ed,
heav′y⸗gāit′ed (hev′),
in′sti-gāt-ed, in-ter′rō-gāt-ed,
in-ves′ti-gāt-ed, ir′ri-gāt-ed,
lev′i-gāt-ed, mit′i-gāt-ed,
nav′i-gāt-ed, ob′li-gāt-ed,
pro′pà-gāt-ed, rel′ē-gāt-ed,
se′grē-gāt-ed, sub′jū-gāt-ed,
un-mit′i-gāt-ed, vār′i-e-gāt-ed.
gr: dis-in′tē-grāt-ed,
em′i-grāt-ed, grāt′ed,
im′mi-grāt-ed, mī′grāt-ed.
h: hāt′ed.
k(ç): ab′di-çāt-ed, ab′lō-çāt-ed,
ad-jū′di-çāt-ed, ad′vō-çāt-ed,
al′lō-çāt-ed, au-then′ti-çāt-ed,
bī′fūr-çāt-ed, cĕr-tif′i-çāt-ed,
çol′lō-çāt-ed, çŏm-mū′ni-çāt-ed,
çom′pli-çāt-ed, çon′fis-çāt-ed,
ded′i-çāt-ed, de′prē-çāt-ed,
dis′lō-çāt-ed, dō-mes′ti-çāt-ed,
dū′pli-çāt-ed, ed′ū-çāt-ed,
ē-quiv′ō-çāt-ed, ē-rad′i-çāt-ed,
ex-çŏm-mū′ni-çāt-ed,
ex′tri-çāt-ed, fab′ri-çāt-ed,
im′pli-çāt-ed, im′prē-çāt-ed,

(Choose only one word out of each group)

in'di-c̣āt-ed, in-tox'i-c̣āt-ed,
in'vō-c̣āt-ed, lō'c̣āt-ed,
lū'bri-c̣āt-ed, mas'ti-c̣āt-ed,
med'i-c̣āt-ed, plā'c̣āt-ed,
plī'c̣āt-ed, pre'di-c̣āt-ed,
prē-var'i-c̣āt-ed,
prog-nos'ti-c̣āt-ed,
rē-cip'rō-c̣āt-ed, rus'ti-c̣āt-ed,
sil'i-c̣āt-ed, sō-phis'ti-c̣āt-ed,
spif'fli-c̣āt-ed, suf'fō-c̣āt-ed,
sup'pli-c̣āt-ed, syn'di-c̣āt-ed,
un-au-then'ti-c̣āt-ed,
un-sō-phis'ti-c̣āt-ed, vā-c̣āt'ed,
vin'di-c̣āt-ed.

kr: c̣on'sē-c̣rāt-ed, des'ē-c̣rāt-ed
ex'ē-c̣rāt-ed.

kw: an'ti-quāt-ed.

l: ac̣-c̣ū'mū-lāt-ed, ac-id'ū-lāt-ed,
an-nī'hil-āt-ed, an'nū-lāt-ed,
är'mil-lāt-ed, är-tic̣'ū-lāt-ed,
as-sim'i-lāt-ed, as-sim'ū-lāt-ed,
bē-lāt'ed, c̣al'c̣ū-lāt-ed,
c̣ap-it'ū-lāt-ed, c̣as'tel-lāt-ed,
cīr'c̣ū-lāt-ed, c̣ō-ag'ū'-lāt-ed,
c̣ol'lāt-ed, c̣ŏn-fab'ū-lāt-ed,
c̣ŏn-grat'ū-lāt-ed, cop'ū-lāt-ed,
c̣or're-lāt-ed, c̣ren'el-lāt-ed,
dē-pop'ū-lāt-ed, des'ō-lāt-ed.
dī'lāt-ed, dis-sim'ū-lāt-ed,
ē-jac̣'ū-lāt-ed, ē-lāt'ed,
ē-mas'c̣ū-lāt-ed, e'mū-lāt-ed,
ē-vac̣'ū-āt-ed, ex-pos'tū-lāt-ed,
flaġ'el-lāt-ed, fŏr'mū-lāt-ed,
ġes-tic̣'ū-lāt-ed, gran'ū-lāt-ed,
grat'ū-lāt-ed, im'mō-lāt-ed,
in-c̣as'tel-lāt-ed, in-oc̣'ū-lāt-ed,
in'sū-lāt-ed, in-tēr'pō-lāt-ed,
ī'sō-lāt-ed, leġ'is-lāt-ed,
man-ip'ū-lāt-ed,
mà-tric̣'ū-lāt-ed,
men'thō-lāt-ed, me-thy-lāt'ed,

mod'ū-lāt-ed, mūt'i-lāt-ed,
nū'c̣lē-āt-ed, os'cil-lāt-ed,
os'c̣ū-lāt-ed, pēr-am'bū-lāt-ed
pēr'c̣ō-lāt-ed, pop'ū-lāt-ed,
pos'tū-lāt-ed, rē-c̣ap-it'ū-lāt-ed,
reg'ū-lāt-ed, rē-lāt'ed,
scin'til-lāt-ed, sib'i-lāt-ed,
sim'i-lāt-ed, spec̣'ū-lāt-ed,
stim'ū-lāt-ed, stip'ū-lāt-ed,
tab'ū-lāt-ed, tes'sel-lāt-ed,
ti'til-lāt-ed, trans-lāt'ed,
trī-añ'gū-lāt-ed, ū'lū-lāt-ed,
un'dū-lāt-ed, un-rē-lāt'ed,
va'cil-lāt-ed, ven'ti-lāt-ed,
vī'ō-lāt-ed.

m: a-mal'ġà-māt-ed,
ap-prox'i-māt-ed,
c̣on'sum-māt-ed, c̣rē'māt-ed,
dec'i-māt-ed, es'ti-māt-ed,
in'ti-māt-ed, māt'ed,
sub'li-māt-ed.

n: ab-om'i-nāt-ed, ā'li-e-nāt-ed,
ạl'tēr-nāt-ed, as-sas'si-nāt-ed,
c̣är'bŏ-nāt-ed, c̣om'mi-nāt-ed,
c̣ŏn-tam'i-nāt-ed,
c̣ō=or'di-nāt-ed, c̣or'ō-nāt-ed,
c̣ul'mi-nāt-ed, dē-nom'i-nāt-ed,
deṣ'ig-nāt-ed, de'tō-nāt-ed,
dis-c̣rim'i-nāt-ed,
dis-sem'i-nāt-ed,
dom'i-nāt-ed, ē-lim'i-nāt-ed,
e'mà-nāt-ed, ex-tēr'mi-nāt-ed,
fas'ci-nāt-ed, fōre-or'di-nāt-ed,
ful'mi-nāt-ed, ġēr'mi-nāt-ed,
il-lū'mi-nāt-ed,
im-pēr'sŏ-nāt-ed,
in-c̣rim'i-nāt-ed,
in-doc̣'tri-nāt-ed, mar'i-nāt-ed,
nom'i-nāt-ed,
ō-pin'iŏn-āt-ed ('yun-),
ōr-iġ'i-nāt-ed, per'ē-gri-nāt-ed,

(Choose only one word out of each group)

pēr′sŏ-nāt-ed, prē-des′ti-nāt-ed,
prē-dom′i-nāt-ed,
prō-çras′ti-nāt-ed,
rē-çrim′i-nāt-ed, rē-jủ′vē-nāt-ed,
rủ′mi-nāt-ed, sub-ọr′di-nāt-ed,
tēr′mi-nāt-ed,
un-il-lū′mi-nāt-ed, vaç′ci-nāt-ed.

p: ad′dle-pāt′ed, an-ti′ci-pāt-ed,
dis′si-pāt-ed, dun′dēr-pāt-ed,
ē-man′ci-pāt-ed, ī′dle⹀pāt′ed,
pär-tic′i-pāt-ed, rat′tle-pāt′ed,
shal′lōw-pāt′ed, syñ′çō-pāt-ed.

pl: är′mŏr-plāt-ed,
çon′tem-plāt-ed,
çop′pēr-plāt-ed,
ēl-eç′trō-plāt-ed,
nick′el⹀plāt′ed, plāit′ed,
plāt′ed, sil′vēr⹀plāt′ed.

pr: prāt′ed.

r: aç-cel′ē-rāt-ed,
ad-ul′tē-rāt-ed, ā′ē-rāt-ed,
ag-glom′ē-rāt-ed,
à-mē′li-ō-rāt-ed,
an-nu′mē-rāt-ed*, as′pi-rāt-ed,
as-sev′ē-rāt-ed, au′gū-rāt-ed,
au′rāt-ed, bē′rāt-ed,
çam′phŏ-rāt-ed,
çŏm-mem′ō-rāt-ed,
çŏm-miṣ′ē-rāt-ed,
çŏn-fed′ē-rāt-ed,
çŏn-glom′ē-rāt-ed,
çō⹀op′ē-rāt-ed, çŏr-ro′bō-rāt-ed,
de′çō-rāt-ed, dē-ġen′ē-rāt-ed,
dē-lib′ē-rāt-ed, dē-sid′ē-rāt-ed,
dē-tē′ri-ō-rāt-ed, ē-lab′ō-rāt-ed,
ē-nū′mē-rāt-ed, ē-vap′ō-rāt-ed,
ex-aġ′ġē-rāt-ed, ex-as′pē-rāt-ed,
ex-hil′à-rāt-ed, ex-on′ē-rāt-ed,
ex-peç′tō-rāt-ed, fed′ē-rāt-ed,
ġen′ē-rāt-ed, in-au′gū-rāt-ed,
in-çär′çē-rāt-ed, in-cin′ē-rāt-ed,

in-çọr′pō-rāt-ed, in′dū-rāt-ed,
in-vig′ŏ-rāt-ed, i′tē-rāt-ed,
jas′pē-rāt-ed, lib′ē-rāt-ed,
mac′ē-rāt-ed, mod′ē-rāt-ed,
nar′rāt-ed, ob-lit′ē-rāt-ed,
op′ē-rāt-ed, ō-vēr-rāt′ed,
pēr′fō-rāt-ed, rāt′ed,
rē-çū′pē-rāt-ed, rē-friġ′ē-rāt-ed,
rē-ġen′ē-rāt-ed, rē-it′ē-rāt-ed,
rē-mū′nē-rāt-ed,
rē-vēr′bē-rāt-ed, sat′ū-rāt-ed,
sep′à-rāt-ed, tol′ē-rāt-ed,
trī′tū-rāt-ed, un-deç′ō-rāt-ed,
un-dēr-rāt′ed, ven′ē-rāt-ed,
vī-tū′pē-rāt-ed, vō-cif′ē-rāt-ed.

s: çom′pen-sāt-ed, sāt′ed,
tēr′ġiv-ēr-sāt-ed.

sk: skāt′ed.

sl: slāt′ed.

st: in-stāt′ed, ō-vēr-stāt′ed,
rē-in-stāt′ed, stāt′ed,
un-dēr-stāt′ed, un-stāt′ed.

str: dem′ŏn-strāt-ed,
un-dem′ŏn-strāt-ed.

t: aġ′i-tāt-ed, am′pū-tāt-ed,
an′nō-tāt-ed, çà-pac′i-tāt-ed,
çoġ′i-tāt-ed, çrep′i-tāt-ed,
dē-bil′i-tāt-ed, dē-çap′i-tāt-ed,
de′văs-tāt-ed, diç′tāt-eᶁ,
ex-ọr′bi-tāt-ed, fà-cil′i-tāt-ed,
grav′i-tāt-ed, heṣ′i-tāt-ed,
im′i-tāt-ed, in-çà-pac′i-tāt-ed,
ir′ri-tāt-ed, med′i-tāt-ed,
mil′i-tāt-ed, nē-ces′si-tāt-ed,
pal′pi-tāt-ed, prē-cip′i-tāt-ed,
prē-med′i-tāt-ed,
rē-hab-il′i-tāt-ed,
rē-sus′ci-tāt-ed,
un-prē-med′i-tāt-ed,
veġ′ē-tāt-ed.

tr: är′bi-trāt-ed, çon cen-trāt-ed,

AT'ED
ĀT'EST

fāte, fär, fȧst, fall, finăl, cãre, at; mēte, prey, hẽr, met; pīne,
marĭne, bĭrd, pin; nōte, mŏve, fŏr, atŏm, not; mŏŏn, book;

394

(Choose only one word out of each group)

frus'trāt-ed, il'lus-trāt-ed,
pen'ē-trāt-ed, pĕr'pē-trāt-ed.
v: ag'grȧ-vāt-ed, ċap'ti-vāt-ed,
ċul'ti-vāt-ed, el'ē-vāt-ed,
ex'ċȧ-vāt-ed, in'nō-vāt-ed,
re'nō-vāt-ed, Rē'nō-vāt-ed,
sal'i-vāt-ed, tit'i-vāt-ed.
w: ȧ-wāit'ed,
heav'y-weight-ed (hev'i-wāt-),
wāit'ed, weight'ed (wāt').
Plus say, Ted, etc.
Plus plate, Ed, etc.

AT'ED

Vowel: ċar-y-at'id.
b: bat'ted.
ch: chat'ted.
dr: drat'ted.
f: fat'ted.
h: hat'ted, hīgh'⸗hat'ted (hī'),
top'⸗hat'ted.
m: mat'ted.
p: pat'ted.
pl: plait'ed, plat'ted.
Plus that, Ed, etc.

AT'EN

b: bat'ten.
f: fat'ten.
fl: flat'ten.
p: pat'en.
r: rat'ten.
Cf. at'in.

ĀT'ENT, AT'ENT

p: pāt'ent.
Plus play-tent, etc.
Cf. mate tent, flat tent, etc.

ĀT'EST

Vowel: al-lē'vi-āt-est*,
ap-prē'ci-āt-est ('shi-)*,
as-sō'ci-āt-est ('shi-)*,
crē'āt-est*, grad'ū-āt-est*,
rād'i-āt-est*, rē-pū'di-āt-est*.
b: ȧ-bāt'est*, bāit'est*,
dē-bāt'est*.
br: cel'ē-brāt-est*.
d: aċ-ċom'mō-dāt-est*.
g: ċon'jū-gāt-est*.
gr: grāt'est*, greāt'est.
h: hāt'est*.
k(ċ): ab'di-ċāt-est*,
ad'vō-ċāt-est*,
ċom-mū'ni-ċāt-est*,
dē-prē-ċāt-est*, in'di-ċāt-est*,
vā'ċāt-est*.
kr: ċon'sē-ċrāt-est*.
l: aċ-ċū'mū-lāt-est*,
an-nī'hi-lāt-est*,
är-tiċ'ū-lāt-est*,
as-sim'ū-lāt-est*, ċal'ċū-lāt-est*,
dī-lāt'est*, ē-jaċ'ū-lāt-est*,
em'ū-lāt-est*, lāt'est,
reg'ū-lāt-est*, rē-lāt'est*,
trans-lāt'est*, vī'ō-lāt-est*.
m: an'i-māt-est*, māt'est*.
n: ċon-tam'i-nāt-est*,
fas'ci-nāt-est*.
p: an-ti'ci-pāt-est*.
pl: ċon'tem-plāt-est*, plāit'est*.
pr: prāt'est*.
r: ȧ-dul'tē-rāt-est*, bē-rāt'est*,
ċom-mem'ō-rāt-est*,
deċ'ō-rāt-est*, ex-ag'gē-rāt-est*,
lib'ē-rāt-est*, nar-rāt'est*,
ō-vĕr-rāt'est*, rāt'est*,
tol'ē-rāt-est*, un-dĕr-rāt'est*.
sk: skāt'est*.
sl: slāt'est*.
st: stāt'est*.
t: ag'i-tāt-est*, ċog'i-tāt-est*,
de'văs-tāt-est*, diċ'tāt-est*,
heṣ'i-tāt-est*, im'i-tāt-est*.

(Choose only one word out of each group)

ir′ri-tāt-est*, nē-ces′si-tāt-est*.
tr: frus′trāt-est*.
v: ag′grȧ-vāt-est*,
ça̧p′ti-vāt-est*, çu̧l′ti-vāt-est*,
el′ē-vāt-est*.
w: ȧ-wāit′est*, wāit′est*, etc.
Plus play test, etc.

AT′EST

b: bat′test*.
ch: chat′test*.
f: fat′test.
fl: flat′test.
p: pat′test*.
Cf. mat test, etc.

ĀT′ETH

Vowel: al-lē′vi-āt-eth*,
ap-prē′ci-āt-eth (′shi-)*,
as-sō′ci-āt-eth (′shi-)*,
c̦rē-āt′eth*, grad′ū-āt-eth*,
rād′i-āt-eth*, rē-pū′di-āt-eth*.
b: ȧ-bāt′eth*, bāit′eth*,
dē-bāt′eth*.
br: cel′ē-brāt-eth*.
d: ac̦-c̦om′mō-dāt-eth*.
g: c̦on′jū-gāt-eth*.
gr: grāt′eth*.
h: hāt′eth*.
k(c̦): ab′di-c̦āt-eth*,
ad′vō-c̦āt-eth*,
c̦ŏm-mū′ni-c̦āt-eth*,
de′prē-c̦āt-eth*, in′di-c̦āt-eth*,
vā′c̦āt-eth*.
kr: c̦on′sē-c̦rāt-eth*.
l: ac̦-c̦ū′mū-lāt-eth*,
an-nī′hi-lāt-eth*,
är-tic̦′ū-lāt-eth*,
as-sim′ū-lāt-eth*,
c̦al′c̦ū-lāt-eth*, dī-lāt′eth*,
ē-jac̦′ū-lāt-eth*, em′ū-lāt-eth*,
reg′ū-lāt-eth*, rē-lāt′eth*,

trans-lāt′eth*, vī′ō-lāt-eth*.
m: an′i-māt-eth*, māt′eth*.
n: c̦ŏn-tam′i-nāt-eth*,
fas′ci-nāt-eth*.
p: an-ti′ci-pāt-eth*.
pl: c̦on′tem-plāt-eth*, plāit′eth*.
pr: prāt′eth*.
r: ȧ-dul′tē-rāt-eth*, bē-rāt′eth*,
c̦ŏm-mem′ō-rāt-eth*,
dec̦′ō-rāt-eth*, ex-ag̣′g̣ē-rāt-eth*,
lib′ē-rāt-eth*, nar-rāt′eth*,
ō-vĕr-rāt′eth*, rāt′eth*,
tol′ē-rāt-eth*, un-dĕr-rāt′eth*.
sk: skāt′eth*.
sl: slāt′eth*.
st: stāt′eth*.
t: ag̣-i-tāt′eth*, c̦og̣′i-tāt-eth*,
de′vǎs-tāt-eth*, dic̦′tāt-eth*,
heṣ′i-tāt-eth*, im′i-tāt-eth*,
ir′ri-tāt-eth*, nē-ces′si-tāt-eth*.
tr: frus′trāt-eth*.
v: ag′grȧ-vāt-eth*,
ça̧p′ti-vāt-eth*, çu̧l′ti-vāt-eth*,
el′ē-vāt-eth*.
w: ȧ-wāit′eth*, wāit′eth*, etc.

AT′ETH

b: bat′teth*.
ch: chat′teth*.
f: fat′teth*.
p: pat′teth*.

ĀT′ĒZ

n: pē-nāt′ēṣ.
Plus rate ease *or* E's, etc.
Plus play tease *or* T's, etc.

AT′FOOT

fl: flat′foot.
Plus that foot, etc.

AT′FǪRM

pl: plat′fǫrm.
Plus that form, etc.

(Choose only one word out of each group)

ĀT'FŬL

f: fāte'fŭl.
gr: grāte'fŭl, un-grāte'fŭl.
h: hāte'fŭl.
Plus plate full, etc.

ÄT'HȦ

n: Jag-ăn-näi'hȧ.
Cf. mä-rȧ-näth'ȧ.

Ā'THĂN

n: El-nā'thăn, Nā'thăn.
Cf. "hāy'than".
Plus faith, an, etc.

AT'HED

f: fat'head.
fl: flat'head.
Plus cat head, etc.

ATH'EN

l: lath'en.
Cf. wrath, an, etc.

ATH'ENZ

Vowel: Ath'ens̩.

ĀTH'FŬL

f: fāith'fŭl.
Plus wraith full, etc.

ÄTH'FŬL, ȦTH'FŬL

r: wräth'fŭl.
Plus lath full, etc.

ATH'IK

m: c̦hrest-ō-math'ic̦,
  phil-ō-math'ic̦, pol-y-math'ic̦.
n: or-thog-nath'ic̦, prog-nath'ic̦.
p: al-lō-path'ic̦, an"ti-path'ic̦,

ēl-ec̦-trō-path'ic̦, fels-path'ic̦,
het"ẽr-ō-path'ic̦,
hō"mē-ō-path'ic̦, hȳ-drō-path'ic̦,
id-i-ō-path'ic̦, neū-rō-path'ic̦,
os"tē-ō-path'ic̦,
psȳ-c̦hō-path'ic̦ (sī-),
tel-ē-path'ic̦, thē-ō-path'ic̦.
sp: spath'ic̦.
Cf. wrath thick, etc.

ĀTH'ING

b: bāTH'ing.
sw: swāTH'ing, un-swaTH'ing.

Ā'THING

pl: plāy'thing.
Cf. scath'ing.
Plus stray thing, etc.

ĀTH'ING

b: bāth'ing.
l: lāth'ing.

ĀTH'LES

f: fāith'less.
sk(sc̦): sc̦āthe'less.
Plus wraith less *or* Les, etc.

ATH'LES

b: bath'less.
p: path'less.
r: wrath'less.
Plus lath, less *or* Les, etc.

ĀTH'ŎM

f: faTH'ŏm.

ATH'ŎMD

f: faTH'ŏmed, un-faTH'ŏmed.

(Choose only one word out of each group)

ĀTH′OS

b: bāth′os.
p: pāth′os.

ATH′Ū

m: Mat′thew (math′).
Plus path you *or* ewe, etc.

ĀTH′ŪR

b: bāTH′ĕr.
sw: swāTH′ĕr.
Plus scathe her *or* err, etc.

ATH′ŪR

bl: blaTH′ĕr.
g: for-gaTH′ĕr, gaTH′ĕr,
un-gaTH′ĕr, up-gaTH′ĕr.
l: laTH′ĕr.

ÄTH′ŪR, ȦTH′ŪR

f: fäTH′ĕr.
r: räTH′ĕr.
Cf. oTH′ŭr.

ATH′ŪRZ

sl: slaTH′ĕrṣ.
Plus aTH′ŭr+s.

ĀT′I, Ā′TI

Vowel: Ā′tē, eight′y (āt′).
h: Hāi′ti, Hāy′ti.
k: Kā′tie (′ti).
l: Jù-bi-lāt′ē.
m: māt′y.
pl: plāt′y.
sl: slāt′y.
t: ex nē-ces′si-tā-tē.
w: weight′y (wāt′).
Plus state he, etc.
Plus play tea *or* T, etc.

ĀT′Ī

n: an-tē-nā′tī, il-lū-mi-nā′tī.
r: lit-e-rā′tī.
Plus plate, I *or* eye, etc.
Plus stray tie, etc.

AT′I

b: bat′ty.
ch: chat′ty.
f: fat′ty.
h: Hat′ty.
k(c): cat′ty, Kat′ty.
m: Mat′tie (′ti), mat′ty.
n: Cin-cin-nat′i, nat′ty.
p: Pat′tie, pat′ty.
r: rat′ty.
Plus skat, he, etc.

AT′ĪD

b: bat′=eȳed′.
k(c): cat′=eȳed′.
Plus flat, I′d *or* eyed, etc.

AT′ID

Vowel: car-y-at′id.
Cf. at′ed.
Cf. flat hid, etc.

Ā′TIF

k(c): cāi′tiff.
Plus play tiff, etc.
Plus plate, if, etc.

AT′IK

Vowel: a-crō-at′ic, Ād-ri-at′ic,
Ā-si-at′ic (-zhi-), at′tic,
car-y-at′ic, E-lē-at′ic,
flù-vi-at′ic, Han-sē-at′ic,
mūr-i-at′ic, pan-crē-at′ic,
scī-at′ic (sī-), vī-at′ic.

(Choose only one word out of each group)

b: ac̦-rō-bat′ic̦, ad″i-ȧ-bat′ic̦,
ec̦-bat′ic̦*, hȳ-pẽr-bat′ic̦,
īs″ō-dī-ȧ-bat′ic̦, sab-bat′ic̦.

f: em-phat′ic̦, lym-phat′ic̦,
phos-phat′ic̦, sul-phat′ic̦.

kr: ar-is-tō-c̦rat′ic̦,
ar-ith-mō-c̦rat′ic̦, ạu-tō-c̦rat′ic̦,
bū-reau-c̦rat′ic̦ (-rō-),
dem-ō-c̦rat′ic̦, id″i-ō-c̦rat′ic̦,
id″i-ō-syn-c̦rat′ic̦, mob-ō-c̦rat′ic̦,
oc̦h-lō-c̦rat′ic̦, pan-c̦rat′ic̦,
pan″tī-sō-c̦rat′ic̦, plu̇-tō-c̦rat′ic̦,
Sō-c̦rat′ic̦, thē-ō-c̦rat′ic̦,
tim-ō-c̦rat′ic̦.

kw: ȧ-quat′ic̦, sub-ȧ-quat′ic̦.

l: pȧ-lat′ic̦, prē-lat′ic̦, vil-lat′ic̦.

m: a-c̦hrō-mat′ic̦, a-c̦öus-mat′ic̦,
ac̦″rō-mon″ō-gram-mat′ic̦,
an″ȧ-gram-mat′ic̦,
a-phōr-iș-mat′ic̦,
ap″ō-phtheg-mat′ic̦ (-theg-),
ar-ō-mat′ic̦, așth-mat′ic̦ (az-),
ạu-tō-mat′ic̦, ax-i-ō-mat′ic̦,
c̦at″ē-gor-ē-mat′ic̦, c̦hrō-mat′ic̦,
c̦lī-mat′ic̦, c̦ŏm-mat′ic̦,
dal-mat′ic̦, dī″ȧ-gram-mat′ic̦,
dī″ȧ-phrag-mat′ic̦,
dī-c̦hrō-mat′ic̦, di-lem-mat′ic̦,
di-plō-mat′ic̦, dog-mat′ic̦,
drȧ-mat′ic̦, em-ble-mat′ic̦,
en-dẽr-mat′ic̦, ē-nig-mat′ic̦,
ep″i-gram-mat′ic̦, gram-mat′ic̦,
hī″ẽr-ō-gram-mat′ic̦,
id″i-ō-mat′ic̦, ī″sō-c̦hrō-mat′ic̦,
kin-ē-mat′ic̦, lip″ō-gram-mat′ic̦,
math-ē-mat′ic̦,
mel″ō-drȧ-mat′ic̦, mī-aș-mat′ic̦,
mon″ō-c̦hrō-mat′ic̦,
mon″ō-gram-mat′ic̦,
nō-ē-mat′ic̦*, nū-miș-mat′ic̦,
par″ȧ-dig-mat′ic̦,

par″al-lel″ō-gram-mat′ic̦,
path-ē-mat′ic̦, phan-tō-mat′ic̦,
phleg-mat′ic̦, plē-ō-c̦hrō-mat′ic̦,
pneū-mat′ic̦ (nū-), pō-ē-mat′ic̦,
pol″y-c̦hrō-mat′ic̦, prag-mat′ic̦,
priș-mat′ic̦, prob-lē-mat′ic̦,
pro″c̦ē-leūs-mat′ic̦, rhē-mat′ic̦,
rheū-mat′ic̦, Sär-mat′ic̦,
sc̦hē-mat′ic̦, schiș-mat′ic̦ (siz-),
smeg-mat′ic̦, sō-mat′ic̦,
stig-mat′ic̦, strō-mat′ic̦,
symp-tō-mat′ic̦, sys-te-mat′ic̦,
thē-mat′ic̦, thē-ō-mat′ic̦,
trạu-mat′ic̦, trī-gram-mat′ic̦,
tru̇-is-mat′ic̦, zeūg-mat′ic̦,
zȳ-gō-mat′ic̦.

n: ag-nat′ic̦, a-plȧ-nat′ic̦,
fȧ-nat′ic̦, mọr-gȧ-nat′ic̦.

p: hē-pat′ic̦.

pl: plat′ic̦.

r: er-rat′ic̦, hī-ē-rat′ic̦,
op-ē-rat′ic̦, pī-rat′ic̦,
quäd-rat′ic̦.

st: ā″ē-rō-stat′ic̦,
an-ȧ-stat′ic̦, ā-stat′ic̦,
ec̦-stat′ic̦, ġē-ō-stat′ic̦,
hȳ-drō-stat′ic̦, hȳ-pō-stat′ic̦,
prō-stat′ic̦, stat′ic̦,
thẽr-mō-stat′ic̦.

t: ma-jes-tat′ic̦*, prō-tat′ic̦.

tr: maġ-is-trat′ic̦.

v: lȧ-vat′ic̦, syl-vat′ic̦, **vat′ic̦.**

y: hal′lē-lu̇-jat′ic̦ (-yat′).

Plus that tick, etc.

ÄT′IK

kw: ȧ-quät′ic̦.

Cf. ot′ik.

Plus ma tick, etc.

399 ūse, bṳll, brúte, tŭrn, **up;** cr̂ŷ, myth; ça̱t, maçhine, ace, church, çhord; ġem, añger, (Fr.) boṅ, aṣ; THis, thin; azure

AT′IKS
ĀT′ING

(Choose only one word out of each group)

AT′IKS

m: math-ē-mat′iç̱s,
   pneū-mat′iç̱s (nū-).

st: ā″ēr-ō-stat′iç̱s,
   ēl-eç̱-trō-stat′iç̱s, hȳ-drō-stat′iç̱s,
   hȳ-grō-stat′iç̱s, stat′iç̱s.

Plus at′ik+s.

Ā′TĪM

d: dāy′tīme.
m: Māy′tīme.
pl: plāy′tīme.
Plus hay time, etc.
Plus hate, I'm, etc.

ĀT′IM

Vowel: sēr-i-āt′im.
b: vēr-bāt′im.
r: lit-e-rāt′im.
Plus hate him, etc.
Plus play, Tim, etc.

AT′IN

l: Lat′in.
m: mat′in.
p: pat′ine.
pl: plat′en.
s: sat′in.
Cf. Man-hat′tăn.
Cf. at′en.
Plus flat in *or* inn, etc.

ĀT′ING

Vowel: ab-brē′vi-āt-ing,
   aç̱-cen′tū-āt-ing, al-lē′vi-āt-ing,
   ap-prē′ci-āt-ing (′shi-),
   ap-prō′pri-āt-ing,
   as-sō′ci-āt-ing (′shi-),
   at-ten′ū-āt-ing, ça̱l-um′ni-āt-ing,
   çŏn-cil′i-āt-ing, çrē-āt′′ing,
   dē-lin′ē-āt-ing,
   dē-prē′ci-āt-ing (′shi-),

dē′vi-āt-ing,
   dif-fēr-en′ti-āt-ing (′shi-),
   dis-sō′ci-āt-ing (′shi-),
   ē-mā′ci-āt-ing (′shi-),
   ē-vaç̱′ū-āt-ing,
   ex-ç̱rù′ci-āt-ing (′shi-),
   ex-pā′ti-āt-ing (′shi-),
   ex′pi-āt-ing, ex-ten′ū-āt-ing,
   fluç̱′tū-āt-ing, grad′ū-āt-ing,
   hū-mil′i-āt-ing, in-ē′bri-āt-ing,
   in-fat′ū-āt-ing, in-fū′ri-āt-ing,
   in-grā′ti-āt-ing (′shi-),
   in-i′ti-āt-ing (′shi-),
   in-sin′ū-āt-ing, ir-rā′di-āt-ing,
   lux-ūr′i-āt-ing, mēd′i-āt-ing,
   nē-gō′ti-āt-ing (′shi-),
   ob′vi-āt-ing, pal′li-āt-ing,
   pēr′mē-āt-ing, pēr-pet′ū-āt-ing,
   prō-pi′ti-āt-ing (′shi-),
   punç̱′tū-āt-ing, rād′i-āt-ing,
   re′ç̱rē-āt-ing, sā′ti-āt-ing (′shi-),
   un-dē′vi-āt-ing,
   vit′i-āt-ing (vish′).

b: a̱-bāt′ing, bāit′ing, bāt′ing,
   dē-bāt′ing, in′ç̱ū-bāt-ing,
   rē′bāt-ing, un-a̱-bāt′ing.

br: cel′ē-brāt-ing.

d: aç̱-ç̱om′mō-dāt-ing, dāt′ing,
   di-lap′i-dāt-ing, ē-lū′ci-dāt-ing,
   in-tim′i-dāt-ing, in′un-dāt-ing,
   in-val′i-dāt-ing, li′qui-dāt-ing,
   un-aç̱-ç̱om′mō-dāt-ing,
   val′i-dāt-ing.

f: fe̱t′ing.
fl: in-flāt′ing.
fr: freight′ing (frāt′).
g: ab′nē-gāt-ing, ag′grē-gāt-ing,
   ça̱s′ti-gāt-ing, ç̱on′grē-gāt-ing,
   ç̱on′jū-gāt-ing, ç̱or′rū-gāt-ing,
   del′ē-gāt-ing, der′ō-gāt-ing,
   fūm′i-gāt-ing, in′sti-gāt-ing,

ĀT'ING

fāte, fär, fàst, fₐll, finăl, cāre, at; mēte, prₑy, hȇr, met; pīne,
marīne, bȋrd, pȋn; nōte, mŏve, fₒr, atŏm, not; mₒₒn, book;

400

(Choose only one word out of each group)

in-ter'rō-gāt-ing,
in-ves'ti-gāt-ing, ir'ri-gāt-ing,
nav'i-gāt-ing, prō-mul'gāt-ing,
ᴠro'pà-gāt-ing, re'lē-gāt-ing,
sub'jù-gāt-ing, vȧr'i-e-gāt-ing.
gr: dis-in'tē-grāt-ing,
em'i-grāt-ing, grāt'ing,
im'mi-grāt-ing, mȋ'grāt-ing.
h: hāt'ing.
k(c̱): ab'di-c̱āt-ing,
ad'vō-c̱āt-ing,
ạu-then'ti-c̱āt-ing, c̱ol'lō-c̱āt-ing,
c̱ŏm-mū'ni-c̱āt-ing,
com'pli-c̱āt-ing, c̱on'fis-c̱āt-ing,
ded'i-c̱āt-ing, de'prē-c̱āt-ing,
dis'lō-c̱āt-ing, dū'pli-c̱āt-ing,
ed'ū-c̱āt-ing, ē-quiv'ō-c̱āt-ing,
ē-rad'i-c̱āt-ing,
ex-c̱ŏm-mū'ni-c̱āt-ing,
ex'tri-c̱āt-ing, fab'ri-c̱āt-ing,
fₒr'ni-c̱āt-ing, im'pli-c̱āt-ing,
im'prē-c̱āt-ing, in'di-c̱āt-ing,
in-tox'i-c̱āt-ing, in'vō-c̱āt-ing,
lō'c̱āt-ing, lū'bri-c̱āt-ing,
mas'ti-c̱āt-ing, prē-var'i-c̱āt-ing,
prog-nos'ti-c̱āt-ing,
quäd-rù'pli-c̱āt-ing,
rē-cip'rō-c̱āt-ing, rus'ti-c̱āt-ing,
sō-phis'ti-c̱āt-ing, suf'fō-c̱āt-ing,
sup'pli-c̱āt-ing, vā'c̱āt-ing,
vin'di-c̱āt-ing.
kr: c̱on'sē-c̱rāt-ing,
des'ē-c̱rāt-ing, ex'ē-c̱rāt-ing.
l: ac̱-c̱ū'mū-lāt-ing,
an-nī'hi-lāt-ing, är-tic̱'ū-lāt-ing,
as-sim'ū-lāt-ing, c̱al'c̱ū-lāt-ing,
c̱ap-it'ū-lāt-ing, c̱ȋr'c̱ū-lāt-ing,
c̱ō-ag'ū-lāt-ing,
c̱ŏn-fab'ū-lāt-ing,
c̱ŏn-grat'ū-lāt-ing,
dē-pop'ū-lāt-ing, dȋ'lāt-ing,

dis-sim'ū-lāt-ing, ē-jac̱'ū-lāt-ing,
em'ū-lat-ing, ex-pos'tū-lāt-ing,
flaġ'el-lāt-ing, fₒr'mū-lāt-ing,
ġes-tic̱'ū-lāt-ing, gran'ū-lāt-ing,
grat'ū-lāt-ing, im'mō-lāt-ing,
in-oc̱'ū-lāt-ing, in'sū-lāt-ing,
in-tȇr'pō-lāt-ing, ȋ'sō-lāt-ing,
leġ'is-lāt-ing, man-ip'ū-lāt-ing,
mȧ-tric̱'ū-lāt-ing, mod'ū-lāt-ing,
mūt'i-lāt-ing, os'cil-lāt-ing,
os'c̱ū-lāt-ing, pȇr-am'bū-lāt-ing,
pȇr'c̱ō-lāt-ing, pop'ū-lāt-ing,
pos'tū-lāt-ing,
rē-c̱ap'it-ū-lāt-ing, reg'ū-lāt-ing,
rē-lāt'ing, scin'til-lāt-ing,
sim'ū-lāt-ing, spec̱'ū-lāt-ing,
stim'ū-lāt-ing, stip'ū-lāt-ing,
tab'ū-lāt-ing, tit'il-lāt-ing,
trans'lāt-ing, un'dū-lāt-ing,
vac̱'il-lāt-ing, ven'ti-lāt-ing,
vȋ'ō-lāt-ing.
m: ȧ-mal'gȧ-māt-ing,
an'i-māt-ing, ap-prox'i-māt-ing,
c̱on'sum-māt-ing, c̱rē'māt-ing,
dec̱'i-māt-ing, es'ti-māt-ing,
in'ti-māt-ing, māt'ing.
n: ȧ-bom'i-nāt-ing, ā'li-e-nāt-ing,
ạl'tȇr-nāt-ing, as-sas'si-nāt-ing,
c̱ŏn-tam'i-nāt-ing,
c̱rim'i-nāt-ing, c̱ul'mi-nāt-ing,
dē-nom'i-nāt-ing, des'ig-nāt-ing,
dē-tȇr'mi-nāt-ing, de'tō-nāt-ing,
dis-c̱rim'i-nāt-ing,
dis-sem'i-nāt-ing, dom'i-nāt-ing,
ē-lim'i-nāt-ing, e'mȧ-nāt-ing,
fas'ci-nāt-ing, ful'mi-nāt-ing,
ġȇr'mi-nāt-ing, il-lū'mi-nāt-ing,
im-pȇr'sŏ-nāt-ing,
im-preg'nāt-ing,
in-c̱rim'i-nāt-ing,
in-dis-c̱rim'i-nāt-ing,

(Choose only one word out of each group)

nom'i-nāt-ing, ō-riġ'i-nāt-ing,
per'ē-gri-nāt-ing, pēr'sŏ-nāt-ing,
prē-dom'i-nāt-ing,
rē-ҫrim'i-nāt-ing,
rē-jù've̅-nāt-ing, rủ'mi-nāt-ing,
tēr'mi-nāt-ing,
un-dis-ҫrim'i-nāt-ing,
vaҫ'ci-nāt-ing.

p: an-ti'ci-pāt-ing, dis'si-pāt-ing,
ē-man'ci-pāt-ing,
in-fan-tic'i-pāt-ing,
pär-tic'i-pāt-ing, syṅ'ҫō-pāt-ing.

pl: är'mŏr plāt'ing,
ҫon'tem-plāt-ing,
ҫop'pēr-plāt-ing,
ēl-eҫ'trō-plāt-ing,
nick'el-plāt-ing, plāit'ing,
plāt'ing.

pr: prāt'ing.

r: aҫ-cel'ē-rāt-ing,
à-dul'tē-rāt-ing, ā'ē-rāt-ing,
à-mēl'i-ō-rāt-ing,
an-nū'mēr-āt-ing*,
au̯'gū-rāt-ing, bē-rāt'ing,
ҫŏm-mem'ō-rāt-ing,
ҫŏn-fed'ē-rāt-ing,
ҫō-op'ē-rāt-ing,
ҫŏr-ro'bō-rāt-ing, de'ҫō-rāt-ing,
dē-ġen'ē-rāt-ing, dē-lib'ē-rāt-ing,
dē-tē'ri-ō-rāt-ing, ē-lab'ō-rāt-ing,
ē-nū'mē-rāt-ing, ē-vap'ō-rāt-ing,
ex-aġ'ġē-rāt-ing,
ex-as'pē-rāt-ing,
ex-hil'à-rāt-ing, ex-on'ē-rāt-ing,
ex-peҫ'tō-rāt-ing, fed'ē-rāt-ing,
ġen'ē-rāt-ing, in-au̯'gū-rāt-ing,
in-ҫär'cē-rāt-ing,
in-vig'ō-rāt-ing, i'tē-rāt-ing,
lib'ē-rāt-ing, mod'ē-rāt-ing,
nar'rāt-ing, ob-lit'ē-rāt-ing,
op'ē-rāt-ing, ō-vēr-rāt'ing,

pēr'fō-rāt-ing, rāt'ing,
rē-ҫū'pē-rāt-ing,
rē-friġ'ē-rāt-ing, rē-i'tē-rāt-ing,
rē-mū'nē-rāt-ing,
rē-vēr'bē-rāt-ing, sat'ū-rāt-ing,
sep'à-rāt-ing, tol'ē-rāt-ing,
un-dēr-rāt'ing, ven'ē-rāt-ing,
vēr'bē-rāt-ing, vī-tū'pē-rāt-ing,
vō-ci'fē-rāt-ing.

s: ҫom'pen-sāt-ing, sāt'ing.

sk: skāt'ing.

sl: slāt'ing.

st: ō-vēr-stāt'ing, rē-in-stāt'ing,
stāt'ing, un-dēr-stāt'ing.

str: de'mŏn-strāt-ing,
frus'trāt-ing, il'lus-trāt-ing.

t: aġ'i-tāt-ing, am'pū-tāt-ing,
ҫoġ'i-tāt-ing, dē-bil'i-tāt-ing,
dē-ҫap'i-tāt-ing, de'vǎs-tāt-ing,
diҫ'tāt-ing, fà-cil'i-tāt-ing,
fē-lic'i-tāt-ing, grav'i-tāt-ing,
heṣ'i-tāt-ing, im'i-tāt-ing,
in-ҫap-aҫ'i-tāt-ing, ir'ri-tāt-ing,
med'i-tāt-ing, mil'i-tāt-ing,
mit'i-gāt-ing, nē-ces'si-tāt-ing,
pal'pi-tāt-ing, prē-cip'i-tāt-ing,
prē-med'i-tāt-ing,
rē-sus'ci-tāt-ing, veġ'ē-tāt-ing.

tr: är'bi-trāt-ing,
ҫon'cen-trāt-ing, pen'ē-trāt-ing,
pēr'pē-trāt-ing.

v: ag'grà-vāt-ing, ҫul'ti-vāt-ing,
de'ri-vāt-ing, el'ē-vāt-ing,
ex'ҫà-vāt-ing, in'nō-vāt-ing,
re'nō-vāt-ing, tit'i-vāt-ing.

w: à-wāit'ing, wāit'ing,
weight'ing (wāt').

AT'ING

b: bat'ting.
ch: chat'ting.

(Choose only one word out of each group)

f: fat′ting.
m: mat′ting.
p: pat′ting.
pl: plat′ting.
r: rat′ting.
t: tat′ting.
v: vat′ting.

AT′ĪR

s: sat′īre.
Plus that ire, etc.
Cf. flat tire, etc.

ĀT′IS

gr: grāt′is.
Cf. Katie's, plate is, etc.

AT′IS

br: brat′tice.
l: lat′tice.
Cf. Pattie's, that is, etc.

AT′ISH

f: fat′tish.
fl: flat′tish.
k(c̣): c̣at′tish.

ĀT′IV

Vowel: al-lē′vi-āt-ive,
an-nun′ci-āt-ive (′shi-),
ap-prē′ci-āt-ive (′shi-),
ap-prō′pri-āt-ive,
as-sō′ci-āt-ive (′shi-),
c̣ŏn-tin′ū-āt-ive, c̣rē-āt′ive,
dē-nun′ci-āt-ive (′shi-),
dē-prē′ci-āt-ive (′shi-),
ē-nun′ci-āt-ive (′shi-),
in-it′i-āt-ive (-ish′),
in-sin′ū-āt-ive, pal′li-āt-ive,
prō′c̣rē-āt-ive,
prō-nun′ci-āt-ive (′shi-),

rād′i-āt-ive, re′c̣rē-āt-ive,
rē-tal′i-āt-ive.
b: ap′prō-bāt-ive, in′c̣ū-bāt-ive,
re′prō-bāt-ive.
d: c̣ŏn-sol′i-dāt-ive, dāt′ive,
ē-lū′ci-dāt-ive.
g: ab′rō-gāt-ive, ag′grē-gāt-ive,
in-ves′ti-gāt-ive, mit′i-gāt-ive,
pro′pȧ-gāt-ive.
k(c̣): c̣ŏm-mū′ni-c̣āt-ive,
de′prē-c̣ā-tive, dū′pli-c̣āt-ive,
ē-rad′i-c̣āt-ive, ex′pli-c̣āt-ive,
im′bri-c̣āt-ive, im′pli-c̣āt-ive,
in-c̣ŏm-mū′ni-c̣āt-ive,
jus′ti-fi-c̣āt-ive,
mod′if-i-c̣āt-ive,
prog-nos′ti-c̣āt-ive,
pūr′if-i-c̣āt-ive,
quäl′i-fi-c̣āt-ive, re′pli-c̣āt-ive,
sig-nif′i-c̣āt-ive, suf′fō-c̣āt-ive,
sup′pli-c̣āt-ive, vel′i-c̣āt-ive,
ver′i-fi-c̣āt-ive, vin′di-c̣āt-ive,
viv′i-fi-c̣āt-ive.
kr: ex′ē-c̣rāt-ive.
l: ac̣-c̣ū′mū-lāt-ive,
as-sim′i-lāt-ive, c̣ō-ag′ū-lāt-ive,
c̣ŏl-lāt′ive, c̣op′ū-lāt-ive,
c̣ū′mū-lāt-ive, dī-lāt′ive,
em′ū-lāt-ive, leg′is-lāt-ive,
man-ip′ū-lāt-ive, os′cil-lāt-ive,
spec̣′ū-lāt-ive, stim′ū-lāt-ive,
trans-lāt′ive, un′dū-lāt-ive,
ven′ti-lāt-ive, vī′ō-lāt-ive.
m: an′i-māt-ive,
ap-prox′i-māt-ive, es′ti-māt-ive.
n: ag-glū′ti-nāt-ive,
c̣ŏn-tam′i-nāt-ive,
c̣ō-ọr′di-nāt-ive, c̣rim′i-nāt-ive,
dē-nom′i-nāt-ive, de′sig-nāt-ive,
dē-tēr′mi-nāt-ive,
dis-c̣rim′i-nāt-ive,

(Choose only one word out of each group)

dis-sem'i-nāt-ive,
dom'i-nāt-ive, e'mȧ-nāt-ive,
ġēr'mi-nāt-ive, glu̇'ti-nāt-ive,
il-lū'mi-nāt-ive, im-aġ'i-nāt-ive,
in-çrim'i-nāt-ive,
in-dis-çrim'i-nāt-ive, nāt'ive,
ōp-in'iŏn-āt-ive ('yun-),
ōr-iġ'i-nāt-ive,
prē-des'ti-nāt-ive,
rat″i-o-ci'nāt-ive (rash″),
rē-çrim'i-nāt-ive,
sub-ọr'di-nāt-ive,
tēr'mi-nāt-ive.
p: an-ti'çi-pāt-ive,
pär-tic'i-pāt-ive.
r: aç-cel'ē-rāt-ive,
ag-glom'ē-rāt-ive,
al-lit'ē-rāt-ive, ạl'tē-rāt-ive,
ȧ-mē'li-o-rāt-ive,
cŏm-mem'ō-rāt-ive
cŏm-miṣ'ē-rāt-ive,
cŏn-fed'ē-rāt-ive,
cō*op'ē-rāt-ive,
cor-rob'ō-rāt-ive, de'çō-rāt-ive,
dē-ġen'ē-rāt-ive,
dē-lib'ē-rāt-ive,
dē-sid'ē-rāt-ive,
ē-dul'çō-rāt-ive,
ē-lab'ō-rāt-ive, ē-nū'mē-rāt-ive,
ē-vap'ō-rāt-ive, ex-aġ'ġē-rāt-ive,
ex-on'ē-rāt-ive, fed'ē-rāt-ive,
ġen'ē-rāt-ive, in-cor'pō-rā-tive,
in-op'ē-rāt-ive, i'tē-rāt-ive,
lac'ē-rāt-ive, op'ē-rāt-ive,
pēr'fō-rāt-ive, rē-çū'pē-rāt-ive,
rē-friġ'ē-rāt-ive,
rē-ġen'ē-rāt-ive,
rē-i'tē-rāt-ive,
rē-mū'nē-rāt-ive,
rē-vēr'bē-rāt-ive, sep'ȧ-rāt-ive,
sup'pū-rāt-ive, vī-tū'pē-rāt-ive.

s: sāt'ive*.
st: stāt'ive.
t: aġ'i-tāt-ive,
au-thor'i-tāt-ive, çoġ'i-tāt-ive,
grav'i-tāt-ive, heṣ'i-tāt-ive,
im'i-tāt-ive, in-çoġ'i-tāt-ive,
in-tēr'prē-tāt-ive,
ir'ri-tāt-ive, med'i-tāt-ive,
quäl'i-tāt-ive, quän'ti-tāt-ive,
rē-sus'ci-tāt-ive, veġ'ē-tāt-ive.
tr: ad-min'is-trāt-ive,
in-tēr-pen'ē-trāt-ive,
min'is-trāt-ive, pen'ē-trāt-ive.
v: in'nō-vāt-ive.

AT'KINZ

Vowel: At'kinṣ.
b: Bat'kinṣ.
(But not Watkins.)
Plus flat kin's, etc.

AT'L

Vowel: Sē-at'tle.
b: bat'tel, bat'tle, em-bat'tle.
ch: chat'tel.
k(ç): çat'tle.
pr: prat'tle.
r: death rat'tle (deth), rat'tle.
t: tat'tle, tit'tle*tat'tle.
Plus that'll, etc.

AT'LĂS, AT'LES

Vowel: at'lăs.
h: hat'less.
v: crȧ-vat'less.
Plus at+less.
Plus flat, less, *or* Les, etc.

ĀT'LES

b: bāit'less.
d: dāte'less.

(Choose only one word out of each group)

fr: freight'less (frāt').
g: gāit'less, gāte'less.
gr: grāte'less.
h: hāte'less.
m: māte'less.
r: rāte'less.
st: stāte'less.
t: es-tāte'less.
w: weight'less (wāt').
Plus skate, less or Les, etc.

ĀT'LI

Vowel: ap-prō'pri-āte-ly,
  in-ap-prō'pri-āte-ly.
d: sē-dāte'ly.
gr: greāt'ly.
k(ç): del'i-çāte-ly,
  in-del'i-çāte-ly.
kw: ad'ē-quāte-ly,
  in-ad'ē-quāte-ly.
l: är-tiç'ū-late-ly, des'ō-lāte-ly,
  dis-çŏn'sō-lāte-ly,
  im-maç'ū-lāte-ly,
  in-är-tiç'ū-lāte-ly, lāte'ly.
m: ap-prox'i-māte-ly,
  çon'sum-māte-ly,
  il-lē-ġit'i-māte-ly, in'ti-māte-ly,
  lē-ġit'i-māte-ly, ul'ti-māte-ly.
n: af-feç'tio-nāte-ly,
  ạl'tẽr-nāte-ly,
  çom-pas'sio-nāte-ly,
  ef-fem'i-nāte-ly,
  ex-tọr'tio-nāte-ly,
  fọr'tū-nāte-ly,
  un-fọr'tū-nāte-ly.
r: aç'çū-rāte-ly,
  çon-sid'ē-rāte-ly,
  des'pē-rāte-ly, ē-lab'ō-rāte-ly,
  il-lit'ē-rāte-ly,
  im-mod'ē-rāte-ly,
  in-çon-sid'ē-rāte-ly,

in-tem'pē-rāte-ly, ī'rāte-ly,
lit'ē-rāte-ly, mod'ē-rāte-ly,
tem'pē-rāte-ly.
st: stāte'ly.
str: strāight'ly (strāt'),
  strāit'ly.
Plus fate, Lee or lea, etc.

AT'LI

f: fat'ly.
fl: flat'ly.
p: pat'ly.
r: rat'tly.
Plus that, Lee or lea, etc.

AT'LING

b: bat'tling.
f: fat'ling.
g: gat'ling.
k(ç): çat'ling.
pr: prat'tling.
r: rat'tling.
t: tat'tling.

AT'LŨR

b: bat'tlẽr.
pr: prat'tlẽr.
r: rat'tlẽr.
st: Stat'lẽr.
t: tat'tlẽr.

ĀT'MENT

b: å-bāte'ment.
fr: af-freight'ment (-frāt').
st: in-stāte'ment,
  ō-vẽr-stāte'ment,
  rē-in-stāte'ment, stāte'ment,
  un-dẽr-stāte ment.
Plus nate, meant, etc.

(Choose only one word out of each group)

ĀT′NES

Vowel: in-ap-prō′pri-āte-ness.
d: sē-dāte′ness.
gr: greāt′ness.
l: lāte′ness.
n: in′nāte-ness, o̱r-nāte′ness.
r: c̩on-sid′ē-rāte-ness.
str: strāight′ness (strāt′nes).

AT′NES

f: fat′ness.
fl: flat′ness.
p: pat′ness.

Ā′TŌ

k(c̱): C̩ā′tō.
m: pō-mā′tō, tō-mā′tō.
pl: Plā′tō.
r: lit-ē-rā′tō.
t: pō-tā′tō.
Plus may toe, etc.
Plus hate owe *or* O, etc.

AT′Ō

l: mū-lat′tō.
pl: plat-eau′ (-ō′).
sh: c̱hât-eau′ (-ō′).
Plus flat owe *or* O, etc.

Ä′TŌ

g: le̱-gä′tō, ob-bli-gä′tō.
k(c̱): piz-zĭ-c̱ä′tō (pit-sē-), stäc̱-c̱ä′tō.
m: pō-mä′tō, tō-mä′tō.
n: än-nät′tō.
r: en-am-ō-rä′tō.
sh: c̱hâ-teau′ (shä-tō′).
Plus shah toe, etc.
Plus yacht owe *or* O, etc.
Cf. ot′ō.

AT′ŎM

Vowel: at′ŏm.
Plus bat ′em, etc.

ĀT′ŎN

d: Dāy′tŏn.
kl: C̩lāy′tŏn.
l: Le̱igh′tŏn (lā′).
p: pe̱y′tŏn.
s: Sā′tăn.
Plus mate on *or* an, etc.
Plus may tun *or* ton, etc.
Plus great ′un, etc.

AT′ŎN

b: bat′ŏn.
h: Hat′tŏn.
Plus flat on *or* an, etc.

Ā′TRȦ

p: C̩lē-ō-pā′trȧ.

Ā′TRĒ

b: bāy tree.
m: māy tree.
Plus spray tree, etc.

ĀT′RED

h: hāt′red.
Plus great red *or* read, etc.
Plus may tread, etc.

Ā′TRES

t: dic̱-tā′tress, im-i-tā′tress, spec̱-tā′tress.
tr: trāit′ress.
w: wāit′ress.
Plus gay tress, etc.

(Choose only one word out of each group)

AT'RES

l: mū-lat'tress.
m: mat'tress.
Plus flat tress, etc.

AT'RIK

Vowel: hip-pi-at'riç, ī-at'riç,
  kin-ēs-i-at'riç, thē-at'riç.
m: mat'riç.
p: Pat'rick, St. Pat'rick.
Plus flat rick, etc.
Cf. hat trick, etc.

ĀT'RIKS

Vowel: āv-i-āt'rix,
  im-prō-pri-āt'rix,
  mēd-i-āt'rix.
k(ç): ci-çāt'rix.
m: māt'rix.
r: ġen-ē-rāt'rix.
t: im'i-tāt-rix, speç-tāt'rix,
  tes-tāt'rix.
tr: ad-min-is-trāt'rix.
Plus hate ricks, etc.
Plus play tricks, etc.

ĀT'RIS, AT'RIS

m: māt'rice.
Cf. at'res.

ĀT'RŎN

m: mā'trŏn.
n: nā'trŏr.
p: pā'trŏn.
Cf. plate run, etc.

ĀTS'MĂN

st: stātes'măn.
Plus plates, man, etc.

ATS'MĂN

b: bats'măn.
Plus flats, man, etc.

AT'SŎN

b: Bat'sŏn.
m: Mat'sŏn.
Plus that son *or* sun, etc.

AT'Ū

st: stat'ūe.
Plus flat, you *or* ewe, etc.

ĀT'UM

d: dāt'um.
l: pos-tu-lāt'um.
m: pō-māt'um, ʉl-ti-māt'um.
r: dē-sid-ē-rāt'um, er-rāt'um.
str: strāt'um, sub-strāt'um,
  sū-pēr-strāt'um.
Plus hate 'em, etc.

AT'UM

str: strat'um, etc.
Plus bat 'em, etc.
Cf. at'ŏm.

ÄT'UM

d: dät'um.
m: pō-mät'um.
Cf. got 'em, etc.

ĀT'ŨR

k(ç): pli-çāt'ūre.
kl: nō'men-çlāt-ūre.
l: leġ'is-lāt-ūre.
n: good nāt'ūre, ill nāt'ūre,
  nāt'ūre, un-nāt'ūre.
Plus fate, you're *or* your, etc.

(Choose only one word out of each group)

ĀT′ŪR

Vowel: ab-brē′vi-āt-ŏr,
al-lē′vi-āt-ŏr, am-ēl′i-ōr-ā-tēr,
an-nun′ci-āt-ŏr ('shi-),
ap-prō′pri-āt-ŏr, ā′vi-āt-ŏr,
çal-um′ni-āt-ŏr,
çŏn-cil′i-āt-ŏr, çrē′āt-ŏr,
dē-lin′ē-āt-ŏr,
dē-nun′ci-āt-ŏr ('shi-),
dē-prē′ci-āt-ŏr ('shi-),
dē′vi-āt-ŏr,
ē-nun′ci-āt-ŏr ('shi-),
ex-pā′ti-āt-ŏr ('shi-),
ex′pi-āt-ŏr, ex-ten′ū-āt-ŏr,
glad′i-āt-ŏr, hū-mil′i-āt-ŏr,
in-i′ti-āt-ŏr ('shi-),
in-sin′ū-āt-ŏr, mēd′i-āt-ŏr,
nē-gō′ti-āt-ŏr ('shi-),
ŏf-fi′ci-āt-ŏr ('shi-), pal′li-āt-ŏr,
pēr′mē-āt-ŏr,
prō-pi′ti-āt-ŏr ('shi-),
rād-i-āt′or, rē-pū′di-ā-tŏr,
rē-tal′i-āt-ŏr.

b: a̤-bāt′ŏr, bāit′ēr, dē-bāt′ēr,
in′çū-bāt-ŏr.

d: çŏn-sol′i-dāt-ēr, dāt′ēr,
de′prē-dāt-ēr, ē-lū′ci-dāt-ŏr,
ē′men-dāt-ŏr, in-tim′i-dāt-ŏr,
la̤u′dāt-ŏr, li′qui-dāt-ŏr,
se-dāt′ēr.

fl: in-flāt′ēr.

fr: af-freight′ēr (-frāt′),
frāt′ēr, freight′ēr (frāt′).

g: ab′nē-gāt-ŏr, ab′rō-gāt-ŏr,
al′li-gāt-ŏr, ças′ti-gāt-ŏr,
çom′pūr-gāt-ŏr, çon′jṳ-gāt-ŏr,
fūm′i-gāt-ŏr, gāit′ēr,
in′sti-gāt-ŏr, in-ter′rō-gāt-ŏr,
in-ves′ti-gāt-ēr, ir′ri-gāt-ŏr,
lit′i-gāt-ŏr, mit′i-gāt-ŏr,
nav′i-gāt-ŏr, prō-mul′gāt-ŏr,

pro′pȧ-gāt-ŏr, sub′jṳ-gāt-ŏr,
sū″pēr-ro-gāt′ŏr.

gr: dis-in′tē-grāt-ŏr, grāt′ēr,
greāt′ēr, mī′grāt-ēr, rē-grāt′ēr.

h: hāt′ēr.

k(ç): ab′di-çāt-ŏr,
ad-jṳ′di-çāt-ŏr,
a̤u-then′ti-çāt-ŏr, çāt′ēr,
çon′fis-çāt-ŏr, ded′i-çāt-ŏr,
dū′pli-çāt-ēr, ed′ū-çāt-ŏr,
ē-quiv′ō-çāt-ēr, ē-rad′i-çāt-ŏr,
ex′tri-çāt-ŏr, fab′ri-çāt-ŏr,
fŏr′ni-çāt-ŏr, hȳ-poth′ē-çāt-ŏr,
in′di-çāt-ŏr, in′vō-çāt-ŏr,
lō′çāt-ēr, lū′bri-çāt-ŏr,
mas′ti-çāt-ŏr, pac-if′i-çāt-ŏr,
pis-çāt′ŏr, prē-var′i-çāt-ŏr,
prog-nos′ti-çāt-ŏr,
rē-cip′rō-çāt-ēr, rus′ti-çāt-ŏr,
sō-phis′ti-çāt-ŏr, sup′pli-çāt-ŏr,
vēr′si-fi-çāt-ŏr, vin′di-çāt-ŏr.

kr: çon′sē-çrāt-ŏr, çrāt′ēr,
ex′ē-çrāt-ēr.

kw: ē-quāt′ŏr.

l: aç-çū′mū-lāt-ŏr, ad′ū-lāt-ŏr,
an-nī′hi-lāt-ŏr, as-sim′i-lāt-ŏr,
çal′çū-lāt-ŏr, dē-pop′ū-lāt-ŏr,
dis-sim′ū-lāt-ŏr, ē-jaç′ū-lāt-ŏr,
flaġ′el-lāt-ŏr, fŏrm′mū-lāt-ŏr,
ġes-tiç′ū-lāt-ŏr, hū-mil′i-āt-ŏr,
in-oç′ū-lāt-ŏr, in′sū-lāt-ŏr,
in-tēr′pō-lāt-ŏr, lāt′ēr,
leġ′is-lāt-ŏr, man-ip′ū-lāt-ŏr,
mod′ū-lāt-ŏr, mūt′i-lāt-ŏr,
os′cil-lāt-ŏr, os′çū-lāt-ŏr,
pēr-am′bū-lāt-ŏr,
pēr′çō-lāt-ŏr, reg′ū-lāt-ŏr,
rē-lāt′ēr, scin′til-lāt-ŏr,
sim′ū-lāt-ŏr, speç′ū-lāt-ŏr,
stim′ū-lāt-ŏr, stip′ū-lāt-ŏr,
tab′ū-lāt-ŏr, tit′il-lāt-ŏr,

(Choose only one word out of each group)

trans'lāt-ŏr, va'cil-lāt-ŏr, ven'ti-lāt-ŏr, vī'ō-lāt-ŏr.

m: al'mȧ māt'ẽr, a-mal'gȧ-māt-ẽr, crē'māt-ŏr, dū'rȧ māt'ẽr, im-pri-māt'ūr, mā'tẽr, pī'ȧ māt'ẽr, Stā'bat Mā'tẽr.

n: ā'li-e-nāt-ŏr, com'mi-nāt-ŏr, cŏn-tam'i-nāt-ŏr, crim'i-nāt-ŏr, dē-nom'i-nāt-ŏr, de'ṣig-nāt-ŏr, dis-sem'i-nāt-ŏr, ē-lim'i-nāt-ŏr, e'mȧ-nāt-ŏr, ex-tẽr'mi-nāt-ŏr, fas'ci-nāt-ŏr, ġer'mi-nāt-ŏr, il-lū'mi-nāt-ŏr, im-pẽr'sŏ-nāt-ŏr, in-crim'i-nāt-ŏr, nom'i-nāt-ŏr, ōr-iġ'i-nāt-ŏr, per'ē-gri-nāt-ŏr, pẽr'sŏ-nāt-ŏr, prē-dom'i-nāt-ŏr, prō-cras'ti-nāt-ŏr, rù'mi-nāt-ŏr, vac'ci-nāt-ŏr, vat-i'ci-nāt-ŏr.

p: ē-man'ci-pāt-ŏr, pāt'ẽr.

pl: con'tem-plāt-ŏr, plāit'ẽr, plāt'ẽr.

pr: prāt'ẽr.

r: ac-cel'ē-āt-ŏr, as'pi-rāt-ŏr, as-sev'ē-rāt-ŏr, bē-rāt'ẽr, cŏl-lab'ō-rāt-ŏr, cŏm-mem'ō-rāt-ŏr, cŏm-miṣ'ē-rāt-ŏr, cō=op'ē-rāt-ŏr, cor-rob'ō-rāt-ŏr, dec'ō-rāt-ŏr, dē-lib'ē-rāt-ŏr, ēl-ab'ō-rāt-ŏr, ē-nūm'ē-rāt-ŏr, ē-vap'ō-rāt-ŏr, ex-aġ'ġē-rāt-ŏr, ex-hil'ȧ-rāt-ŏr, ex-on'ē-rāt-ŏr, ex-pec'tō-rāt-ŏr, fed'ē-rāt-ŏr, fĭrst=rāt'ẽr, ġen'ē-rāt-ŏr, im'per-ā-tŏr, in-cär'cē-rāt-ŏr, in-cọr'pō-rāt-ŏr,

in-vig'ō-rāt-ŏr, lib'ē-rāt-ŏr, mod'ē-rāt-ŏr, nar-rāt'ŏr, ob-lit'ē-rāt-ŏr, op'ē-rāt-ŏr, pẽr'fō-rāt-ŏr, prō'cū-rāt-ŏr, rāt'ẽr, rē-frig'ē-rāt-ŏr, rē-ġen'ē-rāt-ŏr, rē-it'ē-rāt-ŏr, res'pi-rāt-ŏr, sec-ŏnd=rāt'ẽr, sep'ȧ-rāt-ŏr, thĭrd=rāt'ẽr, ven'ē-rāt-ŏr, vī-tū'pē-rāt-ŏr, vō-cif'ē-rāt-ŏr.

s: sāt'yr ('ẽr), tẽr'ġiv-ẽr-sāt-ŏr.

sk(sc): skāt'ẽr.

sl: slāt'ẽr.

st: Free Stāt'ẽr, rē-in-stāt'ẽr, stāt'ẽr.

str: ad-min'is-trāt-ŏr, de'mŏn-strāt-ŏr, il'lus-trāt-ŏr, rē-mon'strāt-ŏr, strāight'ẽr (strāt'), strāit'ẽr.

t: aġ'i-tāt-ŏr, an'nō-tāt-ŏr, coġ'i-tāt-ŏr, com'men-tā-tŏr, com'pō-tā-tŏr, com'pū-tāt-ŏr, dē-cap'i-tāt-ŏr, de'văs-tāt-ŏr, dic-tāt'ẽr, dic-tāt'ŏr, fȧ-cil'i-tāt-ŏr, fē-lic'i-tāt-ŏr, heṣ'i-tāt-ŏr, im'i-tāt-ŏr, ir'ri-tāt-ŏr, med'i-tāt-ŏr, pal'pi-tāt-ẽr, prē-cip'i-tāt-ŏr, pres-ti-diġ'i-tāt-ŏr, rē-sus'ci-tāt-ŏr, scrù-tāt'ŏr, spec-tāt'ŏr, "tāt'ẽr", tes-tā'tẽr.

tr: är'bi-trāt-ŏr, ärch trāi'tŏr, con'cen-trāt-ŏr, frus'trāt-ŏr, pẽr'pē-trāt-ŏr, trāi'tŏr.

v: aġ'grȧ-vāt-ŏr, cap'ti-vāt-ŏr, con'sẽr-vāt-ŏr, cul'ti-vāt-ŏr, el'ē-vāt-ŏr, ex'cȧ-vāt-ŏr,

(Choose only one word out of each group)

in′nō-vāt-ŏr, re′nō-vāt-ŏr,
tit′ti-vāt-ŏr.
w: a̱-wāit′ēr,
dumb′=wāit′ēr (dum′),
wāit′ēr.
Plus mate her *or* err, etc.

AT′Ū̆R

st: stat′ūre.
Plus at your *or* you're, etc.

AT′Ū̆R

Vowel: at′tă̆r.
b: bat′tēr.
bl: blat′tēr.
ch: chat′tēr.
f: fat′tēr.
fl: bē-flat′tēr, flat′tēr.
h: hat′tēr, Mad Hat′tēr.
kl: c̨lat′tēr, c̨lit′tēr=c̨lat′tēr.
l: lat′tēr.
m: mat′tēr, sub′jec̨t mat′tēr.
p: bē-pat′tēr, pat′tēr.
pl: plat′tēr.
r: rat′tēr.
s: sat′yr (′ēr).
sh: shat′tēr.
sk(sc̨): be-sc̨at′tēr, sc̨at′tēr.
sm: smat′tēr.
sp: bē-spat′tēr, spat′tēr.
spl: splat′tēr.
t: tat′tēr.
Plus bat her *or* err, etc.

ÄT′Ū̆R

m: äl′má mät′ēr, mät′ēr,
Stä′bät Mät′ēr.
p: pät′ēr.
Plus swat her *or* err, etc.

AT′Ū̆RN

p: pat′tĕrn, wil′lōw pat′tĕrn.
s: Sat′ūrn.
sl: slat′tĕrn.
Cf. that turn, etc.
Plus that urn, erne *or* earn, etc.

ĀT′US

Vowel: hī-āt′us, mē-āt′us.
fl: af-flāt′us.
n: sē-nāt′us.
r: ap-pá-rāt′us, lit-e-rāt′us,
sal-e-rāt′us.
st: stāt′us.
str: strāt′ous, strāt′us.
Plus hate us, etc.

AT′US

r: ap-pá-rat′us.
Plus bat us, etc.

AT′ŪT

st: stat′ūte.
Plus that Ute, etc.

ĀT′WĀ

g: gāte′wāy.
st: stāte′wāy.
str: strāight′wāy (strāt′).
Plus late weigh *or* way, etc.

Ā′Ū̆R

b: dis-ō-bey̱′ēr, ō-bey̱′ēr.
br: brāy′ēr.
fl: flāy′ēr.
fr: af-frāy′ēr, dē-frāy′ēr.
g: gāy′ēr.
gr: grāy′ēr, grey̱′ēr.

(Choose only one word out of each group)

h: hāy'ẽr.

l: al-lāy'ẽr, bē-lāy'ẽr,
dē-lāy'ẽr, in'lāy-ẽr,
in'tẽr-lāy-ẽr, lāy'ẽr, mis-lāy'ẽr,
out'lāy-ẽr, ō-vẽr-lāy'ẽr,
rē-lāy'ẽr, wāy-lāy'ẽr.

m: dis-māy'ẽr, māy'ŏr.

n: mat-i-nẹ'ẽr, nẹigh'ẽr (nā').

p: pāy'ẽr, prē-pāy'ẽr,
rē-pāy'ẽr, un-dẽr-pāy'ẽr.

pl: dis-plāy'ẽr, plāy'ẽr,
un-dẽr-plāy'ẽr.

pr: prāy'ẽr, prẹy'ẽr.

r: ar-rāy'ẽr, dis-ar-rāy'ẽr,
họọ-rāy'ẽr.

s: as-sāy'ẽr, es-sāy'ẽr,
gāin-sāy'ẽr, mis-sāy'ẽr,
sọọth'sāy-ẽr.

sl: slāy'ẽr.

sp: spāy'ẽr.

spr: sprāy'ẽr.

st: out-stāy'ẽr, stāy'ẽr.

str: strāy'ẽr.

sw: swāy'ẽr.

tr: bē-trāy'ẽr, pōr-trāy'ẽr.

v: cọn-vẹy'ẽr,
in-vẹigh'ẽr (-vā'), pũr-vẹy'ŏr,
sũr-vẹy'ŏr.

w: out-wẹigh'ẽr (-wā'),
wẹigh'ẽr (wā').

z: vĭ-sẹ́'ẽr.

Plus betray her *or* err, etc.

Ä'VÀ

br: brä'vȧ.

gw: guä'vȧ (gwä').

j: Jä'vȧ.

l: lä'vȧ.

s: cas-sä'vȧ.

Plus salve a, etc.

AV'ĀL

tr: trav'āil.

Plus have ale *or* ail, etc.

Ā'VĒ

Vowel: ā'vē.

g: ȧ-gā'vē.

Plus shave, he, etc.

Ä'VĒ

Vowel: ä'vē.

Plus salve, he, etc.

ĀV'EL

g: gāv'el.

n: nāv'ăl, nāv'ĕl.

Plus slave 'll, etc.

AV'EL

g: gav'el.

gr: grav'el.

r: rav'el, un-rav'el.

tr: trav'el.

Cf. cav'il.

Plus Slav'll, etc.

AV'ELD

gr: grav'elled.

r: rav'elled, un-rav'elled.

tr: trav'elled, un-trav'elled.

Plus gavel'd, etc.

ĀV'EN

gr: en-grāv'en*, grāv'en.

h: hāv'en.

kr: crāv'en.

sh: shāv'en.

Cf. save an, etc.

(Choose only one word out of each group)

ĀV′EST

br: brāv′est.
g: for-gāv′est*, gāv′est*.
gr: en-grāv′est*, grāv′est.
h: bē-hāv′est*.
kr: ᴄrāv′est*.
l: lāv′est*.
p: pāv′est*.
pr: dē-prāv′est*.
r: rāv′est*.
s: sāv′est*.
sh: shāv′est*.
sl: bē-slāv′est*, en-slāv′est*, slāv′est.
sw: suāv′est (swāv′).
w: wāiv′est*, wāv′est*.
Plus play vest, etc.

ĀV′ETH

br: brāv′eth*.
g: for-gāv′eth*, gāv′eth*.
gr: en-grāv′eth*, grāv′eth*.
h: bē-hāv′eth*.
kr: ᴄrāv′eth*.
l: lāv′eth*.
p: pāv′eth*.
pr: dē-prāv′eth*.
r: rāv′eth*
s: sāv′eth*.
sh: shāv′eth*.
sl: bē-slāv′eth*, en-slāv′eth*, slāv′eth*.
w: wāiv′eth*, wāv′eth*.

ĀV′ĒZ

d: Dāv′iēṣ.
Plus gravy's, etc.
Plus grave ease, etc.

ĀV′I

d: af-fi-dāv′y, Dāv′ie, Dāv′y.
gr: grāv′y.
k(ᴄ): ᴄav′y, peᴄ-ᴄāv′i.
n: nāv′y.
r: rāv′y.
sl: slāv′ey.
w: wāv′y.
Plus shave, he, etc.

AV′I

n: nav′vy.
s: nō sav′vy, sav′vy.
sl: slav′ey.
Cf. peᴄ-ᴄav′i.
Plus Slav, he, etc.

ĀV′ID

d: Dāv′id.
Cf. āv+d* (en-grāv′ed, etc.).
Cf. slave hid, etc.

AV′ID

Vowel: av′id.
gr: grav′id.
p: im-pav′id, pav′id.
Cf. Slav hid, etc.

AV′IJ

r: rav′ăġe.
s: sav′ăġe.
sk(sᴄ): sᴄav′ăġe.
Cf. Slav age, etc.

AV′IK

gr: grav′iᴄ.
sl: Pan=Slav′iᴄ, Slav′iᴄ.

AV'IN
ĀV'LI

fāte, fär, fȧst, fạll, finăl, cãre, at; mēte, prẹy, hẽr, met; pīne,
marïne, bȋrd, pin; nōte, mŏve, fọr, atŏm, not; mọọn, book;

412

(Choose only one word out of each group)

AV'IN

s: sav'in.
sp: spav'in.
Cf. have inn *or* in, etc.

ĀV'ING

br: brāv'ing, out-brāv'ing.
gr: en-grāv'ing, grāv'ing,
steel en-grāv'ing,
wood en-grāv'ing.
h: bē-hāv'ing, mis-bē-hāv'ing.
k(c): cāv'ing.
kr: crāv'ing.
l: bē-lāv'ing, lāv'ing.
p: pāv'ing.
pr: dē-prāv'ing.
r: rāv'ing.
s: lā'bŏr-sāv-ing, līfe'sāv-ing,
sāv'ing, tīme'sāv-ing.
sh: shāv'ing.
sl: bē-slāv'ing, en-slāv'ing,
slāv'ing.
st: stāv'ing.
w: fiñ'gẽr wāv'ing, flag wāv'ing,
mär-cel' wāv'ing, wāiv'ing,
wāv'ing.

AV'ING

h: hav'ing.
s: salv'ing (sav').

ÄV'ING

h: hälv'ing (häv').
k(c): cälv'ing (käv').
s: sälv'ing (säv').

ĀV'IS

Vowel: rā'rȧ äv'is.
d: Dāv'is.
kl: clāv'is.

m: māv'is.
Cf. slave is, navy's, etc.

ĀV'ISH

br: brāv'ish.
n: knāv'ish (nāv').
sl: slāv'ish.

AV'ISH

l: lav'ish.
r: en-rav'ish, rav'ish.
t: Mc-Tav'ish.

ĀV'IT

d: af-fi-dāv'it.
k: in-di-cāv'it.
Plus shave it, etc.

AV'IT

d: dav'it.
Plus salve it, etc.

ĀV'LES

gr: grāve'less.
k(c): cāve'less.
sl: slāve'less.
st: stāve'less.
w: wāve'less.
Plus brave less *or* Les, etc.

ĀV'LI

br: brāve'ly.
gr: grāve'ly.
n: knāve'ly (nāv').
sw: suāve'ly (swāv').
Plus shave, Lee, etc.

413 ūse, bṳll, brúte, tŭrn, up; crȳ, myth; çat, maçhine, ace,
church, çhord; ġem, aṅger, (Fr.) boṅ, aṣ; THis, thin; aẓure

ÄV′LI
ĀV′ŪRD

(Choose only one word out of each group)

ÄV′LI

Vowel: soú-äve′ly.
sw: suäve′ly (swäv′).
Plus Slav, Lee *or* lea, etc.

AV′LIN

j: jav′elin.
r: rav′elin.
Plus have, Lynn, etc.

ĀV′LING

sh: shāve′ling.

ĀV′MENT

gr: en-grāve′ment.
l: lāve′ment.
p: pāve′ment.
pr: dē-prāve′menт.
sl: en-slāve′ment.
Plus shave meant, etc.

ĀV′NES

br: brāve′ness.
gr: grāve′ness.
sw: suāve′ness (swāv′).

Ā′VŌ, Ä′VŌ

br: brā′vō.
t: oc̣-tā′vō.
Plus shave owe *or* O, etc.

AV′ŎK

h: hav′ŏc̣.

ĀV′ŪR

br: brāv′ēr.
d: c̣à-dāv′ēr.
f: dis-fāv′ŏr, fāv′ŏr,
mar′riăġe fāv′ŏr, mis-fāv′ŏr.

fl: flāv′ŏr.
gr: en-grāv′ēr, grāv′er,
steel en-grāv′ēr,
wood en-grāv′ēr.
kl: c̣lāv′ēr.
kr: c̣rāv′ēr.
kw: dem′i-quāv-ēr, quāv′ēr,
sem′i-quāv-ēr.
l: lāv′ēr.
p: Pà-pāv′ēr, pāv′ēr.
pr: dē-prāv′ēr.
r: rāv′ēr.
s: līfe′sāv-ēr, sāv′ēr, sāv′ŏr,
tīme′sāv-ēr.
sh: shāv′ēr.
sl: en-slāv′ēr, slāv′ēr.
sw: suāv′ēr (swāv′).
w: fiṅ′gēr wāv′ēr,
mär-cel′ wāv′ēr, wāiv′ēr,
wāv′ēr.
Plus enslave her *or* err, etc.

AV′ŪR

d: c̣à-dav′ēr.
h: hav′ēr.
l: pà-lav′ēr.
sl: be-slav′ēr.
Plus have her *or* err, etc.

ÄV′ŪR

l: pà-läv′ēr.
sw: suäv′ēr.
Plus Slav err *or* her, etc.

ĀV′ŪRD

f: fāv′ŏred, ill′⸗fāv′ŏred,
well′⸗fāv′ŏred.
fl: flāv′ŏred.
kw: quāv′ēred.

AV'ŪRN
AZ'À

fāte, fär, fȧst, fᶏll, finăl, cãre, at; mēte, prey, hẽr, met; pīne,
marĭne, bĭrd, pin; nōte, mŏve, fȯr, atŏm, not; mᴏᴏn, book;

414

(Choose only one word out of each group)

s: sāv'ŏred.
w: wăv'ẽred.
Plus shaver'd, etc.

AV'ŪRN

k(ç): çav'ẽrn.
t: tav'ẽrn.
Plus Slav urn, erne *or* earn, etc.

ÄV'US

t: Gus-täv'us.
Plus salve us, etc.

ĀV'YŪR

h: bē-hāv'iŏr ('yẽr), hāv'iŏr,
mis-bē-hāv'iŏr.
p: Pāv'iẽr, pāv'iŏr.
s: sāv'iŏr.
z: Xāv'iẽr.
Cf. çlā'vi-ẽr.

Ā'WĂRD

h: Hey'wărd.
w: wāy'wărd.
Plus play ward, etc.

Ä'WĂRD

v: vä'wărd*.

Ā'WĪR

h: hāy'wīre.
Plus play wire, etc.

Ā'WŌRN

spr: sprăy'⸗wōrn″.
w: wāy'wōrn″.
Plus day worn. etc.

Ā'YÀ

Vowel: āy'yȧ.
gl: À-glā'iȧ.
n: nā'iȧ.
s: çal-i-sā'yȧ.
z: Ī-ṣā'iȧh.
Cf. play a, etc.

Ā'YĂN

l: Him-ȧ-lāy'an, Mȧ-lāy'ăn.
t: Al-tāi'an, Çȧ-tāi'ăn.
Cf. play an, etc.

Ā'YĂN

l: Him-ȧ-lāy'ăn.

Ā'YĂRD

b: Bā'yărd.
Plus play yard, etc.

Ā'YŌ

m: Mā'yō.
Cf. kāy'ō, K. O.
Cf. play owe *or* O, etc.

Ā'YŪ

g: gāy'yoū.
v: Vā'yū.
Cf. pay you, etc.

Ā'ZÀ

g: Gā'zȧ.
Cf. raise a, etc.

AZ'À

Vowel: pi-az'zȧ.
pl: plaz'ȧ.
z: ça-zaz'zȧ.
Plus jazz a, etc.

415 ūse, bu̯ll, brúte, tu̇rn, up; crȳ, myth; c̦at, mac̦hine, ace, church, c̦hord; ġem, aṅger, (Fr.) boṅ, aș; THis, thin; aᶎure

**ĀZ'ĂL
Ā'ZHUN**

(Choose only one word out of each group)

ĀZ'ĂL

h: hāz'el, witch hāz'el.
n: nāș'ăl.
pr: ap-prāiș'ăl.
Plus raise, Al, etc.

AZ'ĂRD

h: hap-haz'ărd, haz'ărd.
m: maz'ărd*, maz'zărd.
Cf. jazz hard, etc.

ĀZ'EST

bl: blāz'est*.
br: brāiș'est*.
d: dāz'est*.
fr: par'à-phrāș-est*
  phrāș'est*.
g: gāz'est*.
gl: glāz'est*.
h: hāz'est*.
m: à-māz'est*.
pr: bē-prāiș'est*, prāiș'est*.
r: rāiș'est*, rāz'est*,
  up-rāiș'est*.
Plus gay zest, etc.

ĀZ'ETH

bl: blāz'eth*.
br: brāiș'eth*.
d: dāz'eth*.
fr: par-à-phrāș'eth*,
  phrāș'eth*.
g: gāz'eth*.
gl: glāz'eth*.
h: hāz'eth*.
m: à-māz'eth*.
pr: bē-prāiș'eth*, prāiș'eth*.
r: rāiș'eth*, rāz'eth*,
  up-rāiș'eth*.

ĀZ'EZ, ĀZ'IZ

b: bāiz'eș.
bl: blāz'eș, greāt blúe blāz'eș.
br: brāiș'eș.
d: dāiș'ieș ('iz), dāz'eș.
f: phāș'eș.
fr: par'à-phrāș-eș, phrāș'eș.
g: gāz'eș, stär'gāz-eș.
gl: glāz'eș.
gr: grāz'eș.
h: hāz'eș, smōke hāz'eș.
kr: crāz'eș.
m: à-māz'eș, bē-māz'eș*,
  māz'eș.
n: māy-ŏn-nāiș'eș.
pr: prāiș'eș.
r: rāiș'eș, rāz'eș.
sh: c̦hāiș'eș.
v: vāș'eș.
Plus craze is, etc.

ÄZH'ING

fl: c̦am-ou̯-fläġ'ing,
  pĕr'si-fläġ-ing.
r: gà-räġ'ing.

AZ'HOUND

j: jazz'hound.
Plus has hound, etc.

Ā'ZHUN

br: à-brā'șiŏn.
k(c̦): oc̦-c̦ā'șiŏn.
r: ē-rā'șiŏn.
sw: dis-suā'șiŏn, pĕr-suā'șiŏn,
  suā'șiŏn.
v: ē-vā'șiŏn, in-vā'șiŏn.
Cf. C̦au-c̦āș'ian.
Cf. ā'zhi-ăn.

Ā′ZHŬR
AZ′LING

fāte, fär, fȧst, fąll, finăl, cãre, at; mēte, prey, hẽr, met; pīne,
marĭne, bĭrd, pin; nōte, mŏve, fôr, atŏm, not; mǫǫn, book;

416

(Choose only one word out of each group)

Ā′ZHŬR

Vowel: ā′ẓūre.
br: brā′ẓiẽr, em-brā′ṣūre.
fr: Frā′ṣiẽr, Frā′ẓiẽr.
gl: glā′ẓiẽr.
gr: grā′ẓiẽr.
r: ē-rā′ṣūre (′zhẽr), rā′ẓūre.
Cf. praise your, you're *or* "yer,"
etc.

AZH′ŬR

Vowel: a′ẓūre.

ĀZ′I

bl: blāz′y.
d: Af′ri-căn dāi′ṣy, dāi′ṣy,
lack′ȧ-dāis-y.
fr: par′ȧ-phrāṣ-y, phrāṣ′y.
h: hāz′y.
j: jāṣ′ey.
kr: crāz′y.
l: lāz′y.
m: māz′y.
Plus maze, he, etc.
Plus say Z *or* Zee, etc.

ÄZ′Ï

g: ghäz′ï.
w: ghȧ-wäz′ï.
Plus Shiraz, he, etc.

AZ′IL

b: Baṣ′il.
Cf. az′l.
Cf. jazz ill, etc.

ĀZ′IN

r: rāiṣ′in.
Plus praisin', etc.
Plus stays in *or* inn, etc.

ĀZ′ING

bl: ȧ-blāz′ing, blāz′ing,
out′blāz-ing, trāil blāz′ing,
up′blāz-ing.
br: brāiṣ′ing, brāz′ing.
d: dāz′ing.
fr: par′ȧ-phrāṣ-ing, phrāṣ-ing.
g: gāz′ing, out-gāz′ing,
stär′gāz-ing.
gl: glāz′ing.
gr: grāz′ing.
h: hāz′ing.
l: lāz′ing.
m: ȧ-māz′ing, bē-māz′ing*.
pr: bē-prāiṣ′ing, prāiṣ′ing,
self′⸗prāiṣ′ing.
r: flag rāiṣ′ing, hell-rāiṣ′ing,
rāiṣ′ing, up-rāiṣ′ing.

AZ′L

b: Baṣ′il.
d: bē-daz′zle, daz′zle,
raz′zle⸗daz″zle.
fr: fraz′zle.
Plus jazz′ll, etc.

ĀZ′LES

bl: blāze′less.
h: hāze′less.
m: māize′less, māze′less.
pr: prāiṣe′less.
v: vāṣe′less.
Plus craze less *or* Les, etc.

AZ′LING

d: daz′zling.
fr: fraz′zling.

(Choose only one word out of each group)

AZ'MÅ

Vowel: aṣth'må (az'),
mī-aṣ'må.
f: Phaṣ'må.
pl: plaṣ'må, prō-tō-plaṣ'må.
t: phan-taṣ'må.
Plus jazz, ma, etc.

AZ'MĂL

Vowel: mī-aṣ'măl.
pl: prō-tō-plaṣ'măl.
t: phan-taṣ'măl.

ĀZ'MENT

m: à-māze'ment.
pr: ap-prāiṣe'ment,
prāiṣe'ment.
Plus craze meant, etc.

AZ'MI

k(ç): çhaṣ'my.
Plus has me, etc.

AZ'MIK

Vowel: mī-aṣ'miç.
pl: bī-ō-plaṣ'miç,
prō-tō-plaṣ'miç.
Plus jazz, Mick, etc.

AZ'MUS

r: Ē-raṣ'mus.
Plus jazz muss, etc.

ĀZ'ŎN

bl: blāz'ŏn, em-blāz'ŏn.
br: brāz'en.
gl: glāz'en.
p: dī-à-pāṣ'ŏn.
sk: skāz'ŏn.
Plus blaze on *or* an, etc.

ĀZ'ŪR

Vowel: El-ē-āz'ēr.
bl: blāz'ēr.
fr: Frāṣ'ēr, par'à-phrāṣ-ēr,
phrāṣ'ēr.
g: gāz'ēr, geẏ'ṣēr, stär'gāz-ēr,
up-gāz'ēr.
gl: glāz'ēr.
h: hāz'ēr.
l: lāz'ēr.
pr: ap-prāiṣ'ēr, dis-prāiṣ'ēr,
prāiṣ'ēr, self=prāiṣ'ēr.
r: rāiṣ'ēr, rāz'ēr, up-rāiṣ'ēr.
Plus daze her *or* err, etc.

Ē′Ȧ
Ē′ĂN
fāte, fär, fȧst, fạll, finȧl, cãre, at; mēte, prĕy, hẽr, met; pīne,
marïne, bĩrd, pin; nōte, mŏve, fŏr, atŏm, not; mọọn, book;
418

(Choose only one word out of each group)

E

The accented vowel sounds included are listed under **E** in Single
Rhymes.

Ē′Ȧ

b: dä-hä-bē′ȧh, ō-bē′ȧh.
ch: Lū-cī′ȧ (-chē′).
d: ī-dē′ȧ, Mē-dē′ȧ.
f: rat-ȧ-fī′ȧ.
j: Hȳ-ġēi′ȧ.
k: La-tȧ-kī′ȧ.
m: C̣rī-mē′ȧ.
n: dysp-nē′ȧ.
p: C̣as-si-ō-pē′ȧ, mel-ōe-pī′ȧ.
pr: Cȳ-praē′ȧ.
r: Ä′vẹ Mä-rï′ȧ,
c̣ä″väl-lẹ-rï′ȧ, dī-ȧr-rhē′ȧ,
gon-ŏr-rhē′ȧ, log-ŏr-rhē′ȧ,
Mä-rï′ȧ, rhē′ȧ, spī-raē′ȧ.
s: pan-ȧ-cē′ȧ.
th: Aﬂ-thaē′ȧ, Dor-ō-thē′ȧ.
tr: As-traē′ȧ.
y: o″nō-mat-ō-poē′iȧ,
path-ō-poē′iȧ,
phär-mȧ-c̣ō-poē′iȧ.
z: Hō-s̟ē′ȧ, Zē′ȧ.
Plus see a, etc.

Ē′ĂL

d: beau ī-dē′ȧl (bō), ī-dē′ăl,
un-ī-dē′ȧl.
j: Ärc̣-tō-ġaē′ăl, lar-yn-ġē′ăl,
phar-yn-ġē′ăl.
n: hȳ-me-nē′ăl.
r: em-py-rē′ăl, rē′ăl, un-rē′ăl.
Plus see, Al, etc.

Ē′ĂN

b: ȧ-moē′bē-ăn, C̣ar-ib-bē′ăn,
Mac̣-c̣ȧ-bē′ăn, Mel-i-bē′ăn,
Nï-ō-bē′ăn, plē-bēi′ăn,
Sā-baē′ăn.
bl: Hȳ-blaē′ăn.
ch: Man-i-chaē′ăn,
Med-i-cē′ăn (-chē′).
d: An-dē′ăn, an-ti-pō-dē′ăn,
Är-c̣hi-mē-dē′ăn, As-si-dē′ăn,
C̣hal-dē′ăn, Jū-dē′ăn,
Pan-dē′ăn, Ven-dē′ăn.
f: nym-phē′ăn, Ọr-phē′ăn,
Sis-y-phē′ăn.
j: Aē-ġē′ăn, am-phi-ġē′ăn,
ap-ō-ġē′ăn, Är-ġē′ăn, Ạu-ġē′ăn,
lar-yn-ġē′ăn, Pal-ē-ō-ġaē′ăn,
per-i-ġē′ăn, phal-an-ġē′ăn,
phar-yn-ġē′ăn.
k(c̣): Ȧ-c̣hē′ăn, dī trō′c̣hē-ăn,
trō′c̣hē-ăn.
l: Gal-i-lē′ăn, Mạu-sō-lē′ăn,
Zōi′lē-ăn.
m: An-ō-moē′ăn, C̣ad′mē-ăn,
C̣rī-mē′ăn, Nē-mē′ăn.
n: A-dō-nē′ăn, Et-nē′ăn,
Haṣ-mō′naē-ăn, hȳ-mē-nē′ăn,
Lin-naē′ăn, Py-re-nē′ăn.
p: cȳ-c̣lō-pē′ăn, Eū-rō-pē′ăn,
In′dō꞊Eū-rō-pē′ăn, paē′ăn,
pam-pē′ăn, Pär-then-ō′pē-ăn.
pr: Cy′praē-ăn.
r: Be-rē′ăn, Cyth-ē-rē′ăn,
em-py-rē′ăn, ep-i-c̣ū′rē-ăn,
Py-thag-ō-rē′ăn,
tẽrp-si-c̣hō′rē-ăn.
s: C̣ĩr-cē′ăn, c̣ol-os-sē′ăn,
Lā-o-di-cē′ăn, lyn-cē′ăn,
Med-i-cē′ăn, Phar-i-sē′ăn,

(Choose only one word out of each group)

Sad-dū-cē′ăn, Ten-nes-sē′ăn, the-o-di-cē′ăn.
t: ad-a-man-tē′ăn, At-lan-tē′ăn, ġi-gan-tē′ăn, prō′tē-ăn.
th: le-thē′ăn.
tr: as-traē′ăn.
Plus see an *or* Ann, etc.

Ē′ĂS

k(ç): Zaç-çhē′us.
n: Ae-nē′ăs.
Cf. fee us, etc.

Ē′BÅ

m: a̶-moē′bå.
r: Rē′bå, zȧ-rē′bå.
s: Sē′bå.
sh: Bath Shē′bå, Shē′bå.
Plus glēbe′å, etc.

Ē′BĒ

f: Phoē′bē.
h: Hē′bē.
j: hee″bee=jee′bee.
t: T B, Tee′biē″.
Plus we be, etc.

ĒB′EN

Vowel: Ēb′en.
Cf. grebe hen, etc.

EB′ING

Vowel: ebb′ing, un-ebb′ing.
w: web′bing.

ĒB′L

f: en-fee′ble, fee′ble.
Plus see bull, etc.
Plus glebe ′ll, etc.

EB′L

j: djeb′el.
p: peb′ble.
r: ärch-reb′el, reb′el.
tr: tre′ble.
Plus web ′ll, etc.

Ē′BŌ

n: Nē′bō.
s: pla-cē′bō.
z: ga-zē′bō.
Plus see beau, bow *or* bo, etc.
Plus glebe owe, etc.

EB′ŎN

Vowel: eb′ŏn.
Plus web on, etc.

Ē′BŌRD

fr: free′bōard.
k: kēy′bōard.
s: sēa′bōard.
Plus tree bored *or* board, etc.

Ē′BŌRN

fr: free′bōrn.
s: sēa′bōrn.
Plus we born, etc.

ĒB′RÅ

z: zē′brå.

ĒB′ROK

p: pï′broçh (pē′).
Plus glebe rock, etc.

Ē′BRU̇

h: Hē′brew.
Plus we brew, etc.

(Choose only one word out of each group)

ĒB′ŪR

g: Ghē′bẽr.
Plus see burr, etc.
Plus glebe err *or* her, etc.

EB′ŪR

Vowel: ebb′ẽr.
w: von Web′ẽr, web′bẽr,
 Web′ẽr.
Plus web her, etc.

Ē′BUS

f: Phoē′bus.
gl: glē′bous.
r: rē′bus.
Plus glebe us, etc.

ECH′ED

r: wretch′ed.
Plus ech+ed*.

ĒCH′EST

bl: blēach′est*.
p: im-pēach′est*.
pr: prēach′est*.
r: fōre-rēach′est*,
 ō-vẽr-rēach′est*, rēach′est*.
s: bē-seech′est*, sēa chest.
skr(scr): screech′est*.
t: tēa chest, tēach′est*.
Plus see chest, etc.

ECH′EST

Vowel: etch′est*.
f: fetch′est*.
r: retch′est*.
sk: sketch′est*.
str: out-stretch′est*,
 stretch′est*.

ĒCH′ETH

bl: blēach′eth*.
p: im-pēach′eth*.
pr: prēach′eth*.
r: fōre-rēach′eth*,
 ō-vẽr-rēach′eth*, rēach′eth*.
s: bē-seech′eth*.
skr(scr): screech′eth*.
t: tēach′eth*.

ECH′ETH

Vowel: etch′eth*.
f: fetch′eth*.
r: retch′eth*.
sk: sketch′eth*.
str: out-stretch′eth*,
 stretch′eth*.

ĒCH′EZ

b: bēach′es, beech′es.
bl: blēach′es.
br: brēach′es, breech′es.
l: leech′es.
p: im-pēach′es, pēach′es.
pr: prēach′es.
r: fōre-rēach′es,
 ō-vẽr-rēach′es, rēach′es,
 sēa-rēach′es.
s: bē-seech′es.
skr(scr): screech′es.
sp: speech′es.
t: tēach′es.
Cf. peach is, etc.

ECH′EZ

Vowel: etch′es.
f: fet′ches.
fl: flet′ches.
k: ketch′es.

(Choose only one word out of each group)

r: retch'eṣ, wretch'eṣ.
sk: sketch'eṣ.
str: out-stretch'eṣ, stretch'eṣ.
v: vetch'eṣ.
Cf. ketch is, etc.

ĒCH'Ï

b: bēach'y, beech'y.
bl: blēach'y.
br: brēach'y.
kw: quēach'y.
p: çam-peech'y, pēach'y.
pr: prēach'y,
  tēach'y-prēach'y.
r: rēach'y, reech'y.
skr(sçr): sçreech'y.
sp: speech'y.
t: tēach'y.
tr: Bēa-trï'çē ('chē).
Plus beach, he, etc.

ECH'Ï

f: fetch'y.
sk: sketch'y.
str: stretch'y.
t: tetch'y.
v: vetch'y.
Plus vetch, he, etc.

ĒCH'ING

b: bēach'ing.
bl: blēach'ing.
br: brēach'ing, breech'ing.
l: lēach'ing, leech'ing.
p: im-pēach'ing, pēach'ing.
pr: prēach'ing.
r: fōre-rēach'ing,
  ō-vẽr-rēach'ing, rēach'ing.
s: bē-seech'ing.
skr(sçr): sçreech'ing.
t: fōre-tēach'ing, tēach'ing.

ECH'ING

Vowel: etch'ing.
f: fetch'ing.
r: retch'ing.
sk: sket'ching.
str: out-stretch'ing, stretch'ing.

ĒCH'LES

b: bēach'less, beech'less.
br: brēach'less.
p: pēach'less.
r: rēach'less.
sp: speech'less.
t: tēach'less.
Plus impeach less, etc.

ĒCH'MENT

p: im-pēach'ment.
pr: prēach'ment.
s: bē-seech'ment.
Plus peach meant, etc.

ECH'UP

k(ç): çatch'up, ketch'up.
Plus fetch up, etc.

ĒCH'ŪR

b: Beech'ẽr.
bl: blēach'ẽr.
br: brēach'ẽr, breech'ẽr.
f: fēa'tūre.
kr: çrēa'tūre.
l: lēach'ẽr, leech'ẽr.
p: im-pēach'ẽr, pēach'ẽr.
pr: prēach'ẽr.
r: fōre-rēach'ẽr, ō-vẽr-rēach'ẽr,
  rēach'ẽr.
s: bē-seech'ẽr.
skr(sçr): sçreech'ẽr.

ECH'ŪR
ED'ED

fāte, fär, fȧst, fạll, finăl, cãre, at; mēte, prey, hẽr, met; pīne,
marïne, bïrd, pin; nōte, mŏve, fọr, atŏm, not; mọọn, book;

422

(Choose only one word out of each group)

t: tēach'ẽr.
Plus reach her, err *or* er, etc.

ECH'ŪR

Vowel: etch'ẽr.
f: fetch'ẽr.
fl: fletch'ẽr.
l: lech'ẽr.
r: retch'ẽr.
sk: sketch'ẽr.
str: stretch'ẽr.
tr: treach'ẽr*.
Plus stretch her *or* err, etc.

Ē'DȦ

dr: ol-lȧ pō-drï'dȧ.
l: Lē'dȧ.
th: Thē'dȧ.
v: Vē'dȧ, Vï'dȧ.
w: Oui'dȧ (wē').
Plus need a, etc.

ED'Ȧ

Vowel: Ed'dȧ.
n: Ned'dȧ.
Plus spread a, etc.

ED'ĂNT

p: ped'ănt.
Plus red ant *or* aunt, etc.

ĒD'BED

r: reed'bed.
s: seed'bed.
w: weed'bed.
Plus need bed, etc.

ED'BĒT

d: dead'bēat (ded').
Plus red beet, etc.

ED'BREST

r: red'breast ('brest).
Plus dead breast, etc.

ED'BUG

b: bed'bug.
r: red'bug.
Plus spread bug, etc.

ĒD'ED

b: bēad'ed.
d: deed'ed.
h: heed'ed, un-heed'ed.
n: knēad'ed, need'ed.
p: im-pēd'ed, stam-pēd'ed.
pl: plēad'ed.
r: reed'ed.
s: ac-cēd'ed, an-tē-cēd'ed,
cēd'ed, cọn-cēd'ed,
ex-ceed'ed, in-tẽr-cēd'ed,
prē-cēd'ed, prō-ceed'ed,
rē-cēd'ed, re-trō-cēd'ed,
sē-cēd'ed, seed'ed,
suc-ceed'ed, sū-pẽr-sēd'ed.
sp: speed'ed.
w: un-weed'ed, weed'ed.
Plus she did, etc.
Cf. need did, etc.

ED'ED

b: bed'ded, em-bed'ded,
im-bed'ded.
dr: dread'ed, un-dread'ed.
h: ad'dle⸗head"ed (-hed"),
ar"rōw-head"ed, bãre'⸗head"ed.
bee'tle⸗head"ed, bē-head'ed,
blun'dẽr⸗head"ed, bull'head"ed,
chuck'le-head"ed, clēar'head"ed,
dun'dẽr⸗hēad"ed, fat'head"ed,
feaTH'ẽr⸗head"ed (feTH'),
fid'dle⸗head"ed, flat'head"ed,
gid'dy⸗head"ed,

(Choose only one word out of each group)

grōss′=head″ed, head′ed,
heav′y=head″ed (hev′),
hōar′y=head″ed, hot′head″ed,
hȳ′drȧ=head″ed, ĭ′dle=head″ed,
Jā′nus=head″ed,
līght′=head″ed (līt′),
lo̱ng′=head″ed,
man′y-head-ed (men′),
mud′dle-head-ed, pig′head-ed,
pud′ding-head-ed,
puz′zle-head-ed,
rat′tle-head-ed, shock′head-ed,
sleek′head-ed, soft′head-ed,
thick′head-ed, trun′dle-head-ed,
wa̱rm′head-ed, wēak′head-ed,
wro̱ng′head-ed.
l: lead′ed (led′).
sl: sled′ded.
shr: shred′ded.
t: ted′ded.
thr: thread′ed (thred′),
un-thread′ed.
w: un-wed′ded, wed′ded.
Cf. head did, etc.
Cf. head dead, etc.
Plus lead, Ed, etc.

Ē′DEN

Vowel: Ē′den.
r: reed′en.
sw: Swē′den.
Plus sea den, etc.
Cf. reed hen, etc.

ED′EN

d: dead′en.
l: lead′en (led′).
r: red′den.
thr: thread′en (thred′).
Cf. red′den, etc.

Ē′DENZ

kr: c̣rē′dence.
s: an-tē-cē′dence, in-tēr-ce′dence, prē-cē′dence.
Cf. an-tē-cē′dents, etc.

Ē′DENT

kr: c̣rē′dent.
n: need′n't.
s: an-tē-cē′dent, dē-cē′dent, in-tēr-cē′dent, prē-cē′dent, rē-trō-cē′dent, sē′dent.
Plus knee dent, etc.

Ē′DĒP

n: knee′deep.
s: sēa′deep.
thr: three deep.
Plus tree deep, etc.

ED′EST

bl: bleed′est*.
br: breed′est*.
d: deed′est*.
f: feed′est*, ō-vēr-feed′est*, un-dēr-feed′est*.
h: heed′est*.
l: lēad′est*, mis-lēad′est*.
n: knēad′est*, need′est*.
p: im-pēd′est*, stam-pēd′est*.
pl: plēad′est*.
r: rēad′est*.
s: ac̱-cēd′est*, cēd′est*, c̣on-cēd′est*, ex-ceed′est*, in-tēr-cēd′est*, prē-cēd′est*, prō-ceed′est*, rē-cēd′est*, sē-cēd′est*, seed′est*, suc̣-ceed′est*, sū-pēr-cēd′est*.
sp: speed′est*.
w: weed′est*.

ED'EST
ED'I

fāte, fär, fàst, fạll, finăl, cãre, at; mēte, prey, hẽr, met; pïne,
marïne, bïrd, pin; nōte, mŏve, fọr, atŏm, not; mọọn, book;

424

(Choose only one word out of each group)

ED'EST

dr: dread'est.
h: bē-head'est*.
r: red'dest.
sh: shed'dest*.
spr: out-spread'est*,
spread'est*.
thr: thread'est*.
tr: tread'est*.
w: wed'dest*.

ĒD'ETH

bl: bleed'eth*.
br: breed'eth*.
d: deed'eth*.
f: feed'eth*, ō-vẽr-feed'eth*,
un-dẽr-feed'eth*.
h: heed'eth*.
l: lēad'eth*, mis-lēad'eth*.
n: knēad'eth*, need'eth*.
p: im-pēd'eth*, stam-pēd'eth*.
pl: plēad'eth*.
r: rēad'eth*.
s: aç-cēd'eth*, cēd'eth*,
çon-cēd'eth*, ex-ceed'eth*,
in-tẽr-cēd'eth*, prē-cēd'eth*,
prō-ceed'eth*, rē-cēd'eth*,
sē-cēd'eth*, seed'eth*,
suç-ceed'eth*, sū-pẽr-cēd'eth*.
sp: speed'eth*.
w: weed'eth*.
Cf. Ē'dith.
Plus see death, etc.

ED'ETH

dr: dread'eth*.
h: bē-head'eth*, head'eth*.
sh: shed'deth*.
shr: shred'deth*.
spr: out-spread'eth*,
ō-vẽr-spread'eth*, spread'eth*.

thr: thread'eth*.
tr: tread'eth*.
w: wed'deth*.
Cf. led death, etc.

ED'FÀST

st: stead'fàst.
Plus tread fast, etc.

ĒD'FỤL

d: deed'fụl.
h: heed'fụl, un-heed'fụl.
m: meed'fụl.
n: need'fụl, un-need'fụl.
sp: speed'fụl.
Plus reed full, etc.

ED'FỤL

dr: dread'fụl.
Plus bed full, etc.

ĒD'GRŌN

r: reed'grōwn.
s: seed'grōwn.
w: weed'grōwn.
Plus we'd groan, etc.
Plus he'd grown, etc.

ED'HED

d: dead'head.
r: red'head.
Plus spread head, etc.

ED'HĒT

d: dead'⸗hēat.
r: red'⸗hēat.
Plus fed heat, etc.

ĒD'I

b: bēad'y.
d: deed'y, in-deed'y.

(Choose only one word out of each group)

gr: greed'y.
h: heed'y, un-heed'y.
kr: çreed'y.
l: Lee'dy.
n: need'y.
p: en-cȳ-çlō-pē'dy.
pr: prē'dy*.
r: reed'y.
s: seed'y.
sp: speed'y.
Plus bleed, he, etc.
Plus wee D, etc.

ED'Ï

Vowel: Ed'diē, ed'dy.
fr: Fred'dy.
l: lead'y.
r: al-read'y, read'y, red'dy, un-read'y.
shr: shred'dy.
st: stead'y, un-stead'y.
t: ted'dy.
thr: thread'y.
Plus said he, etc.

Ē'DIK

m: çō-mē'diç.
p: cȳ-çlō-paē'diç, en-cȳ-çlō-paē'diç.
v: Vē'diç.
Plus see, Dick, etc.

ED'IK

Vowel: Ed'diç.
y: Sa-mō-yed'iç.
Cf. red, Dick, etc.

Ē'DIKT

Vowel: ē'diçt.

ĒD'ING

b: bēad'ing.
bl: bleed'ing, lŏve'⸗līes⸗bleed'ing, un-bleed'ing.
br: breed'ing, in-breed'ing, in-tĕr-breed'ing.
d: deed'ing.
f: feed'ing, ō-vĕr-feed'ing, un-dĕr-feed'ing.
h: heed'ing, un-heed'ing.
l: lēad'ing, mis-lēad'ing.
n: knēad'ing, need'ing.
p: im-pēd'ing, stam-pēd'ing.
pl: in-tĕr-plēad'ing, plead'ing.
r: mis-rēad'ing, reed'ing, reed'ing.
s: aç-cēd'ing, cēd'ing, çon-cēd'ing, ex-ceed'ing, in-tĕr-cēd'ing, prē-cēd'ing, prō-ceed'ing, rē-cēd'ing, ret-rō-cēd'ing, sē-cēd'ing, seed'ing, suç-ceed'ing, sū-pĕr-sēd'ing.
sp: God-speed'ing, out-speed'ing, speed'ing.
w: weed'ing.

ED'ING

b: bed'ding, em-bed'ding.
dr: dread'ing.
h: bē-head'ing, head'ing.
l: lead'ing.
r: red'ding.
sh: shed'ding.
shr: shred'ding.
sl: sled'ding.
spr: bē-spread'ing, out-spread'ing, ō-vĕr-spread'ing, spread'ing.
st: stead'ing.
t: ted'ding.

ĒD'ISH
ED'LES

fāte, fär, fȧst, fạll, finăl, cãre, **at**; mēte, prĕy, hẽr, met; pīne,
marïne, bĭrd, pin; nōte, mŏve, fọr, atŏm, not; mọọn, book;

426

(Choose only one word out of each group)

thr: thread'ing.
tr: tread'ing.
w: wed'ding.

ĒD'ISH

sw: Swēd'ish.

ED'ISH

Vowel: ed'dish.
d: dead'ish.
r: red'dish.
Cf. spread dish, etc.

ED'IT

Vowel: ed'it, sub=ed'it.
kr: ac̯-c̯red'it, c̯red'it,
dis-c̯red'it, mis-c̯red'it.
Plus you said it, etc.

ĒD'ITH

Vowel: Ē'dith.
Cf. ēd'eth.

ED'ÏZ

t: ted'dïeṣ.
Plus ed'ï+s.

Ē'D'L

b: bēa'dle.
d: daē'dăl.
hw: whee'dle.
n: nee'dle.
p: bī-pē'dăl, cen-ti-pē'dăl,
mil-li-pē'dăl, sem-i-pē'dăl.
tw: twee'dle.
Plus feed 'll, etc.
Cf. see dull, etc.

ED'L

h: hed'dle.
m: in-tēr-med'dle, med'ăl,
med'dle.
p: bĭ-ped'ăl, ped'ăl, ped'dle,
trĭ-ped'ăl.
r: red'dle.
tr: tread'le.
Plus bed 'll, etc.
Cf. dead dull, etc.

ED'LĂM

b: Bed'lăm.
Plus dead lamb, etc.

ED'LAND

h: head'land.
Plus red land, etc.

ĒD'LES

br: breed'less.
d: deed'less.
h: heed'less.
kr: c̯reed'less.
n: need'less.
s: seed'less.
sp: speed'less.
st: steed'less.
w: weed'less.
Plus impede less, etc.

ED'LES

b: bed'less.
br: bread'less.
dr: dread'less.
h: head'less.
l: lead'less.
Plus spread less, etc.

(Choose only one word out of each group)

ED'LI

d: dead'ly.
m: chance=med'ley, med'ley.
r: red'ly.
Plus dead lea *or* Lee, etc.

ED'LĪN

br: bread'līne.
d: dead'līne.
h: head'līne.
Plus spread line, etc.

ĒD'LING

hw: wheed'ling.
n: need'ling.
r: reed'ling.
s: seed'ling.

ED'LING

m: in-tēr-med'dling, med'dling.
p: ped'dling.

ED'LĪT

d: dead'līght.
r: red'līght.
Plus spread light, etc.

ED'LOK

d: dead'lock.
h: head'lock.
w: wed'lock.
Plus dread lock, etc.

ĒD'LŪR

hw: wheed'lēr.
n: need'lēr.

ED'LŪR

m: in-tēr-med'dlēr, med'dlēr,
   med'lăr.

p: ped'lăr, ped'dlēr, ped'lēr.
tr: tread'lēr.

ĒD'MAN

fr: Frīed'man.
s: seed'man.
Plus need man, etc.

ED'MĂN

Vowel: Ed'măn.
d: dead'măn.
h: head'măn.
r: red'măn.
st: Sted'măn.
Plus spread man, etc.

ED'NÅ

Vowel: Ed'nȧ.

ED'NES

d: dead'ness.
r: red'ness.

Ē'DŌ

b: li-bï'dō.
kr: ċrē'dō.
l: Lï'dō, Tō-lē'dō.
p: stam-pē'dō, tọr-pē'dō.
r: Lȧ-rē'dō, te-rē'dō.
Plus see dough *or* doe, etc.
Plus need owe *or* O, etc.

ED'Ō

m: mead'ōw.
Plus bed owe *or* O, etc.

ĒD'RÅ

s: ex-ēd'rȧ.
th: ex=ċa-thēd'rȧ.

(Choose only one word out of each group)

ĒD'RĂL

Vowel: dī-ēd'rȧl.
h: dec̣-ȧ-hēd'rȧl,
dī-dec̣-ă-hēd'rȧl, dī-hēd'rȧl.
th: c̣a-thēd'rȧl, prō-c̣ȧ-thēd'rȧl.

ED'REST

b: bed'rest.
h: head'rest.
Plus dead rest, etc.

ED'STŌN

h: head'stōne.
Plus dead stone, etc.
Plus bed's tone, etc.

ĒD'TĪM

f: feed'tīme.
s: seed'tīme.
Plus need time, etc.

Ē'DUM

fr: free'dŏm.
s: c̣ē'dum.
Plus need 'em, etc.
Plus we dumb, etc.

ĒD'ŪR

s: prō-c̣ēd'ūre, sū-pẽr-sēd'ūre.
Cf. need your, etc.

ĒD'ŨR

bl: bleed'ẽr.
br: breed'ẽr, in-breed'ẽr,
in-tẽr-breed'ẽr.
f: feed'ẽr, ō-vẽr-feed'ẽr,
un-dẽr-feed'ẽr.
h: heed'ẽr, un-heed'ẽr.

l: lēad'ẽr, mis-lēad'ẽr,
ring-lēad'ẽr.
n: knēad'ẽr (nēd'), need'ẽr.
p: im-pēd'ẽr, stam-pēd'ẽr.
pl: im-plēad'ẽr,
in-tẽr-plēad'ẽr, plēad'ẽr.
r: rēad'ẽr,
sc̣rip'tūre=rēad'ẽr,
Tal'mud=rēad'ẽr.
s: ac̣-cēd'ẽr, an-tē-c̣ēd'ẽr,
c̣ē'dȧr, c̣ē'dẽr.
c̣on-cēd'ẽr, ex-ceed'ẽr,
in-tẽr-c̣ē'dẽr, prē-c̣ē'dẽr,
prō-ceed'ẽr, rē-c̣ēd'ẽr,
ret-rō-c̣ēd'ẽr, sē-cēd'ẽr, seed'ẽr,
suc̣-ceed'ẽr, sū-pẽr-sēd'ẽr.
sp: speed'ẽr.
w: weed'ẽr.
Plus lead her *or* err, etc.

ED'ŨR

Vowel: ed'dẽr.
b: bed'dẽr, em-bed'dẽr.
ch: Ched'dȧr.
d: dead'ẽr.
dr: dread'ẽr.
h: bē-head'ẽr, dŏu'ble=head'ẽr,
head'ẽr, tri'ple=head'ẽr.
l: lead'ẽr (led').
r: red'dẽr.
sh: shed'dẽr.
shr: shred'dẽr.
spr: bē-spread'ẽr, spread'ẽr.
t: ted'dẽr.
thr: thread'ẽr, un-thread'ẽr.
tr: tread'ẽr.
Plus spread her, etc.

ED'WĀ

h: head'wāy.
Plus bread weigh *or* way, etc.

(Choose only one word out of each group)

ED'WĂRD

Vowel: Ed'wărd.
b: bed'wărd.
Plus dead ward, etc.

ED'WOOD

d: dead'wood.
r: red'wood.
Plus spread wood, etc.

ĒDZ'MĂN

b: bēadṣ'măn, bēdeṣ'măn.
s: seedṣ'măn.
Plus needs man, etc.

EDZ'MĂN

h: headṣ'măn.
l: leadṣ'măn.
Plus spreads man, etc.

ED'ZŌ

m: in-tēr-mez'zō, mez'zō.
Plus beds owe *or* O, etc.

Ē'EST

f: fē'est*.
fl: flē'est*.
fr: frē'est.
gr: à-grē'est*.
r: ref-e-rē'est*.
s: fōre-sē'est*, ō-vēr-sē'est*,
sē'est*.
w: wē'est*.

Ē'ETH

f: fē'eth*.
fl: flē'eth*.
fr: frē'eth*.
gr: à-grē'eth*.
r: reí-e-rē'eth*.

s: fōre-sē'eth*, ō-vēr-sē'eth*,
sē'eth*.

ĒF'ĂS

s: Cē'phăs.
Cf. Jō-sē'phus.

ĒF'DŎM

ch: chiēf'dŏm.
Plus grief dumb, etc.

EF'EN

d: deaf'en.
Cf. Streph'ŏn.

ĒF'I

b: beef'y.
l: lēaf'y.
r: reef'y.
sh: shēaf'y.
Plus grief, he, etc.

ĒF'IJ

l: lēaf'ăġe.
Cf. grief age, etc.

EF'IK

l: mȧ-lef'iç.
str: pēr-i-strepb'iç.

ĒF'LES

br: briēf'less.
ch: chiēf'less.
gr: griēf'less.
l: lēaf'less.
sh: shēaf'less.
Plus leaf less, etc.

EF'NES

d: deaf'ness.

Ĕ'FŌM
Ĕ'G'L

fāte, fär, fåst, fall, finăl, cãre, at; mēte, prey, hẽr, met; pīne,
marïne, bĭrd, pin; nōte, mŏve, fọr, atŏm, not; mọọn, book;

430

(Choose only one word out of each group)

Ē'FŌM

s: sēa'fōam.
Plus tree foam, etc.

Ē'FOUL

p: pēa'fowl.
s: sēa'fowl.
Plus she foul *or* fowl, etc.

EFT'NES

d: deft'ness.

EF'RI

j: Ġeof'frey (jef'ri), Jef'frey.

ĒF'STĀK

b: beef'steāk.
Plus reef stake *or* steak, etc.

ĒF'TIN

ch: chiēf'tăin.
Plus leafed in, etc.
Plus leaf tin, etc.

EF'ŪJ

r: ref'ūġe.
Cf. deaf, huge, etc.

Ē'FUL

gl: glee'ful.
Plus tree full, etc.

ĒF'ŨR

b: beef'ẽr.
br: briēf'ẽr.
ch: chiēf'ẽr.
l: liēf'ẽr.
r: reef'ẽr.
Plus enfeoff her *or* err, etc.
Cf. me for. etc.

EF'ŨR

d: deaf'ẽr.
f: feof'fŏr (fef').
h: heif'ẽr (hef').
z: zeph'yr (zef'ẽr).
Plus clef err *or* her, etc.

Ē'GÅ

d: Tal-là-dē'gà.
m: ō-mē'gà.
r: Rï'gà.
v: Vē'gà.
Plus league a, etc.

EG'I

Vowel: eg'gy.
dr: dreg'gy.
l: leg'gy.
p: peg'gy.
Plus beg he, etc.

ĒG'ING

l: lēagu'ing.
t: fa-tïgu'ing.
tr: in-trïgu'ing.

EG'ING

Vowel: eg'ging.
b: beg'ging.
k: keg'ging, un-keg'ging.
l: leg'ging.
p: peg'ging, un-peg'ging.

Ē'G'L

Vowel: bald ēa'gle, ēa'gle,
  sēa ēa'gle.
b: bēa'gle.
gr: grē'găl.
kl: klēa'gle.
l: il-lē'găl, lē'găl.

(Choose only one word out of each group)

r: rē′găl, vīce-rē′găl.
v: in-vēi′gle.
Cf. sēa′gull.
Plus McTeague'll, etc.

ĒG′LŪR

b: bēag′lĕr.
v: in-vēig′lĕr.

EG′MENT

s: seg′ment.
Plus leg meant, etc.

EG′NĂNT

pr: im-preg′nănt, preg′nănt.
r: queen-reg′nănt, reg′nănt.

Ē′GŌ

Vowel: ē′gō.
s: Ot-sē′gō.
w: Os-wē′gō.
Plus fee go, etc.

Ē′GRĒN

p: pēa′=green″.
s: sēa′=green″.
Plus tree green, etc.

Ē′GRESS

Vowel: ē′gress.
n: Nē′gress.
r: rē′gress.

Ē′GRŌ

n: Nē′grō.
Plus league row, etc.

ĒG′ŪR

Vowel: ēag′ẽr, ēag′re (′ẽr),
ō-vẽr-ēag′ẽr.

l: bē-lēagu′ẽr, lēagu′ẽr.
m: mēa′gre (mē′gẽr).
t: fa-tĭgu′ẽr (-tēg′).
tr: in-trĭgu′ẽr (-trēg′).
Plus league her *or* err, etc.

EG′ŨR

Vowel: eg′gẽr.
b: beg′găr.
l: book′leg″gẽr, boot′leg″gẽr,
leg′gẽr.
p: peg′gẽr.
s: seg′găr.
Plus peg her *or* err, etc.

Ē′GŨRT

s: sēa′gĩrt.
Plus tree girt, etc.

Ē′IK

f: çaf-fē′iç.
p: my-thō-poē′iç.
r: rhē′iç.
t: xan-thō-prō-tē′iç.

Ē′IN

d: çō-dē′ine.
f: çaf-fē′ine.
z: zē′in.
Plus see in *or* inn, etc.

Ē′ING

b: bē′ing, in-bē′ing,
well″=bē′ing.
dr: dree′ing.
f: fee′ing.
fl: flee′ing.
fr: free′ing.
gr: à-gree′ing, dis-à-gree′ing.
j: ġee′ing.

(Choose only one word out of each group)

kr: dē-ċree′ing.
n: knee′ing (nē′).
r: ref-e-ree′ing.
s: ċlēar″=see′ing, fōre-see′ing,
ō-vẽr-see′ing, see′ing,
un-fōre-see′ing, un-see′ing.
sh: skī′ing (shē′).
sk: skī′ing.
spr: spree′ing.
t: guar-ăn-tee′ing (gar-),
tee′ing.
tr: tree′ing.

Ē′IST

d: dē′ist.
k(ċ): man-i-ċhē′ist.
th: an-ti-thē′ist, hȳ-lō-thē′ist,
mon-ō-thē′ist, pol-y-thē′ist,
thē′ist.

Ē′IT

b: al-bē′it, sō bē it.
Plus see it, etc.

Ē′IZM

d: dē′iṣm.
k(ċ): Man-i-ċhē′iṣm.
s: Pär-see′iṣm, Phar-i-see′iṣm,
Sad-dū-cee′iṣm.
t: ab-sen-tee′iṣm, Sut-tee′iṣm.
th: an-ti-thē′iṣm, ạu-tō-thē′iṣm,
ċoṣ-mō-thē′iṣm, hen-ō-thē′iṣm,
hȳ-lō-thē′iṣm, mon-ō-thē′iṣm,
pol-y-thē′iṣm, scī-ō-thē′iṣm (sī-),
thē′iṣm.
w: wē′iṣm.

Ē′JȦ

w: ouï′jȧ (wē′).
Plus siege, a, etc.
Plus see Jah, etc.

Ē′JĂNS

l: al-lē′ġiȧnce.
Cf. see, gents, etc.

EJ′BŪRD

h: hedġe′bĭrd.
s: sedġe′bĭrd.
Plus ledge bird, etc.
Plus hedge burred, etc.

Ē′JĒ

f: Fï′jï.
Plus knee, gee *or* G, etc.
Plus siege, he, etc.

EJ′END

l: leġ′end.
Plus hedge end, etc.

Ē′JENT

r: rē′ġent.
Plus see, gent, etc.

EJ′EST

dr: dredġ′est*.
fl: fledġ′est*.
h: hedġ′est*.
l: al-leġ′est*.
pl: im-pledġ′est*, pledġ′est*.
w: wedġ′est*.

EJ′ETH

dr: dredġ′eth*.
fl: fledġ′eth*.
h: hedġ′eth*.
l: al-leġ′eth*.
pl: im-pledġ′eth*, pledġ′eth*.
w: wedġ′eth*.

(Choose only one word out of each group)

EJ′EZ

Vowel: edġ′eṣ.
dr: dredġ′eṣ.
h: hedġ′eṣ.
k: kedġ′eṣ.
l: al-leġ′eṣ, ledġ′eṣ.
pl: pledġ′eṣ.
sl: sledġ′eṣ.
w: wedġ′eṣ.

EJ′Ï

Vowel: edġ′y.
h: hedġ′y.
kl: çledġ′y.
l: ledġ′y.
s: sedġ′y.
w: wedġ′y.
Plus sledge, he, etc.

EJ′ING

Vowel: edġ′ing.
dr: dredġ′ing.
fl: fledġ′ing.
h: en-hedġ′ing, hedġ′ing.
k: kedġ′ing.
l: al-leġ′ing, ledġ′ing.
pl: mis-pledġ′ing, in-tēr-pledġ′ing, pledġ′ing.
sl: sledġ′ing.
w: wedġ′ing.

EJ′LING

fl: fledġe′ling.
h: hedġe′ling.

ĒJ′MĂN

l: liēġe′măn.
Plus siege, man, etc.

ĒJ′MENT

s: bē-siēġe′ment.
Plus liege meant, etc.

Ē′JUN

l: çol-lē′ġiăn, lē′ġiŏn.
r: rē′ġiŏn, un′dēr₌rē″ġiŏn.
Cf. ē′ji-ăn.

EJ′ŨR

Vowel: edġ′ēr.
dr: dredġ′ēr.
h: hedġ′ēr.
l: al-leġ′ēr, ledġ′ēr, leġ′ēr*.
pl: pledġ′ēr.
sl: sledġ′ēr.
Plus dredge her *or* err, etc.

ĒJ′US

gr: ē-grē′ġiŏus.
l: saç-ri-lē′ġiŏus.
Cf. obleege us, etc.

EJ′WOOD

Vowel: Edġe′wood.
w: Wedġe′wood.
Plus hedge wouıd *or* wood, etc.

Ē′KÀ

ch: Chï′çà.
m: Mee′kà.
n: Dō-min-ï′çà.
p: Tō-pē′kà.
pr: pa-prï′kà.
r: Ços-tà Rï′çà, eū-rē′kà, Fred-e-rï′çà, Fred-rï′kà, Ul-rï′çà.
sp: Spï′çà.
th: bib-li-ō-thē′çà, glyp-tō-thē′çà, zō-ō-thē′çà.
y: Tañ-găn-yï′kà.
Plus wreak a, etc.

(Choose only one word out of each group)

EK'Å

b: Rē-beç'çȧ.
m: Meç'çȧ.
Plus wreck a, etc.

EK'ĀD

d: deç'āde.
Plus wreck aid, etc.

ĒK'ĂL

f: faē'çăl.
s: caē'çăl.
th: bib-lĭ-ō-thē'çăl, thē'çăl.
tr: trēa'çle.
Plus meek'll, etc.
Plus we cull, etc.
Cf. see, Cal, etc.

ĒK'ĂNT

k(ç): pĭ'quănt, prē'çănt, sē'çănt.
Plus he can't, etc.
Plus flee Kant or cant, etc.
Plus meek ant or aunt, etc.

EK'ĂNT

p: ım-peç'çănt, peç'çănt.
Plus wreck ant or aunt, etc.

ĒK'EN

w: wēak'en.
Cf. ēk'ŏn.

ĒK'EST

bl: blēak'est.
l: lēak'est*.
m: meek'est.
n: ū-nĭqu'est (nēk').
p: peek'est*.
r: reek'est*.
s: seek'est*.

sh: shiēk'est.
shr: shriēk'est*.
skw: squēak'est*.
sl: sleek'est.
sn: snēak'est*.
sp: bē-spēak'est*, spēak'est*.
str: strēak'est*.
w: wēak'est.

EK'EST

ch: check'est*.
d: bē-deck'est*, deck'est*.
r: reck'est*, wreck'est*.

ĒK'ETH

l: lēak'eth*.
r: reek'eth*, wrēak'eth*.
s: seek'eth*.
shr: shriēk'eth*.
skw: squēak'eth*.
sn: snēak'eth*.
sp: bē-spēak'eth*, spēak'eth*.
str: strēak'eth*.

EK'ETH

ch: check'eth*.
d: bē-deck'eth*, deck'eth*.
r: reck'eth*, wreck'eth*.

ĒK'I

bl: blēak'y.
ch: cheek'y, cheek=tö=cheek'y.
fr: frēak'y.
kl: clïque'y.
kr: çrēak'y.
l: çock=ă=leek'ĭē, lēak'y.
p: peek'y.
r: reek'y.
s: hīde=and=seek'y.
sh: shēik'y.

(Choose only one word out of each group)

shr: shriēk´y.
skw: squēak´y.
sl: sleek´y.
sn: snēak´y.
str: strēak´y.
t: tēak´y.
v: Bol-she-vī´kī, Men-shē-vī´kī.
w: vē´nī, vī´dï, vī´çï.
Plus see key, etc.
Plus seek, he, etc.

ĒK´ĪD

bl: ō-blïque´⸗eȳed″.
m: meek´⸗eȳed″.
w: wēak´⸗eȳed″.
Plus cheek, I'd or eyed, etc.

ĒK´ING

Vowel: ēk´ing.
ch: cheek´ing,
  cheek⸗tö⸗cheek´ing.
kl: çlïque´ing.
kr: çrēak´ing.
l: lēak´ing.
p: peek´ing.
r: reek´ing, wrēak´ing.
s: seek´ing, self″⸗seek´ing.
sh: shēik´ing.
shr: shriēk´ing.
skw: squēak´ing.
sl: sleek´ing.
sn: snēak´ing.
sp: bē-spēak´ing, fōre-spēak´ing,
  spēak´ing.
str: strēak´ing.
tw: twēak´ing.
Plus see, king, etc.

EK´ING

ch: check´ing.
d: bē-deck´ing, deck´ing.
fl: fleck´ing.
n: neck´ing.
p: hen´peck″ing, peck´ing.
r: bē-wreck´ing, reck´ing,
  wreck´ing.
tr: trek´king.
Cf. neck, king, etc.

ĒK´ISH

bl: blēak´ish.
fr: frēak´ish.
gr: Greek´ish.
kl: çlïqu´ish.
m: meek´ish.
p: pēak´ish.
sn: snēak´ish.
w: wēak´ish.

EK´ISH

p: hen´peck″ish, peck´ish.

ĒK´L

tr: trēa´çle.
Plus also ēk´ăl.

EK´L

d: deck´le.
fr: bē-freck´le, freck´le.
h: heck´le.
j: Jeck´yll.
k: keck´le.
s: Seck´el.
sh: shek´el.
sp: bē-speck´le, speck´le.
Plus wreck ´ll, etc.

EK'LES
Ē'KŎN
fāte, fär, fȧst, fall, finăl, cāre, at; mēte, prey, hȇr, met; pīne,
marĭne, bĭrd, pin; nōte, mŏve, fŏr, atŏm, not; moon, book; **436**

(Choose only one word out of each group)

EK'LES

f: feck'less.
fl: fleck'less.
n: neck'lȧce.
r: reck'less.
sp: speck'less.
Plus check less, etc.

ĒK'LI

bl: blēak'ly, ō-blïque'ly.
m: meek'ly.
n: ū-nïque'ly.
sl: sleek'ly.
tr: trēac'ly.
w: bī-week'ly, trī-week'ly,
wēak'ly, week'ly.
Plus weak Lee *or* lea, etc.

EK'LĬ

fr: freck'ly.
sp: speck'ly.
Plus wreck, Lee *or* lea, etc.

ĒK'LING

w: wēak'ling.

EK'LING

fr: freck'ling.
h: heck'ling.
k: keck'ling.
sp: speck'ling.

EK'LŬR

fr: freck'lĕr.
h: heck'lĕr.

EK'MĀT

ch: check'māte.
d: deck'māte.
Plus wreck mate, etc.

ĒK'NES

bl: blēak'ness, ō-blïque'ness.
m: meek'ness.
n: ū-nïque'ness.
sl: sleek'ness.
t: an-tïque'ness.
w: wēak'ness.

EK'NIK

t: phil-ō-tech'nic,
pol-y-tech'nic, pȳ-rō-tech'nic,
tech'nic, thē-ō-tech'nic.
Plus deck nick *or* Nick, etc.

EK'NING

b: beck'ning.
r: reck'ning, un-reck'ning.

Ē'KŌ

f: bec-cȧ-fï'cō, fï'cō.
kl: Clï'quōt ('kō).
n: Nĭk'kō.
Plus clique owe *or* O, etc.

EK'Ō

Vowel: ech'ō, rē-ech'ō.
g: geck'ō.
s: sec'cō.
Plus wreck owe *or* O, etc.

Ē'KOK

l: Lēa'cock.
m: mēa'cock*.
p: pēa'cock.
Plus see cock, etc.

Ē'KŎN

b: bēa'cŏn.
d: ärch-dēa'cŏn, dēa'cŏn.
m: meek'en.

(Choose only one word out of each group)

w: wēak'en.
Plus speak an *or* on, etc.

EK'ŎN

b: beck'ŏn.
r: reck'ŏn.
Plus fleck on *or* an, etc.

EK'ŎND

s: sec̱'ŏnd.
Plus ek'ŏn+ed.

Ē'KRAB

p: pēa'₌crab.
s: sēa'₌crab.
tr: tree'₌crab.
Plus flee crab, etc.
Plus weak Rab, etc.

Ē'KRET

s: sē'c̱ret.

EK'SĂS

t: tex'ăs.
Cf. vex us, etc.
Plus vex ass, etc.
Plus wreck sass, etc.

EK'SEST

fl: flex'est*.
n: an-nex'est*.
pl: pēr-plex'est*.
s: un-sex'est*.
v: vex'est*.

EK'SETH

fl: flex'eth*.
n: an-nex'eth*.
pl: pēr-plex'eth*.
s: un-sex'eth*.
v: vex'eth*.
Plus wreck Seth, etc.

EK'SHUN

f: af-fec̱'tion, c̱on-fec̱'tion,
dē-fec̱'tion, dis-af-fec̱'tion,
dis-in-fec̱'tion, ef-fec̱'tion,
im-pēr-fec̱'tion, in-fec̱'tion,
pēr-fec̱'tion.

fl: dē-flec̱'tion, flec̱'tion,
ġen-ū-flex'ion, in-flec̱'tion,
ir-rē-flec̱'tion, rē-flec̱'tion.

j: ab-jec̱'tion, ad-jec̱'tion,
dē-jec̱'tion, ē-jec̱'tion,
in-jec̱'tion, in-sub-jec̱'tion,
in-tēr-jec̱'tion, ob-jec̱'tion,
prō-jec̱'tion, rē-jec̱'tion,
sub-jec̱'tion, trá-jec̱'tion.

l: bī-el-ec̱'tion, c̱ol-lec̱'tion,
dī-lec̱'tion, ē-lec̱'tion,
in-tel-lec̱'tion, lec̱'tion,
pre-di-lec̱'tion, prē-lec̱'tion,
re-c̱ol-lec̱'tion. rē-el-ec̱'tion,
se-lec̱'tion.

n: c̱on-nec̱'tion.

pl: c̱om-plex'ion.

r: c̱or-rec̱'tion, dī-rec̱'tion,
ē-rec̱'tion, in-c̱or-rec̱'tion,
in-dī-rec̱'tion, in-sūr-rec̱'tion,
mis-dī-rec̱'tion, rec̱'tion,
re-sūr-rec̱'tion.

s: bī-sec̱'tion, dis-sec̱'tion,
in-sec̱'tion, in-tēr-sec̱'tion,
sec̱'tion, trī-sec̱'tion,
ven-ē-sec̱'tion, viv-i-sec̱'tion.

sp: cīr-c̱um-spec̱'tion,
in-spec̱'tion, in-trō-spec̱'tion,
prō-spec̱'tion, re-trō-spec̱'tion.

t: dē-tec̱'tion, prō-⁺ec̱'tion.

v: cīr-c̱um-vec̱'tion,
c̱on-vec̱'tion, ē-vec̱'tion,
prō-vec̱'tion.
Plus wreck shun, etc.

EK'SHUS
EK'SŪR

fāte, fär, fȧst, fạll, fīnăl, cãre, at; mēte, prẹy, hēr, met; pīne,
marīne, bĭrd, pĭn; nōte, mŏve, fọr, atŏm, not; mọọn, book;

438

(Choose only one word out of each group)

EK'SHUS

f: in-feç'tious.

EK'SI

k: kex'y.
l: ky″rĭ-ō-lex'y.
pl: ap-ō-plex'y.
pr: prex'y.
r: pȳ-rex'y.
Plus wreck see, etc.
Plus wrecks he, etc.

EK'SĪL

Vowel: ex'īle.
fl: flex'īle.
Plus decks aisle *or* isle, etc.
Plus wrecks, I'll, etc.

EK'SING

fl: flex'ing, in-flex'ing.
n: an-nex'ing.
pl: pĕr-plex'ing.
s: un-sex'ing.
v: vex'ing.

EK'SIS

l: Ả-lex'is.
Plus neck, sis, etc.

EK'SIT

Vowel: ex'it.
Plus wrecks it, etc.
Plus deck, sit, etc.

EK'STĂNT

Vowel: ex'tănt.
s: sex'tănt.
Plus wrecks ant *or* aunt, etc.

EK'STIL

s: bīs-sex'tile, sex'tile.
t: tex'tile.
Plus wreck still, etc.
Plus wrecks till, etc.

EK'STŎN

s: sex'tŏn.
Plus wrecks ton *or* tun, etc.
Plus wreck stun, etc.

EK'STRIN

d: dex'trin.
t: tex'trine.

EK'STRUS

d: am-bi-dex'trous, dex'trous.
s: am-bi-sex'trous.

EKS'TŪR

t: in-tēr-tex'tūre, tex'tūre.

EKS'TŨR

d: am-bi-dex'tẽr, dex'tẽr.
Plus wreck stir, etc.

EK'SŪR

fl: dē-flex'ūre, flex'ūre,
in-flex'ūre.
pl: plex'ūre.
Plus wrecks your, etc.

EK'SŨR

fl: flex'ŏr.
n: an-nex'ẽr.
pl: pĕr-plex'ẽr.
s: un-sex'ẽr.
v: vex'ẽr.
Plus wrecks her *or* err, etc.
Plus wreck, sir, etc.

(Choose only one word out of each group)

EK'SUS

n: nex'us.
pl: plex'us.
Cf. Tex'ăs.
Plus wrecks us, etc.

EK'TĂNT

f: dis-in-feç'tănt.
fl: rē-fleç'tănt.
m: hū-meç'tănt.
n: an-neç'tent.
pl: am-plex'tănt.
sp: a-speç'tănt, ex-peç'tănt,
in-ex-peç'tănt, rē-speç'tănt,
su-speç'tănt, un-ex-peç'tănt.
Plus wrecked ant *or* aunt, etc.

EK'TED

f: af-feç'ted, çon-feç'ted,
dē-feç'ted, dis-af-feç'ted,
dis-in-feç'ted, ef-feç'ted,
ill'⸗af-feç'ted, in-feç'ted,
pēr-feç'ted, un-af-feç'ted.
fl: dē-fleç'ted, fleç'ted*,
in-fleç'ted, rē-fleç'ted.
gl: nē-gleç'ted.
j: dē-jeç'ted, ē-jeç'ted,
in-jeç'ted, in-tēr-jeç'ted,
ob-jeç'ted, prō-jeç'ted,
rē-jeç'ted, sub-jeç'ted.
l: çol-leç'ted, ē-leç'ted,
prē-leç'ted, re-çol-leç'ted,
se-leç'ted.
n: çon-neç'ted, dis-çon-neç'ted,
un-çon-neç'ted.
p: ex-peç'ted, sus-peç'ted,
un-ex-peç'ted, un-sus-peç'ted.
pl: çom-pleç'ted,
därk'⸗çom-pleç'ted,
līght'⸗çom-pleç'ted (līt').

r: çor-reç'ted, dī-reç'ted,
ē-reç'ted, mis-dī-reç'ted,
re-ṣūr-reç'ted.
s: bī-seç'ted, dis-seç'ted,
in-tēr-seç'ted, viv-i-seç'ted.
sp: in-speç'ted, rē-speç'ted.
t: dē-teç'ted, ob-teç'ted,
prō-teç'ted, un-prō-teç'ted.
v: in-veç'ted.
Plus wreck, Ted, etc.
Plus wrecked, Ed, etc.

EK'TEST

f: af-feç'test*, dis-in-feç'test*,
ef-feç'test*, in-feç'test*.
gl: nē-gleç'test*.
fl: rē-fleç'test*.
j: ab-jeç'test, ē-jeç'test*,
in-jeç'test*, in-tēr-jeç'test*,
ob-jeç'test*, prō-jeç'test*,
rē-jeç'test*, sub-jeç'test*.
l: çol-leç'test*, ē-leç'test*,
re-çol-leç'test*, se-leç'test*.
n: çon-neç'test*.
p: ex-peç'test*, sus-peç'test*.
r: dī-reç'test, ē-reç'test,
re-ṣūr-reç'test*.
s: bī-seç'test, dis-seç'test*,
viv-i-seç'test*.
sp: in-speç'test*, rē-speç'test*.
t: dē-teç'test*, prō-teç'test*.
Plus wreck test, etc.

EK'TETH

f: af-feç'teth*, dis-in-feç'teth*,
ef-feç'teth*, in-feç'teth*.
fl: rē-fleç'teth*.
gl: nē-gleç'teth*.
j: ē-jeç'teth*, in-jeç'teth*,
in-tēr-jeç'teth*, ob-jeç'teth*,

EKT'FŲL
EK'TIV

fāte, fär, fast, fạll, finăl, cãre, at; mēte, prey, hẽr, met; pīne, marĭne, bĭrd, pin; nōte, mŏve, fọr, atŏm, not; mọọn, book;

440

(Choose only one word out of each group)

prō-jeç'teth*, rē-jeç'teth*, sub-jeç'teth*.
l: çol-leç'teth*, ē-leç'teth*, re-çol-leç'teth*, se-leç'teth*.
n: çon-neç'teth*.
p: ex-peç'teth*, sus-peç'teth*.
r: dī-reç'teth*, ē-reç'teth*, mis-dī-reç'teth*, re-ş̧ur-reç'teth*.
s: bī-seç'teth*, dis-seç'teth*, trī-seç'teth*, viv-i-seç'teth*.
sp: in-speç'teth*, rē-speç'teth*.
t: dē-teç'teth*, prō-teç'teth*.

EKT'FŲL

gl: nē-gleçt'fŭl.
sp: dis-rē-speçt'fŭl, rē-speçt'fŭl.
Plus object full, etc.

EK'TIK

h: heç'tiç.
k(ç): çà-cheç'tiç.
kl: e-çleç'tiç.
l: a-çat-à-leç'tiç, an-à-leç'tiç, brach"y-çat-à-leç'tiç, çat-à-leç'tiç, dī-à-leç'tiç, hȳ"pẽr-çat-à-leç'tiç.
p: peç'tiç.
pl: ap-ō-pleç'tiç.
Plus wreck tick, etc.

EK'TIKS

l: dī-à-leç'tiçs.
Plus ek'tik+s.

EK'TIL

j: prō-jeç'tile.
s: in-seç'tile, seç'tile.
Plus wreck till, etc.
Plus recked ill, etc.

EK'TIN

p: peç'tin.
Plus wrecked in *or* inn, etc.
Plus wreck tin, etc.

EK'TING

f: af-feç'ting, dis-in-feç'ting, ef-feç'ting, in-feç'ting.
fl: dē-fleç'ting, rē-fleç'ting.
gl: ne-gleç'ting.
j: ē-jeçt'ing, in-jeç'ting, in-tẽr-jeç'ting, ob-jeç'ting, prō-jeç'ting, rē-jeç'ting, sub-jeç'ting.
l: çol-leç'ting, e-leç'ting, re-çol-leç'ting, sē-leç'ting.
n: çon-neç'ting, dis-çon-neç'ting.
p: ex-peç'ting, sus-peç'ting, un-sus-peç'ting.
r: dī-reç'ting, e-reç'ting, mis-dī-reç'ting, re-ş̧ur-reç'ting.
s: bī-seç'ting, dis-seç'ting, trī-seç'ting, viv-i-seç'ting.
sp: in-speç'ting, rē-speç'ting, self'-rē-speç'ting.
t: dē-teç'ting, prō-teç'ting.

EK'TIV

f: af-feç'tive, dē-feç'tive, ef-feç'tive, in-ef-feç'tive, in-feç'tive, pẽr-feç'tive, rē-feç'tive.
fl: dē-fleç'tive, in-fleç'tive, ir-rē-fleç'tive, rē-fleç'tive.
gl: ne-gleç'tive.
j: in-jeç'tive, ob-jeç'tive, rē-jeç'tive, sub-jeç'tive.
l: çol-leç'tive, ē-leç'tive, rē-çol-leç'tive, se-leç'tive.
m: hū-meç'tive.

(Choose only one word out of each group)

n: c̤on-nec̤′tive.
r: c̤or-rec̤′tive, dī-rec̤′tive,
ē-rec̤′tive.
s: sec̤′tive.
sp: cĭr-c̤um-spec̤′tive,
in-spec̤′tive, in-trō-spec̤′tive,
ir-rē-spec̤′tive, pēr-spec̤′tive,
prō-spec̤′tive, rē-spec̤′tive,
re-trō-spec̤′tive.
t: dē-tec̤′tive, prō-tec̤′tive.
v: in-vec̤′tive.

EK′TIZM

kl: ec̤-c̤lec̤′tis̤m.
s: sec̤′tis̤m.

EKT′MENT

j: ē-jec̤t′ment, prō-jec̤t′ment,
rē-jec̤t′ment.
Plus neglect meant, etc.

EKT′NES

j: ab-jec̤t′ness.
l: sē-lec̤t′ness.
r: c̤or-rec̤t′ness, dī-rec̤t′ness,
ē-rec̤t′ness, in-c̤or-rec̤t′ness,
in-dī-rec̤t′ness.

EK′TŎR

h: Hec̤′tŏr.
n: nec̤′tăr.
r: rec̤′tŏr.
s: sec̤′tŏr, viv-i-sec̤′tŏr.
v: vec̤′tŏr.
Plus ek′tūr.
Plus wrecked, or, etc.

EK′TŎRD

h: hec̤′tŏred.
n: nec̤′tăred.
r: rec̤′tŏred.

EK′TRĂL

sp: spec̤′trăl.

EK′TRES

l: ē-lec̤′tress.
r: dī-rec̤′tress, rec̤′tress.
sp: in-spec̤′tress.
t: prō-tec̤′tress.
Plus wreck tress, etc.

EK′TRIK

l: an-à-lec̤′tric̤, dī-e-lec̤′tric̤,
ē-lec̤′tric̤, id″i-ō-ē-lec̤′tric̤.
Plus wreck trick, etc.
Plus wrecked rick, etc.

EK′TRŎN

l: ē-lec̤′trŏn.
Plus select run, etc.

EK′TRUM

l: ē-lec̤′trum.
pl: plec̤′trum.
sp: spec̤′trum.
Plus wrecked rum, etc.

EK′TŪR

f: c̤on-fec̤′ture.
j: c̤on-jec̤′ture, prō-jec̤′ture.
l: bē-lec̤′ture, lec̤′ture.
t: är-c̤hi-tec̤′ture.
Plus protect your, etc.

EK′TŪR

f: dis-in-fec̤′tēr, in-fec̤′tēr.
fl: dē-flec̤′tŏr, flec̤′tŏr,
rē-flec̤′tŏr.
gl: ne-glec̤′tēr.
h: hec̤′tŏr.

EK'TUS
ĒK'ŪRZ

fāte, fär, fȧst, fạll, finăl, cãre, at; mēte, prẹy, hẽr, met; pīne,
marīne, bĭrd, pin; nōte, mŏve, fọr, atŏm, not; mọọn, book;

442

(Choose only one word out of each group)

j: ē-jeç'tŏr, in-jeç'tẽr,
in-tẽr-jeç'tẽr, ob-jeç'tŏr,
prō-jeç'tŏr, rē-jeç'tẽr,
sub-jeç'tẽr.
l: çol-leç'tŏr, ē-leç'tŏr, leç'tŏr,
prē-leç'tŏr, re-çol-leç'tẽr,
sē-leç'tŏr.
n: çon-neç'tŏr, neç'tăr.
p: ex-peç'tẽr, pros-peç'tŏr,
sus-peç'tẽr.
r: çọr-reç'tŏr, dī-reç'tŏr,
ē-reç'tẽr, mis-dī-reç'tŏr,
reç'tŏr, re-ṣ̣ũr-reç'tẽr.
s: bī-seç'tẽr, dis-seç'tẽr,
seç'tŏr, trī-seç'tŏr.
sp: dis-rē-speç'tŏr, in-speç'tŏr,
rē-speç'tẽr, speç'tre ('tẽr).
t: dē-teç'tŏr, prō-teç'tŏr.
v: veç'tŏr.
Plus wrecked, or, etc.
Plus wrecked her *or* err, etc.

EK'TUS

p: peç'tous.
sp: çon-speç'tus, prō-speç'tus.
Plus inspect us, etc.

Ē'KUM

m: vä-dē‑mē'çum.
s: cae'çum.
Plus we come, etc.
Plus streak 'em, etc.

ĒK'UND

f: fē'çund, in-fē'çund.

EK'UND

s: seç'ŏnd.
Cf. ek'ŏnd.

ĒK'ŪR

b: ‾ bēak'ẽr.
bl: blēak'ẽr, Bleeck'ẽr.
ch: cheek'ẽr,
chïç'quẽr (chē'kẽr).
kl: çlïqu'ẽr.
kr: çrēak'ẽr.
l: lēak'ẽr.
m: meek'ẽr.
p: peek'ẽr.
r: reek'ẽr.
s: seek'ẽr, self"=seek'ẽr,
shr: shriēk'ẽr.
skw: squēak'ẽr.
sl: sleek'ẽr.
sn: snēak'ẽr.
sp: bē-spēak'ẽr, spēak'ẽr,
stump'=spēak'ẽr.
tw: twēak'ẽr.
w: wēak'ẽr.
Plus tweak her *or* err, etc.
Plus see cur, etc.

EK'ŪR

b: Beck'ẽr.
br: brek'kẽr.
ch: check'ẽr, chequ'ẽr,
ex-chequ'ẽr.
d: be-deck'ẽr, deck'ẽr,
twö'=deck'ẽr (tọọ'),
three'=deck'ẽr.
fl: fleck'ẽr.
p: hen'peck"ẽr, peck'ẽr,
wood'peck"ẽr.
r: wreck'ẽr.
tr: trek'kẽr.
Plus wreck her *or* err, etc.

ĒK'ŪRZ

sn: snēak'ẽrṣ.
Plus ēk'ũr+s.

443 ūse, bṳll, brúte, tũrn, **up;** crȳ, myth; çat, maçhine, ace, church, çhord; ġem, aṅger, (Fr.) boṅ, aṣ; THis, thin; aᶎure

EK′ŪRZ
EL′ĀT

(Choose only one word out of each group)

EK′ŪRZ

ch: check′ērṣ.
Plus ek′ūr+s.

Ē′KWĂL

Vowel: çō͙=ē′quăl, ē′quăl, in-ē′quăl.
s: sē′quel.
Plus peek well, etc.
Plus we quell, etc.

Ē′KWENS

fr: frē′quence, in-frē′quence.
s: sē′quence.
Cf. seek whence, etc.

Ē′KWENT

fr: frē′quent, in-frē′quent.
s: sē′quent.
Plus creek went, etc.

Ē′LÅ

Vowel: Ven-e-zū-ē′là.
b: Bē′là.
d: sẹ-guī-dĭl′là.
g: när-ghī′là, när-ghī′le (′là).
h: gī′là (hē′).
kw: sē-quēl′à.
l: Lēi′là.
m: phil-ō-mē′là.
s: Sē′lah.
sh: Shiē′là.
st: stē′le (′là).
Plus squeal a, etc.
Plus knee, la!, etc.

EL′Å

Vowel: Ā-el′là, El′là, Loù-el′là.
b: Bel′là, Iṣ-à-bel′là, Ros-à-bel′là, um-bel′là.

br: um-brel′là.
d: Å-del′à, Del′là.
f: fel′làh.
m: là-mel′là.
n: Fī-fi-nel′là, ġen″ti-à-nel′là (″shi-), Nel′là, Pim-pi-nel′là, prù-nel′là.
p: ä ça-pel′là, çä-pel′là.
r: li-rel′là, Lit-tōr-el′là.
s: Mär-cel′là.
st: stel′là.
t: fen-es-tel′là, pà-tel′là, sçū-tel′là, tär-ăn-tel′là.
Plus tell a, etc.

EL′ĂN

j: Má-ġel′lăn.
kl: Mc̣-C̣lel′lăn.
t: Å-tel′lăn.
Plus tell Ann *or* an, etc.

EL′ĂNT

p: ap-pel′lănt, im-pel′lănt, in-tēr-pel′lănt, prō-pel′lănt, rē-pel′lănt.
v: di-vel′lănt, rē-vel′lănt.
Plus swell ant *or* aunt, etc.

EL′ĂRZ

s: Sel′lărṣ, Sel′lērṣ.
Plus el′ūr+s.

EL′ĀT

b: dē-bel′lāte, flà-bel′lāte.
p: ap-pel′lāte, in-tēr-pel′lāte.
pr: pre′lāte.
s: ō-cel′lāte.
st: çon-stel′lāte, stel′lāte.
Plus Nell ate *or* eight, etc.
Cf. Nell late, etc.

EL'BÅ
ĒL'DETH

fāte, fär, fȧst, fall, fĭnȧl, cãre, at; mēte, prey, hẽr, met; pīne,
marïne, bĩrd, pĭn; nōte, mŏve, fǒr, atŏm, not; mọọn, book;

444

(Choose only one word out of each group)

EL'BÅ

Vowel: El'bȧ.
m: Mel'bȧ, pēach Mel'bȧ.
Cf. El'be.
Plus smell, bah!, etc.

EL'BORN

h: hell'=born″.
w: well'=born″.
Plus shell born, etc.

EL'BOUND

h: hell'bound.
sp: spell'bound.
Plus well bound, etc.

EL'BŪRT

Vowel: El'bẽrt.
Plus smell, Bert, etc.

ELCH'EST

b: belch'est*.
skw: squelch'est*.
w: welch'est*.
Plus swell chest, etc.

ELCH'ETH

b: belch'eth*.
skw: squelch'eth*.
w: welch'eth*.

ELCH'ING

b: belch'ing.
skw: squelch'ing.
w: welch'ing.

EI CH'ŪR

b: belch'ẽr.
skw: squelch'ẽr.

w: welch'ẽr.
Plus squelch her *or* err, etc.

EL'DÅ

n: Nel'dȧ.
s: Gri-sel'dȧ.
z: Gri'sel'dȧ, Zel'dȧ.
Plus held a, etc.

ĒL'DĂNS

y: yēld'ănce.
Plus heel dance, etc.
Cf. field ants *or* aunts, etc.

ĒLD'ED

f: fiēld'ed.
sh: shiēld'ed, un-shiēld'ed.
w: wiēld'ed.
y: yiēld'ed.
Plus wheel dead, etc.
Cf. wheel did, etc.
Plus concealed, Ed, etc.

ĒL'DEST

sh: shiēl'dest*.
w: wiēl'dest*.
y: yiēl'dest*.

EL'DEST

Vowel: el'dest.
h: held'est*.
w: weld'est*.

ĒL'DETH

sh: shiēl'deth*.
w: wiēl'deth*.
y: yiēl'deth*.
Plus feel death. etc.

(Choose only one word out of each group)

EL′DETH

h: hel′deth*.
w: wel′deth*.
Plus tell death, etc.

EL′DŪR

Vowel: el′dẽr.
g: Gel′dẽr, Van Gel′dẽr.
m: mel′dẽr.
w: wel′dẽr.
Plus held her, etc.

ĒLD′FÃR

f: fiēld′fãre.
Plus yield fair *or* fare, etc.

ĒL′DI

w: un-wiēl′dy.
Plus concealed, he, etc.

ĒL′DING

f: fiēl′ding.
sh: en-shiēl′ding, shiēl′ding,
   un-shiēl′ding.
w: wiēl′ding.
y: un-yiēl′ding, yiēl′ding.

EL′DING

g: gel′ding.
m: mel′ding.
w: wel′ding.
Plus bell ding, etc.

EL′DŎM

s: ṣel′dŏm.
sw: swell′dŏm.
Plus smell dumb, etc.
Plus meld 'em, etc.

EL′EN

Vowel: El′len.
h: Hel′en.
m: Mel′len.
w: Llē-wel′lyn.
Cf. Mel′lŏn.
Cf. tell an *or* on, etc.

ĒL′EST

d: dēal′est*.
f: feel′est*.
h: hēal′est*.
hw: wheel′est*.
j: çon-ġēal′est*.
l: lēal′est.
n: an-nēal′est*, kneel′est*.
p: ap-pēal′est*, pēal′est*,
   peel′est*, rē-pēal′est*.
r: reel′est*.
s: çon-cēal′est*, sēal′est*.
skw: squēal′est*.
sp: spiēl′est*.
st: stēal′est*, steel′est*.
t: ġen-teel′est.
r: rē-vēal′est.
Plus sea, lest, etc.

EL′EST

b: rē-bel′lest*.
ch: cel′list (chel′ist),
   vï-ō-lon-cel′list (-chel′).
dw: dwel′lest*.
f: fel′lest*.
kw: quel′lest*.
n: knel′lest*.
p: çom-pel′lest*, dis-pel′lest*,
   ex-pel′lest*, im-pel′lest*,
   prō-pel′lest*, rē-pel′lest*.
s: ex-cel′lest*, sel′lest*,
   un-dẽr-sel′lest*.
sh: shel′lest*.

(Choose only one word out of each group)

sm: smel'lest*.
sp: spel'lest*.
sw: swel'lest*.
t: fōre-tel'lest*, tel'lest*.
y: yel'lest*.
Cf. yell, lest, etc.

ĒL'ETH

d: dēal'eth*, dŏu'ble=dēai'eth*.
f: feel'eth*.
h: hēal'eth*.
hw: wheel'eth*.
j: con-ġēal'eth*.
n: an-nēal'eth*, kneel'eth*.
p: ap-pēal'eth*, pēal'eth*,
    peel'eth*, rē-pēal'eth*.
r: reel'eth*.
s: con-cēal'eth*, sēal'eth*.
skw: squēal'eth*.
st: stēal'eth*, steel'eth*.
v: rē-vēal'eth*.

EL'ETH

b: rē-bel'leth*.
dw: dwel'leth*.
f: fel'leth*.
kw: quel'leth*.
sm: smel'leth*.
n: knel'leth*.
p: com-pel'leth*, dis-pel'leth*,
    ex-pel'leth*, im-pel'leth*,
    prō-pel'leth*, rē-pel'leth.
s: ex-cel'leth*, sel'leth*,
    un-dẽr-sel'leth*.
sh: shel'leth*.
sp: spel'leth*.
sw: swel'leth*.
t: fōre-tel'leth*, tel'leth*.
y: yel'leth*.

EL'FÃR

w: wel'fãre.
Plus spell fair *or* fare, etc.
Plus elf air *or* heir, etc.

EL'FIK

d: Del'phiͅc.
gw: Guelph'iͅc.

EL'FIN

Vowel: el'fin.
d: del'phin*, del'phine.
Plus pelf in *or* inn, etc.

EL'FĪR

h: hell'fïre.
Plus smell fire, etc.

EL'FISH

Vowel: el'fish.
p: pel'fish.
s: sel'fish, un-sel'fish.
sh: shell'fish.
Plus tell fish, etc.

EL'FRI

b: bel'fry.
p: pel'fry.
Cf. sell free, etc.

ĒL'FỤL

s: seel'fụl.
w: wēal'fụl.
z: zēal'fụl.
Plus meal full, etc.

Ē'LĪ

Vowel: Ē'lī.
Plus we lie *or* lye, etc.
Plus wheel eye *or* I, etc.

447 ūse, bu̯ll, brúte, tŭrn, up; crȳ, myth; çat, maçhine, ace, church, çhord; ġem, aṅger, (Fr.) boṅ, aṣ; THis, thin; aẓure

ĒL'Ꞓ
ĒL'ING

(Choose only one word out of each group)

ĒL'I

Vowel: Ēal'ey, Ēl'y.
fr: free'ly.
h: Hēa'ley,
hw: wheel'y.
k(ç): Kee'ley.
m: mēal'y.
r: Ba-rēill'y, Ba-rē'li.
s: seel'y.
st: steel'y.
Cf. ġen-teel'ly.
Plus wheel, he, etc.
Plus see Lee *or* lea, etc.

EL'I

Vowel: El'ly.
b: bel'ly, çās'us bel'li, pot-bel'ly.
ch: Bot-ti-cel'li (-chel').
d: Del'hi (del'i), Ō-Del'ly.
f: fel'ly.
h: hel'ly*, rāke'hel''ly.
j: jel'ly.
k(ç): Kel'ly, Ō'-Kel'ly.
n: Nel'lie.
r: Bȧ-rel'ly, Çō-rel'li.
s: çan-cel'li, vĕr-mi-cel'lī.
sh: Shel'ley, shel'ly.
sk: Skel'ly.
sm: smel'ly.
t: Don-ȧ-tel'li.
Plus tell, he, etc.

EL'ID

b: bel'lied.
j: ġel'id, jel'lied.
Cf. shell lid, etc.

ĒL'IJ

hw: wheel'äġe.
k: keel'äġe.
Plus feel age, etc.

EL'IJ

p: pel'lȧġe.
Cf. smell age, etc.

ĒL'IK

h: pär-hēl'iç.
Plus bee lick, etc.

EL'IK

b: bel'liç.
h: pär-hel'iç.
j: an-ġel'iç, ärçh-an-ġel'iç, ē-van-ġel'iç, sū''pēr-an-ġel'iç.
k(ç): nick-el'iç.
m: mel'iç, pi-mel'iç.
r: rel'iç.
t: Ar-is-tō-tel'iç, Pen-tel'iç, phil-ȧ-tel'iç, tel'iç.
Cf. smell, lick, etc.

ĒL'IKS

f: Fē'lix.
h: hē'lix.
Plus sea licks, etc.

Ē'LĪN

b: bee'līne.
f: fē'līne.
s: sēa'līne.
Plus me line, etc.

ĒL'ING

Vowel: Ēal'ing.
b: au̯''tō-mō-bïl'ing.

EL'ING
ĔL'MENT

fāte, fär, fàst, fạll, finăl, cãre, at; mēte, prey, hẽr, met; pīne,
marïne, bïrd, pin; nōte, mŏve, fọr, atŏm, not; mọọn, book;

448

(Choose only one word out of each group)

d: dēal'ing, dŏu'ble=dēal'ing,
in-tẽr-dēal'ing, mis-dēal'ing,
New=Dēal'ing, un-dẽr-dēal'ing.

f: feel'ing, fel"lōw=feel'ing,
un-feel'ing.

h: hēal'ing, heel'ing,
self"=hēal'ing, un-hēal'ing.

hw: wheel'ing, free'=wheel'ing.

j: con-ġēal'ing, Där-jeel'ing,
un-con-ġēal'ing.

k(c): keel'ing.

n: an-nēal'ing, kneel'ing.

p: ap-pēal'ing, pēal'ing,
peel'ing, rē-pēal'ing.

r: reel'ing.

s: cēil'ing, con-cēal'ing,
sēal'ing, un-sēel'ing.

sh: shēal'ing.

skw: squēal'ing.

st: stēal'ing, stēel'ing.

v: rē-vēal'ing.

EL'ING

b: bel'ling, rē-bel'ling.

dw: dwel'ling.

f: fel'ling.

j: jel'ling.

kw: quel'ling.

l: par-ăl-lel'ing.

n: knel'ling, sen-ti-nel'ling.

p: cloud'=com-pel'ling,
com-pel'ling, dis-pel'ling,
ex-pel'ling, im-pel'ling,
prō-pel'ling, rē-pel'ling.

s: ex-cel'ling, sel'ling,
un-dẽr-sel'ling.

sh: Schel'ling (shel'), shel'ling.

shm: Schmel'ing (shmel').

sm: smel'ling.

sp: mis-spel'ling, spel'ling.

sw: swel'ling.

t: fōre-tel'ling, fōr"tūne=tel'ling,
tel'ling.

w: wel'ling.

y: yel'ling.

EL'IS

Vowel: El'lis.

tr: trel'lis.

Cf. smell is, etc.

EL'ISH

b: em-bel'lish.

h: hel'lish.

r: dis-rel'ish, rel'ish.

sw: swel'lish.

EL'KUM

w: wel'cŏme.

Plus whelk 'em, etc.

Plus smell come, etc.

EL'MÅ

Vowel: El'må.

s: Sel'må.

th: Thel'må.

v: Vel'må.

Plus well, ma, etc.

Plus overwhelm a, etc.

EL'MĂN

Vowel: El'măn.

b: bell'măn.

w: Well'măn.

Plus smell, man, etc.

Plus overwhelm Ann or an, etc.

ĒL'MENT

j: con-ġēal'ment.

p: rē-pēal'ment.

s: con-cēal'ment.

449 ūse, bu̯ll, brúte, tûrn, up; crȳ, myth; c̦at, mac̦hi̯ne, ace, church, c̦hord; ġem, añger, (Fr.) boṅ, aṣ; THis, thin; aẓure

EL'MET
EL'PÏ

(Choose only one word out of each group)

v: rē-vēal'ment.
Plus steal meant, etc.

EL'MET

h: hel'met.
Plus well met, etc.
Cf. helm it, etc.

EL'MING

h: dis-hel'ming, hel'ming, un-hel'ming.
hw: ō-vēr-whel'ming, whel'ming.
Plus tell Ming, etc.

EL'MŪR

Vowel: El'mēr.
Plus overwhelm her *or* err, etc.

ĒL'NES

l: lēal'ness.
t: ġen-teel'ness.

EL'NES

f: fell'ness.
w: well'ness.

EL'Ō

Vowel: dū-el'lō, nĭ-el'lō.
b: bel'lōw.
ch: cel'lō (chel'), Mon-ti-cel'lō, vi-ō-lŏn-cel'lō (-chel').
d: Sōr-del'lō.
f: fel'lōe, fel'lōw, good fel'lōw, plāy'≈fel″lōw.
h: hel'lō.
j: Jel'lō.
m: mel'lōw.
n: prù-nel'lō, pun-chi-nel'lō.
p: a c̦a-pel'lō, c̦ŏ.″brȧ≈dī≈c̦a-pel'lō

r: mō-rel'lō, sal-tȧ-rel'lō.
t: broc̦-ȧ-tel'lō, Don-ȧ-tel'lō.
v: sc̦ri-vel'lō.
y: yel'lōw.
Plus smell owe *or* O, etc.
Cf. smell low, etc.

EL'ŌD

m: un-mel'lōwed.
Plus el'ō+ed.

EL'ŎN

f: en-fel'ŏn, fel'ŏn.
m: Mel'lŏn, mel'ŏn, wa̯'tēr-mel″ŏn.
Cf. el'en.
Plus smell on *or* an, etc.

EL'ŎP

v: dē-vel'ŏp, en-vel'ŏp.
Cf. smell up, etc.

EL'ŎT

h: hel'ŏt.
z: zeal'ŏt.
Cf. tell Lot, etc.

EL'ŌZ

b: bel'lōwṣ.
Plus el'ō+s.

ELP'FU̯L

h: help'fu̯l, self″≈help'fu̯l, un-help'fu̯l.
Plus whelp full, etc.

EL'PÏ

k: kel'piē.
Plus whelp, he, etc.

EL'PING
EL'TING

fāte, fär, fȧst, fạll, finăl, cāre, at; mēte, prey, hẽr, met; pīne,
marïne, bĭrd, pin; nōte, mŏve, fọr, atŏm, not; mọọn, book;

450

(Choose only one word out of each group)

EL'PING

h: hel'ping.
y: yel'ping.

ELP'LES

h: help'less.
hw: whelp'less.
y: yelp'less.
Plus help less, etc.

EL'PŨR

h: hel'pẽr, self″=hel'pẽr.
y: yel'pẽr.
Plus help her or err, etc.

EL'SȦ

Vowel: El'sȧ.
Cf. melts a, etc.

ĒL'SKIN

Vowel: eel'skin.
s: sēal'skin.
Plus feel skin, etc.

EL'SŎN

k: kel'sŏn.
n: hȧlf=Nel'sŏn (hȧf-), Nel'sŏn.
Plus well, son or sun, etc.

EL'TȦ

d: del'tȧ.
p: pel'tȧ.
Plus pelt a, etc.

EL'TED

b: bel'ted, un-bel'ted.
f: fel'ted.
m: mel'ted.
p: pel'ted.
sm: smel'ted.

w: wel'ted.
Plus well, Ted, etc.
Plus felt, Ed, etc.

EL'TEST

b: bel'test*.
f: fel'test*.
m: mel'test*.
p: pel'test*.
sm: smel'test*.
w: wel'test*.
Plus swell test, etc.

EL'TETH

b: bel'teth*.
f: fel'teth*.
m: mel'teth*.
p: pel'teth*.
sm: smel'teth*.
w: wel'teth*.

EL'THI

h: heal'thy.
st: steal'thy.
w: weal'thy.
Plus wealth, be, etc.

EL'TIK

k(ç): Çel'tiç, Kel'tiç.
Plus swell tick, etc.

EL'TING

b: bel'ting, un-bel'ting.
f: fel'ting.
m: mel'ting.
p: pel'ting.
sm: smel'ting.
w: wel'ting.

451 ūse, bu̧ll, brůte, tůrn, up; crȳ, myth; ça̧t, ma̧chine, ace, church, ҫhord; ġem, aṅger, (Fr.) boṅ, a̧s; THis, thin; a̧zure

ELT′LES
EL′ŨR

(Choose only one word out of each group)

ELT′LES

b: belt′less.
f: felt′less.
k(ç): Çelt′less.
p: pelt′less.
w: welt′less.
Plus felt less, etc.

EL′TRI

p: pel′try.
w: wel′try.
Cf. swell tree, etc.

EL′TŨR

b: bel′tĕr.
f: fel′tĕr.
k(ç): kel′tĕr.
m: mel′tĕr.
p: pel′tĕr.
sh: in-shel′tĕr, shel′tĕr.
sk: hel′tĕr⸗skel′tĕr.
sm: smel′tĕr.
sp: spel′tĕr.
sw: swel′tĕr.
w: wel′tĕr.
Plus felt err *or* her, etc.

EL′TŨRD

sh: un-shel′tĕred.
Plus el′tĕr+ed.

EL′ŪD

pr: pre′lūde.
Plus well, you′d, etc.

EL′ŪJ

d: del′ūġe.
Cf. well, huge, etc.

EL′UM

b: an-tē-bel′lum,
cer-ē-bel′lum, flȧ-bel′lum.
j: flȧ-ġel′lum.
v: vel′lum.
Plus tell ′em, etc.
Plus well, Lum, etc.

ĒL′ŨR

d: dēal′ĕr, dŏu′ble⸗dēal′ĕr,
in-tĕr-dēal′ĕr, mis-dēal′ĕr,
New⸗Dēal′ĕr.
f: feel′ĕr.
h: hēal′ĕr, heel′ĕr,
wa̧rd-heel′ĕr.
hw: fōur′⸗wheel′ĕr, wheel′ĕr.
j: ҫon-ġēal′ĕr.
k(ç): keel′ĕr.
n: an-nēal′ĕr, kneel′ĕr.
p: ap-pēal′ĕr, pēal′ĕr, peel′ĕr,
rē-pēal′ĕr.
r: reel′ĕr.
s: ҫon-cēal′ĕr, seel′ĕr.
skw: squeal′ĕr.
sp: spiēl′ĕr.
st: stēal′ĕr, steel′ĕr.
v: rē-vēal′ĕr.
Plus steal her *or* err, etc.

EL′ŨR

b: rē-bel′lĕr.
dw: ҫȧve′⸗dwel″lĕr, dwel′lĕr.
f: fel′lĕr.
g: Gel′lĕr.
h: hel′lĕr.
k: Kel′lĕr.
kw: quel′lĕr.
m: lȧ-mel′lȧr, "mel′lĕr."
p: ap-pel′lŏr,
ҫloud′⸗ҫom-pel′lĕr, ҫom-pel′lĕr,
dis-pel′lĕr, ex-pel′lĕr,

EL'US
Ē'MȦ

fāte, fär, fȧst, fạll, finăl, cãre, at; mēte, prĕy, hẽr, met; pīne,
marïne, bĭrd, pin; nōte, mŏve, fọr, atŏm, not; mọọn, book;

452

(Choose only one word out of each group)

im-pel'lẽr,   prō-pel'lẽr,
rē-pel'lẽr,   sₑcrew'=prō-pel'lŏr,
twin'=prō-pel'lẽr.

s: cel'lăr, ex-cel'lẽr, Sel'lăr,
sel'lẽr, un-dẽr-sel'lẽr,
wīne'=cel'lăr.

sh: shel'lẽr.

sm: smel'lẽr.

sp: spel'lẽr.

st: in-tẽr-stel'lăr, stel'lăr.

sw: swel'lẽr.

t: fōre-tel'lẽr, fōr'tūne=tel'lẽr,
tāle'=tel'lẽr, tel'lẽr.

w: Wel'lẽr.

y: yel'lẽr.

Plus tell her *or* err, etc.

EL'US

j: jeal'ous.

p: ȧ-pel'lous.

s: prō-cel'lous.

t: en-tel'lus, vī-tel'lus.

z: ō"vẽr-zeal'ous, zeal'ous.

Plus sell us, etc.

EL'VET

v: vel'vet.

Plus swell vet, etc.

EL'VING

d: del'ving.

h: hel'ving.

sh: shelv'ing.

EL'VISH

Vowel: el'vish.

EL'VŨR

d: del'vẽr.

h: hel'vẽr.

sh: shel'vẽr.

Plus shelve her, etc.

ĒL'YA

b: lō-bē'liȧ.

d: Be-dē'liȧ, Ꞓor-dē'liȧ,
Dē'liȧ.

f: Ō-phē'lia (-fē').

l: Lē'liȧ.

m: Ȧ-mē'liȧ, ꞔa-mēl'liȧ,
Rù-mē'liȧ.

n: Ꞓor-nē'liȧ.

r: ᶏu-rē'liȧ.

s: Cē-cē'liȧ, Cē'liȧ,
St. Cē-cē-liȧ.

ĒL'YĂL

b: Bēl'iăl.

ĒL'YŎN

d: Dē'liăn, Men-dē'liăn.

m: ꞔȧ-mēl'eŏn.

Cf. ē'li-ŏn.

EL'YUN

b: rē-bel'liŏn.

h: hel'liŏn.

Cf. el'i-ăn.

EL'YUS

b: rē-bel'lious.

EL'ZȦ

Vowel: El'ṣȧ.

Plus smells a, etc.

Ē'MȦ

Vowel: em-pȳ-ē'mȧ,
sē-ri-ē'mȧ.

b: bē'mȧ.

(Choose only one word out of each group)

d: ē-dē′mȧ, myx-e-dē′mȧ.
l: Lĭ′mȧ.
r: Rĭ′mȧ, ter′zȧ rĭ′mȧ (′tsȧ).
sk(sc̨): sc̨hē′mȧ.
t: blas-tē′mȧ, Fä-tĭ′mȧ.
th: e-ry-thē′mȧ.
z: ec̨-zē′mȧ.
Plus seem a, etc.

EM′Ȧ

Vowel: Em′mȧ.
j: ġem′mȧ.
l: an-ȧ-lem′mȧ, di-lem′mȧ,
  lem′mȧ, neū′ri-lem′mȧ,
  trī-lem′mȧ.
r: mȧ-rem′mȧ.
st: stem′mȧ.
Plus hem a, etc.
Plus hem, ma, etc.

Ē′MĀL

f: fē′māle.
sh: shē′māle.
Plus see male, etc.

ĒM′ĂL

h: hē′mᾰl.
t: blas-tē′mᾰl.
Plus dream, Al, etc.
Cf. deem all, etc.

Ē′MĂN

b: bee′mᾰn.
fr: free′mᾰn.
g: G′=mᾰn.
h: hē mᾰn.
l: lē′mᾰn.
s: ā′ble sēa′mᾰn,
  mẽr′c̨hᾰnt sēa′mᾰn, sēa′mᾰn,
  sē′men.

t: tēa′mᾰn.
Cf. Brē′men.
Plus fee man, etc.
Plus dream an *or* Ann, etc.

EM′B′L

s: as-sem′ble, dis-sem′ble,
  sem′ble.
tr: trem′ble.
z: rē-s̩em′ble.

EM′BLĂNS

s: as-sem′blᾰnce,
  dis-sem′blᾰnce, sem′blᾰnce.
z: rē-s̩em′blᾰnce.

EM′BLĂNT

s: sem′blᾰnt.
z: rē-s̩em′blᾰnt.

EM′B′LD

s: un-dis-sem′bled.
Plus em′b′l+d.

EM′BLEM

Vowel: em′blem.

EM′BLI

s: as-sem′bly.
tr: trem′bly.

EM′BLIJ

s: as-sem′blᾰġe.

EM′BLING

s: as-sem′bling, dis-sem′bling.
tr: trem′bling.
z: rē-s̩em′bling.

(Choose only one word out of each group)

EM'BLŬR

s: as-sem'blẽr, dis-sem'blẽr.
tr: trem'blẽr.
z: rē-ṣem'blẽr.

EM'BRĂL

m: bī-mem'brăl, trī-mem'brăl.

EM'BRANS

m: rē-mem'brănce.

EM'BŬR

Vowel: em'bẽr.
m: dis-mem'bẽr,
dis-rē-mem'bẽr, mem'bẽr,
rē-mem'bẽr.
s: Dē-cem'bẽr.
v: Nō-vem'bẽr.
Plus stem burr, etc.

EM'BŬRD

m: dis-mem'bẽred.
Plus em'bŭr+ed.

EM'ENZ

kl: Ꞓlem'enṣ.
Cf. lemons.

Ē'MENT

gr: ȧ-gree'ment,
dis-ȧ-gree'ment.
kr: dē-ꞓree'ment.
Plus sea meant, etc.

EM'ENT

kl: ꞓlem'eṅṭ, iṅ-ꞓlem'ent.
Cf. hem meant, etc.

ĒM'EST

b: bēam'est*.
d: deem'est*, mis-deem'est*,
rē-deem'est*.
dr: drēam'est*.
f: blas-phēm'est*.
gl: glēam'est*.
kr: ꞓream'est*.
pr: sū-prēm'est.
s: seem'est*.
skr(sꞓr): sꞓrēam'est*.
st: stēam'est*.
str: strēam'est*.
t: es-teem'est*, teem'est*.
tr: ex-trēm'est.

EM'EST

d: ꞓon-demn'est*.
h: hem'mest*.
j: bē-ġem'mest*.
st: stem'mest*.

EM'ET

Vowel: Em'mett.
Plus Lem et, etc.
Cf. condemn it, etc.

ĒM'ETH

b: bēam'eth*.
d: deem'eth*, mis-deem'eth*,
rē-deem'eth*.
dr: drēam'eth*.
f: blas-phēm'eth*.
gl: glēam'eth*.
kr: ꞓream'eth*.
s: seem'eth.
skr(sꞓr): sꞓrēam'eth*.
st: stēam'eth*.
str: strēam'eth*.
t: es-teem'eth*, teem'eth*.

(Choose only one word out of each group)

EM'ETH

d: c̣on-demn'eth*.
h: hem'meth*.
j: bē-g̣em'meth*.
st: stem'meth*.
t: c̣on-temn'eth*.

ĒM'FU̧L

b: bēam'fu̧l.
dr: drēam'fu̧l.
sk(sc̣): sc̣hēme'fu̧l.
t: teem'fu̧l.
Plus dream full, etc.

ĒM'I

b: bēam'y.
dr: day-drēam'y, drēam'y.
gl: glēam'y.
kr: c̣rēam'y.
m: Mī'mī.
s: sēam'y.
skr(sc̣r): sc̣rēam'y.
st: stēam'y.
str: strēam'y.
t: teem'y.
Plus see me, etc.
Plus dream he, etc.

EM'I

d: dem'i.
j: g̣em'my, jem'my.
kl: C̣lem'my.
l: lem'mē.
s: sem'i.
Cf. hem me, etc.

Ē'MIC̣

n: a̓-nē'mic̣.
s: ra̓-cē'mic̣.
t: sys-tē'mic̣.
Plus see Mick, etc.

EM'IC̣

d: ac̣-a̓-dem'ic̣, en-dem'ic̣,
ep-i-dem'ic̣, pan-dem'ic̣.
j: strat-ă-g̣em'ic̣.
k(c̣): al-c̣hem'ic̣, c̣hem'ic̣.
l: pō-lem'ic̣.
r: thē-ō-rem'ic̣.
t: sys-tem'ic̣, tō-tem'ic̣.
Cf. hem Mick, etc.

ĒM'ING

b: bēam'ing.
d: deem'ing, rē-deem'ing.
dr: dāy'=drēam''ing,
drēam'ing.
f: blas-phēm'ing.
gl: glēam'ing.
kr: c̣rēam'ing.
s: bē-seem'ing, seem'ing,
sum'mēr=seem'ing,
un-bē-seem'ing.
sk(sc̣): sc̣hēm'ing.
skr(sc̣r): sc̣rēam'ing.
st: stēam'ing.
str: ō-vĕr-strēam'ing,
strēam'ing.
t: es-teem'ing, teem'ing.

EM'ING

d: c̣on-demn'ing,
self'=c̣on-demn'ing.
fl: Flem'ing.
h: hem'ming.
j: bē-g̣em'ming, g̣em'ming.
l: lem'ming.
st: stem'ming.
t: c̣on-temn'ing.

EM'ISH

b: bēam'ish.
Cf. ice-creamish, etc.

EM'ISH
EM'P'L

fāte, fär, fȧst, fạll, finǎl, cãre, at; mēte, prey, hẽr, met; pīne,
marïne, bĭrd, pin; nōte, mŏve, fọr, atŏm, not; mọọn, book;

456

(Choose only one word out of each group)

EM'ISH

bl: blem'ish, un-blem'ish.
fl: flem'ish.

EM'ISHT

bl: blem'ished, un-blem'ished.

ĒM'IST

sk(sc): schēm'ist.
tr: ex-trēm'ist.
Plus see mist *or* missed, **etc.**

EM'IST

k(c): chem'ist.
Cf. hem mist *or* missed, **etc.**

EM'ĪT, ĒM'ĪT

s: Sem'īte.
Cf. hem might *or* mite, **etc.**

ĒM'LAND

dr: drēam'land.
Plus deem land, **etc.**

ĒM'LES

b: bēam'less.
dr: drēam'less.
kr: crēam'less.
s: sēam'less.
sk(sc): schēme'less.
str: strēam'less.
Plus esteem less, **etc.**

ĒM'LET

str: strēam'let.
Plus dream let *or* Lett, **etc.**

ĒM'LI

pr: sū-prēme'ly.
s: seem'ly, un-seem'ly.

tr: ex-trēme'ly.
Plus dream, Lee *or* lea, **etc.**

EM'NON

m: Ag-ȧ-mem'non, Mem'non.

Ē'MŌ

kr: Crē'mō.
n: Nē'mō.
pr: ä tem'pō prï'mō, prï'mō,
sū-prē'mō.
Plus dream owe *or* O, **etc.**
Plus see, Mo, **etc.**

EM'Ō

m: mem'ō.
Plus hem owe *or* O, **etc.**

ĒM'ŎN

d: a-gȧ-thȧ-daē'mŏn,
cā-cō-dē'mŏn, dē'mŏn,
eū-daē'mŏn.
Cf. ē'mǎn.
Plus seem an *or* on, **etc.**

EM'ŎN

l: lem'ŏn.
Cf. "gem'man".
Plus hem on *or* an, **etc.**

EM'PEST

t: tem'pest.
Plus hem pest, **etc.**

EM'PĪR

Vowel: em'pīre.
Plus condemn pyre, **etc.**

EM'P'L

s: Sem'ple.
st: stem'ple.

(Choose only one word out of each group)

t: tem'ple.
Plus hemp 'll, etc.

EM'PLĂR

t: tem'plăr.
z: ex-em'plăr.

EM'PLĀT

t: con-tem'plāte, tem'plāte.
Plus them plate, etc.
Plus Kemp, late, etc.

EMP'SHUN

Vowel: cō-emp'tion, emp'tion, prē-emp'tion.
d: a-demp'tion, rē-demp'tion.
r: dī-remp'tion.
z: ex-emp'tion.
Plus hemp shun, etc.

EMP'STŨR

d: demp'stẽr.
s: semp'stẽr.
Plus hemp stir, etc.

EMP'TED

Vowel: prē-emp'ted.
t: at-temp'ted, temp'ted,
un-at-temp'ted, un-temp'ted.
z: ex-emp'ted.
Plus hemp, Ted, etc.

EMP'TEST

t: at-temp'test*, temp'test*.
z: ex-emp'test*.
Plus hemp test, etc.

EMP'TETH

t: at-temp'teth*, temp'teth*.
z: ex-emp'teth*

EMP'TI

Vowel: emp'ty.
Plus hemp tea, etc.

EMP'TING

Vowel: prē-emp'ting.
t: at-temp'ting, temp'ting.
z: ex-emp'ting.

EMP'TIV

Vowel: prē-emp'tive.
d: rē-demp'tive.

EMP'TRES

d: rē-demp'tress.
t: temp'tress.
Plus hemp tress, etc.

EMP'TŨR

Vowel: prē-emp'tŏr.
k(c): un-kemp'tẽr.
t: at-temp'tẽr, temp'tẽr.
z: ex-emp'tẽr.
Plus tempt her *or* err, etc.

EM'PŨR

s: Sem'pẽr.
t: at-tem'pẽr, dis-tem'pẽr,
tem'pẽr, un-tem'pẽr.
Plus Kemp err *or* her, etc.

EM'PŨRD

t: ill'-tem'pēred, tem'pēred,
un-tem'pēred.
Plus Kemp erred, etc.
Plus Shem purred, etc.

EM'SŎN

Vowel: Emp'sŏn.
kl: Clem'sŏn.
Plus condemn son *or* sun, etc.

(Choose only one word out of each group)

ĒM'SǫNG

dr: drēam sǫng.
th: thēme sǫng.
Plus scheme song, etc.

ĒM'STŪR

d: deem'stẽr.
s: sēam'stẽr.
t: tẹam'stẽr.
Plus scheme stir, etc.

ĒM'ŨR

b: bēam'ẽr.
d: rē-deem'ẽr.
dr: dāy'＝dream"ẽr, drēam'ẽr.
f: blas-phēm'ẽr, fē'mŭr.
gl: glēam'ẽr.
l: lē'mŭr.
r: rēam'ẽr.
s: sēam'ẽr, seem'ẽr.
sk(sç): sçhēm'ẽr.
skr(sçr): sçrēam'ẽr.
st: stēam'ẽr.
str: strēam'ẽr.
t: teem'ẽr.
Cf. ēm'ĭr.
Plus dream err *or* her, etc.
Plus see myrrh, etc.

EM'ŨR

d: çon-demn'ẽr.
h: hem'mẽr.
j: bē-ġem'mẽr.
st: stem'mẽr.
t: çon-temn'ẽr.
Plus gem her *or* err, etc.

Ē'MUS

d: Ni-çō-dē'mus.
r: Rē'mus.

Plus dream us, etc.
Plus see muss, etc.

ĒM'YẼR

pr: prē'miẽr ('yẽr).
Cf. dream yer, etc.

Ē'NȦ

Vowel: hȳ-ē'nȧ.
b: vẽr-bē'nȧ.
d: Me-dĭ'nȧ, Mō-dē'nȧ.
dr: al-ex-an-drĭ'nȧ.
g: Gĭ'nȧ.
j: ġē'nȧ, Ġeǫr-ġĭ'nȧ.
k(ç): çō-quĭ'nȧ.
kw: Queen'ȧ.
l: ga-lē'nȧ, He-lē'nȧ, Lē'nȧ,
  Mag-dȧ-lē'nȧ, Pạu-lĭ'nȧ,
  Se-lē'nȧ, se-mō-lĭ'nȧ.
m: Wil-hel-mĭ'nȧ, Mĭ'nȧ.
p: phil-ō-pē'nȧ, sub-poē'nȧ.
r: a-rē'nȧ, czä-rĭ'nȧ (zär-),
  fȧ-rĭ'nȧ, Rĭ'nȧ, Sē-rē'nȧ,
  sig-nō-rĭ'nȧ, tsä-rĭ'nȧ.
s: Mes-sĭ'nȧ, scē'nȧ,
  Ter-e-sĭ'nȧ.
t: Är-ġen-tĭ'nȧ, ça-tē'nȧ,
  ça-vȧ-tĭ'nȧ, Ce-les-tĭ'nȧ,
  Çhris-tĭ'nȧ, Çle-men-tĭ'nȧ,
  çon-cẽr-tĭ'nȧ, Fạus-tĭ'nȧ,
  Jus-tĭ'nȧ, sçär-lȧ-tĭ'nȧ,
  ses-tĭ'nȧ.
tr: Ka-trĭ'nȧ.
th: Ȧ-thē'nȧ.
z: māi-zē'nȧ.
Plus wean a, etc.

EN'Ȧ

Vowel: dủ-en'nȧ, Sï-en'nȧ,
  Vï-en'nȧ.

(Choose only one word out of each group)

h: Gē-hen'nȧ, hen'nȧ.
s: sen'nȧ.
t: an-ten'nȧ.
v: Rȧ-ven'nȧ.
Plus when a, etc.

ĒN'ĂL

p: pēn'ăl.
pl: plēn'ăl*.
r: ad-rē'nȧl, rēn'ăl.
sh: mȧ-çhin'ăl.
v: vēn'ăl.
w: wēan'el.
Plus mean, Al, etc.

EN'ĂL

t: an-ten'năl.
Plus when, Al, etc.
Cf. when all, etc.

EN'ĂNT

p: pen'nănt.
t: lieū-ten'ănt,
   sub'-lieū-ten″ănt, ten'ănt,
   Ten'nănt.
Plus then ant or aunt, etc.

EN'ĂRD

l: Leon'ard.
t: ten'ŏred.
Cf. en'ūr+d.
Plus tenor'd.

Ē'NĂS

Vowel: Ē'năs.
z: Zē'năs.
Cf. seen us, etc.
Cf. ēn'us.

EN'ĂS

m: men'ăce.
t: ten'ăce.
Cf. ten'nis.

EN'ĀT

p: brev-i-pen'nāte,
   im-pen'nāte, lọn-ġi-pen'nāte,
   pen'nāte, trī-pen'nāte.
Plus then ate or eight, etc.
Cf. T'hen, Nate, etc.

EN'CHĂNT

tr: tren'chant.
Plus men'chănt, etc.
Plus bench aunt or ant, etc.

ENCH'EST

bl: blench'est*.
dr: bē-drench'est*,
   drench'est*.
fl: flench'est*.
kl: çlench'est*, un-çlench'est*.
kw: quench'est*.
r: wrench'est*.
tr: in-trench'est*,
   rē-trench'est*, trench'est*.
Plus pen chest, etc.

ENCH'ETH

bl: blench'eth*.
dr: bē-drench'eth*,
   drench'eth*.
fl: flench'eth*.
kl: çlench'eth*, un-çlench'eth*.
kw: quench'eth*.
r: wrench'eth*.
tr: in-trench'eth*,
   rē-trench'eth*, trench'eth*.

ENCH'ING
EN'DĂNT

fāte, fär, fȧst, fạll, finăl, cãre, at; mēte, prey, hẽr, met; pīne,
marīne, bird, pin; nōte, mŏve, fǫr, atŏm, not; mọọn, book;

460

(Choose only one word out of each group)

ENCH'ING

b: bench'ing.
bl: blench'ing.
dr: bē-drench'ing, drench'ing.
fl: flench'ing.
kl: çlench'ing, un-çlench'ing.
kw: quench'ing, un-quench'ing.
r: wrench'ing.
tr: in-trench'ing,
rē-trench'ing, trench'ing.

ENCH'LES

kw: quencn less.
Plus ench+less.
Plus French, Les or less, etc.

ENCH'MĂN

fr: French'măn.
h: hench'măn.
Plus stench, man, etc.

ENCH'MENT

tr: in-trench'ment,
rē-trench'ment.
Plus French meant, etc.

ENCH'ŪR

b: bench'ẽr.
bl: blench'ẽr.
dr: bē-drench'ẽr, drench'ẽr.
fl: flench'ẽr.
kl: çlench'ẽr, un-çlench'ẽr.
kw: quench'ẽr.
r: wrench'ẽr.
tr: in-trench'ẽr, rē-trench'ẽr,
trench'ẽr.
Plus French err, etc.
Plus wrench her, etc.

EN'DȦ

Vowel: hac-ï-en'dȧ.
b: Ben'dȧ.
br: Bren'dȧ.
j: a-ġen'dȧ, çor-ri-ġen'dȧ.
l: dē-len'dȧ.
z: Zen'dȧ.
Plus lend a, etc.

EN'DĂL

b: prē-ben'dăl.
s: sen'dăl.
tr: tren'dle.
Plus mend, Al, etc.

EN'DĂNS

p: dē-pen'dence, ım-pen'dence,
in-dē-pen'dence,
in″tēr-dē-pen'dence,
pen'dence*.
s: as-cen'dănce,
çon-dē-scen'dănce (-sen'),
dē-scen'dănce, tran-scen'dănce.
spl: rē-splen'dence.
t: at-ten'dănce,
sū″pēr-in-ten'dence, ten'dănce.
Cf. dē-fen'dănts.
Plus men dance, etc.
Cf. lend aunts or ants, etc.

EN'DĂNT, EN'DENT

f: dē-fen'dănt.
p: ap-pen'dănt, dē-pen'dănt,
dē-pen'dent, e-qui-pen'dent,
im-pen'dent, in-dē-pen'dent,
in″tēr-dē-pen'dent, pen'dănt,
pen'dent.
s: as-cen'dănt, des-cen'dănt,
des-cen'dent,
tran-scen'dent (-sen').

(Choose only one word out of each group)

spl: rē-splen′dent, splen′dent,
tran-splen′dent.

t: at-ten′dănt, c̦on-ten′dănt,
in-ten′dănt, sū-pēr-in-ten′dent.
Plus send aunt *or* ant. etc.

EN′DED

Vowel: en′ded.
b: ben′ded.
bl: blen′ded, in-tēr-blen′ded,
un-blen′ded.
f: dē-fen′ded, fen′ded,
of-fen′ded, un-dē-fen′ded.
fr: bē-frien′ded (-fren′),
frien′ded, un-bē-frien′ded,
un-frien′ded.
h: ap-prē-hen′ded,
c̦om-prē-hen′ded,
mis″ap-prē-hen′ded,
re-prē-hen′ded.
m: a-men′ded, c̦om-men′ded,
ē-men′ded, men′ded,
re-c̦om-men′ded.
p: ap-pen′ded, dē-pen′ded,
ex-pen′ded, im-pen′ded,
sus-pen′ded.
r: ren′ded*.
s: as-cen′ded, c̦on-dē-scen′ded,
dē-scen′ded, rē-as-cen′ded,
tran-scen′ded.
t: at-ten′ded, c̦on-ten′ded,
dis-ten′ded, ex-ten′ded,
in-ex-ten′ded, in-ten′ded,
por-ten′ded, prē-ten′ded,
sub-ten′ded, sū″pēr-in-ten′ded,
ten′ded, un-at-ten′ded,
un-ex-ten′ded.
tr: tren′ded.
w: wen′ded.

Cf. splen′did.
Plus men dead, etc.
Plus send, Ed, etc.
Cf. then did, etc.

EN′DEST

Vowel: en′dest*.
b: ben′dest*, un-ben′dest*.
bl: blen′dest*,
in-tēr-blen′dest*.
f: dē-fen′dest*, fen′dest*,
of-fen′dest*.
fr: bē-frien′dest*.
h: ap-prē-hen′dest*,
c̦om-prē-hen′dest*,
re-prē-hen′dest*.
l: len′dest*.
m: a̦-men′dest*,
c̦om-men′dest*, ē-men′dest*,
men′dest*, re-c̦om-men′dest*.
p: ap-pen′dest*, dē-pen′dest*,
ex-pen′dest*, sus-pen′dest*.
r: ren′dest*.
s: as-cen′dest*,
c̦on-dē-scen′dest*,
dē-scen′dest*, sen′dest*.
sp: spen′dest*.
t: at-ten′dest*, c̦on-ten′dest*,
ex-ten′dest*, in-ten′dest*,
prē-ten′dest*, sub-ten′dest*,
sū″pēr-in-ten′dest*, ten′dest*.
v: ven′dest*.
w: wen′dest*.

EN′DETH

Vowel: en′deth*.
b: ben′deth*, un-ben′deth*.
bl: blen′deth*,
in-tēr-blen′deth*.
f: dē-fen′deth*, fen′deth*,
of-fen′deth*.

EN'DI
END'LES

fāte, fär, fȧst, fạll, finăl, cãre, at; mēte, prey, hêr, met; pīne,
marïne, bĭrd, pin; nōte, mŏve, fọr, atŏm, not; mọọn, book;

462

(Choose only one word out of each group)

fr: bē-frien'deth (-fren')*.
h: ap-prē-hen'deth*,
com-prē-hen'deth*,
re-prē-hen'deth*.
l: len'deth*.
m: ȧ-men'deth*,
com-men'deth*, ē-men'deth*,
men'deth*, re-com-men'deth*.
p: ap-pen'deth*, dē-pen'deth*,
ex-pen'deth*, sus-pen'deth*.
r: ren'deth*.
s: as-cen'deth*,
con-dē-scen'deth (-sen')*,
dē-scen'deth*, sen'deth*.
sp: spen'deth*.
t: at-ten'deth*, con-ten'deth*,
ex-ten'deth*, in-ten'deth*,
prē-ten'deth*, sub-ten'deth*,
sū″pêr-in-ten'deth*, ten'deth*.
v: ven'deth*.
w: wen'deth*.
Plus then death, etc.

EN'DI

b: ben'dy.
f: Ef-fen'di.
w: Wen'dy.
Plus friend, he, etc.
Plus then Dee *or* D, etc.

EN'DIK

w: Wen'dic.
z: zen'dik.
Plus then, Dick, etc.

EN'DING

Vowel: en'ding, un-end'ing.
b: ben'ding, un-ben'ding.
bl: blen'ding, in-têr-blen'ding.
f: dē-fen'ding, fōr-fen'ding*,
of-fen'ding*, un-of-fen'ding.

fr: bē-frien'ding (-fren'),
un-frien'ding.
h: ap-prē-hen'ding,
com-prē-hen'ding,
re-prē-hen'ding.
l: fōre-len'ding*, len'ding.
m: ȧ-men'ding, com-men'ding,
ē-men'ding, men'ding,
re-com-men'ding.
p: ap-pen'ding, dē-pen'ding,
ex-pen'ding, im-pen'ding,
pen'ding, pêr-pen'ding,
sus-pen'ding.
r: heärt'-ren'ding, ren'ding.
s: as-cen'ding,
con-dē-scen'ding, dē-scen'ding,
sen'ding, tran-scen'ding.
sp: fōre-spen'ding*,
mis-spen'ding, spen'ding.
t: at-ten'ding, con-ten'ding,
dis-ten'ding, ex-ten'ding,
in-ten'ding, pọr-ten'ding,
prē-ten'ding, sub-ten'ding,
sū″pêr-in-ten'ding, ten'ding,
un-at-ten'ding,
un-prē-ten'ding.
tr: tren'ding.
v: ven'ding.
w: wen'ding.

ĒND'ISH

f: fiēnd'ish.
Plus clean dish, etc.

END'LES

Vowel: end'less.
fr: friend'less (frend').
Plus lend less, etc.

(Choose only one word out of each group)

END'LI

fr: friend'ly (frend'),
un-friend'ly.
Plus lend, Lee *or* lea, etc.

END'MENT

fr: bē-friend'ment (-frend').
m: à-mend'ment.
t: in-tend'ment.
Plus bend meant, etc.

EN'DŌ

Vowel: di-min″ū-en'dō,
in-nū-en'dō.
s: çres-cen'dō, dē″çres-cen'dō.
Plus then dough *or* doe, etc.
Plus lend, owe *or* O, etc.

EN'DRŎN

d: lir″i-ō-den'drŏn,
lith-ō-den'drŏn,
rhō-dō-den'drŏn,
tox″i-çō-den'drŏn.
Cf. end run, etc.

END'SHIP

fr: friend'ship (frend').
Plus lend ship, etc.

EN'DUM

d: ad-den'dum, çrē-den'dum.
j: a-ġen'dum, çor-ṛi-ġen'dum.
r: re-fēr-en'dum.
Plus lend 'em, etc.
Plus men dumb, etc.

EN'DŨR

Vowel: en'dẽr, tāil'⸗en'dẽr,
week'⸗en'dẽr.
b: ben'dẽr.

bl: blen'dẽr, in-tēr-blen'dẽr.
f: dē-fen'dẽr, fen-dẽr,
of-fen'dẽr.
fr: bē-frien'dẽr (-fren').
h: ap-prē-hen'dẽr,
çom-prē-hen'dẽr,
re-prē-hen'dẽr.
j: en-ġen'dẽr, ġen'dẽr.
l: len'dẽr, mŏn-ey-len'dẽr.
m: à-men'dẽr, çom-men'dẽr,
ē-men'dẽr, men'dẽr,
re-çom-men'dẽr.
p: dē-pen'dẽr, ex-pen'dẽr,
pēr-pen'dẽr, sus-pen'dẽr.
r: ren'dẽr, sũr-ren'dẽr.
s: as-cen'dẽr,
dē-scen'dẽr (-sen'), sen'dẽr.
sl: slen'dẽr.
sp: spen'dẽr.
spl: splen'dŏr.
t: at-ten'dẽr, çon-ten'dẽr,
en-ten'dẽr*, ex-ten'dẽr,
in-ten'dẽr, prē-ten'dẽr,
ten'dẽr.
v: ven'dŏr.
w: wen'dẽr.
Plus send her, Ur, err *or* er, etc.

EN'DŨRD

r: un-sũr-ren'dẽred.
Plus en'dũr+ed.

EN'DUS, not EN'JUS

m: trē-men'dous.
p: stū-pen'dous.
Plus defend us, etc.

END'WĀZ

Vowel: end'wāyṣ.
Plus defend ways *or* weighs, etc.

EN'EL
Ē'NI

fāte, fär, fàst, fạll, fĭnăl cãre, at; mēte. prẹy; hẽr, met; pīne, marĭne, bĭrd, pin; nōte, mŏve, fọr, atŏm, not; mọọn, boọk;

464

(Choose only one word out of each group)

EN'EL

f: fen'nel, Fen'nell.
k: ken'nel, un-ken'nel.
Plus men'll, etc.

EN'ELM

k: Ken'elm.
Plus glen elm, etc.

ĒN'EST

gl: glēan'est*.
gr: green'est.
k: keen'est.
kl: çlēan'est.
l: lēan'est.
m: dē-mēan'est*, mēan'est.
r: se-rēn'est.
skr(sçr): bē-sçreen'est*, sçreen'est*.
v: çon-trà-vēn'est*, çon-vēn'est*, in-tēr-vēn'est*, sū-pēr-vēn'est*.
w: wēan'est*, ween'est*.
Plus sea nest, etc.

EN'EST

d: den'nest*.
k: ken'nest*.
p: pen'nest*, un-pen'nest.

EN'ET

b: Ben'nett.
j: jen'net.
r: ren'net.
s: sen'ăte.
t: ten'et.
Plus men et, etc.
Cf. then it, etc.
Cf. then net, etc.

ĒN'ETH

gl: glēan'eth*.
k: keen'eth*.
kl: çlēan'eth*.
l: lēan'eth*.
m: dē-mēan'eth*, mēan'eth*.
skr: bē-sçreen'eth*, sçreen'eth*.
v: çon-trà-vēn'eth*, çon-vēn'eth*, in-tēr-vēn'eth*, sū-pēr-vēn'eth*.
w: wēan'eth*, ween'eth*.

EN'ETH

d: den'neth*.
k: Ken'neth.
p: pen'neth*, un-pen'neth*.

ENG'THI

l: leng'thy.

ĒN'HỌRN

gr: green'họrn.
Plus seen horn, etc.

Ē'NI

Vowel: ee'ni.
ch: Chē'ney, Chēy'ney, fan-tōc-cĭ'nĭ (-tō-chĭ'), fet-ūc-cĭ'nĭ (-ū-chĭ').
n: fĭ'nĭs (fē'nē), Mç-Fee'ney.
gr: green'y.
j: ġē'niē.
kr: Hip-pō-çrē'nē.
kw: Queen'iē.
l: Se-lē'nē.
m: mēan'y, mee'nĭ.
s: gris-sĭ'nĭ.
sh: shee'ny.
spl: spleen'y.

465 ūse, bull, brůte, tůrn, up; crȳ, myth; ċat, maċhine, ace, church, ċhord; ġem, añger, (Fr.) boñ, aș; THis, thin; aȥure

EN'I
EN'IM

(Choose only one word out of each group)

sw: Swee'ney.
t: teen'y.
v: vis'nē (vē'nē).
w: ween'y.
z: Te-trȧ-zī'nī.
Plus bee knee, etc.
Plus 16 E, etc.

EN'I

Vowel: ăn'y.
b: Ben'ny.
d: Den'ny.
f: fen'ny.
j: jen'ny, spiṅ'ning jen'ny.
k: Ken'ny, Kil-ken'ny.
m: măn'y.
p: Heṅ'ny⸗Pen'ny, Pen'ney, pen'ny, trủe-pen'ny.
r: Ren'nie.
t: ten'ney.
w: wen'ny.
Plus then he, etc.

ĒN'ĪD

gr: green'eȳed.
k: keen'eȳed.
Plus clean eyed, etc.

ĒN'IJ

gr: green'ăġe.
r: cȧ-reen'ăġe.
t: teen'ăġe.
Plus mean age, etc.

ĒN'IK

f: phēn'iċ.
s: scēn'iċ (sēn').
Plus me, Nick, etc.

EN'IK

ch: li-chen'iċ.
d: Ē-den'iċ.
f: al-phen'iċ, phen'iċ.
fr: phren'iċ.
j: an″thrō-pō-ġen'iċ, chron-ō-ġen'iċ, crys″-tăl-lō-ġen'iċ, deü″tēr-ō-ġen'iċ, Dī-ō-ġen'iċ, di-plō-ġen'iċ, em-bry-ō-ġen'iċ, eū-ġen'iċ, glȳ-ċō-ġen'iċ, hys-tēr-ō-ġen'iċ, met-ȧ-ġen'iċ, nī-trō-ġen'iċ, or-gan-ō-ġen'iċ, ox-y-ġen'iċ, par-ȧ-ġen'iċ, pär-then-ō-ġen'iċ, path-ō-ġen'iċ, phos-phor-ō-ġen'iċ, phō-tō-ġen'iċ, prō-tō-ġen'iċ, pȳ-rō-ġen'iċ, pȳ-thō-ġen'iċ, thēr-mō-ġen'iċ, zō-ō-ġen'iċ.
k(ċ): lī-chen'iċ.
l: gȧ-len'iċ, ġē″ō-se-len'iċ, Hel-len'iċ, Pan-hel-len'iċ, Phil-hel-len'iċ, se-len'iċ.
m: e-ċū-men'iċ.
r: ī-ren'iċ.
s: Sar-ȧ-cen'iċ, scen'iċ.
spl: splen'iċ.
st: tung-sten'iċ.
sth: sthen'iċ.
t: Prủ-ten'iċ*.
th: as-then'iċ, ċal-lis-then'iċ, De-mos-then'iċ, neū-răs-then'iċ, pär-then'iċ.
Plus pen nick *or* Nick, etc.

EN'IM

d: den'im.
Plus pen him, etc.

EN′IN
EN′JŪR

fāte, fär. fàst, fạll, finăl, cāre, at; mēte, prẹy, hêr, met; pīne,
marĭne, bĭrd, pĭn; nōte, mȯve, fọr, atŏm, not; mọọn, book;

466

(Choose only one word out of each group)

EN′IN

l: Len′in.
Plus ten in, etc.

ĒN′ING

Vowel: ēan′ing.
b: shē-been′ing.
gl: glēan′ing.
gr: green′ing.
k(c̣): keen′ing.
kl: c̣lēan′ing.
kw: queen′ing.
l: lēan′ing, up-lēan′ing.
m: bē-mēan′ing, dē-mēan′ing,
dŏu′ble mēan′ing, mēan′ing,
un-mēan′ing, well′=mēan′ing.
pr: preen′ing.
s: scēn′ing.
sh: mà-c̣hïn′ing.
skr(sc̣r): sc̣reen′ing.
v: ad-vēn′ing, c̣on-trà-vēn′ing,
c̣on-vēn′ing, in-tēr-vēn′ing,
sub-vēn′ing, sū-pēr-vēn′ing.
w: ō-vēr-ween′ing, wēan′ing,
ween′ing.
y: yēan′ing.

ĒN′INGZ

skr(sc̣r): sc̣reen′ings.
Plus ēn′ing+s.

EN′INGṢ

j: Jen′ningṣ.
Plus en′ing+s.

EN′IS

d: Den′nis.
t: ten′nis.
Cf. menace, tenace.

ĒN′ISH

gr: green′ish.
k: keen′ish.
kl: c̣lēan′ish.
kw: queen′ish.
l: lēan′ish.
m: mēan′ish.
spl: spleen′ish.

EN′ISH

pl: plen′ish, rē-plen′ish.
r: Rhen′ish.
w: wen′nish.

ĒN′IST

pl: plēn′ist.
sh: mà-c̣hïn′ist.
t: röu-tïn′ist.
z: mag-à-zïn′ist.

EN′IZ

b: ben′nieṣ.
j: spin′ning jen′nieṣ.
p: pen′nieṣ.
Plus fen is, etc.

EN′JĂNS

v: ven′ġeănce.

EN′JIN

Vowel: en′ġine.
Plus then gin, djinn *or* jinn, etc.

EN′JING

v: à-ven′ġing, rē-ven′ġing,
ven′ġing*.

EN′JŪR

v: à-ven′ġer.
Plus avenge her *or* err, etc.

(Choose only one word out of each group)

ĒN′LI

gr: green′ly.
k(c̱): keen′ly.
kl: c̱lēan′ly.
kw: queen′ly.
l: lēan′ly.
m: mēan′ly.
r: se-rēne′ly.
s: ob-scēne′ly.
Plus green lea *or* Lee, etc.

EN′LI

h: Hen′ley.
kl: c̱lean′ly (klen′), un-c̱lean′ly.
s: Sen′ley.
sh: Sc̱hen′ley.
Plus then lea *or* Lee, etc.

ĒN′LING

w: wēan′ling.
y: yēan′ling.

EN′MĂN

f: fen′măn.
p: pen′măn.
Plus then man, etc.

ĒN′NES

gr: green′ness.
k: keen′ness.
kl: c̱lēan′ness, un-c̱lēan′ness.
l: lēan′ness.
m: mēan′ness.
r: se-rēne′ness.
s: ob-scēne′ness.

Ē′NŌ

Vowel: Ē′nō.
b: bam-bī′nō, bēan′ō.
d: ton-dī′nō.

k: bal̯-dȧ-c̱hī′nō, kē′nō, ma-răs-c̱hī′nō.
n: pï-ȧ-nï′nō.
p: Fil-i-pï′nō.
r: me-rï′nō, pēach-e-rï′nō, pep-e-rï′nō, Rē′nō, San Mȧ-rï′nō, Se-rē′nō, vet-tū-rï′nō.
s: C̦ȧ-sï′nō.
t: an-dan-tï′nō, fes-tï′nō, Val-en-tï′nō.
Plus see no *or* know, etc.
Plus clean owe *or* O, etc.

Ē′NOK

Vowel: Ē′noc̱h.
Plus we knock, etc.

EN′ŌLD

r: Rey′nōld.
Plus then old, etc.

EN′ŌLZ

r: Rey′nōlds̱.

EN′ŎM

v: en-ven′ŏm, ven′ŏm.
Cf. den′im.
Plus pen ′em, etc.

EN′ŎN

p: pen′nŏn.
t: ten′ŏn.
Plus den on *or* an, etc.

Ē′NŌS

Vowel: Ē′nōs.

EN′RI

d: Den′ry.
h: Hen′ry.

EN'SĂL
EN'SHĂL

fāte, fär, fást, fạll, finăl, cãre, at; mēte, prey, hēr, met; pīne,
marïne, bïrd, pĭn; nōte, mŏve, fọr, atŏm, not; mọọn, book;

468

(Choose only one word out of each group)

EN'SĂL

m: bī-men'săl, cọn-men'săl,
men'săl.
r: fō-ren'săl.
Plus expense, Al, etc.
Cf. expense, all, etc.

EN'SĀT

d: cọn-den'sāte.
p: cọm-pen'sāte.
s: in-sen'sāte.
t: in-ten'sāte.
Plus men sate, etc.
Plus expense ate *or* eight, **etc.**

EN'SEST

d: cọn-den'sest*, den'sest.
f: fen'cest*.
m: cọm-men'cest*.
p: dis-pen'sest*,
rē-cọm-pen'sest*.
s: in-cen'sest*.
t: in-ten'sest.

EN'SETH

d: cọn-den'seth*.
f: fen'ceth*.
m: cọm-men'ceth*.
p: dis-pen'seth*,
rē-cọm-pen'seth*.
s: in-cen'seth*.
Plus then saith *or* Seth, **etc.**

EN'SĒZ

Vowel: à-man-ū-en'sēş.
j: Al-bi-ġen'sēş.
m: men'sēş.
Plus then sees, etc.
Plus expense ease, etc.

ENS'FŌRTH

h: hence'fōrth.
hw: whence'fōrth.
TH: THence'fōrth.
Plus fence fourth *or* forth, **etc.**

EN'SHĂL

Vowel: ex-pēd-i-en'tiăl,
ex-per-i-en'tiăl, in-flū-en'tiăl,
ō-bē-di-en'tiăl, sap-i-en'tiăl,
scī-en'tiăl (sī-).
d: cọn-fi-den'tiăl, crē-den'tiăl,
ev-i-den'tiăl, jù-riş-prù-den'tiăl,
pre-cē-den'tiăl, preş-i-den'tiăl,
prov-i-den'tiăl, prù-den'tiăl,
reş-i-den'tiăl, rō-den'tiăl.
j: à-ġen'tiăl, bī-ġen'tiăl,
in-dul-ġen'tiăl*,
in-tel-li-ġen'tiăl, ten-ġen'tiăl.
kw: cọn-sē-quen'tiăl,
in-cọn-sē-quen'tiăl,
sē-quen'tiăl.
l: pes-ti-len'tiăl,
quer-ū-len'tiăl,
n: ex-pō-nen'tiăl.
r: cọn-fē-ren'tiăl, de-fē-ren'tiăl,
dif-fē-ren'tiăl, in-fē-ren'tiăl,
ir-rev-ē-ren'tiăl, pre-fē-ren'tiăl,
re-fē-ren'tiăl, re-vē-ren'tiăl,
tọr-ren'tiăl, trans-fē-ren'tiăl,
s: cō-es-sen'tiăl, es-sen'tiăl,
in-es-sen'tiăl, non-es-sen'tiăl,
quin-tes-sen'tiăl,
re-min-is-cen'tiăl,
sū″pēr=es-sen'tiăl,
un-es-sen'tiăl.
t: e″qui-pō-ten'tiăl,
ex-iş-ten'tiăl, pen-i-ten'tiăl,
pō-ten'tiăl, sen-ten'tiăl.
v: Prō-ven'ciăl.

(Choose only one word out of each group)

z: om″ni-prē-s̩en′tiăl.
Plus men shall, etc.
Plus bench, Al, etc.
Cf. bench all, etc.

ĒN′SHIP

d: dēan′ship.
kw: queen′ship.
Plus clean ship, etc.

EN′SHUN

h: ap-prē-hen′sion,
c̞om-prē-hen′sion,
de-prē-hen′sion*,
in-ap-prē-hen′sion,
in-c̞om-prē-hen′sion,
mis-ap-prē-hen′sion,
prē-ap-prē-hen′sion,
prē-hen′sion, re-prē-hen′sion.
j: bot′tle ġen′tiăn, ġen′tiăn.
kl: dē-c̞len′sion.
m: di-men′sion, men′tion.
p: pen′sion, prō-pen′sion,
sus-pen′sion.
s: ac̞-cen′sion, as-cen′sion,
c̞on-dē-scen′sion (-sen′),
dē-scen′sion (-sen′),
dis-sen′sion, rē-cen′sion.
st: ab-sten′tion.
t: at-ten′tion, c̞ō′⸗ex-ten′sion,
c̞on-ten′tion, dē-ten′tion,
dis-ten′tion, ex-ten′sion,
in-at-ten′tion, in-ex-ten′sion,
in-ten′sion, in-ten′tion,
ob-ten′tion, os-ten′sion,
por-ten′tion, prē-ten′sion,
rē-ten′tion, ten′sion,
thĕr-mō-ten′sion.
v: cīr-c̞um-ven′tion,
c̞on-trà-ven′tion, c̞on-ven′tion,
in-tĕr-ven′tion, in-ven′tion,

ob-ven′tion, prē-ven′tion,
sub-ven′tion, sū-pĕr-ven′tion.
z: prē-s̩en′tion*.
Plus pen shun, etc.

EN′SHUND

m: un-men′tioned.
p: un-pen′sioned.
t: well′⸗in-ten′tioned.
Plus en′shun+ed.

EN′SHUS

Vowel: c̞on-sci-en′tious (-shi-)
l: pes-ti-len′tious, sī-len′tious.
s: dis-sen′tious, lī-cen′tious.
t: c̞on-ten′tious, prē-ten′tious,
sen-ten′tious.
Cf. drench us, etc.

EN′SIL

h: prē-hen′sile.
p: pen′cil, pen′sile.
st: sten′cil.
t: ex-ten′sile, ten′sile,
ū-ten′sil.
Plus hence, ill, etc.
Plus pen sill, etc.
Plus fence ′ll, etc.

EN′SILD

p: pen′cilled.
st: sten′cilled.
t: ū-ten′silled.

EN′SING

d: c̞on-den′sing.
f: fen′cing.
m: c̞om-men′cing.
p: dis-pen′sing,
re-c̞om-pen′sing.
s: in-cen′sing.

EN'SIV
EN'TĂL

fāte, fär, fȧst, fạll, finăl, cãre, at; mēte, prey, hẽr, met; pīne,
marĭne, bĭrd, pin; nōte, mŏve, fọr, atŏm, not; mọọn, bŏok;

470

(Choose only one word out of each group)

EN'SIV

Vowel: in-flū-en'cive.
d: cọn-den'sive.
f: dē-fen'sive, in-dē-fen'sive*,
in-of-fen'sive, of-fen'sive,
self'=dē-fen'sive.
h: ap-prē-hen'sive,
cọm-prē-hen'sive,
in-ap-prē-hen'sive,
in-cọm-prē-hen'sive,
re-prē-hen'sive,
un-ap-prē-hen'sive.
p: ex-pen'sive, in-ex-pen'sive,
pen'sive, re-cọm-pen'sive,
sus-pen'sive.
s: as-cen'sive, cọn-des-cen'sive,
des-cen'sive, in-cen'sive*.
t: dis-ten'sive, ex-ten'sive,
in-ten'sive, os-ten'sive,
prō-ten'sive, ten'sive.
Plus men sieve, etc.

ENS'LES

f: dē-fense'less, fence'less,
of-fense'less.
p: ex-pense'less.
s: sense'less.
Plus dense less, etc.
Cf. tents less, etc.

ENS'MENT

m: cọm-mence'ment.
s: in-cense'ment.
Plus dense meant, etc.
Cf. tents meant, etc.

ENS'NES

d: dense'ness.
m: im-mense'ness.
p: prō-pense'ness.
t: in-tense'ness, tense'ness.

EN'SŎN

b: Ben'sŏn.
h: Hen'sŏn.
Plus then, son *or* sun, etc.

EN'SŪR

s: cen'sūre.
Plus hence your *or* you're, etc.

EN'SŨR

d: cọn-den'sẽr, den'sẽr.
f: fen'cẽr.
h: prē-hen'sẽr.
m: cọm-men'cẽr.
p: dis-pen'sẽr, re-cọm-pen'sẽr.
s: cen'sẽr, cen'sŏr, in-cen'sŏr*.
sp: spen'cẽr, Spen'sẽr.
t: ex-ten'sŏr, in-ten'sẽr,
ten'sŏr.
Plus men, sir, etc.
Plus condense her, err *or* Ur, etc.

EN'SUS

s: cen'sus.
Plus fence us, etc.

EN'TA

j: mȧ-ġen'tȧ.
l: pō-len'tȧ.
m: Pĭ-men'tȧ.
s: plȧ-cen'ta.
Plus sent a, etc.

EN'TĂL

Vowel: ō-ri-en'tăl.
d: aç-ci-den'tăl,
an"tē-cē-den'tăl, bī-den'tăl,
cō-in-ci-den'tăl, den'tăl,
den'til, den'tile, in-ci-den'tăl,
lāb"i-ō-den'tăl,

471 ūse, bṳll, brúte, tūrn, up; crȳ, myth; c̦at, mac̦hine, ace, church, c̦hord; ġem, añger, (Fr.) boṅ, aș; THis, thin; azure

EN′TĂNS
EN′TED

(Choose only one word out of each group)

liñ-guȧ-den′tăl (-gwȧ),
oc̦-ci-den′tăl,
tran-scen-den′tăl (-sen-),
trī-den′tăl.
j: är-ġen′tăl, fạl-c̦ŏn ġen′tle,
ġen′tle, un-ġen′tle.
k: ken′tle*.
l: Len′tăl.
m: al-i-men′tăl, är-gū-men′tăl,
at-rȧ-men′tăl, c̦om-plē-men′tăl,
c̦om-pli-men′tăl,
dē-pärt-men′tăl,
de-tri-men′tăl,
dē-vel-ŏp-men′tăl,
doc̦-ū-men′tăl, el-ē-men′tăl,
ex-c̦rē-men′tăl, ex-per-i-men′tăl,
fīr-mȧ-men′tăl, frag-men′tăl,
fun-dȧ-men′tăl,
gŏv-ērn-men′tăl,
im-ped-i-men′tăl,
in-strṳ-men′tăl, lig-ȧ-men′tăl,
med″ic-ȧ-men′tăl, men′tăl,
mon-ū-men′tăl, nū-tri-men′tăl,
ọr-nȧ-men′tăl, pär-li-ȧ-men′tăl,
ped-i-men′tăl, pig-men′tăl,
prē-dic̦-ȧ-men′tăl,
re-c̦rē-men′tăl, reġ-i-men′tăl,
rȯd-i-men′tăl, sac̦-rȧ-men′tăl,
seg-men′tăl, sen-ti-men′tăl,
sup-plē-men′tăl,
tem″pēr-ȧ-men′tăl,
ten-ē-men′tăl, tes-tȧ-men′tăl.
n: c̦on-ti-nen′tăl,
in″tēr-c̦on-ti-nen′tăl.
r: pȧ-ren′tăl, ren′tăl.
s: cen′tăl, plȧ-cen′tăl.
tr: tren′tăl.
Plus bent, Al, etc.
Plus gent ′ll, etc.
Cf. men tall, bent all, etc.
Cf. len′til.

EN′TĂNS
p: rē-pen′tănce,
un-rē-pen′tănce.
s: sen′tence.
Cf. bent ants *or* aunts, etc.

EN′TĂNT
p: rē-pen′tănt, un-rē-pen′tănt.
z: re-prē-șen′tănt.
Plus lent aunt *or* ant, etc.

EN′TĀT
d: bī-den′tāte, den′tāte,
ē-den′tāte, quäd-ri-den′tāte,
trī-den′tāte.
m: c̦om-men′tāte, dē-men′tāte.
Plus Lent ate *or* eight, etc.
Plus then Tate, etc.

EN′TĒ
Vowel: Ä-guȧ C̦al-i-en′tē (′gwȧ-),
ä-guär-dï-en′tē (-gwär-),
dōl′ce̦ fär ni-en′tē (′chä).
d: preș-i-den′tē.
l: fes-tï′nō len′tē.
p: dī-ȧ-pen′tē.
s: c̦og-nōs-cen′tē.
Cf. en′ti.
Plus then tea, etc.
Plus lent, he, etc.

EN′TED
d: den′ted, in-den′ted,
prec-ē-den′ted,
un-pre′cē-den″ted.
kw: frē-quen′ted,
un-frē-quen′ted.
l: rē-len′ted.
m: ạug-men′ted,
bat′tle-men″ted, cē-men′ted,

(Choose only one word out of each group)

com-men'ted, com-pli-men'ted,
dē-men'ted, fẽr-men'ted,
fō-men'ted, là-men'ted,
or-nȧ-men'ted,
sup'plē-men″ted, tor-men'ted,
un-là-men'ted,
un-or'nȧ-men″ted,
un-tor-men'ted.
p: rē-pen'ted, un-rē-pen'ted.
r: ren'ted.
s: ab-sen'ted, ac-cen'ted,
as-sen'ted, con-sen'ted,
dis-sen'ted, scen'ted,
sweet'=scen'ted.
t: con-ten'ted, dis-con-ten'ted,
ill'=con-ten'ted, ten'ted,
un-ten'ted, well'=con-ten'ted.
v: cĩr-cum-ven'ted, in-ven'ted,
prē-ven'ted, un-prē-ven'ted,
ven'ted.
z: mis-rep-rē-sen'ted,
prē-sen'ted, re-prē-sen'ted,
rē-sen'ted.
Plus then, Ted, etc.
Plus rent, Ed, etc.

EN'TEST

b: ben'test*.
d: in-den'test*.
kw: frē-quen'test*.
l: rē-len'test*.
m: aug-men'test*, cē-men'test*,
com-men'test*,
com-plē-men'test*,
com-pli-men'test*,
fẽr-men'test*, fō-men'test*,
là-men'test*, or-nȧ-men'test*,
sup-plē-men'test*,
tor-men'test*.
p: rē-pen'test*.
r: ren'test*.

s: ab-sen'test*, ac-cen'test*,
as-sen'test*, con-sen'test*,
dis-sen'test*, sen'test*,
scen'test*.
t: con-ten'test*.
v: cĩr-cum-ven'test*,
in-ven'test*, prē-ven'test*,
ven'test*.
z: mis″rep-rē-sen'test*,
prē-sen'test*, re-prē-sen'test*,
rē-sen'test*.
Plus hen test, etc.
Cf. en'tist.

EN'TETH

b: ben'teth*.
d: in-den'teth*.
kw: frē-quen'teth*.
l: rē-len'teth*.
m: aug-men'teth*,
cē-men'teth*, com-men'teth*,
com-plē-men'teth*,
com-pli-men'teth*,
fẽr-men'teth*, fō-men'teth*,
là-men'teth*, or-nȧ-men'teth*,
sup-plē-men'teth*,
tor-men'teth*.
p: rē-pen'teth*.
r: ren'teth*.
s: ab-sen'teth*, ac-cen'teth*,
as-sen'teth*, con-sen'teth*,
dis-sen'teth*, scen'teth*.
t: con-ten'teth*.
v: cĩr-cum-ven'teth*,
in-ven'teth*, prē-ven'teth*,
ven'teth*.
z: mis″rep-rē-sen'teth*,
prē-sen'teth*, re-prē-sen'teth*,
rē-sen'teth*.

(Choose only one word out of each group)

ENT'FUL

v: ē-vent'ful, un-ē-vent'ful.
z: rē-ṣent'ful.
Plus tent full, etc.

ENT'HOUS

p: pent'house.
Plus rent house, etc.

EN'TI

Vowel:
Ä-guȧ-Çal-i-en'tē ('gwȧ-),
ä-guär-dï-en'tē (-gwär-),
dōl'çe̱ fär nĭ-en'tē ('chä).
d: preṣ-i-den'tē.
h: Hen'ty.
k: çon-trȧ-dī-çen'tē.
l: fēs-tĭ'nō len'tē.
m: tor-men'ty.
p: dī-ȧ-pen'tē.
pl: plen'ty.
s: çog-nōs-cen'tē.
tw: ŏne'=and=twen'ty (wun'),
twö'=and=twen'ty (toọ'), etc.,
twen'ty.
Plus scent, he, etc.
Plus then tea, etc.

EN'TIJ

s: pẽr-cen'tăġe.
v: ven'tăġe.
Cf. lent age, etc.

EN'TIK

d: ī-den'tiç.
j: är-ġen'tiç.
th: a̱u-then'tiç.
Plus then tick, etc.

EN'TĪL

j: Ġen'tīle.
Plus men tile, etc.
Plus sent aisle *or* isle, etc.
Plus scent, I'll, etc.

EN'TIL

l: len'til.
Cf. en'tăl.

EN'TIN

d: den'tine, trī-den'tine.
kw: Quen'tin, San-Quen'tin.
r: tor-ren'tine.
Plus went in, sent inn, etc.
Plus then tin, etc.

EN'TING

d: den'ting, in-den'ting.
kw: frē-quen'ting.
l: rē-len'ting, un-rē-len'ting.
m: a̱ug-men'ting, cē-men'ting,
çom-men'ting,
çom-ple-men'ting,
çom-pli-men'ting, dē-men'ting,
fẽr-men'ting, fō-men'ting,
lȧ-men'ting, or-nȧ-men'ting,
self'=tor-men'ting,
sup'ple-men"ting, tor-men'ting.
p: rē-pen'ting, un-rē-pen'ting.
r: ren'ting.
s: ab-sen'ting, aç-cen'ting,
as-sen'ting, çon-sen'ting,
dis-sen'ting, scen'ting (sen'),
un-çon-sen'ting.
t: çon-ten'ting, ten'ting.
v: cīr-çum-ven'ting, in-ven'ting,
prē-ven'ting, ven'ting.
z: mis"re-prē-ṣen'ting,
prē-ṣen'ting, re-prē-ṣen'ting,
rē-ṣen'ting.

EN'TIS
EN'TOR

fāte, fär, fàst, fạll, finăl, cāre, at; mēte, prey, hěr, met; pīne,
marīne, bĭrd, pin; nōte, mŏve, fọr, atŏm, not; mọọn, book;

474

(Choose only one word out of each group)

EN'TIS

m: non cọm'pŏs men'tis.
p: ap-pen'tice*, pen'tice*.
pr: ap-pren'tice, pren'tice,
  Pren'tiss.

EN'TIST

d: den'tist.
pr: ap-pren'ticed.
v: prē-ven'tist.
Cf. en'test.

EN'TIV

d: pen-den'tive.
s: as-sen'tive, in-cen'tive.
t: at-ten'tive, in-at-ten'tive,
  ir-rē-ten'tive, rē-ten'tive.
v: ad-ven'tive, cĭr-cum-ven'tive,
  in-ven'tive, prē-ven'tive.
z: prē-ṣen'tive, rē-ṣen'tive*.

ENT'LES

d: dent'less.
l: rē-lent'less.
m: cē-ment'less, là-ment'less.
r: rent'less.
s: cent'less, scent'less.
t: tent'less.
Plus accidentless, etc.
Plus meant less, etc.

ENT'LI

d: ev-i-dent'ly.
j: ġen'tly.
l: in'sō-lent"ly.
n: em'i-nent"ly.
s: in'nō-cent"ly.
t: im'pō-tent"ly, in-tent'ly.
Plus ent + ly.
Plus scent, Lee or lea, etc.

ENT'MENT

l: rē-lent'ment.
t: cọn-tent'ment,
  dis-cọn-tent'ment.
z: prē-ṣent'ment,
  re-prē-ṣent'ment, rē-ṣent'ment.
Plus scent meant, etc.

ENT'NES

t: in-tent'ness.

EN'TŌ

ch: cin-quē-cen'tō (-chen'),
  quät-trō-cen'tō.
l: len'tō, pō-len'tō.
m: di-vĕr-ti-men'tō,
  mē-men'tō, pi-men'tō,
  pōr-tȧ-men'tō,
  prō-nun-cĭ-ȧ-men'tō,
  rĭ-fäc-ĭ-men'tō (-fäsh-),
  Saç-rà-men'tō.
s: cen'tō.
Plus then toe, etc.
Plus cent owe or O, etc.

EN'TŎN

b: Ben'tŏn.
d: Den'tŏn.
f: Fen'tŏn.
tr: Tren'tŏn.
Plus ten ton or tun, etc.
Plus intent on or an, etc.

EN'TOR

m: men'tọr.
s: bū-cen'tạur, cen'tạur,
  suç-cen'tọr.
st: sten'tọr.
Cf. en'tūr.
Plus scent, or, etc.
Plus fen tor, etc.

475 ūse, bull, brúte, tūrn, up; crȳ, myth; çat, machine, ace, church, çhord; ġem, añger, (Fr.) boñ, aṣ; THis, thin; aẓure

EN′TRĂL
EN′TÛRD

(Choose only one word out of each group)

EN′TRĂL

s: cen′trăl.
v: ven′trăl.

EN′TRĂNS

Vowel: en′trănce.
Plus again trance, etc.
Plus dent Rance, etc.

EN′TRĀT

s: çon-cen′trate.
Plus rent rate, etc.

ENT′RES

m: tor-men′tress.
v: in-ven′tress.
Plus again tress.

EN′TRI

Vowel: en′try.
j: ġen′try.
s: sen′try.
Plus again tree, etc.

EN′TRIK

s: à-cen′triç,
an″thrō-pō-cen′triç,
an-drō-cen′triç, bar-y-cen′triç,
cen′triç, çon-cen′triç,
eç-cen′triç, ġē-ō-cen′triç,
ġȳ-nē-çō-cen′triç,
hē-li-ō-cen′triç, par-à-cen′triç,
sel-en-ō-cen′triç.
Plus men trick, etc.
Plus bent rick, etc.

EN′TUM

m: mō-men′tum, sär-men′tum.
r: Tà-ren′tum.
Plus bent ′em, etc.
Plus again tum, etc.

EN′TŪR

b: dē-ben′tūre.
d: in-den′tūre.
t: ten′tūre.
v: ad-ven′tūre, mis-ad-ven′tūre,
pĕr-ad-ven′tūre, ven′tūre.
Plus sent your, etc.
Plus scent you′re, etc.

EN′TÛR

Vowel: en′tẽr, rē-en′tẽr.
d: den′tẽr, in-den′tẽr.
kw: frē-quen′tẽr.
l: len′tŏr, rē-len′tẽr.
m: aug-men′tẽr, cē-men′tẽr,
çom-men′tẽr, ex-per′i-men″tẽr,
fĕr-men′tẽr, fō-men′tẽr,
là-men′tẽr, or-nà-men′tẽr,
sup-plē-men′tẽr, tor-men′tẽr.
p: rē-pen′tẽr.
r: ren′tẽr.
s: as-sen′tẽr, cen′tẽr,
çon-cen′tẽr,
dead cen′tẽr (ded),
dis-sen′tẽr, prē-cen′tŏr.
t: çon-ten′tẽr, ten′tẽr.
v: cĩr-çum-ven′tŏr, in-ven′tẽr,
prē-ven′tẽr, ven′tẽr.
z: mis-rep-rē-ṣen′tẽr,
prē-ṣen′tẽr, rep-rē-ṣen′tẽr,
rē-ṣent′ẽr.
Plus bent her *or* err, etc.
Cf. en′tŏr.

EN′TÛRD

Vowel: en′tẽred.
s: self′=cen′tẽred.
Plus en′tûr+ed.
Plus scent erred, etc.

EN'TUS
ĒN'YOR

fāte, fär, fȧst, fall, finăl, cãre, at; mēte, prey, hẽr, met; pīne,
marïne, bĭrd, pĭn; nōte, mŏve, fọr, atŏm, not; mọọn, book;

476

(Choose only one word out of each group)

EN'TUS

gw: un-guen'tous (-gwen').
m: im-mō-men'tous,
  lig-ȧ-men'tous, mō-men'tous,
  pig-men'tous, sär-men'tous.
t: pē-dē-ten'tous, pōr-ten'tous.
Plus sent us, etc.

Ē'NUM

fr: frē'num.
pl: plē'num.
Plus be numb, etc.
Plus gasoline 'em, etc.

ĒN'ŪR

b: shē-been'ẽr.
gl: glēan'ẽr.
gr: green'ẽr.
k: keen'ẽr.
kl: clēan'ẽr.
l: lēan'ẽr.
m: dē-mēan'ŏr, mēs'nẽr (mē'),
  mis-dē-mēan'ŏr.
r: sē-rēn'ẽr.
s: ob-scēn'ẽr (-sēn'), sēin'ẽr.
sh: mȧ-chĭn'ẽr.
skr(scr): screen'ẽr.
v: con-trȧ-vēn'ẽr, con-vēn'ẽr,
  in-tẽr-vēn'ẽr, sū-pẽr-vēn'ẽr.
w: wēan'ẽr, wiēn'ẽr.
z: mag-ȧ-zīn'ẽr.
Plus seen her, err, Ur or er, etc.

EN'ŪR

f: Fen'nẽr.
p: pen'nẽr.
t: con'trȧ=ten'ŏr,
  coun'tẽr-ten'ŏr, fĭrst ten'ŏr,
  sec'ŏnd ten'ŏr, ten'nẽr, ten'ŏr.
Plus den her, err or Ur. etc.

Ē'NUS

j: ġē'nus.
l: Si-lē'nus.
v: vēn'ous, Vē'nus.
Plus wean us, etc.

EN'VI

Vowel: en'vy.

EN'VIL

Vowel: Bī-en'ville.
gl: Glen'ville.
gr: Gren'ville.

EN'VŪR

d: Den'vẽr.

ĒN'YĂL

j: con-ġēn'ial.
Cf. eñ'i-ăl.

ĒN'YĂN

m: Är-mēn'ian.
Cf. ēn'i-ăn.

ĒN'YENS

l: lēn'ience.
Cf. ēn'i-ens.

ĒN'YENT

v: con-vēn'ient.
Cf. ēn'i-ent.

ĒN'YOR

s: mon-sïg'nọr (-sēn'yọr),
  sēig'nior (sēn'yọr), sēn'iŏr,
  sïg'nọr (sēn'yọr).
Cf. demean your, etc.

477

ūse, bu̯ll, brūte, tũrn, up; crȳ, myth; c̨at, mac̨hine, ace,
church, c̨hord; ġem, aṅger, (Fr.) boṅ, as̨; THis, thin; azure

ĒN′YUS
ĒP′EST

(Choose only one word out of each group)

ĒN′YUS

j: ġēn′ius.
Cf. ēn′i-us.

EN′ZÅ

Vowel: in-flu̇-en′zȧ.
d: c̨ȧ-den′zȧ.
Plus when's a, etc.
Plus hens a, etc.

ENZ′DĀ

w: Wednes̨′dāy (wenz′).
Plus hens day, etc.

EN′ZEZ

kl: c̨lean′s̨es̨ (klen′).
l: len′s̨es̨.
Cf. hens is, etc.

EN′ZI

Vowel: Rī-en′zi.
fr: fren′zy.
k: Mc̨-Ken′zie.
Plus hens, he, etc.

EN′ZŌ

r: Lō-ren′zō.
Plus hens owe *or* O, etc.

EN′ZŎN

t: ten′s̨ŏn.
v: ven′is̨ŏn (ven′zŏn).
Plus hens on *or* an, etc.

Ē′Ō

Vowel: Ē′ō.
d: dē′ō.
kl: C̨lē′ō.
l: Lē′ō.
n: nē′ō.

r: Rï′ō.
th: Thē′ō.
tr: trï′ō.
Plus we owe *or* O, etc.

Ē′ŌL

kr: C̨rē′ōle.
Plus see Ole, etc.

Ē′ŎN

Vowel: aē′ŏn.
d: ō-dē′ŏn.
f: phē′ŏn.
kr: C̨rē′ŏn.
l: Lē′ŏn, Pon′ce dē Lē′ŏn,
    Rich′ȧrd C̨oeūr dē Lï′ŏn (kũr).
n: nē′ŏn.
p: paē′ŏn, pē′ŏn.
th: pan-thē′ŏn.
Plus we on *or* an, etc.
Cf. ē′ăn.

EP′ĂRD

j: jeo′părd (jep′).
l: leo′părd (lep′).
p: pep′pēred.
sh: shep′hērd (′ĕrd).
Cf. step hard, etc.
Plus step erred, etc.

ĒP′EN

ch: chēap′en.
d: deep′en.
st: steep′en.
Cf. creep, hen, etc.

ĒP′EST

ch: chēap′est, cheep′est*.
d: deep′est.
h: hēap′est*.
k: keep′est*.

ĒP'ETH
ĒP'ING

fāte, fär, fást, fạll, finăl, cãre, at; mēte, prẹy, hẽr, met; pīne,
marïne, bĭrd, pin; nōte, mȯve, fọr, atŏm, not; mọọn, book;

478

(Choose only one word out of each group)

kr: creep'est*.
l: lēap'est*, ō-vẽr-lēap'est*.
p: peep'est*.
r: rēap'est*.
sl: out-sleep'est*,
  ō-vẽr-sleep'est*, sleep'est*.
st: steep'est.
sw: sweep'est*.
w: weep'est*.
Plus tree pest, etc.

ĒP'ETH

ch: cheep'eth*.
h: hēap'eth*.
k: keep'eth*.
kr: creep'eth*.
l: lēap'eth*, ō-vẽr-lēap'eth*.
p: peep'eth*.
r: rēap'eth*.
sl: out-sleep'eth*,
  ō-vẽr-sleep'eth*, sleep'eth*.
sw: sweep'eth*.
w: weep'eth*.
Cf. tree pith, etc.

ĒP'I

ch: cheep'y.
h: hēap'y.
k: kē'pi.
kr: creep'y.
s: seep'y.
sh: sheep'y.
sl: sleep'y.
st: steep'y.
sw: sweep'y.
t: tē'pee.
w: weep'y.
Plus tree pea, etc.
Plus T. P., etc.

EP'I

Vowel: Ep'pie.
k: kep'i.
p: pep'py.
st: ŏne'=step'py (wun'),
  twö'=step'py (tö').
t: tep'ee.
Plus step, he, etc.

EP'ID

l: lep'id.
t: tep'id.
tr: in-trep'id, trep'id.
Cf. step hid, etc.

ĒP'IJ

s: seep'ăġe.
sw: sweep'ăġe.
Cf. deep age, etc.

EP'IÇ

Vowel: ep'iç, ọr-thō-ep'iç.
Cf. step pick, etc.

ĒP'ING

ch: cheep'ing.
d: Deep'ing.
h: hēap'ing.
k: house-keep'ing, keep'ing,
  sāfe-keep'ing.
kr: creep'ing.
l: lēap'ing, ō-vẽr-lēap'ing.
p: peep'ing.
r: rēap'ing.
s: seep'ing, sēip'ing.
sl: out-sleep'ing,
  ō-vẽr-sleep'ing, sleep'ing,
  un-sleep'ing.
st: steep'ing.

(Choose only one word out of each group)

sw: sweep'ing.
w: un-weep'ing, weep'ing.
Plus we ping, etc.

ĒP'ISH

d: deep'ish.
sh: sheep'ish.
st: steep'ish.

ĒP'L

p: em-pēo'ple*, pēo'ple,
un-pēo'ple.
st: stee'ple.
Plus reap 'll, etc.
Cf. tree pull, etc.

ĒP'LES

sl: sleep'less.
w: weep'less.
Plus creep less *or* Les, etc.

ĒP'NES

ch: chēap'ness.
d: deep'ness.
sl: sleep'ness.
st: steep'ness.

EP'ŎN

w: weap'ŏn (wep').
Plus step on *or* an, etc.

EP'SHUN

r: ab-rep'tion*, ar-rep'tion*,
ē-rep'tion, ob-rep'tion,
sub-rep'tion, sûr-rep'tion.
s: ap-pēr-cep'tion, ċon-cep'tion,
ċon-trȧ-cep'tion, dē-cep'tion,
ex-cep'tion, im-pēr-cep'tion,
in-cep'tion, in-tēr-cep'tion,
in″trō-sus-cep'tion,

in″tus-sus-cep'tion,
mis-ċon-cep'tion, pēr-cep'tion,
prē-ċon-cep'tion,
prē-pēr-cep'tion, rē-cep'tion,
self'=dē-cep'tion.
Plus step shun, etc.

EP'SI

l: ċat-ȧ-lep'sy, ep-i-lep'sy,
nym-phō-lep'sy.
p: ȧ-pep'sy, dys-pep'sy,
eū-pep'sy.
Plus step see, etc.

EP'SIS

l: an-ȧ-lep'sis, ep-an-ȧ-lep'sis,
met-ȧ-lep'sis, par-ȧ-lep'sis,
prō-lep'sis, syl-lep'sis.
s: ȧ-sep'sis.
sk: skep'sis.
Plus step, sis, etc.

ĒP'SKIN

sh: sheep'skin.
Plus keep skin, etc.

EP'TĂNS

s: aċ-cep'tănce.
Plus kept ants *or* aunts, etc.

EP'TĂNT

r: rep'tănt.
s: aċ-cep'tănt, ex-cep'tănt.
Plus kept aunt *or* ant, etc.

EP'TED

s: aċ-cep'ted, ex-cep'ted,
in-tēr-cep'ted.
Plus step, Ted, etc.
Plus kept, Ed, etc.

EP'TEST
EP'ÛR
fāte, fär, fàst, fąll, finăl, cāre, at; mēte, prey, hĕr, met; pīne,
marīne, bĭrd, pin; nōte, mŏve, fọr, atŏm, not; mọọn, book;   **480**

(Choose only one word out of each group)

EP'TEST

d: à-dept'est.
s: aç-cep'test*, ex-cep'test*,
in-tēr-cep'test*.
Plus pep test, etc.

EP'TETH

s: aç-cep'teth*, ex-cep'teth*,
in-tēr-cep'teth*.

EP'TIK

kl: klep'tiç.
l: à-çat-à-lep'tiç, an-à-lep'tiç,
çat-à-lep'tiç, ep-i-lep'tiç,
met-à-lep'tiç, nym-phō-lep'tiç,
ọr-gan-ō-lep'tiç, prō-lep'tiç,
syl-lep'tiç.
p: brā-dy-pep'tiç, dys-pep'tiç,
eū-pep'tiç, pep'tiç.
s: an-ti-sep'tiç, à-sep'tiç,
sep'tiç.
sk(sç): sçep'tiç.
Plus step tick, etc.

EP'TING

s: aç-cep'ting, ex-cep'ting,
in-cep'ting, in-tēr-cep'ting.

EP'TIV

s: aç-cep'tive, çon-cep'tive,
çon-trà-cep'tive, dē-cep'tive,
ex-cep'tive, im-pēr-cep'tive,
in-cep'tive, in-sus-cep'tive,
in-tēr-cep'tive,
in"tus-sus-cep'tive,
ir-rē-cep'tive, pēr-cep'tive,
prē-cep'tive, rē-cep'tive,
sus-cep'tive.

EPT'NES

Vowel: in-ept'ness.

EP'TŪN

n: Nep'tūne.
Plus pep tune, etc.

EP'TŨR

d: à-dep'tẽr.
s: aç-cep'tẽr, ex-cep'tẽr,
in-cep'tŏr, in-tēr-cep'tẽr,
prē-cep'tŏr, scep'tẽr (sep'),
sus-cep'tŏr.
Plus kept her, Ur, err or er, etc.

ĒP'ŨR

Vowel: Y'pres (ē'pẽr).
ch: chēap'ẽr, cheep'ẽr.
d: deep'ẽr.
h: hēap'ẽr.
k: hedġe'-keep'ẽr,
house'keep"ẽr, keep'ẽr,
shop'keep"ẽr, wick'et-keep'ẽr.
kr: çreep'ẽr, wạll'çreep"ẽr.
l: lēap'ẽr.
p: peep'ẽr.
r: rēap'ẽr.
sl: sleep'ẽr.
st: steep'ẽr.
sw: sweep'ẽr.
w: weep'ẽr.
Plus we purr or per, etc.
Plus keep her, err or Ur, etc.

EP'ŨR

h: hep'pẽr.
l: lep'ẽr.
p: pep'pẽr.
st: hīgh'-step'pẽr (hī'),

(Choose only one word out of each group)

ŏne'=step'pĕr (wun),
ō-vĕr-step'pĕr,
twö'=step'pĕr (tọọ), step'pĕr.
Plus pep her, err *or* Ur, etc.

ĒP'WOK

sh: sheep'wạlk.
sl: sleep'wạlk.
Plus creep, walk, etc.

Ē'RÅ

Vowel: C̣a-ïr'å, ē'rå.
d: Må-dēi'rå.
g: gē'råh.
h: Hē'rå.
k: Kï'råh.
l: lï'rå, tïr-rå=lï'rå.
m: c̣hï-mē'rå.
v: Vē'rå.
Cf. here a, etc.

ER'ÅF

s: ser'ăph.
t: ter'ăph.
Cf. sher'iff.

ĒR'ÅL

f: fēr'ăl.
sf: sphēr'ăl.
Cf. ēr'il.
Plus here, Al, etc.
Cf. hear all, etc.

ER'ÅLD

j: Ġer'ăld.
h: her'ăld, Her'rŏld.
Cf. imperilled, etc.

ĒR'ÅNS

b: å-bēr'rănce.
Cf. ēr'ens.
Cf. near ants *or* aunts, etc.

ĒR'ÄNT

b: å-bēr'ränt.
Plus near aunt *or* ant, etc.
Cf. ēr'ent.

ER'ĂS

t: ter'răce.
Cf. er'is.

ER'ĀT

s: sēr'rāte.
Plus near rate, etc.
Plus here ate *or* eight, etc.

ĒR'DED

b: bēar'ded.
Plus deer dead, etc.
Cf. deer did, etc.
Cf. reared, hid, etc.

ĒRD'LI

w: wiērd'ly.
Plus beard, Lee *or* lea, etc.

ĒR'ENS

f: in-tēr-fēr'ence.
h: ad-hēr'ence, c̣ō-hēr'ence,
in-c̣ō-hēr'ence, in-hēr'ence.
kl: c̣lēar'ănce.
p: ap-pēar'ănce,
dis-ap-pēar'ănce,
rē-ap-pēar'ănce.
r: ar-rēar'ănce.
v: pēr-sē-vēr'ănce.
Cf. ēr'ăns.
Cf. Ter'ence.
Cf. near hence, etc.

(Choose only one word out of each group)

ĒR'ENT

j: vīce-ġēr'ent.
h: ad-hēr'ent, cō-hēr'ent,
in-ad-hēr'ent, in-cō-hēr'ent,
in-hēr'ent.
kw: quēr'ent.
v: pễr-sē-vēr'ent.
Cf. near rent, etc.

ĒR'EST

ch: cheer'est*.
d: dēar'est, en-dēar'est*.
dr: drēar'est.
f: fēar'est*, in-tēr-fēr'est*.
g: gēar'est*.
h: ad-hēr'est*, cō-hēr'est*,
hēar'est*, ō-vēr-hēar'est*.
j: jeer'est*.
kl: clēar'est.
kw: queer'est.
l: leer'est*.
m: mēr'est.
n: nēar'est.
p: ap-pēar'est*, dis-ap-pēar'est*,
peer'est*, rē-ap-pēar'est*.
r: cạ-reer'est*, rēar'est*,
un-rēar'est*, up-rēar'est*.
s: in-sin-cēr'est, sēar'est*,
sēr'est, sin-cēr'est.
sh: shēar'est*, sheer'est.
sm: bē-smēar'est*, smēar'est*.
sn: sneer'est*.
sp: spēar'est*.
st: steer'est*.
t: ạus-tēr'est.
v: pễr-sē-vēr'est*, rē-vēr'est*,
sē-vēr'est, veer'est*.
Cf. dear, rest, etc.

ĒR'ET

f: fer'ret.
t: ter'ret.
Cf. er'it.

ĒR'ETH

ch: cheer'eth*.
d: en-dēar'eth*.
f: fēar'eth*, in-tēr-fēr'eth*.
g: gēar'eth*.
h: ad-hēr'eth*, hēar'eth*,
ō-vēr-hēar'eth*.
j: jeer'eth*.
kl: clēar'eth*.
l: leer'eth.
p: ap-pēar'eth, dis-ap-pēar'eth*,
peer'eth*, rē-ap-pēar'eth*.
r: cạ-reer'eth, rēar'eth,
up-rēar'eth*.
s: sēar'eth*.
sh: shēar'eth*.
sm: bē-smēar'eth*, smēar'eth*.
sn: sneer'eth*.
sp: spēar'eth*.
st: steer'eth*.
v: pễr-sē-vēr'eth*, rē-vēr'eth*,
veer'eth*.

ĒR'FŌN

Vowel: ēar'phōne.
Plus near phone, etc.

ĒR'FŲL

Vowel: ēar'fŭl.
ch: cheer'fŭl, un-cheer'fŭl.
f: fēar'fŭl, un-fēar'fŭl.
sn: sneer'fŭl.
t: tēar'fŭl.
Plus beer full, etc.

(Choose only one word out of each group)

Ē'RI

Vowel: aē'rie, ee'rie, Ē'rie.
b: beer'y.
bl: blēar'y.
ch: cheer'y, un-cheer'y.
d: dēar'ie, dēar'y.
dr: drēar'y, Dun-drēar'y.
j: jeer'y.
k: ha'rà-kī'rĭ.
kw: quaē'rē, quēr'y.
l: C̩av-à-liē'rĭ, lēar'y, leer'y, Ō-Lēar'y.
p: pē'rĭ.
r: mi̱s-e-rē'rē.
sf: sphēr'y.
sm: smēar'y.
sn: sneer'y.
t: tēar'y.
v: veer'y.
w: à-wēar'y, fo̱r-wēar'y*, līfe'⸗wēar'y, ō-vēr-wēar'y, wēar'y.
Plus dear, he, etc.

ER'I

b: ber'i-ber'i, ber'ry, black'ber"ry, blūe'ber"ry, bur'y (ber'), dew'ber"ry, huck"le-ber"ry, Jūne'ber"ry, lō'găn-ber"ry, mul'ber"ry, ra̱sp'ber"ry (raz'), straw'ber"ry, who̱r'tle⸗ber"ry.
ch: cher'ry, chōke'cher"ry, Pon-di-cher'ry.
d: Der'ry.
f: fer'ry.
g: Ger'ry.
hw: wher'ry.

j: G̊er'ry, Jer'ry, Tom and Jer'ry.
k: Ker'ry.
m: mer'ry.
n: mil'li-ne"ry, stā'tion-er"y.
p: Pea'ry (per'), per'ry.
s: la'mà-se"ry.
sh: sher'ry.
sk: sker'ry.
t: cem'ē-te"ry, mon'ăs-ter"y, pres̩'by-ter"y, Ter'ry.
v: ver'y.
Cf. ā'ri.

ĒR'ĪD

bl: blēar'ey̅ed.
kl: c̩lēar'ey̅ed.
t: tēar'ey̅ed.
Plus near eyed *or* I'd, etc.
Cf. near ride, etc.

ĒR'ID

kw: quēr'ied.
v: vir'id.
w: un-wēar'ied, wa̱r'⸗wēar'ied, wēar'ied, wŏrld'⸗wēar'ied.
Cf. near hid, etc.

ER'ID

b: ber'ried, bur'ied (ber'), un-bur'ied.
ch: cher'ried.
f: fer'ried.
hw: wher'ried.
s: ser'ried.

ER'IF

sh: sher'iff.
Cf. er'ăf.

ĒR'IJ
ĒR'ING
fāte, fär, fȧst, fạll, fīnăl, cāre, at; mēte, prẹy, hēr, met; pīne,
marīne, bĭrd, pĭn; nōte, mŏve, fọr, atŏm, not; mọọn, book;
484

(Choose only one word out of each group)

ĒR'IJ

kl: clēar'ăġe.
p: peer'ăġe, piēr'ăġe.
r: ar-rēar'ăġe.
st: steer'ăġe.
Cf. near age, etc.
Cf. peer rage, etc.

ER'IK

Vowel: Er'ic.
b: sū-ber'ic.
d: der'rick.
f: at-mos-pher'ic,
chrō-mŏs-pher'ic, fer'ric,
hel-is-pher'ic, hem-is-pher'ic,
per-i-pher'ic, per-is-pher'ic.
h: Her'rick.
kl: cler'ic.
l: vȧ-ler'ic.
m: an-i-sō-mer'ic, chi-mer'ic,
Hō-mer'ic, ī-sō-mer'ic,
mes-mer'ic, nū-mer'ic.
n: ġe-ner'ic.
p: si-per'ic.
sf: spher'ic.
t: al-ex-i-ter'ic, am-phō-ter'ic,
cli-mac-ter'ic, en-ter'ic,
es-ō-ter'ic, ex-ō-ter'ic,
hys-ter'ic, ic-ter'ic,
mas-sē-ter'ic, nē-ō-ter'ic,
phȳ-lac-ter'ic.

ER'IKS

t: e-sō-ter'ics, hys-ter'ics.
Plus er'ik+s.

ER'IL

b: ber'yl, chrys-ō-ber'yl.
m: Mer'rill.

p: per'il.
st: ster'ile.
Cf. er'ăl.

Ē'RIN

Vowel: Ē'rin.
Plus see, Rinn, etc.

ĒR'ING

Vowel: ēar'ing.
b: Bē'ring.
bl: blēar'ing.
ch: cheer'ing, up-cheer'ing*.
d: Dēar'ing, en-dēar'ing.
f: fēar'ing, in-tēr-fēr'ing.
g: gēar'ing, un-gēar'ing.
h: ad-hēr'ing, cō-hēr'ing,
hēar'ing, ō-vĕr-hēar'ing,
rē-hēar'ing.
j: jeer'ing.
kl: clēar'ing.
kw: queer'ing.
l: gon-dō-liēr'ing,
Ed'wărd Lēar'ing, leer'ing.
n: ạuc-tio-neer'ing,
cạn-nŏn-eer'ing, dom-i-neer'ing,
el-ec-tion-eer'ing, en-gi-neer'ing,
moun-tăin-eer'ing, nēar'ing,
pī-ō-neer'ing, ve-neer'ing.
p: ap-pēar'ing, dis-ap-pēar'ing,
peer'ing, rē-ap-pēar'ing.
r: cȧ-reer'ing, rēar'ing,
up-rēar'ing.
s: sēar'ing.
sh: cash-iēr'ing, shēar'ing.
sk: skeer'ing.
sm: bē-smēar'ing, smēar'ing.
sn: sneer'ing.
sp: spēar'ing.
st: steer'ing.

485 ūse, bu̧ll, brute, tûrn, up; crȳ, myth; çat, ma̧chine, ace, church, çhord; g̣em, añger, (Fr.) boṅ, a̧s; THis, thin; a̧zure

ER'IS
ĒR'NES

(Choose only one word out of each group)

t: prī-va̧-teer'ing, vol-un-teer'ing.
v: pêr-sē-vēr'ing, re-vēr'ing, veer'ing.
Cf. ear'ring.
Cf. hear ring, etc.

ER'IS

f: fer'ris.
t: ter'răce, ter'ris.

ER'ISH

ch: cher'ish.
p: per'ish.

ER'IT

h: dis-her'it, dis-in-her'it, in-her'it.
m: dē-mer'it, im-mer'it*, mer'it.
Cf. hear it, etc.
Cf. er'et.

ĒR'IZ

d: dēar'iȩs.
kw: quēr'iȩs.
s: sē'riȩs.
w: ō-vêr-wēar'iȩs, wēar'iȩs.
Plus here is, etc.

ER'IZ

b: ber'riȩs, bur'iȩs (ber').
ch: cher'riȩs.
f: fer'riȩs.
hw: wher'riȩs.
sh: sher'riȩs.

ĒR'LES

Vowel: ēar'less.
ch: cheer'less.
f: fēar'less.
g: gēar'less.
j: jeer'less.
p: peer'less.
sp: spēar'less.
t: tēar'less.
y: yēar'less.
Plus smear less, etc.

ĒR'LI

ch: cheer'ly.
d: dēar'ly.
kl: çlēar'ly.
kw: queer'ly.
l: çav-a̧-liēr'ly.
m: mēre'ly.
n: nēar'ly.
s: sin-cēre'ly.
t: a̧us-tēre'ly.
v: sē-vēre'ly.
y: yēar'ly.
Plus clear, Lee *or* lea, etc.

ĒR'LING

sh: shēar'ling.
st: steer'ling.
y: yēar'ling.

ĒR'MENT

d: en-dēar'ment.
s: cēre'ment.
Plus cheer meant, etc.

ĒR'NES

d: dēar'ness.
kl: çlēar'ness.

ĒR'Ō
ĒR'ÛR

fāte, fär, fȧst, fạll, finăl, cãre, at; mēte, prẹy, hẽr, met; pīne,
marĭne, bĭrd, pin; nōte, mŏve, fọr, atŏm, not; mọọn, book;

486

(Choose only one word out of each group)

kw: queer'ness.
n: nēar'ness.
s: sin-cēre'ness.
t: ạus-tēre'ness.
v: sē-vēre'ness.

ĒR'Ō

h: hē'rō.
l: lil-li-bul-lē'rō.
n: Nē'rō.
s: Cī'rō.
z: zē'rō.
Plus she row *or* roe, etc.

ẼR'ŎN

h: hẽr'ŏn.

Ē'ROOM

s: sēa'room.
t: tēa'room.
Plus we room, etc.

ER'ŎR

Vowel: er'rŏr.
t: ter'rŏr.

ĒR'ŌS

Vowel: Ēr'ōs.

ĒRS'NES

f: fiērce'ness.

ĒR'SÛR

f: fiēr'cẽr.
p: piēr'cẽr.
Plus here, sir, etc.
Plus pierce her, err *or* Ur, etc.

ĒR'SING

p: ēar'⸗piēr'cing, piēr'cing,
trans-piēr'cing.
Plus hear sing, etc.

ĒR'SŎN

gr: Griẽr'sŏn.
m: Mēar'sŏn.
p: Pēar'sŏn, Piēr'sŏn.
Plus cheer son *or* sun, etc.

ER'UB

ch: cher'ub.

ER'ÚL

f: fer'rùle, fer'ùle.
p: per'ùle.
sf: spher'ùle.

ĒR'ÛR

ch: cheer'ẽr.
d: dēar'ẽr, en-dēar'ẽr.
f: fēar'ẽr, in-tẽr-fēr'ẽr.
fl: fleer'ẽr.
h: ad-hẽr'ẽr, hēar'ẽr,
ō-vẽr-hēar'ẽr.
j: jeer'ẽr.
kl: cĮēar'ẽr.
kw: queer'ẽr.
l: leer'ẽr.
n: e-lec̣-tion-eer'ẽr, nēar'ẽr.
p: ap-pēar'ẽr, dis-ap-pēar'ẽr,
peer'ẽr.
r: rēar'ẽr.
s: sēar'ẽr.
sh: shēar'ẽr.
sm: bē-smēar'ẽr, smēar'ẽr.
sn: sneer'ẽr.
sp: spēar'ẽr.
st: steer'ẽr.
t: ạus-tēr'ẽr, teer'ẽr.
v: pẽr-sē-vēr'ẽr, rē-vēr'ẽr,
sē-vēr'ẽr, veer'ẽr.
Cf. mir'rŏr.
Plus cheer her, Ur *or* err, etc.

487 ūse, bu̧ll, brúte, tûrn, up; crȳ, myth; c̱at, mac̱hine, ace, church, c̱hord; ġem, añger, (Fr.) boṅ, as̱; THis, thin; azure

ĒR'US
ES'ENS

(Choose only one word out of each group)

ĒR'US

s: sēr'ous.
skl(sc̱l): sc̱lēr'ous.
Plus cheer us, etc.

ER'US

f: fer'rous.

ĒRZ'MĂN

st: steers̱'măn.
t: prī-vȧ-teers̱'măn.
Plus nears man, etc.

Ē'SȦ

l: Ē-lĭ'sȧ, Fē-lĭ'cȧ.
m: mē'sȧ.
r: The-rē'sȧ (te-).

Ē'SĀJ

pr: prē'sāġe.
Plus he, sage, etc.
Plus peace age, etc.

ES'CHUN

j: c̱on-ġes'tion, dī-ġes'tion,
in-dī-ġes'tion, in-ġes'tion,
sug-ġes'tion.
kw: ques'tion.

ES'CHUND

j: well'⸗dī-ġes'tioned.
kw: ques'tioned, un-ques'tioned.

ES'ED

bl: bles'sed.
Plus es+ed*.
Plus Yes, Ed, etc.
Cf. Tess said, etc.

ĒS'EL

d: Diē'sel.
Plus peace 'll, etc.

ES'EN

l: les'sen.
Cf. les'son.

ĒS'ENS

d: in-dē'cence.

ES'ENS

Vowel: ac̱-qui-es'cence,
es'sence, qui-es'cence.
b: c̱on-tȧ-bes'cence,
er-ū-bes'cence,
ex-a-cēr-bes'cence*,
sū-bes'cence, rú-bes'cence.
d: c̱an-des'cence, fron-des'cence,
in-c̱an-des'cence, ir-i-des'cence,
lap-i-des'cence*,
rē-c̱rú-des'cence,
vir-i-des'cence.
j: tūr-ġes'cence.
k(c̱): glau-c̱es'cence.
kr: ac̱-c̱res'cence,
c̱on-c̱res'cence, ex-c̱res'cence,
sū-pēr-c̱res'cence.
kw: de-li-ques'cence.
l: ad-ō-les'cence, c̱ȧ-les'cence,
c̱ō-ȧ-les'cence, c̱on-vȧ-les'cence,
em-ōl-les'cence, hȳ-ȧ-les'cence,
in-c̱al-es'cence, in-c̱ō-ȧ-les'cence,
ob-sō-les'cence, ō-pȧ-les'cence,
re-vȧ-les'cence, vir-i-les'cence.
m: dē-tū-mes'cence,
frē-mes'cence, in-tū-mes'cence,
spū-mes'cence, tū-mes'cence.
n: ē-vȧ-nes'cence,
jú-ve-nes'cence,
rē-jū-ve-nes'cence,
sē-nes'cence.

(Choose only one word out of each group)

p: tọr-pes′cence.

r: är-bō-res′cence,
cạl-ō-res′cence, ef-flō-res′cence,
flō-res′cence, flū-ō-res′cence,
in-flō-res′cence,
phos-phō-res′cencẹ,
re-flō-res′cence, re-vi-res′cence.

t: de-li-tes′cence, fruc-tes′cence,
frù-tes′cence, lac-tes′cence,
lā-tes′cence, quin-tes′sence.

tr: pē-tres′cence, pū-tres′cence,
vi-tres′cence.

v: dē-fẽr-ves′cence,
ef-fẽr-ves′cence,
in-ef-fẽr-ves′cence.

Cf. less sense, etc.

Ē′SENT

d: dē′cent, in-dē′cent.

r: rē′cent.

Plus sea scent *or* cent, etc.

ES′ENT

Vowel: ac′qui-es′cent,
qui-es′cent.

b: al-bes′cent, e-rù-bes′cent,
hẽr-bes′cent, pū-bes′cent,
rù-bes′cent.

d: in-cạn-des′cent, ir-i-des′cent,
lap-i-des′cent,
rē-crù-des′cent,
vir-i-des′cent.

f: rù-fes′cent.

gr: ni-gres′cent.

gw: lañ-gues′cent (-gwes′).

j: jes′sănt, tūr-ges′cent,
sū-ges′cent.

k(c): glạu-ces′cent.

kr: ac-cres′cent, cres′cent,

dē-cres′cent, ex-cres′cent,
in-cres′cent, sū-pēr-cres′cent.

kw: dē-li-ques′cent,
li-ques′cent.

l: ad-ō-les′cent, al-kȧ-les′cent,
cō-ȧ-les′cent, con-vȧ-les′cent,
in-cȧ-les′cent, ob-sō-les′cent,
ō-păl-es′cent, re-vȧ-les′cent,
spī-nū-les′cent, vī-ō-les′cent.

m: dē-tū-mes′cent, frē-mes′cent,
spū-mes′cent, tū-mes′cent.

n: ē-van-es′cent,
gañ-grēn-es′cent, ig-nes′cent,
jū-vē-nes′cent, rē-jū-vē-nes′cent,
sē-nes′cent, spī-nes′cent.

p: tọr-pes′cent.

pr: dē-pres′sănt.

r: är-bō-res′cent, ef-flōr-es′cent,
flō-res′cent, flū-ō-res′cent,
mȧ-tū-res′cent,
phos-phō-res′cent, vǐ-res′cent.

s: ces′sant, in-ces′sant,
mär-ces′cent.

t: de-li-tes′cent, fruc-tes′cent,
frù-tes′cent, lac-tes′cent,
lā-tes′cent, lū-tes′cent,
suf-frù-tes′cent.

tr: pe-tres′cent, pū-tres′cent,
vī-tres′cent.

v: ef-fẽr-ves′cent, fẽr-ves′cent,
flā-ves′cent, in-ef-fẽr-ves′cent.

Cf. dress sent, etc.

Ē′SEPT

pr: prē′cept.

ĒS′EST

fl: fleec′est*.

gr: grēas′est*.

(Choose only one word out of each group)

kr: c̲rēas′est*, dē-c̲rēas′est*, in-c̲rēas′est*.
l: lēas′est*, rē-lēas′est*.
s: cēas′est*.

ES′EST

Vowel: ac̲-qui-es′cest*.
bl: bles′sest*.
dr: ad-dres′sest*, dres′sest*, rē-dres′sest*, un-dres′sest*.
f: c̲on-fes′sest*, prō-fes′sest*.
g: gues′sest (ges′)*.
gr: dī-gres′sest*, prō-gres′sest*, trans-gres′sest*.
pr: c̲om-pres′sest*, dē-pres′sest*, ex-pres′sest*, im-pres′sest*, op-pres′sest*, pres′sest*, rē-pres′sest*, sup-pres′sest*.
r: c̲à-res′sest*.
s: as-ses′sest*.
tr: dis-tres′sest*.
z: pōṣ-ṣes′sest*.

ĒS′ETH

fl: fleec′eth*.
gr: grēas′eth*.
kr: c̲rēas′eth*, dē-c̲rēas′eth*, in-c̲rēas′eth*.
l: lēas′eth*, rē-lēas′eth*.
s: cēas′eth*.

ES′ETH

Vowel: ac̲-qui-es′ceth*.
bl: bles′seth*.
dr: ad-dres′seth*, dres′seth*, rē-dres′seth*, un-dres′seth*.
f: c̲on-fes′seth*, prō-fes′seth*.
g: gues′seth (ges′)*.

gr: dī-gres′seth*, prō-gres′seth*, trans-gres′seth*.
pr: c̲om-pres′seth*, dē-pres′seth*, ex-pres′seth*, im-pres′seth*, op-pres′seth*, pres′seth*, rē-pres′seth*, sup-pres′seth*.
r: c̲à-res′seth*.
s: as-ses′seth*.
tr: dis-tres′seth*.
z: poṣ-ṣes′seth*.

ĒS′EZ

fl: fleec′eṣ.
gr: grēas′eṣ.
kr: c̲rēas′eṣ, dē-c̲rēas′eṣ, in-c̲rēas′eṣ, krïs′eṣ.
l: lēas′eṣ, pe-lïs′seṣ, rē-lēas′eṣ, và-lïs′eṣ.
n: niē′ceṣ.
p: bat′tle=piēc′eṣ, man′tel-piēc″eṣ, pēac′eṣ, piēc′eṣ.
pr: c̲a-prïc′eṣ.
s: cēas′eṣ.
Plus police's, etc.
Cf. peace is, etc.

ES′EZ

Vowel: ac̲-qui-es′ceṣ.
bl: bles′seṣ.
dr: ad-dres′seṣ, dres′seṣ, rē-dres′seṣ, un-dres′ṣeṣ.
f: c̲on-fes′seṣ, prō-feṣ′seṣ.
g: gues′seṣ (ges′).
gr: dī-gres′seṣ, prō-gres′seṣ, rē-gres′seṣ.
j: jes′seṣ.
kr: c̲res′seṣ, wa̱t′ẽr-c̲res″seṣ.

(Choose only one word out of each group)

l: cō-ȧ-les'ces, con-vȧ-les'ces.
m: mes'ses.
n: fĭ-nes'ses.
pr: com-pres'ses, dē-pres'ses,
  ex-pres'ses, im-pres'ses,
  op-pres'ses, pres'ses,
  rē-pres'ses, sup-pres'ses.
r: cȧ-res'ses.
s: as-ses'ses, ex-ces'ses,
  ob-ses'ses, rē-ces'ses,
  S-Ō-S's, suc-ces'ses.
str: stres'ses.
tr: dis-tres'ses, tres'ses.
v: ef-fẽr-ves'ces.
z: dis-pōṣ-ṣes'ses, pōṣ-ṣes'ses,
  rē-pōṣ-ṣes'ses.
Plus Yes's, tress's, etc.
Cf. yes is, etc.
Plus words ending in es+es.

ĒS'FŬL

p: pēace'fŭl, un-pēace'fŭl.
pr: cȧ-prïce'fŭl.
Plus niece full, etc.

ES'FŬL

s: suc-cess'fŭl.
Plus es+full.

ESH'ĂL

p: es-pec'iăl.
sp: spec'iăl.
Plus fresh, Al, etc.

Ē'SHĂN

gr: Grē'ciăn.
Cf. ēsh'un.

ESH'EST

fr: fresh'est, rē-fresh'est*.
m: en-mesh'est*, im-mesh'est*.
thr: thresh'est*.

ESH'ETH

fr: rē-fresh'eth*.
m: en-mesh'eth*, im-mesh'eth*,
  mesh'eth*.
thr: thresh'eth*.

Ē'SHĒZ

sp: spē'ciēs.
Plus see she's, etc.

ESH'I

fl: flesh'y.
m: mesh'y.
Plus fresh, he, etc.

ESH'ING

fr: rē-fresh'ing.
m: mesh'ing.
thr: thresh'ing.

ESH'INGZ

fl: flesh'ings.
Plus esh'ing+s.

ESH'LES

fl: flesh'less.
m: mesh'less.
Plus fresh less, etc.

ESH'LI

fl: flesh'ly, un-flesh'ly.
fr: fresh'ly.
Plus mesh, Lee or lea, etc.

(Choose only one word out of each group)

ESH'MĂN

fr: fresh'măn.
Plus flesh, man, etc.

ESH'MENT

fr: rē-fresh'ment.
Plus flesh meant, etc.

ESH'NES

fr: fresh'ness.

Ē'SHŌR

s: sēa'shōre.
Plus flee shore, etc.

Ē'SHUN

gr: Grē'ciăn ('shun).
kr: aç-çrē'tion, çon-çrē'tion, sē-çrē'tion.
l: dē-lē'tion.
n: in-tĕr-nē'cion ('shun).
pl: çom-plē'tion, dē-plē'tion, im-plē'tion, in-çom-plē'tion, rē-plē'tion.
Cf. ē'shi-ăn.
Plus we shun, etc.

ESH'UN

f: çon-fes'sion, prō-fes'sion.
fr: fresh'en.
gr: ag-gres'sion, dī-gres'sion, ē-gres'sion, in-gres'sion, in-trō-gres'sion, prō-gres'sion, rē-gres'sion, re-trō-gres'sion, trans-gres'sion.
h: Hes'siăn.
kr: dis-çre'tion, in-dis-çre'tion.
pr: çom-pres'sion, dē-pres'sion, ex-pres'sion, im-pres'sion,
in-trō-pres'sion, op-pres'sion, rē-im-pres'sion, rē-pres'sion, sup-pres'sion.
s: aç-ces'sion, ces'sion, çon-ces'sion, in-ses'sion*, in-tĕr-ces'sion, ob-ses'sion, prē-ces'sion, prō-ces'sion, rē-ces'sion, re-trō-ces'sion, sē-ces'sion, ses'sion, suç-ces'sion, sū-pĕr-ses'sion.
z: dis-pōṣ-ṣes'sion, pōṣ-ṣes'sion, prē-poṣ-ṣes'sion, rē-poṣ-ṣes'sion, self'=poṣ-ṣes'sion.
Cf. less shun, etc.
Plus fresh un, etc.

ESH'UNZ

s: quar'tĕr-ses'sionṣ.
Plus esh'un+s.

ESH'ŨR

fl: flesh'ẽr.
fr: fresh'ẽr, rē-fresh'ẽr.
m: mesh'ẽr.
pr: pres'sūre.
thr: thresh'ẽr.
tr: tres'sūre.
Plus refresh her *or* err, etc.

Ē'SHUS

s: fà-cē'tious.
sp: spē'cious.
Plus unleash us, etc.

ESH'US

pr: pre'cious.
Plus enmesh us, etc.

ĔS'I
Ē'SIS
fāte, fär, fȧst, fạll, fĭnăl, cãre, at; mēte, prey, hẽr, met; pīne,
marīne, bĭrd, pĭn; nōte, mŏve, fọr, atŏm, not; mọọn, book;
492

(Choose only one word out of each group)

ĒS'I

fl: fleec'y.
gr: grēas'y.
kr: Crē'cy, crēas'y.
Plus tree see, etc.
Plus peace, he, etc.

ES'I

b: Bes'sie.
dr: dres'sy, un-dres'sy.
j: Jes'sē, Jes'siē.
kr: Cres'sy.
m: mes'sy.
t: Tes'siē.
tr: tres'sy.
Cf. in es'se.
Plus dress, he, etc.
Cf. dress, see?, etc.

Ē'SĪD

l: lee'sīde.
s: sēa'sīde.
Plus she sighed, etc.
Plus tree side, etc.
Plus fleece, I'd *or* eyed, etc.

ES'IJ

m: mes'săge.
p: pes'ăge.
pr: ex-pres'săge, pre'săge.
Cf. long dress age, etc.

ES'IK

d: ġē-ō-des'ic̣.
n: eū-ġen-es'ic̣.
Cf. less hick, etc.

Ē'SIL, ES'IL, IS'IL

s: Cē'cil.
Plus see sill, etc.

ĒS'ING

fl: fleec'ing.
gr: grēas'ing.
kr: crēas'ing, dē-crēas'ing,
in-crēas'ing.
l: lēas'ing, pō-lïc'ing,
rē-lēas'ing.
p: piēc'ing.
s: cēas'ing, sūr-cēas'ing,
un-cēas'ing.

ES'ING

Vowel: ac̣-qui-es'cing.
bl: bles'sing.
dr: ad-drēs'sing, dres'sing,
rē-dres'sing, un-dres'sing,
wạt'ẽr=dres"sing.
f: c̣on-fes'sing, prō-fes'sing.
g: gues'sing (ges').
gr: dī-gres'sing, prō-gres'sing,
re-trō-gres'sing.
j: jes'sing*, un-jes'sing*.
l: c̣ō-ăl-es'cing, c̣on-vȧ-les'cing.
m: mes'sing.
pr: c̣om-pres'sing, dē-pres'sing,
ex-pres'sing, im-pres'sing,
op-pres'sing, pres'sing,
rē-pres'sing, sup-pres'sing.
r: c̣ȧ-res'sing.
s: as-ses'sing, ex-ces'sing.
str: stres'sing.
tr: dis-tres'sing.
y: yes'sing.
z: dis-pōṣ-ṣes'sing, pōṣ-ṣes'sing,
prē-pōṣ-ṣes'sing, rē-pōṣ-ṣes'sing
un-prē-pōṣ-ṣes'sing.

Ē'SIS

Vowel: dī-ē'sis, dē-ē'sis.
j: ex-ē-ġē'sis.

493 ūse, bu̯ll, brúte, tŭrn, up; crȳ, myth; çat, maçhine, ace,
church, çhord; ġem, anger, (Fr.) boṅ, aṣ; THis, thin; aẓure

Ē′SIV`
ES′L

(Choose only one word out of each group)

kr: çat-à-çhrē′sis.
l: och-lē′sis.
m: mī-mē′sis.
n: am-nē′sis, an-ăm-nē′sis.
p: ap″ō-sī″ō-pē′sis.
r: dī″à-phō-rē′sis, per″i-çhō-rē′sis,
  syn-te-rē′sis.
sk(sç): sçhē′sis.
t: er-ō-tē′sis, par″à-cen-tē′sis.
th: an-es-thē′sis, an-thē′sis,
  hȳ″pēr-es-thē′sis, mà-thē′sis,
  thē′sis.
tm: tmē′sis.
Cf. ē′sus.
Plus spree, sis, etc.
Cf. fleeces, etc.

Ē′SIV

h: ad-hē′sive, çō-hē′sive.
Plus he sieve, etc.

ES′IV

dr: rē-dres′sive.
gr: ag-gres′sive, çoñ-gres′sive,
  dī-gres′sive, prō-gres′sive,
  rē-gres′sive, re-trō-gres′sive,
  trans-gres′sive.
kr: çon-çres′cive, çres′cive.
pr: çom-pres′sive, dē-pres′sive,
  ex-pres′sive, im-pres′sive,
  in-ex-pres′sive, op-pres′sive,
  rē-pres′sive, sup-pres′sive,
  un-ex-pres′sive.
s: aç-ces′sive, çon-ces′sive,
  ex-ces′sive, rē-ces′sive,
  suç-ces′sive.
z: pōṣ-ṣes′sive.
Cf. Bess sieve, etc.

ES′KÀ

j: Mod-jes′kà.
l: Và-les′kà.
tr: Tres′çà.
Plus desk, a, etc.

ES′KI

p: pes′ky.
r: dē Res′zkē.
Plus desk, he, etc.
Plus dress key, etc.

ESK′NES

Vowel: stat-ū-esque′ness (-esk′).
r: piç-tū-resque′ness.
t: grō-tesque′ness.

ES′KŌ

d: tē-des′çō.
fr: al fres′çō, fres′çō.
Plus desk owe *or* O, etc.

ES′KŪ

f: fes′çūe.
r: res′çūe.
Plus bless cue *or* queue, etc.
Plus desk you, etc.

Ē′SKWÃR

t: T′squãre.
Plus see square, etc.

Ē′S′L

Cf. ē′sil.

ES′L

ch: ches′sel.
dr: rē-dres′săl.
j: Jes′sel.
n: nes′tle, un-nes′tle.

(Choose only one word out of each group)

p: pes'tle.
r: wres'tle (res').
s: Cec'il.
tr: tres'tle.
v: ves'sel.
Plus mess 'll, etc.

ĒS'LES

fl: fleece'less.
kr: c̨rēase'less.
l: lēase'less.
p: pēace'less.
pr: c̨ȧ-prīce'less.
s: cēase'less.
Plus piece less, etc.

ES'LING

n: nest'ling.
p: pest'ling.
r: rest'ling.

ES'LŨR

n: nest'lẽr.
r: wrest'lẽr (res').

ĒS'MĂN

l: pō-lïce'mǎn.
Plus fleece, man, etc.

ES'MĂN

pr: press'mǎn.
y: yes'mǎn.
Plus bless man, etc.

ES'MĀT

m: mess'māte.
Plus bless mate, etc.

ĒS'MĒL

p: piēce'mēal.
Plus release meal, etc.

ES'MENT

dr: rē-dress'ment.
pr: im-press'ment.
s: as-sess'ment.
Plus undress meant, etc.

ĒS'NES

b: ō-bēse'ness.

Ē'SŎN

gl: Glēa'sŏn.
l: Lēi'sen.
Plus see, son *or* sun, etc.

ES'ŎN

l: les'sen, les'sŏn.
Plus dress on *or* an, etc.

ES'PIT

r: res'pite.
Plus cress pit, etc.
Cf. yes, spit, etc.

ES'PŨR

h: Hes'pẽr.
v: ves'pẽr.
Plus yes, purr *or* per, etc.

ES'TȦ

Vowel: sĭ-es'tȧ.
d: pō-des'tȧ.
v: Ves'tȧ, Zend Ȧ-ves'tȧ.
Plus detest a, etc.

(Choose only one word out of each group)

ES'TĂL

f: fes'tăl.
v: ves'tăl.
Plus rest, Al, etc.
Cf. rest all *or* awl, etc.

ES'TĂN

b: sē-bes'ten.
v: Å-ves'tăn.
Plus rest an *or* Ann, etc.

ES'TĂNT

j: ġes'tănt.
t: çon-tes'tănt.
Plus rest, aunt *or* ant, etc.

ES'TĀT

t: in-tes'tāte, tes'tāte.
Plus rest ate *or* eight, etc.
Plus dress, Tate, etc.
Cf. less, state, etc.

ES'TED

b: bes'ted.
br: breas'ted,
chick'en=breas"ted,
dŏu"ble=breas'ted,
mär'ble=breas"ted,
piġ'eŏn=breas"ted,
sin"gle=breas'ted, un-breas'ted.
ch: ches'ted.
f: in-fes'ted, man-i-fes'ted,
un-in-fes'ted.
j: çon-ġes'ted, dī-ġes'ted,
in-dī-ġes'ted, in-ġes'ted,
jes'ted, prē-dī-ġes'ted,
rē-dī-ġes'ted, sug-ġes'ted,
un-dī-ġes'ted.

kr: ċas'tle=ċres"ted, ċres'ted,
fōam'=ċres"ted, un-ċres'ted.
kw: ques'ted, rē-ques'ted.
l: mō-les'ted, un-mō-les'ted.
n: nes'ted.
r: ar-res'ted, dis-in'tēr-es"ted,
in'tēr-es"ted, res'ted,
un-res'ted, wres'ted (res').
t: at-tes'ted, çon-tes'ted,
dē-tes'ted, prō-tes'ted, tes'ted.
v: dī-ves'ted, in-ves'ted,
sā'ble=ves"ted, ves'ted.
Plus bless Ted, etc.
Plus rest, Ed, etc.

ES'TEST

b: bes'test*.
br: breas'test*.
f: in-fes'test*, man-i-fes'test*.
j: dī-ġes'test*, jes'test*,
sug-ġes'test*.
kr: ċres'test*.
kw: ques'test*, rē-ques'test*.
l: mō-les'test*.
n: nes'test*.
r: ar-res'test*, in'tēr-es"test*,
res'test*, wres'test (res')*.
t: at-tes'test*, çon-tes'test*,
dē-tes'test*, prō-tes'test*,
tes'test*.
v: dī-ves'test*, in-ves'test*.
Plus dress test, etc.

ES'TETH

b: bes'teth*.
br: breas'teth*.
f: in-fes'teth*, man-i-fes'teth*.
j: dī-ġes'teth*, jes'teth*,
sug-ġes'teth*.

(Choose only one word out of each group)

kr: cres'teth*.
kw: ques'teth*, rē-ques'teth*.
l: mō-les'teth*.
n: nes'teth*.
r: ar-res'teth*, in'tẽr-es"teth*,
   res'teth*, wres'teth (res')*.
t: at-tes'teth*, con-tes'teth*,
   dē-tes'teth*, prō-tes'teth*,
   tes'teth*.
v: dī-ves'teth*, in-ves'teth*.

ES'TĒZ

Vowel: Es'tēs.
Cf. test is, etc.

EST'FUL

bl: blest'ful.
j: jest'ful.
r: rest'ful, un-rest'ful.
Plus chest full, etc.

ĒS'TI

b: bēas'tie, bhees'ty (bees').
y: yēas'ty.
Plus peace, tea, etc.
Plus feast, he, etc.

ES'TĬ

ch: ches'ty.
kr: cres'ty.
r: res'ty.
t: tes'ty.
y: yes'ty*.
Plus bless tea, etc.
Plus dressed, he, etc.
Cf. ȧ-des'tē.

ES'TĬJ

pr: pres'tĭge.
v: ves'tĭge.

ES'TIK

b: aṣ-bes'tic.
gr: ȧ-gres'tic.
h: al-kȧ-hes'tic.
j: ġes'tic, mȧ-jes'tic.
kr: cat-ȧ-chres'tic.
l: tē-les'tic, tel-es'tich.
m: dō-mes'tic.
n: a-năm-nes'tic.
p: an-ȧ-pes'tic.
Plus success tick, etc.
Cf. bless stick, etc.

ES'TIN

b: aṣ-bes'tine.
d: clan-deṣ'tine, des'tine,
   Des'tinn, prē-des'tine.
s: ses'tine.
t: in-tes'tine.
Plus dressed in or inn, etc.
Plus bless tin, etc.

ES'TIND

d: des'tined, prē-des'tined,
   un-des'tined.
Plus cress tinned, etc.

ĒS'TING

Vowel: ēas'ting.
f: fēas'ting.
pr: un-priēs'ting.
y: yēas'ting.

ES'TING

b: bes'ting.
br: breas'ting.
f: in-fes'ting, man-i-fes'ting.
j: con-ġes'ting, dī-ġes'ting,
   in-ġes'ting, jes'ting,
   sug-ġes'ting.

(Choose only one word out of each group)

kr: çres'ting.
kw: ques'ting, rē-ques'ting.
l: mō-les'ting.
n: nes'ting.
r: ar-res'ting, dis-in'tēr-es"ting, in'tēr-es"ting, res'ting, un-in'tēr-es"ting, un-res'ting, wres'ting (res').
t: at-tes'ting, çon-tes'ting, dē-tes'ting, prō-tes'ting, tes'ting.
v: dī-ves'ting, in-ves'ting, rē-in-ves'ting, ves'ting.
w: wes'ting.

ES'TIV

f: fes'tive, in-fes'tive.
j: çon-ġes'tive, dī-ġes'tive, sug-ġes'tive.
p: tem-pes'tive.
r: res'tive.
t: at-tes'tive.

EST'LES

br: breast'less.
g: guest'less.
j: jest'less.
kr: çrest'less.
kw: quest'less.
r: rest'less.
Plus dressed less, etc.

ĒST'LI

b: bēast'ly.
pr: prïest'ly, un-prïest'ly.
Plus east lea *or* Lee, etc.

EST'LING

n: nest'ling.
r: wrest'ling (rest').
w: west'ling.

EST'MENT

r: ar-rest'ment.
v: dī-vest'ment, in-vest'ment, vest'ment.
Plus chest meant, etc.

ES'TŌ

f: man-i-fes'tō.
pr: pres'tō.
Plus dress toe, etc.
Plus best owe *or* O, etc.

Ē'STŌN

fr: free'stōne.
k: kēy'stōne.
Plus see stone, etc.
Plus cease tone, etc.

ES'TŎN

b: Bes'tŏn.
h: Hes'tŏn.
w: Wes'tŏn.
Plus best on *or* an, etc.
Plus bless ton *or* tun, etc.

ES'TRĂL

k: kes'trel, ōr-çhes'trăl.
m: trī-mes'trăl.
n: fē-nes'trăl.
p: çam-pes'trăl.
s: an-çes'trăl.
Plus dress trull, etc.

ES'TRĀT

kw: sē-ques'trāte.
n: fe-nes'trāte.

(Choose only one word out of each group)

Plus best rate, etc.
Plus success trait, etc.

ES'TRIK

k(c): ōr-ches'tric.
l: pà-laes'tric (-les').
Plus dress trick, etc.
Plus blessed rick, etc.

ES'TŪR

j: ġes'tūre.
pr: pūr-pres'tūre.
v: dī-ves'tūre, in-ves'tūre,
  rē-ves'tūre, ves'tūre.
Plus dressed your *or* you're, etc.

ĒS'TŪR

Vowel: down'-ēas'tẽr, Ēas'tẽr,
  nọrth-ēas'tẽr, south-ēas'tẽr.
f: fēas'tẽr.
n: Dniēs'tẽr.
Plus feast her *or* err, etc.
Plus she stir, etc.

ES'TŨR

Vowel: es'tẽr, Es'thẽr ('tẽr).
b: Bes'tẽr, Bes'tŏr.
br: breas'tẽr, dŏu"ble=breas'tẽr,
  sin"gle=breas'tẽr.
ch: Ches'tẽr.
f: fes'tẽr, in-fes'tẽr.
h: Hes'tẽr.
j: dī-ġes'tẽr, jes'tẽr,
  sug-ġes'tẽr.
kw: ques'tẽr, rē-ques'tẽr,
  sē-ques'tẽr.
l: Leices'tẽr (les'), Les'tẽr,
  mō-les'tẽr.
m: mid'=sē-mes'tẽr, sē-mes'tẽr,
  trī-mes'tẽr.

n: Dnes'tẽr, nes'tŏr.
p: pes'tẽr, Les'tẽr dē Pes'tẽr.
pr: pres'tẽr*.
r: ar-res'tẽr, res'tẽr,
  wres'tẽr (res').
t: at-tes'tẽr, con-tes'tẽr,
  prō-tes'tẽr, tes'tẽr.
v: dī-ves'tẽr, in-ves'tŏr,
  Syl-ves'tẽr, ves'tẽr.
w: nọr'-wes'tẽr, sou'-wes'tẽr.
y: yes'tẽr*.
Plus blessed her, etc.
Plus Bess stir, etc.

ES'TŨRD

kw: sē-ques'tẽred,
  un-sē-ques'tẽred.
Plus es'tũr+ed.

ĒS'TŨRN

Vowel: ēas'tẽrn.
Plus pieced urn, earn *or* erne, etc.
Plus cease, tern *or* turn, etc.
Plus see stern, etc.

ES'TŨRN

h: hes'tẽrn*.
w: nọrth-wes'tẽrn,
  south-wes'tẽrn, wes'tẽrn.
y: yes'tern*.
Plus mess turn *or* tern, etc.
Plus blessed urn, earn *or* erne, etc.

ES'TUS

b: aş-bes'tŏs, aş-bes'tus.
s: ces'tus.
Plus infest us, etc.

ĒST'WĂRD

Vowel: ēast'wărd.
Plus policed ward, etc.

(Choose only one word out of each group)

EST'WĂRD

w: west'wărd.
Plus best ward, etc.

ĒS'ŪR

fl: fleec'ẽr.
gr: grēas'ẽr.
kr: c̱rēas'ẽr, dē-c̱rēas'ẽr,
  in-c̱rēas'ẽr.
l: lēas'ẽr, rē-lēas'ẽr.
p: piēc'ẽr.
Plus niece, her *or* err, etc.
Plus see, sir, etc.

ES'ŪR

Vowel: ac̱-qui-es'ẽr.
bl: bles'sẽr.
dr: ad-dres'sẽr, dres'sẽr,
  rē-dres'sẽr, un-dres'sẽr.
f: c̱on-fes'sŏr, prō-fes'sŏr.
g: gues'sẽr.
gr: ag-gres'sŏr, dī-gres'sŏr,
  prō-gres'sŏr, trans-gres'sŏr.
l: les'sẽr.
m: mes'sẽr.
pr: c̱om-pres'sŏr, dē-pres'sŏr,
  im-pres'sŏr, op-pres'sŏr,
  pres'sẽr, rē-pres'sẽr,
  sup-pres'sŏr.
r: c̱a̱-res'sẽr.
s: an-tē-ces'sŏr, as-ses'sŏr,
  ces'sẽr, ex-ces'sẽr,
  in-tẽr-ces'sŏr, pre-dē-ces'sŏr,
  suc̱-ces'sŏr.
tr: dis-tres'sẽr.
z: pōṣ-ṣes'sŏr.
Plus possess her *or* err, etc.
Plus yes, sir, etc.

Ē'SUS

kr: C̱roē'sus (krē').
r: Rhē'sus (rē').
Plus fleece us, etc.

Ē'TÀ

Vowel: ē'tȧ.
b: bē'tȧ.
ch: chee'tah.
fl: Flē'tȧ.
k: Chi-quī'tȧ, Mär-quī'tȧ.
l: Lē'tȧ.
m: Mē'tȧ.
n: A-nī'tȧ, Juän-ī'tȧ (wän-),
  Nī'tȧ.
r: Rī'tȧ.
s: C̱är-men-cī'tȧ.
t: Tī'tȧ.
th: thē'tȧ.
z: zē'tȧ, Zī'tȧ.
Plus beat a, etc.

ET'À

Vowel: a-ri-et'tȧ,
  c̱om-e̱-dĭ-et'tȧ, Et'tȧ,
  Hen-ri-et'tȧ.
ch: c̱on-cet'tȧ (-chet').
d: c̱ō-det'tȧ, ven-det'tȧ.
gr: Gret'ȧ.
l: būr-let'tȧ.
m: an-i-met'tȧ, la̱-met'tȧ.
n: Mi-net'tȧ, Net'tȧ.
r: bi-ret'tȧ, op-e-ret'tȧ,
  Ret'tȧ.
y: Yet'tȧ.
z: mō-ṣet'tȧ, Rō-ṣet'tȧ.
Plus met a, etc.

ĒT'ED

bl: blēat'ed.
ch: chēat'ed, es-chēat'ed.

ET′ED
ĒT′EST

fāte, fär, fȧst, fąll, fĭnăl, cãre, at; mēte, prĕy, hẽr, met; pĭne,
marĭne, bĭrd, pin; nōte, mŏve, fŏr, atŏm, nọt; mọọn, book;

500

(Choose only one word out of each group)

f: dē-fēat′ed, un-dē-fēat′ed.
gl: gleet′ed.
gr: greet′ed.
h: hēat′ed, rē-hēat′ed,
ō-vẽr-hēaṭ′ed, wĭne′⸗hēat′ed.
kl: çleat′ed.
kr: aç-çrēt′ed, ex-çrēt′ed,
sē-çrēt′ed.
l: dē-lēt′ed.
m: mēt′ed, un-meet′ed,
un-mēt′ed.
n: nēat′ed.
p: çom-pēt′ed, rē-pēat′ed.
pl: çom-plēt′ed, dē-plēt′ed,
un-çom-plēt′ed.
s: çon-cēit′ed, rē-cēipt′ed (sēt′),
sēat′ed, self′⸗çon-cēit′ed (-sēt′),
un-sēat′ed.
sh: sheet′ed.
sl: sleet′ed.
tr: en-trēat′ed, ēv′il⸗trēat′ed,
ill″⸗trēat′ed, mal-trēat′ed,
rē-trēat′ed, trēat′ed.
Cf. fē′tid.
Plus heat, Ed, etc.
Plus see, Ted, etc.

ET′ED

Vowel: pi-roù-et′ted.
b: ȧ-bet′ted, bet′ted.
bl: blet′ted.
d: in-deb′ted (-det′).
fr: fret′ted, in-tẽr-fret′ted,
un-fret′ted.
gr: rē-gret′ted.
hw: whet′ted.
j: jet′ted.
k: çō-quet′ted (-ket′).
n: bāy-ō-net′ted, bē-net′ted,
çŏr-ō-net′ted, çŏr-net′ted.
net′ted, un-net′ted.

p: pet′ted, un-pet′ted.
sw: sweat′ed.
v: brē-vet′ted, çũr-vet′ted.
w: wet′ted.
z: gȧ-zet′ted.
Cf. fet′id.
Plus met, Ed, etc.

ET′EN

Vowel: ēat′en, Ēt′ŏn,
moth′⸗ēat″en, ōv-ēr-ēat′en,
un-ēat′en, wŏrm′⸗ēat″en.
b: bēat′en, stŏrm′⸗bēat″en,
tem′pest⸗bēat″en, un-bēat′en,
weaTH′ẽr-bēat″en (weTH′).
hw: whēat′en.
k(ç): çhĭ′tŏn, Kēa′tŏn
kr: Çrē′tăn, çrē′tin.
sw: sweet′en.
Cf. ēt′ŏn.
Cf. sweet hen, etc.
Plus see ten, etc.

ET′EN

br: Bret′ŏn, Bret′tŏn.
fr: fret′ten*.
thr: threat′en.
Cf. fret hen, etc.

ĒT′EST

Vowel: ēat′est*, ō-vẽr-ēat′est*.
b: bēat′est*.
bl: blēat′est*.
ch: chēat′est*.
f: dē-fēat′est*, ef-fēt′est.
fl: fleet′est.
gr: greet′est*.
h: hēat′est*, ō-vẽr-hēat′est*.
kr: dis-çreet′est.
l: dē-lēt′est*, ę-lĭt′est.
m: meet′est*.

501 ūse, bụll, brûte, tûrn, up; crȳ, myth; çat, maçhine, ace, church, çhord; ġem, añger, (Fr.) boṅ, aṣ; THis, thin; aẓure

ET'EST
ĒTH'ĂL

(Choose only one word out of each group)

n: nēat′est.
p: çom-pēt′est*, rē-pēat′est*.
pl: çom-plēt′est, rē-plēt′est*, in-çom-plēt′est, plēat′est*, rē-plēt′est.
s: rē-cēipt′est (-sēt′)*, sēat′est*, un-sēat′est*.
sw: sweet′est.
tr: en-trēat′est*, ill″=trēat′est*, mȧl-trēat′est*, rē-trēat′est*, trēat′est*.
Cf. ēt′ist; e.g., dē-fēat′ist, etc.

ET'EST

b: ȧ-bet′test*, bet′test*.
fr: fret′test*.
g: bē-get′test*, fọr-get′test*, get′test*.
gr: rē-gret′test*.
hw: whet′test*.
k: çō-quet′test (-ket′)*.
l: let′test*.
n: bāy-ō-net′test*, bē-net′test*, net′test*.
p: pet′test*.
s: back″=set′test*, bē-set′test*, ō-vēr-set′test*, set′test*, up-set′test*.
w: wet′test.
Cf. wet test, etc.

ĒT'ETH

Vowel: ēat′eth*, ō-vēr-ēat′eth*.
b: bēat′eth*.
bl: blēat′eth*.
ch: chēat′eth*.
f: dē-fēat′eth*.
gr: greet′eth*.
h: hēat′eth*, ō-vēr-hēat′eth*.
l: dē-lēt′eth*.
m: meet′eth*, mēt′eth*.

p: çom-pēt′eth*, rē-pēat′eth*.
pl: çom-plēt′eth*, dē-plēt′eth*, plēat′eth*.
s: rē-cēipt′eth (-sēt′)*, sēat′eth*, un-sēat′eth*.
tr: en-trēat′eth*, mal-trēat′eth*, rē-trēat′eth*. trēat′eth*.

ET'ETH

b: ȧ-bet′teth*, bet′teth*.
fr: fret′teth*.
g: bē-get′teth*, fọr-get′teth*, get′teth*.
gr: rē-gret′teth*.
hw: whet′teth*.
k: çō-quet′teth (-ket′)*.
l: let′teth*.
n: bāy-ō-net′teth*, bē-net′teth*, net′teth*.
p: pet′teth*.
s: set′teth*, bē-set′teth*.
w: bē-wet′teth*, wet′teth*.

ĒT'FỤL

s: dē-cēit′fụl (-sēt′), sēat′fụl.
Plus treat full, etc.

ET'FỤL

fr: fret′fụl.
g: fọr-get′fụl.
gr: rē-gret′fụl.
Plus net full, etc.

ĒTH'ĂL

kw: bē-quēaTH′ăl (kwēTH′).
Plus seethe, Al, etc.

ĒTH'ĂL

Vowel: ēth′ăl.
l: lēth′ăl.
Plus underneath, Al, etc.

(Choose only one word out of each group)

Ē'THĂN

Vowel: Ē'thăn.
b: Ē-liz-ȧ-bēth'ăn.
Plus beneath, Ann *or* an, etc.

ETH'EL

Vowel: eth'ăl, Eth'ĕl.
b: Beth'ĕl.
Cf. eth'il.
Plus breath 'll, etc.

ĒTH'EN

h: hēaTH'en.
r: wrēaTH'en.
Cf. seethe hen, etc.
Cf. seethe an *or* Ann, etc.

ĒTH'I

h: hēath'y.
l: Lē'thē, lēth'y.
Plus underneath, he, etc.

ETH'I

d: death'y (deth').
Plus breath, he, etc.

ETH'IL

Vowel: eth'yl.
m: meth'yl.
Cf. death 'll, etc.
Plus death ill, etc.

ĒTH'ING

br: brēaTH'ing,
in-brēaTH'ing,
in'cense=brēaTH'ing,
ter'rŏr=brēaTH'ing.
kw: bē-quēaTH'ing.

r: en-wrēaTH'ing,
in-tẽr-wrēaTH'ing,
in-wrēaTH'ing, wrēaTH'ing.
s: seeTH'ing.
sh: en-shēaTH'ing, shēaTH'ing,
un-shēaTH'ing.
t: teeTH'ing.

ĒTH'LES

r: wrēath'less.
sh: shēath'less.
Plus beneath less, etc.

ETH'LES

br: breath'less.
d: death'less.
Plus shibboleth less, etc.

ETH'LI

d: death'ly.
Plus breath, Lee, etc.

ĒTH'MENT

kw: bē-quēaTH'ment.
r: wrēaTH'ment.
sh: en-shēaTH'ment.
Plus seethe meant, etc.

ETH'NIK

Vowel: eth'nic̣.
l: hō-leth'nic̣.
Plus death nick *or* Nick, etc.

ETH'ŎD

m: meth'ŏd.
Plus death odd, etc.

ETH'REN

br: breTH'ren.

(Choose only one word out of each group)

ĒTH′ŪR

Vowel: ēiTH′ēr.
br: brēaTH′ēr,
lung′꞊brēath″ēr,
mud′꞊brēath″ēr,
wạ′tēr꞊brēaTH′ēr.
kw: bē-quēaTH′ēr.
n: nēiTH′ēr.
r: en-wrēaTH′ēr, wrēaTH′er.
s: seeTH′ēr.
sh: shēaTH′ēr.
Plus seethe her *or* err, etc.

ĒTH′ŪR

Vowel: ēth′ēr.
Plus beneath her, etc.

ETH′ŪR

bl: bleTH′ēr.
f: feaTH′ēr (feTH′),
pin′꞊feaTH′ēr, tāil′꞊feaTH′ēr,
un-feaTH′ēr, whīte feaTH′ēr.
g: ạl-tö-geTH′ēr, tö-geTH′ēr.
h: heaTH′ēr (heTH′).
hw: wheTH′ēr.
l: hell′꞊fọr꞊leaTH′ēr (-leTH′),
leaTH′ēr, pat′ent leaTH′ēr
whit-leaTH′ēr.
n: neTH′ēr.
t: teTH′ēr, un-teTH′ēr.
w: ȧ-weaTH′ēr, bell-weTH′ēr,
weaTH′ēr, weTH′ēr.

ETH′ŪRD

f: un-feaTH′ēred.
w: weaTH′ēred.
Plus eTH′ūr+ed.

Ē′TI

m: mēat′y.
p: pēat′y.
s: spēr-mȧ-cē′ti.
sl: sleet′y.
sw: sweet′ie, sweet′y.
tr: en-trēat′y, trēat′y.
Plus street, he, etc.

ET′I

Vowel: Et′tie.
b: Bet′tie, bet′ty.
br: li-bret′tĭ.
ch: çon-cet′tĭ (-chet′).
d: Ven-det′tĭ.
f: çon-fet′tĭ, Ī-rish çon-fet′tĭ.
fr: fret′ty.
g: spȧ-ghet′tĭ (-get′).
gr: Al-li-gret′tĭ.
h: Het′tie, Het′ty.
j: jet′ty.
l: Let′tie, Let′ty.
n: Net′tie, net′ty.
p: pet′it (′ĭ), pet′ty,
Rē-pet′tĭ.
pr: "pret′ty".
s: spēr-mȧ-cet′ĭ.
sw: sweat′y.
z: Don-i-zet′tĭ, Roṣ-ṣet′tĭ,
Van-i-zet′tĭ.
Plus sweat, he, etc.

ET′ID, ĒT′ID

f: fet′id, fēt′id.
Cf. et′ed, ēt′ed.

ĒT′IJ

Vowel: ēat′ȧge.
ch: chēat′ȧge, es-chēat′ȧge.
kl: çlēat′ȧge.

(Choose only one word out of each group)

m: mēt′ăge.
Cf. sweet age, etc.

ĒT′IK

kr: Crēt′ic̨.
r: Rhaēt′ic̨ (rēt′).
s: ȧ-cēt′ic̨, cēt′ic̨.
Plus pea tick, etc.

ET′IK

Vowel: ab-i-et′ic̨, al-ō-et′ic̨,
dī″ȧ-nō-et′ic̨, gal-ac̨t″ō-poi-et′ic̨,
myth″ō-pō-et′ic̨, nō-et′ic̨,
on″ō-mat″ō-pō-et′ic̨, pō-et′ic̨.
b: al-phȧ-bet′ic̨, quod-li-bet′ic̨,
tȧ-bet′ic̨.
d: ġē-ō-det′ic̨.
f: Ja-phet′ic̨, prō-phet′ic̨.
j: ap-ol-ō-ġet′ic̨, en-ēr-ġet′ic̨,
En′nȧ Jet′tick, ex-ē-ġet′ic̨,
Gan-ġet′ic̨, in-ēr-ġet′ic̨,
strat-ē-ġet′ic̨.
k(c̨): c̨at-ē-c̨het′ic̨.
kr: syn-c̨ret′ic̨.
l: am-ū-let′ic̨, ath-let′ic̨,
ₐu-let′ic̨, c̨ol-let′ic̨,
hom-i-let′ic̨, Let′tic̨,
oc̨h-let′ic̨.
m: ar-ith-met′ic̨, Baph-ō-met′ic̨,
c̨ō-met′ic̨, c̨os-met′ic̨, ē-met′ic̨,
hēr-met′ic̨, log″ȧ-rith-met′ic̨,
met′ic̨, mi-met′ic̨.
n: ȧb″i-ō-ġē-net′ic̨,
ȧ-gam″ō-ġē-net′ic̨,
bī″ō-ġen-et′ic̨, bī″ō-mag-net′ic̨,
dī″ăm-ag-net′ic̨,
el-ec̨″trō-mag-net′ic̨,
ep″i-ġē-net′ic̨, eū-ġe-net′ic̨,
frē-net′ic̨, ġē-net′ic̨,
his″tō-ġē-net′ic̨,

hō″mō-ġen-et′ic̨, ki-net′ic̨,
mag-net′ic̨, on″tō-ġē-net′ic̨,
pal″i-nō-ġē-net′ic̨,
pan-ġē-net′ic̨,
pär-then′ō-ġē-net′ic̨,
path″ō-ġē-net′ic̨, phō-net′ic̨,
phrē-net′ic̨, phȳ″lō-ġe-net′ic̨,
pol″y-ġē-net′ic̨, splē-net′ic̨,
thrē-net′ic̨.
r: ȧ-lex″i-pȳ-ret′ic̨,
an-c̨hō-ret′ic̨, dī″ȧ-phō-ret′ic̨,
dī-ū-ret′ic̨, em-pō-ret′ic̨,
Ma-sō-ret′ic̨, pȧ-ret′ic̨,
pleth-ō-ret′ic̨, thē-ō-ret′ic̨.
s: as-cet′ic̨, dō-cet′ic̨,
quēr-cet′ic̨.
t: dī-e-tet′ic̨, er-ō-tet′ic̨,
per″i-pȧ-tet′ic̨, zē-tet′ic̨.
th: aes-thet′ic̨ (es-),
al″lō-pȧ-thet′ic̨, an-es-thet′ic̨,
an″ti-pȧ-thet′ic̨, an-ti-thet′ic̨,
a-pȧ-thet′ic̨, bȧ-thet′ic̨,
ep-i-thet′ic̨, hȳ-pō-thet′ic̨,
id″i-ō-pȧ-thet′ic̨,
nom-ō-thet′ic̨,
pär-ȧ-thet′ic̨, par-en-thet′ic̨,
pȧ-thet′ic̨, pol″y-syn-thet′ic̨,
sym-pȧ-thet′ic̨, syn-thet′ic̨,
thē″ō-pȧ-thet′ic̨.
v: Hel-vet′ic̨.
Cf. yet tick, etc.

ET′IKS

Vowel: pō-et′ic̨s.
j: ap-ol-ō-ġet′ic̨s, ex-ē-ġet′ic̨s.
l: ath-let′ic̨s, hom-i-let′ic̨s.
t: dī-e-tet′ic̨s.
th: aes-thet′ic̨s (es-).
Plus et′ik+s.

(Choose only one word out of each group)

ĒT′ING

Vowel: beef′=ēat′ing,
clāy′=ēat′ing, crōw′=ēat′ing,
dĭrt′=ēat′ing, dung′=ēat′ing,
ēat′ing, fīre-ēat′ing,
flesh′=ēat′ing, frŏg′=ēat′ing,
hum′ble pie=ēat′ing,
gràss′=ēat′ing, hāy′=ēat′ing,
lō′tus=ēat′ing, man′=ēat′ing,
ō-vẽr-ēat′ing, smōke′=ēat′ing,
tōad′=ēat′ing, un-dẽr-ēat′ing.

b: bēat′ing, brow′bēat″ing,
drum′=bēat′ing,
juñ′gle=bēat′ing, rug′=bēat′ing,
slāve′=bēat′ing, swift′=bēat′ing,
wīfe′=bēat′ing.

bl: blēat′ing.

ch: chēat′ing, es-chēat′ing.

f: dē-fēat′ing.

fl: fleet′ing.

ɜr: greet′ing.

h: hēat′ing, ō-vẽr-hēat′ing,
un-dẽr-hēat′ing.

k: Kēat′ing.

kl: clēat′ing.

kr: con-crēt′ing, sē-crēt′ing.

m: meet′ing, mēt′ing.

n: nēat′ing.

p: com-pēt′ing, rē-pēat′ing.

pl: com-plēt′ing, plēat′ing.

s: rē-cēipt′ing (-sēt′), sēat′ing,
un-sēat′ing.

sh: sheet′ing.

sl: sleet′ing.

sw: bit′tẽr=sweet′ing,
sweet′ing.

tr: en-trēat′ing, ill′=trēat′ing,
màl-trēat′ing, rē-trēat′ing,
trēat′ing.

ET′ING

Vowel: min-ū-et′ting.

b: à-bet′ting, bet′ting.

bl: blet′ting.

fr: fret′ting.

g: bē-get′ting, fọr-get′ting,
get′ting.

gr: rē-gret′ting.

hw: whet′ting.

j: jet′ting.

k(c): cō-quet′ting (-ket′),
crō-quet′ting.

l: let′ting.

n: bē-net′ting,
mŏs-quï′tō net′ting, net′ting.

p: pet′ting.

r: ret′ting.

s: back-set′ting, bē-set′ting,
in-tẽr-set′ting, ō-vẽr-set′ting,
set′ting, sŏm′ẽr-set″ting.
un-dẽr-set′ting, up-set′ting.

sw: sweat′ing.

v: brē-vet′ting, cũr-vet′ting.

w: wet′ting.

z: gà-zet′ting.

ĒT′IS

th: Thē′tis.
Cf. ē′tus.

ET′IS

l: Let′tice, let′tuce.

ET′ISH

f: fet′ish.

k(c): cō-quet′tish (-ket′),
crō-quet′tish.

l: Let′tish.

p: pet′tish.

w: wet′tish.
Cf. pet, tish!, etc.

ĒT′IST
ĒT′MENT

fāte, fär, fȧst, fᶏll, finăl, cãre, at; mēte, prᵉy, hẽr, met; pīne,
marïne, bĭrd, pin; nōte, mȯve, fᴑr, atŏm, not; mᴑᴑn, book; **506**

(Choose only one word out of each group)

ĒT′IST

f: dē-fēat′ist.
kr: aꞔ-ꞔrē′tist.
s: ꞔon-cēit′ist,
ꞔoun′ty=sēat′ist,
mẽr′cy=sēat′ist,
self′=ꞔon-cēit′ist,
self′=dē-cēit′ist.
sw: hŏn-ey=sweet′ist.
tr: Dutch′=trēat′ist.
Cf. ēt′est.

ĒT′IT

b: bēat′it.
Plus ēt′it.

Ē′TIV

kr: aꞔ-ꞔrē′tive, ꞔon-ꞔrē′tive,
dē-ꞔrē′tive, dis-ꞔrē′tive,
sē-ꞔrē′tive.
pl: ꞔom-plē′tive, dē-plē′tivᵉ,
rē-plē′tive.

ĒT′IZ

sw: sweet′ieṣ.
tr: en-trēat′ieṣ, trēat′ieṣ,
trēat′iṣe.
Plus Crete is, etc.
Plus see ′tis*, etc.

ĒT′L

b: bee′tle, bē′tel.
f: fē′tăl.
kr: dē-crē′tăl.
Plus meet Al, etc.

ET′L

b: ȧ-bet′tăl.
ch: Chet′tle.
f: fet′tle.
gr: Gret′el.
k: ket′tle.
m: Bab′bitt met′ăl, met′ăl,
met′tle, Mō-nel′ met′ăl,
tȳpe met′ăl, whīte met′ăl.
n: net′tle, sting′ing net′tle.
p: pet′ăl, Pō-pō-ꞔat′ȧ-pet″l.
s: rē-set′tle, set′tle.
Plus pet ′ll, etc.

ET′LD

m: hīgh′=met′tled (hī′).
n: net′tled.
p: pet′ălled.
s: set′tled, un-set′tled.
Plus et′l+d *or* +ed.

ET′LES

d: debt′less (det′).
thr: threat′less.
Plus wet less, etc.

ĒT′LI

f: fēat′ly*.
fl: fleet′ly.
kr: ꞔon-ꞔrēte′ly, dis-ꞔreet′ly,
in-dis-ꞔreet′ly.
l: ob-sō-lēte′ly.
m: meet′ly, un-meet′ly.
n: nēat′ly.
pl: ꞔom-plēte′ly, in-ꞔom-plēte′ly.
sw: sweet′ly.
Plus feet, Lea *or* lea, etc.

ET′LING

n: net′tling.
s: set′tling, un-set′tling.

ĒT′MENT

tr: en-trēat′ment,
ill′=trēat′ment, mal-trēat′ment,
mis-trēat′ment, trēat′ment.
Plus sweet meant, etc.

(Choose only one word out of each group)

ET′MENT

b: à-bet′ment.
d: in-debt′ment.
s: bē-set′ment.
v: brē-vet′ment, rē-vet′ment.
Plus pet meant, etc.

ĒT′NES

f: ef-fēte′ness, fēat′ness.
fl: fleet′ness.
kr: çon-çrēte′ness,
 dis-çreet′ness.
l: ob-sō-lēte′ness.
m: meet′ness.
n: nēat′ness.
pl: çom-plēte′ness,
 in-çom-plēte′ness,
 rē-plēte′ness.
sw: sweet′ness.

ET′NES

ᴣ: set′ness.
w: wet′ness.

Ē′TŌ

l: Lē′tō.
k: mŏs-quī′tō (-kē′).
n: Be-nī′tō, bō-nī′tō,
 San Be-nī′tō.
t: Tī′tō.
v: vē′tō.
Plus see toe, etc.
Plus sweet owe or O, etc.

ET′Ō

br: li-bret′tō.
ch: çon-cet′tō (-chet′).
g: ghet′tō (get′).
gr: al-lē-gret′tō.
k(ç): zuç-çhet′tō.
l: sti-let′tō.
m: pal-met′tō.

n: son-net′tō.
p: ris-pet′tō.
r: a-mō-ret′tō, laz-à-ret′tō.
s: fa̧l-set′tō.
z: tĕr-zet′tō.
Plus wet toe, etc.

ĒT′ŎN

Vowel: Ēat′ŏn, Ē′tŏn.
b: Bēat′ŏn.
j: Zyz-zō-ġē′tŏn.
k: Kēat′ŏn, Kēy′tŏn.
s: Sēat′ŏn, Sēy′tŏn.
Cf. ēt′en.
Plus street on, or an, etc.
Plus see ton or tun, etc.

ET′ŎN

br: Bret′ŏn, Bret′tŏn.
Cf. et′en.
Plus sweat on or an, etc.

ET′RĂL, ĒT′REL

m: dī-à-met′răl.
p: pē′trel, sto̧r′my pē′trel.

Ē′TRI

p: Pē′trie.
Plus bee tree, etc.

ET′RIK

m: aç-tin-ō-met′riç,
 al-kà-li-met′riç,
 an-ē-mō-met′riç,
 an-ī″sō-met′riç,
 au″di-ō-met′riç, bar-ō-met′riç,
 bath-y-met′riç,
 ça̧l-o̧r″i-met′riç, çlī-nō-met′riç,
 çhlōr-ō-met′riç,
 çhron-ō-met′riç, dī-à-met′riç,
 dī-met′riç, el-eç-trō-met′riç,

ĒT′ROK
ĒT′ŪR

fāte, fär, fȧst, fall, finăl, cãre, at; mēte, prey, hẽr, met; pīne,
marīne, bĭrd, pĭn; nōte, mŏve, fọr, atŏm, not; mọọn, book;

508

(Choose only one word out of each group)

en-dos-mō-met′rĭc,
eū″di-ō-met′rĭc, gas-ō-met′rĭc,
ġē-ō-met′rĭc, gon″i-ō-met′rĭc,
grav-i-met′rĭc, hex-ȧ-met′rĭc,
hȳ-drō-met′rĭc, hȳ-grō-met′rĭc,
hyp-sō-met′rĭc,
i″sō-bar″ō-met′rĭc, ī-sō-met′rĭc,
log-ō-met′rĭc,
mag-nēt-ō-met′rĭc, met′rĭc,
mī-crō-met′rĭc, mon-ō-met′rĭc,
ō-zon-ō-met′rĭc, ped-ō-met′rĭc,
phō-tō-met′rĭc, stēr″ē-ō-met′rĭc.
sym-met′rĭc, tas-i-met′rĭc,
thẽr-mō-met′rĭc,
trig″ō-nō-met′rĭc, trī-met′rĭc,
vol-ū-met′rĭc.

st: ob-stet′rĭc.
Plus wet rick, etc.
Cf. wet trick, etc.

ĒT′ROK

sh: sheet′rock.
Plus fleet′rock, etc.

ET′RUS, ĒT′RUS

kw: tri-quet′rous (-ket′).
p: pēt′rous, salt-pēt′rous.

Ē′TUM

b: zī-bē′tum.
fr: frē′tum.
n: pī-nē′tum.
r: är-bō-rē′tum.
Plus meet ′em, etc.

ĒT′ŪR

f: fēa′tūre.
kr: crēa′tūre.
Cf. ēch′ūr.
Plus feet, you're *or* your, etc.

ĒT′ŪR

Vowel: beef′=ēat′ẽr,
cāke′=ēat′ẽr, clāy′=ēat′ẽr,
crōw′=ēat′ẽr, dĭrt′=ēat′ẽr,
dung′=ēat′ẽr, ēat′ẽr,
fīre′ēat′ẽr, flesh′=ēat′ẽr,
frog′=ēat′ẽr, grȧss′=ēat′ẽr,
hāy′=ēat′ẽr, hum′ble pīe=ēat′ẽr,
lō′tus=ēat′ẽr, man′=ēat′ẽr,
ō-vẽr-ēat′ẽr, smōke′=ēat′ẽr,
tōad′-ēat′ẽr, un-dẽr-ēat′ẽr.

b: bēat′ẽr, brow-bēat′ẽr,
drum′=bēat′ẽr, gold′bēat″ẽr,
juñ′gle=bēat′ẽr, rug′=bēat′ẽr,
slāve′=bēat′ẽr, wīfe′=bēat′ẽr.

bl: blēat′ẽr.
ch: chēat′ẽr, es-chēat′ẽr.
f: dē-fēat′ẽr.
gr: greet′ẽr.
h: hēat′ẽr, ō-vẽr-hēat′ẽr,
sū-pẽr-hēat′ẽr, wat′ẽr hēat′ẽr.
j: Jeet′ẽr.
kr: sē-crēt′ẽr.
l: de′cȧ-lït″ẽr, hec′tō-lït″ẽr,
lït′ẽr.
m: cen′ti-mēt″ẽr, De-mēt′ẽr,
gas mēt′ẽr, kil′ō-mēt″ẽr,
meet′ẽr, mēt′ẽr, mē′tre (′tẽr),
wat′ẽr mēt′ẽr.
n: nēat′ẽr.
p: com-pēt′ẽr, Pēt′ẽr,
rē-pēat′ẽr, St. Pēt′ẽr,
salt-pēt′ẽr.
pl: com-plēt′ẽr, dē-plēt′ẽr,
rē-plēt′ẽr.
pr: praēt′ọr (prēt′ẽr).
s: ŏne′=sēat′ẽr (wun),
rē-cēipt′ẽr (-sēt′), sēat′ẽr,
three′=sēat′ẽr, twö′=sēat′ẽr (tọọ),
un-sēat′ẽr.
sk: skeet′ẽr.

(Choose only one word out of each group)

sw: sweet'ēr.

t: teet'ēr.

tr: en-trēat'ēr, ill'=trēat'ēr,
mal-trēat'ēr, mis-trēat'ēr,
rē-trēat'ēr, trēat'ēr.
Plus greet her, err *or* Ur, etc.

ET'ŪR

Vowel: Et'tŏr.

b: à-bet'tēr, bet'tēr.

bl: blet'tēr.

d: deb'tŏr.

f: en-fet'tēr, fet'tēr.

fr: fret'tēr.

g: bē-get'tēr, fȯr-get'tēr,
get'tēr, gō'=get'tēr.

gr: rē-gret'tēr.

hw: whet'tēr.

j: jet'tēr.

l: dead let'tēr (ded'), let'tēr,
red let'tēr.

n: net'tēr.

p: pet'tēr.

r: c̦är-bū-ret'ŏr.

s: bē-set'tēr, Ī'rish set'tēr,
set'tēr, sŏm'ēr-set"tēr,
tȳpe'set"tēr.

sw: sweat'ēr (swet').

v: c̦ūr-vet'tēr.

w: wet'tēr.
Plus get her *or* err, etc.

ĒT'ŪRD

f: fēa'tūred, härd'=fēa'tūred,
ill'=fēa'tūred, well'=fēa'tūred.
Cf. ēch'ūr+ed.
Plus creature'd, etc.

ET'ŪRD

f: fet'tēred, un-fet'tēred.

l: let'tēred, un-let'tēred.
Plus et'ūr+ed.

ĒT'ŪRZ

p: Pēt'ērṣ, St. Pēt'ērṣ.
Plus ēt'ūr+s.
Plus cheater 's, etc.

ĒT'US

Vowel: quī-ēt'us.

f: fē'tus.

s: à-cē'tous, Cē'tus.
Plus greet us, etc.
Plus ēt'is.

ET'WURK

fr: fret'wŏrk.

n: net'wŏrk.
Plus get work, etc.

Ē'UM

b: a-mōe-baē'um.

d: Tē Dē'um.

l: ma̦u-sō-lē'um.

n: ath-ē-naē'um,
per"i-tō-nē'um, prȳ-tà-nē'um.

s: c̦ol-os-sē'um, lȳ-cē'um.

t: bron-tē'um.

z: mū-ṣē'um.
Plus fee 'em, etc.

Ē'ŪR

f: fē'ēr.

fl: flē'ēr.

fr: frē'ēr.

gr: à-grē'ēr.

s: ō-vēr-sē'ēr, sē'ēr,
sīght-sē'ēr (sīt).
Plus free her *or* err, etc.

(Choose only one word out of each group)

Ē′US

b: plum-bē′ous, sċar-ȧ-baē′us.
f: ċor-y-phē′us.
p: on″ō-mat″ō-poē′ous.
r: ċhō-rē′us.
t: glū-tē′us.
Plus see us, etc.

Ē′VȦ

Vowel: Ē′vȧ.
d: dĭ′vȧ, Ka-mȧ-dē′vȧ,
　Mä-hä-dē′vȧ.
k: Kĭ′vah.
n: Ġe-nē′vȧ.
v: vĭ′vȧ.
Plus cleave a, etc.

ĒV′ĂL

Vowel: ċō-ēv′ăl, mē-di-ēv′ăl.
h: up-hēav′ăl.
j: lon-ġē′văl.
m: prī-mē′văl.
shr: shriēv′ăl.
tr: rē-triēv′ăl.
Cf. wee′vil, ē′vil.

EV′ĂN

Vowel: Ev′ăn.
d: Dev′ŏn.
Cf. ev′en.

ĒV′ANS

ch: ȧ-chiēv′ănce.
gr: griēv′ănce.
s: pẽr-cēiv′ănce.
tr: rē-triēv′ănce.
Plus believe aunts *or* ants, etc.
Cf. Lē′vănt's.

EV′EL, EV′L

b: bev′el.
d: bē-dev′il, dev′il.
gr: Grev′ille.
k: kev′el.
l: lev′el, sēa lev′el,
　spir′it lev′el, wạt′ẽr lev′el.
n: Nev′ille.
r: rev′el.
sh: di-shev′el.
Plus Bev′ll, etc.

ĒV′EN

Vowel: ēv′en, good-ēv′en*,
　Hal-lōw-ēv′en, un-ēv′en,
　yes-tẽr-ēv′en*.
r: un-bē-rēav′en*.
st: Stē′phen, Stēv′en.

EV′EN

h: heav′en (hev′).
l: ē-lev′en, leav′en (lev′).
s: sev′en.
Cf. Dev′ŏn.

EV′END

l: leav′ened, un-leav′ened.

EV′ENTH

l: ē-lev′enth.
s: sev′enth.

ĒV′ENZ

st: Stē′venṣ, St. Stē′venṣ.
Plus even's, etc.

ĒV′EST

ch: ȧ-chiēv′est*.
gr: griēv′est*.

511 ūse, bᵤll, brúte, tûrn, up; crȳ, myth; çat, maçhine, ace, church, çhord; ġem, aṅger, (Fr.) boṅ, aş; THis, thin; aᵶure

ĒV'ETH
ĒV'ING

(Chosoe only one word out of each group)

h: hēav′est*, up-hēav′est*.
kl: çlēav′est*.
l: bē-liēv′est*, dis-bē-liēv′est*, lēav′est*, rē-liēv′est*.
pr: rē-priēv′est*.
r: bē-rēav′est*.
s: çon-cēiv′est*, dē-cēiv′est*, pēr-cēiv′est*, rē-cēiv′est*.
th: thiēv′est*.
tr: rē-triēv′est*.
w: in-wēav′est*, wēav′est*.

ĒV'ETH

ch: a-chiēv′eth*.
gr: griēv′eth*.
h: hēav′eth*, up-hēav′eth*.
kl: çlēav′eth*.
l: bē-liēv′eth*, dis-bē-liēv′eth*, lēav′eth*, rē-liēv′eth*.
pr: rē-priēv′eth*.
r: bē-rēav′eth*.
s: çon-cēiv′eth*, dē-cēiv′eth*, pēr-cēiv′eth*, rē-cēiv′eth*.
th: thiēv′eth*.
tr: rē-triēv′eth*.
w: in-wēav′eth*, wēav′eth*.

Ē′VĪ

l: Lē′vī.
Plus grieve eye, etc.
Plus grieve, I, etc.

Ē′VI

Vowel: Ē′vie.
ch: Chee′vy.
l: Lē′vy, Mç-Lē′vy.
Plus weave, he, etc.
Plus see V, etc.

EV′I

b: bev′y.
ch: chev′y.
h: heärt′=heav″y, heav′y, top′heav″y.
kl: çlev′y.
l: lev′ee, lev′y.
n: nev′vy.
sh: Çhev′vy.

ĒV′IJ

kl: çlēav′ăġe.
l: lēav′ăġe.
Cf. grieve, age, etc.

Ē′VIL

Vowel: ē′vil, king′ş ē′vil.
w: wee′vil.
Cf. ē′văl.
Plus sleeve′ll, etc.
Plus leave ill, etc.

EV′IL

d: de′vil, etc.
gr: Grev′ille.
n: Nev′ille.
Plus ev′el.
Plus Chev′ll, etc.

EV′ILZ

d: blūe=dev′ilş.
Plus ev′il+s.

EV′IN

l: lev′in*.
pl: rē-plev′in.
Cf. ev′ăn, ev′en.

ĒV′ING

ch: a-chiēv′ing.
gr: ag-griēv′ing, griēv′ing.

(Choose only one word out of each group)

h: hēav'ing, up-hēav'ing.

kl: clēav'ing.

l: bē-liēv'ing, dis-bē-liēv'ing,
lēav'ing, rē-liēv'ing,
un-bē-liēv'ing.

pr: rē-priēv'ing.

r: bē-rēav'ing.

s: con-cēiv'ing, dē-cēiv'ing,
mis-con-cēiv'ing, pẽr-cēiv'ing,
prē-con-cēiv'ing, rē-cēiv'ing,
un-dē-cēiv'ing.

sh: shēav'ing.

st: steev'ing.

th: thiēv'ing.

tr: rē-triēv'ing.

w: in-tẽr-wēav'ing, in-wēav'ing,
un-wēav'ing, wēav'ing.

ĒV'INGZ

l: lēav'ingṣ.

Plus ēv'ing+s.

ĒV'ISH

p: peev'ish.

th: thiēv'ish.

ĒV'LES

l: lēave'less.

sh: shēave'less.

sl: sleeve'less.

Plus grieve less *or* Les, etc.

ĒV'MENT

ch: ȧ-chiēve'ment.

r: bē-rēave'ment.

tr: rē-triēve'ment.

Plus sleeve meant, etc.

ĒV'NING

Vowel: ēve'ning.

EV'RY

Vowel: eve'ry.

Ē'VŪ

pr: prē'view ('vū).

Plus sea view, etc.

Plus deceive you, etc.

ĒV'ŨR

Vowel: nä-ïv'ẽr.

b: bēav'ẽr.

br: brēv'ẽr*.

ch: ȧ-chiēv'ẽr.

d: Dan'ny Deev'ẽr.

f: en-fēv'ẽr, fē'vẽr, hāy fēv'ẽr,
juñ-gle fē'vẽr, sēa fēv'ẽr,
spring fēv'ẽr, yel'low fēv'ẽr.

gr: ag-griēv'ẽr, griēv'ẽr.

h: bal'lȧst hēav'ẽr,
cōal hēav'ẽr,
Guäd-ȧl-quï'vẽr (-hē'),
hēav'ẽr, up-hēav'ẽr.

k: keev'ẽr.

kl: clēav'ẽr.

l: bē-liēv'ẽr, can-ti-lēv'ẽr,
dis-bē-liēv'ẽr, in-tẽr-lēav'ẽr,
lēav'ẽr, lēv'ẽr, liēv'ẽr,
li'vre ('vẽr), māke'=bē-liēv'ẽr,
rē-liēv'ẽr, un-bē-liēv'ẽr.

pr: rē-priēv'ẽr.

r: bē-rēav'ẽr, rēav'ẽr, reev'ẽr,
rēiv'ẽr.

s: con-cēiv'ẽr, dē-cē-v'ẽr,
mis-con-cēiv'ẽr, pẽr-cēiv'ẽr,
prē-con-cēiv'ẽr, rē-cēiv'ẽr,
un-dē-cēiv'ẽr.

sh: shēav'ẽr.

tr: rē-triēv'ẽr.

w: in-tẽr-wēav'ẽr, wēav'ẽr,
weev'ẽr.

Plus grieve her, err *or* Ur, etc.

513 ūse, bṳll, brûte, tûrn, up; crȳ, myth; ҫat, maҫhine, aᴄe, church, ҫhord; ġem, añger, (Fr.) boṅ, aṣ; THis, thin; aẓure

EV′ŪR
EZ′DĀL

(Choose only one word out of each group)

EV′ŪR

Vowel: ev′ĕr, foͅr-ev′ĕr,
how-ev′ĕr, how-sō-ev′ĕr,
whät-ev′ĕr, whät-sō-ev′ĕr,
whence-sō-ev′ĕr, when-ev′ĕr,
when-sō-ev′ĕr, where-ev′ĕr,
where-sō-ev′ĕr, which-ev′ĕr,
which-sō-ev′ĕr,
whiTH′ĕr-sō-ev′ĕr, whö-ev′ĕr,
whöm-sō-ev′ĕr,
whöṣe-sō-ev′ĕr, whö-sō-ev′ĕr.
d: en-deav′ŏr (-dev′).
kl: cͅlev′ĕr.
l: caͅn-ti-lev′ĕr, lev′ĕr.
n: nev′ĕr.
s: as-sev′ĕr, dis-sev′ĕr,
sev′ĕr, un-sev′ĕr.

EV′ŪRD

s: sev′ĕred, un-sev′ĕred.
Plus ev′ūr+ed.

ĒV′US

gr: griēv′ous.
j: lon-ġēv′ous.
m: prī-mēv′ous.
Plus leave us, etc.

Ē′WĀ

l: lee′wāy.
s: sēa′wāy.
Plus tree way, etc.

Ē′WĂRD

l: lee′wărd.
s: sēa′wărd.
Plus Marie, ward, etc.

Ē′WIT

p: pee′wit.
Plus see wit. etc.

Ē′YĂ

p: Caͅs-si-ō-pē′iȧ, etc.
See ē′ȧ.

Ē′YĂN

p: Tär-pē′iăn, etc.
See ē′ăn.

Ē′ZȦ

Vowel: Loū-ī′ṣȧ.
l: Lï′zȧ.
p: Pï′ṣȧ.
Plus sees a, etc.

ĒZ′ĂNṢ

Vowel: ēaṣ′ănce.
f: dē-fēaṣ′ănce, mal-fēaṣ′ănce,
mis-fēaṣ′ănce.
Plus please aunts *or* ants, etc.

EZ′ĂNS, EZ′ENS

pl: pleaṣ′ănce (plez′).
pr: om′ni-preṣ″ence, preṣ′ence.
Cf. ez′ănt+s, ez′ent+s.
Plus fez, aunts *or* ants.

EZ′ĂNT, EZ′ENT

f: pheaṣ′ănt.
p: peaṣ′ănt.
pl: dis-pleaṣ′ănt, pleaṣ′ănt,
un-pleaṣ′ănt,
pr: om′ni-preṣ″ent, preṣ′ent.
Plus says, aunt *or* ant, etc.

ĒZ′DĀL

t: Tēaṣ′dāle.
Plus freeze dale, etc.

EZ′DĀL

Vowel: Eṣ′dāle.
Plus says, Dale, etc.

ĒZ'EL
EZ'ING

fāte, fär, fàst, fạll, finăl, cãre, at; mēte, prḙy, hĕr, met; pīne,
marïne, bĭrd, pĭn; nōte, mŏve, fọr, atŏm, not; mọọn, book; **514**

(Choose only one word out of each group)

ĒZ'EL

Vowel: ēaṣ'el.
t: tēaṣ'el, Tēaz'le.
w: wēaṣ'el.
Plus these 'll, etc.

EZ'EL

b: bez'el.
Cf. ez'l.

ĒZ'ELZ

Vowel: ēaṣ'elṣ.
m: mēa'ṣleṣ.
Plus ēz'el+s.

Ē'ZHÅ

n: mag-nē'ṣiȧ ('zhȧ).
Cf. ēz'i-ȧ.

Ē'ZHĂN

l: Mī-lē'ṣiăn.
Cf. ēz'i-ăn.

Ē'ZHUN

h: ad-hē'ṣion, çō-hē'ṣion,
in-ad-hē'ṣion, in-hē'ṣion.
l: lē'ṣion, Sī-lē'ṣiăn.
p: tra-pē'ziăn.
Cf. ēz'i-ăn.

Ē'ZHŪR

l: lēi'ṣure.
s: sēiz'ūre.
Plus squeeze your *or* you're, etc.

EZH'ŪR

l: lei'ṣure (le').
m: ad-meaṣ'ūre (-mezh'),
meaṣ'ūre, out-meaṣ'ūre.
pl: dis-pleaṣ'ūre, pleaṣ'ūre.

tr: en-treaṣ'ūre, treaṣ'ūre.
Plus fez, you're *or* your, etc.

Ē'ZHŪRD

l: lēi'ṣured, un-lēi'ṣured.
Plus seizure'd, etc.

E'ZHŪRD

l: lei'ṣured (le'),
un-lei'ṣured (-le').
m: im-meaṣ'ūred, meaṣ'ūred,
un-meaṣ'ūred.
pl: pleaṣ'ūred, un-pleaṣ'ūred.
tr: treaṣ'ūred, un-treaṣ'ūred.
Plus treasure'd, etc.

ĒZ'I

Vowel: ēaṣ'y, free=and=ēaṣ'y,
spēak'ēaṣ"y, un-ēaṣ'y.
b: Zam-bē'zi.
br: breez'y.
ch: cheeṣ'y.
fr: freez'y.
gr: grēaṣ'y.
hw: wheez'y.
kw: quēaṣ'y.
sl: slēaz'y.
sn: sneez'y.
Plus trees he, etc.

ĒZ'IKS

sk: skeez'iks.

ĒZ'IN

s: sēi'zin.
Cf. ēz'ŏn.

ĒZ'ING

Vowel: ēaṣ'ing.
br: breez'ing.

(Choose only one word out of each group)

fr: freez'ing.
gr: grēaṣ'ing.
hw: wheez'ing.
p: ap-pēaṣ'ing.
pl: dis-plēaṣ'ing, plēaṣ'ing, self'=plēaṣ'ing, un-plēaṣ'ing.
s: fōre-sēiz'ing, sēiz'ing.
skw: squeez'ing.
sn: sneez'ing.
t: tēaṣ'ing.

ĒZ'IT

ch: cheeṣe'it.
Plus breeze, it, etc.

EZ'L

b: em-bez'zle.
Cf. ez'el.
Plus fez'll, etc.

EZ'LŪR

b: em-bez'zlĕr.

ĒZ'MENT

Vowel: ēaṣe'ment.
p: ap-pēaṣe'ment.
Plus trees meant, etc.

ĒZ'ŎN

kw: Quē'zŏn.
r: rēaṣ'ŏn, un-rēaṣ'ŏn.
s: sēaṣ'ŏn, un-sēaṣ'ŏn.
tr: trēaṣ'ŏn.
Cf. ēz'in.
Plus trees on *or* an, etc.

EZ'RÅ

Vowel: Ez'rȧ.
Plus fez, Ra, etc.

ĒZ'ŨR

Vowel: ēaṣ'ẽr.
b: beez'ẽr.
fr: freez'ẽr, friēz'ẽr.
g: geez'ẽr.
gr: grēaṣ'ẽr.
hw: wheez'ẽr.
l: lēaṣ'ẽr.
n: E-ben-ē'zẽr.
p: ap-pēaṣ'ẽr.
pl: plēaṣ'ẽr.
s: Caē-ṣăr (sēz').
skw: squeez'ẽr.
sn: sneez'ẽr.
t: tēaṣ'ẽr.
tw: tweez'ẽr.
Plus squeeze her *or* err, etc.

EZ'ŨRT

d: deṣ'ẽrt.
Cf. says hurt, etc.

ĒZ'ŨRZ

tw: tweez'ẽrs.
Plus ēz'ũr+s.

ĒZ'US

j: Jē'ṣus.
Plus tease us, etc.

Ĭ′Å
Ĭ′ĂN

fāte, fär, fȧst, fạll, finăl, cãre, at; mēte, prey, hẽr, met; pīne,
marïne, bïrd, pin; nōte, mŏve, fọr, atŏm, not; mọọn, book;

516

(Choose only one word out of each group)

I

The accented vowel sounds included are listed under **I** in Single
Rhymes.

Ī′Å

b: Tō-bī′ȧh.
d: Jed-ē-dī′ȧh, Ō-bȧ-dī′ȧh,
Zeb-ē-dī′ȧh.
f: St. Sō-phī′ȧ, Sō-phī′ȧ.
k: Hez-ē-kī′ȧh, Zed-ē-kī′ȧh.
l: Thȧ-lī′ȧ,
m: Jer-ē-mī′ȧh.
n: as-thē-nī′ȧ, Bē-nī′ȧh,
gọr-gō-neī′ȧ, Zeph-ȧ-nī′ȧh.
r: Am-ȧ-rī′ȧh, Ā′vē Mȧ-rī′ȧ,
Az-ȧ-rī′ȧh, Bē-rī′ȧh,
Black Mȧ-rī′ȧ,
Mȧ-rī′ȧ, Ū-rī′ȧh, Zach-ȧ-rī′ȧh.
s: Jō-sī′ȧh, mes-sī′ȧh.
str: strī′ȧ.
tr: lȧ-trī′ȧ.
v: vī′ȧ.
z: Ī-saī′ȧh, Kē-zī′ȧh.
Plus buy a, etc.

Ī′AD

d: dȳ′ad.
dr: drȳ′ad, ham-ȧ-drȳ′ad.
m: Jer-ē-mī′ad.
pl: Pleī′ad.
tr: trī′ad.
Plus why add *or* ad, etc.

Ī′ADZ

h: Hȳ′adṣ.
Plus ī′ad+s.

Ī′AK

gw: guī′ac (gwī′).
j: el-ē-ġī′ac.

k: kaȳ′ak.
z: phren-ē-ṣī′ac.

Ī′ĂL, Ī′ŎL

d: dī′ăl, mọọn dī′ăl, sun′dī-ăl.
f: phī′ăl.
h: bās-i-hȳ′ăl.
kr: dē-crī′ăl, des-crī′ăl.
n: dē-nī′ăl, ġē-nī′ăl,
self-dē-nī′ăl.
p: es-pī′ăl.
pl: sup-plī′ăl.
r: rī′ăl*.
tr: rē-trī′ăl, trī′ăl.
v: bāss vī′ŏl, vī′ăl, vī′ŏl.

Ī′AM

pr: Prī′am.
s: Sī′am.
Plus I am, etc.
Cf. ī amb.

Ī′AMB

Vowel: ī′amb.
Cf. ī′am.

Ī′ĂN

br: Brī′ăn, Brȳ′ăn.
k(c): Chī′ăn.
l: thȧ-lī′ăn.
n: ġē-nī′ăn.
r: Ō-rī′ŏn, Ō′-Rȳ′ăn, Rȳ′ăn.
st: stȳ′ăn.
t: al-taī′ăn.
Plus try an, etc.

(Choose only one word out of each group)

Ī′ĂND

v: vī′ănd.
Plus try and, etc.

Ī′ĂNDZ

v: vī′ăndṣ.
Cf. try hands, etc.

Ī′ĂNS

f: af-fī′ănce, dē-fī′ănce.
l: al-lī′ănce, meṣ-al-lī′ănce, mis-al-lī′ănce, rē-lī′ănce, self=rē-li′ănce.
pl: ap-plī′ănce, çŏm-plī′ănce, in-çŏm-plī′ănce, sup-plī′ănce.
s: scī′ence.
Cf. ī′ant+s.
Plus sly ants *or* aunts, etc.

Ī′ĂNT

f: af-fī′ănt, ça̱l-o̱r-i-fī′ent, dē-fī′ănt.
j: ġī′ănt.
kl: çlī′ent.
l: al-lī′ănt, rē-lī′ănt, self=rē-lī′ănt.
pl: çŏm-plī′ănt, plī′ănt.
s: scī′ent.
Plus spy ant *or* aunt, etc.

Ī′ĂS

Vowel: eȳ′ăs.
b: bī′ăs, Tō-bī′ăs, un-bī′ăs.
l: Ē-lī′ăs, Lī′ăs.
m: Jer-ē-mī′ăs.
n: An-á-nī′ăs.
s: Jō-sī′ăs, Mes-sī′ăs.
th: Mat-thī′ăs.
Cf. ī′us.
Cf. try us, etc.

Ī′ĂT

f: fī′ăt.
m: Mȳ′ătt.
Cf. ī′et.
Plus try at, etc.

Ī′AZM

m: mī′aṣm.

Ī′BA

p: çō-paī′ba̱.
z: Zī′ba̱.
Plus describe a, etc.

IB′ĂLD

r: rib′ăld.
t: Theo′băld (ti′).

IB′DIS

r: C̱ha̱-ryb′dis.

ĪB′EST

b: im-bīb′est*.
j: ġīb′est.
skr(sç̱r): a̱-sç̱rīb′est*, cīr-çum-sç̱rīb′est*, dē-sç̱rīb′est*, in-sç̱rīb′est*, prē-sç̱rīb′est*, prō-sç̱rīb′est*, sub-sç̱rīb′est*, sū-pĕr-sç̱rīb′est*, tran-sç̱rīb′est*.
Plus buy best, etc.

IB′EST

f: fib′best*.
gl: glib′best.
j: jib′best*.
Plus rib best, etc.

IB′ET

j: flib′bĕr-ti-ġib-bet, ġib′bet.
t: Tib′bett.
z: zib′et.

ĪB'ETH
IB'LEST

fāte, fär, fȧst, fạll, finȧl, cãre, at; mēte, prẹy, hẽr, met; pīne, marïne, bīrd, pin; nōte, mȯve, fọr, atŏm, not; mọọn, book; **518**

(Choose only one word out of each group)

Cf. ib'it.
Cf. glib bet, etc.
Plus sib et, etc.

ĪB'ETH

b: im-bīb'eth*.
j: g̣īb'eth*.
br: brīb'eth*.
skr(sc̣r): ȧ-sc̣rīb'eth*,
  cïr-c̣um-sc̣rīb'eth*,
  dē-sc̣rīb'eth*, in-sc̣rīb'eth*,
  prē-sc̣rīb'eth*, prō-sc̣rīb'eth*,
  sub-sc̣rīb'eth*,
  sū-pẽr-sc̣rīb'eth*,
  tran-sc̣rīb'eth*.
Plus lie, Beth, etc.

IB'ETH

f: fib'beth*.
j: jib'beth*.
Cf. rib, Beth, etc.

IB'I

k: Kib'bee.
l: Lib'bey, Lib'by.
t: Tib'bie.
Plus bib, he, etc.

ĪB'ING

b: im-bīb'ing.
br: brīb'ing.
j: g̣īb'ing.
skr(sc̣r): ȧ-sc̣rīb'ing,
  cïr-c̣um-sc̣rīb'ing, dē-sc̣rīb'ing,
  in-sc̣rīb'ing, prē-sc̣rīb'ing,
  prō-sc̣rīb'ing, sub-sc̣rīb'ing,
  sū-pẽr-sc̣rīb'ing,
  tran-sc̣rīb'ing.
Plus buy, Byng, etc.

IB'ING

f: fib'bing.
j: jib'bing.
r: rib'bing.
skw: squib'bing.

IB'IT

h: ad-hib'it, c̣ō-hib'it,
  ex-hib'it, in-hib'it, prō-hib'it.
Cf. ib'et.

I'BL

b: Bī'ble.
l: lī'bel.
tr: trīb'ăl.
Plus jibe'll, etc.
Plus sly bull, etc.

IB'L

b: ish'kȧ-bib-ble.
d: dib'ble.
dr: drib'ble.
fr: frib'ble.
gr: grib'ble.
k: Kib'ble.
kr: c̣rib'ble.
kw: quib'ble.
n: nib'ble.
skr(sc̣r): sc̣rib'ble.
thr: thrib'ble.
Plus bib'll, etc.

IB'LD

cr: c̣rib'bled.
r: rib'ăld.
th: Theo'băld (ti').
Plus ib'l+d.

IB'LEST

d: dib'blest*.
dr: drib'blest*.

519 ūse, bṳll, brúte, tǖrn, up; crȳ, myth; c̣at, maçhine, ace, church, c̣hord; ġem, aṅger, (Fr.) boṅ, aṣ; THis, thin; aᶎure

IB′LET
IB′ŎNZ

(Choose only one word out of each group)

kw: quib′blest*.
n: nib′blest*.
skr(sc̣r): sc̣rib′blest*.
Plus ib′l+est*.
Plus ribblest, etc.

IB′LET

dr: drib′let.
j: ġib′let.
tr: trib′let.
Plus fib let, etc.

IB′LETH

d: dib′bleth*.
dr: drib′bleth*.
kw: quib′bleth*.
n: nib′bleth*.
skr(sc̣r): sc̣rib′bleth*.
Plus ib′l+eth*.

IB′LI

dr: drib′bly.
gl: glib′ly.
kw: quib′bly.
n: nib′bly.
skr(sc̣r): sc̣rib′bly.
thr: thrib′bly.
tr: trib′bly.
Cf. rib, Lee or lea, etc.

IB′LIK

n: nib′lick.
Plus rib lick, etc.

IB′LING

d: dib′bling.
dr: drib′bling.
fr: frib′bling.
k: kib′bling.
kr: c̣rib′bling.
kw: quib′bling.
n: nib′bling.

skr(sc̣r): sc̣rib′bling.
str: Strib′ling.
tr: trib′bling.

Ī′BLŌ

b: bȳ′=blōw.
fl: flȳ′blōw.
Plus why blow, etc.
Plus tribe low or lo, etc.

IB′L̇ŪR

d: dib′blĕr.
dr: drib′blĕr.
fr: frib′blĕr.
k: kib′blĕr.
kr: c̣rib′blĕr.
kw: quib′blĕr.
n: nib′blĕr.
skr(sc̣r): sc̣rib′blĕr, tran-sc̣rib′blĕr.

Ī′BOL

Vowel: eȳe′bạll.
h: hīgh′bạll (hĭ).
sk: skȳ′bạll.
Plus why bawl or ball, etc.
Plus tribe all or awl, etc.

Ī′BOLD

p: pīe′bạld.
Plus ī′bol+ed.
Plus why bald, balled or bawled, etc.

IB′ŎN

g: gib′bŏn.
r: blũe rib′bŏn, red rib′bŏn, rib′bŏn, whīte rib′bŏn.
Plus rib on or an, etc.

IB′ŎNZ

g: Fitz-gib′bŏnṣ, Gib′bŏnṣ.
Plus ib′ŏn+s.

Ī'BORN
ICH'EN

fāte, fär, fåst, fąll, finăl, cãre, at; mēte, prĕy, hẽr, met; pīne,
marīne, bĭrd, pĭn; nōte, mŏve, fŏr, atŏm, not; mọọn, book;

520

(Choose only one word out of each group)

Ī'BORN

h: hīgh'born (hī).
sk: skȳ'=born.
Plus why born, etc.

ĪB'RĂNT

v: vī'brănt.
Plus tribe rant, etc.
Plus why, Brant, etc.

ĪB'RĀT

l: ē-qui-lī'brāte, lī'brāte.
v: vī'brāte.
Plus tribe rate, etc.

Ī'BROU

Vowel: eȳe'brow.
h: hīgh'brow (hī).
Plus try brow, etc.
Plus tribe row, etc.

IB'SEN

Vowel: Ib'sen.
Cf. ib'sŏn.

IB'SŎN

Vowel: Ib'sŏn.
d: Dib'sŏn.
g: Gib'sŏn.
Plus rib, son *or* sun, etc.

IB'ŪN

tr: trib'ūne.

ĪB'UR

b: im-bīb'ẽr.
br: brīb'ẽr.
f: fī'bẽr.
j: ġīb'ẽr.
l: Leī'bẽr, līb'ẽr.
skr(scr): à-scrīb'ẽr,
cĭr-cum-scrīb'ẽr, dē-scrīb'ẽr,

in-scrīb'ẽr, prē-scrīb'ẽr,
prō-scrīb'ẽr, scrīb'ẽr,
sub-scrīb'ẽr, tran-scrīb'ẽr.
t: Tī'bẽr.
Plus why burr, etc.
Plus tribe err, er, Ur *or* her, etc.

IB'ŨR

b: bib'bẽr, wīne'bib-bẽr.
d: dib'bẽr.
f: fib'bẽr.
gl: glib'bẽr.
j: flib'bẽr-ġib-bẽr, ġib'bẽr,
jib'bẽr.
kr: crib'bẽr.
l: ad lib'bẽr.
n: nib'bẽr.
skw: squib'bẽr.
Plus rib her *or* err, etc.

IB'ŪT

tr: at-trib'ūte, cŏn-trib'ūte,
dis-trib'ūte, rē-dis-trib'ūte,
rē-trib'ūte, trib'ūte.
Plus rib Ute, etc.

ICH'ĂRD

pr: Pritch'ărd.
r: Rich'ărd.

ICH'EL

k: Kitch'ell.
m: Mitch'ell.
sw: switch'el.
tw: Twich'ell.
Plus switch'll, etc.

ICH'EN

k: kitch'en.
l: lich'en.
Cf. rich hen, etc.
Cf. rich in, etc.

(Choose only one word out of each group)

ICH'EST

h: hitch'est*.
p: pitch'est*.
r: en-rich'est*, rich'est.
st: stitch'est*.
sw: switch'est*.
w: bē-witch'est*, witch'est*.

ICH'ET

f: fit'chet, Fit'chett.
pr: Pritch'ett.
tw: Twich'ett.
w: witch'et.
Plus witch et, etc.
Cf. bewitch it, etc.

ICH'ETH

h: hitch'eth*.
p: pitch'eth*.
r: en-rich'eth*.
st: stitch'eth*.
sw: switch'eth*.
w: bē-witch'eth*, witch'eth*.

ICH'EZ

Vowel: itch'eṣ.
b: bitch'eṣ.
br: breech'eṣ, britch'eṣ.
d: ditch'eṣ.
fl: flitch'eṣ.
h: hitch'eṣ.
n: nich'eṣ.
p: pitch'eṣ.
r: en-rich'eṣ, rich'eṣ.
skr(sçr): sçritch'eṣ.
st: stitch'eṣ.
sw: switch'eṣ.
tw: twitch'eṣ.
w: bē-witch'eṣ, witch'eṣ.
Cf. which is, etc.

ICH'I

Vowel: itch'y.
b: bitch'y.
f: fitch'y.
p: pitch'y.
r: Rich'ie.
st: stitch'y.
sw: switch'y.
w: witch'y.
Plus which he, etc.

ICH'ING

Vowel: itch'ing.
d: ditch'ing.
h: hitch'ing.
m: mich'ing.
p: pitch'ing.
r: en-rich'ing.
st: stitch'ing.
sw: switch'ing.
tw: twitch'ing.
w: bē-witch'ing, witch'ing.

ICH'LES

Vowel: itch'less.
h: hitch'less.
st: stitch'less.
sw: switch'less.
w: witch'less.
Plus pitch less, etc.

ICH'MENT

r: en-rich'ment.
w: bē-witch'ment.
Plus which meant, etc.

ICH'NES

r: rich'ness.

(Choose only one word out of each group)

ICH'ŪR

Vowel: itch'ẽr.
d: ditch'ẽr.
h: hitch'ẽr.
p: pitch'ẽr.
r: en-rich'ẽr, rich'ẽr.
st: stitch'ẽr.
sw: switch'ẽr.
tw: twitch'ẽr.
w: bē-witch'ẽr.
Plus bewitch her *or* err, etc.

Ī'CHUS

r: rīght'eous.

Ī'DẢ

Vowel: Ī'dȧ.
l: Lĭ'dȧ.
n: Ō-neī'dȧ.
r: Rī'dȧ.
v: Vī'dȧ.
Plus I'd a, spied a, etc.

ĪD'ĂNS

b: ȧ-bīd'ănce.
g: guīd'ănce (gīd'),
  mis-guīd'ănce.
s: sub-sīd'ence.
Plus deride aunts *or* ants, etc.
Plus why dance, etc.

ID'ĂNS

b: fŏr-bid'dănce.
r: rid'dănce.
Cf. kid dance, etc.
Plus rid aunts *or* ants, etc.

ĪD'ĂNT

g: guīd'ănt (gīd').
v: di-vīd'ănt.
Plus guide aunt *or* ant, etc.

ĪD'ED

b: ȧ-bīd'ed, bīd'ed.
br: brīd'ed.
ch: chīd'ed.
f: cŏn-fīd'ed.
g: guīd'ed (gīd'), mis-guīd'ed,
  un-guīd'ed.
gl: glīd'ed.
l: cŏl-līd'ed, ē-līd'ed.
pr: prīd'ed.
r: dē-rīd'ed.
s: cō-in-cīd'ed, dē-cīd'ed,
  lop'sīd-ed, man'y-sīd'ed (men'),
  ŏne'-sīd'ed (wun'), sīd'ed,
  slab'-sīd'ed, sub-sīd'ed,
  twō'-sīd'ed (tö'), un-dē-cīd'ed.
sl: back-slīd'ed, land'slīd-ed.
str: strīd'ed.
t: bē-tīd'ed, tīd'ed.
v: di-vīd'ed, prō-vīd'ed,
  sub-di-vīd'ed, un-di-vīd'ed,
  un-prō-vīd'ed.
z: prē-ṣīd'ed, rē-ṣīd'ed.
Cf. tī'died.
Plus pride, Ed, etc.
Plus why dead, etc.
Cf. why did, etc.

ID'ED

b: bid'ded, ō-vẽr-bid'ded,
  un-dẽr-bid'ded.
k: kid'ded.
l: in'vȧ-lid-ed, lid'ded.
m: pyr'ȧ-mid-ed.
r: rid'ded.
sk: skid'ded.
Plus did, Ed, etc.

Ī'DEN

dr: Drȳ'den.
l: Leȳ'den.

(Choose only one word out of each group)

w: wīd′en.
Cf. īd′ŏn.
Plus my den, etc.
Cf. wide hen, etc.

ID′EN

b: bid′den, fŏr-bid′den,
God′=fŏr-bid-den, un-bid′den,
un-fŏr-bid′den.
ch: chid′den.
h: hid′den.
m: kitch′en mid′den, mid′den.
r: hag′rid-den, ō-vĕr-rid′den,
priēst′=rid-den, rid′den,
un-rid′den, wīfe′rid-den.
sl: slid′den.
str: strid′den.

Ī′DENT

b: bī′dent.
r: rī′dent.
str: strīd′ent.
tr: trī′dent.
Plus why dent, etc.

ĪD′EST

b: ȧ-bīd′est*, bīd′est*.
br: brīd′est*.
ch: chīd′est*.
f: c̦ŏn-fīd′est*.
fr: frīed′est.
g: guīd′est (gīd′)*.
gl: glīd′est*.
h: hīd′est*.
l: c̦ŏl-līd′est*, ē-līd′est*.
pr: prīd′est*.
r: dē-rīd′est*, ō-vĕr-rīd′est*,
rīd′est*.
s: c̦ō-in-cīd′est*, dē-cīd′est*,
sīd′est*, sub-sīd′est*.

sl: back-slīd′est*, slīd′est*.
str: strīd′est*.
t: tīd′est*.
v: di-vīd′est*, prō-vīd′est*,
sub-di-vīd′est*.
w: wīd′est.
z: prē-ṣīd′est*, rē-ṣīd′est*.

ID′EST

b: bid′dest*, for-bid′dest*,
ō-vĕr-bid′dest*,
un-dĕr-bid′dest*.
k: kid′dest*.
l: lid′dest*.
m: pyr′ȧ-mid-est*.
r: rid′dest*.
sk: skid′dest*.

ĪD′ETH

b: ȧ-bīd′eth*, bīd′eth*.
br: brīd′eth*.
ch: chīd′eth*.
f: c̦ŏn-fīd′eth*.
g: guīd′eth (gīd′)*.
gl: glīd′eth*.
h: hīd′eth*.
l: c̦ŏl-līd′eth*, ē-līd′eth*.
pr: prīd′eth*.
r: dē-rīd′eth*, ō-vĕr-rīd′eth*,
rīd′eth*.
s: c̦ō-in-cīd′eth*, dē-cīd′eth*,
sīd′eth*, sub-sīd′eth*.
sl: slīd′eth*.
str: strīd′eth*.
t: bē-tīd′eth*, tīd′eth*.
v: di-vīd′eth*, prō-vīd′eth*,
sub-di-vīd′eth*.
z: prē-ṣīd′eth*, rē-ṣīd′eth*.
Plus why death, etc.

ID'ETH
ID'ING

fāte, fär, fâst, fâll, finăl, cãre, at; mēte, prĕv, hẽr, met; pīne, marïne, bĭrd, pin; nōte, mŏve, fŏr, atŏm, not; mŏŏn, book;

524

(Choose only one word out of each group)

ID'ETH

b: bid'deth*, fŏr-bid'deth*, ō-vẽr-bid'deth*, un-dẽr-bid'deth*.
k: kid'deth.
l: lid'deth*.
m: pyr'ȧ-mid-eth*.
r: rid'deth*.
sk: skid'deth*.

ĪD'I

d: dī'dy.
f: bō'nȧ fī'dē.
fr: Frī'day.
l: Leī'dy.
t: tī'dy, un-tī'dy.
v: vī'dē.
Plus why'd he *or* side, he, etc.
Plus try Dee *or* D, etc.

ID'I

b: bid'dy, chick'ȧ-bid-dy.
d: Did'dy.
g: gid'dy.
k: kid'dy.
m: mid'dy.
st: stid'dy.
w: Din-wid'die, "wid'dy".
Plus did he, etc.

ĪD'ID

t: tīd'ied.
Cf. īd'ed.
Plus why did, etc.

ĪD'IJ

g: guīd'ăġe.
h: hīd'ăġe.
Cf. hide age, etc.

ID'IK

Vowel: drù-id'ic.
m: pyr-ȧ-mid'ic.

r: jù-rid'ic.
t: fȧ-tid'ic.

ĪD'IL, ID''L

Vowel: īd'yll.
Cf. ī'dl.
Plus guide ill, I'd ill, etc.
Plus try dill, etc.

ĪD'ING

b: ȧ-bīd'ing, bīd'ing, law'≠ȧ-bīd-ing.
br: brīd'ing.
ch: chīd'ing.
f: çŏn-fīd'ing.
g: guīd'ing (gīd'), mis-guīd'ing.
gl: glīd'ing.
h: hīd'ing.
l: çŏl-līd'ing, ē-līd'ing.
n: nīd'ing.
pr: prīd'ing.
r: dē-rīd'ing, out-rīd'ing, ō-vẽr-rīd'ing, rīd'ing.
s: çō-in-cīd'ing, dē-cīd'ing, sīd'ing, sub-sīd'ing.
sl: back-slīd'ing, slīd'ing.
str: bē-strīd'ing, out-strīd'ing, strīd'ing.
t: bē-tīd'ing.
v: di-vīd'ing, prō-vīd'ing.
z: prē-ṣīd'ing, rē-ṣīd'ing.

ID'ING

b: bid'ding, fŏr-bid'ding, out-bid'ding, ō-vẽr-bid'ding, un-dẽr-bid'ding, un-fŏr-bid'ding.
k: kid'ding, nō kid'ding.
l: lid'ding.
r: rid'ding.
sk: skid'ding.

(Choose only one word out of each group)

ĪD′INGZ

t: tīd′ingṣ.
Plus īd′ing+s.

ID′INGZ

g: Gid′dingṣ.
Plus id′ing+s

ĪD′L

Vowel: ī′dle, ī′dŏl.
br: brīd′ăl, brīd′le.
s: frat-ri-cīd′ăl, hom-i-cīd′ăl,
in-fan′ti-cīd-ăl, mā′tri-cīd-ăl,
par′ri-cīd-ăl, pa′tri-cīd-ăl,
reġ-i-cīd′ăl, sī′dle, sū-i-cīd′ăl,
ux-or′i-cīd-ăl, tyr-ran-i-cīd′ăl.
t: tīd′ăl.
Plus wide, Al, etc.
Cf. īd′yll.
Plus bride 'll, etc.

ID′L

b: Bid′dle.
d: did′dle, flum′à-did-dle.
f: fid′dle.
gr: grid′dle.
kw: quid′dle.
l: Lid′dle.
m: mid′dle.
p: pid′dle.
r: rid′dle, un-rid′dle.
t: rum′tum tid′dle, tid′dle.
tw: twid′dle.
y: yid′dle.
Plus kid′ll, etc.

ĪD′LD

br: brīd′led, un-brīd′led.
Plus īd′l+d.

ID′LD

f: fid′dled.
Plus id′l+d.

ĪD′LEST

Vowel: īd′lest.
br: brīd′lest*.
Plus hide, lest, etc.

ID′LEST

f: fid′dlest*.
r: rid′dlest*, un-rid′dlest*.
tw: twid′dlest*.
Plus hid, lest, etc.

ĪD′LETH

Vowel: īd′leth*.
br: brīd′leth*.

ID′LETH

f: fid′dleth*.
r: rid′dleth*, un-rid′dleth*.
tw: twid′dleth*.

ĪD′LY

br: brīde′ly.
w: wīde′ly.
Plus pride, Lee *or* lea, etc.

ĪD′LING

Vowel: īd′ling.
br: brīd′ling.
s: sīd′ling.

ID′LING

d: did′dling.
f: fid′dling.
k(ç): kid′ling.
m: mid′dling.
p: pid′dling.
r: rid′dling.
tw: twid′dling.

ID′LINGZ

m: mid′dlingṣ.
Plus id′ling+s.

(Choose only one word out of each group)

ĪD′LĪT

g: guīde līght.
s: sīde līght.
Plus spied light, etc.

ĪD′LŨR

Vowel: īd′lẽr.
br: brīd′lẽr.

ID′LŨR

d: did′dlẽr.
f: fid′dlẽr.
p: pid′dlẽr.
r: rid′dlẽr.
t: tid′dlẽr, Tom Tid′dlẽr.
tw: twid′dlẽr.

ĪD′NES

p: pīed′ness.
w: wīde′ness.

ID′NI

k(ç): kid′ney.
s: Sid′ney, Syd′ney.
Plus hid knee, etc.

Ī′DŌ

d: Dī′dō.
f: Fī′dō.
Plus try dough *or* doe, etc.
Plus bride owe *or* O, etc.

ID′Ō

k(ç): kid′dō.
w: wid′ōw.
Plus did owe *or* O, etc.

Ī′DŎN

g: guī′dŏn (gī′).
s: Pō-seī′dŏn, Sī′dŏn.
Cf. wīd′en, Leyden.
Plus spied on *or* an, etc.
Plus Hi, Don, etc.

ID′ŎNZ

s: Sid′dŏnṣ.
Cf. id′ăns.

Ī′DŎR

n: nī′dŏr.
str: strī′dŏr.
Plus tried, or *or* Orr, etc.
Cf. id ur.

ĪD′RŮL

sl: slīde′⸗rùle.
Plus abide rule, etc.
Plus why drool, etc.

ĪD′ŨR

Vowel: eīd′ẽr.
ch: chīd′ẽr.
f: çŏn-fīd′ẽr.
g: guīd′ẽr (gīd′), mis-guīd′ẽr.
gl: glīd′ẽr.
h: hīd′ẽr.
l: çŏl-līd′ẽr, ē-līd′ẽr.
r: dē-rīd′ẽr, out′rīd-ẽr, rīd′ẽr,
    Rŏugh Rīd′ẽr (ruf).
s: cī′dẽr, çō-in-cīd′ẽr, dē-cīd′ẽr,
    in-sīd′ẽr, ŏne′⸗sīd′ẽr (wun′),
    out-sīd′ẽr, sīd′ẽr, sub-sīd′ẽr.
shn: Ṣchneīd′ẽr.
sl: back-slīd′ẽr, slīd′ẽr.
sn: Snī′dẽr, Snȳ′dẽr.
sp: spī′dẽr.
str: bē-strīd′ẽr, strīd′ẽr.
v: di-vīd′ẽr, prō-vīd′ẽr,
    sub-di-vīd′ẽr.
w: Ful-en-wīd′ẽr, wīd′ẽr.
z: prē-ṣīd′ẽr, rē-ṣīd′ẽr.
Plus tied her, etc.

ID′ŨR

b: bid′dẽr, fŏr-bid′dẽr,
    out-bid′dẽr, ō-vẽr-bid′dẽr,
    un-dẽr-bid′dẽr.

527 ūse, bṳll, brúte. tŭrn, up; crȳ, myth; çat, maçhine, ace,
church, çhord; ġem, aṅger, (Fr.) boṅ, aṣ; THis, thin; aẓure

ID′ŪRD
Ī′ET

(Choose only one word out of each group)

k(ç): kid′dẽr.
r: rid′dẽr.
s: çon-sid′ẽr.
sk: skid′dẽr.
Plus slid her, etc.

ID′ŪRD

s: çŏn-sid′ẽred,
 ill′=çŏn-sid′ẽred, un-çŏn-sid′ẽred.
Plus skidder′d, etc.

Ī′E

w: Hä-waī′ĭ (-wī′ē).
Cf. Hatay.

Ī′ENS

s: scī′ence.
Cf. ī′ăns.

Ī′ENT

f: çȧ-lor-i-fī′ent.
kl: çlī′ent.
s: in-scī′ent, scī′ent.
Cf. ī′ant.

Ī′EST

Vowel: eȳ′est*.
b: buȳ′est*.
d: bē-dȳ′est*, dī′est*, dȳ′est*.
dr: drī′est.
f: am′pli-fī-est*, beaū′ti-fī-est*,
 brút′i-fī-est*, cẽr′ti-fī-est*,
 çlar′i-fī-est*, çlas′si-fī-est*,
 çrú′ci-fī-est*, dē-fī′est*,
 dē′i-fī-est*, dig′ni-fī-est*,
 di-vẽr′si-fī-est*, ed′i-fī-est*,
 ē-leç′tri-fī-est*, fạl′si-fī-est*,
 for′ti-fī-est*, glōr′i-fī-est*,
 grat′i-fī-est*, hor′ri-fī-est*,
 ī-den′ti-fī-est*, jus′ti-fī-est*,
 li′quē-fī-est*, mag′ni-fī-est*,
 mod′i-fī-est*, mol′li-fī-est*,

 mor′ti-fī-est*, mys′ti-fī-est*,
 nōt′i-fī-est*, nul′li-fī-est*,
 os′si-fī-est*, pac′i-fī-est*,
 pẽr-son′i-fī-est*, pūr′i-fī-est*,
 quäl′i-fī-est*, rat′i-fī-est*,
 reç′ti-fī-est*, sañç′ti-fī-est*,
 sat′is-fī-est*, sig′ni-fī-est*,
 sim′pli-fī-est*, spec′i-fī-est*,
 stū′pē-fī-est*, ter′ri-fī-est*,
 tes′ti-fī-est*, typ′i-fī-est*,
 ver′i-fī-est*, vẽr′si-fī-est*,
 vil′i-fī-est*, vi′tri-fī-est*.
fl: flī′est*.
fr: frī′est*.
h: hī′est*, hīgh′est (hī′).
kr: çrī′est*, dē-çrī′est*.
l: al-lī′est*, bē-lī′est*, lī′est*,
 rē-lī′est*.
n: dē-nī′est*, nīgh′est (nī′).
p: oç′çū-pī-est*.
pl: ap-plī′est*, çŏm-plī′est*,
 im-plī′est*, mul′ti-plī-est*,
 plī′est*, rē-plī′est*, sup-plī′est*.
pr: prȳ′est*.
r: aw-rȳ′est, wrȳ′est.
s: pro′phē-sī-est*, sīgh′est (sī′)*.
sh: shȳ′est.
skr(sçr): dē-sçrī′est*.
sl: slȳ′est.
sp: bē-spȳ′est*, es-pī′est*,
 spȳ′est*.
spr: sprȳ′est.
t: tī′est*, un-tī′est*.
tr: trȳ′est*.
v: out-vī′est*, vī′est*.

Ī′ET

d: dī′et.
kw: dis-quī′et, in-quī′et,
 quī′et, un-quī′et.
p: pī′et.

(Choose only one word out of each group)

r: rī′ŏt.
Cf. ī′ăt.
Plus pie et, etc.

Ī′ETH

Vowel: eȳ′eth*.
b: buȳ′eth*.
d: bē-dȳ′eth*, dī′eth*, dȳ′eth*.
dr: drī′eth*.
f: am′pli-fī-eth*, plus all words in
   the F group under i′est, with
   termination changed to eth.
fl: flī′eth*.
fr: frī′eth*.
h: hī′eth*.
kr: c̗rī′eth*, dē-c̗rī′eth*.
l: al-lī′eth*, bē-lī′eth*, lī′eth*,
   rē-lī′eth*.
n: dē-nī′eth*.
p: oc̗-c̗ū-pī′eth*.
pl: ap-plī′eth*, c̗ŏm-plī′eth*,
   im-plī′eth*, mul′ti-plī-eth*,
   plī′eth*, rē-plī′eth*,
   sup-plī′eth*.
pr: prȳ′eth*.
s: pro′phē-sī-eth*, sīgh′eth (sī′)*.
sh: shȳ′eth*.
skr(sc̗r): dē-sc̗rī′eth*.
sp: bē-spȳ′eth*, es-pī′eth*,
   spȳ′eth*.
t: tī′eth*, un-tī′eth*.
tr: trȳ′eth*.
v: out-vī′eth*, vī′eth*.

ĬF′EN, ĬF′ŎN

h: hȳ′phen.
s: sī′phŏn.
t: Tȳ′phŏn.
Plus wife on *or* an, etc.
Plus dry fen, etc.

IF′EN, IF′ŎN

gr: grif′fŏn.
st: stif′fen.
Cf. if′n.
Cf. if an *or* on, etc.

IF′EST

hw: whif′fest*.
sn: snif′fest*.
st: stif′fest.

IF′ET

hw: whif′fet.
Cf. sniff it, etc.

IF′ETH

hw: whif′feth.
sn: snif′feth.

IF′I

j: jif′fy.
kl: c̗lif′fy.
sn: snif′fy.
sp: spif′fy.
skw: squif′fy.
Plus if he, etc.

IF′IK

Vowel: dē-if′ic̗.
b: mọr-bif′ic̗, rů-bif′ic̗,
   tȧ-bif′ic̗.
br: ten-ē-brif′ic̗.
d: ac̗-i-dif′ic̗, gran-dif′ic̗,
   lap-i-dif′ic̗.
gl: an-ȧ-glyph′ic̗, dī-ȧ-glyph′ic̗,
   glyph′ic̗, hī″ĕr-ō-glyph′ic̗,
   lith-ō-glyph′ic̗, pe-trō-glyph′ic̗,
   phō-tō-glyph′ic̗, phȳ-tō-glyph′ic̗,
   trī-glyph′ic̗.
j: al-ġif′ic̗.
l: mel-lif′ic̗, prō-lif′ic̗.

(Choose only one word out of each group)

n: çor-nif'iç, dam-nif'iç, fi-nif'iç, mag-nif'iç, om-nif'iç, som-nif'iç, vul-nif'iç.

r: ạu-rif'iç, çal-ō-rif'iç, çŏl-ŏ-rif'iç, do-lŏr-if'iç, friġ-ō-rif'iç, hon-ŏ-rif'iç, hor-rif'iç, hū-mŏ-rif'iç, mī-rif'iç, saç-rif'iç, son-ō-rif'iç, sap-ō-rif'iç, sō-pō-rif'iç, sū-dŏ-rif'iç, ter-rif'iç, tor-pŏ-rif'iç, vāp-ŏ-rif'iç.

s: çlas-sif'iç, lū-cif'iç, mū-cif'iç, os-sif'iç, pạ-cif'iç, pul-sif'iç, sen-sif'iç, siç-cif'iç, spē-cif'iç.

t: bē-ạ-tif'iç, in″çō-hē-ren-tif'iç, laç-tif'iç, pon-tif'iç, scī-en-tif'iç.

tr: pē-trif'iç.

v: sal-vif'iç, vī-vif'iç.

IF'IN

b: bif'fin.
gr: grif'fin.
t: tif'fin.
Cf. if'en, if'on.
Plus stuff in *or* inn, etc.
Cf. stiff fin, etc.

IF'ING

hw: whif'fing.
sn: snif'fing.
t: tif'fing.

IF'ISH

m: mif'fish.
sn: snif'fish.
st: stif'fish.
t: tif'fish.

skw: squif'fish.
Cf. if fish, etc.

I'FL

Vowel: Eif'fel.
r: rī'fle.
st: stī'fle.
tr: trī'fle.
Plus eye full, I full, etc.
Cf. life full, etc.
Plus wife'll, etc.

IF'L

hw: whif'fle.
p: pif'fle.
r: rif'fle.
sn: snif'fle.
Plus tiff'll, etc.
Cf. Riff full, etc.

ĪF'LES

f: fīfe'less.
l: līfe'less.
n: knīfe'less (nīf').
str: strīfe'less.
w: wīfe'less.
Plus fife less, etc.

ĪF'LI

r: rīfe'ly.
w: wīfe'ly.
Plus strife, Lee *or* lea, etc.

ĪF'LĪK

l: līfe'līke.
w: wīfe'līke.
Plus strife like, etc.

ĪF'LING

r: rī'fling.
st: stī'fling.
tr: trī'fling.

IF'LING
IF'TŎN

fāte, fär, fȧst, fȧll, finăl, cãre, at; mēte, prĕy, hẽr, met; pīne,
marïne, bĭrd, pin; nōte, mȯve, fȯr, atŏm, not; mo͞on, book;

530

(Choose only one word out of each group)

IF'LING

hw: whif'fling.
p: pif'fling.
r: rif'ffing.
sn: snif'fling.

ĪF'LŨR

r: rīf'lẽr.
st: stīf'lẽr.
tr: trīf'lẽr.

IF'LŨR

hw: whif'flẽr.
p: pif'flẽr.
r: rif'flẽr.
sn: snif'flẽr.

ĪF'ŎN, ĪF'EN

h: hȳ'phen.
s: sī'phŏn.
t: Tȳ'phŏn.
Plus wife on *or* an, etc.

IF'TED

dr: drif'ted.
g: gif'ted, un-gif'ted.
l: lif'ted, up-lif'ted.
r: rif'ted.
sh: shif'ted.
s: sif'ted.
Plus if, Ted.

IF'TEST

dr: drif'test*.
l: lif'test*, up-lif'test*.
r: rif'test*.
sh: shif'test*.
s: sif'test*.
sw: swif'test.
Plus sniff test, etc.

IF'TETH

dr: drif'teth*.
l: lif'teth*, up-lif'teth*.
r: rif'teth*.
sh: shif'teth*.
s: sif'teth*.

IF'TI

dr: drif'ty.
f: fif'ty, fif-ty⸗fif'ty.
kl: c̦lif'ty.
n: nif'ty.
r: rif'ty.
sh: shif'ty.
thr: thrif'ty.
Plus drift, he, etc.
Plus sniff tea, etc.

IF'TING

dr: drift'ing.
l: lif'ting, shop'lif-ting,
up-lif'ting.
r: rif'ting.
sh: shift'ing.
s: sif'ting.

IFT'LES

dr: drift'less.
r: rift'less.
sh: shift'less.
thr: thrift'less.
Plus sniffed less, etc.

IFT'NES

sw: swift'ness.

IF'TŎN

kl: C̦lif'tŏn.
Plus drift on *or* an, etc.
Plus if ton *or* tun, etc.

(Choose only one word out of each group)

IF'THO̧NG

d: diph'tho̧ng.
tr: triph'tho̧ng.
Plus sniff thong, etc.

IF'TŪR

dr: drif'tẽr.
l: lif'tẽr, shop'lif-tẽr, up-lif'tẽr.
s: sif'tẽr.
sh: scēne'shif-tẽr, shif'tẽr.
sw: swift'ẽr.
Plus sniffed her *or* err, etc.

ĪF'ŨR

f: fīf'ẽr.
l: līf'ẽr.
n: knīf'ẽr (nīf').
r: rīf'ẽr.
s: cī'phẽr, dē-cī'phẽr.
Plus strife her *or* err, etc.
Plus try fur *or* fir, etc.
Cf. try for, etc.

IF'ŨR

d: dif'fẽr.
sn: snif'fẽr.
st: stif'fẽr.
Plus biff her *or* err, etc.

Ī'GÅ

s: saī'gà.

IG'AND

br: brig'ănd.
Plus fig and, etc.

IG'ĂT

fr: frig'ăte.
Cf. big'ŏt.
Cf. dig it, etc.
Plus pig ate *or* eight, etc.
Cf. big gate, etc.

IG'BI

d: Dig'by.
Plus big bee *or* be, etc.

IG'EST

b: big'gest.
d: dig'gest*.
j: jig'gest*.
n: rē-neg'est (-nig')*.
r: rig'gest*.
sw: swig'gest*.
tr: trig'gest.

IG'ETH

d: dig'geth*
j: jig'geth*.
n: rē-neg'eth (-nig')*.
r: rig'geth*.
sw: swig'geth*.

IG'I

b: big'gy.
p: pig'gy.
spr: sprig'gy.
tw: twig'gy.
w: pig'gy=wig'gy.
Plus big he, etc.

IG'ING

d: dig'ging.
g: gig'ging.
j: jig'ging.
r: rig'ging, thim'ble-rig-ging,
  un-rig'ging.
spr: sprig'ging.
sw: swig'ging.
tr: trig'ging.
tw: twig'ging.
w: wig'ging.

IG'INZ
IG'NĂNT

fāte, fär, fȧst, fȧll, finăl, cãre, at; mēte, prey, hẽr, met; pīne,
marïne, bĭrd, pin; nōte, mōve, fọr, atŏm, not; mọọn, book;

532

(Choose only one word out of each group)

IG'INZ

dw: Dwig′ginṣ.
h: Hig′ginṣ.
w: Wig′ginṣ.

IG'ISH

hw: whig′gish.
p: pig′gish.
pr: prig′gish.
Plus swig, Gish, etc.

IG'L

g: gig′gle.
h: hig′gle.
j: jig′gle.
n: nig′gle.
r: wrig′gle.
skw: squig′gle.
sn: snig′gle.
w: wig′gle.
Plus pig'll, etc.

Ī'GLAS

Vowel: eȳe′glass.
sp: spȳ′glass.
Plus try glass, etc.

IG'LD

g: gig′gled.
h: hig′gled.
j: jig′gled.
n: nig′gled.
r: wrig′gled.
skw: squig′gled.
sn: snig′gled.
w: wig′gled.

IG'LEST

g: gig′glest*, etc. See list above.
Cf. pig, lest, etc.

IG'LETH

g: gig′gleth*, etc. See list above.

IG'LI

g: gig′gly, etc. See list above.
w: Pig′gly Wig′gly.
Plus fig, Lee or lea, etc.

ĪG'LIF

d: dī′glyph.
tr: mon-ō-trī′glyph, trī′glyph.

IG'LING

g: gig′gling, etc. See list above.

IG'LŪR

g: gig′glẽr, etc. See list above.

IG'MȦ

n: ē-nig′mȧ.
s: sig′mȧ.
st: stig′mȧ.
Plus pig, ma, etc.

IG'MENT

f: fig′ment.
p: pig′ment.
Plus sprig meant, etc.

IG'MI

p: pyg′my.
Cf. big me, etc.

IG'NĂL

s: sig′năl.

IG'NANS

l: mȧ-lig′nănce.
Plus pig, Nance, etc.

IG'NĂNT

d: in-dig′nănt.
l: mȧ-lig′nănt.
n: bē-nig′nănt.

(Choose only one word out of each group)

IG'NET

s: cyg'net, sig'net.
Plus big net, etc.

IG'NĪT

l: lig'nīte.
Plus big night, etc.

IG'NUM

l: lig'num.
s: eç'çē sig'num.
Plus pig numb, etc.

Ī'GŌ

Vowel: Ī'gōe.
sl: Slī'gō.
Plus why go, etc.

IG'O

l: çà-lig'ō, fū-lig'ō, Lō-lig'ō.
t: im-pē-tig'ō, vēr-tig'ō.
Plus pig owe *or* O, etc.

Ī'GǪN

b: bȳ'gǫne.
tr: trī'gǫne.
Plus sky gone, etc.

IG'ǑN

b: big"un.
l: Lig'ŏn.
Plus pig on *or* an, etc.

IG'ǑR

r: rig'ŏr.
v: vig'ŏr.
Cf. ig'ūr.
Plus pig, or, etc.

IG'ǑT

b: big'ŏt.
j: ġig'ŏt.

sp: spig'ŏt.
Cf. frig'ate.
Cf. rig it *or* at, etc.

Ī'GRES

t: tī'gress.
Cf. dī'gress.

Ī'GŪR

n: Nī'gēr.
t: tī'gēr.

IG'ŪR

f: çǒn-fig'ūre, dis-fig'ūre, fig'ūre, prē-fig'ūre, trans-fig'ūre.
l: lig'ūre.
Plus rig your *or* you're, etc.

IG'ŨR

b: big'gēr.
ch: chig'gēr.
d: dig'gēr, gōld dig'gēr, grāve'dig-gēr.
f: "fig'gēr".
g: gig'gēr.
j: jig'gēr.
l: lig'gēr.
n: nig'gēr.
pr: prig'gēr.
r: mär'ket rig'gēr, out'rig-gēr, rig'gēr, rig'ŏr, thim'ble-rig-gēr.
sn: snig'gēr.
spr: sprig'gēr.
sw: swig'gēr.
tr: trig'gēr.
tw: twig'gēr.
v: vig'ŏr.
Plus twig her *or* err, etc.

IG'ŨRD

f: "fig'gēred".
j: bē-jig'gēred, jig'gēred.
n: nig'gărd, un-nig'gărd.

Ī'ING

fāte, fär, fȧst, fạll, fină̇l, cāre, at; mēte, prey, hẽr, met; pīne,
marīne, bĭrd, pĭn; nōte, mŏve, fọr, atŏm, nŏt; moon, book;

534

(Choose only one word out of each group)

sn: snig'gẽred.
Plus vigor'd, etc.

Ī'ING

Vowel: eȳe'ing, Ī'ing.
b: al'i-bī-ing, buȳ'ing, bȳ'ing,
hush'ȧ-bȳ-ing, lul'lȧ-bȳ-ing,
un-dẽr-buȳ'ing.
d: bē-dȳ'ing, dȳe'ing, dȳ'ing,
un-dȳ'ing.
dr: ȧ-drȳ'ing, drȳ'ing.
f: ac-id'i-fȳ-ing, am'pli-fȳ-ing,
bē-at'i-fȳ-ing, beaū'ti-fȳ-ing,
brŭ'ti-fȳ-ing, çan'di-fȳ-ing,
cẽr'ti-fȳ-ing, çlar'i-fȳ-ing,
çlas'si-fȳ-ing, çod'i-fȳ-ing,
çŏun'tri-fȳ-ing, çrŭ'ci-fȳ-ing,
dam'ni-fȳ-ing, dan'di-fȳ-ing,
dē-fȳ'ing, dē'i-fȳ-ing,
dig'ni-fȳ-ing, dis-quäl'i-fȳ-ing,
dis-sat'is-fȳ-ing, di-vẽr'si-fȳ-ing,
dul'ci-fȳ-ing, ed'i-fȳ-ing,
ē-leç'tri-fȳ-ing, ē-mul'si-fȳ-ing,
ex-em'pli-fȳ-ing, fạl'si-fȳ-ing,
fọr'ti-fȳ-ing, French'i-fȳ-ing,
fruç'ti-fȳ-ing, fȳ'ing,
glō'ri-fȳ-ing, grat'i-fȳ-ing,
hor'ri-fȳ-ing, hū-man'i-fȳ-ing.
ī-den'ti-fȳ-ing, in-dem'ni-fȳ-ing,
in-ten'si-fȳ-ing, jus'ti-fȳ-ing,
lab'i-fȳ-ing, li'quē-fȳ-ing,
mag'ni-fȳ-ing, mod'i-fȳ-ing,
mol'li-fȳ-ing, mọr'ti-fȳ-ing,
mys'ti-fȳ-ing, nōt'i-fȳ-ing,
nul'li-fȳ-ing, os'si-fȳ-ing,
pac'i-fȳ-ing, pẽr-son'i-fȳ-ing,
pe'tri-fȳ-ing, preach'i-fȳ-ing,
pū'ri-fȳ-ing, pū'trē-fȳ-ing,
quäl'i-fȳ-ing, ram'i-fȳ-ing,
rãr'ē-fȳ-ing, rat'i-fȳ-ing,

reç'ti-fȳ-ing, rē-viv'i-fȳ-ing,
sañç'ti-fȳ-ing, sat'is-fȳ-ing,
sçar'i-fȳ-ing, sçōr'i-fȳ-ing,
self=sat'is-fȳ-ing, sig'ni-fȳ-ing,
sim'pli-fȳ-ing, sol-id'i-fȳ-ing,
spec'i-fȳ-ing, stul'ti-fȳ-ing,
stū'pē-fȳ-ing, ter'ri-fȳ-ing,
tes'ti-fȳ-ing, tọr'pi-fȳ-ing,
tor'rē-fȳ-ing, typ'i-fȳ-ing,
ūn'i-fȳ-ing, un-sat'is-fȳ-ing,
ver'i-fȳ-ing, vẽr'si-fȳ-ing,
vil'i-fȳ-ing, vi'tri-fȳ-ing,
viv'i-fȳ-ing.
fl: but'tẽr-flȳ-ing, flȳ'ing,
kīte'flȳ-ing.
fr: frȳ'ing.
g: guȳ'ing (gī').
h: hīe'ing.
kr: çrȳ'ing, dē-çrȳ'ing,
out-çrȳ'ing, un-çrȳ'ing.
l: al-lȳ'ing, bē-lȳ'ing, lȳ'ing,
out'lȳ-ing, rē-lȳ'ing,
self=rē-lȳ'ing, un'dẽr-lȳ-ing.
n: dē-nȳ'ing, self=dē-nȳ'ing.
p: oç'çū-pȳ-ing, pī'ing,
prē-oç'çū-pȳ-ing.
pl: ap-plȳ'ing, çŏm-plȳ'ing,
im-plȳ'ing, mul'ti-plȳ-ing,
plȳ'ing, rē-plȳ'ing,
sup-plȳ'ing, un-çŏm-plȳ'ing.
pr: prȳ'ing.
s: pro'phē-sȳ-ing,
sīgh'ing (sī'), un-sīgh'ing.
sh: shȳ'ing.
sk: skȳ'ing.
skr(scr): dē-sçrȳ'ing.
sp: bē-spȳ'ing, e-spȳ'ing,
spȳ'ing.
t: tīe'ing, un-tȳ'ing.
tr: trȳ'ing.
v: out-vȳ'ing, vīe'ing.

(Choose only one word out of each group)

Ĭ'JÅ

b: Å-bĭ'jàh.
l: Ē-lĭ'jàh.
Plus oblige a, etc.

Ĭ'JAK

h: hĭgh'jack (hĭ'),
Plus try, Jack or jack, etc.

Ĭ'JEST

bl: dis-ō-blĭġ'est*, ō-blĭġ'est*.
d: dĭ'ġest.
Plus try jest, etc.

IJ'ID

fr: frĭġ'id.
r: riġ'id.

IJ'IL

s: siġ'il.
str: striġ'il.
v: viġ'il.
Plus midge'll, etc.

ĪJ'ING

bl: dis-ō-blĭġ'ing, ō-blĭġ'ing.

IJ'ING

br: à-bridġ'ing, bridġ'ing.
r: ridġ'ing.

IJ'IT

Vowel: "ij'jit".
br: Bridġ'et, Brĭġ'it.
d: diġ'it.
f: fidġ'et.
m: midġ'et.
Plus bridge it, etc.

IJ'ŎN

l: ir-rē-liġ'iŏn, rē-liġ'iŏn.
p: piġ'eŏn.

w: widġ'eŏn.
Plus bridge on or an, etc.

IJ'ŪR

br: à-bridġ'ẽr, bridġ'ẽr.
Plus midge err or her, etc.

IJ'US

d: prō-diġ'ious.
l: ir-rē-liġ'ious, rē-liġ'ious.
t: lĭ-tiġ'ious.
Cf. saç-ri-lēġ'ious.
Plus bridge us, etc.

Ī'KÅ

l: bal-à-laĭ'kà.
m: mĭ'çà, Mĭ'çàh.
p: pĭ'çà,· pĭ'kà.
r: lō-rĭ'çà.
sp: spĭ'çà.
Plus strike a, etc.

ĪK'ÅL

m: Çär-mĭçh'ăel, Mĭçh'ăel.
Plus strike'll, etc.
Cf. ĭk'l.

IK'ÅRD

l: liqu'ŏred.
p: Pick'ărd.
r: Rick'ărd.
Plus picker'd, etc.
Cf. pick hard, etc.
Cf. ik'ūrà.

IK'ĀT

s: ex'siç-çāte*, siç'çāte.
Cf. tick, Kate, etc.
Plus tick ate or eight, etc.

IK'ED

w: wick'ed.
Plus nick, Ed, etc.
Plus ik+ed*.

ĬK'EN
IK'I

fāte, fär, fȧst, fạll, finăl, cãre, at; mēte, prĕy, hẽr, met; pīne,
marĭne, bĭrd, pin; nōte, mŏve, fọr, atŏm, not; mọọn, book;   536

(Choose only one word out of each group)

ĪK'EN

l: līc̲h'en, lĭk'en, un-lĭk'en.
Plus my ken, etc.
Cf. strike hen, etc.

IK'EN

ch: chick'en.
kw: quick'en.
s: sick'en.
str: hor'rŏr=strick-en, strick'en,
  ter'rŏr=strick-en,
  wŏn'dĕr=strick-en.
th: thick'en.
w: wick'en.
Cf. stick hen, etc.

IK'ENZ

ch: chick'ens̲.
d: Dick'ens̲, the dick'ens̲.
sl: slick'ens̲.
Plus ik'en+s.

ĪK'EST

bl: ō-blīqu'est.
l: dis-lĭk'est*, lĭk'est*.
sp: spĭk'est*.
str: strīk'est*.

IK'EST

kl: c̲lick'est*.
fl: flick'est*.
k(c̲): kick'est*.
kw: quick'est.
l: lick'est*.
p: pick'est*.
pr: prick'est*.
sl: slick'est.
st: stick'est*.
t: tick'est*.
th: thick'est.
tr: trick'est*.

IK'ET

kl: c̲lick'et.
kr: c̲rick'et.
p: pick'et, Pick'ett.
pr: prick'et, Prick'ett.
r: Rick'ett.
t: tick'et, wạlk'ing tick'et (wạk').
th: thick'et.
w: wick'et, wick'et.
Plus stick et, etc.
Cf. stick it, etc.

ĪK'ETH

l: dis-lĭk'eth*, lĭk'eth*.
sp: spĭk'eth*.
str: strĭk'eth*.

IK'ETH

fl: flick'eth*.
k: kick'eth*.
kl: c̲lick'eth*.
l: lick'eth*.
p: pick'eth*.
pr: prick'eth*.
st: stick'eth*.
t: tick'eth*.
tr: trick'eth*.

IK'ETS

r: rick'ets.
Plus ik'et+s.
Plus Pickett's, etc.

Ī'KI

sp: spĭk'y.
Cf. Psy'che.
Plus like, he, etc.
Plus my key, etc.

IK'I

br: brick'y.
d: dick'ey.

(Choose only one word out of each group)

f: Fick′ē.
h: do̦o̦′hick-ey.
kw: quick′ie.
n: Nick′y.
r: ġin rick′ey, rick′ey.
st: stick′y.
t: Rik′ki=Tik-ki.
tr: trick′y.
v: Vick′i.
Plus trick he, etc.

Ī′KIK

s: psȳ′c̦hic̦ (sī′).
Plus try kick, etc.

Ī′KIKS

s: psȳ′c̦hic̦s (sī′).
Plus sly kicks, etc.

ĪK′ING

b: bīk′ing.
d: dȳk′ing.
h: hīk′ing, hitch′hīk-ing.
l: dis-līk′ing, līk′ing, mis-līk′ing,
well′=līk′ing.
p: pīk′ing.
sp: spīk′ing.
str: strīk′ing.
v: vīk′ing.
Plus my king, etc.

IK′ING

br: brick′ing.
fl: flick′ing.
k: hīgh kick′ing (hī′), kick′ing.
kl: c̦lick′ing.
kr: c̦rick′ing.
l: lick′ing.
n: nick′ing.
p: hand′=pick-ing, pick′ing,
pock′et pick′ing.

pr: prick′ing.
s: sic̦′c̦ing.
sl: slick′ing.
sn: snick′ing.
st: bē-stick′ing, pig′stick-ing,
stick′ing,
wa̦lk′ing stick′ing (wa̦k′).
t: tick′ing.
th: thick′ing.
tr: trick′ing.
w: wick′ing.

IK′ISH

br: brick′ish.
s: sick′ish.
sl: slick′ish.
th: thick′ish.

ĪK′L

m: Mīc̦h′ăel.
s: cȳ′c̦le, ep′i-cȳ-c̦le,
psȳ′c̦hăl (sī′).
Plus strike ′ll.

IK′L

ch: chic̦′le.
f: fick′le.
m: mick′le.
n: nick′el.
p: pick′le.
pr: prick′le.
s: sick′le.
st: stick′le.
str: strick′le.
t: tick′le.
tr: trick′le.
Plus flick′ll, etc.

IK′LEST

f: fick′lest.
p: pick′lest*.
pr: prick′lest*.
s: sick′lest*.

(Choose only one word out of each group)

st: stick'lest*.
t: tick'lest*.
tr: trick'lest*.
Plus quick, lest, etc.

IK'LETH

p: pick'leth*.
pr: prick'leth*.
s: sick'leth*.
st: stick'leth*.
t: tick'leth*.
tr: trick'leth*.

ĪK'LI

bl: ō-blīque'ly.
l: bē-līke'ly, līke'ly, un-līke'ly.
Plus strike Lee *or* lea, etc.

IK'LI

kw: quick'ly.
pr: prick'ly.
s: sick'ly.
sl: slick'ly.
st: stick'ly.
th: thick'ly.
tr: trick'ly.
Plus quick, Lee *or* lea, etc.

ĪK'LIK

s: bī-cȳc'liç, cȳc'liç, en-cȳc'liç,
ep-i-cȳc'liç, gē-ō-cȳc'liç.
Plus Mike lick, etc.
Plus my click, etc.

ĪK'LING

s: cȳc'ling.

IK'LING

ch: chick'ling.
p: pick'ling.
pr: prick'ling.
t: tick'ling.
tr: trick'ling.

IK'LISH

pr: prick'lish.
t: tick'lish.

ĪK'LIST

s: cȳ'çlist.
Plus strike list, etc.

Ī'KLŌN

s: cȳ'çlōne.
Plus Mike, lone *or* loan, etc.

IK'LŨR

f: fick'lêr.
pr: prick'lêr.
st: stick'lêr.
str: strick'lêr.
t: tick'lêr.

ĪK'NES

bl: ō-blīque'ness.
l: līke'ness, un-līke'ness.

IK'NES

kw: quick'ness.
s: lŏve'sick-ness, sick'ness.
sl: slick'ness.
th: thick'ness.

IK'NIK

p: piç'niç.
str: strych'niç.
Plus stick Nick *or* nick, etc.

IK'NIN

str: strych'nine.

IK'NING

kw: quicke'ning.
s: sicke'ning.
th: thicke'ning.

(Choose only one word out of each group)

Ī'KON

Vowel: ī'ċon.
Plus strike on, etc.
Plus sky con, etc.

Ī'KOR

Vowel: ī'ċhor.
Plus strike, or, etc.

Ī'KOUNT

v: vīs'ċount (vī').
Plus my count, etc.

IK'SEN

m: mix'en.
v: vix'en.
Cf. sticks an, etc.
Plus sticks on, etc.

IK'SEST

f: af-fix'est*, fix'est*,
  prē-fix'est*, trans-fix'est*.
m: in-tēr-mix'est*, mix'est.

IK'SET

kw: quick'set.
th: thick'set.
Plus trick set, etc.

IK'SETH

f: af-fix'eth*, fix'eth*,
  prē-fix'eth*, trans-fix'eth*.
m: in-tēr-mix'eth*, mix'eth*.

IK'SHUN

d: ad-diċ'tion, ben-ē-diċ'tion,
  ċon-trȧ-diċ'tion, diċ'tion,
  in-diċ'tion, in-tēr-diċ'tion,
  jṳ-ris-diċ'tion, mal-ē-diċ'tion,
  prē-diċ'tion, val-ē-diċ'tion.

f: af-fix'iŏn, ċrṳ-ci-fix'iŏn,
  fiċ'tion, prē-fix'iŏn,
  suf-fix'iŏn, trans-fix'iŏn.
fl: af-fliċ'tion, ċŏn-fliċ'tion,
  in-fliċ'tion.
fr: af-friċ'tion, friċ'tion.
l: der-e-liċ'tion, rē-liċ'tion.
p: dē-piċ'tion.
str: ab-striċ'tion, ċŏn-striċ'tion,
  ob-striċ'tion, rē-striċ'tion.
v: ċŏn-viċ'tion, ē-viċ'tion.
Plus trick shun, etc.

IK'SHUS

d: ċon-trȧ-diċ'tious.
f: fiċ'tious*.

IK'SI

d: Dix'ey, Dix'ie.
n: nix'ie, waṭ'ēr nix'ie.
p: pix'ie.
tr: trick'sy, Trix'ie.
Plus kicks, he, etc.
Plus trick, see, etc.

IK'SING

f: af-fix'ing, fix'ing,
  prē-fix'ing, trans-fix'ing.
m: ad-mix'ing, in-tēr-mix'ing,
  mix'ing.
Plus trick sing, etc.
Cf. tricks sing, etc.

IK'SŎN

d: Dick'sŏn, Dix'ŏn.
h: Hick'sŏn, Hix'ŏn.
Plus wicks on *or* an, etc.
Plus trick sun *or* son, etc.

IK'STI

s: ạll six'ty, six'ty.
Plus mix tea, etc.
Plus fixed, he, etc.

(Choose only one word out of each group)

IK'STŪR

f: af-fix'tūre, fix'tūre.

m: ad-mix'tūre, im-mix'tūre,
in-cŏm-mix'tūre,
in-tēr-mix'tūre, mix'tūre.
Plus mixed your *or* you're, etc.

IK'STŪR

tr: trick'stẽr.
Plus fixed her, etc.
Plus quick, stir, etc.

IK'SŨR

f: af-fix'ẽr, fix'ẽr, prē-fix'ẽr,
trans-fix'ẽr.

l: ē-lix'ïr.

m: in-tẽr-mix'ẽr, mix'ẽr.
Plus trick, sir, etc.
Plus tricks her *or* err, etc.

IK'TĀT

d: diç'tāte.

n: niç'tāte.
Plus quick, Tate, etc.
Plus tricked, ate *or* eight, etc.

IK'TED

d: ad-diç'ted, con-trȧ-diç'ted,
in-tẽr-diç'ted, prē-diç'ted.

fl: af-fliç'ted, cŏn-fliç'ted,
in-fliç'ted, self=in-fliç'ted.

l: rē-liç'ted.

p: dē-piç'ted.

str: cŏn-striç'ted, rē-striç'ted,
un-rē-striç'ted.

v: cŏn-viç'ted, ē-viç'ted.
Plus quick, Ted, etc.
Plus picked Ed, etc.

IK'TEST

d: ad-diç'test*, con-trȧ-diç'test*,
in-tẽr-diç'test*, prē-diç'test*.

fl: af-fliç'test*, cŏn-fliç'test*,
in-fliç'test*.

p: dē-piç'test*.

str: cŏn-striç'test*, rē-striç'test*,
striç'test.

v: cŏn-viç'test*, ē-viç'test*.
Plus quick test, etc.

IK'TETH

d: ad-diç'teth*, con-trȧ-diç'teth*,
in-tẽr-diç'teth*, prē-diç'teth*.

fl: af-fliç'teth*, cŏn-fliç'teth*,
in-fliç'teth*.

p: dē-piç'teth*.

str: cŏn-striç'teth*,
rē-striç'teth*.

v: cŏn-viç'teth*, ē-viç'teth*.

IK'TIK

Vowel: dē-iç'tiç, en-dē-iç'tiç,
ep-i-dē-iç'tiç, iç'tiç.

d: ap-ō-diç'tiç.
Plus quick tick, etc.

IK'TIM

v: viç'tim.
Plus quick, Tim, etc.
Plus tricked him, etc.

IK'TING

d: ad-diçt'ing, con-trȧ-diçt'ing,
in-tẽr-diçt'ing, prē-diçt'ing.

fl: af-fliç'ting, cŏn-fliçt'ing,
in-fliçt'ing.

p: dē-piçt'ing.

str: cŏn-striç'ting, rē-striç'ting.

v: cŏn-viçt'ing, ē-viç'ting.

IK'TIV

d: ad-diç'tive, ben-ē-diç'tive,
con-trȧ-diç'tive, in-diç'tive,

(Choose only one word out of each group)

in-tēr-diċ′tive, jṳ-ris-diċ′tive, prē-diċ′tive, vin-diċ′tive.
f: fiċ′tive.
fl: af-fliċ′tive, ċŏn-fliċ′tive, in-fliċ′tive.
p: dē-piċ′tive.
str: ċŏn-striċ′tive, rē-striċ′tive, un-rē-striċ′tive.
v: ċŏn-viċ′tive, ē-viċ′tive.

IKT′LI

l: der′e-liċt-ly.
str: striċt′ly.
Plus picked Lee *or* lea, etc.

IKT′NES

str: striċt′ness.

IK′TŎR

Cf. ik′tūr.

IK′TUM

d: diċ′tum, o′bi-tēr diċ′tum.
Plus restrict 'em, etc.
Plus kick tum, etc.

IK′TŪR

p: dē-piċ′tūre, im-piċ′tūre, piċ′tūre, wŏrd piċ′tūre.
str: striċ′tūre.
Plus kicked your *or* you're, etc.

IK′TŪR

d: ċon-trȧ-diċ′tēr, prē-diċ′tēr.
f: fiċ′tŏr*.
fl: af-fliċ′tēr, ċŏn-fliċ′tēr, in-fliċ′tēr.
l: liċ′tŏr.
p: dē-piċt′ēr, Piċ′tŏr.
str: bō′ȧ ċŏn-striċ′tŏr, ċŏn-striċ′tŏr, rē-striċ′tēr, striċ′tēr.

v: ċŏn-viċ′tēr, ē-viċ′tŏr, viċ′tŏr.
Plus picked her *or* err, etc.

IK′TUS

Vowel: iċ′tus.
d: Ben-ē-diċ′tus.
n: aċ-rō-nyċ′tous.
Plus picked us, etc.

ĪK′ŪR

b: bīk′ēr.
bl: ō-blīqu′ēr.
d: dīk′ēr.
h: hīk′ēr, hitch′hīk-ēr.
l: līk′ēr.
p: pīk′ēr.
r: Rīk′ēr.
sp: spīk′ēr.
str: strīk′ēr.
Plus like her *or* err, etc.
Plus why cur *or* Kerr, etc.

IK′ŨR

b: bick′ēr.
d: dick′ēr.
fl: flick′ēr.
k: hīgh kick′ēr (hĭ), kick′ēr.
kl: ċlick′ēr.
kw: quick′ēr.
l: lick′ēr, li′quŏr ('kēr).
n: dom′i-nick-ēr, knick′ēr (nik′), nick′ēr.
p: ber′ry-pick′ēr, pick′ēr.
pr: prick′ēr.
s: sick′ēr.
sl: slick′ēr.
sn: snick′ēr.
st: stick′ēr.
t: tick′ēr.
th: thick′ēr.
tr: trick′ēr.

IK′ŨRD
Ī′LÄRK

fāte, fär, fȧst, fạll, finăl, cāre, at; mēte, prey, hẽr, met; pīne,
marïne, bĭrd, pĭn; nōte, mŏve, fọr, atŏm,. not, mọọn, book;

542

(Choose only one word out of each group)

v: viç′ăr.
w: wick′ẽr.
Plus pick her *or* err, etc.

IK′ŨRD

l: liqu′ŏred (′kẽrd).
Plus ik′ũr+d.
Cf. ik′ărd.

IK′ŨRZ

n: knick′ẽrṣ (nik′).
Plus ik′ũr+s.

ĪK′US

p: Pīç′us.
sp: spīç′ous.
Plus like us, etc.
Plus why cuss, etc.

IK′WID

l: li′quid.
Plus pick wid, etc.

Ī′LȦ

Vowel: Ī′lȧ.
h: Hȳ′lȧ.
l: Dē-lī′lȧh, Lī′lȧ, Lī′lȧh.
Plus smile a, etc.

IL′Ȧ

Vowel: Il′lȧ.
b: Sy-bil′lȧ.
d: Bob′ȧ-dil-lȧ, cē-dil′lȧ,
çō-dil′lȧ, gran-ȧ-dil′lȧ,
sab-ȧ-dil′lȧ, sap-ō-dil′lȧ,
sẹ-guï-dil′lȧ (-gē-).
l: Lil′lȧ, Lil′lȧh.
m: är-mil′lȧ, bis-mil′lȧh,
Çȧ-mil′lȧ.
n: ȧ-nil′lȧ, grȧ-nil′lȧ, mȧ-nil′ȧ,
mȧ-nil′lȧ, vȧ-nil′lȧ.

r: bȧ-ril′lȧ, çam-ȧ-ril′lȧ,
ças-çȧ-ril′lȧ, gō-ril′lȧ,
guer-ril′lȧ (ge-), sär-sȧ-pȧ-ril′lȧ,
sas-pȧ-ril′lȧ.
s: Drú-sil′lȧ, Max-il′lȧ,
Pris-cil′lȧ, Scyl′lȧ.
t: flō-til′lȧ, man-til′lȧ, Til′lȧ.
v: vil′lȧ.
Plus kill a, etc.

Ī′LĂK

l: lī′lăç.
Plus why lack, etc.

Ī′LĂKS

l: lī′lăçs.
sm: smī′lăx.
Plus style ax *or* acts, etc.
Plus why lax, etc.

IL′ĂN

v: ärch vil′lăin, vil′lăin,
vil′lein.
Cf. il′ŏn.
Plus kill an *or* Ann, etc.

Ī′LĂND

Vowel: īs′lănd (ī′),
Lọng Īs′lănd, Rhōde Īs′lănd, etc.
h: hīgh′lănd (hī′).
r: Rȳ′lănd.
sk: skȳ land.
th: Thaī′land (thī′land).
Plus my land, etc.
Plus smile and, etc.

Ī′LÄRK

f: phȳ′lärch.
sk: skȳ′lärk.
Plus buy lark, etc.
Plus style ark *or* arc, etc.

(Choose only one word out of each group)

Ī'LĂS

s: Sī'lăs.
v: Vī'lăs.
Plus my lass, etc.
Plus Nile ass, etc.

Ī'LASH

Vowel: eȳe'lash.
Plus try lash, etc.
Plus style ash, etc.

IL'ĀT

s: pen-i-cil'lāte.
t: dis-til'lāte.
Plus ill eight *or* ate, etc.
Cf. Will, late, etc.

IL'BŬRT

f: fil'bẽrt.
g: Gil'bẽrt.
w: Wil'bẽrt.
Plus thrill Bert, etc.

IL'DȦ

h: Hil'dȧ.
t: Mȧ-thil'dȧ (-til'), Mȧ-til'dȧ.
Plus killed a, etc.

IL'DED

b: buil'ded (bil').
g: bē-gil'ded, gil'ded,
  guil'ded (gil'), un-gil'ded.
Plus still dead, etc.
Cf. Phil did, etc.
Plus stilled, Ed, etc.

ĪL'DEST

m: mīl'dest.
w: wīl'dest.

IL'DEST

b: buil'dest (bil')*.
g: bē-gil'dest*, gil'dest*.

IL'DETH

b: buil'deth (bil')*.
g: bē-gil'deth*, gil'deth*.
Plus still death, etc.

ĪLD'HOOD

ch: chīld'hood.
Plus styled hood, etc.

ĪL'DING

ch: chīl'ding.
w: wīl'ding.

IL'DING

b: buil'ding (bil'),
  ça̧s'tle⸗buil-ding,
  house'buil-ding, rē-buil'ding,
  ship'buil-ding, un-buil'ding.
g: bē-gil'ding, gil'ding,
  rē-gil'ding, un-gil'ding.

ĪL'DISH

ch: chīl'dish.
m: mīl'dish.
w: wīl'dish.
Plus style dish, etc.

ĪLD'LES

ch: chīld'ness.
m: mīld'less.
Plus styled less *or* Les, etc.

ĪLD'LI

ch: chīld'ly.
m: mīld'ly.
w: wīld'ly.
Plus styled, Lee *or* lea, etc.

ĪLD'LĬK
Ī'LET

fāte, fär, fȧst, fạll, fĭnăl, cãre, at; mēte, prĕy, hẽr, met; pīne,
marĭne, bĭrd, pin; nōte, mŏve, fọr, atŏm, not; mọọn, book;

544

(Choose only one word out of each group)

ĪLD'LĪK

ch: chĭld'līke.
Plus mild like, etc.

ĪLD'NES

m: mīld'ness, un-mīld'ness.
r: rīled'ness.
w: wīld'ness.

IL'DRED

m: Mil'dred.
Plus still dread, etc.

IL'DREN

ch: chil'dren.
Plus killed wren, etc.

ĪL'DŬR

m: mīld'ẽr.
w: wīl'dẽr.
Plus styled her *or* err, etc.

IL'DŬR

b: build'ẽr (bil'),
  cȧs'tle=buil-dẽr,
  hōme buil'dẽr, house'buil-dẽr,
  rē-buil'dẽr, ship'buil-dẽr,
  un-buil'dẽr.
ch: chil'dẽr*.
g: bē-gil'dẽr, gil'dẽr,
  guil'dẽr (gil').
w: bē-wil'dẽr, wil'dẽr*.
Plus filled her *or* err, etc.

ĪLD'WOOD

w: wīld'wood.
Plus mild wood *or* would, etc.

Ī'LENS

s: sī'lence.
Cf. vī'ō-lence.
Cf. style hence, etc.

Ī'LENT

s: sī'lent.
Cf. vī'o-lent.
Plus sky lent, etc.

ĪL'EST

f: dē-fīl'est*, fīl'est*.
g: bē-guīl'est (-gīl')*.
hw: whīl'est*.
p: cọm-pīl'est*, pīl'est*.
r: rīl'est*.
s: re'cọn-cīl-est*.
sm: smīl'est*.
st: stȳl'est*.
v: rē-vīl'est*, vīl'est.
w: wīl'est*.
Plus try, lest, etc.

IL'EST

Vowel: il'lest.
ch: chil'lest.
dr: dril'lest.
f: fil'lest*, fụl-fil'lest*,
  ō-vẽr-fil'lest*.
fr: bē-fril'lest*, fril'lest*.
gr: gril'lest*.
k: kil'lest*.
m: mil'lest*.
shr: shril'lest.
sp: spil'lest*.
st: in-stil'lest*, stil'lest.
sw: swil'lest*.
t: dis-til'lest*, til'lest*.
thr: en-thril'lest*, thril'lest*.
tr: tril'lest*.
w: wil'lest*.
Cf. kill, lest, etc.

Ī'LET, Ī'LŎT

Vowel: eȳe'let, ĭs'let (ī').
p: pī'lŏt. skȳ pī'lŏt.

(Choose only one word out of each group)

st: stȳ'let.
Plus sky let, etc.
Plus try lot, etc.

IL'ET

b: bil'let.
f: fil'let.
m: mil'let.
r: ril'let.
sk: skil'let.
w: wil'let, Wil'lett.
Plus still et, etc.

ĪL'ETH

f: dē-fīl'eth*, fīl'eth*.
g: bē-guīl'eth (-gīl')*.
hw: whīl'eth*.
p: çŏm-pīl'eth*,
pīl'eth*, up'pīl-eth*.
r: rīl'eth*.
s: re'çŏn-cīl-eth*.
sm: smīl'eth*.
st: stȳl'eth*.
t: tīl-eth*.
v: rē-vīl'eth*.
w: wīl'eth*.

IL'ETH

ch: chil'leth*.
dr: dril'leth*.
f: fil'leth*, ful-fil'leth*,
ō-vĕr-fil'leth*.
fr: bē-fril'leth*, fril'leth*.
gr: gril'leth*.
k(ç): kil'leth*.
m: mil'leth.
sp: spil'leth*.
st: in-stil'leth*.
sw: swil'leth*.
t: dis-til'leth*, til'leth*.
thr: en-thril'leth*, thril'leth*.

tr: tril'leth*.
w: wil'leth*.

ĪL'FUL

g: guīle'ful (gīl').
sm: smīle'ful.
w: wīle'ful.
Plus style full, etc.

IL'FUL

sk: skil'ful, un-skil'ful.
w: wil'ful.
Plus still full, etc.

IL'FŨR

p: pil'fĕr.
Plus sylph err *or* her, etc.
Cf. ill for, etc.
Plus still fur *or* fir, etc.

IL'GRIM

m: Mil'grim.
p: pil'grim.
Plus still grim, etc.

Ī'LI

dr: drī'ly.
h: hīgh'ly (hī').
r: O'-Reīl'ly, Reīl'ly, Rī'ley,
wrȳ'ly.
s: an-cī'lē.
sh: shȳ'ly.
sl: slī'ly.
w: wī'ly.
Plus while he, etc.

IL'I

Vowel: il'ly.
b: Bil'lee, Bil'lie, bil'ly.
ch: Chil'ē, chil'i, chil'ly.
d: daf'fy-down-dil'ly,
Piç-çà-dil'ly.

(Choose only one word out of each group)

f: fil′ly.
fr: fril′ly.
g: gil′lie.
gr: gril′ly.
h: hil′ly.
l: dāy li′ly, li′ly,
   mead′ōw li′ly (med′),
   piç′çȧ-lil-li, pond li′ly,
   tī′gẽr li′ly, wạ′tẽr li′ly,
   wood li′ly.
m: Mil′lie, Mil′ly.
n: wil′ly⸗nil′ly.
s: sil′ly.
shr: shril′ly.
sk: skil′ly.
st: stil′ly.
t: Til′lie, Til′ly.
thr: thril′ly.
tr: tril′ly.
w: Wil′lie, Wil′ly.
Plus still he, etc.

Ī′LID

Vowel: eȳe′lid.
Plus sky lid, etc.

IL′ID

l: lil′ied.
Cf. still hid, etc.

IL′IJ

gr: gril′lȧġe.
p: pil′lȧġe.
t: til′lȧġe.
thr: thril′lȧġe.
v: vil′lȧġe.
Cf. will age, etc.

IL′IK

d: ĭ-dyl′liç, ō-dyl′iç.
m: ȧ-myl′iç.
r: Cy-ril′liç.

s: bȧ-sil′iç, sal′i-cyl-iç.
t: daç-tyl′iç, maç″rō-daç-tyl′iç,
   zȳ″gō-daç-tyl′iç.
th: mē-thyl′iç.
Cf. still lick, etc.

Ī′LĬN

sk: skȳ′līne.
st: stȳ′līne.
Plus try line, etc.

IL′IN

kw: Mç-Quil′lin.
m: Maç-Mil′lin.
Cf. il′ăn, il′ŏn, etc.
Plus still in *or* inn, etc.

ĪL′ING

f: dē-fīl′ing, fīl′ing.
g: bē-guīl′ing (-gīl′), guīl′ing,
   tīme bē-guīl′ing.
hw: whīl′ing.
p: çŏm-pīl′ing, pīl′ing,
   rē-pīl′ing, un-pīl′ing, up-pīl′ing.
r: rīl′ing.
s: re′çŏn-cīl-ing.
sm: smīl′ing.
st: stȳl′ing.
t: tīl′ing.
v: rē-vīl′ing.
w: wīl′ing.

IL′ING

b: bil′ling.
ch: chil′ling.
dr: dril′ling.
f: fil′ling, fụl-fil′ling,
   ō-vẽr-fil′ling, rē-fil′ling,
   up-fil′ling.
fr: bē-fril′ling, fril′ling.
gr: gril′ling.
h: hil′ling.

(Choose only one word out of each group)

k: kil′ling.
m: mil′ling.
sh: shil′ling.
shr: shril′ling.
sp: spil′ling.
st: in-stil′ling, stil′ling.
sw: swil′ling.
t: dis-til′ling, til′ling.
thr: en-thril′ling, thril′ling.
tr: tril′ling.
w: un-wil′ling, wil′ling.

IL'INGZ

b: Bil′lings.
Plus il′ing+s.

IL'IP

f: fil′lip, Phil′ip.
Cf. still lip, etc.

IL'IPS

f: fil′lips, Phil′ips, Phil′ipse.
Cf. still lips, etc.

IL'IS

f: Phyl′lis.
r: Am-à-ryl′lis.
t: Myr-til′lis (mẽr-).
w: Wil′lis, Wyl′lis.

ĪL'ISH

st: stȳl′ish.

Ī'LĪT

dr: drȳ light.
h: hīgh light.
sk: skȳ′light.
st: stȳ′līte.
tw: twī′līght.
z: xȳ′līte.
Plus why light, etc.

IL'IZ

ch: chil′ieṣ.
f: fil′lieṣ.
g: gil′lieṣ.
l: lil′ieṣ, etc.
s: sil′lieṣ.
w: THē Wil′lieṣ.
Plus il′i+s.

ĪL'IZM

h: hȳ′liṣm.
l: Çär-lȳl′iṣm.

IL'JOI

k(ç): kill′-joy.
Plus still joy, etc.

IL'KEN

m: mil′ken.
s: sil′ken.
Cf. milk an *or* on, etc.

IL'KI

m: mil′ky.
ç: sil′ky.
w: Will′kie.
Plus milk, he, etc.
Plus will key, etc.

IL'KING

b: bil′king.
m: mil′king.

IL'KOKS

f: Phil′çox.
s: Sil′çox.
w: Wil′çox.
Plus still cocks, etc.

ĪL'LES

g: guīle′less (gīl′).
sm: smīle′less.
w: wīle′less.
Plus style, Les *or* less, etc.

IL'MĂN
ĪL'ŎM

fāte, fär, fȧst, fạll, finăl, cãre, at; mēte, prḙy, hẽr, met; pīne,
marïne, bĩrd, pin; nōte, mŏve, fọr, atŏm, nọt; mọọn, book;

548

(Choose only one word out of each group)

IL'MĂN

b: bill'măn.
g: Gil'măn.
gr: grill'măn.
h: hill'măn.
m: mill'măn, Mil'măn.
st: Still'măn.
Plus kill man, etc.

ĪL'MENT

f: dē-fīle'ment.
g: bē-guīle'ment (-gīl').
s: ex'īle-ment,
ir-reç'ŏn-cīle-ment,
re'çŏn-cīle-ment.
v: rē-vīle'ment.
Plus style meant, etc.

IL'MENT

f: fụl-fil'ment.
st: in-stil'ment.
t: dis-til'ment.
Plus skill meant, etc.

IL'MI

f: fil'my.
Plus thrill me, etc.

IL'MŌR

f: Fil'mōre.
g: Gil'mōre.
Plus thrill more, etc.
Plus film oar *or* o'er, etc.

ĪL'NES

n: jů've̅-nīle-ness.
v: vīle'ness.

IL'NES

Vowel: ill'ness.
ch: chill'ness.
shr: shrill'ness.
st: still'ness.

IL'NŨR

m: Mil'nẽr.

Ī'LŌ

h: hīgh'=lōw.
m: mī'lō.
s: sī'lō.
Plus try low *or* Lowe, etc.
Plus smile owe *or* O, etc.

IL'Ō

b: bil'lōw, em-bil'lōw.
d: är-må-dil'lō, gren-å-dil'lō,
peç-ça-dil'lō.
gr: nē-gril'lō.
k(ç): kil'lōw*, ki'lō.
p: pil'lōw.
v: pul-vil'lō*.
w: weep'ing wil'lōw, wil'lōw.
Plus still owe *or* O, etc.
Cf. fill low, etc.

IL'ŌD

p: pil'lōwed, un-pil'lōwed.
Plus il'ō+ed.

Ī'LOID

st: stȳ'loid.
z: xȳ'loid.
Plus why, Lloyd, etc.

Ī'LOK

sh: Shȳ'lock.
Plus try lock, etc.

IL'ŎK

h: hil'lŏck.
Cf. will lock, etc.

ĪL'ŎM

hw: whīl'ŏm.
Plus beguile 'em, etc.

549 ūse, bṳll, brúte, tũrn, up; crȳ, myth; çat, maçhine, ace, church, çhord; ġem, aṅger, (Fr.) boṅ, aṣ; THis, thin; aᴢure

ĪL'ON
IL'TING

(Choose only one word out of each group)

ĪL'ON

n: nȳ'lon.
p: pȳ'lon.
tr: trȳ'lon.
Plus smile on, etc.
Plus why, Lon, etc.

IL'ŎN

d: Dil'lŏn.
Cf. il'ăn.

ĪL'ŎT

p: pī'lŏt, skȳ pī'lŏt.
Cf. ī'let.

IL'PIN

g: Gil'pin.
Plus still pin, etc.

IL'RǪǪM

gr: grill'rǫǫm.
st: still'rǫǫm.
Plus thrill room, etc.

IL'SĪD

h: hill'sīde.
r: rill sīde.
Plus still side *or* sighed, etc.

IL'SŎN

g: Gil'sŏn.
st: Stil'sŏn.
w: Wil'sŏn.
Plus fill son *or* sun, etc.

IL'TED

h: hil'ted.
j: jil'ted.
k(ç): kil'ted.
kw: quil'ted.
l: lil'ted.
s: sil'ted.
st: stil'ted.
t: ō-vẽr-til'ted, til'ted, tip'til-ted.
w: wil'ted.
Plus wilt, Ed, etc.
Plus skill, Ted, etc.

IL'TEST

j: jil'test*.
k(ç): kil'test*.
kw: quil'test*.
l: lil'test*.
t: til'test*.
w: wil'test*.
Plus skill test, etc.

IL'TETH

j: jil'teth*.
k(ç): kil'teth*.
kw: quil'teth*.
l: lil'teth*.
t: til'teth*.
w: wil'teth*.

IL'THI

f: fil'thy.
Plus spilth, he, etc.

IL'TI

g: guil'ty (gil').
s: sil'ty.
st: stil'ty.
Plus milt, he, etc.

IL'TING

j: jil'ting.
k(ç): kil'ting.
kw: quilt'ing.
l: lil'ting.
s: sil'ting.
t: til'ting.
w: wil'ting.

(Choose only one word out of each group)

IL'TŎN

ch: Chil'tŏn.
h: Hil'tŏn.
m: Mil'tŏn.
st: Stil'tŏn.
t: Til'tŏn.
Plus fill ton *or* tun, etc.
Plus wilt on, etc.

IL'TŨR

f: fil'tẽr, in-fil'tẽr, phil'tẽr.
j: jil'tẽr.
k(c̣): kil'tẽr.
kw: quil'tẽr.
t: til'tẽr.
w: wil'tẽr.
Plus tilt her *or* err, etc.

Ī'LUM

f: phȳ'lum.
s: ȧ-sȳ'lum.
w: Wȳ'lăm.
Plus file 'em, etc.
Plus why, Lum, etc.

ĪL'ŨR

f: bē-fīl'ăr, dē-fīl'ẽr, fīl'ăr, fīl'ẽr.
g: bē-guīl'ẽr.
h: Huȳ'lẽr.
m: mī'lẽr, half=mī'lẽr,
  quạr'tẽr=mī'lẽr, twö=mī'lẽr, etc.
p: c̣ŏm-pīl'ẽr, pīl'ẽr, up-pīl'ẽr.
r: rīl'ẽr.
s(sc̣): re'c̣ŏn-cīl-ẽr.
sk: Sc̣huȳ'lẽr.
sm: smīl'ẽr.
st: stȳl'ăr.
t: tīl'ẽr, Tȳ'lẽr.
v: rē-vīl'ẽr, vīl'ẽr.
w: Weȳ'ler (wī'), wīl'ẽr.

z: Van Zuȳ'lẽr, Zuȳ'lẽr.
Plus beguile her *or* err, etc.

IL'ŨR

Vowel: il'lẽr.
b: bil'lẽr.
ch: chil'lẽr.
d: kil'lẽr=dil'lẽr.
dr: dril'lẽr.
f: fil'lẽr, fụl-fil'lẽr.
fr: bē-fril'lẽr, fril'lẽr.
gr: gril'lẽr.
k(c̣): kil'lẽr, ġī'ănt kil'lẽr.
  lā'dy=kil-lẽr, man'=kil-lẽr.
m: Jōe Mil'lẽr, mil'lẽr.
p: c̣at'ẽr-pil-lăr, pil'lăr.
s: max'il-lăr, sil'lẽr.
sh: Sc̣hil'lẽr.
shr: shril'lẽr.
sp: spil'lẽr.
st: in-stil'lẽr, stil'lẽr.
sw: swil'lẽr.
t: dis-til'lẽr, til'lẽr.
th: thil'lẽr.
thr: thril'lẽr.
tr: tril'lẽr.
w: ill=wil'lẽr, wil'lẽr.
Plus thrill her *or* err, etc.

IL'US

br: fī'bril-lous.
g: as-pẽr-gil'lus.
j: ọr'ġil-lous.
s: bȧ-cil'lus.
v: fȧ-vil'lous, vil'lus.
Plus thrill us, etc.

IL'VĂN

s: syl'văn.
Plus fill van, etc.
Cf. Kill von, etc.

(Choose only one word out of each group)

IL′VŪR
s: sil′vẽr.
Plus still vẽr*, etc.

IL′YĂM
g: Gil′liăm.
w: Wil′liăm.
Plus still yam, etc.

IL′YĂNS
br: bril′liăńce.
Cf. il′i-ăns, il′i-ens.

IL′YĂNT
br: bril′liănt.
Cf. il′i-ănt, il′i-ent.

IL′YĂR
b: at-rȧ-bil′iăr.
m: fȧ-mil′iăr.
s: aux-il′iăr, çŏn-cil′iăr,
dom-i-cil′iăr.
Cf. il′i-ūr.

IL′YĂRDZ
b: bil′liărdṣ.
m: mil′liărdṣ.
Plus fill yards, etc.

IL′YUN
b: bil′liŏn, tou̯r-bil′liŏn.
d: man-dil′liŏn, mō-dil′liŏn.
l: Lil′liăn.
m: mil′liŏn, vẽr-mil′iŏn.
n: nō-nil′liŏn.
p: pil′liŏn.
r: çar-il′lŏn, quäd-ril′liŏn.
s: dē-cil′liŏn.
st: stil′liŏn.
t: çō-til′liŏn, oç-til′liŏn,
pōs-til′liŏn, quin-til′liŏn,
sex-til′liŏn.

tr: tril′liŏn.
v: pȧ-vil′liŏn.
Cf. vil′lian (vil′yăn).

IL′YUNTH
b: bil′liŏnth.
m: mil′liŏnth.
n: nō-nil′liŏnth.
r: quäd-ril′liŏnth.
s: dē-cil′liŏnth.
t: oç-til′liŏnth, quin-til′liŏnth,
sex-til′liŏnth.
tr: tril′liŏnth.

Ī′MȦ
Vowel: Ī′mȧ.
l: Lī′mȧ.
m: Jē-mī′mȧ.
s: cȳ′mȧ.
Plus rhyme a, etc.
Plus I'm a, etc.

ĪM′ĂKS
kl: an-ti-çlī′măx, çlī′măx.
Plus rhyme ax, etc.
Plus why, Max, etc.

ĪM′ĂL
k(ç): īs-ō-çheīm′ăl.
kr: īs-ō-çrȳm′ăl.
pr: prīm′ăl.
Plus time, Al, etc.

Ī′MĂN, Ī′MEN, Ī′MŎN
d: daī′măn.
h: Hȳ′men.
p: pīe′măn.
s: Sī′mŏn.
t: Tī′mŏn.
w: Wȳ′măn.

ĬM′ĂT
ĬM′ETH

fāte, fär, fást, fạll, fĭnăl, cãre, at; mēte, prĕy, hẽr, met; pīne,
marïne, bĭrd, pĭn; nōte, mŏve, fŏr, atŏm, nŏt; mọọn, book;

552

(Choose only one word out of each group)

Plus why, man, etc.
Cf. why, men, etc.

ĪM′ĀT

kl: aç-çlīm′āte, çlīm′āte.
pr: prīm′āte.
Plus prime ate *or* eight, etc.
Plus why. mate, etc.

ĬM′BÅ

b: bĭm′băh.
r: má-rĭm′bá.
s: sĭm′băh.

ĬM′BĂL

f: fĭm′ble.
g: gĭm′băl, Gĭm′bel.
n: nĭm′ble.
s: cĭm′băl, sĭm′bŏl.
t: tĭm′băl.
th: thĭm′ble.
w: wĭm′ble.
Plus trim bull, etc.

ĬM′BŌ

b: bĭm′bō.
k(ç): á-kĭm′bō, kĭm′bō.
l: lĭm′bō.
Plus him, beau, bo *or* bow, etc.

ĬM′BREL

hw: whĭm′brel.
t: tĭm′brel.

ĬM′BŨR

Vowel: ĭm′bẽr.
l: lĭm′bẽr, un-lĭm′bẽr.
t: tĭm′bẽr, tĭm′bre.
Plus slim burr, etc.

ĬM′BŨRD

t: tĭm′bẽred, un-tĭm′bẽred.
Plus ĭm′bŨr+ed.

ĬM′BUS

l: lĭm′bus.
n: nĭm′bus.
Plus him buss *or* bus, etc.

ĬM′EL

fr: Frĭm′l.
g: gĭm′măl.
gr: Grĭm′mell.
h: Hĭm′mel.
k(ç): kŭm′mel (kĭm′).
Plus limb ′ll, etc.

Ī′MEN

h: Hȳ′men.
See ī′măn.

ĬM′EN

w: wŏm′en (wĭm′).
Cf. ĭm′ŏn.

ĪM′EST

ch: chīm′est*.
gr: bē-grīm′est*.
kl: çlīmb′est (klīm′)*.
l: sub-līm′est.
pr: prīm′est.
r: bē-rhȳm′est*, rhȳm′est*.
sl: bē-slīm′est*.

ĬM′EST

br: brĭm′mest*.
d: dĭm′mest*.
gr: grĭm′mest.
pr: prĭm′mest.
sk: skĭm′mest*.
sl: slĭm′mest.
sw: swĭm′mest*.
tr: trĭm′mest.

ĪM′ETH

ch: chīm′eth*.
gr: bē-grīm′eth*.

(Choose only one word out of each group)

kl: çlīmb′eth*.
pr: prīm′eth*.
r: bē-rhȳm′eth*, rhȳm′eth*.
sl: bē-slīm′eth*.

IM′ETH

br: brim′meth*.
d: dim′meth*.
sk: skim′meth*.
sw: swim′meth*.
tr: trim′meth*.

IM′FLAM

fl: flim′flam.
Plus nymph lam *or* lamb, etc.

ĪM′I

bl: blīm′y.
gr: grī′my.
l: līm′ey, līm′y.
r: rīm′y, rhȳm′y.
sl: bē-slīm′y, slīm′y.
st: stȳ′mie.
th: thȳm′y.
Plus try me, etc.
Plus rhyme, he, etc.

IM′I

g: gim′mē.
hw: whim′my.
j: jim′my.
sh: shim′my.
Plus gi′ me, etc.
Plus trim, he, etc.

IM′ID

t: tim′id.
Cf. Jim hid, etc.

IM′IJ

Vowel: im′ăġe.
skr(sçr): sçrim′măġe.
Cf. dim age, etc.

IM′IK

b: cher-ū-bim′iç.
k(ç): al-çhim′iç, çaç-ō-çhym′iç.
m: mim′iç, pan-tō-mim′iç.
n: ep-ō-nym′iç, hōm-ō-nym′iç,
met-ō-nym′iç, met-rō-nym′iç,
pat-rō-nym′iç, syn-ō-nym′iç.
t: e-tym′iç.
th: līp-ō-thym′iç.
z: zy′miç (also zȳ′miç).
Plus try Mick, etc.

ĪM′ING

ch: chīm′ing.
gr: bē-grīm′ing, grīm′ing.
kl: çlīmb′ing.
l: bē-līm′ing, līm′ing.
pr: prīm′ing, pump prīm′ing.
r: bē-rhȳm′ing, rhȳm′ing.
sl: bē-slīm′ing, slīm′ing.
t: tīm′ing.
Plus buy Ming, etc.

IM′ING

br: brim′ming.
d: bē-dim′ming, dim′ming.
gr: grim′ming.
sk: skim′ming.
sl: slim′ming.
sw: swim′ming.
tr: bē-trim′ming, trim′ming.

ĪM′IST

r: rhȳm′ist.
t: tīm′ist.
Plus pie missed *or* mist, etc.

IM′IT

l: lim′it.
Plus dim it, etc.

(Choose only one word out of each group)

IM'JAMṢ

j: jim'jamṣ.
Plus hymn jams, etc.

IM'KRAK

j: ġim'ᴄrack.
Plus him crack, etc.

ĪM'LES

ch: chīme'less.
gr: grīme'less.
kr: ᴄrīme'less.
l: līme'less.
r: rhȳme'less, rīme'less.
sl: slīme'less.
t: thȳme'less (tīm'), tīme'less,
   ō-vẽr-tīme'less.
Plus lime less *or* Les, etc.
Plus I'm less *or* Les, etc.

IM'LES

br: brim'less.
h: hymn'less.
hw: whim'less.
l: limb'less.
r: rim'less.
sw: swim'less.
v: vim'less.
Plus skim less *or* Les, etc.

ĪM'LI

l: sub-līme'ly.
pr: prīme'ly.
t: tīme'ly, un-tīme'ly.
Plus rhyme, Lee *or* lea, etc.

IM'LI

d: dim'ly.
gr: grim'ly.
pr: prim'ly.
sl: slim'ly.

tr: trim'ly.
Plus him, Lee *or* lea, etc.

IM'NĂL, IM'NEL

h: hym'năl.
s: sim'nel.

ĪM'NES

l: sub-līme'ness.
pr: prīme'ness.

IM'NES

d: dim'ness.
gr: grim'ness.
pr: prim'ness.
sl: slim'ness.
tr: trim'ness.

IM'NI

ch: chim'ney.
Plus slim knee, etc.

Ī'MŎN

s: Sī'mŏn.
t: Tī'mŏn.
Plus i'măn.

I'MŎND

d: dīa'mŏnd.
Plus Wyman'd, etc.

IM'ŎN

r: Rim'mŏn.
s: pẽr-sim'mŏn.
Cf. wom'en.
Plus limb on *or* an, etc.

IM'ŎNZ

s: pẽr-sim'mŏnṣ, Sim'mŏnṣ.
Plus Rimmon's.

(Choose only one word out of each group)

IM′PET

l: lim′pet.
Plus him, pet, etc.

IM′PI

Vowel: im′pi, im′py.
kr: çrim′py.
sk: skim′py.

ĪMP′ING

Vowel: imp′ing.
bl: blimp′ing.
kr: çrimp′ing.
l: limp′ing.
pr: primp′ing.
shr: shrimp′ing.
sk: skimp′ing.
skr(sçr): sçrimp′ing.
Plus him ping, etc.

IM′PISH

Vowel: im′pish.
Plus him? Pish!, etc.

ĪM′PIT

l: līme′pit.
sl: slīme′pit.
Plus rhyme pit *or* Pitt, etc.

IM′PL

d: dim′ple.
kr: çrim′ple.
p: pim′ple.
r: rim′ple.
s: sim′ple.
w: bē-wim′ple, wim′ple.
Plus limb pull, etc.

IM′PLEST

d: dim′plest*.
kr: çrim′plest*.
p: pim′plest*.

r: rim′plest*.
s: sim′plest.
w: wim′plest*.
Plus limp, lest, etc.

IM′PLETH

d: dim′pleth*.
kr: çrim′pleth*.
p: pim′plet*.
r: rim′pleth*.
s: sim′pleth*.
w: wim′pleth*.

IMP′LI

d: dimp′ly.
kr: çrimp′ly.
l: limp′ly.
p: pimp′ly.
s: simp′ly.
Plus limp, Lee *or* lea, etc.

IMP′LING

Vowel: imp′ling.
d: dimp′ling.
kr: çrimp′ling.
p: pimp′ling.
r: rimp′ling.
shr: shrimp′ling.
w: wimp′ling.

IMP′LŪR

d: dimp′lẽr.
kr: çrimp′lẽr.
r: rimp′lẽr.
s: simp′lẽr.
w: wimp′lẽr.

IMP′ŪR

hw: whimp′ẽr.
kr: çrimp′ẽr.
l: limp′ẽr.
shr: shrimp′ẽr.

(Choose only one word out of each group)

skr(c̣): sc̣rimp'ẽr.
s: simp'ẽr.
sk: skimp'ẽr.
Plus skimp her *or* err, etc.

IM'RŌZ

pr: prim'rōṣe.
Plus limb rose, etc.

IM'SHI

Vowel: im'shi.
Plus limb, she, etc.

IM'SŎN

j: jim'sŏn.
Plus him, son *or* sun, etc.

ĪM'STŪR

r: rhȳme'stẽr.
Plus time stir, etc.

ĪM'ŪR

ch: chīm'ẽr.
gr: bē-grīm'ẽr.
h: Hẽr'ges-heīm-ẽr,
   Laub'en-heīm-ẽr.
kl: c̣līmb'ẽr.
l: sub-līm'ẽr.
pr: prīm'ẽr.
r: rhȳm'ẽr.
t: ōld'‗tīm'ẽr, tīm'ẽr.
Plus time her *or* err, etc.

IM'ŪR

Vowel: im'mẽr.
br: brim'mẽr.
d: dim'mẽr.
g: gim'mẽr.
gl: glim'mẽr.
gr: grim'mẽr.
h: hymn'ẽr.

l: limn'ẽr.
pr: prim'ẽr, prim'mẽr.
s: sim'mẽr.
sh: shim'mẽr.
sk: skim'mẽr.
sl: slim'mẽr.
sw: swim'mẽr.
tr: trim'mẽr.
z: zim'mẽr.
Plus limn her, etc.
Cf. trim myrrh, etc.

ĪM'US

pr: prīm'us.
r: rīm'ous.
s: Sīm'ous.
t: tīme'ous, un-tīme'ous.
Plus beslime us, etc.

IM'ZI

fl: flim'ṣy.
hw: whim'ṣey.
sl: slim'ṣy.
Plus limbs, he, etc.
Cf. him see, etc.

IM'ZŎN

kr: c̣rim'ṣŏn, en-c̣rim'ṣŏn.
Plus limbs on *or* an, etc.

Ī'NȦ

Vowel: Ī'nȧ.
b: Sȧ-bī'nȧ.
br: Sȧ-brī'nȧ.
ch: Chī'nȧ.
d: Dī'nȧh.
gr: Mel″ē-ȧ-grī'nȧ.
h: Heï'ne.
j: Jaīn'ȧ, Rē-ġīn'ȧ.
k(c̣): Shē-kī'nȧ, tri-c̣hī'nȧ.
l: Ad-e-lī'nȧ, An-ġe-lī'nȧ,
   C̣ar-ō-lī'nȧ, Cat-ȧ-lī'nȧ,

557 ūse, bụll, brúte, tŭrn, **up**; crȳ, myth; çat, maçhine, **a**ce,
church, ᴄhord; ġem, aṅger, (Fr.) boṅ, aṣ; THis, thin; aᴢure   IN'Å
IN'DED

(Choose only one word out of each group)

Ev-e-lī'nȧ, Mes-sȧ-lī'nȧ,
North Çar-ō-lī'nȧ, sȧ-lī'nȧ,
sem-ō-lī'nȧ, South Çar-ō-lī'nȧ.
m: Mī'nȧ.
n: Nī'nȧ.
r: fȧ-rī'nȧ, Pla-ty-rhȳ'nȧ.
s: Lū-cī'nȧ.
t: Tī'nȧ.
tr: Kȧ-trī'nȧ.
Plus fine a, etc.

IN'Å

m: Min'nȧ.
r: Çō-rin'nȧ, E-rin'nȧ.
Plus tin a, etc.

ĪN'ĂL

b: bīn'ăl.
f: fīn'ăl, sem-i-fīn'ăl.
kl: aᴄ-ᴄlīn'ăl, an-ti-ᴄlīn'ăl,
dē-ᴄlīn'ăl, īs-ō-ᴄlin'ăl,
per-i-ᴄlīn'ăl, syn-ᴄlīn'ăl.
kr: ᴄrīn'ăl, en-dō-ᴄrīn'ăl.
kw: ē-quī'năl*.
n: ᴄȧ-nīn'ăl.
r: rhī'năl.
s: of-fi-cīn'ăl, pis-cī'năl.
sp: cer″ē-brō-spīn'ăl, spīn'ăl.
t: ma-tū-tīn'ăl.
tr: trīn'ăl.
v: Vīn'ăl.
Plus mine, Al, etc.

IN'ĂS

p: pin'năce.

ĪN'ĀT

b: bīn'āte.
kw: quīn'āte.
Plus mine ate *or* eight, etc.

IN'CHEST

fl: flin'chest*.
kl: ᴄlin'chest*.
l: lyn'chest*.
p: pin'chest*.
Plus skin chest, etc.

IN'CHETH

fl: flin'cheth*.
kl: ᴄlin'cheth*.
l: lyn'cheth*.
p: pin'cheth*.

IN'CHING

fl: flin'ching, un-flin'ching.
kl: ᴄlin'ching.
l: lyn'ching.
p: pin'ching.

IN'CHŪR

fl: flin'chēr.
kl: ᴄlin'chēr.
l: lyn'chēr.
p: pin'chēr.
Plus pinch her, etc.

IN'CHŪRZ

p: pin'chērṣ.
Plus in'chūr+s.

IN'DÅ

l: Bē-lin'dȧ, E-thel-in'dȧ,
Lin'dȧ.
r: Çhlō-rin'dȧ, Dō-rin'dȧ.
s: Lū-cin'dȧ.
Plus skinned a, etc.

ĪN'DED

bl: blīn'ded, self=blīn'ded,
snōw'=blīn-ded.

IN'DED
ĪND'ING
fāte, fär, fȧst, fạll, finăl, cãre, ạt; mēte, prẹy, hẽr, met; pīne,
marïne, bĩrd, pin; nōte, mŏve, fọr, atŏm, not; mọọn, book;
558

(Choose only one word out of each group)

m: ȧ-līke'=mĭn'ded,
blood'y=mĭn'ded (blud'),
çär'năl=mĭn'ded,
dŏu'ble=mĭn'ded,
ĕarth'ly=mĭn'ded,
ĕv'en-mĭn'ded, ē'vil=mĭn'ded,
fãir'=mĭn'ded, fee'ble=mĭn'ded,
flesh'ly=mĭn'ded,
free'=mĭn'ded,
hīgh'=mĭn'ded (hī),
lĭght'=mĭn'ded (lĭt),
līke'=mĭn'ded,
lōw'=mĭn'ded, mĭn'ded,
nar'rōw=mĭn'ded,
pub'liç=mĭn'ded, rē-mĭn'ded,
sim'ple=mĭn'ded,
siñ'gle=mĭn'ded,
sō'bẽr=mĭn'ded,
strọng'=mĭn'ded,
wŏrld'ly=mĭn'ded.
r: rĭn'ded.
w: wĭn'ded.
Plus shine dead, etc.
Cf. mine did, etc.
Plus dined, Ed, etc.

IN'DED

br: brĭn'ded*.
s: ab-scĭn'ded, ex-scĭn'ded,
in-tẽr-scĭn'ded, rē-scĭn'ded.
w: lọng'=wind'ed,
shọrt'=win'ded, win'ded.
Plus kin dead, etc.
Cf. kin did, etc.

IN'DEN

l: lin'den, Lin'dŏn.
m: Min'den.
Plus inn (or in) den, etc.

ĪN'DEST

b: bīn'dest*.
bl: blīn'dest*.
f: fīn'dest*.
gr: grīn'dest*.
k: kīn'dest.
m: rē-mīn'dest*.
w: wīn'dest*.

ĪN'DETH

b: bīn'deth*.
bl: blīn'deth*.
f: fīn'deth*.
gr: grīn'deth*.
m: mīn'deth*, rē-mīn'deth*.
w: wīn'deth*.
Plus wine, death, etc.

ĪND'FỤL

m: mīnd'fụl, rē-mīnd'fụl,
un-mīnd'fụl.
Plus dined full, etc.

IN'DI

l: Lin'dy.
s: Lū-çin'dy.
sh: shin'dy.
w: win'dy.
Plus thinned, he, etc.

IN'DIG

sh: shin'dig.
Plus kin dig, etc.

IN'DIK

Vowel: in'diç.
s: syn'diç.
Plus win, Dick, etc.

ĪND'ING

b: bīnd'ing, in-bīnd'ing,
un-bīnd'ing, up-bīnd'ing.

(Choose only one word out of each group)

bl: blīnd'ing.
f: fīnd'ing.
gr: grīnd'ing.
m: mīnd'ing, rē-mīnd'ing.
w: un-wīnd'ing, up-wīnd'ing.

IN'DL

br: brin'dle.
dw: dwin'dle.
k: en-kin'dle, kin'dle,
rē-kin'dle.
sp: spin'dle.
sw: swin'dle.
Plus wind'll, etc.
Plus kin dull, etc.

IN'DLD

br: brin'dled.
Plus in'd'l+d.

IN'DLEST

br: brin'dlest*.
dw: dwin'dlest*.
k: en-kin'dlest*, kin'dlest*,
rē-kin'dlest*.
sw: swin'dlest*.
Plus wind, lest, etc.

IN'DLETH

br: brin'dleth*.
dw: dwin'dleth*.
k: en-kin'dleth*, kin'dleth*,
rē-kin'dleth*.
sw: swin'dleth*.

ĪND'LI

bl: blīnd'li.
k: kīnd'ly, un-kīnd'ly.
Plus mind, Lee or lea, etc.

IND'LI

h: Hind'ley ('li).
sp: spin'dly.
Plus thinned, Lee or lea, etc.

IND'LING

br: brind'ling.
dw: dwind'ling.
k: en-kind'ling, kind'ling,
rē-kind'ling.
sw: swind'ling.

IND'LŪR

dw: dwind'lẽr.
k: kind'lẽr.
sw: swind'lẽr.

ĪND'NES

bl: blīnd'ness, çŏl'ŏr blīnd'ness.
k: kīnd'ness, lŏv'ing kīnd'ness,
un-kīnd'ness.

IN'DŌ

w: win'dōw.
Plus inn dough or doe, etc.

IN'DRĂNS

h: hin'drănce.

IN'DRED

k: kin'dred.
Plus inn dread, etc.
Plus thinned red, etc.

ĪND'ŪR

b: bīnd'ẽr, spell'bīnd-ẽr.
bl: blīnd'ẽr.
f: fault'fīnd-ẽr, fīnd'ẽr,
path'fīnd-ẽr, wạt'ẽr-fīnd-ẽr.
gr: grīnd'ẽr, ọr'găn=grīnd-ẽr.

(Choose only one word out of each group)

h: hīnd′ẽr.
k: kīnd′ẽr.
m: mīnd′ẽr, rē-mīnd′ẽr.
w: sīde′wĭnd-ẽr, stem′-wĭnd′ẽr,
    wĭnd′ẽr.
Plus bind her *or* err, etc.

IN′DŬR

fl: flin′dẽr.
h: hin′dẽr.
p: pin′dẽr.
s: cin′dẽr, rē-scin′dẽr.
t: tin′dẽr.
Plus skinned her *or* err, etc.

IN′EN

l: lin′en.
Cf. thin hen, etc.
Cf. win in, etc.

Ī′NES

dr: drȳ′ness.
h: hīgh′ness.
n: nīgh′ness.
r: wrȳ′ness.
sh: shȳ′ness.
sl: slȳ′ness.
spr: sprȳ′ness.

IN′ES

Vowel: In′ness.
g: Guin′ness.
Cf. pin′năce.

ĪN′EST

b: cǫm-bīn′est*.
d: cǫn-dīgn′est*, dīn′est*.
f: cǫn-fīn′est*, dē-fīn′est*,
    fīn′est, rē-fīn′est*,
    sū′pẽr-fīn-est.
hw: whīn′est*.
kl: dē-clīn′est*, in-clīn′est*,
    rē-clīn′est*.

l: mȧ-līgn′est, out′līn-est*,
    un-dẽr-līn′est*.
m: mīn′est*, un-dẽr-mīn′est*.
n: bē-nīgn′est.
p: pīn′est*, sū-pīn′est.
s: as-sīgn′est*, cǫn-sīgn′est*,
    coun-tẽr-sīgn′est*,
    rē-as-sīgn′est*, sīgn′est*,
    un-dẽr-sīgn′est*.
sh: out-shīn′est*, shīn′est*.
shr: en-shrīn′est*.
tw: en-twīn′est*,
    in-tẽr-twīn′est*,
    ō-vẽr-twīn′est*, twīn′est*,
    un-twīn′est*.
v: di-vīn′est*.
w: wīn′est*.
z: dē-sīgn′est*, rē-sīgn′est*.
Plus high nest, etc.

IN′EST

d: din′nest*.
g: bē-gin′nest*.
gr: grin′nest*.
p: pin′nest*.
s: sin′nest*.
sk: skin′nest*.
sp: spin′nest.
th: thin′nest.
w: win′nest.
Cf. thin nest, etc.

IN′ET

l: lin′net.
m: min′ute (′it).
sp: spin′et.
Cf. thin net, etc.
Cf. in it, etc.

ĬN′ETH

b: cǫm-bīn′eth*.
d: dīn′eth*.

(Choose only one word out of each group)

f: cŏn-fīn'eth*, dē-fīn'eth*,
rē-fīn'eth*.
hw: whīn'eth*.
kl: dē-clīn'eth*, in-clīn'eth*,
rē-clīn'eth*.
l: mȧ-līgn'eth*, out'līn-eth*,
un-dēr-līn'eth*.
m: mīn'eth*, un-dēr-mīn'eth*.
p: pīn'eth*, rē-pīn'eth*.
s: as-sīgn'eth*, cŏn-sīgn'eth*,
coun-tēr-sīgn'eth*,
rē-as-sīgn'eth*, sīgn'eth*,
un-dēr-sīgn'eth*.
sh: out-shīn'eth*, shīn'eth*.
shr: en-shrīn'eth*.
tw: en-twīn'eth*,
in-tēr-twīn'eth*,
ō-vēr-twīn'eth*, twīn'eth*,
un-twīn'eth*.
v: di-vīn'eth*.
w: wīn'eth*.
z: dē-ṣīgn'eth*, rē-ṣīgn'eth*.

IN'ETH

d: din'neth*.
g: bē-gin'neth*.
gr: grin'neth*.
j: ġin'neth*.
p: pin'neth*.
s: sin'neth*.
sk: skin'neth*.
sp: spin'neth*.
w: win'neth*.

IN'FĂNT

Vowel: in'fănt.

IN'FṲL

s: sin'fṳl.
Plus skin full, etc.

ING'ĂM

b: Bing'hăm.
Plus bring 'em, etc.

ING'BŌLT

k: king'bōlt.
r: ring'bōlt, wring'bōlt.
Plus bring bolt, etc.

ING'DŎM

k: king'dŏm.
Plus sting dumb, etc.

ING'DUV

r: ring'dŏve.
Plus bring dove, etc.

ING'ED

w: wing'ed.
Plus ing+ed*.
Plus bring, Ed, etc.

ING'EST

br: bring'est*.
fl: fling'est*.
kl: cling'est*.
r: ring'est*, wring'est*.
s: sing'est*.
sl: sling'est*.
spr: spring'est*.
st: sting'est*.
str: string'est*.
sw: swing'est*.
w: out-wing'est*, wing'est*.

ING'ETH

br: bring'eth*.
fl: fling'eth*.
kl: cling'eth*.
r: ring'eth*, wring'eth*.

ING'GÅ
ING'GŌ

fāte, fär, fȧst, fall, final, cãre, at; mēte, prey, hẽr, met; pīne,
marīne, bĭrd, pin; nōte, mŏve, fŏr, atŏm, nŏt; mọọn, book;

562

(Choose only one word out of each group)

s: sing'eth*.
sl: sling'eth*.
spr: spring'eth*.
st: sting'eth*.
str: string'eth*.
sw: swing'eth*.
w: out-wing'eth*, wing'eth*.

ING'GÅ

h: an-hiñg'ȧ.

ING'GI

d: diñgh'y.
Cf. Fer-ing'hee.

ING'GL

Vowel: iñ'gle.
d: diñ'gle.
j: jiñ'gal, jiñ'gle.
kr: çriñ'gle, Kriss Kriñ'gle.
m: çŏm-miñ'gle, im-miñ'gle,
  in-tẽr-miñ'gle, miñ'gle.
s: siñ'gle, sũr'ciñ-gle.
sh: shiñ'gle.
spr: spring'ȧl.
sw: swiñ'gle.
t: 'iñ'gle.
tr: triñ'gle.
Plus sing, gull, etc.

ING'GLD

m: un-miñ'gled.
Plus springald.
Plus ing'l+d.

ING'GLEST

j: jiñ'glest*.
m: miñ'glest*.
t: tiñ'glest*.

IN'GLETH

j: jiñ'gleth*.
m: miñ'gleth*.
t: tiñ'gleth*.

ING'GLI

j: jiñ'gly.
m: miñ'gly.
s: siñ'gly.
sh: shiñ'gly.
t: tiñ'gly.
Plus sing glee, etc.

ING'GLING

j: jiñ'gling.
k: king'ling.
m: in-tẽr-miñ'gling, miñ'gling.
s: siñ'gling.
t: tiñ'gling.
w: wiñ'gling.

ING'GLISH

Vowel: Eñg'lish.
t: tiñ'glish.

ING'GLŪR

j: jiñ'glẽr.
m: in-tẽr-miñ'glẽr, miñ'glẽr.
sh: shiñ'glẽr.
t: tiñ'glẽr.

ING'GŌ

b: biñ'gō.
d: diñ'gō.
gr: griñ'gō.
j: jiñ'gō.
l: liñ'gō.
m: flȧ-miñ'gō.
r: Riñġ'gō.
st: stiñ'gō.
Plus wing go, etc.

(Choose only one word out of each group)

ING′GŪR

f: fiñ′gẽr, fōre′fiñ-gẽr,
in′dex fiñ′gẽr.
l: liñ′gẽr, mȧ-liñ′gẽr.

ING′GŪRD

f: līght′=fiñ′gẽred (līt′),
rō′ṣy=fiñ′gẽred, web′=fiñ′gẽred.
Plus ing′gŭr+ed.

ING′GUS

d: diñ′gus.
Plus sing, Gus, etc.

ING′GWĂL

l: bī-liñ′guăl, liñ′guăl.

ING′GWISH

t: çon″trȧ-dis-tiñ′guish,
dis-tiñ′guish, ex-tiñ′guish.

ING′I

kl: çling′y.
spr: spring′y.
st: sting′y.
str: string′y.
sw: swing′y.
w: wing′y.
Plus bring, he, etc.

ING′ING

br: bring′ing, up-bring′ing.
d: ding′ing.
fl: fling′ing.
kl: çling′ing.
r: en-ring′ing, ring′ing,
wring′ing.
s: plāin sing′ing, sing′ing.
sl: sling′ing, un-sling′ing.
spr: spring′ing.
st: sting′ing.

str: rē-string′ing, string′ing,
un-string′ing, up-string′ing.
sw: swing′ing.
w: out-wing′ing, wing′ing.

INGK′EST

Vowel: iñk′est*.
bl: bliñk′est*.
ch: chiñk′est*.
dr: driñk′est*.
kl: çliñk′est*.
l: liñk′est*.
p: piñk′est.
s: siñk′est*.
shr: shriñk′est*.
sl: sliñk′est*.
st: stiñk′est*.
th: bē-thiñk′est*, thiñk′est*.
w: hood′wiñk-est*, wiñk′est*.

INGK′ET

tr: triñ′ket.
Cf. think it, etc.

INGK′ETH

Vowel: iñk′eth*.
bl: bliñk′eth*.
ch: chiñk′eth*.
dr: driñk′eth*.
kl: çliñk′eth*.
l: liñk′eth*.
p: piñk′eth*.
s: siñk′eth*.
shr: shriñk′eth*.
sl: sliñk′eth*.
st: stiñk′eth*.
th: bē-thiñk′eth*, thiñk′eth*.
w: hood′wiñk-eth*, wiñk′eth*.

INGK′GŌ

g: giñk′gō.
Plus sink go, etc.

(Choose only one word out of each group)

INGK'I

Vowel: iñk'y.
bl: bliñk'y.
d: diñk'y.
k: kiñk'y.
p: piñk'y.
z: ziñck'y.
Plus think, he, etc.

INGK'ĪD

bl: bliñk'=eȳed.
p: piñk'=eȳed.
Plus think, I'd or eyed, etc.

INGK'ING

Vowel: iñk'ing.
bl: bliñk'ing, un-bliñk'ing.
ch: chiñk'ing.
dr: driñk'ing.
kl: cliñk'ing.
l: en-liñk'ing, in-tẽr-liñk'ing,
liñk'ing, rē-liñk'ing,
un-liñk'ing.
pr: priñk'ing.
r: riñk'ing.
s: siñk'ing.
shr: shriñk'ing, un-shriñk'ing.
sl: sliñk'ing.
st: stiñk'ing.
th: bē-thiñk'ing,
free'thiñk'ing, thiñk'ing,
un-thiñk'ing.
w: hood'wiñk-ing, un-wiñk'ing,
wiñk'ing.
Plus bring kind, etc.

INGK'L

Vowel: iñk'le.
kw: criñk'le.
r: wriñk'le.

spr: bē-spriñk'le, spriñk'le.
t: tiñk'le.
tw: twiñk'le.
w: per'i-wiñk-le, wiñk'le.
Plus pink'll, etc.

INGK'LD

r: un-wriñk'led.
Plus ingk'l+d.

INGK'LEST

kr: criñk'lest*.
r: wriñk'lest*.
spr: spriñk'lest*.
t: tiñk'lest*.
tw: twiñk'lest*.
Plus think, lest, etc.

INGK'LETH

kr: criñk'leth*.
r: wriñk'leth*.
spr: spriñk'leth*.
t: tiñk'leth*.
tw: twiñk'leth*.

INGK'LI

kr: criñk'ly.
p: piñk'ly.
r: wriñk'ly.
t: tiñk'ly.
tw: twiñk'ly.
Plus think, Lee or lea, etc.

INGK'LING

Vowel: iñk'ling.
kr: crink'ling.
r: wriñk'ling.
spr: bē-spriñk'ling,
spriñk'ling.
t: tiñk'ling.
tw: twiñk'ling.

(Choose only one word out of each group)

INGK′LŪR

r: wriñk′lẽr.
spr: spriñk′lẽr.
t: tiñk′lẽr.
tw: twiñk′lẽr.

INGK′Ō

st: stiñk′ō.
Plus drink owe *or* O, etc.

INGK′ŎN

l: Liñ′cŏln (′kun).
p: piñk″un.
Plus think an *or* on, etc.

INGK′SHUN

t: con″trȧ-dis-tiñc′tion,
dis-tiñc′tion, ex-tiñc′tion,
in-dis-tinc′tion, in-tiñc′tion.
Plus drink shun, etc.

INGK′TIV

t: con″trȧ-dis-tiñc′tive,
dis-tiñc′tive, in-stiñc′tive.

INGKT′NES

s: sục-ciñct′ness.
t: dis-tiñct′ness,
in-dis-tiñct′ness.

INGK′TŪR

s: ciñc′tūre, en-ciñc′tūre.
t: tiñc′ture.
Plus winked you're *or* your, etc.

INGK′TŪRD

s: ciñc′tūred, en-ciñc′tūred,
un-ciñc′tūred.
t: tiñc′tūred, un-tiñc′tūred.

INGK′ŬR

Vowel: iñk′ẽr.
bl: bliñk′ẽr.
dr: driñk′ẽr.
kl: cliñk′ẽr.
l: en-liñk′ẽr, liñk′ẽr.
p: piñk′ẽr.
pr: priñk′ẽr.
r: riñk′ẽr.
s: siñk′ẽr.
shr: shriñk′ẽr.
sl: sliñk′ẽr.
st: stiñk′ẽr.
t: tiñk′ẽr.
th: bẽ-thiñk′ẽr, free′thiñk′ẽr,
thiñk′ẽr.
w: hood′wiñk-ẽr,
tid′dle-dy-wiñk-ẽr, wiñk′ẽr.
Plus shrink her *or* err, etc.

INGK′US

r: or″nith-ō-rhyñ′chus,
ox-y-rhyñ′chus.
s: sciñ′cus.
z: ziñ′cous.
Plus shrink us, etc.

ING′LES

k: king′less.
r: ring′less.
spr: spring′less.
st: sting′less.
w: wing′less.
Plus bring less *or* Les, etc.

ING′LET

k: king′let.
r: ring′let.
spr: spring′let.
w: wing′let.
Plus bring Lett *or* let, etc.

(Choose only one word out of each group)

ING'LĬK

k: king'lĭke.
spr: spring'lĭke.
w: wing'lĭke.
Plus thing like, etc.

IN'GRAM

Vowel: In'gram.
Plus thin gram, etc.

ING'SŎNG

s: sing'sọng.
spr: spring sọng.
Plus bring song, etc.

ING'TĪM

r: ring'tīme.
spr: spring'tīme.
Plus bring time, etc.

ING'ŨR

br: bring'ẽr, fīre bring'ẽr,
news bring'ẽr.
d: ding'ẽr, hum-ding'ẽr.
fl: fling'ẽr.
hw: whing'ẽr.
kl: çling'ẽr.
r: bell ring'ẽr, çlōTHeṣ'wring'ẽr,
ring'ẽr, wring'ẽr.
s: bal'lăd sing'ẽr,
mȧs'tẽr-sing-ẽr,
Meïs'tẽr-sing-ẽr,
min'nē-sing-ẽr, sing'ẽr.
sl: mud'sling-ẽr, sling'ẽr,
un-sling'ẽr.
spr: spring'ẽr.
st: sting'ẽr.
str: string'ẽr.
sw: swing'ẽr.
w: wing'ẽr.
Plus bring her, Ur *or* err, etc.

ĪN'I

br: brīn'y.
ch: chīn'ie.
h: Heīn'e.
hw: whīn'ey.
l: līn'ey, out'līn-ey.
m: mīn'y.
p: pīn'ey.
sh: mọọn'shīn-y, shīn'y,
sun'shīn-y.
sp: spīn'y.
t: tīn'y.
tw: twīn'ey.
v: vīn'y.
w: wīn'y.
Plus mine, he, etc.

IN'I

b: Bin'ney.
ch: chin'ny.
d: Din'ny.
f: fin'ny.
g: guin'ea ('i),
New Guin'ea.
gr: grin'ny.
h: hin'ny.
hw: whin'ney.
j: jin'ny, Vĭr-ġin'ny.
m: ig'nō-min-y, Min'nie.
n: nin'ny, pick'ȧ-nin-ny.
p: pin'ny.
pl: Plin'y.
sh: shin'ney.
sk: skin'ny.
skw: squin'ny.
sp: spin'ney.
t: Tin'ney, tin'ny.
v: vin'ny.
Plus din, he, etc.

(Choose only one word out of each group)

ĪN′IK

k(ç): kī′niç.
p: pī′niç.
v: vī′niç.
Plus try, Nick *or* nick, etc.

IN′IK

b: Jaç-ō-bin′iç, rab-bin′iç.
d: Ō-din′iç.
f: del-phin′iç, fin′iç.
j: pol-y-ġyn′iç.
kl: ā-çlin′iç, çlin′iç, īs-ō-çlin′iç, mon-ō-çlin′iç.
kw: quin′iç.
l: Frank-lin′iç.
m: Bräh-min′iç, ful-min′iç.
p: pin′iç.
r: man-dà-rin′iç.
s: cyn′iç.
t: aç-tin′iç, ad″i-aç-tin′iç, dī-aç-tin′iç, när-çō-tin′iç, niç-ō-tin′iç, plat-in′iç.
v: vin′iç.
Plus win, Nick *or* nick, etc.

IN′IM

m: min′im.
Cf. Houyhn′hmn (hwin′im).
Plus win him, etc.

ĪN′ING

b: çŏm-bīn′ing.
br: brīn′ing.
d: dīn′ing.
f: çŏn-fīn′ing, dē-fīn′ing, fīn′ing, rē-fīn′ing, trē-phīn′ing.
hw: whīn′ing.
j: j′īn′ing.
kl: dē-çlīn′ing, in-çlīn′ing, rē-çlīn′ing.
l: à-līgn′ing (-līn′), in-tĕr-līn′ing, līn′ing,

mà-līgn′ing (-līn′), out′līn-ing, rē-līn′ing, un-dĕr-līn′ing.
m: çoun-tĕr-mīn′ing, in-tĕr-mīn′ing, mīn′ing, un-dĕr-mīn′ing.
p: ō-pīn′ing, pīn′ing, rē-pīn′ing.
s: as-sīgn′ing, çŏn-sīgn′ing, çoun-tĕr-sīgn′ing, sīgn′ing, sub-sīgn′ing.
sh: bē-shīn′ing, mo̧o̧n′shīn-ing, out-shīn′ing, shīn′ing.
shr: en-shrīn′ing, shrīn′ing.
tw: en-twīn′ing, in-tĕr-twīn′ing, ō-vĕr-twīn′ing, twīn′ing, un-twīn′ing.
v: di-vīn′ing.
w: wīn′ing.
z: dē-s̤īgn′ing, rē-s̤īgn′ing.

IN′ING

Vowel: in′ning.
ch: chin′ning.
d: din′ning.
g: bē-gin′ning.
gr: grin′ning.
j: çot′tŏn ġin′ning, ġin′ning.
p: pin′ning, un-dĕr-pin′ning, un-pin′ning.
s: sin′ning, un-sin′ning.
sh: shin′ning.
sk: skin′ning.
sp: spin′ning.
t: tin′ning.
th: thin′ning.
tw: twin′ning.
w: win′ning.

IN′INGZ

Vowel: in′nings̤.
Plus in′ing+s.

(Choose only one word out of each group)

IN'ISH

f: fin'ish, Fin'nish.
m: di-min'ish.
t: tin'nish.
th: thin'nish.

IN'ISHT

m: di-min'ished,
un-di-min'ished.
Plus in'ish+ed.

IN'IST

l: vī-ō-lin'ist.
Cf. in+est.

Ī'NĪT

f: fī'nīte.
kr: crī'nīte.
Plus try night *or* knight, etc.

IN'JENS

t: cŏn-tin'gence.
Cf. in'gent+s.

IN'JENT

f: fin'gent.
fr: rē-frin'gent.
p: im-pin'gent.
r: rin'gent.
str: ȧ-strin'gent, cŏn-strin'gent.
rē-strin'gent, strin'gent.
t: cŏn-tin'gent, tin'gent*.
Plus thin gent, etc.

IN'JEST

fr: bē-frin'gest*, frin'gest*,
im-frin'gest*, in-frin'gest*.
h: hin'gest*, un-hin'gest*.
kr: crin'gest*.
s: sin'gest*.
sw: swin'gest*.

t: tin'gest*.
tw: twin'gest*.
Plus thin jest, etc.

IN'JETH

fr: bē-frin'geth*, frin'geth*,
im-frin'geth*, in-frin'geth*.
h: hin'geth*, un-hin'geth*.
kr: crin'geth*.
s: sin'geth*.
sw: swin'geth*.
t: tin'geth*.
tw: twin'geth*.

IN'JEZ

b: bin'ges.
d: din'ges.
fr: bē-frin'ges, frin'ges,
in-frin'ges.
h: hin'ges, un-hin'ges.
kr: crin'ges.
p: im-pin'ges.
s: sin'ges.
skr(scr): scrin'ges.
spr: sprin'ges.
str: cŏn-strin'ges,
pẽr-strin'ges.
sw: swin'ges.
t: tin'ges.
tw: twin'ges.
Cf. hinge is, etc.
Plus thin jizz, etc.

IN'JI

d: din'gy.
fr: frin'gy.
kr: cring'gy.
st: stin'gy.
sw: swin'gy.
tw: twin'gy.
Plus binge, he, etc.

(Choose only one word out of each group)

IN'JING

fr: frin'ġing, in-frin'ġing.
h: hin'ġing, un-hin'ġing.
kr: çrin'ġing.
s: sinġe'ing.
sw: swinġe'ing.
t: tinġe'ing.
tw: twinġe'ing.

INJ'LES

fr: frinġe'less.
h: hinġe'less.
sw: swinġe'less.
t: tinġe'less.
tw: twinġe'less.
Plus cringe, Les *or* less, etc.

INJ'MENT

fr: in-frinġe'ment.
h: un-hinġe'ment.
p: im-pinġe'ment.
Plus binge meant, etc.

IN'JŬR

Vowel: in'jŭre.
fr: frin'ġẽr, in-frin'ġẽr.
h: hin'ġẽr.
j: ġin'ġẽr.
kr: çrin'ġẽr.
s: sin'ġẽr.
sw: swin'ġẽr.
tw: twin'ġẽr.
Plus unhinge her *or* err, etc.

IN'KÅ

Vowel: In'çà.
Cf. Katinka, Katrinka.
Plus think a, etc.

ĪN'KLAD

p: pīne'=çlad.
v: vīne'=çlad.
Plus mine clad, etc.

IN'KŎM

Vowel: in'çŏme.
Plus skin come, etc.

IN'KRĒS

Vowel: in'çrēase.
Plus skin crease, etc.

ĪN'KROUND

p: pīne'=çrowned.
v: vīne'=çrowned.
Plus shine, crowned, etc.

IN'KWENT

l: dē-lin'quent, rē-lin'quent.
Cf. ink went, etc.

IN'KWISH

l: rē-lin'quish.
v: vin'quish.
Cf. think wish, etc.

ĪN'LAND

r: Rhīne'land.
v: Vīne'land.
Plus wine land, etc.

IN'LĂND

Vowel: in'lănd.
f: Fin'lănd.
Plus thin land, etc.

IN'LES

d: din'less.
f: fin'less.

ĪN'LI
IN'SES
fāte, fär, fȧst, fạll, finăl, cāre, at; mē⁺e, prey, hẽr, met; pīne,
marïne, bĩrd, pin; nōte, mȯve, fọr, atŏm, not; mọọn, book; 570

(Choose only one word out of each group)

j: ġin'less.
k(ç): kin'less.
p: pin'less.
s: sin'less.
sk: skin'less
t: tin'less.
w: win'less.
Plus din less *or* Les, etc.

ĪN'LI

d: çŏn-dīgn'ly (-dīn').
f: fīne'ly, sū'pẽr-fīne-ly.
l: a'qui-līne-ly,
   mȧ-līgn'ly (-līn').
n: bē-nīgn'ly (-nīn'),
   çā'nīne-ly, sat'ūr-nīne-ly.
p: sū-pīne'ly.
v: di-vīne'ly.
Plus fine, Lee *or* lea, etc.

IN'LI

Vowel: in'ly.
f: Fin'ley.
g: Mç-Gin'ley.
k(ç): Mç-Kin'ley.
th: thin'ly.
Plus skin, Lee *or* lea, etc.

ĪN'MENT

f: çŏn-fīne'ment, rē-fīne'ment.
kl: in-çlīne'ment.
l: ȧ-līgn'ment (-līn'),
   in-tẽr-līne'ment.
s: as-sīgn'ment, çŏn-sīgn'ment.
tw: en-twīne'ment.
z: dē-sīgn'ment, rē-sīgn'ment.
Plus mine meant, etc.

ĪN'NES

d: çŏn-dīgn'ness (-dīn').
f: fīne'ness, sū'pẽr-fīne-ness.
l: sā-līne'ness.

p: sū-pīne'ness.
v: di-vīne'ness.

IN'NES

th: thin'ness.
Cf. in'es.

Ī'NO

Vowel: Aī'nō.
b: al-bī'nō.
f: dam-fī'nō.
r: rhī'nō.
d: jụ'rē di-vī'nō.
Plus why no, *or* know, etc.
Plus mine owe *or* O, etc.

IN'Ō

m: min'nōw.
w: win'nōw.
Plus inn owe *or* O, etc.
Cf. inn know *or* no, etc.

ĪN'ỌF

s: sīgn (sīn) ọff.
Plus mine off, etc.

IN'SEL

t: tin'sel.
Cf. Insull.
Plus skin sell, etc.
Plus prince 'll, etc.

IN'SENS

Vowel: in'cense.
Plus skin sense, etc.
Cf. St. Vincent's.

IN'SENT

v: St. Vin'cent, vin'cent.
Plus inn sent *or* scent, etc.

IN'SES

pr: prin'cess.

(Choose only one word out of each group)

IN'SEST

Vowel: in'cest.
m: min'cest*.
pr: prin'cessed ('sest).
r: rin'sest*.
v: çŏn-vin'cest*, ē-vin'cest*.
w: win'cest*.

IN'CETH

m: min'ceth*.
r: rin'seth*.
v: çŏn-vin'ceth*, ē-vin'ceth*.
w: win'ceth*.
Plus kin, Seth, etc.

IN'SHĂL

v: prō-vin'cial ('shăl).
Plus kin shall, etc.
Plus winch, Al, etc.

IN'SI

kw: Quin'cy.
r: rin'sey ('si).
Plus skin, see, etc.
Plus prince, he, etc.

IN'SING

m: min'cing.
r: rin'sing.
v: çŏn-vin'cing, ē-vin'cing, un-çŏn-vin'cing.
w: win'cing.
Plus skin sing, etc.

IN'SIV

v: ē-vin'cive.
Plus skin sieve, etc.

INS'LI

pr: prince'ly.
Plus quince, Lee or lea, etc.

INS'MENT

v: çŏn-vince'ment, ē-vince'ment.
Plus quince meant, etc.

IN'SŎM

w: win'sŏme.
Plus skin some or sum, etc.
Plus convince 'em, etc.

IN'STREL

m: min'strel.

IN'STŬR

m: min'stĕr, West'min-stĕr.
sp: spin'stĕr.
Plus skin stir, etc.

IN'SŨR

m: min'cĕr.
r: rin'cĕr.
v: çŏn-vin'cĕr.
w: win'cĕr.
Plus tin, sir, etc.
Plus convince her or err, etc.

IN'SŨRZ

p: pin'cĕrṣ.
Plus in'sũr+s.

IN'TED

d: din'ted.
gl: glin'ted.
h: hin'ted.
m: min'ted.
pr: im-prin'ted, mis-prin'ted, prin'ted.
skw: squin'ted.
spr: sprin'ted.
st: stin'ted.

IN'TEST
IN'TL

fāte, fär, fȧst, fạll, finăl, cãre, at; mēte, prey, hêr, met; pīne,
marïne, bĭrd, pin; nōte, mȯve, fọr, atŏm, nͅot; mọọn, book;

572

(Choose only one word out of each group)

t: rāin'bōw=tin'ted,
rō'ṣy=tin'ted, tin'ted.
v: vin'ted.
Plus print, Ed, etc.
Plus kin, Ted, etc.

IN'TEST

gl: glin'test*.
h: hin'test*.
m: min'test*.
pr: im-prin'test*,
mis-prin'test*, prin'test*.
spr: sprin'test*.
st: stin'test*.
t: tin'test*.
Plus skin test, etc.

IN'TETH

gl: glin'teth*.
h: hin'teth*.
m: min'teth*.
pr: im-prin'teth*,
mis-prin'teth*, prin'teth*.
spr: sprin'teth*.
st: stin'teth*.
t: tin'teth*.

ĪN'TI

n: nīne'ty.
Plus fine tea, etc.
Plus pint, he, etc.

IN'TI

d: Din'ty.
fl: flin'ty.
g: Mͅc-Gin'ty.
gl: glin'ty.
l: lin'ty.
skw: squin'ty.
Plus thin tea, etc.

INT'ĪD

fl: flint'=eȳed.
skw: squint'=eȳed.
Plus thin tied or tide, etc.
Plus print, I'd *or* eyed, etc.

IN'TIJ

m: min'tăge ('tij).
v: vin'tăge ('tij).
Cf. print age, etc.

IN'THIK

r: lab-y-rin'thiͅc.
s: ab-sin'thiͅc.
Plus skin thick, etc.

IN'THIN

b: ter-ē-bin'thine.
r: lab-y-rin'thine.
s: hȳ-ȧ-cin'thine.
Plus skin thin, etc.

IN'TING

d: din'ting.
gl: glin'ting.
h: hin'ting.
m: min'ting.
pr: im-prin'ting, mis-prin'ting,
prin'ting.
skw: squin'ting.
spr: sprin'ting.
st: stin'ting.
t: a'quȧ-tin-ting, tin'ting.

IN'TL

kw: quin'tăl.
l: lin'tle.
p: pin'tle.
Plus hint 'll, etc.
Plus twin tell, etc.

573 ūse, bull, brûte, tũrn, up; crȳ, myth; çat, maçhine, ace, church, çhord; ġem, aṅger, (Fr.) boṅ, aṣ; THis, thin; aẓure

IN'TŌ
IN'ŪR

(Choose only one word out of each group)

IN'TŌ

p: pin'tō.
sh: Shin'tō.
t: mez-zō-tin'tō (med-).
Plus skin toe, or tow, etc.
Plus print owe or O, etc.

IN'TREST

Vowel: in'terest, self'₌in'terest.
spl: splin'terest.
w: win'terest*.
Plus hint rest, etc.

IN'TRY

spl: splin'try.
v: vin'try.
w: win'try.
Plus thin tree, etc.

IN'TŨR

d : din'tẽr.
h: hin'tẽr.
m: min'tẽr.
pr: im-prin'tẽr, prin'tẽr.
skw: squin'tẽr.
spl: splin'tẽr.
spr: sprin'tẽr.
st: stin'tẽr.
t: a'quà-tin-tẽr, tin'tẽr.
w: win'tẽr.
Plus print her or err, etc.

IN'Ū

s: sin'ew, un-sin'ew.
t: çŏn-tin'ūe, dis-çŏn-tin'ūe, re'tin-ūe.
Plus skin ewe or you, etc.
Cf. skin new, etc.

IN'ŪD

s: sin'ewed, un-sin'ewed.
t: çŏn-tin'ūed, dis-çŏn-tin'ūed.
Plus win, you'd, etc.

ĪN'ŪR

b: çŏm-bīn'ẽr.
d: dīn'ẽr.
f: çŏn-fīn'ẽr, dē-fīn'ẽr, fīn'ẽr, rē-fīn'ẽr.
hw: whīn'ẽr.
kl: dē-çlīn'ẽr, in-çlīn'ẽr, rē-çlīn'ẽr.
l: līn'ẽr, mà-līgn'ẽr (-līn'), pen'ny₌à₌līn″ẽr, rē-līn'ẽr, un-dẽr-līn'ẽr.
m: çal'çi-mīn-ẽr, mīn'ẽr, mīn'ŏr, un-dẽr-mīn'ẽr.
n: bē-nīgn'ẽr (-nīn').
p: pīn'ẽr, rē-pīn'ẽr, sū-pīn'ẽr.
s: as-sīgn'ẽr (-sīn'), çal-çīn'ẽr, çŏn-sīgn'ẽr, sīgn'ẽr.
sh: shīn'ẽr.
shr: en-shrīn'ẽr, shrīn'ẽr.
st: Steīn'ẽr.
tw: en-twīn'ẽr, in-tẽr-twīn'ẽr, twīn'ẽr.
v: di-vīn'ẽr.
w: wīn'ẽr.
z: ärch-dē-ṣīgn'ẽr (-zīn'), dē-ṣīgn'ẽr, rē-ṣīgn'ẽr.
Plus fine her or err, etc.

IN'ŨR

Vowel: in'nẽr.
b: Byn'nẽr.
ch: chin'nẽr.
d: din'nẽr, àf'tẽr₌din-nẽr.
f: fin'nẽr.

ĬN'ŬS
Ī'ŎR

fāte, fär, fȧst, fąll, finăl, cãre, at; mēte, prey, hẽr, met; pīne,
marine. b́ĩrd, pĭn; nōte, mŏve, fŏr, atŏm, nŏt; mo͞on, book;

574

(Choose only one word out of each group)

g: bĕ-ġĭn'nẽr.
gr: grĭn'nẽr.
j: c̣ŏt'tŏn ġin'nẽr, ġin'nẽr.
p: pin'nẽr, un-pin'nẽr.
s: sin'nẽr.
sh: shin'nẽr.
sk: skin'nẽr.
sp: spin'nẽr.
t: tin'nẽr.
th: thin'nẽr.
tw: twin'nẽr.
w: bread'win-nẽr (brĕd'),
win'nẽr.
Plus inn her *or* err, etc.

ĪN'ŬS

b: bīn'ous.
k(c̣): ē-c̣hĭn'us.
l: lĭn'ous, Lĭn'us, sȧ-lĭn'ous.
m: mĭn'us.
p: lū-pĭn'us, Pīn'us.
r: Rhȳn'us.
s: sĭn'us.
sp: spĭn'ous.
Plus fine us, etc.

ĬN'WĂRD

Vowel: in'wărd.
Plus thin ward, etc.

ĬN'YŎN

b: Bin'yŏn.
m: dō-min'iŏn ('yun),
min'iŏn.
p: ō-pin'iŏn, pin'iŏn.
Cf. in'i-ăn.
Plus skin yon*, etc.

ĬN'YŎND

m: dō-min'iŏned, min'iŏned.
p: ō-pin'iŏned, pin'iŏned,
self=ō-pin'iŏned.

ĬN'ZĬ

kw: quin'sey.
l: Lind'ṣay, Lind'ṣey,
lin'ṣey.
Plus pins, he, etc.

ĬN'ZĬK

tr: ex-trin'ṣic̣, in-trin'ṣic̣.

ĬNZ'MĂN

k(c̣): kins'măn.
Plus pins, man, etc.

ĬN'ZŎR

w: Wind'ṣŏr.
Plus pins or, etc.

Ī'Ō

Vowel: Ī'ō.
h: heīgh'≠hō (hī').
kl: C̣lī'ō.
r: Rī'ō.
tr: trī'ō.
Plus why owe *or* O, etc.

Ī'ŎL

v: bȧss vī'ŏl.
Cf. ī'al.
Cf. try all, etc.

Ī'ŎN

Vowel: ī'ŏn.
l: dan'dē-lī-ŏn, lī'ŏn, sēa lī'ŏn.
r: Ō-rī'ŏn.
s: Ix-ī'ŏn, scī'ŏn.
z: Zī'ŏn.
Plus ī'an.
Plus try on, etc.

Ī'ŎR

pr: prī'ŏr.
Cf. ī'ūr.
Plus sky or, etc.

(Choose only one word out of each group)

Ī'ŎT

Vowel: eȳ'ŏt.
kw: quī'et.
p: pī'ŏt.
s: Scī'ŏt (sī').
Cf. try it *or* at, etc.

IP'Å

l: Phi-lip'på.
p: Pip'på.
Plus skip a, etc.

Ī'PĂL, Ī'PL

s: dis-cī'ple.
t: eç-tȳ'păl.
Plus why, pal, etc.
Plus tripe, Al, etc.
Cf. stripe all, etc.

IP'ĂNT

fl: flip'pănt.
tr: trip'pănt.
Plus ship pant, etc.
Plus skip ant *or* aunt, etc.

ĪP'EN

r: en-rīp'en, rīp'en.
Cf. swipe hen, etc.
Plus my pen, etc.

ĪP'END

r: rīp'ened.
st: stī'pend.
Plus why penned, etc.
Plus stripe end, etc.

ĪP'EST

p: pīp'est*.
r: rīp'est.
t: tȳp'est*, tȳp'ist.
w: wīp'est*.
Plus why pest, etc.

IP'EST

ch: chip'pest*.
d: dip'pest*.
dr: drip'pest*.
fl: flip'pest.
gr: grip'pest*.
hw: horse'whip-pest*,
    whip'pest*.
j: ġyp'pest*.
kl: çlip'pest*.
kw: ē-quip'pest*.
n: nip'pest*.
r: rip'pest*.
s: sip'pest*.
sh: ship'pest*.
sk: skip'pest*.
sl: slip'pest*.
sn: snip'pest*.
str: out-strip'pest*,
    strip'pest*.
t: tip'pest*.
tr: trip'pest*.
Cf. ship pest, etc.

IP'ET

s: sip'pet.
sk: skip'pet.
sn: snip'pet.
t: tip'pet.
Plus skip it, etc.

ĪP'ETH

gr: grīp'eth*.
p: pīp'eth*.
t: tȳp'eth*.
w: wīp'eth*.

IP'ETH

ch: chip'peth*.
d: dip'peth*.
dr: drip'peth*.

(Choose only one word out of each group)

fl: flip'peth*.
gr: grip'peth*.
hw: horse'whip-peth*,
   whip'peth*.
j: ġyp'peth*.
kl: c̣lip'peth*.
kw: ē-quip'peth*.
n: nip'peth*.
r: rip'peth*.
s: sip'peth*.
sh: ship'peth*.
sk: skip'peth*.
sl: slip'peth*.
sn: snip'peth*.
str: out-strip'peth*,
   strip'peth*.
t: tip'peth*.
tr: trip'peth.

ĪP'Ī

Vowel: I. P.
p: pīp'y.
sw: swīp'ey ('i).
Plus stripe, he, etc.

IP'Ī

ch: chip'py.
d: dip'py.
gr: grip'py.
l: Lip'pō Lip'pi, lip'py.
n: nip'py.
s: Mis-sis-sip'pi.
sh: ship'py.
sn: snip'py.
z: zip'py.
Plus ship he, etc.

IP'ID

s: in-sip'id.

IP'IJ

k(c̣): kip'păġe.
skr(sc̣r): sc̣rip'păġe.

str: strip'păġe.
Cf. skip age, etc.

IP'IK

h: hip'pic̣.
l: phi-lip'pic̣.
t: ā-typ'ic̣,
   dȧ-guer'reō-typ-ic̣ (-ger'),
   ē-lec̣'trō-typ-ic̣, hō-mō-typ'ic̣,
   id-i-ō-typ'ic̣, mon-ō-typ'ic̣,
   phō-nō-typ'ic̣, ster-ē-ō-typ'ic̣.
Cf. ship pick, etc.

IP'IN

p: pip'pin.
Cf. skippin', etc.
Plus ship in *or* inn, etc.

ĪP'ING

gr: grīp'ing.
p: Peī'ping, pīp'ing.
str: strīp'ing.
sw: swīp'ing.
t: ster'ē-ō-tȳp-ing, tȳp'ing.
w: wīp'ing.
Plus I ping, etc.

IP'ING

ch: chip'ping.
d: dip'ping.
dr: drip'ping.
fl: flip'ping.
gr: grip'ping.
hw: horse'whip-ping,
   whip'ping.
j: ġyp'ping.
kl: c̣lip'ping.
kw: ē-quip'ping, quip'ping.
n: nip'ping.
p: pip'ping.
r: rip'ping.
s: sip'ping.

(Choose only one word out of each group)

sh: ship'ping, tran-ship'ping.
sk: skip'ping.
sl: slip'ping.
sn: snip'ping.
str: out-strip'ping,
 ō"vēr-strip'ping, strip'ping.
t: tip'ping.
tr: à-trip'ping, trip'ping.

IP'ISH

gr: grip'pish.
h: hip'pish, hyp'pish.
sn: snip'pish.
Cf. strip, pish!

IP'L

gr: grip'păl.
kr: bē-çrip'ple, çrip'ple.
n: nip'ple.
r: rip'ple.
s: sip'ple.
st: stip'ple.
sw: swi'ple.
t: tip'ple.
tr: tri'ple.
Plus ship'll, etc.
Cf. ship pull, etc.

IP'LET

l: lip'let.
r: rip'plet.
s: sip'let.
tr: trip'let.
Plus ship let or Lett, etc.

IP'LI

kr: çrip'ply.
r: rip'ply.
st: stip'ply.
tr: tri'ply.
Plus ship, Lee or lea, etc.

IP'LING

k(ç): Kip'ling.
kr: çrip'pling.
r: rip'pling.
st: stip'pling.
str: strip'ling.
t: tip'pling.

IP'LŨR

kr: çrip'plĕr.
t: tip'plĕr.

IP'MENT

kw: ē-quip'ment.
sh: ship'ment, tran-ship'ment.
Plus quip meant, etc.

ĪP'NES

r: dead⸗rīpe'ness (ded⸗),
 ō-vēr-rīpe'ness, rīpe'ness,
 un-dĕr-rīpe'ness, un-rīpe'ness.

IP'Ō

h: hip'pō.
j: ġip'pō*.
l: Lip'pō.
Plus ship owe or O, etc.

Ī'PRES

s: cȳ'press.
Plus my press, etc.

IP'SHUN

j: Ē-ġyp'tiăn.
n: çŏn-nip'tion.
skr(sçr): ā-sçrip'tion,
 cīr-çum-sçrip'tion,
 çŏn-sçrip'tion, dē-sçrip'tion,
 in-sçrip'tion, prē-sçrip'tion,
 prō-sçrip'tion, rē-sçrip'tion,
 sub-sçrip'tion,

IP'SI
IP'ŬR

fāte, fär, fȧst, fạll, finăl, cãre, ⱥt; mēte, prẹy, hẽr, met; pīne,
marïne, bĭrd, pin; nōte, mŏve, fọr, atŏm, not; mọọn, book;

578

(Choose only one word out of each group)

sū-pẽr-sc̜rip'tion,
tran-sc̜rip'tion.
Plus ship shun, etc.

IP'SI

j: ġyp'sy.
k(c̜): Pŏugh-keep'sie (pō-kip'si).
sk: Skip'sey ('si).
t: tip'sy.
Plus ships, he, etc.
Plus ship, see, etc.

IP'SIS

l: el-lip'sis.
tr: trip'sis.
Plus skip, sis, etc.

IP'TIK

d: dip'tyc̜h.
gl: an-ȧ-glyp'tic̜, glyp'tic̜.
kl: ē-c̜lip'tic̜.
kr: c̜ryp'tic̜, hol-ō-c̜ryp'tic̜.
l: ap-oc̜-ȧ-lyp'tic̜,
ī-ȧ-trȧ-lip'tic̜.
st: styp'tic̜.
tr: trip'tyc̜h.
Plus ship tick, etc.

IP'TIV

skr(sc̜r): ad-sc̜rip'tive,
ās-c̜rip'tive*, c̜īr-c̜um-sc̜rip'tive,
dē-sc̜rip'tive, in-dē-sc̜rip'tive,
in-sc̜rip'tive, prē-sc̜rip'tive,
prō-sc̜rip'tive, rē-sc̜rip'tive,
tran-sc̜rip'tive.

IP'TŪR

skr(sc̜r): sc̜rip'tūre.
Plus clipped your *or* you're, etc.

ĪP'ŬR

d: dī''pẽr.
gr: grīp'ẽr.

l: Leīp'ẽr.
p: bag'pīp-ẽr, pīp'ẽr.
r: rīp.'ẽr.
sn: snīp'ẽr.
str: strīp'ẽr.
sw: swīp'ẽr.
t: dȧ-guer'reō-tȳp-ẽr (-ger'),
ĕl-ec̜'trō-tȳp-ẽr, līn'ō-tȳp-ẽr,
mon'ō-tȳp-ẽr, ster'ē-ō-tȳp-ẽr,
tȳp'ẽr.
v: vī'pẽr.
w: wī'pẽr.
Plus why purr *or* per, etc.
Plus stripe her *or* err, etc.

IP'ŬR

ch: chip'pẽr.
d: Big Dip'pẽr, dip'pẽr.
dr: drip'pẽr.
fl: flip'pẽr.
fr: frip'pẽr*.
gr: grip'pẽr.
hw: horse'whip-pẽr, whip'pẽr.
j: ġyp'pẽr.
k(c̜): kip'pẽr, Yōm Kip'pūr.
kl: c̜lip'pẽr.
n: gal'li-nip-pẽr, nip'pẽr.
p: pip'pẽr.
r: Jack the Rip'pẽr, rip'pẽr.
s: sip'pẽr.
sh: ship'pẽr, tran-ship'pẽr.
sk: skip'pẽr.
sl: lā'dy's slip'pẽr, slip'pẽr.
sn: snip'pẽr.
str: out-strip'pẽr,
ō-vẽr-strip'pẽr, strip'pẽr.
sw: swip'pẽr*.
t: tip'pẽr.
tr: trip'pẽr.
z: zip'pẽr.
Plus whip her *or* err, etc.

579
ūse, bṳll, brute, tûrn, up; crȳ, myth; çat, maçhine, ace, church, ҫhord; ġem, aṅger, (Fr.) boṅ, aṣ; THis, thin; azure

IP'ŪRD
ĪR'ENT

(Choose only one word out of each group)

IP'ŪRD

k: kip'pēred.
sk: skip'pēred.
sl: slip'pēred.
Plus zipper'd, etc.

Ī'RÅ

Vowel: Ī'rȧ.
f: Sap-phī'rȧ.
j: hē-ġī'rȧ.
k: Kī'rȧh.
l: Lȳ'rȧ.
m: Al-mī'rȧ, El-mī'rȧ, Mȳ'rȧ, Pal-mȳ'rȧ.
th: Thȳ'rȧ.
Plus hire a, etc.

IR'ÅH

s: sir'rȧh.

ĪR'ĂL

j: ġȳr'ăl.
sp: spīr'ăl.
t: rē-tīr'ăl.
Plus inquire, Al, etc.

Ī'RĂM

h: Hī'răm.
Plus buy ram, etc.
Plus fire 'em, etc.

ĪR'ĂNT

j: ġȳ'ränt.
sp: a-spīr'ănt, ҫŏn-spīr'ănt, ex-pīr'ănt, spīr'ănt.
t: ärch'tȳ'ränt, tȳ'ränt.
Plus why rant, etc.
Plus fire aunt or ant, etc.

ĪR'ÅT

Vowel: ī'rāte.
j: cīr-ҫum-ġȳ'rāte, dex-trō-ġȳ'rāte, ġȳ'rāte.

l: lȳr'āte.
Plus fire ate or eight, etc.
Plus why rate, etc.
Cf. fire rate, etc.

Ī'RĂT

p: pī'răte.
Cf. fire at, etc.

Ī'RĒ

Vowel: Dī'ēṣ Ī'raē.
n: praē-mū-nī'rē.
Cf. ī'ri.
Plus fire, he, etc.

IR'EL

b: Bir'rell.
skw: squir'rel.
t: Tir'rell.
Cf. Cyr'il, Tyr'ol, vir'ile.
Plus stir L or ell, etc.

Ī'RĒM

b: bī'rēme.
tr: trī'rēme.
Plus buy ream, etc.

ĪR'ĒN

p: pȳr'ēme.
skw: squīr'een.

Ī'REN

s: lep″i-dō-sī'ren, sī'ren.
Plus why wren, etc.
Cf. fire hen, etc.

ĪR'ENT

kw: in-quīr'ent.
v: sem-pi-vīr'ent, vīr'ent.
Plus īr'ănt.

ĪR'EST
ĪR'ING

fāte, fär, fȧst, fạll, fīnăl, cãre, at; mēte, pₑ₋y, hẽr, met; pīne,
marïne, bĩrd, pin; nōte, mŏve, fọr, atŏm, not; mọọn, book;

580

(Choose only one word out of each group)

ĪR'EST

d: dīr'est.
f: fīr'est*.
h: hīr'est*.
kw: ac̦-quīr'est*, en-quīr'est*,
in-quīr'est*, rē-quīr'est*.
m: ad-mīr'est*, bē-mīr'est*,
mīr'est*.
p: pȳr'est*, um-pīr'est*.
sp: a-spīr'est*, c̦ŏn-spīr'est*,
ex-pīr'est*, in-spīr'est*,
pĕr-spīr'est*, rē-spīr'est*,
sus-pīr'est*, tran-spīr'est*.
t: at-tīr'est*, rē-tīr'est*, tīr'est*.
w: wīr'est*.
z: dē-șīr'est*.
Plus why rest, etc.

ĪR'ETH

f: fīr'eth*.
h: hīr'eth*.
kw: ac̦-quīr'eth*, en-quīr'eth*,
in-quīr'eth*, rē-quīr'eth*.
m: ad-mīr'eth*, bē-mīr'eth*,
mīr'eth*.
p: pȳr'eth*, um-pīr'eth*.
sp: a-spīr'eth*, c̦ŏn-spīr'eth*,
ex-pīr'eth*, in-spīr'eth*,
pĕr-spīr'eth*, rē-spīr'eth*,
sus-pīr'eth*, tran-spīr'eth*.
t: at-tīr'eth*, rē-tīr'eth*,
tīr'eth*.
w: wīr'eth*.
z: dē-șīr'eth*.

ĪR'FLĪ

f: fīre'flȳ.
Plus desire fly, etc.

ĪR'FUL

Vowel: īre'fu̧l.
d: dīre'fu̧l.
Plus desire full, etc.

ĪR'I

d: daī'ri, dīa'ry.
kw: ac̦-quīr'y*, en-quīr'y,
in-quīr'y.
m: mīr'y.
skw: squīr'y.
sp: spīr'y.
w: wīr'y.
Cf. īr'e.
Cf. fiery, and i'ūr-i.
Plus squire, he, etc.

ĪR'I

Vowel: eȳr'ie ('i).
Cf. Ē'rie, and ē'ri.

IR'ID

Vowel: ir'id.
v: vir'id.
Cf. he rid, etc.

IR'IK

j: pan-ē-ġyr'ic̦.
l: lyr'ic̦.
p: em-pir'ic̦, Pyr'rhic̦.
t: bū-tyr'ic̦, sa-tir'ic̦,
sa-tyr'ic̦.
Cf. Vier'eck.

IR'IL

s: Cyr'il.
v: vir'ile.
Cf. ir'el.

ĪR'ING

f: fīr'ing.
h: hīr'ing.
kw: ac̦-quīr'ing, en-quīr'ing,
in-quīr'ing, rē-quīr'ing.
l: lȳr'ing.
m: ad-mīr'ing, bē-mīr'ing,
mīr'ing.

(Choose only one word out of each group)

p: pȳr′ing.
skw: squīr′ing.
sp: a-spīr′ing, c̩ŏn-spīr′ing,
ex-pīr′ing, in-spīr′ing,
pĕr-spīr′ing, rē-spīr′ing,
sus-pīr′ing, tran-spīr′ing,
un-a-spīr′ing.
t: at-tīr′ing, rē-tīr′ing, tīr′ing,
un-tīr′ing.
z: dē-s̩īr′ing, un-dē-s̩īr′ing.

ĪR′IS
Vowel: īr′is.
s: Ō-sīr′is.
Cf. desire is, etc.

ĪR′ISH
Vowel: Īr′ish.
Cf. mīr′ish, etc.

ĪR′IST
Vowel: īr′ised (′ist).
l: lȳ′rist.
Plus why wrist, etc.

IR′IST
j: pan-ē-ġyr′ist.
l: lyr′ist.

IR′IT
sp: di-spir′it, in-spir′it,
mȧs′tĕr spir′it, pär′ty spir′it,
spir′it.
Cf. fear it, etc.

ĪR′LING
h: hīre′ling.
skw: squīre′ling.

ĪR′MĂN
f: fīre′măn.
Plus desire, man, etc.

ĪR′MENT
kw: ac̩-quīre′ment,
rē-quīre′ment.
m: bē-mīre′ment.
sp: a-spīre′ment.
t: rē-tīre′ment.
Plus fire meant, etc.

ĪR′NES
d: dīre′ness.
t: en-tīre′ness.

ĪR′Ō
j: a̩u-tō-ġī′rō, ġȳ′rō.
k(c̩): C̩aī′rō.
t: tȳ′rō.
Plus why row *or* roe, etc.
Plus fire owe *or* O, etc.

Ī′RŌD
b: bȳ′rōad.
h: hīgh′rōad (hī′).
Plus sky road, etc.
Plus fire ode *or* owed, etc.

Ī′RON
b: Bȳ′rŏn.
ch: Chī′rŏn.
j: ġȳ′rŏn.
v: en-vī′rŏn, vī′rŏn.
Plus fire on *or* an, etc.
Cf. why run, etc.

ĪR′ŌS
j: ġȳr′ōse.
v: vīr′ōse.
Plus why rose, etc.
Cf. squire hose, etc.

ĪR′SĪD
f: fīre′sīde.
Plus desire sighed *or* side, etc.

(Choose only one word out of each group)

ĪR'SŎM

Vowel: īre're'sŏme.
t: tīre'sŏme.
Plus fire some *or* sum, etc.

IR'UP

ch: chir'rup.
st: stir'rup.
s: syr'up.
Plus her *or* err up, etc.

ĪR'ŨR

f: fīr'ẽr.
h: hīr'ẽr.
kw: aç-quīr'ẽr, en-quīr'ẽr,
  in-quīr'ẽr, rē-quīr'ẽr.
m: ad-mīr'ẽr, bē-mīr'ẽr, mīr'ẽr.
p: pȳr'ẽr.
skw: squīr'ẽr.
sp: a-spīr'ẽr, çŏn-spīr'ẽr,
  ex-pīr'ẽr, in-spīr'ẽr,
  pẽr-spīr'ẽr, rē-spīr'ẽr,
  tran-spīr'ẽr, un-a-spīr'ẽr.
t: at-tīr'ẽr, rē-tīr'ẽr, tīr'ẽr.
z: dē-ṣīr'ẽr.
Plus desire her *or* err, etc.

IR'ŨR

m: mir'rŏr.
Cf. ẽr'ũr.

ĪR'US

p: ā-pȳr'ous, Ē-pī'rus,
  pȧ-pȳr'us.
s: Cȳ'rus.
v: vīr'us.
z: dē-ṣīr'ous.
Plus hire us, etc.

ĪR'WŨRKS

f: fīre'wŏrks.
w: wīre'works.
Plus desire works, etc.

IS'Ȧ

l: Ē-lis'ȧ, Lis'ȧ, Mē-lis'ȧ.
r: Çlȧ-ris'ȧ, Nē-ris'ȧ.
Plus miss a, etc.

Ī'SĀL

sk: skȳ'sāil.
tr: trȳ'sāil.
Plus why sale *or* sail, etc.
Plus ice ail *or* ale, etc.

ĪS'ĂL

d: par-ȧ-dīs'ăl.
Plus ice, Al, etc.
Plus why, Sal, etc.

IS'CHIF

m: mis'chief ('chif).

IS'CHĂN

kr: an-ti-Çhris'tiăn ('chăn),
  Çhris'tiăn ('chăn).
Plus miss Chan, etc.

Ī'SENS

l: dog lī'cense, fish'ing lī'cense,
  hunt'ing lī'cense, lī'cense,
  mar'riăġe lī'cense ('ij),
  pō-e'tiç lī'cense.
Plus buy sense, scents *or* cents,
  etc.
Cf. lice, hence, etc.

IS'ENS

h: dē-his'cence, in-dē-his'cence.
n: re-mi-nis'cence.
p: çon-çū-pis'cence,
  re-si-pis'cence.
t: fȧ-tis'cence.
v: re-vi-vis'cence.
Cf. bliss sense, scents *or* cents, etc.

583 ūse, bu̱ll, brúte, tū̆rn, up; crȳ, myth; c̱at, ma̱chine, ace, church, c̱hord; ġem, añger, (Fr.) boṅ, a̱s; THis, thin; a̱zure

IS′ENT
I′SHĂL

(Choose only one word out of each group)

IS′ENT

h: dē-his′cent, in-dē-his′cent.
n: re-mi-nis′cent.
v: re-vi-vis′cent.
Cf. bliss sent, scent or cent, etc.

ĪS′EST

f: sa̱c-ri-fīc′est*, suf-fīc′est*.
n: nīc′est.
pr: prīc′est*.
s: c̱ŏn-cīs′est, prē-cīs′est.
sl: slīc′est*.
sp: bē-spīc′est*, spīc′est*.
spl: splīc′est*.
t: en-tīc′est*.

IS′EST

h: his′sest*.
k(c̱): kis′sest*.
m: dis-mis′sest*, mis′sest*.

ĪS′ETH

f: sa̱c-ri-fīc′eth*, suf-fīc′eth*.
pr: prīc′eth*.
sl: slīc′eth*.
sp: bē-spīc′eth*, spīc′eth*.
spl: splīc′eth*.
t: en-tīc′eth*.
Plus why, Seth, etc.

IS′ETH

h: his′seth*.
k(c̱): kis′seth*.
m: dis-mis′seth*, mis′seth*.

IS′ĒZ

l: Ū-lys′sēs.
Cf. is′ez.
Cf. miss seas or seize, etc.

IS′EZ

b: a̱-bys′ses.
bl: blis′ses.

d: pre′ju̱-dic-es.
f: är′ti-fic-es, ben′ē-fic-es, ed′i-fic-es.
h: his′ses.
k(c̱): kis′ses.
m: dis-mis′ses, mis′ses.
p: prec′i-pic-es.
sw: Swiss′es.
tr: c̱ock′a̱-tric-es.
Plus this is, etc.

IS′FU̱L

bl: bliss′fu̱l, un-bliss′fu̱l.
m: rē-miss′fu̱l.
Plus kiss full, etc.

Ī′SHȦ

l: Ē-lī′shȧ.

I′SHA

l: Dē-li′ciȧ.
t: Le-ti′tiȧ.
Plus wish a, etc.

I′SHĂL

d: ex″trȧ-ju̱-di′ciăl, ju̱-di′ciăl, pre-ju̱-di′ciăl.
f: är-ti-fi′ciăl, ben-ē-fi′ciăl, ed-i-fi′ciăl, in-är-ti-fi′ciăl, of-fi′ciăl, sa̱c-ri-fi′ciăl, sū-pēr-fi′ciăl.
l: ġen-ti-li′tiăl, nat-ȧ-li′tiăl, pō-li′ciăl.
m: c̱ō-mi′tiăl.
n: i-ni′tiăl, tri-bū-ni′ciăl.
s: ex-i′tiăl*.
st: in-tēr-sti′tiăl, vōl-sti′tiăl.
t: a̱c-c̱rē-men-ti′tiăl, re-c̱rē-men-ti′tiăl, sus-ti′ciăl.
Cf. we shall, etc.
Plus wish, Al, etc.

(Choose only one word out of each group)

I'SHĂN

j: lō-ġi'ciăn, mȧ-ġi'ciăn.
m: aç-a-de-mi'ciăn.
t: op-ti'ciăn, etc.
Plus i'shun.
Plus wish an, etc.

I'SHENS

f: dē-fi'cience, ef-fi'cience,
in-suf-fi'cience, mal-ē-fi'cience,
prō-fi'cience, self=suf-fi'cience.
n: om-ni'science.
sp: pẽr-spi'cience,
prō-spi'cience.

I'SHENT

f: ben-ē-fi'cient, çal-or-i-fi'cient,
çō-ef-fi'cient, dē-fi'cient,
ef-fi'cient, in-dē-fi'cient,
in-ef-fi'cient, in-suf-fi'cient,
mal-ē-fi'cient, pẽr-fi'cient*,
prō-fi'cient, self=suf-fi'cient,
suf-fi'cient.
j: ob-ji'cient.
l: vō-li'tient.
n: om-ni'scient.

ISH'EST

d: dish'est*.
f: fish'est*.
sw: swish'est*.
w: wish'est*.

ISH'ETH

d: dish'eth*.
f: fish'eth*.
sw: swish'eth*.
w: wish'eth*.

ISH'FŲL

d: dish'fųl.
w: wish'fųl.
Plus knish full, etc.

ISH'I

f: fish'y.
sw: swish'y.

ISH'ING

d: dish'ing.
f: fish'ing.
sw: swish'ing.
w: ill=wish'ing, well'=wish'ing,
wish'ing.

ISH'ŎP

b: bish'ŏp.
Cf. fish up, etc.

I'SHUN

Vowel: cĭr-çū-i'tion*, frū-i'tion,
in-tū-i'tion, tū-i'tion.
b: ad-hi-bi'tion, am-bi'tion,
ex-hi-bi'tion, im-bi-bi'tion,
in-hi-bi'tion, prō-hi-bi'tion.
br: Hē-bri'ciăn, rū-bri'ciăn.
d: ad-di'tion, ạu-di'tion,
çŏn-di'tion, dē-pẽr-di'tion*,
ē-di'tion, e-rụ-di'tion,
ex-pē-di'tion, ex-trȧ-di'tion,
pẽr-di'tion, prē-çŏn-di'tion,
red-di'tion, rē-di'tion*,
ren-di'tion, sē-di'tion,
sū″pẽr-ad-di'tion, trȧ-di'tion,
ven-di'tion.
f: fis'sion.
j: lō-ġi'ciăn, mȧ-ġi'ciăn.
l: ab-ō-li'tion, çō-ȧ-li'tion,
de-mō-li'tion, e-bul-li'tion,
Gȧ-li'ciăn, nō-li'tion,
Pạu-li'ciăn, rē-ṣi-li'tion,
vō-li'tion.
m: ȧ-ça-de-mi'ciăn, ad-mis'sion,
ad-ō-mi'ciăn, çom-mis'sion,
dē-mis'sion, dis-mis'sion,
ē-mis'sion, im-mis'sion,
in-sub-mis'sion, in-tẽr-mis'sion,

(Choose only one word out of each group)

in-trō-mis′sion, ir-rē-mis′sion,
man-ū-mis′sion, mis′sion,
ob-dọr-mi′tion, ō-mis′sion,
pĕr-mis′sion, rē-ad-mis′sion,
rē-mis′sion, sub-mis′sion,
trans-mis′sion, vō-mi′tion.

n: a-ban-ni′tion*, ad-mō-ni′tion,
af-fi-ni′tion, am-mū-ni′tion,
çog-ni′tion, de-fi-ni′tion,
ep-i-ni′ciǎn, ig-ni′tion,
il-li-ni′tion, in-à-ni′tion,
in-i′tion, me-çhà-ni′ciǎn,
mō-ni′tion, mū-ni′tion,
nē″ō-plā-tō-ni′ciǎn,
Phoē-ni′ciǎn, prē-çog-ni′tion,
prē-mō-ni′tion, pū-ni′tion,
pȳ″rō-teçh-ni′ciǎn,
re-çog-ni′tion, rē-ū-ni′tion,
sub-mō-ni′tion, tri-bū-ni′tion.

p: Ā-pi′ciǎn, sus-pi′ciŏn.

pl: sim-pli′ciǎn*.

r: ab-li-gū-ri′tion*, ap-pà-ri′tion,
fū-tū-ri′tion, pär-tū-ri′tion,
pre-tē-ri′tion, rhet-ō-ri′ciǎn.

s: in-si′tion.

st: sū-pĕr-sti′tion.

t: aç-çrē-men-ti′tion,
a-çöus-ti′ciǎn, a-glụ-ti′tion,
à-rith-me-ti′ciǎn, bī-pär-ti′tion,
çom-pē-ti′tion, dē-glụ-ti′tion,
den-ti′tion, dē-pär-ti′tion,
dī-à-leç-ti′ciǎn,
hȳ-drō-stà-ti′ciǎn,
mag-ne-ti′ciǎn,
math″ē-mà-ti′ciǎn, op-ti′ciǎn,
pär-ti′tion, pē-ti′tion,
pol-i-ti′ciǎn, praç-ti′ciǎn,
re-pe-ti′tion, sọr-ti′tion,
sta-tis-ti′ciǎn, taç-ti′ciǎn,
tra-là-ti′tion, trī-pär-ti′tion.

tr: at-tri′tion, çŏn-tri′tion,

dē-tri′tion, ēl-eç-tri′ciǎn,
ġē-o-me-tri′ciǎn, mē-tri′ciǎn,
nū-tri′tion, ob-ste-tri′ciǎn,
pà-tri′ciǎn.

z: aç-qui-ṣi′tion, ap-pō-ṣi′tion,
çom-pō-ṣi′tion,
çon″trà-pō-ṣi′tion,
dē-çom-pō-ṣi′tion, dis-pō-ṣi′tion,
dis-qui-ṣi′tion, ex-pō-ṣi′tion,
im-pō-ṣi′tion, in-dis-pō-ṣi′tion,
in-qui-ṣi′tion, in″tēr-pō-ṣi′tion,
jux″tà-pō-ṣi′tion, mū-ṣi′ciǎn,
op-pō-ṣi′tion, pĕr-qui-ṣi′tion,
phy-ṣi′ciǎn, pō-ṣi′tion,
prē-dis-pō-ṣi′tion,
pre-pō-ṣi′tion,
prē-sup-pō-ṣi′tion,
prop-ō-ṣi′tion,
rē-çom-pō-ṣi′tion, rē-pō-ṣi′tion,
re-qui-ṣi′tion, sū″pĕr-pō-ṣi′tion,
sup-pō-ṣi′tion, trans-pō-ṣi′tion,
tran-ṣi′tion.

ISH′ŪR

d: dish′ĕr.

f: Fis′çhĕr, fish′ĕr, fis′sūre,
king′fish-ĕr.

sw: swish′ĕr.

w: ill‹wish′ĕr, well′‹wish′ĕr,
wish′ĕr.

Plus swish her *or* err, etc.

I′SHUS

b: am-bi′tious.

d: ex-pē-di′tious, in-jù-di′cious,
jù-di′cious, sē-di′tious.

f: ben-ē-fi′cious, in-of-fi′cious,
of-fi′cious, ven-ē-fi′cious.

j: flà-ġi′tious.

l: ci-li′cious*, dē-li′cious,
ġen-ti-li′tious*, mà-li′cious,

ĬS′I
ĬS′ISH
fāte, fär, fȧst, fạll, finăl, cãre, at; mēte, prĕy, hẽr, met; pīne,
marĭne, bĭrd, pin; nōte, mŏve, fọr, atŏm, nọt; mọọn, book;
586

(Choose only one word out of each group)

nā-tȧ-li′tious, sa-tel-li′tious,
si-li′cious.
m: pū-mi′cious, vẽr-mi′cious.
n: pẽr-ni′cious, pū-ni′ceous.
p: ạus-pi′cious, in-ạu-spi′cious,
pi′ceous, prō-pi′tious,
sus-pi′cious.
pl: mul-ti-pli′cious.
pr: cạ-pri′cious.
r: av-ȧ-ri′cious, lat-e-ri′tious,
sē-ri′ceous.
s: ex-i′tious*.
st: sū-pẽr-sti′tious.
t: ad-di-ti′tious, ad-jec-ti′tious,
ad-sci-ti′tious, ad-ven-ti′tious,
ar-rep-ti′tious*, as-ci-ti′tious,
as-crip-ti′tious, dē-glu-ti′tious,
fac-ti′tious, fic-ti′tious,
ob-rep-ti′tious, prō-fec-ti′tious,
sē-crē-ti′tious, stil-lȧ-ti′tious,
sup-pōṣ-i-ti′tious,
sũr-rep-ti′tious, tra-lȧ-ti′tious.
tr: mer-ē-tri′cious, nū-tri′tious,
ob-ste-tri′cious*.
v: vi′cious.
z: sup-pō-ṣi′tious.
Plus wish us, etc.

ĪS′I

Vowel: īc′y.
n: nī′si.
sp: spīc′y.
t: Dȧ-tī′si.
Plus why see, etc.

IS′I

m: mis′si.
s: sis′sy.
Plus kiss, he, etc.

IS′IK

l: sȧ-lic′ic̣.
t: mas-tic′ic̣.

IS′IL

f: fis′sile.
m: mis′sile.
s: scis′sile.
Cf. is′l.
Plus kiss ill, etc.

IS′ID

v: vis′cid.

IS′IN

t: dȧ-tis′cin.
v: vis′cin.
Plus bliss in, etc.

ĪS′ING

Vowel: īc′ing.
d: dīc′ing.
f: sac̣′ri-fīc-ing,
self⸗sac̣′ri-fīc-ing,
self⸗suf-fīc′ing, suf-fīc′ing.
pr: prīc′ing.
sl: slīc′ing.
sp: bē-spīc′ing, spīc′ing.
spl: splīc′ing.
t: en-tīc′ing.
Plus why sing, etc.

IS′ING

h: dē-hisc′ing, his′sing.
k(c̣): kis′sing.
m: dis-mis′sing, mis′sing.

ĪS′IS

Vowel: Īs′is.
kr: crīs′is.
t: phthīs′is (tī′).
Cf. īs+es.
Cf. rice is, etc.

IS′ISH

m: mis′sish.

587 ūse, bull, brūte, tūrn, up; crȳ, myth; cat, machine, ace, church, chord; ġem, añger, (Fr.) boñ, aṣ; THis, thin; aẓure

IS'IT
IS'KING

(Choose only one word out of each group)

IS'IT

l: ē-lic′it, il-lic′it, lic′it, sō-lic′it.
pl: ex-plic′it, im-plic′it.
Plus kiss it, etc.

Ī'SIV

l: cōl-lī′sive.
r: dē-rī′sive.
s: de-cī′sive, in-ci′sive, in-dē-cī′sive.
tr: cic-à-trīs′ive.
v: di-vīs′ive.
Plus why sieve, etc.

IS'IV

m: ad-mis′sive, cŏm-mis′sive, dē-mis′sive*, ē-mis′sive, in-tĕr-mis′sive, ir-rē-mis′sive, mis′sive, non-sub-mis′sive, ō-mis′sive, pĕr-mis′sive, prō-mis′sive, rē-mis′sive, sub-mis′sive, trans-mis′sive.
Cf. this sieve, etc.

IS'KÁ OR ISH'KÁ

r: Mà-ris′kà.

IS'KĂL

d: dis′căl.
f: fis′căl.
l: ob-e-lis′căl.
Plus kiss, Cal, etc.
Plus whisk, Al, etc.

IS'KĀT

f: con′fis-cāte.
v: in-vis′cāte.
Plus bliss, Kate, etc.
Plus disc eight *or* ate, etc.

IS'KEST

br: bris′kest.
fr: fris′kest*.
hw: whis′kest*.
r: ris′kest*.

IS'KET

br: bris′ket.
fr: fris′ket.
t: tis′ket.
Cf. risk it, etc.

IS'KETH

fr: fris′keth*.
hw: whis′keth*.
r: ris′keth*.

ISK'FUL

fr: frisk′ful.
r: risk′ful.
Plus risk full, etc.

IS'KI

fr: fris′ky.
hw: whis′key, Ī′rish whis′key, etc.
r: ris′ky.
Plus this key, etc.
Plus whisk, he.

IS'KIN

gr: gris′kin.
s: sis′kin.
Plus this kin, etc.
Plus whisk ín *or* inn, etc.

IS'KING

br: brisk′ing.
fr: frisk′ing.
hw: whisk′ing.
r: risk′ing.
Plus this king, etc.

(Choose only one word out of each group)

IS′KIT

b: bis′c̣uit.
Plus bliss, Kit, etc.
Plus risk it, etc.

IS′KŌ

kr: C̣ris′c̣ō.
s: Fran-cis′c̣ō, San Fran-cis′c̣ō.
Plus risk owe *or* O, etc.
Cf. this Co., etc.

IS′KŪR

br: bris′kẽr.
fr: fris′kẽr.
hw: bē-whis′kẽr, whis′kẽr.
r: ris′kẽr.
Plus risk her *or* err, etc.

IS′KŪRZ

hw: whis′kẽrṣ.
Plus is′kūr+ṣ.

IS′KUS

b: hī-bis′c̣us.
d: dis′c̣ous, dis′c̣us.
k(c̣): trō-c̣his′c̣us.
n: lem-nis′c̣us, mē-nis′c̣us.
s: ab-ȧ-cis′c̣us.
t: len-tis′c̣us.
v: vis′c̣ous.
Plus risk us, etc.

IS′L

b: ȧ-bys′săl.
br: bris′tle.
gr: gris′tle.
hw: whis′tle.
m: dis-mis′săl, mis′săl.
p: ē-pis′tle.
s: scis′sel.
th: this′tle.
Cf. is′il.
Plus this′ll, etc.

ĪS′LES

Vowel: īce′less.
d: dīce′less.
m: mīce′less.
pr: prīce′less.
sp: spīce′less.
spl: splīce′less.
v: ad-vīce′less, vīce′less, etc.
Plus price less *or* Les, etc.

ĪS′LI

n: nīce′ly.
s: C̣īce′ly, c̣ŏn-c̣īse′ly,
  prē-c̣īse′ly.
Plus price, Lee *or* lea, etc.

IS′LI

br: bris′tly.
gr: gris′tly.
th: this′tly.
Plus bliss, Lee *or* lea, etc.

IS′LING

br: bris′tling.
hw: whis′tling.

ĪS′MENT

f: suf-fīce′ment,
  self′=suf-fīce′ment.
t: en-tīce′ment.
Plus lice meant, etc.

IS′MUS

Vowel: isth′mus.
Cf. Christ′măs (kris′).
Plus this muss, etc.

IS′N

gl: glis′ten.
kr: c̣hris′ten.
l: lis′ten, rē-lis′ten.

(Choose only one word out of each group)

Plus this'n, etc.
Cf. this sun *or* sun, etc.

ĪS'NES

n: nīce'ness, ō-vēr-nīce'ness.
s: çŏn-cīse'ness, prē-cīse'ness.

IS'NES

m: rē-miss'ness.
TH: THis'ness.

IS'NING

gl: glis'tening.
kr: Chris'tening.
l: lis'tening.

IS'ŎM

l: lis'sŏme.
Cf. this sum *or* some, etc.

Ī'SŎN

b: bī'sŏn.
d: Dȳ'sŏn.
gr: grī'sŏn.
h: hȳ'sŏn.
t: Tȳ'sŏn.
v: vī'sŏn.
Plus why, son *or* sun, etc.

IS'PEST

kr: cris'pest.
l: lis'pest*.
Plus this pest, etc.

IS'PETH

kr: cris'peth*.
l: lis'peth*.

IS'PI

kr: cris'py.
l: lis'py.

IS'PIN

kr: Cris'pin, St. Cris'pin.
Plus this pin, etc.

IS'PING

kr: cris'ping.
l: lis'ping.
Plus this ping, etc.

IS'PŪR

hw: stāġe whis'pēr, whis'pēr.
kr: cris'pēr.
l: lis'pēr.
Plus this purr *or* per, etc.
Plus crisp her *or* err, etc.

IS'TÀ

l: bal-lis'tà, Çal-lis'tà.
n: ġē-nis'tà.
t: Bap-tis'tà.
v: Buęn'ä Vis'tà, vis'tà.
Plus assist a, etc.

IS'TĂL, IS'TL

kr: crys'tăl.
l: lis'tel.
p: pis'tŏl, pock'et pis'tŏl, wạt'ēr pis'tŏl.
Plus kissed, Al, etc.

IS'TĂN

tr: Tris'tăn.
Plus this tan, etc.

IS'TĂNS

d: dis'tănce, ē"qui-dis-tănce.
s: as-sis'tănce, çŏn-sis'tence, in-çŏn-sis'tence, in-sis'tence, sub-sis'tence.
z: çō-ex-is'tănce, dē-ṣis'tănce, ex-is'tence, in-ex-is'tence,

(Choose only one word out of each group)

non-ex-is'tence, pĕr-ṣis'tence,
prē⸗ex-is'tence, rē-ṣis'tănce.
Cf. is'tănt+s.
Cf. kissed aunts *or* ants, etc.

IS'TĂNT, IS'TENT

d: dis'tănt, ē-qui-dis'tănt.
s: as-sis'tănt, çŏn-sis'tent,
  in-çŏn-sis'tent, in-sis'tent,
  sub-sis'tent.
z: çō-ex-is'tent, ex-is'tent,
  in-ex-is'tent, non-ex-is'tent,
  non-rē-ṣis'tănt, pĕr-ṣis'tent,
  prē⸗ex-is'tent, rē-ṣis'tănt.
Plus this tent, etc.
Plus kissed aunt *or* ant, etc.

ĪST'DŎM

kr: Ç͟hrīst'dŏm.
Plus sliced dumb, etc.

IS'TED

f: çlōse'fis'ted, fis'ted,
  härd'fis'ted, ïr'ŏn-fis'ted (ī'ẽrn-),
  tīght'fis'ted (tīt'),
  twö'⸗fis'ted (tooͦ').
l: black'⸗lis-ted, en-lis'ted,
  lis'ted, whīte'⸗lis-ted.
m: mis'ted.
s: as-sis'ted, çŏn-sis'ted,
  cys'ted, en-cys'ted, in-sis'ted,
  sub-sis'ted, un-as-sis'ted.
tw: en-twis'ted, in-tĕr-twis'ted,
  twis'ted, un-twis'ted.
z: dē-ṣis'ted, ex-is'ted,
  pĕr-ṣis'ted, prē⸗ex-is'ted,
  rē-ṣis'ted.
Plus kiss Ted, etc.
Plus missed Ed, etc.

IS'TEM

s: sys'tem.
Plus kissed 'em, etc.
Cf. miss tum, etc.

IS'TEST

l: en-lis'test*, lis'test*.
s: as-sis'test*, çŏn-sis'test*,
  in-sis'test*, sub-sis'test*.
tw: twis'test*.
z: dē-ṣis'test*, ex-is'test*,
  pĕr-ṣis'test*, rē-ṣis'test*.
Plus this test, etc.

IS'TETH

l: en-lis'teth*, lis'teth*.
m: mis'teth*.
s: as-sis'teth*, çŏn-sis'teth*,
  in-sis'teth*, sub-sis'teth*.
tw: twis'teth*.
z: dē-ṣis'teth*, ex-is'teth*,
  pĕr-ṣis'teth*, rē-ṣis'teth*.

IST'FUͦL

m: mist'fuͦl.
w: wist'fuͦl.
Plus fist full, etc.

IS'TIK

Vowel: al-trù-is'tiç,
  āth-ē-is'tiç,
  çaṣ-ū-is'tiç (kazh-), dē-is'tiç,
  ē-gō-is'tiç, Hē-brā-is'tiç,
  Jù-dā-is'tiç, mon″ō-thē-is'tiç,
  pan-thē-is'tiç, pol-y-thē-is'tiç,
  thē-is'tiç, trī-thē-is'tiç.
d: Buͦd-dhis'tiç, meth-ŏ-dis'tiç,
  sa-dis'tiç, Tal-mu-dis'tiç.
f: fis'tiç, phil-o-sō-phis'tiç,
  sō-phis'tiç.
gw: lin-guis'tiç.

(Choose only one word out of each group)

h: El-ō-his′tiċ.

j: āph-lō-ġis′tiċ,
bib-lē-op-ē-ġis′tiċ,
dī-à-lō-ġis′tiċ, ep-i-lō-ġis′tiċ,
eū-lō-ġis′tiċ, lō-ġis′tiċ,
nē-o-lō-ġis′tiċ, pal-ō-ġis′tiċ,
syl-lō-ġis′tiċ.

k(ċ): an-är-ċhis′tiċ,
ċat-ē-ċhis′tiċ.

kr: pāl″ē-ö-ċrys′tiċ.

l: an-na-lis′tiċ, à-nom-à-lis′tiċ,
bal-lis′tiċ, bib″li-o-pōl-is′tiċ,
ċa-băl-is′tiċ, ċam″ēr-à-lis′tiċ,
ċūr″i-à-lis′tiċ, dū-à-lis′tiċ,
ēl-eċ″trō-bal-lis′tiċ,
ē-van-ġe-lis′tiċ, fam-i-lis′tiċ,
fā-tà-lis′tiċ, ī-dē-à-lis′tiċ,
in-di-vid″ū-à-lis′tiċ,
joūr-nà-lis′tiċ, lib-ēr-à-lis′tiċ,
mà-tē″ri-à-lis′tiċ, nat-ū-rà-lis′tiċ,
nī-hi·lis′tiċ, nom-i-nà-lis′tiċ,
par-ål·le-lis′tiċ, pūġ-i-lis′tiċ,
ra-tion-à-lis′tiċ, rē-à-lis′tiċ,
rit-ū-à-lis′tiċ, scī-ō-lis′tiċ,
sen-sṳ-à-lis′tiċ (-shoo-),
sō-cià-lis′tiċ (-shà-),
som-nam-bū-lis′tiċ,
spir″i-tū-à-lis′tiċ, stȳ-lis′tiċ,
ūn-i-vēr-sà-lis′tiċ.

m: al-ċhē-mis′tiċ, an-i-mis′tiċ,
eū-phē-mis′tiċ, in″tēr-i-mis′tiċ,
mys′tiċ, op-ti-mis′tiċ,
pes-si-mis′tiċ.

n: ag-ō-nis′tiċ, an-a-ċhrō-nis′tiċ,
an-tag-ō-nis′tiċ, Ċal-vi-nis′tiċ,
ċan-ŏ-nis′tiċ,
ċhau-vi-nis′tiċ (shō-),
ċŏm-mū-nà-lis′tiċ,
ċom-mū-nis′tiċ,
eū-dē-mon-is′tiċ, Hel-le-nis′tiċ,
hū-mà-nis′tiċ, il-lū-mi-nis′tiċ,

Lat-i-nis′tiċ, mō-nis′tiċ,
syñ-ċhrō-nis′tiċ, ūn-iŏn-is′tiċ.

p: pà-pis′tiċ, phil-an-thrō-pis′tiċ.

pl: sim-plis′tiċ.

r: ad-i-a-phō-ris′tiċ, ā-ō-ris′tiċ,
aph-ō-ris′tiċ, ċhar-ăċ-tē-ris′tiċ,
e-ris′tiċ, Eū-ċhà-ris′tiċ,
eū-hē-mē-ris′tiċ,
for″mū-la-ris′tiċ, hū-mŏ-ris′tiċ,
jù-ris′tiċ, pō-lă-ris′tiċ,
pū-ris′tiċ, töu-ris′tiċ.

s: cys′tiċ, sol-ē-cis′tiċ.

sh: fēt-i-ċhis′tiċ, sċhis′tiċ.

t: ab″sō-lū-tis′tiċ,
an″à-bap-tis′tiċ, är-tis′tiċ,
bap-tis′tiċ, ē-gō-tis′tiċ,
pī-e-tis′tiċ, quī-e-tis′tiċ,
stà-tis′tiċ.

tr: bel-le-tris′tiċ, pà-tris′tiċ.

v: at-à-vis′tiċ, Jē-hō-vis′tiċ.

Plus this tick, etc.

IS′TIKS

j: sphrà-ġis′tiċs.

l: bal-lis′tiċs.

m: mys′tiċs.

n: ag-ō-nis′tiċs.

t: stà-tis′tiċs.

Plus is′tik+s.

Plus dismiss ticks, etc.

Cf. dismiss sticks *or* Styx, etc.

IS′TIL

p: pis′til.

Plus wrist ill, etc.

Plus this till, etc.

Cf. this still, etc.

IS′TIN

j: an″ti-phlō-ġis′tine,
phlō-ġis′tine.

l: Phi-lis′tine.

IS'TING
IS'Ū

fāte, fär, fåst, fall, finăl, cāre, at; mēte, prey, hẽr, met; pīne,
marĭne, bĭrd, pĭn; nōte, mŏve, fŏr, atŏm, not; mŏŏn, book;

592

(Choose only one word out of each group)

pr: pris'tine.
s: Sis'tine.
th: am-ē-thys'tine.
Plus this tin, etc.
Plus kissed in *or* inn, etc.

IS'TING

l: en-list'ing, list'ing.
m: mist'ing.
s: as-sist'ing, cŏn-sist'ing,
  in-sist'ing, sub-sis'ting.
tw: en-twist'ing, in-tẽr-twist'ing,
  twist'ing, un-twist'ing.
z: dē-ṣist'ing, ex-ist'ing,
  prē=ex-ist'ing, pẽr-ṣist'ing,
  rē-ṣist'ing, un-rē-ṣist'ing.

IS'TIV

z: pẽr-ṣis'tive, rē-ṣis'tive.

IST'LES

l: list'less.
tw: twist'less.
z: rē-ṣist'less.
Plus missed less *or* Les, etc.

IST'MĂS

kr: Christ'măs.
Cf. isth'mus.
Plus missed mass, etc.

IST'MENT

j: à-ġist'ment.
l: en-list'ment.
Plus wrist meant, etc.

IS'TRAL

m: mis'trăl.

IS'TRĂM

tr: tris'trăm.
Plus this tram, etc.
Plus missed ram, etc.

IS'TRES

m: mis'tress.
Plus this tress, etc.

IS'TŪR

Vowel: Is'tăr.
b: bis'tẽr.
bl: blis'tẽr, wat'ẽr blis'tẽr.
gl: glis'tẽr.
j: à-ġis'tŏr, mà-ġis'tẽr.
l: en-lis'tẽr, lis'tẽr.
m: mis'tẽr.
s: as-sis'tẽr, fŏs'tẽr sis'tẽr,
  hälf sis'tẽr (häf), in-sis'tẽr,
  sis'tẽr, step'sis-tẽr,
  sob sis'tẽr, sub-sis'tẽr.
tw: in-tẽr-twis'tẽr, twis'tẽr,
  un-twis'tẽr.
w: Wis'tẽr.
z: e-xis'tẽr, non-rē-ṣis'tẽr,
  pas'sive rē-ṣis'tẽr, pẽr-ṣis'tẽr,
  rē-ṣis'tẽr.
Plus missed her *or* err, etc.

IS'TŪRN

s: cis'tẽrn.
Plus bliss turn, etc.

IS'TUS

sh: schis'tous.
th: a-çà-this'tus.
Plus missed us, etc.

IS'Ū

Vowel: is'sūe.
t: tis'sūe.
Plus miss you *or* ewe, etc.

(Choose only one word out of each group)

ĪS′ŪR

d: dīc′ẽr.
f: saç-ri-fīc′ẽr.
g: geȳ′sẽr.
n: nīc′ẽr.
s: çŏn-cīs′ẽr, prē-cīs′ẽr.
sl: mēat slīc′ẽr,
po̅-tā′to̅ slīc′ẽr, slīc′ẽr.
sp: spīc′ẽr.
spl: splīc′ẽr.
t: en-tīc′ẽr.
Plus why, sir, etc.
Plus ice her *or* err, etc.

IS′ŪR

h: dē-his′cẽr, his′sẽr.
k: kis′sẽr.
m: dis-mis′sẽr, mis′sẽr,
rē-mis′sẽr.
Plus hiss her *or* err, etc.

IS′US

Vowel: Is′sus.
b: bys′sus.
m: "mis′sus".
s: när-cis′sus.
Plus kiss us, etc.

ĪT′ĂL

kw: rē-quīt′ăl.
s: cīt′ăl*, par-à-sīt′ăl, rē-cīt′ăl.
t: en-tīt′le, tīt′le.
tr: dē-trīt′ăl.
v: vīt′ăl.
Plus fight′ll, etc.
Plus smite, Al, etc.

ĪT′ĂLZ

v: vīt′ăls̱.
Plus īt′ăl+s.

Ī′TĂN

t: Tī′tăn.
Plus smite an, etc.
Plus why tan, etc.
Cf. īt′en.

IT′ĂN, IT′EN

br: Brit′ăin, Brit′ŏn, Brit′ten.
Plus hit an *or* on, etc.

IT′ĂNS

kw: aç-quit′tănce, quit′tănce.
m: ad-mit′tănce, o̅-mit′tănce,
pēr-mit′tănce, rē-mit′tănce,
trans-mit′tănce.
p: pit′tănce.
Cf. hit aunts *or* ants, etc.

Ī′TĒ

d: Aph-ro̅-dī′tē.
tr: Am-phi-trī′tē.
v: är-bŏr-vī′taē, lig′num vī′taē.
Cf. ī′ti.

ĪT′ED

b: bīght′ed.
bl: blīght′ed.
d: bē-dīght′ed (-dīt′), dīght′ed*,
in-dīct′ed (-dīt′), in-dīt′ed,
un-dīght′ed*.
fl: ēag′le⸗flīght′ed.
fr: af-frīght′ed, frīght′ed,
un-af-frīght′ed, un-frīght′ed.
k: kīt′ed.
kw: rē-quīt′ed, un-rē-quīt′ed.
l: à-līght′ed, dē-līght′ed,
līght′ed, un-līght′ed.
m: dȳ-nà-mīt′ed.
n: bē-knīght′ed (-nīt′),
bē-nīght′ed, ig-nīt′ed,
knīght′ed (nīt′), nīght′ed,
rē-ū-nīt′ed, un-bē-nīght′ed,
ū-nīt′ed.

IT'ED
IT'EN
fāte, fär, fȧst, fạll, fĭnăl, cãre, at; mēte, prẹy, hêr, met; pīne,
marīne, bĭrd, pin; nōte, mŏve, fọr, atŏm, not; mọọn, book;   **594**

(Choose only one word out of each group)

pl: plīght'ed, troth'plīght-ed,
un-plīght'ed.
r: rīght'ed, un-rīght'ed.
s: cīt'ed, clēar'=sīght'ed,
ēag'le=sīght'ed, ex-cīt'ed,
fär'sīght'ed, fōre-sīght'ed,
in-cīt'ed, lọng'=sīght'ed,
nēar'sīght'ed, ō'vẽr-sīght-ed,
quick'=sīght'ed, rē-cīt'ed,
sec'ŏnd=sīght'ed,
shärp'=sīght'ed, shọrt'sīght'ed,
sīght'ed, sīt'ed, un-sīght'ed.
sl: slīght'ed.
sp: dē-spīt'ed, spīt'ed.
tr: at-trīt'ed, dē-trīt'ed.
v: in-vīt'ed.
Plus bright, Ed, etc.
Plus tie, Ted, etc.

IT'ED

b: bit'ted, un-bit'ted.
d: dit'tied.
f: bē-fit'ted, ben-ē-fit'ed,
coun-tẽr-feit'ed, fit'ted,
rē-fit'ted, un-ben-ē-fit'ed,
un-fit'ted.
fl: flit'ted.
g: git'ted.
gr: grit'ted.
kw: ac-quit'ted, quit'ted.
m: ad-mit'ted, cŏm-mit'ted,
ē-mit'ted, in-tẽr-mit'ted,
man-ū-mit'ted, ō-mit'ted,
pẽr-mit'ted, rē-cŏm-mit'ted,
rē-mit'ted, sub-mit'ted,
trans-mit'ted, un-rē-mit'ted.
n: in-tẽr-knit'ted (-nit'),
knit'ted (nit').
p: pit'ied, pit'ted.
r: writ'ted.
s: cit'ied.

sl: slit'ted.
sp: spit'ted.
spl: split'ted.
spr: bōw'sprit-ted.
t: tit'ted.
tw: twit'ted.
w: af'tẽr-wit-ted, blunt'=wit-ted,
fat'=wit-ted, hälf'=wit'ted (häf'),
lēan'=wit-ted, nim'ble=wit-ted,
out-wit'ted, quick'=wit'ted,
read'y=wit'ted (red'),
shärp'=wit'ted, shọrt'=wit'ted,
sub'tle=wit-ted (sut'),
un'dẽr-wit-ted, wit'ted.
Plus hit, Ed, etc.

Ī'TEM

Vowel: ī'tem.
Plus smite 'em, etc.
Cf. ad in-fi-nī'tum.

ĪT'EN

br: brīght'en.
fr: frīght'en.
h: hēight'en.
hw: whīt'en.
k(c): chī'tin, chī'tŏn.
l: en-līght'en, līght'en.
t: tīght'en, Tī'tăn.
tr: trī'tŏn.
Plus fight on, _or_ an, etc.
Plus why ten, etc.
Cf. why tan _or_ ton, etc.

IT'EN

b: bit'ten, flēa'=bit-ten,
flÿ'=bit-ten, huñ'gẽr=bit-ten,
weaTH'ẽr=bit-ten (weTH').
br: Brit'ain, Brit'ten, Brit'ŏn.
f: Fit'tŏn.
k: kit'ten.

(Choose only one word out of each group)

l: lit′ten*, red′=lit-ten*.
m: mit′ten.
r: un-dĕr-writ′ten, un-writ′ten, writ′ten.
sm: çŏn′science=smit′ten ('shens=), heärt′=smit-ten, smit′ten, sun′smit-ten, ter′rŏr=smit-ten, un-smit′ten.
Cf. hit′ten, etc.
Plus lit on *or* an, etc.

IT′ENT

m: ē-mit′tent, in-tĕr-mit′tent, in-trō-mit′tent, rē-mit′tent.
Cf. hit tent, etc.

ĪT′EST

b: bīt′est*.
bl: blīght′est*.
br: brīght′est.
d: in-dīct′est*, in-dīt′est*.
f: fīght′est*.
fr: af-frīght′est*.
hw: whīt′est.
kw: rē-quīt′est*.
l: à-līght′est*, dē-līght′est*, im-pō-līt′est, līght′est, pō-līt′est.
m: mīght′est*.
n: bē-knīght′est (-nīt′)*, knīght′est (nīt′)*, rē-ū-nīt′est*, ū-nīt′est*.
pl: plīght′est*.
r: rīght′est, up-rīght′est, wrīt′est*.
s: cīt′est*, ex-cīt′est*, in-cīt′est*, rē-cīt′est*, sīght′est*
sl: sleīght′est*, slīght′est.
sm: smīt′est*.
sp: spīt′est*.

t: tīght′est.
tr: trīt′est.
v: in-vīt′est*.
Plus high test, etc.

IT′EST

b: bit′test*, un-bit′test*.
f: ben-ē-fit′est*, fit′test, rē-fit′test*.
fl: flit′test*.
h: hit′test*.
kw: aç-quit′test*, quit′test*.
m: ad-mit′test*, çŏm-mit′test*, ō-mit′test*, pĕr-mit′test*, rē-mit′test*, sub-mit′test*.
n: knit′test (nit′)*.
p: pit′test*.
s: sit′test*.
sl: slit′test*.
sp: spit′test*.
spl: split′test*.
tw: twit′test*.
w: out-wit′test*.

ĪT′ETH

b: bīt′eth*.
bl: blīght′eth*.
d: in-dīct′eth*, in-dīt′eth*.
f: fīght′eth*.
fr: af-frīght′eth*.
kw: rē-quīt′eth*.
l: à-līght′eth*, dē-līght′eth*, līght′eth*.
m: mīght′eth*.
n: bē-knīght′eth (-nīt′)*, knīght′eth (nīt′)*, rē-ū-nīt′eth*, ū-nīt′eth*.
pl: plīght′eth*.
r: rīght′eth*, wrīt′eth*.
s: cīt′eth*, ex-cīt′eth*, in-cīt′eth*, rē-cīt′eth*, sīght′eth*.

(Choose only one word out of each group)

sl: sleīght'eth*, slīght'eth*.
sm: smīt'eth*.
sp: spīt'eth*.
v: in-vīt'eth*.

IT'ETH

b: bit'teth*, un-bit'teth*.
f: ben-ē-fit'eth*, fit'teth*,
rē-fit'teth*.
fl: flit'teth*.
h: hit'teth*.
kw: ac̦-quit'teth*, quit'teth*.
m: ad-mit'teth*, c̦ŏm-mit'teth*,
ō-mit'teth*, pẽr-mit'teth*,
rē-mit'teth*, sub-mit'teth*.
n: knit'teth (nit')*.
p: pit'teth*.
s: sit'teth*.
sl: slit'teth*.
sp: spit'teth*.
spl: split'teth*.
tw: twit'teth*.
w: out-wit'teth*.

ĪT'ĒZ

r: pȳ-rīt'ēṣ, sō-rīt'ēṣ.
Plus fight ease, etc.
Plus why tease *or* teas, etc.

ĪT'FỤL

fr: frīght'fụl.
l: dē-līght'fụl.
m: mīght'fụl.
r: rīght'fụl.
sp: dē-spīte'fụl, spīte'fụl.
spr: sprīght'fụl.
Plus bright full, etc.

IT'FỤL

f: fit'fụl.
w: wit'fụl.
Plus knit full, etc.

ITH'Ē

pr: priTH'ee.
Plus with, he, etc.

ĪTH'EN

r: bat'tle-wrīTH-en*,
wrīTH'en*.
Cf. lithe hen, etc.

ĪTH'EST

bl: blīTH'est.
l: līTH'est.
r: wrīTH'est*.

ĪTH'ETH

r: wrīTH'eth*.

ĪTH'FỤL

bl: blīTHe'fụl.
l: līTHe'fụl.
Plus scythe full, etc.

ĪTH'I

bl: blīTH'y.
l: līTH'y.
Plus why the *or* thee*, etc.
Plus scythe, he, etc.

ITH'I

p: pith'y.
sm: smith'y.
st: stith'y.
w: with'y.
Plus myth, he, etc.

ITH'IK

l: ē-ō-lith'ic̦, lith'ic̦,
me-gȧ-lith'ic̦, mī-c̦rō-lith'ic̦,
mon-ō-lith'ic̦, nē-ō-lith'ic̦,
pāl-aē-ō-lith'ic̦, trī-lith'ic̦.
m: myth'ic̦.
n: ọr-nith'ic̦.

597 ūse, bu̱ll, brúte, tū̆rn, up; crȳ, myth; c̱at, ma̱chine, ace, church, c̱hord; g̱em, añger, (Fr.) boṅ, as̱; THis, thin; azure

ĪTH′ING
IT′I

(Choose only one word out of each group)

ĪTH′ING

n: nĭTH′ing*.
r: wrīTH′ing.
s: scȳTH′ing.
t: tĭTH′ing.
tr: trīTH′ing.

ITH′M

r: lo̱g′a̱-riTH-m, pol′y-rhyTH-m, rhyTH′m.
Plus with ′em, etc.

ITH′MIK

r: lo̱g-a̱-rhyTH′mi̱c, pol-y-rhyTH′mi̱c, rhyTH′mi̱c.
Plus with Mick, etc.

ĪTH′NES

bl: blīTHe′ness.
l: līTHe′ness.

Ī′THON

p: pȳ′thon.
Plus stithe on *or* an, etc.

ĪTH′SUM

bl: blīTHe′sŏme.
l: līTHe′sŏme.
Plus scythe some *or* sum, etc.

ĪTH′ŪR

Vowel: eīTH′ēr.
bl: blīTH′ēr.
n: neīTH′ēr.
r: wrīTH′ēr.
t: tīTH′ēr.
Plus scythe her *or* err, etc.

ITH′ŪR

bl: bliTH′ēr.
d: diTH′ēr.

h: bē-hiTH′ēr*, hiTH′ēr.
hw: an′y-whiTH-ēr (en′), nō′whiTH-ēr, sŏme′whiTH-ēr, whiTH′ēr.
sl: sliTH′ēr.
sw: swiTH′ēr.
TH: THiTH′ēr.
w: wiTH′ēr.
Plus with her *or* err, etc

ITH′ŪRD

w: un-wiTH′ēred, wiTH′ēred.
Plus iTH′ūr+ed.

ITH′ŪRZ

w: wiTH′ērs̱.
Plus iTH′ūr+s̱.

ĪT′I

bl: blīght′y.
d: Aph-rō-dī′tē.
fl: flīght′y.
hw: whīt′y.
m: a̱l-mīght′y, mīght′y, mīt′y.
tr: Am-phi-trī′tē.
v: är′bŏr-vī-taē, lig′num vī′taē.
Plus might he, etc.
Plus my tea, etc.

IT′I

d: ban-dit′ti, dit′ty.
fl: flit′ty.
gr: grit′ty.
k: kit′ty.
m: c̱ŏm-mit′tee, Mit′tie.
p: pit′y, self′⸗pit′y.
pr: pret′ty.
s: cit′y.
w: wit′ty.
Plus with, he, etc.

(Choose only one word out of each group)

IT'ID

d: dit'tied.
p: pit'ied, un-pit'ied
s: cit'ied.
Cf. it'ed.

IT'IK

Vowel: Je-ṣū-it'ic̗, Sī-nā-it'ic̗.
b: cen-ō-bit'ic̗, Jac̗-ō-bit'ic̗,
trī-lō-bit'ic̗.
d: hẽr-maph-rō-dit'ic̗,
trog-lō-dyt'ic̗.
dr: den-drit'ic̗.
f: an″thrō-pō-mọr-phit'ic̗,
ē-ō-phit'ic̗, ep-i-phyt'ic̗,
mē-phit'ic̗, nec̗-rō-phyt'ic̗,
xē-rō-phyt'ic̗, zō-ō-phyt'ic̗.
j: ġin-ġit'ic̗.
k(c̗): coïï-c̗hit'ic̗, rȧ-c̗hit'ic̗.
kl: eū-c̗lit'ic̗, he-tẽr-ō-c̗lit'ic̗,
prō-c̗lit'ic̗.
kr: c̗rit'ic̗, dī-ȧ-c̗rit'ic̗,
hȳ-pẽr-c̗rit'ic̗, hȳ-pō-c̗rit'ic̗,
ō-neī-rō-c̗rit'ic̗.
l: ac-tin-ō-lit'ic̗, ac-rō-lit'ic̗,
an-ȧ-lyt'ic̗, bī-ō-lyt'ic̗,
c̗at-ȧ-lyt'ic̗, dī-ȧ-lyt'ic̗,
ē-lec̗-trō-lyt'ic̗,
Iṣ-ra-e-lit'ic̗ (-ri-),
num-mū-lit'ic̗, ō-ö-lit'ic̗ (-ō-),
par-ȧ-lyt'ic̗, thē-o-dō-lit'ic̗,
ton-sil-lit'ic̗, tox-o-phi-lit'ic̗,
vãr-i-ō-lit'ic̗, zē-ō-lit'ic̗.
m: Ad-a-mit'ic̗, dol-ō-mit'ic̗,
er-ē-mit'ic̗, Ham-it'ic̗,
Is-la-mit'ic̗, pal-mit'ic̗,
prē≠Ad-a-mit'ic̗, Sē-mit'ic̗,
She-mit'ic̗, Sta-lag-mit'ic̗.
n: ac̗-ō-nit'ic̗, gra-nit'ic̗,
lig-nit'ic̗, saġ-ē-nit'ic̗,
sel-ē-nit'ic̗, sȳ-e-nit'ic̗,

Tīt-ȧ-nit'ic̗, tym-pȧ-nit'ic̗,
ūr-ȧ-nit'ic̗,
r: C̗a-bi-rit'ic̗, diph-the-rit'ic̗,
mär-gȧ-rit'ic̗, Naz-ȧ-rit'ic̗,
phos-pho-rit'ic̗, pleu̇-rit'ic̗,
pọr-phy-rit'ic̗, sy-bȧ-rit'ic̗.
s: an-thrȧ-cit'ic̗, par-ȧ-sit'ic̗.
t: hem-ȧ-tit'ic̗, stȧ-lac̗-tit'ic̗,
stē-ȧ-tit'ic̗, stron-tit'ic̗.
thr: ạr-thrit'ic̗.
v: Lē-vit'ic̗.

IT'IKS

l: an-ȧ-lyt'ic̗s.
Plus it'ic̗+s.

ĪT'IN

k(c̗): c̗hīt'in.
Cf. īt'en, īt'ŏn.

ĪT'ING

b: back'bīt-ing, bīt'ing.
bl: blīght'ing.
d: ex-pē-dīt'ing, in-dīct'ing,
in-dīt'ing.
f: cock'fīght-ing, fīght'ing,
fist fīght'ing.
fr: af-frīght'ing, frīght'ing.
hw: whīt'ing.
k(c̗): kīt'ing.
kw: rē-quīt'ing.
l: ac̗-ō-lȳt'ing, ȧ-līght'ing,
dē-līght'ing, līght'ing.
m: dȳ-nȧ-mīt'ing.
n: bē-knīght'ing (-nīt'),
dis-ū-nīt'ing, ig-nīt'ing,
knīght'ing (nīt'), rē-ū-nīt'ing,
ū-nīt'ing.
pl: plīght'ing.
r: cop'y-rīght-ing,
cop'y wrīt'ing, hand'wrīt-ing,
rīght'ing, un-dẽr-wrīt'ing,
wrīt'ing.

599 ūse, oull, brūte, tŭrn, up; crȳ, myth; çat, machine, ace, church, çhord; ġem, añger, (Fr.) boṅ, aṣ; THis, thin; aȥure

IT'ING
IT'L

(Choose only one word out of each group)

s: cīt'ing, ex-cīt'ing, in-cīt'ing, rē-cīt'ing, sīght'ing.
sl: slīght'ing.
sm: smīt'ing.
sp: spīt'ing.
v: in-vīt'ing.

IT'ING

b: bit'ting, un-bit'ting.
f: bē-fit'ting, ben-ē-fit'ting, coun'tẽr-feit'ing, fit'ting, mis-fit'ting, rē-fit'ting, stēam fit'ting, un-bē-fit'ting, un-fit'ting.
fl: flit'ting.
gr: grit'ting.
h: härd'-hit-ting, hit'ting, pinch'-hit-ting.
kw: ac-quit'ting, quit'ting.
m: ad-mit'ting, cŏm-mit'ting, ē-mit'ting, man-ū-mit'ting, ō-mit'ting, pẽr-mit'ting, pre-tẽr-mit'ting, rē-cŏm-mit'ting, rē-mit'ting, sub-mit'ting, trans-mit'ting, un-rē-mit'ting, un-sub-mit'ting.
n: knit'ting (nit').
p: pit'ting.
s: out-sit'ting, sit'ting.
sk: skit'ting.
sl: slit'ting.
sp: spit'ting.
spl: hãir'split-ting, rāil split'ting, split'ting.
tw: twit'ting.
w: out-wit'ting, un-wit'ting, wit'ting.

ĪT'IS

b: phle-bīt'is (flē-).
d: cär-dīt'is, en″dō-cär-dīt'is, per″i-cär-dīt'is.

fr: nē-phrīt'is.
j: lar-yn-ġīt'is, men-in-ġīt'is, phar-yn-ġīt'is.
k(c): broñ-chīt'is, rà-chīt'is, trà-chīt'is.
l: cō-līt'is, hȳ-à-līt'is, ton-sil-līt'is.
r: neū-rīt'is.
s: ap-pen-di-cīt'is.
thr: är-thrīt'is.
tr: gas-trīt'is.
Cf. īt'us.

ĪT'ISH

hw: whīt'ish.
l: Ish-mà-e-līt'ish, Is-ra-e-līt'ish (-ri-), līght'ish.
m: er-ē-mīt'ish.
n: Çā-naa-nīt'ish.
r: añ-chō-rīt'ish.
t: tīght'ish.

IT'ISH

br: Brit'ish.
sk: skit'tish.

ĪT'IV

d: ex-pē-dī'tive.
t: ap-pē-tī'tive.

Ī'TL

t: en-tī'tle, tī'tle.
Cf. īt'ăl.
Plus light 'll, etc.

IT'L

Vowel: 'it'tle.
br: brit'tle, pēa'nut brit'tle.
hw: whit'tle.
kw: ac-quit'tăl.
l: bē-lit'tle, lit'tle.

(Choose only one word out of each group)

m: cŏm-mit'tăl,
non-cŏm-mit'tăl, rē-mit'tăl,
trans-mit'tăl.
n: knit'tle (nit').
sk: skit'tle.
sp: lick'spit-tle, spit'ăl*,
spit'tle*.
t: tit'tle.
v: vic'tuăl (vit'l).
Plus bit'll, etc.

ĪT'LES

f: fīght'less.
fr: frīght'less.
h: heīght'less.
l: dē-līght'less, līght'less.
n: knīght'less (nīt'), nīght'less.
r: rīte'less.
s: sīght'less.
sp: spīte'less.
spr: sprīght'less.
Plus write less, etc.

IT'LES

w: wit'less.
Plus it+less.
Plus hit less, etc.

IT'LEST

br: brit'tlest.
hw: whit'tlest*.
l: bē-lit'tlest*, lit'tlest.
v: vic'tuălest (vit'lest)*.
Plus hit, lest, etc.

IT'LETH

hw: whit'tleth*.
l: bē-lit'tleth*.
v: vic'tuăleth (vit'leth)*.

ĪT'LI

br: brīght'ly.
hw: Whīte'ley, whīte'ly.

l: im-pō-līte'ly, līght'ly,
pō-līte'ly.
n: Kneīght'ly (nīt'),
knīght'ly (nīt'), nīght'ly,
un-knīght'ly (-nīt').
r: fọrth-rīght'ly, rīght'ly,
up-rīght'ly.
s: sīght'ly, un-sīght'ly.
sl: slīght'ly.
spr: sprīght'ly.
t: tīght'ly.
tr: trīte'ly.
Plus write, Lee *or* lea, etc.

IT'LI

f: fit'ly, un-fit'ly.
Plus hit Lee *or* lea, etc.

ĪT'LING

t: en-tīt'ling, tīt'ling.

IT'LING

hw: whit'tling.
k: kit'ling.
t: tit'ling.
w: wit'ling.

IT'LŨR

br: brit'tlēr.
h: Hit'lēr.
hw: whit'tlēr.
l: bē-lit'tlēr, lit'tlēr.
v: vic'tuăl-lēr (vit'lũr).

IT'LZ

sk: skit'tles̩.
v: vic'tuăls̩ (vit'lz).
Plus it'l+s̩.

ĪT'MENT

d: in-dīct'ment.
fr: af-frīght'ment, frīght'ment.
s: ex-cīte'ment, in-cīte'ment.

(Choose only one word out of each group)

v: in-vīte′ment.
Plus light meant, etc.

IT'MENT

f: fit′ment, rē-fit′ment.
kw: ac-quit′ment.
m: cŏm-mit′ment, rē-mit′ment.
Plus grit meant, etc.

ĪT'NES

br: brīght′ness.
hw: whīte′ness.
l: im-pō-līte′ness, līght′ness, pō-līte′ness.
r: rīght′ness, up-rīght′ness.
sl: slīght′ness.
t: tīght′ness.
tr: trīte′ness.

IT'NES

f: fit′ness, un-fit′ness.
w: eȳe′wit′ness, wit′ness.

IT'NI

hw: Mt. Whit′ney, Whit′ney.
j: jit′ney.
Plus hit knee, etc.

ĪT'NING

br: brīght′ening.
fr: frīght′ening.
h: hēight′ening.
hw: whīt′ening.
l: līght′ening, līght′ning, sheet līght′ning.
t: tīght′ening.

ĪT'NUR

br: brīght′enēr.
fr: frīght′enēr.
h: hēight′enēr.
hw: whīt′enēr.

l: līght′enēr.
Cf. whiten her *or* err, etc.

IT'ŎL

w: wit′tŏl.
Cf. it′l.

ĪT'ŎN

k(c): chīt′ŏn.
tr: trīt′ŏn.
Cf. īt′en, īt′in.
Plus light on *or* an, etc.

Ī'TRĀT

n: nī′trāte.
t: tī′trāte.
Plus bright rate, etc.

ĪT'RI

m: mīt′ry.
n: nīt′ry*.

ĪT'RIK

n: nīt′ric.
Plus bright rick, etc.

IT'RIK

s: cit′ric.
v: vit′ric.
Plus hit rick, etc.

IT'SI

b: it′sy bit′sy.
fr: Frit′zy.
r: Rit′zy.
Plus his, he, etc.

ĪT'STIK

n: nīghtstick.
Plus bright stick, etc.

ĪT'ŪR

Vowel: īt′ēr.
b: är-beī′tēr, back′bīt-ēr, bīt′ēr.

IT'ŪR
IT'ŪRZ

fāte, fär, fȧst, fạll, finăl, cāre, at; mēte, prey, hẽr, met; pīne,
marĭne, bĩrd, pĭn; nōte, mŏve, fôr, atŏm, not; mọọn, book;

602

(Choose only one word out of each group)

bl: blīght'ẽr.
br: brīght'ẽr.
d: in-dīct'ẽr, in-dīt'ẽr.
f: cọck'fīght-ẽr, fīght'ẽr,
fist fīght'ẽr.
fl: fĩrst'=flīght-ẽr, flīght'ẽr,
seç'ŏnd=flīght'ẽr, etc.
hw: whīt'ẽr.
k: check kīt'ẽr, kīt'ẽr.
kw: rē-quīt'ẽr,
l: à-līght'ẽr, cig-à-rette' līght'ẽr,
dē-līght'ẽr, im-pō-līt'ẽr,
lamp'līght-ẽr, līght'ẽr,
mọọn'līght-ẽr, pō-līt'ẽr.
m: bē-mīt're, dȳ-nà-mīt'ẽr,
mīt'ẽr, un-mīt'ẽr.
n: ig-nīt'ẽr, nīt'ẽr.
pl: plīght'ẽr.
r: cọp'y-rīght-ẽr,
cọp'y wrīt'ẽr, rīght'ẽr,
tȳpe'wrīt-ẽr, un'dẽr-wrīt-ẽr,
wrīt'ẽr.
s: cīt'ẽr, ex-cīt'ẽr, in-cīt'ẽr,
rē-cīt'ẽr, sīght'ẽr.
sl: slīght'ẽr.
sm: smīt'ẽr.
t: tīght'ẽr.
tr: trīt'ẽr.
v: in-vīt'ẽr.
Plus smite her *or* err, etc.

IT'ŪR

b: bit'tẽr, em-bit'tẽr.
f: bē-fit'tẽr, ben-ē-fit'ẽr,
cọun'tẽr-feit-ẽr, fit'tẽr,
mis-fit'tẽr, rē-fit'tẽr,
stēam fit'tẽr, un-fit'tẽr.
fl: flit'tẽr.
fr: frit'tẽr.
g: gō'=git'tẽr.
gl: glit'tẽr.

gr: grit'tẽr.
h: hit'tẽr.
j: jit'tẽr.
kr: crit'tẽr.
kw: aç-quit'tẽr, quit'tẽr.
l: lit'tẽr.
m: ad-mit'tẽr, cŏm-mit'tẽr,
ē-mit'tẽr, in-tẽr-mit'tẽr,
in-trō-mit'tẽr, man-ū-mit'tẽr,
ō-mit'tẽr, pẽr-mit'tẽr,
pre-tẽr-mit'tẽr, rē-cŏm-mit'tẽr,
rē-mit'tẽr, sub-mit'tẽr,
trans-mit'tẽr.
n: knit'tẽr (nit').
p: pit'tẽr.
s: out-sit'tẽr, sit'tẽr.
sl: slit'tẽr.
sp: spit'tẽr.
spl: lọg split'tẽr, rāil split'tẽr,
split'tẽr.
t: tit'tẽr.
tw: à-twit'tẽr, twit'tẽr.
w: out-wit'tẽr, wit'tẽr.
Plus hit her *or* err, etc.

IT'ŪRD

b: em-bit'tẽred,
un-em-bit'tẽred.
Plus it'ūr+ed.

IT'ŪRN

b: bit'tẽrn.
fl: flit'tẽrn.
g: git'tẽrn.
Plus hit urn, erne *or* earn, etc.

IT'ŪRZ

b: Añ-gŏ-stū'rà bit'tẽrṣ,
bit'tẽrṣ, or'ăṅġe bit'tẽrṣ, etc.
Plus it'ūr+s.

603 ūse, bull, brúte, tûrn, up; crȳ, myth; çat, maçhine, ace,
     church, çhord; ġem, añger, (Fr.) boń, aṣ; THis, thin;ᵉaẓure

ĬT'US
Ī'UR

(Choose only one word out of each group)

ĪT'US

t: Tīt'us.
tr: dē-trīt'us.
v: St. Vīt'us, Vīt'us.
Plus smite us, etc.

ĪT'WĀT

l: līght'weight.
Plus might wait *or* weight, etc.

IT'WIT

n: nit'wit.
Plus hit wit, etc.

IT'ZI

b: it'sy=bit'sy.
fr: Frit'zy.
r: Rit'zy.

Ī'UMF

tr: trī'umph.
Plus sky, umph, etc.

Ī'ŪN

tr: trī'ūne.

Ī'UR

Vowel: eȳ'ẽr.
b: Baȳ'ẽr, Beȳ'ẽr, buȳ'ẽr.
br: brī'ăr, brī'ẽr, sweet'brī-ẽr.
d: dȳ'ẽr, nev'ẽr=sāy=dī'ẽr.
dr: drī'ẽr.
f: am'pli-fī-ẽr, beaū'ti-fī-ẽr,
  cẽr'ti-fī-ẽr, çlar'i-fī-ẽr,
  çlás'si-fī-ẽr, çod'i-fī-ẽr,
  crú'ci-fī-ẽr, dē-fī'ẽr, dē-fȳ'ẽr,
  dē'i-fī-ẽr, dig'ni-fī-ẽr,
  dis-quäl'i-fī-er, di-vẽr'si-fī-ẽr,
  ed'i-fī-ẽr, ēl-eç'tri-fī-ẽr,
  ex-em'pli-fī-ẽr, fạl'si-fī-ẽr,
  fọr'ti-fī-ẽr, fruç'ti-fī-ẽr,
  glõr'i-fī-ẽr, grat'i-fī-ẽr,
  hor'ri-fī-ẽr, ī-den'ti-fī-ẽr,

in-dem'ni-fī-ẽr, in-ten'si-fī-ẽr,
jus'ti-fī-ẽr, li'quē-fī-ẽr,
mag'ni-fī-ẽr, mod'i-fī-ẽr,
mol'li-fī-ẽr, mọr'ti-fī-ẽr,
mys'ti-fī-er, nōt'i-fī-ẽr,
nul'li-fī-ẽr, paç'i-fī-ẽr,
pẽr-son'i-fī-ẽr, pet'ri-fī-ẽr,
pūr'i-fī-ẽr, pū'trē-fī-ẽr,
quäl'i-fī-ẽr, ram'i-fī-ẽr,
rat'i-fī-ẽr, reç'ti-fī-ẽr,
rē-viv'i-fī-ẽr, sañç'ti-fī-ẽr,
sat'is-fī-ẽr, sçar'i-fī-ẽr,
sçōr'i-fī-ẽr, sig'ni-fī-ẽr,
sim'pli-fī-ẽr, speç'i-fī-ẽr,
speech'i-fī-ẽr, stul'ti-fī-ẽr,
stū'pē-fī-ẽr, ter'ri-fī-ẽr,
tes'ti-fī-ẽr, typ'i-fī-ẽr,
ver'i-fī-ẽr, vẽr'si-fī-ẽr,
vil'i-fī-ẽr, viv'i-fī-ẽr.
fl: flī'ẽr, hīgh'flī-ẽr, kīte'flī-ẽr.
fr: black frī'ăr, frī'ăr, frī'ẽr,
  grāy frī'ẽr, whīte frī'ăr.
g: lam'mẽr-geī-ẽr.
h: hī'ẽr, hīgh'ẽr.
kr: çrī'ẽr, çrȳ'ẽr, dē-çrȳ'ẽr,
  des-çrī'ẽr, town çrī'ẽr.
l: lī'ăr, lī'ẽr, rē-lī'ẽr.
m: Biē'dẽr-meī-ẽr, Maȳ'ẽr,
  Meī'ẽr, Meȳ'ẽr, Mȳ'ẽr,
  Un'tẽr-meȳ-ẽr, Un'tẽr-mȳ-ẽr.
n: dē-nī'ẽr, nīgh'ẽr.
p: oç'çū-pī-ẽr.
pl: ap-plī'ẽr, çǒm-plī'ẽr, im-plī'ẽr,
  mul'ti-plī-ẽr,
  rē-plī'ẽr, sup-plī'ẽr.
pr: prī'ǒr, prȳ'ẽr.
r: wrȳ'ẽr.
s: pro'phē-sī-ẽr, sīgh'ẽr.
sh: shȳ'ẽr.
sk: skȳ'ẽr.
sl: slȳ'ẽr.

Ĭ'ŪRN
IV'EN

fāte, fär, fȧst, fạll, fīnăl, cãre, at; mēte, prey, hẽr, met; pīne,
marïne, bïrd, pĭn; nōte, mŏve, fọr, atŏm, not; mọọn, book;   **604**

(Choose only one word out of each group)

sp: spȳ'ẽr.
spr: sprȳ'ẽr.
t: tī'ẽr, tȳ'ẽr, un-tī'ẽr.
tr: trī'ẽr, trī'ŏr.
v: vī'ẽr.
Plus why her or err, etc.

Ĭ'ŪRN

Vowel: grap'pling ĭ'rŏn, ĭ'rŏn,
lŏft'ing ĭ'rŏn.
Plus my urn, erne or earn, etc.

Ī'ŪRZ

m: Meȳ'ẽrṣ, Mȳ'ẽrṣ.
pl: plī'ẽrṣ.
Plus ī'ūr+s.

Ī'US

k(ç): an"ti-baç-çhī'us,
baç-çhī'us.
p: pī'ous, Pī'us.
pr: nī'si prī'us.
r: Dȧ-rī'us.
Cf. Ē-lī'ăs and ī'ăs.

Ī'VȦ

l: sȧ-lī'vȧ.
s: Saī'vȧ, Sī'vȧ.
Plus I've a, shrive a, etc.

ĪV'ĂL

k(ç): är-çhīv'ăl.
l: sȧ-līv'ăl.
r: ar-rīv'ăl, non-ar-rīv'ăl,
out-rīv'ăl, rīv'ăl.
t: ad-jeç-tīv'ăl, çon-junç-tīv'ăl,
es-tīv'ăl, im-per-ȧ-tīv'ăl,
nom-i-nȧ-tīv'ăl.
v: rē-vīv'ăl, sūr-vīv'ăl.
Plus alive, Al, etc.
Plus why, Val, etc.

Ī'VĂN

Vowel: Ī'văn.
Cf. en-liv'en.
Plus why van or von, etc.

ĪV'ĂNS

n: çŏn-nīv'ănce.
r: ar-rīv'ănce.
tr: çŏn-trīv'ănce.
v: sūr-vīv'ănce.
Cf. thrive, ants or aunts, etc.
Plus Why, Vance, etc.

ĪV'ĂNT

tr: trīv'ănt.
Plus arrive, aunt or ant, etc.

Ī'VĀT

pr: prī'vāte.
Plus I've ate, or eight, etc.
Cf. deprive it, etc.

ĪV'EN

l: en-līv'en.
Cf. Ī'văn.
Cf. deprive hen, etc.

IV'EN

b: Biv'en.
dr: driv'en, ō-vẽr-driv'en,
stọrm'=driv'en, un-dẽr-driv'en,
un-driv'en,
weaTH'ẽr=driv-en (weTH').
g: fŏr-giv'en, giv'en,
un-fŏr-giv'en.
r: riv'en.
shr: shriv'en, un-shriv'en.
skr(sçr): sçriv'en.
str: striv'en.
thr: thriv'en.
Cf. give hen, etc.

(Choose only one word out of each group)

ĪV'ENT

n: çŏn-nīv'ent.
Plus why vent, etc.

ĪV'EST

d: dīv'est*.
dr: drīv'est*.
l: līv'est.
n: çŏn-nīv'est*.
pr: dē-prīv'est*.
r: ar-rīv'est*, dē-rīv'est*, rīv'est*.
shr: shrīv'est*.
str: strīv'est*.
thr: thrīv'est*.
tr: çŏn-trīv'est*.
v: rē-vīv'est*, sūr-vīv'est*.
Plus my vest, etc.

IV'EST

g: fŏr-giv'est*, giv'est*, mis-giv'est*.
l: liv'est*, out-liv'est*, rē-liv'est*.

IV'ET

gr: griv'et.
pr: priv'et.
r: riv'et, un-riv'et.
s: civ'et.
tr: triv'et.
Plus Biv'et, etc.
Cf. give it, etc.

ĪV'ETH

d: dīv'eth*.
dr: drīv'eth*.
n: çŏn-nīv'eth*.
pr: dē-prīv'eth*.
r: ar-rīv'eth*, dē-rīv'eth*, rīv'eth*.
shr: shrīv'eth*.

str: strīv'eth*.
thr: thrīv'eth*.
tr: çŏn-trīv'eth*.
v: rē-vīv'eth*, sūr-vīv'eth*.

IV'ETH

g: fŏr-giv'eth*, giv'eth*, mis-giv'eth*.
l: liv'eth*, out-liv'eth*, rē-liv'eth*.

I'VI

Vowel: i'vy.
Plus thrive, he, etc.

IV'I

ch: chiv'vy.
d: di'vi=di'vi, div'vy.
l: Liv'y.
pr: priv'y.
t: tan-tiv'y, tiv'y.
Plus forgive, he, etc.

Ī'VID

Vowel: ī'vied.
Plus thrive, he'd, etc.

IV'ID

ch: chiv'vied.
d: div'vied.
l: liv'id.
pr: priv'ied.
v: viv'id.
Plus Livy'd, etc.

IV'IK

s: civ'iç.

IV'IL, IV'EL

dr: driv'el.
r: riv'el*.
s: civ'il, un-civ'il.
shr: shriv'el.

ĪV'ING
IV'ŬR
fāte, fär, fȧst, fȧll, fĭnăl, cāre, at; mēte, prey, hêr, met; pīne,
marīne, bĭrd, pin; nōte, mŏve, fŏr, atŏm, not; mŏŏn, book; **606**

(Choose only one word out of each group)

sn: sniv'el.
sw: swiv'el.
Plus forgive 'll, etc.

ĪV'ING

d: dīv'ing.
dr: drīv'ing.
h: hīv'ing.
n: cŏn-nīv'ing.
pr: dē-prīv'ing.
r: ar-rīv'ing, dē-rīv'ing.
shr: shrīv'ing.
str: strīv'ing.
thr: thrīv'ing.
tr: cŏn-trīv'ing, un-cŏn-trīv'ing.
v: sŭr-vīv'ing.
w: wīv'ing.

IV'ING

g: fŏr-giv'ing, giv'ing,
law'giv-ing, life'=giv-ing,
mis-giv'ing, thanks'giv-ing,
un-fŏr-giv'ing.
l: ev-ẽr-liv'ing, liv'ing,
out-liv'ing.

ĪV'LI

l: līve'ly.
Plus thrive, Lee or lea, etc.

IV'LI

t: ab'sō-tive-ly, pos'i-tive-ly.

IV'LING

shr: shriv'elling.
sn: sniv'elling.

ĪV'MENT

pr: dē-prīve'ment.
v: rē-vīve'ment.
Plus Clive meant, etc.

IV'NES

g: for-give'ness,
un-for-give'ness.

IV'ŎT

d: div'ŏt.
p: piv'ŏt.
Cf. give at, etc.

IV'RING

kw: quiv'ering.
l: dē-liv'ering.
sh: shiv'ering.
sl: sliv'ering.
Plus give ring, etc.

ĪV'ŬR

d: dīv'ẽr, pẽarl dīv'ẽr.
dr: drīv'ẽr, slāve drīv'ẽr.
f: fīv'ẽr.
h: hīv'ẽr.
j: gȳv'ẽr.
l: ȧ-līv'ẽr, līv'ẽr.
n: cŏn-nīv'ẽr.
pr: dē-prīv'ẽr.
r: ar-rīv'ẽr, dē-rīv'ẽr, **rīv'ẽr**.
shr: shrīv'ẽr.
sk: skīv'ẽr.
sl: slīv'ẽr.
st: stīv'ẽr.
str: strīv'ẽr.
thr: thrīv'ẽr.
tr: cŏn-trīv'ẽr.
v: rē-vīv'ẽr, sŭr-vīv'ẽr.
Plus shrive her or err, etc.

IV'ŬR

fl: fliv'vẽr.
g: for-giv'ẽr, giv'ẽr,
In'di-ăn giv'ẽr, mis-giv'ẽr.
kw: quiv'ẽr.

607 ūse, bųll, brute, tŭrn, up; crȳ, myth; ċat, maċhine, ace,
church, ċhord; ġem, aṅger, (Fr.) boṅ, aṣ; THis, thin; aẓure

IV'ŪRD
IZ'EN

(Choose only one word out of each group)

l: ċan'ti-liv-ēr, dē-liv'ēr,
free liv'ēr, liv'ēr, out-liv'ēr.
r: riv'ēr, Spọọn Riv'ēr, etc.
sh: shiv'ēr.
sk: skiv'ēr.
sl: sliv'ēr.
st: stiv'ēr.
t: tiv'ēr.
Plus give her *or* err, **etc.**

IV'ŪRD

kw: quiv'ēred.
l: dē-liv'ēred, li'ly=liv-ēred,
piġ'eŏn=liv'ēred, whīte=liv'ēred,
yel'lōw=liv'ēred.
sh: shiv'ēred, un-shiv'ēred.
sl: sliv'ēred.
Plus giver'd, etc.

ĪV'US

kl: aċ-ċlīv'ous, dē-ċlīv'ous,
prō-ċlīv'ous.
l: sȧ-līv'ous.
Plus shrive us, etc.

IV'YĂL

tr: triv'iăl.
Cf. iv'i-ăl.

Ī'WĀ

b: bȳ'wāy.
h: hīgh'wāy.
sk: skȳ'wāy.
Plus try way *or* weigh, **etc.**

Ī'ZȦ

Vowel: Ī'ṣȧ, Ī'zȧ
l: Ē-lī'zȧ, Lī'zȧ.
r: ċō-rȳ'zȧ.
Plus why's a, etc.
Plus realize a, etc.

Ī'ZAK

Vowel: Ī'ṣaaċ.

ĪZ'ĂL

pr: ċŏm-prīṣ'ăl, sūr-prīṣ'ăl.
v: rē-vīṣ'ăl.
Plus skies, Al, etc.

IZ'ĂRD

Vowel: iz'zărd.
bl: bliz'zărd.
g: giz'zărd.
l: liz'ărd, lounġe liz'ărd.
s: sciṣ'ṣŏred.
v: viṣ'ŏred, viz'ărd.
w: wiz'ărd.
Cf. is hard, etc.

IS'DĀL

gr: Gris'dāle.
Plus is dale, etc.

IZ'DŎM

w: wiṣ'dŏm.
Plus is dumb, etc.

ĪZ'EN

d: bē-dīz'en, dīz'en.
p: pī''zen.
Cf. wise hen, etc.

IZ'EN, IZ'ŎN

d: bē-diz'en, diz'en.
m: miz'zen.
pr: im-priṣ'ŏn, priṣ'ŏn.
r: ȧ-riṣ'en, rē-ȧ-riṣ'en, riṣ'en.
t: ptiṣ'ăn (tiz').
w: wiz'en.
Cf. his'n.
Cf. is on *or* an, etc.

ĪZ'EST
I'ZHUN

fāte, fär, fȧst, fạll, finăl, cãre, at; mēte, prey, hẽr, met; pīne,
marïne, bĭrd, pin; nōte, mŏve, fọr, atŏm, not; mọọn, book;

608

(Choose only one word out of each group)

ĪZ'EST

d: mẽr'chăn-dīṣ-est*.

g: dis-guīṣ'est (-gīz')*.

j: ȧ-pol'ō-ġīz-est*,
eū'lō-ġīz-est*.

k(c): cat'ē-chīz-est*.

l: civ'i-līz-est*, mō'bi-līz-est*,
mōn-op'ō-līz-est*,
rē'ăl-īz-est*.

m: com'prō-mīṣ-est*,
prē-mīṣ'est*, sŭr-mīs'est*.

n: ag'ō-nīz-est*, ọr'gȧ-nīz-est*,
pa'trō-nīz-est*, re'cŏg-nīz-est*,
sol'em-nīz-est*, tyr'an-nīz-est*.

pr: cŏm-prīṣ'est*, prīz'est*,
sŭr-prīṣ'est*.

r: ȧ-rīṣ'est*, rē-ȧ-rīṣ'est*,
rīṣ'est*, thē'ō-rīz-est*,
up-rīṣ'est*.

s: crit'i-cīz-est*,
em'phȧ-sīz-est*, ex-cīṣ'est*,
ex'ēr-cīṣ-est*, ex'ọr-cīṣ-est*.
sīz'est*.

sp: dē-spīṣ'est*.

t: ad'vẽr-tīṣ-est*, bap-tīz'est*,
chas-tīṣ'est*, dram'ȧ-tīz-est*.

th: sym'pȧ-thīz-est*.

v: ad-vīṣ'est*, dē-vīṣ'est*,
im'prō-vīṣ-est*, rē-vīṣ'est*,
sū-pẽr-vīṣ'est*.

w: wīṣ'est.

IZ'EST

f: fiz'zest*, ġin fiz'zest*.

fr: friz'zest*.

hw: whiz'zest*.

kw: quiz'zest*.

s: siz'zest*.

IZ'ETH

d: mẽr'chăn-dīṣ-eth*.

g: dis-guīṣ'eth (-gīz')*.

j: ȧ-pol'ō-ġīz-eth*,
eū'lō-ġīz-eth*.

k(c): cat'ē-chīz-eth*.

l: civ'i-līz-eth*, mō'bi-līz-eth*,
mōn-op'ō-līz-eth*, rē'ăl-īz-eth*.

m: com'prō-mīṣ-eth*,
prē-mīṣ'eth*, sŭr-mīs'eth*.

n: ag'ō-nīz-eth*, ọr'gȧ-nīz-eth*,
pa'trō-nīz-eth*, re'cŏg-nīz-eth*,
sol'em-nīz-eth*,
tyr'an-nīz-eth*

pr: cŏm-prīṣ'eth*, prīz'eth*,
sŭr-prīṣ'eth*.

r: ȧ-rīṣ'eth*, rē-ȧ-rīṣ'eth*,
rīṣ'eth*, thē'ō-rīz-eth*,
up-rīṣ'eth*.

s: crit'i-cīz-eth*,
em'phȧ-sīz-eth*, ex-cīṣ'eth*,
ex'ēr-cīṣ-eth*, ex'ọr-cīṣ-eth*,
sīz'eth*.

sp: dē-spīṣ'eth*.

t: ad'vẽr-tīṣ-eth*, bap-tīz'eth*,
chas-tīṣ'eth*, dram'ȧ-tīz-eth*.

th: sym'pȧ-thīz-eth*.

v: ad-vīṣ'eth*, dē-vīṣ'eth*,
im'prō-vīṣ-eth*, rē-vīṣ'eth*,
sū-pẽr-vīṣ'eth*.

IZ'ETH

f: fiz'zeth*, ġin fiz'zeth*.

fr: friz'zeth*.

hw: whiz'zeth*.

kw: quiz'zeth*.

s: siz'zeth*.

I'ZHUN

i: aȧ-li'ṣiŏn, col-li'ṣiŏn,
ē-li'ṣiŏn, il-li'ṣiŏn.

pr: mis-pri'ṣiŏn.

r: dē-ri'ṣiŏn, ir-ri'ṣiŏn.

(Choose only one word out of each group)

s: ab-scis'ṣiŏn, c̣ŏn-ci'ṣiŏn,
dē-ci'ṣiŏn, ex-ci'ṣiŏn,
im-prē-ci'ṣiŏn, in-ci'ṣiŏn,
in-dē-ci'ṣiŏn, prē-ci'ṣiŏn,
rē-ci'ṣiŏn, rē-scis'ṣiŏn,
scis'ṣiŏn.

v: di-vi'ṣiŏn, en-vi'ṣiŏn,
prē-vi'ṣiŏn, prō-vi'ṣiŏn,
rē-vi'ṣiŏn, sub-di-vi'ṣiŏn,
su-pēr-vi'ṣiŏn, tel-ē-vi'ṣiŏn,
vi'ṣiŏn.
Cf. iz'i-ăn.

IZH'UND

v: prō-vi'ṣiŏned, vi'ṣiŏned.
Plus i'zhun+ed.

IZH'ŪR

s: sciṣ'ṣūre.
Plus is your *or* you're, etc.

ĪZ'I

s: sīz'y.
Plus cries, he, etc.

IZ'I

b: buṣ'y.
d: diz'zy.
fr: friz'zy.
j: jiz'zy.
l: Liz'zie, Liz'zy, tin liz'zie.
t: tiz'zy.
Plus is he, etc.

IZ'ID

b: buṣ'ied, un-buṣ'ied.
d: diz'zied.
Cf. is hid, etc.
Plus Lizzie'd, etc.

IZ'IJ

v: viṣ'ăge.
Cf. whizz age, etc.

IZ'IK

d: par-à-diṣ'ic̣.
f: met-à-phys'ic̣, phyṣ'ic̣.
t: phthiṣ'ic̣ (tiz').

IZ'IKS

f: met-à-phyṣ'ic̣s, phyṣ'ic̣s.
t: phthiṣ'ic̣s (tiz').

ĪZ'ING

Vowel: Hē'brā-īz-ing.
d: ag'gran-dīz-ing,
gor'măn-dīz-ing, hȳ'bri-dīz-ing,
jeo'păr-dīz-ing (je'),
me'thŏ-dīz-ing, stan'dăr-dīz-ing,
sub'si-dīz-ing.
g: dis-guīṣ'ing (-gīz').
j: à-pol'ō-ġīz-ing, eū'lō-ġīz-ing.
k(c̣): c̣at'ē-c̣hīz-ing.
kw: sō-lil'ō-quīz-ing.
l: an'à-lȳz-ing, brú'tà-līz-ing,
c̣ap'i-tà-līz-ing, cen'trà-līz-ing,
civ'i-līz-ing, c̣rys'tăl-līz-ing,
dē-mor'à-līz-ing, ē'quà-līz-ing,
ē-tēr'nà-līz-ing, ē-van'ġe-līz-ing,
fēr'ti-līz-ing, ġēn'ēr-à-līz-ing,
ī-dē'à-līz-ing, ī'dŏ-līz-ing,
im-mor'tà-līz-ing,
joūr'nà-līz-ing, lō-c̣à-līz-ing,
mà-tēr'i-à-līz-ing, mō'bi-līz-ing,
mōn-op'ō-līz-ing, mor'à-līz-ing,
neū'trà-līz-ing, par'à-lȳz-ing,
rat'ion-à-līz-ing, rē'à-līz-ing,
ru'rà-līz-ing, sc̣an'dà-līz-ing,
sig'nà-līz-ing,
spec'ià-līz-ing (spesh'à-),
ster'i-līz-ing, sym'bŏ-līz-ing,
tan'tà-līz-ing, tō'tà-līz-ing,
tran'quil-līz-ing, ū'ti-līz-ing,
viṣ'ū-à-līz-ing (vizh'),

IZ'ING
IZ'LD

fāte, fär, fàst, fạll, finăl, cāre, at; mēte, prey, hẽr, met; pīne,
marīne, bĭrd, pin; nōte, mŏve, fọr, atŏm, not; mọọn, book;

610

(Choose only one word out of each group)

vī'tȧ-līz-ing, vō'c̣ȧ-līz-ing,
vol'ȧ-ti-līz-ing.
m: c̣om'prō-mĭṣ-ing, dē-mĭṣ'ing,
ē-c̣on'ō-mīz-ing,
mȧc̣-ad'ȧ-mīz-ing,
min'i-mīz-ing, prē-mĭṣ'ing,
sūr-mĭṣ'ing,
un-c̣om'prō-mĭṣ-ing.
n: ag'ō-nīz-ing,
an-tag'ō-nīz-ing, c̣an'ŏ-nīz-ing,
c̣ol'ō-nīz-ing, dis-ọr'gȧ-nīz-ing,
gal'vȧ-nīz-ing, här'mō-nīz-ing,
mod'ēr-nīz-ing, ọr'gȧ-nīz-ing,
pa'trō-nīz-ing, re'c̣ŏg-nī-zing,
rev-ō-lū'tio-nīz-ing,
sc̣rū'tī-nīz-ing, sẽr'mŏ-nīz-ing,
sol'em-nī-zing, tyr'ăn-nīz-ing.
pr: ap-prĭṣ'ing, c̣ŏm-prĭṣ'ing,
en'tẽr-prĭṣ-ing, prīz'ing,
sūr-prĭṣ'ing, un-dẽr-prīz'ing.
r: ȧ-rīṣ'ing, ạu'thŏ-rīz-ing,
c̣äu'tē-rīz-ing,
char'ăc̣-tē-rīz-ing,
dē-ō'dŏ-rīz-ing,
fam-il'iăr-īz-ing,
meṣ'mē-rīz-ing, pạu'pē-rīz-ing,
plā'ġi-ȧ-rīz-ing, pul'vē-rīz-ing,
rīṣ'ing, se'c̣ū-lȧ-rīz-ing,
sum'mȧ-rīz-ing, tem'pō-rīz-ing,
ter'rŏ-rīz-ing, thē'ō-rīz-ing,
up-rīṣ'ing, vā'pō-rīz-ing,
vul'gȧ-rīz-ing.
s: Añ'gli-cīz-ing, c̣ap'sīz-ing,
C̣ȧ-thol'i-cīz-ing, c̣rit'i-cīz-ing,
em'phȧ-sīz-ing, ex'ẽr-cīṣ-ing,
ex'ọr-cīṣ-ing, it-al'i-cīz-ing,
sīz'ing.
sp: dē-spīṣ'ing.
t: ad'vẽr-tīṣ-ing,
ap-os'tȧ-tīz-ing, ap'pē-tīz-ing,
bap-tīz'ing, chas-tīz'ing,

dram'ȧ-tīz-ing, hyp'nō-tīz-ing,
mag'ne-tīz-ing, stig'mȧ-tīz-ing,
sys'te-mȧ-tīz-ing.
th: sym'pȧ-thīz-ing.
v: ad-vīṣ'ing, dē-vīṣ'ing,
im'prō-vīṣ-ing, rē-vīṣ'ing,
sū-pẽr-vīṣ'ing.

IZ'ING

f: fiz'zing, ġin fiz'zing,
phiz'zing.
fr: bē-friz'zing, friz'zing.
hw: whiz'zing.
kw: quiz'zing.

IZ'IT

Vowel: whät iṣ it.
v: viṣ'it.
Plus is it, etc.

ĪZ'KRAK

w: wīṣe'c̣rack.
Plus skies crack, etc.

IZ'L

ch: chiṣ'el, en-chiṣ'el.
dr: driz'zle.
f: fiz'zle.
fr: friz'zle.
gr: griz'zle.
kr: c̣riz'zle.
m: miz'zle.
s: siz'zle.
sw: swiz'zle.
tw: twiz'zle.
Plus Liz'll, etc.

IZ'LD

gr: griz'zled.
Plus iz'l+d.

(Choose only one word out of each group)

IZ′LI

ch: chiṣ′elly.
dr: driz′zly.
fr: friz′zly.
gr: griṣ′ly, griz′zly.
Plus is, Lee *or* lea, etc.

IZ′LING

ch: chiṣ′eling.
dr: driz′zling.
f: fiz′zling.
fr: bē-friz′zling, friz′zling.
gr: griz′zling.
m: miz′zling.
s: siz′zling.
sw: swiz′zling.

IZ′M

w: iz′zum wiz′zum.
Plus izm.

IZ′MĂL

b: à-byṣ′măl.
d: diṣ′măl, Greāt Diṣ′măl.
k(c̱): ça̤t-ē-chiṣ′măl.
kl: ça̤t-à-c̱lyṣ′măl.
kr: c̱hriṣ′măl.
l: em-bō-liṣ′măl.
r: a-neū-riṣ′măl.
s: par-ox-yṣ′măl.
t: bap-tiṣ′măl, rheū-mà-tiṣ′măl.
Plus prism, Al, etc.

ĪZ′MĂN

pr: prīze′măn.
s: ex-cīṣe′măn.
Plus wise man, etc.

ĪZ′MENT

d: ag-gran′dīze-ment.
pr: ap-prīze′ment.

s: as-sīze′ment.
t: bap-tīze′ment.
Plus skies meant, etc.

IZ′MET

k: kiṣ′met.
Plus Liz met, etc.

IZ′MI

pr: priṣ′my.
Plus is me, etc.

IZ′MIK

kl: ça̤t-à-c̱lyṣ′mi̤c̱, c̱lyṣ′mi̤c̱.
l: em-bō-liṣ′mic̱.
r: aph-ō-riṣ′mic̱.
s: par-ox-yṣ′mi̤c̱.
Plus is, Mick, etc.

IZ′MUS

b: strà-biṣ′mus.
s: a̤c̱-ciṣ′mus.
t: tar-an-tiṣ′mus*.
tr: triṣ′mus.
Plus Liz muss, etc.

ĪZ′NES

w: wīṣe′ness.

IZ′NES

b: buṣ′iness.
Cf. iz′i-nes.

IZ′ŎM

kr: c̱hriṣ′ŏm.
Cf. izm.

ĪZ′ŎN

l: Kȳ′rie ē-leī′ṣŏn.
r: hōr-ī′zŏn.
Plus eyes on *or* an, etc.

ĪZ'ŎRD
IZ'URZ

fāte, fär, fȧst, fạll, finăl, cāre, at; mēte, prev,·hēr, met; pīne,
marīne, bîrd, pin; nōte, mŏve, fọr, atŏm, not; mọọn, book;   **612**

(Choose only one word out of each group)

ĪZ'ŎRD

v: vīṣ'ŏred.

IZ'ŎRD

Cf. iz'ărd.

ĪZ'ŪR

d: ag'gran-dīz-ēr,
  gọr'măn-dīz-ēr, hȳ'bri-dīz-ēr.

g: dis-guĭṣ'ēr (-gīz'), geȳ'ṣēr,
  guĭṣ'ēr (gīz').

j: a-pol'ō-ġīz-ēr, eū'lō-ġiz-ēr.

k(c): cat'ē-chīz-ēr, Kaī'ṣēr,
  Keȳ'ṣēr, Kȳ'ṣēr.

l: an'ȧ-lȳz-ēr, civ-i-līz'er,
  dī'ȧ-lȳ-ṣēr, ē-līṣ'ŏr,
  ē'quȧ-līz-ēr, fēr'ti-līz-ēr,
  ġen'ēr-ȧ-līz-ēr, ī'dŏ-līz-ēr,
  mor'ȧ-līz-ēr, rē'ȧ-līz-ēr,
  sçan'dȧ-līz-ēr, ster'i-līz-ēr,
  tan'tȧ-līz-ēr, tran'quil-līz-ēr,
  vī'tȧ-līz-ēr, vō'çȧ-līz-ēr.

m: at'ŏ-mīz-ēr, ē-çon'ō-mīz-ēr,
  ep-i'tō-mīz-ēr, ī'te-mīz-ēr,
  mīṣ'ēr, sūr-mīṣ'ēr,
  viç'ti-mīz-ēr.

n: ag'ō-nīz-ēr, çan'ŏ-nīz-ēr,
  çol'ō-nīz-ēr, dis-ọr'gȧ-nīz-ēr,
  gal'vȧ-nīz-ēr, här'mō-nīz-ēr,
  hū'mȧ-nīz-ēr, lī'ŏ-nīz-ēr,
  ọr'gȧ-nīz-ēr, sçrù'ti-nīz-ēr,
  sēr'mŏ-nīz-ēr, sol'em-nīz-ēr,
  syñ'chrō-nīz-ēr, tyr'ăn-nīz-ēr,
  vul'çȧ-nīz-ēr.

pr: ap-prīṣ'ēr, prīz'ēr,
  sūr-prīṣ'ēr.

r: ạu'thŏ-rīz-ēr, çạu'tĕ-rīz-ēr,
  dē-ō'dŏ-rīz-ēr, ex-tem'pō-rīz-ēr,
  pạu'pĕ-rīz-ēr, pō'lȧ-rīz-ēr,
  pul'vĕ-rīz-ēr, rīṣ'ēr,
  tem'pō-rīz-ēr, ter'rŏ-rīz-ēr,
  thē'ō-rīz-ēr, up-rīṣ'ēr,
  vā'pō-rīz-ēr, vul'gȧ-rīz-ēr.

s: as-sīz'ēr, çap-sīz'ēr,
  ex'ēr-cīṣ-ēr, ex'ọr-cīṣ-ēr,
  in-cīṣ'ŏr, sīz'ēr.

sp: dē-spīṣ'ēr.

t: ad'vēr-tīṣ-ēr, ap'pē-tīz-ēr,
  bap-tīz'ēr, chas-tīṣ'ēr,
  dog'mȧ-tīz-ēr, mag'ne-tīz-ēr,
  pros'e-ly-tīz-ēr, stig'mȧ-tīz-ēr.

th: sym'pȧ-thīz-ēr.

v: ad-vīṣ'ēr, dē-vīṣ'ēr,
  dē-vīṣ'ŏr, di-vīṣ'ŏr,
  im'prō-vīṣ'ēr, rē-viṣ'ēr,
  sū-pēr-vīṣ'ēr.

w: wīṣ'ēr.

Plus tries her, etc.

IZ'ŪR

fr: bē-friz'zēr, friz'zēr.

kw: quiz'zēr.

s: sciṣ'ṣọr.

v: viṣ'ọr.

IZ'URZ

s: sciṣ'ṣọrṣ.

Plus iz'ūr + ṣ.

613

ūse, bụll, brúte, tũrn, **up**; crȳ, myth; çat, maçhine, ace, church, çhord; ġem, añger, (Fr.) boṅ, aṣ; THis, thin; aᶎure

**Ō′Å
OB′ET**

(Choose only one word out of each group)

O

The accented vowel sounds included are listed under **O** in Single Rhymes.

Ō′Å

b: bō′å, Gil-bō′å, jĕr-bō′å.
m: mō′å, Sa-mō′å.
n: Ġe-nō′å, Nō′åh, quin-ō′å.
pr: prō′å.
st: stō′å.
z: en-tō-zō′å, ep′i-zō′å, met-å-zō′å, prō-tō-zō′å, spĕr″må-tå-zō′å.
Cf. Al-ō′hå.
Plus owe *or* O, a, etc.

Ō′AB

j: Jō′ab.
m: Mō′ab.
Plus so, Ab, etc.

Ō′ĂL

st: bē-stōw′ăl.
Plus go, Al, etc.

Ọ′ĂL

dr: with-draw′ăl.
Plus straw, Al, etc.

Ō′BÅ

g: da-gō′bå.
r: ar-rō′bå, bō″nå-rō′bå*.
t: Man-i-tō′bå.
Plus globe, a, etc.

Ọ′BÅ

h: Çå-hå′bå.
t: Çä-taw′bå.
Plus daub a, etc.

Ō′BALL

n: nō ball.
sn: snōw′ball.
Plus throw ball, etc.

Ō′BĀT

gl: glō′bāte.
l: lō′bāte.
pr: prō′bāte.
Plus globe eight *or* ate, etc.
Plus throw bait, etc.

ŌB′EST

pr: prōb′est*.
r: dis-rōb′est*, en-rōb′est*, rōb′est*, un-rōb′est*.
Plus throw best, etc.

ỌB′EST

d: bē-dạub′est*, dạub′est*.
Plus saw best, etc.

OB′EST

r: rob′best*.
s: sob′best*.
thr: throb′best*.
Cf. job best, etc.

OB′ET

k(ç): Çob′bett.
Plus mob et, etc.
Cf. job it, etc.

ŌB'ETH
OB'ING

fāte, fär, fàst, fall, finăl, cãre, at; mēte, prey, hĕr, met; pīne,
marĭne, bĭrd, pin; nōte, mŏve, fọr, atŏm, not; mọọn, book;

614

(Choose only one word out of each group)

ŌB'ETH

pr: prōb'eth*.
r: dis-rōb'eth*, en-rōb'eth*,
rōb'eth*, un-rōb'eth*.
Plus glow, Beth, etc.

ỌB'ETH

d: bē-dạub'eth*, dạub'eth*.
Plus saw Beth, etc.

OB'ETH

r: rob'beth*.
s: sob'beth*.
thr: throb'beth*.
Cf. job, Beth, etc.

Ō'BĪ

g: gō bȳ.
Plus so buy, by, or bye, etc.
Plus globe, I or eye, etc.

Ō'BĒ, Ō'BI

Vowel: ō'bi.
d: a-dō'bē.
f: hȳ-drō-phō'by.
g: Gō'bi.
gl: glōb'y.
k: Kō'bē.
Plus so be or bee, etc.
Plus globe, he, etc.

OB'I

b: bob'by.
h: hob'by.
k(ç): çob'by.
l: Hob'by Lob'by, lob'by.
m: mob'by.
n: knob'by, nob'by.
sk(sç): sçob'by.
skw: squäb'by.
sn: snob'by.

Plus job, be, etc.
Cf. job, be or bee, etc.
Plus bah, be or bee, etc.

Ō'BIL, Ō'BĒL

m: ạu-tō-mō'bile, im-mō'bile,
mō'bile.
Plus owe bill or O Bill, etc.
Cf. so, Beale, etc.
Plus globe ill, etc.

OB'IN

b: bob'bin.
d: dob'bin.
r: rag'ged rob'in, rob'bin,
rob'in, round rob'in,
wāke rob'in.
Cf. throb'bin', etc.
Plus job in or inn, etc.

ŌB'ING

gl: glōb'ing.
pr: prōb'ing.
r: dis-rōb'ing, en-rōb'ing,
rōb'ing, un-rōb'ing.
Plus so, Byng, etc.

OB'ING

b: bob'bing.
bl: blob'bing.
j: job'bing.
k(ç): çob'bing.
l: lob'bing.
m: mob'bing.
n: hob-nob'bing, knob'bing.
r: rob'bing.
s: sob'bing.
sn: snob'bing.
sw: swäb'bing.
thr: throb'bing.

615 ūse, bu̱ll, brúte, tūrn, u̇p; crȳ, myth; ça̱t, machine, ace, church, ç̱hord; ġem, a̐nger, (Fr.) bon̊, a̱ş; THis, thin; azure

OB'INZ
Q'BŌNZ

(Choose only one word out of each group)

OB'INZ

j: Job'bins̱.
r: Rob'bins̱.
Plus ob'in+s.

OB'ISH

b: bob'bish.
m: mob'bish.
n: nob'bish.
skw: squäb'bish.
sn: snob'bish.

OB'JEKT

Vowel: ob'jec̱t.

Ō'B'L

n: en-nō'ble, ig-nō'ble, nō'ble, un-nō'ble.
s: Sō'bel.
Plus throw bull, etc.
Plus globe 'll, etc.

Q'B'L

b: ba̱u'ble.
Plus saw bull, etc.
Plus daub 'll, etc.

OB"L

g: gob'ble.
h: hob'ble.
k(c̱): c̱ob'ble, c̱o'ble.
n: nob'ble.
skw: squäb'ble.
w: wäb'ble.
Plus stob'll, etc.

OB'LI

k(c̱): c̱ob'bly.
skw: squäb'bly.
w: wäb'bly, Wob'bly.
Plus job, Lee *or* lea, etc.

OB'LIN

g: gob'lin.
Plus rob Lynn, etc.

OB'LING

g: gob'bling.
h: hob'bling.
k(c̱): c̱ob'bling.
n: nob'bling.
sn: snob'ling.
skw: squäb'bling.
w: wäb'bling.

OB'LŬR

g: gob'blĕr, tŭr'key gob'blĕr.
h: hob'blĕr.
k(c̱): c̱ob'blĕr,
black'bĕr-ry c̱ob'blĕr,
pēach c̱ob'blĕr,
sher'ry c̱ob'blĕr.
n: knob'blĕr, nob'blĕr.
skw: squäb'blĕr.
w: wäb'blĕr.

Ō'BŌ

Vowel: ō'bōe.
h: hō'bō.
l: lō'bō.
z: zō'bō.
Plus so, bo, beau *or* bow, etc.
Plus robe owe *or* O, etc.

Ō'BOI

Vowel: Ō boy!
d: dōugh'boy (dō').
Plus show boy, etc.
Plus robe, oi!, etc.

Q'BŌNZ

j: jaw bōnes̱.
s: saw'bōnes̱.

(Choose only one word out of each group)

Plus straw bones, etc.
Plus daub owns, etc.

Ō′BŌT

sh: shōw′bōat.
Plus so boat, etc.

Ō′BRȦ

k(ç): çō′brȧ.

Ō′BROU

l: lōw′brow.
n: nō′brow.
Plus show brow *or* brau, etc.

ŌB′SŎN

j: Jōb′sŏn.
r: Rōbe′sŏn, Rōb′sŏn.
Plus globe, son *or* sun, etc.

OB′SŎN

d: dob′sŏn.
j: Job′sŏn.
r: Rob′sŏn.
Plus job, son *or* sun, etc.

OB′STŨR

l: lob′stẽr.
m: mob′stẽr.
Plus job stir, etc.

OB′ŪL

gl: glob′ūle.
l: lo′būle.
Plus job, you'll *or* Yule, etc.

ŌB′ŨR

k: Kō′bẽr.
pr: prōb′ẽr.
r: dis-rōb′ẽr, en-rōb′ẽr, rōb′ẽr.
s: sōb′ẽr.
t: Oç-tō′bẽr.
Plus no burr, etc.
Plus globe her *or* err, etc.

ọB′ŨR

d: bē-dạub′ẽr, dạub′ẽr.
k(ç): Mi-çaw′bẽr.
Plus raw burr, etc.
Plus daub her, etc.

OB′ŨR

bl: blob′bẽr.
j: job′bẽr.
k(ç): çob′bẽr.
kl: çlob′bẽr.
l: lob′bẽr.
n: knob′bẽr.
r: rob′bẽr.
s: sob′bẽr.
sl: bē-slob′bẽr, slob′bẽr.
sn: snob′bẽr.
sw: swäb′bẽr.
thr: throb′bẽr.
Cf. Fä′bre.
Plus mob her *or* err, etc.

ọ′BŨRN

Vowel: ạu′būrn.
Plus daub ûrn, earn *or* erne, etc.
Plus saw burn, etc.

ŌB′US

Vowel: ōb′us.
gl: glōb′us.
k(ç): ja-çō′bus.
Plus owe bus *or* buss, etc.
Plus enrobe us, etc.

OB′WEB

k(ç): çob′web.
Plus rob web, etc.

ŌCH′EST

br: brōach′est*.
kr: en-çrōach′est*.

(Choose only one word out of each group)

p: pōach'est*.
pr: ap-prōach'est*, rē-prōach'est*.
Plus slow chest, etc.

ỌCH'EST

b: dē-bạuch'est*.
Plus saw chest, etc.

OCH'EST

b: botch'est*.
bl: blotch'est*.
n: notch'est*.
w: wätch'est*.

OCH'ET

kr: çrotch'et.
r: rotch'et*.
Plus Scotch et, etc.
Cf. scotch it, etc.

ŌCH'ETH

br: brōach'eth*.
kr: en-çrōach'eth*.
p: pōach'eth*.
pr: ap-prōach'eth*, rē-prōach'eth*.

ỌCH'ETH

b: dē-bạuch'eth*.

OCH'ETH

b: botch'eth*.
bl: blotch'eth*.
n: notch'eth*.
w: wätch'eth*.

ŌCH'EZ

br: brōach'eş, brōoch'eş.
k(ç): çōach'eş, trāin çōach'eş, stāġe çōach'eş.

kr: en-çrōach'eş.
l: lōach'eş.
p: pōach'eş.
pr: ap-prōach'eş, rē-prōach'eş, self rē-prōach'eş.
r: rōach'eş.
Cf. roach is, etc.

ŌCH'FỤL

pr: rē-prōach'fụl.

OCH'I

b: botch'y.
bl: blotch'y.
n: notch'y.
spl: splotch'y.
Plus watch he, etc.

ŌCH'ING

br: brōach'ing.
k(ç): çōach'ing.
kr: en-çrōach'ing.
p: pōach'ing.
pr: ap-prōach'ing, rē-prōach'ing.

ỌCH'ING

b: dē-bạuch'ing.

OCH'ING

b: botch'ing.
bl: blotch'ing.
n: notch'ing.
sk(sç): sçotch'ing.
spl: splotch'ing.
w: wätch'ing.

OCH'MĂN

sk(sç): Sçotch'măn.
w: wätch'măn.
Plus notch'măn. etc.

(Choose only one word out of each group)

ŌCH′MENT

kr: en-c̦rōach′ment.
pr: ap-prōach′ment.
Plus coach meant, etc.

ŌCH′ŪR

br: brōach′ẽr.
kr: en-c̦rōach′ẽr.
p: pōach′ẽr.
pr: ap-prōach′ẽr, rē-prōach′ẽr,
  self rē-prōach′ẽr.
Plus coach her *or* err, etc.

QCH′ŪR

b: dē-bạuch′ẽr.

OCH′ŪR

b: botch′ẽr.
bl: blotch′ẽr.
n: not′chẽr, top′=not′chẽr. }
spl: splotch′ẽr.
w: wätch′ẽr.
Plus scotch her *or* err, etc.

OCH′WŪRD

w: wätch′wŏrd.
Plus notch word, etc.

Ō′DÀ

g: pȧ-gō′då.
k(c̦): c̦ō′då.
n: trī-nō′då.
r: Bȧ-rō′då, Rhō′då (rō′).
s: bāk′ing sō′då,
  bran′dy and sō′då,
  īce′c̦rēam sō′då, sō′då,
  whis′key and sō′då (hwis′).
Plus owed a, etc.

ŌD′ĂL

m: mōd′ăl.
n: in-tẽr-nōd′ăl, nōd′ăl,
  trī-nōd′ăl.
y: yōd′el.
Plus code′ll, etc.

QD′ĂL

d: daw′dle.
k(c̦): bī-c̦ạu′dăl, c̦ạu′dăl,
  c̦ạu′dle.
Plus gaud′ll, etc.

OD′ĂRD

f: fod′dẽred.
g: God′dărd.
s: sol′dẽred (sod′ẽrd).
st: Stod′dărd.
Cf. trod hard, etc.

ŌD′ED

b: bōd′ed, fōre-bōd′ed.
g: gōad′ed.
k(c̦): c̦ōd′ed, dē-c̦ōd′ed.
l: lōad′ed, lōd′ed,
  ō″vẽr-lōad′ed, un-lōad′ed.
m: out-mō′ded.
pl: ex-plōd′ed.
r: c̦ǫr-rōd′ed, ē-rōd′ed.
w: wōad′ed.
Cf. tōad′ied.
Plus show dead, etc.
Cf. show did, etc.
Plus code, Ed.

QD′ED

fr: dē-frạud′ed.
l: bē-lạud′ed, lạud′ed.
pl: ap-plạud′ed.
r: mȧ-rạud′ed.
Plus saw dead, etc.
Plus sawed, Ed, etc.

(Choose only one word out of each group)

OD′ED

n: nod′ded.
p: pod′ded.
pl: plod′ded.
pr: prod′ded.
s: sod′ded.
w: wäd′ded.
Cf. od′id.
Plus sod dead, etc.
Cf. sod, Ed, etc.

ŌD′EL

y: yōd′el.
Cf. ōd′ăl.

ŌD′EN

b: fōre-bōd′en*.
w: Wōd′en.
Cf. Ō′din, Bō′din.
Plus low den, etc.

ǪD′EN

br: brǫad′en.
Plus saw den, etc.

OD′EN

h: hod′den.
s: sod′den, wạt′ĕr⸗sod′den.
tr: trod′den, un-trod′den.
Cf. äd′en.
Plus pod den, etc.

ŌD′ENT

pl: ex-plōd′ent.
r: cǫr-rō′dent, ē-rō′dent, rō′dent.
Plus slow dent, etc.

OD′ES

g: god′dess.
Cf. bod′ice.

ŌD′EST

b: bōd′est*, fōre-bōd′est*.
g: gōad′est*.
l: lōad′est*, ō″vēr-lōad′est*,
un-lōad′est*.
pl: ex-plōd′est*.
r: cǫr-rōd′est*.

ǪD′EST*

br: brǫad′est.
fr: dē-frạud′est*.
l: bē-lạud′est*, lạud′est*.
pl: ap-plạud′est*.
r: mạ̀-rạud′est*.

OD′EST

Vowel: od′dest.
m: im-mod′est, mod′est.
n: nod′dest*.
pl: plod′dest*.
pr: prod′dest*.
w: wäd′dest*.

ŌD′ETH

b: bōd′eth*, fōre-bōd′eth*.
g: gōad′eth*.
l: lōad′eth*, ō″vēr-lōad′eth*,
un-lōad′eth*.
pl: ex-plōd′eth*.
r: cǫr-rōd′eth*.
Plus slow death, etc.

ǪD′ETH

fr: dē-frạud′eth*.
l: bē-lạud′eth*, lạud′eth*.
pl: ap-plạud′eth*.
r: mạ̀-rạud′eth*.
Plus law death, etc.

OD'ETH
OD'ING

fāte, fär, fåst, fall, finăl, cāre, at; mēte, prey, hēr, met; pīne,
marĭne, bĭrd, pin; nōte, mŏve, fŏr, atŏm, not; mōon, book;

620

(Choose only **one** word out of each group)

OD'ETH

n: nod'deth*.
pl: plod'deth*.
pr: prod'deth*.
w: wäd'deth*.
Cf. God, death, etc.

ŌD'I

t: tōad'y.
w: wōad'y.
Plus road, he, etc.

OD'I

b: baw'dy.
d: daw'dy.
g: gaud'y.
m: Maud'ie.
Plus outlawed, he, etc.
Plus saw Dee, etc.

OD'I

b: bod'y, bus'y=bod"y (biz'),
  em-bod'y, nō'bod-y,
  sŏme'bod-y.
h: hod'dy.
kl: clod'dy.
m: Mäh'di.
n: nod'dy.
r: rod'dy.
s: sod'dy.
sh: shod'dy.
skw: squäd'dy.
t: tod'dy.
w: wäd'dy.
Cf. äd'i.
Plus clod, he, etc.

OD'ID

b: ā'ble=bod'ied, bod'ied,
  dis"em-bod'ied, em-bod'ied,
  un-bod'ied, un"em-bod'ied.

t: tod'died, well'=tod'died.
Cf. od'ed.

OD'IC

Vowel: ōd'ic.
Plus so, Dick, etc.

OD'IC

Vowel: hy̆-dri-od'ic, ī-od'ic,
  od'ic, pē-ri-od'ic.
k(c): sär-cod'ic.
l: mel-od'ic.
m: spas-mod'ic.
n: ā-nod'ic, hel-là-nod'ic,
  syn-od'ic.
p: ē-pod'ic.
r: pà-rod'ic.
s: ep-i-sod'ic, ex-od'ic,
  kin-ē-sod'ic, rhap-sod'ic (rap-).
th: me-thod'ic.

ŌD'IN

Vowel: Ōd'in.
b: Bō-din.
w: Wōd'in.
Cf. ōd'en.
Plus low din, etc.
Plus load in *or* inn, etc.

ŌD'ING

b: bōd'ing, fōre-bōd'ing.
g: gōad'ing.
l: lōad'ing, ō"vēr-lōad'ing,
  un-lōad'ing.
m: out-mōd'ing.
pl: ex-plōd'ing.
r: cor-rōd'ing, ē-rōd'ing.

OD'ING

fr: dē-fraud'ing.
l: bē-laud'ing, laud'ing.
pl: ap-plaud'ing.
r: mà-raud'ing.

621 ūse, bṳll, brûte, tŭrn, up; crȳ, myth; çat, maçhine, ace, church, çhord; ġem, aṅger, (Fr.) boṅ, aṣ; THis, thin; aᶎure

OD'ING
OD'ŎM

(Choose only one word out of each group)

OD'ING

k(c̦): c̦od'ding.
n: nod'ding.
p: pod'ding.
pl: plod'ding.
pr: prod'ding.
w: wäd'ding.

OD'IS

b: bod'ice.
Cf. god'dess.

OD'ISH

g: god'dish.
kl: c̦lod'dish.

ŌD'IST

k(c̦): c̦ōd'ist.
m: mōd'ist.
n: pal″i-nōd'ist.

ǪD'IT

Vowel: ạud'it.
pl: plạud'it.
Plus outlawed it, etc.

ǪD'KȦST

br: broạd'c̦ȧst.
Plus gaud cast, etc.

OD″L

k(c̦): c̦od'dle, mol'ly-c̦od″dle.
m: mod'el, rē-mod'el.
n: nod'dle.
sw: swäd'dle.
t: tod'dle.
tw: twäd'dle.
w: wäd'dle.
Plus God'll, etc.

OD'LI

g: god'ly, un-god'ly.
tw: twäd'dly.
w: wäd'dly.
Plus sod, Lee or lea, etc.

ǪD'LIN

m: mạud'lin.
Plus laud Lynn, etc.

OD'LING

g: god'ling.
k(c̦): c̦od'dling, c̦od'ling.
m: mod'elling, rē-mod'elling.
sw: swäd'dling.
t: tod'dling.
tw: twäd'dling.
w: wäd'dling.

OD'LŪR

k(c̦): c̦od'dlẽr, mol'ly-c̦od″dlẽr.
m: mod'ellẽr.
sw: swäd'dlẽr.
t: tod'dlẽr.
tw: twäd'dlẽr.
w: wäd'dlẽr.

OD'NES

Vowel: odd'ness.

Ō'DŌ

d: dō'dō.
m: Quä″si-mō'dō.
Plus slow dough or doe, etc.
Plus code owe or O, etc.

OD'ŎM

s: Sod'ŏm.
Plus wad 'em, etc.

(Choose only one word out of each group)

ǑD'RI

b: bawd'ry.
t: tawd'ry.

OD'RŎN

skw: squäd'rŏn.
Plus sod run, etc.

OD'SŎN

d: Dod'sŏn.
h: Hod'sŏn.
Plus god, sun *or* son, etc.

ŌD'STÄR

l: lōde'stär.
Plus showed star, etc.
Plus goads tar, etc.

ŌD'STŌN

l: lōad'stōne, lōde'stōne.
t: tōad'stōne.
Plus road stone, etc.
Cf. road's tone, etc.

ŌD'STŨR

g: gōad'stẽr.
r: rōad'stẽr.
Plus mode stir, etc.

OD'UKT

pr: prod'uċt.
Cf. ma ducked *or* duct, etc.
Cf. sod ducked *or* duct, etc.

OD'ŪL

m: mod'ūle.
n: nod'ūle.
Plus sod, you'll *or* Yule, etc.

ŌD'ŨR

Vowel: mal-ōd'ŏr, Ō'dẽr, ōd'ŏr.
b: bōd'ẽr, fōre-bōd'ẽr.

g: gōad'ẽr.
l: lōad'ẽr, muz'zle=lōad''ẽr,
    un-lōad'ẽr.
pl: ex-plōd'ẽr.
r: cọr-rōd'ẽr, ē-rōd'ẽr.
Plus goad her *or* err, etc.

ǑD'ŨR

br: broạd'ẽr.
fr: dē-frạud'ẽr.
l: bē-lạud'ẽr, lạud'ẽr.
pl: ap-plạud'ẽr.
r: må-rạud'ẽr.
s: sạw'dẽr, sọft sạw'dẽr.
Plus awed her *or* err, etc.

OD'ŨR

Vowel: od'dẽr.
d: dod'dẽr.
f: fod'dẽr.
k(ċ): ċod'dẽr.
n: nod'dẽr.
p: pod'dẽr.
pl: plod'dẽr.
pr: prod'dẽr.
s: sol'dẽr (sod'ẽr).
Plus wad her *or* err, etc.

OD'ŨRN

m: mod'ẽrn, un-mod'ẽrn.
Plus sod urn, earn *or* erne, etc.

ŌD'US

m: mōd'us.
n: nōd'ous.
Plus owed us, etc.

Ō'ED

k(ċ): ċō'ed.
Plus beau, Ed, etc.
Cf. tow head, etc.

(Choose only one word out of each group)

Ō′EL

j: Jō′el.
kr: Çrōw′ell.
l: Lōw′ell.
n: Nō′el.
Plus slow el, ell *or* L, etc.

Ō′EM

p: pō′em.
pr: prō′em.
Plus throw 'em, etc.

Ō′EN

Vowel: Ōw′en.
b: Bōw′en.
k(ç): Çō′hen (kō′en).
Cf. Rōw′ăn.

Ō′EST

Vowel: ōw′est*.
bl: blōw′est*.
fl: flōw′est*, ō″vĕr-flōw′est*.
g: fōre-gō′est*, gō′est*,
    out-gō′est*, un″dĕr-gō′est*.
gl: glōw′est*.
gr: grōw′est*, out-grōw′est*,
    ō″vĕr-grōw′est*.
h: hō′est*.
kr: çrōw′est*, out-çrōw′est*,
    ō″vĕr-çrōw′est*.
l: lōw′est.
m: mōw′est*.
n: fōre-knōw′est*, knōw′est*.
r: rōw′est*.
s: sew′est (sō′)*, sōw′est*.
sh: fōre-shōw′est*, shōw′est*.
sl: slōw′est.
sn: snōw′est*.
st: bē-stōw′est*, stōw′est*.
t: tōw′est*, un-dĕr-tōw′est*.
thr: ō″vĕr-thrōw′est*,
    thrōw′est*, up-thrōw′est*.
tr: trōw-est*.

Ǫ′EST

Vowel: aw′est*, ō′vĕr-aw′est*.
dr: draw′est*, with-draw′est*.
l: out-law′est*.
r: raw′est.

Ō′ET

p: pō′et.
Cf. go it, etc.

Ō′ETH

Vowel: ōw′eth*.
bl: blōw′eth*.
fl: flōw′eth*, ō″vĕr-flōw′eth*.
g: fōre-gō′eth*, gō′eth*,
    out-gō′eth*, un″dĕr-gō′eth*.
gl: glōw′eth*.
gr: grōw′eth*, out-grōw′eth*,
    ō″vĕr-grōw′eth*.
h: hō′eth*.
kr: çrōw′eth*, out-çrōw′eth*,
    ō″vĕr-çrōw′eth*.
l: lōw′eth*.
m: mōw′eth*.
n: fōre-knōw′eth*, knōw′eth*.
r: rōw′eth*.
s: sew′eth (sō′)*, sōw′eth*.
sh: fōre-shōw′eth*, shōw′eth*.
sn: snōw′eth*.
st: bē-stōw′eth*, stōw′eth*.
t: tōw′eth*, un″dĕr-tōw′eth*.
thr: ō″vĕr-thrōw′eth*,
    thrōw′eth*, up-thrōw′eth*.
tr: trōw′eth*.

Ǫ′ETH

Vowel: aw′eth*, ō″vĕr-aw′eth*.
dr: draw′eth*, with-draw′eth*.
l: out-law′eth*.

Ō′FÅ

s: sō′få.
Plus loaf a, etc.

(Choose only one word out of each group)

OF'ĂL

Vowel: ọf'făl.
Plus toff'll, etc.
Cf. ọ'fụl, ọf''l.

Ō'FET

t: Tō'phet.
Plus loaf et, etc.
Cf. loaf it, etc.

OF'ET, OF'IT

pr: ärch'proph''et, prof'it,
proph'et.
weaTH'ẽr proph'et (weTH').
s: sof'fit.
Plus doff it, etc.
Plus prof et, etc.

Ō'FI

s: Sō'phie.
str: strō'phe.
tr: trō'phy.
Plus loaf, he, etc.
Plus low fee, etc.

OF'Ï

k(ç): çof'feē.
sp: spof'fy.
t: tof'fy.
Plus off, he, etc.

OF'IK

s: phil''ō-soph'iç (fil''ō-sof'ik),
thē''ō-soph'iç,
thē''ō-phil''ō-soph'iç.
str: an''ti-stroph'iç,
ap''ŏs-troph'iç, çat''à-stroph'iç.
tr: hȳ''pẽr-troph iç.

Ō'FĪL

pr: prō'fïle.
Plus slow file, etc.
Plus loaf, I'll, aisle *or* isle, etc.

OF'IN

k(ç): çof'fin, en-çof'fin.
g: Mç-Gof'fin.
Plus trough in *or* inn, etc.

OF'ING

Vowel: ọf'fing.
d: dọf'fing.
g: gọlf'ing (gawf').
k(ç): çough'ing (kawf').
sk(sç): scọf'fing.

OF'IS

Vowel: of'fice, wạr of'fice.

OF'ISH

Vowel: stand''ọf'fish.
kr: crạw'fish.
Plus law, fish, etc.

OF'ISH

Vowel: of'fish.
sp: spof'fish.
Plus prof fish, etc.

OF''L

Vowel: ọf'făl.
w: wạf'fle.
Cf. ọ'fụl.
Plus cough'll, etc.

OF'N

Vowel: ọf'ten.
s: sọf'ten.

OF'TED

l: lọf'ted.
Plus scoff, Ted, etc.
Plus scoffed, Ed, etc.

(Choose only one word out of each group)

ǪF'TEST

l: lǫf'test*.
s: sǫf'test.
Plus soph test, etc.

ǪF'TI

l: lǫf'ty.
s: sǫf'ty.
Plus oft* he, etc.
Plus cough tea, etc.

ǪFT'LI

s: sǫft'ly.
Plus scoffed, Lee or lea, etc.

ǪF'TŪR

kr: c̦rǫf'tēr.
l: lǫf'tēr.
s: sǫf'tēr.
Plus scoffed her or err, etc.

Ō'FU̯L

w: wōe'fu̯l.
Plus snow full, etc.

Ǫ'FU̯L

Vowel: aw'fu̯l.
l: law'fu̯l, un-law'fu̯l.
w: wa̯f'fle
Cf. ǫf''l.
Plus craw full, etc.

ŌF'ŪR

Vowel: Ō'phĭr.
g: gōph'ēr (gōf').
l: lōaf'ēr.
sh: c̦hauf'fēur (shō').
Plus oaf her or err, etc.
Plus owe for, fur or fir, etc.

ǪF'ĒR

Vowel: ǫf'fēr.
d: dǫf'fēr.
g: gǫf'fēr, gǫl'fēr (gawf').
k(c̦): c̦ǫf'fēr, c̦ough'ēr (kawf').
pr: prǫf'fēr.
sk(sc̦): sc̦ǫf'fēr.
Plus scoff her or err, etc.

Ō'GȦ

r: Tĭ-c̦on''de-rō'gȧ.
sn: snō'gȧ.
t: Sar''ȧ-tō'gȧ, tō'gȧ.
y: yō'gȧ.
Plus prō-rōgue a, etc.

ǪG'Ȧ

k(c̦): Syl''ȧ-c̦au'gȧ.
m: Chic̦''ȧ-ma̯u'gȧ.
t: A̯u-ta̯u'gȧ.

ŌG'ĂL

d: dōg'ăl.
Plus rogue, Al, etc.
Plus slow gal, etc.

OG'ĂL

g: syn''ȧ-gog'ăl.
Plus frog, Aĭ, etc.

Ō'GĂN

br: brō'găn.
h: Hō'găn.
sl: slō'găn.
Plus prorogue an, etc.

OG'ĂN

b: tō-bog'găn.
g: Mc̦-Gog'găn.
Plus dog an, etc.

OG'HWIP
Ō'GRAM

fāte, fär, fȧst, fȧll, finăl, cāre, at; mēte, prey, hẽr, met; pīne,
marῑne, bȋrd, pȋn; nōte, mȯve, fǫr, atŏm, not; mǫǫn, book;

626

(Choose only one word out of each group)

OG'HWIP

d: dog whip.
Plus hog whip, etc.

Ō'GI

b: bō'gey ('gi), bō'gie.
d: dō'gie.
f: fō'gey, ōld fō'gey.
st: stō'gie.
y: yō'gi.
Plus rogue, he, etc.

OG'I

b: bog'gy.
d: dog'gy.
f: fog'gy.
fr: frog'gy.
gr: grog'gy.
j: jog'gy.
kl: clog'gy.
s: sog'gy.
Plus frog, he, etc.

OG'IN

n: nog'gin.
Plus frog in *or* inn, etc.

OG'ING

b: bog'ging.
d: dog'ging.
f: bē-fog'ging, fog'ging.
fl: flog'ging.
j: jog'ging.
k(c): cog'ging.
kl: clog'ging, un-clog'ging.
n: nog'ging.
sl: slog'ging.
t: tog'ging.

ŌG'ISH

r: rōgue'ish (rōg').
Plus rogue, Gish, etc.

OG'ISH

d: dog'gish.
h: hog'gish.
Cf. tog, Gish, etc.

Ō'GLE

Vowel: ō'gle.
b: bō'gle.
f: fō'gle.
Cf. slow gull, etc.
Plus rogue'll, etc.

OG''L

b: bog'gle.
d: boon'dog-gle.
g: gog'gle.
j: jog'gle.
k(c): cog'gle.
t: tog'gle.
Plus dog'll, etc.

OG'LING

b: bog'gling.
d: boon'dog-gling.
g: gog'gling.
j: jog'gling.

Ō'GLŨR

Vowel: ō'glẽr.

OG'LŨR

b: bog'glẽr.
d: boon'dog-glẽr.
g: gog'gler.
j: jog'gler.

OG'MῙR

kw: quäg'mῑre.
Plus frog mire, etc.

Ō'GRAM

pr: prō'gram, prō'gramme.
Plus slow gram, etc.
Plus rogue ram, etc.

627 ūse, bull, brúte, tūrn, up; crȳ, myth; çat, machine, ace,
church, çhord; ġem, añger, (Fr.) boṅ, aṣ; THis, thin; aẓure

Ō'GRES
Ō'I

(Choose only one word out of each group)

Ō'GRES

Vowel: ō'gress.
pr: prō'gress.

OG'RES

pr: prog'ress.

OG'STÄR

d: dog'stär.
Plus hog star, etc.
Plus hogs tar, etc.

OG'TROT

d: dog'trot.
j: jog'trot.
Plus frog trot, etc.
Plus water-logged, rot, etc.

Ō'GŬR

Vowel: ō'gre.
Plus rogue her *or* err, etc.

OG'ŬR

Vowel: aug'ēr, aug'ūr.
m: maug'ēr.
n: i-naug'ēr.

OG'ŬR

d: dog'gēr.
f: bē-fog'gēr, pet'ti-fog″gēr.
fl: flog'gēr.
h: hog'gēr, whōle'=hog'gēr.
j: jog'gēr.
k(ç): çog'gēr.
kl: çlog'gēr.
l: log'gēr.
sl: slog'gēr.
t: tog'gēr.
Plus flog her *or* err, etc.

Ō'GUS

b: bō'gus.
Plus prorogue us, etc.
Plus so, Gus, etc.

O'GUST

Vowel: Au'gust.
Plus raw gust, etc.

OG'WOOD

b: bog'wood.
d: dog'wood.
l: log'wood.
Plus clog wood *or* would, etc.

Ō'HED

t: tōw'head.
Cf. çō'ed.
Plus no head, etc.

Ō'HEN

k(ç): Çō'hen.
Plus throw hen, etc.

Ō'HUNK

b: Bō'hunk.
Plus no hunk, etc.

Ō'I

b: Bō'wie.
bl: blōw'y.
d: dōugh'y (dō').
fl: Flō'ey.
gl: glōw'y.
j: Jō'ey.
k(ç): Çō'wie.
kl: Çhlō'ē.
m: Mō'ē.
sh: shōw'y.
sn: snōw'y.
t: tōw'y.

Q'I
OI'DEN

fāte, fär, fȧst, fạll, fīnăl, cãre, at; mēte, prẹy, hẽr, met; pīne,
marĭne, bĭrd, pin; nōte, mŏve, fọr, atŏm, not; mọọn, book;

628

(Choose only one word out of each group)

v: ē-vō'ē.
z: Zō'ē.
Plus owe *or* O, he, etc.

Q'I

fl: flaw'y.
j: jaw'y.
str: straw'y.
th: thaw'y.
Cf. ạ'i.
Plus saw he, etc.

OI'Ȧ

g: Goy'ȧ.
Plus employ a, etc.

OI'ĂL

l: dis-loy'ăl, loy'ăl.
r: chap'el roy'ăl, pen″ny-roy'ăl,
  roy'ăl, sūr-roy'ăl.
Plus employ Al, etc.

OI'ĂNS

b: buoy'ănce (boy').
j: joy'ănce.
n: an-noy'ănce.
v: clãir-voy'ănce.
Cf. enjoy ants, *or* aunts, etc.

OI'ĂNT

b: buoy'ănt (boy'), flam-boy'ănt.
n: an-noy'ănt.
t: cha-toy'ănt.
v: clãir-voy'ănt, prē-voy'ănt.
Plus enjoy aunt *or* ant, etc.

OI'B'I

f: foi'ble.
Plus toy bull, etc.

OID'ĂL

Vowel: ō-oid'ăl.
b: rhom-boid'ăl (rom-).
dr: den-droid'ăl.
f: tȳ-phoid'ăl.
gr: nē-groid'ăl.
k(c): con-choid'ăl, dis-coid'ăl,
  trō-choid'ăl.
kl: cȳ-cloid'ăl.
l: col-loid'ăl, cor″ăl-loid'ăl,
  met″ăl-loid'ăl, par″ȧ-bō-loid'ăl.
m: priṣ-moid'ăl, sig-moid'ăl.
n: cō-noid'ăl, cri-noid'ăl,
  eth-noid'ăl, gȧ-noid'ăl.
r: as″tē-roid'ăl,
  hem″is-phē″roid'ăl,
  sac″chȧ-roid'ăl, sphē-roid'ăl.
s: el″lip-soid'ăl.
t: el″ē-phan-toid'ăl,
  plan″ē-toid'ăl, priṣ″mȧ-toid'ăl.
th: li-thoid'ăl.
v: ō-void'ăl.
Plus employed Al, etc.

OID'ĂNS

v: ȧ-void'ănce.
Plus boy dance, etc.
Plus destroyed ants *or* aunts, etc.

OID'ED

v: ȧ-void'ed, void'ed.
Plus boy dead, etc.
Cf. boy did, etc.

OI'DEN

h: hoy'den.
Plus boy den, etc.
Cf. avoid hen, etc.

(Choose only one word out of each group)

OID′ŪR

br: broid′ēr, em-broid′ēr
m: "moid′ēr".
v: à-void′ēr, void′ēr.
Plus cloyed her *or* err, etc.

OI′Ē

pl: em-ploy′ē, em-ploy′eē.
Plus joy he, etc.

OI′EST

b: buoy′est (boy′)*.
j: en-joy′est*, joy′est*.
k(c̦): c̦oy′est, dē-c̦oy′est*.
kl: cloy′est*.
n: an-noy′est*.
pl: dē-ploy′est*, em-ploy′est*.
str: dē-stroy′est*.
t: toy′est*.
v: c̦on-voy′est*.

OI′ETH

b: buoy′eth (boy′)*.
j: en-joy′eth*, joy′eth*.
k(c̦): dē-c̦oy′eth*.
kl: cloy′eth*.
n: an-noy′eth*.
pl: dē-ploy′eth*, em-ploy′eth*
str: dē-stroy′eth*.
t: toy′eth*.
v: c̦on-voy′eth*.

OI′FṲL

j: joy′fṳl.
Plus boy full, etc.

OI′IJ

b: buoy′ăġe (boy′).
l: al-loy′ăġe.
v: voy′ăġe.
Cf. boy age, etc.

OI′ING

b: buoy′ing (boy′)
j: en-joy′ing, joy′ing.
k(c̦): dē-c̦oy′ing.
kl: cloy′ing.
n: an-noy′ing.
pl: dē-ploy′ing, em-ploy′ing.
str: dē-stroy′ing.
t: toy′ing.
v: c̦on-voy′ing.

OI′ISH

b: boy′ish.
k(c̦): c̦oy′ish.
t: toy′ish.

Ō′IJ

fl: flōw′ăġe.
st: stōw′ăġe.
t: tōw′ăġe.
Cf. throw age, etc.

Ō′IK

kr: dī-c̦hrō′ic̦, mel″à-nō-c̦hrō′ic̦,
plē″ō-c̦hro′ic̦,
xan″thō-c̦hrō′ic̦ (zan″).
n: dyp-nō′ic̦.
r: hē-rō′ic̦, mock′⸗hē-rō′ic̦,
un-hē-rō′ic̦.
st: Stō′ic̦.
tr: Trō′ic̦.
z: à-zō′ic̦, ben-zō′ic̦,
Cen″ō-zō′ic̦, Ē″ō-zō′ic̦,
hȳ″lō-zō′ic̦, hyp″nō-zō′ic̦,
Mez″ō-zō′ic̦, Nē″ō-zō′ic̦,
Pal″aē-ō-zō′ic̦, prō″tō-zō′ic̦.

OIL′EST

b: boil′est*.
br: broil′est*, em-broil′est*.
f: foil′est*.

(Choose only one word out of each group)

k(c͜): c͜oil'est*, rē-c͜oil'est*,
 un-c͜oil'est*.
r: roil'est*.
s: soil'est*.
sp: dē-spoil'est*, spoil'est*.
t: toil'est.
Plus boy, lest, etc.
Cf. toil, lest, etc.

OIL'ET

Vowel: oil'let.
t: toi'let.
Plus boy let *or* Lett, etc.
Plus Hoyle et, etc.
Cf. spoil it, etc.

OIL'ETH

b: boil'eth*.
br: broil'eth*, em-broil'eth*.
f: foil'eth*.
k(c͜): c͜oil'eth*, rē-c͜oil'eth*,
 un-c͜oil'eth*.
r: roil'eth*.
s: soil'eth*.
sp: dē-spoil'eth*, spoil'eth*.
t: toil'eth*.

OIL'I

Vowel: oil'y.
d: doil'y.
k(c͜): c͜oy'ly.
r: roil'y.
Plus toil, he, etc.
Plus boy, Lee *or* lea, etc.

OIL'ING

b: boil'ing.
br: broil'ing, em-broil'ing,
 pan broil'ing.
f: foil'ing.
k(c͜): c͜oil'ing, rē-c͜oil'ing,
 un-c͜oil'ing.

m: moil'ing.
r: roil'ing.
s: as-soil'ing, soil'ing.
sp: dē-spoil'ing, spoil'ing.
t: toil'ing.

OIL'MENT

br: em-broil'ment.
k(c͜): rē-c͜oil'ment.
sp: dē-spoil'ment.
Plus toil meant, etc.

OIL'ŪR

Vowel: oil'ẽr.
b: boil'ẽr.
br: broil'ẽr, em-broil'ẽr.
f: foil'lẽr.
k(c͜): c͜oil'ẽr, rē-c͜oil'ẽr,
 un-c͜oil'ẽr.
r: roil'ẽr.
s: soil'ẽr.
sp: dē-spoil'ẽr, spoil'ẽr.
t: toil'ẽr.
Plus roil her *or* err, etc.

OI'MĂN

h: hoy'măn.
k(c͜): dē-c͜oy'măn.
t: toy'măn.
Plus joy, man, etc.

OI'MENT

j: en-joy'ment.
pl: dē-ploy'ment, em-ploy'ment.
Plus coy meant, etc.

OIN'DŪR

j: rē-join'dẽr.
Plus coined her *or* err, etc.

OI'NES

k(c͜): c͜oy'ness.

(Choose only one word out of each group)

Ō'ING

Vowel: Ōh'ing, ōw'ing.
b: beau'ing (bō'), bōw'ing,
ō'bōe-ing.
bl: blōw'ing, bū'gle=blōw'ing,
gláss=blōw'ing, horn=blōw'ing,
nōşe=blōw'ing,
trum'pet blōw'ing.
fl: flōw'ing, in'flōw-ing,
out'flōw-ing, ō"vĕr-flōw'ing,
un-flōw'ing.
g: ēaş"y-gō'ing, fōre-gō'ing,
gō'ing, out'gō-ing, sēa'gō-ing,
thŏr'ough-gō"ing (thĕr'ō-),
un"dĕr-gō'ing.
gl: glōw'ing.
gr: grōw'ing, out-grōw'ing,
ō"vĕr-grōw'ing, up-grōw'ing.
h: hōe'ing.
kr: cock c̦rōw'ing, c̦rōw'ing,
ō"vĕr-c̦rōw'ing.
l: hel-lō'ing, lōw'ing.
m: mōw'ing.
n: fōre-knōw'ing (-nō'),
knōw'ing, self'=knōw'ing,
un-knōw'ing.
r: rōw'ing.
s: sew'ing (sō'), sōw'ing.
sh: fōre-shōw'ing, shōw'ing.
sl: slōw'ing.
sn: snōw'ing.
st: bē-stōw'ing, stōw'ing.
str: strōw'ing*.
t: tip'tōe-ing, tōe'ing, tōw'ing,
un"dĕr-tōw'ing.
thr: ō"vĕr-thrōw'ing, thrōw'ing.

Q'ING

Vowel: aw'ing, ō"vĕr-aw'ing.
ch: chaw'ing.

dr: draw'ing, ō"vĕr-draw'ing,
wīre draw'ing, with-draw'ing.
f: guf-faw'ing.
h: hee=haw'ing.
j: jaw'ing.
k(c̦): c̦aw'ing.
kl: c̦law'ing.
l: law'ing, out-law'ing.
g: bē-gnaw'ing (-naw'),
gnaw'ing (naw').
p: paw'ing.
s: saw'ing, see'saw-ing.
sh: pshaw'ing (shaw').
str: straw'ing.
t: taw'ing.
th: thaw'ing.
y: yaw'ing.

OIN'IJ

k(c̦): c̦oin'ăġe.
Cf. loin age, etc.

OIN'ING

gr: groin'ing.
j: ad-join'ing, c̦on-join'ing,
dis-join'ing, en-join'ing,
join'ing, rē-join'ing,
sub-join'ing.
k(c̦): c̦oin'ing.
l: pūr-loin'ing.

OIN'TED

j: c̦on-join'ted, dis-join'ted,
join'ted, un-join'ted.
n: à-noin'ted, un"à-noin'ted.
p: ap-poin'ted, dis"ap-poin'ted,
poin'ted, un-poin'ted.
Plus coin, Ted, etc.

OIN'TING

j: dis-join'ting, join'ting.
n: à-noin'ting.

OINT′LES
OIS′TŬR

fāte, fär, fåst, f̧ll, finăl, cãre, at; mēte, prĕy, hẽr, met; pīne,
marïne, bïrd, pin; nōte, mŏve, fo̧r, atŏm, not; mo̧o̧n, book;

632

(Choose only one word out of each group)

p: ap-poin′ting, dis″ap-poin′ting,
poin′ting.

OINT′LES

j: joint′less.
p: point′less.
Plus anoint Les *or* less, etc.

OINT′MENT

Vowel: oint′ment.
j: dis-joint′ment.
n: à-noint′ment.
p: ap-point′ment,
dis″ap-point′ment.
Plus counterpoint meant, etc.

OIN′TŬR

j: dis-join′tẽr, join′tẽr.
n: à-noin′tẽr.
p: ap-poin′tẽr, dis″ap-poin′tẽr,
poin′tẽr.
Plus disjoint her *or* err, etc.

OIN′ŪR

j: co̧n-join′ẽr, en-join′ẽr,
join′ẽr.
k(ç): çoin′ẽr.
l: pūr-loin′ẽr.
Plus purloin her *or* err, etc.

OI′RĪD

j: joy′rĭde.
Plus boy ride, etc.

Ō′IS

l: Lō′is.

Ō′ISH

sh: nīght⸗shōw′ish (nīt⸗),
shōw′ish.
sn: snōw′ish.
Cf. so wish, etc.

OIS′ING

j: rē-joic′ing, un″rē-joic′ing.
v: voic′ing.
Plus boy sing, etc.

OIS′LES

ch: choice′less.
v: voice′less.
Plus rejoice less, etc.

OI′SŎM

n: noi′sŏme.
t: toy′sŏme.
Plus cloy some *or* sum, etc.

OIS′TI

f: fois′ty.
m: mois′ty.
Plus choice tea, etc.
Plus rejoiced, he, etc.

OI′STIK

j: joy′stick.
Plus boy stick, etc.
Plus voice tick, etc.

OIS′TING

f: fois′ting.
h: hois′ting.
j: jois′ting.
Plus boy sting, etc.

OIS′TRĂL

k(ç): çoy′strel.
kl: çlois′trăl.

OIS′TŬR

Vowel: oy′stẽr, pēarl oy′stẽr.
d: Rålph Rois′tẽr Dois′tẽr.
f: fois′tẽr.
h: hois′tẽr.
kl: çlois′tẽr, en-çlois′tẽr,
un-çlois′tẽr.

(Choose only one word out of each group)

m: mois′tẽr.
r: roy′stẽr.
Plus joy stir, etc.
Plus rejoiced her *or* err, etc.

OIT′ED
d: doit′ed.
kw: quoit′ed.
pl: ex-ploit′ed, un″ex-ploit′ed.
Plus boy Ted, etc.
Plus adroit, Ed, etc.

OIT′I
k(ç): då-çoit′y.
t: hoit′y⸗toit′y.
Plus enjoy tea, etc.
Plus quoit, he, etc.

OIT′RING
l: loit′ering.
n: rē-çŏn-noit′ring.
Plus quoit ring, etc.

OIT′ŪR
pl: ex-ploit′ūre.
v: voit′ūre.
Plus quoit, you′re *or* your, etc.

OIT′ŨR
dr: å-droit′ẽr.
g: goit′ẽr.
l: loit′ẽr.
n: rē″çŏn-noit′ẽr.
pl: ex-ploit′ẽr.
Plus quoit her *or* err, etc.

OI′ŨR
b: Boy′år, Boy′ẽr.
j: en-joy′ẽr.
k(ç): çoy′ẽr, dē-çoy′ẽr.
n: an-noy′ẽr.

pl: dē-ploy′ẽr, em-ploy′ẽr.
str: dē-stroy′ẽr,
　self′⸗dē-stroy′ẽr.
t: toy′ẽr.
Plus enjoy her *or* err, etc.

OI′US
j: joy′ous.
Plus destroy us, etc.

OIZ′EZ
b: boy′ṣeṣ.
n: noiṣ′eṣ.
p: poiṣ′eṣ.
Cf. noise is, etc.

OIZ′I
n: noiṣ′y.
Plus joys, he, etc.

OIZ′ING
n: noiṣ′ing.
p: poiṣ′ing.

OI′ZŎN
f: foi′ṣŏn*.
p: em-poi′ṣŏn*, poi′ṣŏn.
t: toi′ṣŏn*.
Plus annoys an *or* on, etc.

OIZ′ŎNZ
f: foi′ṣŏnṣ.
p: poi′ṣŏnṣ.

Ō′JĂN
tr: Trō′jăn.
Plus show Jan, etc.

OJ′EZ
d: dodġ′eṣ (doj′ez).
h: Hodġ′eṣ.
l: dis-lodġ′eṣ, hōr-ō-loġ′eṣ,
　lodġ′eṣ.
p: hodġe⸗podġ′eṣ.
Cf. Dodge is, etc.

Ō′JĒ
ŌK′Ȧ

fāte, fär, fȧst, fạll, finăl, cāre, at; mēte, prẹy, hĕr, met; pīne,
marīne, bĭrd, pin; nōte, mȯve, fọr, atŏm, not; mọọn, book; **634**

(Choose only one word out of each group)

Ō′JĒ

g: an″ȧ-gō′ġē, ap″ȧ-gō′ġē,
e″pȧ-gō′ġē, par″ȧ-gō′ġē.
Plus doge, he, etc.
Plus O, Gee, etc.

Ō′ĠENT

k(c): cō′ġent.
Plus slow gent, etc.

OJ′I

g: ped′ȧ-goġ-y.
p: podġ′y.
st: stodġ′y.
Plus lodge, he, etc.

OJ′IK

g: an″ȧ-goġ′ic, dem″ȧ-goġ′ic,
ep″ȧ-goġ′ic, ī″sȧ-goġ′ic,
mys″tȧ-goġ′ic, par″ȧ-goġ′ic,
ped″ȧ-goġ′ic.
l: āer″ō-loġ′ic,
an″thrō-pō-loġ′ic,
är-chaē-ō-loġ′ic, as″trō-loġ′ic,
bī″ō-loġ′ic, chron″ō-loġ′ic,
cūr″i-ō-loġ′ic, dē″mŏn-ō-loġ′ic,
dī″ȧ-loġ′ic, en″tō-mō-loġ′ic,
ep″i-loġ′ic, eth″nō-loġ′ic,
eth″ō-loġ′ic, et″y-mō-loġ′ic,
eū-loġ′ic, ġē″ō-loġ′ic,
gnom-ō-loġ′ic (nom-),
hī″ēr-ō-loġ′ic, his″tō-loġ′ic,
họr″ō-loġ′ic, ich″thy-ō-loġ′ic,
ī′dē-a-loġ-ic, lith″ō-loġ′ic, loġ′ic,
mär″tyr-ō-loġ′ic,
mēt″ē-ọr-ō-loġ′ic,
min″ēr-ȧ-loġ′ic,
mọr″phō-loġ′ic (″fō-),
mȳ-cō-loġ′ic, mȳ-ō-loġ′ic,
myth″ō-loġ′ic, ne″crō-loġ′ic,
nē″ō-loġ′ic, on″tō-loġ′ic,

ō″phi-ō-loġ′ic, path″ō-loġ′ic,
phil″ō-loġ′ic, phōn″ō-loġ′ic,
phō″tō-loġ′ic, phrās″ē-ō-loġ′ic,
phys′i-ō-loġ′ic,
psȳch″ō-loġ′ic (sīk′),
sär″cō-loġ′ic, sō″ci-ō-loġ′ic,
tạu″tō-loġ′ic, thē″ō-loġ′ic,
trop″ō-loġ′ic, zȳ″mō-loġ′ic.

OJ′IKS

g: ped″ȧ-goġ′ics.
Plus oj′ik+s.

OJ′ING

d: dodġ′ing.
l: dis-lodġ′ing, lodġ′ing.

OJ′ŪR

d: ′corn dodġ′ēr, dodġ′ēr.
k(c): codġ′ēr.
l: dis-lodġ′ēr, lodġ′ēr.
r: roġ′ēr.
Plus lodge her *or* err, etc.

Ō′JŪRN

s: sō′joŭrn.
Plus doge earn, urn *or* erne, etc.

Ō′KĀ

Vowel: O.K., ō′kāy.
kr: crō-quet′ (-kā′).
r: rō-quet′ (-kā′).
t: Tō′kāy.
Plus slow, Kay *or* K, etc.

ŌK′Ȧ

Vowel: tap″i-ō′cȧ.
b: Bōc′ȧ.
k(c): cō′cȧ.
m: mō′chȧ.
p: pōlk′ȧ (pōk′)
Plus joke a, etc.

(Choose only one word out of each group)

ŌK'ĂL

b: bō'çăl.
f: bī-fōç'ăl, fōç'ăl, phōç'ăl.
l: lōç'ăl.
s: sō'çle.
v: vōç'ăl.
y: yōk'el.
Plus joke'll, etc.

Ō'KĒ

tr: trō'çhē, trō'çhēe.
Cf. ōk'i.
Plus slow key, etc.
Plus joke, he, etc.

ŌK'EN

Vowel: ōak'en.
b: Hō-bōk'en.
br: brōk'en, heärt'brōk"en, un-brōk'en.
sp: bē-spōk'en, fãir'=spōk"en, fīne'=spōk"en, fōre'=spōk"en, free'=spōk"en, out-spōk'en, soft'=spōk"en, spōk'en, un-spōk'en.
t: bē-tōk'en, fōre-tōk'en, tōk'en.
Cf. spoke an *or* on, etc.
Cf. Shà-mōk'in.

OK'EN

br: Brock'en.
h: Çon-shō-hock'en.
Cf. shock hen, etc.

ŌK'EST

ch: chōk'est*.
j: jōk'est*.
kl: çlōak'est*.
kr: çrōak'est[1].
s: sōak'est*.
sm: smōk'est*.

sp: spōk'est*.
v: çon-vōk'est*, ē-vōk'est*, in-vōk'est*, prō-vōk'est*, rē-vōk'est*.
y: un-yōk'est*, yōk'est*.

QK'EST

b: balk'est (bawk')*.
st: stalk'est*.
t: talk'est*.
w: walk'est*.

OK'EST

bl: block'est*.
d: dock'est*.
fl: flock'est*.
fr: frock'est*, un-frock'est*.
l: lock'est*, un-lock'est*.
m: bē-mock'est*, mock'est*.
n: knock'est*.
s: sock'est*.
sh: shock'est*.
sm: smock'est*.
st: stock'est*.

OK'ET

br: brock'et.
d: dock'et.
k(ç): çock'et.
kr: crock'et, Çrock'ett.
l: lock'et, Lock'ett.
p: ãir pock'et, hip pock'et, im-pock'et, pick'pock-et, pock'et, vest pock'et, wätch pock'et.
r: rock'et, skȳ'rock-et.
s: sock'et.
spr: sprock'et.
Cf. cock it, etc.

ŌK'ETH
OK'ĪD

fāte, fär, fȧst, fạll, fīnăl, cãre, at; mēte, prey, hẽr, met; pīne,
marĭne, bĭrd, pin; nōte, mōve, fọr, atŏm, not; mọọn, book;

636

(Choose only one word out of each group)

ŌK'ETH

ch: chōk'eth*.
j: jōk'eth*.
kl: clōak'eth*.
kr: crōak'eth*.
s: sōak'eth*.
sm: smōk'eth*.
sp: spōk'eth*.
v: cọn-vōk'eth*, ē-vōk'eth*,
  in-vōk'eth*, prō-vōk'eth*,
  rē-vōk'eth*.
y: un-yōk'eth*, yōk'eth*.

OK'ETH

b: bạlk'eth (bawk')*.
st: stạlk'eth*.
t: tạlk'eth*.
w: wạlk'eth*.

OK'ETH

bl: block'eth*.
d: dock'eth*.
fl: flock'eth*.
fr: frock'eth*, un-frock'eth*.
l: lock'eth*, un-lock'eth*.
m: bē-mock'eth*, mock'eth*.
n: knock'eth*.
s: sock'eth*.
sh: shock'eth*.
sm: smock'eth*.
st: stock'eth*.

OK'HED

bl: block'head.
sh: shock'head.
Plus stock head, etc.

ŌK'I

Vowel: ōak'y.
ch: chōk'y.
d: ō'key⸗dōk'ey.

h: hōk'ey.
j: jōk'ey.
k(c): cōk'ey.
kr: crōak'y.
l: Lō'ki.
m: mōk'y.
p: hō'cy⸗pō'cy, pōk'y,
  slōw'pōk-y.
r: rōk'y.
s: sōak'y.
sm: smōk'y.
y: yōk'y.
Cf. ō'kē.
Plus joke, he, etc.

OK'I

b: bạlk'y (bawk').
ch: chạlk'y.
g: gạwk'y.
p: pạwk'y.
skw: squạwk'y.
st: stạlk'y.
t: tạlk'ie, tạlk'y.
w: Mil-wạu'kēe, wạlk'ie.
Plus saw key, etc.
Plus talk, he, etc.

OK'I

fl: flock'y.
h: fiēld hock'ey, hock'ey,
  īce hock'ey.
j: jock'ey.
k(c): cock'y.
kr: crock'y.
l: lock'y.
r: rock'y.
st: stock'y.
Plus shock, he, etc.

OK'ĪD

k(c): cock'eȳed.
Plus flock, I'd _or_ eyed, etc.

637　　ūse, bu̱ll, brúte, tŭrn, up; crȳ, myth; c̨at, mac̨hine, ace,
　　　church, c̨hord; ġem, añger, (Fr.) boṅ, as̱; THis, thin; azure

ŌK'IJ
OK"L

(Choose only one word out of each group)

ŌK'IJ

br: brōk'ăġe.
kl: c̨lōak'ăġe.
s: sōak'ăġe.
Cf. joke age, etc.
Plus low cage, etc.

OK'IJ

d: dock'ăġe.
l: lock'ăġe.
s: soc̨'c̨ăġe.
Cf. shock age, etc.

Ō'KIN

m: Shȧ-mō'kin.
Cf. ōk'en.

ŌK'ING

ch: chōk'ing.
j: jōk'ing.
kl: c̨lōak'ing, un-c̨lōak'ing.
kr: c̨rōak'ing.
p: pōk'ing.
s: sōak'ing.
sm: bē-smōk'ing, smōk'ing.
st: stōk'ing.
str: strōk'ing.
tr: trōc̨h'ing.
v: c̨on-vōk'ing, ē-vōk'ing,
　in-vōk'ing, prō-vōk'ing,
　rē-vōk'ing.
y: un-yōk'ing, yōk'ing.
Plus no king, etc.

O̱K'ING

b: ba̱lk'ing (bawk').
h: hawk'ing, jāy'hawk-ing.
k: c̨alk'ing.
skw: squa̱wk'ing.
st: sta̱lk'ing.
t: ta̱lk'ing.

w: jāy'wa̱lk"ing, wa̱lk'ing.
Plus saw king, etc.

OK'ING

bl: block'ing.
d: dock'ing.
fl: flock'ing.
fr: frock'ing, un-frock'ing.
h: hock'ing.
k(c̨): c̨ock'ing.
kl: c̨lock'ing.
kr: c̨rock'ing.
l: in"tēr-lock'ing, lock'ing,
　un-lock'ing.
m: bē-mock'ing, mock'ing.
n: knock'ing.
p: pock'ing.
r: rock'ing.
s: sock'ing.
sh: shock'ing.
sm: smock'ing.
st: stock'ing.

O̱K'INZ

d: Daw'kins̱.
h: Haw'kins̱.
w: wa̱lk'=ins̱ (wawk').
Plus talk inns or ins, etc.

O̱K'ISH

h: hawk'ish.
m: mawk'ish.

OK'ISH

bl: block'ish.
k(c̨): c̨ock'ish.
m: mock'ish.
st: stock'ish.

OK"L

h: hock'le.
k(c̨): c̨ock'le.

ŌK′LES
OK′SHUS

fāte, fär, fȧst, fạll, finăl, cãre, at; mēte, prey, hẽr, met; pīne,
marïne, bïrd, pin; nōte, mŏve, fọr, atŏm, not; mọọn, book;

638

(Choose only one word out of each group)

s: soç′le.
str: strock′lə.
Plus flock ’ll, etc.

ŌK′LES

j: jōke′less.
kl: çlōak′less.
sm: smōke′less.
y: yōke′less, yōlk′less (yōk′).
Plus choke less *or* Les, etc.

OK′LING

fl: flock′ling.
k(ç): çock′ling.
r: rock′ling.

ŌK′LŌR

f: fōlk′lōre (fōk′).
Plus joke lore, etc.

OK′MĂN

br: Brock′măn.
l: Lock′măn.
s: soç′măn.
Plus shock man, etc.

ŌK′MENT

v: in-vōke′ment, prō-vōke′ment,
rē-vōke′ment.
Plus joke meant, etc.

OK′NI

k(ç): çock′ney.
Plus knock knee, etc.

OK′NID

k(ç): çock′neyed.
Cf. knock kneed, etc.

Ō′KŌ

f: lō′çō=fō′çō.
k(ç): çō′çō, çō′çōa, kō′kō,
rō-çō′çō.

l: lō′çō.
n: Ō″ri-nō′çō.
r: bȧ-rō′çō.
tr: trō′çō.
Plus joke owe *or* O, etc.

OK′Ō

j: Jock′ō.
r: Mō-roç′çō, si-roç′çō.
Plus shock owe *or* O, etc.

OK′PŌRT

br: Brock′pōrt.
l: Lock′pōrt.
st: Stock′pōrt.
Plus hock port, etc.

ŌK′RȦ

Vowel: ōk′rȧ.
Plus joke Ra, etc.

OK′SEN, OK′S′N

Vowel: ox′en.
k(ç): çock′swain (kok′s′n).
Cf. ok′sin.

OK′SHĂL

n: ē″qui-noç′tiăl, trī-noç′tiăl.
Plus flock shall, etc.

OK′SHUN

Vowel: ạuç′tion.
Plus squawk shun, etc.

OK′SHUN

k(ç): çon-çoç′tion, dē-çoç′tion.
Plus flock shun, ętc.

OK′SHUS

n: in-nox′ious, nox′ious,
ob-nox′ious.

(Choose only one word out of each group)

OK'SI

d: çaç'ō-dox-y, dox'y, het'ēr-ō-dox″y, or'thō-dox-y, par'à-dox-y.
f: fox'y.
k(ç): Çox'ey.
l: Bi-lox'i.
pr: prox'y.
Plus shock see, etc.
Plus shocks, he, etc.

OK'SĪD

Vowel: ox'=ēyed', ox'īde.
f: fox'=ēyed″.
r: pēr-ox'īde.
Plus locks, I'd or eye'd, etc.
Plus lock, sighed or side, etc.

OK'SIK

t: an″ti-tox'iç, tox'iç.
Plus stock sick, etc.

OK'SIKS

k(ç): çoç'cyx.
t: an″ti-tox'içs, tox'içs.
Plus flock sicks or six, etc.

OK'SIN

t: an″ti-tox'in, toç'sin, tox'in.
Cf. ok'sen.
Plus flocks in or inn, etc.
Plus flock sin, etc.

ŌK'SING

h: hōax'ing.
k(ç): çōax'ing.
Plus folk sing, etc.

OK'SING

b: box'ing.
f: fox'ing.
Plus flock sing, etc.

ŌKS'MĂN

sp: spōkes'măn.
str: strōkes'măn.
Plus folks, man.

ŌK'SMITH

j: jōke'smith.
Plus poke smith, etc.
Plus folks myth, etc.

ŌK'SŨR

h: hōax'ēr.
k(ç): çōax'ēr.
Plus cloak, sir.
Plus cloaks her or err, etc.

OK'SŨR

Vowel: ox'ēr.
b: box'ēr.
f: fox'ēr.
Plus flock, sir.
Plus shocks her or err, etc.

OK'TIL

Vowel: trī-oç'tile.
k(ç): çoç'tile.
Plus shock till, etc.
Plus shocked, ill, etc.

OK'TIV

k(ç): çon-çoç'tive, dē-çoç'tive.

OK'TŎN

bl: Bloç'tŏn.
br: Brock'tŏn.
st: Stock'tŏn.
Plus shock ton or tun, etc.
Plus shocked 'un, etc.

OK'TRIN

d: doç'trine.

(Choose only one word out of each group)

OK'TŬR

d: dŏç'tŏr.
k(ç): çon-çoç'tẽr, dē-çoç'tẽr.
pr: proç'tŏr.
Plus shocked her *or* err, etc.

OK'TŬRN

n: noç'tŭrne.
Plus shocked urn, earn *or* erne, etc.
Plus flock turn, etc.

Ō'KUM

Vowel: ōak'um.
h: hōk'um.
Plus soak 'em, etc.
Plus so come, etc.

Ō'KUND

j: jō'çund.

ŌK'ŬR

Vowel: mē"di-ōç're, ō'çhẽr.
br: brōk'ẽr, stock'brōk"ẽr.
ch: chōk'ẽr.
j: jōk'ẽr.
kl: çlōak'ẽr, un-çlōak'ẽr.
kr: çrōak'ẽr.
p: pōk'ẽr.
s: sōak'ẽr.
sm: smōk'ẽr.
st: stōk'ẽr.
str: strōk'ẽr.
v: çon-vōk'ẽr, ē-vōk'ẽr,
  in-vōk'ẽr, prō-vōk'ẽr,
  rē-vōk'ẽr.
y: yōk'ẽr.
Plus choke her *or* err, etc.

ǪK'ŬR

b: bȧlk'ẽr (bawk').
ch: chȧlk'ẽr.
g: gawk'ẽr.

OK'TŬR (cont.)

h: hawk'ẽr, jāy'hawk-ẽr,
  tom'ȧ-hawk-ẽr.
k(ç): çȧlk'ẽr.
m: mawk'ẽr.
skw: squawk'ẽr.
st: deel stȧlk'ẽr, stȧlk'ẽr.
t: tȧlk'ẽr.
w: jāy'wȧlk-ẽr, shop'wȧlk-ẽr,
  sleep'wȧlk-ẽr, street'wȧlk-ẽr,
  wȧlk'ẽr.
Plus stalk her *or* err, etc.

OK'ŬR

b: Knick'ẽr-bock-ẽr (nik').
bl: block'ẽr.
d: dock'ẽr.
f: Fok'kẽr.
fl: flock'ẽr.
h: hock'ẽr, hough'ẽr (hok').
k(ç): çock'ẽr.
kl: çlock'ẽr.
l: lock'ẽr.
m: mock'ẽr.
n: knock'ẽr.
r: pat'ent rock'ẽr, rock'ẽr.
s: soç'çẽr, sock'ẽr.
sh: shock'ẽr, shil'ling shock'ẽr.
sm: smock'ẽr.
st: stock'ẽr.
Plus unlock her *or* err, etc.

OK'ŬRZ

b: knick'ẽr-bock-ẽrṣ.
Plus ok'ŭr+s.

ŌK'US

f: fōç'us.
h: hōç'us, Hō-hōk'us.
kr: au'tumn çrō'çus, çrō'çus.
l: lōç'us.
p: hōç'us=pōç'us.

(Choose only one word out of each group)

Plus stroke us, etc.
Plus slow cuss, etc.

QK'US

d: Dauç'us.
gl: glauç'ous.
k(ç): çauç'us.
r: rauç'ous.
Cf. Bauç'is.
Plus outtalk us, etc.
Plus straw cuss, etc.

Ō'KUST

f: fō'çussed, un-fō'çussed.
l: hŏn'ey lō'çust, lō'çust,
sweet lō'çust.
Plus ok'us+ed.

QK'WĂRD

Vowel: awk'wărd.
Plus talk, ward, etc.

Ō'LÅ

Vowel: Lē-ō'là, Ō'là,
sçag-li-ō'là, vī-ō'là.
b: çär-am-bō'là.
d: gon-dō'là.
g: An-gō'là, gō'là.
k(ç): Ap″pà-lach″i-çō'là, çō'là,
Çō'çà-Çō'là, kō'là,
Pen″sà-çō'là.
l: Lō'là.
m: Rà-mō'là, Rō-mō'là.
n: Nō'là, Sem″i-nō'là.
r: py-rō-là, Sà-von″à-rō'là.
sk(sç): sçhō'là.
st: stō'là.
z: Gor″gon-zō'là, Mà-zō'là,
Zō'là.
Plus stole a, etc.

QL'Å

f: Eū-faul'à.
m: Guät″à-mal'à.
p: Paul'à.
Plus tall a, etc.

OL'Å

h: hol'là.
m: mol'là.
r: çō-rol'là.
Plus parasol a, etc.

ŌL'AK

p: Pōl'ack.
Plus show lack, etc.

Ō'LĂN

d: Dō'lăn.
n: Nō'lăn.
Plus droll an *or* on, etc.

Ō'LĂND

b: Bō'lănd, Bōw'lănd.
l: lōw'lănd.
n: Nō'lănd.
r: Rō'lănd, Rōw'lănd.
Plus stole, and, etc.
Plus glow, land, etc.

OL'ĂR

d: dol'lăr.
k(ç): çol'lăr.
sk(sç): sçhol'ăr.
Plus ol'ŭr.

OL'ĂRD

b: bol'lărd.
d: dol'lăred.
k(ç): çol'lărd, çol'lăred.
l: Lol'lărd.
p: pol'lărd.
sk(sç): sçol'lărd.
Plus collar'd, etc.

OL'ĀS
ŌL'DI

fāte, fär, fȧst, fạll, finăl, cãre, at; mēte, prey, hẽr, met; pïne,
marïne, bïrd, pin; nōte, mŏve, fọr, atŏm, nọt; mọọn, book;

642

(Choose only one word out of each group)

OL'ĀS

s: sol'āce.
Plus gun moll ace, etc.
Cf. doll lace, etc.

ỌL'CHUN

f: fạl'chiŏn.
Plus Balch 'un, etc.

ỌL'DẢ

Vowel: Ạl'dȧ.
Plus called a, etc.

ŌL'DED

f: blīnd'-fōl″ded, en-fōl'ded,
 in-fōl'ded, man'i-fōl″ded,
 rē-fōl'ded, un-fōl'ded.
m: mōl'ded.
sk(sç): sçōl'ded.
Plus foal dead, etc.
Cf. soul did, etc.
Plus cold, Ed, etc.

ŌL'DEN

Vowel: ōl'den.
b: em-bōl'den.
g: gōl'den.
h: bē-hōl'den, hōl'den,
 mis″bē-hōl'den, with-hōl'den.
Plus coal den, etc.

ỌL'DEN

Vowel: Ạl'den.
Plus call den, etc.

ŌL'DEST

Vowel: ōl'dest.
b: bōl'dest.
f: en-fōl'dest*, fōl'dest*,
 in-fōl'dest*, in″tẽr-fōl'dest*,
 rē-fōl'dest*, un-fōl'dest*.

h: bē-hōl'dest*, hōl'dest*,
 up-hōl'dest*, with-hōl'dest*.
k(ç): çōl'dest.
m: mōl'dest*.
sk(sç): sçōl'dest*.
t: tōl'dest*.

ỌL'DEST

b: bạl'dest.
sk(sç): sçạl'dest*.

ŌL'DETH

f: en-fōl'deth*, fōl'deth*,
 in-fōl'deth*, in″tẽr-fōl'deth*,
 rē-fōl'deth*, un-fōl'deth*.
h: bē-hōl'deth*, hōl'deth*,
 up-hōl'deth*, with-hōl'deth*.
m: mōl'deth*.
sk(sç): sçōl'deth*.
Plus soul death, etc.

ỌL'DETH

sk(sç): sçạl'deth*.
Plus call death, etc.

ŌLD'HĂM

Vowel: Ōld'hăm.
Plus scold 'em, etc.
Cf. whole, dumb, etc.

ŌLD'FȦST

h: hōld fȧst.
Plus sold fast, etc.

ŌL'DI

f: fōl'dy.
m: mōl'dy.
Plus bold, he, etc.
Plus shoal Dee, etc.

(Choose only one word out of each group)

ŌL′DING

f: en-fōl′ding, fōl′ding, in-fōl′ding, in″tēr-fōl′ding, rē-fōl′ding, un-fōl′ding.

h: bē-hōl′ding, hōl′ding, slāve hōl′ding, up-hōl′ding, with-hōl′ding.

m: mōl′ding, mōul′ding, weaTH′ēr mōld′ing (weTH′).

sk(sç): sçōl′ding.

ǪL′DING

b: Ba̧l′ding.
p: Pa̧ul′ding.
sk(sç): sça̧l′ding.
sp: Spa̧ul′ding.

ŌL′DISH

Vowel: ōl′dish.
k(ç): çōl′dish.
Plus whole dish, etc.

ŌLD′LY

b: bōld′ly.
f: man′i-fōld″ly.
k(ç): çōld′ly.
Plus controlled lea *or* Lee, etc.

ŌLD′MĂN

Vowel: Ōld′măn.
g: Gōld′măn.
Plus told man, etc.

ŌLD′MENT

f: en-fōld′ment.
h: with-hōld′ment.
Plus cold meant, etc.

ŌLD′NES

Vowel: ōld′ness.
b: bōld′ness.
k(ç): çōld′ness.

ǪL′DRŎN

k(ç): ça̧l′drŏn.
p: pa̧ul′drŏn.
Cf. called run, etc.

ŌL′DRUMZ

d: dōl′drums.
Plus parasol drums, etc.

ŌLD′SMITH

g: gōld′smith.
Plus bold smith, etc.

ŌL′DŬR

Vowel: ōl′dēr.
b: bōl′dēr, bōul′dēr.
f: bill fōl′dēr, en-fōl′dēr, fōl′dēr, in-fōl′dēr, in″tēr-fōl′dēr, rē-fōl′dēr, un-fōl′dēr.
h: bē-hōl′dēr, bond hōl′dēr, bot′tle hōl′dēr, free′hōl-dēr, hand hōl′dēr, hōl′dēr, house′hōl-dēr, land′hōl-dēr, lēase′hōl-dēr, shāre′hōl-dēr, slāve′hōl-dēr, stock′hōl-dēr, up-hōl′dēr, with-hōl′dēr.
k(ç): çōl′dēr.
m: mōl′dēr, pat′tērn mōl′dēr.
p: pōl′dēr.
sh: shōul′dēr.
sk(sç): sçōl′dēr.
sm: smōl′dēr.
Plus told her *or* err, etc.

ǪL′DŬR

Vowel: a̧l′dēr.
b: ba̧l′dēr, Ba̧l′dŭr.
sk(sç): sça̧l′dēr.
Plus called her *or* err, etc.

ŌL'DŪRD
ǪL'EST

fāte, fär, fȧst, fąll, finăl, cãre, at; mēte, prey, hẽr, met; pīne, marïne, bĭrd, pin; nōte, mŏve, fŏr, atŏm, not; mọọn, book;

644

(Choose only one word out of each group)

ŌL'DŪRD

b: bōul'dēred.
m: mōl'dēred.
sh: broạd shōul'dēred, shōul'dēred.
sm: smōl'dēred.
Plus boulder'd, etc.

ǪLD'WIN

b: Bạld'win.
Plus called, win *or* Wynn, etc.

OL'ĒG

k(c̲): c̲ol'lēague.
Plus doll, league, etc.

OL'EJ

k(c̲): c̲ol'lege.
n: ack-now'ledġe, fōre-know'ledġe, know'ledġe, self'⁼know'ledġe.
Plus doll edge, etc.

OL'EJD

n: ack-now'ledġed, un"ack-now'ledġed.
Plus doll edged, etc.

OL'EM, OL'UM

k(c̲): c̲ol'umn.
s: sol'emn.
Plus alcohol 'em, etc.

ŌL'EN

st: stōl'en.
sw: swōl'len.
Cf. ōl'ŏn.

ǪL'EN

f: chop'⁼fạl'len, fạl'len, wind'fạl"len.
Cf. call an *or* on, etc.

OL'EN

p: pol'len.
st: stol'len, stol'ŏn.
Cf. doll an, etc.

ŌL'ENT

s: Sōl'ent.
v: non vō'lent.
Plus no Lent, etc.

OL'ENT

p: ē"qui-pol'lent, prē-pol'lent.

ŌL'ẼR

Cf. ōl'ũr.

Ǫ'LES

fl: flaw'less.
j: jaw'less.
kl: c̲law'less.
l: law'less.
m: maw'less.
s: saw'less.
Plus gnaw less *or* Les, etc.

ŌL'EST

b: bōwl'est*.
d: c̲on-dōl'est,* dōl'est*.
dr: drōll'est.
j: c̲à-jōl'est*.
p: pōl'lest*.
r: en-rōl'lest*, Hō'ly Rōl'lest*, rōl'lest*, un-rōl'lest*, up-rōl'lest*.
s: c̲on-sōl'est*.
str: strōl'lest*.
t: tōl'lest*.
tr: c̲on-trōl'lest*, pà-trōl'lest*, trōl'lest*.
Plus grow, lest, etc.

ǪL'EST

b: bawl'est*.
br: brawl'est*.
dr: drawl'est*.

645 ūse, bu̱ll, brúte, tũrn, up; crȳ, myth; c̱at, ma̱chine, ace, church, c̱hord; ġem, añger, (Fr.) boṅ, a̱ş; THis, thin; aẕure

**OL'ET
Ō'LI**

(Choose only one word out of each group)

f: fa̱l'lest*.
h: ha̱ul'est*.
k(c̱): c̱al'lest*, ō"vĕr-c̱al'lest*, rē-c̱al'lest*.
kr: c̱rawl'est*.
m: bē-ma̱ul'est*, ma̱ul'est*.
p: ap-pa̱l'lest*.
skr(sc̱r): sc̱rawl'est*.
skw: squa̱l'lest*.
sm: sma̱l'lest.
spr: sprawl'est*.
st: fōre-sta̱l'lest*, sta̱l'lest*.
t: ta̱l'lest.
thr: en-thra̱l'lest*.
tr: trawl'est*.
Cf. call, lest, etc.

OL'ET

f: Là Fol'lette.
k(c̱): c̱ol'let.
w: wäl'let.
Plus doll, et, etc.
Cf. alcohol it, etc.

ŌL'ETH

b: bōwl'eth*.
d: c̱on-dōl'eth*, dōl'eth*.
j: c̱à-jōl'eth*.
p: pōl'leth*.
r: en-rōl'leth*, Hō'ly Rōl'leth*, rōl'leth*, un-rōl'leth*.
s: c̱on-sōl'eth*.
str: strōl'leth*.
t: tōl'leth*.
tr: c̱on-trōl'leth*, pà-trōl'leth*, trōl'leth*.

O̱L'ETH

b: bawl'eth*.
br: brawl'eth*.
dr: drawl'eth*.
f: fa̱l'leth*.

h: ha̱ul'eth*.
k(c̱): c̱al'leth*, ō"vĕr-c̱al'leth*, rē-c̱al'leth*.
kr: c̱rawl'eth*.
m: bē-ma̱ul'eth*, ma̱ul'eth*.
p: ap-pa̱l'leth*.
skr(sc̱r): sc̱rawl'eth*.
skw: squa̱l'leth*.
spr: sprawl'eth*.
st: fōre-sta̱l'leth*, sta̱l'leth*.
thr: en-thra̱l'leth*.
tr: trawl'eth*.

OL'FIN

d: dol'phin.
Plus alcohol fin, etc.
Plus golf in or inn, etc.

OL'FING

g: gol'fing.

ŌL'FU̱L

b: bōwl'fu̱l.
d: dōle'fu̱l.
s: sōul'fu̱l.
Plus hole full, etc.

OL'FŨR

g: gol'fẽr.
Cf. alcohol fur, fir *or* for, etc.

OL'FUS

d: Å-dol'phus, Doll'fuss, Rō-dol'phus, Rù-dol'phus.
Cf. golf us, etc.

ŌL'HOUS

p: pōll'house.
t: tōll'house.
Plus soul house, etc.

Ō'LI, ŌL'I

Vowel: Ōl'ē.
b: Strom-bō'li.

OL'I
OL'IK

fāte, fär, fȧst, fạll, finăl, cãre, at; mēte, prey, hẽr, met; pīne,
marĭne, bĭrd, pĭn; nōte, mŏve, fọr, atŏm, not; mọọn, book;

646

(Chosoe only one word out of each group)

f: Fō'ley.
h: hōl'ey, hō'ly, un-hō'ly, whōl'ly (hōl').
k(c̣): c̣ōal'y.
kr: C̣rō'ley, Crōw'ley.
l: lōw'ly.
m: Mō'ley, mō'ly.
p: pō'ly, rō'ly-pō'ly.
sh: shōal'y, shō'ly.
sl: slōw'ly.
str: strōl'ly.
Cf. ōl'li.
Plus so Lee *or* lea, etc.
Plus soul, he, etc.

ỌL'I

hw: whạl'ly.
k(c̣): Mȧ-c̣aul'ay, Mȧ-c̣aul'ey.
skw: squạl'ly.
spr: sprawl'y.
Plus tall, he, etc.
Plus saw Lee *or* lea, etc.

OL'I

Vowel: Ä'li, Ol'lie.
b: Bä'li.
ch: Chol'ly.
d: Dol'lie, dol'ly.
f: fol'ly.
g: gol'ly.
h: Hol'ley, hol'ly.
j: jol'ly.
k(c̣): C̣ol'ley, c̣ol'lie, mel'ăn-c̣hol-y.
l: lob'lol''ly.
m: hot tȧ-mä'lē, Mol'lie, Mol'ly, tȧ-mä'lē.
n: fi-nä'lē.
p: Pol'ly.
r: päs-tō-rä'lē, rol'ley.
t: Tol'ley.

tr: trol'ley.
v: vol'ley.
w: Wäl'ly.
Cf. äl'ē, äl'i.
Plus doll, he, etc.

OL'ID

Vowel: ol'id.
j: jol'lied.
s: sol'id.
skw: squäl'id.
st: stol'id.
v: vol'leyed.
Plus collie'd, etc.

Ō'LĪF

l: lōw'līfe.
Plus no life, etc.

ỌL'IJ

h: hạl'lăge*, haul'ăge.
st: stạl'lăge.
Cf. call age, etc.

ỌL'IK

Vowel: ạul'ic̣, in''tẽr-ạul'ic̣.
dr: hȳ-drạul'ic̣.
g: Gạl'lic̣.
Plus saw lick, etc.

OL'IK

Vowel: Aē-ol'ic̣, vär''i-ol'ic̣, vit''ri-ol'ic̣.
b: c̣är-bol'ic̣, dī''ȧ-bol'ic̣, em-bol'ic̣, hȳ''pẽr-bol'ic̣, met''ȧ-bol'ic̣, par''ȧ-bol'ic̣, sym-bol'ic̣.
fr: frol'ic̣.
h: al''c̣ō-hol'ic̣.
k(c̣): bū-c̣ol'ic̣, c̣ol'ic̣, mel''ăn-c̣hol'ic̣.
p: bib''li-ō-pol'ic̣, ep''i-pol'ic̣.

647 ūse, bṵll, brúte, tũrn, **up;** crȳ, **myth;** c̣at, mac̣hine, ace, church, c̣hord; ġem, aṅger, (Fr.) boṅ, aṣ; THis, thin; aẓure

QL'IN
ŌL'ISH

(Choose only one word out of each group)

r: rol'lick.

t: ap″os-tol'ic̣, dī″as-tol'ic̣,
ep″is-tol'ic̣, sys-tol'ic̣,
vic̣'ăr≠ap″os-tol'ic̣.

tr: pe-trol'ic̣.

QL'IN

p: tär-pḁul'in.
Plus haul in or inn, etc.
Plus saw Lynn, etc.

ŌL'ING

b: bōll'ing, bōwl'ing.

d: c̣on-dōl'ing, dōl'ing.

dr: drōll'ing.

f: fōal'ing.

g: gōal'ing.

h: hōl'ing.

j: c̣à-jōl'ing.

k(c̣): c̣ar″à-c̣ōl'ing, c̣ōal'ing.

p: pōl'ing, pōll'ing.

r: en-rōll'ing, Hō'ly Rōl'ling,
pà-rōll'ing, rōll'ing,
un-rōll'ing, up-rōll'ing.

s: c̣on-sōl'ing, hȧlf sōl'ing (hȧf),
sōl'ing.

sh: shōal'ing.

sk: skōal'ing.

skr(sc̣r): in-sc̣rōll'ing, sc̣rōll'ing.

str: strōll'ing.

t: ex-tōll'ing, tōll'ing.

tr: c̣on-trōl'ing, pà-trōll'ing,
trōll'ing.

QL'ING

b: bḁll'ing, bāse'bḁll-ing,
bawl'ing, bas'ket-bḁll″ing,
black'bḁll-ing, foot'bḁll-ing,
snōw'bḁll-ing.

br: brawl'ing.

dr: drawl'ing.

f: bē-fḁll'ing, fḁll'ing.

g: gḁll'ing.

h: hḁul'ing, ō″vẽr-hḁul'ing.

k(c̣): c̣ḁll'ing, mis-c̣ḁll'ing,
ō″vẽr-c̣ḁll'ing, rē-c̣ḁll'ing,
un″dẽr-c̣ḁll'ing.

kr: c̣rawl'ing.

m: bē-mḁul'ing, mḁul'ing.

p: ap-pḁll'ing, pḁll'ing,
Pawl'ing.

sh: shawl'ing.

skr(sc̣r): sc̣rawl'ing.

skw: squḁll'ing.

spr: sprawl'ing.

st: fōre-stḁll'ing, stḁll'ing,
in-stḁll'ing.

thr: en-thrḁll'ing, thrḁll'ing.

tr: trawl'ing.

w: c̣at'ẽr-wḁul″ing,
un-wḁll'ing, wḁll'ing.

OL'ING

d: bā'by≠doll'ing.

k(c̣): c̣ar″à-c̣oll'ing.

l: loll'ing.

t: ex-toll'ing.

OL'INZ

h: Hol'linṣ.

k(c̣): C̣ol'linṣ, rum C̣ol'linṣ,
Tom C̣ol'linṣ.

r: Rol'linṣ.
Plus ḋoll inns *or* ins, etc.

OL'IS

h: Hol'lis.

k(c̣): C̣ol'lis.

w: C̣orn-wäl'lis, Wäl'lȧce,
Wäl'lis.

ŌL'ISH

dr: drōll'ish.

p: Pōl'ish.

(Choose only one word out of each group)

ǑL'ISH

g: Gạul'ish.
skw: squạll'ish.
sm: smạll'ish.
t: tạll'ish.

OL'ISH

b: ȧ-bol'ish.
m: dē-mol'ish.
p: pol'ish.

OL'ISHT

b: ȧ-bol'ished.
m: dē-mol'ished,
un"dē-mol'ished.
p: pol'ished, un-pol'ished.

OL'IV

Vowel: green ol'ive, ol'ive,
rīpe ol'ive.

ŌL'JŪR

s: sōl'diẽr.

ŌL'KÅ

p: pōl'kȧ.
Plus stole Kaa, etc.

ǑL'KŎN

f: fạl'cŏn, ġẽr-fạl'cŏn,
sōar fạl'cŏn, sōre fạl'cŏn.
Plus talc on *or* an, etc.

ǑL'KNŪR

f: fạl'conẽr ('knūr).

ŌL'LI

dr: drōl'ly.
h: whōl'ly.
s: sōle'ly.
Cf. ō'li, ōl'i.
Plus soul, Lee *or* lea, **etc.**

ŌL'MĂN

h: Hōl'măn.
k(c̨): c̨ōal'măn, C̨ōle'măn,
C̨ōl'măn.

t: tōll'man.
Plus soul, man, etc.

ŌL'MENT

d: c̨on-dōle'ment.
j: c̨ȧ-jōle'ment.
r: en-rōll'ment.
tr: c̨on-trōl'ment.
Plus soul meant, etc.

ǑL'MENT

p: ap-pạll'ment, ē-pạule'ment.
st: in-stạl'ment, in-stạll'ment.
thr: dis"en-thrạll'ment,
en-thrạll'ment.
Plus call meant, etc.

ǑL'MŌST

Vowel: ạl'mōst.
Plus call most, etc.

ŌL'NES

dr: drōll'ness.
h: whōle'ness.
s: sōle'ness.

ǑL'NES

Vowel: ạll'ness.
sm: smạll'ness.
t: tạll'ness.

Ō'LŌ

b: bō'lō.
p: pō'lō, wạt'ẽr pō'lō.
s: sō'lō.
Plus grow low, etc.
Plus goal owe *or* O, etc.

OL'Ō

f: fol'lōw.
h: hol'lō, hol'lōw.
p: A-pol'lō.
sw: swäl'lōw.

(Choose only one word out of each group)

w: wäl′lōw.
Plus doll owe *or* O, etc.

Ō′LOK
m: Mō′loçh.
r: rōw′lock.
Plus throw lock, etc.

ŌL′ŎN
d: eī-dōl′ŏn.
k(ç): çōl′ŏn, sem′i-çōl″ŏn.
s: Sōl′ŏn.
st: stōl′ŏn.
Cf. ōl′ăn, ōl′en.
Plus stroll on *or* an, etc.

OL′OP
d: dol′lop.
k(ç): çol′lop.
l: lol′lop.
sk(sç): e-sçäl′ŏp, sçäl′lŏp.
tr: trol′lŏp.
w: wäl′lŏp.
Cf. doll up, etc.

ŌL′ŎR
d: dōl′ŏr.
Plus mole or, etc.
Plus O, Lor', etc.

ǪLS′HOOD
f: fạlse′hood.
Plus waltz, Hood, etc.

ǪL′SID
p: pạl′sied.
Plus small, Sid, etc.

ǪLS′NES
f: fạlse′ness.

ǪL′SŌ
Vowel: ạl′sō.
Plus small, so, etc.

ŌL′SŎM
d: dōle′sŏme.
h: whōle′sŏme.
Plus troll some *or* sum, etc.

ŌL′SŎN
Vowel: Ōl′sen, Ōl′sŏn.
j: Jōl′sŏn.
t: Tōl′sŏn, Tōul′sŏn.
Plus bowl, son *or* sun, etc.

ŌL′STÄR
p: pōle′stär.
Plus whole star, etc.

ǪL′STŌN
g: gạll′stōne.
Plus small stone, etc.

ǪL′STŎN
Vowel: Ạl′stŏn.
b: Bạl′stŏn.
r: Rạl′stŏn.
Plus hall stun, etc.

ŌL′STŨR
b: bōl′stẽr.
h: hōl′stẽr, up-hōl′stẽr.
Plus soul stir, etc.

ŌL′TED
b: bōl′ted, un-bōl′ted.
j: jōl′ted, un-jōl′ted.
m: mōl′ted, un-mōl′ted.
v: rē-vōl′ted.
Plus colt, Ed, etc.
Plus soul, Ted, etc.

ǪL′TED
f: dē-fạul′ted, fạul′ted, foot fạul′ted.
h: hạl′ted.

ŌL'TEN
ŌL'TISH

fāte, fär, fȧst, fạll, finȧl, cãre, at; mēte, prey, hẽr, met; pīne, marïne, bĭrd, pin; nōte, mŏve, fọr, atŏm, not; mọọn, book;

650

(Choose only one word out of each group)

m: mạl'ted.
s: as-sạul'ted, sạl'ted.
v: vạul'ted.
z: ex-ạl'ted.
Plus small, Ted, etc.
Plus malt, Ed, etc.

ŌL'TEN

m: mōl'ten.
Plus goal ten, etc.

ŌL'TEST

b: bōl'test*, un-bōl'test*.
j: jōl'test*.
m: mōl'test*.
v: rē-vōl'test*.
Plus soul test, etc.

ǪL'TEST

f: dē-fạul'test*, fạul'test*,
foot fạul'test*.
h: hạl'test*.
m: mạl'test*.
s: as-sạul'test*, sạl'test*.
v: vạul'test*.
z: ex-ạlt'est*.
Plus small test, etc.

ŌL'TETH

b: bōl'teth*, un-bōl'teth*.
j: jōl'teth*.
m: mōl'teth*.
v: rē-vōl'teth*.

ǪL'TETH

f: dē-fạult'eth*, fạul'teth*,
foot fạul'teth*.
h: hạl'teth*.
m: mạl'teth*.
s: as-sạul'teth*, sạl'teth*.
v: vạul'teth*.
z: ex-ạlt'eth*.

ǪL'TI

f: fạul'ty.
m: mạl'ty.
s: sạl'ty.
v: vạul'ty.
Plus small tee, etc.
Plus fault, he, etc.

ŌL'TIJ

v: vōl'tȧġe.
Cf. çolt'ăġe, etc.

ǪL'TIJ

m: mạl'tăġe.
v: vạul'tăġe.
Cf. hạlt'ăġe, etc.

ǪL'TIK

b: Bạl'tiç, çō-bạl'tiç.
f: as-phạl'tiç (-fạl').
s: bȧ-sạl'tiç.
st: per"i-stạl'tiç.
Plus small tick, etc.

ŌL'TING

b: bōl'ting, un-bōl'ting.
j: jōl'ting.
m: mōl'ting, un-mōl'ting.
v: rē-vōl'ting.

ǪL'TING

f: dē-fạult'ing, fạul'ting,
foot fạul'ting.
h: hạlt'ing.
m: mạlt'ing.
s: as-sạult'ing, sạlt'ing.
v: vạult'ing.
z: ex-ạlt'ing.

ŌL'TISH

d: dōl'tish.
k(ç): çōl'tish.

(Choose only one word out of each group)

ǪLT'LES

f: fạult'less.
m: mạlt'less.
s: sạlt'less.
Plus fault, less *or* Les, etc.

ŌL'TŎN

b: Bōl'tŏn.
k(c): Cōl'tŏn.
m: Mōl'tŏn, Mōul'tŏn.
Plus whole ton *or* tun, etc.
Plus bolt on *or* an, etc.

ǪL'TŎN

d: Dạl'tŏn.
w: Wạl'tŏn.
Plus fault on *or* an, etc.
Plus small tun *or* ton, etc.

ŌL'TRI

p: pōul'try.
Plus whole tree, etc.

ŌL'TŨR

b: bōlt'ẽr, un-bōlt'ẽr.
j: jōlt'ẽr.
k(c): cōlt'ẽr.
v: rē-vōlt'ẽr.
Plus bolt her *or* err, etc.

ǪL'TŨR

Vowel: ạl'tăr, ạl'tẽr, un-ạl'tẽr.
br: Ġi-brạl'tăr.
f: dē-fạult'ẽr, fạult'ẽr,
  foot fạult'ẽr.
h: hạlt'ẽr.
m: mạlt'ẽr.
p: pạl'tẽr.
s: as-sạult'ẽr, psạlt'ẽr (sạlt'),
  sạlt'ẽr.
v: vạult'ẽr.

w: Mc-Wạl'tẽr, Wạl'tẽr.
z: ex-ạlt'ẽr.
Plus halt her *or* err, etc.

ǪL'TŨRN

Vowel: sub-ạl'tẽrn.
s: sạl'tẽrn.
Plus small tern *or* turn, etc.
Plus fault, earn, erne *or* urn, etc.

ǪLT'SŨR

f: fạl'sẽr.
w: wạltz'ẽr.
Plus fault, sir, etc.

OL'ŪM

k(c): cọl'yūm.
v: vol'ūme.

OL'UM

k(c): Cọl'um, cọl'umn.
s: sol'emn.
Plus baby doll 'em, etc.

ŌL'ŨR

b: bōwl'ẽr.
d: cọn-dōl'ẽr, dōl'ẽr, dōl'ŏr.
dr: drōl'lẽr.
f: fōal'ẽr.
g: gōal'ẽr, ŏne'⸗gōal'ẽr (wun'),
  twö⸗gōal'ẽr (tö'), etc.
j: cạ-jōl'ẽr.
k(c): cōal'ẽr, kōhl'ẽr (kōl').
m: mōl'ăr.
p: cĩr-cum-pōl'ẽr, pōl'ăr,
  pōl'ẽr, pōll'ẽr, ūn″i-pōl'ăr.
r: en-rōll'ẽr, Hō'ly Rōll'ẽr,
  rōl'lẽr, un-rōll'ẽr, up-rōll'ẽr.
s: cọn-sōl'ẽr, sōl'ăr.
sh: shōal'ẽr.
skr(scr): scrōll'ẽr.
str: strōll'ẽr.

(Choose only one word out of each group)

t: tōll'ẽr.
tr: comp-trōl'lẽr, con-trōl'lẽr,
pȧ-trōl'lẽr, trōll'ẽr.
Plus shoal her *or* err, etc.

OL'ŪR

b: bawl'ẽr, bāse'ball''ẽr,
bas'ket-ball''ẽr, foot'ball-ẽr,
hĭgh'ball-ẽr (hĭ').
br: brawl'ẽr.
dr: drawl'ẽr.
f: fall'ẽr.
h: haul'ẽr, ō''vẽr-haul'ẽr.
k(c): call'ẽr, hog call'ẽr,
trāin call'ẽr.
kr: crawl'ẽr.
m: bē-maul'ẽr, maul'ẽr.
skr(scr): scrawl'ẽr.
skw: squall'ẽr.
sm: small'ẽr.
spr: sprawl'ẽr.
st: fōre-stall'ẽr, stall'ẽr.
t: tall'ẽr.
thr: en-thrall'ẽr.
tr: trawl'ẽr.
w: cat'ẽr-waul''ẽr.
y: yawl'ẽr.
Plus haul her *or* err, etc.

OL'ŪR

d: dol'lȧr.
k(c): chol'ẽr, col'lȧr.
l: lol'lẽr.
s: sol'lȧr.
sk(sc): schol'ȧr.
skw: squäl'ŏr.
t: ex-toll'ẽr, Tol'lẽr.

ŌL'US

Vowel: glad-i-ōl'us.
b: bōl'us, hōl'us=bōl'us.

s: sōl'us.
Plus goal us, etc.

OL'USK

m: mol'lusk.
Plus doll, Lusk, etc.

OL'VENT

s: in-sol'vent, sol'vent.
v: ē-vol'vent.
z: dis-sol'vent, rē-sol'vent.
Plus doll vent, etc.

OL'VEST

s: ab-sol'vest*, sol'vest*.
v: dē-vol'vest*, ē-vol'vest*,
in-vol'vest*, rē-vol'vest*.
z: dis-sol'vest*, rē-sol'vest*.
Plus doll vest, etc.

OL'VETH

s: ab-sol'veth*, sol'veth*.
v: dē-vol'veth*, ē-vol'veth*,
in-vol'veth*, rē-vol'veth*.
z: dis-sol'veth*, rē-sol'veth*.

OL'VING

s: ab-sol'ving, sol'ving.
v: dē-vol'ving, ē-vol'ving,
in-vol'ving, rē-vol'ving.
z: dis-sol'ving, rē-sol'ving.

OLV'MENT

v: dē-volve'ment, ē-volve'ment,
in-volve'ment.
Plus resolve meant, etc.

OLV'ŪR

s: ab-sol'vẽr, sol'vẽr.
v: ē-vol'vẽr, in-vol'vẽr,
rē-vol'vẽr.

(Choose only one word out of each group)

z: diṣ-ṣol′vẽr, rē-ṣol′vẽr.
Plus resolve her *or* err, etc.

ǪL′WĂRT

st: stạl′wᴀrt.
Plus small wart, etc.

ǪL′WĀZ

Vowel: ạl′wāyṣ.
h: hạll′wāyṣ.
Plus stall weighs *or* ways, etc.

Ō′MȦ

Vowel: Ō′mȧ.
b: ȧ-bō′mȧ.
br: thē″ō-brō′mȧ.
g: zȳ-gō′mȧ.
k(ᴄ): çō′mȧ, sär-çō′mȧ,
   Tȧ-çō′mȧ.
l: Point Lō′mȧ.
n: Sō-nō′mȧ.
pl: di-plō′mȧ.
r: ȧ-rō′mȧ, Rō′mȧ.
s: sō′mȧ.
st: stō′mȧ.
t: Nȧ-tō′mȧ.
Plus home, a, etc.

OM′Ȧ

k(ᴄ): çom′mȧ.
m: mom′mȧ.
Plus from a, etc.

Ō′MAD

Vowel: ōhm′ad*.
n: nō′mad.
Plus so mad, etc.
Plus Rome ad *or* add, etc.

Ō′MĂN

b: bōw′mᴀn.
f: fōe′mᴀn.

r: Rō′mᴀn.
sh: shōw′mᴀn.
y: yeō′mᴀn.
Plus snow, man, etc.

OM′ĂS

t: Thom′ᴀs (tom′).
Cf. from us, etc.

OM′BAT

k(ᴄ): çom′bat.
w: wom′bat.
Plus from bat, etc.

OM′BI

d: Dom′bey.
kr: A′bẽr-ᴄrom″bie.
z: zom′bie.
Plus from bee *or* be, etc.

OM′BRUS

s: som′brous.

OM′BŨR

Vowel: om′bẽr, om′bre.
h: hom′bre.
s: som′bẽr.
sk(sᴄ): Sᴄom′bẽr.
Plus from burr, etc.

ŌM′EN, Ō′MEN

Vowel: ō′men.
b: bōw′men.
d: ab-dō′men.
f: fōe′men.
n: ag-nō′men, ᴄog-nō′men,
   praē-nō′men.
y: yeō′men.
Plus show men, etc.

Ō'MEND
OM'IS

fāte, fär, fást, fạll, fināl, cãre, at; mēte, prey, hẽr, met; pīne,
marïne, bïrd, pin; nōte, mŏve, fọr, atŏm, not; mọọn, book; **654**

(Choose only one word out of each group)

Ō'MEND

Vowel: ill'=ō'mened, ō'mened.
Plus Rome end, etc.
Plus so mend, etc.

Ō'MENT

m: mō'ment.
st: bē-stōw'ment.
Plus glow meant, etc.

OM'ET

d: dom'ett.
gr: grom'met.
k(c̲): c̲om'et.
Cf. from it, etc.
Cf. mamma met, etc.

ŌM'I

Vowel: Na-ō'mi, Ōh'mē.
f: fōam'y.
h: hōm'ey, hōm'y.
l: lōam'y.
r: rōam'y.
Plus show me, etc.

Ọ'MI

m: Mạu'mee.
Plus saw me, etc.

OM'I

m: mom'my.
t: Tom'mie, Tom'my.
Plus blah me, etc.

OM'IJ

Vowel: hom'ȧg̣e.
Cf. bomb'ȧg̣e, etc.

ŌM'IK

br: brōm'ic̲, hȳ"drō-brōm'ic̲.
kr: c̲hrōm'ic̲, pol"y-c̲hrōm'ic̲.
n: gnōm'ic̲ (nōm').
Plus slow, Mick, etc.

OM'IK

dr: hip"pō-drom'ic̲,
or"thō-drom'ic̲, pal"in-drom'ic̲.
k(c̲): c̲om'ic̲, sē'ri-ō=c̲om'ic̲,
trag̣'i-c̲om'ic̲.
kr: hē"li-ō-c̲hrom'ic̲,
stēr"ē-ō-c̲hrom'ic̲.
m: cin"nȧ-mom'ic̲*.
n: ag"rō-nom'ic̲, as"trō-nom'ic̲,
ạu"tō-nom'ic̲, ē"c̲ō-nom'ic̲,
gas"trō-nom'ic̲, ī"sō-nom'ic̲,
met"rō-nom'ic̲, nom'ic̲,
phys̲"i-og-nom'ic̲ (fiz"),
tax"o-nom'ic̲.
t: an"ȧ-tom'ic̲, ȧ-tom'ic̲,
dī"ȧ-tom'ic̲, dys-tom'ic̲,
en-tom'ic̲, mī"c̲rō-tom'ic̲,
mon"ȧ-tom'ic̲,
phan-tom'ic̲ (fan-),
stēr"ē-ō-tom'ic̲, trī"ȧ-tom'ic̲.
v: vom'ic̲.

OM'IKS

n: ē-c̲ō-nom'ic̲s, phọr"ō-nom'ic̲s.
Plus om'ik+s.

Ō'MĪN

br: brō'mīne, thē"ō-brō'mīne.
Plus know mine, etc.

ŌM'ING

f: bē-fōam'ing, fōam'ing.
gl: glōam'ing.
h: hōm'ing.
k(c̲): c̲ōam'ing, c̲ōmb'ing.
r: rōam'ing.
Plus show Ming, etc.

OM'IS

pr: prom'ise.
Cf. ma miss, etc.

655 ūse, bull, brúte, tūrn, up; crȳ, myth; çat, maçhine, ace,
church, çhord; ġem, añger, (Fr.) boñ, aş; THis, thin; azure

ŌM'ISH
OM'ŪR

(Choose only one word out of each group)

ŌM'ISH

r: Rōm'ish.

OM'IT

v: vom'it.
Plus from it, etc.

ŌM'LES

f: fōam'less.
h: hōme'less.
k(ç): çōmb'less.
Plus Rome less, etc.

ŌM'LET

h: hōme'let.
t: tōme'let.
Plus Nome let, etc.

OM'LET

Vowel: om'elet.
Plus from Lett or let, etc.

ŌM'LI

h: hōme'ly.
Plus roam, Lee or lea, etc.

Ō'MŌ

d: mā'jŏr-dō'mō.
h: Eç'çē Hō'mō, hō'mō.
k(ç): Çō'mō.
kr: çhrō'mō.
Plus show Mo, etc.
Plus Rome owe or O, etc.

OM'ŎN

k(ç): çom'mŏn, un-çom'mŏn.
Plus bomb on or an, etc.

OM'PI

p: Pom'pey.
Plus swamp, he, etc.

OMP'ISH

r: romp'ish.
sw: swämp'ish.
Plus bomb, pish!, etc.

OM'PLISH

k(ç): aç-çom'plish.
Plus pomp, Lish, etc.

OMP'TED

pr: promp'ted, un-promp'ted.
Plus pomp, Ted, etc.
Plus prompt, Ed, etc.

OMP'TŎN

br: Bromp'tŏn.
k(ç): Çomp'tŏn, Le-çomp'tŏn.
p: Pomp'tŏn.
Plus romp, ton or tun, etc.
Plus prompt 'un, etc.

OM'PUS

p: pom'pous.
Plus swamp us, etc.

ŌM'SPUN

h: hōme'spun.
Plus Rome spun, etc.

ŌM'STED

h: hōme'stead.
Plus Nome stead, etc.

ŌM'ŪR

Vowel: ōm'ẽr.
g: gōm'ẽr.
h: hōm'ẽr, Hōm'ẽr.
k(ç): bēach'çōmb-ẽr, Çōm'ẽr,
çōmb'ẽr, wool çōmb'ẽr.
n: mis-nōm'ẽr.
r: rōam'ẽr.
v: vōm'ẽr.
Plus roam her or err, etc.

OM'ŪR

b: bomb'ẽr (bom').
Plus from her or err, etc.

OM'ŪRS
ON'DED

fāte, fär. fȧst, fall, finȧl; cāre, at; mēte, prey, hẽr, met; pīne,
marïne, bïrd, pin; nōte, mōve, fọr, atŏm, not; mọọn, book;

656

(Choose only one word out of each group)

OM'ŪRS

k(c): com'mẽrce.
Plus from Erse, etc.

ŌM'WĂRD

h: hōme'wȧrd.
Plus Rome ward, etc.

Ō'NȦ

Vowel: Ī-ō'nȧ, Ō'nȧ.
b: bō'nȧ (dē'ȧ), Cär-bō'nȧ.
ch: cin-chō'nȧ.
d: Dō'nȧ.
j: Jō'nȧh ('nȧ).
l: Bär-cē-lō'nȧ, Bel-lō'nȧ,
Bō-lōgn'ȧ (-lōn').
m: Crē-mō-nȧ, Deṣ"dē-mō'nȧ,
mō'nȧ, Pō-mō'nȧ, Rȧ-mō'nȧ.
n: an-nō'nȧ, Å-nō'nȧ, Nō'nȧ.
r: cō-rō'nȧ.
z: Ar"ï-zō'nȧ, Zō'nȧ.
Plus own a, etc.

ỌN'Å

f: faun'ȧ.
l: Laun'ȧh.
m: Maun'ȧ.
Plus fawn a, etc.

ON'Å

d: bel"lȧ-don'nȧ, don'nȧ,
Mȧ-don'nȧ, prï"mȧ-don'nȧ.
Plus on a, etc.

ŌN'ĂL

b: sub"um-bōn'ăl.
r: cō-rōn'ȧl.
t: tōn'ȧl.
z: zōn'ăl.
Plus phone, Al, etc.

ON'ĂLD

d: Don'ăld, Mac-Don'ăld,
Mc-Don'ăld.
r: Ron'ȧld.

ŌN'ĂNT

s: in"tẽr-sōn'ănt, sōn'ănt.
Cf. ōn'ent.
Plus throne aunt *or* ant, etc.

ON'ÄRK

m: mon'ärch.
Plus on ark *or* arc, etc.

ŌN'ĂS

j: Jōn'ăs.
Cf. throne us, etc.

ŌN'ĀT

d: dōn'āte.
z: zōn'āte.
Plus throne ate *or* eight, etc.
Plus go, Nate, etc.

ON'DÅ

f: Fon'dȧ.
k(c): an"ȧ-con'dȧ.
r: Dē-ron'dȧ.
Plus bionde a, etc.

ỌN'DĒ

r: ar-rọn'di.
Plus fawned, he, etc.

ON'DĒ

sp: dï-spon'dee, spon'dee.
Plus fond, he, etc.
Plus on Dee, etc.

ON'DED

b: bon'ded.
sk(sc): ab-scon'ded.

(Choose only one word out of each group)

sp: cọr-rē-spon'ded,
dē-spon'ded, rē-spon'ded.
Plus Don dead, etc.
Cf. Don did, etc.

ŌN'DEF

st: stōne'=deaf'.
t: tōne'=deaf'.
Plus throne deaf, etc.
Plus throned F, etc.

ON'DEL

r: ron'del.
Plus beyond L or el, etc.
Plus Don Dell, etc.
Cf. on'd'l.

ON'DENS

sp: cọr"res-pon'dence,
dē-spon'dence, rē-spon'dence.
Cf. fond, hence, etc.
Plus Don, dense or dents, etc.

ON'DENT

fr: fron'dent.
sp: cō"rē-spon'dent,
cọr"rē-spon'dent, dē-spon'dent.
rē-spon'dent.
Plus Don dent, etc.

ON'DEST

b: bon'dest*, vag"à-bon'dest*.
f: fon'dest.
sk(sç): ab-sçon'dest*.
sp: cọr"rē-spon'dest*,
dē-spon'dest*.
rē-spon'dest*.

ON'DETH

b: bon'deth*, vag"à-bon'deth*.
sk(sç): ab-sçon'deth*.

sp: cọr"rē-spon'deth*,
dē-spon'deth*, rē-spon'deth*.
Plus on death, etc.

ON'DIJ

b: bon'dăġe, vag"à-bon'dăġe.
fr: fron'dăġe.
Cf. beyond age, etc.

ON'DING

b: bon'ding, vag"à-bon'ding.
sk(sç): ab-sçon'ding.
sp: cō"rē-spon'ding,
cọr"rē-spon'ding, dē-spon'ding,
rē-spon'ding.

ON'D'L

f: fon'dle.
r: ron'dle.
Cf. Don, dull, etc.
Plus beyond'll, etc.

OND'LI

f: fond'ly.
Plus beyond Lee or lea, etc.

OND'LING

b: bond'ling.
f: fond'ling.

OND'NES

bl: blond'ness.
f: fond'ness.

ON'DRÀ

s: Son'drà.

ON'DŪ

f: fon'dū.
Cf. cheese fon'dūe, etc.
Plus Don do, etc.

(Choose only one word out of each group)

QN'DŪR

m: Mạun'dẽr.
Plus pawned her, *or* err, etc.

ON'DŪR

b: bon'dẽr.
bl: blon'dẽr.
f: fon'dẽr.
k(c): hȳ"pō-chon'dẽr*.
l: Uit-län'dẽr (oit-).
p: pon'dẽr.
sk(sc): ab-scon'dẽr.
skw: squän'dẽr.
sp: cō"rē-spon'dẽr,
cọr"rē-spon'dẽr, dē-spon'dẽr.
rē-spon'dẽr.
w: wän'dẽr.
y: yon'dẽr.
Cf. con'dŏr.
Plus bond her *or* err, etc.

QN'DŪRZ

m: mạun'dẽrṣ.
s: Sạun'dẽrṣ.
Plus pawned hers *or* errs, etc.

QN'Ē

p: Paw'nee.
sh: Shaw'nee.
sw: Swạ'nee.
t: Punx"à-taw'nee.
w: Sē-wä'nee.
Cf. ọn'i.
Plus lawn, he, etc.

ŌN'ENT

p: com-pōn'ent, dē-pōn'ent,
ex-pōn'ent, in"tẽr-pōn'ent,
op-pōn'ent, prō-pōn'ent.
Cf. ō'nănt.

Ō'NES

l: lōw'ness.
sl: slōw'ness.

ŌN'EST

Vowel: dis-ōwn'est*, ōwn'est*.
d: con-dōn'est*.
dr: drōn'est*.
gr: grōan'est*, grōwn'est.
h: hōn'est*.
l: lōan'est*, lōn'est.
m: bē-mōan'est*, mōan'est*.
p: pōst-pōn'est*.
st: stōn'est*.
t: à-tōn'est*, in-tōn'est*,
tōn'est*.
thr: dē-thrōn'est*,
en-thrōn'est*, thrōn'est*.
Plus low nest, etc.

ON'EST

Vowel: dis-hon'est (-on'),
hon'est (on').
d: don'nest*.
k(c): con'nest*.
n: non'est.
w: wän'nest.
Plus ma nest, etc.

ON'ET

b: blūe'bon"net, bon'net,
grāy'bon"net, un-bon'net.
s: son'net.
Plus Don et, etc.
Cf. don it, etc.

ŌN'ETH

Vowel: dis-ōwn'eth*, ōwn'eth*.
d: con-dōn'eth*.
dr: drōn'eth*.
gr: grōan'eth*.

(Choose only one word out of each group)

h: hōn'eth*.
l: lōan'eth*.
m: bē-mōan'eth*, mōan'eth*.
p: pōst-pōn'eth*.
st: stōn'eth*.
t: à-tōn'eth*, in-tōn'eth*, tōn'eth*.
thr: dē-thrōn'eth*, en-thrōn'eth*, thrōn'eth*.

ON'ETH

d: don'neth*.
k(ç): çon'neth*.

ONG'EST

l: long'est.
str: strong'est.

ONG'FṲL

r: wrong'fṵl (rong').
s: song'fṵl.
thr: throng'fṵl.
Plus gong full, etc.

ONG'GŌ

b: Boṅg'ō.
k(ç): Çoṅg'ō.
Plus wrong go, etc.

ONG'GŬR

k(ç): çoṅg'ēr.
l: long'ēr.

ONG'ING

l: bē-long'ing, long'ing, prō-long'ing.
r: wrong'ing (rong').
thr: throng'ing.

ONG'ISH

l: long'ish.
pr: prong'ish.
s: song'ish.
str: strong'ish.

ONG'KI

d: doṅ'key.
Plus strong key, etc.

ONG'KŬR

h: hoṅk'ēr.
k(ç): çoṅk'ēr, çoṅ'quēr ('kēr).
Plus honky-tonk her.

ONG'KŬRZ

h: hoṅk'ērṣ.
k(ç): çoṅ'quērṣ.
y: Yoṅk'ērṣ.
Plus honky-tonk errs *or* hers, etc.
Plus wrong curs, etc.

ONG'LI

l: long'ly.
r: wrong'ly (rong').
Plus song, Lee *or* lea, etc.

ONG'NES

l: long'ness.
r: wrong'ness.

ONG'STŬR

s: song'stēr.
Plus wrong stir, etc.
Plus wrong'st* her *or* err, etc.

ONG'ŬR

l: prō-long'ēr.
r: wrong'ēr (rong').
Plus strong err *or* her, etc.

ONG'WĀV

l: long wāve.
Plus song wave *or* waive, etc.

ŌN'HED

b: bōne'head.
Plus own head, etc.

(Choose only one word out of each group)

Ō′NI

Vowel: Ō′ney.
b: bōn′y.
dr: drōn′y.
f: phō′ny.
h: Mȧ-hōn′ey.
k(c̯): C̯ōn′ey, c̯ō′ny.
kr: c̯rō′ny.
l: ȧ-lōn′ey, bȧ-lō′ney,
bō-lōgn′y (-lōn′), Ma-lō′ney.
m: al″i-mō′ny, an′ti-mō″ny,
mat′ri-mō″ny, pär′si-mo″ny,
pat′ri-mō″ny, sañc̯′ti-mō″ny,
tes′ti-mō″ny.
p: pō′ny.
r: cic″e-rō′nē, laz″zȧ-rō″ni,
mac̯″ȧ-rō′ni.
st: stō′ny.
t: tō′ny.
tr: min″is-trō′nē.
Plus known he, etc.
Plus slow knee *or* nee, etc.

ON̯′I

br: brawn′y.
l: lawn′y.
s: saw′ney.
skr(sc̯r): sc̯rawn′y.
t: mul″li-gȧ-taw′ny,
or′ănge-taw′ny, taw′ny.
y: yawn′y.
Plus saw knee, etc.
Plus lawn, he, etc.

ON′I

b: bon′nie, bon′ny.
k: C̯on′nie.
l: Lon′nie.
r: Rä′nee, Ron′nie.
Plus Don, he, etc.
Cf. ma, knee, etc.

ŌN′IK

f: phōn′ic̯ (fōn′), tel″ē-phōn′ic̯.
y: yōn′ic̯.
z: zōn′ic̯.
Plus slow nick, etc.

ON′IK

Vowel: Am-phic̯″ty-on′ic̯ (-fik″),
em″bry-on′ic̯, gang″li-on′ic̯,
his″tri-on′ic̯, in″tēr-gang″li-on′ic̯,
Ī-on′ic̯, Ō-lym″pi-on′ic̯,
Phā-rā-on′ic̯ (fā-), zō-on′ic̯.
b: bu̇-bon′ic̯, c̯är-bon′ic̯.
d: Ȧ-don′ic̯, C̯hal″ce-don′ic̯,
hē-don′ic̯, sär-don′ic̯.
f: an″ti-phon′ic̯ (-fon′),
cac̯″ō-phon′ic̯, c̯at″ȧ-phon′ic̯*,
c̯ol″ō-phon′ic̯, dī″ȧ-phon′ic̯,
eū-phon′ic̯, hōm″ō-phon′ic̯,
mon′ō-phon′ic̯, phon′ic̯,
phō″tō-phon′ic̯ (fō″tō-fon′ik),
pol″y-phon′ic̯, sym-phon′ic̯,
tel″ē-phon′ic̯.
g: ȧ-gon′ic̯, ġē″ō-gon′ic̯,
jär-gon′ic̯, thē″ō-gon′ic̯.
k(c̯): c̯on′ic̯, drȧ-c̯on′ic̯,
lā-c̯on′ic̯, Tȳ-c̯hon′ic̯.
kl: cy-c̯lon′ic̯.
kr: ȧ-c̯ron′yc̯, c̯hron′ic̯,
mon″ō-c̯hron′ic̯.
l: Bab″y-lon′ic̯, c̯ō-lon′ic̯.
m: an″här-mon′ic̯, daē-mon′ic̯,
dē-mon′ic̯, gnō-mon′ic̯ (nō-),
här-mon′ic̯, heg-e-mon′ic̯,
mnē-mon′ic̯ (nē-),
path″ō-gnō-mon′ic̯ (-nō-),
phil″här-mon′ic̯ (fil″),
pneu̇-mon′ic̯ (nu̇-), pu̇l-mon′ic̯,
sēr-mon′ic̯, Sol″ō-mon′ic̯.
n: c̯a-non′ic̯.
p: ġē″ō-pon′ic̯, hȳ″drō-pon′ic̯.

661 ūse, bᵤll, brûte, tᵘ̃rn, up; crȳ, myth; c̨at, mac̨hine, ace, church, c̨hord; g̊em, an̊ger, (Fr.) bon̊, as̨; THis, thin; azure

ON'IKS
ŌN'LES

(Choose only one word out of each group)

r: Aã-ron'ic̨, ī-ron'ic̨,
mac̨"à-ron'ic̨,
Pyr-rhon'ic̨ (-ron'),
sten"tō-ron'ic̨.

s: mà-son'ic̨, pär-son'ic̨.

t: är"c̨hi-tec̨-ton'ic̨, à-ton'ic̨,
c̨rō-ton'ic̨, dī"à-ton'ic̨,
Hous"à-ton'ic̨, ī"sō-ton'ic̨,
Mē-ton'ic̨, Mil-ton'ic̨,
mon"ō-ton'ic̨, nē"ō-plà-ton'ic̨,
par"à-ton'ic̨, plà-ton'ic̨,
Plù-ton'ic̨, sem"i-ton'ic̨,
strà-ton'ic̨, tec̨-ton'ic̨,
Teù-ton'ic̨, ton'ic̨.

th: pȳ-thon'ic̨.

v: Slà-von'ic̨.

Cf. ma nick, etc.

ON'IKS

Vowel: his"tri-on'ic̨s, on'yx.

d: hē-don'ic̨s.

f: phon'ic̨s (fon').

l: Meg"à-lon'yx.

m: mnē-mon'ic̨s (nē-).

p: g̊ē"ō-pon'ic̨s, hȳ"drō-pon'ic̨s.

Plus on'ik+s.

ŌN'ING

Vowel: dis-ōwn'ing, ōwn'ing.

b: bōn'ing.

dr: drōn'ing.

f: phōn'ing (fōn'),
tel'e-phōn"ing.

gr: grōan'ing.

h: hōn'ing.

l: lōan'ing.

m: bē-mōan'ing, mōan'ing.

p: pōn'ing, pōst-pōn'ing.

st: stōn'ing.

t: à-tōn'ing, in-tōn'ing,
tōn'ing.

thr: dē-thrōn'ing, en-thrōn'ing,
thrōn'ing.

z: zōn'ing.

ON'ING

Vowel: awn'ing.

d: dawn'ing, un-dawn'ing.

f: fawn'ing.

p: pawn'ing.

sp: spawn'ing.

y: yawn'ing.

ON'ING

d: don'ning.

k(c̨): c̨on'ning.

ŌN'IS

d: Å-dōn'is.

r: Cō-rō'nis.

ŌN'ISH

dr: drōn'ish.

l: Bab"y-lōn'ish.

Plus no knish, etc.

ON'ISH

m: ad-mon'ish.

st: à-ston'ish.

t: ton'nish.

w: wän'nish.

ŌN'ĪT

z: Zōn'īte.

Plus no night, etc.

ON'JE

k(c̨): c̨on'g̊ee.

p: pon'g̊ee.

Plus on, Gee!, *or* G, etc.

ŌN'LES

b: bōne'less.

t: tōne'less.

ŌN'LI
ON'TĂL

fāte, fär, fȧst, fạll, finăl, cãre, at; mēte, prey, hẽr, met; pīne,
marïne, bïrd, pin; nōte, mŏve, fọr, ·atŏm, not; mọọn, book;

662

(Choose only one word out of each group)

thr: thrōne'less.
z: zōne'less.
Plus own less, etc.

ŌN'LI

Vowel: ōn'ly.
l: lōne'ly.
Plus known, Lee or lea, etc.

ŌN'MENT

Vowel: dis-ōwn'ment.
d: ҫon-dōne'ment.
p: pōst-pōne'ment.
t: ȧ-tōne'ment.
thr: dē-thrōne'ment,
en-thrōne'ment.
Plus cone meant, etc.

ŌN'NES

l: lōne'ness.
n: un-knōwn'ness.
pr: prōne'ness.

ŌN'ŎR

d: dōn'ŏr.
Cf. ōn'ūr.
Plus loan, or etc.

ON'RAD

k(ҫ): Ҫon'rad.

ON'SHENS

k(ҫ): ҫon'science.

ON'SHUS

k(ҫ): ҫon'scious, self-ҫon'scious,
sub-ҫon'scious, un-ҫon'scious.
Cf. launch us, etc.

ON'SIV

sp: ҫō″rē-spon'sive,
ҫor″rē-spon'sive, ir″rē-spon'sive,
rē-spon'sive.
Plus don sieve. etc.

ŌN'SŎM

l: lōne'sŏme.
Plus own some or sum, etc.

ON'SON

j: John'son, Jon'son.
Cf. Wis-ҫon'sin.
Plus Don, son or sun, etc.

ON'SŎR

sp: spon'sŏr.
t: ton'sŏr.

ON'STANT

k(ҫ): ҫon'stănt, in-ҫon'stănt.

ON'STŎN

j: John'stŏn.
Plus Don stun, etc.

ON'STRĂNCE

m: mon'strănce, rē-mon'strănce.
Cf. Don's trance, etc.

ON'STRĀTE

m: dē-mon'strāte*,
rē-mon'strāte.
Plus Don, straight or strait, etc.

ON'STROUS

m: mon'strous.
Cf. Don's truss, etc.

ON'STŬR

m: mon'stẽr.
Plus Don stir, etc.

ON'TĂL

d: per-i-don'tăl.
f: fon'tăl.

663 ūse, bṵll, brûte, tûrn, up; crȳ, myth; c̣at, mac̣hine, ace, church, c̣hord; ġem, añger, (Fr.) boṅ, aṣ; THis, thin; aᶻure

ON'TĀN
ON'TING

(Choose only one word out of each group)

fr: fron'tăl.
z: hor″i-zon'tăl.
Plus font, Al, etc.

ON'TĀN

m: cis-mon'tāne, trȧ-mon'tāne, ul″trȧ-mon'tāne.

ON'TED

d: dạunt'ed, un-dạunt'ed.
fl: flạunt'ed.
h: hạunt'ed.
t: tạunt'ed.
v: vạunt'ed.
w: help wạnt'ed, wạnt'ed.
Plus flaunt, Ed, etc.
Plus lawn, Ted, etc.

ON'TED

w: wont'ed.
Plus on, Ted, etc.
Plus font, Ed, etc.

ON'TEST

d: dạunt'est*.
fl: flạunt'est*.
h: hạunt'est*.
t: tạunt'est*.
v: vạunt'est*.
w: wạnt'est*.
Plus lawn test, etc.

ON'TETH

d: dạunt'eth*.
fl: flạunt'eth*.
h: hạunt'eth*.
t: tạunt'eth*.
v: vạunt'eth*.
w: wạnt'eth*.

ON'TI

fl: flaunt'y.
j: jạunt'y.
Plus haunt, he, etc.
Plus lawn tea, etc.

ON'TIF

p: pon'tiff.
Plus Don, tiff, etc.

ON'TIJ

w: wạn'tăġe.
Cf. flaunt age, etc.

ON'TIJ

p: pont'ăġe.
w: wänt'ăġe.
Cf. font, age, etc.

ON'TIK

Vowel: An″ȧ-c̣rē-on'tic̣.
d: mas'tō-don'tic̣.
k(c̣): är-c̣hon'tic̣.
kw: quän'tic̣.
p: pon'tic̣.
Plus Don, tick, etc.

ON'TIN

k(c̣): drȧ-c̣on'tine.
p: Hel″les-pon'tine, pon'tine.
Cf. ton'tine.
Plus font in *or* inn, etc.
Plus con tin, etc.

ON'TING

d: dạunt'ing.
fl: flạunt'ing.
h: hạunt'ing.
j: jạunt'ing.
t: tạunt'ing.
v: vạunt'ing.
w: wạnt'ing.

ON'TING
ON'ÜRD
fāte, fär, fȧst, fạll, finăl, cãre, at; mēte, prĕy, hẽr, met; pīne,
marïne, bĭrd, pin; nōte, mōve, fọr, atŏm, not; mọọn, book;   **664**

(Choose only one word out of each group)

ON'TING

w: wont'ing.

ǪNT'LES

d: dạunt'less.
t: tạunt'less.
v: vạunt'less.
Plus jaunt, Les *or* less, etc.

ǪNT'LET

g: gạnt'let, gaunt'let.
Plus flaunt Lett *or* let, etc.

ON'TǑN

w: wän'tŏn.
Cf. fron'tŏn.
Plus Don, ton *or* tun, etc.

ON'TRĪT

k(ç): çon'trīte, un-çon'trīte.
Plus Don, trite, etc.
Plus font right *or* write, etc.

ON'TUM

kw: quän'tum.
Plus font 'em, etc.

ǪN'TŨR

d: dạunt'ẽr.
fl: flạunt'ẽr.
g: gạunt'ẽr.
h: hạunt'ẽr.
j: jạunt'ẽr.
s: sạunt'ẽr.
t: tạunt'ẽr.
v: vạunt'ẽr.
Plus flaunt her *or* err, etc.

ŌN'ÜR

Vowel: ōwn'ẽr.
b: bōn'ẽr.
d: çon-dōn'ẽr, dōn'ŏr.
dr: drōn'ẽr.
f: phōn'ẽr, tel'e-phōn"ẽr (-fōn").
gr: grōan'ẽr.
h: hōn'ẽr.
m: bē-mōan'ẽr, mōan'ẽr.
p: pōst-pōn'ẽr.
st: stōn'ẽr.
t: á-tōn'ẽr, in-tōn'ẽr.
thr: dē-thrōn'ẽr, en-thrōn'ẽr.
Plus own her *or* err, etc.

ǪN'ŨR

Vowel: ạwn'ẽr, bär'ley ạwn'ẽr.
br: brạwn'ẽr.
f: fạwn'ẽr.
p: pạwn'ẽr.
sp: spạwn'ẽr.
y: yạwn'ẽr.
Plus lawn her *or* err, etc.

ON'ŨR

Vowel: dis-hon'ŏr (-on'),
hon'ŏr.
b: Bon'nẽr.
g: gon'ẽr.
k(ç): çon'nẽr, Çon'nŏr,
Ō'-Çon'nẽr, Ō'-Çon'nŏr.
w: Wän'nẽr.
Plus on her *or* err, etc.

ON'ŨRD

Vowel: dis-hon'ŏred (-on'),
hon'ŏred, tīme'⹀hon'ŏred,
un-hon'ŏred.

665

ūse, bṳll, brúte, tűrn, **up**; crȳ, **myth**; çat, maçhine, ace,
church, çhord; ġem, aṅger, (Fr.) boṅ, aᶎ; THis, thin; aᶎure

**ON´ŪRZ
OOK´ED**

(Choose only one word out of each group)

ON´ŪRZ

k(c̲): C̲on´nḗrᶊ, C̲on´nŏrᶊ,
Ō´-C̲on´nḗrᶊ, Ō´-C̲on´nŏrᶊ.
Plus on´ŭr+s.

ŌN´US

Vowel: ōn´us.
b: bōn´us.
t: tōn´ous.
Plus telephone us, etc.

ŌN´YÄRD

b: bōne´yärd.
Plus own yard, etc.

ON´YĂRD

p: pon´iărd.
Plus con yard, etc.

ON´ZŌ

f: Al-phon´ᶊō (-fon´),
Al-phon´zō.
l: Ȧ-lon´zō.
Plus dons owe *or* O, etc.

Ō´ON

z: en″tō-zō´on, ep″i-zō´on,
phȳ″tō-zō´on, zō´on.
Plus and so on, etc.

OOD´ED

h: hood´ed.
w: un-wood´ed, wood´ed.
Plus hood, Ed, etc.
Cf. good dead, etc.

OOD´EN

w: wood´en.
Cf. good den, etc.
Plus good N *or* en, etc.

OOD´I

g: good´y, good´y=good´y.
w: wood´y.
Plus should, he, etc.

OOD´ING

g: good´ing.
h: hood´ing.
p: bag pṳd´ding,
In´di-ăn pṳd´ding, pṳd´ding.

OOD´ISH

g: good´ish.
w: wood´ish.
Cf. should dish, etc.

OOD´LI

g: good´ly.
Plus wood, lea *or* Lee, etc.

OOD´MĂN

g: good´măn.
h: hood´măn.
w: wood´măn.
Plus should man, etc.

OOD´NES

g: good´ness.

OOG´I

w: boo´gie woo´gie.

OOG´ŪR

b: boog´ŭr.
s: beet sṳg´ăr (shṳg´),
lōaf sṳg´ăr, mā´ple sṳg´ăr,
sṳg´ăr.

OOK´ED

kr: c̲rook´ed.
Plus ook+ed*.

(Choose only one word out of each group)

OOK'I

b: book'ie.
h: hook'ey, hook'y.
k(ͼ): ͼook'y,
  sụg'ăr ͼook'y (shụg').
r: rook'y.
Plus cook, he, etc.
Cf. took key, etc.

OOK'ING

b: book'ing.
br: brook'ing.
h: hook'ing, un-hook'ing.
k(ͼ): ͼook'ing, hōme ͼook'ing.
kr: ͼrook'ing.
l: ill'⸗look'ing, look'ing,
  ō″vẽr-look'ing, well'⸗look'ing.
r: rook'ing.
Cf. look, king, etc.

OOK'LET

b: book'let.
br: brook'let.
Plus crook let or Lett, etc.

OOK'UP

h: hook'up.
Plus cook up, etc.

OOK'ŨR

h: hook'ẽr.
k(ͼ): ͼook'ẽr, el-eͼ'triͼ ͼook'ẽr,
  fīre'less ͼook'ẽr.
l: look'ẽr, ō″vẽr-look'ẽr.
st: stook'ẽr.
Plus crook her or err, etc.

OOL'BOOL

b: bụl'bụl.
Plus pull bull, etc.

OOL'EN

w: wool'len.
Cf. pull hen, etc.
Plus pull N or en, etc.

OOL'ET

b: bụl'let.
p: pụl'let.
Cf. pull it, etc.
Plus bull et, etc.
Cf. bull let, etc.

OOL'I

b: bụl'ly.
f: fụl'ly.
p: pụl'ley.
w: wool'ly.
Plus full, Lee or lea, etc.

OOL'ID

b: bụl'lied.
p: pụl'lied.
Cf. wool hid, etc.
Cf. pull lid, etc.

OOL'ING

b: bụl'ling.
p: pụl'ling.

OOL'ISH

b: bụl'lish.
f: fụl'lish.

OOL'MAN

p: Pụll'măn.
w: Wool'măn.
Plus full, man, etc.

OOL'NES

f: fụl'ness.

(Choose only one word out of each group)

OOL′ŬR

b: bu̯ll′lêr.
f: fu̯ll′lêr.
p: pu̯ll′lêr, wīre pu̯ll′lêr.
Plus pull her *or* err, etc.

OOM′ĂN

w: wom′ăn.
Cf. room an, etc.

OOR′BUN

b: Bou̯r′bŏn.

OOS′I

p: pu̯s′sy.

OOT′ED

f: foot′ed, nim′ble-foot′ed.
Plus put, Ed, etc.

OOT′ING

f: foot′ing.
p: pu̯t′ting.

OOT′ŬR

f: foot′êr.
p: pu̯t′têr.
Plus foot her *or* err, etc.

Ō′PÀ

r: Eü-rōp′à.
Plus grope a, etc.

OP′À

gr: grop′pà.
j: Jop′pà.
p: pop′pà.
Plus stop a, etc.

Ō′PĂL, Ō′P′L

Vowel: ō′păl.
b: Bhō′păl (bō′).

g: Ghō′păl (gō′).
n: Ād″ri-à-nō′ple,
  Çon-stan″ti-nō′ple, nō′păl.
Plus pope′ll, etc.
Cf. no pull, etc.

Ō′PAZ

t: tō′paz.
Cf. Lō′pez.
Cf. ŏp′i+s.

Ō′PEN

Vowel: ō′pen.
Plus slow pen, etc.

ŌP′EST

gr: grōp′est*.
h: hōp′est*.
k(ç): çōp′est*.
l: ē-lōp′est*, in″tĕr-lōp′est*,
  lōp′est*.
m: mōp′est*.
r: rōp′est*.
s: sōap′est*.
Plus no pest, etc.

OP′EST

ch: chop′pest*.
dr: drop′pest*.
h: hop′pest*.
l: lop′pest*.
m: mop′pest*.
p: pop′pest*.
pr: prop′pest*.
sh: shop′pest*.
st: stop′pest*.
t: ō″vĕr-top′pest*, top′pest*.
Cf. drop′pest*, etc.

OP'ET
OP'IC

fāte. fär, fȧst, fạll, finăl, cãre, at; mēte, prey, hẽr, met; pīne,
marïne, bïrd, pĭn; nōte, mŏve, fọr, atŏm, nŏt; mọọn, book;

668

(Choose only one word out of each group)

OP'ET

m: mop'pet.
p: pop'pet.
Plus pop et, etc.
Cf. stop it, etc.

ŌP'ETH*

gr: grōp'eth*.
h: hōp'eth*.
k(c): cōp'eth*.
l: ē-lōp'eth*, in″tẽr-lōp'eth*,
  lōp'eth*.
m: mōp'eth*.
r: rōp'eth*.
s: sōap'eth*.

OP'ETH

ch: chop'peth*.
dr: drop'peth*.
h: hop'peth*.
l: lop'peth*.
m: mop'peth*.
p: pop'peth*.
pr: prop'peth*.
sh: shop'peth*.
st: stop'peth*.
t: ō″vẽr-top'peth*, top'peth*.

ŌP'FUL

h: hōpe'ful, un-hōpe'ful.
Plus soap full, etc.

OP'HED

h: hop'head.
Plus stop head, etc.

ŌP'I

d: dōp'ey.
h: Hō'pi.

m: mōp'y.
s: sōap'y.
sl: slōp'y.
Plus hope he, etc.

OP'Ī

p: Pop'eȳe.
Plus stop, I or eye, etc.
Cf. flop pie, etc.

OP'I

ch: chop'py.
dr: drop'py.
fl: flop'py.
h: hop'py.
k(c): cop'y.
kr: crop'py.
l: lop'py.
m: mop'py.
p: ō'pi-um pop'py, pop'py.
s: sop'py.
sh: shop'py.
sl: slop'py.
Plus top, he, etc.

OP'IJ

pr: prop'păge.
st: stop'păge.
Cf. drop age, etc.

OP'IC

Vowel: Ē″thi-op'ic, mȳ-op'ic,
  pres″by-op'ic.
k(c): ȧ-cop'ic.
kl: Cȳ-clop'ic.
n: cȧ-nop'ic.
sk: dī″chrō-scop'ic,
  ē-lec″trō-scop'ic,
  gal-van″ō-scop'ic,

(Choose only one word out of each group)

hē"li-ō-sçop'iç, họr"ō-sçop'iç,
hȳ"drō-sçop'iç, hȳ"grō-sçop'iç,
kȧ-leī"dō-sçop'iç,
lȧ-ryn̄"gō-sçop'iç, met"ō-sçop'iç,
mī"çrō-sçop'iç, ne"çrō-sçop'iç,
pan"tȧ-sçop'iç, per"i-sçop'iç,
speç"trō-sçop'iç, stēr"ē-ō-sçop'iç,
steth"ō-sçop'iç, tel"ē-sçop'iç.

t: met"ȧ-top'iç, top'iç

thr: an-throp'iç,
mis"an-throp'iç,
phil"an-throp'iç,
psī"lan-throp'iç (sī"),
thē"an-throp'iç,
thē"ō-phil"an-throp'iç (-fil").

tr: al"lō-trop'iç, ġē"ō-trop'iç,
hē"li-ō-trop'iç, ī"sō-trop'iç,
trop'iç.

Cf. drop pick, etc.

OP'IKS

t: top'içs.
tr: trop'içs.
Plus op'ik+s
Cf. stop hicks, etc.

ŌP'ING

d: dōp'ing.
gr: grōp'ing.
h: hōp'ing.
k(ç): çōp'ing.
l: ē-lōp'ing, in"tēr-lōp'ing,
lōp'ing.
m: mōp'ing.
r: rōp'ing.
s: sōap'ing.
sl: slōp'ing.
st: stōp'ing.
t: tōp'ing.
Plus no ping, etc.

OP'ING

ch: chop'ping.
dr: bē-drop'ping, drop'ping,
ēaveṣ"drop'ping.
fl: flop'ping.
h: hop'ping.
hw: whop'ping (hwop').
k(ç): çop'ping.
kl: çlip'=çlop'ping.
kr: çrop'ping.
l: lop'ping.
m: mop'ping.
p: pop'ping.
pl: plop'ping.
pr: prop'ping.
s: sop'ping.
sh: shop'ping.
sl: slop'ping.
st: stop'ping.
str: strop'ping.
sw: swäp'ping.
t: ō"vēr-top'ping, top'ping.
w: Wäp'ping.

ŌP'ISH

m: mōp'ish.
p: pōp'ish.
Plus slow, pish!, etc.

OP'ISH

f: fop'pish.
sh: shop'pish.
Cf. stop, pish!, etc.

OP"L

h: hop'ple.
p: pop'ple.
st: es-top'pel, stop'ple.
t: ō"vēr-top'ple, top'ple.
Plus mop'll, etc.
Cf. crop pull, etc.

ŌP'LES
ǪP'ŪR

fāte, fär, fàst, fǎll, finǎl, cāre, at; mēte, prey, hēr, met; pīne,
marïne, bïrd, pin; nōte, mǒve, fǫr, atǒm, not; mǫǫn, book;   **670**

(Choose only one word out of each group)

ŌP'LES

h: hōpe'less.
p: pōpe'less.
s: sōap'less.
Plus dope less, etc.

OP'LING

f: fop'ling.
t: ō"vĕr-top'pling, top'pling.

ŌP'MENT

l: ē-lōpe'ment.
Plus soap meant, etc.

OP'NOT

t: top'knot.
Plus crop not, *or* knot, etc.

Ǫ'PǪ

p: paw'paw.
Plus gnaw paw, etc.

Ō'PŌK

sl: slōw'pōke.
Plus no poke, etc.

OP'SHUN

Vowel: op'tion.
d: ȧ-dop'tion.
Plus crop shun, etc.

OP'SI

dr: drop'sy.
k(ç): çop'sy.
m: Mop'sy.
t: Top'sy.
Plus drop, see, etc.

OP'SIS

k(ç): lȳ-çop'sis.
l: am"pē-lop'sis.
n: sy-nop'sis.
t: than"ȧ-top'sis.
Plus stop, sis, etc.

ŌP'STŪR

d: dōpe'stẽr.
Plus soap stir, etc.

OP'TED

Vowel: çō=op'ted.
d: ȧ-dop'ted.
Plus cop, Ted, etc.
Plus dropped, Ed, etc.

OP'TIK

Vowel: op'tiç.
k(ç): Çop'tiç.
n: sy-nop'tiç.
t: ạu-top'tiç.
Plus stop tick, etc.

ŌP'ŪR

d: dōp'ẽr.
gr: grōp'ẽr.
k(ç): çōp'ẽr.
l: ē-lōp'ẽr, lōp'ẽr.
m: mōp'ẽr.
r: rōp'ẽr.
s: sōap'ẽr.
sl: slōp'ẽr.
t: tōp'ẽr.
Plus soap her *or* err, etc.

ǪP'ŪR

p: pạup'ẽr.
sk(sç): sçạup'ẽr.
y: yawp'ẽr.

(Choose only one word out of each group)

OP′ŪR

Vowel: Op′pĕr.
ch: chop′pĕr, mēat chop′pĕr.
dr: drop′pĕr, ēave̞s′drop″pĕr, eȳe drop′pĕr.
fl: flop′pĕr.
gr: Grop′pĕr.
h: c̨lod′hop-pĕr, fi-na′lē hop′pĕr, grass′hop-pĕr, hop′pĕr.
hw: whop′pĕr (hwop′).
k(c̨): c̨op′pĕr.
kl: c̨lop′pĕr.
kr: c̨rop′pĕr, shãre′c̨rop-pĕr.
l: lop′pĕr.
m: mop′pĕr.
p: pop′pĕr.
pl: plop′per.
pr: im-prop′ĕr, prop′ĕr, prop′pĕr.
s: sop′pĕr.
sh: shop′pĕr, win′dōw shop′pĕr.
sl: slop′pĕr.
st: stop′pĕr.
str: strop′pĕr.
sw: swäp′pĕr.
t: ō″vĕr-top′pĕr, tip″top′pĕr, top′pĕr.
Plus chop her or err, etc.

Ō′PUS

Vowel: ō′pus.
g: là-gō′pous, Là-gō′pus.
n: C̨à-nō′pus.
Plus so, puss, etc.

Ō′RÀ

Vowel: Ō′rà.
d: Dō′rà, dumb꞊Dō′rà, El-dō′rà, En-dō′rà, Eū-dō′rà, Flō″rà-dō′rà, Pan-dō′rà, Thē″ō-dō′rà.

fl: flō′rà, pas″si-flō′rà.
g: An-gō′rà.
h: hō′rà.
k(c̨): C̨ō′rà.
m: Mär-mō′rà.
l: El″ē-ō-nō′rà, Lē″ō-nō′rà, Nō′rà, sig-nō′rà.
r: A̞u-rō′rà.
s: Mà-sō′rà.
t: Tō′ràh (′rà).
z: Zō′rah (′rà).
Plus glow, Ra, etc.
Plus adore a, etc.

QR′À

Vowel: a̞u′rà.
l: La̞u′rà.
m: Ma̞u′rà.
s: C̨ham″aē-sa̞u′rà.
Plus for a, etc.
Plus saw Ra, etc.

Ō′RĀ

f: fō′rāy.
Plus so, ray or Rae, etc.

OR′À

d: An-dor′rà.
m: Gō-mor′ràh (′rà).
Cf. are a, etc.

Ō′RAKS

b: bō′rax.
k(c̨): c̨ō′rax.
st: stō′rax.
th: thō′rax.
Plus so wracks or racks, etc.
Plus store ax or acts, etc.

(Choose only one word out of each group)

Ō'RĂL

Vowel: ō'răl.
fl: flō'răl, trī-flō'răl.
h: hō'răl.
k(c̠): c̠hō'răl.
kl: c̠hlō'răl.
r: au̠-rō'răl, sō-rō'răl.
th: thōr'ăl.
Plus sore, Al, etc.

ǪR'ĂL, ǪR'EL

Vowel: au̠r'ăl.
l: lau̠'rel.
n: bī-nau̠r'ăl.
Plus war, Al, etc.

OR'ĂL, OR'EL

k(c̠): c̠or'ăl.
kw: quär'rel.
m: im-mor'ăl, mor'ăl,
un-mor'ăl.
s: sor'rel.

OR'ĂNJ

Vowel: mock or'ănge, or'ănge.
Cf. mar, Inge, etc.

ŌR'ĂNT

s: sōar'ănt.
v: vōr'ănt.
Plus core, aunt or ant, etc.
Plus go rant, etc.

Ō'RĀT

fl: dē-flō'rāte.
kl: c̠hlō'rāte, pẽr-c̠hlō'rāte.
Plus so rate, etc.
Plus adore eight *or* ate, etc.

ǪR'ĀT

n: i-nau̠r'āte.
st: in-stau̠r'āte*.
Plus war eight, *or* ate, etc.
Plus straw rate, etc.

ǪR'BI

Vowel: ǫr'by.
k(c̠): c̠or'bie.
Plus war, be *or* bee, etc.

ǪR'BID

m: mor'bid.
Plus war bid, etc.

ǪR'BING

Vowel: ǫrb'ing.
s: ab-sǫrb'ing, rē-sǫrb'ing.
Plus war, Byng, etc.

ǪR'B'L

k(c̠): c̠or'bel.
w: war'ble.
Cf. war, bull, etc.

ǪR'BLŨR

w: war'blẽr.

ǪR'CHĂRD, ǪR'CHŨRD

Vowel: ǫr'chărd.
t: tor'tūred ('chũrd),
un-tor'tūred.
Plus for, Chard, etc.

ǪRCH'ŨR

sk(sc̠): sc̠orch'ẽr.
t: torch'ẽr.
Plus scorch her *or* err, etc.

673 ūse, bull, brúte, tũrn, up; crȳ, myth; çat, machine, ace, church, çhord; ġem, aṅger, (Fr.) boṅ, aş; THis, thin; aᶽure

** OR'DĂN
ŌR'DIJ**

(Choose only one word out of each group)

OR'DĂN

j: Jọr'dăn.

Cf. ọr'dŏn.

OR'DĂNS

k(ç): aç-çọr'dănce, çon-çọr'dănce, dis-çọr'dănce.

Plus war dance, etc.

Plus ward, aunts *or* ants, etc.

OR'DĂNT

k(ç): aç-çọr'dănt, çon-çọr'dănt, dis"aç-çọr'dănt, dis-çọr'dănt, in"aç-çọr'dănt.

m: mọr'dănt.

Plus ward aunt *or* ant, etc.

ŌR'DED

b: bōar'ded.

f: af-fōr'ded, fōr'ded, un-fōr'ded.

h: hōar'ded, un-hōar'ded, up-hōar'ded.

s: swōr'ded (sōr').

Plus store dead, etc.

Plus soared, Ed, etc.

OR'DED

k(ç): aç-çọr'ded, çhọr'ded, çọr'ded, rē-çọr'ded, un"rē-çọr'ded.

l: bē-lọr'ded, lọr'ded, un-lọr'ded.

s: sọr'did.

sw: swạr'ded.

w: à-wạr'ded, rē-wạr'ded, un"rē-wạr'ded, wạr'ded.

Plus war dead, etc.

Plus lord, Ed, etc.

Cf. war did, etc.

OR'DEN

w: wạr'den, wāy'wạr"den.

Cf. ọr'dŏn.

Plus Thor den, etc.

ŌR'DEST

b: bōar'dest*.

f: fōr'dest*.

h: hōar'dest*.

OR'DEST

k(ç): aç-çọr'dest*, rē-çọr'dest*.

l: bē-lọr'dest*, lọr'dest*.

w: à-wạr'dest*, rē-wạr'dest*, wạr'dest*.

ŌR'DETH

b: bōar'deth*.

f: fōr'deth*.

h: hōar'deth*.

Plus more death, etc.

OR'DETH

k(ç): aç-çọr'deth*, rē-çọr'deth*.

l: bē-lọr'deth*, lọr'deth*.

w: à-wạr'deth*, rē-wạr'deth*, wạr'deth*.

Plus for death, etc.

ORD'FUL

k(ç): dis-çord'ful.

w: à-wạrd'ful.

Plus lord full, etc.

OR'DID

s: sọr'did.

Cf. ọr'ded.

ŌR'DIJ

b: bōar'dăge, bōr'dăge.

Cf. stored age, etc.

ǪR'DIJ
ǪR'ENS

fāte, fär, fåst, fall, finăl, cãre, at; mēte, prey, hẽr, met; pīne,
marïne, bĭrd, pin; nōte, mŏve, fǫr, atŏm, not; mǫǫn, book;

674

(Choose only one word out of each group)

ǪR'DIJ

k(c̣): cǫr'dăġe.
Cf. lord age, etc.

ŌR'DING

b: bōar'ding, un-bōar'ding,
weaTH'ẽr bōar'ding (weTH').
f: af-fōr'ding, fōr'ding.
h: hōar'ding, un-hōar'ding,
up-hōar'ding.

ǪR'DING

k(c̣): ac̣-cǫr'ding, cǫr'ding,
rē-cǫr'ding, un"rē-cǫr'ding.
l: bē-lǫr'ding, lǫr'ding,
un-lǫr'ding.
w: à-war'ding, rē-war'ding,
un"rē-war'ding, war'ding.

ǪRD'LI

l: lǫrd'ly, un-lǫrd'ly.
Plus award, Lee or lea, etc.

ǪR'DŎN

g: Gǫr'dŏn.
j: Jǫr'dăn.
k(c̣): cǫr'dŏn.
w: war'den.
Plus warred on or an, etc.

ǪRD'SHIP

l: lǫrd'ship.
w: ward'ship.
Plus cord, ship, etc.

ŌR'DŨR

b: bōar'dẽr, pär'lŏr bōar'dẽr.
f: fōr'dẽr.
h: hōar'dẽr.
Plus board her, or err, etc.

ǪR'DŨR

Vowel: dis-ǫr'dẽr,
mŏn'ey ǫr'dẽr, ǫr'dẽr,
rē-ǫr'dẽr, un-ǫr'dẽr.
b: bǫr'dẽr, em-bǫr'dẽr.
k(c̣): ac̣-cǫr'dẽr, chǫr'dẽr,
cǫr'dẽr, rē-cǫr'dẽr.
w: à-war'dẽr, rē-war'dẽr,
war'dẽr.
Plus lord her or err, etc.

ǪR'DŨRD

Vowel: dis-ǫr'dẽred, ǫr'dẽred,
rē-ǫrd'ered, well'=ǫr'dẽred.
Plus ǫr'dũr+ed.

ŌRDZ'MĂN

s: swōrds̩'măn (sǫrdz').
Plus fords, man, etc.

ŌR'ED

f: fōre'head.
Cf. ōr'id.

ǪR'EL, OR'EL

l: lau'rel.
Cf. ǫr'ăl, or'ăl.

ǪR'EN, ǪR'ĂN

sp: spǫr'răn.
w: rab'bit war'ren, war'ren.
Cf. fǫr'eign (fǫr'en).
Plus for an, etc.

ǪR'ENS

h: ab-hǫr'rence.
l: Law'rence, St. Law'rence.
Cf. or'ens.
Cf. straw rents, etc.

(Choose only one word out of each group)

OR'ENS

d: Dor'răn̄ce.
fl: Flor'ence.
t: tor'rents.
w: wär'rants.
Cf. o̯r'ens.

OR'ENT, OR'ĂNT

h: hor'rent.
t: tor'rent.
w: death wär'rănt (deth),
    wär'rănt.
Cf. ab-ho̯r'rent.

ŌR'EST

b: bōr'est*.
d: à-dōr'est*.
fl: floōr'est*.
g: gōr'est*.
h: hōar'est, whōr'est (hōr')*.
k(c̭): eñ-c̭ōr'est (äng-kōr'est)*.
n: ig-nōr'est*.
p: pōr'est*, pōur'est*.
pl: dē-plōr'est*, ex-plōr'est*,
    im-plōr'est*.
r: rōar'est*.
s: out-sōar'est*, sōar'est*,
    sōr'est.
sk(sc̭): sc̭ōr'est*.
sn: snōr'est*.
st: rē-stōr'est*, stōr'est*.
Plus no rest, etc.

O̯R'EST

h: ab-ho̯r'rest*.
w: wa̯r'rest*.
Plus saw rest, etc.

OR'EST

f: af-for'est, dis"af-for'est,
    en-for'est, for'est.
Cf. car rest, etc.

ŌR'ETH

b: bōr'eth*.
d: à-dōr'eth*.
fl: floōr'eth*.
g: gōr'eth*.
h: whōr'eth (hōr')*.
k(c̭): eñ-c̭ōr'eth (äng-kōr'eth)*.
n: ig-nōr'eth*.
p: pōr'eth*, pōur'eth*.
pl: dē-plōr'eth*, ex-plōr'eth*,
    im-plōr'eth*.
r: rōar'eth*.
s: out-sōar'eth*, sōar'eth*.
sk(sc̭): sc̭ōr'eth*.
sn: snōr'eth*.
st: rē-stōr'eth*, stōr'eth*.

O̯R'ETH

h: ab-ho̯r'reth*.
w: wa̯r'reth*.

O̯R'FĂN

Vowel: o̯r'phăn ('făn).
Plus war fan, etc.
Plus wharf, Ann *or* an, etc.

O̯R'FIK

Vowel: O̯r'phic̭.
m: al"lō-mo̯r'phic̭,
    an"thrō-pō-mo̯r'phic̭,
    a̯u"tō-mo̯r'phic̭, dī-mo̯r'phic̭,
    en"dō-mo̯r'phic̭,
    het"ēr-ō-mo̯r'phic̭,
    ic̭h"thy-ō-mo̯r'phic̭,
    id"i-ō-mo̯r'phic̭, ī"sō-mo̯r'phic̭,
    met"à-mo̯r'phic̭, mo̯r'phic̭,
    ō"phi-ō-mo̯r'phic̭,
    pan"tà-mo̯r'phic̭,
    pol"y-mo̯r'phic̭,
    prō"tō-mo̯r'phic̭,

(Choose only one word out of each group)

pseū″dō-mȯr'phic (sū″),
thē″ō-mȯr'phic,　trī-mȯr'phic,
zō″ō-mȯr'phic.

QR'FING

dr: dwȧr'fing.
hw: whȧr'fing.

QR'FIST

hw: whȧr'fist.
m: an″thrō-pō-mȯr'phist ('fist),
met″ȧ-mȯr'phist, etc.
Plus war fist, etc.

QR'FIT

f: fȯr'feit.
Plus wharf it, etc.

QR'FIZM

m: al″lō-mȯr'phism,
ȧ-mȯr'phism,　an″ȧ-mȯr'phism,
an″thrō-pō-mȯr'phism,
au″tō-mȯr'phism,　dī-mȯr'phism,
ī″sō-dī-mȯr'phism,
ī″sō-mer″ō-mȯr'phism,
ī″sō-mȯr'phism,
ī″sō-trī-mȯr'phism,
met″ȧ-mȯr'phism,
mon″ō-mȯr'phism,
plē″ō-mȯr'phism,
plō″y-mȯr'phism,
trī-mȯr'phism, zō′ō-mȯr'phism.
Plus war fizz 'em, etc.

QR'FŪS

Vowel: Qr'pheūs.
m: Mȯr'pheūs.

QR'FUS

m: ȧ-mȯr'phous,
an″thrō-pō-mȯr'phous,

dī-mȯr'phous,　ī″sō-dī-mȯr'phous,
ī″sō-mȯr'phous,
ī″sō-trī-mȯr'phous,
o″phi-ō-mȯr'phous,
par″ȧ-mȯr'phous,
pol″y-mȯr'phous,
trī-mȯr'phous.
Plus wharf us, etc.
Plus war fuss, etc.

QR'GĂN, QR'GŎN

Vowel: bar'rel ȯr'găn,　ȯr'găn.
d: Dȯr'găn.
g: Dem″ō-gȯr'gŏn,　Gȯr'gŏn.
m: Mȯr'găn,　mȯr'gen.
Plus morgue an, *or* on, etc.

ŌR'HAND

f: ȧ-fōre'hand,　bē-fōre'hand,
fōre'hand.
Plus sore hand, etc.

ŌR'HOUS

h: whōre'house (hōr').
st: stōre'house.
Plus adore house, etc.

Ō'RI

Vowel: ā fōr″ti-ō'ri (″shi-),
ā pōs-tēr″i-ō'ri,　ā pri-ō'ri,
ōar'y.
d: dō'ry,　hun'ky dō'ry.
fl: flō'ry.
g: al'lē-gō'ry,　cat'ē-gō'ry, gō'ry.
gl: glō'ry,　Ōld Glō'ry,
vāin'glō-ry.
h: hōar'y,　whōr'y (hōr').
j: Mag-giōr'ē (jōr').
l: lō'ry.
s: prom'is-sō-ry.

677

ūse, bu̧ll, brúte, tŭrn, up; crȳ, myth; ça̧t, ma̧chine, ace,
church, çhord; g̈em, an̄ger, (Fr.) bon̄, as̩; THis, thin; aȥure

Ō′RI

(Choose only one word out of each group)

sh: shōr′y.
sn: snōr′y.
st: bāse′ment stō′ry,
shōrt stō′ry, stō′ry.
t: ab-brē′vi-a̧-tō″ry,
ad-jū′ra̧-tō″ry, ab-sol′ū-tō″ry,
a̧ç-cel′ēr-a̧-tō″ry,
a̧ç-çlam′a̧-tō″ry,
a̧ç-cū′s̩a̧-tō″ry, ad′di-tō″ry,
ad-ho̧r′ta̧-tō″ry, ad-jū′ra̧-tō″ry,
ad-mon′i-tō″ry, ad′ū-la̧-tō″ry,
am′a̧-tō″ry, am-bag̈′i-tō″ry,
am′bū-la̧-tō″ry, a̧-men′da̧-tō″ry,
an-nō′ta̧-tō″ry,
an-nun′ci-a̧-tō″ry (′shi-),
ap-pel′la̧-tō″ry, ap-pliç′a̧-tō″ry,
ap-prē′ci-a̧-tō″ry (′shi-),
ap-prōb′a̧-tō″ry, ar″a̧-tō″ry,
as′pir-a̧-tō″ry,
as-sev″ēr-a̧-tō″ry,
as-sim′i-la̧-tō″ry, a̧u′di-tō″ry,
a̧ux-il′i-a̧-tō″ry, bib′i-tō″ry,
ça-çhin′na̧-tō″ry,
çal′çū-la̧-tō″ry,
çal-um′ni-a̧-tō″ry,
ças′ti-ga̧-tō″ry, cĭr′çū-la̧-tō″ry,
çom-man′da̧-tō″ry,
çom-men′ō-ra̧-tō″ry,
çom-men′da̧-tō″ry,
çom-min′a̧-tō″ry,
çom-mū′ni-ça̧-tō″ry,
çom-pel′la̧-tō″ry,
çom-pen′sa̧-tō″ry,
çon-cil′i-a̧-tō″ry,
çon-dem′na̧-tō″ry,
çon-fab′ū-la̧-tō″ry,
çon-fīr′ma̧-tō″ry,
çon-fis′ça̧-tō″ry,
çon-grat′ū-la̧-tō″ry,
çon-sēr′va̧-tō″ry,
çon-sōl′a̧-tō″ry,

çon-trib′ū-tō″ry,
ço̧r-rob′ō-ra̧-tō″ry,
çrē′ma̧-tō″ry, çrim′i-na̧-tō″ry,
dam′na̧-tō″ry, dē-çlam′a̧-tō″ry,
dē-clar′a̧-tō″ry, ded′i-ça̧-tō″ry,
dē-fam′a̧-tō″ry,
dē-lin′ē-a̧-tō″ry,
dē-mon′strà-tō″ry,
dē-nun′ci-a̧-tō″ry (′shi-),
dē-pil′a̧-tō″ry, dē-pos̩′i-tō″ry,
dep′re-ça̧-tō″ry,
dē-prē′ci-a̧-tō″ry (′shi-),
dē-pred′a̧-tō″ry, dē-ro̧g′a̧-tō″ry,
dē-sig′na̧-tō″ry, des′ul-tō″ry,
dis′ta̧-tō″ry, dil′a̧-tō″ry,
dis″ap-prōb′a̧-tō″ry,
dis-çrim′i-na̧-tō″ry,
dis-pen′sa̧-tō″ry, do̧r′mi-tō″ry,
ed″i-fiç′a̧-tō″ry,
ē-jaç′ū-la̧-tō″ry, ē-men′da̧-tō″ry,
em′ū-la̧-tō″ry, ex-ag̈′g̈ēr-a̧-tō″ry,
ex-çlam′a̧-tō″ry, ex-çul′pa̧-tō″ry,
ex′e-çra̧-tō″ry, ex-eç′ū-tō″ry,
ex-ho̧r′ta̧-tō″ry (-o̧r′),
ex′pi-a̧-tō″ry, ex-pīr′a̧-tō″ry,
ex-plan′a̧-tō″ry,
ex-pos′tū-la̧-tō″ry,
ex-pūr′ga̧-tō″ry,
ex-ten′ū-a̧-tō″ry,
ex-tēr′min-a̧-tō″ry,
ex-tīr′pa̧-tō″ry, feū′da̧-tō″ry,
frig̈′ēr-a̧-tō″ry,
fū-nam′bū-la̧-tō″ry,
g̈es-tiç′ū-la̧-tō″ry,
glad′i-a̧-tō″ry, grad′a̧-tō″ry,
gral′la̧-tō″ry, grat′ū-la̧-tō″ry,
gus′ta̧-tō″ry, g̈ȳ′ra̧-tō″ry.
hab-il′a̧-tō″ry,
hal-lū′cin-a̧-tō″ry, ho̧r′ta̧-tō″ry,
im-per′a̧-tō″ry,
im′prē-ça̧-tō″ry,

OR'I
OR'I

fāte, fär, fȧst, fạll, finăl, cãre, at; mēte, prey, hẽr, met; pīne, marïne, bĭrd, pin; nōte, mȯve, fọr, atŏm, not; mọọn, book;

678

(Choose only one word out of each group)

im-prō-vīṣ'ȧ-tō"ry,
in-can'tȧ-tō"ry,
in-crim'i-nȧ-tō"ry,
in-cū'bȧ-tō"ry, in-cul'pȧ-tō"ry,
in-dic'ȧ-tō"ry, in-flam'mȧ-tō"ry,
in-i'ti-ȧ-tō"ry ('shi-),
in-spīr'ȧ-tō"ry,
in"tẽr-loc'ū-tō"ry,
in"tẽr-rog'ȧ-tō"ry,
in'ven-tō"ry, in-ves'ti-gȧ-tō"ry,
in-vīt'ȧ-tō"ry, in-voc'ȧ-tō"ry,
jac'ū-lȧ-tō"ry, jūd'i-cȧ-tō"ry,
lab'ō-rȧ-tō"ry, lau'dȧ-tō"ry,
lī'bȧ-tō"ry, lib'ẽr-ȧ-tō"ry,
man'dȧ-tō"ry, mas'ti-cȧ-tō"ry,
mī'grȧ-tō"ry, mon'i-tō"ry,
nar'rȧ-tō"ry, nat'ȧ-tō"ry,
neg'ȧ-tō"ry,
nē-gō'ti-ȧ-tō"ry ('shi-),
nū'gȧ-tō"ry, ob-jūr'gȧ-tō"ry,
ob'lig-ȧ-tō"ry, ob-ṣẽr'vȧ-tō"ry,
of'fẽr-tō"ry, ọr'ȧ-tō"ry,
os-cil'lȧ-tō"ry, os'cū-lȧ-tō"ry,
pȧ-cif'i-cȧ-tō"ry, pal'li-ȧ-tō"ry,
pẽr'emp-tō"ry, pẽr-fūm'ȧ-tō"ry,
pẽr-spīr'ȧ-tō"ry, pis'cȧ-tō"ry,
plau'di-tō"ry, pos'tū-lȧ-tō"ry,
pō'tȧ-tō"ry, pred'ȧ-tō"ry,
prē-dic'ȧ-tō"ry, pref'ȧ-tō"ry,
prē-mon'i-tō"ry,
prē-pãr'ȧ-tō"ry, prō'bȧ-tō"ry,
prō-cras'ti-nȧ-tō"ry,
prō-cū'rȧ-tō"ry,
prō-fan'ȧ-tō"ry, prō-hib'i-tō"ry,
prom'on-tō"ry,
prō-nun'ci-ȧ-tō"ry ('shi-),
prō-pi'ti-ȧ-tō"ry ('shi-),
pūn'i-tō"ry, pūr'gȧ-tō"ry,
pūr-if'i-cȧ-tō"ry,
rec"om-men'dȧ-tō"ry,
rē-crim'i-nȧ-tō"ry,

rē-fọr'mȧ-tō"ry,
rē-frig'ẽr-ȧ-tō"ry,
rē-fū'tȧ-tō"ry, rē-ġen'ẽr-ȧ-tō"ry,
rē-mūn'ẽr-ȧ-tō"ry,
rep'ẽr-tō"ry, rē-poṣ'i-tō"ry,
rē-prō'bȧ-tō"ry, rep'tȧ-tō"ry,
rē-quiṣ'i-tō"ry, rē-spīr'ȧ-tō"ry,
rē-stōr'ȧ-tō"ry, rē-tal'i-ȧ-tō"ry,
rē-tär'dȧ-tō"ry, rē-trib'ū-tō"ry,
rē-vẽr'bẽr-ȧ-tō"ry,
rē-vō'cȧ-tō"ry, rog'ȧ-tō"ry,
rō'tȧ-tō"ry, sac'ri-fi-cā"tō-ry,
sal'tȧ-tō"ry, san'i-tō"ry,
si-bil'i-tō"ry, sig'nȧ-tō"ry,
sig-nif'i-cȧ-tō"ry, sim'ū-lȧ-tō"ry,
spec'ū-lȧ-tō"ry, stẽr-nū'tȧ-tō"ry,
stil'lȧ-tō"ry, strid'ū-lȧ-tō"ry,
sub-lim'ȧ-tō"ry, sūd'ȧ-tō"ry,
sup-plic'ȧ-tō"ry,
tẽr'min-ȧ-tō"ry, ter'ri-tō"ry,
tō'ry, tran'si-tō"ry,
tran-spīr'ȧ-tō"ry,
un'dū-lȧ-tō"ry, ū-ṣūr'pȧ-tò"ry,
vȧ-cil'lȧ-tō"ry, vē-hic'ū-lȧ-tō"ry,
vī'brȧ-tō"ry, vin'dic-ȧ-tō"ry,
vom'i-tō"ry.

Plus also cac'ci-ȧ-tō-re,
Il Trōv'ȧ-tō'rē,
im-prov-vīs'ȧ-tō-re, etc.
Plus shore, he, etc.

OR'I

l: An'nie Lau'rie, Lau'rie.
m: Mau'ry.
Plus war, he, etc.

OR'I

fl: Flor'rie.
k(c): Cor'rie.
kw: quär'ry.
l: lor'ry.

(Choose only one word out of each group)

s: sor'ry.
Cf. par, he, etc.
Cf. är'i.

OR'ID

kl: bī-çhlō'rīde, çhlō'ride,
pẽr-çhlō'rīde.
s: sōre'⸗eȳed' (-īd').
Plus more, I'd or eyed, etc.
Plus show ride, etc.

ŌR'ID

gl: glōr'ied.
st: stōr'ied.
Plus so rid, etc.
·Cf. sorehead.

OR'ID

fl: flor'id.
h: hor'rid.
t: tor'rid.
Cf. forehead.

ŌR'IJ

sh: shōr'ăġe.
st: stōr'ăġe.
Cf. more age, etc.

OR'IJ

b: bor'ăġe.
f: for'ăġe.
p: por'ridġe.
Cf. scär'ăġe, etc.
Cf. ma rage, etc.

Ō'RIK

k(ç): çhō'riç.
kl: çhlōr'iç, eū-çhlōr'iç,
hȳ″drō-çhlōr'iç, pẽr-çhlōr'iç.
r: rōr'iç, Rōe'riçh.
Plus no rick, etc.

OR'IK

Vowel: mēt″ē-or'iç, thē-or'iç.
d: Dor'iç, el″y-dor'iç.

f: am-phor'iç, çam-phor'iç,
lith″ō-phos-phor'iç,
met″à-phor'iç,
phos-phor'iç (fos-),
prō-phor'iç, sem″à-phor'iç,
zö″ō-phor'iç.
g: al″lē-gor'iç, am″phi-gor'iç,
par'ē-gor'iç,
phan-tas″mà-gor'iç (fan-),
Pyth-à-gor'iç.
l: çà-lor'iç, pē-lor'iç, pȳ-lor'iç.
m: är-mor'iç, soph″ō-mor'iç.
sp: zō″ō-spor'iç.
t: his-tor'iç, piç-tor'iç,
prē″his-tor'iç, un″his-tor'iç.
th: plē-thor'iç.
y: Yor'içk.
Cf. far rick, etc.

OR'IN

f: for'eign.
fl: flor'in.
Cf. or'en.

ŌR'ING

Vowel: ōar'ing,
dǒu'ble ōar'ing (du'),
siñ'gle ōar'ing.
b: bōr'ing.
ch: chōr'ing.
d: à-dōr'ing.
fl: floōr'ing.
g: Gōe'ring, gōr'ing.
h: à-whōr'ing (-hōr'), whōr'ing.
k(ç): eñ-çōr'ing (äng-kōr').
l: Lōr'ing.
m: Mōe'ring.
n: ig-nōr'ing.
p: pōr'ing, pōur'ing.
pl: dē-plōr'ing, ex-plōr'ing,
im-plōr'ing.
r: rōar'ing.

(Choose only one word out of each group)

s: out-sōar'ing, sōar'ing, up-sōar'ing.
sh: shōr'ing.
sk(sc̱): sc̱ōr'ing.
sn: snōr'ing.
sp: spōr'ing.
st: rē-stōr'ing, stōr'ing.
Plus so ring, etc.

ỌR'ING

h: ab-họr'ring.
w: wạr'ring.
Plus Thor ring, etc.

ŌR'IS

d: Dōr'is.
l: lōr'is.

ỌR'IS

d: Dọr'is.

OR'IS

Vowel: or'ris.
d: doc̱h an dor'ris, Dor'is.
h: Hor'ăce.
l: lor'is.
m: mor'ris.

ỌR'JĂ

b: Bọr'ġiȧ.
g: Ġeȯr'ġiȧ.
Plus gorge a, etc.

ỌR'JĂL, ỌRD'YĂL

k(c̱): c̱ọr'diăl.
Plus gorge, Al, etc.

ỌR'JI

Vowel: ọr'ġy.
p: Ġeȯr'ġy Pȯr'ġy, pọr'ġy.
st: stȯr'ġy.
Plus gorge, he, etc.

ŌR'JING

f: fōr'ġing.

ỌR'JING

g: dis-gọr'ġing, en-gọr'ġing, gọr'ġing, rē-gọr'ġing.

ỌR'JIZ

Vowel: ọr'ġieṣ.
g: gọr'ġeṣ.
j: Ġeọr'ġeṣ.
p: pọr'ġieṣ.
st: stọr'ġeṣ.
Plus George's, etc.
Plus George is, etc.
Plus war jizz, etc.

ŌR'JŨR

f: fōr'ġẽr.

ỌR'JUS

g: gọr'ġeous.
Plus George us.

ỌR'KĂS

d: Dọr'c̱ăs.
Cf. war kiss, etc.
Cf. stork us, etc.
Cf. ọr'chis.

ỌR'KI

f: fọr'ky.
k(c̱): c̱ọr'ky.
Plus stork, he, etc.
Plus war key, etc.

ỌR'KID

Vowel: ọr'c̱hid.
Plus war, kid, etc.

ỌR'KING

d: Dọr'king.
f: fọr'king.
k(c̱): c̱ọr'king, un-c̱ọr'king.
Plus war king, etc.

(Choose only one word out of each group)

QR'KIS

Vowel: or'ċhis.
Cf. Dor'ċăs.
Plus war kiss, etc.

ŌR'LES

Vowel: ōar'less, ōre'less.
b: bōar'less, bōre'less.
d: doōr'less.
fl: floōr'less.
g: gōre'less.
k(ċ): ċōre'less, en-ċōre'less.
sh: shōre'less.
sk(sċ): sċōre'less.
sn: snōre'less.
sp: spōre'less.
st: stōre'less.
Plus ignore less *or* Les, etc.

QR'LI

m: Mor'ley.
sk(sċ): sċhor'ly.
w: war'ly*.
Plus Thor, Lee *or* lea, etc.

ŌR'LING

sh: shōre'ling.

ŌR'LOK

Vowel: ōar'lock.
f: fōre'lock.
Plus more lock, etc.

QR'LOK

w: war'lock.
Plus Thor lock, etc.

QR'MĂL

f: for'măl, in-for'măl,
ūn"i-for'măl.

k(ċ): cor'măl, cor'mel.
n: ab-nor'măl, ā-nor'măl,
nor'măl.
Plus warm, Al, etc.

ŌR'MĂN

d: dōor'măn.
f: fōre'măn.
fl: flōor'măn.
sh: loṅg"shōre'măn, shōre'măn.
Plus more, man, etc.

QR'MĂN, QR'MŎN

g: Gor'măn, Ō'-Gor'măn.
m: Mor'mŏn.
n: Nor'măn.
Plus war, man, etc.

QR'MĂNS

d: dor'mănce.
f: con-for'mănce, pēr-for'mănce.
Plus swarm ants *or* aunts, etc.

QR'MĂNT

d: dor'mănt.
f: con-for'mănt, in-for'mănt.
Plus swarm aunt *or* ant, etc.

ŌR'MENT

d: à-dōre'ment.
n: ig-nōre'ment.
pl: dē-plōre'ment,
ex-plōre'ment, im-plōre'ment.
st: rē-stōre'ment.
Plus snore meant, etc.

QR'MENT

t: tor'ment.
Plus war meant, etc.

ORM'EST
OR'NÅ

fāte, fär, fȧst, fạll, fĭnăl, cãre, at; mēte, prĕy, hẽr, met; pīne,
marĭne, bĭrd, pĭn; nōte, mŏve, fọr, atŏm, not; mọọn, book; **682**

(Choose only one word out of each group)

ORM'EST

f: ̣con-fọrm'est*, dē-fọrm'est*,
fọrm'est*, in-fọrm'est*,
pẽr-fọr'mest*, rē-fọrm'est*,
trans-fọrm'est*.
st: stọrm'est*.
sw: swạrm'est*.
w: wạrm'est.
Plus war messed, etc.

OR'METH

f: ̣con-fọrm'eth*, dē-fọrm'eth*,
fọrm'eth*, in-fọrm'eth*,
pẽr-fọrm'eth*, rē-fọrm'eth*,
trans-fọrm'eth*.
st: stọrm'eth*.
sw: swạrm'eth*.
w: wạrm'eth*.

OR'MI

d: dọr'my.
st: stọr'my.
w: wạr'my.
Plus for me, etc.
Plus swarm, he, etc.

ORM'ING

f: ̣con-fọrm'ing, dē-fọrm'ing,
fọrm'ing, in-fọrm'ing,
non"̣con-fọrm'ing, pẽr-fọrm'ing,
rē-fọrm'ing, trans-fọrm'ing.
st: bē-stọrm'ing, stọrm'ing.
sw: swạrm'ing.
w: wạrm'ing.
Plus war, Ming, etc.

OR'MIST

f: ̣con-fọrm'ist, non"̣con-fọrm'ist,
rē-fọrm'ist.
Cf. ọrm'est.
Plus war mist, or missed, etc.

ORM'LES

f: fọrm'less.
st: stọrm'less.
sw: swạrm'less.
Plus warm, less or Les, etc.

ORM'LI

f: ūn-i-fọrm'ly.
w: wạrm'ly.
Plus swarm, Lee or lea, etc.

ŌR'MŌST

f: fōre'mōst,
head'=fōre'mōst (hed').
Plus floor most, etc.

ORM'ŪR

f: ̣con-fọrm'ẽr, dē-fọrm'ẽr,
fọrm'ẽr, in-fọrm'ẽr,
pẽr-fọrm'ẽr, rē-fọrm'ẽr,
trans-fọrm'ẽr.
st: bärn'stọrm"ẽr, stọrm'ẽr.
sw: swạrm'ẽr.
w: bed wạrm'ẽr, foot wạrm'ẽr,
wạrm'ẽr.
Plus warm her or err, etc.

OR'MUS

f: mul"ti-fọr'mous.
k(c): ̣cọr'mous, ̣cọr'mus.
n: ab-nọr'mous, ē-nọr'mous.
Plus swarm us, etc.
Plus war muss, etc.

OR'NÅ

l: Lọr'nȧ.
m: crō-mọr'nȧ.
n: Nọr'nȧ.
Plus adorn a, etc.

(Choose only one word out of each group)

ǪR′NĀT

Vowel: ǫr′nāte.
Plus war, Nate, etc.
Plus warn eight *or* ate, etc.

ŌR′NES

s: sōre′ness.

ǪRN′EST

b: sub-ǫrn′est*.
d: à-dǫrn′est*.
sk(sç): bē-sçǫrn′est*, sçorn′est*.
w: fōre-wa̧rn′est*, wa̧rn′est*.
Plus Thor nest, etc.

ǪR′NET

h: hǫr′net.
k(ç): çǫr′net.
Cf. warn it, etc.
Plus war net, etc.

ǪR′NETH

b: sub-ǫrn′eth*.
d: à-dǫrn′eth*.
sk(sç): bē-sçǫrn′eth*,
sçorn′eth*.
w: fōre-wa̧rn′eth*, wa̧rn′eth*.

ŌRN′FṲL

m: mōurn′fṳl.
Plus sworn full, etc.

ǪRN′FṲL

sk(sç): sçǫrn′fṳl.
Plus warn full, etc.

ǪR′NI

h: Hǫr′nie, hǫr′ny.
k(ç): çǫr′ny.
th: thǫr′ny.
Plus for knee, etc.
Plus warn, he, etc.

ŌRN′ING

m: mōurn′ing.

ǪRN′ING

b: sub-ǫrn′ing.
d: à-dǫrn′ing.
h: dē-hǫrn′ing, dis-hǫrn′ing,
hǫrn′ing.
m: good mǫrn′ing, mǫrn′ing,
yes′tēr mǫrn′ing*.
sk(sç): bē-sçǫrn′ing, sçorn′ing.
w: fōre-wa̧rn′ing, wa̧rn′ing.

ǪR′NIS

Vowel: Aē″py-ǫr′nis (ē′pi-),
Hē″li-ǫr′nis, Içh″thy-ǫr′nis.
k(ç): çǫr′nice.
n: Dī-nǫr′nis.
t: Gas-tǫr′nis.

ǪRN′ISH

h: hǫrn′ish.
k(ç): Çǫrn′ish.

ǪRN′LES

h: hǫrn′less.
sk(sç): sçǫrn′less.
th: thǫrn′less.
Plus warn less *or* Les, etc.

ǪRN′MENT

d: à-dǫrn′ment.
Plus corn meant, etc.

ŌR′NÚN

f: fōre′nōon.
Plus score noon, etc.

ŌR′NŨR

m: mōur′nẽr.
Plus borne her *or* err, etc.

ŎR'NÛR
ŎR'SETH   fāte, fär, fàst, fall, finăl, cãre, at; mēte, prey, hêr, met; pīne,
marīne, bîrd, pin; nōte, mōve, fŏr, atŏm, not; mọọn, book;   **684**

(Choose only one word out of each group)

ŎR'NÛR

b: sub-ọr'nêr.
d: à-dọr'nêr.
h: họr'nêr, Lit'tle Jack Họr'nêr.
k: chim'ney cọr'nêr, cọr'nêr.
sk(sc): bē-scọr'nêr, scọr'nêr.
w: fōre-war'nêr, war'nêr.
Plus warn her *or* err, etc.

Ō'RŌ

Vowel: Ō'rō.
d: Rĭ'ō d' Ō'rō.
m: Mō'rō.
t: tō'rō.
Plus so row *or* roe, etc.
Plus score owe *or* O, etc.

OR'Ō

b: bor'rōw.
m: à-mor'rōw, good mor'row,
Mor'rō, mor'rōw, tö-mor'rōw.
s: sor'rōw.
Cf. scar owe *or* O, etc.
Cf. ma row *or* roe, etc.

OR'ŌD

b: bor'rōwed.
s: sor'rōwed, un-sor'rōwed.
Cf. car ode *or* owed, etc.
Cf. ma rode *or* road, etc.

OR'ŎLD

th: Thor'ŏld.
Cf. quär'relled.
Cf. car old, etc.

OR'ŎR

h: hor'rŏr.
Cf. car or etc.

ŎR'PID

t: tọr'pid.
Cf. dorp, hid, etc.

ŎR'PŎR

t: tọr'pŏr.
Plus dorp, or, etc.
Plus warp her *or* err, etc.

ŎR'SĂL

d: dọr'săl, dọr'sel.
m: mọr'sel.
t: tọr'sel.
tr: dex-trọr'săl.
Plus war, Sal *or* sell, etc.
Plus Morse L *or* el, etc.

ŌR'SEN

h: hōar'sen.
k(c): cōar'sen.

ŌR'SEST

f: en-fōr'cest*, fōr'cest*,
rē"in-fōr'cest*.
h: hōar'sest.
k(c): cōar'sest, cōur'sest*,
dis-cōur'sest*.
v: di-vōr'cest*.

ŎR'SEST

d: en-dọr'sest*.
h: họr'sest*, un-họr'sest*.

ŌR'SETH

f: en-fōr'ceth*, fōr'ceth*,
rē"in-fōr'ceth*.
k(c): cōur'seth*, dis-cōur'seth*.
v: di-vōr'ceth*.
Plus more, Seth, etc.

ŎR'SETH

d: en-dọr'seth*.
h: họr'seth*, un-họr'seth*.
Plus war, Seth, etc.

(Choose only one word out of each group)

ŌRS'FṴL

f: fōrce'fṵl.
s: rē-sōurce'fṵl.
Plus course full, etc.

ǪRS'FṴL

m: rē-mǫrse'fṵl.
Plus gorse full, etc.

ŌR'SHUN

p: ap-pōr'tion, dis″prō-pōr'tion,
pōr'tion, prō-pōr'tion.
Plus score shun, etc.

ǪR'SHUN

b: a̤-bǫr'tion.
s: c̣on-sǫr'tion.
t: c̣on-tǫr'tion, dē-tǫr'tion,
dis-tǫr'tion, ex-tǫr'sion,
in-tǫr'sion, rē-tǫr'sion,
tǫr'sion.
Plus war, shun, etc.

ŌR'SHUND

p: ap-pōr'tioned,
dis″prō-pōr'tioned, pōr'tioned,
prō-pōr'tioned, un-pōr'tioned.
Plus score shunned, etc.

ǪRS'HWIP

h: hǫrse'whip.
Plus Norse whip, etc.

ǪR'SI

g: gǫr'sy.
h: hǫr'sy.
Plus war, see, etc.

ŌR'SING

f: en-fōr'cing, fōr'cing,
rē″in-fōr'cing.
k(c̣): c̣ōur'sing, dis-c̣ōur'sing.

v: di-vōr'c̣ing.
Plus floor sing, etc.

ŌR'SIV

f: en-fōr'cive.
k(c̣): dis-c̣ōur'sive.
v: di-vōr'cive.
Plus more sieve.

ŌRS'LES

f: fōrce'less.
s: rē-sōurce'less, sōurce less.
Plus coarse less *or* Les, etc.

ǪRS'LES

h: hǫrse'less.
m: rē-mǫrse'less.
Plus gorse, less *or* Les, etc.

ǪRS'MĂN

h: hǫrse'măn,
līght'=hǫrse″măn (līt').
n: Nǫrse'măn.
Plus gorse, man, etc.

ŌRS'MENT

f: dē-fōrce'ment, en-fōrce'ment,
fōrce'ment, rē″in-fōrce'ment.
v: di-vōrce'ment.
Plus course meant, etc.

ǪRS'MENT

d: en-dǫrse'ment.
Plus gorse meant, etc.

ŌRS'NES

h: hōarse'ness.
k(c̣): c̣ōurse'ness.

ŌR'SŎM

f: fōur'sŏme.
Plus score some *or* sum. etc.

OR'SŎN
ŌR'TENT

fāte, fär, fȧst, fall, finăl, cãre, at; mēte, prĕy, hẽr, met; pīne,
marĭne, bĩrd, pin; nōte, mŏve, fŏr, atŏm, not; mŏŏn, book; **686**

(Choose only one word out of each group)

OR'SŎN

Vowel: Or'sŏn.
Plus war, sun *or* son, etc.

OR'SONG

w: war song.
Plus Thor song, etc.

ŌR'SŪR

f: en-fōr'cẽr, fōr'cẽr,
  rē"in-fōr'cẽr.
h: hōar'sẽr.
k(c): cōar'sẽr, cōur'sẽr,
  dis-cōur'sẽr.
v: di-vōr'cẽr.
Plus divorce her *or* err, etc.

OR'SŪR

d: en-dor'sẽr.
h: hor'sẽr, un-hor'sẽr.
Plus gorse err *or* her, etc.

ŌR'TĂL

p: pōr'tăl, trans-pōr'tăl.
Plus fort, Al, etc.

OR'TĂL

Vowel: ā-or'tăl.
ch: chor'tle.
m: im-mor'tăl, mor'tăl.
Cf. or't'l.
Plus quart 'll, etc.
Cf. war till, etc.

ŌR'TĂNS

p: sup-pōr'tănce,
  trans-pōr'tănce.
Plus support aunts *or* ants, etc.

OR'TĂNS

p: im-por'tance.
Plus quart, ants *or* aunts, etc.

OR'TĂNT

p: im-por'tant.
Plus quart, aunt *or* ant, etc.

ŌR'TED

k(c): cōur'ted.
p: dis-pōr'ted, ex-pōr'ted,
  im-pōr'ted, rē-pōr'ted,
  sup-pōr'ted, trans-pōr'ted.
sp: spōr'ted.
Plus more, Ted, etc.
Plus fort, Ed, etc.

OR'TED

b: à-bor'ted.
k(c): es-cor'ted.
s: as-sor'ted, con-sor'ted,
  sor'ted, un-sor'ted.
sn: snor'ted.
t: con-tor'ted, dē-tor'ted,
  dis-tor'ted, ex-tor'ted,
  rē-tor'ted.
thw: thwar'ted.
z: ex-hor'ted, re-sor'ted.
Plus war, Ted, etc.
Plus quart, Ed, etc.

OR'TEKS

k(c): cor'tex.
v: vor'tex.
Plus war, Tex, etc.
Plus quart, Exe *or* ex, etc.

OR'TEM

m: pōst-mor'tem.
Plus sort 'em, etc.

OR'TEN

sh: shor'ten.
Plus war, ten, etc.

ŌR'TENT

p: pōr'tent.
Plus more tent, etc.

(Choose only one word out of each group)

ŌR′TEST

k(ċ): cōur′test*.
p: dis-pōr′test*, ex-pōr′test*,
 im-pōr′test*, rē-pōr′test*,
 sup-pōr′test*, trans-pōr′test*.
sp: spōr′test*.
Plus floor test, etc.

ǪR′TEST

b: à-bǫr′test*.
k(ċ): es-cǫr′test*.
s: as-sǫr′test*, con-sǫr′test*,
 sǫr′test*.
sh: shǫr′test.
sn: snǫr′test*.
sw: swǫr′test.
t: con-tǫr′test*, dē-tǫr′test*,
 dis-tǫr′test*, ex-tǫr′test*,
 rē-tǫr′test*.
thw: thwǫr′test*.
z: ex-hǫr′test*, rē-sǫr′test*.
Plus war test, etc.

ŌR′TETH

k(ċ): cōur′teth*.
p: dis-pōr′teth*, ex-pōr′teth*,
 im-pōr′teth*, rē-pōr′teth*,
 sup-pōr′teth*, trans-pōr′teth*.
sp: spōr′teth*.

ǪR′TETH

b: à-bǫr′teth*.
k(ċ): es-cǫr′teth*.
s: as-sǫr′teth*, con-sǫr′teth*,
 sǫr′teth*.
sn: snǫr′teth*.
t: con-tǫr′teth*, dē-tor′teth*,
 dis-tǫr′teth*, ex-tǫr′teth*,
 rē-tǫr′teth*.
thw: thwǫr′teth*.
z: ex-hǫr′teth*, rē-sǫr′teth*.

ŌRT′GĪD

k(ċ): cōurt guīde.
p: pōrt guīde.
Plus sport guide *or* guyed, etc.

ǪR′THI

sw: swǫr′thy.
Plus north, he, etc.

ŌR′TI

f: fōr′tē.
Plus more tea, etc. (Also ǫr′tä.)

ǪR′TI

f: fǫr′ty, pi-an′ō-fǫr″tē.
s: sǫr′tie.
sn: snǫr′ty.
sw: swǫr′ty*.
w: wǫr′ty.
Plus for tea, etc.

ǪR′TIJ

sh: shǫr′tăge.
Cf. quart age, etc.

ŌR′TĪM

f: à-fōre′tīme, bē-fōre′tīme.
Plus more time, etc.
Plus court, I'm, etc.

ŌR′TING

k(ċ): cōur′ting.
p: dē-spōrt′ing, dis-pōrt′ing,
 ex-pōrt′ing, im-pōrt′ing,
 rē-pōrt′ing, sup-pōrt′ing,
 trans-pōrt′ing.
sp: spōrt′ing.

ǪR′TING

b: à-bǫr′ting.
k(ċ): es-cǫr′ting.

(Choose only one word out of each group)

s: as-sǫr′ting, cǫn-sǫr′ting,
sǫr′ting.
sn: snǫr′ting.
t: cǫn-tǫr′ting, dē-tǫr′ting,
dis-tǫr′ting, ex-tǫr′ting,
rē-tǫr′ting.
thw: thwȧr′ting.
z: ex-hǫr′ting, rē-sǫr′ting.

ŌR′TIV

p: trans-pōr′tive.
sp: spōr′tive.

ǪR′TIV

Vowel: ǫr′tive.
b: à-bǫr′tive.
t: cǫn-tǫr′tive, dis-tǫr′tive,
rē-tǫr′tive, tǫr′tive.

ǪR′T′L

ch: chǫr′tle.
hw: whǫr′tle (hwǫr′)*.
Cf. ǫr′tăl.
Plus quart ′ll, etc.

ŌRT′LĂND

k(c): Cōurt′lănd.
p: Pōrt′lănd.
Plus sport land, etc.

ŌRT′LI

k(c): cōurt′ly, un-cōurt′ly.
p: pōrt′ly.
Plus sport, Lee, or lea, etc.

ǪRT′LI

sh: shǫrt′ly.
Plus quart, Lee, or lea, etc.

ŌRT′MENT

p: cǫm-pōrt′ment,
dē-pōrt′ment, dis-pōrt′ment,
trans-pōrt′ment.
Plus sport meant, etc.

ǪRT′MENT

s: as-sǫrt′ment.
Plus short meant, etc.

ǪRT′NES

sw: swȧrt′ness.
thw: thwȧrt′ness.

ǪRT′NIT

f: fǫrt′night.
Plus sort nit, etc.

ǪR′TŎN

g: Gǫr′tŏn.
h: Hǫr′tŏn.
m: Mǫr′tŏn.
n: Nǫr′tŏn.
Plus war ton or tun, etc.

ŌR′TRĀT

p: pōr′trāit.
Plus floor trait, etc.
Plus court rate, etc.

ǪR′TRES

f: fǫr′tress.
Plus Thor tress, etc.

ŌRT′SHIP

k(c): cōurt′ship.
Plus sport ship, etc.

ŌRTS′MĂN

sp: spōrts′măn.
Plus court's man, etc.

ǪR′TŪN

f: bē-fǫr′tūne, en-fǫr′tūne,
fǫr′tūne, mis-fǫr′tūne.
p: im-pǫr′tūne.
Plus war tune, etc.

(Choose only one word out of each group)

ŌR′TŪR

k(ç): çōur′tẽr.
p: dis-pōr′tẽr, ex-pōr′tẽr,
im-pōr′tẽr, pōr′tẽr, rē-pōr′tẽr,
sup-pōr′tẽr, trans-pōr′tẽr.
sp: spōr′tẽr.
Plus court her *or* err, etc.

ǪR′TŪR

t: tǫr′tūre.
Plus short, you're *or* your, etc.
Cf. scorch your *or* you're, etc.

ǪR′TŨR

b: à-bǫr′tẽr.
k(ç): es-çǫr′tẽr.
kw: làst quạr′tẽr, quạr′tẽr,
weaTH′ẽr quạr′tẽr (weTH′).
m: mǫr′tăr.
s: as-sǫr′tẽr, çon-sǫr′tẽr,
sǫr′tẽr, wool sǫr′tẽr.
sh: shǫr′tẽr.
sn: snǫr′tẽr.
t: çon-tǫr′tẽr, dē-tǫr′tẽr,
dis-tǫr′tẽr, ex-tǫr′tẽr,
rē-tǫr′tẽr.
thw: thwạr′tẽr.
z: ex-hǫr′tẽr, rē-sǫr′tẽr.
Plus thwart her *or* err, etc.

ǪR′TŪRD, ǪR′CHĂRD

Vowel: ǫr′chărd.
t: tǫr′tūred.

ǪR′TŪRZ

kw: quạr′tẽrṣ,
sum′mẽr quạr′tẽrṣ,
win′tẽr quạr′tẽrṣ.
Plus ǫr′tūr+s.

ǪRT′WĀV

sh: shǫrt′wāve.
Plus quart wave *or* waive, etc.

Ō′RUM

Vowel: vā″ri-ō′rum.
f: fō′rum.
j: jō′rum.
k(ç): dē-çō′rum, in″dē-çō′rum.
kw: quō′rum.
l: ad vȧ-lō′rem.
Plus shore 'em, etc.
Plus no rum, etc.

ŌR′ŨR

b: bōr′ẽr, wood bōr′ẽr.
d: à-dōr′ẽr.
fl: flōor′ẽr.
g: gōr′ẽr.
k(ç): çōr′ẽr, dē-çōr′ẽr*,
eñ-çōr′ẽr (äng-).
n: ig-nōr′ẽr.
p: out-pōur′ẽr, pōr′ẽr, pōur′ẽr.
pl: dē-plōr′ẽr, ex-plōr′ẽr,
im-plōr′ẽr.
r: rōar′ẽr.
s: out-sōar′ẽr, sōar′ẽr, sōr′ẽr.
sh: shōr′ẽr.
sk(sç): sçōr′ẽr.
sn: snōr′ẽr.
st: rē-stōr′ẽr, stōr′ẽr.
Plus restore her *or* err, etc.

Ō′RUS

h: Hō′rus.
k(ç): çhō′rus, dē-çō′rous,
in″dē-çō′rous.
l: pȳ-lō′rus.
n: çȧ-nō′rous, sō-nō′rous.
p: im-pō′rous, pō′rous.
t: tō′rous, tō′rus.
Plus implore us, etc.

OR'US
OS'FĀT

fāte, fär, fȧst, fall, fināl, cãre, at; mēte, prey, hẽr, met; pīne,
marïne, bĩrd, pin; nōte, mõve, fŏr, atŏm, not; mọọn, book;

690

(Choose only one word out of each group)

OR'US

s: bron″tō-saur′us,
dol″i-cho̅-saur′us,
had″rō-saur′us,
ich″thy-ō-saur′us,
meg″ȧ-lō-saur′us, mos″ō-saur′us,
nan″ō-saur′us, plēi″ō-saur′us,
ples″i-ō-saur′us, prō″tō-saur′us,
reg″nō-saur′us
saur′us, tel″ē-ō-saur′us,
thē-saur′us, ty-ran″ō-saur′us.
t: Mē-taur′us, Taur′us.
Plus war us, etc.

ŌR'WȦRD

f: fōre′wȧrd.
sh: shōre′wȧrd.
Plus score ward, etc.

OR'WĂRD

f: fŏr′wȧrd, hence″fŏr′wȧrd,
straight-fŏr′wȧrd,
THence″fŏr′wȧrd.
n: nŏr′wȧrd.
Plus war ward, etc.

OR'WORN

w: war′worn.
Plus Thor worn, etc.

ŌR'WŨRD

f: fōre′wŏrd.
Plus shore word, etc.

ŌRZ'MĂN

Vowel: ōars′măn.
Plus implores man, etc.

Ō'SȦ

m: For-mō′sȧ, mi-mō′sȧ.
r: am″ō-rō′sȧ.
Plus gross a, etc.

OS'CHUN

z: ex-haus′tion (eg-zaus′chun).

ŌS'EST

d: dōs′est*, ō″vẽr-dōs′est*.
gr: grōs′sest.
k(c): jō-c̱ōs′est.
kl: c̱lōs′est.
n: di″ag-nōs′est*.
r: mō-rōs′est.

OS'EST

b: em-bos′sest*.
gl: glos′sest*.
kr: c̱ros′sest*.
t: tos′sest*.

OS'ET

f: fau′cet.
Plus straw set, etc.
Cf. sauce it, etc.

OS'ET

b: bos′set.
k(c): c̱os′set.
p: pos′set, sack pos′set.
Cf. toss it, etc.

ŌS'ETH

d: dōs′eth*, ō″vẽr-dōs′eth*.
n: dī″ag-nōs′eth*.
Plus no, Seth, etc.

OS'ETH

b: em-bos′seth*.
gl: glos′seth*.
kr: c̱ros′seth*.
t: tos′seth*.

OS'FĀT

f: phos′phāte.
Plus cross fate, etc.

691 ūse, bṵll, brúte, tũrn, up; crȳ, myth; ċat, maċhine, ace,
church, çhord; ġem, aṅger, (Fr.) boṅ, aṣ; THiṣ, thin; aẓure

Ō′SHĂL
OS′I

(Choose only one word out of each group)

Ō′SHĂL

s: an″ti-sō′ciăl, in″tēr-sō′ciăl,
sō′ciăl, un-sō′ciăl.
Plus throw shall, etc.
Plus gauche, Al, etc.

OSH′I

b: Bosċh′y, bosh′y.
skw: squäsh′y.
sl: slosh′y.
sw: swäsh′y.
t: tosh′y.
w: wäsh′y, wish′y=wäsh′y.
Plus wash, he, etc.
Cf. ma, she, etc.

OSH′ING

skw: squäsh′ing.
sl: slosh′ing.
sw: swäsh′ing.
w: wäsh′ing.

ŌSH′ŨR

g: gauċh′ēr (gōsh′).
k(ċ): kōsh′ēr.

OSH′ŨR

j: josh′ēr.
k: ċosh′ēr.
skw: squäsh′ēr.
sw: swäsh′ēr.
w: wäsh′ēr.
Plus slosh her, etc.

Ō′SHUN

Vowel: Boē-ō′tiăn, ō′ceăn.
g: Gō′shen.
gr: grō′sċhen.
k(ċ): ni-ċō′tiăn.
l: lō′tion.

m: ċom-mō′tion, ē-mō′tion,
lō″ċō-mō′tion, mō′tion,
prō-mō′tion, rē-mō′tion.
n: nō′tion, prē-nō′tion.
p: pō′tion.
v: dē-vō′tion, in″dē-vō′tion,
self′=dē-vō′tion.
Plus so shun, etc.

Ọ′SHUN

k(ċ): ċau′tion, in-ċau′tion,
prē-ċau′tion.
Plus law shun, etc.

Ō′SHUS

k(ċ): prē-ċō′cious.
p: nē-pō′tious.
r: fē-rō′cious.
tr: a-trō′cious.
Plus gauche us, etc.

Ọ′SHUS

k(ċ): ċau′tious, in-ċau′tious,
prē-ċau′tious.

Ō′ZI

j: Jō′ṣie.
l: Lō′sey.
Plus go see, etc.

ỌS′I

s: ṣauc′y.
Plus straw see, etc.
Plus sauce, he, etc.

OS′I

b: bos′sy.
dr: dros′sy.
fl: Flos′sie, flos′sy.
gl: glos′sy.
m: mos′sy.
p: pos′se.

OS'IJ
Ō'SIV

fāte, fär, fȧst, fạll, finăl, cãre, at; mēte, prey, hẽr, met; pīne,
marïne, bĭrd, pin; nōte, mŏve, fọr, atŏm, not; mọọn, book;

692

(Choose only one word out of each group)

t: tos'sy.
Cf. cross, see, etc.
Plus cross he, etc.

OS'IJ

s: sạus'ăġe.

OS'IK

f: fọs'sick.
gl: glọs'sic.
Cf. loss, sick, etc.

Ō'SIL

d: dō'cile, in-dō'cile.
Plus no sill, etc.
Plus dose'll, etc.

OS'IL

d: doc'ile, dos'sil.
f: fos'sil.
Plus cross'll, etc.
Plus cross ill, etc.

ŌS'ING

d: dōs'ing.
gr: en-grōs'sing.
Plus go sing, etc.

OS'ING

b: bos'sing, em-bos'sing.
d: dos'sing.
gl: glos'sing.
kr: cros'sing, grāde cros'sing,
rāil'rōad cros'sing.
t: tos'sing.

OS'IP

g: gos'sip.
Cf. cross hip, etc.
Cf. moss sip, etc.

Ō'SIS

Vowel: ȧ-poth″ē-ō'sis,
ē-nan″ti-ō'sis, hē″li-o'sis,
ich″thy-ō'sis, meī-ō'sis.
f: an″ȧ-mọr-phō'sis (-fō'),
mọr-phō'sis.
g: zȳ-gō'sis.
k(c): met″em-psȳ-chō'sis (-sī-),
när-cō'sis, psȳ-chō'sis (sī-),
sär-cō'sis.
kr: nē-crō'sis.
l: añ″ky-lō'sis, tū-bẽr″cū-lō'sis.
n: en″dos-mō'sis, ex″os-mō'sis,
os-mō'sis, zȳ-mō'sis.
n: cär-ci-nō'sis, dī″ag-nō'sis,
ġē″og-nō'sis, hyp-nō'sis,
prog-nō'sis.
p: hȳ″pō-tȳ-pō'sis.
pl: an″ȧ-dī-plō'sis,
ē-pan″ȧ-dī-plō'sis.
r: chō-rō'sis, cĭr-rhō'sis (-rō'),
het″ē-rō'sis, mō-rō'sis,
neū-rō'sis, sȳ-rō'sis,
scĭr-rhō'sis (sĭr-rō'), sō-rō'sis.
t: hal″i-tō'sis,
met″ȧ-sōm-ȧ-tō'sis,
met″emp-tō'sis,
met″en-sōm″ȧ-tō'sis,
prō″emp-tō'sis, ptō'sis (tō').
th: ē-pan″ọr-thō'sis.
Plus no, sis, etc.

OS'IS

b: prō-bos'cis.
Cf. loss, sis, etc.

Ō'SIV

pl: ex-plō'sive, in″ex-plō'sive.
r: cọr-rō'sive, ē-rō'sive.
Plus no sieve, etc.

693

ūse, bụll, brúte, tûrn, **up**; crȳ, myth; çat, maçhine, ace, church, çhord; ġem, aṅger, (Fr.) boṅ, aş; THis, thin; aẕure

OS'KĂR
OS'TĂL

(Choose only one word out of each group)

OS'KĂR

Vowel: Os'çăr.
Cf. hoss car, etc.
Cf. cross scar, etc.

OS'KI

b: bos'ky.
Plus cross key, etc.

OS"L

d: dos'el*, dos'sil.
f: fos'sil.
gl: hȳ-pō-glos'săl.
j: jos'tle.
l: çō-los'săl.
p: a̱-pos'tle.
t: tos'sel.
thr: thros'tle.
w: wäs'sail.
Plus cross'll, etc.

OS'LŬR

h: hos'tlĕr.
j: jos'tlĕr.
r: Ross'lĕr.

OS'LI

kr: çross'ly.
Plus loss, Lee *or* lea, etc.

ŌS'NES

b: vĕr-bōse'ness.
gr: grōss'ness.
k(ç): jō-çōse'ness.
kl: çlōse'ness.
r: mō-rōse'ness.

Ō'SŌ

Vowel: ar"i-ō'sō,
grāc"i-ō'sō (grā"shi-),
vĭr"tū-ō'sō.

fr: Phrō'sō (frō').

r: ä"mō-rō'sō, dō"lō-rō'sō.
s: sō'sō.
Plus go so, sow *or* sew, etc.
Plus gross owe *or* O, etc.

OS'ŎM

bl: blos'sŏm, o̱r'ănġe blos'sŏm.
gl: ō-don"tō-glos'sum.
p: ō-pos'sum, pos'sum.
Plus boss 'em, etc.

O'SŎN

d: Daw'sŏn.
l: Law'sŏn.
r: Raw'sŏn.
Plus craw, son *or* sun, etc.

OS'PEL

g: gos'pel.
Plus wasp'll, etc.

OS'PISH

w: wäs'pish.
Plus toss, pish!, etc.

OS'PŬR

pr: pros'pĕr.
Plus cross per *or* purr, etc.
Plus wasp her *or* err, etc.

ŌS'TĂL

k(ç): çōas'tăl.
p: pōs'tăl.
Plus most, Al, etc.

OS'TĂL

k(ç): ços'tăl, in"frà-ços'tăl,
in"tĕr-ços'tăl, Pen"tē-ços'tăl,
sū"prà-ços'tăl.
Plus lost, Al, etc.

(Choose only one word out of each group)

OS'TĀT

k(c̡): lat″i-c̡os'tāte,
  quäd″ri-c̡os'tāte.
p: ȧ-pos'tāte.
pr: pros'tāte.
Plus crossed eight *or* ate, **etc.**
Plus cross, Tate, etc.

ŌS'TED

b: bōas'ted.
k(c̡): c̡ōas'ted.
p: pōs'ted, un-pōs'ted.
r: rōas'ted.
t: tōas'ted.
Plus gross, Ted, etc.
Plus grossed, Ed, etc.

QS'TED

z: ex-hȧus'ted (egz-ȧus').
Plus sauce, Ted, etc.

OS'TED

fr: fros'ted.
k(c̡): ȧc̡-c̡os'ted.
Plus cross, Ted, etc.
Plus crossed, Ed, etc.

OS'TEL, OS''L

h: hos'tel.
Plus cost'll, etc. *or* cross'll, **etc.**

QS'TEN, QS'TIN

Vowel: Ạus'ten, Ạus'tin.
Plus cross ten, etc.
Plus cross tin, etc.
Plus lost in, etc.
Cf. Bos'ton.

ŌS'TES

h: hōs'tess.
Plus gross, Tess, etc.

ŌS'TEST

b: bōas'test*.
k(c̡): c̡ōas'test*.
p: pōs'test*.
r: rōas'test*.
t: tōas'test*.
Plus gross test, etc.

ŌS'TETH

b: bōas'teth*.
k(c̡): c̡ōas'teth*.
p: pōs'teth*.
r: rōas'teth*.
t: tōas'teth*.

ŌST'HOUS

Vowel: ōast'house*.
p: pōst'house.
Plus boast house, etc.

OS'TI

fr: fros'ty.
Plus cross tea *or* T, etc.
Plus crossed, he, etc.

ŌS'TIJ

p: pōs'tăġe.
Cf. coast age, etc.

OS'TIJ

h: hos'tăġe.
Cf. lost age, etc.

QS'TIK

k(c̡): c̡at″ȧ-c̡ạus'tic̡, c̡ạus'tic̡,
  dī″ȧ-c̡ạus'tic̡, en-c̡ạus'tic̡.
Plus sauce tick, etc.
Plus straw stick, etc.

OS'TIK

Vowel: et″ē-os'tic̡*.
k(c̡): pen″tȧ-c̡os'tic̡.

(Choose only one word out of each group)

kr: a̤-çros´tiç, par″a̤-çros´tiç.
n: ag-nos´tiç, dī″ag-nos´tiç,
ġē-og-nos´tiç, gnos´tiç (nos´),
prog-nos´tiç.
Plus loss tick, etc.
Cf. lost stick, etc.

OS´TIL

h: hos´tile.
Plus loss till, etc.

ŌS´TING

b: bōas´ting.
k(ç): çōas´ting.
p: pōs´ting.
r: rōas´ting.
t: tōas´ting.
Plus no sting, etc.

Q̧S´TING

z: ex-ha̤us´ting.
Plus saw sting, etc.

OS´TING

fr: fros´ting.
k(ç): a̤ç-çost´ing, çost´ing.
Cf. loss sting, etc.

Q̧S´TIV

z: ex-ha̤us´tive (eg-za̤us´),
in″ex-ha̤us´tive.

OS´TIV

k(ç): ços´tive.

ŌST´LI

g: ghōst´ly.
m: mōst´ly.
Plus coast, Lee or lea, etc.

OST´LI

k(ç): çost´ly.
Plus crossed, Lee or lea, etc.

ŌST´MĂN

p: pōst´măn.
Plus ghost, man, etc.

ŌST´MÄRK

p: pōst´märk.
Plus ghost, mark!, etc.

OS´TON

b: Bos´ton.
Cf. o̧s´ten.

Ō´STORM

sn: snōw´sto̧rm.
Plus go, storm, etc.

Q̧S´TRĂL

Vowel: a̤us´trăl.
kl: cla̤us´trăl.

OS´TRĂL, OS´TREL

k(ç): ços´trel.
r: lá-mel″li-ros´trăl,
lon″ġi-ros´trăl, ros´trăl.
Cf. nos´tril.

OS´TRĀT

pr: pros´trāte.
r: ros´trāte.
Plus frost rate, etc.
Plus cross straight or strait, etc.

OS´TRICH

Vowel: os´trich.
Plus lost rich, etc.

OS´TRIL

n: nos´tril.
Cf. os´trăl.
Plus crossed rill, etc.
Plus loss trill, etc.

(Choose only one word out of each group)

OS'TRUM

n: nos'trum.
r: ros'trum.
Plus lost rum, etc.

OS'TŪM

k(c̣): c̣os'tūme.

ŌS'TŪR

b: bōas'tẽr.
k(c̣): c̣ōas'tẽr.
p: fōur'=pōs'tẽr, pōs'tẽr.
r: rōas'tẽr.
t: tōas'tẽr.
thr: thrōw'stẽr.
Plus roast her *or* err, etc.
Plus no stir, etc.

ǪS'TŪR

Vowel: a̧us'tẽr.
z: ex-ha̧us'tẽr (eg-za̧us').
Plus saw stir, etc.
Plus holocaust her *or* err, etc.

OS'TŪR

p: im-pos'tūre, pos'tūre.
Plus lost your *or* you're, etc.

OS'TŪR

f: fos'tẽr.
gl: Glos'tẽr, Glouces'tẽr (glos').
k(c̣): ac̣-c̣os'tẽr, c̣os'tẽr,
  pen″tē-c̣os'tẽr.
n: Pāt'ẽr-nos″tẽr.
r: ros'tẽr.
Plus bossed her *or* err, etc.
Cf. loss stir, etc.

OS'TŪRN

p: pos'tẽrn.
Plus loss turn, *or* tern, etc.
Cf. cross stern, etc.
Plus crossed urn, erne *or* earn, etc.

ǪS'TUS

f: Fa̧us'tus.
Plus sauced us, etc.
Plus straw stuss, etc.

ŌS'ŨR

d: dōs'ẽr.
gr: en-grōs'sẽr, grō'cẽr,
  grōs'sẽr.
k(c̣): jō-c̣ōs'ẽr.
kl: c̣lōs'ẽr.
r: mō-rōs'ẽr.
Plus dose her *or* err, etc.
Plus no, sir, etc.

ǪS'ŨR

ch: Cha̧uc'ẽr.
s: sa̧uc'ẽr.
Plus naw, sir, etc.
Plus sauce her *or* err, etc.

OS'ŨR

b: bos'ẽr, em-bos'sẽr.
d: dos'ẽr.
gl: glos'ẽr.
j: jos'ẽr.
kr: c̣ros'ẽr.
t: tos'ẽr.
Plus toss her *or* err, etc.
Cf. toss, sir, etc.

OS'US

l: c̣ō-los'sus, mō-los'sus.
Plus cross us, etc.

Ō'TȦ

Vowel: ī-ō'tȧ.
fl: flō'tȧ.
k(c̣): Dȧ-kō'tȧ, North Dȧ-kō'tȧ,
  South Dȧ-kō'tȧ.
kw: quō'tȧ.
r: rō'tȧ.
s: Min″nē-sō'tȧ.
Plus quote a. etc.

(Choose only one word out of each group)

OT'Å

k(c̱): ter″rȧ-çot'tȧ.

l: C̱är-lot'tȧ, Lot'tȧ.

Plus what a, etc.

ŌT'ĂL

d: an″eç-dōt'ăl, an″ti-dōt'ăl, dōt'ăl, ex″trȧ-dōt'ăl, sac″ēr-dōt'ăl.

n: nōt'ăl.

r: rōt'al, sc̱lē-rō'tăl.

t: tee″tōt'ăl, tōt'ăl.

Plus quote, Al, etc.

ŌT'ĂL

Cf. ōt″l.

ŌT'ĂNT, ŌT'ENT

fl: flōt'ănt.

p: pōt'ent, prē-pōt'ent.

Plus no tent, etc.

Ō'TĀT

n: dē-nō'tate*, nō'tāte.

r: rō'tāte.

Plus go, Tate, etc.

Plus note eight *or* ate, etc.

OT'ASH

p: pot'ash.

Plus got ash, etc.

ŌT'ED

Vowel: ōat'ed.

b: bōat'ed, stēam'bōat″ed.

bl: blōat'ed.

d: dōt'ed, an'eç-dōt″ed.

fl: flōat'ed, rē-flōat'ed.

g: gōat'ed.

gl: glōat'ed.

k(c̱): c̱ōat'ed, frock c̱oat'ed, pär'ti-c̱ōat″ed, pet'ti-c̱ōat″ed.

kw

kw: mis-quōt'ed, quōt'ed.

m: dē-mōt'ed, mōat'ed, prō-mōt'ed.

n: dē-nōt'ed, nōt'ed, un-nōt'ed.

t: tōt'ed.

thr: li'ly꞊thrōat'ed, swän'꞊thrōat'ed, thrōat'ed.

v: dē-vōt'ed, self'꞊dē-vōt'ed, vōt'ed.

Plus so, Ted, etc.

Plus quote, Ed, etc.

OT'ED

n: Är'gō-naut″ed, Jug'gēr-naut″ed.

th: mer'ry꞊thought'ed.

Plus brought, Ed, etc.

Plus saw, Ted, etc.

OT'ED

Vowel: chev'i-ot″ted.

bl: blot'ted, un-blot'ted.

d: dot'ted, un-dot'ted.

j: jot'ted.

kl: c̱lot'ted, un-c̱lot'ted.

l: al-lot'ted, lot'ted.

n: knot'ted (not'), un-knot'ted.

p: pot'ted, un-pot'ted.

pl: plot'ted, un″dēr-plot'ted, un-plot'ted.

r: c̱ȧ-rot'id, gȧ-rot'ted, rot'ted, un-rot'ted.

s: bē-sot'ted, sot'ted.

sh: shot'ted.

sk(sc̱): wāin'sc̱ot-ted.

skw: squät'ted.

sl: slot'ted.

sp: bē-spot'ted, blood'꞊bē-spot'ted (blud'), blood'꞊spot'ted, spot'ted, un-spot'ted.

(Choose only one word out of each group)

t: tot'ted.
tr: trot'ted.
Plus not, Ed, etc.

ŌT'EN

Vowel: ōat'en.
Plus so ten, etc.

OT'EN, OT'ŎN

g: bē-got'ten, fīrst'=bē-got'ten,
for-got'ten, got'ten,
härd'=got'ten, ill'=got'ten,
mis″be-got'ten, mis-got'ten,
un″bē-got'ten, un″for-got'ten,
un-got'ten.
gr: Grot'ŏn.
k(c): cot'tŏn,
sēa'=is'lănd cot'tŏn (=ī').
r: rot'ten.
t: Fōrt Tot'ten, Tot'ten.
Cf. hot ten, etc.
Cf. got hen, etc.

ŌT'EST

d: dōt'est*.
fl: flōat'est*.
gl: glōat'est*.
kw: mis-quōt'est*, quōt'est*.
m: dē-mōt'est*, prō-mōt'est*.
n: dē-nōt'est*, nōt'est*.
v: dē-vōt'est*, vōt'est*.
Plus no test, etc.

ỌT'EST

k(c): caught'est*.
n: Är'gō-naut'est*,
Jug'gẽr-naut″est*.
th: mer'ry=thought'est*, etc.
Plus saw test, etc.

OT'EST

bl: blot'test*.
d: dot'test*.

g: bē-got'test*, got'test*.
h: hot'test.
j: jot'test*.
kl: clot'test*.
l: al-lot'test*.
n: knot'test (not')*.
pl: plot'test*.
r: gȧ-rot'test*, rot'test*.
s: bē-sot'test*.
sh: shot'test*.
skw: squät'test*.
tr: trot'test*.
w: wot'test*.
y: yächt'est (yät')*, etc.
Cf. yacht test, etc.

ŌT'ETH

d: dōt'eth*.
fl: flōat'eth*.
gl: glōat'eth*.
kw: mis-quōt'eth*, quōt'eth*.
m: dē-mōt'eth*, prō-mōt'eth*.
n: dē-nōt'eth*, nōt'eth*.
v: dē-vōt'eth*, vōt'eth*.

ỌT'ETH

k(c): caught'eth*.
n: Är″gō-naut'eth*,
Jug'gẽr-naut″eth*.
th: mer'ry=thought'eth*, etc.

OT'ETH

bl: blot'teth*.
d: dot'teth*.
g: bē-got'teth*, got'teth*.
j: jot'teth*.
kl: clot'teth*.
l: al-lot'teth*.
n: knot'teth (not')*.
pl: plot'teth*.
r: gȧ-rot'teth*, rot'teth*.

(Choose only one word out of each group)

s: bē-sot'teth*.
sh: shot'teth*.
skw: squät'teth*.
tr: trot'teth*.
w: wot'teth*.
y: yächt'eth*.

QT'FUL

th: thought'ful.
Plus brought full, etc.

Ō'THÅ

kw: quō'thå.

ŌTH'ĂL

tr: bē-trōth'ăl.
Plus quoth Al, etc.

Ō'THĂM

g: Gō'thăm.
j: Jō'thăm.
Plus sloth, am, etc.

OTH'ĂM

g: Goth'ăm.
Plus wroth, am, etc.

ŌTH'EST

kl: çlōTH'est*.
l: lōaTH'est*.

ŌTH'ETH

kl: çlōTH'eth*.
l: lōaTH'eth*.

ŌTH'FUL

l: lōaTH'ful.
Plus clothe, full, etc.

ŌTH'FUL

sl: slōth'ful.
Plus growth full, etc.

OTH'FUL

r: wräth'ful.
Plus swath full, etc.

OTH'I

fr: froth'y.
m: moth'y.
Plus cloth, he, etc.

OTH'IK

g: Goth'iç, Moē"sō-goth'iç,
Os"trō-goth'iç, Viṣ"i-goth'iç.
Cf. cloth thick, etc.

ŌTH'ING

kl: çlōTH'ing.
l: lōaTH'ing.

OTH'MENT

tr: bē-troth'ment.
Plus Thoth meant, etc.

Ō'THŌ

Vowel: Ō'thō.
kl: Çlō'thō.
Plus Thoth owe *or* O, etc.

ŌT'HOOK

b: bōat'hook.
k(ç): çōat'hook.
Plus note hook, etc.
Cf. so took, etc.

Q'THORN

h: haw'thorn.
k(ç): Çaw'thorn.
Plus saw thorn, etc.

ŌTH'SŎM

l: lōaTH'sŏme.
Plus clothe some *or* sum, etc.

(Choose only one word out of each group)

QTH'ŪR

Vowel: au'thŏr.
Plus wroth, her *or* err, etc.

OTH'ŪR

b: boTH'ẽr.
f: foTH'ẽr.
p: poTH'ẽr.
Cf. fä'THẽr, rä'THẽr.

Ō'TI

Vowel: ōat'y̆.
bl: blōat'y̆.
d: dhō'ty (dō'), Dōt'y, Dōt'ey,
    dōugh'ty.
fl: flōat'y̆.
g: gōat'y̆.
k(c): Cō'ty.
l: Lō'ti.
thr: thrōat'y̆.
y: coy̆-ō'tē.
Plus quote, he, etc.
Plus no tea, etc.

QT'I

h: haught'y̆.
n: naught'y̆.
Plus caught, he, etc.
Plus saw tea, etc.

OT'I

d: dot'ty̆.
kl: clot'ty̆.
l: Lot'tie.
n: knot'ty̆ (not').
sp: spot'ty̆.
t: tot'ty̆.
Plus what he, etc.
Cf. hot tea, etc.

OT'ID

r: cȧ-rot'id, pȧ-rot'id.
Cf. ot'ed.

ŌT'IJ

d: an″ec-dōt'ăge, dōt'ăge.
fl: flōat'ăge, flōt'ăge.
Cf. quote age, etc.

OT'IJ

k(c): cot'tăge.
p: pot'tăge.
w: wät'tăge.
Cf. what age, etc.

ŌT'IK

Vowel: ō'tic.
Plus no tick, etc.

QT'IK

n: äer″ō-naut'ic, Är″gō-naut'ic,
    naut'ic.
Plus straw tick, etc.

OT'IK

Vowel: an″tī-pā″tri-ot'ic,
    chā-ot'ic, ep″i-zō-ot'ic,
    id″i-ot'ic, mac″rō-bī-ot'ic,
    ot'ic, pā″tri-ot'ic, sē″meī-ot'ic,
    zō·ot'ic.
d: an″ec-dot'ic.
dr: hī-drot'ic.
gl: ep″i-glot'ic, glot'tic.
k(c): när-cot'ic, sär-cot'ic,
    psȳ-chot'ic (sī).
kr: ȧ-crot'ic.
kw: ȧ-quät'ic.
l: añ″ky-lot'ic, cū-lot'tic,
    Nī-lot'ic, sans'⸗cū-lot'tic.
m: dē-mot'ic, en″dos-mot'ic,
    os-mot'ic, zȳ-mot'ic.
n: hē-not'ic, hyp-not'ic.
p: des-pot'ic, nē-pot'ic.
r: cȧ-rot'ic, chlō-rot'ic,
    cīr-rhot'ic (-rot'), ē-rot'ic,
    es″chä-rot'ic, neū-rot'ic,

(Choose only one word out of each group)

pȳ-rot'iç̣, sç̣lē-rot'iç̣.
s: ex-ot'iç̣ (ek-sot'), quix-ot'iç̣.
t: an"à-plot'iç̣, ap-tot'iç̣.
z: ex-ot'iç̣ (eg-zot').

ŌT'ING

b: bōat'ing, stēam'bōat"ing.
bl: blōat'ing.
d: an'eç̣-dōt"ing, dōt'ing.
fl: flōat'ing, non-flōat'ing,
   un-flōat'ing.
gl: glōat'ing, un-glōat'ing.
k(ç̣): ç̣ōat'ing, un-ç̣ōat'ing.
kw: mis-quōt'ing, quōt'ing,
   un-quōt'ing.
m: dē-mōt'ing, prō-mōt'ing.
n: dē-nōt'ing, nōt'ing,
   un-nōt'ing.
t: tōt'ing.
thr: thrōat'ing.
v: dē-vōt'ing, vōt'ing.

Q̇T'ING

n: Är'gō-nạut"ing,
   Jug'gēr-nạut"ing.
th: mer'ry=thọught'ing.

OT'ING

bl: blot'ting.
d: dot'ting.
j: jot'ting.
kl: ç̣lot'ting, un-ç̣lot'ting.
l: al-lot'ting.
n: knot'ting (not'),
   un-knot'ting, rē-knot'ting.
p: pot'ting, un-pot'ting.
pl: plot'ting, un"dēr-plot'ting,
   un-plot'ting.
r: gà-rot'ting, rot'ting.
s: bē-sot'ting, sot'ting.
skw: squät'ting.

sp: spot'ting, sun'spot"ting.
t: tot'ting.
tr: trot'ting.
y: yächt'ing.

OT'IS

gl: ep"i-glot'tis, glot'tis.

ŌT'ISH

d: dōt'ish.
g: gōat'ish.

OT'ISH

s: sot'tish.
sk(sç̣): Sç̣ot'tish.

ŌT'IST

d: an"eç̣-dōt'ist.
n: nōt'iced, un-nōt'iced.
sk(sç̣): Sç̣ōt'ist.

OT'IST

l: sanṣ=ç̣ū-lot'tist.

ŌT'IV

m: ē-mō'tive, lō"ç̣ō-mō'tive,
   mō'tive, prō-mō'tive.
v: vō'tive.

OT'KINZ

Vowel: Ot'kinṣ.
w: Wät'kins.
Plus not kin's, etc.

OT"L

b: bot'tle.
d: dot'tle.
gl: ep"i-glot'tăl, glot'tăl.
m: mot'tle.
p: pot'tle.
t: tot'tle.
thr: throt'tle.
tw: twät'tle.
w: wät'tle.
Plus hot'll, etc.

OT'LES
OT'ŎM

fāte, fär, fåst, fąll, finăl, cãre, at; mēte, prey, hẽr, met; pīne,
marīne, bĭrd, pĭn; nōte, mŏve, fǫr, atŏm, not; mōon, book;

702

(Choose only one word out of each group)

OT'LES

th: thǫught'less.
Plus brought less, etc.

OT'LES

bl: blot'less.
d: dot'less.
j: jot'less.
k(c): cot'less.
kl: clot'less.
l: lot'less.
n: knot'less (not').
p: pot'less.
r: rot'less.
s: sot'less.
sp: spot'less.
t: tot'less.
tr: trot'less.
Plus what less *or* Les, etc.

OT'LI

h: hot'ly.
m: mot'ley.
Plus not, Lee *or* lea, etc.

OT'LING

b: bot'tling
m: mot'tling
thr: throt'tling.
tw: twät'tling.
w: wät'tling.

ŌT'MĂN

b: bōat'măn.
g: gōat'măn.
Plus quote, man, etc.

OT'MĂN

Vowel: Ott'măn.
k(c): Cot'măn.
Plus got man, etc.

ŌT'MENT

m: dē-mōte'ment.
n: dē-nōte'ment.
v: dē-vōte'ment.
Plus quote meant, etc.

OT'MENT

l: al-lot'ment.
s: bē-sot'ment.
Plus what meant, etc.

OT'NES

h: hot'ness.
hw: whät'ness.

Ō'TŌ

Vowel: Kī-ō'tō.
f: phō'tō (fō').
g: få-gōt'tō.
s: Dē Sō'tō.
t: in tō'tō.
v: di-vō'tō, ex vō'tō.
Plus note owe *or* O, etc.
Plus so toe, etc.

OT'Ō

Vowel: ot'tō.
bl: blot'tō.
d: ri-dot'tō.
gr: grot'tō.
k(c): stac-cä'tō.
l: lot'tō.
m: mot'tō.
s: ri-sot'tō.
w: Wat'teau.
Plus not owe *or* O, etc.

OT'ŎM

b: bot'tŏm.
Plus got 'em, etc.
Cf. hot tum, etc.

(Choose only one word out of each group)

Ō′TŎN

Vowel: ōat′en.
kr: Çrō′tŏn.
pr: prō′ton.
Plus float on *or* an, etc.
Plus no ton *or* tun, etc.
Plus taught an, etc.

Ǫ′TŎN

l: Law′tŏn.
r: Raw′tŏn.
Plus claw ton *or* tun, etc.

OT′ŎN

gr: Grot′ŏn.
k(ç): çot′tŏn.
Cf. ot′en.

OT′REL

d: dot′trel.
k(ç): Çot′trell.

OT′SI

m: Mot′sie.
t: hot′sy=tot′sy.
Plus what see, etc.

OTS′MĂN

sk(sç): Sçots′măn.
y: yăchts′măn.
Plus blots, man, etc.

OT′SŎN

w: Wät′sŏn.
Plus what son *or* sun, etc.

Ō′TUM

kw: quō′tum.
skr(sçr): scrō′tum.
t: tee-tōt′um.
Plus note ′em, etc.

Ǫ′TUM

Vowel: ąu′tumn.
Plus caught ′em, etc.

ŌT′ŪR

b: bōat′ēr.
bl: blōat′ēr.
d: dot′ēr.
fl: flōat′ēr.
gl: glōat′ēr.
k(ç): çōat′ēr, frock çōat′ēr.
kw: mis-quōt′ēr, quōt′ēr.
m: dē-mōt′ēr, hȳ″drō-mōt′ŏr,
lō″çō-mōt′ŏr, mag-nēt″ō-mōt′ŏr,
mōt′ŏr, prō-mōt′ēr, pųl′mō-tŏr,
rōt′ō-mō″tŏr, trī′mōt″ŏr,
vas′ō-mō″tŏr.
n: dē-nōt′ēr, nōt′ēr.
r: rōt′ŏr.
sk(sç): sçōt′ēr.
t: tōt′ēr.
v: dē-vōt′ēr, fag′ŏt vōt′ēr,
vōt′ēr.
Plus devote her *or* err, etc.

ǪT′ŪR

d: dąught′ēr.
sl: sląught′ēr.
w: back′wąt″ēr, fīre′wąt″ēr,
fizz wąt′ēr, gig′gle wąt′ēr,
milk′=and=wąt′ēr, sō′dà wąt′ēr.
wąt′ēr.
Plus caught her *or* err, etc.

OT′ŪR

Vowel: ot′tăr, ot′tēr.
bl: blot′tēr.
d: dot′tēr.
h: hot′tēr.
j: jot′tēr.
k(ç): çot′tăr, çot′tēr.

(Choose only one word out of each group)

kl: ̣clot'tẽr.

n: knot'tẽr (not'), un-knot'tẽr.

p: pot'tẽr.

pl: ̣com-plot'tẽr, plot'tẽr,
un"dẽr-plot'tẽr, un-plot'tẽr.

r: gȧ-rot'tẽr, rot'tẽr.

skw: squät'tẽr.

sp: spot'tẽr.

sw: swät'tẽr.

t: tot'tẽr.

tr: bog'trot"tẽr, glōbe'trot"tẽr,
trot'tẽr.

y: yächt'ẽr.

Plus got her *or* err, etc.

ŌT'US

kr: mȧ-c̣rō'tous.

l: lō'tus.

n: G̣ym-nō'tus.

Plus quote us, etc.

OT'WĀ

Vowel: Ot'wāy.

Plus what way, etc.

OU'ĂL

v: ȧ-vow'ăl, dis"ȧ-vow'ăl.

Cf. ou'el.

Plus plough, Al, etc.

OU'ĂN

g: gow'ăn, Ṃc-Gow'ăn.

r: row'ăn, row'en.

Plus allow an, etc.

OU'ANS

l: al-low'ănce, dis"al-low'ănce.

v: ȧ-vow'ănce, dis"ȧ-vow'ănce.

Plus plough ants *or* aunts, etc.

OU'ĂRD

h: How'ărd.

k: c̣ow'ărd.

Cf. ou'ũrd.

OUCH'EST

k(c̣): c̣ouch'est*.

kr: c̣rouch'est*.

p: pouch'est*.

v: ȧ-vouch'est*, vouch'est*.

Plus allow chest, etc.

OUCH'ETH

k(c̣): c̣ouch'eth*.

kr: c̣rouch'eth*.

p: pouch'eth*.

v: ȧ-vouch'eth*, vouch'eth*.

OUCH'ING

gr: grouch'ing.

k(c̣): c̣ouch'ing.

kr: c̣rouch'ing.

p: pouch'ing.

sl: slouch'ing.

v: ȧ-vouch'ing, vouch'ing.

OUCH'ŨR

g: Gouch'ẽr.

gr: grouch'ẽr.

k(c̣): c̣ouch'ẽr.

kr: c̣rouch'ẽr.

p: pouch'ẽr.

sl: slouch'ẽr.

v: ȧ-vouch'ẽr, vouch'ẽr.

Plus avouch her *or* err, etc.

OU'DÅ

h: how'dȧh ('dȧ).

Plus crowd a, etc.

(Choose only one word out of each group)

OUD'ED

kl: bē-çloud'ed, çloud'ed,
ō"vẽr-çloud'ed, un"bē-çloud'ed,
un-çloud'ed.
kr: çrow'ded, ō"vẽr-çrow'ded,
un"dẽr-çrow'ded.
shr: en-shroud'ed, shroud'ed,
un-shroud'ed.
Plus vow dead, etc.
Plus vowed, Ed, etc.
Cf. scow did, etc.

OUD'EST

bl: bē-çloud'est*, çloud'est*,
ō"vẽr-çloud'est*.
kr: çrowd'est*, ō"vẽr-çrowd'est*.
l: loud'est.
pr: proud'est.
shr: en-shroud'est*,
shroud'est*.

OUD'ETH

bl: bē-çloud'eth*, çloud'eth*,
ō"vẽr-çloud'eth*.
kr: çrowd'eth*,
ō"vẽr-çrow'deth*.
shr: en-shroud'eth*,
shroud'eth*.
Plus vow death, etc.

OUD'I

d: dow'dy, pan-dow'dy.
g: Gou'dy.
h: how'die, how'dy.
kl: çloud'y, un-çloud'y.
kr: çrowd'y.
pr: proud'y.
r: row'dy.
shr: shroud'y.
Cf. sụm'mä çụm laud'ē.
Plus vowed he, etc.
Plus vow Dee or D, etc.

OUD'ING

kl: bē-çloud'ing, çloud'ing,
ō"vẽr-çloud'ing.
kr: çrowd'ing, ō"vẽr-çrowd'ing.
shr: bē-shroud'ing,
en-shroud'ing, shroud'ing,
un-shroud'ing.

OUD'ISH

l: loud'ish.
pr: proud'ish.
Plus allow dish, etc.

OUD'LI

l: loud'ly.
pr: proud'ly.
Plus vowed, Lee or lea, etc.

OUD'NES

l: loud'ness.
pr: proud'ness.

OUD'ŨR

ch: çlam chow'dẽr, chow'dẽr.
kr: çrowd'ẽr.
l: loud'ẽr.
p: bāk'ing pow'dẽr, bē-pow'dẽr,
pow'dẽr,
seid'litz pow'dẽr (sed').
pr: proud'ẽr.
Plus allowed her or err, etc.

OU'EL

b: bow'el, em-bow'el.
d: dow'el.
h: How'ell.
p: Pow'ell.
pr: Prow'ell.
r: row'el.
t: tow'el.
tr: trow'el.

OU'ES
OUL'ING   fāte, fär, fàst, fạll, finăl, cãre, at; mēte, prey, hẽr, met; pīne,
marïne, bĭrd, pin; nōte, mŏve, fọr, atŏm, not; mọọn, book;   **706**

(Choose only one word out of each group)

v: vow'el.
Cf. ou'ăl.
Cf. plough will, etc.
Cf. plough well, etc.

OU'ES

pr: prow'ess.
Cf. now, West, etc.

OU'EST

b: bow'est*.
d: en-dow'est*.
k(c): cow'est*.
l: al-low'est*, dis"al-low'est*.
pl: plough'est*.
v: à-vow'est*, dis"à-vow'est*,
vow'est*.
Cf. now west, etc.

OU'ET

h: How'ett.
j: Jow'ett.
Cf. plough wet, etc.
Cf. plough it, etc.

OU'ETH

b: bow'eth*.
d: en-dow'eth*.
k(c): cow'eth*.
l: al-low'eth*, dis"al-low'eth*.
pl: plough'eth*.
v: à-vow'eth*, dis"à-vow'eth*,
vow'eth*.

OU'HAND

k(c): cow'hand.
pl: plough'hand.
Plus vow hand, etc.

OU'I

d: Dow'ie.
z: zow'ie.
Plus now he, etc.
Plus now we, etc.

OU'ING

b: bow'ing.
d: en-dow'ing.
k(c): cow'ing.
l: al-low'ing, dis"al-low'ing.
pl: plough'ing, plow'ing.
r: row'ing.
v: à-vow'ing, dis"à-vow'ing,
vow'ing.

OUL'EST

f: foul'est.
gr: growl'est*.
h: howl'est*.
pr: prowl'est*.
sk(sc): scowl'est*.
Plus now, lest, etc.

OUL'ET

Vowel: owl'et.
h: howl'et*.
Plus now let *or* Lett, etc.
Cf. prowl it, etc.

OUL'ETH

gr: growl'eth*.
h: howl'eth*.
pr: prowl'eth*.
sk(sc): scowl'eth*.

OU'LI

k(c): Cow'ley.
kr: Crow'ley.
p: Pow'ley.
r: Row'ley.
Plus bow, Lee *or* lea, etc.

OUL'ING

f: foul'ing, fowl'ing.
gr: growl'ing.
h: howl'ing.
pr: prowl'ing.
sk(sc): scowl'ing.

(Choose only one word out of each group)

OUL'ISH

Vowel: owl'ish.
f: foul'ish.

OUL'UR

f: foul'ẽr, fow'lẽr.
gr: grow'lẽr.
h: howl'ẽr.
pr: prowl'ẽr.
sk(sç): sçowl'ẽr.
y: yowl'ẽr.
Plus howl her *or* err, etc.

OU'MENT

d: en-dow'ment.
v: à-vow'ment.
Plus plough meant, etc.

OUN'DED

b: à-boun'ded, boun'ded,
rē-boun'ded,
sū″pēr-à-boun'ded,
un-boun'ded.
d: rē-doun'ded.
dr: "drown'ded".
f: çon-foun'ded, dum-foun'ded,
foun'ded, un-foun'ded,
well'⸗foun'ded.
gr: groun'ded, un-groun'ded.
h: houn'ded.
m: moun'ded.
p: çom-poun'ded, ex-poun'ded,
im-poun'ded, poun'ded,
prō-poun'ded.
r: roun'ded, sūr-roun'ded.
s: soun'ded, un-soun'ded.
t: as-toun'ded.
w: woun'ded.
z: rē-ṣoun'ded.
Plus clown dead, etc.
Cf. clown did, etc.
Plus clowned, Ed, etc.

OUN'DEL

r: roun'del.
Plus down dell, etc.
Plus sound L *or* el, etc.

OUN'DEN

b: boun'den.
Plus clown den, etc.

OUN'DEST

b: à-boun'dest*, boun'dest*,
rē-boun'dest*,
sū″pēr-à-boun'dest*.
f: çon-foun'dest*, foun'dest*,
prō-foun'dest.
gr: groun'dest*.
h: houn'dest*.
p: çom-poun'dest*,
ex-poun'dest*, im-poun'dest*,
poun'dest*, prō-poun'dest*.
r: roun'dest, sūr-roun'dest*.
s: soun'dest.
t: as-toun'dest*.
w: woun'dest*.
z: rē-ṣoun'dest*.

OUN'DETH

b: à-boun'deth*, boun'deth*,
rē-boun'deth*,
sū″pēr-à-boun'deth*.
f: çon-foun'deth*, foun'deth*.
gr: groun'deth*.
h: houn'deth*.
p: çom-poun'deth*,
ex-poun'deth*,
im-poun'deth*, poun'deth*,
prō-poun'deth*.
r: roun'deth*, sūr-roun'deth*.
s: soun'deth*.
t: as-toun'deth*.

(Choose only one word out of each group)

w: woun'deth*.
z: rē-ṣoun'deth*.
Plus go down, death, etc.

OUN'DIJ

gr: groun'dăġe.
p: poun'dăġe.
s: soun'dăġe.
Cf. clowned age, etc.

OUN'DING

b: à-boun'ding, boun'ding,
  rē-boun'ding,
  sū″pĕr-à-boun'ding,
  un-boun'ding.
d: rē-doun'ding.
f: çon-foun'ding,
  dum-foun'ding, foun'ding.
gr: groun'ding.
h: houn'ding.
p: çom-poun'ding,
  ex-poun'ding, im-poun'ding,
  poun'ding, prō-poun'ding.
r: roun'ding, sūr-roun'ding.
s: big′=soun'ding,
  hīgh′=soun'ding (hī′), soun'ding.
t: as-toun'ding.
w: woun'ding.
z: rē-ṣoun'ding.

OUND'LES

b: bound'less.
gr: ground'less.
s: sound'less.
Plus crowned less or Les, etc.

OUND'LI

f: prō-found'ly.
r: round'ly.
s: sound'ly, un-sound'ly.
Plus crowned, Lee or lea, etc.

OUND'LING

f: found'ling.
gr: ground'ling.

OUND'NES

f: prō-found'ness.
r: round'ness.
s: sound'ness, un-sound'ness.

OUN'DREL

sk(sç): sçoun'drel.

OUN'DRY

f: foun'dry.

OUN'DŪR

b: boun'dĕr, rē-boun'dĕr.
f: çon-foun'dĕr,
  dum-foun'dĕr, foun'dĕr,
  ïr'on foun'dĕr (ï'ĕrn),
  prō-foun'dĕr, tȳpe foun'dĕr.
fl: floun'dĕr.
h: houn'dĕr.
p: çom-poun'dĕr, ex-poun'dĕr,
  fōur′=poun″dĕr, etc.,
  im-poun'dĕr, poun'dĕr,
  prō-poun'dĕr.
r: roun'dĕr, sūr-roun'dĕr.
s: soun'dĕr.
t: as-toun'dĕr.
z: rē-ṣoun'dĕr.
Plus bound her or err, etc.

OUN'EST

br: brown'est.
dr: drown'est*.
fr: frown'est*.
kr: çrown'est*.
Plus now nest, etc.

(Choose only one word out of each group)

OUN'ETH

br: brown'eth*.
dr: drown'eth*.
fr: frown'eth*.
kr: Çrown'eth*.

OUN'I

br: brown'ie, brown'i.
d: down'y.
fr: frown'y.
kl: çlown'y.
t: town'y.
Plus down, he, etc.

OUN'ING

br: brown'ing.
d: down'ing.
dr: drown'ing.
fr: frown'ing.
g: gown'ing, un-gown'ing.
kl: çlown'ing, un-çlown'ing.
kr: çrown'ing, dis-çrown'ing,
 un-çrown'ing.
t: in-town'ing.

OUN'ISH

br: brown'ish.
fr: frown'ish.
kl: çlown'ish.

OUN'JEST

l: loun'ġest*.
Plus clown jest, etc.

OUN'JETH

l: loun'ġeth*.

OUN'JING

l: loun'ġing.

OUN'JŬR

l: loun'ġẽr.

OUN'LES

fr: frown'less.
g: gown'less.
kr: çrown'less.
Plus down, Les or less, etc.

OUN'SEST

b: boun'cest*.
fl: floun'cest*.
n: an-noun'cest*,
 dē-noun'cest*, prō-noun'cest*,
 rē-noun'cest*.
p: poun'cest*.

OUN'SETH

b: boun'seth*.
fl: floun'ceth*.
n: an-noun'ceth*,
 dē-noun'ceth*, prō-noun'ceth*,
 rē-noun'ceth*.
p: poun'ceth*.
Plus down, Seth, etc.

OUN'SEZ

Vowel: oun'çeṣ.
b: boun'çeṣ.
fl: floun'çeṣ.
n: an-noun'çeṣ, dē-noun'çeṣ,
 prō-noun'çeṣ, rē-noun'çeṣ.
p: poun'çeṣ.
tr: troun'çeṣ.
Plus clown says, etc.
Plus bounce, Ez, etc.

OUN'SING

b: boun'çing.
fl: floun'çing.

(Choose only one word out of each group)

n: an-noun'cing, dē-noun'cing,
prō-noun'cing, rē-noun'cing.
p: poun'cing.
tr: troun'cing.
Plus clown sing, etc.

OUNS'MENT

n: an-nounce'ment,
dē-nounce'ment,
prō-nounce'ment,
rē-nounce'ment.
Plus bounce meant, etc.

OUN'SŪR

b: boun'cẽr.
fl: floun'cẽr.
n: an-noun'cẽr, dē-noun'cẽr,
prō-noun'cẽr, rē-noun'cẽr.
p: poun'cẽr.
tr: troun'cẽr.
Plus down, sir, etc.
Plus counts err *or* her, etc.

OUN'TED

k(c̲): ac̲-c̲oun'ted, c̲oun'ted,
dis-c̲oun'ted, mis-c̲oun'ted,
rē-c̲oun'ted, un-c̲oun'ted,
un"rē-c̲oun'ted.
m: à-moun'ted, dis-moun'ted,
moun'ted, rē-moun'ted,
sũr-moun'ted, un-moun'ted.
Plus down, Ted, etc.
Plus mount, Ed, etc.

OUN'TES

k(c̲): c̲oun'tess.
Plus down, Tess, etc.

OUN'TEST

k(c̲): ac̲-c̲oun'test*, c̲oun'test*,
dis-c̲oun'test*, mis-c̲oun'test*,
rē-c̲oun'test*.

m: à-moun'test*,
dis-moun'test*, moun'test*,
rē-moun'test*,
sũr-moun'test*.
Plus clown test, etc.

OUN'TETH

k(c̲): ac̲-c̲oun'teth*, c̲oun'teth*,
dis-c̲oun'teth*, mis-c̲oun'teth*,
rē-c̲oun'teth*.
m: à-moun'teth*,
dis-moun'teth*, moun'teth*,
rē-moun'teth*, sũr-moun'teth*.

OUN'TI

b: boun'ty.
k(c̲): c̲oun'ty, vīs'c̲oun"ty (vī').
m: moun'ty.
Plus mount, he, etc.
Plus down tea, etc.

OUN'TIN

f: foun'tain.
m: c̲at"à-moun'tain, moun'tain.
Plus mount in, etc.
Plus down tin, etc.

OUN'TING

k(c̲): ac̲-c̲oun'ting, c̲oun'ting,
dis-c̲oun'ting, mis-c̲oun'ting,
rē-c̲oun'ting.
m: à-moun'ting, dis-moun'ting,
moun'ting, rē-moun'ting,
sũr-moun'ting.

OUN'TŪR

k(c̲): ac̲-c̲oun'tẽr, c̲oun'tẽr,
dis-c̲oun'tẽr, en-c̲oun'tẽr,
rē-c̲oun'tẽr, rē"en-c̲oun'tẽr.
m: moun'tẽr, rē-moun'tẽr,
sũr-moun'tẽr.
Plus mount her *or* err, etc.

(Choose only one word out of each group)

OUN′ŪR

br: brown′ẽr.
dr: drown′ẽr.
fr: frown′ẽr.
kr: crown′ẽr.
Plus down her *or* err, etc.

OUN′WĂRD

d: down′wărd.
t: town′wărd.
Plus gown ward, etc.

OUNZ′MĂN

g: gownş′măn.
t: townş′măn.
Plus downs man, etc.

Ō′ŪR

Vowel: ōw′ẽr.
bl: blōw′ẽr, glass blōw′ẽr.
fl: flōw′ẽr.
g: fōre-gō′ẽr, gō′ẽr, out′gō-ẽr, un″dẽr-gō′ẽr.
gl: glōw′ẽr.
gr: flow′ẽr grōw′ẽr, grōw′ẽr, wīne grōw′ẽr.
h: hō′ẽr.
l: lōw′ẽr.
m: mōw′ẽr.
n: fōre-knōw′ẽr, knōw′ẽr.
s: sew′ẽr (sō′), sōw′ẽr.
sh: fōre-shōw′ẽr, shōw′ẽr.
sl: slōw′ẽr.
st: bē-stōw′ẽr, stōw′ẽr.
t: tōw′ẽr.
thr: ō″vẽr-throw′ẽr, throw′ẽr.
Plus know her *or* err, etc.

Ọ′ŪR

Vowel: ō″vẽr-aw′ẽr.
dr: draw′ẽr, wīre draw′ẽr, with-draw′ẽr.

f: guf-faw′ẽr.
j: "jaw′ẽr".
k(ç): çaw′ẽr.
kl: çlaw′ẽr.
n: gnaw′ẽr (naw′).
p: paw′ẽr.
r: raw′ẽr.
s: saw′ẽr.
t: taw′ẽr.
Plus draw her *or* err, etc.

Ō′ŪRD, Ō′ĂRD

l: lōw′ẽred.
t: tō′wărd, un-tō′wărd.
Cf. snow heard, or herd, etc.
Cf. so ward, etc.

OUR′EST

fl: dē-flower′est*.
s: sour′est.
sk(sç): bē-sçour′est*, sçour′est*.
b: dē-vour′est*.
Plus now rest, etc.

OUR′ETH

fl: dē-flower′eth*.
s: sour′eth*.
sk(sç): bē-sçour′eth*, sçour′eth*.
v: dē-vour′eth*.

OUR′I

d: dow′ry.
fl: flour′y, flower′y.
h: hou′ri.
k(ç): çow′rie.
v: à-vow′ry.
Cf. ou′ūr-i.
Plus shower, he, etc.

OUR′ING

fl: dē-flower′ing, flour′ing.
s: sour′ing.

(Choose only one word out of each group)

sk(sc): bē-scour'ing,
off'-scour'ing, scour'ing.
v: dē-vour'ing.
Plus now ring, or wring, etc.
Cf. ou'ūr-ing.

OUR'LI

Vowel: hour'ly.
s: sour'ly.
Plus flower, Lee *or* lea, etc.

OUR'NES

s: sour'ness.

OUR'ŪR

fl: dē-flower'ẽr.
s: sour'ẽr.
sk(sc): scour'ẽr.
v: dē-vour'ẽr.
Plus sour her *or* err, etc.

OU'SŎN

d: Dow'sŏn.
Plus how, son *or* sun, etc.

OUS'TING

Vowel: ous'ting.

OUT'ED

Vowel: out'ed.
b: bout'ed.
d: doubt'ed, mis-doubt'ed,
rē-doubt'ed, un-doubt'ed.
fl: flout'ed.
g: gout'ed.
gr: grout'ed.
kl: clout'ed.
kr: sau'ẽr-kraut"ed.
n: knout'ed (nout').
p: pout'ed.
sh: shout'ed.

sk(sc): scout'ed.
sn: snout'ed.
sp: spout'ed.
spr: sprout'ed, rē-sprout'ed,
un-sprout'ed.
t: tout'ed.
tr: trout'ed.
Plus lout, Ed, etc.
Plus now, Ted, etc.

OUT'EST

d: doubt'est*.
fl: flout'est*.
kl: clout'est*.
p: pout'est*.
sh: shout'est*.
sk(sc): scout'est*.
sp: spout'est*.
spr: sprout'est*.
st: stout'est.
v: dē-vout'est.
Plus now test, etc.

OUT'ETH

d: doubt'eth*.
fl: flout'eth*.
kl: clout'eth*.
p: pout'eth*.
sh: shout'eth*.
sk(sc): scout'eth*.
sp: spout'eth*.
spr: sprout'eth*.

OUT'I

d: dought'y.
dr: drought'y.
g: gout'y.
gr: grout'y.
l: lout'y.
m: "mought'y".
p: pout'y.
sn: snout'y.

(Choose only one word out of each group)

t: tout'y.
Plus, out, he, etc.
Plus now tea, etc.

OUT'ING

Vowel: out'ing.
b: bout'ing.
d: doubt'ing, un-doubt'ing.
fl: flout'ing.
gr: grout'ing.
kl: çlout'ing.
kr: sau'ẽr-kraut"ing.
l: lout'ing.
n: knout'ing (nout').
p: pout'ing.
r: rout'ing.
sh: bē-shout'ing, shout'ing.
sk(sç): sçout'ing.
sp: bē-spout'ing, spout'ing.
spr: bē-sprout'ing,
  rē-sprout'ing, sprout'ing,
  un-sprout'ing.
t: tout'ing.
tr: trout'ing.

OUT'LET

Vowel: out'let.
tr: trout'let.
Plus clout let or Lett, etc.

OUT'LI

st: stout'ly.
v: dē-vout'ly.
Plus shout, Lee or lea, etc.

OUT'NES

st: stout'ness.
v: dē-vout'ness.

OUT'ŪR

Vowel: down'=and=out'ẽr,
  out'=and=out'ẽr, out'ẽr.
b: bout'ẽr.

d: doubt'ẽr, non"doubt'ẽr.
fl: flout'ẽr.
j: jowt'ẽr.
kl: çlout'ẽr.
kr: sau'ẽr-kraut"ẽr.
n: knout'ẽr (nout').
p: pout'ẽr.
r: rout'ẽr.
sh: shout'ẽr.
sk(sç): sçout'ẽr.
sp: spout'ẽr.
spr: sprout'ẽr.
st: stout'ẽr.
t: tout'ẽr.
v: dē-vout'ẽr.
w: Wout'ẽr.
Plus clout her or err, etc.

OU'ŪR

b: bau'ẽr, bow'ẽr, em-bow'ẽr,
  im-bow'ẽr.
br: Brow'ẽr.
d: dow'ẽr, en-dow'ẽr.
fl: bē-flow'ẽr, çau'li-flow"ẽr,
  dāy flow'ẽr, dē-flow'ẽr,
  en-flow'ẽr, flow'ẽr,
  gil'li-flow"ẽr, Māy'flow"ẽr,
  moon'flow"ẽr,
  pas'sion flow'ẽr (pash'ŏn),
  sun'flow-ẽr, wall'flow-ẽr,
  wind'flow-ẽr.
g: Gow'ẽr.
gl: glow'ẽr.
k(ç): çow'ẽr.
l: al-low'ẽr, low'ẽr.
p: çan'dle-pow"ẽr, em-pow'ẽr,
  horse'pow-ẽr, man'pow-ẽr,
  ō"vẽr-pow'ẽr, pow'ẽr,
  wat'ẽr-pow"ẽr.
pl: plough'ẽr, plow'ẽr.
r: row'ẽr.

OU'ŪRD
OUZ'ING

fāte, fär, fåst, fạll, finăl, cãre, at; mēte, prey, hẽr, met; pīne,
marïne, bĭrd, pin; nōte, mŏve, fọr, atŏm, not; mọọn, book;

714

(Choose only one word out of each group)

sh: show'ẽr, thun'dẽr-show"ẽr.
t: bēa'çon tow'ẽr,
chŭrch'tow-ẽr, fīre tow'ẽr,
ō"vẽr-tow'ẽr, tow'ẽr,
wätch'tow-ẽr.
v: à-vow'ẽr, vow'ẽr.
Cf. our.
Plus endow her *or* err, etc.

OU'ŪRD

sh: show'ẽred, un-show'ẽred.
t: tow'ẽred, un-tow'ẽred.
Plus ou'ūr+ed.

OU'ŪRZ

p: Pow'ẽrṣ.
Plus ou'ūr+s.

OU'WOU

b: bow'wow.
p: pow'wow.
w: wow wow.
Plus now wow, etc.

OU'ZĂL, OU'ZEL, OU'Z'L

Vowel: ou'ṣel.
h: hou'ṣel.
r: à-rou'ṣăl, çà-rou'ṣăl.
sp: ē-spou'ṣăl, spou'ṣăl.
t: tou'ṣle.
Plus drowse'll, etc.

OU'ZĂND

th: thou'ṣănd.
Plus rouse and, etc.

OUZ'EST

b: bouṣ'est*.
br: browṣ'est*.
dr: drowṣ'est*.
h: un-houṣ'est*.

r: à-rouṣ'est*, çà-rouṣ'est*.
rouṣ'est*, up-rouṣ'est*.
sp: ē-spouṣ'est*.

OUZ'ETH

b: bouṣ'eth*.
br: browṣ'eth*.
dr: drowṣ'eth*.
h: un-houṣ'eth*.
r: à-rouṣ'eth*, çà-rouṣ'eth*,
rouṣ'eth*.
up-rouṣ'eth*.
sp: ē-spouṣ'eth*.

OUZ'EṢ

bl: blouṣ'eṣ.
br: browṣ'eṣ.
h: houṣ'eṣ.
r: à-rouṣ'eṣ, çà-rouṣ'eṣ,
rouṣ'eṣ.
sp: ē-spouṣ'eṣ, spouṣ'eṣ.
Cf. browse is, etc.

OUZ'I

b: bow'ṣie.
bl: blouṣ'y.
dr: drowz'y.
fr: frowz'y.
l: louṣ'y.
m: mouṣ'y.
Plus allows he, etc.
Plus now Z *or* Zee, etc.

OUZ'IJ

h: houṣ'ăġe.
sp: ē-spouṣ'ăġe, spouṣ'ăġe.
Cf. blouse age, etc.

OUZ'ING

b: bouz'ing.
bl: blouṣ'ing.
br: browṣ'ing.

(Choose only one word out of each group)

h: hous̟′ing.
r: a̍-rous̟′ing, ça̍-rous̟′ing,
rous̟′ing.

OUZ′ŪR

b: bouz′ēr.
br: brows̟′ēr.
h: hous̟′ēr.
m: mau′s̟ēr, mous̟′ēr.
r: a̍-rous̟′ēr, rous̟′ēr.
shn: şchnau′zēr.
t: Tows̟′ēr.
tr: trous̟′ēr.
y: yow′zēr.
Plus rouse her *or* err, etc.

OUZ′ŪRZ

tr: trous̟′ērs̟.
Plus ouz′ūr+s.

Ō′VȦ

h: Jē-hō′vȧh.
n: Ça-nō′va, Ças-sȧ-nō′vȧ,
nō′va, Vil′la Nō′vȧ.
Plus clove a, etc.

Ō′VĂL

Vowel: ō′văl.
Plus rove, Al, etc.

OV′EL

gr: grov′el.
h: hov′el.
n: nov′el.
Plus of′ll, etc.

ŌV′EN

h: hōv′en.
k: Dē Kōv′en.
kl: c̲lōv′en, un-c̲lōv′en.
w: in″tēr-wōv′en, in-wōv′en,
wōv′en.
Cf. clove hen, etc.

ŌV′I

ch: an-chō′vy.
gr: grōv′y.
k(c̲): c̲ōv′y.
Plus clove, he, etc.

Ō′VĪN

Vowel: ō′vīne.
b: bō′vīne.
Plus no vine, etc.

ŌV′ING

r: rōv′ing.
shr: shrōv′ing.

Ō′VŌ

Vowel: ab ō′vō.
n: dē nō′vō.
Plus clove owe *or* O, etc.

ŌV′ŪR

Vowel: flop′ō-vēr,
hälf⸗sēas̟⸗ō′vēr (häf),
mōre-ō′vēr, ō′vēr, pu̧sh′ō-vēr,
wa̧lk′ō-vēr (wa̧k′).
d: Dōv′ēr.
dr: drōv′ēr.
kl: c̲lōv′ēr, sweet c̲lōv′ēr.
pl: plōv′ēr.
r: rōv′ēr, sēa rōv′ēr.
st: stōv′ēr.
tr: trōv′ēr.
Plus drove her *or* err, etc.

OV′ŪRB

pr: prov′ērb.
Cf. Slav herb, etc.

ŌV′ŪRZ

t: es-tōv′ērs̟.
Plus ōv′ūr+s.

Ō'WĂRD
ŌZ'ETH

fāte, fär, fȧst, fạll, finăl, cãre, at; mēte, prey, hẽr, met; pīne,
marïne, bîrd, pin; nōte, mŏve, fọr, atŏm, not; mọọn, book; **710**

(Choose only one word out of each group)

Ō'WĂRD

fr: frō'wărd.
Plus go, ward, etc.
Cf. toward.

Ō'WHÃR

n: nō'where ('hwãr).
Plus go where, etc.

Ō'YEZ

Vowel: ō'yez.
Plus go, "yez," etc.

Ō'YŨR

Vowel: ō'yẽr.
b: bōw'yẽr.

Ọ'YUR

l: law'yẽr.
s: saw'yẽr, top″saw″yẽr.

Ō'ZÀ

n: Spi-nōz'ȧ.
r: Rōṣ'ȧ.
Plus glows a, etc.

ŌZ'ĂL

p: des-pō'ṣal*, dis-pōṣ'ăl,
in″tẽr-pōṣ'ăl, op-pōṣ'ăl,
prē″sup-pōṣ'ăl, rē-pōṣ'ăl,
sup-pōṣ'ăl, trans-pōṣ'ăl.
r: rōṣ'ăl.
Plus knows, Al, etc.

ŌZ'BUD

r: rōṣe'bud.
Plus nose bud, etc.

ŌZ'DĪV

n: nōṣe'dīve.
Plus foes, dive, etc.

ŌZ'EN

ch: chōṣ'en, fōre-chōṣ'en.
fr: frōz'en.
h: hōṣ'en*.
p: Pōṣ'en.
r: rōṣ'en*.
skw: "squōz'en".

OZ'ENJ

l: loz'enġe.

ŌZ'EST

d: dōz'est*.
kl: c̣lōṣ'est*, dis-c̣lōṣ'est*,
en-c̣lōṣ'est*, in-c̣lōṣ'est*.
p: c̣om-pōṣ'est*,
dē″c̣om-pōṣ'est*, dē-pōṣ'est*,
dis″c̣om-pōṣ'est*, dis-pōṣ'est*,
ex-pōṣ'est*, in″tẽr-pōṣ'est*,
jux″tȧ-pōṣ'est*, op-pōṣ'est*,
pōṣ'est*, prē″sup-pōṣ'est*,
prō-pōṣ'est*, rē″c̣om-pōṣ'est*,
rē″im-pōṣ'est*, rē-pōṣ'est*,
sū″pẽr-im-pōṣ'est*, sup-pōṣ'est*,
trans-pōṣ'est*.
Plus no zest, etc.

ŌZ'ETH

d: dōz'eth*.
kl: c̣lōṣ'eth*, dis-c̣lōṣ'eth*,
en-c̣lōṣ'eth*, in-c̣lōṣ'eth*.
p: c̣om-pōṣ'eth*,
dē″c̣om-pōṣ'eth*, dē-pōṣ'eth*,
dis″c̣om-pōṣ'eth*, dis-pōṣ'eth*,
ex-pōṣ'eth*, in″tẽr-pōṣ'eth*,
jux″tȧ-pōṣ'eth*, op-pōṣ'eth*,
prē″sup-pōṣ'eth*, prō'pōṣ'eth*,
rē″c̣om-pōṣ'eth*,
rē″im-pōṣ'eth*, rē-pōṣ'eth*,
sū″pẽr-im-pōṣ'eth*,
sup-pōṣ'eth*, trans-pōṣ'eth*.

(Choose only one word out of each group)

ŌZ'EṢ

ch: chōṣ'eṣ.
d: dōz'eṣ.
gl: glōz'eṣ.
kl: c̣lōṣ'eṣ, dis-c̣lōṣ'eṣ, en-c̣lōṣ'eṣ, fōre-c̣lōṣ'eṣ, in-c̣lōṣ'eṣ, un-c̣lōṣ'eṣ.
m: Mōṣ'eṣ.
n: nōṣ'eṣ.
p: c̣om-pōṣ'eṣ, dē″c̣om-pōṣ'eṣ, dē-pōṣ'eṣ, dis″c̣om-pōṣ'eṣ, dis-pōṣ'eṣ, ex-pōṣ'eṣ, im-pōṣ'eṣ, in″dis-pōṣ'eṣ, in″tēr-pōṣ'eṣ, jux″tȧ-pōṣ'eṣ, op-pōṣ'eṣ, pōṣ'eṣ, prē″dis-pōṣ'eṣ, prē″sup-pōṣ'eṣ, prō-pōṣ'eṣ, rē″c̣om-pōṣ'eṣ, rē″im-pōṣ'eṣ, rē-pōṣ'eṣ, sū″pēr-im-pōṣ'eṣ, sū″pēr-pōṣ'eṣ, sup-pōṣ'eṣ, trans-pōṣ'eṣ.
r: bram'ble rōṣ'eṣ, dam'ȧsk rōṣ'eṣ, moss rōṣ'eṣ, rōṣ'eṣ, tūbe'rōṣ-eṣ, wīld rōṣ'eṣ.
Cf. nose is, etc.
Plus Joe says, etc.

OZ'EZ

g: gạuz'eṣ.
k(c̣): c̣ạuṣ'eṣ.
kl: c̣lạuṣ'eṣ.
p: pạuṣ'eṣ.
v: vạṣ'eṣ.
Cf. gauze is, etc.
Plus maw says, etc.

ŌZ'GĀ

n: nōse'gāy.
Plus rose gay, etc.

Ō'ZHĂN

br: am-brō'ṣiăn.
Cf. ō'zi-ăn, etc.

Ō'ZHUN

pl: ex-plō'ṣion, im-plō'ṣion.
r: c̣or-rō'ṣion, ē-rō'ṣion.
Cf. ō'zi-ăn, etc.

Ō'ZHŨR

Vowel: ō'ṣiĕr.
d: Dō'ziĕr.
h: hōṣ'iĕr.
kr: c̣rōṣ'iĕr.

ŌZ'I

d: dōz'y.
k(c̣): c̣ōz'y.
n: nōṣ'y.
p: pōṣ'y.
pr: prōṣ'y.
r: Rōṣ'ie, rōṣ'y.
Plus rose, he, etc.

OZ'I

g: gạuz'y.
k(c̣): c̣ạuṣ'ey, c̣ạuṣe'way.
l: law'ṣie.
Plus claws, he, etc.

ŌZ'ID

p: pōṣ'ied.
r: rōṣ'ied.
Cf. nose hid, etc.

ŌZ'ING

d: dōz'ing.
h: hōṣ'ing.
kl: c̣lōṣ'ing, dis-c̣lōṣ'ing, en-c̣lōṣ'ing, fōre-c̣lōṣ'ing, in-c̣lōṣ'ing, un-c̣lōṣ'ing.
n: nōṣ'ing.

OZ'ING
OZ'ÜR

fāte, fär, fȧst, fᴀll, finăl, cāre, at; mēte, prĕy, hêr, met; pīne,
marĭne, bĭrd, pin; nōte, mŏve, fᴏr, atŏm, not; mᴏᴏn, book; **718**

(Choose only one word out of each group)

p: çom-pōş'ing, dē"çom-pōş'ing,
dē-pōş'ing, dis"çom-pōş'ing,
dis-pōş'ing, ex-pōş'ing,
im-pōş'ing, in"tēr-pōş'ing,
jux"tȧ-pōş'ing, op-pōş'ing,
pōş'ing, prē"dis-pōş'ing,
prē"sup-pōş'ing, prō-pōş'ing,
rē"çom-pōş'ing, rē-pōş'ing,
sup-pōş'ing, trans-pōş'ing,
un-im-pōş'ing.

OZ'ING

k(ç): çauş'ing.
p: pauş'ing.

OZ'IT, OZ'ET

kl: çloş'et.
p: dē-poş'it, in"tēr-poş'it,
jux"tȧ-poş'it, poş'it, rē-poş'it.
Cf. was it, etc.

OZ'IV

pl: ap-plauş'ive, plauş'ive,
un"ap-plauş'ive.
Plus claw sieve, etc.

OZ"L

n: noz'zle.
s: soz'zle.
shn: sçhnoz'zle.
Plus Boz'll, etc.

OZ'MIK

d: en-doş'miç.
k(ç): çoş'miç, maç"rō-çoş'miç,
mī"çrō-çoş'miç.
Cf. was Mick, etc.

Ō'ZŌ

b: bō'zō.
Plus rose owe, *or* O, etc.

ŌZ'ŌN

Vowel: ōz'ōne.
Plus rose own, etc.

ŌZ'ÜR

kl: çlōş'ūre, dis-çlōş'ūre,
fōre-çlōş'ūre, in-çlōş'ūre.
p: çom-pōş'ūre,
dis-çom-pōş'ūre, dis-pōş'ūre,
ex-pōş'ūre, rē-pōş'ūre.
Plus foes, your *or* you're, etc.

ŌZ'ÜR

d: bull'dōz-ēr, dōz'ēr.
gl: glōz'ēr.
h: hōş'ēr.
kl: çlōş'ēr, dis-çlōş'ēr,
en-çlōş'ēr, fōre-çlōş'ēr,
in-çlōş'ēr, un-çlōş'ēr.
p: çom-pōş'ēr, dē-pōş'ēr,
dis-pōş'ēr, ex-pòş'ēr,
im-pōş'ēr, in"tēr-pōş'ēr,
jux"tȧ-pōş'ēr, op-pōş'ēr,
pōş'ēr, prē"dis-pōş'ēr,
prē"sup-pōş'ēr, prō-pōş'ēr,
rē"im-pōş'ēr, rē-pōş'ēr,
sü"pēr-im-pōş'ēr, sup-pōş'ēr,
trans-pōş'ēr.
r: rōş'ēr.
Plus close her *or* err, etc.

OZ'ÜR

h: haw'şēr.
k(ç): çauş'ēr, fîrst çauş'ēr.
p: pauş'ēr.
Plus claws her *or* err, etc.

(Choose only one word out of each group)

U

The accented vowel sounds included are listed under **U** in Single Rhymes.

Ū′ĂL

ch: es-chew′ăl.
d: dū′ăl, sub-dū′ăl.
n: rē-new′ăl.
s: pŭr-sū′ăl.
v: rē-view′ăl.
Cf. ū′el.
Plus two, Al, etc.

Ū′ĂN

ch: Choū′ăn.
d: dū′ăn.
g: Pĕr-gū′ăn.
Plus view an, etc.

Ū′ĂNS

ch: es-chew′ănce.
n: rē-new′ănce.
s: pŭr-sū′ănce.
Plus view ants *or* aunts, etc.

Ū′ĂNT

s: pŭr-sū′ănt.
tr: trū′ănt.
Plus new ant, or aunt, etc.

Ū′ĂRD

l: lee′wărd (lū′ărd).
st: stew′ărd.
Cf. ū′ŭrd.
Cf. view hard, etc.

Ū′ĂRT

st: Stew′ărt, Stū′ărt.
Plus new art, etc.

Ū′BÀ

j: jū′bà.
k(ᴄ): Ꞓū′bà.
t: tū′bà.
Plus cube a, etc.
Plus new, bah!, etc.

Ū′BAL

k(ᴄ): ᴄue ball.
skr(sᴄr): sᴄrew ball.
Plus new ball, etc.
Plus rube all, etc.

Ū′BĂL

j: Jū′bal.
t: Tū′bal.
Cf. Ū′b′l.

Ū′BEN

r: Reū′ben.
st: Steū′ben.
Cf. Lū′bin.
Plus you, Ben, etc.
Cf. tube in, etc.

Ú′BI

b: bᴏᴏ′by.
l: lᴏᴏ′by.
r: rú′by.
Plus you be *or* bee, etc.
Plus Rube, he, etc.

UB′I

b: bub′by.
ch: chub′by.
f: fub′by.
gr: grub′by.
h: hub′by.

Ŭ′BID
UB′LETH

fāte, fär, fȧst, fạll, finăl, cãre, at; mēte, prĕy, hẽr, met; pīne,
marĭne, bĭrd, pĭn; nōte, mŏve, fŏr, atŏm, not; mọọn, book;

720

(Choose only one word out of each group)

k(ç): çub′by.
n: nub′by.
r: rab′ĭ (rub′ē), rub′by.
shr: shrub′by.
skr(sçr): sçrub′by.
st: stub′by.
t: tub′by.
Plus tub, he, etc.

Ŭ′BID

r: rŭ′bied.
Plus you bid, etc.

ŪB′IK

k(ç): çūb′iç.
p: pūb′iç.
r: chē-rŭ′biç.

ŪB′ING

k(ç): çūb′ing.
t: tūb′ing.
Plus you, Byng, etc.

UB′ING

blī: blub′bing.
d: dub′bing.
dr: drub′bing.
gr: grub′bing.
kl: çlub′bing.
n: nub′bing.
r: rub′bing.
s: sub′bing.
skr(sçr): sçrub′bing.
sn: snub′bing.
st: stub′bing.
t: tub′bing.

UB′ISH

gr: grub′bish.
k(ç): çub′bish.
kl: çlub′bish.
r: rub′bish.
t: tub′bish.

Ū′BIT

k(ç): çū′bit.
Plus you bit, etc.
Plus tube it, etc.

UB′JEKT

s: sub′jeçt.

Ŭ′B′L

r: rŭ′ble.
Cf. you bull, etc.
Plus tube′ll, etc.

UB′L

b: bub′ble, hub′ble=bub′ble.
d: doub′le, rē-doub′le.
gr: grub′ble*.
h: Hub′bell.
n: nub′ble.
r: rub′ble.
st: stub′ble.
tr: troub′le (trub′).
Plus tub′ll, etc.

UB′LD

b: bub′bled.
d: doub′led, rē-doub′led.
st: stub′bled.
tr: troub′led, un-troub′led.
Plus rubble′d, etc.

UB′LEST

b: bub′blest*.
d: doub′lest*, rē-doub′lest*.
tr: troub′lest*.
Plus tub, lest, etc.

UB′LET

d: doub′let.
Plus tub let, *or* Lett, etc.

UB′LETH

b: bub′bleth*.
d: doub′leth*, rē-doub′leth*.
tr: troub′leth*.

721   ūse, bᴜll, brúte, tŭrn, up; crȳ, myth; çat, maçhine, ace,
church, çhord; ġem, añger, (Fr.) boṅ, aṣ; THis, thin; āᴢure   **UB'LI**
Ú'CHĒ

(Choose only one word out of each group)

UB'LI

b: bub'bly.
d: doub'ly.
n: knub'bly, nub'bly.
r: rub'bly.
st: stub'bly.
Plus tub, Lee, *or* lea, etc.

UB'LIK

p: pub'liç, rē-pub'liç.
Plus cub lick, etc.

UB'LING

b: bub'bling.
d: doub'ling, rē-doub'ling.
tr: troub'ling.

UB'LISH

p: pub'lish, rē-pub'lish.

UB'LŪR

b: bub'blēr.
d: doub'lēr.
tr: troub'lēr.

UB'LUS

tr: troub'lous.

UB'ŎRN

st: stub'bŏrn.
Cf. cub born, etc.

ŪB'RIK

l: lūb'riç.
r: rùb'riç.
Plus tube rick, etc.
Plus new brick, etc.

UB'STĀK

gr: grub'stāke.
Plus cubs take, etc.
Plus tub stake *or* steak, etc.

UB'STANS

s: sub'stance.
Plus cub stance, etc.

UB'ŨR

bl: blub'bũr.
d: dub'bēr.
dr: drub'bēr, tub drub'bēr.
gr: grub'bēr, mŏn'ey⹀grub'bēr.
kl: çlub'bēr.
l: land'lub″bēr, lub'bēr.
r: in″di-à-rub'bēr, rub'bēr.
skr(sçr): sçrub'bēr.
sl: slub'bēr.
sn: snub'bēr.
st: stub'bēr.
t: tub'bēr.
Plus rub her *or* err, etc.

ŪB'ŨR

g: goo'bēr.
h: Hŭ'bēr.
t: tū'bēr.
Plus new burr, etc.

UB'ŨRD

bl: blub'bēred.
h: Hub'bărd,
mŏ'THēr hub'bărd.
k(ç): çup'boărd (çub'ărd).
r: rub'bēred.

Ū'BŪRT

h: Hŭ'bērt.
Plus knew, Bert, etc.

Ú'CHĒ

d: Il Dū'çē.
Plus brooch, he, etc.
Cf. Úch'i.

UCH'ES
ŪD'ED

fāte, fär, fȧst, fall, fĭnȧl, cãre, at; mēte, prĕy, hẽr, met; pīne,
marĭne, bĭrd, pin; nōte, mŏve, fŏr, atŏm, not; mŏŏn, book;

722

(Choose only one word out of each group)

UCH'ES

d: ärch'duch'ess, duch'ess,
Dutch'ess.
Cf. such chess, etc.

UCH'EST

kl: c̣lutch'est*.
sm: smutch'est*.
t: rē-touch'est*, touch'est*.

UCH'ETH

kl: c̣lutch'eth*.
sm: smutch'eth*.
t: rē-touch'eth*, touch'eth*.

UCH'EZ

h: hutch'eṣ.
kl: c̣lutch'eṣ.
kr: crutch'eṣ.
sk(sc̣): sc̣utch'eṣ.
sm: smutch'eṣ.
t: rē-touch'eṣ, touch'eṣ.
Cf. Dutch is, etc.

ŮCH'I

d: Il Dū'ce ('chi).
g: Nō-gū'chi.
k(c̣): c̣ooch'y, hooch'y-c̣ooch'y.
n: pan-ou'chi, pē-nū'chi.
Plus brooch, he, etc.

UCH'I

d: ärch'duch'y, duch'y.
kl: c̣lutch'y.
sm: smutch'y.
t: touch'y.
Plus crutch, he, etc.

UCH'ING

kl: c̣lutch'ing.
sk(sc̣): sc̣utch'ing.
sm: smutch'ing.
t: rē-touch'ing, touch'ing.

UCH'ŎN

k(c̣): es-c̣ut'cheŏn,
Mc̣-C̣ut'cheŏn.
Plus much on *or* an, etc.

UCH'ŨR

d: Dutch'ẽr.
kl: c̣lutch'ẽr.
sk(sc̣): sc̣utch'ẽr.
sm: smutch'ẽr.
t: rē-touch'ẽr, touch'ẽr.
Plus touch her *or* err, etc.

Ū'DȦ

b: Bär-bū'dȧ, Būd'dhȧ ('dȧ).
j: Jū'dȧh.
k(c̣): bar'ra-c̣ū'dȧ, Ish-koo'dȧ.
m: Bẽr-mū'dȧ.
Plus stewed a, etc.

Ů'DAD

d: doo'dad.
Plus new dad, etc.

ŪD'ĂL

f: feūd'ăl.
l: pȧ-lūd'ăl.
y: ūd'ăl.
Plus rude, Al, etc.

ŪD'ED

br: brood'ed.
d: dūd'ed.
kl: c̣on-c̣lūd'ed, ex-c̣lūd'ed,
in-c̣lūd'ed, oc̣-c̣lūd'ed,
prē-c̣lūd'ed, rē-c̣lūd'ed*,
sē-c̣lūd'ed.
l: al-lūd'ed, c̣ol-lūd'ed,
dē-lūd'ed, ē-lūd'ed, il-lūd'ed,
in"tēr-lūd'ed, prē-lūd'ed,
un"dē-lūd'ed.

(Choose only one word out of each group)

n: dē-nūd'ed.
s: tran-sūd'ed.
sn: snọọd'ed.
tr: dē-trúd'ed, ex-trúd'ed, in-trúd'ed, ob-trúd'ed, prō-trúd'ed, rē-trúd'ed, sub-trúd'ed.
z: ex-ūd'ed.
Plus you dead, etc.
Cf. you did, etc.

UD'ED

b: bud'ded.
bl: blood'ed.
fl: flood'ed.
sk(sç): sçud'ded.
sp: spud'ded.
st: bē-stud'ded, stud'ded.
th: thud'ded.
Cf. ud'id.
Cf. stud dead, etc.

UD'EN

s: sud'den.
Plus blood den, etc.

Ú'DENS

pr: jù″ris-prú'dence, prú'dence.
Plus new dense *or* dents, etc.
Cf. ú'dent+s.

ŪD'ENT

kl: çon-çlūd'ent, oç-çlūd'ent.
pr: im-prú'dent, jù″ris-prú'dent, prú'dent.
st: stū'dent.
Plus new dent, etc.

ŪD'EST

br: brọọd'est*.
kl: çon-çlūd'est*, ex-çlūd'est*, in-çlūd'est*, prē-çlūd'est*, rē-çlūd'est*, sē-çlūd'est*.

kr: çrúd'est.
l: al-lūd'est*, dē-lūd'est*, ē-lūd'est*, il-lūd'est*, lewd'est, prē-lūd'est*.
n: dē-nūd'est*, nūd'est.
r: rúd'est.
shr: shrewd'est.
tr: dē-trúd'est*, ex-trúd'est*, in-trúd'est*, ob-trúd'est*, prō-trúd'est*, rē-trúd'est*, sub-trúd'est*.
z: ex-ūd'est*.
Cf. ū'dist.

UD'EST

b: bud'dest*.
fl: flood'est*.
sk: sçud'dest*.
st: stud'dest*.
th: thud'dest*.

ŪD'ETH

br: brọọd'eth*.
j: Jū'dith.
kl: çon-çlūd'eth*, ex-çlūd'eth*, in-çlūd'eth*, prē-çlūd'eth*, rē-çlūd'eth*, sē-çlūd'eth*.
l: al-lūd'eth*, dē-lūd'eth*, ē-lūd'eth*, il-lūd'eth*, prē-lūd'eth*.
n: dē-nūd'eth*.
tr: dē-trúd'eth*, ex-trúd'eth*, in-trúd'eth*, ob-trúd'eth*, prō-trúd'eth*, rē-trúd'eth*, sub-trúd'eth*.
z: ex-ūd'eth*.
Plus new death, etc.

UD'ETH

b: bud'deth*.
fl: flood'eth*.
sk(sç): sçud'deth*.

ŬD′I
UD″L

fāte, fär, fȧst, fạll, finăl, cãre, at; mēte, prĕy, hẽr, met; pīne,
marine, bĩrd, pin; nōte, mȯve, fŏr, atŏm, not; mọọn, book;

724

(Choose only one word out of each group)

st: stud′deth*.
th: thud′deth*.
Cf. blood death, etc.

ŬD′I

br: brọọd′y.
m: mọọd′y.
sk(sç): sçụ′di.
Plus rude, he, etc.

UD′I

b: bud′dy.
bl: blood′y.
k(ç): çud′dy.
m: mud′dy.
p: pud′dy.
r: rud′dy.
st: stud′dy, stud′y.
Plus blood, he, etc.

UD′ID

bl: blood′ied.
m: mud′died.
r: rud′died.
st: stud′ied, un-stud′ied.
Cf. ud′ed.
Cf. blood did, etc.

ŪD′ING

br: ȧ-brọọ′ding, brọọd′ing.
kl: çon-çlūd′ing, ex-çlūd′ing,
in-çlūd′ing, oç-çlūd′ing,
prē-çlūd′ing, rē-çlūd′ing,
sē-çlūd′ing.
l: al-lūd′ing, dē-lūd′ing,
ē-lūd′ing, il-lūd′ing,
prē-lūd′ing.
n: dē-nūd′ing.
s: tran-sūd′ing.
sn: snọọd′ing.
tr: dē-trụd′ing, ex-trụd′ing,
in-trụd′ing, ob-trụd′ing,

prō-trụd′ing, rē-trụd′ing,
sub-trụd′ing.
z: ex-ūd′ing.

UD′ING

b: bud′ding.
fl: flood′ing.
sk(sç): sçud′ding.
sp: spud′ding.
st: bē-stud′ding, stud′ding.

UD′ISH

pr: prụd′ish.
r: rụd′ish.
shr: shrewd′ish.
Plus new dish, etc.

ŪD′IST

n: nūd′ist.
pr: prụd′ist.
Cf. rīd′est.

Ụ′DITH

j: Jụ′dith.
Cf. ụ′deth.

Ụ′D′L

b: bọọ′dle, çȧ-bọọ′dle.
d: flap′dọọ″dle,
Yañ′kee dọọ′dle.
n: çȧ-nọọ′dle, nọọ′dle.
p: pọọ′dle.
y: kī-yọọ′dle.
Plus food′ll, etc.

UD″L

b: bud′dle.
f: fud′dle.
h: hud′dle.
k(ç): çud′dle.
m: bē-mud′dle, mud′dle.
n: nud′dle.
p: pud′dle.

(Choose only one word out of each group)

r: rud′dle.
sk(sç): sçud′dle.
Plus mud′ll, etc.

UD′LEST

h: hud′dlest*.
k(ç): çud′dlest*.
m: bē-mud′dlest*, mud′dlest*.
p: pud′dlest*.
Plus mud, lest, etc.

UD′LETH

h: hud′dleth*.
k(ç): çud′dleth*.
m: bē-mud′dleth*, mud′dleth*.
p: pud′dleth*.

ŪD′LI

kr: çrūde′ly.
l: lewd′ly.
n: nūde′ly.
r: rùde′ly.
shr: shrewd′ly.
Plus brood, Lee *or* lea, etc.

UD′LI

d: Dud′ley.
Plus blood, Lee, *or* lea, etc.

UD′LING

f: fud′dling.
h: hud′dling.
k(ç): çud′dling.
m: bē-mud′dling, mud′dling.
p: pud′dling.
sk(sç): sçud′dling.

ÙD′LUM

h: họod′lum.
Plus brood, Lum, etc.

UD′LŪR

f: fud′dlẽr.
h: hud′dlẽr.
k(ç): çud′dlẽr.
m: mud′dlẽr.
p: pud′dlẽr.

ŪD′NES

kr: çrūde′ness.
l: lewd′ness.
n: nūde′ness.
r: rùde′ness.
shr: shrewd′ness.

UD′OK

p: pud′dock.
r: rud′dock.
Plus mud, dock, etc.

Ū′DOS

k: kū′dos.

UD′SŎN

h: Hud′sŏn.
j: Jud′sŏn.
Plus blood, son *or* sun, etc.

ŪD′ŪR

br: brọod′ẽr.
kl: çon-çlūd′ẽr, ex-çlūd′ẽr,
in-çlūd′ẽr, oç-çlūd′ẽr,
prē-çlūd′ẽr, rē-çlūd′ẽr,
sē-çlūd′ẽr.
kr: çrùd′ẽr.
l: al-lūd′ẽr, dē-lūd′ẽr, ē-lūd′ẽr,
il-lūd′ẽr, prē-lūd′ẽr.
n: dē-nūd′ẽr.
r: rùd′ẽr.
s: tran-sūd′ẽr.
shr: shrewd′ẽr.
t: Tūd′ŏr.
tr: dē-trùd′ẽr, ex-trùd′ẽr,
in-trùd′ẽr, ob-strùd′ẽr,

UD′ŪR
Ū′ET

fāte, fär, fȧst, fạll, finăl, cāre, at; mēte, prey, hẽr, met; pīne,
marĭne, bĭrd, pin; nōte, mŏve, fọr, atŏm, not; mọọn, book;

726

(Choose only one word out of each group)

prō-trŭd′ẽr, rē-trŭd′ẽr,
sub-trŭd′ẽr.
z: ex-ūd′ẽr.
Plus exclude her *or* err, etc.

UD′ŪR

Vowel: ud′dẽr.
br: "brŭd′dẽr".
d: dud′dẽr.
fl: flood′ẽr.
m: mud′dẽr.
p: pud′dẽr.
r: rud′dẽr.
sh: shud′dẽr.
sk(sc): scud′dẽr.
Plus flood her *or* err, etc.

UD′ZI

s: sud′sy.
Plus buds, he, etc.

Ú′Ē

k(c): cọọ′ee.
Cf. ú′i.

Ū′EL

d: dū′el.
f: fū′el.
gr: grŭ′el.
h: Hew′ell.
j: bē-jew′el, jew′el.
kr: crew′el (krŭ′), crŭ′el.
n: new′el.
r: Reú′el.
s: Sew′ell.
t: tew′el.
Cf. ū′ăl.
Plus new el *or* L, etc.

Ū′ES

j: Jew′ess.
Plus new S, etc.

Ū′EST

b: im-bū′est*.
bl: blū′est.
br: brew′est*, im-brew′est*.
ch: chew′est*, es-chew′est*.
d: bē-dew′est*, dö′est*,
en-dū′est*, sub-dū′est*,
un-dö′est*.
dr: drew′est*, with-drew′est*.
f: few′est.
fl: flew′est*.
gl: glū′est*, un-glū′est*.
gr: grew′est*.
h: hew′est*, hū′est*.
k(c): cọọ′est*.
kr: ac-crŭ′est*.
l: hal-lọọ′est*.
m: mew′est*.
n: knew′est*, new′est,
rē-new′est*.
p: sham-pọọ′est*.
r: rŭ′est*.
s: en-sū′est*, pŭr-sū′est*, sū′est*.
sh: shö′est*, shọọ′est*
shr: bē-shrew′est*.
skr(scr): screw′est*,
un-screw′est*.
sl: slew′est*.
sp: spew′est*.
st: stew′est*.
t: tat-tọọ′est*.
tr: trŭ′est, un-trŭ′est.
thr: threw′est*.
v: in″tẽr-view′est*,
rē-view′est*, view′est*.
w: wọọ′est*.

Ū′ET

kr: crŭ′et.
s: sū′et.
Plus who et, etc.
Cf. do it. etc.

(Choose only one word out of each group)

Ū'ETH

b: im-bū'eth*.
bl: blū'eth*.
br: brew'eth (brū')*,
    im-brew'eth*.
ch: chew'eth*, es-chew'eth*.
d: bē-dew'eth*, dö'eth*,
    en-dū'eth*, sub-dū'eth*,
    un-dö'eth*.
dr: drew'eth*, with-drew'eth*.
fl: flew'eth*.
gl: glū'eth*, un-glū'eth*.
gr: grew'eth*.
h: hew'eth*, hū'eth*.
k(ç): çoọ'eth*.
kr: aç-çrú'eth*.
l: hal-loọ'eth*.
m: mew'eth*.
n: knew'eth*, rē-new'eth*.
p: sham-poọ'eth*.
r: rú'eth*.
s: en-sū'eth*, pŭr-sū'eth*, sū'eth*.
sh: shö'eth*, shoọ'eth*.
shr: bē-shrew'eth*.
skr(sçr): sçrew'eth*,
    un-sçrew'eth*.
sl: slew'eth*.
sp: spew'eth*
st: stew'eth*.
t: tat-toọ'eth*.
thr: threw'eth*.
v: in"tēr-view'eth*,
    rē-view'eth* view'eth*
w: woọ 'eth*.

Ú'FÅ

ch: chù'få.
st: stù'få.
t: tú'få.
y: ū'få.
Plus roof a, etc.

Ū'FĒLD

bl: Blūe'fiēld.
n: New'field.
Plus strew field, etc.

UF'EN

r: rough'en.
t: tough'en.

UF'EST

b: rē-buf'fest*.
bl: bluf'fest.
gr: gruf'fest.
k(ç): çuf'fest*.
l: luf'fest*.
m: muf'fest*.
p: bē-puf'fest*, puf'fest*.
r: rough'est.
sl: slough'est*.
sn: snuf'fest*.
st: stuf'fest.
t: tough'est.
Cf. snuff fest, etc.

UF'ET

b: buf'fet.
m: Muf'fett.
t: tuf'fet.
Cf. rough it, etc.

UF'ETH

b: rē-buf'feth*.
bl: bluf'feth*.
k(ç): çuf'feth*.
l: luf'feth*.
m: muf'feth*.
p: bē-puf'feth*, puf'feth*
r: rough'eth*.
sl: slough'eth*.
sn: snuf'feth*.
st: stuf'feth*.

UF'HOUS
UF'LEST

fāte, fär, fȧst, fạll, finăl, cãre, at; mēte, prey, hẽr, met; pīne,
marïne, bïrd, pin; nōte, mŏve, fŏr, atŏm, not; mŏŏn, book;

728

(Choose only one word out of each group)

UF'HOUS

r: rough'house.
Plus tough house, etc.

UF'I

g: goof'y.
r: roof'y.
sp: spoof'y.
w: woof'y.
Plus who fee, etc.
Plus roof, he, etc.

UF'I

b: buf'fy.
bl: bluf'fy.
ch: chuf'fy.
fl: fluf'fy.
h: huf'fy.
p: puf'fy.
pl: pluf'fy.
sl: slough'y.
sn: snuf'fy.
st: stuf'fy.
Plus rough, he, etc.

UF'IN

m: muf'fin, rag″ȧ-muf'fin.
p: puf'fin.
Plus enough in, *or* inn, etc.
Cf. tough fin *or* Finn, etc.

ÙF'ING

pr: wȧt″ẽr=proof'ing.
r: roof'ing.
sp: spoof'ing.
w: woof'ing.

UF'FING

bl: bluf'fing.
fl: fluf'fing.
h: huf'fing.

k(c): cuf'fing.
l: luf'fing.
p: puf'fing.
r: rough'ing.
sl: slough'ing.
sn: snuf'fing.
st: stuf'fing.

UF'ISH

Vowel: uf'fish.
gr: gruf'fish.
h: huf'fish.
r: rough'ish.
t: tough'ish.
Cf. tough fish, etc.

UF″L

b: buf'fle.
d: duf'fle.
m: bē-muf'fle, muf'fle,
un-muf'fle.
r: ruf'fle, un-ruf'fle.
sh: dŏu'ble shuf'fle, shuf'fle.
sk(sc): scuf'fle.
sn: snuf'fle.
tr: truf'fle.
Plus tough'll, etc.

UF'L'D

m: bē-muf'fled, muf'fled,
un-muf'fled.
r: ruf'fled, un-ruf'fled.
sh: shuf'fled.
sk(sc): scuf'fled.
Plus truffle'd, etc.

UF'LEST

m: bē-muf'flest*, muf'flest*,
un-muf'flest*.
r: ruf'flest*.
sh: shuf'flest*.

(Choose only one word out of each group)

sk(sċ): sċuf′flest*.
Plus snuff, lest, etc.

UF′LETH

m: bē-muf′fleth*, muf′fleth*,
un-muf′fleth*.
r: ruf′fleth*.
sh: shuf′fleth*.
sk(sċ): sċuf′fleth*.

UF′LI

bl: bluff′ly.
gr: gruff′ly.
m: muf′fly.
r: rough′ly, ruf′fly.
sk(sċ): sċuff′ly.
sl: sluff′ly.
sn: snuff′ly.
t: tough′ly.
tr: truff′ly.
Plus enough, Lee or lea, etc.

UF′LING

m: bē-muf′fling, muf′fling,
un-muf′fling.
r: ruf′fling, un-ruf′fling.
sh: shuf′fling.
sk(sċ): sċuf′fling.
sn: snuf′fling.

UF′FLŨR

m: muf′flẽr, un-muf′flẽr.
r: ruf′flẽr.
sh: shuf′flẽr.
sk(sċ): sċuf′flẽr.
sn: snuf′flẽr.

UF′NES

bl: bluff′ness.
gr: gruff′ness.
r: rough′ness.
t: tough′ness.

UF′TED

t: tuf′ted.
Plus rough, Ted, etc.
Plus snuffed, Ed, etc.

UF′TI

m: muf′ti.
t: tuf′ty.
Plus enough tea, etc.

ŪF′ŨR

h: hoof′ẽr.
l: à-loof′ẽr.
r: roof′ẽr.
sp: spoof′ẽr.
Plus new fur or fir, etc.
Cf. who, for, etc.
Plus roof her or err, etc.

UF′ŨR

b: buf′fẽr.
bl: bluf′fẽr.
d: duf′fẽr.
gr: gruf′fẽr.
h: huf′fẽr.
k(ċ): ċuf′fẽr.
l: luf′fẽr.
m: muf′fẽr.
p: puf′fẽr.
r: rough′ẽr.
s: suf′fẽr.
sk(sċ): sċuf′fẽr.
sn: snuf′fẽr.
st: stuf′fẽr.
t: tough′ẽr.
Plus rough her or err, etc.
Cf. rough fur or fir, etc.

Ú′FUS

g: goof′us.
r: rúf′ous, Rúf′us.
Plus roof us, etc.

ŬG'Á
UG'ĬNZ

fāte, fär, fåst, fall, final, cãre, at; mēte, prey, hẽr, met; pine,
marïne, bĭrd, pin; nōte, mŏve, fôr, atŏm, not; mọọn, book;

730

(Choose only one word out of each group)

ŬG'Á

sh: mē-shŭg'gåh.
Plus fugue a, etc.

Ŭ'GÄR

k(ç): çoü'gär.
Plus knew gar, etc.

UG'ÄRD

sl: slug'gärd.
Cf. ug'ûr+ed.

UG'BI

r: Rug'by.
Plus bug be *or* bee, etc.

UG'ED

r: rug'ged.
Cf. ug+ed*.

UG'EST

dr: drug'gest*.
h: hug'gest*.
j: jug'gest*.
l: lug'gest*.
m: mug'gest*.
pl: plug'gest*.
shr: shrug'gest*.
sl: slug'gest*.
sm: smug'gest.
sn: snug'gest.
t: tug'gest*.
Cf. drug'gist.

UG'ET

dr: drug'get.
n: nug'get.
Cf. rug get, etc.
Cf. slug it, etc.

UG'ETH

dr: drug'geth*.
h: hug'geth*.

j: jug'geth*.
l: lug'geth*.
m: mug'geth*.
pl: plug'geth*.
shr: shrug'geth*.
sl: slug'geth*.
t: tug'geth*.

UG'HOUS

b: bug'house.
Plus rug house, etc.

ŬG'I

w: bọọ'gie=wọọ'gie.
Plus knew ghee, etc.
Plus fugue E, etc.

UG'I

b: bug'gy.
m: mug'gy.
p: pug'gi, pug'gy.
sl: slug'gy.
Plus drug, he, etc.

UG'IJ

l: lug'gåġe.
Cf. drug age, etc.

UG'ING

dr: drug'ging.
h: hug'ging.
j: jug'ging.
l: lug'ging.
m: mug'ging.
pl: plug'ging.
shr: shrug'ging.
sl: slug'ging.
t: tug'ging.

UG'INZ

m: Mug'gins.
Plus drug inns *or* ins, etc.

(Choose only one word out of each group)

UG'ISH

m: mug'gish.
sl: slug'gish.
sm: smug'gish.
sn: snug'gish.

UG'IST

dr: drug'gist.
Cf. ug'est.

ŪG"L

b: bū'gle.
d: Mac̦-Doū'gȧll.
f: feb-ri-fūg'ăl, fūg'ăl,
vĕr-mi-fūg'ăl.
fr: frů̇g'ăl, in-frů'găl.
j: jů̇g'ăl.
Plus fugue 'll, etc.
Cf. new gull, etc.

UG"L

g: gug'gle.
j: jug'gle.
sm: smug'gle.
sn: snug'gle.
str: death strug'gle (deth),
strug'gle.
Plus bug'll, etc.

UG'LEST

j: jug'glest*.
sm: smug'glest*.
sn: snug'glest*.
str: strug'glest*.
Plus drug, lest, etc.

UG'LETH

j: jug'gleth*.
sm: smug'gleth*.
sn: snug'gleth*.
str: strug'gleth*.

UG'LI

Vowel: plug'=ug'ly, ug'ly.
g: gug'gly.
j: jug'gly.
sm: smug'ly.
sn: snug'gly.
str: strug'gly.
Plus drug, Lee *or* lea, etc.

UG'LING

g: gug'gling.
j: jug'gling.
sm: smug'gling.
sn: snug'gling.
str: strug'gling.

Ū'GLŬR

b: bū'glẽr.
f: fū'glẽr.

UG'LŬR

j: jug'glẽr.
sm: smug'glẽr.
sn: snug'glẽr.
str: strug'glẽr.

UG'NES

sm: smug'ness.
sn: snug'ness.

Ū'GO

h: Hū'gō.
Plus you go, etc.

UG'OUT

d: dug'out.
Plus jug out, etc.

UG'ŬR

b: bug'gẽr.
dr: drug'gẽr.
h: hug'gẽr.
l: lug'gẽr.
m: hug'gẽr=mug"gẽr, mug'gẽr.

(Choose only one word out of each group)

pl: plug'gẽr.
r: rug'gẽr.
shr: shrug'gẽr.
sm: smug'gẽr.
sn: snug'gẽr.
t: tug'gẽr.
Plus hug her *or* err, etc.

UG'WUMP

m: mug'wump.

Ū'I

Vowel: ọọ'ey.
b: Böw'ie, bu'oy.
bl: blū'ey, blọọ'ie.
ch: chew'y.
d: bē-dew'y, Dew'ey, dew'y.
f: fọọ'ey, pfu'i (fu').
fl: flọọ'ey, flu'ey.
g: gọọ'ey.
gl: glū'ey.
h: họọ'ey.
k(c): cọọ'ee, Cou'ē.
l: Lou'is (lu'i).
s: chop-su'ey.
skr(scr): screw'y.
th: thew'y.
v: view'y.
Plus knew he, etc.

Ū'ĪD

bl: blūe'⸗eȳed'.
tr: trūe'⸗eȳed'.
Plus knew I'd *or* eyed, etc.

U'ID

dr: dru'id.
fl: flu'id.

U'IJ

br: brew'ăġe.
s: sew'ăġe.
Cf. knew age, etc.

Ū'IK

ch: cat"ȧ-chū'ic.
l: tō-lū'ic.

Ū'IN

br: bru'in.
r: blūe ru'in, ru'in.
s: sew'en.
Plus crew in *or* inn, etc.

Ū'ING

b: im-bū'ing.
bl: blūe'ing.
br: brew'ing, im-brū'ing.
ch: chew'ing, es-chew'ing.
d: bē-dew'ing, dö'ing,
  en-dū'ing, mil'dew"ing,
  mis-dö'ing, out-dö'ing,
  ō"vẽr-dö'ing, sub-dū'ing,
  un-dö'ing, well'⸗dö'ing,
  wrong'⸗dö'ing (rong').
gl: glū'ing.
h: hew'ing.
k(c): bar'bē-cū"ing, cọọ'ing,
  cūe'ing.
kl: clew'ing, clūe'ing.
kr: ac-cru'ing, fụll crew'ing.
l: hal-lọọ'ing, lọọ'ing.
m: mew'ing, mọọ'ing.
n: cȧ-nöe'ing, rē-new'ing.
p: pọọh'⸗pọọh'ing,
  sham-pọọ'ing.
r: rùe'ing.
s: en-sū'ing, pūr-sū'ing, sū'ing.
sh: shöe'ing.
shr: bē-shrew'ing.
skr(scr): screw'ing,
  un-screw'ing.
sp: spew'ing.
st: stew'ing.
str: bē-strew'ing, con-strū'ing,
  mis"con-strū'ing, strew'ing.

733 ūse, bu̥ll, brûte, tū̄rn, up; crȳ, myth; c̦at, ma̧chine, ace,
church, c̦hord; ġem, añger, (Fr.) bon̊, as̱; THis, thin; azure

Ū'INGZ
UJ'ING

(Choose only one word out of each group)

t: tat-too̥'ing.
tr: trūe'ing.
v: in'tĕr-view"ing, rē-view'ing, view'ing.
w: woo̥'ing.
y: ewe'ing (yū').
z: zoo̥'ing.

Ū'INGZ

d: dö'ings̱, mis-dö'ings̱.
Plus ū'ing+s.

Ŭ'IS

l: Lew'is, Loŭ'is, St. Loŭ'is.
Cf. Jew'ess.

Ū'ISH

bl: blūe'ish.
gl: glūe'ish.
j: Jew'ish.
n: new'ish.
shr: shrew'ish.
tr: trŭ'ish.

UJ'EL

k(c̦): c̦ud'ġel.
Plus drudge'll, etc.

UJ'EST

b: budġ'est*.
dr: drudġ'est*.
gr: bē-grudġ'est*.
j: ad-judġ'est*, judġ'est*, mis-judġ'est*, prē-judġ'est*.
n: nudġ'est*.
sl: sludġ'est*.
sm: smudġ'est*.
tr: trudġ'est*.

UJ'ET

b: budġ'et.
Cf. grudge it, etc.

UJ'ETH*

b: budġ'eth*.
dr: drudġ'eth*.

gr: bē-grudġ'eth*.
j: ad-judġ'eth*, judġ'eth*, mis-judġ'eth*, prē-judġ'eth*.
n: nudġ'eth*.
sl: sludġ'eth*.
sm: smudġ'eth*.
tr: trudġ'eth*.

UJ'EZ

b: budġ'es̱.
dr: drudġ'es̱.
f: fudġ'es̱.
gr: bē-grudġ'es̱, grudġ'es̱.
j: ad-judġ'es̱, fōre-judġ'es̱, judġ'es̱, mis-judġ'es̱, prē-judġ'es̱, rē-judġ'es̱.
n: nudġ'es̱.
sl: sludġ'es̱.
sm: smudġ'es̱.
tr: trudġ'es̱.
Cf. judge is, etc.

UJ'I

p: pudġ'y.
sl: sludġ'y.
sm: smudġ'y.
Plus judge, he, etc.

UJ'ING

b: budġ'ing.
dr: drudġ'ing.
f: fudġ'ing.
gr: bē-grudġ'ing, grudġ'ing, un-grudġ'ing.
j: ad-judġ'ing, fōre-judġ'ing, judġ'ing, mis-judġ'ing, prē-judġ'ing, rē-judġ'ing.
n: nudġ'ing.
sl: sludġ'ing.
sm: smudġ'ing.
tr: trudġ'ing.

(Choose only one word out of each group)

UJ'MENT

j: judġ'ment.
Plus grudge meant, etc.

UJ'ŎN

bl: blud'ġeŏn.
d: dud'ġeŏn.
g: gud'ġeŏn.
m: çūr-mud'ġeŏn.
Plus judge on *or* an, etc.

UJ'ŪR

b: budġ'ẽr.
dr: drudġ'ẽr.
f: fudġ'ẽr.
gr: bē-grudġ'ẽr, grudġ'ẽr.
j: ad-judġ'ẽr, fōre-judġ'ẽr,
judġ'ẽr, mis-judġ'ẽr,
prē-judġ'ẽr, rē-judġ'ẽr.
n: nudġ'ẽr.
sl: sludġ'ẽr.
sm: smudġ'ẽr.
tr: trudġ'ẽr.

Ū'KA

b: būç'çȧ, sam-böu'kȧ.
l: fē-lùç'çȧ, pȧ-lọọk'ȧ.
r: gȧ-rọọk'uh.
t: fes-tùç'çȧ, fis-tùç'çȧ.
y: yūk'kȧ.
Plus rebuke a, etc.

UK'Å

ch: chuk'kȧ.
Plus pluck a, etc.

ŪK'ĂL

d: ärch'dūç'ăl, dūç'ăl.
l: noç"ti-lūch'ăl.
n: nū'chăl.
t: Pen"tȧ-teūch'ăl.

Plus duke'll, etc.
Plus spook, Al, etc.

ŪK'ĂN

l: an"tē-lūç'ăn.
t: töu'çăn.
Plus you can, etc.

Ū'KĀS

y: ū'kāse.
Plus new case, etc.
Plus uke ace, etc.

Ù'KAS

kl: Çlù'çăs.
l: Lù'çăs.

ŪK'EST

b: rē-būk'est*.
p: pūk'est*.

UK'EST

b: buck'est*.
d: duck'est*.
pl: pluck'est*.
s: suck'est*.

UK'ET

b: buck'et.
l: Luck'ett.
p: Puck'ett.
s: suck'et.
t: Nan-tuck'et, Paw-tuck'et,
tuck'et.
Cf. pluck it, etc.

ŪK'ETH

b: rē-būk'eth*.
p: pūk'eth*.

UK'ETH

b: buck'eth*.
d: duck'eth*.

(Choose only one word out of each group)

pl: pluck'eth*.
s: suck'eth*.

ŬK'I

fl: flŭk'y.
sn: snọọk'y.
sp: spọọk'y.
Plus duke, he, etc.
Plus new key, etc.

UK'I

d: duck'y.
l: luck'y, un-luck'y.
m: muck'y.
pl: pluck'y.
t: Ken-tuck'y.
w: wuck'y.
Plus ruck, he, etc.

ŪK'ING

b: rē-būk'ing.
p: pūk'ing.
Plus new king, etc.

UK'ING

b: buck'ing.
ch: chuck'ing.
d: duck'ing.
kl: çluck'ing.
m: muck'ing.
pl: pluck'ing.
sh: shuck'ing.
s: suck'ing.
t: tuck'ing.
tr: truck'ing.

UK'ISH

b: buck'ish.
m: muck'ish.
p: puck'ish.

UK"L

b: buck'le, par'buck"le,
un-buck'le.

br: bruck'le.
ch: chuck'le.
h: huck'le.
m: muck'le.
n: knuck'le.
s: suck'le, hŏn'ey-suck'le.
tr: truck'le.
Plus luck'll, etc.

UK"LD

b: buck'led, un-buck'led.
ch: chuck'led.
k(ç): çuck'ŏld.
n: knuck'led (nuk').
s: suck'led.
tr: truck'led.

UK'LES

l: luck'less.
Plus pluck less, etc.

UK'LEST

b: buck'lest*, un-buck'lest*.
ch: chuck'lest*.
s: suck'lest*.
Plus duck, lest, etc.

UK'LETH

b: buck'leth*, un-buck'leth*.
ch: chuck'leth*.
s: suck'leth*.

UK'LING

b: buck'ling, un-buck'ling.
ch: chuck'ling.
d: duck'ling, ug'ly duck'ling.
n: knuck'ling (nuk').
s: suck'ling.
tr: truck'ling.

UK'LŪR
ŪK'TEST   fāte, fär, fåst, fall, fǐnăl, cãre, at; mēte, prey, hẽr, met; pīne,
marïne, bĭrd, pin; nōte, mōve, fǫr, atŏm, not; mǫǫn, book;   **736**

(Choose only one word out of each group)

UK'LŪR

b: buck'lẽr, swäsh'buck"lẽr.
ch: chuck'lẽr.
n: knuck'lẽr (nuk').
s: suck'lẽr.
tr: truck'lẽr.

Ū'KŌ

b: Pẽr"nam-bū'çō.
d: Dū'çō.
Plus spook owe *or* O, etc.

UK'ŎLD

k(ç): çuck'ŏld.
Cf. uk"'ld.
Plus luck, old, etc.

UK'RĀK

m: muck'rāke.
Plus pluck rake, etc.

UK'SI

l: Bi-lŏx'i.
Plus bucks, he, etc.

UK'SIV

fl: in-flux'ive.
Plus pluck sieve, etc.

UK'SŎM

b: bux'ŏm.
l: luck'sŏme.
Plus pluck some *or* sum, etc.

UK'STŪR

h: huck'stẽr.
Plus luck stir, etc.
Plus pluck'st* her *or* err, etc.

UK'SHUN

d: ab-duç'tion, ad-duç'tion,
çon-duç'tion, dē-duç'tion,
di-duç'tion*, ē-duç'tion,
in-duç'tion,
in"trō-duç'tion, man"ū-duç'tion,
non"çon-duç'tion, ob-duç'tion,
ō"vẽr-prō-duç'tion, prō-duç'tion,
rē-duç'tion, rē"prō-duç'tion,
sē-duç'tion, sub-duç'tion,
sū"pẽr-in-duç'tion, trȧ-duç'tion.
fl: af-flux'ion, dē-flux'ion,
ef-flux'ion, flux'ion, in-flux'ion.
r: ruç'tion.
s: suç'tion.
str: çon-struç'tion,
dē-struç'tion, in-struç'tion,
mis"çon-struç'tion,
ob-struç'tion, rē"çon-struç'tion,
self'=des-truç'tion,
sub-struç'tion, sū"pẽr-struç'tion.
Plus luck shun, etc.

UK'TĂNS

l: rē-luç'tănce.
Plus deduct aunts *or* ants, etc.

UK'TĂNT

l: rē-luç'tănt.
Plus plucked ant *or* aunt, etc.

UK'TED

d: ab-duç'ted, çon-duç'ted,
dē-duç'ted, in-duç'ted.
fr: fruç'ted.
str: çon-struç'ted, in-struç'ted,
mis"çon-struç'ted, ob-struç'ted,
sū"pẽr-struç'ted,
un"ob-struç'ted.
Plus pluck Ted, etc.
Plus deduct Ed, etc.

UK'TEST

d: ab-duçt'est*, çon-duçt'est*,
dē-duçt'est*, in-duçt'est*.

(Choose only one word out of each group)

str: c̟on-struc̟′test*,
in-struc̟′test*,
mis″c̟on-struc̟′test*,
ob-struc̟′test*.
Plus muck test, etc.

UK′TETH

d: ab-duc̟t′eth*, c̟on-duc̟t′eth*,
dē-duc̟t′eth*, in-duc̟t′eth*.
str: c̟on-struc̟′teth*,
in-struc̟′teth*,
mis″c̟on-struc̟′teth*,
ob-struc̟′teth*.

UK′TIL

d: duc̟′tile, in-duc̟′tile,
prō-duc̟′tile.
Plus pluck till, etc.

UK′TING

d: ab-duc̟t′ing, c̟on-duc̟t′ing,
dē-duc̟t′ing, in-duc̟t′ing,
mis″c̟on-duc̟t′ing,
non″c̟on-duc̟t′ing.
str: c̟on-struc̟t′ing, in-struc̟t′ing,
non″ob-struc̟t′ing,
ob-struc̟t′ing.

UK′TIV

d: ad-duc̟′tive, c̟on-duc̟′tive,
dē-duc̟′tive, in-duc̟′tive,
in″trō-duc̟′tive,
non″c̟on-duc̟′tive,
ō″vēr-prō-duc̟′tive,
prō-duc̟′tive, rē″c̟on-duc̟′tive,
rē-duc̟′tive, rē″prō-duc̟′tive,
sē-duc̟′tive, sū″pēr-in-duc̟′tive,
trȧ-duc̟′tive,
un″dēr-prō-duc̟′tive.
str: c̟on-struc̟′tive,
dē-struc̟′tive, in-struc̟′tive,

ob-struc̟′tive, rē″c̟on-struc̟′tive,
self′-des-truc̟′tive,
sū″pēr-struc̟′tive.

UK′TRES

d: c̟on-duc̟′tress, sē-duc̟′tress.
str: in-struc̟′tress,
in″trō-duc̟′tress.
Plus pluck tress, etc.

UK′TŪR

str: struc̟′tūre, sub′struc̟″tūre,
sū′pēr-struc̟″tūre.
Plus plucked your *or* you're, etc.

UK′TŬR

d: ab-duc̟′tŏr, ad-duc̟′tŏr,
c̟on-duc̟′tŏr, duc̟′tŏr, ē-duc̟′tŏr,
in-duc̟′tŏr, in″trō-duc̟′tŏr,
man′ū-duc̟″tŏr,
non″c̟on-duc̟′tŏr.
str: c̟on-struc̟′tŏr, dē-struc̟′tŏr,
in-struc̟′tŏr, ob-struc̟′tŏr.
Plus plucked her *or* err, etc.

U′KU, OO′KU

k(c̟): c̟u̇′ckoo.
Plus you coo, etc.

ŪK′ŪR

b: rē-būk′ēr.
fl: flūk′ēr.
l: lu̇′c̟re.
p: pūk′ēr.
y: eū′c̟hre.
Plus spook her *or* err, etc.

UK′ŬR

b: buck′ēr.
ch: chuck′ēr, chuk′kēr.
d: duck′ēr.
kl: c̟luck′ēr.

Ū′KUS
ŪL′ETH

fāte, fär, fȧst, fall, final, cãre, at; mēte, prey, hẽr, met; pine,
marine, bĭrd, pin; nōte, mŏve, fôr, atŏm. not; mọọn, book;

738

(Choose only one word out of each group)

m: muck′ẽr.
p: puck′ẽr.
s: all′=dāy′suck″ẽr, sap′suck″ẽr,
  seer′suck″ẽr, suç′cŏr, suck′ẽr.
t: tuck′ẽr.
tr: truck′ẽr.
Plus tuck her, *or* err, etc.

Ū′KUS

d: çȧ-dū′çous.
f: fū′çus.
l: leū′çous, noç″ti-lū′çous.
m: mū′çous, mū′çus.
r: rù′kus.
Plus rebuke us, etc.
Plus new cuss, etc.

Ū′LÁ

b: Ash″tȧ-bū′lȧ, Beū′lȧh,
  Bọọ′lȧ=Bọọ′lȧ.
h: hù′lȧ=hù′lȧ.
l: Loù′lȧ, Lù′lȧ, Tal-lū′lȧ
  Wạl-lù′lȧ.
y: Eū′lȧ.
z: Mis̹-s̹öu′lȧ.
Plus rule a, etc.

UL′Á

d: mē-dul′lȧ.
m: mul′lȧh.
n: nul′lȧh.
p: am-pul′lȧ.
Plus dull a, etc.

UL′DÁ

h: Hul′dȧ.
Plus sculled a, etc.

UL′EN

k(ç): Çul′len.
m: Mç-Mul′lin, mul′lein.
s: sul′len.
Cf. dull in *or* inn, etc.

Ū′LEP

j: jū′lep.
Cf. tū′lip.

Ū′LES

d: dew′less.
j: Jew′less.
k(ç): çūe′less.
kl: çlūe′less.
m: mew′less.
p: pew′less.
skr(sçr): sçrew′less.
v: view′less.
Plus knew less *or* Les, etc.

ŪL′EST

f: bē-fọọl′est*, fọọl′est.
k(ç): çool′est.
p: pūl′est*.
r: rūl′est*.
Plus new, lest, etc.

UL′EST

d: dul′lest.
k(ç): çul′lest*.
l: lul′lest*.
n: an-nul′lest*.
sk(sç): sçul′lest*.
Plus trull, lest, etc.

UL′ET

g: gul′let.
k(ç): çul′let.
m: mul′let.
Cf. scull it, etc.

ŪL′ETH

f: bē-fọọl′eth*.
k(ç): çool′eth*.
p: pūl′eth*.
r: rúl′eth*.

(Choose only one word out of each group)

UL'ETH

d: dul'leth*.
g: gul'leth*.
l: lul'leth*.
n: an-nul'leth*.
sk(sc̲): sc̲ul'leth*.

UL'FŨR

s: sul'phũr.
Cf. Gulf'ẽr.
Plus dull fur *or* fir, etc.
Cf. scull for, etc.
Plus engulf her *or* err, etc.

UL'GĂR

v: vul'găr.
Plus dull gar, etc.

UL'GĀT

m: prō-mul'gāte.
v: vul'gāte.
Plus dull gate, etc.

U̇'LI

bl: blūe'ly.
ch: pat-chöu'li.
d: Dọọ'ley, dū'ly, un-dū'ly.
dr: drọọl'ly.
g: gūl'y*.
h: Gil-họọ'ley.
k(c̲): C̲ọọ'ley, c̲ọọl'ie, c̲ọọl'ly.
l: Gil-lọọ'ley, Gil-lū'ly.
n: new'ly.
r: un-ru̇'ly.
sk(sc̲): hīgh'=sc̲họọl''y (hī').
t: tu̇'lē.
th: Thū'lē, Ul'ti-mȧ Thū'lē.
tr: tru̇'ly.
Plus few, Lee *or* lea, etc.

UL'I

d: dul'ly.
g: Gul'ley, gul'ly.
h: hul'ly.
k(c): c̲ul'ly.
s: sul'ly.
t: Tul'ly.
Plus dull, he, etc.

UL'ID

g: gul'lied.
s: sul'lied, un-sul'lied.
Cf. trull hid, etc.

U̇L'IJ

k(c̲): C̲ọọl'idġe.
Cf. rule age, etc.

UL'IJ

Vowel: ul'lăġe.
g: gul'lăġe.
s: sul'lăġe.
Cf. dull age, etc.

UL'IN

m: Mc̲-Mul'lin, mul'lein.
Cf. ul'en.
Plus dull in *or* inn, etc.

U̇L'ING

dr: drọọl'ing.
f: bē-fọọl'ing, fọọl'ing, nō fọọl'ing.
k(c̲): c̲ọọl'ing.
m: mewl'ing.
p: pūl'ing.
r: mis-ru̇l'ing, ō''vẽr-ru̇l'ing, ru̇l'ing.
sk(sc̲): sc̲họọl'ing.
sp: spọọl'ing.
t: tọọl'ing.

UL'ING

d: dul'ling.
g: gul'ling.

(Choose only one word out of each group)

h: hul'ling.
k(c): cul'ling.
l: lul'ling.
m: mul'ling.
n: an-nul'ling.
sk(sc): scul'ling.

UL'INZ

m: Mc-Mul'lins, Mul'lins,
   mul'leins.
Plus dull inns *or* ins, etc.

Ū'LIP

t: tū'lip.
Cf. jù'lep.
Plus new lip, etc.
Cf. school hip, etc.

UL'IS

k(c): pōrt-cul'lis.

ÙL'ISH

f: fọọl'ish, pound'=fọọl'ish,
   tom'=fọọl'ish.
k(c): cọọl'ish.
m: mūl'ish.

UL'ISH

d: dul'lish.
g: gul'lish.

Ū'LIKS

d: spon-dū'lix.
Plus new licks, etc.

UL'JENS

d: in-dul'gence,
   self'=in-dul'gence.
f: ef-ful'gence, rē-ful'gence.
Cf. dull gents, etc.
Cf. bulge hence, etc.

UL'JENT

d: in-dul'gent, self'=in-dul'gent.
f: cīr"cum-ful'gent, ef-ful'gent,
   ful'gent, in"tēr-ful'gent,
   prō-ful'gent, rē-ful'gent.
m: ē-mul'gent.
Plus trull, gent, etc.

UL'JEST

b: bul'gest*.
d: in-dul'gest*.
f: ef-ful'gest*.
m: prō-mul'gest*.
v: dī-vul'gest*.
Plus dull jest, etc.

UL'JETH

b: bul'geth*.
d: in-dul'geth*.
f: ef-ful'geth*.
m: prō-mul'geth*.
v: dī-vul'geth*.

UL'JEZ

b: bul'ges.
d: in-dul'ges.
f: ef-ful'ges.
m: prō-mul'ges.
v: dī-vul'ges.
Cf. bulge is, etc.
Plus bulge, Ez, etc.

UL'JING

b: bul'ging.
d: in-dul'ging.
f: ef-ful'ging.
m: prō-mul'ging.
v: dī-vul'ging.

ULJ'MENT

d: in-dulg'ment.
v: dī-vulg'ment.
Plus bulge meant, etc.

741 ūse, bṳll, brûte, tûrn, up; crȳ, myth; cat, machine, ace, church, chord; ġem, añger, (Fr.) boṅ, aṣ; THis, thin; aẓure

UL'JŪR
ULP'TŎR

(Choose only one word out of each group)

UL'JŪR

b: Bul'ġēr.
d: in-dul'ġēr.
m: prō-mul'ġēr.
v: dī-vul'ġēr.
Plus divulge her *or* err, etc.

UL'KĀT

k(c): in-cul'cāte.
s: sul'cāte, trī-sul'cāte.
Plus dull, Kate, etc.
Plus hulk eight *or* ate, etc.

UL'KING

b: bulk'ing.
h: hulk'ing.
s: sulk'ing.
sk: skulk'ing.
Plus dull king, etc.

UL'KI

b: bul'ky.
h: hul'ky.
s: sul'ky.
Plus dull key, etc.
Plus bulk, he, etc.

UL'KŪR

b: bul'kēr.
s: sul'kēr.
sk: skul'kēr.
Plus hulk her *or* err, etc.

UL'MĂN

Vowel: Ull'măn.
Plus dull man, etc.

ŬL'NES

k(c): cool'ness.

UL'NES

d: dull'ness.

UL'Ō

h: hul'lō.
n: nul'lō.
Plus trull owe *or* O, etc.

UL'OK

h: hul'lock*.
r: row'lock (rul').
Cf. dull lock, etc.

UL'PĀT

k(c): dis-cul'pāte, ex-cul'pāte, in-cul'pāte.
Plus dull pate, etc.

UL'PEST

g: gul'pest*.
p: pul'pest*.
sk(sc): sculp'est*.
Plus dull pest, etc.

UL'PETH

g: gul'peth*.
p: pul'peth*.
sk(sc): scul'peth*.

UL'PI

g: gul'py.
p: pul'py.
Plus sculp, he, etc.

UL'PĪN, UL'PIN

v: vul'pīne (*or* 'pin).
Plus dull pine *or* dull pin, etc.
Plus sculp in *or* inn, etc.

UL'PRIT

k(c): cul'prit.
Plus pulp writ, etc.

ULP'TŎR

sk(sc): sculp'tŏr.
Cf. pulped her *or* err, etc.

(Choose only one word out of each group)

ULP'TŪR

sk(sç): sçulp'tūre.
Plus pulped your *or* you're, etc.

UL'SEST

m: mul'sest*.
p: rē-pul'sest*.
v: çon-vul'sest*.

UL'SET

d: dul'cet.
Plus trull set, etc.

UL'SETH

m: mul'seth*.
p: rē-pul'seth*.
v: çon-vul'seth*.

UL'SHUN

m: dē-mul'sion, ē-mul'sion.
p: ap-pul'sion, çom-pul'sion,
ex-pul'sion, im-pul'sion,
prō-pul'sion, pul'sion,
rē-pul'sion.
v: à-vul'sion, çon-vul'sion,
dī-vul'sion, ē-vul'sion,
rē-vul'sion.
Plus trull shun, etc.

UL'SING

p: pul'sing, rē-pul'sing.
v: çon-vul'sing.
Plus trull sing, etc.

UL'SIV

m: ē-mul'sive.
p: ap-pul'sive, çom-pul'sive,
ex-pul'sive, im-pul'sive,
prō-pul'sive, pul'sive,
rē-pul'sive.

v: çon-vul'sive, dī-vul'sive,
rē-vul'sive.
Plus dull sieve, etc.

UL'SUR

Vowel: ul'cẽr.
p: rē-pul'sẽr.
Plus trull, sir, etc.
Plus convulse her *or* err, etc.

UL'TĂN

s: sul'tăn.
Plus dull tan, etc.
Plus occult an *or* Ann, etc.

UL'TĂNS

z: ex-ul'tănce, rē-ṣul'tănce.
Plus consult aunts *or* ants, etc.

UL'TĂNT

z: ex-ul'tănt, rē-ṣul'tănt.
Plus insult aunt *or* ant, etc.

UL'TED

k(ç): oç-çul'ted.
s: çon-sul'ted, in-sul'ted.
z: ex-ul'ted, rē-ṣul'ted.
Plus dull, Ted, etc.
Plus result, Ed, etc.

UL'TEST

k(ç): oç-çul'test*.
s: çon-sul'test*, in-sul'test*.
z: ex-ul'test*, rē-ṣul'test*.
Plus dull test, etc.

UL'TETH

k(ç): oç-çul'teth*.
s: çon-sul'teth*, in-sul'teth*.
z: ex-ul'teth*, rē-ṣul'teth*.

743 ūse, bu̧ll, brúte, tũrn, up; crȳ, myth; çat, maçhine, ace, church, çhord; ġem, aṅger, (Fr.) boṅ, a̧s; THis, thin; aᴢure

UL'TING
UL'YUN

(Choose only one word out of each group)

UL'TING

k(ç): oç-çul'ting.
s: çon-sul'ting, in-sul'ting.
z: ex-ul'ting, rē-s̱ult'ing.

UL'TIV

s: çon-sul'tive.
z: ex-ul'tive.

ULT'NES

d: á-dult'ness.
k(ç): oç-çult'ness.

UL'TRI

s: sul'try.
Cf. "ul'tri".

UL'TŪR

k(ç): ag'ri-çul″tūre, ā'pi-çul″tūre, är-bōr'i-çul″tūre, ā'vi-çul″tūre, çul'tūre, flō'ri-çul″tūre, hor'ti-çul″tūre, in-çul'tūre, pis'çi-çul″tūre, self'-çul'tūre, syl'vi-çul″tūre, ter'rà-çul″tūre, vit'i-çul″tūre.
m: mul'tūre.
v: vul'tūre.
Plus consult your *or* you're, etc.

UL'TŪR

s: çon-sul'tẽr, in-sul'tẽr.
z: ex-ul'tẽr, rē-s̱ul'tẽr.
Plus occult her *or* err, etc.

Ú'LU

l: Hon″ō-lú'lú, Lú'lú.
z: Ᶎú'lú.
Plus new loo *or* Lou, etc.

U̇L'ŪR

dr: dro̦ol'ẽr.
k(ç): çoo̦l'ẽr, rid'i-çul-ẽr, wa̧t'ẽr çoo̦l'ẽr, wīne çoo̦l'ẽr.

m: mewl'ẽr.
p: pūl'ẽr.
r: rúl'ẽr.
sp: spoo̦l'ẽr.
Plus rule her *or* err, etc.

UL'ŪR

d: dul'lẽr, me-dul'lẽr.
g: gul'lẽr.
h: hul'lẽr.
k(ç): çŏl'ŏr, çul'lẽr, dis-çŏl'ŏr, mis-çŏl'ŏr, mul'ti-çŏl″ŏr, rē-çŏl'ŏr, rōs̱e'-çŏl'ŏr, teçh'ni-çŏl″ŏr, trī'çŏl'ŏr, wa̧t'ẽr çŏl'ŏr.
kr: çrul'lẽr.
l: lul'lẽr.
m: Mul'lẽr.
n: an-nul'lẽr.
sk(sç): sçul'ler.
Plus dull her *or* err, etc.

UL'ŪRD

d: dul'lărd.
k(ç): çŏl'ŏred, dis-çŏl'ŏred, hīgh'-çŏl'ŏred (hī'), ō″vẽr-çŏl'ŏred, pär'ti-çŏl″ŏred, pär'ty-çŏl″ŏred, pēaçh'-çŏl″ŏred, rō'sy-çŏl″ŏred, skȳ'-çŏl″ŏred, wīne'-çŏl″ŏred.
Plus cruller'd, etc.

Ú'LŪS

skr(sçr): sçrew'loo̦se.
Plus you loose, etc.

Ū'LYĂR

k(ç): pē-çū'liăr.

UL'YUN

k(ç): çul'lion.
m: mul'lion.
sk(sç): sçul'lion.

ÚL'YUS
UM'BLEST

fāte, fär, fȧst, fạll, finăl, cāre, at; mēte, prey, hẽr, met; pīne,
marīne, bĭrd, pĭn; nōte, mŏve, fọr, atŏm, not; mọọn, book;

744

(Choose only one word out of each group)

ÚL'YUS

j: Jùl'ius.
p: Ȧ-pūl'ius.
Cf. ūl'i-us.

Ū'MȦ

d: dū'ma.
p: pū'mȧ.
y: Yū'mȧ.
z: mȧ-zū'mȧ, Mon"tē-zū'mȧ.
Plus who, ma, etc.
Plus entomb a, etc.

Ū'MĂN

h: hū'măn, in-hū'măn,
sū"pẽr-hū'măn.
n: New'măn.
tr: Trú'măn.
Plus who, man, etc.

ŪM'ĀT

h: ex-hūm'āte, in-hūm'āte.
sp: dē-spūm'āte.
Plus new mate, etc.
Plus room eight *or* ate, etc.

UM'ĂT

s: çon-sum'măte.
Plus dumb eight *or* ate, etc.

UM'BȦ, ÚM'BȦ

r: rum'bȧ (*or* rùm').
Plus dumb, *or* doom, bah!, etc.

UM'BAT

k(ç): çŏm'bat.
Cf. wŏm'bat.
Plus some bat, etc.

UM'BEL

d: dumb'bell.
Plus some bell, etc.

UM'BENT

c: aç-çum'bent, dē-çum'bent,
in-çum'bent, prō-çum'bent,
rē-çum'bent,
sū"pẽr-in-çum'bent.
Plus some bent, etc.

UM'BIÇ

l: çō-lum'biç.
pl: plum'biç.

UM'B'L

Vowel: um'bel, hum'ble (um')*.
b: bum'ble.
f: fum'ble.
gr: grum'ble.
h: hum'ble.
j: bē-jum'ble, jum'ble.
kr: çrum'ble.
m: mum'ble.
r: rum'ble.
sk(sç): sçum'ble.
st: stum'ble.
Cf. some bull, etc.

UM'B'LD

h: hum'bled, un-hum'bled.
Plus um'b'l+d.

UM'BLEST

f: fum'blest*.
gr: grum'blest*.
h: hum'blest.
j: jum'blest*.
kr: çrum'blest*.
m: mum'blest*.
r: rum'blest*.
st: stum'blest*.
t: tum'blest*.
Plus some blest. etc.

(Choose only one word out of each group)

UM'BLETH

f: fum'bleth*.
gr: grum'bleth*.
h: hum'bleth*.
j: jum'bleth*.
kr: с̣rum'bleth*.
m: mum'bleth*.
r: rum'bleth*.
st: sum'bleth*.
t: tum'bleth*.

UM'BLI

h: hum'bly.
j: Jum'bly.
kr: с̣rum'bly.
st: stum'bly.
t: tum'bly.

UM'BLING

f: fum'bling.
gr: grum'bling.
h: hum'bling.
j: jum'bling.
kr: с̣rum'bling.
m: mum'bling.
r: rum'bling.
st: stum'bling.
t: tum'bling.

UM'BLŨR

dr: drum'blẽr.
f: fum'blẽr.
gr: grum'blẽr.
h: hum'blẽr.
j: jum'blẽr.
kr: с̣rum'blẽr.
m: mum'blẽr.
r: rum'blẽr.
st: stum'blẽr.
t: tum'blẽr.

UM'BŌ

g: gum'bō.
j: Jum'bō, Mum'bō=Jum'bō.
m: Mum'bō.
Plus some beau, bo *or* bow, etc.

UM'BRAT

Vowel: in-um'brāte,
   ob-um'brāte.
d: à-dum'brāte.

UM'BRIJ

Vowel: um'brăġe.

UM'BRIL

t: tum'bril.
Plus come, Brill, etc.

UM'BRUS

k(с̣): с̣um'brous.
n: pē-num'brous.
sl: slum'brous, un-slum'brous.

UM'BUG

h: hum'bug.
Plus some bug, etc.

UM'BУ̣L

tr: Trum'bу̣ll.
Plus some bull, etc.

UM'BŨR

h: Hum'bẽr.
k(с̣): с̣um'bẽr, dis″en-с̣um'bẽr,
   en-с̣um'bẽr.
l: lum'băr, lum'bẽr.
n: num'bẽr, out-num'bẽr.
sl: slum'bẽr.
Plus some burr, etc.

UM'BŨRD

n: num'bẽred, out-num'bẽred,
   un-num'bẽred.
Plus um'būr+ed.
Plus some bird, etc.

UM'DRUM fāte, fär, fȧst, fạll, finăl, cāre, at; mēte, prĕy, hẽr, met; pīne,
UM'FĂL marīne, bĭrd, pĭn; nōte, mŏve, fọr, atŏm, not; mọọn, book; **746**

(Choose only one word out of each group)

UM'DRUM
h: hum'drum.
Plus come, drum, etc.

UM'EL
h: hum'mel.
p: bē-pum'mel, pŏm'mel,
pum'mel.
Plus drum'll, etc.

Ū'MEN
b: al-bū'men.
g: lē-gū'men.
k(c): ȧ-cū'men, cat″ē-chū'men.
l: lū'men.
r: rū'men.
t: bi-tū'men.
Cf. ū'min.
Plus you men, etc.

Ū'MENT
b: im-būe'ment.
br: im-brūe'ment.
ch: es-chew'ment.
d: in-dūe'ment, sub-dūe'ment.
kr: ac-crū'ment.
Plus you meant, etc.

ŪM'EST
b: bọọm'est*.
bl: blọọm'est*.
d: dọọm'est*.
f: fūm'est*, pēr-fūm'est*.
gr: grọọm'est*.
h: ex-hūm'est*.
l: il-lūm'est*, lọọm'est*.
pl: plūm'est*.
s: as-sūm'est*, cọn-sūm'est*.
t: cọs-tūm'est*, en-tömb'est*.
z: prē-şūm'est*, rē-şūm'est*.
Plus who messed, etc.

UM'EST
d: dumb'est.
dr: drum'mest*.
g: gum'mest*.
gl: glum'mest.
h: hum'mest*.
k(c): bē-cŏm'est*, cŏm'est*,
ō″vēr-cŏm'est*, suc-cumb'est*.
n: numb'est.
r: rum'mest.
str: strum'mest.
Cf. bum messed, etc.

UM'ET
gr: grum'met.
pl: plum'met.
Cf. sum'mit.
Plus Lum et, etc.
Cf. numb it, etc.

ŪM'ETH
b: bọọm'eth*.
bl: blọọm'eth*.
d: dọọm'eth*.
f: fūm'eth*, pēr-fūm'eth*.
gr: grọọm'eth*.
h: ex-hūm'eth*.
l: il-lūm'eth*, lọọm'eth*.
pl: plūm'eth*.
s: as-sūm'eth*, cọn-sūm'eth*.
t: cọs-tūm'eth*, en-tömb'eth*.
z: prē-şūm'eth*, rē-şūm'eth*.

UM'ETH
dr: drum'meth*.
g: gum'meth*.
h: hum'meth*.
k(c): bē-cŏm'eth*, cŏm'eth*,
ō″vēr-cŏm'eth*, suc-cumb'eth*.
str: strum'meth*.

UM'FĂL
Vowel: trī-um'phăl.

747   ūse, bṳll, brúte, tûrn, up; crȳ, myth; çat, maçhine, ace,
     church, çhord; ġem, aṅger, (Fr.) boṅ, aṣ; THis, thin; aẓure

UM'FĀNT
ŪM'IN

(Choose only one word out of each group)

UM'FĀNT
Vowel: trī-um'phănt.

UM'FIT
k(c): çŏm'fit.
Plus some fit, etc.

UM'FŎRT
k(c): çŏm'fŏrt.
Plus some fort, etc.

UM'FRI
h: Hum'phrey.
Plus some free, etc.

UM'FRIZ
h: Hum'phreyṣ.
Plus some "friz", etc.

ŬM'FṲL
bl: bloọm'fṳl.
d: doọm'fṳl.

ŪM'I
bl: bloọm'y.
br: broọm'y.
f: fūm'y.
gl: gloọm'y.
pl: plūm'y.
r: rheûm'y, roọm'y.
sp: spūm'y.
y: Fi-ū'mē.
Plus who, me, etc.
Plus tomb, he, etc.

UM'I
d: dum'my.
g: gum'my.
kr: crumb'y, crum'mie.
l: lum'my.
m: mum'my.
pl: plum'my.
r: aṳc'tion rum'my,
  Eṅg'lish rum'my,

fōur'-hand' rum'my,
Ja'và rum'my,
Miçh'i-găn rum'my (mish'),
rum'my.
sk(sc): scum'my.
skr(scr): scrum'my.
t: tum'my.
thr: thrum'my.
y: yum'my.
Cf. hum me, etc.

ŪM'ID
h: hūm'id.
t: tūm'id.
Cf. loom hid, etc.
Plus who 'mid*, etc.

ŪM'IJ
f: fūm'ăġe.
pl: plūm'ăġe.
Cf. tomb age, etc.
Cf. new mage, etc.

UM'IJ
ch: chum'măġe.
r: rum'măġe.
skr(scr): scrum'măġe.
Cf. some mage, etc.
Cf. some age, etc.

UM'IM
th: Thum'mim.
z: Ẓam-zum'mim.
Plus drum him, etc.

ŪM'IN
b: al-bū'mim.
l: il-lūm'ine, rē-lūm'ine.
Cf. ūm'en.
Plus tomb in, etc.
Plus who, Min, etc.

UM'IN
UM'LI

fāte, fär, fàst, fạll, finăl, cãre, at; mēte, prẹy, hẽr, met; pīne, marine, bĩrd, pin; nōte, mŏve, fọr, atŏm, not; mọọn, book;

748

(Choose only one word out of each group)

UM'IN

k(ç): çum'in, çum'min.
Plus rum in or inn, etc.

ŪM'ING

b: bọọm'ing.
bl: blọọm'ing, rē-blọọm'ing.
br: brọọm'ing, new'-brọọm'ing.
d: dọọm'ing, prē-dọọm'ing.
f: fūm'ing, pēr-fūm'ing.
gl: glọọm'ing.
gr: grọọm'ing.
h: ex-hūm'ing.
l: il-lūm'ing, lọọm'ing.
pl: plūm'ing.
r: rọọm'ing.
s: as-sūm'ing, çon-sūm'ing, un"as-sūm'ing.
sp: spūm'ing.
t: dis"en-tŏmb'ing, en-tŏmb'ing, tŏmb'ing.
v: vọọm'ing.
w: un-wŏmb'ing, wŏmb'ing.
z: prē-ṣūm'ing, rē-ṣūm'ing, un"prē-ṣūm'ing, zọọm'ing.
Plus new Ming, etc.

UM'ING

b: bum'ming.
ch: chum'ming.
dr: drum'ming.
g: gum'ming.
h: hum'ming.
k(ç): bē-çŏm'ing, çŏm'ing, fõrth-çŏm'ing, ō"vēr-çŏm'ing, shọrt'çŏm"ing, suç-çumb'ing, un"bē-çŏm'ing.
kr: çrumb'ing.
m: mum'ming.
n: bē-numb'ing, numb'ing.
pl: plumb'ing, plum'ming.

s: sum'ming.
skr(sçr): sçrum'ming.
sl: slum'ming.
str: strum'ming.
th: thumb'ing.
Cf. some Ming, etc.

UM'INGZ

k(ç): çŏm'ingṣ, shọrt'çŏm"ingṣ, Çum'mingṣ.
Plus um'ing+s

UM'IS

p: pum'ice.
Cf. come, miss, etc.

UM'IT

s: sum'mit.
Cf. um'et.
Plus dumb it, etc.
Cf. some mitt, etc.

ŪM'LES

bl: blọọm'less.
br: brọọm'less.
d: dọọm'less.
f: fūme'less.
gr: grọọm'less.
l: lọọm'less.
pl: plūme'less.
r: rọọm'less.
t: tŏmb'less.
Plus whom, Les or less, etc.

ŪM'LET

b: bọọm'let.
gr: grọọm'let.
pl: plūme'let.
Plus tomb let, or Lett, etc.

UM'LI

ch: Cholmondes'ley (chum'), Chum'ley.

749 üse, bụll, brûte, tûrn, up; crȳ, myth; çat, maçhine, ace,
church, çhord; ġem, añger, (Fr.) boṅ, aṣ; THis, thin; aẓure

UM'NĂL
UM'PI

(Choose only one word out of each group)

d: dumb'ly.
gl: glum'ly.
n: numb'ly.
r: ruml'y.
s: çum'bẽr-sŏme-ly,
frol'iç-sŏme-ly, hŭm'ŏr-sŏme-ly,
trou'ble-sŏme-ly (trub'), etc.
Plus come, Lee *or* lea, etc.

UM'NĂL

l: çō-lum'năl.
t: ạu-tum'năl.

UM'NES

d: dumb'ness.
gl: glum'ness.
n: numb'ness.

UM'NŨR

s: Sum'nẽr.

UM'ŎK

h: hum'mŏck.
st: stŏm'ăçh.
Cf. some mock, etc.
Cf. some muck, etc.

UM'ŎKS

h: hum'mŏcks.
l: lum'mŏx.
st: stŏm'ăçhs.

UM'ON

k(ç): çŏme on.
s: sum'mŏn.
Plus dumb on *or* an, etc.

UM'ŎND

dr: Drum'mŏnd.
s: sum'mŏned.
Cf. numb and, etc.

UM'PĂS, UM'PUS

k(ç): çŏm'păss, en-çom'păss.
r: rum'pus.
Cf. some pass *or* puss, etc.

UMP'EST

b: bump'est*.
d: dump'est*.
h: hump'est*.
j: jump'est*.
l: lump'est*.
p: pump'est*.
pl: plump'est.
st: stump'est*.
th: bē-thump'est*, thump'est*.
tr: trump'est*.
Plus some pest, etc.

UM'PET

kr: çrum'pet.
str: strum'pet.
tr: trum'pet.
Plus some pet, etc.
Plus chump et, etc.
Cf. trump it, etc.

UMP'ETH

b: bump'eth*.
d: dump'eth*.
h: hump'eth*.
j: jump'eth*.
l: lump'eth*.
p: pump'eth*.
st: stump'eth*.
th: bē-thump'eth*, thump'eth*.
tr: trump'eth*.

UM'PI

b: bum'py.
ch: chum'py.
d: dum'py.

UMP'ING
UM'PŌ

fāte, fär, fåst, fạll, finăl, cãre, at; mēte, prey, hẽr, met; pīne,
marïne, bĩrd, pin; nōte, mŏve, fọr, atŏm, not; mọọn, book;

750

(Choose only one word out of each group)

fr: frum'py.
gr: grum'py.
h: hum'py.
j: jum'py.
kl: c̹lum'py.
kr: c̹rum'py.
l: lum'py.
m: mum'py.
pl: plum'py.
r: rum'py.
sl: slum'py.
st: stum'py.
th: thum'py.
Plus thump, he, etc.

UMP'ING

b: bump'ing.
d: dump'ing.
h: hump'ing.
j: broad'₌jump″ing,
  hīgh'₌jump″ing (hī'), jump'ing.
kl: c̹lump'ing.
l: gȧ-lump'ing, lump'ing.
m: mump'ing.
p: pump'ing.
pl: plump'ing.
sl: slump'ing.
st: stump'ing.
th: bē-thump'ing, thump'ing.
tr: trump'ing.
Plus some ping, etc.

UM'PĪR

Vowel: um'pīre.
Plus chump ire, etc.
Plus some pyre, etc.

UMP'ISH

b: bump'ish.
ch: chump'ish.
d: dump'ish.

fr: frump'ish.
gr: grump'ish.
h: hump'ish.
j: jump'ish.
l: lump'ish.
m: mump'ish.
pl: plump'ish.
sl: slump'ish.
Plus dumb, pish!, etc.

UMP'KIN

b: bump'kin.
p: pump'kin.
Cf. Lum'kin.
Plus thump kin, etc.

UM'P'L

kr: c̹rum'ple.
r: rum'ple, un-rum'ple.
Plus stump'll, etc.
Cf. some pull, etc.

UMP'LEST

kr: c̹rump'lest*.
r: rump'lest*, un-rump'lest*.
Plus trump, lest, etc.

UMP'LETH

kr: c̹rump'leth*.
r: rump'leth*, un-rump'leth*.

UMP'LING

d: dump'ling.
kr: c̹rump'ling.
r: rump'ling, un-rump'ling.

UMP'NES

pl: plump'ness.

UM'PŌ

b: Bum'pō.
Plus some Poe *or* Po, etc.

(Choose only one word out of each group)

UMP'SHUN

g: gump'tion.
s: as-sump'tion, c̣on-sump'tion, sub-sump'tion.
z: prē-ṣump'tion, rē-ṣump'tion.
Plus trump shun, etc.

UMP'SHUS

b: bump'tious.
skr(sc̣r): sc̣rump'tious.

UMP'TIV

s: as-sump'tive, c̣on-sump'tive, sub-sump'tive.
z: prē-ṣump'tive, rē-ṣump'tive.

UMP'ŪR

b: bump'ēr.
d: dump'ēr.
j: broad'꞊jump″ēr, c̣oun'tēr꞊jump″ēr, hīgh'꞊jump'ēr (hī'), jump'ēr.
l: lump'ēr.
m: mump'ēr.
p: pump'ēr.
pl: plump'ēr.
sl: slump'ēr.
st: stump'ēr.
th: bē-thump'ēr, thump'ēr, tub'꞊thump'ēr.
tr: trump'ēr.
Plus trump her *or* err, etc.
Plus some purr *or* per, etc.

UM'PUS

r: rum'pus.
Cf. um'pǎs.
Plus some puss, etc.

U̇M'STŌN

t: tömb'stōne.
Plus room stone, etc.

UM'TŪR

s: Fōrt Sum'tēr, sum'tēr.
Cf. trumped her *or* err, etc.

ŪM'ŪR

b: boom'ēr.
bl: bloom'ēr.
d: doom'ēr.
f: fūm'ēr, pēr-fūm'ēr.
h: good'꞊hūm'ŏr, hūm'ŏr, ill'꞊hūm'ŏr.
l: il-lūm'ēr.
pl: os'trich plūm'ēr, plūm'ēr.
r: room'ēr, rùm'ŏr.
s: as-sūm'ēr, c̣on-sūm'ēr.
t: en-tōmb'ēr, tūm'ŏr.
z: prē-ṣūm'ēr, rē-ṣūm'ēr.
Plus new myrrh, etc.
Plus tomb her *or* err, etc.

UM'ŪR

d: dumb'ēr.
dr: drum'mēr.
g: gum'mēr.
gl: glum'mēr.
gr: grum'mēr.
h: hum'mēr.
k(c̣): c̣öm'ēr, C̣um'mēr, in'c̣öm-ēr, lāte'꞊c̣öm'ēr, new'c̣öm-ēr.
m: mum'mēr.
n: numb'ēr.
pl: plumb'ēr.
r: rum'mēr.
s: mid'sum″mēr, sum'mēr.
sk(sc̣): sc̣um'mēr.
skr(sc̣r): sc̣rum'mēr.
str: strum'mēr.
Cf. some myrrh, etc.
Plus numb her *or* err, etc.

(Choose only one word out of each group)

ŪM'ŪRD

h: gọọd'=hūm'ŏred, hūm'ŏred,
ill'=hūm'ŏred.
r: rům'ŏred.
t: tům'ŏred.
Cf. tomb herd *or* heard, etc.

ŪM'ŪRZ

bl: blọọm'ẽrṣ.
Plus ūm'ūr+s.

UM'ŪRZ

s: Sŏm'ẽrṣ.
Plus um'ūr+s.

ŮM'US

br: brům'ous.
d: dūm'ous.
f: fūm'ous.
gr: grům'ous.
h: hūm'ous, hūm'us.
pl: im-plūm'ous, plūm'ous.
sp: spūm'ous.
Plus bloom us, etc.

ŮMZ'DĀ

d: dọọmṣ'dāy.
Plus perfumes day, etc.

UM'ZI

kl: clum'ṣy.
m: mum'ṣie.
Plus some Z *or* Zee, etc.

ŮMZ'MĂN

d: dọọmṣ'măn.
gr: grọọmṣ'măn.
Plus tombs man, etc.

Ū'NĄ

k(c): Á-cū'nạ, là-cū'nạ,
vī-cū'nạ.
l: lū'nạ.
p: pū'nạ.

r: Pē-rú'nạ.
t: fōr-tū'nạ.
y: ū'nạ.
Plus tune a, etc.

ŪN'ĂL

b: trī-būn'ăl.
k(c): là-cūn'ăl.
Plus tune, Al, etc.

UNCH'EST

b: bunch'est*.
h: hunch'est*.
kr: crunch'est*.
l: lunch'est*.
m: munch'est*.
p: punch'est*.
skr(scr): scrunch'est*.
Plus one chest, etc.

UNCH'ETH

b: bunch'eth*.
h: hunch'eth*.
kr: crunch'eth*.
l: lunch'eth*.
m: munch'eth*.
p: punch'eth*.
skr(scr): scrunch'eth*.

UN'CHEZ

b: bun'cheṣ.
br: brun'cheṣ.
h: hun'cheṣ.
kr: crun'cheṣ.
l: lun'cheṣ.
m: mun'cheṣ.
p: pun'cheṣ.
skr(scr): scrun'cheṣ.

UN'CHI

b: bun'chy.
h: hun'chy.

(Choose only one word out of each group)

kr: c̯run'chy.
p: pun'chy.
Plus lunch, he, etc.

UN'CHING

b: bun'ching.
br: brun'ching.
h: hun'ching.
kr: c̯run'ching.
l: lun'ching.
m: mun'ching.
p: pun'ching.
skr(sc̯r): sc̯run'ching.

UN'CHUN

br: brun'cheon.
l: lun'cheon.
n: nun'cheon.
p: pun'cheon.
sk(sc̯): sc̯un'cheon.
tr: trun'cheon.

UNCH'ŪR

b: bunch'ēr.
br: brunch'ēr.
h: hunch'ēr.
kr: c̯runch'ēr.
l: lunch'ēr.
m: munch'ēr.
p: c̯ow'punch″ēr, punch'ēr.
skr(sc̯r): sc̯runch'ēr.
Plus lunch her or err, etc.

UN'DĀN

m: an″tē-mun'dāne,
ex″trà-mun'dāne,
in″frà-mun'dāne,
in″tēr-mun'dāne,
in″trà-mun'dāne, mun'dāne,
sū″pēr-mun'dāne,
sū″prà-mun'dāne,
ul″trà-mun'dāne.
Plus stun Dane or deign, etc.

UN'DĂNS

b: à-bun'dănce,
sū″pēr-à-bun'dănce.
d: rē-dun'dănce.
Plus sun dance, etc.
Plus stunned aunts or ants, etc.

UN'DĂNT

b: à-bun'dănt,
sū″pēr-à-bun'dănt.
d: rē-dun'dănt.
Plus stunned aunt or ant, etc.

UN'DĀT

k(c̯): fē-c̯un'dāte, sē-c̯ŏn'dāte.
Plus one date, etc.
Plus stunned ate or eigh̲t, etc.

ŬN'DED

w: un-wöun'ded, wöun'ded.
Plus loon dead, etc.
Cf. loon did, etc.

UN'DED

Vowel: un'dead.
f: fun'ded, rē-fun'ded.
t: rē-tun'ded*.
Plus one dead, etc.
Cf. one did, etc.
Plus gunned, Ed, etc.

ŬN'DEST

kr: c̯roo̲n'dest*, etc.
w: wöund'est*.

UN'DEST

f: fun'dest*.

ŬN'DETH

kr: c̯roo̲n'deth*, etc.
w: wöun'deth*.
Plus noon death, etc.

(Choose only one word out of each group)

UN′DETH

f: fun′deth*.
Plus one death, etc.

UN′DI

b: Bun′dy.
f: fun′di, Fun′dy.
g: sal″mȧ-gun′di.
gr: Grun′dy, Mrs. Grun′dy.
l: Lun′dy.
m: Mŏn′day.
s: Sun′day.
Plus sunned, he, etc.
Cf. shun day, etc.

UN′DIN

r: hī-run′dine.
Plus begun din, etc.
Plus stunned in, etc.

UN′DING

f: fund′ing, rē-fund′ing.

UN′DIT

k(ç): çŏn′duit.
p: pun′dit.
Plus stunned it, etc.

UN′D′L

b: bun′dle, un-bun′dle.
tr: trun′dle.
Plus fund′ll, etc.
Cf. one dull, etc.

UND′LEST

b: bund′lest*, un-bund′lest*.
tr: trund′lest*.
Plus fund, lest, etc.

UND′LETH

b: bund′leth*, un-bund′leth*.
tr: trund′leth*.

UND′LING

b: bund′ling, un-bund′ling.
tr: trund′ling.

UN′DRED

h: hun′dred.
Plus one dread, etc.

UN′DRI

s: sun′dry.
th: thun′dry*.

UN′DRUS

w: wŏn′drous.
Plus fund, Russ, etc.

UN′DUM

r: çär-bō-run′dum.
Cf. çŏn′dŏm.
Plus fund ′em, etc.
Plus one dumb, etc.

UN′DUN

l: Lŏn′dŏn.
Cf. un-dŏne′.
Plus fun done, etc.
Plus stunned an, etc.

UN′DŪR

Vowel: down′⹀un′dẽr,
　THere-un′dẽr, un′dẽr.
bl: blun′dẽr.
d: dun′dẽr.
f: rē-fund′ẽr.
g: Gun′dẽr.
pl: plun′dẽr.
s: ȧ-sun′dẽr, dis-sun′dẽr,
　sun′dẽr.
t: rō-tund′ẽr.
th: en-thun′dẽr, thun′dẽr.
w: wŏn′dẽr.
Plus stunned her *or* err, etc.

(Choose only one word out of each group)

UN′EL

f: fun′nel.
g: gun′wale (′nl).
r: run′nel.
t: tun′nel.
tr: trun′nel.
Plus gun′ll, etc.

UN′ET

p: pun′net.
r: run′net.
Cf. fun it, etc.
Cf. dun net, etc.

Ū′NES

bl: blūe′ness.
f: few′ness.
n: new′ness.
tr: trúe′ness.
Plus moon S, etc.

ŪN′EST

kr: c̣rọọn′est*.
m: c̣om-mūn′est*, mọọn′est*.
p: här-pọọn′est*, im-pūgn′est*,
  op-pūgn′est*.
pr: prún′est*.
s: sọọn′est.
sp: spọọn′est*.
sw: swọọn′est*.
t: at-tūn′est*, en-tūn′est*,
  im-pọr-tūn′est*, tūn′est*.
Plus new nest, etc.

UN′EST

f: fun′nest*.
g: gun′nest*.
p: pun′nest*.
r: out-run′nest*,
  ō″vẽr-run′nest*, run′nest*.
sh: shun′nest*.
st: stun′nest*.
w: wŏn′nest*.

ŪN′ETH

kr: c̣rọọn′eth*.
m: c̣om-mūn′eth*, mọọn′eth*.
p: här-pọọn′eth*, im-pūgn′eth*,
  op-pūgn′eth*.
pr: prún′eth*.
sp: spọọn′eth*.
sw: swọọn′eth*.
t: at-tūn′eth*, en-tūn′eth*,
  im″pọr-tūn′eth*, tūn′eth*.

UN′ETH

f: fun′neth*.
g: gun′neth.
p: pun′neth*.
r: out-run′neth*,
  ō″vẽr-run′neth*, run′neth*.
sh: shun′neth*.
st: stun′neth*.
w: wŏn′neth*.

ŪN′FṵL

r: rúne′fṵl.
sp: spọọn′fṵl.
t: tūne′fṵl.
Plus dune full, etc.

UNG′G′L

b: buñ′gle.
j: juñ′gle.
Cf. one guu, etc.

UNG′GLING

b: buñ′gling.
j: juñ′gling.

UNG′GŪR

h: en-huñ′ger, huñ′gẽr.
m: bal′lăd mŏñ′gẽr,
  bŏr′ōugh mŏñ′gẽr,
  fish′mŏñ″gẽr, gos′sip mŏñ′gẽr,

(Choose only one word out of each group)

īr'ŏn-mŏñ″gẽr (ī'ẽrn), mŏñ'gẽr,
Muñ'gẽr, sçan'dăl-mŏñ″gẽr.
y: youñ'gẽr.

UNGK'ĂL

Vowel: uñ'çle.
b: çär'buñ″çle.
d: pē-duñ'çle.
r: çȧ-ruñ'çle.
tr: truñ'çăl.
Plus monk, Al.
Plus hung, Cal, etc.

UNGK'ĀT

r: av″ẽr-ruñ'çāte.
tr: dē-truñ'çāte, truñ'çāte.
Plus monk ate or eight, etc.
Plus rung, Kate, etc.

UNGK'EN

dr: druñk'en.
s: suñk'en.
shr: shruñk'en.
Plus hung, Ken, etc.
Cf. drunk hen, etc.

UNGK'ET

j: juñ'ket.
pl: Pluñ'kett.
Cf. drunk it, etc.
Plus drunk, et, etc.

UNGK'I

ch: chuñk'i.
f: fuñk'y.
fl: fluñk'ey.
h: huñk'y.
m: mŏñk'ey, pow'dẽr mŏñk'ey,
  spī'dẽr mŏñk'ey.
p: puñk'ie.
sp: spuñk'y.
Plus drunk, he, etc.
Plus hung key, etc.

UNG'KIN

p: puñ'kin.
Cf. ungk'en.
Plus hung kin, etc.
Plus chunk in or inn, etc.

UNGK'ISH

f: fuñk'ish.
m: mŏñk'ish.
sk: skuñk'ish.
Plus hung Kish, etc.

UNGK'Ō

b: buñ'çō.
j: juñ'çō.
Plus drunk owe or O, etc.

UNGK'SHUN

Vowel: ex-trēme'uñç'tion,
  in-uñç'tion, uñç'tion.
f: dē-fuñç'tion, fuñç'tion.
j: ad-juñç'tion, çon-juñç'tion,
  dis-juñç'tion, in-juñç'tion,
  in″tẽr-juñç'tion, juñç'tion,
  sē-juñç'tion*, sub-juñç'tion*.
p: çom-puñç'tion, ex-puñç'tion,
  in″tẽr-puñç'tion, puñç'tion.
Plus drunk shun, etc.

UNGK'SHUS

Vowel: uñç'tious.
b: ram-buñç'tious.
p: çom-puñç'tious.

UNGK'TIV

j: ab-juñç'tive, ad-juñç'tive,
  çon-juñç'tive, dis-juñç'tive,
  sub-juñç'tive.
p: çom-puñç'tive.

(Choose only one word out of each group)

UNGK'TŨR

j: c̦on-juñc̦'tũre, juñc̦'tūre.
p: ac̦'ū-puñc̦"tūre, puñc̦'tūre.
Plus chunked your *or* you're, etc.

UNGK'UM

b: Buñ'c̦ŏmbe, buñ'kum.
Plus chunk 'em, etc.
Plus rung come, etc.

UNGK'ŨR

b: buñk'ẽr.
d: duñk'ẽr.
dr: druñk'ẽr.
f: fuñk'ẽr.
fl: fluñk'ẽr.
h: huñk'ẽr.
j: juñk'ẽr.
p: puñk'ẽr.
t: tuñk'ẽr.
Plus dunk her *or* err, etc.

UNGK'ŨRD

b: buñk'ẽred.
d: Duñk'ărd.
dr: druñk'ărd.
Cf. drunk hard, etc.
Plus flung curd *or* Kurd, etc.

UNGK'US

d: à-duñ'c̦ous.
h: dö'huñ"kus.
j: juñ'c̦ous.
Plus shrunk us, etc.
Plus hung cuss, etc.

UNG'LING

y: young'ling.

UNG'RI

h: huñ'gry.

UNG'STŨR

t: tŏngue'stẽr.
y: yŏung'stẽr.
Plus dung stir, etc.

UNG'ŨR

l: lung'ẽr, ŏne'-lung'ẽr (wun').
Plus hung her *or* err, etc.

ŪN'I

d: Do̧o̧n'ey.
l: lo̧o̧n'y.
m: Mo̧o̧n'ey, mo̧o̧n'y, Mūn'i.
p: pūis'nē, pū'ny.
r: Ro̧o̧n'ey.
sp: spo̧o̧n'y.
t: tūne'y.
Plus croon he, etc.

UN'I

b: bun'ny.
f: dö'fun"ny, fun'ny.
g: gun'ny.
h: hŏn'ey, wĭld hŏn'ey.
m: ac̦'ri-mŏn"y, ag'ri-mŏn"y,
al'i-mŏn"y, an'ti-mŏn"y,
mat'ri-mŏn"y, mŏn'ey,
pär'si-mŏn"y, pat'ri-mŏn"y,
sañc̦'ti-mŏn"y.
r: run'ny.
s: sŏn'ny, sun'ny, un-sun'ny.
t: Tun'ney, tun'ny.
Plus fun he, etc.
Cf. stun knee, etc.

UN'IJ

d: dun'năġe.
g: gun'năġe.
t: tŏn'năġe.
Cf. stun age, etc.

(Choose only one word out of each group)

ŪN'IK

m: Mūn'ich.
p: Pūn'ic̣.
r: rȗn'ic̣.
t: tūn'ic̣
Plus you, Nick *or* nick, etc.

UN'IN

r: run'=in".
Plus sun in *or* inn, etc.

ŪN'ING

kr: croon'ing.
l: bal-loon'ing.
m: com-mūn'ing, moon'ing.
n: noon'ing.
p: ex-pūgn'ing, här-poon'ing,
im-pūgn'ing, op-pūgn'ing.
pr: prȗn'ing.
sp: spoon'ing.
sw: swoon'ing.
t: tūn'ing.

UN'ING

d: dun'ning.
f: fun'ning.
g: gun'ning.
k(c̣): cun'ning.
p: pun'ning
r: gun run'ning, out-run'ning,
ō"vẽr-run'ning, run'ning.
s: sun'ning.
sh: shun'ning.
st: stun'ning.

Ū'NIS

t: Tū'nis.
y: Eū'nice.

ŬN'ISH

f: buf-foon'ish.
tr: pol-troon'ish.

UN'ISH

h: Hun'nish.
p: pun'ish.

ŪN'IST

l: bal-loon'ist.
p: här-poon'ist.
s: bas-soon'ist.
t: op-pọr-tūn'ist.

ŪN'IT

y: ūn'it.
Plus few knit *or* nit, etc.
Plus tune it, etc.

ŪN'IZM

f: buf-foon'ism.
t: op-pọr-tūn'ism.
tr: pol-troon'ism.

UN'JENT

p: pun'gent.
Plus fun gent, etc.

UN'JEST

l: lun'gest*.
p: ex-pun'gest*.
pl: plun'gest*.
sp: spŏn'gest*.
Plus one jest, etc.

UN'JETH

l: lun'geth*.
p: ex-pun'geth*.
pl: plun'geth*.
sp: spŏn'geth*.

UN'JEZ

l: lun'geṣ.
p: ex-pun'geṣ.
pl: plun'geṣ.
sp: spŏn'geṣ.

(Choose only one word out of each group)

UN'JI

pl: plun'ġy.
sp: spŏn'ġy.
Plus lunge, he, etc.

UN'JING

l: lun'ġing.
p: ex-pun'ġing.
pl: plun'ġing.
sp: spŏn'ġing.

UN'JUN

d: dun'ġeŏn.
pl: plun'ġeŏn*.
Cf. none, John, etc.

UN'JŨR

bl: ⸂blun'ġēr.
l: lun'ġēr.
p: ex-pun'ġēr.
pl: plun'ġēr.
sp: spŏn'ġēr.
Plus plunge her *or* err, etc.

UN'KĂN

d: Dun'çăn.
Cf. ung'kin.
Plus one can, etc.
Plus drunk an *or* on, etc.

ŪN'LES

j: Jūne'less.
m: mo̧o̧n'less.
r: rúne'less.
t: tūne'less.
Plus spittoon less *or* Les, etc.

UN'LES

r: run'less.
s: sŏn'less, sun'less.
Plus none less *or* Les, etc.

ŬN'LĪT

m: mo̧o̧n'līght.
n: no̧o̧n līght.
Plus June light, etc.

UN'MĂN

g: gun'măn.
Plus one man, etc.

ŪN'NES

j: jē-jùne'ness, Jūne'ness.
t: in-op-po̧r-tūne'ness,
op-po̧r-tūne'ness.

Ū'NŌ

br: Brú'nō.
j: Jū'nō.
Plus you know *or* no, etc.
Plus croon owe *or* O, etc.

ŬN'RĪZ

m: mo̧o̧n'rīṣe.
Plus June rise, etc.

UN'SI

d: dunce'y.
m: Mun'sey.
Plus fun, see, etc.

UN'STĂN, UN'STŎN

d: Dun'stăn.
f: fun'stŏn.
Plus dunced an *or* on, etc.
Plus once tan, ton *or* tun, **etc.**

UN'STŨR

g: gun'stēr.
p: pun'stēr.
Plus fun stir.
Plus dunced her *or* err, etc.
Cf. Mun'ster.

(Choose only one word out of each group)

UN'TĂL

fr: frŏn'tăl.
gr: dis-grun'tle, grun'tle.
p: çon-trȧ-pun'tăl.
Plus punt, Al, etc.

UN'TED

b: bun'ted.
bl: blun'ted, un-blun'ted.
fr: af-frŏn'ted, çon-frŏn'ted,
frŏn'ted.
gr: grun'ted.
h: hun'ted.
p: pun'ted.
sh: shun'ted.
st: stun'ted.
w: un-wŏn'ted, wŏn'ted.
Plus runt, Ed, etc..
Plus none, Ted, etc.

UNT'EST

b: bunt'est*.
bl: blunt'est.
fr: af-frŏnt'est*, çon-frŏnt'est*.
gr: grunt'est*.
h: hunt'est*.
p: punt'est*.
sh: shunt'est*.
st: stunt'est*.
Plus one test, etc.

UNT'ETH

b: bunt'eth*.
bl: blunt'eth*.
fr: af-frŏnt'eth*, çon-frŏnt'eth*.
gr: grunt'eth*.
h: hunt'eth*.
p: punt'eth*.
sh: shunt'eth*.
st: stunt'eth*.

UNT'I

p: punt'y.
r: runt'y.
st: stunt'y.
Plus bunt, he, etc.
Plus one tea, etc.

UNT'ING

b: bunt'ing, red bunt'ing,
yel'lōw bunt'ing.
fr: af-frŏnt'ing, çon-frŏnt'ing,
frŏnt'ing.
gr: grunt'ing.
h: brush hunt'ing,
head'⸗hunt"ing (hed'), hunt'ing,
lï'ŏn hunt'ing, sçalp hunt'ing,
tāil hunt'ing.
p: punt'ing.
sh: shunt'ing.
st: stunt'ing.

UNT'LES

fr: frŏnt'less.
w: wŏnt'less.
Plus stunt less or Les, etc.

UNT'NES

bl: blunt'ness.
st: stunt'ness.

UN'TŌ

j: jun'tō.
Plus one toe, etc.
Plus runt owe or O, etc.

UN'TRI

k(ç): çŏun'try.
Plus one tree, etc.

UN'TÖ

Vowel: un'tö.
Plus won, two, to, or too, etc.

(Choose only one word out of each group)

UNT'ŨR

b: bunt'ẽr.
bl: blunt'ẽr.
fr: af-frŏnt'ẽr, çon-frŏnt'ẽr.
g: Gunt'ẽr.
gr: grunt'ẽr.
h: fŏr'tūne-hunt″ẽr, head'hunt″ẽr (hed'), hunt'ẽr, leg'à-cy hun'tẽr, lī'ŏn hunt'ẽr, sçalp hunt'ẽr.
p: punt'ẽr.
sh: shunt'ẽr.
st: stunt'ẽr.
Plus bunt her *or* err, etc.

UNTS'VIL

bl: Blŏunts'ville.
h: Hunts'ville.

Ū'NUK

y: eū'nuçh.

UN'ŨR

g: drà-gǫǫn'ẽr.
k(ç): là-çūn'ăr.
kr: crǫǫn'ẽr.
b: bal-lǫǫn'ẽr, in-tẽr-lūn'ăr, lūn'ăr, nō-vi-lūn'ăr, plen-i-lūn'ăr, sem-i-lūn'ăr, sub-lūn'ăr, trans-lūn'ăr.
m: çom-mūn'ẽr, mǫǫn'ẽr.
p: här-pǫǫn'ẽr, im-pūgn'ẽr, lam-pǫǫn'ẽr, op-pūgn'ẽr.
pr: prùn'ẽr.
s: sǫǫn'ẽr.
sk(sç): sçhǫǫn ẽr.
sp: spǫǫn'ẽr.
sw: swǫǫn'ẽr.
t: at-tūn'ẽr, im-pŏr-tūn'ẽr, pi-an'ō tūn'ẽr, tūn'ẽr.
Plus croon her *or* err, etc.

UN'ŨR

d: dun'nẽr.
g: gun'nẽr.
p: pun'nẽr.
r: gun'run″nẽr, out-run'nẽr, ō″vẽr-run'nẽr, rum'run″nẽr, run'nẽr.
st: stun'nẽr.
Plus dun her *or* err, etc.

ŪN'YŎN

m: çom-mūn'iŏn, ex-çom-mūn'iŏn, in″tẽr-çom-mūn'iŏn.
y: dis-ūn'iŏn, lā'bŏr ūn'iŏn, rē-ūn'iŏn, trādeṣ-ūn'iŏn, ūn'iŏn.

UN'YŎN

Vowel: ŏn'iŏn, wīld ŏn'iŏn.
b: bun'iŏn, Bun'yăn.
m: mun'niŏn.
r: rŏn'yŏn*.
tr: trun'niŏn.

ŪN'YŎR

j: jùn'iŏr.
Cf. croon your, etc.

Ū'PÀ

p: pū'pà.
s: sù'pà.
Plus group a, etc.

UP'ĂNS

Vowel: çŏme″-up'pănce.
thr: thrup'pence.
Plus sup ants *or* aunts, etc.

Ū'PĒ

hw: whǫǫ'pee (hwǫǫ').
Cf. ùp'i.

ŪP′EST
UP′ING

fāte, fär, fàst, fạll, finăl, cãre, at; mēte, prĕy, hẽr, met; pīne,
marīne, bĭrd, pin; nōte, mŏve, fọr, atŏm, not; mọọn, book;

762

(Choose only one word out of each group)

ŪP′EST

d: dūp′est*.
dr: drọọp′est*.
gr: gröup′est*.
hw: whọọp′est*.
k(c̱): c̱ọọp′est*, rē-c̱öup′est*.
l: lọọp′est*.
sk(sc̱): sc̱ọọp′est*.
st: stọọp′est*.
sw: swọọp′est*.
tr: trọọp′est*.
Plus new pest, etc.

UP′EST

k(c̱): c̱up′pest*.
s: sup′pest*.
t: tup′pest*.
Cf. pup pest, etc.

UP′ET

p: pup′pet.
Cf. cup it, etc.
Cf. cup, pet, etc.

UP′ETH

d: dūp′eth*.
dr: drọọp′eth*.
gr: gröup′eth*.
hw: whọọp′eth*.
k(c̱): c̱ọọp′eth*, rē-c̱öup′eth*.
l: lọọp′eth*.
sk(sc̱): sc̱ọọp′eth*.
st: stọọp′eth*.
sw: swọọp′eth*.
tr: trọọp′eth*.

UP′ETH

k(c̱): c̱up′peth*.
ꜱ: sup′peth*.
t: tup′peth*.

ŪP′I

dr: drọọp′y.
kr: c̱röup′y.
s: söup′y.
sw: swọọp′y.
Cf. whọọ′pee.
Plus group, he, etc.

UP′I

g: gup′py.
k(c̱): c̱up′py, hic̱′c̱ough″y,
hic̱′c̱up″y.
p: pup′py.
Plus up, he, etc.

Ū′PID

k(c̱): C̱ū′pid.
st: stū′pid.
Cf. group hid, etc.

Ū′PIL

p: pū′pil.
Cf. ū′p′l.
Plus new pill, etc.
Plus group ill, etc.

ŪP′ING

d: dūp′ing.
dr: drọọp′ing.
gr: gröup′ing.
h: họọp′ing.
hw: whọọp′ing (hwọọp′).
k(c̱): c̱ọọp′ing, rē-c̱öup′ing.
l: lọọp′ing, lọọp′≠THĕ≠lọọp′ing.
sk(sc̱): sc̱ọọp′ing.
st: stọọp′ing.
sw: swọọp′ing.
tr: trọọp′ing.
Plus you ping, etc.

UP′ING

k(c̱): c̱up′ping.
s: sup′ping.
t: tup′ping.

(Choose only one word out of each group)

UP'ISH

Vowel: up'pish.
p: pup'pish.

Ū'PL

d: sub-dū'ple.
dr: quäd-rú'ple.
skr(sc̨): sc̨rú'ple.
t: oc̨-tū'ple, quin-tū'ple,
  sep-tū'ple, sex-tū'ple.
Cf. pū'pil.
Plus group'll, etc.

UP'L

k(c̨): c̨ŏu'ple, un-c̨ŏu'ple.
s: sup'ple.
Plus pup'll, etc.

U'PLEST

skr(sc̨r): sc̨rú'plest*.

UP'LEST

k(c̨): c̨ŏup'lest*, un-c̨ŏup'lest*.
s: sup'plest.

ŪP'LET

dr: quäd-rú'plet.
t: oc̨-tū'plet, quin-tū'plet,
  sep-tū'plet, sex-tū'plet.
Plus group let *or* Lett, etc.

UP'LETH

skr(sc̨): sc̨rú'pleth*.

UP'LETH

k(c̨): c̨ŏup'leth*, un-c̨ŏup'leth*.

UP'LŬR

k(c̨): c̨ŏup'lĕr, un-c̨ŏup'lĕr.
s: sup'plĕr.

ŪP'MENT

gr: ag-gröup'ment.
k(c̨): rē-c̨öup'ment.
Plus swoop meant, etc.

Ū'PON

j: jū'pon.
k(c̨): c̨ōū'pon.
Plus group on, etc.

ŪP'ŎR

st: stūp'ŏr.
Cf. ūp'ūr.
Plus group, or, etc.

UP'SHĂL

n: an-tē-nup'tiăl, nup'tiăl,
  pōst-nup'tiăl.
Plus cup shall, etc.

UP'SHUN

r: ab-rup'tion, c̨or-rup'tion,
  dis-rup'tion, ē-rup'tion,
  in-c̨or-rup'tion, in-tēr-rup'tion,
  ir-rup'tion, rup'tion.
Plus pup shun, etc.

UP'TED

r: ab-rup'ted, c̨or-rup'ted,
  dis-rup'ted, in-tēr-rup'ted,
  ir-rup'ted.
Plus pup, Ted, etc.
Plus supped, Ed, etc.

UP'TEST

br: à-brup'test.
r: c̨or-rup'test, in-tēr-rup'test*.
Plus pup test, etc.

UP'TETH

r: c̨or-rup'teth*,
  in-tēr-rup'teth*.

UP'TING
ŪR'ĂL

fāte, fär, fȧst, fạll, fĭnȧl, cãre, ạt; mēte, prẹy, hẽr, met; pīne,
marĭne, bĭrd, pĭn; nōte, mŏve, fọr, atŏm, not; mọọn, book;

764

(Choose only one word out of each group)

UP'TING

r: cọr-rup'ting, ē-rup'ting,
in-tēr-rup'ting.

UP'TIV

r: cọr-rup'tive, dis-rup'tive,
ē-rup'tive, in-cọr-rup'tive,
in-tēr-rup'tive, ir-rup'tive.

UPT'LI

br: ȧ-brupt'ly.
r: cọr-rupt'ly, in-cọr-rupt'ly.
Plus supped, Lee *or* lea, etc.

UPT'NES

br: ȧ-brupt'ness.
r: cọr-rupt'ness,
in-cọr-rupt'ness.

UP'TŪR

br: ȧ-brup'tēr.
r: cọr-rup'tēr, dis-rup'tēr,
ē-rup'tēr, in-cọr-rup'tēr,
in-tēr-rup'tēr, ir-rup'tēr.
Plus supped her *or* err, etc.

ŪP'ŪR

d: dūp'ēr.
dr: drọọp'ēr.
gr: gröup'ēr.
h: họọp'ēr.
hw: whọọp'ēr.
k(c): cọọp'ēr, rē-cöup'ēr.
kr: cröup'ēr.
l: lọọp'ēr, lọọp'=THē=lọọp'ēr.
s: söup'ēr, sūp'ēr.
sk(sc): scọọp'ēr.
sn: snọọp'ēr.
st: stọọp'ēr, stūp'ŏr.
sw: swọọp'ēr.
tr: trọọp'ēr.
Plus group her *or* err, etc.

UP'ŪR

Vowel: up'pēr.
k(c): cup'pēr.
kr: crup'pēr.
s: sup'pēr.
sk(sc): scup'pēr.
t: Tup'pēr.
Plus sup her *or* err, etc.

Ū'PĒRT

r: Rú'pērt.
Plus new pert, etc.

UP'WĂRD

Vowel: up'wărd.
Plus cup ward, etc.

Ū'RȦ

d: pi-ẹt'rȧ dù'rȧ.
k(c): Cū-ti-cū'rȧ.
p: pūr-pū'rȧ.
pl: pleū'rȧ.
s: caē-sū'rȧ (sē-), cē-sū'rȧ,
fis-sū'rȧ, flex-ū'rȧ, sū'rȧ,
sūr'rȧ, sūr'rȧh.
st: An"gō-stū'rȧ.
t: ap-pọġ"gi-ȧ-tū'rȧ,
cọl'ŏr-ȧ-tū'rȧ, dā-tū'rȧ,
Kē-tū'rȧh, vel-ȧ-tū'rȧ,
vet-tū'rȧ.
v: brä-vū'rȧ.
z: caē-ṣū'rȧ (sē-), cē-ṣū'rȧ.
Plus you're a, etc.

ŪR'ĂL

j: jūr'ăl.
k(c): sĭn-e-cūr'ăl.
kr: crūr'ăl.
l: tel-lūr'ăl.
m: an-tē-mūr'ăl, ex-trȧ-mūr'ăl,
in-tēr-mūr'ăl, in-trȧ-mūr'ăl,
mūr'ăl.

765 ūse, bṳll, brûte, tûrn, up; crȳ, myth; çat, maçhine, ace, church, çhord; ġem, añger, (Fr.) boṅ, aṣ; THis, thin; aẓure

ŪR′ĂNS
ŪR′BID

(Choose only one word out of each group)

n: in-tēr-neū′răl, neū′răl.
pl: pleūr′ăl, plū′răl.
r: rú′răl.
s: caē-sūr′ăl (sē-), cē-ṣūr′ăl, çom-mis-sūr′ăl, sūr′ăl.
y: Ū′răl.
z: caē-ṣūr′ăl (sē-), cē-ṣūr′ăl.
Plus pure, Al, etc.

ŪR′ĂNS

d: dūr′ănce, en-dūr′ănce, pēr-dūr′ănce.
l: al-lūr′ănce.
sh: as-sūr′ănce, in-sūr′ănce, rē-as-sūr′ănce, rē-in-sūr′ănce.
Plus pure ants, *or* aunts, etc.
Plus who rants, etc.

ŪR′ĀT

k(ç): çūr′āte.
Plus demure eight *or* ate, etc.
Plus you rate, etc.

ŪR′AT

j: jùr′at.
Plus you rat, etc.
Plus pure at, etc.

ŪR′BĂL

h: hēr′băl.
v: vēr′băl.
Plus curb Al, etc.

ŪR′BĂN

Vowel: ūr′băn.
b: sub-ūr′băn.
t: tūr′băn.
Plus curb an, etc.
Plus her ban etc.

ŪR′BĂNS

t: dis-tūr′bănce.
Plus çur′bănts, etc.
Plus curb ants *or* aunts, etc.

ŪR′BÄR

d: dūr′bär.
Plus stir bar, etc.

ŪR′BĀT

s: à-cēr′bāte.
t: pēr-tūr′bāte.
Plus curb eight *or* ate, etc.
Plus cur bait, etc.

ŪRB′EST

bl: blūrb′est*.
k(ç): çurb′est*.
t: dis-tūrb′est*, pēr-tūrb′est*.
Plus stir best, etc.

ŪR′BET

sh: shēr′bet.
Plus Herb et, etc.
Plus her bet, etc.

ŪR′BETH

bl: blūrb′eth*.
k(ç): çūrb′eth*.
t: dis-tūrb′eth*, pēr-tūrb′eth*.
Plus stir, Beth, etc.

ŪR′BI

d: Dēr′by.
h: hēr′by.
k: Kǐr′by.
t: I-tūr′bi.
Plus stir bee *or* be, etc.
Plus curb, he, etc.

ŪR′BID

h: hēr′bid.
t: tūr′bid.

(Choose only one word out of each group)

Plus stir bid, etc.
Cf. curb hid, etc.

ŪR'BIN

t: tŭr'bine.
Cf. ŭr'băn.
Plus cur been, etc.
Plus curb in *or* inn, etc.

ŪRB'ING

bl: blŭrb'ing.
k(c̨): c̨ŭrb'ing.
t: dis-tŭrb'ing, pẽr-tŭrb'ing.
Plus err, Byng, etc.

ŪR'BŎT

b: bŭr'bŏt.
t: tŭr'bŏt.
Cf. curb hot, etc.
Plus curb Ott, etc.

ŪR'BUN

b: Boŭr'bŏn.
Plus pure bun, etc.

ŪRB'ŪR

b: Bẽr'bẽr.
bl: blŭrb'ẽr.
f: Fẽr'bẽr.
g: Gẽr'bẽr.
k(c̨): c̨ŭrb'ẽr.
p: sū-pẽrb'ẽr.
t: dis-tŭrb'ẽr, pẽr-tŭrb'ẽr.
Plus her burr, etc.
Plus curb her *or* err, etc.

ŪR'BŬRT

h: Hẽr'bẽrt.
Plus stir, Bert *or* Burt, etc.
Cf. curb hurt, etc.

ŪR'CHĂNT

m: mẽr'chănt.
p: pẽr'chănt*.
Plus myrrh chant, etc.
Plus church ant *or* aunt, etc.

ŪR'CHĀS, ŪR'CHĂS

p: pŭr'chāse (*or* 'chăs).
Cf. her chase, etc.
Plus church ass, etc.

ŪR'CHĀST, ŪR'CHĂST

p: pŭr'chāsed (*or* 'chăst).
Plus her chaste *or* chased, etc.

ŪRCH'EN

b: bĭrch'en.
Cf. ŭr'chin.
Cf. church hen, etc.

ŪRCH'EST

b: bĭrch'est*.
l: lŭrch'est*.
p: pẽrch'est*.
s: sẽarch'est*.
sm: smĭrch'est*.
Cf. pŭr'chāsed.
Plus her chest, etc.

ŪRCH'ETH

b: bĭrch'eth*.
l: lŭrch'eth*.
p: pẽrch'eth*.
s: sẽarch'eth*.
sm: smĭrch'eth*.

ŪR'CHEZ

b: bĭr'ches̨.
ch: chŭr'ches̨.
l: lŭr'ches̨.
p: pẽr'ches̨.

(Choose only one word out of each group)

s: rē-sēar'cheṣ, sēar'cheṣ.
sm: bē-smîr'cheṣ, smîr'cheṣ.
Cf. church is, etc.

ŪR'CHIF

k: kẽr'chief.

ŪRCH'ING

b: bĩrch'ing.
ch: chŭrch'ing.
l: lŭrch'ing.
p: pẽrch'ing.
s: sẽarch'ing.
sm: bē-smîrch'ing, smîrch'ing.

ŪRCH'LES

ch: chŭrch'less.
sm: smĩrch'less.
Plus perch less or Les, etc.

ŪR'CHUR

b: bĩr'chẽr.
l: lũr'chẽr.
p: pẽr'chẽr.
s: sēar'chẽr, bē-smĩr'chẽr,
   smîr'chẽr.
Cf. nũr'tūre.
Plus birch her or err, etc.

ŪRD'BOOK

h: hẽrd'book.
w: wõrd'book.
Plus stirred book, etc.

ŪR'DED

g: bē-gĩr'ded, en-gĩr'ded,
   gĩr'ded.
h: hẽr'ded.
k(ç): çũr'ded.
sh: shẽr'ded.

w: wõr'ded.
Plus her dead, etc.
Plus bird, Ed, etc.

ŪR'DEN

b: bũr'den, Bũr'dŏn,
   dis-bũr'den, ō-vẽr-bũr'den,
   un-bũr'den.
g: guẽr'dŏn (gẽr').
Plus heard an or on, etc.
Plus Jõr'dan (Jũr).

ŪRD'EST

g: bē-gĩrd'est*, en-gĩrd'est*,
   gĩrd'est*.
h: hẽard'est*, hẽrd'est*.
s: ab-sũrd'est.

ŪRD'ETH

g: bē-gĩrd'eth*, en-gĩrd'eth*,
   gĩrd'eth*,
h: hẽard'eth*, hẽrd'eth*.
Plus stir death, etc.

ŪRD'I

b: bĩrd'y.
g: hũrd'y⹀gũrd'y.
k(ç): çũrd'y.
st: stũr'dy.
w: wõrd'y.
Plus heard, he, etc.

ŪR'DIKT

v: vẽr'dict.

ŪR'DING

g: bē-gĩrd'ing, en-gĩrd'ing,
   gĩrd'ing, un-gĩrd'ing.
h: hẽrd'ing.
w: wõrd'ing.

ŪR'D'L

g: bē-gĩr'dle, en-gĩr'dle, gĩr'dle.
   hũr'dle.

(Choose only one word out of each group)

k(ç): çûr'dle.
Plus word'll, etc.
Cf. cur dull, etc.

ŬR'DŎN

b: Bŭr'dŏn.
g: guêr'dŏn (gêr').
Cf. ûr'den.

ŬR'DŪR

v: vêr'dūre.
Cf. pêr'jūre.
Plus heard your *or* you're, etc.

ŬR'DŪR

b: Bŭr'dẽr.
g: en-gĩr'dẽr, gĩr'dẽr.
h: gōat'=hẽr"dẽr, hẽr'dẽr,
   sheep'=hẽr"dẽr.
m: mŭr'dẽr, self'=mŭr'dẽr.
s: ab-sŭr'dẽr.
th: thĩr'dẽr.
Plus bird her *or* err, etc.

ŬRDZ'MAN

h: hẽrdṣ'măn.
w: wŏrdṣ'măn.
Plus birds, man, etc.

ŬR'EL

b: Bŭr'rell.
skw: squĩr'rel.
Cf. ĩr'el.

ŬR'ENS

k(ç): çon-çûr'rence,
   in-çûr'rence, in-tẽr-çûr'rence,
   oç-çûr'rence, rē-çûr'rence.
f: trans-fẽr'ence.
t: dē-tẽr'rence.
Plus her rents, etc.

ŬR'ENT, ŬR'ĂNT

k(ç): çon-çûr'rent, çûr'rănt,
   çûr'rent, dē-çûr'rent,
   in-tẽr-çûr'rent, rē-çûr'rent,
   un-dẽr-çûr'rent.
s: sū-sûr'rănt.
t: dē-tẽr'rent.
Plus fir rent, etc.
Plus stir aunt *or* ant, etc.

ŬR'EST

d: en-dûr'est*.
j: ab-jūr'est*, ad-jūr'est*,
   çon-jūr'est*.
k(ç): çûr'est*, prō-çûr'est*,
   sē-çûr'est.
l: al-lūr'est*, lūr'est*.
m: dē-mûr'est, im-mûr'est*,
   mōͅor'est*, un-mōͅor'est*.
p: im-pūr'est, pōͅor'est,
   pūr'est.
sh: as-sûr'est*, en-sûr'est*,
   in-sûr'est*, rē-as-sûr'est*,
   rē-in-sûr'est*, sûr'est.
sk(sç): ob-sçûr'est.
t: im-mȧ-tūr'est, mȧ-tūr'est,
   toûr'est*.
Cf. ûr'ist.
Plus who rest, etc.
Cf. pure rest, etc.

ŬR'EST

Vowel: ẽr'rest*.
bl: blūr'rest*.
f: çon-fẽr'rest*, dē-fẽr'rest*,
   in-fẽr'rest*, prē-fẽr'rest*,
   rē-fẽr'est*, trans-fẽr'rest*.
k(ç): çon-çûr'rest*, in-çûr'rest*.
m: dē-mûr'rest*.
p: pûr'rest*.

(Choose only one word out of each group)

sh: shĭr'rest*.
sl: slŭr'rest*.
st: bē-stĭr'rest*, stĭr'rest*.
t: in-tẽr'rest*.
Cf. her rest, etc.

ŪR'ET

t: tũr'ret.
Cf. fir it, etc.

ŪR'ETH

d: en-dūr'eth*.
j: ab-jūr'eth*, ad-jūr'eth*,
çon-jūr'eth*.
k(ç): çūr'eth*, prō-çūr'eth*,
sē-çūr'eth*.
l: al-lūr'eth*, lūr'eth*.
m: im-mūr'eth*, moͅor'eth*,
un-moͅor'eth*.
sh: as-sūr'eth*, en-sūr'eth*,
in-sūr'eth*, rē-as-sūr'eth*,
rē-in-sūr'eth*.
sk(sç): ob-sçūr'eth*.
t: mȧ-tūr'eth*.

ŪR'ETH

Vowel: ẽr'reth*
bl: blŭr'reth*.
f: çon-fẽr'reth*, dē-fẽr'reth*,
in-fẽr'reth*, prē-fẽr'reth*,
rē-fẽr'reth*, trans-fẽr'reth*.
k(ç): çon-çŭr'reth*, in-çŭr'reth*.
m: dē-mŭr'reth*.
p: pŭr'reth*.
sh: shĭr'reth*.
sl: slŭr'reth*.
st: bē-stĭr'reth*, stĭr'reth*.
t: in-tẽr'reth*.

ŪR'FĂS

s: sūr'făce.

UR'FEKT

p: im-pẽr'feçt, pẽr'feçt.

ŪR'FI

d: Dūr'fey.
m: Mũr'phy.
s: sūr'fy.
sk(sç): sçũr'fy.
t: tũr'fy.
Plus her fee, etc.
Plus serf, he, etc.

ŨR'FIT

s: sũr'feit.
Plus fir ·fit, etc.
Plus turf it, etc.

ŨR'FŌR

hw: whẽre'fōre.
TH: THẽre'fōre.
Plus share four *or* fore, etc.

ŨR'FŪM

p: pẽr'fūme.
Plus stir fume, etc.

ŨR'GAT

j: ob-jũr'gāte.
p: ex-pũr'gāte.
v: vĭr'gāte.
Plus her gate, etc.
Plus erg eight *or* ate, etc.

UR'G'L

b: bũr'gle.
g: gũr'gle.
Plus erg'll, etc.
Cf. her gull, etc.

ŨR'GLĂR

b: bũr'glăr.
g: gũr'glẽr.

ŪR′GŌ
ŪR′IM

fāte, fär, fȧst, fᶏll, finᶏl, cãre, at; mēte, prᶒy, hẽr, met; pīne,
marïne, bïrd, pin; nōte, mŏve, fȯr, atŏm, nᴑt; mᴑᴑn, book;

770

(Choose only one word out of each group)

ŪR′GŌ

Vowel: ẽr′gō.
t: ȧ-tẽr′gō.
v: Vïr′gō.
Plus her go, etc.
Plus erg owe *or* O, etc.

ŪR′GŪR

b: bũr′ghẽr.
j: jẽr′guẽr*.
Plus erg her *or* err, etc.

ŪR′GUS

Vowel: dem-i-ũr′gus.
m: Mẽr′gus.
t: thᶏu-mȧ-tũr′gus.
Plus myrrh, Gus, etc.
Plus erg us, etc.

Ū′RI

dr: Drú′ry.
f: fū′ry.
h: hoú′ri.
j: dē jú′re, Jew′ry, jú′ry.
k(ç): Çū′rie.
y: ēw′ry.
z: Miṣ-ṣoú′ri.
Plus pure, he, etc.

ŪR′I

b: bũr′ry.
bl: blũr′ry.
f: fïr′ry, fũr′ry.
fl: flũr′ry.
h: hũr′ry.
hw: whïr′ry.
k(ç): Çū′rie, çũr′ry.
l: lũr′ry.
m: Mũr′ray.
s: sũr′rey.
sk(sç): hũr′ry=sçũr′ry, sçũr′ry.
sl: slũr′ry.

w: wŏr′ry.
Plus myrrh, he, etc.

Ū′RID

l: lū′rid.
Plus who rid, etc.
Cf. you′re hid, etc.

ŪR′ID

fl: flũr′ried, un-flũr′ried.
h: hũr′ried, un-hũr′ried.
k(ç): çũr′ried, un-çũr′ried.
sk(sç): sçũr′ried.
w: un-wŏr′ried, wŏr′ried.
Cf. myrrh hid, etc.

ŪR′IJ

m: mᴑᴑr′ȧge, mũr′ȧge.
Cf. your age, etc.
Cf. you rage, etc.

ŪR′IJ

k(ç): çoũr′ȧge, dis-çoũr′ȧge,
en-çoũr′ȧge.
m: dē-mũr′rȧge.
Cf. her age, etc.
Cf. her rage, etc.

ŪR′IK

f: hȳ″drō-sul-phũr′iç,
sul-phũr′iç.
p: pũr-pūr′iç.
t: hȳ″drō-tel-lūr′iç, tel-lūr′iç.
Plus new rick, etc.

ŪR′IK

m: myr′rhiç.
Cf. her rick, etc.

ŪR′IM

p: pùr′im.
y: ūr′im.

771 ūse, bu̧ll, brûte, tŭrn, up; crȳ, myth; çat, ma̧chine, ace, church, çhord; ġem, añger, (Fr.) boṅ, a̧s; THis, thin; azure

ŪR′IN
ŪR′IZ

(Choose only one word out of each group)

Plus new rim, etc.
Plus cure him, etc.

ŪR′IN

b: būr′in.
n: neūr′in, neūr′ine.
t: da̧-tūr′in.
y: ūr′ine.
Plus pure in, etc.

ŪR′ING

d: dūr′ing, en-dūr′ing, ev-ēr-dūr′ing.
j: ab-jūr′ing, ad-jūr′ing, çon-jūr′ing, jūr′ing, non-jūr′ing.
k(ç): çūr′ing, prō-çūr′ing, sē-çūr′ing.
l: al-lūr′ing, lūr′ing.
m: im-mūr′ing, mo̧or′ing, un-mo̧or′ing.
n: ma̧-nūr′ing.
sh: as-sūr′ing, en-sūr′ing, in-sūr′ing, rē-as-sūr′ing, rē-in-sūr′ing.
sk(sç): ob-sçūr′ing.
sp: spo̧or′ing.
t: ma̧-tūr′ing, toūr′ing.
y: in-ūr′ing.
Plus new ring, etc.

ŪR′ING

Vowel: ēr′ring, un-ēr′ring.
bl: blūr′ring.
f: çon-fēr′ring, dē-fēr′ring, in-fēr′ring, prē-fēr′ring, rē-fēr′ring, trans-fēr′ring.
g: Goēr′ing.
hw: whīr′ring.
k(ç): çon-çūr′ring, in-çūr′ring, non-çon-çur′ring, oç-çūr′ring, rē-çūr′ring.

m: dē-mūr′ring.
p: pūr′ring.
sh: shīr′ring.
sl: slūr′ring.
sp: spūr′ring.
st: a̧-stīr′ring, bē-stīr′ring, stīr′ring.
t: dis-in-tēr′ring, in-tēr′ring.
Cf. hēr′ring.
Cf. her ring, etc.

ŪR′ISH

b: bo̧or′ish.
m: Mo̧or′ish.
p: po̧or′ish.
t: am″a̧-teūr′ish.

ŪR′ISH

b: būr′rish.
fl: floūr′ish.
k(ç): çūr′rish.
n: noūr′ish, ō-vēr-noūr′ish, un-dēr-noūr′ish.

ŪR′ISHT

fl: floūr′ished.
n: noūr′ished, ō-vēr-noūr′ished, un-dēr-noūr′ished.

Ū′RIST

j: jü′rist.
p: pū′rist.
t: çar″i-ça̧-tū′rist, toū′rist.
Plus new wrist, etc.

ŪR′IZ

fl: flūr′rieş.
h: hūr′rieş.
k(ç): çūr′rieş.
sk(sç): sçūr′rieş.
w: wŏr′rieş.
Plus surrey's, etc.
Plus myrrh is, etc.

(Choose only one word out of each group)

ŪR'IZM

p: pūr'ism.
t: toùr'ism.

ŪR'JENS

m: ē-mēr'ġence, sub-mēr'ġence.
s: rē-sūr'ġence.
t: dē-tūr'ġence.
v: ọon-vēr'ġence, dī-vēr'ġence.
Plus her gents, etc.
Cf. urge hence, etc.

ŪR'ĠENT

Vowel: ūr'ġent.
m: ē-mēr'ġent.
s: as-sūr'ġent, in-sūr'ġent,
    rē-sūr'ġent.
spl: splūr'ġent.
st: ab-stēr'ġent.
t: dē-tēr'ġent, tūr'ġent.
v: ọon-vēr'ġent, dī-vēr'ġent,
    vēr'ġent.
Plus her gent, etc.

ŪR'JEST

Vowel: ūr'ġest*.
d: dīr'ġest*.
m: ē-mēr'ġest*, mēr'ġest*,
    sub-mēr'ġest*.
p: pūr'ġest*.
s: sūr'ġest*.
sk(sç): sçoūr'ġest*.
spl: splūr'ġest*.
v: ọon-vēr'ġest*, dī-vēr'ġest*,
    vēr'ġest*.
Plus her jest, etc.

ŪR'ĠETH

Vowel: ūr'ġeth*.
d: dīr'ġeth*.

m: ē-mēr'ġeth*, mēr'ġeth*,
    sub-mēr'ġeth*.
p: pūr'ġeth*.
s: sūr'ġeth*.
sk(sç): sçoūr'ġeth*.
spl: splūr'ġeth*.
v: ọon-vēr'ġeth*, dī-vēr'ġeth*,
    vēr'ġeth*.

UR'JEZ

Vowel: ūr'ġeṣ.
d: dīr'ġeṣ.
m: ē-mēr'ġeṣ, mēr'ġeṣ,
    sub-mēr'ġeṣ.
n: Bō-à-nēr'ġeṣ.
p: aṣ-pēr'ġeṣ, pūr'ġeṣ.
s: sēr'ġeṣ, sūr'ġeṣ.
sp: spūr'ġeṣ.
spl: splūr'ġeṣ.
v: ọon-vēr'ġeṣ, dī-vēr'ġeṣ,
    vēr'ġeṣ.
Cf. serge is, etc.

UR'JI

Vowel: ac'i-ūr-gy, per'i-ēr-ġy*.
d: dīr'ġie.
kl: çlēr'ġy.
l: met'ăl-lūr-ġy.
t: dram'à-tūr-ġy,
    thạu'mà-tūr-ġy.
Plus urge, he, etc.

UR'JID

t: tūr'ġid.
Cf. verge hid, etc.

ŪR'JIK

Vowel: dem-i-ūr'ġiç, thē-ūr'ġiç.
l: met-ăl-lūr'ġiç.
n: ē-nēr'ġiç.
r: çhī-rūr'ġiç.
t: dram-à-tūr'ġiç, li-tūr'ġiç,
    thạu-mà-tūr'ġiç.

ūse, bu̯ll, brúte, tŭrn, up; crȳ, myth; c̦at, mac̦hine, ace,
church, c̦hord; ġem, aṅger, (Fr.) boṅ, aṣ; THis, thin; aᴢure

773

ŪR′JIN
ŪR′KI

(Choose only one word out of each group)

ŪR′JIN

v: vīr′ġin.
Cf. ūr′ġin′, etc.
Plus her gin, etc.
Plus serge in, *or* inn, etc.

ŪR′JING

Vowel: ūr′ġing.
d: dīr′ġing.
m: ē-mēr′ġing, im-mēr′ġing,
  mēr′ġing, sub-mēr′ġing.
p: pūr′ġing.
s: sūr′ġing.
sk(sc̦): sc̦oūr′ġing.
spl: splūr′ġing.
v: c̦on-vēr′ġing, dī-vēr′ġing,
  vēr′ġing.

ŪR′JIST

l: met′ăl-lūr-ġist.
t: dram′ȧ-tūr-ġist,
  thau̯′mȧ-tūr-ġist.
Plus her gist, etc.

ŪR′JUN

b: būr′ġĕon.
s: sūr′ġĕon.
sp: spūr′ġĕon.
st: stūr′ġĕon.
Cf. vīr′ġin.
Plus urge on *or* an, etc.
Plus her, John *or* Jan, etc.

ŪR′JŪR

p: pēr′jūre.
Cf. vēr′dūre.
Cf. urge her *or* err, etc.

ŪR′JŪR

Vowel: ūrġ′ēr.
d: dīr′ġēr.
m: ē-mēr′ġēr, mēr′ġēr,
  sub-mēr′ġēr.

p: pūr′ġēr.
sk(sc̦): sc̦oūr′ġēr.
spl: splūr′ġēr.
v: c̦on-vēr′ġēr, dī-vēr′ġēr,
  vēr′ġēr.
Plus dirge her *or* err, etc.

ŪR′JUS

v: vēr′jùice.
Plus myrrh juice, etc.

ŪR′KĂL

p: Lū-pēr′c̦ăl.
v: nō-vēr′c̦ăl.
Cf. ūr′k′l.
Plus myrrh, Cal, etc.
Plus work, Al, etc.

ŪR′KEST

j: jēr′kest*.
kl: c̦lēr′kest*.
l: lūr′kest*.
sh: shīr′kest*.
sm: smīr′kest*.
w: wŏr′kest*.

ŪR′KETH

j: jēr′keth*.
kl: c̦lēr′keth*.
l: lūr′keth*.
sh: shīr′keth*.
sm: smīr′keth*.
w: wŏr′keth*.

ŪR′KI

d: Dūr′kee.
j: jēr′ky.
kw: quīr′ky.
l: lūr′ky.
m: mīr′ky, mūr′ky.
p: pēr′ky.
sh: shīr′ky.

(Choose only one word out of each group)

sm: smîr′ky.
t: tạlk tŭr′key (tawk), tŭr′key.
Plus work, he, etc.
Plus her key, etc.

ŪR′KIN

f: fîr′kin.
g: ghẽr′kin (gẽr′).
j: jẽr′kin.
m: mẽr′kin*.
Plus work in *or* inn, etc.
Plus her kin, etc.

ŪR′KINZ

f: Fĭr′kinṣ.
p: Pẽr′kinṣ.
Plus ūr′kin+s.
Plus her kin's, etc.
Plus work inns *or* ins, etc.

ŪRK′ING

j: jẽrk′ing.
kl: çlẽrk′ing.
l: lŭrk′ing.
p: pẽrk′ing.
sh: shĭrk′ing.
sm: smîrk′ing.
w: ȧ-wŏrk′ing, härd′-wŏrk′ing, wŏrk′ing.
Plus her king, etc.

ŪRK′ISH

kw: quĭrk′ish.
t: Tŭrk′ish.

ŪR′KIT

s: cîr′çuit.
Plus her kit, etc.
Plus work it, etc.

ŪR′K′L

m: Mẽr′kle.
s: cĭr′çle, en-cĭr′çle, sem′i-cĭr″çle.

t: tŭrk′le.
Plus work′ll, etc.

ŪRK′LET

s: cîrç′let.
Plus Turk let *or* Lett, etc.

ŪRK′LI

kl: çlẽrk′ly.
s: cîrç′ly.
Plus work, Lee *or* lea, etc.

ŪRK′LING

s: cîrç′ling.
Plus her cling, etc.

ŪRK′MĂN

t: Tŭrk′măn.
w: wŏrk′măn.
Plus shirk, man, etc.

ŪRK′SŎM

Vowel: ĭrk′sŏme.
m: mĭrk′sŏme.
Plus work some, etc.
Cf. works 'em, etc.

ŪRK′ŪR

b: bŭrk′ẽr.
j: jẽrk′ẽr, jẽr′quẽr.
l: lŭrk′ẽr.
sh: shĭrk′ẽr.
sm: smîrk′ẽr.
w: wŏn′dẽr wŏrk′ẽr, wŏrk′ẽr.
Plus work her *or* err, etc.
Plus her cur, etc.

ŪRK′US

f: bī-fŭrç′ous.
kw: Quẽr′çus.
s: cîr′çus.
Cf. work house.
Plus her cuss, etc.
Plus work us, etc.

(Choose only one word out of each group)

ŪR′KWOIZ

t: tūr′quoiṣe.

URLD′LI

w: un-wŏrld′ly, wŏrld′ly.
Plus furled, Lee *or* lea, etc.

ŪRLD′LING

w: wŏrld′ling.

ŪRL′EST

f: fūrl′est*, un-fūrl′est*.
h: hūrl′est*.
hw: whĩrl′est*.
k(ç): çūrl′est*.
sw: swĩrl′est*.
tw: twĩrl′est*.
Plus myrrh, lest, etc.

ŪRL′ETH

f: fūrl′eth*, un-fūrl′eth*.
h: hūrl′eth*.
hw: whĩrl′eth*.
k(ç): çūrl′eth*.
sw: swĩrl′eth*.
tw: twirl′eth*.

URL′HOOD

g: gĩrl′hood.
Plus whirl hood, etc.

ŪRL′I

k: sē-çūre′ly.
m: dē-mūre′ly.
p: poọr′ly, pūre′ly.
sk(sç): ob-sçūre′ly.
t: ma-tūre′ly.
Plus sure, Lee *or* lea, etc.

ŪR′LI

Vowel: ēar′ly.
b: Būr′leigh, būr′ly,
hūr′ly⹀būr″ly.
ch: chūr′ly.
g: gĩrl′ie, gĩr′ly.
h: Hūr′ley.
hw: whĩr′ly.
k(ç): çūr′ly.
n: knūr′ly (nūr′)*.
p: pēar′ly*.
s: sūr′ly.
sw: swĩr′ly.
sh: Shĩr′ley.
tw: twĩr′ly.
Plus her, Lee *or* lea, etc.

ŪR′LIN

m: mēr′lin.
p: pēar′lin.
Plus pearl in *or* inn, etc.
Plus her, Lynn, etc.

ŪRL′ING

f: fūrl′ing, un-fūrl′ing.
h: hērl′ing, hūrl′ing.
hw: up-whĩrl′ing, whĩrl′ing.
k(ç): çūrl′ing, un-çūrl′ing,
up-çūrl′ing.
p: pēarl′ing, pūrl′ing.
sk: skĩrl′ing.
sp: Spērl′ing.
st: stērl′ing, Stĩrl′ing.
sw: swĩrl′ing.
tw: twĩrl′ing.

ŨRL′ISH

ch: chūrl′ish.
g: gĩrl′ish.
p: pēarl′ish.

(Choose only one word out of each group)

ŬR'LOIN

p: pŭr'loin.
s: sĭr'loin.
Plus her loin, etc.

ŬR'LŪ

k(c̣): c̣ŭr'lew.
p: pŭr'lieū.
Plus Pearl, who, etc.
Plus myrrh, Lou *or* loo, **etc.**

ŬRL'ŬR

b: bŭrl'ẽr.
f: fŭrl'ẽr.
h: hŭrl'ẽr.
hw: whĭrl'ẽr.
k(c̣): c̣ŭrl'ẽr.
p: pĕarl'ẽr, pŭrl'ẽr.
sk: skĭrl'ẽr.
sw: swĭrl'ẽr.
tw: twĭrl'ẽr.
Plus whirl her, etc.

ŬR'MȦ

Vowel: Ĭr'mȧ.
b: Bŭr'mȧ.
d: dẽr'mȧ.
f: ter'ra fir'ma.
s: syr'mȧ.
w: Bŭr'mȧ=Wŭr'mȧ.
Plus term a, etc.

ŬR'MĀD

m: mẽr'māid.
Plus her maid *or* made, **etc.**

ŬR'MĂL

d: dẽr'măl, ep-i-dẽr'măl,
hȳ-pō-dẽr'măl, pac̣h-y-dẽr'măl,
tax-i-dẽr'măl.
th: dī-ȧ-thẽr'măl, ġē-ō-thẽr'măl,
hȳ-drō-thẽr'măl,

i"sō-ġē"ō-thẽr'măl,
ī-sō-thẽr'măl, syn-thẽr'măl,
thẽr'măl.
Plus squirm, Al, etc.

ŬR'MĂN

f: fĭr'măn.
g: c̣ŏu'ṣin ġer'măn, Ġẽr'măn.
m: mẽr'măn.
s: sẽr'mŏn.
Plus her man, etc.

ŬR'MĂNS

f: af-fĭr'mănce, c̣on-fĭr'mănce,
dis-af-fĭr'mănce.
Plus her manse, etc.
Plus term aunts *or* ants, etc.

ŪR'MENT

j: ab-jūre'ment, c̣on-jūre'ment.
k(c̣): prō-c̣ūre'ment.
l: al-lūre'ment.
m: im-mūre'ment.
sk(sc̣): ob-sc̣ūre'ment.
Plus pure meant, etc.

ŬR'MENT, UR'MANT

f: af-fĭr'mănt, dē-fẽr'ment,
fẽr'ment, prē-fẽr'ment,
rē-fẽr'ment.
t: dē-tẽr'ment, dis-in-tẽr'ment,
in-tẽr'ment.
v: ȧ-vẽr'ment.
Plus myrrh meant, etc.

ŬRM'EST

f: c̣on-fĭrm'est*, fĭrm'est,
in-fĭrm'est.
skw: squirm'est*.
t: tẽrm'est*.
w: wŏrm'est*.
Plus purr messed, etc.

(Choose only one word out of each group)

ŪRM'ETH

f: c̦on-fĭrm'eth*.
skw: squĭrm'eth*.
t: tẽrm'eth*.
w: wŏrm'eth*.

ŪR'MĒZ

h: Hẽr'mēṣ.
k: kẽr'mēṣ.
Plus term ease *or* E's, **etc.**

ŪRM'I

d: tax'i-dẽrm″y.
g: ġẽrm'y.
n: Nũr'mi.
w: wŏrm'y.
Plus firm, he, etc.
Plus stir me, etc.

ŪR'MIK

d: dẽr'mic̦, en·dẽr'mic̦,
ep-i-dẽr'mic̦, hȳ-drō-dẽr'mic̦,
hȳ-pō-dẽr'mic̦, pac̦h-y-dẽr'mic̦,
sc̦ler-ō-dẽr'mic̦, tax-i-dẽr'mic̦.
th: ā″di-à-thẽr'mic̦,
dī-à-thẽr'mic̦, ġē-ō-thẽr'mic̦,
ī″sō-ġē″ō-thẽr'mic̦, thẽr'mic̦.
Plus her Mick, etc.

ŪR'MIN

Vowel: ẽr'mine.
d: dē-tẽr'mine.
v: vẽr'min.
Cf. ũr'măn.
Plus worm in *or* inn, **etc.**
Plus stir Min, etc.

ŪR'MIND

Vowel: ẽr'mined.
t: dē-tẽr'mined,
un-dĕ-tẽr'mined.
Plus worm inned, etc.

ŪRM'ING

f: af-fĭrm'ing, c̦on-fĭrm'ing,
fĭrm'ing.
skw: squĭrm'ing.
t: tẽrm'ing.
w: wŏrm'ing.
Plus her Ming, etc.

ŪR'MIS

d: dẽr'mis, ep-i-dẽr'mis.
Plus her miss, etc.

ŪR'MISH

sk: skĭr'mish.
w: wŏrm'ish.

ŪR'MĪT

t: tẽr'mīte.
Plus myrrh might *or* mite, etc.

ŪR'MIT

h: hẽr'mit.
p: pẽr'mit.
Plus term it, etc.
Plus her mitt, etc.

ŪRM'LI

f: fĭrm'ly.
t: tẽrm'ly.
Plus squirm, Lee *or* lea, **etc.**

ŪR'MOIL

t: tûr'moil.
Plus her moil, etc.
Plus sperm oil, etc.

ŪRM'ŪR

f: af-fĭrm'ẽr, c̦on-fĭrm'ẽr,
fĭrm'ẽr, in-fĭrm'ẽr.
m: bē-mûr'mûr, mûr'mûr.
skw: squĭrm'ẽr.

ŪR′NÀ
ŪR′NEST

fāte, fär, fȧst, fall, finăl, cāre, at; mēte, prey, hĕr, met; pīne, marïne, bĭrd, pin; nōte, mŏve, fŏr, atŏm, not; mōͻn, book;

778

(Choose only one word out of each group)

t: tĕrm′ēr, tĕrm′ŏr.
w: wŏrm′ēr.
Plus squirm her, etc.
Plus her myrrh, etc.

ŪR′NÀ

m: Myr′nȧ.
sm: Smyr′nȧ.
v: Vĕr′nȧ.
Plus turn a, etc.

ŪR′NĂL

Vowel: dī-ūr′năl, hō-di-ēr′năl,
sem″i-dī-ūr′năl, ūr′năl.
b: hī-bĕr′năl.
f: in-fĕr′năl, par-ȧ-phĕr′năl.
j: joŭr′năl.
k(c̣): c̣olo′nel (kĕr′), kĕr′nel.
p: sū-pĕr′năl.
s: lū-cĕr′năl.
st: stĕr′năl.
t: c̣ō-ē-tĕr′năl, dī-ū-tĕr′năl,
ē-tĕr′năl, ex-tĕr′năl,
frȧ-tĕr′năl, hes-tĕr′năl,
in-tĕr′năl, mȧ-tĕr′năl,
noc̣-tūr′năl, pȧ-tĕr′năl,
sem-pi-tĕr′năl.
v: c̣a-vĕr′năl, vĕr′năl.
Plus burn, Al, etc.

ŪR′NĂNT, ŪR′NENT

s: sē-cĕr′nănt.
t: al-tĕr′nant.
v: vĕr′nănt.
Plus turn aunt *or* ant, etc

ŪR′NĂRD

b: Bĕr′nărd.
Plus myrrh, nard, etc.
Cf. burn hard, etc.

ŪR′NĂS

f: fūr′năce.
Cf. burn ace, etc.

ŪR′NĀT

t: al-tĕr′nāte, sub-al′tĕr-nāte,
tĕr′nāte.
th: c̣ō-thūr′nāte.
Plus tern ate *or* eight, etc.
Plus her. Nate, etc.

ŪR′NED

l: lĕarn′ed, un-lĕarn′ed.
Plus urn+ed*.

ŪR′NES

k(c̣): in-sē-c̣ūre′ness,
sē-c̣ūre′ness.
m: dē-mūre′ness.
p: im-pūre′ness, poor′ness,
pūre′ness.
sh: sūre′ness.
sk(sc̣): ob-sc̣ūre′ness.
t: im-mȧ-tūre′ness,
mȧ-tūre′ness.

ŪR′NES

f: Fūr′ness.
Cf. fur′nace.
Plus turn S, etc.

ŪR′NEST

Vowel: ēar′nest, Ér′nest,
ō-vĕr-ēar′nest.
b: būr′nest*.
ch: chūr′nest*.
j: ad-joŭr′nest*, sō-joŭr′nest*.
l: lĕar′nest*.
s: c̣on-cĕr′nest*, dis-cĕr′nest*.
sp: spūr′nest*.
st: stĕr′nest.

(Choose only one word out of each group)

t: ō-vĕr-tūr′nest*, rē-tūr′nest*, tūr′nest*.
y: yĕar′nest*.
z: diṣ-cĕr′nest*.
Plus her nest, etc.
Cf. erne nest, etc.

ŪR′NETH

Vowel: ēar′neth*.
b: būr′neth*.
ch: chūr′neth*.
j: ad-joūr′neth*, sō-joūr′neth*.
l: lēar′neth*.
s: çon-cĕr′neth*, dis-cĕr′neth*.
sp: spūr′neth*.
t: ō-vĕr-tūr′neth*, rē-tūr′neth*, tūr′neth*.
y: yĕar′neth*.
z: diṣ-cĕr′neth*.

ÚR′NI

b: Bĕr′ney, Bĭr′ney, būr′ny≠būr′ny.
f: fĕr′ny.
g: Gūr′ney.
j: joūr′ney.
t: at-tŏr′ney, toūr′ney, Tūr′ney.
Plus earn, he, etc.
Plus her knee, etc.

ŪRN′ING

Vowel: ēarn′ing, ūrn′ing.
b: būrn′ing, heärt′≠būrn″ing, ō-vĕr-būrn′ing, sun′būrn″ing.
ch: chūrn′ing.
j: ad-joūrn′ing, sō-joūrn′ing.
l: book lēarn′ing, lēarn′ing, un-lēarn′ing.
s: çon-cĕrn′ing, dis-cĕrn′ing, un-dis-cĕrn′ing.

sp: spūrn′ing.
t: ō-vĕr-tūrn′ing, rē-tūrn′ing, tā′ble≠tūrn″ing, tūrn′ing, up-tūrn′ing.
y: yĕarn′ing.
z: diṣ-cĕrn′ing, un-diṣ-cĕrn′ing.

ŪR′NISH

b: būr′nish.
f: fūr′nish.

ŪR′NISHT

b: būr′nished, un-būr′nished.
f: fūr′nished, un-fūr′nished.

ŪRN′MENT

j: ad-joūrn′ment, sō-joūrn′ment.
s: çon-cĕrn′ment, dis-cĕrn′ment, sē-cĕrn′ment.
t: at-tŏrn′ment.
z: diṣ-cĕrn′ment.
Plus erne meant, etc.

ŪRN′NES

st: stĕrn′ness.

ŪR′NŌ

f: in-fĕr′nō.
st: Stĕr′nō.
Plus burn owe *or* O, etc.
Plus fir no *or* know, etc.

ŪR′NUM

b: lả-būr′num.
Plus turn ′em, etc.
Plus her numb, etc.

ŪRN′ŪR

Vowel: ēarn′ẽr.
b: bärn būrn′ẽr, būr′nẽr.
j: ad-joūrn′ẽr, sō-joūrn′ẽr.

ŪR'NUS
ŪRP'ŪR

fāte, fär, fȧst, fạll, finăl, cãre, at; mēte, prĕv, hẽr, met; pīne,
marïne, bïrd, pin; nōte, mŏve, fŏr, atŏm, nŏt; mọọn, book;

780

(Choose only one word out of each group)

l: lẽarn'ẽr.

s: dis-cẽrn'ẽr.

sp: spŭrn'ẽr.

st: stẽrn'ẽr.

t: ō-vẽr-tŭrn'ẽr, rē-tŭrn'ẽr,
tŭrn'ẽr.

y: yẽarn'ẽr.

z: dis̟-cẽrn'ẽr.

Plus burn her *or* err, etc.

ŪR'NUS

th: çō-thŭr'nus.

Plus burn us, etc.

Ū'RŌ

b: bū'reau.

d: mȧ-dū'rō.

sk(sç): çhi"ȧ-rō-sçu'rō.

tr: Trū'rō.

Plus you row *or* roe, etc.

Plus pure owe *or* O, etc.

ŪR'Ō

b: bŏr'ōugh, bŭr'rōw

f: fŭr'rōw.

th: thŏr'ōugh.

Plus her owe *or* O, etc.

Cf. her roe *or* row, etc.

ŪR'ŌD

b: bŭr'rōwed.

f: fŭr'rōwed, un-fŭr'rōwed.

Plus her ode, etc.

Cf. her road *or* rode, etc.

ŪR'ŎR

f: fŭr'ŏr.

j: jŭr'ŏr, grand jŭr'ŏr,
non-jŭr'ŏr, pet'ty jŭr'ŏr,
trī'ăl jŭr'ŏr.

Cf. ŭr'ŭr.

Plus pure, or, etc.

ŪR'PENT

s: sẽr'pent.

Plus her pent, etc.

ŪRP'EST

b: bŭrp'est*.

ch: chïrp'est*.

z: ū-s̟ŭrp'est*.

Plus her pest, etc.

ŪRP'ETH

b: bŭrp'eth*.

ch: chïrp'eth*.

t: tŭr'peth.

z: ū-s̟ŭr'peth*.

ŪR'PĒZ

b: Bŭr'pee's̟.

Plus deter peas, etc.

ŪRP'ING

b: bŭrp'ing.

ch: chïrp'ing.

z: ū-s̟ŭrp'ing.

Plus her ping, etc.

ŪR'P'L

p: em-pŭr'ple, pŭr'ple.

Plus chirp'll, etc.

Cf. her pull, etc.

UR'PŎS

p: pŭr'pŏse.

Plus her puss, etc.

Cf. chirp us, etc.

ŪRP'ŪR

b: bŭrp'ẽr.

ch: chïrp'ẽr.

z: ū-s̟ŭr'pẽr.

Plus twirp err *or* her, etc.

(Choose only one word out of each group)

ŪR'SÅ

Vowel: ūr'så.
v: vī'ce-vẽr'så.
Plus immerse a, etc.

ŪR'SĂL

Vowel: ūr'săl.
h: rē-hẽar'săl.
t: tẽr'cel.
v: çon-trō-vẽr'săl, rē-vẽr'săl,
   trans-vẽr'săl, ūn-i-vẽr'săl,
   vẽr'săl*.
Plus curse, Al, etc.
Plus her Sal, etc.

UR'SĂNT

k(ç): rē-çûr'sănt.
v: à-vẽr'sănt, vẽr'sănt.
Plus curse aunt *or* ant, etc.

ŪRS'ED

k(ç): aç-çûrs'ed.
Plus ūrs+d*.

ŪRS'EST

Vowel: ço-ẽrc'est*.
b: dis-būrs'est*, rē-im-būrs'est*.
h: rē-hẽars'est*.
k(ç): aç-çûrs'est*, bē-çûrs'est*,
   çûrs'est*.
m: im-mẽrs'est*.
n: nûrs'est*.
p: dis-pẽrs'est*.
sp: in-tẽr-spẽrs'est*.
v: çon-vẽrs'est*, rē-vẽrs'est*,
   trà-vẽrs'est*.

ŪR'SET

t: tẽr'cet.
Plus her set, etc.
Cf. nurse it, etc.

ŪRS'ETH

Vowel: çō-ẽrc'eth*.
b: dis-būrs'eth*,
   rē-im-būrs'eth*.
h: rē-hẽars'eth*.
k(ç): aç-çurs'eth*, bē-çûrs'eth*,
   çûrs'eth*.
m: im-mẽrs'eth*.
n: nûrs'eth*.
p: dis-pẽrs'eth*.
sp: in-tẽr-spẽrs'eth*.
v: çon-vẽrs'eth*, rē-vẽrs'eth*,
   trà-vẽrs'eth*.
Plus her. Seth, etc.

ŪR'SEZ

Vowel: çō-ẽr'ceṣ.
b: dis-būr'seṣ, rē-im-būr'seṣ.
h: hẽar'seṣ, rē-hẽar'seṣ.
k(ç): aç-çûr'seṣ, bē-çûr'seṣ,
   çûr'seṣ.
m: à-mẽr'ceṣ, im-mẽr'seṣ,
   sub-mẽr'seṣ.
n: nûr'seṣ.
p: dis-pẽr'seṣ, pûr'seṣ.
sp: in-tẽr-spẽr'seṣ.
t: tẽr'ceṣ.
v: çon-vẽr'seṣ, rē-vẽr'seṣ,
   trà-vẽr'seṣ, vẽr'seṣ.
Plus myrrh says, etc.
Plus hearse, Ez, etc.

ŪR'SHĂL

m: çom-mẽr'ciăl,
   un-çom-mẽr'ciăl.
t: tẽr'tiăl.
v: çon-trō-vẽr'siăl.
Plus myrrh shall, etc.
Plus Hirsch, Al, etc.

ŪR'SHIP

w: wŏr'ship.
Plus her ship, etc.

(Choose only one word out of each group)

ŬR′SHUM

t: nas-tŭr′tium.
Plus Hirsch 'em, etc.

ŬR′SHUN

Vowel: ҫō-ēr′cion.
k(ҫ): dis-ҫūr′sion, ex-ҫūr′sion,
   in-ҫūr′sion, rē-ҫūr′sion.
m: dē-mēr′sion, ē-mēr′sion,
   im-mēr′sion, mer′sion*,
   sub-mēr′sion.
p: ȧ-pēr′tion*, as-pēr′sion,
   dis-pēr′sion.
s: as-sēr′tion, ҫon-cēr′tion*,
   dis-ҫon-cēr′tion, in-sēr′tion,
   in-tēr-sēr′tion*,
   self′=as-sēr′tion.
sp: in-spēr′sion*, in-tēr-spēr′sion.
st: ab-stēr′sion.
t: ex-tēr′sion*, nas-tŭr′tion,
   tēr′tiăn.
v: an″i-mad-vēr′sion, a-vēr′sion,
   cĩr″ҫum-vēr′sion*,
   ҫon′trȧ-vēr′sion,
   ҫon″trō-vēr′sion, ҫon-vēr′sion,
   dī-vēr′sion, ē-vēr′sion,
   in-trō-vēr′sion, ob-vēr′sion,
   pēr-vēr′sion, rē-trō-vēr′sion,
   rē-vēr′sion, sub-vēr′sion,
   vēr′sion.
z: dē-ṣēr′tion, ex-ēr′tion.
Plus fur shun, etc.
Cf. ūr′si-ăn.

ŬR′SI

m: grȧ-mēr′cy, mēr′cy, Mēr′sey.
p: Pēr′cy, pūr′sy.
s: Cĩr′ce, Sēar′cy.
v: ҫon′trō-vēr″sy.
Plus her see, etc.
Plus purse, he, etc.

ŬR′SING

Vowel: ҫō-ēr′cing.
b: dis-bũr′sing, rē-im-bũr′sing.
h: rē-hēar′sing.
k(ҫ): aҫ-ҫūr′sing, bē-ҫūr′sing,
   ҫūr′sing.
m: im-mēr′sing.
n: nũr′sing.
p: dis-pēr′sing.
v: ҫon-vēr′sing, rē-vēr′sing,
   trans-vēr′sing, trȧ-vēr′sing,
   vēr′sing.
Plus her sing, etc.

ŬR′SIV

Vowel: ҫō-ēr′cive.
k(ҫ): ҫūr′sive, dē-ҫūr′sive,
   dis-ҫūr′sive, ex-ҫūr′sive,
   in-ҫūr′sive, prē-ҫūr′sive.
p: as-pēr′sive, dis-pēr′sive.
st: ab-stēr′sive.
t: dē-tēr′sive.
v: an″i-mad-vēr′sive, ȧ-vēr′sive,
   ҫon-vēr′sive, ē-vēr′sive,
   pēr-vēr′sive, sub-vēr′sive.
Plus her sieve, etc.

ŬRS′MENT

b: dis-bũrse′ment,
   im-bũrse′ment,
   rē-im-bũrse′ment.
m: ȧ-mērce′ment.
Plus purse meant, etc.

ŬRS′NES

t: tērse′ness.
v: ad-vērse′ness, ȧ-vērse′ness,
   pēr-vērse′ness.

(Choose only one word out of each group)

ŪR′SŎN

f: Mc̜-Phēr′sŏn.
g: Gēr′sŏn.
p: pēr′sŏn.
Plus her son, etc.

ŪR′STED

b: būr′sted.
th: thĭr′sted.
w: wŏr′sted.
Plus first, Ed, etc.
Plus purse, Ted, etc.
Plus her stead, etc.

ŪRST′EST

b: būrst′est*.
th: thĭrst′est*.
w: wŏrst′est*.
Plus purse test, etc.

ŪRST′ETH

b: būrst′eth*.
th: thĭrst′eth*.
w: wŏrst′eth*.

ŪR′STI

th: thĭr′sty.
Plus burst, he, etc.
Plus worse tea, etc.

ŪR′STING

b: būr′sting.
th: thĭr′sting.
w: wŏr′sting.

ŪR′STŪR

b: būr′stēr.
th: thĭr′stēr.
w: wŏr′stēr.
Plus her stir, etc.
Plus cursed her *or* err, etc.

ŪR′SŪR

Vowel: c̜ō-ēr′cēr.
b: būr′săr, dis-būr′sēr,
rē-im-būr′sēr.
h: hēar′sēr, rē-hēar′sēr.
k(c̜): ac̜-c̜ūr′sēr, an-tē-c̜ūr′sŏr*,
c̜ūr′sēr, c̜ūr′sŏr, prē-c̜ūr′sŏr.
m:- à-mēr′cēr, c̜om-mēr′cēr,
im-mēr′sēr, mēr′cēr.
n: nūr′sēr.
p: dis-pēr′sēr, pūr′sēr.
v: c̜on-vēr′sēr, pēr-vēr′sēr,
rē-vēr′sēr, trȧ-vēr′sēr, vēr′sēr.
w: wŏr′sēr.
Plus curse her, etc.

ŪR′SUS

Vowel: ūr′sus.
k(c̜): ex-c̜ūr′sus.
th: thyr′sus.
v: vēr′sus.
Plus curse us, etc.

ŪR′TÅ

b: Al-bēr′tȧ, El-bēr′tȧ.
Plus pert a, etc.

ŪR′TĂN

k(c̜): c̜ūr′tăin, en-c̜ūr′tăin.
s: cēr′tăin, in-cēr′tăin*,
un-cēr′tăin.
Plus hurt an *or* on, etc.
Cf. her tan, etc.

ŪR′TED

bl: blūr′ted.
fl: flĭr′ted.
kw: quĭr′ted.
s: as-sēr′ted, c̜on-cēr′ted,
dis-c̜on-cēr′ted, in-sēr′ted,
in-tēr-sēr′ted, prē-c̜on-cēr′ted.

(Choose only one word out of each group)

sh: shĭr'ted, un-shĭr'ted.
sk: skĭr'ted, un-skĭr'ted.
skw: squĭr'ted.
sp: spŭr'ted.
v: ad-vẽr'ted, ȧ-vẽr'ted,
   cọn-vẽr'ted, dī-vẽr'ted,
   in-vẽr'ted, pẽr-vẽr'ted,
   rē-vẽr'ted, sub-vẽr'ted,
   un-dī-vẽr'ted, un-pẽr-vẽr'ted.
z: dē-ṣẽr'ted, ex-ẽr'ted.
Plus her Ted, etc.
Plus hurt Ed, etc.

ŪR'TĒN

th: thĭr'teen.
Plus spurt e'en*, etc.

ŪR'TENS

v: ad-vẽr'tence, in-ad-vẽr'tence,
   mis-ad-vẽr'tence.
Plus her tents *or* tense, etc.
Cf. squirt, hence, etc.

ŪR'TEST

bl: blŭr'test*.
h: hŭr'test*.
k(ç): çūr'test.
p: pẽr'test.
s: as-sẽr'test*, cọn-cẽr'test*,
   dis-cọn-cẽr'test*, in-sẽr'test*.
sk: skĭrt'est*.
skw: squĭrt'est*.
sp: spŭrt'est*.
v: ad-vẽr'test*, ȧ-vẽr'test*,
   cọn-trō-vẽr'test*, cọn-vẽr'test*,
   dī-vẽr'test*, in-vẽr'test*,
   pẽr-vẽr'test*, rē-vẽr'test*,
   sub-vẽr'test*.
z: dē-ṣẽr'test*, ex-ẽr'test*.
Plus her test, etc.

ŪR'TETH

bl: blŭr'teth*.
h: hŭr'teth*.
s: as-sẽr'teth*, cọn-cẽr'teth*,
   dis-cọn-cẽr'teth*, in-sẽr'teth*.
sk: skĭr'teth*.
skw: squĭr'teth*.
sp: spŭr'teth.
v: ad-vẽr'teth*, ȧ-vẽr'teth*,
   cọn-trō-vẽr'teth*, cọn-vẽr'teth*,
   dī-vẽr'teth*, in-vẽr'teth*,
   pẽr-vẽr'teth*, rē-vẽr'teth*,
   sub-vẽr'teth*.
z: dē-ṣẽr'teth*, ex-ẽr'teth*.

ŪR'THȦ

b: Bẽr'thȧ.
h: Hẽr'thȧ.
Plus worth a, etc.

ŪR'THEN

b: bŭr'THen, dis-bŭr'THen,
   un-bŭr'THen.
Plus myrrh then, etc.

ŪRTH'EN

Vowel: ẽarth'en
Cf. mirth, hen, etc.

ŪR'THŪR

f: fŭr'THẽr.

ŪR'THEST

f: fŭr'THest.

ŪRTH'FŮL

m: mĭrth'fůl.
w: wŏrth'fůl.
Plus berth full, etc.

(Choose only one word out of each group)

ŪRTH′LES

b: bĭrth′less.
m: mĭrth′less.
w: wŏrth′less.
Plus earth less *or* Les, etc.

ŪR′THI

w: nōte′wŏr″THy, sēa′wŏr″THy,
trust′wŏr″THy, wŏr″THy,
un-wŏr″THy.
Cf. stir the *or* thee*, etc.

ŪR′THI

Vowel: ēar′thy.
Plus worth, he, etc.

ŪR′TI

ch: chẽr′ty.
d: dĭr′ty.
fl: flĭr′ty.
g: Gẽr′tie.
th: thĭr′ty.
Plus hurt, he, etc.
Plus her tea, etc.

ŪR′TING

bl: blŭr′ting.
fl: flĭr′ting.
h: hŭr′ting.
s: as-sẽr′ting, çon-cẽr′ting,
dis-çon-cẽr′ting, in-sẽr′ting,
in-tẽr-sẽr′ting, prē-çon-cẽr′ting,
self′=as-sẽr′ting.
sh: shĭr′ting, un-shĭr′ting.
sk: skĭr′ting, un-skĭr′ting.
skw: squir′ting.
sp: spŭr′ting.
v: ad-vẽr′ting, à-vẽr′ting,
çon-trō-vẽr′ting, çon-vẽr′ting,
dī-vẽr′ting, in-tẽr-vẽr′ting,

in-vẽr′ting, pẽr-vẽr′ting,
rē-trō-vẽr′ting, rē-vẽr′ting,
sub-vẽr′ting.
z: dē-ṣẽr′ting, ex-ẽr′ting.

ŪR′TIV

f: fŭr′tive.
s: as-sẽr′tive, self′=as-sẽr′tive.
v: dī-vẽr′tive, rē-vẽr′tive.
z: ex-ẽr′tive.

ŪR′TIS

k: Çūr′tis.
Cf. Gertie's, hurt his, etc.

ŪR′T′L

f: fẽr′tile.
h: hŭr′tle.
hw: whŏr′tle.
k: kĭr′tle.
m: myr′tle.
sp: spŭr′tle.
t: tŭr′tle.
Plus squirt'll, etc.
Cf. her, till, etc.

ŪRT′LES

sh: shĭrt′less.
sk: skĭrt′less.
Plus hurt, Les *or* less, etc.

ŪRT′LI

Vowel: in-ẽrt′ly.
k(ç): çúrt′ly.
l: à-lẽrt′ly.
p: ex-pẽrt′ly, in-ex-pẽrt′ly,
pẽrt′ly.
Plus hurt, Lee *or* lea, etc.

ÛRT′NES
ÛR′ÛR

fāte, fär, fȧst, fall, finăl, cāre, at; mēte, prey, hêr, met; pīne,
marïne, bîrd, pin; nōte, mŏve, fôr, atŏm, nŏt; mọọn, book;

786

(Choose only one word out of each group)

ÛRT′NES

Vowel: in-ērt′ness.
k(c): çūrt′ness.
l: ȧ-lērt′ness.
p: ex-pērt′ness, in-ex-pērt′ness,
pērt′ness.

ÛR′TŎN

b: Bēr′tŏn.
g: Gūr′tŏn.
l: Lūr′tŏn.
m: Mēr′tŏn.
Plus her ton *or* tun, etc.
Plus chert on *or* an, etc.

ÛR′TRŪD

g: Gēr′trūde.
Plus Bert, rude, etc.

ÛRT′SI

k(c): çūrt′sey.
Plus Bert, see, etc.

ÛR′TŪ

v: vīr′tūe.
Plus hurt you, etc.

ÛR′TŪR

n: nūr′tūre.
Cf. ūr′chŭr.
Plus hurt, you're *or* your, etc.

ÛR′TÛR

bl: blūr′tēr.
fl: flīr′tēr.
h: hūr′tēr.
k(c): çūr′tēr.
p: pēr′tēr.
s: as-sēr′tēr, dis-çon-cēr′tēr,
in-sēr′tēr, prē-çon-cēr′tēr.

skw: squîr′tēr.
sp: spūr′tēr.
v: ad-vēr′tēr, an″i-mad-vēr′tēr,
ȧ-vēr′tēr, çon-vēr′tēr,
dī-vēr′tēr, in-vēr′tēr,
pēr-vēr′tēr, sub-vēr′tēr.
z: ex-ēr′tēr.
Plus hurt her, etc.

ÛR′UP

st: stîr′rup.
Cf. îr′up.
Plus her up, etc.

ÛR′ÛR

d: en-dūr′ēr.
j: ab-jūr′ēr, ad-jūr′ēr,
çon-jūr′ēr, jūr′ŏr, non″jūr′ŏr.
k(c): çūr′ēr, prō-çūr′ēr,
sē-çūr′ēr.
l: al-lūr′ēr, lūr′ēr.
m: dē-mūr′ēr, im-mūr′ēr,
mọọr′ēr, un-mọọr′ēr.
n: mȧ-nūr′ēr.
p: im-pūr′ŏr, pọọr′ēr, pūr′ēr.
sh: as-sūr′ēr (ȧ-shūr′),
en-sūr′ēr, in-sūr′ēr,
rē-as-sūr′ēr, rē-in-sūr′ēr,
sūr′ēr.
sk(sc): ob-sçūr′ēr.
t: mȧ-tūr′ēr, toûr′ēr.
y: in-ūr′ēr.
Cf. ūr′ŏr.
Plus procure her *or* err, etc.

ÛR′ÛR

bl: blūr′rēr.
f: çon-fēr′rēr, dē-fēr′rēr,
in-fēr′rēr, prē-fēr′rēr,
trans-fēr′rēr.
k(c): çon-çūr′rer, in-çūr′rēr.

787 ūse, bṳll, brūte, tŭrn, up; crȳ, myth; çat, machine, ace, church, çhord; ġem, aṅger, (Fr.) boṅ, aṣ; THis, thin; aᴢure

Ū′RUS
ŪR′VI

(Choose only one word out of each group)

m: dē-mūr′rēr.
p: pūr′rēr.
sh: shĭr′rēr.
sl: slŭr′rēr.
sp: spūr′rēr.
st: bē-stĭr′rēr, stĭr′rēr.
t: in-tēr′rēr.
v: à-vēr′rēr.
Plus spur her *or* err, etc.

Ū′RUS

k(ç): dol-i-çhū′rus.
n: à-nū′rous.
t: Arç-tū′rus.
y: Eū′rus, ū′rus.
Plus assure us, etc.

ŪR′US

s: sū-sŭr′rous.
w: wŭr′rus.
Plus blur us, etc.

ŪR′ŌZ

b: Bŭr′rōughṣ, Bŭr′rōwṣ.
Plus ŭr′ō+s.
Plus her rows *or* roes, etc.

ŪR′VÀ

n: Mi-nēr′và, Nēr′và.
Plus serve a, etc.

ŪR′VĂL

k(ç): çŭr′văl*.
s: à-cēr′văl*.
Plus swerve, Al, etc.

ŪR′VĂNS, ŪR′VENS

f: fēr′vence*.
z: in-ob-ṣēr′vănce, ob-ṣēr′vănce, un-ob-ṣēr′vănce.
Cf. ŭr′vănt+s.
Plus stir Vance *or* vents, etc.
Plus swerve ants *or* aunts, etc.

ŪR′VĂNT, ŪR′VENT

f: fēr′vent.
k(ç): çŭr′vănt, rē-çŭr′vănt.
s: çon-sēr′vănt, sēr′vănt.
z: in-ob-ṣēr′vănt, ob-ṣēr′vănt, un-ob-ṣēr′vănt.
Plus stir vent, etc.
Plus swerve aunt *or* ant, etc.

ŪR′VĀT

k(ç): çŭr′vāte, in-çŭr′vāte, rē-çŭr′vāte.
n: ē-nēr′vāte, trī-nēr′vāte.
s: à-cēr′vāte.
Plus conserve eight *or* ate, etc.

ŪR′VĒN

n: nēr′vïne.

UR′VEST

k(ç): çŭr′vest*.
n: un-nēr′vest*.
s: çon-sēr′vest*, sēr′vest*.
sw: swēr′vest*.
z: dē-ṣēr′vest*, ob-ṣēr′vest*, prē-ṣēr′vest*, rē-ṣēr′vest*.
Plus her vest, etc.

ŪR′VETH

k(ç): çŭr′veth*.
n: un-nēr′veth*.
s: çon-sēr′veth*, sēr′veth*.
sw: swēr′veth*.
z: dē-ṣēr′veth*, ob-ṣēr′veth*, prē-ṣēr′veth*, rē-ṣēr′veth*.

ŪR′VI

n: nēr′vy.
sk(sç): sçŭr′vy.
t: top′sy-tŭr′vy.
Plus swerve, he, etc.

(Choose only one word out of each group)

ŪR'VID

f: fẽr'vid, pẽr-fẽr'vid.
t: top'sy=tũr'vied.
Cf. curve hid, etc.

ŪR'VĪL

s: sẽr'vīle.
Plus her vile, etc.
Plus swerve, I'll, isle *or* aisle, etc.

ŪR'VIL

ch: chẽr'vil.
s: sẽr'vile.
Plus curve ill, etc.
Cf. swerve hill, etc.

ŪR'VIN

n: nẽr'vine.
s: cẽr'vine.
Plus swerve in *or* inn, etc.

ŪR'VING

Vowel: Ĩr'ving.
k(c): cũr'ving, in'cũr"ving,
    out'cũr"ving.
n: nẽr'ving, un-nẽr'ving.
s: con-sẽr'ving, sẽr'ving,
    tīme'=sẽr"ving.
sw: swẽr'ving, un-swẽr'ving.
z: dē-sẽr'ving, ob-sẽr'ving,
    prē-sẽr'ving, rē-sẽr'ving,
    un-dē-sẽr'ving, un-ob-sẽr'ving.

ŪR'VIS

p: Pũr'vis.
s: dis-sẽr'vice, lip sẽr'vice,
    mẽr'chant sẽr'vice, sēa sẽr'vice,
    sẽr'vice, un-sẽr'vice.

ŪRV'LES

k(c): cũrve'less.
n: nẽrve'less.

sw: swẽrve'less.
Plus deserve less, etc.

ŪR'VUR

f: fẽr'vŏr.
n: nẽr'vẽr, un-nẽr'vẽr.
s: con-sẽr'vẽr, sẽr'vẽr,
    tīme'=sẽr"vẽr.
sw: swẽr'vẽr.
z: dē-sẽr'vẽr, gāme prē-sẽr'vẽr,
    līfe prē-sẽr'vẽr, ob-sẽr'vẽr,
    prē-sẽr'vẽr, rē-sẽr'vẽr.
Plus swerve her *or* err, etc.

ŪR'VUS

k(c): rē-cũr'vous.
n: nẽr'vous.
Plus swerve us, etc.

ŪR'WIN

Vowel: Ẽr'win, Ĩr'win.
m: Mẽr'win.
Plus her win *or* Wynn, etc.

ŪRZ'DĀ

th: Thũrṣ'dāy.
Plus furze day *or* dey, etc.

ŪR'ZHȦ

p: Pẽr'ṣiȧ.

ŪR'ZHUN

k(c): dis-cũr'ṣion, ex-cũr'ṣion,
    in-cũr'ṣion.
m: dē-mẽr'ṣion.
p: as-pẽr'ṣion, dis-pẽr'ṣion,
    Pẽr'ṣiăn.
v: an"i-mad-vẽr'ṣion, a-vẽr'ṣion,
    con-vẽr'ṣion, dī-vẽr'ṣion,
    in-trō-vẽr'ṣion, in-vẽr'ṣion,
    pẽr-vẽr'ṣion, rē-vẽr'ṣion,
    sub-vẽr'ṣion, vẽr'ṣion.

(Choose only one word out of each group)

ŨR′ZI

f: fũr′zy.
j: jẽr′ṣey.
k: kẽr′ṣey.
m: Mẽr′ṣey.
Plus furze, he, etc.
Plus stir Zee *or* Z, etc.

Ū′SÅ

d: Mē-dū′sȧ.
k(c̨): C̨o̤o̤′sȧ.
l: Tus-c̨ȧ-lo̤o̤′sȧ.
p: Tal-lȧ-po̤o̤′sȧ.
s: Soṳ′sȧ, Sṳ′sȧ.
th: Ar-ē-thū′sȧ.
Plus reduce a, etc.

ŪS′ĂL

n: hȳ-pot-ē-nūs′ăl.
Plus reduce, Al, etc.

US′CHUN

b: c̨om-bus′tion.
d: ȧ-dus′tion*.
f: fus′tiăn.

ŪS′ED

d: deūc′ed.
Plus ūs+d*.
Cf. ūs′id.

ŪS′EN

l: lo̤o̤s′en, un-lo̤o̤s′en.
Cf. reduce hen, etc.

Ū′SENS, Ū′SĂNS

l: trans-lū′cence.
n. nūi′sănce.
Plus few scents, cents, *or* sense,
  etc.

Ū′SENT

d: ab-dū′cent, ad-dū′cent,
  c̨on-dū′cent, prō-dū′cent,
  rē-dū′cent, trȧ-dū′cent.
l: in-tẽr-lū′cent, lū′cent,
  rē-lū′cent, trȧ-lū′cent*,
  trans-lū′cent, un-lū′cent.
Plus new scent *or* cent, etc.
Cf. Tous′saint.

ŪS′EST

d: ad-dū′cest*, c̨on-dū′cest*,
  dē-dū′cest*, in-dū′cest*,
  in-trō-dū′cest*, prō-dū′cest*,
  rē-dū′cest*, rē-prō-dū′cest*,
  sē-dū′cest*, trȧ-dū′cest*.
f: prō-fūs′est.
l: lo̤o̤s′est, un-lo̤o̤s′est*.
spr: sprṳc′est.
str: ab-strṳs′est.

US′EST

b: bus′sest*.
k(c̨): c̨us′sest*, dis-c̨us′sest*.
f: fus′sest*.
m: mus′sest*.
tr: trus′sest*.

US′ET

g: gus′set.
r: rus′set.
Cf. discuss it, etc.
Cf. bus set, etc.

ŪS′ETH

d: ad-dū′ceth*, c̨on-dū′ceth*,
  dē-dū′ceth*, in-dū′ceth*,
  in-trō-dūc′eth*, prō-dū′ceth*ᵣ
  rē-dūc′eth*, rē-prō-dūc′eth*,
  sē-dū′ceth*, trȧ-dū′ceth*.

(Choose only one word out of each group)

l: lọọs'eth*, un-lọọs'eth*.
spr: sprủc'eth*.
Plus new, Seth, etc.

US'ETH

b: bus'seth*.
k(ç): çus'seth*, dis-çus'seth*.
f: fus'seth*.
m: mus'seth*.
tr: trus'seth*.

Ū'SEZ

b: å-bū'ses, çå-bọọ'ses.
d: ad-dū'çeṣ, çon-dū'çeṣ,
dē-dū'çeṣ, deūc'eṣ, ē-dūc'eṣ,
in-dūc'eṣ, in-trō-dūc'eṣ,
prō-dū'çeṣ, rē-dū'çeṣ,
rē-prō-dū'çeṣ, sē-dū'çeṣ,
trå-dū'çeṣ.
dr: Drủ'seṣ.
j: jủi'çeṣ.
k(ç): ex-çū'seṣ.
l: lọọ'seṣ, un-lọọ'seṣ.
n: bŭr-nọọ'seṣ, nọọ'seṣ.
sl: slủi'çeṣ.
spr: sprủ'çeṣ.
tr: trủ'çeṣ.
y: ū'seṣ.
Plus who says, etc.
Plus truce, Ez, etc.
Cf. noose is, etc.

US'EZ

b: bus'eṣ, bus'seṣ.
f: fus'seṣ.
k(ç): çus'seṣ, dis-çus'seṣ.
m: mus'seṣ.
tr: trus'seṣ, un-trus'seṣ.
Plus Gus's, etc.
Plus buss, Ez, etc.

ŪS'FỤL

j: jủice'fụl.
y: ūse'fụl.
Plus reduce full, etc.

Ū'SHÅ

r: Jē-rủ'shå.
Plus new shah, etc.
Plus debouch a, etc.

·USH'A

pr: Prus'siå.
r: Rus'siå.
Plus crush a, etc.

U'SHĂL

d: fĭ-dū'ciăl.
kr: çrủ'ciăl.
Plus you shall, etc.
Plus barouche, Al, etc.

USH'AN

pr: Prus'siăn.
r: Rus'siăn.
Plus crush an *or* Ann, etc.

USH'EST

bl: blush'est*.
br: brush'est*.
fl: flush'est*.
g: gush'est*.
h: hush'est*.
kr: çrush'est*.
r: rush'est*.

USH'ETH

bl: blush'eth*.
br: brush'eth*.
fl: flush'eth*.
g: gush'eth*.

(Choose only one word out of each group)

h: hush′eth*.
kr: çrush′eth*.
r: rush′eth*.

USH′EZ

bl: blush′eṣ.
br: brush′eṣ.
fl: flush′eṣ.
g: gush′eṣ.
h: hush′eṣ.
kr: çrush′eṣ.
l: lush′eṣ.
m: mush′eṣ.
pl: plush′eṣ.
r: on′rush″eṣ, rush′eṣ,
up-rush′eṣ.
t: tush′eṣ.
thr: thrush′eṣ.
Plus hush, Ez, etc.

USH′I

bl: blush′y.
br: brush′y.
g: gush′y.
l: lush′y.
m: mush′y.
r: rush′y.
sl: slush′y.
Plus crush, he, etc.

ÚSH′ING

d: doûçh′ing.
r: rúçh′ing.

USH′ING

bl: blush′ing, un-blush′ing.
br: brush′ing.
fl: flush′ing.
g: gush′ing.
h: hush′ing.
kr: çrush′ing.
l: lush′ing.
r: on′rush″ing, rush′ing,
up-rush′ing.

Ū′SHUN

b: at-tri-bū′tion, çon-tri-bū′tion,
dis-tri-bū′tion, ret-ri-bū′tion.
g: rē-där-gū′tion.
k(ç): al-lō-çū′tion,
çīr″çum-lō-çū′tion,
çol-lō-çū′tion, ē-leç-trō-çū′tion,
el-ō-çū′tion, ex-ē-çū′tion,
in-sē-çū′tion, in″tēr-lō-çū′tion,
lō-çū′tion, pēr-sē-çū′tion.
pros-ē-çū′tion,
ven-tril-ō-çū′tion.
l: ab-lū′tion, ab-sō-lū′tion,
çīr″çum-vō-lū′tion,
çon-vō-lū′tion, dev-ō-lū′tion,
dī-lū′tion, dis-sō-lū′tion,
ev-ō-lū′tion, in-vō-lū′tion,
ir-reṣ-ō-lū′tion, ob-vō-lū′tion,
pol-lū′tion, reṣ-ō-lū′tion,
rev-ō-lū′tion, self′-pol-lū′tion,
sō-lū′tion, vō-lū′tion.
n: çom-mi-nū′tion,
dim-i-nū′tion, im-mi-nū′tion.
p: Lil-li-pū′tiăn.
t: çon-sti-tū′tion, des-ti-tū′tion,
in-sti-tū′tion, pros-ti-tū′tion,
res-ti-tū′tion, sub-sti-tū′tion.
Plus you shun, etc.

USH′UN

k: çon-çus′sion, dis-çus′sion,
in-çus′sion, pēr-çus′sion,
rē-çus′sion, rē-pēr-çus′sion,
suç-çus′siăn.
pr: Prus′siăn.
r: Rus′siăn.

USH′ŪR

Vowel: ush′ēr.
bl: blush′ēr.

Ŭ'SHUS
Ŭ'SIV

fāte, fär, fȧst, fạll, finăl, cãre, at; mēte, prẹy, hẽr, met; pīne,
marīne, bĭrd, pin; nōte, mŏve, fọr, atŏm, not; mọọn, book;

792

(Choose only one word out of each group)

br: brush'ẽr.
fl: flush'ẽr, fōur'⸗flush″ẽr.
g: gush'ẽr.
h: hush'ẽr.
kr: c̦rush'ẽr.
l: lush'ẽr.
m: mush'ẽr.
pl: plush'ẽr.
r: rush'ẽr.
Plus crush her *or* err, etc.

Ū'SHUS

l: Lū'cius.
Plus debouch us, etc.

USH'US

l: lus'cious.
Plus crush us, etc.

Ū'SI

b: Dē-būs'sy.
d: Il Dū'cē.
g: gọọ'sy.
j: jüi'cy.
l: Lü'cy.
sl: slüi'cy.
Plus you see, etc.
Plus reduce, he, etc.

US'I

f: fus'sy.
h: hus'sy.
m: mus'sy.
Plus cuss, he, etc.

Ū'SID

l: lū'cid, pel-lū'cid,
trans-lū'cid.
m: mū'cid.
Cf. ūs'ed.
Plus you, Sid, etc.
Cf. goose hid, etc.

ŪS'IJ

b: ȧ-būs'ăg̣e*.
y: ūs'ăg̣e.
Cf. goose age, etc.
Cf. new sage, etc.

ŪS'IL

tr: prō-trü'sile.
Plus new sill, etc.
Plus goose ill, etc.

Ū'SING

d: ad-dū'cing, c̦on-dū'cing,
dē-dū'cing, ē-dū'cing,
in-dū'cing, in-trō-dū'cing,
prō-dū'cing, rē-dū'cing,
rē-prō-dū'cing, sē-dū'cing,
trȧ-dū'cing.
l: lọọs'ing, un-lọọs'ing.
spr: sprüc'ing.
Plus you sing, etc.

US'ING

b: bus'ing, bus'sing.
f: fus'sing.
k(c̦): c̦us'sing, dis-c̦us'sing.
m: mus'sing.
tr: trus'sing, un-trus'sing.

Ū'SIV

b: ȧ-bū'siv.
d: c̦on-dū'cive, dē-dū'cive,
ē-dū'cive.
f: c̦on-fū'sive, dif-fū'sive,
ef-fū'sive, in-fū'sive,
pẽr-fū'sive, trans-fū'sive.
kl: c̦on-c̦lū'sive, ex-c̦lū'sive,
in-c̦lū'sive, in″c̦on-c̦lū'sive,
rē-c̦lū'sive, sē-c̦lū'sive.
l: al-lū'sive, c̦ol-lū'sive,

(Choose only one word out of each group)

dē-lū′sive, ē-lū′sive, il-lū′sive.

t: çon-tū′sive.

tr: in-ob-trü′sive, in-trü′sive, ob-trú′sive.

Plus new sieve, etc.

US′IV

k(c̟): çon-çus′sive, dis-çus′sive, pĕr-çus′sive, rē-pĕr-çus′sive, suç-çus′sive.

Cf. muss sieve, etc.

US′KAN

d: dus′ken.

kr: Del′la Çrus′çăn.

l: mol-lus′çăn.

t: Tus′çăn.

tr: Ē-trus′çăn.

Plus bus′çăn, etc.

Plus musk an, etc.

US′KĀT

f: in-fus′çāte, ob-fus′çāte.

r: çō-rus′çāte.

Plus muss Kate, etc.

Plus musk ate *or* eight, etc.

US′KEST

d: dus′kest*.

h: hus′kest*.

US′KET

b: bus′ket.

m: mus′ket.

US′KETH

d: dus′keth*.

h: hus′keth*.

US′KI

d: dus′ky.

h: hus′ky.

m: mus′ky.

t: tus′ky.

Plus musk, he, etc.

Plus thus key, etc.

US′KIN

b: bus′kin.

r: Rus′kin.

Plus thus kin, etc.

Plus husk in *or* inn, etc.

US′KING

d: dus′king.

h: hus′king.

t: tus′king.

Plus muss king, etc.

US′KŪL

j: mȧ-jus′çūle.

n: mi-nus′çūle.

p: çrē-pus′çūle, ō-pus′çūle.

Plus husk, you'll, etc.

Cf. us cool, etc.

US′KŬR

h: hus′kĕr.

t: tus′kĕr.

Plus tusk her *or* err, etc.

Plus muss cur, etc.

US″L

b: bus′tle.

h: hus′tle.

j: jus′tle.

m: mus′cle, mus′sel.

p: çor-pus′cle, ō-pus′cle.

r: rus′tle.

t: tus′sle.

(Choose only one word out of each group)

Plus muss′ll, etc.
Cf. thus sell, etc.

ŪS′LES

j: jüice′less.
y: ūse′less.
Plus goose less *or* Les, etc.

US′LEST

b: bus′tlest*.
h: hus′tlest*.
r: rus′tlest*.
t: tus′slest*.
Plus crust, lest, etc.

US′LETH

b: bus′tleth*.
h: hus′tleth*.
r: rus′tleth*.
t: tus′sleth*.

US′LING

b: bus′tling.
h: hus′tling.
m: mus′cling.
r: rus′tling.
t: tus′sling.
Cf. us sling, etc.

US′LŨR

b: bus′tlẽr.
h: hus′tlẽr.
r: rus′tlẽr.
t: tus′slẽr.

US″LZ

br: Brus′selș.
Plus us″l+s.

ŪS′MENT

d: con-dūce′ment,
dē-dūce′ment, in-dūce′ment,

rē-dūce′ment, sē-dūce′ment,
sū″pẽr-in-dūce′ment,
trȧ-dūce′ment.
Plus goose meant, etc.

ŪS′NES

f: dif-fūse′ness, prō-fūse′ness.
kl: rē-cluse′ness.
l: loọse′ness.
spr: spruce′ness.
str: ab-struse′ness.
t: ob-tūse′ness.

Ů′SŌ

hw: whŏ′sō.
kr: Cru′sōe.
r: Cā-ru′sō.
tr: trous′seau (trů′sō).
Plus you sew, sow, *or* so, etc.
Plus goose owe *or* O, etc.

US′TȦ

g: Au-gus′tȧ.
j: Just′ȧ.
Plus must a, etc.

ŪS′TĂS

y: Eūs′tăce.
Plus boost ace, etc.

US′TĀT

kr: in-crus′tāte.
Plus just ate *or* eight, etc.
Plus muss, Tate, etc.

US′TED

b: bus′ted, com-bus′ted.
d: bē-dus′ted, dus′ted.
f: fus′ted.
g: dis-gus′ted.
j: ad-jus′ted, cō-ad-jus′ted,
self′‑ad-jus′ted.

(Choose only one word out of each group)

kr: c̱rus′ted, en-c̱rus′ted.
l: lus′ted.
r: rus′ted.
tr: bē-trus′ted, dis-trus′ted,
en-trus′ted, mis-trus′ted,
ō-vēr-trus′ted, trus′ted.
Plus must, Ed, etc.
Plus fuss, Ted, etc.

US′TEST

b: rō-bus′test.
d: dus′test*.
g: dis-gus′test*.
j: ad-jus′test*, jus′test.
kr: en-c̱rus′test*.
l: lus′test*.
r: rus′test*.
thr: thrus′test*.
tr: dis-trus′test*, en-trus′test*,
mis-trus′test*, trus′test*.
Plus fuss test, etc.

US′TETH

d: dus′teth*.
g: dis-gus′teth*.
j: ad-jus′teth*.
kr: en-c̱rus′teth*.
l: lus′teth*.
r: rus′teth*.
thr: thrus′teth*.
tr: dis-trus′teth*, en-trus′teth*,
mis-trus′teth*, trus′teth*.

UST′FU̱L

l: lust′fu̱l.
tr: dis-trust′fu̱l, mis-trust′fu̱l,
ō-vēr-trust′fu̱l, trust′fu̱l,
un-trust′fu̱l.
Plus just full, etc.

US′TI

d: dus′ty.
f: fus′tie, fus′ty.
g: gus′ty.
kr: c̱rus′ty.
l: lus′ty.
m: mus′ty.
r: rus′ty.
tr: trus′ty.
Plus bust, he, etc.

US′TIK

f: fus′tic̱.
r: rus′tic̱.
Plus us tick, etc.

US′TIN

d: Dus′tin.
j: Jus′tin.
Plus rust in *or* inn, etc.
Plus us tin, etc.

US′TING

b: bus′ting.
d: bē-dus′ting, dus′ting.
g: dis-gus′ting.
j: ad-jus′ting, c̱ō-ad-jus′ting,
self′⸗ad-jus′ting.
kr: c̱rus′ting, en-c̱rus′ting.
l: lus′ting.
r: rus′ting.
thr: thrus′ting.
tr: bē-trus′ting, dis-trus′ting,
en-trus′ting, mis-trus′ting,
ō-vēr-trus′ting, trus′ting,
un-mis-trus′ting.

US′TINGZ

d: dus′tingṣ.
h: hus′tingṣ.
l: lus′tingṣ.
thr: thrus′tingṣ.

US'TIS
US'TÜR

fāte, fär, fȧst, fạll, finăl, cãre, at; mēte, prĕy, hẽr, met; pīne,
marïne, bĭrd, pin; nōte, mŏve, fọr, atŏm, not; mọọn, book; **796**

(Choose only one word out of each group)

US'TIS

j: in-jus'tice, jus'tice.
k(c): Cus'tis.
Cf. dust is, etc.
Cf. rusty's, etc.

US'TIV

b: com-bus'tive.
j: ad-jus'tive.

UST'LI

b: rō-bust'ly.
g: au-gust'ly.
j: just'ly, un-just'ly.
Plus must, Lee or lea, etc.

UST'MENT

j: ad-just'ment.
mal-ad-just'ment.
kr: en-crust'ment.
Plus rust meant, etc.

UST'NES

b: rō-bust'ness.
g: au-gust'ness.
j: just'ness.

US'TŌ

b: bas'sō rō-bus'tō, rō-bus'tō.
g: gus'tō.
Plus just owe or O, etc.
Plus muss toe, etc.

US'TRĂL

k(c): là-cus'trăl.
l: lus'trăl, pà-lus'trăl.

US'TRĀT

fr: frus'trāte.
l: il-lus'trāte.

Plus must rate, etc.
Plus fuss trait, etc.
Cf. cuss straight, etc.

US'TRIN

k(c): là-cus'trine.
l: pà-lus'trine.

US'TRUM

fl: flus'trum.
l: lus'trum.
Plus must rum, etc.
Cf. us strum, etc.

US'TRUS

bl: blus'trous.
l: lus'trous.

US'TUM

k(c): cus'tŏm.
r: Rus'tum.
Plus bust 'em, etc.

ÚS'TŨR

b: bọọs'tẽr.
br: brew'stẽr.
f: Few'stẽr.
j: joús'tẽr.
r: rọọs'tẽr.
w: Wörces'tẽr (wús'tẽr).
Plus few stir, etc.
Plus loosed her or err, etc.

US'TŨR

b: bus'tẽr, fil'i-bus"tẽr,
rō-bus'tẽr, trust bus'tẽr.
bl: blus'tẽr.
d: dus'tẽr,
knuck'le dus'tẽr (nuk').
fl: flus'tẽr.
j: ad-jus'tẽr, cō-ad-jus'tẽr,
jus'tẽr.

797　　　üse, bu̱ll, brúte, tŭrn, **up**; crȳ, myth; ça̱t, maç̱hine, ace,
church, ç̱hord; ġem, añger, (Fr.) bon̄, aş; THis, thin; aᶎure

US′TŪRD
ÚT′ED

(Choose only one word out of each group)

k(ç̱): C̱us′tĕr.
kl: ç̱lus′tĕr.
l: lack′lus″tre, lus′tĕr, lus′tre.
m: mus′tĕr.
thr: thrus′tĕr.
tr: dis-trus′tĕr, trus′tĕr.
Plus thrust her *or* err, etc.

US′TŪRD

b: bus′tărd.
bl: blus′tēred.
fl: flus′tēred.
k(ç̱): c̱us′tărd.
kl: ç̱lus′tēred.
l: lus′tēred.
m: mus′tărd, mus′tēred.
Plus Custer′d, etc.
Cf. just stirred, etc.

US′TUS

g: A̱u-gus′tus.
j: Jus′tus.
Plus fussed us, etc.

Ú′SUM

gr: grúe′sŏme.
t: twö′sŏme (to̱o̱).
Plus through some *or* sum, etc.

ŪS′ŪR

d: ad-dūc′ĕr, c̱on-dūc′er,
dē-dūc′ĕr, in-dūc′ĕr,
in-trō-dūc′ĕɾ, prō-dūc′ĕr,
rē-dūc′ĕr, rē-prō-dūc′ĕr,
sē-dūc′ĕr, trà-dū′cĕr.
l: lo̱os′ĕr.
spr: sprúc′ĕr.
str: ab-strús′ĕr.
Plus who, sir, etc.
Plus loose her *or* err, etc.

US′ŪR

f: fus′sĕr.
k(ç̱): c̱us′sĕr, dis-c̱us′sĕr.
m: mus′sĕr.
tr: trus′sĕr.
Plus fuss her *or* err, etc.
Cf. fuss, sir, etc.

UT′ĂL

br: brút ăl.
f: fo̱o̱t′le.
t: to̱o̱t′le.
Cf. ūt′il.
Plus suit, Al, etc.

UT′ĀT

m: im-mū′tāte.
n: cĭr-c̱um-nū′tāte.
sk(sç̱): sc̱ū′tāte.
Plus you, Tate, etc.
Plus brute eight *or* ate, etc.

ŪT′Ē

b: bo̱o̱t′ee.
Plus new tea *or* T, etc.
Plus newt, he, etc.

ÚT′ED

b: bē-bo̱o̱t′ed, bo̱o̱t′ed,
un-bo̱o̱t′ed.
br: brúit′ed.
f: c̱on-fūt′ed, rē-fūt′ed,
un-c̱on-fūt′ed.
fl: flút′ed.
fr: frúit′ed.
h: ho̱o̱t′ed.
k(ç̱): al′lō-c̱ut-ed, el′ō-c̱ut-ed,
ē-lec′trō-c̱ut-ed, ex′ē-c̱ut-ed,
pēr′sē-c̱ut-ed, pros′ē-c̱ut-ed,
un-pēr′sē-c̱ut-ed,
un-pros′ē-c̱ut-ed.
kr: rē-c̱rúit′ed.

UT′ED
ŪT′ETH

fāte, fär, fȧst, fạll, finăl, cãre, at; mēte, prey, hẽr, met; pīne,
marïne, bĭrd, pin; nōte, mŏve, fọr, atŏm, not; mọọn, book; **798**

(Choose only **one** word out of each group)

l: con′vō-lūt-ed, dĭ-lūt′ed,
in′vō-lūt-ed, loọt′ed, pol-lūt′ed,
sȧ-lūt′ed, un-pol-lūt′ed,
vō-lūt′ed.

m: com-mūt′ed, im-mūt′ed,
moọt′ed, trans-mūt′ed.

n: com′mi-nūt-ed.

p: com-pūt′ed, dē-pūt′ed,
dis-pūt′ed, im-pūt′ed,
rē-pūt′ed, un-dis-pūt′ed.

r: roọt′ed, un-roọt′ed,
up-roọt′ed.

s: soọt′ed, sùit′ed, un-sùit′ed.

sk(sc): scoọt′ed.

t: con′sti-tù-ted, in′sti-tù-ted,
pros′ti-tūt-ed,
self′=con′sti-tū-ted,
sub′sti-tūt-ed, toọt′ed.

Cf. ūt′id.

Plus fruit, Ed, etc.

Plus you, Ted, etc.

UT′ED

b: ȧ-but′ted, but′ted,
rē-but′ted.

g: gut′ted.

gl: glut′ted.

j: jut′ted.

p: put′ted.

r: rut′ted.

str: strut′ted.

Plus strut, Ed, etc.

ŪT′EST

b: boọt′est*.

f: con-fūt′est*, rē-fūt′est*.

h: hoọt′est*.

k(c): ȧ-cūt′est, cūt′est,
ex′ē-cūt-est*, pẽr′sē-cūt-est*.

kr: rē-crùit′est*.

l: dĭ-lūt′est*, loọt′est*,

pol-lūt′est*, reṣ′ō-lūt-est,
sȧ-lūt′est*.

m: com-mūt′est*, mūt′est,
trans-mūt′est*.

n: mĭ-nūt′est.

p: dē-pūt′est*, dis-pūt′est*,
im-pūt′est*.

r: roọt′est*, up-roọt′est*.

sh: shoọt′est*.

t: as-tūt′est, con′sti-tūt-est*,
in′sti-tūt-est*, sub′sti-tūt-est*.

Plus new test, etc.

UT′EST

b: ȧ-but′test*, but′test*,
rē-but′test*.

g: gut′test*.

gl: glut′test*.

j: jut′test*.

p: put′test*.

r: rut′test*.

str: strut′test*.

Cf. smut test, etc.

ŪT′ETH

b: boọt′eth*.

f: con-fūt′eth*, rē-fūt′eth*.

h: hoọt′eth*.

k(c): ex′ē-cūt-eth*,
pẽr′sē-cūt-eth*.

kr: rē-crùit′eth*.

l: dĭ-lūt′eth*, loọt′eth*,
pol-lūt′eth*, sȧ-lūt′eth*.

m: com-mūt′eth*, mūt′eth*,
trans-mūt′eth*.

p: dē-pūt′eth*, dis-pūt′eth*,
im-pūt′eth*

r: roọt′eth*, up-roọt′eth*.

sh: shoọt′eth*.

t: con′sti-tūt-eth*,
in′sti-tūt-eth*, sub′sti-tūt-eth*.

(Choose only one word out of each group)

UT'ETH

b: à-but'teth*, but'teth*,
   rē-but'teth*.
g: gut'teth*.
gl: glut'teth*.
j: jut'teth*.
p: put'teth*.
r: rut'teth*.
str: strut'teth*.

ŪT'FU̧L

fr: frúit'fu̧l.
Plus snoot full, etc.

ŪTH'EST

s: soọTH'est.
sm: smoọTH'est.

ŪTH'FU̧L

r: rúth'fu̧l.
t: toọth'fu̧l.
tr: trúth'fu̧l, un-trúth'fu̧l.
y: yoúth'fu̧l.
Plus tooth full, etc.

ŪTH'ING

s: soọTH'ing.
sm: smoọTH'ing.

ŪTH'ING

t: toọth'ing.
Plus new thing, etc.

UTH'ING

d: dŏth'ing*.
n: nŏth'ing.

ŪT̠H'LES

r: rúth'less.
t: toọth'less.
tr: trúth'less.
Plus Ruth, less or Les, etc.

ŪTH'NES

sm: smoọTH'ness.

ŪTH'NES

k(c̣): un-c̣oúth'ness.

ŪTH'SUM

t: toọth'sŏme.
y: yoúth'sŏme.
Plus Ruth, some or sum, **etc.**

ŪTH'ŪR

s: soọTH'ẽr.
sm: smoọTH'ẽr.
Plus soothe her or err, **etc.**

ŪTH'ŪR

k(c̣): un-c̣oúth'ẽr.
l: Lú'thẽr.
Plus truth, her, etc.

UTH'ŪR

Vowel: ŏTH'ẽr.
br: brŏTH'ẽr,
   Chär'tẽr brŏTH'ẽr,
   fos'tẽr brŏTH'ẽr,
   half brŏTH'ẽr (haf),
   lodġe brŏTH'ẽr.
m: fõre'mŏTH"ẽr,
   fos'tẽr mŏTH'ẽr, mŏTH'ẽr,
   step'mŏTH-ẽr.
n: à-nŏTH'ẽr.
sm: smŏTH'ẽr.
t: t'ŏTH'ẽr.

UTH'ŪRN

s: SŏTH'ẽrn, sŏuTH'ẽrn.

Ū'TI

b: boọ'ty, beaū'ty,
   Dji-boú'ti (ji), free'boọ"ty,
   Ji-boú'ti.

UT'I
UT'ING

fāte. fär, fåst, fạll, finăl, cãre, at; mēte, prẹy, hẽr, met; pīne,
marĭne, bĭrd, pĭn; nōte, mŏve, fọr, atŏm, not; mọọn, book;

800

(Choose only one word out of each group)

d: dū'ty.

fl: flū'ty.

fr: frùit'y, tūt'ti=frùt'ti.

g: à-goù'ti.

k(c): cọọ'tie, cū'tie.

l: lọọ'ty.

r: rọọ'ty.

s: sọọ'ty.

sn: snọọ'ty.

Plus brute, he, etc.

UT'I

b: but'ty.

g: gut'ty.

j: jut'ty.

n: nut'ty.

p: put'ty.

r: rut'ty.

sm: smut'ty.

t: tut'ty.

Plus but he, etc.

ŪT'ID

b: bọọt'ied.

p: pūt'id.

Cf. ūt'ed.

Cf. boot hid, etc.

UT'IJ

fr: frùit'ăge.

m: mūt'ăge.

sk(sc): scùt'ăge.

Cf. flute age, etc.

ŪT'IK

b: scọr-būt'ic.

d: prō-paē-deū'tic.

n: hẽr-mē-neū'tic.

p: ther-à-peū'tic.

t: em-phy-teū'tic.

y: māi-ē-ūt'ic, tọr-ē-ūt'ic.

z: dī-à-zeū'tic.

Plus you tick, etc.

Ū'TIL

f: fū'tile.

r: rù'tile.

s: sū'tile.

y: in-ū'tile.

Plus few till, etc.

Plus brute ill, etc.

ŪT'ING

b: bọọt'ing, un-bọọt'ing.

f: con-fūt'ing, rē-fūt'ing.

fl: flūt'ing.

fr: frùit'ing.

h: họọt'ing.

k(c): ex'ē-cūt"ing,
pẽr'sē-cūt"ing, pros'ē-cūt"ing.

kr: rē-crùit'ing.

l: dī-lūt'ing,
hīgh'=fà-lūt'ing (hī'), lọọt'ing,
pol-lūt'ing, sà-lūt'ing.

m: com-mūt'ing, mọọt'ing,
pẽr-mūt'ing, trans-mūt'ing.

n: com-mi-nūt'ing.

p: com-pūt'ing, dē-pūt'ing,
dis-pūt'ing, im-pūt'ing.

r: rọọt'ing, un-rọọt'ing,
up-rọọt'ing.

s: sùit'ing.

sk(sc): scọọt'ing.

sh: off'=shọọt"ing,
out'=shọọt"ing, ō-vẽr-shọọt'ing,
shọọt'ing.

t: con'sti-tūt"ing,
därn'=tọọt'ing, in'sti-tūt"ing,
pros'ti-tūt"ing,
rē-con'sti-tūt"ing,
sub'sti-tūt"ing, tọọt'ing.

UT'ING

b: à-but'ting, but'ting,
rē-but'ting.

(Choose only one word out of each group)

g: gut'ting.
gl: glut'ting.
j: jut'ting.
k(c̲): c̲ross'-c̲ut″ting, c̲ut'ting, gláss c̲ut'ting.
n: nut'ting.
p: put'ting.
r: rut'ting.
sh: shut'ting.
str: strut'ting.

ŪT'ISH

br: brůt'ish.
s: so̱o̱t'ish.
Plus you, Tish, etc.

UT'ISH

r: rut'tish.
sl: slut'tish.

UT'IST

fl: flūt'ist.
l: lūt'ist.
n: hĕr-mē-neūt'ist,
p: ther-a̱-peūt'ist.
s: phär-ma̱-ceūt'ist.

ŪT'IV

d: in-dūt'ive.
j: cō-ad-jūt'ive.
k(c̲): pĕr-sē-c̲ūt'ive.
l: res̱-ō-lūt'ive.
t: c̲on-sti-tūt'ive.

ŪT'IZM

br: brůt'is̱m.
m: mūt'is̱m.
Plus cute ism, etc.

UT″L

b: a̱-but'tăl, rē-but'tăl.
g: gut'tle.
k(c̲): c̲ut'tle.

r: rut'tle.
s: sub'tle (sut″l), sut'tle.
sh: shut'tle.
sk(sc̲): sc̲ut'tle.
t: Tut'tle.
Plus Tutt'll, etc.

UT'LĂS

k(c̲): c̲ut'lăss.
Plus strut, lass, etc.

ŪT'LES

b: bo̱o̱t'less.
fr: frůit'less.
Plus suit less, etc.

UT'LEST

s: sut'tlest*.
sk(sc̲): sc̲ut'tlest*.
Plus cut, lest, etc.

UT'LET

k(c̲): c̲ut'let.
Plus butt Lett or let, etc.

UT'LETH

s: sut'tleth*.
sk(sc̲): sc̲ut'tleth*.

ŪT'LI

l: ab-sō-lūte'ly, po̱s̱-i-lūte'ly
Plus cute, Lee or lea, etc.

ŪT'LING

f: fo̱o̱t'ling.
t: to̱o̱t'ling.

UT'LING

g: gut'ling.
s: sut'ling.
sk(sc̲): sc̲ut'tling

(Choose only one word out of each group)

UT'LŪR

b: but'lẽr.
k(c̨): c̨ut'lẽr.
s: sub'tlẽr (sut'lūr), sut'lẽr.
sk(sc̨): sc̨ut'tlẽr.

ŪT'MENT

br: im-brùte'ment.
f: c̨on-fūte'ment.
kr: rē-c̨rùit'ment.
Plus suit meant, etc.

ŪT'NES

k(c̨): à-c̨ūte'ness, c̨ūte'ness.
l: ab-sō-lūte'ness.
m: mūte'ness.
n: mī-nūte'ness.
s: hīr-sūte'ness.
st: à-stūte'ness.

Ū'TŌ

pl: Plū'tō.
t: sos-ten-tū'tō.
Plus you toe *or* tow, etc.
Plus brute owe *or* O, etc.

Ū'TŎN

br: Brew'tŏn.
n: New'tŏn.
t: Teū'tŏn.
Plus brute on *or* an, etc.
Plus brew ton *or* tun, etc.

UT'ŎN

b: bach'el-ŏr but'tŏn, but'tŏn.
d: Dut'tŏn.
gl: glut'tŏn.
h: Hut'tŏn.
m: mut'tŏn.
n: nut"n.
s: Sut'tŏn.
Plus strut on *or* an, etc.

ŪT'ŎR

s: sùit'ŏr.
t: tūt'ŏr.
Cf. ūt'ūr.
Plus flute, or, etc.

ŪT'RĂL

n: neūt'rȧl.

UT'RES

b: but'tress.
Plus cut tress, etc.

Ū'TRID

p: pū'trid.
Plus brute rid, etc.

Ū'TRIKS

k(c̨): pẽr-sē-c̨ū'trix.
t: tū'trix.
Plus new tricks, etc.
Plus cute ricks, etc.

ŪT'RON

n: neūt'ron.
Cf. brute run, etc.

ŪT'SI

w: tọọt'sie⸗wọọt'sie.
Plus brute see, etc.
Plus lutes, he, etc.

Ū'TŪR

f: fū'tūre.
p: pū'tūre.
s: sū'tūre.
Plus suit your *or* you're, etc.

ŪT'ŪR

b: bọọt'ẽr, free'⸗bọọt'ẽr.
f: c̨on-fūt'ẽr, foùt'ẽr, rē-fūt'ẽr.
fl: flūt'ẽr.

(Choose only one word out of each group)

h: hoot′ēr.

j: cō-ad-jú′tŏr.

k(ç): aç-coút′re,
à-cūt′ēr, çūt′ēr,
ex′ē-çūt″ŏr, pēr′sē-çūt″ŏr,
pros′ē-çūt″ŏr.

kr: rē-çrúit′ēr.

l: dī-lūt′ēr, loot′ēr, lūt′ēr,
pol-lūt′ēr, sà-lūt′ēr.

m: çom-mūt′ēr, moot′ēr,
mūt′ēr, pēr-mūt′ēr,
trans-mūt′ēr.

n: mī-nūt′ēr, neūt′ēr.

p: çom-pūt′ēr, dē-pūt′ēr,
dis-pūt′ēr, im-pūt′ēr, pew′tēr.

r: root′ēr, up-root′ēr.

s: súit′ŏr.

sh: chút′ēr, par′a-chút″ēr,
pēa′shoot″ēr, shärp′shoot″ēr,
shoot′ēr.

sk(sç): scoot′ēr.

t: as-tūt′ēr, çon′sti-tūt″ēr,
in′sti-tūt″ēr, pros′ti-tūt″ēr,
res′ti-tū″tŏr, ring′=tāiled′toot′ēr,
sub′sti-tūt″ēr, toot′ēr, tūt′ŏr.
Plus loot her *or* err, etc.

UT′Ū̃R

Vowel: ut′tēr.

b: à-but′tēr,
bread′=and=but′tēr (bred′),
but′tēr, pēa′nut but′tēr,
rē-but′tēr.

f: fut′tēr.

fl: flut′tēr.

g: gut′tēr.

gl: glut′tēr.

k(ç): çut′tēr, pī′lŏt çut′tēr,
wood′çut″tēr.

kl: çlut′tēr.

m: mut′tēr.

n: nut′tēr.

p: put′tēr.

r: rut′tēr.

s: sut′tēr.

sh: shut′tēr.

sk(sç): scut′tēr.

sp: sput′tēr.

spl: splut′tēr.

st: stut′tēr.

str: strut′tēr.

Plus but her *or* err, etc.

UT′URD

Vowel: ut′tēred, un-ut′tēred.
Plus ut′ūr+ed.

Ū′Ū̃R

b: im-bū′ēr.

bl: blū′ēr.

br: brew′ēr.

ch: chew′ēr, es-chew′ēr,
gum′chew″ēr, tō-baç′çō chew′ēr.

d: bē-dew′ēr, derr′ing=dö′ēr,
dö′ēr, en-dū′ēr, ē′vil=dö″ēr,
mis-dö′ēr, out-dö′ēr,
ō-vēr-dö′ēr, sub-dū′ēr, un-dö′ēr,
well′=dö″ēr, wrong′=dö″ēr.

f: few′ēr.

gl: glū′ēr.

h: hew′ēr.

k(ç): coo′ēr.

l: hal-loo′ēr.

m: mew′ēr.

n: çà-nö′ēr, new′ēr, rē-new′ēr.

p: sham-poo′ēr.

r: rù′ēr.

s: pūr-sù′ēr, sew′ēr, sū′ēr.

sh: horse′shö″ēr, shö′ēr.

sk: skew′ēr.

skr(sçr): sçrew′ēr, un-sçrew′ēr.

st: stew′ēr.

(Choose only one word out of each group)

str: bē-strew'ẽr, mis-çon-strŭ'ẽr,
strew'ẽr.
t: tat-tọọ'ẽr.
tr: trŭ'ẽr.
v: in'tẽr-view″ẽr, rē-view'ẽr,
view'ẽr.
w: wọọ'ẽr.
y: ew'ẽr.
Plus due her *or* err, etc.

Ū'ŬRD

l: lee'wărd (lū'wărd).
s: Sew'ărd, sew'ẽred.
sk: skew'ẽred.
st: stew'ărd.
Cf. new ward, etc.

ŪV'ĂL

m: rē-mŏv'ăl.
pr: ap-prŏv'ăl, dis-ap-prŏv'ăl,
dis-prŏv'ăl, rē-prŏv'ăl.
Plus groove, Al, etc.
Plus you, Val, etc.

UV'ED

l: bē-lŏv'ed.
Plus uv+d*.
Plus shove, Ed, etc.

UV'EL

sh: shŏv'el.
sk(sç): sçŏv'el.
Cf. ŏv'el.
Plus dove'll, etc.

ŪV'EN

h: họọv'en.
pr: prŏv'en.
Cf. improve hen, etc.

UV'EN

Vowel: ŏv'en.
k(ç): çŏv'en.

sl: slŏv'en.
Cf. shove hen, etc.

ŪV'EST

m: mŏv'est*, rē-mŏv'est*.
pr: ap-prŏv'est*,
dis-ap-prŏv'est*, dis-prŏv'est*,
prŏv'est*, rē-prŏv'est*.
Plus new vest, etc.

UV'EST

gl: glŏv'est*, un-glŏv'est*.
l: lŏv'est*.
sh: shŏv'est*.

ŪV'ETH

m: mŏv'eth*, rē-mŏv'eth*.
pr: ap-prŏv'eth*,
dis-ap-prŏv'eth*, dis-prŏv'eth*,
prŏv'eth*, rē-prŏv'eth*.

UV'ETH

gl: glŏv'eth*, un-glŏv'eth*.
l: lŏv'eth*.
sh: shŏv'eth*.

ŪV'I

m: mŏv'ie.
Plus prove he, etc.
Plus knew, Vee *or* V, etc.

UV'I

d: dŏv'ey, lŏv'ey≈dŏv'ey.
k(ç): çŏv'ey.
l: lŏv'ey.
Plus shove he, etc.

ŪV'ING

gr: grọọv'ing.
m: mŏv'ing, rē-mŏv'ing,
un-mŏv'ing.

(Choose only one word out of each group)

pr: ap-pröv′ing, dis-ap-pröv′ing,
dis-pröv′ing, im-pröv′ing,
pröv′ing, rē-pröv′ing.

UV′ING

gl: glŏv′ing, un-glŏv′ing.
l: lŏv′ing, self′⸗lŏv′ing,
un-lŏv′ing.
sh: shŏv′ing.

UV′LES

gl: glŏve′less.
l: lŏve′less.
Plus shove, Les or less, etc.

ŪV′MENT

m: möve′ment.
p: ap-pröve′ment,
im-pröve′ment.
Plus behoove meant, etc.

ŪV′ŨR

gr: grọọv′ẽr.
h: Họọv′ẽr.
k(ç): Van-çöu′vẽr.
l: Löu′vre.
m: möv′ẽr, rē-möv′ẽr.
n: mȧ-neūv′ẽr.
pr: ap-pröv′ẽr, dis-ap-pröv′ẽr,
dis-pröv′ẽr, im-pröv′ẽr,
pröv′ẽr, rē-pröv′ẽr.
Plus groove her or err, etc.

UV′ŨR

gl: glŏv′ẽr.
k(ç): çŏv′ẽr, dis-çŏv′ẽr,
rē-çŏv′ẽr, rē-dis-çŏv′ẽr,
tā′ble-çŏv″ẽr, un-çŏv′ẽr.
l: lŏv′ẽr.
pl: plŏv′ẽr.
sh: shŏv′ẽr.
Plus love her or err, etc.

UV′ŨRN

g: gŏv′ẽrn.
Plus love urn, erne or earn, etc.

Ū′YȦ

l: al″lē-lú′iȧ.
Cf. who "yuh," etc.
Cf. through you, etc.

Ū′YĂNS

b: boú′yănce.

Ū′YĂNT

b: boú′yănt.

Ū′ZA

l̵: lal″lȧ-pȧ-lọọ′zȧ.
Plus who's a, etc.

ŪZ′ĂL

f: rē-fūṣ′ăl.
m: mūṣ′ăl.
Cf. fūṣ′il.
Plus brews, Al, etc.

ŪZ′ĂN

s: Sú′şăn.
Plus who's an, etc.
Plus rues an, etc.

UZ′ĂRD

b: buz′zărd, tûr′key buz′zărd.
Cf. fuzz hard, etc.

UZ′BĂND

h: huş′bănd.
Plus fuzz band, etc.

ŪZ′DI

t: Tūes′day.
Plus bruised, he, etc.
Plus cruise Dee, etc.

(Choose only one word out of each group)

ŪZ′EST

Vowel: ọọz′est*.
b: ȧ-būṣ′est*, bọọz′est*.
br: brüiṣ′est*.
ch: chọọṣ′est*.
f: cọn-fūṣ′est*, dif-fūṣ′est*,
  fūṣ′est*, in-fūṣ′est*,
  rē-fūṣ′est*, suf-fūṣ′est*,
  trans-fūṣ′est*.
k(c̱): a̱c̱-c̱ūṣ′est*, ex-c̱ūṣ′est*.
kr: c̱rüiṣ′est*.
l: lös′est*.
m: ȧ-mūṣ′est*, mūṣ′est*.
r: pē-rùṣ′est*.
sn: snọọz′est*.
y: ūṣ′est*.
Plus new zest, etc.

UZ′EST

b: buz′zest*.
f: fuz′zest*.

ŪZ′ETH

Vowel: ọọz′eth*.
b: ȧ-būṣ′eth*, bọọz′eth*.
br: brüiṣ′eth*.
ch: chọọṣ′eth*.
f: cọn-fūṣ′eth*, dif-fūṣ′eth*,
  fūṣ′eth*, in-fūṣ′eth*,
  rē-fūṣ′eth*, suf-fūṣ′eth*,
  trans-fūṣ′eth*.
k(c̱): a̱c̱-c̱ūṣ′eth*, ex-c̱ūṣ′eth*.
kr: c̱rüiṣ′eth*.
l: lös′eth*.
m: ȧ-mūṣ′eth*, mūṣ′eth*.
r: pē-rùṣ′eth*.
sn: snọọz′eth*.
y: ūṣ′eth*.

UZ′ETH

b: buz′zeth*.
f: fuz′zeth*.

ŪZ′EZ

Vowel: ọọz′ez.
b: ȧ-būṣ′ez, dis-ȧ-būṣ′ez.
br: brüiṣ′ez.
ch: chọọṣ′ez.
dr: drùṣ′ez.
f: cĭr-c̱um-fūṣ′ez, cọn-fūṣ′ez,
  dif-fūṣ′ez, fūṣ′ez, in-fūṣ′ez,
  in-tēr-fūṣ′ez, rē-fūṣ′ez,
  suf-fūṣ′ez, trans-fūṣ′ez.
k(c̱): a̱c̱-c̱ūṣ′ez, ex-c̱ūṣ′ez.
kr: c̱rüiṣ′ez, c̱rúz′ez.
l: lös′ez.
m: ȧ-mūṣ′ez, bē-mūṣ′ez,
  mūṣ′ez.
n: nọọṣ′ez.
r: pē-rùṣ′ez, rùṣ′ez.
sn: snọọz′ez.
t: cọn-tūṣ′ez.
y: dis-ūṣ′ez, mis-ūṣ′ez, ūṣ′ez.
Plus lose, Ez, etc.

UZ′EZ

b: buz′zes.
f: fuz′zes.

Ū′SHUN

b: ȧ-bū′ṣion.
f: af-fū′ṣion, cĭr″c̱um-fū′ṣion,
  cọn-fū′ṣion, dif-fū′ṣion,
  ef-fū′ṣion, fū′ṣion, in-fū′ṣion,
  in″tēr-fū′ṣion, pẽr-fū′ṣion,
  prō-fū′ṣion, rē-fū′ṣion,
  suf-fū′ṣion, trans-fū′ṣion.
kl: cọn-c̱lú′ṣion, ex-c̱lú′ṣion,
  in-c̱lú′ṣion, in″tēr-c̱lú′ṣion*,
  o̱c̱-c̱lú′ṣion, prē-c̱lú′ṣion,
  rē-c̱lú′ṣion, sē-c̱lú′ṣion.
l: al-lū′ṣion, cọl-lū′ṣion,
  dē-lū′ṣion, dis″il-lū′ṣion,

(Choose only one word out of each group)

ē-lū′s̜ion, il-lū′s̜ion,
prō-lū′s̜ion, self′=dē-lū′s̜ion.
str: ab-strú′s̜ion.
t: c̜on-tū′s̜ion, pĕr-tū′s̜ion*.
tr: dē-trú′s̜ion, ex-trú′s̜ion,
in-trú′s̜ion, ob-trú′s̜ion,
prō-trú′s̜ion, rē-trú′s̜ion,
trú′s̜ion.
th: Mal-thú′s̜iăn.
Cf. ūz′i-ăn.

Ū′ZI

Vowel: o̜o̜′zy.
b: bo̜o̜′zy.
fl: flū′zie.
w: wo̜o̜′zy.
Plus cruise, he, etc.
Plus knew Zee *or* Z, etc.

UZ′I

b: buz′zy.
f: fuz′zy.
h: hus̜′s̜y.
Plus does he, etc.

Ū Z′IK

m: mūs̜′ic̜.

UZ′IN

d: dŏz′en.
k(c̜): c̜o̜us̜′in, c̜ŏz′en.
Cf. buzzin′, etc.
Plus buzz in *or* inn, etc.

Ū Z′ING

Vowel: o̜o̜z′ing.
b: à-būs̜′ing, bo̜o̜z′ing.
br: brúis̜′ing.
ch: cho̜o̜s̜′ing.
f: c̜on-fūs̜′ing, dif-fūs̜′ing,
fūs̜′ing, in-fūs̜′ing,

in-tēr-fūs̜′ing, rē-fūs̜′ing,
suf-fūs̜′ing, trans-fūs̜′ing.
k(c̜): ac̜-c̜ūs̜′ing, ex-c̜ūs̜′ing,
self′=ac̜-c̜ūs̜′ing.
kr: c̜rúis̜′ing.
l: lös′ing.
m: à-mūs̜′ing, mūs̜′ing.
p: pē-rús̜′ing.
sn: sno̜o̜z′ing.
t: c̜on-tūs̜′ing.
y: dis-ūs̜′ing, ūs̜′ing.

UZ′ING

b: buz′zing.
f: fuz′zing.

UZ′INZ

d: dŏz′ens̜.
k(c̜): c̜ŏu′s̜ins̜, c̜ŏz′ens̜, c̜ŏuz′ens̜.
Plus buzz ins *or* inns, etc.

Ū Z′IV

m: à-mūs̜′ive, un-à-mūs̜′ive.

Ū Z″L, Ū Z′ĂL

b: bam-bo̜o̜′zle.
f: fo̜o̜′zle, gum-fo̜o̜′zle,
rē-fūs̜′ăl.
r: pē-rú′s̜ăl.
Plus lose, Al, etc.

UZ″L

f: fuz′zle*.
g: guz′zle.
m: bē-muz′zle, muz′zle,
un-muz′zle.
n: nuz′zle.
p: moñ′key puz′zle, puz′zle.
Plus buzz′ll, etc.

(Choose only one word out of each group)

UZ'LEST

g: guz'zlest*.
m: bē-muz'zlest*, muz'zlest*,
un-muz'zlest*.
n: nuz'zlest*.
p: puz'zlest*.
Plus buzz lest, etc.

UZ'LETH

g: guz'zleth*.
m: bē-muz'zleth*, muz'zleth*,
un-muz'zleth*.
n: nuz'zleth*.
p: puz'zleth*.

UZ'LIN

m: muş'lin.
Plus buzz, Lynn, etc.

UZ'LING

g: guz'zling.
m: bē-muz'zling, muz'zling,
un-muz'zling.
n: nuz'zling.
p: puz'zling.

ŪZ'LŨR

b: bam-bọọz'lẽr.
f: fọọz'lẽr.

UZ'LŨR

g: guz'zlẽr.
m: muz'zlẽr.
n: nuz'zlẽr.
p: puz'zlẽr.

ŪZ'MĂN

n: newş'măn.
tr: trewş'măn.
Plus whose man, etc.

ŪZ'MENT

m: à-mūşe'ment.
Plus news meant, etc.

ŪZ'RĒL

n: newş'reel.
Plus booze reel, etc.

ŪZ'UM

b: bŏş'ŏm.
Plus lose 'em, etc.

UZ'UM

w: iz'zum=wuz'zum.
Plus does 'em, etc.

ŪZ'ŨR

Vowel: ọọz'ẽr.
b: à-būş'ẽr, bọọz'ẽr.
br: brüiş'ẽr.
ch: chọọş'ẽr.
f: çon-fūş'ẽr, dif-fūş'ẽr, fūş'ẽr,
in-fūş'ẽr, in-tẽr-fūş'ẽr,
rē-fūş'ẽr, suf-fūş'ẽr,
trans-fūş'ẽr.
k(ç): aç-çūş'ẽr, ex-çūş'ẽr.
kr: çrüiş'ẽr.
l: läl″là-pà-lọọz'ẽr, lŏş'ẽr.
m: à-mūş'ẽr, mūş'ẽr.
sn: snọọz'ẽr.
y: mis-ūş'ẽr, non-ūş'ẽr, ūş'ẽr.
Plus bruise her *or* err, etc.

UZ'UR

b: buz'zẽr.
f: fuz'zẽr.
Plus buzz her *or* err, etc.

(Choose only one word out of each group)

TRIPLE RHYMES

(Words Accented on the Antepenult, the Second Syllable from the Last)

A

The accented vowel sounds included are listed under **A** in Single Rhymes.

Archaic Verb-Forms among Triple Rhymes.—Archaic verb forms ending in **-eth** and **-est,** which form triple rhymes, are not listed. They can easily be located, if desired, by locating present participles of verbs which form triple rhymes (**neighboring, carrying,** etc.) and altering the suffixes to the desired archaic forms: **neighborest*, neighboreth*, carryest,* carryeth.***

Ā′Á-B′L

fr: dē-frāy′à-ble.
p: im-pāy′à-ble, pāy′à-ble,
　rē-pāy′à-ble, un-pāy′à-ble.
pr: prāy′à-ble, un-prāy′à-ble.
sw: swāy′à-ble, un-swāy′à-ble.
tr: por-trāy′à-ble,
　un-por-trāy′à-ble.
v: çon-veẏ′à-ble,
　un-çon-veẏ′à-ble.
Cf. weigh a bull, etc.

AB′A-SIS

n: à-nab′à-sis.
t: çà-tab′à-sis, mē-tab′à-sis.
Plus grab a sis, etc.

ĀB′EL-ŪR

g: gā′bel-ĕr.
l: lā′bel-lĕr.
Plus label her, etc.

ĀB′I-Á

l: lāb′i-à.
r: Á-rāb′i-à.
sw: Suāb′i-à.
Plus baby a, etc.

AB′I-ĂN

f: Fāb′i-ăn.
r: Á-rāb′i-ăn, Sō-rāb′i-ăn.
s: Sāb′i-ăn.
sw: Swāb′i-ăn.
Plus baby an, etc.

AB′ID-NES

r: rab′id-ness.
t: tab′id-ness.

AB′I-EST

fl: flab′bi-est.
sh: shab′bi-est.

ĀB′I-ĒZ

r: rāb′i-ēṣ.
sk(sç): sçāb′i-ēṣ.
Plus maybe ease, etc.

AB′I-FĪ

l: lab′ē-fȳ, dis-syl-lab′i-fȳ,
　syl-lab′i-fȳ.
t: tab′ē-fȳ.
Plus cabby, fie!, etc.

(Choose only one word out of each group)

AB'I-KĂL

l: mon″ō-syl-lab'i-çal.
    pol″y-syl-lab'i-çal.
r: Ȧ-rab'i-çal*.
Plus crabby Cal, etc.

AB'I-LY

fl: flab'bi-ly.
sh: shab'bi-ly.
Plus slabby lea, etc.

AB'I-NES

fl: flab'bi-ness.
sh: shab'bi-ness.
sk(sç): sçab'bi-ness.
sl: slab'bi-ness.

AB'I-NET

k(ç): çab'i-net.
t: tab'i-net.
Plus flabby net, etc.

AB'I-TŪD

h: hab'i-tūde.
t: tab'i-tūde.
Plus cab etude, etc.

AB'I-ŨR

fl: flab'bi-ẽr.
g: gab'bi-ẽr.
sh: shab'bi-ẽr.
Plus tabby, her, etc.

AB'LȦ-TIV

Vowel: ab'lȧ-tive.
b: bab'lȧ-tive.

AB'L-MENT

b: bab'ble-ment
br: brab'ble-ment.

d: dab'ble-ment.
g: gab'ble-ment.
r: rab'ble-ment.
Plus babble meant, etc.

ĀB'L-NES

s: sāb'le-ness.
st: stāb'le-ness, un-stāb'le-ness.

AB'Ō-LȦ

r: pȧ-rab'ō-là.
t: Me-tab'ō-là.

AB'Ū-LĂR

f: çon-fab'ū-lăr.
n: tin-tin-nab'ū-lăr.
p: pab'ū-lăr.
t: tab'ū-lăr.

AB'Ū-LĀT

f: çon-fab'ū-lāte.
t: tab'ū-lāte.
Plus grab you, late, etc.

AB'Ū-LIST

f: fab'ū-list.
k(ç): vō-çab'ū-list.
Plus nab you, list, etc.

AB'Ū-LUM

n: tin-tin-nab'ū-lum.
p: pab'ū-lum.
t: ac-ē-tab'ū-lum.
Plus grab you, Lum, etc.

AB'Ū-LUS

f: fab'ū-lous.
n: tin-tin-nab'ū-lous.
p: pab'ū-lous.
s: sab'ū-lous.

(Choose only one word out of each group)

ĀB′ŪR-ING

l: bē-lāb′ŏr-ing, lāb′ŏr-ing,
un-lāb′ŏr-ing.
n: nẹigh′bŏr-ing (nā′).
Plus say, Bo, ring, etc.
Plus May beau ring, etc.

ĀB′ŪR-ŪR

l: lāb′ŏr-ēr.
t: tāb′ŏr-ēr.

ACH′Å-B′L

k(ç): çatch′å-ble.
m: im-match′å-ble,
match′å-ble, un-match′å-ble.
skr(sçr): sçratch′å-ble.
t: at-tach′å-ble, dē-tach′å-ble.
Plus catch a bull, etc.

ĀD′Å-B′L, ĀD′I-B′L

sh: shād′å-ble.
sw: pēr-suād′å-ble.
tr: trād′å-ble.
v: ē-vād′i-ble.
w: wād′å-ble.
Plus trade a bull, etc.

AD′ED-NES

f: fād′ed-ness.
gr: dē-grād′ed-ness.
j: bē-jād′ed-ness, jād′ed-ness.
sh: shād′ed-ness.
sw: pēr-suād′ed-ness.

AD′E-US

m: A-mad′ē-us.
th: Thad′dē-us.
Plus caddie us, etc.

ĀD′I-ĂN

b: Bär-bād′i-ăn.
k(ç): Å-çād′i-ăn, Är-çād′i-ăn,
Ọr-çād′i-ăn.
l: Pal-lād′i-ăn.
m: nō-mād′i-ăn.
n: Çå-nād′i-ăn.
Plus shady an.

ĀD′I-ĂNT, ĀD′I-ENT

gr: grād′i-ent.
r: ir-rād′i-ănt, rād′i-ănt.
Plus lady aunt, etc.

AD′I-TIV

Vowel: ad′di-tive.
tr: trad′i-tive.

ĀD′I-UM

l: pal-lād′i-um.
n: vå-nād′i-um.
r: rād′i-um.
st: stād′i-um.
Plus lady, um, etc.

AD′Ō-ING

sh: fōre-shad′ōw-ing,
ō-vēr-shad′ōw-ing,
shad′ōw-ing.

AF′Å-NUS

Vowel: dī-aph′å-nous.

AF′I-KĂL

gr: au″tō-bī-ō-gráph′i-çăl,
au-tō-gráph′i-çăl,
bib″li-ō-gráph′i-çăl,
bī-ō-gráph′i-çal,
çal-li-gráph′i-çăl,
çär-tō-gráph′i-çăl,

(Choose only one word out of each group)

cos̹-mō-gráph'i-căl,
dī-a-gráph'i-căl,
eth-nō-gráph'i-căl,
gē-ō-gráph'i-căl,
glos-sō-gráph'i-căl,
gráph'i-căl, lex''i-cō-gráph'i-căl,
lex-i-gráph'i-căl,
ọr-thō-gráph'i-căl,
pā''lē-on''tō-gráph'i-căl,
phō-tō-gráph'i-căl,
phys̹''i-ō-gráph'i-căl,
phȳ-tō-gráph'i-căl,
pter''yl-ō-gráph'i-căl (ter''),
top-ō-gráph'i-căl,
tȳ-pō-gráph'i-căl.
r: sē-ráph'i-căl.
Plus traffic, Al, etc.
Cf. traffic all, etc.
Plus daffy Cal, etc.

AF'TI-LI

dr: draught'i-ly (draf'ti-li).
kr: craf'ti-ly.
Plus crafty lea, etc.

AG'ED-LI

j: jag'ged-ly.
r: rag'ged-ly.
Plus cragged lea, etc.

AG'ED-NES

j: jag'ged-ness.
kr: crag'ged-ness.
r: rag'ged-ness.

AG'I-NES

b: bag'gi-ness.
kr: crag'gi-ness.
n: knag'gi-ness (nag').
sh: shag'gi-ness.
skr(scr): scrag'gi-ness.

AG'ŎN-IST

Vowel: ag'ŏn-ist.
t: an-tag'ŏn-ist, prō-tag'ŏn-ist.

AG'ŌN-ĪZ

Vowel: ag'ōn-īz.
t: an-tag'ōn-īze.
Plus dragon eyes, etc.

AG'ŎN-IZM

Vowel: ag'ŏn-is̹m.
t: an-tag'ŏn-is̹m.

ĀG'RĂN-SI

fl: flāg'răn-cy.
fr: frāg'răn-cy.
v: vāg'răn-cy.

AG'ŨR-I

f: fag'gẽr-y.
j: jag'gẽr-y.
r: rag'gẽr-y.
w: wag'gẽr-y.
z: zig-zag'gẽr-y.

AG'ŨR-ING

st: stag'gẽr-ing.
sw: swag'gẽr-ing.
Plus dagger ring, etc.

AG'ŨR-ŨR

st: stag'gẽr-ẽr.
sw: swag'gẽr-ẽr.
Plus dagger her, etc.

Ā'IK-ĂL

br: al-gē-brā'i-căl, Hē-brā'i-căl.
k(c): är-chā'i-căl.
l: lā'i-căl.
s: par''ȧ-di-sā'i-căl,
ᴐhar-i-sā'i-că!

(Choose only one word out of each group)

Ā'IT-I

g: gāi'e-ty.
l: lā'i-ty.

ĀJ'Á-B'L

g: gāuġe'à-ble (gāj').
sw: as-suāġe'à-ble (-swāj').
Plus enrage a bull, etc.

ĀJ'I-ĂN

l: pē-lāġ'i-ăn.
m: māġ'i-ăn.
n: Brob-dig-nāġ'i-ăn.
Cf. c̱on-tāġ'i-ŏn, etc.

AJ'I-KAL

m: maġ'i-c̱ăl.
tr: traġ'i-c̱ăl.

AJ'IL-NES

Vowel: aġ'ile-ness.
fr: fraġ'ile-ness.

AJ'IN-AL

m: im-aġ'i-năl.
p: paġ'i-năl.
v: vaġ'i-năl.

AJ'I-NUS

Vowel: ō-lē-aġ'i-nous.
b: lum-baġ'i-nous.
l: c̱är-ti-laġ'i-nous,
 mū-ci-laġ'i-nous.
r: far-raġ'i-nous, vō-raġ'i-nous.
Plus imagine us, etc.

ĀJ'US-NES

br: um-brāġe'ous-ness.
p: ram-pāġe'ous-ness.
r: c̱öu-rāġe'ous-ness,
 out-rāġe'ous-ness.

t: ad-van-tāġe'ous-ness,
 dis"ad-van-tāġe'ous-ness.

ĀK'Á-B'L

Vowel: āc̱he'à-ble (āk'à-b'l).
br: breāk'à-ble, un-breāk'à-ble.
p: im-pāc̱'à-ble, pāc̱'à-ble.
pl: im-plāc̱'à-ble, plāc̱'à-ble.
sh: shāk'à-ble, un-shāk'à-ble.
t: mis-tāk'à-ble,
 un-dēr-tāk'à-ble,
 un-mis-tāk'à-ble.
Plus make a bull, etc.

AK'ET-ED

br: brack'et-ed.
j: jack'et-ed.
r: rack'et-ed.
Plus packet, Ed, etc.

AK'ET-ING

br: brack'et-ing.
j: jack'et-ing.
r: rack'et-ing.

AK'I-ĂN

Vowel: Nō-ac̱h'i-ăn.
t: eūs-tac̱h'i-ăn.
tr: bà-trac̱h'i-ăn.
Plus wacky an, etc.

ĀK'I-NES

fl: flāk'i-ness.
kw(qu): quāk'i-ness.
sh: shāk'i-ness.
sn: snāk'i-ness.

AK'ISH-NES

br: brack'ish-ness.
n: knack'ish-ness (nak').
sl: slack'ish-ness.

AK'RI-TY
AK'TŬR-ING
fāte, fär, fȧst, fᶏll, finȧl, cãre, at; mēte, prꬴy, hẽr, met; pīne,
marïne, bïrd, pin; nōte, mȯve, fọr, atŏm, not; mọọn, book;   **814**

(Choose only one word out of each group)

AK'RI-TY

Vowel: aꞔ'ri-ty*.
l: ȧ-laꞔ'ri-ty.

AK'RŎN-IṢM

n: ȧ-naꞔh'rŏn-iṣm.
t: mē-taꞔh'rŏn-iṣm.

AK'SȦ-B'L

l: rē-lax'ȧble.
t: tax'ȧ-ble.
Plus packs a bull, etc.

AK'SHUN-ĂL

f: faꞔ'tion-ăl.
fr: fraꞔ'tion-ăl.
p: paꞔ'tion-ăl.
Plus exaction, Al, etc.

AK'SHUS-NES

f: faꞔ'tiŏus-ness.
fr: fraꞔ'tiŏus-ness.

AK'TȦ-B'L, AK'TI-B'L

fr: in-fraꞔ'ti-ble, ir-rē-fraꞔ'ti-ble,
rē-fraꞔ'ti-ble.
p: ꞔom-paꞔ'ti-ble.
t: in-taꞔ'ti-ble, taꞔ'tȧ-ble.
tr: at-traꞔ'ti-ble,
ꞔon-traꞔ'tȧ-ble, dē-traꞔ'ti-ble,
dis-traꞔ'ti-ble, ex-traꞔ'ti-ble.
in-traꞔ'tȧ-ble, rē-traꞔ'tȧ-ble,
traꞔ'tȧ-ble.
Plus tracked a bull, etc.

AK'TED-NES

str: ab-straꞔ'ted-ness.
tr: ꞔon-traꞔ'ted-ness,
dis-traꞔ'ted-ness,
prō-traꞔ'ted-ness.

AK'TI-KĂL

d: di-daꞔ'ti-ꞔăl.
pr: praꞔ'ti-ꞔăl.

AK'TI-LUS

d: dī-daꞔ'ty-lŏus,
hex-ȧ-daꞔ'ty-lŏus,
lep-tō-daꞔ'ty-lŏus,
paꞔh-y-daꞔ'ty-lŏus,
pter-ō-daꞔ'ty-lŏus (ter-).
Plus tactile, us, etc.

AK'TIV-NES

Vowel: aꞔ'tive-ness.
f: pū-trē-faꞔ'tive-ness.
fr: rē-fraꞔ'tive-ness.
str: ab-straꞔ'tive-ness.
tr: at-traꞔ'tive-ness,
ꞔon-traꞔ'tive-ness,
dē-traꞔ'tive-ness,
dis-traꞔ'tive-ness,
prō-traꞔ'tive-ness.

AK'TŎ-RI

f: dis"sat-is-faꞔ'tŏ-ry, faꞔ'tŏ-ry,
man-ū-faꞔ'tŏ-ry, ol-faꞔ'tŏ-ry.
sat-is-faꞔ'tŏ-ry,
un"sat-is-faꞔ'tŏ-ry.
fr: rē-fraꞔ'tŏ-ry.
l: laꞔ'tȧ-ry, phy-laꞔ'tē-ry.
tr: dē-traꞔ'tŏ-ry, traꞔ'tŏ-ry.

AK'TŪ-ĂL

Vowel: aꞔ'tū-ăl.
f: faꞔ'tū-ăl.
t: taꞔ'tū-ăl.
Plus smacked you, Al, etc.

AK'TŪR-ING

f: man-ū-faꞔ'tūr-ing.
fr: fraꞔ'tūr-ing.
Plus manufacture, ring, etc.

(Choose only one word out of each group)

AK′Ū-LĂR

Vowel: pī-ac̦′ū-lăr.
n: sū-pēr-nac̦′ū-lăr,
tab-ēr-nac̦′ū-lăr, vēr-nac̦′ū-lăr.
r: ō-rac̦′ū-lăr.
t: spec̦-tac̦′ū-lăr, ten-tac̦′ū-lăr.

AK′Ū-LĀT

j: ē-jac̦′ū-lāte, jac̦′ū-lāte.
m: bī-mac̦′ū-lāte,
im-mac̦′ū-lāte, mac̦′ū-lāte.
Plus track, you late!, etc.

AK′Ū-LUS

Vowel: pī-ac̦′ū-lŏus.
b: ȧ-bac̦′ū-lus.
n: vēr-nac̦′ū-lŏus.
r: mi-rac̦′ū-lŏus, ō-rac̦′ū-lŏus.

ĀK′ŬR-I

b: bāk′ēr-y.
f: fāk′ēr-y, fāk′ĭr-y.
r: rāk′ēr-y.

ĀK′ŬR-I

h: hack′ēr-y.
j: hī-jack′ēr-y.
kw(qu): quack′ēr-y (kwak′).
n: knick′=knack′ēr-y (nik′=nak′).
th: Thack′ēr-ay.
z: Zach̦′ăr-y.

ĀK′ŬR-IZM

f: fāk′ĭr-ism.
kw(qu): Quāk′ēr-ism (kwāk′).
sh: Shāk′ēr-ism.

ĀK′WĒ-US

Vowel: ā′quē-ous,
sub-ā′quē-ous.
r: ter-rā′quē-ous.

ĀL′Ȧ-B'L

b: bāil′ȧ-ble.
h: ex-hāl′ȧ-ble, in-hāl′ȧ-ble.
m: māil′ȧ-ble, un-māil′ȧ-ble.
s: as-sāil′ȧ-ble, sāil′ȧ-ble,
sāle′ȧ-ble, un-as-sāil′ȧ-ble,
un-sāil′ȧ-ble, un-sāle′ȧ-ble.
t: rē-tāil′ȧ-ble.
v: ȧ-vāil′ȧ-ble, un-ȧ-vāil′ȧ-ble.
Plus for sale, a bull, etc.

ĀL′Ē-Ȧ

z: ȧ-zāl′ē-ȧ.
Cf. ā′li-ȧ.

AL′Ē-ĀT, AL′I-ĀT

m: mal′lē-āte.
p: pal′li-āte.
t: rē-tal′i-āte.
Plus Hally ate, etc.
Plus Sallie, eight, etc.

AL′EN-TĪN

b: Bal′lăn-tīne.
v: Val′en-tīne.

Ā′LI-Ȧ

d: Ȧ-dā′li-ȧ, Fī-de̦′li-ȧ,
Sē-dā′li-ȧ.
g: rē-gā′li-ȧ.
l: ech-ō-lā′li-ȧ, Eū-lā′li-ȧ.
t: At-tā′li-ȧ.
th: Ȧ-thā′li-ȧ, Thā′li-ȧ.
tr: A̧us-trā′li-ȧ, Cen-trā′li-ȧ.
z: ȧ-zā′lē-ȧ, Rō-şā′li-ȧ.
Cf. āl′yȧ.
Plus Bailey, a, etc.

AL′I-BŪR

k(c̦): c̦al′i-bēr, Ex-c̦al′i-bŭr.
Plus valley burr, etc.

(Choose only one word out of each group)

AL'ID-NES
p: im-pal'lid-ness, pal'lid-ness.
v: in-val'id-ness, val'id-ness.

AL'I-FĪ
k(c̦): al-kal'i-fy, c̦al'ē-fy*.
s: sal'i-fȳ.
Plus Sallie, fie!, etc.

AL'I-ING
d: dal'ly-ing.
r: ral'ly-ing.
s: sal'ly-ing.
t: tal'ly-ing.

ĀL'I-NES
d: dāil'i-ness.
sk(s): sc̦āl'i-ness.

AL'I-SIS
Vowel: dī-al'y-sis.
n: à-nal'y-sis.
r: pà-ral'y-sis.
t: c̦à-tal'y-sis.
Plus rally, sis!, etc.

AL'I-SŎN
Vowel: Al'i-sŏn.
k(c̦): C̦al'li-sŏn.
m: Mal'li-sŏn.
Plus rally, son, etc.

AL'I-TI
Vowel: ac̦-tū-al'i-ty,
är"ti-fic̦-i-al'i-ty (-fish-),
bes-ti-al'i-ty,
cir"c̦um-stan"ti-al'i-ty ("shi-),
c̦on"fi-den"ti-al'i-ty ("shi-),
c̦on-g̣ēn-i-al'i-ty,
c̦on-nū-bi-al'i-ty,
c̦on"sub-stan"ti-al'i-ty ("shi-),
c̦on-viv-i-al'i-ty, c̦or-di-al'i-ty,

c̦or-pō-rē-al'i-ty, c̦ū-ri-al'i-ty,
dū-al'i-ty,
es-sen-ti-al'i-ty (-shi-),
ē-thēr-ē-al'i-ty, ē-ven-tū-al'i-ty,
ex-ter"ri-tōr"i-al'i-ty,
g̣ēn-i-al'i-ty, grad-ū-al'i-ty,
ī-dē-al'i-ty, im-mà-tēr-i-al'i-ty,
im-pär-ti-al'i-ty (-shi-),
im-pēr-i-al'i-ty,
in-c̦on"sē-quen"ti-al'i-ty ("shi-),
in"di-vid"ū-al'i-ty,
in"ef-fec̦"tū-al'i-ty,
in"tel-lec̦"tū-al'i-ty,
jŏv-i-al'i-ty, lin-ē-al'i-ty,
mà-tēr-i-al'i-ty, mū-tū-al'i-ty,
of-fi-ci-al'i-ty (-shi-),
pà-rōc̦h-i-al'i-ty,
pär-ti-al'i-ty (-shi-),
pō-ten-ti-al'i-ty (-shi-),
prō-vin-ci-al'i-ty (-shi-),
prù-den-ti-al'i-ty (-shi-),
punc̦-tū-al'i-ty, rē-al'i-ty,
sen-sū-al'i-ty, sēr-i-al'i-ty,
sex-ū-al'i-ty, sō-ci-al'i-ty (-shi-),
spec-i-al'i-ty (spesh-),
spir"it-ū-al'i-ty,
sub-stan-ti-al'i-ty (-shi-),
sū"pēr-fi"ci-al'i-ty ("shi-),
trī-al'i-ty, triv-i-al'i-ty,
un-ūș-ū-al'i-ty (-ūzh-),
vēn-i-al'i-ty,
viș-ū-al'i-ty (vizh-).
b: vēr-bal'i-ty.
d: à-là-mō-dal'i-ty,
feū-dal'i-ty, mō-dal'i-ty,
pē-dal'i-ty, ses"qui-pē-dal'i-ty,
sō-dal'i-ty.
g: c̦on-jù-gal'i-ty, ē-gal'i-ty,
frù-gal'i-ty, il-lē-gal'i-ty,
lē-gal'i-ty, rē-gal'i-ty.
gr: in-tē-gral'i-ty.

(Choose only one word out of each group)

k(c̣): Bib-li-c̣al′i-ty,
c̣las-si-c̣al′i-ty, c̣om-i-c̣al′i-ty,
c̣oṣ-mi-c̣al′i-ty,
fan-tas-ti-c̣al′i-ty,
fin-i-c̣al′i-ty, in-im-i-c̣al′i-ty,
in-trin-si-c̣al′i-ty, lā-i-c̣al′i-ty,
lō-c̣al′i-ty, loġ-i-c̣al′i-ty,
prac̣-ti-c̣al′i-ty, rad-i-c̣al′i-ty,
ras-c̣al′i-ty, rē-cip-rō-c̣al′i-ty,
tec̣h-ni-c̣al′i-ty,
thē″ō-ret″i-c̣al′i-ty,
ver-ti-c̣al′i-ty, vō-c̣al′i-ty,
whim-ṣi-c̣al′i-ty (hwim″),
m: ab-nọr-mal′i-ty,
an-i-mal′i-ty, fọr-mal′i-ty,
in-fọr-mal′i-ty.
n: bà-nal′i-ty, c̣är-nal′i-ty,
c̣on″sti-tū″tio-nal′i-ty (″shu-),
c̣on-ven-tio-nal′i-ty (-shu-),
c̣rim-i-nal′i-ty, ex-tēr-nal′i-ty,
fem-i-nal′i-ty, fī-nal′i-ty,
im-pēr-sŏ-nal′i-ty,
in-ten-tio-nal′i-ty (-shu-),
ir-ra-tio-nal′i-ty (-shu-),
mer-id″i-ō-nal′i-ty,
mēs-nal′i-ty (mē-),
na-tio-nal′i-ty (-shu-),
nō-tiŏ-nal′i-ty (-shu-),
ōr-iġ″i-nal′i-ty, pē-nal′i-ty,
pēr-sŏ-nal′i-ty,
prō-pọr-tio-nal′i-ty (-shu-),
ra-tio-nal′i-ty (-shu-),
sec̣-tiŏ-nal′i-ty (-shu-),
sep-ten″tio-ō-nal′i-ty (″shu-),
sig-nal′i-ty, tō-nal′i-ty,
trà-di-tio-nal′i-ty (-shu-),
vē-nal′i-ty.
p: mū-nic-i-pal′i-ty,
prin-ci-pal′i-ty.
r: c̣on-jec̣-tū-ral′i-ty,
c̣ọr-pō-ral′i-ty, ē-phem-ē-ral′i-ty,

ġen-ē-ral′i-ty, gut-tē-ral′i-ty,
im-mō-ral′i-ty, lat-ē-ral′i-ty,
lib-ē-ral′i-ty, lit-ē-ral′i-ty,
mō-ral′i-ty, nat-ū-ral′i-ty,
plù-ral′i-ty,
prē″tēr-nat″ū-ral′i-ty,
rù-ral′i-ty, sev-ē-ral′i-ty,
spī-ral′i-ty,
sū-pēr-nat″ū-ral′i-ty,
tem-pō-ral′i-ty.
s: ọr″thō-dox-al′i-ty,
ūn-i-vēr-sal′i-ty.
t: ac̣″ci-den-tal′i-ty,
brù-tal′i-ty, el-ē-men-tal′i-ty,
fā-tal′i-ty, fun″dà-men-tal′i-ty,
họr″i-zŏn-tal′i-ty,
hos-pi-tal′i-ty,
im-mōr-tal′i-ty,
in″strù-men-tal′i-ty,
men-tal′i-ty, mọr-tal′i-ty,
oc̣″ci-den-tal′i-ty,
ō″ri-en-tal′i-ty,
sen″ti-men-tal′i-ty, tō-tal′i-ty,
tran″scen-den-tal′i-ty,
vī-tal′i-ty, veġ-ē-tal′i-ty.
tr: cen-tral′i-ty, dex-tral′i-ty,
maġ-is-tral′i-ty, neū-tral′i-ty,
spec̣-tral′i-ty.
v: rī-val′i-ty.
z: c̣au-ṣal′i-ty, nā-ṣal′i-ty.
Plus bally tea, etc.

AL′I-UM

p: pal′li-um.
th: thal′li-um.

AL′I-ŪR

d: dal′li-ēr.
r: ral′li-ēr.
s: sal′li-ēr.
t: tal′li-ēr.
Plus rally her, etc.

Ā′LI-US
ĀL′YEN-IZM   fāte, fär, fȧst, fᾳll, finăl, cãre, at; mēte, prᵉy, hėr, met; pīne,
marīne, bĭrd, pin; nōte, mŏve, fᴏr, atŏm, not; mᴏᴏn, book;   **818**

(Choose only one word out of each group)

Ā′LI-US

b: Si-bᵉ′li-us.
d: Dᵉ′li-us.
Cf. āl′i-ăs.
Plus scaly, us, etc.

AL′JI-Å

r: neū-ral′ġi-ȧ.
t: nos-tal′ġi-ȧ.

AL′Ō-EST

h: hal′lōw-est.
k(ç): çal′lōw-est.
s: sal′lōw-est.
sh: shal′lōw-est.

AL′Ō-JI

Vowel: ġen-ē-al′ō-ġy,
    ġen-eth″li-al′ō-ġy.
b: pȳ-rō-bal′lō-ġy*.
m: mam-mal′ō-ġy.
n: ȧ-nal′ō-ġy.
r: min-ē-ral′ō-ġy, pȧ-ral′ō-ġy,
    pet-ral′ō-ġy, tet-ral′ō-ġy.
t: çrus-tal′ō-ġy.
Plus pal? O, Gee! etc.

AL′Ō-JIST

Vowel: dī-al′ō-ġist,
    ġen-ē-al′ō-ġist.
k(ç): dē-çal′ō-ġist.
m: mam-mal′ō-ġist.
n: ȧ-nal′ō-ġist, pē-nal′ō-ġist.
r: min-ē-ral′ō-ġist.
Plus shallow ġist, etc.

AL′Ō-JĪZ

Vowel: dī-al′ō-ġīze,
    ġen′ē-al′ō-ġīze.
n: ȧ-nal′ō-ġize.
r: pȧ-ral′ō-ġize.

AL′Ō-JIZM

Vowel: dī-al′ō-ġiṣm.
n: ȧ-nal′ō-ġiṣm.
r: pȧ-ral′ō-ġiṣm.

AL′Ō-ISH

s: sal′lōw-ish.
sh: shal′lōw-ish.
t: tal′lōw-ish.

AL′Ō-NES

k(ç): çal′lōw-ness.
f: fal′lōw-ness.
s: sal′lōw-ness.
sh: shal′lōw-ness.

AL′Ō-ŪR

k(ç): çal′lōw-ẽr.
h: hal′lōw-ẽr.
s: sal′lōw-ẽr.
sh: shal′lōw-ẽr.
t: tal′lōw-ẽr.
Plus hallow her.

ĀL′ŪR-I

n: nāil′ẽr-y.
r: rāil′lẽr-y.

AL′ŪR-I

g: gal′lẽr-y.
r: rail′lẽr-y*.
s: sal′ăr-y.

ĀL′YEN-IZM, ĀL′YĂN-IZM

Vowel: āl′ien-iṣm.
d: ses″quip-ē-dāl′iăn-iṣm.
n: baç-çhȧ-nāl′iăn-iṣm,
    sat-ūr-nāl′iăn-iṣm.
p: ē-pis″çō-pāl′iăn-iṣm.
s: ūn″i-vẽr-sāl′iăn-iṣm.

(Choose only one word out of each group)

ĀM'Å-B'L

bl: blām'å-ble (-b'l),
un-blām'å-ble.
fr: frām'å-ble.
kl: çlāim'å-ble,
ir-rē-çlāim'å-ble,
rē-çlāim'å-ble,
un-rē-çlāim'å-ble.
n: nām'å-ble, un-nām'å-ble.
t: tām'å-ble, un-tām'å-ble.

AM'Å-RI

gr: gram'å-rye*.
m: mam'må-ry.
Plus slam Marie, etc.

AM'Å-TIST

dr: dram'å-tist,
mel-ō-dram'å-tist.
gr: ep-i-gram'må-tist,
gram'må-tist,
hī″ēr-ō-gram'må-tist,
lip-ō-gram'må-tist.

AM'Å-TIV

Vowel: am'å-tive.
kl: ex-çlam'å-tive.

AM'Å-TĪZ

dr: dram'å-tize.
gr: an-å-gram'må-tīze,
dī-å-gram'må-tīze,
ep-i-gram'må-tize.
Plus Alabama ties, etc.

AM'BŪ-LĀT

Vowel: am'bū-lāte,
dē-am'bū-lāte.
n: fū-nam'bū-lāte,
som-nam'bū-lāte.
r: pē-ram'bū-lāte.

AM'BŪ-LIST

n: fū-nam'bū-list,
som-nam'bū-list.
t: noç-tam'bū-list.

AM'BŪ-LIZM

n: fū-nam'bū-lişm,
som-nam'bū-lişm.
t: noç-tam'bū-lişm.

AM'ĒT-ÊR

Vowel: dī-am'ē-tēr,
plūv-i-am'ē-tēr, vī-am'ē-tēr.
n: dȳ-nam'ē-tēr.
r: på-ram'ē-tēr, peī-ram'ē-tēr,
tet-ram'ē-tēr.
s: hex-am'ē-tēr.
t: oç-tam'ē-tēr, pen-tam'ē-tēr,
vōl-tam'ē-tēr.

ĀM'FṵL-NES

bl: blāme'fṵl-ness.
sh: shāme'fṵl-ness.

Ā'MI-Å

l: lā'mi-å.
t: Mes″ō-pō-tā'mi-å.
Plus Mamie, a, etc.

AM'I-KĂL

Vowel: am'i-çăl.
n: dȳ-nam'i-çăl.
s: bal-sam'i-çăl.
Plus mammy, Cal, etc.
Plus ceramic, Al, etc.

AM'IN-Å

l: lam'in-å.
st: stam'in-å.
Plus famine, a, etc.

(Choose only one word out of each group)

AM′I-NĀTE

l: lam′i-nāte.
t: c̦on-tam′i-nāte.
Plus clammy, Nate, etc.

ÄM′IS-TRI

p: pälm′is-try (päm′).
s: psälm′is-try (säm′).

AM′I-TY

Vowel: am′i-ty.
l: c̦ȧ-lam′i-ty.
Plus mammy, tea, etc.

ĀM′LES-NES

Vowel: āim′less-ness.
bl: blāme′less-ness.
d: dāme′less-ness.
f: fāme′less-ness.
n: nāme′less-ness.
sh: shāme′less-ness.
t: tāme′less-ness.

AM′ŎN-ĪT

Vowel: Am′mŏn-īte.
m: Mam′mŏn-īte.
Cf. backgammon night, etc.

AM′ŎN-IZM

m: Mam′mŏn-iṣm.
sh: Sha′măn-iṣm.

AM′ŎR-US

Vowel: am′ōr-ŏus.
gl: glam′ōr-ŏus.
kl: c̦lam′ŏr-ŏus.
Plus ham′mẽr us, etc.

AM′PI-ŎN

ch: cham′pi-ŏn.
k(c̦): c̦am′pi-ŏn.
t: tam′pi-ŏn.

AM′PŨR-ING

h: ham′pẽr-ing.
p: pam′pẽr-ing.
sk(sc̦): sc̦am′pẽr-ing.
t: tam′pẽr-ing.
Plus damper ring, etc.

AM′PŨR-ẼR

h: ham′pẽr-ẽr.
p: pam′pẽr-ẽr.
sk(sc̦): sc̦am′pẽr-ẽr.
t: tam′pẽr-ẽr.
Plus vamper, her, etc.

AM′ŪL-US

f: fam′ūl-us.
h: ham′ūl-us.
r: ram′ū-lous.

AM′ŨR-ING

h: ham′mẽr-ing.
kl(c̦l): c̦lam′ŏr-ing.
st: stam′mẽr-ing.
y: yam′mẽr-ing.
Plus hammer ring, etc.
Plus slam her ring, etc.

AM′ŨR-ŎN

k(c̦): Dē-c̦am′ẽr-ŏn.
t: Hep-tam′ẽr-ŏn.
Plus grammar on, etc.
Plus ram her on, etc.

AM′ŨR-ŨR

h: ham′mẽr-ẽr.
kl: c̦lam′ŏr-ẽr.
st: stam′mẽr-ẽr.
y: yam′mẽr-ẽr.
Plus hammer her, etc.

821 ūse, b̥ull, brûte, tŭrn, up; crȳ, myth; c̥at, ma̱chine, ace,
church, c̱hord; ġem, añger, (Fr.) boṅ, a̱ş; THis, thin; a̱zure

ĀN′Å-B′L
AN′DŪR-SŎN

(Choose only one word out of each group)

ĀN′Å-B′L

ch: chāin′à-ble.
d: o̱r-dāin′à-ble.
dr: drāin′à-ble, un-drāin′à-ble.
g: gāin′à-ble.
pl: ex-plāin′à-ble,
un-ex-plāin′à-ble.
spr: sprāin′à-ble.
str: c̱on-strāin′à-ble,
ō-vĕr-strāin′à-ble,
strāin′à-ble.
t: as-cĕr-tāin′à-ble,
at-tāin′à-ble, c̱on-tāin′à-ble,
dē-tāin′à-ble, māin-tāin′à-ble,
ob-tāin′à-ble, sus-tāin′à-ble,
un-at-tāin′à-ble,
un-ob-tāin′à-ble.
tr: res-trāin′à-ble, trāin′à-ble.
Plus gain a bull, etc.

AN′Å-B′L

k(c̱): c̱an′ni-bǎl.
s: in-san′à-ble*, san′à-ble.
t: tan′nà-ble.
Plus can a bull, etc.

ĀN′ĀR-I

k(c̱): chi-c̱ān′er-y.
l: lān′ār-y*.
pl: plān′ār-y.

AN′Å-RI

gr: gran′à-ry.
p: pan′à-ry.
Cf. an′ūr-i.

AN′CHES-TER

gr: Gran′ches-tĕr.
m: Man′ches-tĕr.
Plus branchy stir.

AND′Å-B′L

m: c̱om-mand′à-ble,
c̱oun-tĕr-mand′à-ble,
dē-mand′à-ble,
re-pri-mand′à-ble.
s: sand′à-ble.
st: un-dĕr-stand′à-ble.
Plus stand a bull, etc.

AN′DI-FI

d: dan′di-fy.
k(c̱): c̱an′di-fy.
Plus brandy? Fie!, etc.

AN′DI-NES

d: dan′di-ness.
h: han′di-ness.
s: san′di-ness.

AN′DRI-ĂN

Vowel: mē-an′dri-ăn*.
n: Mē-nan′dri-ăn.
z: Al-ex-an′dri-ăn.

AN′DŪR-ING

Vowel: mē-an′dĕr-ing.
l: phi-lan′dĕr-ing.
p: pan′dĕr-ing.
sl: slan′dĕr-ing.
Plus gander ring, etc.

ÄN′DŪR-ING

w: wän′dĕr-ing.
Cf. on′dūr-ing.

AN′DŪR-SŎN

Vowel: An′dĕr-sŏn.
s: San′dĕr-sŏn.
Plus gander, son, etc.
Plus grander sun, etc.

AN'DŪR-ŪR
ANG'Ū-LĂR

fāte, fär, fȧst, fạll, finăl, cãre, at; mēte, prĕy, hẽr, met; pīne, marïne, bïrd, pin; nōte, mŏve, fọr, atŏm, not; mọọn, book;

822

(Choose only one word out of each group)

AN'DŪR-ŪR

Vowel: mē-an'dẽr-ẽr.
l: phi-lan'dẽr-ẽr.
p: pan'dẽr-ẽr.
sl: slan'dẽr-ẽr.
Plus slander her, etc.

ÄN'DŪR-ŪR

l: läun'dẽr-ẽr.
w: wän'dẽr-ẽr.
Cf. on'dŭr-ŭr.

AN'DŪR-US

p: pan'dẽr-ous.
sl: slan'dẽr-ous.
Plus slander us, etc.

AN'EL-ING

ch: chan'nel-ing.
p: pan'el-ling.

ĀN'Ē-US

br: mem-brān'ē-ous.
d: an″tē-cē-dān'ē-ous,
suc̣-cē-dān'ē-ous,
l: mis-cel-lān'ē-ous,
pọr-cē-lān'ē-ous.
r: ar-rān'ē-ous,
cir″c̣um-fō-rān'ē-ous,
c̣on-tem″pō-rān'ē-ous,
ex-tem″pō-rān'ē-ous,
ex-tẽr-rān'ē-ous,
med″i-tẽr-rān'ē-ous*,
sub-tẽr-rān'ē-ous,
tem-pō-rān'nē-ous,
ter-rān'ē-ous.
t: cō-ē-tān'ē-ous, c̣u-tān'ē-ŏus,
dis-sen-tān'ē-ous,
in-stan-tān'ē-ous,
mō-men-tān'ē-ous,

sī-mul-tān'ē-ous,
spon-tān'ē-ous,
sub-c̣ū-tān'ē-ous.
tr: ex-trān'ē-ous.
Plus brainy, us, etc.

ĀN'FỤL-I

b: bāne'fụl-ly.
d: dis-dāin'fụl-ly.
p: pāin'fụl-ly.

ĀN'FỤL-NES

d: dis-dāin'fụl-ness.
g: gāin'fụl-ness.
p: pāin'fụl-ness.

ANGK'ŪR-ING

Vowel: añ'c̣hŏr-ing.
h: hañ'kẽr-ing.
k(c̣): c̣añ'kẽr-ing,
en-c̣añ'kẽr-ing.
Plus rancor ring, etc.

ANGK'ŪR-US

k(c̣): c̣añk'ẽr-ous.
t: c̣an-tañk'ẽr-ŏus.
Plus anchor us, etc.

ANG'L-SOM

Vowel: ang'le-sŏme.
r: wrang'le-sŏme (rang').
t: tang'le-sŏme.
Plus mangle some, etc.

ANG'Ū-LĂR

Vowel: ang'ū-lăr, trī-ang'ū-lăr.
r: quäd-rang'ū-lăr.
sl: slang'ū-lăr.
t: oc̣-tang'ū-lăr,
pen-tang'ū-lăr,
rec̣-tang'ū-lăr.

823 ūse, bụll, brúte, tûrn, up; crȳ, myth; çat, maçhine, ace, church, çhord; ġem, añger, (Fr.) boñ, aṣ; THis, thin; aẓure

Ā′NI-Ȧ
AN′I-KĂL

(Choose only one word out of each group)

Ā′NI-Ȧ

Vowel: Lith-ū-ā′ni-ȧ.
b: Al-bā′ni-ȧ.
d: suç-cē-dā′nē-ȧ*.
kr: Ū-krāi′ni-ȧ.
l: mis-cel-lā′nē-ȧ.
m: Añ-glō-mā′ni-ȧ,
bib″li-ō-mā′ni-ȧ,
dē-çal″çō-mā′ni-ȧ,
dē″mŏn-ō-mā′ni-ȧ*,
dip-sō-mā′ni-ȧ,
el-eū″thēr-ō-mā′ni-ȧ,
ē-rōt-ō-mā′ni-ȧ, Gal-lō-mā′ni-ȧ,
klep-tō-mā′ni-ȧ, log-ō-mā′ni-ȧ,
mā′ni-ȧ, meg″ȧ-lō-mā′ni-ȧ,
met-rō-mā′ni-ȧ, mon-ō-mā′ni-ȧ,
nym-phō-mā′ni-ȧ,
py-rō-mā′ni-ȧ, Rú-mā′ni-ȧ,
Taṣ-mā′ni-ȧ.
r: Ū-rā′ni-ȧ.
t: A-qui-tā′ni-ȧ,
Lū-ṣi-tā′ni-ȧ,
Maụ-rē-tā′ni-ȧ, Rúr-i-tā′ni-ȧ,
Ti-tā′ni-ȧ, Tri-pol-i-tā′ni-ȧ.
v: Penn-syl-vā′ni-ȧ, Syl-vā′ni-ȧ,
Tran-syl-vā′ni-ȧ.

Ā′NI-AK

m: bib″li-ō-mā′ni-aç,
dip-sō-mā′ni-aç,
el-eū″thēr-ō-mā′ni-aç,
klep-tō-mā′ni-aç, mā′ni-aç,
meg″ȧ-lō-mā′ni-aç,
mon-ō-mā′ni-aç,
nym-phō-mā′ni-aç,
py-rō-mā′ni-aç.

Ā′NI-AL

kr: çrā′ni-ăl.
m: dō-mā′ni-ăl.
r: sub-tēr-rā′nē-ăl.
Plus zany, Al, etc.

Ā′NI-ĂN

Vowel: cȳ-ā′nē-ăn,
Li-thū-ā′ni-ăn.
b: Al-bā′ni-ăn.
k(ç): vol-çā′ni-ăn.
kr: Ū-krāi′ni-ăn.
m: Alç-mā′ni-ăn, Rú-mā′ni-ăn,
San-dē-mā′ni-ăn, Taṣ-mā′ni-ăn.
r: cir-çum-fō-rā′nē-ăn,
ex-tem-pō-rā′nē-ăn, I-rā′ni-ăn,
Med″i-tēr-rā′nē-ăn,
sub-tēr-rā′nē-ăn, Tū-rā′ni-ăn,
Ū-rā′ni-ăn.
t: A-qui-tā′ni-ăn,
Maụ-rē-tā′ni-ăn,
Tri-pol-i-tā′ni-ăn.
v: Penn-syl-vā′ni-ăn,
Tran-syl-vā′ni-ăn.
Plus zany, an, etc.

AN′I-BĂL

h: Han′ni-băl.
k(ç): çan′ni-băl.
Cf. an′ȧ-b'l.

AN′I-EL

d: Dan′i-el.
h: Han′i-el.
s: San′i-el.
th: Nȧ-than′i-el.
Cf. spaniel.

AN′I-GĂN

br: Bran′ni-găn.
fl: Flan′ni-găn.
l: Mul-lan′i-găn.
n: she-nan′ni-găn.

AN′I-KĂL

k(ç): mē-çhan′i-çăl.
m: Bräh-man′i-çăl.

AN'I-FI
AN'Ō-SKŌP

fāte, fär, fȧst, fạll, finăl, cāre, at; mēte, prẹy, hêr, met; pīne,
marïne, bĩrd, pin; nōte, möve, fọr, atŏm, not; mọọn, book;

824

(Choose only one word out of each group)

p: pan'i-cle.
r: ty-ran'ni-căl.
t: bō-tan'i-căl, chär-là-tan'i-căl.
v: gal-van'i-căl.
Plus canny Cal, etc.
Plus panic, Al, etc.

AN'I-FI

m: hū-man'i-fy.
s: in-san'i-fy, san'i-fy.
Plus Fannie? Fie!

AN'I-MUS

Vowel: an'i-mus.
l: pù-sil-lan'i-mous.
n: mag-nan'i-mous,
ū-nan'i-mous.
t: mul-tan'i-mous.
Plus Annie muss, etc.

AN'ISH-ING

b: ban'ish-ing.
pl: plan'ish-ing.
v: van'ish-ing.

AN'ISH-MENT

b: ban'ish-ment.
v: ē-van'ish-ment,
van'ish-ment.
Plus Spanish meant, etc.

AN'IS-TŨR

b: ban'is-tẽr.
g: gan'is-tẽr.
k(c): can'is-tẽr.
Plus Fannie stir, etc.

AN'I-TY

Vowel: Chris-ti-an'i-ty,
in-an'i-ty.
b: in-ũr-ban'i-ty, ũr-ban'i-ty.
d: mun-dan'i-ty.

f: prō-fan'i-ty.
g: in-ọr-gan'i-ty, pā-gan'i-ty.
k(c): vol-can'i-ty
m: ạl-dẽr-man'i-ty,
gig-man'i-ty, hū-man'i-ty,
im-man'i-ty, in-hū-man'i-ty.
r: sub-tẽr-ran'i-ty.
s: in-san'i-ty, san'i-ty.
v: van'i-ty.
Plus Fannie, tea *or* T., etc.

ĀN'I-UM

d: suc-cē-dā'nē-um.
kr: crā'ni-um, per-i-crā'ni-um.
r: ġē-rā'ni-um, ū-rā'ni-um.
t: tī-tā'ni-um.

AN'JEN-SI

pl: plan'ġen-cy.
t: tan'ġen-cy.

AN'JI-B'L

fr: fran'ġi-ble, in-fran'ġi-ble,
rē-fran'ġi-ble.
t: in-tan'ġi-ble, tan'ġi-ble.

AN'I-KIN

m: man'i-kin.
p: pan'i-kin.
Plus panic in, etc.
Plus Fannie kin, etc.

AN'Ō-GRȦF

Vowel: pi-an'ō-grȧph.
v: gal-van'ō-grȧph.

AN'Ō-SKŌP

f: dī-à-phan'ō-scōpe.
v: gal-van'ō-scōpe.

(Choose only one word out of each group)

AN′SHI-AN

z: Bȳ-zan′ti-ăn.
Cf. an′shun.

AN′SHI-ĀT

st: cir-ċum-stan′ti-āte,
sub-stan′ti-āte,
tran-sub-stan′ti-āte.
Plus man, she ate, etc.

AN′SIV-NES

p: ex-pan′sive-ness.
v: ad-van′cive-ness.

AN′SŎM-EST

h: hand′sŏm-est.
r: ran′sŏm-est*.

AN′SŎM-UR

h: hand′sŏm-ẽr.
r: ran′sŏm-ẽr.
Plus plan summer, etc.

ANT′Å-B′L

gr: grant′å-ble.
pl: plant′å-ble.

AN′TŬR-ING

b: ban′tẽr-ing.
k(ċ): ċan′tẽr-ing.
Plus plant her ring, etc.
Plus grant a ring, etc.

ANT′ŨR-ŨR

b: ban′tẽr-ẽr.
k(ċ): ċan′tẽr-ẽr.
Plus enchanter, her, etc.

AN′THRŌ-PI

Vowel: phyṣ-i-an′thrō-py,
thē-an′thrō-py, zō-an′thrō-py.
k(ċ): lȳ-ċan′thrō-py.
l: a-phi-lan′thrō-py,
phi-lan′thrō-py,
thē″ō-phi-lan′thrō-py.
p: à-pan′thrō-py.
s: mi-san′thrō-py.
Plus can throw pea, etc.

AN′THRŌ-PIST

l: phi-lan′thrō-pist,
psȳ-lan′thrō-pist (sī-),
thē″ō-phi-lan′thrō-pist.
s: mi-san′thrō-pist.

AN′THRŌ-PIZM

Vowel: thē-an′thrō-piṣm.
l: psī-lan′thrō-piṣm (sī-),
thē″ō-phi-lan′thrō-piṣm.

AN′TI-SĪD

f: in-fan′ti-cīde.
g: ġi-gan′ti-cīde.
Plus aunty sighed, etc.
Plus anti side, etc.
Plus ant, he sighed, etc.

AN′TIK-NES

fr: fran′tiċ-ness.
g: ġi-gan′tiċ-ness.
m: rō-man′tiċ-ness.

AN′Ū-ĂL

Vowel: an′nū-ăl.
m: man′ū-ăl.
Cf. Manuel, Immanuel.
Plus can you, Al, etc.
Cf. can you all.

AN′Ū-LÅ
ĀP′ŪR-I

fāte, fär, fåst, fạll, finăl, cãre, at; mēte, prẹy, hẽr, met; pǐne, marïne, bǐrd, pǐn; nōte, mŏve, fọr, atŏm, not; mọọn, book;

826

(Choose only one word out of each group)

AN′Ū-LÅ

gr: gran′ū-lå.
k(ç): çan′nū-lå.

AN′Ū-LĂR

Vowel: an′nū-lăr.
k(ç): çan′nū-lăr.
n: pē-nan′nū-lăr.

AN′Ū-LĀT

Vowel: an′nū-lāte.
gr: gran′ū-lāte.
p: çam-pan′ū-lāte.
Plus fan you, late, etc.

AN′ŨR-ET

b: ban′nẽr-et.
l: lan′nẽr-et.
Plus manner, et, etc.

AN′ŨR-I

gr: gran′å-ry.
k(ç): çan′nẽr-y.
p: pan′å-ry.
st: stan′nå-ry.
t: çhär-lå-tan′ẽr-y, tan′nẽr-y.
Plus manner, he, etc.

ĀP′Å-B'L

dr: drāp′å-ble.
k(ç): çāp′å-ble, es-çāp′å-ble,
in-çāp′å-ble, in-es-çāp′å-ble.
p: pāp′å-ble.
sh: shăp′å-ble.
Plus drape a bull, etc.

AP′ID-LI

r: rap′id-ly.
s: sap′id-ly.
v: vap′id-ly.

AP′ID-NES

r: rap′id-ness.
s: sap′id-ness.
v: vap′id-ness.

AP′I-EST

h: hap′pi-est.
s: sap′pi-est.
sn: snap′pi-est.

AP′I-LI

h: hap′pi-ly.
s: sap′pi-ly.
sn: snap′pi-ly.
Plus happy Lee, etc.

AP′I-NES

h: hap′pi-ness.
s: sap′pi-ness.
sn: snap′pi-ness.

AP′I-ŨR

h: hap′pi-ẽr.
s: sap′pi-ẽr.
sn: snap′pi-ẽr.

AP′Ō-LIS

Vowel: Min-nē-ap′ō-lis.
n: An-nap′ō-lis,
In″di-å-nap′ō-lis.

ĀP′ŨR-I

Vowel: āp′ẽr-y.
dr: drāp′ẽr-y.
gr: grāp′ẽr-y.
n: nāp′ẽr-y.
p: pāp′ẽr-y.
v: vāp′ŏr-y.
Plus caper, he, etc.

(Choose only one word out of each group)

ĀP'ŨR-ING

k(ç): çāp'ẽr-ing.
p: pāp'ẽr-ing.
t: tāp'ẽr-ing.
v: vāp'ŏr-ing.
Plus paper ring, etc.

ĀP'ŨR-ŨR

k(ç): çāp'ẽr-ẽr.
p: pāp'ẽr-ẽr.
v: vāp'ŏr-ẽr.
Plus taper her, etc.

ÃR'Å-B'L

Vowel: ãir'å-ble.
b: beãr'å-ble, un-beãr'å-ble.
d: dãre'å-ble.
kl: dē-çlãr'å-ble.
p: pãir'å-ble, rē-pãir'å-ble.
sw: sweãr'å-ble.
t: teãr'å-ble.
w: un-weãr'å-ble, weãr'å-ble.
Plus tear a bull, etc.

AR'Å-B'L

Vowel: ar'å-ble.
p: par'å-ble.

ÃR'Å-DĪS

p: im-păr'å-dīse, pãr'å-dīse.
Plus share a dice, etc.

AR'ĂS-ING

b: em-bar'răs-sing.
h: har'ăs-sing.
Plus Tara, sing, etc.

AR'ĂS-MENT

b: em-bar'răss-ment.
h: har'ăss-ment.
Plus ar'răs meant, etc.

AR'Å-TIV

kl: dē-çlar'å-tive.
n: nar'rå-tive.
p: çom-par'å-tive, prē-par'å-tive, rē-par'å-tive.

ÄR'BŨR-ING

b: bär'bẽr-ing.
h: här'bŏr-ing.
Plus garb, a ring, etc.

ÄR'DI-ĂN

g: guär'di-ăn (gär').
k(ç): per-i-çär'di-ăn.
Plus tardy, an, etc.
Plus tardy Ann, etc.

ÄR'DI-NES

h: fọol-här'di-ness, här'di-ness.
t: tär'di-ness.

Ā'RĒ-Å

Vowel: ā'rē-å.
Cf. ā'ri-å.

ÃR'FỤL-I

k(ç): çãre'fụl-ly, un-çãre'fụl-ly.
pr: prãyer'fụl-ly (prãr').
Plus share fully.

ÃR'FỤL-NES

k(ç): çãre'fụl-ness, un-çãre'fụl-ness.
pr: prãyer'fụl-ness (prãr').
sp: spãre'fụl-ness.
w: wãre'fụl-ness.

(Choose only one word out of each group)

Ā′RI-Å

Vowel: ā′rē-å.
g: Bul-gā′ri-å.
k(c): Cā′ri-å.
l: cå-bal-le′ri-å,
Cal″cē-ō-lā′ri-å, Hī-lā′ri-å,
må-lā′ri-å.
r: cin-ē-rā′ri-å.
s: ad-vẽr-sā′ri-å.
t: da-tā′ri-å, diġ-i-tā′ri-å,
wis-tā′ri-å.
Cf. pãr′i-åh.
Plus Mary a, etc.
Plus gay rhea, etc.

ĀR′I-ĂL

Vowel: ac-tū-ār′i-ăl, ār′ē-ăl.
d: cal-en-dār′i-ăl, dī-ār′i-ăl*.
k(c): vi-cār′i-ăl.
l: må-lār′i-ăl.
p: pů-pār′i-ăl.
s: com-mis-sār′i-ăl,
glos-sār′i-ăl.
t: nec-tār′i-ăl, nō-tār′i-ăl,
sec-rē-tār′i-ăl.
v: ov-ār′i-ăl.
Plus stay real, etc.

ĀR′I-ĂN

Vowel: āp-i-ār′i-ăn, Ār-i-ăn,
Ār′y-ăn, Brī-ār′ē-ăn,
dī-ār′i-ăn, es-tū-ār′i-ăn.
sen-ten″ti-ār-i-ăn.
b: bär-bār′i-ăn.
br: lī-brār′i-ăn.
d: ā″bē-cē-dār′i-ăn, Dā′ri-en,
lap-i-dār′i-ăn, stī-pen-dār′i-ăn.
g: Bul-gār′i-ăn, Huñ-gār′i-ăn,
Mē-gār′i-ăn, vul-gār′i-ăn.
gr: å-grār′i-ăn.

k(c): Cā′ri-ăn, Ī-cār′i-ăn.
kw(qu): an-ti-quār′i-ăn,
å-quār′i-ăn, ūb-i-quār′i-ăn.
l: at″rå-bi-lār′i-ăn.
m: gram-mār′i-ăn.
n: å-des″sē-nār′i-ăn,
al″ti-tū-di-nār′i-ăn,
Å-pol-li-nār′i-ăn,
at″ti-tū-di-nār′i-ăn,
cen-tē-nār′i-ăn,
dis″cip-li-nār′i-ăn,
doc-tri-nār′i-ăn,
lat″i-tū-di-nār′i-ăn,
lū-nār′i-ăn, mil-lē-nār′i-ăn,
mis-cel″lē-nār′i-ăn,
non″ē-ġē-nār′i-ăn,
oc″tō-ġē-nār′i-ăn,
plat″i-tū-di-nār′i-ăn,
plen″i-tū-di-nār′i-ăn,
prē-des-ti-nār′i-ăn,
sep″tū-å-ġē-nār′i-ăn,
sex″å-ġē-nār′i-ăn,
val″ē-tū-di-nār′i-ăn,
vet″ẽr-i-nār′i-ăn.
p: Pār′i-ăn, rī-pār′i-ăn.
s: ne-ces-sār′i-ăn,
sub-lap-sār′i-ăn.
sū″prå-lap-sār′i-ăn.
t: al″phå-bē-tār′i-ăn,
an″ec-dō-tār′i-ăn,
an″ti-sab″bå-tār′i-ăn,
an″ti-trin″i-tār′i-ăn,
dī-e-tār′i-ăn, ē-quäl-i-tār′i-ăn,
ex-per″i-men-tār′i-ăn,
fū-til-i-tār′i-ăn,
hū-man-i-tār-i-ăn,
li-bẽr-tār′i-ăn, lim-i-tār′i-ăn,
nē-ces-si-tār′i-ăn, nec-tār′i-ăn,
pär″liå-men-tār′i-ăn (-lyå-),
prō-lē-tār′i-ăn, sab-bå-tār-i-ăn,
sac″rå-men-tār′i-ăn,

829

üse, bull, brúte, tûrn, **up;** crȳ, myth; çat, maçhine, ace,
church, çhord; ġem, aṅger, (Fr.) boṅ, aṣ; **TH**is, thin; aẓure

ĀR′I-ĂNT
ĀR′I-NES

(Choose only one word out of each group)

Tär-tär′ē-ăn, traç-tär′i-ăn,
trin-i-tār′i-ăn,
ū-bi-qui-tār′i-ăn, ūn-i-tār′i-ăn,
ū-til-i-tār′i-ăn, veġ-ē-tār′i-ăn.
v: Bȧ-vār′i-ăn, ō-vār′i-ăn,
Vā′ri-ăn.
z: Caē-ṣär′i-ăn, Jan-i-zär′i-ăn.
Plus Mary Ann, etc.
Plus vary an, etc.

ĀR′I-ĂNT

p: om-ni-pār′i-ent.
tr: çon-trār′i-ănt.
v: vār′i-ănt.
Plus Mā′ry, aunt, etc.
Plus wā′ry ant, etc.

ĀR′I-ĀT

k(ç): vī-çār′i-āte.
v: vār′i-ate.
Plus Mary ate, etc.
Plus nary eight, etc.

AR′I-AT

l: lär′i-at.
s: çom-mi-sär′i-at.
t: prō-lē-tār′i-at,
prō″thō-nō-tār′i-at,
seç-rē-tār′i-at.
Plus tarry at, etc.
Cf. ar′i-et.

ĀR′I-EST

ch: chär′i-est.
v: vār′i-est*.
w: wär′i-est.

AR′I-ET, AR′I-ŎT

h: Har′ri-et.
k(ç): Is-çar′i-ŏt.
m: Mar′ry-ătt, Mar′ri-ŏtt.
Plus tarry at, etc.
Cf. är′i-at.

Ā′RI-ĒZ

Vowel: Ā-ri-ēṣ.
k(ç): çā-ri-ēṣ.
Plus fragmentary ease, etc.

AR′I-FI

k(ç): saç-çhar′i-fy.
kl: çlar′i-fy.
sk(sç): sçar′i-fy.
Plus Carrie, fie!, etc.

ÃR′I-FǪRM

l: sçȧ-lär′i-fǫrm.
p: peär′i-fǫrm.
Plus nary form, etc.
Plus spare reform, etc.

AR′I-GAN

g: Gar′ri-gan.
h: Har′ri-gan.
l: Lar′ri-gan.

AR′I-ING

h: har′ry-ing.
k(ç): çar′ry-ing.
m: mar′ry-ing.
t: tar′ry-ing.

ÃR′I-NES, ĀR′I-NES

Vowel: âir′i-ness,
tū-mul-tū-âr′i-ness.
ch: chär′i-ness.
gl: glär′i-ness.
h: hâir′i-ness.
n: sañ-gui-när′i-ness (-gwi-).
r: tem-pō-rär′i-ness.
t: sal-ū-tär-i-ness,
sed-en-tār′i-ness,
sol-i-tär′i-ness,

ÄR′I-NES
AR′I-TI
fāte, fär, fȧst, fạll, fĭnăl, cãre, at; mēte, prẹy, hẽr, met; pīne,
marïne, bĭrd, pĭn; nōte, mŏve, fọr, atŏm, nọt; mọọn, book;

830

(Choose only one word out of each group)

ū-bi-qui-tār′i-ness,
vol-un-tār′i-ness.
tr: är-bi-trār′i-ness,
cọn-trār′i-ness.
w: wār′i-ness.

ÄR′I-NES

st: stär′ri-ness.
t: tär′ri-ness.

ÃR′ING-LI

bl: blãr′ing-ly.
d: dãr′ing-ly.
fl: flãr′ing-ly.
gl: glãr′ing-ly.
sp: spãr′ing-ly.
t: teãr′ing-ly.
Plus pairing Lee, etc.

AR′ING-TŎN

b: Bar′ring-tŏn,
Great Bar′ring-tŏn.
f: Far′ring-tŏn.
h: Har′ring-tŏn.
k(c): Car′ring-tŏn.
Cf. bearing ton, etc.

ÄR′I-Ō

n: scē-när′i-o (sē-).
s: im-prẹ-sär′i-ō.
Cf. Lō-thär′i-ō.
Plus starry, Oh, etc.
Plus starry, owe, etc.

AR′I-ŎN

k(c): car′ri-ŏn.
kl: clar′i-ŏn.
m: Mar′i-ăn, Mar′i-ŏn.
Plus carry an, etc.

AR′I-SŎN

g: gar′ri-sŏn.
h: Har′ri-sŏn.
Plus marry, son, etc.
Plus tarry, sun, etc.

ÃR′I-TI

n: dē-bō-när′i-ty.
r: rãr′i-ty.
Plus fairy tea, etc.

AR′I-TI

Vowel: fȧ-mil-i-ar′i-ty,
pē-cū-li-ar′i-ty,
rec″ti-lin″ē-ar′i-ty.
b: bär-bar′i-ty.
ch: char′i-ty, un-char′i-ty.
d: sol-i-dar′i-ty.
g: vul-gar′i-ty.
kl: clar′i-ty.
l: añ-gū-lar′i-ty,
cir-cū-lar′i-ty,
dis-sim-i-lar′i-ty,
glob-ū-lar′i-ty, hī-lar′i-ty,
in-sū-lar′i-ty, ir-reg-ū-lar′i-ty,
joc-ū-lar′i-ty, mol-ec-ū-lar′i-ty,
mus-cū-lar′i-ty,
pär-tic-ū-lar′i-ty,
per″pen-dic-ū-lar′i-ty,
pi″ȧ-cū-lar′i-ty, pō-lar′i-ty,
pop-ū-lar′i-ty, pū-pi-lar′i-ty,
rec-tañ-gū-lar′i-ty,
reg-ū-lar′i-ty, sec-ū-lar′i-ty,
sim-i-lar′i-ty, siñ-gū-lar′i-ty,
tit-ū-lar′i-ty, trī-añ-gū-lar′i-ty,
vas-cū-lar′i-ty.
p: dis-par′i-ty, fis-si-par′i-ty,
ġem-mi-par′i-ty, im-par′i-ty,
om-ni-par′i-ty, par′i-ty,
viv-i-par′i-ty.

831 ūse, bull, brúte, tũrn, up; crÿ, myth; çat, maçhine, ace,
church, çhord; ġem, aṅger, (Fr.) boṅ, aṣ; THis, thin; aẓure

AR'I-TŪD
ÄR'MING-LI

(Choose only one word out of each group)

pl: ex-em-plar'i-ty.
Plus carry tea, etc.

AR'I-TŪD

kl: çlar'i-tūde*.
m: à-mar'i-tūde*.

ĀR'I-UM

Vowel: glā-ci-ār'i-um (-shi-).
b: bār'i-um, çol-um-bār'i-um,
  hēr-bār'i-um.
d: tep-i-dār'i-um.
kw: à-quār'i-um.
r: hon-ō-rār'i-um (on-),
  saç-rār'i-um, ter-rār'i-um,
  xer-ō-tēr-rār'i-um (zer-).
t: san-i-tār'i-um,
  tēr-mi-tār'i-um.
v: a″quà-vi-vār'i-um,
  vi-vār'i-um.
Plus vary 'em, etc.
Plus vary, um, etc.

ĀR'I-ŪR

ch: chār'i-ēr.
w: wār'i-ēr.
Plus Mary err, etc.
Plus Carey, er, etc.
Plus vary her, etc.

AR'I-ŪR

b: bar'ri-ēr.
f: far'ri-ēr.
h: har'ri-ēr.
k(ç): çar'ri-ēr.
m: mar'ri-ēr.
t: tar'ri-er.
Plus carry her, etc.
Plus Harry err, etc.
Plus Harry, er, etc.

ĀR'I-US

f: mul-ti-fār'i-ŏus, nē-fār'i-ŏus,
  om-ni-fār'i-ŏus.
g: grē-gār'i-ŏus, và-gār'i-ŏus,
k(ç): çal-çār'ē-ŏus,
  prē-çār'i-ŏus, vī-çār'i-ŏus.
kw(qu): À-quā'ri-us (-kwā').
l: at-rà-bi-lār'i-ŏus, hī-lār'i-ŏus,
  mà-lār'i-ŏus.
n: är-ē-nār'i-ŏus, dē-nār'i-us,
  quäd″rà-ġē-nār'i-ŏus,
  tes″ti-tū″di-nār'i-ŏus,
  val″ē-tū″di-nār'i-ŏus.
p: vī-pār'i-ŏus.
r: hon-ō-rār'i-ŏus (on-),
  tem-ē-rār'i-ŏus.
t: frù-men-tār'i-ŏus,
  neç-tār'i-ŏus, Saġ-it-tār'i-us,
  tär-tār'ē-ŏus.
tr: är-bi-trār'i-ŏus,
  çon-trār'i-ŏus.
v: vār'i-ous.
Plus vary us, etc.

ÄR'KI-KĂL

Vowel: är'çhi-çăl.
l: hÿ-lär'çhi-çăl.
n: mō-när'çhi-çăl.
r: hīe-rär'çhi-çăl,
  tet-rär'çhi-çăl.
Plus darky, Cal, etc.

ÄR'LÀ-TĂN

sh: çhär'là-tăn.
t: tär'là-tăn.

ÄR'MING-LI

ch: chär'ming-ly.
f: fär'ming-ly.
h: här'ming-ly.

ÄR′NISH-ING
ÄRT′LES-LI

fāte, fär, fȧst, fạll, fĭnăl, cãre, at; mēte, prey, hẽr, met; pĭne, marĭne, bĭrd, pĭn; nōte, mŏve, fọr, atŏm, not; mọọn, book; 832

(Choose only one word out of each group)

l: ȧ-lär′ming-ly.
Plus harming Lee, etc.
Plus farming lea, etc.

ÄR′NISH-ING

g: gär′nish-ing.
t: tär′nish-ing.
v: vär′nish-ing.

ÄR′NISH-ŨR

g: gär′nish-ẽr.
t: tär′nish-ẽr.
v: vär′nish-ẽr.
Plus varnish err, *or* er.
Plus varnish her.

AR′Ō-EST

h: har′rōw-est*.
n: nar′rōw-est.

AR′Ō-I

Vowel: ar′rōw-y.
m: mar′rōw-y.
sp: spar′rōw-y.
y: yar′rōw-y.
Plus farrōw, wē, etc.

AR′Ō-ING

b: wheel-bar′rōw-ing.
h: har′rōw-ing.
n: nar′rōw-ing.

Ā′RŎN-ĪT

Vowel: Āa′rŏn-īte.
m: Mā′rŏn-īte.
Cf. Çhā′rŏn night, etc.

AR′Ō-ŨR

h: har′rōw-ẽr.
n: nar′rōw-ẽr.
Plus sparrow err, *or* er.
Plus harrow her, etc.

ÄR′SEN-I

l: lär′cen-y.
p: çō-pär′cen-y.
Plus arson, he, etc.

ÄR′SEN-ŨR

l: lär′cen-ẽr.
p: çō-pär′cen-ẽr, pär′cen-ẽr.
Plus parson, her, etc.

ÄR′SHĂL-IZM

m: mär′tiăl-iṣm.
p: pär′tiăl-iṣm.

ÄR′TED-NES

h: fạlse′⸗heärt″ed-ness,
fick′le⸗heärt″ed-ness,
frank′⸗heärt″ed-ness,
free′⸗heärt″ed-ness,
härd′⸗heärt″ed-ness,
kīnd′⸗heärt″ed-ness,
līght′⸗heärt″ed-ness,
ō′pen⸗heärt″ed-ness,
soft′⸗heärt″ed-ness,
ten′dẽr⸗heärt″ed-ness,
trùe′⸗heärt″ed-ness,
wärm′⸗heärt″ed-ness.
p: dē-pärt′ed-ness.

ÄR′TI-K′L

Vowel: är′ti-çle.
p: pär′ti-çle.

ÄR′TI-ZĂN

Vowel: är′ti-ṣăn.
b: bär′ti-ẓăn.
p: pär′ti-ṣăn.

ÄRT′LES-LI

Vowel: ärt′less-ly.
h: heärt′less-ly.

(Choose only one word out of each group)

Plus smart, Leslie, etc.
Plus start, Les; Lee, etc.

ÄRT′LES-NES

Vowel: ärt′less-ness.
h: heärt′less-ness.

ÄRT′ŪR-ING

b: bär′tēr-ing.
ch: chär′tēr-ing.
m: mär′tȳr-ing.
Plus gär′tēr-ring, etc.

ÄRT′ŪR-ŪR

b: bär′tēr-ēr.
ch: chär′tēr-ēr.
Plus martyr her, etc.
Plus garter err, *or* er, etc.

AS-Å-B'L

ch: chās′å-ble (-b'l).
f: ef-fāce′å-ble, in-ef-fāce′å-ble.
r: ē-rās′i-ble.
tr: rē-trāce′å-ble,
  trāce′å-ble.
v: ē-vās′i-ble.
Plus race a bull, etc.

ĀS′EN-SI

j: ad-jāc′en-cy, in-tēr-jāc′en-cy.
pl: com-plāc′en-cy.
Plus renascence, he, etc.

ĀS′FUL-NES

gr: dis-grāce′ful-ness,
  grāce′ful-ness, un-grāce′ful-ness.

Ā′SHI-Å

Vowel: Ā-si-å.
k(c): å-cā′ci-å.

p: As-pā′si-å.
r: Eū-rā′si-å.
(Cf. ā′zhi-å, ā′zi-å, ā′shå, ā′zhå.
So in all similar sounds.)
Cf. crazy a, etc.

ASH′I-Å

k(c): cas′si-å.
kw(qu): quas′si-å.
n: Pär-nas′si-å.
Plus flashy a, etc.

Ā′SHI-ĂL

b: bā′si-ăl.
Cf. spā′ti-ăl.

Ā′SHI-ĂN

Vowel: Ā-si-ăn.
h: Hāy′ti-ăn.
kr: Pan-crā′ti-ăn.
l: Aus-trå-lā′si-ăn,
  Ga-lā′ti-ăn, Lā′ti-ăn.
n: A-thå-nā′si-ăn.
r: Hiē-rā′ci-ăn, Hō-rā′ti-ăn.
s: Al-sā′ti-ăn.
thr: Thrā′ci-ăn.
Cf. ā′shun, ā′zhun.

ASH′I-ĂN

k(c): Cir-cas′si-ăn.
n: Pär-nas′si-ăn.
Cf. ash′un.
Plus flashy an, etc.

Ā′SHI-ĀT

gl: glā′ci-āte.
gr: in-grā′ti-āte.
m: ē-mā′ci-āte.
p: ex-pā′ti-āte.
s: in-sā′ti-āte, sā′ti-āte.
Plus the way she ate, etc.

Ā'SHI-ENT
Ā'SHUN-IST

fāte, fär, fȧst, fąll, finăl, cãre, at; mēte, prey, hẽr, met; pīne,
marïne; bĭrd, pin; nōte, mŏve, fǫr, atŏm, not; mọọn, book;

834

(Choose only one word out of each group)

Ā'SHI-ENT

f: çal-ē-fā'ci-ent,
dē-lir-ē-fā'ci-ent, fā'ci-ent,
li-quē-fā'ci-ent,
pär-tū-ri-fā'ci-ent,
rū-bē-fā'ci-ent, sen-si-fā'ci-ent,
sǫr-bē-fā'ci-ent,
stū-pē-fā'ci-ent,
tū-mē-fā'ci-ent.
Cf. ā'shent.

ASH'I-NES

Vowel: ash'i-ness.
fl: flash'i-ness.
tr: trash'i-ness.

Ā'SHUN-ĂL

Vowel: as-sō-ci-ā'tion-ăl,
çrē-ā'tion-ăl, ĭ-dē-ā'tion-ăl.
b: prō-bā'tion-ăl.
d: grā-dā'tion-ăl.
g: çon-grē-gā'tion-ăl.
gr: em-i-grā'tion-ăl.
k(ç): ed-ū-çā'tion-ăl.
l: rē-lā'tion-ăl.
n: dē-nom-i-nā'tion-ăl,
tẽr-mi-nā'tion-ăl.
r: ġȳ-rā'tion-ăl,
in-spi-rā'tion-ăl,
re-spi-rā'tion-ăl.
s: çon-vẽr-sā'tion-ăl,
sen-sā'tion-ăl.
st: stā'tion-ăl.
t: dis-sẽr-tā'tion-ăl,
im-i-tā'tion-ăl,
rep-rē-șen-tā'tion-ăl,
rō-tā'tion-ăl.
v: çon-sẽr-vā'tion-ăl,
der-i-vā'tion-ăl.
ob-șẽr-vā'tion-ăl.
Plus nation, Al, etc.

ASH'UN-ĂL

n: in-tẽr-na'tion-ăl, na'tion-ăl.
p: pas'sion-ăl.
r: ir-ra'tion-ăl, ra'tion-ăl.
Plus fashion, Al, etc.

ASH'UN-ĀT

p: çom-pas'sion-āte,
dis-pas'sion-nāte,
im-pas'sion-āte,
in-çom-pas'sion-āte,
pas'sion-āte.
Plus fashion, ate, etc.
Plus Circassian eight, etc.

ASH'UN-ING

f: fash'ion-ing.
p: çom-pas'sion-ing,
pas'sion-ing.

Ā'SHUN-IST

Vowel: rē-pū-di-ā'tion-ist.
fl: in-flā'tion-ist.
gr: em-i-grā'tion-ist,
im-mi-grā'tion-ist.
k(ç): çon-vō-çā'tion-ist,
ed-ū-çā'tion-ist.
l: an-nī-hi-lā'tion-ist,
ĭ-sō-lā'tion-ist.
m: çrē-mā'tion-ist.
p: ē-man-ci-pā'tion-ist.
r: dē-ġen-ē-rā'tion-ist,
in-spi-rā'tion-ist,
res-tō-rā'tion-ist.
s: an-nex-ā'tion-ist,
çon-vẽr-sā'tion-ist.
t: an-nō-tā'tion-ist,
im-i-tā'tion-ist,
trans-mū-tā'tion-ist.
v: in-nō-vā'tion-ist.
z: çau-șā'tion-ist.

835 ūse, bu̧ll, brúte, tûrn, up; crȳ, myth; çat, ma̧chine, ace, church, çhord; ġem, añger, (Fr.) boṅ, a̧s; THis, thin; azure

Ā'SHUN-LES
AS'I-NES

(Choose only one word out of each group)

Ā'SHUN-LES

d: foun-dā'tion-less.
gr: em-i-grā'tion-less,
im-mi-grā'tion-less.
r: in-spi-rā'tion-less.
s: çon-vĕr-sā'tion-less.
t: im-i-tā'tion-less,
temp-tā'tion-less.
Plus one nation less, etc.

Ā'SHUN-ŪR

b: prō-bā'tion-ĕr,
rep-rō-bā'tion-ĕr.
d: foun-dā'tion-ĕr.
l: ob-lā'tion-ĕr.
r: res-tō-rā'tion-ĕr.
st: stā'tion-ĕr.
Plus indignation, her, etc.
Plus nation err, *or* er, etc.

ASH'ŪR-I

d: ha-bĕr-dash'ĕr-y.
f: fash'ĕr-y.
s: sash'ĕr-y.
Plus rasher, he, etc.

Ā'SHUS-NES

d: a̧u-dā'cious-ness,
ē-dā'cious-ness,
men-dā'cious-ness.
f: in-ef-fā'cious-ness.
g: fū-gā'cious-ness,
sa̧-gā'cious-ness.
gr: grā'cious-ness,
un-grā'cious-ness.
k(ç): ef-fi-çā'cious-ness,
pĕr-spi-çā'cious-ness,
kw(qu): lō-quā'cious-ness,
sē-quā'cious-ness.
l: fal-lā'cious-ness,
sa̧-lā'cious-ness.

m: çon-tū-mā'cious-ness.
n: pĕr-ti-nā'cious-ness,
pug-nā'cious-ness,
te-nā'cious-ness.
p: ça-pā'cious-ness,
in-ça̧-pā'cious-ness,
ra-pā'cious-ness.
r: vē-rā'cious-ness,
vō-rā'cious-ness.
s: vex-ā'tious-ness.
sp: spā'cious-ness.
t: dis-pū-tā'tious-ness,
os-ten-tā'tious-ness.
v: vī-vā'cious-ness.

AS'I-B'L

n: rē-nas'ci-ble.
p: im-pas'si-ble, pas'sa̧-ble,
pas'si-ble, sūr-pas'sa̧-ble.
r: i-ras'ci-ble.
Plus classy bull, etc.

AS'I-NĀT

b: ab-bac'i-nāte.
f: fas'ci-nāte.
r: dē-rac'i-nāte.
s: as-sas'si-nāte, ex-ac'i-nāte.
Plus classy, Nate, etc.
Plus class in eight, etc.
Plus mass innate, etc.

ĀS'I-NES

l: lāc'i-ness.
r: rāc'i-ness.

AS'I-NES

br: brass'i-ness.
gl: glass'i-ness.
gr: grass'i-ness.
kl: çlass'i-ness.
m: mass'i-ness.
s: sass'i-ness.

AS'I-TI
AS'TRI-ĂN
fāte, fär, fåst, fạll, finăl, cāre, at; mēte. prẹy, hẽr, met; pīne, marïne, bĭrd, pĭn; nōte, mŏve, fọr, atŏm, not; mọọn, book;

836

(Choose only one word out of each group)

AS'I-TI

b: bī-bac'i-ty.
d: ạu-dac'i-ty, ē-dac'i-ty,
men-dac'i-ty, mọr-dac'i-ty.
g: fū-gac'i-ty, sȧ-gac'i-ty.
k(c̣): dī-c̣ac'i-ty*,
pẽr-spi-c̣ac'i-ty, pẽr-vi-c̣as'i-ty,
prō-c̣ac'i-ty.
kw(qu): lō-quac'i-ty,
sē-quac'i-ty.
l: bel-lac'i-ty, sȧ-lac'i-ty.
m: c̣on-tū-mac'i-ty.
n: mī-nac'i-ty, pẽr-ti-nac'i-ty,
pug-nac'i-ty, sa-pō-nac'i-ty,
tē-nac'i-ty.
p: c̣ȧ-pac'i-ty, in-c̣ȧ-pac'i-ty,
ō-pac'i-ty, rȧ-pac'i-ty.
r: fē-rac'i-ty, vē-rac'i-ty,
vō-rac'i-ty.
v: vī-vac'i-ty.
Plus classy tea, etc.
Plus tacit, he, etc.

AS'IV-LI

m: mas'sive-ly.
p: im-pas'sive-ly, pas'sive-ly.
Plus lascive Lee, etc.

Ā'SIV-NES

sw: dis-suā'sive-ness,
pẽr-suā'sive-ness, suā'sive-ness.
v: ē-vā'sive-ness,
pẽr-vā'sive-ness.

AS'IV-NES

m: mas'sive-ness.
p: im-pas'sive-ness,
pas'sive-ness.

ASP'ING-LI

g: gasp'ing-ly.
r: rasp'ing-ly.
Plus clasping Lee, etc.

AS'TĂR-DI

b: bas'tăr-dy.
d: das'tăr-dy.
Plus bastard, he, etc.

ĀST'FŲL-I

t: dis-tāste'fụl-ly, tāste'fụl-ly.
w: wāste'fụl-ly.
Plus chased fully, etc.

AS'TI-C̣ĂL

Vowel: ec̣-c̣lē-ṣi-as'ti-c̣ăl,
en-c̣ō-mi-as'ti-c̣ăl,
en-thū-ṣi-as'ti-c̣ăl.
l: ē-las'ti-c̣ăl.
n: g̣ym-nas'ti-c̣ăl.
t: fan-tas'ti-c̣ăl.
Plus nasty, Cal, etc.

ĀS'TI-LI

h: hās'ti-ly.
p: pās'ti-ly.
t: tās'ti-ly.
Plus pasty, Lee, etc.

AS'TI-SIZM

Vowel: ec̣-c̣lē-ṣi-as'ti-cism.
l: sc̣hō-las'ti-cism.
n: mō-nas'ti-cism.
t: fan-tas'ti-cism.
Plus nasty schism, etc.

AS'TRI-ĂN

Vowel: Zō-rō-as'tri-ăn.
b: al-a-bas'tri-ăn.
k(c̣): Lan-c̣as'tri-ăn.

(Choose only one word out of each group)

AS'TRŌ-FĒ

n: ep-a-nas'trō-phē.
t: ça-tas'trō-phē.

AS'TŬR-SHIP

m: mas'tẽr-ship.
p: pas'tŏr-ship.
Plus fas'tẽr ship, etc.
Plus passed her ship, etc.

AS'TŬR-I

k: dī-ças'tẽr-y.
m: mas'tẽr-y, self'=mas'tẽr-y.
pl: plas'tẽr-y.

AS'TŬR-ING

m: mas'tẽr-ing,
ō-vẽr-mas'tẽr-ing.
pl: bē-plas'tẽr-ing, plas'tẽr-ing.
Plus faster ring, etc.

AS'ŪR-ĀT

l: lac'ẽr-āte.
m: ē-mac'ẽr-āte, mac'ẽr-āte.
Plus pass her eight, etc.
Plus first classer ate, etc.

AS'UR-I

br: brāc'ẽr-y, em-brāc'ẽr-y.
tr: trāc'ẽr-y.

ĀT'À-B'L

Vowel: çrē-āt'à-ble.
b: à-bāte'à-ble, bāit'à-ble,
dē-bāt'à-ble.
gr: grāt'à-ble.
h: hāt'à-ble.
l: çol-lāt'à-ble, dī-lāt'à-ble,
re-gū-lāt'à-ble, trans-lāt'à-ble,
un-trans-lāt'à-ble.
m: māt'à-ble.

r: bē-rāt'à-ble, rāt'à-ble.
st: stāt'à-ble.
Plus fete a bull, etc.

AT'À-B'L

b: çom-bat'à-ble.
Cf. at'i-b'l.

AT'E-LĪT

p: pat'el-līte*.
s: sat'el-līte.
Plus Mattie, light, etc.
Plus pat, he light, etc.

Ā'TEN-SI

l: lā'ten-cy.
p: pā'ten-cy.
Plus Satan, see, etc.

ĀT'FUL-I

f: fāte'ful-ly.
gr: grāte'ful-ly.
h: hāte'ful-ly.
Plus mate fully, etc.

ĀT'FUL-NES

f: fāte'ful-ness.
gr: grāte'ful-ness.
h: hāte'ful-ness.

Ā'THI-ĂN

b: Sab-bā'thi-ăn.
p: Çär-pā'thi-ăn.

ATH'Ē-SIS

Vowel: dī-ath'ē-sis.
r: pà-rath'ē-sis.

ATH'I-ÇĂL

m: çhres-tō-math'i-çăl.
p: an"thrō-pō-path'i-çăl.

(Choose only one word out of each group)

ATH′ŪR-ING

bl: blaTH′ẽr-ing.
g: fōre-gaTH′ẽr-ing,
gaTH′ẽr-ing, up-gaTH′ẽr-ing,
wool-gaTH′ẽr-ing.
l: laTH′ẽr-ing.
Plus lather, ring, etc.

ATH′ŪR-ŪR

g: fōre-gaTH′ẽr-ẽr,
gaTH′ẽr-ẽr, tax gaTH′ẽr-ẽr,
tōll gaTH′ẽr-ẽr, up-gaTH′ẽr-ẽr.
l: laTH′ẽr-ẽr.
Plus lather her, etc.

AT′I-B′L

Vowel: cŏme-at′à-ble.
b: cọm-bat′à-ble.
p: cọm-pat′i-ble, im-pat′i-ble*,
im-cọm-pat′i-ble, pat′i-ble.
Plus pat a bull, etc.

AT′I-FY

Vowel: bē-at′i-fy.
gr: grat′i-fy.
r: rat′i-fy.
str: strat′i-fy.
Plus Mattie, fie!, etc.
Plus cat, if I, etc.
Plus flat, if eye, etc.

AT′IK-Å

Vowel: At′ti-çà, scī-at′i-çà (sī-).
m: dal-mat′i-çà.
p: hē-pat′i-çà.
Plus attic, a, etc.

AT′IK-ĂL

b: ab-bat′ı-çuı, sab-bat′i-çǎl.
f: em-phat′i-çǎl (-fat′).

kr: ar-is″tō-çrat′i-çǎl,
ạu-tō-çrat′i-çǎl,
bū-reau-çrat′i-çǎl (-rō-),
dem-ō-çrat′i-çǎl, Sō-çrat′i-çǎl.
m: aç″rō-à-mat′i-çǎl,
an-ath-ē-mat′i-çǎl,
an-id″i-ō-mat′i-çǎl,
ap″ō-phleg-mat′i-çǎl,
ap″oph-theg-mat′i-çǎl,
asth-mat′i-çǎl (az-),
ạu-tō-mat′i-çal, ax″i-ō-mat′i-çǎl,
çlī-mat′i-çǎl, di-plō-mat′i-çǎl,
dog-mat′i-çǎl, drà-mat′i-çǎl,
em-blē-mat′i-çǎl,
ē-nig-mat′i-çǎl,
ep″i-gram-mat′i-çǎl,
gram-mat′i-çǎl,
heb-dō-mat′i-çǎl,
id″i-ō-mat′i-çǎl,
math-ē-mat′i-çǎl,
phan-taṣ-mat′i-çǎl,
prag-mat′i-çǎl, prī-mat′i-çǎl,
schiṣ-mat′i-çǎl (siz-),
spaṣ-mat′i-çǎl.
n: fà-nat′i-çǎl.
r: lē-vi-rat′i-çǎl, pī-rat′i-çǎl,
se-pà-rat′i-çǎl.
st: āe-rō-stat′i-çǎl, stat′i-çǎl.
t: ap-os-tat′i-çǎl, eçs-tat′i-çǎl.
v: vat′i-çǎl.
Plus batty, Cal, etc.
Plus attic, Al, etc.

AT′IN-ĀT

l: ġē-lat′i-nāte, Pà-lat′i-nāte.
Plus satin ate, *or* eight, etc.
Plus rat innate, etc.
Plus batty, Nate, etc.

ĀT′I-NES

sl: slāt′i-ness.
w: wẹight′i-ness (wāt′).

(Choose only one word out of each group)

AT′I-NES

ch: chat′ti-ness.
f: fat′ti-ness.
n: nat′ti-ness.

AT′IN-ĪZ

l: ġē-lat′i-nīze, Lat′in-īze.
pl: plat′i-nīze.
Plus satin eyes, etc.

AT′I-NUS

l: ġē-lat′i-nous.
pl: plat′in-ous.
Plus Latin us, etc.
Plus fat in us, etc.

AT′I-SĪZ

m: em-blē-mat′i-cīze,
   gram-mat′i-cīze.
n: fȧ-nat′i-cīze.
Plus Hattie sighs, etc.
Cf. Hattie's eyes, etc.

AT′I-SIZM

Vowel: Ā-si-at′i-cis̗m (-shi-).
m: gram-mat′i-cis̗m.
n: fȧ-nat′i-cis̗m.

AT′I-TŪD

Vowel: at′ti-tūde, bē-at′ti-tūde.
gr: grat′i-tūde, in-grat′i-tūde.
l: lat′i-tūde.
pl: plat′i-tūde.
Plus pat it, you'd, etc.
Plus cat etude, etc.

Ā′TIV-NES

n: nā′tive-ness.
r: al-lit-ē-rā′tive-ness.
t: im-i-tā′tive-ness.
tr: pen-ē-trā′tive-ness.

AT′L-MENT

b: bat′tle-ment,
   em-bat′tle-ment.
pr: prat′tle-ment.
t: tat′tle-ment.
Plus cattle meant, etc.

AT′ŎM-I

Vowel: at′ŏm-y.
n: ȧ-nat′ŏ-my.
Plus hat o' me, etc.

AT′ŎM-IST

Vowel: at′ŏ-mist.
n: ȧ-nat′ŏ-mist.
Plus hat o' mist, etc.

AT′ŎM-ĪZ

Vowel: at′ŏm-īze.
n: ȧ-nat′ŏ-mīze.

AT′ŎM-IZM

Vowel: at′ŏ-mis̗m.
n: ȧ-nat′ŏ-mis̗m.

AT′ŎM-US

Vowel: dī-at′ŏ-mous.
r: pȧ-rat′ŏ-mous.

ĀT′ŎR-I

kr: ob-sē-c̣rāt′ŏ-ry.
l: rē″c̣ap-it″ū-lāt′ŏ-ry.
n: rat″i-oc″i-nāt′ŏ-ry (rash″).

AT′RI-KĂL

Vowel: thē-at′ri-c̣ăl.
l: id-ō-lat′ri-c̣ăl.

(Choose only one word out of each group)

AT'RI-SĪD

fr: frat'ri-cīde.
m: mat'ri-cīde.
p: pat'ri-cīde.

Ā'TRŎN-ĂL

m: mā'trŏn-ăl.
p: pā'trŏn-ăl.
Plus natron, Al, etc.

Ā'TRŎN-IJ

m: mā'trŏn-ăġe.
p: pā'trŏn-ăġe.

Ā'TRŎN-ĪZ

m: mā'trŏn-īze.
p: pā'trŏn-īze.

AT'Ū-LĀT

gr: ҫon-grat'ū-lāte, grat'ū-lāte.
sp: spat'ū-lāte.
Plus Matt, you late?, etc.

AT'ŪR-ĂL

n: nat'ūr-ăl, prē-tẽr-nat'ūr-ăl,
sū-pẽr-nat'ūr-ăl.

AT'ŪR-ĂL

l: bī-lat'ẽr-ăl, ҫol-lat'ẽr-ăl,
ē-qui-lat'ẽr-ăl, lat'ẽr-ăl,
quäd-ri-lat'ẽr-ăl, ūn-i-lat'ẽr-ăl.
Plus matter, Al?, etc.

AT'ŪR-ĂN

k(ҫ): ҫat'ẽr-ăn.
l: Lat'ẽr-ăn.
Plus matter, Ann, etc.

AT'ŪR-ĀT

m: mat'ūr-āte.
s: sat'ūr-āte, sū"pẽr=sat'ūr-āte.
Plus Pat, you're eight, etc.
Plus Mat, you rate, etc.

AT'ŪR-I

b: bat'tẽr-y.
fl: flat'tẽr-y.
sh: shat'tẽr-y.
sl: slat'tẽr-y.
t: tat'tẽr-y.
Plus clatter, he, etc.

AT'ŪR-ING

b: bat'tẽr-ing.
bl: blat'tẽr-ing.
ch: chat'tẽr-ing.
fl: bē-flat'tẽr-ing, flat'tẽr-ing.
kl: ҫlat'tẽr-ing.
p: bē-pat'tẽr-ing, pat'tẽr-ing.
sh: shat'tẽr-ing.
sk(sҫ): bē-sҫat'tẽr-ing,
sҫat'tẽr-ing.
sm: smat'tẽr-ing.
sp: bē-spat'tẽr-ing, spat'tẽr-ing.
spl: splat'tẽr-ing.
Plus patter ring, etc.
Plus pat a ring, etc.

AT'ŪR-ŪR

b: bat'tẽr-ẽr.
bl: blat'tẽr-ẽr.
ch: chat'tẽr-ẽr.
fl: flat'tẽr-ẽr.
kl: ҫlat'tẽr-ẽr.
p: pat'tẽr-ẽr.
sh: shat'tẽr-ẽr.
sk(sҫ): sҫat'tẽr-ẽr.

(Choose only one word out of each group)

sm: smat′tēr-ēr.
spl: splat′tēr-ēr.
Plus batter her, etc.
Plus batter err *or* er, etc.

Ā́ŪR-I

Vowel: ā′ēr-y.
f: fā′ē-rie*.

AV́ĂN-ĒZ

h: Hav́ăn-ēṣe.
j: Jav́ăn-ēṣe.

AV́EL-ING

gr: grav́el-ling.
r: rav́el-ling, un-rav́el-ling.
tr: trav́el-ling.

AV́EL-ŪR

r: rav́el-lēr, un-rav́el-lēr.
tr: trav́el-lēr.
Plus gavel her, etc.
Plus gavel err *or* er, etc.

AV́EN-DŪR

ch: chav́en-dēr.
l: lav́en-dēr.

Ā́VI-À

gr: Bel-grā′vi-à.
n: Sc̨an-di-nā′vi-à.
p: Pā′vi-à.
r: Mō-rā′vi-à.
sl: Jū′gō=Slā′vi-à (yū′).
t: Bà-tā′vi-à, Oc̨-tā′vi-à.
Plus navy, a, etc.
Plus way, via, etc.

Ā́VI-ĂN

Vowel: ā′vi-ăn.
gr: Bel-grā′vi-ăn.
n: Sc̨an-di-nā′vi-ăn.
r: Mō-rā′vi-ăn.
sh: Shā′vi-ăn.
sl: Jū-gō=Slā′vi-ăn (yū-).
t: Bà-tā′vi-ăn.
Plus wavy, Ann *or* an, etc.

AV́IJ-ING

r: rav́ăġ-ing.
sk(sc̨): sc̨av́ăġ-ing.

AV́IJ-ŪR

r: rav́ăġ-ēr.
s: sav́ăġ-ēr.
sk(sc̨): sc̨av́ăġ-ēr.
Plus ravage her, etc.
Plus savage err *or* er, etc.

AV́ISH-ING

l: lav́ish-ing.
r: en-rav́ish-ing, rav́ish-ing.

AV́ISH-MENT

l: lav́ish-ment.
r: en-rav́ish-ment,
rav́ish-ment.

ĀV́ISH-NES

n: knāv́ish-ness (nāv′).
sl: slāv́ish-ness.

AV́ISH-ŪR

l: lav́ish-ēr.
r: rav́ish-ēr.
Plus ravish her, etc.
Plus lavish, err *or* er, etc.

AV'I-TI
ĀZ'I-NES
fāte, fär, fȧst, fạll, fĭnăl, cãre, at; mēte, prey, hẽr, met; pīne,
marῐne, bîrd, pin; nōte, mŏve, fọr, atŏm, not; mọọn, book;
842

(Choose only one word out of each group)

AV'I-TI

gr: grav'i-ty.
k(c): cav'i-ty, con-cav'i-ty.
pr: dē-prav'i-ty, prav'i-ty.
sw: suav'i-ty (swav').
Plus navvy tea, etc.

ĀV'ŨR-I

br: brāv'ẽr-y.
gr: grāv'ẽr-y.
n: knāv'ẽr-y (nāv').
s: sāv'ŏr-y, un-sāv'ŏr-y.
sl: slāv'ẽr-y.

ĀV'ŨR-ING

f: fāv'ŏr-ing.
fl: flāv'ŏr-ing.
kw(qu): quāv'ẽr-ing.
s: sāv'ŏr-ing.
w: un-wāv'ẽr-ing, wāv'ẽr-ing.
Plus braver ring, etc.

ĀV'ŨR-ŨR

f: fāv'ŏr-ẽr.
fl: flāv'ŏr-ẽr.
kw(qu): quāv'ẽr-ẽr.
w: wāv'ẽr-ẽr.
Plus favor her, etc.
Plus flavor err *or* er, etc.

ĀV'ŨR-US

fl: flāv'ŏr-ous.
s: sāv'ŏr-ous.
Plus favor us, etc.

AV'ŨR-US

d: cȧ-dav'ẽr-ous.
p: pȧ-pav'ẽr-ous.
Plus beslaver us, etc.

Ā'ZI-Ȧ

Vowel: A'și-ȧ.
f: ȧ-phā'și-ȧ.
k: Cạu-cā'și-ȧ.
l: Ạus-trȧ-lā'și-ȧ.
m: par"ŏn-ō-mā'și-ȧ.
n: a-thȧ-nā'și-ȧ, eū·thȧ-nā'și-ȧ.
p: As-pā'și-ȧ.
r: Eū-rā'și-ȧ.

Ā-ZI-ĂN

Vowel: Ā-și-ăn.
k(c): Cạu-cā'și-ăn.
l: Ạus-trȧ-lā'și-ăn,
Rab-ē-lāi'și-ăn.
n: A-thȧ-nā'și-ăn.
r: Eū-rā'și-ăn.
Cf. ā'zhun.

ĀZ'I-B'L

pr: prāiș'ȧ-ble.
r: rāiș'ȧ-ble.
sw: pẽr-suā'și-ble (-swā'),
suā'și-ble.
Plus raise a bull, etc.
Plus Gaza bull, etc.

ĀZ'I-NES

h: hāz'i-ness.
kr: crāz'i-ness.
l: lāz'i-ness.
m: māz'i-ness.

(Choose only one word out of each group)

E

The accented vowel sounds included are listed under **E** in single rhymes.

Ē′Á-B'L

f: fee′á-ble.
gr: á-gree′á-ble, dis-á-gree′á-ble.
kr: crē′á-ble*, dē-cree′á-ble.
m: ir-re-mē′á-ble.
Cf. see a bull, etc.

Ē′ĂL-IST

d: ī-dē′ăl-ist.
r: rē′ăl-ist.
Plus see a list, etc.
Plus real list, etc.

Ē′ĂL-ĪZ

d: ī-dē′ăl-īze.
r: rē′ăl-īze.
Plus real eyes, etc.
Plus real lies, etc.

Ē′ĂL-IZM

d: ī-dē′ăl-is̟m.
r: rē′ăl-is̟m.

Ē′ĂL-TI

f: fē′ăl-ty.
r: rē′ăl-ty.
Plus ideal tea, etc.

Ē′ĂN-IZM

b: Sá-baē′ăn-is̟m,
  plē-bēi′ăn-is̟m.
p: pē′ăn-is̟m.
r: ep″i-c̟ū-rē′ăn-is̟m,
  Py-thag-ō-rē′ăn-is̟m.
s: Lā″ō-di-cē′ăn-is̟m.

ĒB′RI-US

Vowel: ē′bri-ous.
n: fū-nē′bri-ous, i-nē′bri-ous,
  te-nē′bri-ous.

ĒCH′Á-B'L

bl: blēach′á-ble.
p: im-pēach′á-ble,
  un-im-pēach′á-ble.
r: rēach′á-ble, un-rēach′á-ble.
t: tēach′á-ble, un-tēach′á-ble.
Plus teach a bull, etc.

ECH′I-NES

sk: sketch′i-ness.
t: tetch′i-ness.

ECH′ŨR-I

l: lech′ẽr-y.
tr: treach′ẽr-y.

ECH′ŨR-US

l: lech′ẽr-ous.
tr: treach′ẽr-ous.
Plus stretcher us, etc.

ĒD′Á-B'L

b: ō-bēd′i-ble.
p: im-pēd′i-ble.
pl: plēad′á-ble, un-plēad′á-ble.
r: rēad′á-ble, un-rēad′á-ble.
s: ex-ceed′á-ble.
Plus feed a bull, etc.
Plus Theda bull, etc.

(Choose only one word out of each group)

ED'Á-B'L

dr: dread'ȧ-ble.
Cf. ed'i-b'l.

ĒD'FỤL-NES

h: heed'fụl-ness,
   un-heed'fụl-ness.
n: need'fụl-ness,
   un-need'fụl-ness.

Ē'DI-ĂL

m: bī-mēd'i-ăl, in-tẽr-mēd'i-ăl,
   mēd'i-ăl, rē-mēd'i-ăl.
p: pēd'i-ăl.
Plus seedy, Al, etc.

Ē'DI-ĂN

j: tra-ġē'di-ăn.
m: cọ-mē'di-ăn, mē'di-ăn.
p: en-cy-clō-pē'di-ăn.
Plus speedy Ann, *or* an, etc.

Ē'DI-ĀT

m: im-mē'di-āte,
   in-tẽr-mē'di-āte, mē'di-āte.
Plus needy āte, *or* eight, etc.

ED'I-B'L

Vowel: ed'i-ble.
dr: dread'ȧ-ble.
kr: cred'i-ble, in-cred'i-ble.
Plus fed a bull, etc.
Plus ready bull, etc.

Ē'DI-ENS

b: dis-ō-bē'di-ence, ō-bē'di-ence.
p: ex-pē'di-ence,
   in-ex-pē'di-ence.

Ē'DI-ENT

b: dis-ō-bē'di-ent, ō-bē'di-ent.
gr: in-grē'di-ent.
p: ex-pē'di-ent, in-ex-pē'di-ent.

ĒD'I-EST

b: bēad'i-est.
gr: greed'i-est.
n: need'i-est.
r: reed'i-est.
s: seed'i-est.
sp: speed'i-est.
w: weed'i-est.

ED'I-EST

h: head'i-est.
r: read'i-est.
st: stead'i-est, un-stead'i-est.

ED'I-KĂL

m: med'i-căl.
p: ped'i-cle.
Plus ready, Cal, etc.
Plus medic, Al, etc.

ED'I-KANT

m: med'i-cant.
pr: pred'i-cant.
Plus ready cant *or* Kant, etc.
Plus encyclopedic ant *or* aunt, etc.

ED'I-KĀT

d: ded'i-cāte.
m: med'i-cāte.
pr: pred'i-cāte.
Plus ready, Kate, etc.
Plus medic ate *or* eight, etc.

ĒD'I-LI

gr: greed'i-ly.
n: need'i-ly.

(Choose only one word out of each group)

sp: speed′i-ly.
Plus weedy lea *or* Lee, etc.
Plus speed alee, etc.

ED′I-LI

h: head′i-ly.
r: read′i-ly.
st: stead′i-ly, un-stead′i-ly.
Plus ready, Lee, etc.
Plus head alee, etc.

ED′I-MENT

p: im-ped′i-ment, ped′i-ment.
s: sed′i-ment.
Plus ready meant, etc.

ĒD′I-NES

gr: greed′i-ness.
n: need′i-ness.
s: seed′i-ness.
sp: speed′i-ness.
w: weed′i-ness.

ED′I-NES

h: head′i-ness.
r: read′i-ness, un-read′i-ness.
st: stead′i-ness, un-stead′i-ness.
thr: thread′i-ness.

ĒD′I-NUS

b: rú-bē′di-nous.
s: mū-cē′di-nous.
tr: pū-trē′di-nous.
Plus weed in us, etc.

ED′IT-ED

Vowel: ed′it-ed.
kr: aç-çred′it-ed, çred′it-ed,
dis-çred′it-ed, mis-çred′it-ed
un-aç-çred′it-ed.
Plus ready, Ted, etc.
Plus credit, Ed, etc.

ED′IT-ING

Vowel: ed′it-ing.
kr: aç-çred′it-ing, çred′it-ing,
dis-çred′it-ing, mis-çred′it-ing.

ED′I-TIV

r: red′di-tive.
s: sed′á-tive.

ED′IT-ŎR

Vowel: ed′it-ŏr.
kr: çred′it-ŏr.
Plus said it, or, etc.
Plus credit, or, etc.

Ē′DI-UM

m: mē′di-um.
t: tē′di-um.
Cf. te deum.

ĒD′I-ŪR

b: bēad′i-ẽr.
gr: greed′i-ẽr.
n: need′i-ẽr.
r: reed′i-ẽr.
s: seed′i-ẽr.
sp: speed′i-ẽr.
w: weed′i-ẽr.
Plus speedy her, etc.
Plus weedy err *or* er, etc.

ED′I-ŪR

h: head′i-ẽr.
r: read′i-ẽr.
st: stead′i-ẽr, un-stead′i-ẽr.
Plus already her, etc.
Plus already err *or* er, etc.

Ē′DI-US

m: in-tẽr-mē′di-ous.
t: tē′di-ous.

(Choose only one word out of each group)

Plus weedy, us, etc.
Cf. see *deus*, etc.

ĒD'LES-LI

h: heed'less-ly.
n: need'less-ly.
Plus heed, Leslie, etc.
Plus heedless Lee, etc.

ĒD'LES-NES

h: heed'less-ness.
n: need'less-ness.

ED'Ū-LUS

kr: cred'ū-lous, in-cred'ū-lous.
s: sed'ū-lous.
Plus schedule us, etc.

ED'ŨR-ǍL

f: fed'ẽr-ǎl.
h: hed'ẽr-ǎl.
Plus double-header, Al, etc.

ĒD'ŨR-SHIP

l: lēad'ẽr-ship.
r: rēad'ẽr-ship.
Plus cedar ship, etc.
Plus feed her ship, etc.

ĒF'I-NES

b: beef'i-ness.
l: lēaf'i-ness.

EF'I-SENS

l: mȧ-lef'i-cence.
n: bē-nef'i-cence.

EF'I-SENT

l: mȧ-lef'i-cent.
n: bē-nef'i-cent.

EF'ŨR-ENS

d: def'ẽr-ence.
pr: pref'ẽr-ence.
r: cross'-ref'ẽr-ence, ref'ẽr-ence.

EF'ŨR-ENT

Vowel: ef'fẽr-ent.
d: def'ẽr-ent.
Plus clef for rent, etc.

EG'Ȧ-B'L

b: beg'gȧ-ble.
l: leg'ȧ-ble.
Plus peg a bull, etc.

Ē'GǍL-IZM

g: rē'gǎl-ism.
l: lē'gȧl-ism.

Ē'GǍL-NES

g: rē'gǎl-ness.
l: il-lē'gǎl-ness, lē'gǎl-ness.

EG'I-NES

dr: dreg'gi-ness.
l: leg'gi-ness.

EG'NǍN-SI

pr: preg'nǎn-cy.
r: reg'nǎn-cy.
Cf. regnant, see, etc.

EG'ŨR-I

Vowel: egg'ẽr-y.
b: beg'gǎr-y.
gr: Greg'ŏr-y.

Ē'GŪR-LI

Vowel: ēa'gẽr-ly,
ō-vẽr-ēa'gẽr-ly.
m: mēa'gẽr-ly.
Plus intriguer, Lee, etc.

847 ūse, bṳll, brûte, tûrn, up; crȳ, myth; ċat, maċhine, ace,
church, ċhord; ġem, aṅger, (Fr.) boṅ, aş; THis, thin; aᶎure

Ē′GŪR-NES
EK′SHUN-ăL

(Choose only one word out of each group)

Ē′GŪR-NES

Vowel: ēa′gēr-ness,
ō-vēr-ēa′gēr-ness.
m: mēa′gēr-ness.

Ē′I-TI

b: plē-bē′i-ty.
d: dē′i-ty, hēr-maph-rō-dē′i-ty.
l: vel-lē′i-ty.
n: ċon-tem″pō-rā-nē′i-ty,
dī″ȧ-thēr″mȧ-nē′i-ty,
ex-trȧ-nē′i-ty, fem-i-nē′i-ty,
he″tēr-ō-ġē-nē′i-ty,
hō″mō-ġē-nē-i-ty,
in-stan-ti-nē′i-ty, om-nē′i-ty,
pēr-sŏ-nē′i-ty, sī-mul-tā-nē′i-ty,
spon-tȧ-nē′i-ty.
r: ċor-pō-rē′i-ty,
in-ċor-pō-rē′i-ty.
s: ȧ-sē′i-ty, gȧ-sē′i-ty, sē′i-ty.
t: mul-tē′i-ty.
Plus see it, he, etc.

Ē′JI-ĂN

Vowel: Fū-ē′ġi-ăn.
l: ċol-lē′ġi-ăn.
w: Nor-wē′ġi-ăn.
Cf. ouija, Ann *or* an, etc.

EJ′I-B'L

l: al-leġe′ȧ-ble, il-leġ′i-ble,
leġ′i-ble.
Plus hedgy bull, etc.

Ē′JUS-NES

gr: ē-grē′ġious-ness.
l: sa-ċri-lēg′ious-ness.

ĒK′À-B'L

sp: spēak′ȧ-ble, un-spēak′ȧ-ble.
Plus weak a bull, etc.

EK′À-B'L

p: im-peċ′ċȧ-ble, peċ′ċȧ-ble.
s: seċ′ċȧ-ble*.
Plus wreck a bull, etc.

ĒK′I-LI

ch: cheek′i-ly.
kr: ċrēak′i-ly.
l: lēak′i-ly.
skw(squ): squēak′i-ly (skwēk′).
sl: sleek′i-ly.
sn: snēak′i-ly.
Plus streaky lea *or* Lee, etc.
Plus streak a lee, etc.

ĒK′I-NES

ch: cheek′i-ness.
kr: ċrēak′i-ness.
l: lēak′i-ness.
skw(squ): squēak′i-ness (skwēk′).
sn: snēak′i-ness.

ĒK′ISH-NES

fr: frēak′ish-ness.
kl: ċlïqu′ish-ness.
sn: snēak′ish-ness.

EK′ŎN-ING

b: beck′ŏn-ing.
r: dead′=reck′ŏn-ing, reck′ŏn-ing.

EK′RĒ-MENT

d: deċ′rē-ment.
r: reċ′rē-ment.

EK′SHUN-ĂL

f: af-feċ′tion-ăl.
fl: in-fleċ′tion-ăl.
j: in-tēr-jeċ′tion-ăl.
pl: ċom-plex′ion-ăl (-plek′).

(Choose only one word out of each group)

r: cọr-reç'tion-ăl,
in-sūr-reç'tion-ăl.
s: in-tẽr-seç'tion-ăl, seç'tion-ăl.
t: prō-teç'tion-ăl.
Plus direction, Al, etc.

EK'SHUN-IST

f: pẽr-feç'tion-ist.
r: in-sūr-reç'tion-ist.
re-ṣūr-reç'tion-ist.
t: prō-teç'tion-ist.

EK'SHUN-ĪZ

r: re-ṣūr-reç'tion-īze.
s: seç-tion'īze.
Plus projection eyes, etc.

EK'SI-B'L

fl: flex'i-ble, in-flex'i-ble,
rē-flex'i-ble.
n: nex'i-ble.
Plus apoplexy, bull, etc.

EK'SI-TI

fl: rē-flex'i-ty.
pl: com-plex'i-ty,
in″tẽr-com-plex'i-ty,
pẽr-plex'i-ty.
v: con-vex'i-ty.
Plus prexy, tea, etc.

EK'SIV-NES

fl: rē-flex'ive-ness.
pl: pẽr-plex'ive-ness.

EK'TȦ-B'L

sp: rēs-peç'tȧ-ble.
Cf. ek'ti-b'l.

EK'TĂR-I

n: neç'tăr-y.
Cf. ek'tŏ-ri.

EK'TED-NES

f: af-feç'ted-ness,
dis-af-feç'ted-ness,
in-feç'ted-ness.
j: ad-jeç'ted-ness,
dē-jeç'ted-ness.
p: sus-peç'ted-ness,
un-sus-peç'ted-ness.

EK'TI-B'L

f: af-feç'ti-ble, dē-feç'ti-ble,
ef-feç'ti-ble, in-dē-feç'ti-ble,
pẽr-feç'ti-ble.
fl: rē-fleç'ti-ble.
j: ob-jeç'tȧ-ble, rē-jeçt'ȧ-ble.
l: çol-leç'ti-ble, dē-leç'tȧ-ble,
in-dē-leç'tȧ-ble.
p: ex-peç'tȧ-ble, rēs-peç'tȧ-ble,
sus-peç'tȧ-ble.
r: cọr-reç'ti-ble, ē-reç'tȧ-ble.
s: dis-seç'ti-ble.
t: dē-teç'ti-ble.
Plus wrecked a bull, etc.

EK'TI-FĪ

j: ob-jeç'ti-fȳ.
r: reç'ti-fȳ.

EK'TI-KĂL

l: dī-ȧ-leç'ti-căl.
pl: ap-ō-pleç'ti-căl.

EK'TI-TŪD

n: sē-neç'ti-tūde.
r: reç'ti-tūde.

EK'TIV-LI

f: af-feç'tive-ly, dē-feç'tive-ly,
ef-feç'tive-ly, in-ef-feç'tive-ly,
in-feç'tive-ly, pẽr-feç'tive-ly,
rē-feç'tive-ly.

(Choose only one word out of each group)

fl: dē-fleç´tive-ly, in-fleç´tively,
ir-rē-fleç´tive-ly, rē-fleç´tive-ly,
un-rē-fleç´tive-ly.
j: in-jeç´tive-ly, ob-jeç´tive-ly,
rē-jeç´tive-ly, sub-jeç´tive-ly.
l: çol-leç´tive-ly, ē-leç´tive-ly,
neg-leç´tive-ly, reç-ŏl-leç´tive-ly,
sē-leç´tive-ly.
m: hū-meç´tive-ly.
n: çon-neç´tive-ly.
r: çor-reç´tive-ly, dī-reç´tive-ly,
ē-reç´tive-ly.
s: seç´tive-ly.
sp: cĭr-çum-speç´tive-ly,
in-speç´tive-ly,
in-trō-speç´tive-ly,
ir-rē-speç´tive-ly,
pĕr-speç´tive-ly,
prō-speç´tive-ly, rē-speç´tive-ly,
ret-rō-speç´tive-ly.
t: dē-teç´tive-ly, prō-teç´tive-ly.
v: in-veç´tive-ly.
Plus detective, Lee, etc.

EK´TIV-NES

f: dē-feç´tive-ness,
ef-feç´tive-ness,
in-ef-feç´tive-ness.
fl: rē-fleç´tive-ness.
j: ob-jeç´tive-ness,
sub-jeç´tive-ness.
l: çol-leç´tive-ness.
sp: prō-speç´tive-ness.
t: prō-teç´tive-ness.

EK´TŎ-RĂL

l: ē-leç´tŏ-răl.
p: peç´tŏ-răl.
r: reç´tŏ-răl.
s: seç´tŏ-răl.
t: prō-teç´tŏ-răl.
Plus Hector, Al, etc.

EK´TŌ-RĀT

l: ē-leç´tō-rāte.
r: di-reç´tō-rāte, reç´tō-rāte.
sp: ex-peç´tō-rāte.
t: prō-teç´tō-rāte.
Plus Hector ate *or* eight, etc.
Plus wrecked a rate, etc.

EK´TŎ-RI

f: rē-feç´tŏ-ry.
n: neç´tăr-y.
r: çor-reç´tŏ-ry, di-reç´tŏ-ry,
reç´tŏ-ry.
s: seç´tă-ry.
Plus rector, he, etc.

EK´TŪ-ĂL

f: ef-feç´tū-ăl, in-ef-feç´tū-ăl.
l: in-tel-leç´tū-ăl, leç´tū-ăl.
Cf. henpecked you all, etc.

EK´TŪR-ĂL

j: çon-jeç´tūr-ăl.
t: är-çhi-teç´tūr-ăl.
Plus lecture, Al, etc.
Cf. lecture all, etc.

EK´TŪR-ŨR

j: çon-jeç´tūr-ẽr.
l: leç´tūr-ẽr.
Plus lecture her, err *or* er, etc.

EK´Ū-LĂR

l: mō-leç´ū-lăr.
s: seç´ū-lăr.
sp: speç´ū-lăr.

EK´Ū-LĀT

p: peç´ū-lāte.
sp: speç´ū-lāte.
Plus wreck, you late, etc.

EK'Ū-TIV
EL'I-KĂL

fāte, fär, fåst, fall, finăl, cãre, at; mēte, prey, hẽr, met; pīne, marĭne, bĭrd, pĭn; nōte, mŏve, fŏr, atŏm, not; mọọn, book;

850

(Choose only one word out of each group)

EK'Ū-TIV

s: con-sec'ū-tive, ex-ec'ū-tive, sub-sec'ū-tive.

ĒL'Å-B'L

h: hēal'å-ble.
j: con-ġeal'å-ble.
p: peel'å-ble, rē-pēal'å-ble.
s: con-cēal'å-ble, in-con-cēal'å-ble.
v: rē-vēal'å-ble.
Plus steal a bull, etc.
Plus Venezuela bull, etc.

EL'Å-TIV

p: com-pel'lå-tive.
r: cor-rel'å-tive, rel'å-tive.

EL'Ē-GĀT

d: del'ē-gāte.
r: rel'ē-gāte.
Plus Kelly gate, etc.

EL'Ē-TŎN

sk: skel'ē-tŏn.
Cf. ġel'å-tin.
Plus smelly ton or tun, etc.
Cf. smell it on, etc.

EL'FISH-NESS

Vowel: el'fish-ness.
s: sel'fish-ness, un-sel'fish-ness.

Ē'LI-Å

Vowel: Ē'li-å.
b: lō-bē'li-å.
d: Bē-dē'li-å, Cor-dē'li-å, Dē'li-å, Fī-dē'li-å.
f: Ō-phē'li-å.
l: Lē'li-å.

m: Å-mē'li-å, Ċå-mē'li-å.
n: Cor-nē'li-å.
r: Åu-rē'li-å.
s: Ce-cē'li-å, Cē'li-å.
v: Vĭ'li-å.
Plus steely a, etc.
Cf. ēl'yå.

ĒL'I-ĂN

Vowel: Is-må-ēl'i-ăn.
d: Dēl'i-ăn.
f: Me"phis-tō-phēl'ē-ăn.
g: Hē-gēl'i-ăn.
gr: Min-grēl'i-ăn.
n: cär-nēl'i-ăn.
t: Ar"is-tō-tēl'i-ăn.
v: Mac"chi-å-vēl'i-ăn.
Plus steely an or Ann, etc.
Plus feel, Ian, etc.
Cf. ēl'yăn.

EL'I-ĂN

j: ē-van-ġel'i-ăn.
s: sel'i-ŏn.
w: Boṣ-wel'li-ăn, Crom-wel'li-ăn.
Plus smelly an or Ann, etc.
Plus smell, Ian, etc.
Cf. el'yăn, el'yun.

EL'I-B'L, EL'Å-B'L

d: del'i-ble, in-del'i-ble.
f: fel'lå-ble.
j: ġel'å-ble, in-ġel'å-ble.
p: com-pel'lå-ble, ex-pel'lå-ble.
sp: spel'lå-ble.
t: tel'lå-ble.
Plus umbrella bull, etc.
Plus tell a bull, etc.

EL'I-KĂL

b: bel'li-căl.
h: hel'i-căl.

(Choose only one word out of each group)

j: an-ġel′i-c̦ăl, ē-van-ġel′i-c̦ăl.
p: pel′li-c̦le.
Plus jelly, Cal, etc.
Plus bellic, Al, etc.

Ē′LI-ŎN

f: a̍-phē′li-ŏn (-fē′).
h: per′i-hē′li-ŏn.
m: c̦ha̍-mē′lē-ŏn.
th: an-thē′li-ŏn.
Plus freely on, an *or* Ann, etc.

EL′ISH-ING

b: em-bel′lish-ing.
r: rel′ish-ing.

EL′ISH-MENT

b: em-bel′lish-ment.
r: rel′ish-ment.
Plus hellish meant, etc.

Ē′LI-US

b: Si-bē′li-us.
d: Dē′li-us.
n: C̦or-ne′li-us.
r: A̍u-rē′li-us.
Plus genteelly us, etc.
Cf. hē′li-ŏs.
Cf. ēl′yus.

EL′Ō-EST

b: bel′lōw-est.
m: mel′lōw-est.
y: yel′lōw-est.

EL′Ō-ING

b: bel′lōw-ing.
ch: cel′lō-ing (chel′).
m: mel′lōw-ing.
y: yel′lōw-ing.

EL′ŎN-I

f: fel′ŏn-y.
m: mel′ŏn-y.
Plus watermelon, he, etc.

EL′Ō-ŪR

b: bel′lōw-ẽr.
ch: cel′lō-ẽr (chel′).
m: mel′lōw-ẽr.
y: yel′lōw-ẽr.
Plus good-fellow her, err *or* er, etc.

EL′THI-EST

h: heal′thi-est.
st: steal′thi-est.
w: weal′thi-est.

EL′THI-LI

h: heal′thi-ly.
st: steal′thi-ly.
w: weal′thi-ly.
Plus wealthy lea *or* Lee, etc.

EL′THI-ŪR

h: heal′thi-ẽr.
st: steal′thi-ẽr.
w: weal′thi-ẽr.
Plus wealthy her, err *or* er, etc.

EL′TŪR-I

sh: shel′tẽr-y.
sm: smel′tẽr-y.
Plus swelter, he.

EL′TŪR-ING

sh: shel′tẽr-ing.
w: wel′tẽr-ing.
Plus felt her ring, etc.
Plus smelter ring, etc.

(Choose only one word out of each group)

EL′TŪR-ŪR

sh: shel′tēr-ēr.
w: wel′tēr-ēr.
Plus shelter her, etc.

EL′Ū-LĂR

s: cel′lū-lăr, in-tēr-cel′lū-lăr, ūn-i-cel′lū-lăr.
st: stel′lū-lăr.

EL′ŪR-I

s: cel′ēr-y.
st: stel′lăr-y.
Plus seller, he, etc.

EL′US-LI

j: jeal′ous-ly.
z: ōv-ēr-zeal′ous-ly, zeal′ous-ly.

ĒM′Ȧ-B'L

d: rē-deem′ȧ-ble.
dr: drēam′ȧ-ble.
t: es-teem′ȧ-ble.
Plus redeem a bull, etc.

Ē′MȦ-TIST

sk(sc̣): sc̣hēm′ȧ-tist.
th: thēm′ȧ-tist.

EM′Ȧ-TIST

bl: em-blem′ȧ-tist.
r: thē-ō-rem′ȧ-tist.

EM′BŪR-ING

m: dis-mem′bēr-ing, mem′bēr-ing, rē-mem′bēr-ing, un-rē-mem′bēr-ing.
s: Dē-cem′bēr-ing.
v: Nō-vem′bēr-ing.
Plus ember ring, etc.

Ē′MI-Ȧ

f: Eū-phē′mi-ȧ.
h: Bō-hē′mi-ȧ.
k(c̣): leu-kē′mi-ȧ.
n: ȧ-nē′mi-ȧ.
r: ū-rē′mi-ȧ.
Plus schemy a, etc.

Ē′MI-ĂL

d: ac̣-ȧ-dē′mi-ăl, en-dē′mi-ăl, vin-dē′mi-ăl.
gr: grē′mi-ăl.
r: ū-rē′mi-ăl.
Plus dreamy, Al, etc.

Ē′MI-ĂN

d: ac̣-ȧ-dē′mi-ăn.
h: Bō-hē′mi-ăn.

EM′I-KĂL

d: ac̣-ȧ-dem′i-c̣ăl, en-dem′i-c̣ăl, ep-i-dem′i-c̣ăl.
k(c̣): al-c̣hem′i-c̣ăl, c̣hem′i-c̣ăl, el-ec̣-trō-c̣hem′i-c̣ăl.
l: pō-lem′i-c̣ăl.
Plus gemmy, Cal, etc.

ĒM′I-LI

b: bēam′i-ly.
dr: drēam′i-ly.
kr: c̣rēam′i-ly.
st: stēam′i-ly.
Plus steamy lea *or* Lee, etc.

EM′I-NĂL

f: fem′i-năl.
j: ġem′i-năl.
s: sem′i-năl.

EM′I-NĀT

f: ef-fem′i-nāte.
j: ġem′i-nāte, in-ġem′i-nāte.

(Choose only one word out of each group)

s: dis-sem′i-nāte, in-sem′i-nāte, sem′i-nāte.
Plus gemmy, Nate, etc.

ĒM'I-NES

dr: drēam′i-ness.
kr: çrēam′i-ness.
st: stēam′i-ness.

Ē'MI-ŎN

Vowel: prō-oē′mi-ŏn.
th: an-thē′mi-ŏn.
Cf. ē′mi-ăn.
Plus steamy on, etc.

ĒM'I-ŬR

b: bēam′i-ẽr.
dr: drēam′i-ẽr.
kr: çrēam′i-ẽr.
pr: prēm′i-ẽr.
Plus steamy, err, er *or* her, etc.

EM'NI-TI

d: in-dem′ni-ty.
l: sō-lem′ni-ty.

EM'Ō-NĒ

n: an-em′ō-nē.
p: Ag-ȧ-pem′ō-nē.
s: Geth-sem′ȧ-nē.
Plus lemon, he, etc.

EM'ŎR-ĂL

f: ē-phem′ẽr-ăl, fem′ŏr-ăl.
n: nem′ŏr-ăl.
Plus condemner, Al, etc.
Plus condemn her, Al, etc.

EM'ŎR-I

Vowel: Em′ẽr-y, Em′ŏr-y.
m: mem′ŏr-y.
Plus tremor, he, etc.

EM'PŎR-ŬR, EM'PŬR-ĒR

Vowel: em′pẽr-ŏr.
t: tem′pẽr-ēr.
Plus sic semper, err, er *or* her, etc.

EM'Ū-LENT

t: tem′ū-lent.
tr: trem′ū-lent.
Plus Clem, you lent, etc.

EM'Ū-LUS

Vowel: em′ū-lous.
tr: trem′ū-lous.

EM'ŨR-ĂLD

Vowel: em′ẽr-ăld.
f: ȧ-phem′ẽr-ălled.

ĒM'ŨR-I

dr: drēam′ẽr-y.
kr: çrēam′ẽr-y.
Plus schemer, he, etc.
Cf. we, Murray, etc.

EM'ŨR-I

j: ġem′mẽr-y.
Cf. em′ŏr-i.

EM'ŨR-IST

f: ē-phem′ẽr-ist.
h: eū-hem′ẽr-ist.
Plus condemn her wrist, etc.

Ē'NȦ-B'L

m: ȧ-mē′nȧ-ble.
v: çon-vē′nȧ-ble.
Plus screen a bull, etc.
Plus hyena bull, etc.

(Choose only one word out of each group)

EN'Ă-RI

d: den'ă-ry.
h: hen'nẽr-y.
s: dē-cen'nă-ry.
t: cen-ten'ă-ry.
Plus tenner, he, etc.

EN'Ȧ-TŎR

j: prō-g̣en'i-tŏr.
s: sen'ȧ-tŏr.
Plus rennet, or, etc.
Plus tenet err *or* er, etc.

END'I-B'L

f: dē-fend'ȧ-ble.
h: c̣om-prē-hend'i-ble,
un-c̣om-prē-hend'i-ble.
l: lend'ȧ-ble.
m: ȧ-mend'ȧ-ble,
c̣om-mend'ȧ-ble, mend'ȧ-ble,
re-c̣om-mend'ȧ-ble.
p: dē-pend'ȧ-ble.
r: rend'i-ble.
s: as-cend'ȧ-ble, dēs-cend'ȧ-ble,
un-as-cend'ȧ-ble.
t: ex-tend'i-ble.
v: in-vend'i-ble, vend'i-ble.
Plus vend a bull, etc.
Plus hä-ci-en'dȧ bull, etc.

END'EN-SI

p: dē-pend'en-cy,
ē-qui-pend'en-cy*,
im-pend'en-cy,
in-dē-pend'en-cy,
in″tẽr-dē-pend'en-cy.
s: as-cend'en-cy,
tran-scend'en-cy.
spl: rē-splend'en-cy.
t: at-tend'en-cy, in-tend'en-cy,
sū-pẽr-in-tend'en-cy, ten'den-cy.
Plus dependence, he, etc.

END'I-US

p: c̣om-pend'i-ous.
s: in-cend'i-ous.

END'LES-LI

Vowel: end'less-ly.
fr: friend'less-ly.
Plus end, Leslie, etc.
Plus endless, he, etc.

END'LES-NES

Vowel: end'less-ness.
fr: friend'less-ness.

EN'DŪR-EST

j: en-g̣en'dẽr-est*.
r: ren'dẽr-est*, sūr-ren'dẽr-est*.
sl: slen'dẽr-est.
t: ten'dẽr-est.
Plus mend her rest, etc.
Plus defender rest, etc.
Plus friend arrest, etc.
Plus mend a rest, etc.

EN'DŪR-ING

j: en-g̣en'dẽr-ing, g̣en'dẽr-ing.
r: ren'dẽr-ing, sūr-ren'dẽr-ing.
t: ten'dẽr-ing.
Plus mend her ring, etc.
Plus mend a ring, etc.
Plus tender ring, etc.

EN'DŪR-LI

sl: slen'dẽr-ly.
t: ten'dẽr-ly.
Plus gender, Lee, etc.

EN'DŪR-NES

sl: slen'dẽr-ness.
t: ten'dẽr-ness.

(Choose only one word out of each group)

EN′DŬR-ŪR

j: en-ġen′dĕr-ēr.
r: ren′dĕr-ēr, sŭr-ren′dĕr-ēr.
sl: slen′dĕr-ēr.
t: ten′dĕr-ēr.
Plus surrender her, etc.

EN′DUS-LI

(NOT en′jus-li).
m: trē-men′dous-ly.
p: stū-pen′dous-ly.

EN′Ē-SIS

j: ab″i-ō-ġen′ē-sis, bī-ō-ġen′ē-sis,
eç-tō-ġen′ē-sis, eū-ġen′ē-sis,
ġen′ē-sis, het″ĕr-ō-ġen′ē-sis,
hō-mō-ġen′ē-sis, on-tō-ġen′ē-sis,
ọr-gan-ō-ġen′ē-sis,
pal-in-ġen′ē-sis, pan-ġen′ē-sis,
par-à-ġen′ē-sis,
pär-then-ō-ġen′ē-sis,
phȳ-lō-ġen′ē-sis,
phō-tō-gen′ē-sis, pol-y-ġen′ē-sis,
psȳ-çhō-ġen′ē-sis,
xen-ō-ġen′ē-sis (zen-).
r: pà-ren′ē-sis.
Plus any sis, etc.
Cf. tennis's, etc.
Cf. menaces, etc.

EN′ET-ING

j: jen′net-ing.
r: ren′net-ing.

Ē′NI-À

d: gär-dē′ni-à.
fr: sçhiz-ō-phrē′ni-à.
j: Eū-ġē′ni-à.
m: Är-mē′ni-à.
th: neū-rōs-thē′ni-à,
Pär-thē′ni-à.

z: Xē′ni-à (zē′).
Plus Sweeny, a, etc.

Ē′NI-ĂL

j: çon-ġē′ni-ăl, ġē′ni-ăl,
prī-mi-ġē′ni-ăl,
un-çon-ġē′ni-ăl.
m: dē-mēs′ni-ăl (-mē′), mē′ni-ăl.
v: vē′ni-ăl.
Plus meany, Al, etc.

EN′I-ĂL

Vowel: bī-en′ni-ăl, trī-en′ni-ăl.
kw: quin-quen′ni-ăl.
l: mil-len′i-ăl.
r: pĕr-en′ni-ăl, quäd-ren′ni-ăl.
s: dē-cen′ni-ăl, dū″ō-dē-cen′ni-ăl,
vī-cen′ni-ăl.
t: cen-ten′ni-ăl, oç-ten′ni-ăl,
sep-ten′ni-ăl.
v: nō-ven′ni-ăl.
Plus penny, Al, etc.

Ē′NI-ĂN

f: Fē′ni-ăn.
l: Hel-lē′ni-ăn, Mad-ri-lē′ni-ăn.
m: Är-mē′ni-ăn,
Es-trē-mē′ni-ăn.
r: Cȳ-rē′ni-ăn.
th: Á-thē′ni-ăn, Rú-thē′ni-ăn.
Plus Selene, an *or* Ann, etc.
Plus mean, Ian, etc.

ĒN′I-ENS

l: lēn′i-ence.
v: çon-vēn′i-ence,
in-çon-vēn′i-ence.
Cf. ēn′yens.

(Choose only one word out of each group)

ĒN'I-ENT

l: lēn'i-ent.
v: ad-vēn'i-ent, con-vēn'i-ent,
in-con-vēn'i-ent, in-tēr-vēn'i-ent,
in-trō-vēn'i-ent,
sūp-ēr-vēn'i-ent.
Cf. ēn'yent.

EN'I-FǪRM

p: pen'ni-fǫrm.
t: an-ten'ni-fǫrm.
Plus penny form, etc.

EN'I-KĂL

m: cat″ē-chū-men'i-căl,
ē-cū-men'i-căl.
r: sī-ren'i-căl.
s: är-sen'i-căl, scen'i-căl (sen').
Plus Hellenic, Al, etc.

EN'I-TI

l: len'i-ty.
m: ȧ-men'i-ty.
r: sē-ren'i-ty, ter-ren'i-ty.
s: ob-scen'i-ty.
Plus penny tea, etc.
Plus pen it, he, etc.

EN'I-TIV

j: gen'i-tive, prī-mō-gen'i-tive.
l: len'i-tive.
spl: splen'i-tive.

EN'I-TŪD

l: len'i-tūde.
pl: plen'i-tūde.
r: sē-ren'i-tūde.
Plus men etude, etc.

ĒN'I-UM

l: sē-lēn'i-um.
s: prō-scēn'i-um (-sēn').
z: xēn'i-um (zēn').

ĒN'I-US

j: ex-trȧ-ġēn'ē-ous, ġēn'i-us,
het″ẽr-ō-ġēn'i-ous,
hō-mō-ġēn'i-ous, in-ġēn'i-ous,
nī-trō-ġēn'i-ous,
prī-mi-ġēn'i-ous.
l: se-lēn'i-ous.
m: pẽr-gȧ-mēn'ē-ous.
s: är-sēn'i-ous.
Plus genie us, etc.

EN'I-ZŎN

b: ben'i-ṣǒn.
d: den'i-zen, en-den'i-zen.
v: ven'i-ṣǒn.
Cf. penny, son *or* sun, etc.

EN'SȦ-B'L

d: con-den'sȧ-ble.
Cf. en'si-b'l.

EN'SȦ-RI

p: dis-pen'sȧ-ry.
Cf. en'sō-ri.

EN'SȦ-TIV

d: con-den'sȧ-tive.
f: dē-fen'sȧ-tive.
p: com-pen'sȧ-tive,
dis-pen'sȧ-tive, pen'sȧ-tive.
s: in-sen'si-tive, sen'si-tive.
t: in-ten'si-tive.

EN'SHÅ-RI

d: re-ṣi-den'tiȧ-ry.
t: pen-i-ten'tiȧ-ry.

857 ūse, bu̲ll, brŭte, tûrn, up; crȳ, myth; c̲at, mac̲hine, ace, church, c̲hord; ġem, añger, (Fr.) boṅ, as̲; THis, thin; azure

EN′SHI-ĀT
ENT′A̓-B′L

(Choose only one word out of each group)

EN′SHI-ĀT

s: es-sen′ti-āte, lī-cen′ti-āte.
t: pō-ten′ti-āte.
Plus then she ate *or* eight, etc.

EN′SHI-ENT

s: as-sen′ti-ent, c̲on-sen′ti-ent, dis-sen′ti-ent, in-sen′ti-ent, prē-sen′ti-ent, sen′ti-ent.

EN′SHUN-ĂL

s: as-cen′sion-ăl, dē-scen′sion-ăl.
t: ex-ten′sion-ăl, in-ten′tion-ăl.
v: c̲on-ven′tion-ăl, prē-ven′tion-ăl.
Plus mention, Al, etc.

EN′SHUN-IST

s: as-cen′sion-ist, rē-cen′sion-ist.
t: ex-ten′sion-ist.

EN′SHUS-NES

Vowel: c̲on-sci-en′tious-ness (-shi-).
s: lī-cen′tious-ness.
t: c̲on-ten′tious-ness, prē-ten′tious-ness.

EN′SI-B′L

d: c̲on-den′sà-ble (-b′l), in-c̲on-den′sà-ble.
f: dē-fen′si-ble, in-dē-fen′si-ble.
h: c̲om-prē-hen′si-ble, de-prē-hen′si-ble, in-c̲om-prē-hen′si-ble, rep-rē-hen′si-ble.
p: dis-pen′sà-ble, in-dis-pen′sà-ble, sus-pen′si-ble.
s: in-sen′si-ble, sen′si-ble, sub-sen′si-ble.
t: dis-ten′si-ble, ex-ten′si-ble, os-ten′si-ble, ten′si-ble.

EN′SI-KĂL

r: fō-ren′si-c̲ăl.
s: non-sen′si-c̲ăl.

EN′SI-TI

d: c̲on-den′si-ty, den′si-ty.
m: im-men′si-ty.
p: prō-pen′si-ty.
t: in-ten′si-ty, ten′si-ty.
Plus men see tea, etc.

EN′SIV-NES

f: in-of-fen′sive-ness, of-fen′sive-ness.
h: c̲om-prē-hen′sive-ness.
p: ex-pen′sive-ness, pen′sive-ness.
t: ex-ten′sive-ness, in-ten′sive-ness.

ENS′LES-LI

f: dē-fense′less-ly.
s: sense′less-ly.
Plus hence, Leslie, etc.
Plus senseless, Lee *or* lea, etc.

ENS′LES-NES

f: dē-fense′less-ness.
s: sense′less-ness.

EN′SŌ-RI

f: dē-fen′sō-ry.
h: prē-hen′sō-ry, re-prē-hen′sō-ry.
p: dis-pen′sà-ry, sus-pen′sō-ry.
s: in-cen′sō-ry, sen′sō-ry.
t: os-ten′sō-ry.

ENT′A̓-B′L

kw(qu): frē-quent′à-ble.
m: fẽr-ment′à-ble.

EN'TÅ-K'L
EN'TÅ-TIVE
fāte, fär, fåst, fall, finăl, cāre, at; mēte, prey, hēr, met; pīne,
marīne, bîrd, pin; nōte, mŏve, fŏr, atŏm, not; mọọn, book; **858**

(Choose only one word out of each group)

r: rent'á-ble.

v: in-vent'i-ble, prē-vent'á-ble.

z: prē-şent'á-ble,
rep-rē-şent'á-ble.

Plus sent a bull, etc.

EN'TÅ-K'L

p: pen'tá-ċle.

t: ten'tá-ċle.

EN'TĂL-I

d: aċ-ci-den'tăl-ly,
in-ci-den'tăl-ly,
tran-scen-den'tăl-ly.

m: ex-per-i-men'tăl-ly,
fun-dá-men'tăl-ly,
in-strú-men'tăl-ly,
sen-ti-men'tăl-ly.

Plus rental lea *or* Lee, etc.

Plus sent alee, etc.

EN'TĂL-IST

Vowel: O-ri-en'tăl-ist.

d: Oċ-ci-den'tăl-ist,
tran-scen-den'tăl-ist.

m: ex-per-i-men'tăl-ist,
fun-dá-men'tăl-ist,
in-strú-men'tăl-ist,
sen-ti-men'tăl-ist.

Plus sent a list, etc.

Plus rental list, etc.

EN'TAL-ĪZ

Vowel: O-ri-en'tăl-ize.

m: ex-per-i-men'tăl-īze,
sen-ti-men'tăl-ize.

Plus monumental lies, etc.

Plus monumental eyes, etc.

EN'TĂL-IZM

Vowel: Ō-ri-en'tăl-işm.

d: aċ-ci-den'tăl-işm,
tran-scen-den'tăl-işm.

m: el-ē-men'tăi-işm,
sen-ti-men'tăl-işm.

EN'TĂL-NES

d: aċ-ci-den'tăl-ness,
in-ci-den'tăl-ness.

j: ġen'tle-ness, un-ġen'tle-ness.

m: fun-dá-men'tăl-ness,
in-strú-men'tăl-ness,
sen-ti-men'tăl-ness.

EN'TÅ-RI

d: aċ-ci-den'tá-ry, den'tá-ry.

m: al-i-men'tá-ry,
ċom-plē-men'tá-ry,
ċom-pli-men'tá-ry,
el-ē-men'tá-ry, fil-á-men'tá-ry,
in-strú-men'tá-ry,
in-teg-ū-men'tá-ry,
pär-li-á-men'tá-ry,
pig-men'tá-ry, rúd-i-men'tá-ry,
saċ-rá-men'tá-ry,
sed-i-men'tá-ry,
teg-ū-men'tá-ry,
ten-ē-men'tá-ry,
tes-tá-men'tá-ry,
un-pär-li-á-men'tá-ry.

s: plá-cen'tá-ry.

Plus enter, he, etc.

EN'TÅ-TIVE

kw: frē-quen'tá-tive.

m: al-i-men'tá-tive,
är-gū-men'tá-tive,
aug-men'tá-tive,
ċom-men'tá-tive,
ċom-pli-men'tá-tive,
ex-per-i-men'tá-tive,
fēr-men'tá-tive.

t: prē-ten'tá-tive, ten'tá-tive.

v: prē-ven'tá-tive.

(Choose only one word out of each group)

z: mis-rep-rē-sen'ta-tive,
prē-ṣen'ta-tive.
re-prē-ṣen'ta-tive.

EN'TI-KĂL

d: den'ti-çle, ī-den'ti-çăl.
th: a̤u-then'ti-çăl.
v: çon-ven'ti-çăl, çon-ven'ti-cle.
Plus twenty, Cal, etc.

EN'TI-KŪL

d: den'ti-çūle.
l: len'ti-çūle.

EN'TI-MENT

s: sen'ti-ment.
z: prē-ṣen'ti-ment.
Plus Henty meant, etc.

EN'TI-NĂL

d: den'ti-năl.
s: sen'ti-năl.
Plus San Quentin, Al, etc.

EN'TI-TI

Vowel: en'ti-ty, non-en'ti-ty.
d: ī-den'ti-ty.
Plus meant it, he, etc.
Plus plenty tea, etc.

EN'TIV-NES

m: al-i-men'tive-ness.
t: at-ten'tive-ness,
in-at-ten'tive-ness,
rē-ten'tive-ness.
v: in-ven'tive-ness.

EN'TŪ-ĂL

s: aç-cen'tū-ăl.
v: ad-ven'tū-ăl, çon-ven'tū-ăl,
ē-ven'tū-ăl.
Plus sent you, Al, etc.

EN'TŪ-ĀT

s: aç-cen'tū-āte.
v: ē-ven'tū-āte.
Plus meant you ate *or* eight, etc.

EN'TUS-LI

m: mō-men'tous-ly.
t: por-ten'tous-ly.
Plus sent us, Lee, etc.

EN'TUS-NES

m: mō-men'tous-ness.
t: por-ten'tous-ness.

EN'Ū-ĂNT

j: ġen'ū-ănt*.
t: at-ten'ū-ănt.
Plus then, you ant *or* aunt, etc.

EN'Ū-ĀT

t: at-ten'ū-āte, ex-ten'ū-āte,
ten'ū-āte.
Plus then you ate *or* eight, etc.

EN'ŨR-ĀT

j: dē-ġen'ēr-āte, ġen'ēr-āte,
in-ġen'ēr-āte, prō-ġen'ēr-āte,
rē-ġen'ēr-āte.
t: in-ten'ēr-āte.
v: ven'ēr-āte.
Plus pen her, ate *or* eight, etc.
Plus tenor ate *or* eight, etc.

ĒN'ŨR-I

d: dēan'ēr-y.
gr: green'ēr-y.
pl: plē'na̤-ry.
s: scēn'ēr-y (sēn').
sh: ma̤-çhin'ēr-y (-shēn').
Plus cleaner, he, etc.

EN'ÛR-I
ÊR'FŬL-NES

fāte, fär, fȧst, fall, finăl, cāre, at; mēte, prĕy, hẽr, met; pīne,
marĭne, bĭrd, pĭn; nōte, mŏve, fŏr, atŏm, not; mo͝on, book;   **860**

(Choose only one word out of each group)

EN'ÛR-I

p: pen'ūr-y.
Plus Then you're he, etc.

EN'ÛR-I

d: den'ȧ-ry.
h: hen'nĕr-y.
s: dē-cen'nȧ-ry, sen'ȧ-ry*.
v: ven'ẽr-y.
Plus tenor, he, etc.
Plus ten *or* he, etc.

EN'Ū-US

j: dis-in-ġen'ū-ŏus, in-ġen'ū-ŏus.
str: stren'ū-ŏus.
t: ten'ū-ŏus.

ĒN'YEN-SI

l: lēn'ien-cy.
v: con-vēn'ien-cy,
in-con-vēn'ien-cy.
Plus mean yen, see?, etc.

ĒP'I-LI

kr: creep'i-ly.
sl: sleep'i-ly.
Plus weepy, Lee *or* lea, etc.
Plus steep alee, etc.

ĒP'I-NES

kr: creep'i-ness.
sl: sleep'i-ness.
st: steep'i-ness.
w: weep'i-ness.

EP'TȦ-B'L

s: ac-cep'tȧ-ble, dē-cep'ti-ble,
im-pẽr-cep'ti-ble,
in-sus-cep'ti-ble, pẽr-cep'ti-ble,
rē-cep'ti-ble, sus-cep'ti-ble.
Plus kept a bull, etc.

EP'TI-KĂL

s: an-ti-sep'ti-căl, ȧ-sep'ti-căl,
rē-cep'tȧ-cle, sep'ti-căl.
sk(sc): scep'ti-căl.

EP'TIV-NES

s: dē-cep'tive-ness,
rē-cep'tive-ness,
sus-cep'tive-ness.

EP'ÛR-US

l: lep'ẽr-ous.
str: ob-strep'ẽr-ous,
pẽr-strep'ẽr-ous*, strep'ẽr-ous.
Plus pepper us, etc.

ER'ĂN-SI

Vowel: ab-er'răn-cy, er'răn-cy,
in-er'răn-cy.

ER'Ȧ-PI

th: bal"nē-ō-ther'ȧ-py,
hȳ-drō-ther'ȧ-py,
kin-ē-si-ther'ȧ-py,
phō-tō-ther'ȧ-py,
rā"di-ō-ther'ȧ-py.

ĒR'FŬL-I

ch: cheer'ful-ly.
f: fēar'ful-ly.
t: tēar'ful-ly.
Plus smear fully, etc.
Plus tearful, he, etc.

ĒR'FŬL-NES

ch: cheer'fŭl-ness.
f: fēar'fŭl-ness.
t: tēar'fŭl-ness.

861

ūse, bṵll, brûte, tŭrn, up; crȳ, myth; c̣at, mac̣hine, ace, church, c̣hord; ġem, aṅger, (Fr.) boṅ, aṣ; THis, thin; aẓure

ĒR′I-Ȧ
ER′I-KĂL

(Choose only one word out of each group)

ĒR′I-Ȧ, Ē′RI-Ȧ

b: Lī-bē′ri-ȧ.
j: Al-ġē′ri-ȧ, Ē-ġē′ri-ȧ, Nī-ġē′ri-ȧ.
k: Val-ky′ri-ȧ.
p: hes-pē′ri-ȧ.
t: hys-tē′ri-ȧ, ic̣-tē′ri-ȧ*, wis-tē′ri-ȧ.
th: diph-thē′ri-ȧ, el-eū-thē′ri-ȧ, Ē-thē′ri-ȧ.
Plus weary a, etc.

ĒR′I-ĂL, Ē′RI-ĂL

Vowel: ā-ēr′i-ăl.
d: sī-dē′ri-ăl.
f: fē′ri-ăl.
j: man-ȧ-gēr′i-ăl.
n: fū-nē′rē-ăl, ma-nē′rē-ăl.
p: im-pē′ri-ăl.
s: cē′rē-ăl, rhī-nō-cē′ri-ăl (rī-), sē′ri-ăl.
t: är-tē′ri-ăl, maġ-is-tē′ri-ăl, mȧ-tē′ri-ăl, min-is-tē′ri-ăl, mon-ăs-tē′ri-ăl, pres-by-tē′ri-ăl.
th: ē-thē′ri-ăl.
z: vi-ziēr′i-ăl (-zēr′).
Plus weary, Al, etc.

ĒR′I-ĂN

Vowel: ā-ēr′i-ăn, Pī-ēr′i-ăn.
b: Celt-i-bēr′i-ăn, Ī-bēr′i-ăn, Sī-bēr′i-ăn.
d: Ab-dēr′i-ăn.
f: Lū-ci-fēr′i-ăn.
j: Al-ġēr′i-ăn.
k: Val-kyr′i-ăn.
l: Kep-lēr′i-ăn, va-lēr′i-ăn.
m: Cim-mēr′i-ăn.
p: Hes-pēr′i-ăn, Shākes-pēar′ē-ăn, Shākes-pēar′i-ăn.

s: Spen-cēr′i-ăn, Spen-sēr′i-ăn.
st: phal-an-stēr′i-ăn.
t: Pres-by-tēr′i-ăn.
th: Wẽr-thēr′i-ăn.
Plus weary an or Ann, etc.

ER′I-DĒZ

Vowel: Pī-er′i-dēṣ.
p: Hes-per′i-dēṣ.
t: An-ter′i-dēṣ.
Plus buried ease or he's, etc.

ĒR′I-EST

Vowel: eer′i-est.
b: beer′i-est.
bl: blēar′i-est.
ch: cheer′i-est.
dr: drēar′i-est.
t: tēar′i-est.
w: wēar′i-est.

ER′I-EST

b: bur′i-est*.
f: fer′ri-est*.
m: mer′ri-est.

ĒR′I-ĒZ

j: c̣on-ġēr′i-ēṣ.
s: sēr′i-ēṣ*.
Plus dreary ease, etc.

ER′I-ING

b: ber′ry-ing, bur′y-ing.
f: fer′ry-ing.
hw: wher′ry-ing.

ER′I-KĂL

f: at-mos-pher′i-c̣ăl.
kl: c̣ler′i-c̣ăl.
m: c̣hī-mer′i-c̣ăl, nū-mer′i-c̣ăl.
s: rhī-nō-cer′i-c̣ăl (rī-).

ĒR′I-LI
ER′I-TI
fāte, fär, fȧst, fạll, finăl, cãre, at; mēte, prey, hẽr, met; pīne,
marïne, bĩrd, pin; nōte, mŏve, fọr, atŏm, not; mọọn, book;

862

(Choose only one word out of each group)

sf: hē″li-ō-spher′i-çăl,
hē-li-spher′i-çăl, spher′i-çăl,
spher′i-çle.
t: ȧ-lix-i-ter′i-çăl,
çlī-maç-ter′i-çăl, es-ō-ter′i-çăl,
ex-ō-ter′i-çăl, hys-ter′i-çăl,
phȳ-laç-ter′i-çăl.
Plus merry, Cal, etc.

ĒR′I-LI

Vowel: eer′i-ly.
ch: cheer′i-ly.
dr: drēar′i-ly.
w: wēar′i-ly.
Plus dreary lea or Lee, etc.
Plus drear alee, etc.

ER′I-LI

m: mer′ri-ly.
v: ver′i-ly.
Plus cherry, Lee or lea, etc.

ER′I-MAN

f: fer′ry-man.
hw: wher′ry-man.
m: Mer′ri-man.
Plus cemetery man, etc.

ER′I-MENT

m: mer′ri-ment.
Cf. ũr′i-ment.
Plus Kerry meant, etc.

ĒR′I-NES

Vowel: eer′i-ness.
b: beer′i-ness.
bl: blēar′i-ness.
dr: drēar′i-ness.
t: tēar′i-ness.
w: wēar′i-ness.

ĒR′I-ŎN

l: al-lēr′i-ŏn.
p: Hȳ-pēr′i-ŏn.
t: çrī-tēr′i-ŏn.
Cf. ēr′i-ăn.
Plus veery on, etc.

ĒR′I-ŎR

f: in-fēr′i-ŏr.
p: sū-pēr′i-ŏr.
t: an-tēr′i-ŏr, ex-tēr′i-ŏr,
in-tēr′i-ŏr, pos-tēr′i-ŏr,
ul-tēr′i-ŏr.
Cf. ēr′i-ūr.
Plus peri, or, etc.

ER′ISH-ING

ch: cher′ish-ing.
p: per′ish-ing, un-per′ish-ing.

ER′IT-ED

f: fer′ret-ed.
h: dis-her′it-ed, dis-in-her′it-ed,
in-her′it-ed.
m: ē-mer′it-ed, mer′it-ed.
Cf. tũr′ret-ed.
Plus mer′it, Ed, etc.

ER′I-TI

j: lē-ġer′i-ty.
l: cē-ler′i-ty.
m: tē-mer′i-ty.
p: as-per′i-ty, pros-per′i-ty.
s: in-sin-cer′i-ty, prō-cer′i-ty,
sin-cer′i-ty.
t: am″bi-dex-ter′i-ty,
ạus-ter′i-ty, dex-ter′i-ty,
in-dex-ter′i-ty, pos-ter′i-ty.
v: sē-ver′i-ty, ver′i-ty.
Plus merit, he, etc.
Plus merry tea, etc.

(Choose only one word out of each group)

ER′IT-ING

f: fer′ret-ing.
h: in-her′it-ing.
m: mer′it-ing.

Ē′RI-UM

t: ac̨-ro-tē′ri-um,
ap″ō-dȳ-tē′ri-um.
th: dī-nō-thē′ri-um,
meg-a̍-thē′ri-um,
pal″ē-ō-thē′ri-um,
tī-tan-ō-thē′ri-um.
Plus weary 'em, etc.

ER′I-ŪR

Vowel: eer′i-ēr.
b: beer′i-ēr.
bl: blēar′i-ēr, bleer′i-ēr.
ch: cheer′i-ēr.
dr: drēar′i-ēr.
t: tēar′i-ēr.
w: wēar′i-ēr.
Cf. ēr-i-ŏr.
Plus weary her, err *or* er, etc.

ER′I-ŪR

b: ber′ri-ēr, bur′i-ēr.
m: mer′ri-ēr.
t: ter′ri-ēr.
Plus bury her, err *or* er, etc.

Ē′RI-US, ER′I-US

d: sī-dēr′i-ous.
p: im-pēr′i-ous.
s: cēr′ē-ous, cēr′ē-us, sēr′i-ous.
t: del-ē-tēr′i-ous, mys-tēr′i-ous.
th: ē-thēr′i-ŏus.
Plus weary us, etc.

ER′LES-NES

ch: cheer′less-ness.
f: fēar′less-ness.
p: peer′less-ness.
t: tēar′less-ness.

ER′Ō-GĀT

t: in-ter′rō-gāte.
Cf. ūr′ō-gāte.

ER′YĂL-IST

p: im-pēr′iăl-ist.
t: im-ma̍-tēr′iăl-ist,
ma̍-tēr′iăl-ist.
Plus material list, etc.

ER′YĂL-IZM

p: im-pēr′iăl-işm.
t: im-ma̍-tēr′iăl-işm,
ma̍-tēr′iăl-işm.

ĒS′Á-B'L

kr: c̨rēas′a̍-ble.
l: rē-lēas′a̍-ble.
p: pēac′a̍-ble, piēce′i-ble.
Plus fleece a bull, etc.

ES′Á-RI

f: c̨on-fes′sa̍-ry, prò-fes′sŏ-ry.
p: pes′sa̍-ry.
s: in-tēr-ces′sŏ-ry, su̧c̨-ces′sa̍-ry.
Plus successor, he, etc.

Ē′SEN-SI

d: dē′cen-cy, in-dē′cen-cy.
r: rē′cen-cy.
Plus Gleason, see, etc.

(Choose only one word out of each group)

ES'EN-SI

Vowel: aç-qui-es'cen-cy,
quī-es'cen-cy.

b: er-ū-bes'cen-cy,
pū-bes'cen-cy.

d: in-çan-des'cen-cy,
rē-çrù-des'cen-cy.

j: tûr-ġes'cen-cy.

kr: ex-çres'cen-cy.

kw(qu): li-ques'cen-cy.

l: ad-ō-les'cen-cy,
al-kà-les'cen-cy.
çon-và-les'cen-cy,
in-çà-les'cen-cy.

r: ef-flọr-es'cen-cy.

s: à-ces'cen-cy.

t: del-i-tes'cen-cy.

v: dē-fẽr-ves'cen-cy,
ef-fẽr-ves'cen-cy.

Cf. effervescent, see, etc.

Ē'SENT-LI

d: dē'cent-ly, in-dē'cent-ly.

r: rē'cent-ly.

Plus decent lea *or* Lee, etc.

Ē'SHI-ĂN

d: ġē-ō-dē'si-ăn*.

gr: Grē'ci-ăn.

l: Meg-à-lē'si-ăn, Sī-lē'si-ăn.

n: ġy-noē'ci-ăn*, Mel-à-nē'si-ăn,
Pel''ō-pon-nē'si-ăn, Vē-nē'ti-ăn.

p: Çà-pē'ti-ăn.

t: E-piç-tē'ti-ăn.

Cf. ēsh'ăn, ēsh'un.

Plus fleecy Ann *or* an, etc.

ESH'I-ENS

n: nes'ci-ence.

pr: pres'ci-ence.

ESH'I-NES

fl: flesh'i-ness.

m: mesh'i-ness.

ESH'LI-NES

fl: flesh'li-ness, un-flesh'li-ness.

fr: fresh'li-ness.

ESH'UN-ĂL

f: çon-fes'sion-ăl, prō-fes'sion-ăl.

gr: çon-gres'sion-ăl,
dī-gres'sion-ăl, prō-gres'sion-ăl,
trans-gres'sion-ăl.

kr: dis-çre'tion-ăl.

pr: ex-pres'sion-ăl (eks-).

s: aç-ces'sion-ăl,
in-tẽr-ces'sion-ăl,
prō-ces'sion-ăl, rē-ces'sion-ăl,
re-trō-ces'sion-ăl, ses'sion-ăl,
suç-ces'sion-ăl.

z: poș-șes'sion-ăl.

Plus confession, Al, etc.

ESH'UN-IST

gr: prō-gres'sion-ist.

pr: im-pres'sion-ist.

s: sē-ces'sion-ist, suç-ces'sion-ist.

ESH'UN-ŨR

s: prō-ces'sion-ẽr, sē-ces'sion-ẽr.

z: poș-șes'sion-ẽr.

Plus procession her, err *or* er, etc.

Ē'SHUS-NES

s: fà-cē'tious-ness.

sp: spē'cious-ness.

ES'I-B'L

dr: rē-dres'si-ble.

gr: trans-gres'si-ble.

kr: çon-çres'ci-ble.

(Choose only one word out of each group)

pr: çom-pres'si-ble,
ex-pres'si-ble, in-çom-pres'si-ble,
in-ex-pres'si-ble,
in-sup-pres'si-ble,
ir-rē-pres'si-ble, rē-pres'si-ble,
sup-pres'si-ble.
s: aç-ces'si-ble, çon-ces'si-ble,
in-aç-ces'si-ble, in-ces'sȧ-ble,
mär-ces'ci-ble.
t: fẽr-men-tes'ci-ble.
tr: im-pū-tres'ci-ble,
pū-tres'ci-ble, vi-tres'ci-ble.
v: ef-fẽr-ves'ci-ble,
ịn"ef-fẽr-ves'ci-ble.
Plus dressy bull, etc.

ES'I-MĂL

d: dec'i-măl.
j: non-ȧ-ġes'i-măl,
quäd-rȧ-ġes'i-măl,
sep"tū-ȧ-ġes'i-măl,
sex-ȧ-ġes'i-măl (seks-).
l: mil-les'i-măl.
t: cen-tes'i-măl,
in"fin-i-tes'i-măl.
Plus dress him, Al, etc.

ĒS'I-TY

b: ō-bē'si-ty.
Plus piece it, he, etc.

ES'I-TI

b: ō-bes'i-ty.
s: nē-ces'si-ty.
Plus dress it, he, etc.

ES'IV-NES

gr: ag-gres'sive-ness,
prō-gres'sive-ness.
pr: dē-pres'sive-ness,
ex-pres'sive-ness (eks-),

im-pres'sive-ness,
in-ex-pres'sive-ness,
op-pres'sive-ness.
s: ex-ces'sive-ness.

ES'TI-ĂL

b: bes'ti-ăl.
gr: ȧ-gres'ti-ăl.
l: cē-les'ti-ăl, sū"pēr-cē-les'ti-ăl.
Plus chesty, Al, etc.

ES'TI-B'L

j: çon-ġes'ti-ble, di-ġes'ti-ble,
in-di-ġes'ti-ble.
m: çō-mes'ti-ble.
t: çon-tes'tȧ-ble, dē-tes'tȧ-ble,
in-çon-tes'tȧ-ble, in-tes'tȧ-ble,
tes'tȧ-ble.
v: dī-ves'ti-ble.
Plus dressed a bull, etc.
Plus siesta, bull, etc.

ES'TIN-ĂL

d: des'tin-ăl.
t: in-tes'tin-ăl.
Plus clandestine, Al, etc.

ES'TIN-ĀT

d: des'tin-āte, prē-des'tin-āte.
f: fes'tin-āte.
Plus dressed in eight *or* ate, etc.
Plus less tin, ate, etc.

ĒS'TI-NES

r: rēas'ti-ness.
y: yēas'ti-ness.

ES'TI-NES

r: res'ti-ness.
t: tes'ti-ness.

ES'TIV-NES
ET'FŬL-I

fāte, fär, fȧst, fạll, finăl, cãre, at; mēte, prey, hẽr, met; pīne,
marīne, bĭrd, pin; nōte, mŏve, fọr, atŏm, not; mọọn, book;

866

(Choose only one word out of each group)

ES'TIV-NES

f: fes'tive-ness.
j: sug-ges'tive-ness.
r: res'tive-ness.

ĒST'LI-NES

b: bēast'li-ness.
pr: priēst'li-ness.

ES'TRI-ĂL

d: pē-des'tri-ăl.
m: trī-mes'tri-ăl.
r: sū″pẽr-ter-res'tri-ăl,
ter-res'tri-ăl.
Plus vestry, Al, etc.

ES'TRI-ĂN

d: pē-des'tri-ăn.
kw(qu): ē-ques'tri-ăn.
l: pȧ-les'tri-ăn.
p: ċam-pes'tri-ăn.
v: syl-ves'tri-ăn.
Plus vestry, Ann *or* an, etc.

ES'TRI-US

d: pē-des'tri-ous.
r: ter-res'tri-ous.
Plus vestry, us, etc.

ES'TŪ-RĂL

j: ges'tū-răl.
v: ves'tū-răl.
Plus vesture, Al, etc.

ES'TŨR-ING

f: fes'tẽr-ing.
p: pes'tẽr-ing.
w: wes'tẽr-ing.
Plus guessed her ring, etc.
Plus jester ring, etc.
Plus at best a ring, etc.

ES'TŪ-US

p: tem-pes'tū-ous.
s: in-ces'tū-ous.

ĒT'Ȧ-B'L

Vowel: ēat'ȧ-ble, un-ēat'ȧ-ble.
b: bēat'ȧ-ble, un-bēat'ȧ-ble.
ch: chēat'ȧ-ble, es-chēat'ȧ-ble.
f: dē-fēat'ȧ-ble.
l: dē-lēt'ȧ-ble.
p: rē-pēat'ȧ-ble.
tr: en-trēat'ȧ-ble.
Plus meet a bull, etc.

ET'Ȧ-B'L

g: bē-get'ȧ-ble, fọr-get'ȧ-ble,
get'ȧ-ble, un-fọr-get'ȧ-ble.
gr: rē-gret'ȧ-ble.
hw: whet'ȧ-ble.
n: bāy-ō-net'ȧ-ble.
p: pet'ȧ-ble.
s: set'ȧ-ble.
Plus met a bull, etc.

ET'ĂL-ĒN

s: ȧ-cet'y-lēne.
Plus met a lean, etc.

ET'Ȧ-LIN

m: met'ăl-line.
p: pet'ȧ-line.
Plus metăl in *or* inn, etc.

ET'ĂL-IZM

m: bī-met'ăl-liṣm,
mon-ō-met'ăl-liṣm.
p: pet'ăl-iṣm.

ET'FŬL-I

fr: fret'fŭl-ly.
g: fọr-get'fŭl-ly.

(Choose only one word out of each group)

gr: rē-gret'fụl-ly.
Plus debt fully, etc.

ET'FỤL-NESS

fr: fret'fụl-ness.
g: fọr-get'fụl-ness.
gr: rē-gret'fụl-ness.

ETH'LES-LI

br: breath'less-ly.
d: death'less-ly.
Plus breath, Leslie, etc.

ETH'LES-NES

br: breath'less-ness.
d: death'less-ness.

ETH'ÛR-I

f: feaTH'ĕr-y.
h: heaTH'ĕr-y.
l: leaTH'ĕr-y.
w: weaTH'ĕr-y.
Plus together, he, etc.

ETH'ÛR-ING

f: feaTH'ĕr-ing.
l: leaTH'ĕr-ing.
t: teTH'ĕr-ing.
w: weaTH'ĕr-ing.
Plus together ring, etc.

ET'I-KĂL

Vowel: a-lō-et'i-çăl, nō-et'i-çăl,
pō-et'i-çăl.
b: al-phȧ-bet'i-çăl.
j: ap-ol-ō-ġet'i-çăl,
en-ēr-ġet'i-çăl, ex-ē-ġet'i-çăl.
k(ç): çat-ē-çhet'i-çăl.
l: hom-i-let'i-çăl.
m: ar-ith-met'i-çăl,
çoṣ-met'i-çăl, hēr-met'i-çăl.

n: plȧ-net'i-çăl.
r: añ-çhō-ret'i-çăl,
em-pō-ret'i-çăl, hē-ret'i-çăl,
thē-ō-ret'i-çăl.
t: dī-e-tet'i-çăl.
th: aes-thet'i-çăl (es-),
an"ti-pȧ-thet'i-çăl,
an-ti-thet'i-çăl, a-pȧ-thet'i-çăl,
ep-i-thet'i-çăl, hȳ-pō-thet'i-çăl.
Plus jetty, Cal, etc.
Plus emetic, Al, etc.

ET'I-KŪL

Vowel: pō-et'i-çule.
r: ret'i-çule.
Plus energetic Yule *or* you'll, etc.

ĒT'I-NES

m: mēat'i-ness.
p: pēat'i-ness.
sl: sleet'i-ness.

ET'I-NES

j: jet'ti-ness.
p: pet'ti-ness.
sw: sweat'i-ness.

ET'IN-Ū

d: det'in-ūe.
r: ret'in-ūe.
Plus met in you, etc.
Plus Wettin, you, etc.

ET'ISH-LY

k(ç): çō-quet'tish-ly (-ket').
p: pet'tish-ly.
Plus Lettish, Lee, etc.

ET'ISH-NES

k(ç): çō-quet'tish-ness (kō-ket').
p: pet'tish-ness.

(Choose only one word out of each group)

ET'I-SIZM

l: ath-let'i-cişm.
s: as-cet'i-cişm.
t: per"i-pà-tet'i-cişm.
th: aes-thet'i-cişm (es-),
es-thet'i-cişm.

ĒT'Ō-RI

kr: sē-çrēt'ō-ry.
pl: çom-plēt'ō-ry, dē-plēt'ō-ry,
rē-plēt'ō-ry.
Plus fetor *or* sweeter, he, etc.

ET'RI-KĂL

m: al"kà-li-met'ri-çăl,
a-sym-met'ri-çăl,
bar-ō-met'ri-çăl,
çrā"ni-ō-met'ri-çăl,
dī-à-met'ri-çăl, ḡē-ō-met'ri-çăl,
gnōm"i-ō-met'ri-çăl (nōm"),
gràph-ō-met'ri-çăl,
họr-ō-met'ri-çăl,
ī"sō-per-i-met'ri-çăl,
met'ri-çăl, per-i-met'ri-çăl,
plan-i-met'ri-çăl,
plū"vi-ō-met'ri-çăl,
stiçh-ō-met'ri-çăl,
sym-met'ri-çăl,
trig"ō-nō-met'ri-çăl.
st: ob-stet'ri-çăl.
Plus photometric, Al, etc.

ET'RI-MENT

d: det'ri-ment.
r: ret'ri-ment*.

ET'ŨR-ING

b: bet'tẽr-ing.
f: fet'tẽr-ing.
l: let'tẽr-ing.
Plus letter ring, etc.

Plus let her ring, etc.
Plus let a ring, etc.

ĒV'À-B'L

ch: à-chiēv'à-ble.
gr: griēv'à-ble.
kl: çlēav'à-ble.
l: bē-liēv'à-ble, rē-liēv'à-ble,
un-bē-liēv'à-ble.
s: çon-cēiv'à-ble, dē-cēiv'à-ble,
im-pẽr-cēiv'à-ble,
in-çon-ceiv'à-ble, pẽr-cēiv'à-ble,
rē-cēiv'à-ble, un-dē-cēiv'à-ble.
tr: ir-rē-triēv'à-ble,
rē-triēv'à-ble.
Plus grieve a bull, etc.
Plus Eva, bull, etc.

EV'EL-EST

b: bev'el-lest*.
d: bē-dev'il-lest*.
l: lev'el-lest.
r: rev'el-lest*.
sh: di-shev'el-lest.
Plus devil, lest, etc.

EV'EL-ETH

b: bev'el-leth*.
d: bē-dev'il-leth*.
l: lev'el-leth*.
r: rev'el-leth*.
sh: di-shev'el-leth*.

EV'EL-ING

b: bev'el-ling.
d: bē-dev'il-ling.
l: le'vel-ling.
r: rev'el-ling.
sh: di-shev'el-ling.

(Choose only one word out of each group)

EV'EL-IZM

d: dev'il-iṣm.
l: lev'el-iṣm.

EV'EL-ŪR

b: bev'el-lĕr.
d: bē-dev'il-lĕr.
l: lev'el-lĕr.
r: rev'el-lĕr.
sh: di-shev'el-lĕr.
Plus level her, err *or* er, etc.

Ē'VI-ĀT

br: ab-brē'vi-āte.
d: dē'vi-āte.
l: al-lē'vi-āte.
Plus Levy ate *or* eight, etc.

EV'IL-MENT

d: bē-dev'il-ment, dev'il-ment.
r: rev'el-ment.
Plus level meant, etc.

EV'IL-RY

d: dev'il-ry.
r: rev'el-ry.

ĒV'ISH-LI

p: peev'ish-ly.
th: thiēv'ish-ly.
Plus thievish, Lee *or* lea, etc.

ĒV'ISH-NES

p: peev'ish-ness.
th: thiēv'ish-ness.

EV'I-TY

br: brev'i-ty.
j: lon-ġev'i-ty.
l: lev'it-y.
Plus heavy tea, etc.

Ē'VI-US

d: dē'vi-ous.
pr: prē'vi-ous.
Plus Levy, us, etc.

EV'ŌL-ENS

l: mȧ-lev'ō-lence.
n: bē-nev'ō-lence.

EV'Ō-LENT

l: mȧ-lev'ō-lent.
n: bē-nev'ō-lent.

EV'ŌL-US

l: mȧ-lev'ō-lŭus.
n: bē-nev'ō-lŭus.
Plus devil us, etc.

EV'Ō-LŪT

Vowel: ev'ō-lute.
r: rev'ō-lūte.

EV'ŪR-EST

Vowel: Ev'ĕr-est.
d: en-deav'ŏr-est (-dev')*.
kl: clev'ĕr-est.
s: sever-est*.
Plus clever rest, etc.

EV'ŪR-MŌR

Vowel: ev'ĕr-mōre.
n: nev'ĕr-mōre.
Plus clever more, etc.

EV'ŪR-ŪR

d: en-dēav'ŏr-ĕr.
kl: clev'ĕr-ĕr.
s: sev'ĕr-ĕr.
Plus sever her, err *or* er, etc.

(Choose only one word out of each group)

ĒZ'À-B'L

f: dē-fēas'i-ble, fēas'i-ble,
  in-dē-fēas'i-ble, in-fēas'i-ble.
fr: freez'à-ble.
h: cō-hēṣ'i-ble.
p: ap-pēas'i-ble,
  in-ap-pēas'à-ble,
  un-ap-pēas'à-ble.
s: sēiz'à-ble.
skw(squ): squeez'à-ble.
Plus freeze a bull, etc.

EZ'ĂN-TRI

f: pheaṣ'ăn-try.
p: peaṣ'ăn-try.
pl: pleaṣ'ăn-try.
Cf. pleasant tree, etc.

Ē'ZHI-À, Ē'ZI-À

b: Zam-bē'ṣi-à.
d: Rhō-dē'ṣi-à.
kl: ec̲-c̲lē'ṣi-à.
l: Si-lē'ṣi-à.
n: am-nē'ṣi-à, mag-nē'ṣi-à.
r: par-rhē'ṣi-à.
th: an-aes-thē'ṣi-à (-es-),
  an-es-thē'ṣi-à, es-thē'ṣi-à.
Plus easy a, etc.

EZH'ŨR-ING

m: meaṣ'ũr-ing.
pl: pleaṣ'ũr-ing.
tr: treaṣ'ũr-ing.
Plus treasure ring, etc.

EZH'ŨR-ŨR

m: meaṣ'ũr-ẽr.
pl: pleaṣ'ũr-ẽr.
tr: treaṣ'ũr-ẽr.
Plus treasure her, err or er, etc.

Ē'ZI-ĂN

f: E-phē'ṣi-ăn.
kl: ec̲-c̲lē'ṣi-ăn.
l: Mī-lē'ṣi-ăn.
n: mag-nē'ṣi-ăn, Pol-y-nē'ṣi-ăn.
p: tra-pē'ṣi-ăn.
t: är-tē'ṣi-ăn, c̲är-tē'ṣi-ăn,
  ē-tē'ṣi-ăn.
Plus easy, Ann or an, etc.

EZ'I-DENT

pr: preṣ'i-dent.
r: reṣ'i-dent.

ĒZ'I-LI

Vowel: ēaṣ'i-ly, un-ēaṣ'i-ly.
br: breez'i-ly.
gr: grēaṣ'i-ly.
hw: wheez'i-ly.
Plus easy lea or Lee, etc.

EZ'I-NES

Vowel: ēaṣ'i-ness, un-ēaṣ'i-ness.
br: breez'i-ness.
ch: chees'i-ness.
gr: grēaṣ'i-ness.
hw: wheez'i-ness.
kw(qu): quēaṣ'i-ness.
sl: slēaz'i-ness.

ĒZ'ING-LI

fr: freez'ing-ly.
hw: wheez'ing-ly.
p: ap-pēaṣ'ing-ly.
pl: plēaṣ'ing-ly.
t: tēaṣ'ing-ly.
Plus pleasing lea or Lee, etc.

Ē'ZŎN-ING

r: rēa'ṣŏn-ing, un-rēa'ṣŏn-ing.
s: sēa'ṣŏn-ing.

871 ūse, bu̥ll, brūte, tûrn, **up**; crȳ, myth; c̣at, mac̣hine, ace, church, c̣hord; ġem, añger, (Fr.) boṅ, aṣ; THis, thin; aᴢure

Ī'À-B'L
Ī'ĂR-IST

(Choose only one word out of each group)

I

The accented vowel sounds included are listed under **I** in Single Rhymes.

Ī'À-B'L

f: ac-id-i-fī'à-ble, c̣las-si-fī'à-ble, di-vēr-si-fī'à-ble, ē-lec̣-tri-fī'à-ble, ex-em-pli-fī'à-ble, fa̠l-si-fī'à-ble, fo̠r-ti-fī'à-ble, jus-ti-fī'à-ble, li-que-fī'à-ble, mag-ni-fī'à-ble, mod-i-fī'à-ble, pac-i-fī'à-ble, pet-ri-fī'à-ble, quäl-i-fī'à-ble, rãr-ē-fī'à-ble, rec̣-ti-fī'à-ble, sa̠-pon-i-fī'à-ble, sat-is-fī'à-ble, sol-id-i-fī'à-ble, ver-i-fī'à-ble, vit-ri-fī'à-ble.
fr: frī'à-ble.
l: lī'à-ble, rē-lī'à-ble.
n: dē-nī'à-ble, un-dē-nī'à-ble.
pl: ap-plī'à-ble, c̣om-plī'à-ble, im-plī'à-ble, plī'à-ble.
tr: trī'à-ble, vī'à-ble.
Plus Hezekiah bull, etc.
Plus try a bull, etc.

Ī'À-BLI

f: jus-ti-fī'a-bly, etc.
l: lī'à-bly, rē-lī'à-bly.
n: dē-nī'à-bly, un-dē-nī'à-bly.
pl: plī'à-bly, etc.

Ī'À-DĒZ

dr: ham-à-drȳ'à-dēṣ.
h: Hȳ'à-dēṣ.
pl: Plei'à-dēṣ.

Ī'À-KĂL

d: c̣är-dī'à-c̣ăl, en-cȳ"c̣lō-pē-dī'à-c̣ăl, pro-sō-dī'à-c̣ăl, zō-dī'à-c̣ăl.

dr: hȳ"pō-c̣hon-drī'à-c̣ăl.
j: el-ē-ġī'à-c̣ăl.
l: hē-lī'à-c̣ăl.
n: bib"li-ō-mà-nī'à-c̣ăl, dē-mō-nī'à-c̣ăl, dip"sō-mà-nī'à-c̣ăl, klep"tō-mā-nī'à-c̣ăl, mā-nī'à-c̣ăl, meg"ăl-ō-mà-nī'à-c̣ăl, mon-ō-mā-nī'à-c̣ăl, nym"phō-mā-nī'à-c̣ăl, pȳ"rō-mā-nī'à-c̣ăl, sī-mō-nī'à-c̣ăl.
s: par-à-dī-sī'à-c̣ăl.
Plus Sophia, Cal, etc.

Ī'ĂN-SI, Ī'EN-SI

kl: c̣lī'en-cy.
pl: c̣om-plī'ăn-cy, plī'ăn-cy.
r: rī'ăn-cy.
Plus Bryan see, etc.
Cf. try and see, etc.

Ī'ĂNT-LI

f: dē-fī'ănt-ly.
l: rē-lī'ănt-ly.
pl: c̣om-plī'ănt-ly, plī'ănt-ly.
Plus giant Lee *or* lea, etc.

Ī'ĂR-I

fr: frī'ăr-y.
Cf. ī'ūr-i.

Ī'ĂR-IST

d: dī'ă-rist.
p: Pī'ă-rist.
Plus higher wrist, etc.
Plus tie a wrist, etc.

Ĭ'ÄR-KI
ĪD·Ä-B'L

fāte, fär, fàst, fạll, finăl, cāre, at; mēte, prey, hẽr, met; pīne,
marïne, bĩrd, pin; nōte, mȯve, fọr, atŏm, not; mọọn, book;

872

(Choose only one word out of each group)

Ī'ÄR-KI

d: dī'är-c͟hy.
tr: trī'är-c͟hy.

Ī'-ÀSIS

dr: hȳ"pō-c͟hon-drī'à-sis.
t: el"ē-phăn-tī'à-sis.
Plus try a sis, etc.
Cf. try her, sis, etc.

Ī'À-SIZM

dr: hȳ"pō-c͟hon-drī'à-cis͟m.
n: dē-mō-nī'à-cis͟m.

Ī'À-TŨR

k(c̲): psȳ-c͟hī'à-tẽr (sī-).
Cf. är-c͟hī'à-tẽr.

ĪB'À-B'L

br: brīb'à-ble.
skr(sc̲r): dē-sc̲rīb'à-ble,
in-dē-sc̲rīb'à-ble, in-sc̲rīb'à-ble,
sc̲rīb'à-ble, sub-sc̲rīb'à-ble,
un-dē-sc̲rīb'à-ble.

IB'I-À

f: am-phib'i-à.
l: Lib'y-à.
t: tib'i-à.

IB'I-ĂL

f: am-phib'i-ăl.
st: stib'i-ăl.
t: tib'i-ăl.

IB'I-ĂN

f: am-phib'i-ăn.
l: Lyb'i-ăn.

IB'IT-ED

h: in-hib'it-ed, prō-hib'it-ed.
z: ex-hib'it-ed (ek-zib').
Plus prohibit, Ed, etc.

IB'IT-ING

h: in-hib'it-ing, prō-hib'it-ing.
z: ex-hib'it-ing (ek-zib').

IB'I-TIVE

h: in-hib'i-tive, prō-hib'i-tive.
z: ex-hib'i-tive (ek-zib').

IB'I-US

f: am-phib'i-ŏus.
st: stib'i-ŏus.
th: ba-thyb'i-us.

IB'Ū-LĂR

d: in-fun-dib'ū-lăr,
man-dib'ū-lăr.
f: fib'ū-lăr.
t: ves-tib'ū-lăr.

ICH'I-NES

b: bitch'i-ness.
i: itch'i-ness.
p: pitch'i-ness.

ICH'ŨR-I

m: mich'ẽr-y*.
st: stitch'ẽr-y.
w: bē-witch'ẽr-y, witch'ẽr-y.

ĪD'À-B'L

f: c̲on-fīd'à-ble.
g: guīd'à-ble (gīd').
h: hīd'à-ble.
l: ē-līd'à-ble.

873

ūse, bull, brúte, tŭrn, up; crȳ, myth; çat, maçhine, ace,   **ID'EN-NES**
church, çhord; ġem, aṅger, (Fr.) boṅ, aṣ; THis, thin; aẓure   **ID'I-TI**

(Choose only one word out of each group)

r: dē-rīd′à-ble, out-rīd′à-ble,
ō-vēr-rīd′à-ble, rīd′à-ble.
s: çō-in-cīd′à-ble, dē-cīd′à-ble,
sub-sīd′à-ble.
str: bē-strīd′à-ble, strīd′à-ble.
v: di-vīd′à-ble, sub-di-vīd′à-ble.
Plus ride a bull, etc.
Plus I'd a bull, etc.

ID'EN-NES

b: fọr-bid′den-ness.
h: hid′den-ness.

ID'Ē-US

h: hid′ē-ŏus.
Cf. id′i-us.

ID'I-ĂL

s: prē-sid′i-ăl.
t: noç-tid′i-ăl.
Plus chickabiddy, Al, etc.

ID'I-ĂN

f: nul-li-fīd′i-ăn, ō-phid′i-ăn.
g: Gid′ē-ŏn.
k(ç): rà-çhid′i-ăn.
l: Lyd′i-ăn.
m: Mid′i-ăn, Nū-mid′i-ăn.
r: an′tē-mē-rid′i-ăn, mē-rid′i-ăn,
pōst mē-rid′i-ăn, vi-rid′i-ăn.
s: ob-sid′i-ăn.
t: quō-tid′i-ăn.
v: Ō-vid′i-ăn.
Plus kiddy, Ann *or* an, etc.

ID'I-ĀT

m: di-mid′i-āte.
s: in-sid′i-āte.
Plus kiddy ate *or* eight, etc.
Plus kid he ate, etc.

ID'I-FĪ

l: sō-lid′i-fȳ.
p: là-pid′i-fȳ.
s: à-cid′i-fȳ.
Plus kiddy, fīe!, etc.

ID'I-KĂL

Vowel: drù-id′i-çăl.
m: pyr-à-mid′i-çăl.
r: jù-rid′i-çăl, vē-rid′i-çăl.
Plus chickabiddy, Cal, etc.

ID'I-NUS

b: li-bid′i-nŏus.
Cf. pin-guid′i-nŏus.
Plus hid in us, etc.
Plus hidden us, etc.

ID'I-TI

b: mọr-bid′i-ty, rà-bid′i-çy,
tūr-bid′i-ty.
br: hȳ-brid′i-ty.
j: fri-ġid′i-ty, ri-ġid′i-ty,
tūr-ġid′i-ty.
k(ç): vis-çid′i-ty.
kr: à-crid′i-ty.
kw(qu): li-quid′i-ty, quid′di-ty.
l: in-sō-lid′i-ty, in-và-lid′i-ty,
ġē-lid′i-ty, pal-lid′i-ty,
sō-lid′i-ty, squà-lid′i-ty,
sto-lid′i-ty, va-lid′i-ty.
m: hū-mid′i-ty, ti-mid′i-ty,
tū-mid′i-ty.
p: çū-pid′i-ty, in-si-pid′i-ty,
in-tre-pid′i-ty, lim-pid′i-ty,
ra-pid′i-ty, sa-pid′i-ty,
stū-pid′i-ty, tọr-pid′i-ty,
tre-pid′i-ty, va-pid′i-ty.
r: a-rid′i-ty, tọr-rid′i-ty,
vi-rid′i-ty.

(Choose only one word out of each group)

s: a-cid′i-ty, lū-cid′i-ty,
mär-cid′i-ty, pel-lū-cid′i-ty,
ran-cid′i-ty.
sp: hi-spid′i-ty.
t: pū-tid′i-ty.
tr: pū-trid′i-ty.
v: a-vid′i-ty, gra-vid′i-ty,
li-vid′i-ty, pȧ-vid′i-ty,
vi-vid′i-ty.
Plus did it, he, etc.

ID′I-ŎM, ID′I-UM

Vowel: id′i-ŏm.
r: i-rid′i-um, pẽr-id′i-um.
Plus kiddy 'em, etc.

ID′I-US

d: splen-did′i-ous.
f: ō-phid′i-ous, pẽr-fid′i-ous,
Phid′i-ăs.
h: hid′ē-ous.
s: in-sid′i-ous, par-rȧ-cid′i-ous,
stil-li-cid′i-ous.
t: fas-tid′i-ous.
v: a-vid′i-ous, in-vid′i-ous.
Plus chickabiddy us, etc.

ID′Ū-ĂL

v: in-di-vid′ū-ăl.
z: rē-ṣid′ū-ăl.
Cf. amid you all, etc.
Plus hid you, Al, etc.

ID′Ū-ĀT

s: as-sid′ū-āte.
v: in-di-vid′ū-āte.
Plus kid, you ate *or* eight, etc.

ID′Ū-LĀT

s: a-cid′ū-lāte.
str: strid′ū-lāte.
Plus kid, you late, etc.

ID′Ū-LUS

s: a-cid′ū-lous.
str: strid′ū-lous.

ID′Ū-US

s: as-sid′ū-ous, dē-cid′ū-ous,
prō-cid′ū-ous, suc̣-cid′ū-ous.
v: vid′ū-ous.
z: rē-ṣid′ū-ous.

Ī′EN-SI

kl: c̣lī′en-cy.
Cf. ī′ăn-si.

Ī′ET-ĂL

d: dī′et-ăl.
h: hȳ′et-ăl.
r: pȧ-rī′et-ăl, vȧ-rī′et-ăl.
Cf. try it, Al, etc.
Plus riot, Al, etc.

Ī′ET-ED

d: dī′et-ed.
kw(qu): dis-quī′et-ed,
quī′et-ed.
r: rī′ŏt-ed.
Plus fiat, Ed, etc.
Plus messiah, Ted, etc.

Ī′ET-EST

d: dī′et-est*.
kw(qu): quī′et-est.
r: rī′ŏt-est*.
Plus messiah test, etc.

Ī′ET-I

b: dū-bī′et-y, nul-li-bī′et-y,
ū-bī′et-y.
br: ē-brī′et-y, in-ē-brī′et-y,
in-sō-brī′et-y, sō-brī′et-y.

875 ūse, bµll, brúte, tũrn, **up**; crȳ, myth; çat, maçhine, ace,
church, çhord; ġem, aṅger, (Fr.) boṅ, aṣ; THis, thin; aẓure **Ī'ET-ING
IF'LÛ-US**

(Choose only one word out of each group)

d: mē-dī'et-y.
l: fi-lī'et-y.
m: ni-mī'et-y.
n: om-nī'et-y.
p: im-pī'et-y, pī'et-y.
pr: im-prō-prī'et-y, prō-prī'et-y.
r: çon-trà-rī'et-y, lux-ū-rī'et-y*,
 nō-tō-rī'et-y, và-rī'et-y.
s: sō-cī'et-y.
t: sà-tī'et-y.
z: añ-xī'et-y (-zī').
Plus riot, he, etc.
Plus Nehemiah, tea!, etc.

Ī'ET-ING

d: dī'et-ing.
kw(qu): dis-quī'et-ing,
 quī'et-ing.
r: rī'ŏt-ing.

Ī'ET-IST

d: dī'et-ist.
kw(qu): quī'et-ist.
p: pī'et-ist.
pr: prō-prī'et-ist.
r: và-rī'et-ist.
z: añ-xī'et-ist (-zī').

Ī'ET-IZM

kw(qu): quī'et-iṣm.
p: pī'et-iṣm.
r: và-rī'et-iṣm.

Ī'ET-ŪR, Ī'ET-ŎR

d: dī'et-ēr.
kw(qu): quī'et-ēr.
pr: prō-prī'et-ŏr.
r: rī'ŏt-ēr.
Plus quiet her, etc.

IF'I-KĂL

n: là-nif'i-çăl*.
r: dō-lō-rif'i-çăl.
n: spē-cif'i-çăl.
t: bē-à-tif'i-çăl, pon-tif'i-çăl.
Plus jiffy, Cal, etc.
Plus terrific, Al, etc.

IF'I-KĂNT

d: mun-dif'i-çănt.
kr: sa-çrif'i-çănt.
n: in-sig-nif'i-çănt, sig-nif'i-çănt.
Plus terrific ant, etc.
Plus sniffy cant or Kant, etc.

IF'I-KĀT

n: sig-nif'i-çāte.
t: cēr-tif'i-çāte, pon-tif'i-çāte.
Plus terrific, ate or eight, etc.
Plus sniffy, Kate, etc.

IF'I-SENS

n: mag-nif'i-cence,
 mū-nif'i-cence.
Plus sniffy sense or cents, etc.

IF'I-SENT

n: mag-nif'i-cent, mū-nif'i-cent.
r: mi-rif'i-cent*.
Plus jiffy sent or cent or scent, etc.
Plus if he sent, etc.

IF'I-SŪR

p: ō-pif'i-cēr.
t: är-tif'i-cēr.
Plus if he, sir, etc.
Plus sniffy sir, etc.

IF'LÛ-US

gw: sañ-guif'lú-ous.
l: fel-lif'lú-ous, mel-lif'lú-ous.

IF'ŎN-I
IF'ŪR-US
fāte, fär, fȧst, fạll, fināl, cãre, at; mēte, prey, hẽr, met; pīne,
marīne, bĩrd, pin; nōte, mȯve, fọr, atŏm, not; mọọn, book;
876

(Choose only one word out of each group)

n: ig-nif′lu̇-ous.
s: cul-cif′lu̇-ous.
Plus a Riff flew us, etc.

IF'ŎN-I

l: pō-lyph′ŏn-y.
s: ox-yph′ŏn-y.
t: an-tiph′ŏn-y.

IF'RȦ-GUS

r: fed-rif′rȧ-gous*.
s: os-sif′rȧ-gous, sax-if′rȧ-gous.

IF'TȦ-B'L

dr: drift′ȧ-ble.
l: lift′ȧ-ble.
s: sift′ȧ-ble.
sh: shift′ȧ-ble.
Plus shift a bull, etc.

IF'TI-LI

n: nif′ti-ly.
sh: shif′ti-ly.
thr: thrif′ti-ly.
Plus thrifty Lee *or* lea, etc.
Plus thrift alee, etc.

IF'TI-NES

n: nif′ti-ness.
sh: shif′ti-ness.
thr: thrif′ti-ness.

IFT'LES-NES

sh: shift′less-ness.
thr: thrift′less-ness.

IF'Ū-GĂL

m: vẽr-mif′ū-găl.
r: feb-rif′ū-găl.
tr: cen-trif′ū-găl.
Plus skiff, you gal, etc.

IF'ŪR-US

Vowel: ō-lē-if′ẽr-ous.
b: bul-bif′ẽr-ous, hẽr-bif′ẽr-ous,
nim-bif′ẽr-ous, nū-bif′ẽr-ous,
plum-bif′ẽr-ous, sē-bif′ẽr-ous.
bl: om-blif′ẽr-ous.
br: um-brif′ẽr-ous.
d: ac-i-dif′ẽr-ous,
dī″ȧ-mŏn-dif′ẽr-ous,
fron-dif′ẽr-ous, ġē-ō-dif′ẽr-ous,
glan-dif′ẽr-ous.
g: fru̇-gif′ẽr-ous.
gw: san-guif′ẽr-ous (-gwif′).
j: tẽr-ġif′ẽr-ous.
k(c): con-chif′ẽr-ous,
sil-i-cif′ẽr-ous, suc-cif′ẽr-ous,
ziñ-cif′ẽr-ous.
kr: lū-crif′ẽr-ous*.
l: al-i′fẽr-ous, chē-lif′ẽr-ous,
cor-ăl-lif′ẽr-ous, fī-lif′ẽr-ous,
fō-lif′ẽr-ous, fos-si-lif′ẽr-ous,
glan-dū-lif′ẽr-ous,
gran-ū-lif′ẽr-ous,
la-mel-lif′ẽr-ous, mȧ-lif′ẽr-ous,
mam-mȧ-lif′ẽr-ous,
mel-lif′ẽr-ous, met-ăl-lif′ẽr-ous,
nick-e-lif′ẽr-ous,
pis-til-lif′ẽr-ous, sȧ-lif′ẽr-ous,
stel-lif′ẽr-ous,
ten-tȧ-cū-lif′ẽr-ous,
um-bel-lif′ẽr-ous,
um-brȧ-cū-lif′ẽr-ous,
vas-cū-lif′ẽr-ous.
m: är-mif′ẽr-ous,
bal-sȧ-mif′ẽr-ous,
flam-mif′fẽr-ous, fū-mif′ẽr-ous,
ġem-mif′ẽr-ous,
mam-mif′ẽr-ous, pal-mif′ẽr-ous,
ra-cē-mif′ẽr-ous, spū-mif′ẽr-ous.
n: al-ū-mi-nif′ẽr-ous,
an-ten-nif′ẽr-ous,

(Choose only one word out of each group)

ba-là-nif′ẽr-ous,
çär-bō-nif′ẽr-ous, çō-nif′ẽr-ous,
lū-mi-nif′ẽr-ous,
mem-brà-nif′ẽr-ous,
om-nif′ẽr-ous, ō-zō-nif′ẽr-ous,
plat-i-nif′ẽr-ous, prù-nif′ẽr-ous,
pul-mō-nif′ẽr-ous,
re-ṣi-nif′ẽr-ous, sa-li-nif′ẽr-ous,
som-nif′ẽr-ous, sō-nif′ẽr-ous,
spī-nif′ẽr-ous, stā-me-nif′ẽr-ous,
stan-nif′ẽr-ous, stol-ō-nif′ẽr-ous.
p: pol-y-pif′ẽr-ous,
sçō-pif′ẽr-ous.
r: au-rif′ẽr-ous,
çal-çà-rif′ẽr-ous, cir-rif′ẽr-ous,
dō-lō-rif′ẽr-ous, fer-rif′ẽr-ous,
flō-rif′ẽr-ous, he-dē-rif′ẽr-ous,
lau-rif′ẽr-ous, neç-tà-rif′ẽr-ous,
ō″-dō-rif′ẽr-ous, rō-rif′ẽr-ous,
saç-chà-rif′ẽr-ous,
sō-pō-rif′ẽr-ous, sū-dō-rif′ẽr-ous,
thū-rif′ẽr-ous, tū-bē-rif′ẽr-ous,
vā-pō-rif′ẽr-ous.
s: çal-cif′ẽr-ous, çrù-ci′fẽr-ous,
en-sif′ẽr-ous*, fūr-cif′ẽr-ous,
ġyp-sif′ẽr-ous, lan-cif′ẽr-ous,
lat-i-cif′ẽr-ous, lū-cif′ẽr-ous,
nū-cif′ẽr-ous, os-sif′ẽr-ous,
sen-sif′ẽr-ous, spī-cif′ẽr-ous,
vō-cif′ẽr-ous.
str: mon-strif′ẽr-ous.
t: am-mō-ni-tif′ẽr-ous,
är-ġen-tif′ẽr-ous,
dī″à-man-tif′ẽr-ous,
fà-tif′ẽr-ous, fluç-tif′ẽr-ous,
gut-tif′ẽr-ous, laç-tif′ẽr-ous,
lig-ni-tif′ẽr-ous,
mag-nē-tif′ẽr-ous,
mär″ġà-ri-tif′ẽr-ous,
mor-tif′ẽr-ous, mul-tif′ẽr-ous,
noç-tif′ẽr-ous, ō″ō-li-tif′ẽr-ous,

pes-tif′ẽr-ous, sal-ū-tif′ẽr-ous,
sçū-tif′ẽr-ous, sē-tif′ẽr-ous.
th: lē-thif′ẽr-ous.
tr: as-tri′fẽr-ous, nī-trif′ẽr-ous,
os-trif′ẽr-ous.
z: quär-ti-zif′ẽr-ous.
Plus differ us, etc.

IG′Å-MY

b: big′à-my.
d: dig′à-my.
l: pō-lyg′à-my.
tr: trig′à-my.

IG′Å-MIST

b: big′à-mist.
l: pō-lyg′à-mist.
tr: trig′à-mist.
Plus big a mist, etc.

IG′Å-MUS

b: big′à-mous.
d: dig′à-mous.
l: pō-lyg′à-mous.
tr: trig′à-mous.

IG′MÅ-TIST

n: ē-nig′mà-tist.
st: stig′mà-tist.

IG′MÅ-TĪZ

d: par-à-dig′mà-tīze.
n: ē-nig′mà-tīze.
st: stig′mà-tīze.

IG′NĂN-SI

d: in-dig′năn-cy.
l: mà-lig′năn-cy.
Plus a pig, Nan, see?, etc.

(Choose only one word out of each group)

IG′NĒ-US

Vowel: ig′nē-ŏus.
l: lig′nē-ŏus.

IG′NI-FĪ

Vowel: ig′ni-fȳ.
d: dig′ni-fy, un-dig′ni-fȳ.
l: lig′ni-fȳ, mȧ-lig′ni-fȳ.
s: sig′ni-fȳ.
Plus big knee? fie!, etc.

IG′NI-TI

l: mȧ-lig′ni-ty.
d: dig′ni-ty, in-dig′ni-ty.
n: bē-nig′ni-ty.

IG′ŎR-US

r: rig′ŏr-ous.
v: vig′ŏr-ous.
Plus trigger us, etc.

IG′RȦ-FI

k(c̠): tȧ-c̠hyg′rȧ-phy.
l: c̠al-lig′rȧ-phy, pō-lig′rȧ-phy.
p: ē-pig′rȧ-phy,
  pseū-dē-pig′rȧ-phy (sū-).
s: lex-ig′rȧ-phy, pȧ-sig′rȧ-phy.
t: strȧ-tig′rȧ-phy.

IG′Ū-LĀT

f: fig′ū-lāte.
l: lig′ū-lāte.
Plus pig, you late, etc.

IG′ŨR-I

hw: Whig′gẽr-y.
p: pig′gẽr-y.
w: wig′gẽr-y.
Plus bigger, he, etc.

IG′Ū-US

b: am-big′ū-ous.
r: ir-rig′ū-ous.
s: ex-ig′ū-ous.
t: c̠on-tig′ū-ous.

IJ′Ē-NUS

b: nū-biġ′ē-nous.
d: in-diġ′ē-nous.
gw: sañ-guiġ′ē-nous (-gwij′)*.
l: al-kȧ-liġ′ē-nous,
  c̠ȯr-ăl-liġ′ē-nous, fū-liġ′i-nous,
  mel-liġ′ē-nous, pō-lyġ′ē-nous,
  ū-liġ′i-nous.
n: ig-niġ′ē-nous, om-niġ′ē-nous,
  ū-niġ′ē-nous.
p: ē-piġ′ē-nous.
r: mȧ-riġ′ē-nous, prù-riġ′ē-nous,
  ter-riġ′ē-nous.
s: ox-yg′ē-nous.
t: ġe-lȧ-tiġ′ē-nous,
  mon-tiġ′ē-nous, vẽr-tiġ′ē-nous,
  vor-tiġ′ē-nous.
Plus bridge in us, etc.

IJ′I-ĂN

br: C̠an-tȧ-briġ′i-ăn.
fr: Phryġ′i-ăn (frij′).
st: Styġ′i-ăn.
v: ves-tiġ′i-ăn.

IJ′ID-LI

fr: friġ′id-ly.
r: riġ′id-ly.

IJ′ID-NES

fr: friġ′id-ness.
r: riġ-id′ness.

(Choose only one word out of each group)

IJ'I-TI

d: diġ'i-ty.
f: fidġ'e-ty.
Plus midget, he, etc.

IJ'ŪR-ĀT

fr: friġ'ē-rāte*, rē-friġ'ē-rāte.
l: bel-liġ'ē-rāte.
Plus bridger ate *or* eight, etc.
Plus ridge, a rate, etc.

IJ'ŪR-ENT

fr: rē-friġ'ēr-ănt.
l: bel-liġ'ēr-ent.
Plus bridger rent, etc.

IJ'ŪR-US

d: pē-diġ'ēr-ous.
k(ç): çrú-ciġ'ēr-ous.
l: á-liġ'ēr-ous, bel-liġ'ēr-ous, çor-ăl-liġ'ēr-ous, pī-liġ'ēr-ous, prō-liġ'ēr-ous.
m: är-miġ'ēr-ous, plū-miġ'ēr-ous.
n: çor-niġ'ēr-ous, lá-niġ'ēr-ous, lī-niġ'ēr-ous, pen-niġ'ēr-ous, spī-niġ'ēr-ous.
p: pal-piġ'ēr-ous.
r: cir-riġ'ēr-ous, im-mō-riġ'ēr-ous*.
t: den-tiġ'ēr-ous, sē-tiġ'ēr-ous.
v: ná-viġ'ēr-ous, ō-viġ'ēr-ous.
Plus bridge a Russ, etc.

IJ'US-NES

d: prō-diġ'ious-ness.
l: rē-liġ'ious-ness.
t: li-tiġ'ious-ness.

IK'Á-MENT

d: me-diç'á-ment, prē-diç'á-ment.

IK'Á-TIV

d: ab-diç'á-tive, in-diç'á-tive, prē-diç'á-tive.
fr: friç'á-tive.
s: dē-siç'çá-tive, ex-siç'çá-tive, siç'çá-tive.

IK'EN-ING

kw(qu): quick'en-ing.
s: sick'en-ing.
th: thick'en-ing.

IK'ET-I

n: pēr-nick'et-ty.
r: rick'et-y.
th: thick'et-y.
Plus lickety-(split), etc.
Plus lick it, he, etc.
Plus picket, he, etc.

IK'ET-ING

kr: çrick'et-ing.
p: pick'et-ing.
t: tick'et-ing.

IK'ET-ŪR

kr: çrick'et-ēr.
p: pick'et-ēr.
Plus thicket, her, err, *or* er, etc.

IK'I-LI

st: stick'i-ly.
tr: trick'i-ly.
Plus wick alee, etc.
Plus trick a Lee, etc.

IK'I-NES

st: stick'i-ness.
tr: trick'i-ness.

(Choose only one word out of each group)

IK'LI-NES

pr: prick'li-ness.
s: sick'li-ness.

IK'Ō-LIST

b: plē-bi'cō-list.
n: ig-nic'ō-list.
r: ag-ric'ō-list.

IK'Ō-LUS

p: sē-pic'ō-lous.
r: ag-ric'ō-lous, ter-ric'ō-lous.
Plus pickle us, etc.

IK'Ō-MUS

r: au-ric'ō-mous.
v: flȧ-vic'ō-mous.

IK'SȦ-B'L

f: fix'ȧ-ble.
m: mix'ȧ-ble.
Plus tricks a bull, etc.

IK'SHUN-ĂL

d: con-trȧ-dic'tion-ăl,
    jū-ris-dic'tion-ăl.
f: fic'tion-ăl.
fr: fric'tion-ăl.
Plus affliction, Al, etc.

IK'SI-TI

f: fix'i-ty.
l: prō-lix'i-ty.
s: sic'ci-ty.
Plus pixie tea, etc.

IK'TIV-LI

d: vin-dic'tive-ly.
str: rē-stric'tive-ly.
Plus vindictive Lee, etc.

IK'TIV-NES

d: vin-dic'tive-ness.
str: rē-stric'tive-ness.

IK'TŌ-RI

d: ben-ē-dic'tō-ry,
    con-trȧ-dic'tō-ry,
    in-tẽr-dic'tō-ry, val-ē-dic'tō-ry.
v: vic'tō-ry.
Plus boa constrictor, he, etc.
Plus picked her, he, etc.

IK'Ū-LȦ

d: fī-dic'ū-lȧ.
n: Cȧ-nic'ū-lȧ.
t: zē-tic'ū-lȧ.

IK'Ū-LĂR

b: cū-bic'ū-lăr, ǫr-bic'ū-lăr.
d: pẽr-pen-dic'ū-lăr,
    rȧ-dic'ū-lăr.
h: vē-hic'ū-lăr.
l: cȧ-lyc'ū-lăr, fol-lic'ū-lăr,
    pel-lic'ū-lăr.
m: vẽr-mic'ū-lăr.
n: ad-mi-nic'ū-lăr, cȧ-nic'ū-lăr,
    fū-nic'ū-lăr.
r: au-ric'ū-lăr.
s: ȧ-cic'ū-lăr, fas-cic'ū-lăr,
    vẽr-sic'ū-lăr, vē-sic'ū-lăr.
sp: spic'ū-lăr.
t: är-tic'ū-lăr, cū-tic'ū-lăr,
    len-tic'ū-lăr, pär-tic'ū-lăr,
    quin-quär-tic'ū-lăr,
    rē-tic'ū-lăr, sub-cū-tic'ū-lăr
tr: ven-tric'ū-lăr.
v: cla-vic'ū-lăr, na-vic'ū-lăr,
    ō-vic'ū-lăr.

(Choose only one word out of each group)

IK′Ū-LĀT

h: vē-hic̩′ū-lāte.
l: c̩a-nȧ-lic̩′ū-lāte.
m: vĕr-mic̩′ū-lāte.
n: fū-nic̩′ū-lāte, g̊ē-nic̩′ū-lāte, pa-nic̩′ū-lāte.
s: fas-cic̩′ū-lāte, vē-sic̩′ū-lāte.
sp: spic̩′ū-lāte.
t: är-tic̩′ū-lāte, den-tic̩′ū-lāte, g̊es-tic̩′ū-lāte, mon-tic̩′ū-lāte, pär-tic̩′ū-lāte, rē-tic̩′ū-lāte.
tr: mȧ-tric̩′ū-lāte.
Plus Nick, you late?, etc.

IK′Ū-LUM

n: g̊ē-nic̩′ū-lum.
r: c̩ur-ric̩′ū-lum.
Plus pick you, Lum, etc.

IK′Ū-LUS

b: ū-bic̩′ū-lous.
d: den-dic̩′ū-lus, pe-dic̩′ūlous, pe-dic̩′ū-lus, ri-dic̩′ū-lous.
l: fol-lic̩′ū-lous.
m: vĕr-mic̩′ū-lous.
s: fas-cic̩′ū-lus, vē-sic̩′ū-lous.
t: den-tic̩′ū-lus, mē-tic̩′ū-lous.
tr: ven-tric̩′ū-lous.

IK′WI-TI

b: ū-bi′qui-ty.
l: ob-li′qui-ty.
n: i-ni′qui-ty.
t: an-ti′qui-ty.
Plus quick wit, he, etc.

IK′WI-TUS

b: ū-bi′qui-tous.
n: i-ni′qui-tous.
Plus slick wit us, etc.

ĪL′A-B'L

f: dē-fīl′ȧ-ble.
g: bē-guīl′ȧ-ble.
p: c̩om-pīl′ȧ-ble.
s: ir-rec̩-on-cīl′ȧ-ble.
v: rē-vīl′ȧ-ble.

IL′Ȧ-B'L

f: fill′ȧ-ble (-b'l), rē-fill′ȧ-ble, un-rē-fill′ȧ-ble.
k: kill′ȧ-ble.
s: syl′lȧ-ble.
sp: spill′ȧ-ble.
t: dis-till′ȧ-ble, till′ȧ-ble, un-till′ȧ-ble.
thr: thrill′ȧ-ble.
Plus kill a bull, etc.
Plus gorilla bull, etc.

Ī′LĂN-DŨR

Vowel: īs′lăn-dẽr (ī′-).
h: hīgh′lăn-dẽr (hī′).
sk: skȳ′lăn-dẽr.
th: Thaī′lăn-dẽr (thī′).
Plus Rȳland, her, err, *or* er, etc.
Plus dry land err, etc.

IL′Ȧ-RI

h: Hil′ȧ-ry.
Cf. il′ūr-i.

IL′ET-ED

b: bil′let-ed.
f: fil′let-ed, un-fil′let-ed.
Plus will it, Ed, etc.
Plus millet, Ed, etc.
Plus silly, Ted, etc.

IL′ET-ING

b: bil′let-ing.
f: fil′let-ing.

ĬL'FŬL-I
ĬL'I-ENS

fāte, fär, fåst, fall, fĭnăl, cāre, at; mēte, prĕy, hẽr, met; pīne,
marīne, bĭrd, pin; nōte, mŏve, fŏr, atŏm, not; mŏŏn, book;

882

(Choose only one word out of each group)

ĪL'FŬL-I

g: guīle'fŭl-ly (gīl').
w: wīle'fŭl-ly.
Plus guileful Lee *or* lea, etc.
Plus pile full, Lee, etc.

ĬL'FŬL-I

sk: skil'fŭl-ly, un-skil'fŭl-ly.
w: wil'fŭl-ly.
Plus mill full, Lee, etc.

ĪL'FŬL-NES

g: guīle'fŭl-ness (gīl').
w: wīle'fŭl-ness.

ĬL'FŬL-NES

sk: skill'fŭl-ness,
  un-skill'fŭl-ness.
w: will'fŭl-ness.

ĬL'I-Å

b: mem″ō-rȧ-bil'i-ȧ,
  nōt-ȧ-bil'i-ȧ.
d: sē-dil'i-ȧ.
f: al″çō-hol″ō-phil'i-ȧ,
  an-drō-phil'i-ȧ,
  Añ-glō-phil'i-ȧ, an-ō-phil'i-ȧ,
  çop-rō-phil'i-ȧ,
  Frañ-çō-phil'i-ȧ,
  gam-ō-phil'i-ȧ,
  ġy-nē-çō-phil'i-ȧ,
  haēm-ō-phil'i-a,
  hēm-ō-phil'i-ȧ,
  phal-lō-phil'i-ȧ,
  Rus-sō-phil'i-ȧ,
  spaṣ-mō-phil'i-ȧ,
  ū″rin-ō-phil'i-ȧ,
  vul-vō-phil-i-ȧ.
Plus chilly a, etc.

ĬL'I-ĂD

Vowel: Il'i-ăd.
ch: chil'i-ăd.
g: Gil'ē-ăd.
Cf. Willy had, etc.

ĬL'I-ĂN

b: pēr-feç-tȧ-bil'i-ăn.
d: çroç-ō-dil'i-ăn.
j: Vēr-ġil-i'ăn, Vĭr-ġil'i-ăn.
l: Lil'i-ăn, Lil'li-ăn.
m: Max-i-mil'i-ăn.
r: Kū-ril'i-ăn.
s: Cē-cil'i-ăn, Si-cil'i-ăn.
t: Ças-til'i-ăn, la-cēr-til'i-ăn,
  rep-til'i-ăn.
v: vil'ly-ăn.
z: Brȧ-zil'i-ăn.
Plus hilly an, etc.
Cf. all words ending in il'yun.

ĬL'I-ĂR

b: at-rȧ-bil'i-ăr.
s: çon-cil'i-ăr, dom-i-cil'i-ăr.
z: ȧux-il'i-ăr.
Cf. il'yăr.

ĬL'I-ĀT

f: af-fil'i-āte, fil'i-āte.
m: hū-mil'i-āte.
s: çon-cil'i-āte, dō-mi-cil'i-āte.
Plus Lily ate *or* eight, etc.
Plus until he ate *or* eight, etc.

ĬL'I-ENS

br: bril'li-ănce.
s: çon-sil'i-ence, dis-sil'i-ence,
  tran-sil'i-ence.
z: rē-ṣil'i-ence.

(Choose only one word out of each group)

IL′I-ENT

br: bril′li-ănt.
s: dis-sil′i-ent, tran-sil′i-ent.
z: rē-ṣil′i-ent.

IL′I-EST

ch: chil′li-est.
h: hil′li-est.
s: sil′li-est.
st: stil′li-est.

IL′I-FĪ

b: nō-bil′i-fȳ, stȧ-bil′i-fȳ.
s: fos-sil′i-fȳ.
v: vil′i-fȳ.
Plus Millie, fie!, etc.
Plus will he? fie, etc.

IL′I-FǪRM

f: fil′i-fǫrm.
m: plū-mil′i-fǫrm.
Plus Willy form, etc.
Plus will he form, etc.

IL′I-GĂN

g: Gil′li-găn.
m: Mc̗-Mil′li-găn, Mil′li-găn.
Plus will again, etc.

IL′IJ-ŬR

p: pil′lăġ-ēr.
v: vil′lăġ-ēr.

IL′I-KȦ

s: bȧ-sil′i-c̗ȧ, sil′i-c̗ȧ.
z: bȧ-ṣil′i-c̗ȧ.
Plus idyllic a, etc.

IL′I-KĂL

b: um-bil′i-c̗ăl.
f: fil′i-c̗ăl.
s: bȧ-sil′i-c̗ăl, sil′i-c̗le.
z: bȧ-ṣil′i-c̗ăl.
Plus silly Cal, etc.
Plus will he, Cal? etc.

IL′I-NES

ch: chil′li-ness.
h: hill′i-ness.
s: sil′li-ness.

IL′ING-LI

k: kil′ling-ly.
thr: thril′ling-ly.
tr: tril′ling-ly.
w: wil′ling-ly.
Plus drilling Lee *or* lea, etc.

IL′I-Ō

t: puñc̗-til′i-ō.
v: pul-vil′li-ō.
Plus Milly owe, etc.
Plus will he owe, etc.

IL′I-TĀT

b: ȧ-bil′i-tāte, dē-bil′i-tāte,
　　hȧ-bil′i-tāte,
　　im-pos-si-bil′i-tāte,
　　nō-bil′i-tāte, rē-hȧ-bil′i-tāte,
　　stȧ-bil′i-tāte.
m: mil′i-tāte.
s: fȧ-cil′i-tāte.
Plus Willy Tate *or* Tait, etc.
Plus skillet ate *or* eight, etc.
Plus fill it eight, etc.

IL′I-TI

b: ȧ-bil′i-ty, ab-ṣǫr-bȧ-bil′i-ty,
　　as-cen-di-bil′i-ty,

(Choose only one word out of each group)

ac-cep-tȧ-bil'i-ty,
ac-ces-si-bil'i-ty,
ac-coun-tȧ-bil'i-ty,
ac-quīr-ȧ-bil'i-ty,
ȧ-dap-tȧ-bil'i-ty, ad-di-bil'i-ty,
ad″mir-ȧ-bil'i-ty,
ad-mis-si-bil'i-ty,
ȧ-dop-tȧ-bil'i-ty,
ȧ-dōr-ȧ-bil'i-ty,
ad-vīṣ-ȧ-bil'i-ty,
af-fȧ-bil'i-ty,
af-fec-ti-bil'i-ty,
ȧ-gree-ȧ-bil'i-ty,
āl″ien-ȧ-bil'i-ty,
al″tẽr-ȧ-bil'i-ty,
ȧ-men-ȧ-bil'i-ty,
ā″mi-ȧ-bil'i-ty,
am″i-cȧ-bil'i-ty,
ȧ-miss-i-bil'i-ty,
ap″pē-ti-bil'i-ty,
ap″pli-cȧ-bil'i-ty,
as-sim″i-lȧ-bil'i-ty,
as-sō″ci-ȧ-bil'i-ty,
at-tāin-ȧ-bil'i-ty,
at-tempt-ȧ-bil'i-ty,
at-trac-tȧ-bil'i-ty,
aud-i-bil'i-ty,
ȧ-vāil-ȧ-bil'i-ty, cāp-ȧ-bil'i-ty,
chānge-ȧ-bil'i-ty,
cog-nos-ci-bil'i-ty,
cō-hēṣ-i-bil'i-ty,
com-bus-ti-bil'i-ty,
com-mū″ni-cȧ-bil'i-ty,
com-mū-tȧ-bil'i-ty,
com-pat-i-bil'i-ty,
com″prē-hen″si-bil'i-ty,
com-pres-si-bil'i-ty,
com″pū-tȧ-bil'i-ty,
con-cēiv-ȧ-bil'i-ty,
con-den-sȧ-bil'i-ty,
con-dū-ci-bil'i-ty,

con-duc-tȧ-bil'i-ty,
con-fŏrm-ȧ-bil'i-ty,
con-fūṣ-ȧ-bil'i-ty,
con-temp-ti-bil'i-ty,
con-trac-ti-bil'i-ty,
con-vẽr-ti-bil'i-ty,
cor″ri-ġi-bil'i-ty,
cor-rōd-i-bil'i-ty,
cor-rōs'i-bil'i-ty,
cred-i-bil'i-ty,
cred″i-tȧ-bil'i-ty,
cul-pȧ-bil'i-ty, cūr-ȧ-bil'i-ty,
dam-nȧ-bil'i-ty, dē-bil'i-ty,
dē-cep-ti-bil'i-ty,
dē-dūc-i-bil'i-ty,
dē-fect-i-bil'i-ty,
dē-mīs-ȧ-bil'i-ty,
dē-mon-strȧ-bil'i-ty,
dē-plōr-ȧ-bil'i-ty,
dēs-cen-di-bil'i-ty,
dē-ṣīr-ȧ-bil'i-ty,
des″pic-ȧ-bil'i-ty,
dēs-truc-ti-bil'i-ty,
dē-tẽrm″in-ȧ-bil'i-ty,
dē-tes-tȧ-bil'i-ty,
dif-fū-ṣi-bil'i-ty,
dī-ġes-ti-bil'i-ty,
dī-lāt-ȧ-bil'i-ty, dis-ȧ-bil'i-ty,
dis-sol-ū-bil'i-ty,
diṣ-ṣol-vȧ-bil'i-ty,
dis-ten-si-bil'i-ty,
di-viṣ-i-bil'i-ty, doc-i-bil'i-ty,
dūr-ȧ-bil'i-ty, ed-i-bil'i-ty,
ed″ū-cȧ-bil'i-ty, el-iġ-i-bil'i-ty,
e-quȧ-bil'i-ty,
ex-chānge'ȧ-bil'i-ty,
ex-cīt-ȧ-bil'i-ty,
ex-haus-ti-bil'i-ty (egs-aus-),
ex-pan-si-bil'i-ty,
ex-ten-si-bil'i-ty, fal-li-bil'i-ty,
fēaṣ-i-bil'i-ty,

(Choose only one word out of each group)

fẽr-men-tá-bil'i-ty,
flex-i-bil'i-ty,
fluç-tū-á-bil'i-ty,
flux-i-bil'i-ty,
fọr"mid-á-bil'i-ty,
fran-ġi-bil'i-ty, frī-á-bil'i-ty,
fūṣ-i-bil'i-ty, ġen-ẽr-á-bil'i-ty,
gul-li-bil'i-ty, hab"it-á-bil'i-ty,
ig-nō-bil'i-ty, il-lá-bil'i-ty,
im"i-tá-bil'i-ty,
im-mē-á-bil'i-ty,
im-meaṣ"ūr-á-bil'i-ty,
im-mis-ci-bil'i-ty,
im-möv-á-bil'i-ty,
im-mūt-á-bil'i-ty,
im-pal-pá-bil'i-ty,
im-pär-ti-bil'i-ty,
im-pas-si-bil'i-ty,
im-peç-çá-bil'i-ty,
im-pen"ē-trá-bil'i-ty,
im"pẽr-cep"ti-bil'i-ty,
im-pẽrd-i-bil'i-ty,
im-pẽr"mē-á-bil'i-ty,
im"pẽr-tūr"bá-bil'i-ty,
im-pẽr"vi-á-bil'i-ty,
im-plá-çá-bil'i-ty,
im-pos-si-bil'i-ty,
im-preg-ná-bil'i-ty,
im"prē-sçrip"ti-bil'i-ty,
im-pres'si-bil'i-ty,
im-pres'siŏn-á-bil'i-ty,
im-prob-á-bil'i-ty,
im-pūt-á-bil'i-ty, in-á-bil'i-ty,
in"aç-ces"si-bil'i-ty,
in-çog"ni-tá-bil'i-ty,
in-çog"nos-ci-bil'i-ty,
in"çom-bus"ti-bil'i-ty,
in-çom-meaṣ"ū-rá-bil'i-ty,
in-çom-mū"ni-çá-bil'i-ty,
in"çom-mū"tá-bil'i-ty,
in"çom-pat"i-bil'i-ty,

in-çom"prē-hen"si-bil'i-ty,
in"çom-pres"si-bil'i-ty,
in"çon-cēiv"á-bil'i-ty,
in"çon-den"sá-bil'i-ty,
in-çon"trō-vẽr"ti-bil'i-ty,
in"çon-vẽr"ti-bil'i-ty,
in-çor"ri-ġi-bil'i-ty,
in"çor-rup"ti-bil'i-ty,
in-çred-i-bil'i-ty,
in-çūr-á-bil'i-ty,
in"dē-fat-i"gá-bil'i-ty,
in"dē-fēaṣ"i-bil'i-ty,
in"dē-feç"ti-bil'i-ty,
in-del-i-bil'i-ty,
in"dē-mon"strá-bil'i-ty,
in"dē-struç"ti-bil'i-ty,
in"di-ġes"ti-bil'i-ty,
in"dis-cẽrn"i-bil'i-ty,
in"dis-cẽrp"ti-bil'i-ty,
in"dis-pen"sá-bil'i-ty,
in"dis-pūt"á-bil'i-ty,
in"dis-sol"ū-bil'i-ty,
in"di-viṣ"i-bil'i-ty,
in-doc-i-bil'i-ty,
in-ef-fá-bil'i-ty,
in-ef"fẽr-ves"ci-bil'i-ty,
in-el"i-ġi-bil'i-ty,
in-ev"i-tá-bil'i-ty,
in"ex-haus"ti'bil-i-ty (-egs aus),
in-ex"ōr-á-bil'i-ty,
in-ex"pli-çá-bil'i-ty,
in-fal-li-bil'i-ty,
in-fēaṣ-i-bil'i-ty,
in-flam-má-bil'i-ty,
in-flex-i-bil'i-ty,
in-fran-ġi-bil'i-ty,
in-fūṣ-i-bil'i-ty,
in-há-bil'i-ty,
in-hab"it-á-bil'i-ty,
in-her"it-á-bil'i-ty,
in-im"i-tá-bil'i-ty,

(Choose only one word out of each group)

in-nūm″ẽr-ȧ-bil′i-ty,
in-san-ȧ-bil′i-ty,
in-sā-ti-ȧ-bil′i-ty (-shi-),
in-sen-si-bil′i-ty,
in-sep″är-ȧ-bil′i-ty,
in-sōc″i-ȧ-bil′i-ty (-sōsh″),
in-sol-ū-bil′i-ty, in-stȧ-bil′i-ty,
in-sūp″ẽr-ȧ-bil′i-ty,
in″sūr-mount″ȧ-bil′i-ty,
in″sus-cep″ti-bil′i-ty,
in-tan-ġi-bil′i-ty,
in-tel″li-ġi-bil′i-ty,
in″tẽr-chānge″ȧ-bil′i-ty,
in-traç-tȧ-bil′i-ty,
in-ven-di-bil′i-ty,
in-vin-ci-bil′i-ty,
in-vī″ō-lȧ-bil′i-ty,
in-viṣ-i-bil′i-ty,
in-vul″nẽr-ȧ-bil′i-ty,
ir-as-ci-bil′i-ty,
ir″rē-çon-cīl″ȧ-bil′i-ty,
ir″rē-duç″ti-bil′i-ty,
ir″rē-möv″ȧ-bil′i-ty,
ir″rē-pär″ȧ-bil′i-ty,
ir″rē-ṣis″ti-bil′i-ty,
ir″rēs-pon″si-bil′i-ty,
ir″ri-tȧ-bil′i-ty, lȧ-bil′i-ty,
la″min-ȧ-bil′i-ty,
lạud-ȧ-bil′i-ty, leġ-i-bil′i-ty,
lī-ȧ-bil′i-ty, mal″lē-ȧ-bil′i-ty,
man″ăġe-ȧ-bil′i-ty,
mem″ōr-ȧ-bil′i-ty,
men″sūr-ȧ-bil′i-ty,
mis-ci-bil′i-ty, mō-bil′i-ty,
mod″i-fī-ȧ-bil′i-ty,
mod-i-fi-çȧ-bil′i-ty,
möv-ȧ-bil′i-ty, mūt-ȧ-bil′i-ty,
nav″i-ġȧ-bil′i-ty,
nē-gō″ti-ȧ-bil′i-ty (-shi-),
nō-bil′i-ty, nōt-ȧ-bil′i-ty,
op-pōṣ-ȧ-bil′i-ty,

ǫr″găn-īz″ȧ-bil′i-ty,
os-ten-si-bil′i-ty,
pal-pȧ-bil′i-ty, pär-ti-bil′i-ty,
pas-si-bil′i-ty, peç-çȧ-bil′i-ty,
pen″ē-trȧ-bil′i-ty,
pẽr-cep-ti-bil′i-ty,
pẽr-dūr-ȧ-bil′i-ty,
pẽr-feç-ti-bil′i-ty,
pẽr-mis-si-bil′i-ty,
pẽr-suā-si-bil′i-ty (-swā-),
pẽr-tūrb-ȧ-bil′i-ty,
plā-çȧ-bil′i-ty, plạu-ṣi-bil′i-ty,
plī-ȧ-bil′i-ty, pon-dẽr-ȧ-bil′i-ty,
pǫr-tȧ-bil′i-ty, pos-si-bil′i-ty,
praç-ti-çȧ-bil′i-ty,
prē-cip″i-tȧ-bil′i-ty,
prē-fẽr-ȧ-bil′i-ty,
prē-sçrip-ti-bil′i-ty,
prē-vent-ȧ-bil′i-ty,
prob-ȧ-bil′i-ty,
prō-dū-ci-bil′i-ty,
quōt-ȧ-bil′i-ty,
rāt-ȧ-bil′i-ty, rēad-ȧ-bil′i-ty,
rē-cēiv-ȧ-bil′i-ty,
rē-cep-ti-bil′i-ty,
rē-deem-ȧ-bil′i-ty,
rē-duç-ti-bil′i-ty,
rē-fleç-i-bil′i-ty,
rē-frag-ȧ-bil′i-ty,
rē-fran-ġi-bil′i-ty,
rē-fūt-ȧ-bil′i-ty, rē-lī-ȧ-bil′i-ty,
rē-mis-si-bil′i-ty,
rē-möv-ȧ-bil′i-ty,
rē-mū″nẽr-ȧ-bil′i-ty,
rē-new-ȧ-bil′i-ty (-nū-),
rē-pär-ȧ-bil′i-ty,
rē-pēal-ȧ-bil′i-ty,
rē-ṣis-ti-bil′i-ty,
rē-ṣol-vȧ-bil′i-ty,
rēs-peç-tȧ-bil′i-ty,
rēs-pon-si-bil′i-ty,

887
ūse, bu̯ll, brúte, tũrn, up; crȳ, myth; c̦at, mac̦hine, ace, church, c̦hord; ġem, añger, (Fr.) boṅ, a̡s; THis, thin; azure

IL̕'I-US
Ī'LŌ-BĀT

(Choose only one word out of each group)

rē-vẽr-si-bil'i-ty,
rē-vō-c̦à-bil'i-ty, ri̡s-i-bil'i-ty,
sāle-à-bil'i-ty, sal-và-bil'i-ty,
san-à-bil'i-ty,
sā-ti-à-bil'i-ty (-shi-),
sen-si-bil'i-ty, sep-ãr-à-bil'i-ty,
sō-ci-à-bil'i-ty, sol-ū-bil'i-ty,
sol-và-bil'i-ty, spo̜rt-à-bil'i-ty,
squeez-à-bil'i-ty, stà-bil'i-ty,
suā-bil'i-ty (swā-),
sūit-à-bil'i-ty (sūt-),
sus-cep-ti-bil'i-ty,
sus-pen-si-bil'i-ty,
tam-à-bil'i-ty, tan-ġi-bil'i-ty,
tax-à-bil'i-ty, temp-tà-bil'i-ty,
ten-à-bil'i-ty, ten-si-bil'i-ty,
tol"ẽr-à-bil'i-ty, to̜r-si-bil'i-ty,
trac̦-tà-bil'i-ty,
trans"fẽr-à-bil'i-ty,
trans-mis-si-bil'i-ty,
trans-mūt-à-bil'i-ty,
trans-po̜rt-à-bil'i-ty,
un"ac̦-c̦oun"tà-bil'i-ty,
un-bē-liēv-à-bil'i-ty,
un-ut"tẽr-à-bil'i-ty,
vā"po̜r-à-bil'i-ty,
vãr"i-à-bil'i-ty,
veġ"ē-tà-bil'i-ty,
ven-di-bil'i-ty, ven"ẽr-à-bil'i-ty,
vẽr-sà-bil'i-ty, vī-à-bil'i-ty,
vin"di-c̦à-bil'i-ty, vi̡s-i-bil'i-ty,
vol-ū-bil'i-ty, vul"nẽr-à-bil'i-ty,
wrīt-à-bil'i-ty.

d: c̦roc̦-ō-dil'i-ty.
h: nī-hil'i-ty.
j: à-ġil'i-ty, frà-ġil'i-ty.
kw: tran-quil'li-ty.
m: hū-mil'i-ty, vẽr-si-mil'i-ty.
n: à-nil'i-ty, jù-vē-nil-i'ty,
sē-nil'i-ty,
vẽr-nil'i-ty.

r: neū-ril'i-ty, pū-ē-ril'i-ty,
sc̦ũr-ril'i-ty, stē-ril'i-ty,
vī-ril'i-ty.
s: dō-cil'i-ty, fà-cil'i-ty,
fos-sil'i-ty, grà-cil'i-ty,
im-bē-cil'i-ty, in-dō-cil'i-ty,
pen-sil'i-ty, ten-sil'i-ty.
t: c̦on-trac̦-til'i-ty, duc̦-til'i-ty,
fẽr-til'i-ty, fic̦-til'i-ty,
fū-til'i-ty, ġen-til'i-ty,
hos-til'i-ty, in-fẽr-til'i-ty,
in-ū-til'i-ty, mō-til'i-ty,
sub-til'i-ty, tac̦-til'i-ty,
to̜r-til'i-ty, trac̦-til'i-ty,
ū-til'i-ty, vẽr-sà-til'i-ty,
vī-brà-til'i-ty, vol-à-til'i-ty.
v: ci-vil'i-ty, in-ci-vil'i-ty,
sẽr-vil'i-ty.
Plus millet, he, etc.
Plus silly tea, etc.

IL̕'I-US

b: at-rà-bil'i-ous, bil'i-ous.
s: sū-pẽr-cil'i-ous.
t: puñc̦-til'i-ous.
Cf. il'yus.
Plus willy-nilly us, etc.

IL̕'KI-EST

m: mil'ki-est.
s: sil'ki-est.

IL̕'KI-ŨR

m: mil'ki-ẽr.
s: sil'ki-ẽr.

Ī'LŌ-BĀT

st: stȳ'lō-bāte.
tr: trī'lō-bate.
Plus silo bait, etc.

IL'Ō-I
IL'Ō-KWIZM

fāte, fär, fȧst, fạll, finăl, cāre, at; mēte, prẹy, hễr, met; pīne, marïne, bȋrd, pin; nōte, mŏve, fọr, atŏm, not; mọọn, book; **888**

(Choose only one word out of each group)

IL'Ō-I

b: bil'lōw-y.
p: pil'lōw-y.
w: wil'lōw-y.
Plus armadillo he, etc.

IL'Ō-ING

b: bil'lōw-ing.
p: pil'lōw-ing.
Plus pecadillo wing, etc.

IL'Ō-JI

d: dil'ō-ġy.
k(ç): brȧ-çhyl'ō-ġy.
l: pȧ-lil'ō-ġy.
s: fos-sil'ō-ġy.
t: an-til'ō-ġy.
tr: tril'ō-ġy.
Plus willow, gee!, etc.
Plus skill, Oh gee!, etc.

IL'Ō-JĪZ

p: e-pil'ō-ġize.
s: syl'lō-gīze.

IL'Ō-JIZM

p: e-pil'ō-ġiṣm.
s: ep-i-syl'lō-ġiṣm, syl'lō-ġiṣm.

IL'Ō-RI

p: pil'lō-ry.
Cf. il'ūr-i.

IL'Ō-KWENS

d: blan-dil'ō-quence,
gran-dil'ō-quence.
n: mag-nil'ō-quence,
som-nil'ō-quence.
t: stul-til'ō-quence.
v: bre-vil'ō-quence.

IL'Ō-KWENT

d: blan-dil'ō-quent,
gran-dil'ō-quent.
l: mel-lil'ō-quent.
n: mag-nil'ō-quent,
som-nil'ō-quent.
r: vē-ril'ō-quent.
s: flex-il'ō-quent,
pạu-cil'ō-quent.
t: sañç-til'ō-quent,
stul-til'ō-quent.
v: bre-vil'ō-quent,
suȧ-vil'ō-quent (swȧ-).
Plus mill oak went, etc.

IL'Ō-KWI

l: sō-lil'ō-quy.
n: som-nil'ō-quy.
r: peç-tō-ril'ō-quy.
s: pạu-cil'ō-quy.
t: den-til'ō-quy, stul-til'ō-quy.
tr: gas-tril'ō-quy,
ven-tril'ō-quy.
v: suȧ-vil'ō-quy.
Plus hillock, we, etc.
Plus hill oak, we, etc.

IL'Ō-KWIST

n: som-nil'ō-quist.
t: den-til'ō-quist.
tr: gas-tril'ō-quist,
ven-tril'ō-quist.

IL'Ō-KWĪZ

l: sō-lil'ō-quize.
tr: ven-tril'ō-quize.

IL'Ō-KWIZM

n: som-nil'ō-quiṣm.
r: peç-tō-ril'ō-quiṣm.

889

ūse, bull, brûte, tūrn, up; crȳ, myth; çat, machine, ace,   **IL′Ō-KWUS**
church, chord; ġem, añger, (Fr.) boñ, aş; THis, thin; aʒure   **IM′I-ĂN**

(Choose only one word out of each group)

tr: gas-tril′ō-quişm,
ven-tril′ō-quişm.

IL′Ō-KWUS

d: gran-dil′ō-quous.
n: mag-nil′ō-quous,
som-nil′ō-quous.
r: peç-tō-ril′ō-quous.
tr: ven-tril′ō-quous.

IL′ŪR-I

f: phyl-lăr-y.
h: Hil′ăr-y.
p: çà-pil′lăr-y, pil′lŏr-y.
s: cil′ēr-y, çō-di-cil′lăr-y,
Sil′lēr-y.
t: är-til′lēr-y, dis-til′lēr-y.
Plus miller, he, etc.

IL′YĂN-SI

br: bril′lian-cy.
s: tran-sil′ien-cy.
z: re-şil′ien-cy.
Plus million, see, etc.

IL′YĂR-I

b: at-rà-bil′iăr-i.
z: aux-il′iăr-y.

IM′À-NUS

d: pē-dim′à-nous.
j: lon-ġim′à-nous.

ĪM′À-TŪR

kl: çlīm′à-tūre.
l: līm′à-tūre*.
Plus I'm at your, etc.

IM′BRI-KĀT

Vowel: im′bri-çāte.
f: fim′bri-çāte.

Ī′MĒR-I

pr: prī′măr-y.
r: rhȳ′mēr-y.
Plus two-timer, he, etc.

IM′ET-RI

j: lon-ġim′et-ry.
l: al-kà-lim′et-ry.
n: plà-nim′et-ry.
r: çal-ō-rim′et-ry,
ī″sō-pē-rim′et-ry,
pō-là-rim′et-ry,
saç-chà-rim′et-ry.
s: à-sym′met-ry, sym′met-ry.
th: bà-thym′et-ry.

IM′ET-ŪR

d: dim′et-ēr
l: al-kà-lim′et-ēr, lim′it-ēr,
sà-lim′et-ēr,
n: plà-nim′et-ēr.
r: çal-ō-rim′et-ēr, pē-rim′et-ēr,
pō-là-rim′et-ēr,
saç-chà-rim′et-ēr.
s: dà-sym′et-ēr, fō-cim′et-ēr,
lī-cim′et-ēr, pul-sim′et-ēr,
rhȳ-sim′et-ēr, scim′et-ēr,
tà-sim′et-ēr, vē-lō-cim′et-ēr,
zȳ-mō-sim′et-ēr.
t: al-tim′et-ēr.
tr: trim′et-ēr.
v: grà-vim′et-ēr, pel-vim′et-ēr.
Plus limit her, err *or* er, etc.
Cf. scim′i-tăr.

IM′I-ĂN, IM′I-ŎN

d: En-dym′i-ŏn.
s: Sim′ē-ŏn, sim′i-ăn.
Plus jimmy an *or* Ann, etc.

IM'I-KĂL
IM'Ŭ-LĂT

fāte, fär, fȧst, fạll, fĭnăl, cãre, at; mēte, prey, hẽr, met; pīne, marïne, bĭrd, pĭn; nōte, mŏve, fọr, atŏm, not; mọọn, book; 890

(Choose only one word out of each group)

IM'I-KĂL

k(ç): al-çhym'i-çăl.
m: mim'i-çăl, pan-tō-mim'i-çăl.
n: an-ō-nym'i-çăl,
hō-mō-nym'i-çăl, i-nim'i-çăl,
met-ō-nym'i-çăl.
Plus shimmy, Cal, etc.

IM'I-NĂL

j: rē-ġim'i-năl.
kr: çrim'i-năl.
l: sub-lim'i-năl.
v: vim'i-năl.
Plus women, Al, etc.
Cf. women all, etc.
Plus vim in Al, etc.
Cf. vim in all, etc.

IM'I-NĀT

kr: aç-çrim'i-nāte*,
çrim'i-nāte, dis-çrim'i-nāte,
in-çrim'i-nāte,
in-dis-çrim'i-nāte,
rē-çrim'i-nāte.
l: ē-lim'i-nāte.
Plus women ate *or* eight, etc.
Plus vim innate, etc.
Plus limb in eight, etc.

ĪM'I-NES

gr: grīm'i-ness.
r: rhȳm'i-ness (rīm').
sl: slīm'i-ness.
t: thȳm'i-ness (tīm').

IM'I-NI

b: Bim'i-ni.
j: jim'i-ny.
l: pōst"-lim'i-ny.

p: nim'i-ni-pim'i-ni.
r: Rim'i-ni.
Plus women, he, etc.
Plus limb in, he, etc.
Plus shimmy, knee, etc.

IM'I-NUS

kr: çrim'i-nous.
l: mō-lim'i-nous*.
Plus women *or* persimmon us, etc.

IM'I-TI

d: dim'i-ty.
l: sub-lim'i-ty.
n: an-ō-nym'i-ty,
equ-ȧ-nim'i-ty (ek-wȧ-),
mag-nȧ-nim'i-ty,
pär-vȧ-nim'i-ty,
pseū-dō-nym'-ity (sū-),
pū"sil-lȧ-nim'i-ty,
sañç-tȧ-nim'i-ty,
ū-nȧn-nim'i-ty.
s: prox-im'i-ty.
Plus limit, he, etc.
Plus dim it, he, etc.

IM'PŨR-ING

hw: whim'pẽr-ing.
s: sim'pẽr-ing.
Plus simper, ring, etc.

IM'PŨR-ŨR

hw: whim'pẽr-ẽr.
s: sim'pẽr-ẽr.
Plus whimper her, etc.

IM'Ū-LĀT

s: as-sim'ū-lāte,
dis-sim'ū-lāte, sim'ū-lāte.
st: stim'ū-lāte.
Plus him, you late, etc.

(Choose only one word out of each group)

IM´Ū-LUS

l: lim´ū-lus.
st: stim´ū-lus.

IM´ŨR-US

d: dim´ẽr-ous.
l: pō-lym´ẽr-ous.
Plus simmer us, etc.

ĪN´A̤-B'L

b: c̱om-bīn´a̤-ble.
f: dē-fīn´a̤-ble, fīn´a̤-ble,
   in-dē-fīn´a̤-ble.
kl: dē-c̱līn´a̤-ble, in-c̱lin´a̤-ble,
   in-dē-c̱līn´a̤-ble.
s: as-sīgn´a̤-ble,
   c̱on-sīgn´a̤-ble,
   sīgn´a̤-ble.
z: dē-ṣīgn´a̤-ble.
Plus assign a bull, etc.
Plus china bull, etc.

ĪN´ĂR-I

b: bīn´ăr-y.
Cf. īn´ũr-i.

ĪN´A̤-TIV

b: c̱om-bīn´a̤-tive.
f: fīn´a̤-tive*.

IN´DI-KĀT

Vowel: in´di-c̱āte.
s: syn´di-c̱āte.
v: vin´di-c̱āte.
Plus windy Kate, etc.

ĪN´DŨR-I

b: bīn´dẽr-y.
gr: grīn´dẽr-y.
Plus blinder, he, etc.

IN´DŨR-I

s: cin´dẽr-y.
t: tin´dẽr-y.
Plus cinder, he, etc.

IN´Ē-ĂL, IN´I-ĂL

f: fin´i-ăl.
gw: c̱on-sañ-guin´ē-ăl (-gwin´),
   sañ-guin´ē-ăl.
l: in-tẽr-lin´ē-ăl, lin´ē-ăl.
m: grȧ-min´ē-ăl, stȧ-min´ē-ăl.
p: pin´ē-ăl.
t: pec̱-tin´ē-ăl.
Plus whinny, Al, etc.

IN´Ē-MA̤

k: kin´ē-ma̤.
s: cin´ē-ma̤.
Plus skinny ma, etc.

IN´Ē-US

d: tes-tū-din´ē-ous.
gw: c̱on-sañ-guin´ē-ous (-gwin´).
   sañ-guin´ē-ous.
j: c̱är″ti-lȧ-g̣in´ē-ous.
m: flȧ-min´ē-ous, ful-min´ē-ous,
   grȧ-min´ē-ous, ig-nō-min´i-ous,
   stȧ-min´ē-ous, strȧ-min´ē-ous,
   vi-min´ē-ous.
Plus shinney us, etc.

ING´GŨR-ING

f: fiñ´gẽr-ing.
l: liñ´gẽr-ing, mȧ-liñ´gẽr-ing.
Plus finger ring, etc.

ING´GŨR-ŨR

f: fiñ´gẽr-ẽr.
l: liñ´gẽr-ẽr, mȧ-liñ´gẽr-ẽr.
Plus finger her, err *or* er, etc.

ING'I-NES
IN'I-K'L

fāte, fär, fȧst, fȧll, finȧl, cãre, at; mēte, prey, hẽr, met; pīne,
marīne, bĩrd, pin; nōte, mōve, fọr, atŏm, nọt; mọọn, book; **892**

(Choose only one word out of each group)

ING'I-NES

r: ring'i-ness.
spr: spring'i-ness.
str: string'i-ness.

INGK'Å-B'L

dr: driñk'ȧ-ble, un-driñk'ȧ-ble.
s: siñk'ȧ-ble, un-siñk'ȧ-ble.
shr: shriñk'ȧ-ble,
un-shriñk'ȧ-ble.
th: thiñk'ȧ-ble, un-thiñk'ȧ-ble.
Plus sink a bull, etc.

INGK'I-NES

Vowel: iñk'i-ness.
k: kiñk'i-ness.
p: piñk'i-ness.
sl: sliñk'i-ness.

INGK'WI-TI

j: lon-ġiñqu'i-ty (-jingk'). *
p: prō-piñqu'i-ty.
Plus pink wit, he, etc.

IN'I-ĂL

f: fin'i-ăl.
Cf. in'ē-ăl.

IN'I-Å

d: Sär-din'i-ȧ.
j: Vĩr-ġin'i-ȧ.
s: Ab-ys-sin'i-ȧ.
v: Lȧ-vin'i-ȧ.
z: zin'ni-ȧ.
Plus whinny a, etc.

IN'I-ĂN

d: Sär-din'i-ăn.
f: Del-phin'i-ăn.

j: an"thrō-pō-phȧ-ġin'i-ăn,
Cär-thȧ-ġin'i-ăn,
vĩr-ȧ-ġin'i-ăn, Vĩr-ġin'i-ăn.
l: Çar-ō-lin'i-ăn.
m: Är-min'i-ăn.
r: czä-rin'i-ăn (zä-).
s: Ab-ys-sin'i-ăn,
El-eū-sin'i-ăn, Hẽr-cyn'i-ăn,
Sō-cin'i-ăn.
t: Au-gus-tin'i-ăn,
Jus-tin'i-ăn, Pal-es-tin'ē-ăn,
sẽr-pen-tin'ē-ăn.
w: Där-win'i-ăn.
Plus skinny, Ann *or* an, etc.

IN'I-ĀT

l: dē-lin'ē-āte, lin'ē-āte.
m: min'i-āte.
s: lȧ-cin'i-āte.
Plus Minnie ate *or* eight, **etc.**
Plus thin, he ate, etc.

ĪN'I-EST

br: brīn'i-est.
sh: shīn'i-est.
sp: spīn'i-est.
t: tīn'i-est.

IN'I-FQRM

m: al-ū-min'i-fọrm.
s: lȧ-cin'i-fọrm.
t: aç-tin'i-fọrm.
Plus finny form, etc.

IN'I-KIN

f: fin'i-kin.
m: min'i-kin.
Plus finny kin, etc.

IN'I-K'L

b: bin'nȧ-çle, bin'ō-çle.
f: fin'i-çăl.

(Choose only one word out of each group)

kl: çlin'i-çăl, syn-çlin'i-çăl.
m: ad-min'i-çle,
Bräh-min'i-çăl.
dō-min'i-çăl, flá-min'i-çăl.
p: pin'ná-çle.
s: cyn'i-çăl, Sin'i-çăl.
Plus skinny, Cal, etc.

IN'I-MENT

l: lin'i-ment.
m: min'i-ment*.
Plus whinny meant, etc.
Plus skin he meant, etc.

IN'ISH-ING

f: fin'ish-ing.
m: di-min'ish-ing.

IN'IS-TRĂL

m: min'is-trăl.
s: sin'is-trăl.

IN'IS-TŪR

m: ad-min'is-tẽr, min'is-tẽr.
s: sin'is-tẽr.
Plus Minnie stir, etc.
Plus violinist, her, err *or* er, etc.

IN'I-TI

f: af-fin'i-ty, in-fin'i-ty.
gr: per-ē-grin'i-ty.
gw: çon-sañ-guin'i-ty,
sañ-guin'i-ty (-gwin').
j: vīr-á-ġin'i-ty, vīr-ġin'i-ty.
l: al-ká-lin'i-ty, fē-lin'i-ty,
mas-çū-lin'i-ty, sá-lin'i-ty.
n: as-i-nin'i-ty, fem-i-nin'i-ty.
s: vi-cin'i-ty.
t: La-tin'i-ty, sa-tin'i-ty.
tr: trin'i-ty.

v: di-vin'i-ty, pa-tá-vin'i-ty.
Plus in it, he, etc.
Plus linnet, he, etc.
Plus guinea tea, etc.

IN'I-TIV

b: çom-bin'i-tive.
f: fin'i-tive, in-fin'i-tive.

ĪN'I-ŪR

br: brīn'i-ẽr.
sh: shīn'i-ẽr.
sp: spīn'i-ẽr.
t: tīn'i-ẽr.
Plus winy, her, err *or* er, etc.

IN'JEN-SI

fr: rē-frin'ġen-cy.
str: strin'ġen-cy.
t: çon-tin'ġen-cy.
tr: as-trin'ġen-cy.

IN'JI-ĂN

r: Thṳ-rin'ġi-an.
v: Çär-lō-vin'ġi-ăn,
Mer-ō-vin'ġi-ăn.
Plus stingy, Ann *or* an, etc.

IN'JI-LI

d: din'ġi-ly.
st: stin'ġi-ly.
Plus fringy, Lee *or* lea, etc.

IN'JI-NES

d: din'ġi-ness.
st: stinġ'i-ness.

ĪN'LĂN-DŪR

r: Rhīne'lăn-dẽr (rīn').
v: Vīne'lăn-dẽr.
Plus mine, land her, etc.

(Choose only one word out of each group)

IN′LĂN-DŬR

Vowel: in′lăn-dẽr.
f: Fin′lăn-dẽr.
Plus Min land her, etc.

IN′Ō-LIN

kr: ̧crin′ō-line.
kw: quin′ō-line.

IN′THI-ĂN

r: ̧Cȧ-rin′thi-ăn, ̧Cō-rin′thi-ăn,
lab-y-rin′thi-ăn.
s: ab-sin′thi-ăn,
hȳ-ȧ-cin′thi-ăn.

IN′TŨR-EST

Vowel: in′tẽr-est.
spl: splin′tẽr-est*.
w: win′tẽr-est*.
Cf. sin to rest, etc.

IN′TŨR-I

pr: prin′tẽr-y.
spl: splin′tẽr-y.
w: win′tẽr-y.
Plus sprinter, he, etc.

ĪN′ŨR-I

b: bī′năr-y.
f: fī′năr-y*, fī′nẽr-y,
rē-fīn′ẽr-y.
kw: quī′năr-y.
p: al-pīn′ẽr-y*, pīn′ẽr-y.
sw: swīn′ẽr-y.
v: vīn′ẽr-y.
Plus miner, he, etc.

IN′Ū-ĀT

s: in-sin′ū-āte, sin′ū-āte.
t: ̧con-tin′ū-āte.
Plus skin you ate *or* eight, etc.
Plus sinew ate, etc.

IN′Ū-US

s: sin′ū-ous.
t: ̧con-tin′ū-ous.
Plus sinew us, etc.

Ī′ŌL-Ȧ

r: vȧ-rī′ōl-ȧ.
v: vī′ōl-ȧ.
Plus bass-viol, a, etc.

Ī′Ō-LET

tr: trī′ō-let.
v: vī′ō-let.
Plus sky, O let, etc.
Plus viol let, etc.
Plus Clio let, etc.

Ī′Ō-LIST

s: scī′ō-list (sī′).
v: vī′ō-list.
Plus try, O list, etc.
Plus Clio, list, etc.

Ī′Ō-LUS

d: glȧ-dī′ō-lus.
r: vȧ-rī′ō-lus.
s: scī′ō-lus (sī′).
Plus bass-viol us, etc.

Ī′Ō-PĒ

b: pres-bȳ′ō-py.
l: ̧Cal-lī′ō-pē.
m: mȳ′ō-pē.

Ī′Ō-TŨR

r: rī′ō-tẽr.
Cf. ī′et-ūr.

(Choose only one word out of each group)

Ī′-Ō-SĒN

m: Mī′ō-cēne.
pl: Plī′ō-cēne,
post″=Plī′ō-cēne.
Plus sky, O scēne *or* seen, etc.

IP′-ĂR-US

Vowel: dē-ip′ăr-ous,
fol-i-ip′ăr-ous.
b: bip′ăr-ous, sē-bip′ăr-ous.
d: fron-dip′ăr-ous.
l: ġe-mel-lip′ăr-ous,
po-lyp′ăr-ous.
m: ġem-mip′ăr-ous,
tō-mip′ăr-ous, vĕr-mip′ăr-ous.
n: çri-nip′ăr-ous,
om-nip′ăr-ous, ū-nip′ăr-ous.
p: ō-pip′ăr-ous,
pol-y-pip′ăr-ous.
r: flō-rip′ăr-ous,
sū-dō-rip′ăr-ous.
s: fis-sip′ăr-ous.
t: fruç-tip′ăr-ous,
mul-tip′ăr-ous.
v: lär-vip′ăr-ous, ō-vip′ăr-ous.
ō-vō-vip′ăr-ous, vi-vip′ăr-ous.
Plus skipper us, etc.

IP′-Á-THI

n: çom-nip′á-thy.
s: kin-ē-sip′á-thy.
t: an-tip′á-thy.
Cf. whippeth thee*, etc.

IP′-Á-THIST

n: som-nip′á-thist.
t: an-tip′á-thist.

IP′-ED-ĂL

kw: ē-quip′e-dăl.
l: sō-lip′e-dăl.

IP′-LI-KĀT

kw: ses-quip′li-çāte.
tr: trip′li-çāte.
Plus triply, Kate, etc.

IP′-Ō-LI

l: Gal-lip′ō-li.
tr: Trip′ō-li.
Plus ship alee, etc.
Plus tipple he, etc.
Plus strip a lea *or* Lee, etc.

IP′-Ō-TENS

m: är-mip′ō-tence.
n: ig-nip′ō-tence,
om-nip′ō-tence,
plē-nip′ō-tence.
Plus hippo, tense *or* tents, etc.

IP′-Ō-TENT

l: bel-lip′ō-tent.
m: är-mip′ō-tent.
n: ig-nip′ō-tent,
om-nip′ō-tent,
plē-nip′ō-tent.
t: mul-tip′ō-tent.
Plus hippo tent, etc.

IP′-TI-KĂL

kr: çryp′ti-çăl.
l: ap-oç-á-lyp′ti-çăl,
el-lip′ti-çăl.
Plus ecliptic, Al, etc.

IP′-TŨR-US

d: dip′tĕr-ous.
r: pē-rip′tĕr-ous.
tr: trip′tĕr-ous.

IP′-Ū-LĀT

n: má-nip′ū-lāte.
st: á-stip′ū-lāte, stip′ū-lāte.
Plus skip, you late, etc.

fāte, fär, făst, fạll, finăl, cãre, at; mēte, prẹy, hẽr, met; pīne, marīne, bĩrd, pĭn; nōte, mŏve, fọr, atŏm, not; mọọn, book;

(Choose only one word out of each group)

IP'ŪR-I

fr: frip'pẽr-y.
sl: slip'pẽr-y.
Plus zipper, he, etc.

ĪR'Á-B'L

kw: aç-quĩr'á-ble, rē-quĩr'á-ble.
sp: ex-pĩr'á-ble, pẽr-spĩr'á-ble, rē-spĩr'á-ble, tran-spĩr'á-ble.
t: un-tĩr'á-ble.
z: dē-sĩr'á-ble.
Plus hire a bull, etc.
Plus Elmira bull, etc.

ĪR'ÁS-I

p: pī'rá-cy.
t: rē-tĩr'á-cy.
Plus acquire a sea, etc.
Plus Mira, see, etc.

IR'ÁS-I

l: dē-lir'á-cy.
sp: çon-spir'á-cy.
Plus Kirah, see, etc.
Plus smear a sea, etc.

ĪR'FỤL-NES

Vowel: īre'fụl-ness.
d: dīre'fụl-ness.

IR'I-ĂN

s: As-syr'i-ăn, Syr'i-ăn.
st: Styr'i-ăn.
t: Tyr'i-ăn.
Cf. ēr'i-ăn.
Plus weary an, etc.
Plus drear, Ian, etc.

IR'I-KĂL

j: pan-ē-ġyr'i-çăl.
l: lyr'i-çăl.

m: mir'á-çle.
p: em-pir'i-çăl.
t: sá-tir'i-çăl.
Plus weary, Cal, etc.
Plus lyric, Al, etc.

IR'I-SIZM

l: lyr'i-cism.
p: em-pir'i-cism.

IR'I-US

l: dē-lir'i-ous.
s: Sir'i-us.
Cf. ēr'i-us.
Plus weary us, etc.

ĪR'ŎN-I

Vowel: īr'ŏn-y.
j: ġȳr'ŏn-y.
Plus Myron, he, etc.
Plus Cairo knee, etc.

IS'EN-ING

gl: glis'ten-ing (glis'en-).
kr: çhris'ten-ing (kris'en-).
l: lis'ten-ing (lis'en-), un-lis'ten-ing.

IS'EN-SI

n: re-mi-nis'cen-cy.
v: rē-vi-vis'cen-cy.
Plus listen, sea *or* see, etc.

IS'EN-ŨR

kr: çhris'ten-ẽr (kris'en-ẽr).
l: lis'ten-ẽr (lis'en-ẽr).
Plus glisten, her *or* er, etc.

ISH'ĂL-I

d: jú-dic'iăl-ly (-dish'ăl-), pre-jú-dic'iăl-ly.

(Choose only one word out of each group)

f: of-fic′iăl-ly (-fish′ăl-),
sū-pēr-fic′iăl-ly.
Plus initial, Lee or lea, etc.
Plus initial, he, etc.

ISH′ĂL-IZM

d: jᵤ-dic′iăl-iṣm (-dish-ăl).
f: of-fic′iăl-iṣm.

ISH′EN-SI

f: ben-ē-fic′ien-cy (-fish′en-),
dē-fic′ien-cy, ef-fic′ien-cy,
in-ef-fic′ien-cy, in-suf-fic′ien-cy,
prō-fic′ien-cy,
self′=suf-fic′ien-cy,
suf-fic′ien-cy.
l: al-lic′ien-cy.
s: in-sit′ien-cy*.
Plus mission, sea or see, etc.

ISH′I-Å

l: A-lic′i-à (-lish′), Dē-lic′i-à,
Fē-lic′i-à.
Plus sissy, a, etc.

ISH′I-ĀT

f: mal-ē-fic′i-āte (-fish′),
of-fic′i-āte.
n: i-nit′i-āte (-nish′).
p: prō-pit′i-āte (-pish′).
tr: pà-tric′i-āte (-trish′).
v: nō-vit′i-āte (-vish′),
vit′i-āte (vish′).
Plus wish he ate, etc.
Plus swishy, ate or eight, etc.

ISH′I-ENS

n: om-nis′ci-ence (-nish′i-).
Cf. ish′ens.

ISH′I-ENT

n: om-nis′ci-ent (-nish′).
Cf. ish′ent.

I′SHUN-ĂL

Vowel: in-tū-i′tiŏn-ăl (-i′shun-ăl).
d: ad-di′tiŏn-ăl,
c̟on-di′tion-ăl, trà-di′tion-ăl.
l: vō-li′tion-ăl.
m: c̟om-mi′sion-al.
n: de-fi-ni′tion-ăl.
t: re-pe-ti′tion-ăl.
z: dis-pō-ṣi′tion-ăl,
dis-qui-si′tion-ăl,
in-qui-ṣi′tion-ăl,
pō-ṣi′tion-ăl, pre-pō-ṣi′tion-ăl,
pro-pō-si′tion-ăl,
sup-pō-ṣi′tion-ăl,
tran-ṣi′tion-ăl,
trans-pō-si′tion-ăl.
Plus mission, Al, etc.

I′SHUN-IST

b: ex-hi-bi′tion-ist,
prō-hi-bi′tion-ist.
d: ex-pē-di′tion-ist,
trà-di′tion-ist.
l: ab-ō-li′tion-ist,
c̟ō-à-li′tion-ist.
z: op-pō-ṣi′tion-ist,
re-qui-ṣi′tion-ist.

I′SHUN-ŪR

b: ex-hi-bi′tion-ēr.
d: trà-di′tion-ēr.
l: c̟ō-à-li′tion-ēr.
m: c̟om-mis′sion-ēr,
mis′sion-ēr.
n: ad-mō-ni′tion-ēr.
t: prac̟-ti′tion-ēr.
Plus patrician her, err or er, ɛtc.

(Choose only one word out of each group)

ISH'US-NES

d: ex-pē-di'tious-ness
(-dish'us-nes),
in-di'cious-ness,
jù-di'cious-ness,
sē-di'tious-ness.
j: flȧ-ġi'tious-ness.
l: dē-li'cious-ness,
mȧ-li'cious-ness.
n: pẽr-ni'cious-ness.
p: ạus-pi'cious-ness,
in-ạus-pi'cious-ness,
prō-pi'tious-ness,
sus-pi'cious-ness.
pr: çȧ-pri'cious-ness.
r: a-vȧ-ri'cious-ness.
st: sū-pẽr-sti'tious-ness.
t: ad-ven-ti'tious-ness,
fiç-ti'tious-ness.
tr: mer-ē-tri'cious-ness.
z: sup-pō-ṣi'tious-ness.

IS'I-B'L

m: ad-mis'si-ble (-b'l),
ȧ-mis'si-ble, dis-mis'si-ble,
im-mis'ci-ble,
in-çom-mis'ci-ble,
ir-rē-mis'sȧ-ble, mis'ci-ble,
ō-mis'si-ble, pẽr-mis'ci-ble,
pẽr-mis'si-ble, rē-mis'si-ble,
trans-mis'si-ble.
s: scis'si-ble.
Plus hiss a bull, etc.

ĪS'I-EST

Vowel: īc'i-est.
sp: spīc'i-est.

Ī'SI-K'L

Vowel: ī'ci-cle.
b: bī'cy-cle.

tr: trī'cy-cle.
Plus spicy, Cal, etc.

ĪS'I-LI

Vowel: īc'i-ly.
sp: spīc'i-ly.
Plus icy Lee *or* lea, etc.

IS'I-MŌ

l: ġen"ẽr-ȧ-lis'si-mō.
n: pĭ-ȧ-nis'si-mō.
t: fọr-tis'si-mō,
pres-tis'si-mō.
v: brä-vis'si-mō.
Plus sissy, Mo, etc.

IS'I-NĂL

d: fi-dic'i-năl, mē-dic'i-năl.
f: of-fic'i-năl.
t: vȧ-tic'i-năl.
v: vic'i-năl.

ĪS'I-NES

Vowel: īc'i-ness.
sp: spīc'i-ness.

IS'I-TI

Vowel: stō-ic'i-ty.
br: lū-bric'i-ty, rù-bric'i-ty.
d: ben-ē-dic'e-tē,
im-mun-dic'i-ty,
im-pū-dic'i-ty, men-dic'i-ty,
pẽr-i-ō-dic'i-ty, pù-dic'i-ty,
spher-oi-dic'i-ty (sfer-).
l: cath-ō-lic'i-ty,
ē-van-ġē-lic'i-ty, fē-lic'i-ty,
in-fe-lic'i-ty, pub-lic'i-ty,
trip-lic'i-ty.
m: en-dē-mic'i-ty.

899 ūse, bu̧ll, brúte, tū̃rn, up; crȳ, myth; c̦at, mac̦hine, ace, church, c̦hord; ġem, an̄ger, (Fr.) bon̂, a̧s; THis, thin; a̧zure

IS'IT-NES
IS'TI-KĂL

(Choose only one word out of each group)

n: can-ō-nic'i-ty, c̦ō-nic'i-ty, ē-lec̦''trō-tō-nic'i-ty, tō-nic'i-ty, ū-nic'i-ty, vol-c̦à-nic'i-ty, vul-c̦à-nic'i-ty.

p: hȳ-grō-scō-pic'i-ty.

pl: ac̦-c̦om-plic'i-ty, c̦om-plic'i-ty, dú-plic'i-ty, mul-ti-plic'i-ty, sim-plic'i-ty.

r: c̦al-ō-ric'i-ty, his-tō-ric'i-ty, splē-ric'i-ty.

t: à-c̦hrō-mà-tic'i-ty, au-then-tic'i-ty, c̦aus-tic'i-ty, dō-mes-tic'i-ty, ē-las-tic'i-ty, el-lip-tic'i-ty, in-ē-las-tic'i-ty, pep-tic'i-ty, plas-tic'i-ty, rus-tic'i-ty, spas-tic'i-ty, styp-tic'i-ty, vĕr-tic'i-ty.

tr: cen-tric'i-ty, ē-lec̦-tric'i-ty.

Plus illicit, he, etc.

Plus kiss it, he, etc.

IS'IT-NES

l: il-lic'it-ness, lic'it-ness.

pl: ex-plic'it-ness, im-plic'it-ness.

IS'I-TŪD

l: sō-lic'i-tūde.

s: vi-cis'si-tude.

sp: spis'si-tūde.

Plus this etude, etc.

I'SI-US

n: Dī-ō-ny'si-us.

Cf. Ly'ci-ăs.

ĪS'IV-LY

r: dē-rīs'ive-ly.

s: dē-cīs'ive-ly, in-cīs'ive-ly, in-dē-cīs'ive-ly.

ĪS'IV-NES

r: dē-rīs'ive-ness.

s: dē-cīs'ive-ness, in-cīs'ive-ness, in-dē-cīs'ive-ness.

IS'KI-EST

fr: fris'ki-est.

r: ris'ki-est.

IS'ŎN-US

n: ū-nis'ŏn-ous.

t: fluc̦-tis'ŏn-ous.

Plus imprison us, etc.

ĪS'ŌR-I, ĪS'ŪR-I

r: dē-rīs'ŏr-y.

s: dē-cīs'ŏr-y, in-cīs'ŏr-y.

sp: spīc'ĕr-y.

Plus nicer, he, etc.

IS'ŎR-I

m: ad-mis'sŏ-ry, dis-mis'sŏ-ry, ē-mis'sŏ-ry, rē-mis'ŏ-ry.

s: rē-scis'sŏ-ry.

Plus dismisser, he, etc.

IS'TEN-SI

d: dis'tăn-cy.

s: c̦on-sis'ten-cy, in-c̦on-sis'ten-cy, sub-sis'ten-cy.

z: ex-is'ten-cy, pĕr-sis'ten-cy, prē-ex-is'ten-cy.

Plus distance, he, etc.

IS'TI-KĂL

Vowel: ā-thē-is'ti-c̦ăl, c̦aș-ū-is'ti-c̦ăl, dē-is'ti-c̦ăl, ē-gō-is'ti-c̦ăl, thē-is'ti-c̦ăl.

(Choose only one word out of each group)

d: me-thō-dis'ti-cȧl.

f: par-ȧ-gra-phis'ti-cȧl,
sō-phis'ti-cȧl,
thē"ō-sō-phis'ti-cȧl.

gw: liñ-guis'ti-cȧl.

j: dī"ȧ-lō-ġis'ti-cȧl,
eū-lō-ġis'ti-cȧl.

k(c̨): an-är-c̨his'ti-cȧl,
ant"an-är-c̨his'ti-cȧl.

l: an-om-ȧ-lis'ti-cȧl,
c̨a-bȧ-lis'ti-cȧl.

m: al-c̨he-mis'ti-cȧl,
c̨he-mis'ti-cȧl,
eū-phe-mis'ti-cȧl,
hē-mis'ti-c̨hăl, mys'ti-cȧl.

n: ag-ō-nis'ti-cȧl,
an-tag-ō-nis'ti-cȧl,
C̨al-vȧ-nis'ti-cȧl.

r: ā-ō-ris'ti-cȧl,
a-phō-ris'ti-cȧl,
c̨har-ac̨-tē-ris'ti-cȧl,
eū-c̨hȧ-ris'ti-cȧl, pū-ris'ti-cȧl.

t: är-tis'ti-cȧl, ē-gō-tis'ti-cȧl,
pī-e-tis'ti-cȧl, stȧ-tis'ti-cȧl.

th: ap-ȧ-this'ti-cȧl.

Plus misty, Cal, etc.

IS'TI-KĀT

f: sō-phis'ti-cāte.

j: dē-phlō-ġis'ti-cāte.

Plus misty, Kate, etc.

Plus mystic ate or eight, etc.

IST'LES-NES

l: list'less-ness.

z: rē-ṣist'less-ness.

IS'TŎ-RI

h: his'tŏ-ry.

m: mys'tẽr-y.

---

s: c̨on-sis'tŏ-ry.

Plus blister, he, etc.

Cf. bis'ton-ry.

ĪT'Ȧ-B'L

d: in-dict'ȧ-bie (-dīt'),
in-dīt'ȧ-ble.

kw: rē-quīt'ȧ-ble.

l: līght'ȧ-ble (līt').

n: ig-nīt'ȧ-ble, ū-nīt'ȧ-ble.

r: wrīt'ȧ-ble (rīt').

s: cīt'ȧ-ble, ex-cīt'ȧ-ble,
in-cīt'ȧ-ble.

Plus fight a bull, etc.

IT'Ȧ-B'L

f: fit'tȧ-ble.

h: Mē-hit'ȧ-ble.

kw: quit'tȧ-ble.

m: ad-mit'tȧ-ble,
ir-rē-mit'tȧ-ble,
trans-mit'tȧ-ble.

Plus hit a bull, etc.

IT'ĂN-I

d: dit'tăn-y.

k: kit'ten-y.

l: lit'ăn-y.

Plus mitten, he, etc.

Plus hit a knee, etc.

ĪT'Ȧ-TIV

r: wrīt'ȧ-tive (rīt').

s: ex-cīt'ȧ-tive, in-cīt'ȧ-tive.

ĪT'FU̯L-I

fr: frīght'fu̯l-ly (frīt').

l: dē-līght'fu̯l-ly.

r: rīght'fu̯l-ly.

sp: spīte'fu̯l-ly.

Plus spiteful, lea or Lee. etc.

(Choose only one word out of each group)

ITH′Ē-SIS

p: ē-pith′ē-sis.
t: an-tith′ē-sis.
Plus pithy, sis, etc.

ĪTH′SUM-LI

bl: blīTHe′sŏme-ly.
l: līTHe′sŏme-ly.
Plus blithesŏme, Lee *or* lea, etc.

ĪTH′SUM-NES

bl: blīTHe′sŏme-ness.
l: līTHe′sŏme-ness.

ITH′ŪR-WĂRD

h: hiTH′ēr-wărd.
hw: whiTH′ēr-wărd.
TH: thiTH′ēr-wărd.
Plus wither, ward, etc.
Plus with her ward, etc.

IT′I-GĂNT

l: lit′i-gănt.
m: mit′i-gănt.

IT′I-GĀT

l: lit′i-gāte.
m: mit′i-gāte.
Plus hit a gāte, etc.

IT′I-KĂL

Vowel: Jeş-ū-it′i-c̣ăl.
kr: à-c̣rit′i-c̣ăl, c̣rit′i-c̣ăl,
  dī-à-c̣rit′i-c̣ăl,
  hȳ-pēr-c̣rit′i-c̣ăl,
  hy-pō-c̣rit′i-c̣ăl.
l: an-à-lyt′i-c̣ăl,
  c̣oş-mō-pō-lit′i-c̣ăl,
  ē-lec̣-trō-lyt′i-c̣ăl, pō-lit′i-c̣ăl.
m: Ā″brà-ha-mit′i-c̣ăl,
  hēr-mit′i-c̣ăl.

p: pṳl-pit′i-c̣ăl.
r: aṅ-c̣hō-rit′i-c̣ăl, sō-rit′i-c̣ăl.
s: thēr-sit′i-c̣ăl.
v: Le-vit′i-c̣ăl.
Plus witty, Cal, etc.
Plus Hamitic, Al, etc.

IT′I-LI

gr: grit′ti-ly.
pr: pret′ti-ly (prit′).
w: wit′ti-ly.
Plus pity, Lee *or* lēa, etc.

ĪT′I-NES

fl: flīght′i-ness.
m: al-mīght′i-ness,
  mīght′i-ness.

IT′I-NES

fl: flit′ti-ness.
gr: grit′ti-ness.
pr: pret′ti-ness.
w: wit′ti-ness.

IT′I-SIZM

br: Brit′i-cişm.
w: wit′ti-cişm.

ĪT′LI-NES

n: knīght′li-ness (nīt′).
s: un-sīght′li-ness (-sīt′).
spr: sprīte′li-ness.

IT′L-NES

br: brit′tle-ness.
l: lit′tle-ness.

IT′Ū-ĂL

b: ha-bit′ū-ăl, ō-bit′ū-ăl.
r: rit′ū-ăl.
Plus hit you, Al, etc.

(Choose only one word out of each group)

IT'Ū-ĀT
b: ha-bit'ū-āte.
s: sit'ū-āte.
Plus bit you ate *or* eight, etc.

IT'Ū-LĂR
p: cạ-pit'ū-lăr.
t: tit'ū-lăr.

IT'ŨR-ĀT
Vowel: it'ẽr-āte, rē-it'ẽr-āte.
l: il-lit'ẽr-āte, lit'ẽr-āte,
ob-lit'ẽr-āte, trans-lit'ẽr-āte.
Plus hit her eight, etc.
Plus wit orate, etc.

IT'ŨR-EST
b: bit'tẽr-est, em-bit'tẽr-est*.
fr: frit'tẽr-est*.
gl: glit'tẽr-est*.
Plus bitter rest, etc.
Plus hit arrest, etc.

IT'ŨR-ING
b: bit'tẽr-ing, em-bit'tẽr-ing.
fr: frit'tẽr-ing.
gl: glit'tẽr-ing.
t: tit'tẽr-ing.
tw: twit'tẽr-ing.
Plus glitter, ring, etc.
Plus hit her ring, etc.

Ī'ŨR-I
br: brī'ẽr-y.
d: dī'ăr-y.
f: fī'ẽr-y.
fr: frī'ăr-y.
pr: prī'ŏr-y.
Plus higher, he, etc.

ĪV'Å-B'L
pr: dē-prīv'å-ble.
r: dē-rīv'å-ble.

tr: con-trīv'å-ble.
v: rē-vīv'å-ble.
Plus drive a bull, etc.

IV'Å-B'L
g: for-giv'å-ble, giv'å-ble,
un-for-giv'å-ble.
l: liv'å-ble.
Plus outlive a bull, etc.

IV'Å-LENT
kw: ē-quiv'å-lent,
quin-quiv'å-lent.
n: om-niv'å-lent, ū-niv'å-lent.
t: mul-tiv'å-lent.
tr: tri'văl-ent.

ĪV'ĂN-SI
n: con-nīv'ăn-cy.
v: sũr-vīv'ăn-cy.

IV'Å-TIV
pr: priv'å-tive.
r: dē-riv'å-tive.

IV'EL-ŨR, IV'IL-ŨR
dr: driv'el-lẽr.
s: civ'il-lẽr.
sn: sniv'el-lẽr.
Plus shrivel her, etc.

IV'I-Å
l: Bō-liv'i-å, Liv'i-å,
Ō-liv'i-å.
tr: triv'i-å.
Plus Livy, a, etc.

IV'I-ĂL
l: ob-liv'i-ăl.
r: quäd-riv'i-ăl.
s: lix-iv'i-ăl.
tr: triv'i-ăl.
v: con-viv'i-ăl.
Plus Livy, Al, etc.

(Choose only one word out of each group)

IV'I-ĂN

l: Bō-liv′i-ăn.
v: Viv′i-ăn, Viv′i-en.
Plus Livy, Ann *or* an, etc.

IV'ID-NES

l: liv′id-ness.
v: viv′id-ness.

IV'I-TI

kl: ac̦-c̦liv′i-ty, dē-c̦liv′i-ty,
   prō-c̦liv′i-ty.
pr: priv′i-ty.
s: im-pas-siv′i-ty,
   pas-siv′i-ty,
t: ab-sorp-tiv′i-ty, ac̦-tiv′i-ty,
   c̦ap-tiv′i-ty, c̦au-ṣà-tiv′i-ty,
   c̦oġ″i-tà-tiv′i-ty,
   c̦ol-lec̦-tiv′i-ty,
   c̦on-duc̦-tiv′i-ty, fes-tiv′i-ty,
   in-c̦oġ″i-tà-tiv′i-ty,
   in-stinc̦-tiv′i-ty, mō-tiv′i-ty,
   nā-tiv′i-ty, neg-à-tiv′i-ty,
   ob-jec̦-tiv′i-ty,
   pêr-cep-tiv′i-ty, poṣ-i-tiv′i-ty,
   prō-duc̦-tiv′i-ty, rē-cep-tiv′i-ty,
   re-là--tiv′i-ty, sen-si-tiv′i-ty,
   sub-jec̦-tiv′i-ty.
Plus civet, he, etc.
Plus privy tea, etc.

IV'I-US

b: biv′i-ous.
l: ob-liv′i-ous.
s: las-civ′i-ous, lix-iv′i-ous.
t: mul-tiv′i-ous.
Plus Livy us, etc.

IV'Ō-KĂL

kw: ē-quiv′ō-c̦ăl.
n: ū-niv′ō-c̦ăl.

IV'Ō-LI

r: Riv′ō-li.
t: Tiv′ō-li.
Plus give, oh Lee, etc.

ĪV'Ŏ-RY, ĪV'À-RY

Vowel: ī′vŏ-ry.
v: vīv′à-ry.
Plus contriver, he, etc.

IV'ŎR-US

b: hĕr-biv′ŏr-ous.
g: frú-giv′ŏr-ous.
k(c̦): pis-c̦iv′ŏr-ous.
kw: ē-quiv′ŏr-ous.
m: vêr-miv′ŏr-ous.
n: c̦är-niv′ŏr-ous,
   gram-i-niv′ŏr-ous,
   gra-niv′ŏr-ous, om-niv′ŏr-ous,
   pa-niv′ŏr-ous,
   sañ-gui-niv′ŏr-ous.
s: fū-civ′ŏr-ous, os-siv′ŏr-ous.
t: in-sec̦-tiv′ŏr-ous,
   phȳ-tiv′ŏr-ous (fĭ-).
Plus deliver us, etc.

IV'ŬR-I

l: dē-liv′ẽr-y,
   ġaol dē-liv′ẽr-y (jāl),
   jāil dē-liv′ẽr-y, liv′ẽr-y.
r: riv′ẽr-y.
sh: shiv′ẽr-y.
Plus liver, he, etc.

IV'ŬR-ING

l: dē-liv′ẽr-ing.
kw: quiv′ẽr-ing.
sh: shiv′ẽr-ing.
Plus quivẽr ring, etc.

IV'ŬR-ŬR
ĬZ'Ŏ-RI

fāte, fär, fȧst, fạll, fĭnăl, cãre, ȧt; mēte, prĕy, hẽr, met; pīne,
marīne, bĭrd, pĭn; nōte, mŏve, fȯr, atŏm, nŏt; mọọn, book;

904

(Choose only one word out of each group)

IV'ŬR-ŬR

l: dē-lĭv'ẽr-ẽr.
kw: quĭv'ẽr-ẽr (kwĭv').
sh: shĭv'ẽr-ẽr.
Plus deliver her, etc.

ĪZ'Ȧ-B'L

d: ŏx-ĭ-dīz'ȧ-ble.
l: ăn-ȧ-lȳṣ'ȧ-ble,
crȳs-tăl-līz'ȧ-ble,
ē-lec̨-trō-lȳṣ'ȧ-ble,
rē-ȧ-līz'ȧ-ble.
m: dē-mīṣ'ȧ-ble.
n: ȯr-gȧ-nīz'ȧ-ble,
re-c̨og-nīz'ȧ-ble.
pr: prīz'ȧ-ble.
r: vā-pō-rīz'ȧ-ble.
s: ex-cīṣ'ȧ-ble, ex-ẽr-cīṣ'ȧ-ble,
sīz'ȧ-ble.
sp: dē-spīṣ'ȧ-ble.
t: mag-nē-tīz'ȧ-ble.
v: ad-vīṣ'ȧ-ble, dē-vīṣ'ȧ-ble.
Plus prize a bull, etc.

IZ'Ȧ-B'L

kw: ac̨-quĭṣ'i-ble.
r: rĭṣ'i-ble.
v: di-vĭṣ'i-ble, in-di-vĭṣ'i-ble,
in-vĭṣ'i-ble, vĭṣ'i-ble.
Plus quiz a bull, etc.

I'ZHUN-ĂL

s: tran-ṣi'tiŏn-al.
v: di-vi'ṣiŏn-al, prō-vi'ṣiŏn-ăl,
rē-vi'ṣiŏn-ăl, vi'ṣiŏn-ăl.
Plus incision, Al, etc.

IZ'I-AN

d: Pär-ȧ-diṣ'ē-ăn.
fr: Friṣ'i-ăn.
l: Ē-lyṣ'i-ăn.
r: Pȧ-riṣ'i-ăn.

s: prē-ciṣ'i-ăn.
Cf. izh'un.
Plus dizzy an *or* Ann, etc.

IZ'I-EST

b: buṣ'i-est.
d: diz'zi-est.

IZ'I-KĂL

d: par-ȧ-diṣ'i-c̨ăl.
f: met-ȧ-phyṣ'i-c̨ăl (-fiz'),
phyṣ'i-c̨ăl (fiz'),
psȳ-c̨hō-phyṣ'i-c̨al (si-kō-fiz'i-
k̈ăl).
t: phthiṣ'i-c̨ăl (tiz'i-kăl).
Plus dizzy, Cal, etc.
Plus physic, Al, etc.

IZ'I-LI

b: buṣ'i-ly.
d: diz'zi-ly.
Plus busy lea *or* Lee, etc.

IZ'I-TŎR

kw: ac̨-quiṣ'i-tŏr, in-quiṣ'i-tŏr,
rē-quiṣ'i-tŏr.
v: viṣ'i-tŏr.
Plus what-is-it, or, etc.

IZ'I-ŬR

b: buṣ'i-ẽr (biz').
d: diz'zi-ẽr.
fr: friz'zi-ẽr.
Plus busy her, err *or* er, etc.
Cf. viz'i-ẽr.

ĪZ'Ŏ-RI

r: ir-rīṣ'ŏr-y.
v: ad-vīṣ'ŏr-y, prō-vīṣ'ŏr-y,
rē-vīṣ'ŏr-y, sū-pẽr-vīṣ'ŏr-y.
Plus miser, he, etc.

(Choose only one word out of each group)

O

The accented vowel sounds included are listed under **O** in Single
Rhymes.

Ō′BI-Å

Vowel: ō′bē-ah.
f: ag″ō-rȧ-phō′bi-ȧ (-fō′),
āir-phō′bi-ȧ, an-drō-phō′bi-ȧ,
Añ-glō-phō′bi-ȧ,
baç-tēr″i-ō-phō′bi-ȧ,
çla̱us-trō-phō′bi-ȧ,
dē″mŏn-ō-phō′bi-ȧ,
dēr″mat-ō-phō′bi-ȧ,
dō-rȧ-phō′bi-ȧ,
dys″mō-phō-phō′bi-ȧ,
Fran-çō-phō′bi-ȧ,
Gal-lō-phō′bi-ȧ, gam-ō-phō′bi-ȧ,
Gēr″măn-ō-phō′bi-ȧ,
ġyn″ē-kō-phō′bi-ȧ,
her″ē-sy-phō′bi-ȧ,
hȳ-drō-phō′bi-ȧ,
lys-sō-phō′bi-ȧ, nē-ō-phō′bi-ȧ,
phär″mȧ-çō-phō′bi-ȧ, phō′bi-ȧ,
phō-bō-phō′bi-ȧ,
phō-tō-phō′bi-ȧ, py-rō-phō′bi-ȧ,
Rus-sō-phō′bi-ȧ, sit-i-phō′bi-ȧ,
sy″phil-ō-phō′bi-ȧ,
than″ȧ-tō-phō′bi-ȧ,
tox″i-çō-phō′bi-ȧ,
zō-ō-phō′bi-ȧ.
n: Zē-nō′bi-ȧ.
Plus adobe a, etc.

OB′IN-ET

b: bob′bin-et.
r: rob′in-et.
Plus Dobbin et, etc.
Plus hobby net, etc.

OB′Ū-LĂR

gl: glob′ū-lăr.
l: lob′ū-lăr.

QB′ŪR-I

d: da̱ub′ẽr-y.
Cf. strawberry.

OB′ŪR-I

b: bob′bẽr-y.
j: job′bẽr-y, stock⸗job′bẽr-y.
r: rob′bẽr-y.
sl: slob′bẽr-y.
sn: snob′bẽr-y.
Plus slobber, he, etc.
Plus rob her, he, etc.

OB′ŪR-ING

kl: çlob′bẽr-ing.
sl: slob′bẽr-ing.
Plus jobber ring, etc.
Plus fob, her ring, etc.
Plus rob a ring, etc.

Ō′DI-ĂL

l: al-lō′di-ăl.
n: pal-i-nō′di-ăl, thre-nō′di-al.
s: ep-i-sō′di-ăl, prō-sō′di-ăl.
t: çus-tō′di-ăl.
Plus toady, Al.

Ō′DI-ĂN

r: He-rō′di-ăn, Rhō′di-ăn (rō′).
s: prō-sō′di-ăn.
t: çus-tō′di-ăn.
Plus toady, Ann *or* an.
Plus load, Ian, etc.

OD′EL-ŪR

m: mod′el-lẽr.
Cf. od′lŭr.
Plus coddle her, etc.

OD'I-FĪ
ÖF'À-GĪ

fāte, fär, fåst, fȧll, finăl, cãre, at; mēte, prĕy, hẽr, met; pīne,
marïne, bïrd, pin; nōte, mȯve, fȯr, atŏm, not; mo͞on, book;

906

(Choose only one word out of each group)

OD'I-FĪ

k(ç): çod'i-fy.
m: mod'i-fy.
Plus body, fie!, etc.
Cf. nod of eye, etc.

OD'I-KĂL

Vowel: pē-ri-od'i-çăl.
k(ç): çod'i-çăl, ep-is-çod'i-çăl.
m: spaṣ-mod'i-çăl.
n: mō-nod'i-çăl, nod'i-çăl,
sȳ-nod'i-çăl.
s: ep-i-sod'i-çăl, pro-sod'i-çăl,
rhap-sod'i-çăl.
th: me-thod'i-çăl.
Plus body, Cal, etc.
Plus melodic, Al, etc.

ǪD'I-NES

b: bạwd'i-ness.
g: gaud'i-ness.

OD'I-TI

Vowel: od'di-ti.
m: çom-mod'i-ty,
in-çom-mod'i-ty.
Plus sod it, he, etc.
Plus toddy, tea, etc.

Ō'DI-UM

Vowel: ō'di-um.
r: rhō'di-um (rō').
s: sō'di-um.
Plus toady 'em.

Ō'DI-US

Vowel: ō'di-ous.
l: mē-lō'di-ous.
m: çom-mō'di-ous,
in-çom-mō'di-ous.
Plus toady us.

ǪD'RI-NES

b: bạwd'ri-ness.
t: tạwd'ri-ness.

OD'Ū-LĂR

m: mod'ū-lăr.
n: nod'ū-lăr.

OD'ŪR-IK

Vowel: Thē-od'ẽr-iç.
r: Rod'ẽr-ick.
Plus fodder rick, etc.
Plus prod a rick, etc.

OD'ŪR-ING

d: dod'dẽr-ing.
f: fod'dẽr-ing.
Plus odder ring, etc.
Plus God, her ring, etc.
Plus trod a ring, etc.

OF'À-GĂN

Vowel: thē-oph'à-găn,
zō-oph'à-găn.
k(ç): sär-çoph'à-găn.
r: sap-roph'à-găn.
Cf. off again, etc.

OF'À-GĪ

Vowel: thē-oph'à̤-gī (-of').
d: çär-doph'à-gī.
dr: an-droph'à-gī.
k(ç): sär-çoph'à-gī.
p: an-thrō-poph'à-gī,
hip-poph'à-gī.
r: het-ē-roph'à-gī.
t: Lō-toph'à-gī, pan-toph'à-gī.
th: li-thoph'à-gī.
Plus off a guy, etc.

(Choose only one word out of each group)

OF'Å-GI

Vowel: iċh-thy-oph'à-gy,
thē-oph'à-gy.
n: chthō-noph'à-gy (thō-).
p: an-thrō-poph'à-gy,
hip-poph'à-gy.
r: zē-roph'à-gy.
t: pan-toph'à-gy,
phy-toph'à-gy (fi-).

OF'Å-GIST

Vowel: ġē-oph'à-gist,
iċh-thy-oph'à-gist.
p: hip-poph'à-gist.
t: ġa-laċ-toph'à-gist,
pan-toph'à-gist.

OF'Å-GUS

Vowel: ġē-oph'à-gous,
oph-i-oph'à-gous,
thē-oph'à-gous, zō-oph'à-gous.
dr: an-droph'à-gous.
k(ç): ba-trà-ċhoph'à-gous,
sär-çoph'à-gus.
l: hȳ-loph'à-gous,
xȳ-loph'à-gous (zī-).
p: an-thrō-poph'à-gous,
hip-poph'à-gous.
r: neċ-roph'à-gous,
sap-roph'à-gous.
s: ē-soph'à-gus.
t: ġà-laċ-toph'à-gous,
pan-toph'à-gous,
phȳ-toph'à-gous (fī-).
th: li-thoph'à-gous.

OF'I-KĂL

s: phil-ō-soph'i-çăl,
thē-ō-soph'i-çăl.
tr: troph'i-çăl.
Plus coffee, Cal, etc.

OF'I-LIST

Vowel: bib-li-oph'i-list,
zō-oph'i-list.
s: Rus-soph'i-list.
Plus coffee list, etc.

OF'I-LIZM

Vowel: bib-li-oph'i-lism.
r: neċ-roph'i-lism.
s: Rus-soph'i-lism.

OF'IL-US

Vowel: Thē-oph'i-lus.
d: ac-i-doph'à-lus.
l: xȳ-loph'i-lous (zī-).
m: an-ē-moph'i-lous.

OF'ŎN-I

Vowel: thē-o'phăn-y ('făn-).
g: lär-yn-goph'ŏn-y.
k(ç): çà-çoph'ŏn-y.
m: hō-moph'ŏn-y.
n: Sä-tà-no'phăn-y ('făn-).
r: mīċ-roph'ŏn-y.
t: phō-toph'ŏn-y (fō-),
tạu-toph'ŏn-y.
th: ọr-thoph'ŏn-y.
Plus off a knee, etc.

OF'ŎN-US

dr: hȳ-dro'phăn-ous ('făn-).
gr: hȳ-gro'phăn-ous.
k(ç): çà-çoph'ŏn-ous.
l: meg-à-loph'ŏn-ous.
m: hō-moph'ŏn-ous.
n: mō-no'phăn-ous.
r: pȳ-ro'phăn-ous.
Plus soften us, etc.
Cf. scoff in us, etc.

(Choose only one word out of each group)

OF'ŌR-US

Vowel: zō-oph'ōr-ous.
g: mas-ti-goph'ōr-ous.
l: phyl-loph'ōr-ous (fil-).
n: ac-ti-noph'ōr-ous,
ad-ē-noph'ōr-ous.
r: py̆-roph'ōr-ous.
s: ĭ-soph'ōr-ous.
t: ġà-lac-toph'ōr-ous.
tr: el-ec-troph'ōr-ous.
Plus offer us, etc.

O'FŬL-I

Vowel: aw'fŭl-ly.
l: law'fŭl-ly, un-law'fŭl-ly.
Plus craw full, Lee, etc.
Plus awful, Lee, etc.

O'FŬL-NES

Vowel: aw'fŭl-ness.
l: law'fŭl-ness, un-law'fŭl-ness.

OF'ŪR-ING

Vowel: of'fēr-ing,
pēace of'fēr-ing (pēs).
k(c): cof'fēr-ing.
pr: prof'fēr-ing.
Plus offer ring, etc.
Plus doff her ring, etc.

OG'Å-MI

d: en-dog'à-my.
n: coē-nog'à-my (sē-),
mō-nog'à-my.
r: deū-tē-rog'à-my (dū-).
s: mi-sog'à-my.
z: ex-og'à-my.

OG'Å-MIST

Vowel: nē-og'à-mist.
n: mō-nog'à-mist.

r: deū-tē-rog'à-mist (dū-).
s: mi-sog'à-mist.
Plus fog, a mist, etc.

OG'Å-MUS

d: en-dog'à-mous.
n: mō-nog'à-mous,
phaē-nog'à-mous (fē-).
r: het-ē-rog'à-mous,
phan-ē-rog'à-mous (fan-).
z: ex-og'à-mous.

OG'Å-TIV

r: dē-rog'à-tive, in-tēr-rog'à-tive,
prē-rog'à-tive.

Ō'GI-IZM

b: bō-gēy'ism.
f: fō'gēy-ism.

OG'NŌ-MI

Vowel: crā-ni-og'nō-my,
phys-i-og'nō-my (fiz-).
th: pa-thog'nō-my
Plus hog know me, etc.

OG'RÅ-FI

Vowel: au-tō-bī-og'rà-phy,
bal-nē-og'rà-phy,
bib-li-og'rà-phy, bī-og'rà-phy,
dac-tyl-i-og'rà-phy,
gē-og'rà-phy, hag-i-og'rà-phy,
hal-i-og'rà-ph-y, hē-li-og'rà-phy,
her-ē-si-og'rà-phy,
his-tor-i-og'rà-phy,
hor"ò-log-i-og'rà-phy,
ich-thy-og'rà-phy,
id-ē-og'rà-phy, nē-og'rà-phy,
ō-phi-og'rà-phy, ō-rē-og'rà-phy,
os-tē-og'rà-phy,
pal-ē-og'rà-phy,
phys-i-og'rà-phy,
scī-og'rà-phy (sī-),

(Choose only one word out of each group)

sem-ē-i-og′rȧ-phy,
ster-ē-og′rȧ-phy,
sym-bol-aē-og′rȧ-phy,
taçh-ē-og′rȧ-phy, zō-og′rȧ-phy.
d: pseū-dog′rȧ-phy (sū-)
dr: den-drog′rȧ-phy,
hȳ-drog′rȧ-phy.
f: gly-phog′rȧ-phy.
g: lō-gog′rȧ-phy.
k(ç): ça-çog′rȧ-phy,
çal-çog′rȧ-phy, lex-i-çog′rȧ-phy,
phär-mȧ-çog′rȧ-phy (fär-),
phȳ-çog′rȧ-phy (fī-),
psȳ-çhog′rȧ-phy (sī-),
zin-çog′rȧ-phy.
l: çhrōm-ox-y-log′rȧ-phy
(krōm-oks-),
çrys-tal-log′rȧ-phy,
ē-pis-tō-log′rȧ-phy,
hȳ-ȧ-log′rȧ-phy,
met-ăl-log′rȧ-phy,
pter-y-log′rȧ-phy (ter-),
stē-log′rȧ-phy, stȳ-log′rȧ-phy,
xȳ-log′rȧ-phy (zī-).
m: ços-mog′rȧ-phy,
dē-mog′rȧ-phy,
mīç-rō-ços-mog′rȧ-phy,
nō-mog′rȧ-phy,
phan-tăs-mog′rȧ-phy (fan-),
pneū-mog′rȧ-phy (nū-),
pen-tȧ-mog′rȧ-phy,
psäl-mog′rȧ-phy (säl),
seīş-mog′rȧ-phy (sīz-),
thẽr-mog′rȧ-phy.
n: Çhris-ti-ȧ-nog′rȧ-phy (kris-),
eth-nog′rȧ-phy,
gal-vȧ-nog′rȧ-phy,
hym-nog′rȧ-phy,
içh-nog′rȧ-phy,
ī-çō-nog′rȧ-phy,
liçh-ē-nog′rȧ-phy,

meçh-ȧ-nog′rȧ-phy,
mō-nog′rȧ-phy,
o̧r-gȧ-nog′rȧ-phy,
pan-ē-ī-çō-nog′rȧ-phy,
phō-nog′rȧ-phy (fō-),
po̧r-nog′rȧ-phy,
scē-nog′rȧ-phy (sē-),
sē-lē-nog′rȧ-phy,
sphē-nog′rȧ-phy (sfē-),
ste-gȧ-nog′rȧ-phy,
ste-nog′rȧ-phy, ū-rȧ-nog′rȧ-phy.
p: an-thrō-pog′rȧ-phy,
stē-ōr″ē-ō-tȳ-pog′rȧ-phy,
tō-pog′rȧ-phy, tȳ-pog′rȧ-phy.
r: çhī-rog′rȧ-phy,
çhō-rog′rȧ-phy,
het-ē-rog′rȧ-phy,
hīe-rog′rȧ-phy (hī-),
hō-rog′rȧ-phy,
neū-rog′rȧ-phy (nū-),
rhȳ-pȧ-rog′rȧ-phy (rī-)
sī-dē-rog′rȧ-phy,
xȳ-lō-py-rog′rȧ-phy (zī-).
s: glos-sog′rȧ-phy,
gyp-sog′rȧ-phy, ī-sog′rȧ-phy,
nō-sog′rȧ-phy.
t: a̧u-tog′rȧ-phy,
çhär-tog′rȧ-phy,
çhrō-mȧ-tog′rȧ-phy,
çhrō″mō-phō-tō-pog′rȧ-phy,
çlī-mȧ-tog′rȧ-phy,
çryp-tog′rȧ-phy,
glyp-tog′rȧ-phy,
hē-li-ō-tog′rȧ-phy,
hē-mȧ-tog′rȧ-phy,
his-tog′rȧ-phy, hȳ-ē-tog′rȧ-phy,
nū-mis-mȧ-tog′rȧ-phy,
ō-don-tog′rȧ-phy,
pal-ē-on-tog′rȧ-phy,
pan-tog′rȧ-phy,
per-speç-tog′rȧ-phy,

(Choose only one word out of each group)

phō-tog′rȧ-phy,
phȳ-tog′rȧ-phy,
plas-tog′rȧ-phy,
stra-tog′rȧ-phy,
tō″rē-um-ȧ-tog′rȧ-phy.
th: an-thog′rȧ-phy,
li-thog′rȧ-phy, ọr-thog′rȧ-phy.
tr: pe-trog′rȧ-phy.

OG′RÅ-FIST

Vowel: mū-sẹ̄-og′rȧ-phist,
pal-aē-og′rȧ-phist,
zō-og′rȧ-phist.
l: me-tăl-log′rȧ-phist.
m: psäl-mog′rȧ-phist (säl-).
n: lich̤-ē-nog′rȧ-phist,
mech̤-ȧ-nog′rȧ-fist,
mō-nog′rȧ-phist,
ọr-gȧ-nog′rȧ-phist,
phō-nog′rȧ-phist (fō-),
sē-lē-nog′rȧ-phist,
sphē-nog′rȧ-phist (sfē-),
steg-ȧ-nog′rȧ-phist,
ste-nog′rȧ-phist,
ū-rȧ-nog′rȧ-phist.
p: tȳ-pog′rȧ-phist.
r: chi-rog′rȧ-phist,
sī-dē-rog′rȧ-phist.
t: phō-tog′rȧ-phist.
th: ọr-thog′rȧ-phist.

OG′RÅ-FŨR

Vowel: ạu-tō-bī-og′rȧ-phẽr,
bib-li-og-rȧ′phẽr,
bī-og′rȧ-phẽr, ġē-og′rȧ-phẽr,
hal-i-og′rȧ-phẽr,
her-ē-si-og′rȧ-phẽr,
his-tō-ri-og′rȧ-phẽr,
họr-ō-log-ix-og′rȧ-phẽr,
os-tē-og′rȧ-phẽr,
pal-aē-og′rȧ-phẽr, zō-og′rȧ-phẽr.
b: ī-ăm-bog′rȧ-phẽr.

dr: hȳ-drog′rȧ-phẽr.
f: gly-phog′rȧ-phẽr.
g: lō-gog′rȧ-phẽr.
k(c̠): c̠al-c̠og′rȧ-phẽr,
lex-i-c̠og′rȧ-phẽr (leks-),
zin-c̠og′rȧ-phẽr.
l: c̠rys-tăl-log′rȧ-phẽr,
zȳ-log′rȧ-phẽr (zī-).
m: c̠os-mog′rȧ-phẽr,
mī-mog′rȧ-phẽr,
nō-mog′rȧ-phẽr,
psäl-mog′rȧ-phẽr (säl-),
n: c̠hrō-nog′rȧ-phẽr,
eth-nog′rȧ-phẽr,
hym-nog′rȧ-phẽr,
lich̤-ē-nog′rȧ-phẽr,
mō-nog′rȧ-phẽr,
phō-nog′rȧ-phẽr,
sē-lē-nog′rȧ-phẽr,
sphē-nog′rȧ-phẽr (sfē-),
ste-nog′rȧ-phẽr.
p: tō-pog′rȧ-pher,
tȳ-pog′rȧ-phẽr.
r: c̠hō-rog′rȧ-phẽr,
hīe-rog′rȧ-phẽr,
s: glos-sog′rȧ-phẽr.
t: c̠är-tog′rȧ-phẽr,
c̠här-tog′rȧ-pher,
c̠ryp-tog′rȧ-phẽr (krip-),
glyp-tog′rȧ-phẽr,
phō-tog′rȧ-phẽr.
th: li-thog′rȧ-phẽr,
my-thog′ra-pher,
ọr-thog′rȧ-phẽr.
tr: pe-trog′rȧ-phẽr.

OI′Å-B'L

j: en-joy′ȧ-ble (-b'l).
pl: em-ploy′ȧ-ble.
Plus destroy a bull, etc.
Cf. Goya bull.

(Choose only one word out of each group)

OI'ĂL-I

l: loy'ăl-ly.
r: roy'ăl-ly.
Plus pennyroyal, he, etc.
Plus destroy a lea, etc.

OI'ĂL-IST

l: loy'ăl-ist.
r: roy'ăl-ist.
Plus royal list, etc.
Plus enjoy a list, etc.

OI'ĂL-IZM

l: loy'ăl-iṣm.
r: roy'ăl-iṣm.

OI'ĂL-TI

l: loy'ăl-ty.
r: roy'ăl-ty, vīce-roy'ăl-ty (vīs-)
Plus pennyroyal tea, etc.

Ō'I-KĂL

g: ē-gō'i-çăl.
r: hē-rō'i-çăl, un-hē-rō'i-çăl.
st: stō'i-çăl.
Plus Mesozoic, Al, etc.
Plus snowy, Cal, etc.

OIN'TED-LI

j: dis-join'ted-ly
p: poin'ted-ly
Plus disappointed Lee *or* lea, etc.
Plus join Ted Lee, etc.

OIS'TŪR-ING

kl: çlois'tẽr-ing.
r: rois'tẽr-ing.
Plus oyster ring, etc.
Plus foist her ring, etc.
Plus foist a ring, etc.

OJ'Ē-NI

Vowel: ab-i-oġ'ē-ny,
bī-oġ'ē-ny, em-brȳ-oġ'ē-ny,
ġē-oġ'ē-ny, os-tō-oġ'ē-ny,
zō-oġ'ē-ny.
l: phī-loġ'ē-ny,
phȳ-loġ'ē-ny (fī-).
m: hō-moġ'ē-ny.
n: eth-noġ'ē-ny,
hy-me-noġ'ē-ny (him-),
mō-noġ'ē-ny.
p: an-thrō-poġ'ē-ny.
pr: proġ'ē-ny.
r: het-ē-roġ'ē-ny.
s: mī-so'ġyn-y.
t: his-toġ'ē-ny, ō-don-toġ'ē-ny,
on-toġ'ē-ny, phō-toġ'ē-ny,
prō-to'ġyn-y.
th: pá-thoġ'ē-ny.
Cf. dodge a knee, etc.
Plus stodgy knee, etc.

OJ'Ē-NIST

Vowel: ab-i-oġ'ē-nist,
bī-oġ'ē-nist.
l: phi-lo'ġyn-ist.
n: mō-noġ'ē-nist.
r: het-ē-roġ'ē-nist.
s: mi-so'ġyn-ist.

OJ'Ē-NUS

d: en-doġ'ē-nous.
dr: hȳ-droġ'ē-nous.
m: ther-moġ'ē-nous.
p: hy-po'ġyn-ous.
r: pȳ-roġ'ē-nous.
s: ex-oġ'ē-nous.
th: li-thoġ'ē-nous.
tr: nī-troġ'ē-nous.

(Choose only one word out of each group)

Ō′JI-ĂN

b: gam-bō′gi-ăn.

l: är-chae-ō-lō′gi-ăn,
as-trō-lō′gi-ăn, ġē-ō-lō′gi-ăn,
myth-ō-lō′gi-ăn, nē-ō-lō′gi-ăn,
phil-ō-lō-ġi′ăn, thē-ō-lō′gi-ăn.
Plus doge, Ian, etc.

OJ′I-KĂL

g: dem-å-goġ′i-căl,
syn-å-goġ-i-căl.

l: ā-ēr-ō-loġ′i-căl,
am-phi-bī-ō-loġ′i-căl,
am-phi-bō-loġ′i-căl,
an-å-loġ′i-căl, an-thō-loġ′i-căl,
an-thrō-pō-loġ′i-căl,
är-chae-ō-loġ′i-căl,
as-trō-loġ′i-căl, bib-li-ō-loġ′i-căl
bī-ō-loġ′i-căl, brȳ-ō-loġ′i-căl,
chron-ō-loġ′i-căl,
clī-măt-ō-loġ′i-căl,
con-chō-loġ′i-căl,
cos-mŏ-loġ′i-căl,
crā-ni-ō-loġ′i-căl,
dē-mŏn-ō-loġ′i-căl,
dē-on-tō-loġ′i-căl,
dī-å-loġ′i-căl,
dox-ō-loġ-i-căl (doks-),
Ē-ġyp-tō-loġ′i-căl,
en-tō-mō-loġ′i-căl,
et-i-ō-loġ′i-căl, et-y-mō-loġ′i-căl,
ġen-ē-å-loġ′i-căl, ġē-ō-loġ′i-căl,
glos-sō-loġ′i-căl,
glot-tō-loġ′i-căl,
hō-mō-loġ′i-căl,
hȳ-drō-loġ′i-căl,
ich-nō-loġ′i-căl,
ī-dē-ō-loġ′i-căl, il-loġ′i-căl,
lith-ō-loġ′i-căl, loġ′i-căl,
maz-ō-loġ′i-căl,
met-å-loġ′i-căl,

met-ē-ōr-ō-loġ′i-căl,
myth-ō-loġ′i-căl,
ne-crō-loġ′i-căl, nē-ō-loġ′i-căl,
neū-rō-loġ′i-căl (nū-),
nō-sō-loġ′i-căl,
ō-don-tō-loġ′i-căl,
or-găn-ō-loġ′i-căl,
or-nith-ō-loġ′i-căl,
ō-rō-loġ′i-căl, os-tē··ō-loġ′i-căl,
pal-ae-on-tō-loġ′i-căl,
pan-tō-loġ′i-căl,
par-ă-loġ′i-căl, pēn-ō-loġ′i-căl,
per-is-sō-loġ′i-căl,
pe-trō-loġ′i-căl, phil-ō-loġ′i-căl
phrăs-ē-ō-loġ′i-căl,
phren-ō-loġ′i-căl (fren-),
physs-i-ō-loġ′i-căl (fiz-),
phȳ-tō-loġ′i-căl,
pneū-mat-ō-loġ′i-căl (nū-),
pom-ō-loġ′i-căl,
psȳ-chō-loġ′i-căl (sī-),
sē-lē-nō-loġ′i-căl,
sē-meī-ō-loġ′i-căl, Sin-ō-loġ′i-căl,
sō″ci-ō-loġ′i-căl,
spec-trō-loġ′i-căl,
sym-bō-loġ′i-căl,
taut-ō-loġ′i-căl,
tech-ni-cō-loġ′i-căl,
tech-nō-loġ′i-căl,
tel-ē-ō-loġ′i-căl,
ter-åt-ō-loġ′i-căl,
tēr-min-ō-loġ′i-căl,
thē-ō-loġ′i-căl,
tox-i-cō-loġ′i-căl (toks-),
trop-ō-loġ′i-căl,
ūn-i-vēr-sō-loġ′i-căl,
zō-ō-loġ′i-căl,
zō″ō-phyt-ō-loġ′i-căl,
zȳ-mō-loġ′i-căl.
Plus pedagogic, Al, etc.
Plus stodgy, Cal, etc.

(Choose only one word out of each group)

OJ´Ō-NI

Vowel: ġē-oġ-ō-ny,
phy-si-oġ´ō-ny, thē-oġ´ō-ny,
zō-oġ´ō-ny.
m: çoṣ-moġ´ō-ny.
t: au-toġ´ō-ny.
th: pà-thoġ´ō-ny.
Cf. dodge a knee, etc.

OJ´Ō-NIST

Vowel: thē-oġ´ō-nist.
m: çoṣ-moġ´ō-nist.

Ō´KÅ-LĪZ

f: fō´căl-īze.
l: lō´căl-īze.
v: vō´căl-īze.
Plus yokel eyes, etc.
Plus tapioca, Lize, etc.

Ō´KĂL-IZM

l: lō-căl-iṣm.
v: vō-căl-iṣm.

OK´Å-TIV

l: loç-à-tive.
v: in-voç´à-tive, prō-voç´à-tive,
voç´à-tive.

Ō´KEN-LI

br: brō´ken-ly.
sp: out-spō´ken-ly.
Plus token, Lee or lea, etc.

OK´I-LI

ch: chạlk´i-ly.
g: gạwk´i-ly.
p: pạwk´i-ly.
skw: squạwk´i-ly (skwạ´).
Plus talky, Lee or lea, etc.
Plus squawk alee, etc.

OK´I-NES

ch: chạlk´i-ness.
g: gạwk´i-ness.
p: pạwk´i-ness.
skw: squạwk´i-ness (skwạ´).
t: tạlk´i-ness.

OK´I-NES

k(ç): çock´i-ness (kok´).
r: rock´i-ness.
st: stock´i-ness.

OK´RÅ-SI

Vowel: hag-i-oç´rà-cy,
id-i-oç´rà-sy, nē-oç´rà-cy,
plou-si-oç´rà-cy, thē-oç´rà-cy,
thē-oç´rà-sy.
b: mob-oç´rà-cy, snob-oç´rà-cy.
g: log-oç´rà-cy.
k(ç): ġy-naē-çoç´rà-cy.
l: och-loç´rà-cy.
m: är-ith-moç´rà-cy,
dē-moç´rà-cy, nō-moç´rà-cy,
tim-oç´rà-cy.
n: cot-tŏn-oç´rà-cy,
mōn-oç´rà-cy.
p: hy-po´çri-sy, shop-oç´rà-cy.
r: hiēr-oç´rà-cy (hēr-).
s: pan-ti-soç´rà-cy.
t: ar-is-toç´rà-cy, au-toç´rà-cy
des-pot-oç´rà-cy,
ger-on-toç´rà-cy,
pe-dănt-oç´rà-cy,
plant-oç´rà-cy, plū-toç´rà-cy,
strat-oç´rà-cy.
v: slāv-oç´rà-cy.

OK´RÅ-TIZM

m: dē-mo´çrà-tiṣm.
s: So´çrà-tiṣm.

(Choose only one word out of each group)

OK'RŌ-MI

Vowel: hē-li-oçh'rō-my,
ster-ē-oçh'rō-my.
l: met-ăl-loçh'rō-my.
n: mō-noçh'rō-my.

OK'RŎN-US

s: ĭ-soçh'rŏn-ous.
t: täu-toch'rŏn-ous.

OK'SI-KĂL

d: ọr-thō-dox'i-çăl (doks-),
par-å-dox'i-çăl.
t: tox'i-çăl.
Plus proxy, Cal, etc.
Plus toxic, Al, etc.

OK'TỌR-SHIP

d: dọç'tọr-ship.
pr: prọç'tọr-ship.
Plus blocked her ship, etc.
Plus concocter, ship, etc.

OK'Ū-LĂR

Vowel: oç'ū-lăr.
j: joç'ū-lăr.
l: loç'ū-lăr.
n: bĭ-noç'ū-lăr, mon-oç'ū-lăr.
v: voç'ū-lăr.

OK'ŪR-I

kr: çrock'ẽr-y.
m: mock'ẽr-y.
r: rock'ẽr-y.
Plus socker, he, etc.

ŌL'À-B'L

r: rōll'å-ble.
s: çon-sōl'å-ble.
t: ex-tōll'å-ble, tōll'å-ble.

tr: çon-trōl'lå-ble,
un-çon-trōl'lå-ble.
Plus toll a bull, etc.
Plus Angola bull, etc.

ỌL'A-B'L

k(ç): rē-çạll'å-ble.
thr: en-thrạll'å-ble.
Plus call a bull, etc.
Plus Eū-fạ'lå bull, etc.

ŌL'À-RI

b: bōl'å-ry.
j: çå-jōl'å-ry.
p: pōl'å-ry.
s: sōl'å-ry.
v: vōl'å-ry.
Plus molar, he, etc.
Cf. so, Larry, etc.

ŌL'À-RĪZ

p: pōl'å-rīze.
s: sōl'å-rīze.
Plus goal arise, etc.
Plus Lola rise, etc.
Plus molar eyes, etc.

OL'À-TRI

Vowel: bib-li-ol'å-try,
ġē-ol'å-try, ġyn-ē-ol'å-try,
hē-li-ol'å-try, iç-thy-ol'å-try,
id-i-ol'å-try, Mā-ri-ol'å-try,
ōph-i-ol'å-try, phyṣ-i-ol'å-try,
zō-ol'å-try.
b: sym-bol'å-try.
d: ĭ-dol'å-try, lọrd-ol'å-try.
kr: nē-çrol'å-try.
m: çoṣ-mol'å-try.
n: dē-mŏn-ol'å-try.
p: an-thrō-pol'å-try,
tō-pol'å-try.

(Choose only one word out of each group)

r: hī-ēr-ol'à-try, pȳ-rol'à-try.
t: thau-mà-tol'à-try.
th: lith-ol'à-try.
tr: as-trol'à-try.
Plus corolla tree, etc.
Plus doll a tree, etc.

OL'Å-TRUS

b: sym-bcl'à-trous.
d: ī-dol'à-trous.
Plus extol a truss, etc.
Plus corolla truss, etc.

OL'Å-TŨR

Vowel: bib-li-ol'à-tẽr,
hē-li-ol'à-tẽr, Mā-ri-ol'à-tẽr.
d: ī-dol'à-tẽr.
n: ī-çon-ol'à-tẽr.
r: pȳ-rol'à-tẽr.
Plus doll ate her, etc.

ŌL'Ē-UM

n: li-nō'lē-um.
tr: pē-trō'lē-um.
Cf. ōl'i-um.

Ō'LI-À

g: Mon-gō'li-à.
k(ç): çō'li-à, mel-an-çhō'li-à.
h: mag-nō'li-à.
t: Aē-tō'li-à, An-à-tō'li-à.
Plus holy a, etc.

Ō'LI-ĂN

Vowel: Aē-ō'li-ăn,
Çrē-ō'li-ăn.
b: met-à-bō'li-ăn.
g: Mon-gō'li-ăn.
k(ç): mel-an-çhō'li-ăn.
m: si-mō'lē-ŏn.
p: Na-pō'lē-ŏn.

t: Aē-tō'li-ăn, An-à-tō'li-ăn,
çap-i-tō'li-ăn, Paç-tō'li-ăn.
Plus holy an, etc.
Plus holy un, etc.
Plus so, Leon, etc.

ŌL'I-ĀT

f: fō'li-āte, in-fō'li-āte.
sp: spō'li-āte.
Plus holy eight or ate, etc.

Ō'LI-ĂZ

ō'li-à+s.

OL'ID-LI

s: sol'id-ly.
skw: squäl'id-ly.
st: stol'id-ly.
Plus solid Lee, etc.

OL'ID-NES

s: sol'id-ness.
skw: squäl'id-ness.
st: stol'id-ness.

Ō'LI-EST

h: hō'li-est, un-hō'li-est.
l: lōw'li-est.

OL'I-FĪ

d: ī-dol'i-fȳ.
k: dis-quäl'i-fȳ, quäl'i-fȳ.
m: mol'li-fȳ.
Plus Polly, fie!, etc.

OL'I-FĪD

d: ī-dol'i-fīed.
kw: dis-quäl'i-fīed,
quäl'i-fīed, un-quäl'i-fīed.
m: mol'li-fīed.
Plus Polly fie'd, etc.

(Choose only one word out of each group)

OL'I-KĂL

b: dī-à-bol'i-çăl,
    hȳ-pẽr-bol'i-çăl,
    par-à-bol'i-çăl,   sym-bol'i-çăl.
f: fol'li-çle.
p: bib″li-ō-pol'i-çăl.
t: a-pos-tol'i-çăl.
th: çà-thol'i-çăl.
Plus colic, Al, etc.
Plus jolly, Cal, etc.

OL'IK-SUM

fr: frol'iç-sŏme.
r: rol'lick-sŏme.
Plus alcoholic sum *or* some, etc.
Plus frolics 'em *or* um, etc.

Ō'LI-NES

h: hō'li-ness, un-hō'li-ness.
l: lōw'li-ness.
sh: shōal'i-ness.

Ō'LI-Ō

Vowel: ō'li-ō.
f: fō'li-ō,   pōrt-fō'li-ō.
p: Sa-pō'li-ō.
Plus holy owe *or* Oh, etc.
Cf. no, Leo, etc.

OL'ISH-ING

b: à-bol'ish-ing.
m: dē-mol'ish-ing.
p: pol'ish-ing.

OL'ISH-ŨR

b: à-bol'ish-ẽr.
m: dē-mol'ish-ẽr.
p: pol'ish-ẽr.
Plus abolish her *or* err, etc.

OL'I-TI

j: jol'li-ty.
kw: ē-quäl'i-ty,   in-ē-ɑuäl'i-ty,
    quäl'i-ty.
p: in-tẽr-pol'i-ty,
    ī-sō-pol'i-ty,   pol'i-ty.
v: fri-vol'i-ty.
Plus holly tea *or* T, etc.
Plus doll it, he, etc.

ŌL'I-UM

f: trī-fō'li-um.
sk(sç): sçhō'li-um.
Plus holy 'em *or* um, etc.
Cf. ōl'ē-um.

Ō'LI-ŨR

Vowel: ō'li-ẽr.
gr: Grō'li-ẽr.
h: hō'li-ẽr,   un-hō'li-ẽr.
l: lōw'li-ẽr.
Plus slowly her *or* err, etc.
Plus soul, he err, etc.

OL'I-VŨR

Vowel: Ol'i-vẽr.
b: Bol'i-vǎr.
t: Tal'iafer-ro (tol'li-vũr),
    Tol'li-vẽr.
Plus olive her *or* err, etc.

OL'Ō-GUS

m: hō-mol'ō-gous.
r: het-ē-rol'ō-gous.
s: ī-sol'ō-gous.
t: tau-tol'ō-gous.
Plus hollow, Gus, etc.

OL'Ō-ING

f: fol'lōw-ing.
h: hol'lō-ing,   hol'lōw-ing.
sw: swäl'lōw-ing.
w: wäl'lōw-ing.

(Choose only one word out of each group)

Plus hollow wing, etc.
Plus doll, O wing, etc.

OL'Ō-JI

Vowel: aes-thē-si-ol'ō-ġy (es-),
ag-ri-ol'ō-ġy, ā-lē-thi-ol'ō-ġy,
am″phib-i-ol'ō-ġy,
är-c̦haē-ol'ō-ġy, är-tēr-i-ol'ō-ġy,
as-trō-thē-ol'ō-ġy,
bal-nē-ol'ō-ġy, bib-li-ol'ō-ġy,
bī-ol'ō-ġy, brȳ-ol'ō-ġy,
c̦on-c̦hy-li-ol'ō-ġy,
c̦rän-i-ol'ō-ġy,
dac̦-tyl-i-ol'ō-ġy, dī-caē-ol'ō-ġy,
ec̦-c̦lē-si-ol'ō-ġy,
el-ec̦″trō-bī-ol'ō-ġy,
el-ec̦″trō-phy̦s-i-ol'ō-ġy,
em-bry-ol'ō-ġy,
en-dem-i-ol'ō-ġy,
en-tō-zō-ol'ō-ġy,
ep-i-dem-i-ol'ō-ġy,
et-i-ol'ō-ġy, ġen-ē-si-ol'ō-ġy,
ġē-ol'ō-ġy, hag-i-ol'ō-ġy,
his-to̧r-i-ol'ō-ġy, hȳ-ġi-ol'ō-ġy,
ic̦h-thy-ol'ō-ġy, ī-dē-ol'ō-ġy,
lit-ūr-ġi-ol'ō-ġy,
mī-c̦rō-gē-ol'ō-ġy, mȳ-ol'ō-ġy,
nē-ol'ō-ġy, nō-ol'ō-ġy, ol'ō-ġy,
ō-ol'ō-ġy, ō-phi-ol'ō-ġy,
os-tē-ol'ō-ġy, pal-aē-ol'ō-ġy,
pal″aē-ō-zō-ol'ō-ġy,
pal-aē-ti-ol'ō-ġy,
pan-thē-ol'ō-ġy,
phrā̧s-ē-ol'ō-ġy, phy̦s-i-ol'ō-ġy,
phȳ″tō-phy̦s-i-ol'ō-ġy,
sem'eī-ol'ō-ġy,
sō-ci-ol'ō-ġy, sō-ter″i-ol'ō-ġy,
spec-i-ol'ō-ġy, stō-i-c̦hi-ol'ō-ġy,
tel-ē-ol'ō-ġy, tes-tȧ-cē-ol'ō-ġy,
thē-ol'ō-ġy, ther-ē-ol'ō-ġy,
zō-ol'ō-ġy.

b: am-phi-bol'ō-ġy (-fi-),
phlē-bol'ō-ġy (flē-),
sym-bol'ō-ġy.
d: meth-od-ol'ō-ġy,
mō-nad-ol'ō-ġy,
o̧r-c̦hid-ol'ō-ġy,
pē-ri-od-ol'ō-ġy,
pter-id-ol'ō-ġy (ter-),
tīd-ol'ō-ġy.
dr: den-drol'ō-ġy, hȳ-drol'ō-ġy.
f: mo̧r-phol'ō-ġy.
fr: nē-phrol'ō-ġy (-frol').
b: bug-ol'ō-ġy, fun-gol'ō-ġy.
lar-yn-ġol'ō-ġy,
phar-yn-ġol'ō-ġy.
k(c̦): c̦ȧ-c̦ol'ō-ġy, c̦on-c̦hol'ō-ġy,
fil-i-c̦ol'ō-ġy, ġyn-ē-c̦ol'ō-ġy,
lex-i-c̦ol'ō-ġy (leks-),
mal-ȧ-c̦ol'ō-ġy, mus-c̦ol'ō-ġy,
mȳ-c̦ol'ō-ġy,
phär-mȧ-c̦ol'ō-ġy, phȳ-c̦ol'ō-ġy,
psȳ-c̦hol'ō-ġy, sär-c̦ol'ō-ġy,
tox-i-c̦ol'ō-ġy (toks-).
kr: mȧ-c̦rol'ō-ġy, mī-c̦rol'ō-ġy,
nē-c̦rol'ō-ġy.
l: ān-ġel-ol'ō-ġy,
ceph-ăl-ol'ō-ġy (sef-),
hȳ-lol'ō-ġy, phi-lol'ō-ġy,
psī-lol'ō-ġy (sī-).
m: at-ŏm-ol'ō-ġy, c̦os-mol'ō-ġy,
des-mol'ō-ġy, en-tō-mol'ō-ġy,
ē-pis-tē-mol'ō-ġy, et-y-mol'ō-ġy,
gnōm-ol'ō-ġy (nōm-),
hō-mol'ō-ġy, mī-ăs-mol'ō-ġy,
nōm-ol'ō-ġy,
oph-thăl-mol'ō-ġy (of-),
ō-ris-mol'ō-ġy, par-ȯ-mol'ō-ġy,
pneūm-ol'ō-ġy (nūm'),
pom-ol'ō-ġy, pot-ȧ-mol'ō-ġy,
seī̧s-mol'ō-ġy (sīz-),
spa̧s-mol'ō-ġy, spērm-ol'ō-ġy,

(Choose only one word out of each group)

syn-des-mol′ō-ġy, thẽr-mol′ō-ġy,
zȳ-mol′ō-ġy.

n: ac̯-ti-nol′ō-ġy,
aph-nol′ō-ġy (of-),
är-ac̯h-nol′ō-ġy, as-then-ol′ō-ġy,
bot-ȧ-nol′ō-ġy, c̯am-pȧ-nol′ō-ġy,
c̯hron-ol′ō-ġy, dē-mŏn-ol′ō-ġy,
ec̯-c̯ri-nol′ō-ġy, em-mē-nol′ō-ġy,
en″tẽr-ȧ-den-ol′ō-ġy,
eth-nol′ō-ġy, gal-vȧ-nol′ō-ġy,
gnō-mŏn-ol′ō-ġy (nō-),
hȳ-men-ol′ō-ġy, hym-nol′ō-ġy,
hyp-nol′ō-ġy,
ic̯h″nō-lith-nol′ō-ġy,
ic̯h-nol′ō-ġy, ī-c̯ŏn-ol′ō-ġy,
kī-nol′ō-ġy, lī-c̯hen-ol′ō-ġy,
mem-brăn-ol′ō-ġy,
mē-nō-nol′ō-ġy
mō-nol′ō-ġy,
neū-ryp-nol′ō-ġy (nū-),
ō-cē-ă-nol′ō-ġy (-shē-),
ō-nol′ō-ġy, ọr-găn-ol′ō-ġy,
ọr″nith-ic̯h-nol′ō-ġy*,
pal″aē-ō-eth-nol′ō-ġy,
pär-then-ol′ō-ġy, pē-nol′ō-ġy,
phē-nom-ē-nol′ō-ġy (fē-),
phō-nol′ō-ġy (fō-),
phrē-nol′ō-ġy (frē-),
pun-nol′ō-ġy, quī-nol′ō-ġy,
rū-nol′ō-ġy, sē-lē-nol′ō-ġy,
sī-nol′ō-ġy, splanc̯h-nol′ō-ġy,
splē-nol′ō-ġy, syn-c̯hrō-nol′ō-ġy,
tec̯h-nol′ō-ġy, tẽr-mi-nol′ō-ġy,
tẽr-mō-nol′ō-ġy, ū-rȧ-nol′ō-ġy,
ū-ri-nol′ō-ġy, ū-rŏn-ō-nol′ō-ġy,
vul-c̯ȧ-nol′ō-ġy.

p: an-thrō-pol′ō-ġy, ȧ-pol′ō-ġy,
tō-pol′ō-ġy, trō-pol′ō-ġy,
ty-pol′ō-ġy.

r: ā-ē-rol′ō-ġy,
as″trō-met-ē-rol′ō-ġy,

bȧ-rol′ō-ġy, en-tē-rol′ō-ġy,
het-ē-rol′ō-ġy, hīe-rol′ō-ġy (hī-),
hō-rol′ō-ġy, hys-tē-rol′ō-ġy,
ic̯h-ō-rol′ō-ġy, mär-ty-rol′ō-ġy,
mē-tē-ō-rol′ō-ġy, neū-rol′ō-ġy,
ō-nē-i-rol′ō-ġy, ō-rol′ō-ġy,
phȧ-rol′ō-ġy (fȧ-),
pō-nē-rol′ō-ġy, pȳ-rol′ō-ġy,
thē-rol′ō-ġy.

s: ad-en″o-c̯hi-răp-sol′ō-ġy,
dō-sol′ō-ġy, dox-ol′ō-ġy,
glos-sol′ō-ġy, ġyp-sol′ō-ġy,
mī-sol′ō-ġy, nō-sol′ō-ġy,
os-mo-nō-sol′ō-ġy,
par-ȧ=dox-ol′ō-ġy,
par-i-sol′ō-ġy, per-is-sol′ō-ġy,
pō-sol′ō-ġy, psȳ″c̯hō-nō-sol′ō-ġy,
tax-ol′ō-ġy, threp-sol′ō-ġy,
ūn″i-vẽr-sol′ō-ġy.

t: aes-thē-mȧ-tol′ō-ġy,
ag-mȧ-tol′ō-ġy, ā-rē-tol′ō-ġy,
ar-is-tol′ō-ġy, bat-tol′ō-ġy,
brō-mȧ-tol′ō-ġy, bron-tol′ō-ġy,
C̯hris-tol′ō-ġy, c̯hrō-mȧ-tol′ō-ġy,
c̯lī-mȧ-tol′ō-ġy, c̯ryp-tol′ō-ġy,
dē-on-tol′ō-ġy, dẽr-mȧ-tol′ō-ġy,
dī″ȧ-lec̯-tol′ō-ġy, dit-tol′ō-ġy,
Ē-ġyp-tol′ō-ġy, em-ē-tol′ō-ġy,
es-c̯hȧ-tol′ō-ġy, ġi-gan-tol′ō-ġy,
glot-tol′ō-ġy, his-tol′ō-ġy,
hȳ-ē-tol′ō-ġy, in-sec̯-tol′ō-ġy,
lep-tol′ō-ġy, man-tol′ō-ġy,
nū″mis-mȧ-tol′ō-ġy,
ō-don-tol′ō-ġy,
ō-nō-mȧ-tol′ō-ġy, on-tol′o-ġy,
ō-tol′ō-ġy, pal-ae-on-tol′ō-ġy,
pal-ae-o-phy-tol′ō-ġy,
pan-tol′ō-ġy, par-a-si-tol′ō-ġy,
pa-trō-nō-mȧ-tol′ō-ġy,
phō-tol′ō-ġy, phy-tol′ō-ġy,
pneūm-ȧ-tol′ō-ġy,

(Choose only one word out of each group)

prō-tō-phȳ-tol′ō-ġy,
py-ri-tol′ō-ġy, sē-mȧ-tol′ō-ġy,
si-tol′ō-ġy, skel-e-tol′ō-ġy,
sō-mȧ-tol′ō-ġy, spēr-mȧ-tol′ō-ġy,
sta-tis-tol′ō-ġy,
strō-mȧ-tol′ō-ġy,
symp-tō-mȧ-tol′ō-ġy,
sys-te-mȧ-tol′ō-ġy, tȧu-tol′ō-ġy,
te-rȧ-tol′ō-ġy, tha-nȧ-tol′ō-ġy,
tor-ē-um-ȧ-tol′ō-ġy,
zō-ō-phy-tol′ō-ġy.

th: an-thol′ō-ġy, e-thol′ō-ġy,
li-thol′ō-ġy, my-thol′ō-ġy,
o̧r-ni-thol′ō-ġy, pa-thol′ō-ġy,
phȳ-tō-li-thol′ō-ġy,
phȳ-tō-pa-thol′ō-ġy.

tr: as-trol′ō-ġy, el-eç-trol′ō-ġy,
gas-trol′ō-ġy, me-trol′ō-ġy,
pe-trol′ō-ġy, speç-trol′ō-ġy.

v: ō-vol′ō-ġy.

z: ma-zol′ō-ġy.

Plus hollow, Gee!, etc.

OL′Ō-JIST

Vowel: ag-ri-ol′ō-ġist,
är-çhaē-ol′ō-ġist,
As-syr-i-ol′ō-ġist, bī-ol′ō-ġist,
çrān-i-ol′ō-ġist,
çrus-tā″cē-ol′ō-ġist,
eç-çlē-ṣi-ol′ō-ġist,
el-eç″trō-bī-ol′ō-ġist,
em-bry-ol′ō-ġist, ġē-ol′ō-ġist,
ha-gi-ol′ō-ġist, iç̧h-thy-ol′ō-ġist,
ī-dē-ol′ō-ġist, mȳ-ol′ō-ġist,
nē-ol′ō-ġist, nō-ol′ō-ġist,
ō-ol′ō-ġist, ō-phi-ol′ō-ġist,
os-tē-ol′ō-ġist, pal-aē-cl′ō-ġist,
pal-aē-ti-ol′ō-ġist,
pan-thē-ol′ō-ġist,
phrāṣ-ē-ol′ō-ġist,
phy-ṣi-ol′ō-ġist, sō-ci-ol′ō-ġist,

tel-ē-ol′ō-ġist, thē-ol′ō-ġist,
ther-ē-ol′ō-ġist, zō-ol′ō-ġist.

b: sym-bol′ō-ġist.

d: o̧r-çhid-ol′ō-ġist,
pseū-dol′ō-ġist (sū-),
pter-i-dol′ō-ġist (ter-).

dr: den-drol′ō-ġist,
hȳ-drol′ō-ġist.

f: mo̧r-phol′ō-ġist.

k(ç): ço̧n-çhol′ō-ġist,
lex-i-ço̧l′ō-ġist (leks-),
mȳ-ço̧l′ō-ġist,
phär-mȧ-ço̧l′ō-ġist,
psȳ-çhol′ō-ġist (sī-),
sär-ço̧l′ō-ġist,
tox-i-ço̧l′ō-ġist (toks-).

kr: nē-ç̧rol′ō-ġist.

l: phi-lol′ō-ġist.

m: ço̧s-mol′ō-ġist,
en-tō-mol′y-ġist,
et-y-mol′ō-ġist, pō-mol′ō-ġist,
seīṣ-mol′ō-ġist (sīz-),
zȳ-mol′ō-ġist.

n: ça̧m-pȧ-nol′ō-ġist,
çhrō-nol′ō-ġist, dē-mŏn-ol′ō-ġist,
eth-nol′ō-ġist, gal-vȧ-nol′ō-ġist,
hym-nol′ō-ġist, hyp-nol′ō-ġist,
mō-nol′ō-ġist,
pal″aē-ō-eth-nol′ō-ġist,
phō-nol′ō-ġist,
phrē-nol′ō-ġist (frē-),
quī-nol′ō-ġist (kwī-),
rù-nol′ō-ġist, sī-nol′ō-ġist,
teç̧h-nol′ō-ġist, vul-ça̧-nol′ō-ġist.

p: an-thrō-pol′ō-ġist,
ȧ-pol′ō-ġist.

r: ā-ē-rol′ō-ġist,
hīe-rol′ō-ġist (hī-), hō-rol′ō-ġist,
mär-ty-rol′ō-ġist,
mēt-ē-ō-rol′ō-ġist,
neū-rol′ō-ġist (nū-),

(Choose only one word out of each group)

ō-neī-rol′ō-ġist,
ō-rol′ō-ġist, pȳ-rol′ō-ġist,
thē-rol′ō-ġist.
s: glos-sol′ō-ġist, ġyp-sol′ō-ġist,
nō-sol′ō-ġist, ūn-i-vẽr-sol′ō-ġist.
t: bat-tol′ō-gist, dē-on-tol′ō-ġist,
dẽr-mȧ-tol′ō-ġist,
Ē-ġyp-tol′ō-ġist, glot-tol′ō-ġist,
his-tol′ō-ġist, man-tol′ō-ġist,
nū″mis-mȧ-tol′ō-gist,
ō-nō-mȧ-tol′ō-ġist, on-tol′ō-ġist,
pal-aē-ŏn-tol′ō-ġist,
pan-tol′ō-ġist,
phō-tol′ō-ġist (fō-),
phȳ-tol′ō-ġist,
pneū-mȧ-tol′ō-ġist (nū-),
sāint-ol′ō-ġist (sānt-),
tạu-tol′ō-ġist, te-rȧ-tol′ō-ġist.
th: e-thol′ō-ġist, li-thol′ō-ġist,
my-thol′ō-ġist, ọr-ni-thol′ō-ġist,
pȧ-thol′ō-ġist,
phȳ-tō-li-thol′ō-ġist,
phȳ-tō-pȧ-thol′ō-ġist.
tr: as-trol′ō-gist, pe-trol′ō-ġist.
z: mȧ-zol′ō-ġist, etc.

OL′Ō-JĪZ
Vowel: ġē-ol′ō-ġīze,
nē-ol′ō-ġīze, sō-ci-ol′ō-ġīze,
thē-ol′ō-ġīze, zō-ol′ō-ġīze.
l: phi-lol′ō-ġīze.
m: en-tō-mol′ō-ġīze,
e-ty-mol′ō-ġīze.
p: ȧ-pol′ō-ġīze.
s: dox-ol′ō-ġīze (doks-).
t: bat-tol′ō-ġīze, tạu-tol′ō-ġīze.
tr: as-trol′ō-ġīze, etc.

OL′Ō-JŨR
Vowel: ġē-ol′ō-ġẽr,
os-tē-ol′ō-ġẽr, phy-ṣi-ol′ō-ġẽr,
thē-ol′ō-ġẽr.

d: sock-dol′ȧ-ġẽr.
l: phil-ol′ō-ġẽr.
m: e-ty-mol′ō-ġẽr.
n: ạck-now′led-ġẽr (no′),
bot-ȧ-nol′ȧ-ġẽr. phō-nol′ō-ġẽr,
phrē-nol′ō-ġer (frē-).
r: hō-rol′ō-ġẽr.
th: my-thol′ō-ġẽr.
tr: as-trol′ō-ġẽr.

OL′Ō-ŨR
f: fol′lōw-ẽr.
h: hol′lōw-ẽr.
sw: swäl′lōw-ẽr.
w: wäl′lōw-ẽr.
Plus swallow her, etc.

OL′TI-EST
f: fạul′ti-est.
s: sạl′ti-est.

OL′TI-NES
f: fạul′ti-ness.
m: mạl′ti-ness.
s: sạl′ti-ness.

OL′TŨR-ING
Vowel: ạl′tẽr-ing, un-ạl′tẽr-ing.
f: fạl′tẽr-ing, un-fạl′tẽr-ing.
p: pạl′tẽr-ing.
Plus Gibralter ring, etc.
Plus exalt her ring, etc.
Plus exalt a ring, etc.

OL′TŨR-ŨR
Vowel: ạl′tẽr-ẽr.
f: fạl′tẽr-ẽr.
p: pạl′tẽr-ẽr.
Plus alter her, etc.

OL′Ū-B′L
s: in-sol′ū-ble, sol′ū-ble.
v: vol′ū-ble.
Plus loll, you bull, etc.

(Choose only one word out of each group)

OL′Ū-TIV

s: sol′ū-tive*.
v: sū-pēr-vol′ū-tive.
Cf. evolutive, revolutive.

OL′VÀ-B'L

s: ab-sol′và-ble, in-sol′và-ble, sol′và-ble.
z: diṣ-ṣol′và-ble, in-diṣ-ṣol′và-ble, rē-ṣol′và-ble.
Plus involve a bull, etc.

OL′VEN-SI

s: in-sol′ven-cy, sol′ven-cy.
v: rē-vol′ven-cy.
Cf. insolvent, see?, etc.

OM′À-KI

Vowel: al-eç-try-om′à-çhy, scī-om′à-çhy (sī-), thē-om′à-çhy.
g: lō-gom′à-çhy.
k(ç): psȳ-çhom′à-çhy (sī-kom′à-ki).
n: ī-çō-nom′à-çhy, mō-nom′à-çhy.
t: ġi-gan-tom′à-çhy.
Plus from a key, etc.
Plus comma key, etc.

OM′À-THI

l: phī-lom′à-thy (fī-).
t: çhres-tom′à-thy.

Ō′MÀ-TIZM

kr: à-çhrō′mà-tiṣm, çhrō′mà-tiṣm.
pl: di-plō′mà-tiṣm.

OM′Ē-NÀ

g: an-ti-lē-gom′ē-nà, prō-lē-gom′ē-nà.

n: phē-nom′ē-nà.
p: par-à-li-pom′ē-nà.
Cf. common a, etc.

OM′Ē-NON

g: prō-lē-gom′ē-non.
n: phē-nom′ē-non.
Cf. common on, etc.

ŌM′Ē-Ō

dr: Drō′mi-ō.
r: Rō′mē-ō.
Plus loamy, O, etc.
Plus show me, Oh, ete.

OM′E-TRI

Vowel: bī-om′ē-try, çrā-ni-om′ē-try, eū-di-om′ē-try (ū-), ġē-om′ē-try, gon-i-om′ē-try, rhē-om′ē-try (rē-), ster-ē-om′ē-try, stō-i-çhi-om′ē-try.
d: ō-dom′ē-try.
dr: hȳ-drom′ē-try.
gr: hȳ-grom′ē-try.
h: Mà-hom′ē-try.
k(ç): hē-li-çom′ē-try, sti-çhom′ē-try.
kr: mī-çrom′ē-try.
m: pneū-mom′ē-try (nū-), seīṣ-mom′ē-try (sīz-),
n: çhrō-nom′ē-try, gal-và-nom′ē-try, ō-zō-nom′ē-try, plà-nom′ē-try, trig-ō-nom′ē-try.
r: ba-rom′ē-try, hō-rom′ē-try, pȳ-rom′ē-try, saç-çhà-rom′ē-try.
s: gà-som′ē-try, hyp-som′ē-try.
t: phō-tom′ē-try (fō-).

OM'Ē-TŪR
OM'I-NĂL

fāte, fär, fȧst, fạll, finăl, cãre, at; mēte, prĕy, hẽr, met; pīne,
marĭne, bĭrd, pin; nōte, mŏve, fọr, atŏm, not; mọọn, book;

922

(Choose only one word out of each group)

th: ọr-thom'ē-try,
pȧ-thom'ē-try
Cf. from a tree, etc.

OM'Ē-TŪR

Vowel: ab-sọrp"ti-om'ē-tẽr,
ạu-di-om'ē-tẽr, c̣rā-ni-om'ē-tẽr,
eū-di-om'ē-tẽr (ū-), g̣ē-om'ē-tẽr,
gō-ni-om'ē-tẽr, hē-li-om'ē-tẽr,
ō-lē-om'ē-tẽr, plū-vi-om'ē-tẽr,
rā-di-om'ē-tẽr,
rhē-om'ē-tẽr (rē-),
ster-ē-om'ē-tẽr.

b: trī-bom'ē-tẽr.

br: om-brom'ē-tẽr.

dr: ō-dom'ē-tẽr, pe-dom'ē-tẽr,
speed-om'ē-tẽr, ū-dom'ē-tẽr.

dr: den-drom'ē-tẽr,
hȳ-drom'ē-tẽr.

f: grȧ-phom'ē-tẽr.

g: lō-gom'ē-tẽr.

gr: hȳ-grom'ē-tẽr.

k(c̣): ē-c̣hom'ē-tẽr,
tȧ-c̣hom'ē-tẽr, trō-c̣hom'ē-tẽr.

kr: mȧ-c̣rom'ē-tẽr,
mī-c̣rom'ē-tẽr.

l: ce-phȧ-lom'ē-tẽr.

m: dȳ-nȧ-mom'ē-tẽr,
en-dos-mom'ē-tẽr,
g̣ē"ō-thẽr-mom'ē-tẽr,
seĭs-mom'ē-tẽr (sīz-),
thẽr-mom'ē-tẽr, zȳ-mom'ē-tẽr.

n: ac̣-ti-nom'ē-tẽr,
c̣hrō-nom'ē-tẽr, c̣lī-nom'ē-tẽr,
dē-c̣lī-nom'ē-tẽr,
gal-vȧ-nom'ē-tẽr,
mī-c̣rō-nom'ē-tẽr, mō-nom'ē-tẽr,
ō-zō-nom'ē-tẽr, phō-nom'ē-tẽr,
plȧ-nom'ē-tẽr, sa-li-nom'ē-tẽr,
sō-nom'ē-tẽr, tan-nom'ē-tẽr,

vī-nom'ē-tẽr,
vol-ūm-e-nom'ē-tẽr.

p: nạu-rō-pom'ē-tẽr.

r: bȧ-rom'ē-tẽr, hō-rom'ē-tẽr,
pȳ-rom'ē-tẽr, sac̣-c̣hȧ-rom'ē-tẽr,
sphē-rom'ē-tẽr (sfē-).

s: drō-som'ē-tẽr, hyp-som'ē-tẽr,
pul-som'ē-tẽr.

t: al-tom'ē-tẽr, chär-tom'ē-tẽr,
c̣hrō-mȧ-tom'ē-tẽr,
lac̣-tom'ē-tẽr, op-tom'ē-tẽr,
pan-tom'ē-tẽr, phō-tom'ē-tẽr,
plȧ-tom'ē-tẽr,
pneū-mȧ-tom'ē-tẽr (nū-),
rē-frac̣-tom'ē-tẽr,
strȧ-tom'ē-tẽr.

th: bȧ-thom'ē-tẽr,
ste-thom'ē-tẽr.

tr: as-trom'ē-tẽr,
el-ec̣-trom'ē-tẽr, spec̣-trom'ē-tẽr.

z: pī-ē-zom'ē-tẽr.
Plus from it, her, err *or* er, etc.
Plus vomit her, etc.

OM'I-KĂL

d: dom'i-c̣ăl.

k(c̣): c̣om'i-c̣ăl,
c̣ox-c̣omb'i-c̣ăl (-kom')
trȧ-g̣i-c̣om'i-c̣al.

n: ag-rō-nom'i-c̣ăl,
as-trō-nom'i-c̣ăl, e-c̣ō-nom'i-c̣ăl,
ī-c̣ō-nom'ăc̣h-ăl.

t: an-ȧ-tom'i-c̣ăl, ȧ-tom'i-c̣ăl,
zō-ō-tom'i-c̣ăl.
Plus from me, Cal, etc.
Plus tommie, Cal, etc.

OM'I-NĂL

d: ab-dom'i-năl.

n: c̣og-nom'i-năl, nom'i-năl,
prē-nom'i-năl, sūr-nom'i-năl.
Plus bomb in, Al, etc.

(Choose only one word out of each group)

OM'I-NĂNS

d: dom'i-nănce,
prē-dom'i-nănce.
pr: prom'i-nence.

OM'I-NĂNT

d: dom'i-nănt, prē-dom'i-nănt.
sub-dom'i-nănt,
sū-pēr-dom'i-nănt.
pr: prom'i-nent.
Plus bomb in aunt *or* ant, etc.

OM'I-NĀT

Vowel: om'i-nāte*
b: ȧ-bom'i-nāte.
d: dom'i-nāte, prē-dom'i-nāte.
k(ç): çom'mi-nāte.
n: ag-nom'i-nāte,
dē-nom'i-nāte, nom'i-nāte,
prē-nom'i-nāte.
Plus bomb in eight *or* ate, etc.

OM'I-NI

d: dom'i-nie.
h: Chiçk-ȧ-hom'i-ni, hom'i-ny.
Cf. Rōm'ȧ-ny.
Plus from a knee, etc.
Plus Tommie, knee, etc.

OM'I-NUS

Vowel: om'i-nous.
d: ab-dom'i-nous, dom'i-nus.
g: prō-lē-gom'ē-nous.
Plus bomb in us, etc.

OM'ŪR-US

gl: glom'ēr-ous*.
s: ī-som'ēr-ous.
Plus bomb her, us, etc.

ŌN'A-B'L

l: lōan'ȧ-ble.
t: tōn'ȧ-ble, un-ȧ-tōn'ȧ-ble.
Plus stone a bull, etc.
Plus Iona bull, etc.

ON-DŪR'ING

p: pon'dēr-ing.
skw: squän'dēr-ing.
w: un-wän'dēr-ing,
wän'dēr-ing.
Plus yonder ring, etc.
Plus beyond her ring, etc.
Plus beyond a ring, etc.

ON'DŪR-ŪR

p: pon'dēr-ēr.
skw: squän'dēr-ēr.
w: wän'dēr-ēr.
Plus fonder, her, etc.
Plus fond o' hēr, etc.

ON'EL-I

d: Don'nel-y.
k(ç): Çon'nŏl-y.
Plus McConnell, he, etc.

Ō'NI-Ȧ

Vowel: brȳ-ō'ni-ȧ, Ī-ō'ni-ȧ.
d: A-dō'ni-ȧ, Dō'ni-ȧ,
Frē-dō'ni-ȧ.
f: ȧ-phō'ni-ȧ, Eū-phō'ni-ȧ.
fr: Sō-phrō'ni-ȧ.
g: bē-gō'ni-ȧ, Pat-ȧ-gō'ni-ȧ.
k(ç): La-çō'ni-ȧ.
l: Ce-phăl-lō'ni-ȧ,
vȧ-lō'ni-ȧ.
m: am-mō'ni-ȧ,
pneū-mō'ni-ȧ (nū-).
n: big-nō'ni-ȧ.

Ō′NI-AK
ON′I-KĂL

fāte, fär, fȧst, fall, finăl, cāre, at; mēte, prey, hēr, met; pīne,
marïne, bïrd, pin; nōte, mȯve, fŏr, atŏm, not; mǫǫn, book;

924

(Choose only one word out of each group)

s: An-sō′ni-ȧ, Sō′ni-ȧ.
t: An-tō′ni-ȧ, Lȧ-tō′ni-ȧ.
v: Sla-vō′ni-ȧ.
Plus pony, a, etc.

Ō′NI-AK

m: dē-mō′ni-aç, sī-mō′ni-aç.
Cf. bony yak, etc.

Ō′NI-ĂL

g: ox-y-gō′ni-ăl* (oks-).
l: çō-lō′ni-ăl,
  in-tēr-çō-lō′ni-ăl,
m: cer-ē-mō′ni-ăl, dē-mō′ni-ăl,
  mat-ri-mō′ni-ăl, mō′ni-ăl,
  pat-ri-mō′ni-ăl, sañç-ti-mō′ni-ăl,
  tes-ti-mō′ni-ăl.
r: bȧ-rō′nĭ-ăl.
Plus macaroni, Al, etc.

Ō′NI-ĂN

Vowel: Ā-ō′ni-ăn,
  hal-cy-ō′ni-ăn, Ī-ō′ni-ăn.
b: Sēr-bō′ni-ăn.
d: Ab-ēr-dō′ni-ăn,
  Çal-ē-dō′ni-ăn, Mac-ē-dō′ni-ăn,
  Myr-mi-dō′ni-ăn,
  Sär-dō′ni-ăn.
f: çol-ō-phō′ni-ăn.
g: Gǫr-gō′nē-ăn, Pat-ȧ-gō′ni-ăn.
k(ç): Bā-çō′ni-ăn, Dra-çō-′ni-ăn,
  Hel-i-çō′ni-ăn, Lȧ-çō′ni-ăn.
kth: Çhthō′ni-ăn.
l: Bab-y-lō′ni-ăn, Chē-lō′ni-ăn,
  Thes-sȧ-lō′ni-ăn.
m: Am-mō′ni-ăn, dē-mō′ni-ăn,
  Sī-mō′ni-ăn.
p: Lap-pō′ni-ăn.
r: Çam-ē-rō′ni-ăn,
  Cic-ē-rō′ni-ăn,
  Nē-rō′ni-ăn,
  Pyr-rhō′ni-ăn (-rō′).

s: Au-sō′ni-ăn,
  Gran-di-sō′ni-ăn,
  John-sō′ni-ăn (jon-),
  Ox-ō′ni-ăn (oks-).
t: Çā-tō′ni-ăn, Çot-tō′ni-ăn,
  Dal-tō′ni-ăn, Ē-tō′ni-ăn,
  Mil-tō′ni-ăn,
  New-tō′ni-ăn (nū-),
  Plù-tō′ni-ăn.
v: De-vō′ni-ăn, Fȧ-vō′ni-ăn,
  Li-vō′ni-ăn, Sla-vō′ni-ăn.
z: Am-ȧ-zō′ni-ăn, bē-zō′ni-ăn.
Plus bony Ann, or an, etc.

ǪN′I-EST

br: braw′ni-est.
t: taw′ni-est.

ON′I-FĪ

p: sȧ-pon′i-fȳ.
s: pēr-son′i-fȳ.
Cf. ō-zon′i-fȳ.
Plus Desdemona, fie!, etc.

ON′I-KȦ

m: här-mon′i-çȧ.
r: vē-ron′i-çȧ.
Plus tonic, a, etc.

ON′I-KĂL

b: Sǫr-bon′i-çăl.
f: an-ti-phon′i-çăl,
  dī-ȧ-phon′i-çăl,
  eū-phon′i-çăl (ū-),
  tau-tō-phon′i-çăl.
k(ç): çon′i-çăl, ī-çon′i-çăl.
kr: ȧ-çron′y-çăl,
  an-ti-çhron′i-çăl, çhron′i-çle,
  syn-çhron′i-çăl.
l: Bab-y-lon′i-çăl.
m: här-mon′i-çăl.

(Choose only one word out of each group)

n: çȧ-non′i-çăl, un-çȧ-non′i-çăl.
p: ġē-ō-pon′i-çăl.
r: ī-ron′i-çăl.
s: thrȧ-son′i-çăl.
t: är″çhi-teç-ton′i-çăl, ton′i-çal.
Plus cyclonic, Al, etc.
Plus bonnie, Cal, etc.

ON′I-KŎN
kr: çhron′i-çŏn.
m: här-mon′i-çŏn.

ON′I-MI
Vowel: pol-y-on′ŏ-my.
m: hō-mon′ŏ-my.
n: sȳ-non′ŏ-my.
r: pȧ-ron′ŏ-my.
t: mē-ton′ŏ-my.
Cf. on′ō-mi.
Plus Ranee me, etc.

ON′I-MUS
Vowel: pol-y-on′y-mous.
d: pseū-don′y-mous (sū-).
m: hō-mon′y-mous.
n: ȧ-non′y-mous,
sy-non′y-mous.
p: ē-pon′y-mous.
r: het-ē-ron′y-mous,
pȧ-ron′y-mous.
t: au̇-ton′y-mous.

ON′ISH-ING
m: ad-mon′ish-ing,
mon′ish-ing*.
st: ȧ-ston′ish-ing.

ON′ISH-MENT
m: ad-mon′ish-ment,
prē-mon′ish-ment.
st: ȧ-ston′ish-ment.
Plus wannish meant, etc.

ON′I-SIZM
Vowel: his-tri-on′i-çiṣm.
k(ç): lȧ-çon′i-çiṣm.
t: Teū-ton′i-çiṣm (tū-).

Ō′NI-UM
g: pē-lăr-gō′ni-um.
k(ç): zir-çō′ni-um.
m: här-mō′ni-um,
pan-dē-mō′ni-um,
strȧ-mō′ni-um.
Plus Coney 'em, etc.

Ō′NI-US
b: Trē-bō′ni-us.
f: eū-phō′ni-ous,
sym-phō′ni-ous.
l: fē-lō′ni-ous.
m: aç-ri-mō′ni-ous,
al-i-mō′ni-ous, cer-ē-mō′ni-ous,
här-mō′ni-ous, in-här-mō′ni-ous,
mat-ri-mō′ni-ous,
pär-si-mō′ni-ous,
quer-i-mō′ni-ous (kwer-),
sañç-ti-mō′ni-ous, sō-mō′ni-ous.
r: er-rō′nē-ous.
t: An-tō′ni-us.
tr: ul-trō′nē-ous.
Plus macaroni us, etc.

ON′Ō-GRȦF
kr: çhron′ō-grȧph.
m: mon′ō-grȧph.
Cf. phōn′ō-grȧph.

ON′Ō-MI
f: mor-phon′ō-my.
k(ç): ē-çon′ō-my.
l: daç-ty-lon′ō-my.

ON′Ō-MIST
OP′I-KĂL
fāte, fär, fȧst, fạll, finăl, cãre, at; mēte, prey, hẽr, met; pīne,
marïne, bĩrd, pin; nōte, mȯve, fọr, atŏm, not; mọọn, book;
926

(Choose only one word out of each group)

r: ag-ron′ō-my, Deū-tē-ron′ō-my,
het-ē-ron′ō-my.
s: ī-son′ō-my, tax-on′ō-my.
t: au-ton′ō-my.
tr: as-tron′ō-my, gas-tron′ō-my.

ON′Ō-MIST

k(c): ē-con′ō-mist.
n: sy-non′y-mist.
p: ē-pon′y-mist.
r: ag-ron′ō-mist.
t: au-ton′ō-mist.
tr: gas-tron′ō-mist.

ON′Ō-MĪZ

k(c): ē-con′ō-mīze.
tr: as-tron′ō-mīze,
gas-tron′ō-mīze.

ON′Ō-MŨR

tr: as-tron′ō-mẽr,
gas-tron′ō-mẽr.

OOD′I-NES

w: wood′i-ness.
Cf. ud′i-nes.

OOK′Ũ-RI

b: book′ẽr-y.
k(c): cook′ẽr-y.
r: rook′ẽr-y.

Ō′Ō-LĪT

Vowel: ō′ō-līte.
z: zō′ō-līte.

OOM′ĂN-LI

w: wom′ăn-ly (woom′).
Cf. ū′măn-li.

OP′Ȧ-THI

Vowel: ē-năn-ti-op′ȧ-thy,
hō-moē-op′ȧ-thy (-mē-),
ī-dē-op′ȧ-thy, os-tē-op′ȧ-thy,
thē-op′ȧ-thy.
dr: hȳ-drop′ȧ-thy.
k(c): psȳ-chop′ȧ-thy (sī-).
l: al-lop′ȧ-thy.
n: som-nop′ȧ-thy.
r: het-e-rop′ȧ-thy,
neū-rop′ȧ-thy (nū-).
s: ī-sop′ȧ-thy.

OP′Ȧ-THIST

Vowel: hō-moē-op′ȧ-thist (-mē-),
os-tē-op′ȧ-thist.
dr: hȳ-drop′ȧ-thist.
l: al-lop′ȧ-thist, hȳ-lop′ȧ-thist.
n: som-nop′ȧ-thist.

Ō′PI-Ȧ

Vowel: Ē-thi-ō′pi-ȧ,
mȳ-ō′pi-ȧ, pres-by-ō′pi-ȧ.
k(c): cor-nū-cō′pi-ȧ.
t: Ū-tō′pi-ȧ.
Plus dopy a, etc.

Ō′PI-ĂN, Ō′PĒ-ĂN

Vowel: Ē-thi-ō′pi-ăn.
l: Fal-lō′pi-ăn.
s: Aē-sō′pi-ăn,
Ē-sō′pi-ăn.
t: Ū-tō′pi-ăn.
Plus ropy an *or* Ann, etc.

OP′I-KĂL

sk(sc): me″tō-pō-scop′i-căl,
mī-crō-scop′i-căl.
t: top′i-căl.
tr: al-lō-trop′i-căl,
sub-trop′i-căl, trop′i-căl.

927 ūse, bụll, brúte, tŭrn, up; crȳ, myth; çat, maçhine, ace, church, çhord; ġem, añger, (Fr.) boṅ, aṣ; THis, thin; azure

ŌP′I-NES
QR′DI-ĂL

(Choose only one word out of each group)

thr: mis-ăn-throp′i-çăl.
Plus floppy, Cal, etc.
Plus kaleidoscopic, Al, etc.

ŌP′I-NES

d: dōp′i-ness.
r: rōp′i-ness.
s: sōap′i-ness.
sl: slōp′i-ness.

OP′I-NES

ch: chop′pi-ness.
s: sop′pi-ness.
sl: slop′pi-ness.

ŌP′ISH-NES

d: dōp′ish-ness.
m: mōp′ish-ness.
p: pōp′ish-ness.

OP′Ō-LIS

Vowel: Hē-li-op′ō-lis.
kr: ȧ-çrop′ō-lis, ne-çrop′ō-lis.
m: ços-mop′ō-lis, Dē-mop′ō-lis.
tr: me-trop′ō-lis.

OP′Ō-LIST

Vowel: bib-li-op′ō-list.
k(ç): phär-mȧ-çop′ō-list.
n: mō-nop′ō-list.

OP′Ō-LĪT

m: ços-mop′ō-līte.
tr: me-trop′ō-līte.
Cf. shah polite, etc.

OP′SI-KĂL

dr: drop′si-çăl.
m: mop′si-çăl.
p: Pop′si-çle.
Plus Topsy, Cal, etc.

OP′TI-KĂL

Vowel: op′ti-çăl.
t: a̤u-top′ti-çăl.
Plus Coptic, Al, etc.

OP′TŪR-US

d: le-pi-dop′tĕr-ous.
kr: mȧ-çrop′tĕr-ous.
th: or-thop′tĕr-ous.

OP′Ū-LĀT

k(ç): çop′ū-lāte.
p: dē-pop′ū-lāte, pop′ū-lāte.
Plus stop, you late, etc.

ŌP′ŪR-I

d: dōp′ĕr-y.
p: pōp′ĕr-y.
r: rōp′ĕr-y.
Plus rope her, he, etc.
Plus eloper, he, etc.

OP′ŪR-I

f: fop′pĕr-y.
k(ç): çop′pĕr-y.
Plus stop her, he, etc.
Plus sharecropper, he, etc.

ŌR′Ȧ-B'L

d: ȧ-dōr′ȧ-ble.
pl: dē-plōr′ȧ-ble, ex-plōr′ȧ-ble.
st: rē-stōr′ȧ-ble.
Plus gore a bull, etc.
Plus Angora bull, etc.

ŌR′Ȧ-TIV

pl: ex-plōr′ȧ-tive.
st: rē-stōr′ȧ-tive.

QR′DI-ĂL

k(ç): çor′di-ăl.
m: prī-mor′di-ăl.
s: ex-or′di-ăl.

(Choose only one word out of each group)

OR'DI-NĀT

Vowel: cō-ọr'di-nāte,
fōre-ọr'di-nāte, ọr'di-nāte.
b: in-su-bọr'di-nāte,
su-bọr'di-nāte.
Cf. Gordon ate *or* eight, etc.
Plus lord innate, etc.

OR'DI-ŎN, OR'DI-ĂN

g: Gọr'di-ăn.
k(c): ạc-cọr'di-ŏn.
Plus Lordy, Ann *or* an, etc.

OR'DŪR-ING

Vowel: ọr'dẽr-ing.
b: bọr'dẽr-ing.
Plus order ring, etc.
Plus award a ring, etc.
Plus award her ring, etc.

OR'Ē-ĀT

Vowel: ạu'rē-āte.
l: bạc-cạ-lạu'rē-āte,
lạu'rē-āte, pō'et lạu'rē-āte.
Plus Maury ate *or* eight, etc.
Plus war, he ate, etc.

OR'Ē-ŌL

Vowel: ạu'rē-ōle.
l: lạu'rē-ōle*.

OR'GĂN-ĪZ

Vowel: or'găn-īze.
g: gọr'gŏn-īze.
Plus Morganize, etc.
Plus gorgon eyes, etc.

Ō'RI-Ȧ

Vowel: Pē-ō'ri-ȧ.
f: dys-phō'ri-ȧ,
eū-phō'ri-ȧ (ū-).

g: phan-taṣ-mȧ-gō'ri-ȧ.
gl: Glō'ri-ȧ.
n: Hō-nō'ri-ȧ (ō-).
p: ȧ-pō'ri-ȧ.
s: in-fū-sō'ri-ȧ.
sk(sc): scō'ri-ȧ.
t: As-tō'ri-ȧ, Cas-tō'ri-ȧ,
lit-tō'ri-ȧ, Prē-tō'ri-ȧ,
viç-tō'ri-ȧ, Wạl'dọrf As-tō'ri-ȧ.
Plus story a, etc.
Cf. slow, rhea, etc.

Ō'RI-ĂL

b: är-bō'rē-ăl, bō'rē-ăl.
d: am-bas-sȧ-dō'ri-ăl.
g: phan-taṣ-mȧ-gō'ri-ăl.
m: är-mō'ri-ăl, im-me-mō'ri-ăl,
märmō'rē-ăl, me-mō'ri-ăl.
n: mȧ-nō'ri-ăl,
sēig-nō'ri-ăl (sē-).
p: cọr-pō'rē-ăl, em-pō'ri-ăl,
in-cọr-pō'rē-ăl.
s: ạc-ces-sō'ri-ăl, as-ses-sō'ri-ăl,
cen-sō'ri-ăl,
com-prō-mis-sō'ri-ăl,
cũr-sō'ri-ăl, fos-sō'ri-ăl,
gres-sō'ri-ăl, in-fū-sō'ri-ăl,
in-ses-sō'ri-ăl,
in-tẽr-ces-sō'ri-ăl,
pro-fes-sō'ri-ăl, rȧ-sō'ri-ăl,
rī-sō'ri-ăl, scan-sō'ri-ăl,
sen-sō'ri-ăl, spon-sō'ri-ăl,
ton-sō'ri-ăl, ux-ō'ri-ăl (uks-).
t: ạc-cū-sȧ-tō'ri-ăl,
ȧ-dap-tō'ri-ăl, ad-mon-i-tō'ri-ăl,
am-ȧ-tō'ri-ăl, an-ces-tō'ri-ăl,
ạu-di-tō'ri-ăl,
com-men-tȧ-tō'ri-ăl,
com-pũr-gȧ-tō'ri-ăl,
con-sis-tō'ri-ăl, ded-i-cȧ-tō'ri-ăl,
diç-tȧ-tō'ri-ăl, dī-reç-tō'ri-ăl,

(Choose only one word out of each group)

dis-quī-tō′ri-ăl (-kwī-),
ed-i-tō′ri-ăl, el-ec̦-tō′ri-ăl,
ē-quȧ-tō′rē-ăl (-kwȧ-),
es-c̦ri-tō′ri-ăl,
ex-ec̦-ū-tō′ri-ăl,
ex-pu̅r-gȧ-tō′ri-ăl,
ex-ter-ri-tō′ri-ăl,
ex-trȧ-ter-ri-tō′ri-ăl,
fac̦-tō′ri-ăl, glad-i-ȧ-tō′ri-ăl,
gral-lȧ-tō′ri-ăl,
gū-ber-nȧ-tō′ri-ăl, his-tō′ri-ăl,
im-per-ȧ-tōr′i-ăl,
im-prō-vi-ṣi-tōr′i-ăl,
in-quiṣ-i-tō′ri-ăl (-kwiz-),
in-ven-tō′ri-ăl, leġ″is-lȧ-tō′ri-ăl,
mē-di-ȧ-tō′ri-ăl, men-tō′ri-ăl,
mon-i-tō′ri-ăl, mō-tō′ri-ăl,
or-ȧ-tō′ri-ăl, pic̦-tō′ri-ăl,
pis-c̦ȧ-tō′ri-ăl, prē-cep-tō′ri-ăl,
prē-fȧ-tō′ri-ăl, proc̦-tō′ri-ăl,
prō-c̦ūr-ȧ-tō′ri-ăl,
prō-prī-e-tō′ri-ăl,
prō-tec̦-tō′ri-ăl, pu̅r-gȧ-tō′ri-ăl,
rap-tō′ri-ăl,
rec̦-tō′ri-ăl, rē-por-tō′ri-ăl,
sär-tō′ri-äl, sec̦-tō′ri-ăl,
sen-ȧ-tō′ri-ăl, spec̦-tȧ-tō′ri-ăl,
spec̦-ū-lȧ-tō′ri-ăl, suc̦-tō′ri-ăl,
ter-ri-tō′ri-ăl, tiñc̦-tō′ri-ăl,
tū-tō′ri-ăl, vic̦-tō′ri-ăl,
viṣ-i-tȧ-tō′ri-ăl.
th: a̠u-thō′ri-ăl.
Plus gory, Al, etc.
Plus no real, etc.

Ō′RI-ĂN

b: hy̅-pēr-bō′rē-ăn.
d: Dō′ri-ăn.
f: Bos-phō′ri-ăn (-fō′).
g: Gre-gō′ri-ăn.
m: mär-mō′rē-ăn.

s: cen-sō′ri-ăn.
t: am-ȧ-tō′ri-ăn,
con-sis-tō′ri-ăn,
dic̦-tȧ-tō′ri-ăn, glad-i-ȧ-tō′ri-ăn,
Hec̦-tō′rē-ăn, his-tō′ri-ăn,
mid꞊Vic̦-tō′ri-ăn, Nes-tō′ri-ăn,
or-ȧ-tō′ri-ăn, praē-tō′ri-ăn (prē-),
pu̅r-gȧ-tō′ri-ăn, sal-ūt-ȧ-tō′ri-ăn,
sen-ȧ-tō′ri-ăn, sten-tō′ri-ăn,
val-ē-dic̦-tō′ri-ăn, Vic̦-tō′ri-ăn.
Plus gory an *or* Ann, etc

ŌR′I-ĀT

k(c̦): ex-c̦ō′ri-āte.
s: prō-fes-sō′ri-āte.
Plus lory ate *or* eight, etc.
Plus more he ate, etc.

OR′ID-LI

fl: flor′id-ly.
h: hor′rid-ly.
t: tor′rid-ly.
Plus forehead, Lee, etc.

Ō′RI-FĪ

gl: glō′ri-fy̅.
sk(sc̦): sc̦ōr′i-fy̅.
Plus tory, fie!, etc.

OR′I-FĪ

h: hor′ri-fy̅.
t: his-tor′i-fy̅, tor′rē-fy̅.
Plus sorry, fie!, etc.

OR′I-KĂL

Vowel: or′ȧ-c̦le.
f: me-tȧ-phor′i-c̦ăl (-for′).
g: al-lē-gor′i-c̦ăl, c̦at-ē-gor′i-c̦ăl,
ta̠ut-ē-gor′i-c̦ăl.
k(c̦): c̦or′ȧ-c̦le.

Ō′RI-NES
ǪR′MI-TI

fāte, fär, fȧst, fǎll, finǎl, cãre, at; mēte, prey, hẽr, met; pīne,
marïne, bĭrd, pin; nōte, mŏve, fọr, atŏm, not; mọọn, book;

930

(Choose only one word out of each group)

t: his-tor′i-çǎl, or-ȧ-tor′i-çǎl,
pic-tor′i-çǎl, rhē-tor′i-çǎl (rē-).
Plus sorry, Cal, etc.
Plus Doric, Al, etc.

Ō′RI-NES

g: gōr′i-ness.
h: hōar′i-ness, whōr′i-ness.
t: de-ṣul-tō′ri-ness,
dil-ȧ-tōr′i-ness,
pẽr-emp-tō′ri-ness.

Ō′RI-ŌL

Vowel: ō′ri-ōle.
gl: glō′ri-ōle, glō′ry hōle.
Plus story, Ole, etc.
Plus lory hole *or* whole, etc.

OR′I-TI

Vowel: an-tẽr-i-or′i-ty,
dē-tẽr-i-or′i-ty, ex-tẽr-i-or′i-ty,
in-fē-ri-or′i-ty, in-tẽr-i-or′i-ty,
mē-li-or′i-ty, pos-tē-ri-or′i-ty, ·
prī-or′i-ty, sū-pēr-i-or′i-ty.
j: mȧ-jor′i-ty.
n: mī-nor′i-ty.
r: sō-ror′i-ty.
th: au-thor′i-ty.
y: jūn-ior′i-ty (-yor′),
sen-ior′i-ty.
Plus Dorrit, he, etc.
Plus sorry tea, etc.

Ō′RI-UM

b: cī-bō′ri-um.
f: trī-fō′ri-um.
k(ç): çō′ri-um.
p: em-pō′ri-um.
s: as-per-sō′ri-um, sen-sō′ri-um.
t: au-di-tō′ri-um,
crē-mȧ-tō′ri-um, diġ-i-tō′ri-um,
fū-mȧ-tō′ri-um, hạus-tō′ri-um,

in-çlin-ȧ-tō′ri-um,
mọr-ȧ-tō′ri-um,
praē-tō′ri-um (prē-),
pros-peç-tō′ri-um,
san-ȧ-tō′ri-um, scrip-tō′ri-um,
sū-dȧ-tō′ri-um.
th: thō′ri-um.
Plus glory ′em, etc.

Ō′RI-US

b: är-bō′rē-ous, la-bō′ri-ous.
gl: glō′ri-ous, in-glō′ri-ous,
vāin=glō′ri-ous (vān=).
n: hip-pi-çȧ-nō′ri-ous.
r: up-rōar′i-ous (-rōr′).
s: cen-sō′ri-ous, lú-sōr′i-ous,
ux-ōr′i-ous (uks-).
sk(sç): sçō′ri-ous.
t: am-ȧ-tō′ri-ous,
cir-çū-là-tō′ri-ous,
de-ṣul-tō′ri-ous,
ex-pi-ȧ-tō′ri-ous,
ex-pūr-gȧ-tō′ri-ous,
in-quiṣ-i-tō′ri-ous,
mer-i-tō′ri-ous, nō-tō′ri-ous,
or-a-tō′ri-ous, pūr-gȧ-tō′ri-ous,
rap-tō′ri-ous, sal-ū-tȧ-tō′ri-ous,
sal-tȧ-tō′ri-ous, sen-ȧ-tō′ri-ous,
sten-tō′ri-ous, stẽr-tō′ri-ous,
suç-tō′ri-ous, ūs-tō′ri-ous,
viç-tō′ri-ous.
Plus glory us, etc.

ǪR′MÅ-TIV

d: dọr′mi-tive.
f: ăf-fọr′mȧ-tive, fọr′mȧ-tive,
in-fọr′mȧ-tive, rē-fọr′mȧ-tive,
trans-fọr′mȧ-tive.

ǪR′MI-TI

f: çon-fọr′mi-ty, dē-fọr′mi-ty,
in-çon-for′mi-ty,

(Choose only one word out of each group)

mul-ti-for′mi-ty,
non-con-for′mi-ty,
ūn-i-for′mi-ty.
n: ab-nor′mi-ty, ē-nor′mi-ty.
Plus storm it, he, etc.
Plus war, Mittie, etc.

OR′Ō-ING

b: bor′rōw-ing.
m: mor′rōw-ing, tö-mor′rōw-ing.
s: sor′rōw-ing.

OR′Ō-ŪR

b: bor′rōw-ẽr.
s: sor′rōw-ẽr.
Plus tomorrow her, etc.
Cf. car, O her, etc.

ŌRS′Ȧ-B'L, ŌRS′I-B'L

f: en-fōrce′ȧ-ble, fōr′ci-ble.
v: di-vōrce′ȧ-ble.
Plus force a bull, etc.

OR′TI-FȲ

f: for′ti-fȳ.
m: mor′ti-fȳ.
Plus warty, fie!, etc.

OR′TI-KĂL

k(ç): cor′ti-căl.
v: vor′ti-căl.
Plus forty, Cal, etc.

ORT′I-NES

sw: swar′ti-ness*.
w: war′ti-ness.

ŌRT′LI-NES

k(ç): cōurt′li-ness (kōrt′),
un-cōurt′li-ness.
p: pōrt′li-ness.

OR′TŪ-NĀT

f: for′tū-nāte, un-for′tū-nāte.
p: im-por′tū-nāte.
Plus fortune ate or eight, etc.
Plus escort you, Nate, etc.

Ō′RUS-LI

k(ç): de-cōr′ous-ly.
n: sō-nōr′ous-ly.
p: pōr′ous-ly.
Plus chorus, Lee or lea, etc.

ŌR′YUS-LI

b: là-bōr′ious-ly.
gl: glōr′ious-ly, in-glōr′ious-ly,
vāin⹀glōr′ious-ly.
n: hip″pi-çà-nōr′ious-ly.
r: up-rōar′ious-ly.
s: ux-ōr′ious-ly (uks-).
t: mer-i-tōr′ious-ly,
nō-tōr′ious-ly, sten-tōr′ious-ly,
vic̣-tōr′ious-ly.

OS′FOR-US

b: Bos′phor-us.
f: phos′phor-ous, phos′phor-us.
Plus loss for us, etc.

Ō′SHI-ĂN

Vowel: Boē-ō′ti-ăn.
k(ç): Ni-cō′ti-ăn.
Cf. ō′shuṇ.

Ō′SHUN-ĂL

m: ē-mō′tion-ăl.
n: nō′tion-ăl.
v: dē-vō′tion-ăl.
Plus emotion, Al, etc.

Ō′SHUS-NES

k(ç): prē-cō′cious-ness (′shus-).
r: fē-rō′cious-ness.
tr: à-trō′cious-ness.

OS'I-NAT
Ō'SIV-NES

fāte, fär, fȧst, fᶏll, finăl, cȧre, at; mēte, prey, hȇr, met; pīne,
marīne, bĩrd, pin; nōte, mȯve, fǫr, atŏm, not; mo͝on, book; **932**

(Choose only one word out of each group)

OS'I-NAT

Vowel: ra-ti-o'cin-āte   (rash-i-).
tr: pā-tro'cin-āte*.
Plus loss innate, etc.
Plus loss in eight *or* ate, etc.
Plus glossy, Nate, etc.

OS'I-NES

dr: dros'si-ness.
fl: flos'si-ness.
gl: glos'si-ness.
m: mos'si-ness.
Cf. sauciness.

OS'I-TI

p: pau'ci-ty.
r: rau'ci-ty.
Cf. craw, city, etc.
Plus cross it, he, etc.
Plus faucet, he, etc.

OS'I-TY

Vowel: aç-tū-os'i-ty,
an-fraç-tū-os'i-ty, çū-ri-os'i-ty,
dī-bū-os'i-ty, ē-bri-os'i-ty,
fō-li-os'i-ty, fū-ri-os'i-ty,
gran-di-os'i-ty, hid-ē-os'i-ty,
im-pē-çū-ni-os'i-ty,
im-pet-ū-os'i-ty, in-ġēn-i-os'i-ty,
el-ē-os'i-ty, ō-ti-os'i-ty (-shi-),
prē-ci-oc'i-ty (-shi-),
prē-ti-os'i-ty, rē-li-ġi-os'i-ty,
sen-sū-os'i-ty, sin-ū-os'i-ty,
spēc-i-os'i-ty, tǫr-tū-os'i-ty,
uñç-tū-os'i-ty, vic-i-os'i-ty,
vīr-tū-os'i-ty, vī-ti-os'i-ty.
b: gib-bos'i-ty, glē-bos'i-ty,
glō-bos'i-ty, vȇr-bos'i-ty.
br: ten-ē-bros'i-ty.
d: doc'i-ty, nō-dos'i-ty.
g: fun-gos'i-ty, rů-gos'i-ty.

k(ç): mus-ços'i-ty, pre-çoc'i-ty,
spī-ços'i-ty, vȧr-i-ços'i-ty,
vis-ços'i-ty.
kw(qu): ȧ-quos'i-ty.
l: an-gū-los'i-ty, çal-los'i-ty,
fab-ū-los'i-ty, glan-dū-los'i-ty,
gů-los'i-ty, mus-çū-los'i-ty,
neb-ū-los'i-ty, pī-los'i-ty,
rid-i-çū-los'i-ty, sa-bū-los'i-ty,
sçrūp-ū-los'i-ty,
tū-mū-los'i-ty, vē-loc'i-ty,
vil-los'i-ty.
m: an-i-mos'i-ty,
an-on-y-mos'i-ty,
fū-mos'i-ty, ġem-mos'i-ty,
gum-mos'i-ty, plū-mos'i-ty,
rī-mos'i-ty.
n: çȧ-liġ-i-nos'i-ty,
çär-nos'i-ty, fū-liġ-i-nos'i-ty,
glū-ti-nos'i-ty, lī-bid-i-nos'i-ty,
lū-mi-nos'i-ty, spī-nos'i-ty,
vī-nos'i-ty.
p: pom-pos'i-ty.
pr: re-ci-proc'i-ty.
r: fē-roc'i-ty, ġen-ē-ros'i-ty,
pon-dē-ros'i-ty, pō-ros'i-ty,
sap-ō-ros'i-ty,
sçir-rhos'i-ty (-ros'),
sē-ros'i-ty, tō-ros'i-ty,
tū-bē-ros'i-ty, vō-ci-fē-ros'i-ty.
str: mon-stros'i-ty.
tr: ȧ-troc'i-ty.
v: nȇr-vos'i-ty.
Plus cross it, he, etc.
Plus Flossie, tea, etc.
Plus posset, he, etc.
Cf. faucet, he, etc.

Ō'SIV-NES

pl: ex-plō'sive-ness (eks-).
r: çor-rō'sive-ness.

933

ūse, bu̧ll, brúte, tũrn, up; crȳ, myth; c̨at, machine, ace, church, c̨hord; ġem, añger, (Fr.) boñ, a̧s; THis, thin; azure

OS′KŌ-PI
ŌT′ED-LI

(Choose only one word out of each group)

OS′KŌ-PI

Vowel: c̨rā-ni-os′c̨ō-py, ġē-os′c̨ō-py, ster-ē-os′c̨ō-py.
l: ġē-los′c̨ō-py.
n: o̧r-ga̧-nos′c̨ō-py, re-ti-nos′c̨ō-py, ūr-a̧-nos′c̨ō-py.
p: me-tō-pos′c̨ō-py.
r: hīe-ros′c̨ō-py, hō-ros′c̨ō-py, me-tē-ō-ros′c̨ō-py, ō-nē-i-ros′c̨ō-py.
t: ō-mō-plá-tos′c̨ō-py.
th: o̧r-ni-thos′c̨ō-py, ste-thos′c̨ō-py.

OS′KŌ-PIST

Vowel: ster-ē-os′c̨ō-pist.
kr: mī-c̨ros′c̨ō-pist.
p: ne-tō-pos′c̨ō-pist.
r: o-nē-ī-ros′c̨ō-pist.
th: o̧r-ni-thos′c̨ō-pist, ste-thos′c̨ō-pist.

OS′Ō-FI

Vowel: thē-os′ō-phy.
l: phi-los′ō-phy, psȳ-los′ō-phy.
n: ġym-nos′ō-phy.
Plus cross off, he, etc.

OS′Ō-FIST

Vowel: thē-os′o-phist.
l: phi-los′ō-phist.
n: dē-ip-nos′ō-phist, ġym-nos′ō-phist.
r: c̨hī-ros′ō-phist.
Plus loss, Oh fist, etc.

OS′Ō-FĪZ

Vowel: thē-os′ō-phīze.
l: phi-los′ō-phīze.

OS′Ō-FŨR

Vowel: thē-os′ō-phĕr (-fẽr).
l: phi-los′ō-phĕr (fi-), psī-los′ō-pher (sī-).
Cf. cross off her, etc.

ŌT′A̧-B′L

fl: flōat′a̧-ble.
kw(qu): quōt′a̧-ble.
n: nōt′a̧-ble.
p: pōt′a̧-ble.
v: vōt′a̧-ble.
Plus tote a bull, etc.
Plus Minnesota bull, etc.

ŌT′A̧-LIZM

d: sa̧c̨-ēr-dō′ta̧-lişm.
t: tee-tōt′a̧-lişm.

OT′ĂN-I

b: bot′ăn-y, bot′ŏ-nee.
k(c̨): c̨ot′tŏn-y.
n: mō-not′ŏ-ny.
Plus rotten, he, etc.
Plus not a knee, etc.

ŌT′Ă-RI

n: nōt′ă-ry.
r: rōt′ă-ry.
v: vōt′ă-ry.
Plus voter, he, etc.
Plus quote her, he, etc.

ŌT′A̧-TIV

n: c̨on-nōt′a̧-tive, dē-nōt′a̧-tive.
r: rōt′a̧-tive.

ŌT′ED-LI

bl: blōat′ed-ly (blōt′).
n: nōt′ed-ly.

OT'I-EST
OT'ÜR-ING
fāte, fär, fȧst, fạll, finǎl, cãre, at; mēte, prẹy, hẽr, met; pīne,
marïne, bĭrd, pin; nōte, mŏve, fọr, atŏm, not; mọọn, book;   **934**

(Choose only one word out of each group)

v: dē-vōt'ed-ly.
Plus quoted Lee, moated lea, etc.
Plus slow, Ted Lee, etc.

OT'I-EST

h: hạught'i-est (hạt').
n: nạught'i-ness (nạt').

OT'I-KĂL

d: an-eç-dot'i-çǎl.
g: bi-got'i-çǎl.
l: zēal-ot'i-çǎl (zēl-).
p: des-pot'i-çǎl.
r: ē-rot'i-çǎl.
s: ex-ot'i-çǎl (eks-).
Plus dotty, Cal, etc.
Plus erotic, Al, etc.

OT'I-LI

h: hạught'i-ly (hạt').
n: nạught'i-ly.
Plus naughty Lee, etc.
Plus brought alee, etc.

OT'I-NES

h: hạught'i-ness (hạt').
n: nạught'i-ness.

OT'I-NES

d: dot'ti-ness.
n: knot'ti-ness (not').
sn: snot'ti-ness.
sp: spot'ti-ness.

OT'I-ÜR

h: hạught'i-ẽr (hạt').
n: nạught'i-ẽr.
Plus haughty, her, err *or* er, etc.

OT'ŎM-I

Vowel: iç h-thy-ot'ŏm-y,
ster-ē-ot'ŏm-y, trȧç h-ē-ot'ŏm-y,
zō-ot'ŏm-y.

b: bot'tŏm-y,
phlē-bot'ŏm-y (flē-).
k(ç): bron-ç hot'ŏm-y,
dī-ç hot'ŏm-y.
l: en-ceph-à-lot'ŏm-y (-sef-).
m: dẽr-mot'ŏm-y.
p: à-pot'ŏm-ē, hip-pō-pot'ăm-y.
sk(sc): sçot'ŏm-y.
t: phȳ-tot'ŏm-y (fī-).
Cf. hip-pō-pot'à-mi.
Plus lot o' me, etc.
Plus blotto me, etc.
Plus bottom, he, etc.

OT'Ō-MIST

Vowel: iç h-thy-ot'ō-mist,
zō-ot'ō-mist.
b: phlē-bot'ō-mist.
t: phȳ-tot'ō-mist, etc.
Plus lot o' mist, etc.
Plus blotto mist *or* missed, etc.

OT'ÜR-I

k(ç): çau'tẽr-y.
w: wạ'tẽr-y.
Plus brought her, he, etc.
Plus daughter, he, etc.

OT'ÜR-I

l: lot'tẽr-y.
p: pot'tẽr-y.
t: tot'tẽr-y.
tr: trot'tẽr-y.
Plus squatter, he, etc.
Plus got her, he, etc.

OT'ÜR-ING

sl: slạught'ẽr-ing.
w: wạ'tẽr-ing.
Plus caught her ring, etc.
Plus caught a ring, etc.
Plus daughter ring, etc.

935 ūse, bụll, brúte, tũrn, up; crȳ, myth; çat, maçhine, ace, church, çhord; ġem, añger, (Fr.) boń, aṣ; THis, thin; aᴢure

QT'ŨR-ŨR
OU'ŨR-I

(Choose only one word out of each group)

QT'ŨR-ŨR

sl: slaught′ẽr-ẽr.
w: wạt′ẽr-ẽr.
Plus daughter, her, etc.
Plus caught her, her, etc.

OU'Å-B'L

d: en-dow′à-ble.
l: al-low′à-ble.
v: à-vow′à-ble.
Plus cow a bull, etc.

OUD'ED-NES

kl: çloud′ed-ness,
un-çloud′ed-ness.
kr: çrowd′ed-ness,
ō-vẽr-çrowd′ed-ness.

OUD'I-IZM

d: dou′dy-iṣm.
r: row′dy-iṣm.

OUD'I-NES

d: dow′di-ness.
kl: çloud′i-ness.
r: row′di-ness.

OUL'ŨR-I

Vowel: owl′ẽr-y.
pr: prowl′ẽr-y.
Plus foul her, he, etc.
Plus growler, he, etc.

OUN'DÅ-B'L

p: çom-poun′dà-ble.
s: soun′dà-ble, un-soun′dà-ble.
z: rē-ṣoun′dà-ble.
Plus surround a bull, etc.

OUN'DED-NES

b: un-boun′ded-ness.
f: çon-foun′ded-ness,
dum-foun′ded-ness.
gr: un-groun′ded-ness.
st: à-stoun′ded-ness.

OUND'LES-LI

b: bound′less-ly.
gr: ground′less-ly.
s: sound′less-ly.
Plus boundless lea or Lee, etc.

OUND'LES-NES

b: bound′less-ness.
gr: ground′less-ness.
s: sound′less-ness.

OUN'TÅ-B'L

k(ç): çoun′tà-ble,
dis-çoun′tà-ble,
un-aç-çoun′tà-ble.
m: in-sŭr-moun′tà-ble,
moun′tà-ble,
sũr-moun′tà-ble.
Plus mount a bull, etc.

OUT'I-NESS

d: dout′i-ness.
dr: drought′i-ness (drout′).
g: gout′i-ness.

OU'ŨR-I

b: bow′ẽr-y.
d: dow′ẽr-y.
fl: flow′ẽr-y.
gl: glow′ẽr-y.
l: low′ẽr-y.
sh: show′ẽr-y.
t: tow′ẽr-y.
Cf. our′i.
Plus flower, he, etc.

OU′ŪR-ING
Ō′ZŪR-I

fāte, fär, fȧst, fąll, finăl, cãre, at; mēte, prĕy, hẽr, met; pīne,
marīne, bĭrd, pin; nōte, mŏve, fŏr, atŏm, not; mọọn, book; **936**

(Choose only one word out of each group)

OU′ŪR-ING

d: dow′ẽr-ing.
fl: dē-flow′ẽr-ing, flow′ẽr-ing.
gl: glow′ẽr-ing.
k(c): çow′ẽr-ing.
l: low′ẽr-ing.
p: em-pow′ẽr-ing,
ō-vẽr-pow′ẽr-ing.
sh: show′ẽr-ing.
t: ō-vẽr-tow′ẽr-ing,
tow′ẽr-ing.

OUZ′I-NES

dr: drow′și-ness.
fr: frow′și-ness.
l: lou′și-ness.

OV′EL-ING

gr: gro′vel-ling.
h: ho′vel-ling.
Cf. sho′vel-ling.

Ō′VI-ĂL

j: jō′vi-ăl.
n: sy-nō′vi-ăl.
Plus Hovey, Al, etc.

Ō′VI-ĂN

j: Jō′vi-ăn.
k(c): Çrȧ-çō′vi-ăn.
Plus Hovey, Ann or an, etc.

Ō′ZHI-Ȧ, Ō′ZI-Ȧ

br: am-brō′și-ȧ.
p: sym-pō′și-ȧ.
Plus posy, a, etc.

Ō′ZHI-ĂL, Ō′ZI-ĂL

br: am-brō′și-ăl.
r: rō′șē-ăl.
Plus dozy, Al, etc.

Ō′ZHI-ĂN, Ō′ZI-ĂN

br: am-brō′și-ăn.
Cf. ō′zhun.

Ō′ZI-EST

k(c): çō′zi-est.
n: nō′și-est.
pr: prō′și-est.
r: rō′și-est.

Ō′ZI-LI

k(c): çō′zi-ly.
n: nō′și-ly.
pr: prō′și-ly.
r: rō′și-ly.
Plus cozy, Lee or lea, etc.
Plus doze alee, etc.

Ō′ZI-NES

d: dō′zi-ness.
k(c): çō′zi-ness.
n: nō′și-ness.
pr: prō′și-ness.
r: rō′și-ness.

O′ZI-ŪR

Vowel: ō′și-ẽr.
d: Dō′zi-ẽr.
h: hō′și-ẽr.
k(c): çō′zi-ẽr.
kr: çrō′și-ẽr.
n: nō′și-ẽr.
pr: prō′și-ẽr.
r: rō′și-ẽr.
Plus posy her, etc.

Ō′ZŪR-I

d: dō′zẽr-y.
p: çom-pō′șẽr-y.
r: rō′șȧr-y.
(*Not* hosiery.)

(Choose only one word out of each group)

U

The accented vowel sounds included are listed under **U** in Single Rhymes.

Ū′Ȧ-B′L

d: dö′ȧ-ble, sub-dū′ȧ-ble, un-dö′ȧ-ble.
n: rē-new′ȧ-ble (-nū′).
s: pūr-sū′ȧ-ble, sū′ȧ-ble, un-pūr-sū′ȧ-ble, un-sū′ȧ-ble.
v: rē-view′ȧ-ble (-vū′), un-rē-view′ȧ-ble.
Plus knew a bull, etc.

Ū′BI-ĂN

n: Dȧ-nū′bi-ăn, Nū′bi-ăn.
r: rů′bi-ăn.
Plus booby, Ann *or* an, etc.

Ū′BI-KĂL

k(ç): çū′bi-çăl.
r: che-rů′bi-çăl.
Plus booby, Cal, etc.
Plus pubic, Al, etc.

Ū′BI-LĀT

j: jů′bi-lāte.
l: vo-lū′bi-lāte*.
n: ē-nū′bi-lāte, nū′bi-lāte, ob-nū′bi-lāte.
Plus booby late, etc.
Plus boob elate, etc.

UB′I-NES

ch: chub′bi-ness.
gr: grub′bi-ness.
shr: shrub′bi-ness.
skr(sçr): sçrub′bi-ness.
st: stub′bi-ness.

Ū′BI-US

d: dū′bi-ous.
r: rů′bi-ous.
Plus booby us, etc.

Ū′BRI-KĀT

l: lū′bri-çāte.
r: rů′bri-çāte.
Plus new Brie Kate, etc.

Ū′BRI-US

g: lů-gū′bri-ous.
l: in-sȧ-lů′bri-ous, sȧ-lů′bri-ous.

Ū′BŬR-US

s: sū′bĕr-ous.
t: prō-tū′bĕr-ous, tū′bĕr-ous.
Plus Huber us, etc.

ŪD′Ȧ-B′L

kl: in-çlūd′ȧ-ble.
l: al-lūd′ȧ-ble, dē-lūd′ȧ-ble.
tr: prō-trůd′ȧ-ble.
Plus brood a bull, etc.
Plus Bermuda bull, etc.

ŪD′EN-SI

kl: çon-çlū′den-cy.
kr: rē-çrů′den-cy.
p: im-pū′den-cy, pū′den-cy.
Cf. students see, etc.
Plus new den, see, etc.

ŪD′I-B′L

kl: in-çlūd′i-ble.
l: in-ē-lūd′i-ble.

UD′I-LI
UF′I-NES
fāte, fär, fȧst, fạll, finăl, cãre, at; mēte, prey, hẽr, met; pīne,
marïne, bĩrd, pin; nōte, mȯve, fọr, atŏm, not; mọọn, book; **938**

(Choose only one word out of each group)

Cf. ūd′ȧ-b'l.
Plus brood a bull, etc.
Plus Barbuda bull, etc.

sō-lic-i-tū′di-nous,
vi-cis-si-tū′di-nous.
Plus food in us, etc.

UD′I-LI

bl: blood′i-ly.
m: mud′di-ly.
r: rud′di-ly.
Plus study, Lee *or* lea, etc.
Plus mud alee, etc.

Ū′DI-TI

kr: c̣ru′di-ty.
n: nū′di-ty.
r: rủ′di-ty.
Plus moody tea, etc.
Plus brood it, he, etc.

Ū′DI-NĂL

t: ap-ti-tū′di-năl, at-ti-tū′di-năl,
c̣on-suē-tū′di-nal (-swē-),
lat-i-tū′di-năl, lon-ġi-tū′di-năl,
tes-ti-tū′di-năl.
Plus brood in, Al, etc.
Cf. brood in all, etc.

Ū′DI-US

l: prē-lū′di-ous.
st: stū′di-ous.

UD′ŨR-I

d: dud′dẽr-y.
sh: shud′dẽr-y.
st: stud′dẽr-y.
Plus udder, he, etc.

Ū′DI-NES

m: mọọ′di-ness.
Cf. ood′i-nes.

Ū′EL-ING

d: dū′el-ling.
f: fū′el-ling, rē-fū′el-ing.
gr: grú′el-ling.
j: bē-jew′el-ling,
jew′el-ling.

UD′I-NES

bl: blood′i-ness.
m: mud′di-ness.
r: rud′di-ness.

Ū′DI-NĪZ

t: at-ti-tū′di-nīze,
plat-i-tū′di-nīze.
Plus food in eyes, etc.

Ū′EL-ŨR

d: dū′el-lẽr.
f: fū′el-lẽr.
j: jew′el-lẽr.
kr: c̣rú′el-lẽr.
Plus newel her, err *or* er, etc.

Ū′DI-NUS

l: pȧ-lū′di-nous.
t: fọr-ti-tū′din-ous,
lat-i-tū′di-nous,
lon-ġi-tū′di-nous,
mul-ti-tū′di-nous,
plat-i-tū′di-nous,

UF′I-NES

fl: fluf′fi-ness.
h: huf′fi-ness.
p: puf′fi-ness.
st: stuf′fi-ness.

(Choose only one word out of each group)

UG′ŪR-I

p: pug′à-ree.
sn: snug′gĕr-y.
th: thug′gĕr-y.
Plus lugger, he, etc.
Plus hug her, he, etc.

Ū′I-NES

d: dew′i-ness.
gl: glūe′y-ness.

Ú′IN-US

br: brú′in-ous.
pr: prú′in-ous.
r: rú′in-ous.
Plus knew in us, etc.
Plus ruin us, etc.

Ū′ISH-NES

j: Jew′ish-ness.
shr: shrew′ish-ness.

Ū′I-TI

d: as-si-dū′i-ty.
fl: sū-pēr-flū′i-ty.
g: am-bi-gū′i-ty, çon-ti-gū′i-ty,
  ex-i-gū′i-ty (eks-).
k(ç): à-çū′i-ty, cir-çū′i-ty,
  çon-spi-çū′i-ty, in-no-çū′i-ty,
  pēr-spi-çū′i-ty, prō-mis-çū′i-ty,
  và-çū′i-ty.
n: an-nū′i-ty, çon-ti-nū′i-ty,
  dis-çon-ti-nū′i-ty, in-ġē-nū′i-ty,
  stre-nū′i-ty, te-nū′i-ty.
s: sū′ē-ty.
t: fà-tū′i-ty, grà-tū′i-ty,
  pēr-pē-tū′i-ty.
Plus suet tea, etc.
Plus suet, he, etc.
Plus sue it, he, etc.

Ū′I-TUS

k(ç): cir-çū′i-tous.
t: fà-tū′i-tous, for-tū′i-tous,
  grà-tū′i-tous, pi-tū′i-tous.
Plus suet us, etc.

ŪJ′I-NUS

n: là-nū′ġi-nous.
r: āe-rū′ġi-nous, fer-rū′ġi-nous.
s: sal-sū′ġi-nous.
Plus huge in us, etc.

UK′I-LI

l: luck′i-ly.
pl: pluck′i-ly.
Plus lucky lea *or* Lee, etc.

UK′SHUN-ĂL

d: in-duç′tiŏn-ăl.
fl: flux′iŏn-ăl.
str: çon-struç′tiŏn-ăl,
  in-struç′tiŏn-ăl.
Plus ruction, Al, etc.

UK′SHUN-IST

fl: flux′iŏn-ist (fluk′shun-).
str: çon-struç′tiŏn-ist,
  dē-struç′tiŏn-ist.

UK′TI-B′L

d: çon-duç′ti-ble.
str: dē-struç′ti-ble,
  in-dē-struç′ti-ble, in-struç′ti-ble.
Plus deduct a bull, etc.

UK′TIV-LĬ

d: in-duç′tive-ly, prō-duç′tive-ly.
str: çon-struç′tive-ly,
  dē-struç′tive-ly, in-struç′tive-ly.
Plus instructive, Lee, etc.

(Choose only one word out of each group)

UK'TIV-NES

d: in-duc̣'tive-ness,
pro͞-duc̣'tive-ness.
str: c̣on-struc̣'tive-ness,
dē-struc̣'tive-ness,
in-struc̣'tive-ness.

UK'TŌ-RI

d: c̣on-duc̣'tō-ry,
in-trō-duc̣'tō-ry,
rē-prō-duc̣'tō-ry.
Plus instructor, he, etc.

Ū'KŪ-LENT

l: lū'c̣ū-lent.
m: mū'c̣ū-lent.
Cf. suc̣'c̣ū-lent.

UK'ŨR-ING

p: puck'ẽr-ing.
s: suc̣'c̣ŏr-ing.
Plus muckẽr ring, etc.
Plus pluck a ring, etc.
Plus pluck her ring, etc.

Ū'LĒ-ĂN, Ū'LI-ĂN

j: Jū'li-ăn, Jū'li-en.
k(c̣): hêr-c̣ū'lē-ăn.
r: cē-rū'lē-ăn.
Plus Dooley, Ann, *or* an, etc.
Plus rule, Ian, etc.

ŪL'ISH-NES

f: fọọl'ish-ness.
m: mūl'ish-ness.

Ū'LI-TI

d: c̣rē-dū'li-ty, in-c̣rē-dū'li-ty,
sē-dū'li-ty.
r: gar-rù'li-ty.
Plus rule it, he, etc.

Ū'LI-US

j: Jū'li-us.
p: Ȧ-pū'li-us.
Plus coolie us, etc.
Cf. ūl'yus.

UL'KI-NES

b: bul'ki-nes.
s: sul'ki-nes.

UL'MI-NĂNT

f: ful'mi-nănt.
k(c̣): c̣ul'mi-nănt.

UL'MI-NĀT

f: ful'mi-nāte.
k(c̣): c̣ul'mi-nāte.
Plus skull me, Nate, etc.

UL'SIV-LI

p: im-pul'sive-ly, rē-pul'sive-ly.
v: c̣on-vul'sive-ly.
Plus emulsive, Lee, etc.

UL'SIV-NES

p: c̣om-pul'sive-ness,
im-pul'sive-ness,
rē-pul'sive-ness.
v: c̣on-vul'sive-ness,
rē-vul'sive-ness.

UL'TŨ-RI

d: ȧ-dul'tẽr-y.
s: c̣on-sul'tăr-y.
Plus consult her, he, etc.
Plus exulter, he, etc.

UL'TŨR-IZM

gr: ȧ-gri-c̣ul'tūr-iṣm, etc.
v: vul'tūr-iṣm.
Cf. ul'tūr plus iṣm.

941 ūse, bu̧ll, brúte, tŭrn, up; crȳ, myth; c̣at, ma̧chine, ace, church, c̣hord; ġem, a̱nger, (Fr.) boṅ, a̱ş; THis, thin; a̱zure

UL′ŪR-I
UMP′ISH-NES

(Choose only one word out of each group)

UL′ŨR-I

d: mē-dul′lär-y.
g: gul′lēr-y.
sk(sc̣): sc̣ul′lēr-y.
Plus color, he, etc.
Plus gull err, he, etc.

UL′VŨR-IN

k(c̣): c̣ul′vẽr-in.
p: pul′vẽr-in.

ŪM′Å-B'L

s: as-sūm′å-ble, c̣on-sūm′å-ble.
z: prē-ṣūm′å-ble, rē-ṣūm′å-ble.
Plus entomb a bull, etc.
Plus Yuma bull, etc.

Ū′MĂN-LI

h: hū′măn-ly, in-hū′măn-ly.
Cf. womanly.
Plus new man, Lee, etc.

UM′BŨR-I

Vowel: um′bẽr-y.
sl: slum′bẽr-y.
Plus number, he, etc.

UM′BŨR-ING

k(c̣): c̣um′bẽr-ing, en-c̣um′bẽr-ing.
l: lum′bẽr-ing.
n: num′bẽr-ing, out-num′bẽr-ing.
sl: slum′bẽr-ing, un-slum′bẽr-ing.
Plus Humber ring, etc.

UM′BŨR-ŨR

k(c̣): c̣um′bẽr-ẽr, en-c̣um′bẽr-ẽr.
l: lum′bẽr-ẽr.
n: num′bẽr-ẽr.
sl: slum′bẽr-ẽr.
Plus number her, err or er, etc.

Ū′MI-NĂNT

l: il-lū′mi-nănt, lū′mi-nănt.
r: rù′mi-nănt.
Plus acumen, aunt or ant, etc.
Plus new men, aunt, etc.

Ū′MI-NĀT

k(c̣): à-c̣ū′mi-nāte, c̣at-ē-c̣hū′men-āte.
l: il-lū′mi-nāte, lū′mi-nāte.
r: fẽr-rù′mi-nāte, rù′mi-nāte.
Plus two men ate, or eight, etc.
Plus gloomy, Nate, etc.
Plus room in eight, etc.

ŪM′I-NES

gl: glo̤o̤m′i-ness.
r: ro̤o̤m′i-ness.
sp: spūm′i-ness.

UM′ING-LI

h: hum′ming-ly.
k(c̣): bē-c̣ŏm′ing-ly, un-bē-c̣ŏm′ing-ly.
n: bē-numb′ing-ly, numb′ing-ly.
str: strum′ming-ly.
Plus strumming, Lee, etc.

Ū′MI-NOUS

fl: flū′mi-nous.
g: lē-gū′mi-nous.
l: à-lū′mi-nous, lū′mi-nous, vō-lū′mi-nous.
t: bi-tū′min-ous.
Plus illumine us, etc.
Plus doom in us, etc.

UMP′ISH-NES

d: dump′ish-ness.
fr: frump′ish-ness.

(Choose only one word out of each group)

gr: grump′ish-ness.
l: lump′ish-ness.
m: mump′ish-ness.

UMP′SHUS-LI

b: bump′tiŏus-ly (′shus-).
skr(sc̨r): sc̨rump′tiŏus-ly.
Plus bumptious, Lee, etc.

UMP′TŪ-OUS

s: sump′tū-ous.
z: prē-s̨ump′tū-ous.

Ū′MŪ-LĀT

k(c̨): ac̨-c̨ū′mū-lāte.
t: tū′mū-lāte.
Plus whom you late, etc.
Plus new mule ate, etc.

Ū′MŪ-LUS

k(c̨): c̨ū′mū-lus.
t: tū′mū-lus.

Ū′MŨR-ĂL

h: hū′mẽr-ăl.
n: nū′mẽr-ăl.
Plus roomer, Al, etc.
Plus groom her, Il, etc.

ŪM′ŨR-I

f: pẽr-fūm′ẽr-y.
pl: plū′mẽr-y.
r: rū′mŏr-y.
Cf. room′ẽr-y.
Plus who, Marie, etc.
Plus humor, he, etc.

UM′ŨR-I

fl: flum′mẽr-y.
m: mum′mẽr-y.

n: num′măr-y.
pl: plumb′ẽr-y (plum′).
s: sum′măr-y, sum′mẽr-y.
Plus dumber, he, etc.
Plus dumb Marie, etc.

Ū′MŨR-US

h: hūm′ẽr-us, hū′mŏr-ous.
n: nū′mẽr-ous.
r: rū′mŏr-ous.
Plus humor us, etc.
Plus groom or us, etc.

UN′Ȧ-B'L

p: ex-pūgn′ȧ-ble (pūn′)*.
t: tū′nȧ-ble.
Plus festoon a bull, etc.
Plus vicuna bull, etc.

Ū′NȦ-RI

l: lū′nȧ-ry.
Cf. ū′nûr-i.

UN′DI-TI

b: mȯr-i-bun′di-ty.
f: prō-fun′di-ty.
k(c̨): fē-c̨un′di-ty, jo-c̨un′di-ty,
     jū-c̨un′di-ty, rṳ-bi-c̨un′di-ty.
t: rō-tun′di-ty.
Plus pundit, he, etc.

UN′DŨR-ING

bl: blun′dẽr-ing.
pl: plun′dẽr-ing.
s: sun′dẽr-ing.
th: thun′dẽr-ing.
w: wŏn′dẽr-ing, un-wŏn′dẽr-ing.
Plus under ring, etc.
Plus shunned her ring, etc.
Plus shunned a ring, etc.

(Choose only one word out of each group)

UN′DŬR SǪNG

Vowel: un′dẽr sǫng.
th: thun′dẽr sǫng.
w: wŏn′dẽr sǫng.
Plus plunder song, etc.
Plus shunned her song, etc.

UN′DŪR-ŪR

bl: blun′dẽr-ẽr.
pl: plun′dẽr-ẽr.
s: sun′dẽr-ẽr.
th: thun′dẽr-ẽr.
w: wŏn′dẽr-ẽr.
Plus plunder her, err *or* er, etc.

UN′DŪR-US

bl: blun′dẽr-ous.
th: thun′dẽr-ous.
w: wŏn′dẽr-ous.
Plus plunder us, etc.

UN′DẼR-WŎRLD

Vowel: un′dẽr-wŏrld.
w: wŏn′dẽr wŏrld.
Plus plunder world, etc.
Plus shunned her world, etc.

UNG′GŪR-ING

h: hun′gẽr-ing.
m: mŏn-gẽr-ing,
  sçan′dăl⸗mŏn′gẽr-ing.
Plus younger ring, etc.

UNGK′SHUN-ĂL

f: fuñç′tiŏn-ăl (′shun-).
j: çon-juñç′tiŏn-ăl.
Plus junction, Al, etc.
Plus monk shun, Al, etc.

UNGK′Ū-LĂR

Vowel: uñ′çū-lăr.
b: çär-buñç′ū-lăr.
d: pē-duñç′ū-lăr.
r: çä-ruñç′ū-lăr.
v: à-vuñç′ū-lăr.

Ū′NI-KĀT

m: çom-mū′ni-çāte,
  ex-çom-mū′ni-çāte.
t: tū′ni-çāte.
Plus loony, Kate, etc.
Plus Punic eight *or* ate, etc.
Plus new knee, Kate, etc.

Ū′NI-FǪRM

k(ç): çū′ni-fǫrm.
l: lū′ni-fǫrm.
y: ū′ni-fǫrm.
Plus puny form, etc.
Plus new knee form, etc.

UN′I-LI

f: fun′ni-ly.
s: sun′ni-ly.
Plus honey, Lee *or* lea, etc.

Ū′NI-TI

m: çom-mū′ni-ty, im-mū′ni-ty,
  in″tẽr-çom-mū′ni-ty.
p: im-pū′ni-ty.
t: im-pǫr-tū′ni-ty,
  in-op-pǫr-tū′ni-ty,
  op-pǫr-tū′ni-ty.
y: trī-ū′ni-ty, ū′ni-ty (yū′).
zh: jē-jū′ni-ty (-zhū′).
Plus loony tea, etc.
Plus spoon o' tea, etc.

Ū′NI-TIV
ŪR′DI-LI

fāte, fär, fȧst, f**a**ll, finăl, cãre, **a**t; mēte, pr**e**y, hẽr. met; pīne,
marĭne, bĭrd, pin; nōte, mŏve, f**o**r, atŏm, not; m**oo**n, book;

944

(Choose only one word out of each group)

Ū′NI-TIV

p: pū′ni-tive.
y: ū′ni-tive.

UNT′ED-LI

fr: af-frŏnt′ed-ly.
st: stunt′ed-ly.
w: un-wŏnt′ed-ly, wŏnt′ed-ly.
Plus bunted, Lee, etc.

ŪN′ŪR-I

f: buf-f**oo**n′ẽr-y.
k(ç): çō-ç**oo**n′ẽr-y.
l: pan-tȧ-l**oo**n′ẽr-y.
tr: pol-tr**oo**n′ẽr-y.
Plus sooner, he, etc.

UN′ŪR-I

g: gun′nẽr-y.
n: nun′nẽr-y.
Plus runner, he, etc.

Ū′PŪR-ĀT

k(ç): rē-çū′pẽr-āte.
t: vi-tū′pẽr-āte.
Plus super-eight *or* ate, etc.
Plus loop her eight, etc.

ŪR′Ȧ-B'L

d: dūr′ȧ-ble, en-dūr′ȧ-ble.
k(ç): çūr′ȧ-ble, in-çūr′ȧ-ble,
prō-çūr′ȧ-ble, sē-çūr′ȧ-ble.
s: as-sūr′ȧ-ble, in-sūr′ȧ-ble.
Plus procure a bull, etc.

ŪR′Ȧ-B'L

f: çon-fẽr′rȧ-ble, in-fẽr′ȧ-ble,
rē-fẽr′ȧ-ble, trans-fẽr′ȧ-ble.
m: dē-mūr′rȧ-ble.
Plus stir a bull, etc.

Ů′RĂL-IST

r: rů′răl-ist.
Cf. plů′răl-ist.
Plus neural list, etc.

Ū′RĂL-IŞM

pl: plů′răl-işm.
r: rů′răl-işm.

Ū′RȦ-TIV

d: in-dūr′ȧ-tive.
k(ç): çūr′ȧ-tive.
p: dē-pūr′ȧ-tive.
t: mȧ-tūr′ȧ-tive.

ŪR′BĂL-IST

h: hẽr′băl-ist.
v: vẽr′băl-ist.
Plus disturb a list, etc.

ŪR′BĂL-IZM

h: hẽr′băl-işm.
v: vẽr′băl-işm.

ŪR′BI-ĂL

b: su-būr′bi-ăl.
v: ad-vẽr′bi-ăl, pro-vẽr′bi·al.
Plus Derby, Al, etc.

ŪR′BŪ-LENT

h: hẽr′bū-lent.
t: tūr′bū-lent.
Plus blurb you lent, etc.

ŪR′DI-LI

st: stūr′di-ly.
w: wŏr′di-ly.
Plus third alee, etc.

945 ūse, bṳll, brûte, tûrn, up; crȳ, myth; çat, maçhine, ace, church, çhord; ġem, añger, (Fr.) boṅ, aṣ; THis, thin; aᶎure

ŪR′DŪR-ŪR
ŪR′I-ING

(Choose only one word out of each group)

ŪR′DŪR-ŪR

m: mūr′dẽr-ẽr.
v: vẽr′dẽr-ẽr.
Plus herder, her, etc.
Plus heard her err, etc.

ŪR′EN-SI

k(ç): çon-çūr′ren-cy, çūr′ren-cy, rē-çūr′ren-cy.
Plus transference, he, etc.

ŪR′ET-ED

t: tûr′ret-ed.
Cf. ẽr′i-ted.

ŪR′FLŪ-OUS

p: sū-pẽr′flū-ous.
t: sub-tẽr′flū-ous.

Ū′RI-Ȧ

ch: Man-chū′ri-ȧ.
m: Lē-mū′ri-ȧ.
tr: Ē-trṳ′ri-ȧ.
Plus fury a, etc.

Ū′RI-ĂL

g: au-gū′ri-ăl, fi-gū′ri-ăl.
k(ç): mẽr-çū′ri-ăl.
m: Mū′ri-el.
n: sēig-nū′ri-ăl (sē-).
p: pūr-pū′rē-ăl.
Plus Missouri, Al, etc.

Ū′RI-ĂN

d: dū′ri-ăn.
l: Sī-lū′ri-ăn.
t: cen-tū′ri-ăn, scrip-tū′ri-ăn.
tr: Ē-trṳ′ri-ăn.
y: Ū′ri-ăn.
z: Miṣ-ṣöu′ri-ăn.
Cf. cen-tū′ri-ŏn.
Plus fury, Ann *or* an, etc.

Ū′RI-ANS

z: lux-ū′ri-ănce.
Plus fūry, ants *or* aunts, etc.

Ū′RI-ĂNT

r: lux-ū′ri-ănt.
Plus fury, ant, etc.

Ū′RI-ĀT

f: in-fū′ri-āte.
m: mū′ri-āte.
t: pär-tū′ri-āte.
z: lux-ū′ri-āte (lugz-).
Plus jury ate *or* eight, etc.

Ū′RI-ENS

pr: prū′ri-ence.
Cf. lux-ūr′i-ănce.

Ū′RI-ENT, Ū′RI-ĂNT

pr: prū′ri-ent.
s: ē-sū′ri-ent.
t: pär-tū′ri-ent, scrip-tū′ri-ent.
z: lux-ūr′i-ănt (lugz-).
Plus Missouri aunt *or* ant, etc.

ŪR′I-EST

f: fūr′ri-est.
h: hūr′ri-est*.
w: wŏr′ri-est*.

Ū′RI-FĪ

p: pū′ri-fȳ.
th: thū′ri-fȳ.
Plus houri, fie!, etc.

ŪR′I-ING

fl: flūr′ry-ing.
h: hūr′ry-ing.
k(ç): çūr′ry-ing.
sk(sç): sçūr′ry-ing.
w: wŏr′ry-ing.

(Choose only one word out of each group)

ŨR'I-MENT

w: wŏr'ri-ment.
Cf. ẽr'i-ment.

ŨR'ISH-ING

fl: floŭr'ish-ing.
n: noŭr'ish-ing.

Ū'RI-TI

k(c̨): in-sē-c̨ū'ri-ty, sē-c̨ū'ri-ty.
m: dē-mū'ri-ty.
p: im-pū'ri-ty, pū'ri-ty.
sk(sc̨): ob-sc̨ū'ri-ty.
t: im-mȧ-tū'ri-ty, mȧ-tū'ri-ty,
  prē-mȧ-tū'ri-ty.
Plus lure it, he, etc.

ŨR'I-ŨR

f: fũr'ri-ẽr.
fl: flũr'ri-ẽr.
h: hũr'ri-ẽr.
k(c̨): c̨ũr'ri-ẽr.
sk(sc̨): sc̨ũr'ri-ẽr.
w: wŏr'ri-ẽr.
Plus worry her, err *or* er, etc.

Ū'RI-US

f: fū'ri-ous, sul-phū'rē-ous (-fū')**.**
g: stran-gū'ri-ous.
j: in-jù'ri-ous, pẽr-jù'ri-ous.
k(c̨): c̨ū'ri-ous, in-c̨ū'ri-ous.
n: pē-nū'ri-ous.
sp: spū'ri-ous.
z: lu-xū'ri-ous (lug-zū').
zh: ū-ṣū'ri-ous (-zhū').
Plus fury, us, etc.

ŨR'JEN-SI

Vowel: ũr'g̈en-cy.
m: ē-mẽr'g̈en-cy.

s: as-sũr'g̈en-cy, in-sũr'g̈en-cy.
t: dē-tẽr'g̈en-cy.
v: c̨on-vẽr'g̈en-cy, dī-vẽr'g̈en-cy,
  vẽr'g̈en-sy.
Plus virgin, see, etc.
Plus divergence, he *or* see, etc.

ŨR'JI-KĂL

Vowel: de-mi-ũr'g̈i-c̨ăl,
  thē-ũr'g̈i-c̨ăl.
kl: c̨lẽr'g̈i-c̨ăl.
n: ē-nẽr'g̈i-c̨ăl.
r: chi-rūr'g̈i-c̨ăl.
s: sũr'g̈i-c̨ăl.
t: li-tūr'g̈i-c̨ăl,
  thȧu-mȧ-tūr'g̈i-c̨ăl.
Plus metallurgy, Cal, etc.
Plus demiurgic, Al, etc.

ŨR'JŨR-I

p: pẽr'jũr-y, pūr'g̈ẽr-y.
r: chi-rūr'g̈ẽr-y.
s: sũr'g̈ẽr-y.
Plus verger, he, etc.
Plus scourge her, he, etc.

ŨR'KŪ-LĂR

b: tū-bẽr'c̨ū-lăr.
f: fũr'c̨ū-lăr.
s: c̨ĩr'c̨ū-lăr.

ŨR'KŪ-LĀT

b: tū-bẽr'c̨ū-lāte.
s: c̨ĩr'c̨ù-lāte.
Plus work, you late, etc.

ŨR'KŪ-LUS

b: tū-bẽr'c̨ū-lous.
s: sũr'c̨ū-lus, sũr'c̨ū-lous.

(Choose only one word out of each group)

ŪR′LI-EST

Vowel: ēar′li-est (ēr′).
b: būr′li-est.
ch: chūr′li-est.
k(c): cūr′li-est.
p: pēar′li-est (pēr′).
s: sūr′li-est.

ŪR′LI-NES

Vowel: ēar′li-ness (ēr′).
b: būr′li-ness.
k(c): cūr′li-ness.
p: pēar′li-ness (pēr′).
s: sūr′li-ness.

ŪR′LISH-LY

ch: chūrl′ish-ly.
g: gĭrl′ish-ly.

ŪR′LISH-NES

ch: chūr′lish-ness.
g: gĭrl′ish-ness.

ŪR′MI-NĂL

j: ġēr′mi-năl.
t: tēr′mi-năl.
Plus ermine, Al, etc.
Plus germ in, Al, etc.
Cf. vermin, all, etc.

ŪR′MI-NĂNT

j: ġēr′mi-nănt.
t: dē-tēr′mi-nănt, tēr′mi-nănt.
Plus ermine aunt or ant, etc.
Plus worm in ant, etc.

ŪR′MI-NĀT

j: ġēr′mi-nāte.
t: dē-tēr′mi-nāte, ex-tēr′mi-nāte,
in-dē-tēr′mi-nāte, in-tēr′mi-nāte,
tēr′mi-nāte.

Plus vermin ate or eight, etc.
Plus worm innate, etc.
Plus squirm in eight or ate, etc.

ŪR′MI-NUS

t: cō-tēr′min-ous, tēr′mi-nus.
v: vēr′min-ous.
Plus ermine us, etc.
Plus term in us, etc.

ŪRN′Å-B'L

b: būrn′å-ble.
l: lēarn′å-ble.
t: ō-vēr-tūrn′å-ble, tūrn′å-ble.
z or s: dis-cērn′i-ble (or -zērn′),
in-dis-cērn′i-ble (or -zērn′).
Plus turn a bull, etc.
Plus Smyrna bull, etc.

ŪR′NĂL-IST

j: joūr′năl-ist.
t: ē-tēr′năl-ist.
Plus infernal list, etc.
Plus Verna list, etc.

ŪR′NĂL-ĪZ

j: joūr′năl-īze.
t: ē-tēr′năl-īze, ex-tēr′năl-īze.
Plus infernal eyes, etc.
Plus Verna lies, etc.

ŪR′NĂL-IZM

j: joūr′năl-iṣm.
t: ē-tēr′năl-iṣm,
ex-tēr′năl-iṣm (eks-).

ŪR′NI-ĂN

b: Hī-bēr′ni-ăn.
l: Få-lēr′ni-ăn.
t: Så-tūr′ni-ăn.

(Choose only one word out of each group)

v: Å-vẽr′ni-ăn.
Plus attorney, an *or* Ann, etc.
Plus spurn, Ian, etc.

ŪR′NISH-ING

b: būr′nish-ing.
f: fūr′nish-ing, rē-fūr′nish-ing.

ŪR′NISH-ŪR

b: būr′nish-ẽr.
f: fūr′nish-ẽr, rē-fūr′nish-ẽr.
Plus furnish her, etc.

ŪR′NI-TY

d: mo-dẽr′ni-ty.
t: al-tẽr′ni-ty, dī-ū-tẽr′ni-ty,
ē-tẽr′ni-ty, frȧ-tẽr′ni-ty,
mȧ-tẽr′ni-ty, pȧ-tẽr′ni-ty,
sem-pi-tẽr′ni-ty, tac-i-tūr′ni-ty.
Plus burn it, he, etc.
Plus ferny tea, etc.

ŪR′NŪR-I

f: fẽr′nẽr-y.
t: tūr′nẽr-y.
Plus burner, he, etc.
Plus spurn her, he, etc.

ŪR′Ō-GĀT

s: sūr′rō-gāte.
Cf. ẽr′ō-gāt.

ŪR′PEN-TĪN

s: sẽr′pen-tīne.
t: tūr′pen-tīne.

ŪR′SĂR-I

b: būr′săr-y.
k(c̣): c̣ur-sŏr-y, pẽr-c̣ur′sŏr-y.
n: nūr′sẽr-y.

p: as-pẽr′sŏr-y.
v: an-ni-vẽr′săr-y,
c̣on-trō-vẽr′sȧ-ry.
Plus disperser, he, etc.
Plus curse her, he, etc.

ŪR′SHI-ĂL

v: c̣on-trō-vẽr′si-ăl.
Cf. ūr′shăl.

ŪR′SHI-ĂN

p: Pẽr′si-ăn.
s: lȧ-cẽr′ti-ăn.
t: Cis-tẽr′ci-ăn.
(also, as-ūr′shăn, ūr′zhăn.)

ŪR′SI-B'L, ŪR′SȦ-B'L

Vowel: c̣ō-ẽr′ci-ble,
in-c̣ō-ẽr′ci-ble.
b: rē-im-būr′sȧ-ble.
m: ȧ-mẽrce′ȧ-ble, im-mẽr′si-ble.
v: c̣on-vẽr′sȧ-ble, c̣on-vẽr′si-ble,
ir-rē-vẽr′si-ble, rē-vẽr′si-ble.
Plus curse a bull, etc.
Plus vice versa, bull, etc.

ŪR′SI-FORM

Vowel: ūr′si-fọrm.
v: dī-vẽr′si-fọrm, vẽr′si-fọrm.
Plus Circe form, etc.

ŪR′SIV-NES

Vowel: c̣ō-ẽr′cive-ness.
k(c̣): dis-c̣ur′sive-ness,
ex-c̣ur′sive-ness.
t: dē-tẽr′sive-ness.

ŪRTH′LES-NES

m: mĭrth′less-ness.
w: wŏrth′less-ness.

(Choose only one word out of each group)

ŪR′TI-TŪD

Vowel: in-ēr′ti-tūde.
s: cēr′ti-tūde, in-cēr′ti-tūde.
Plus assert it, you'd, etc.

ŪR′VĂN-SI

f: fēr′ven-cy.
s: çon-sēr′văn-cy.

ŪR′VȦ-TIV

k(ç): çūr′vȧ-tive.
n: ē-nēr′vȧ-tive.
s: çon-sēr′vȧ-tive.
z: ob-ṣēr′vȧ-tive, prē-ṣēr′vȧ-tive, rē-ṣēr′vȧ-tive.

ŪR′ZHUN-IST

k(ç): ex-çūr′ṣiŏn-ist (′zhun-).
m: im-mēr′ṣiŏn-ist, tō′tȧl-im-mēr′-ṣiŏn-ist.
v: vēr′ṣiŏn-ist.

Ū′SĒ-ĂN, Ū′SI-ĂN

d: Çȧ-dū′cē-ăn.
f: Çon-fū′ci-ăn.
k(ç): Rōs-i-çrū′ci-ăn.
l: Tus-çȧ-lọọs′i-ăn.
Plus juicy, Ann *or* an, etc.

Ū′SED-LY

d: deū′ced-ly (dū′).
l: lū′cid-ly, pel-lū′cid-ly.
m: mū′cid-ly.
Plus lucid, Lee, etc.

Ū′SEN-SI

l: lū′cen-cy, trȧ-lū′cen-cy*, trans-lū′cen-cy.
Cf. nuisancy.

Ū′SHI-ĂL

d: fī-dū′ci-ăl.
kr: çrū′ci-ăl.

Ū′SHUN-ĂL

k(ç): cĭr″çum-lō-çū′tiŏn-ăl (′shun-),
    e-lō-çū′tiŏn-ăl.
l: ev-ō-lū′tiŏn-ăl.
t: çon-sti-tū′tiŏn-ăl, in-sti-tū′tiŏn-ăl, sub-sti-tū′tiŏn-ăl.
Plus diminution, Al, etc.

Ū′SHUN-IST

k(ç): cĭr″çum-lō-çū′tiŏn-ist (′shun-),
    el-ō-çū′tiŏn-ist.
l: ev-ō-lū′tiŏn-ist, reṣ-ō-lū′tiŏn-ist, rev-ō-lū′tiŏn-ist.
t: çon-sti-tū′tiŏn-ist.

Ū′SHUN-ŪR

k(ç): ex-ē-çū′tiŏn-ēr (eks-).
l: ab-lū′tiŏn-ēr, reṣ-ō-lū′tiŏn-ēr, rev-ō-lū′tiŏn-ēr.
Plus institution her, err *or* er, etc.

Ū′SI-B′L

d: ad-dū′ci-ble, çon-dū′ci-ble, dē-dū′ci-ble, ē-dū′ci-ble, in-dū′ci-ble, ir-rē-dū′ci-ble, prō-dū′ci-ble, rē-dū′ci-ble, sē-dū′ci-ble, trȧ-dū′ci-ble.
kr: çrù′ci-ble.
Plus juicy bull, etc.
Plus loose a bull, etc.

Ū′SIV-NES

b: ȧ-bū′sive-ness.
d: çon-dū′cive-ness.

(Choose only one word out of each group)

f: dif-fū'sive-ness, ef-fū'sive-ness.
kl: cọn-clū'sive-ness,
ex-clū'sive-ness (eks-),
in-cọn-clū'sive-ness.
l: al-lū'sive-ness, dē-lū'sive-ness,
ē-lū'sive-ness, il-lū'sive-ness.
tr: in-ob-trū'sive-ness,
in-trū'sive-ness, ob-trū'sive-ness.

US'KI-LI

d: dus'ki-ly.
h: hus'ki-ly.
m: mus'ki-ly.
Plus husky Lee, etc.
Plus musk alee, etc.

US'KŪ-LĂR

m: bī-mus'cū'lăr, mus'cū-lăr.
p: cọr-pus'cū-lăr, crē-pus'cū-lăr.

US'KŪ-LUS

m: mus'cū-lous.
p: cọr-pus'cū-lous,
crē-pus'cū-lous.

Ū'SŌ-RI

kl: cọn-clū'sō-ry,
ex-clū'sō-ry (eks-), rē-clū'sō-ry.
l: cọl-lū'sō-ry, dē-lū'sō-ry,
ē-lū'sō-ry, il-lū'sō-ry, lū'sō-ry,
prē-lū'sō-ry.
tr: ex-trū'sō-ry.
Plus prodūcer, he, etc.
Plus loose her, he, etc.

UST'FỤL-I

l: lust'fụl-ly.
tr: dis-trust'fụl-ly,
mis-trust'fụl-ly, trust'fụl-ly.
Plus trustful, he, etc.

US'TI-B'L, US'TȦ-B'L

b: bust'ȧ-ble, cọm-bus'ti-ble,
in-cọm-bus'ti-ble.
d: dus'ti-ble.
j: ad-jus'ti-ble.
r: rust'ȧ-ble.
thr: thrus'tȧ-ble.
Plus Augusta bull, etc.
Plus thrust a bull, etc.

US'TI-EST

d: dus'ti-est.
f: fus'ti-est.
g: gus'ti-est.
kr: crus'ti-est.
l: lus'ti-est.
m: mus'ti-est.
r: rus'ti-est.
tr: trus'ti-est.

US'TI-LY

d: dus'ti-ly.
f: fus'ti-ly.
g: gus'ti-ly.
kr: crus'ti-ly.
l: lus'ti-ly.
m: mus'ti-ly.
r: rus'ti-ly.
thr: thrus'ti-ly.
Plus trusty, Lee *or* lea, etc.
Plus dust alle, etc.

US'TI-NES

d: dus'ti-ness.
f: fus'ti-ness.
g: gus'ti-ness.
kr: crus'ti-ness.
l: lus'ti-ness.
m: mus'ti-ness.
r: rus'ti-ness.
tr: trus'ti-ness.

(Choose only one word out of each group)

US'TRI-US

d: in-dus'tri-ous.
l: il-lus'tri-ous.

US'TŪR-ING

bl: blus'tēr-ing.
fl: flus'tēr-ing.
kl: çlus'tēr-ing.
m: mus'tēr-ing.
Plus adjuster ring, etc.
Plus thrust her *or* a, ring, etc.

Ū'TÀ-B'L

f: çon-fū'tà-ble, rē-fū'tà-ble.
k(ç): ex-ē-çūt'à-ble.
m: çom-mū'tà-ble, im-mū'tà-ble,
in-çom-mū'tà-ble, moọt'à-ble,
mū'tà-ble, pēr-mū'tà-ble,
trans-mū'tà-ble.
p: çom-pū'tà-ble, dis-pū'tà-ble,
im-pū'tà-ble.
s: sūit'à-ble.
skr(sçr): in-sçrṳ'tà-ble,
sçrṳ'tà-ble.
Plus shoot a bull, etc.

Ū'TÀ-TIV

f: çon-fū'tà-tive.
m: çom-mū'tà-tive.
n: stēr-nū'tà-tive.
p: dis-pū'tà-tive, im-pū'tà-tive,
pū'tà-tive.
sp: spū'tà-tive.

Ū'TĒ-US

b: beaū'tē-ous (bū').
d: dū'tē-ous.
l: lū'tē-ous.
Plus tutti-frutti us, etc.

ŪTH'FṳL-I

r: rúth'fṳl-ly.
tr: trúth'fṳl-ly.
y: youth'fṳl-ly.
Plus toothful, Lee, etc.

ŪTH'FṳL-NES

r: rúth'fṳl-ness.
tr: trúth'fṳl-ness.
y: youth'fṳl-ness.

ŪTH'LES-LI

r: rúth'less-ly.
tr: trúth'less-ly.
y: youth'less-ly.
Plus tooth, Leslie, etc.
Plus toothless, Lee, etc.

UTH'ÛR-HOOD

br: brŏTH'ēr-hood.
m: mŏTH'ēr-hood.
Plus another hood, etc.

UTH'ÛR-I

br: brŏTH'ēr-y.
m: mŏTH'ēr-y.
sm: smŏTH'ēr-y.
Plus other, he, etc.

UTH'ÛR-ING

br: brŏTH'ēr-ing.
m: mŏTH'ēr-ing.
sm: smŏTH'ēr-ing.
w: WuTH'ēr-ing.
Plus another ring, etc.

UTH'ÛR-LI

br: brŏTH'ēr-ly,
un-brŏTH'ēr-ly.
m: mŏTH'ēr-ly, un-mŏTH'ēr-ly.

(Choose only one word out of each group)

s: sŏuTH′ẽr-ly.
Plus smother, Lee *or* Lea, etc.

UTH′ŬR-LĬK

br: brŏTH′ẽr-līke.
m: mŏTH′ẽr-līke.
Plus another like, etc.

Ū′TI-FĪ

b: beaū′ti-fȳ.
br: brū′ti-fȳ.
Plus booty, fie!, etc.

Ū′TI-FỤL

b: beaū′ti-fụl.
d: dū′ti-fụl.
Plus booty full, etc.

Ū′TI-K′L, Ū′TI-KĂL

b: scọr-bū′ti-cạl.
k(ç): çū′ti-çle.
p: ther-ȧ-peū′ti-cạl.
s: phär-mȧ-ceū′ti-cạl.
tr: lȧ-treū′ti-cạl.
Plus duty, Cal, etc.
Plus hermeneutic, Al, etc.

Ū-TI-NĒR′

m: mū-ti-neer′.
skr(sçr): sçrū-ti-neer′.
Cf. beauty near, etc.

Ū′TI-NY

m: mū′ti-ny.
skr(sçr): sçrū′ti-ny.
Plus loot in, he, etc.
Plus gluten, he, etc.

Ū′TI-NOUS

gl: glū′ti-nous.
l: vē-lū′ti-nous.

m: mū′ti-nous.
skr(sçr): sçrū′ti-nous.
Plus boot in us, etc.
Plus gluten us, etc.

UT′LŪR-I

b: but′lẽr-y.
k(ç): çut′lẽr-y.
s: sut′lẽr-y.
Plus butler, he, etc.

UT′ŎN-I

b: but′tŏn-y.
gl: glut′tŏn-y.
m: mut′tŏn-y.
Plus Dutton, he, etc.
Plus smut on, he, etc.

Ū′TŪR-I

b: bọọt′ẽr-y, free′≠bọọt′ẽr-y,
fr: frūit′ẽr-y.
p: pew′tẽr-y (pū′).
r: rọọt′ẽr-y.
Plus looter, he, etc.

UT′ŬR-ING

Vowel: ut′tẽr-ing.
b: but′tẽr-ing.
fl: flut′tẽr-ing.
g: gut′tẽr-ing.
m: mut′tẽr-ing.
sp: sput′tẽr-ing.
spl: splut′tẽr-ing.
st: stut′tẽr-ing.
Plus utter ring, etc.
Plus cut a ring, etc.
Plus cut her ring, etc.

UT′ŬR-ŬR

Vowel: ut′tẽr-ẽr.
b: but′tẽr-ẽr.

(Choose only one word out of each group)

fl: flut'tẽr-ẽr.
m: mut'tẽr-ẽr.
sp: sput'tẽr-ẽr.
spl: splut'tẽr-ẽr.
st: stut'tẽr-ẽr.
Plus utter her *or* err, etc.

Ū'VȦ-B'L

m: im-öv'a̲-ble, ir-rē-möv'a̲-ble, möv'a̲-ble, rē-möv'a̲-ble.
pr: ap-pröv'a̲-ble, im-pröv'a̲-ble, pröv'a̲-ble, rē-pröv'a̲-ble.
Plus behoove a bull, etc.

Ū'VI-ĂL

fl: ef-flū'vi-ăl, flū'vi-ăl.
l: al-lū'vi-ăl, an-tē-di-lū'vi-ăl, di-lū'vi-ăl, pōst⹀di-lū'vi-ăl.
pl: plū'vi-ăl.
z: ex-ū'vi-ăl.
Plus movie, Al.

Ū'VI-ĂN

l: an-tē-di-lū'vi-ăn, di-lu'vi-ăn, pōst⹀di-lū'vi-ăn.
r: Pē-rù'vi-ăn.
s: Vē-sū'vi-ăn.
Plus movie, Ann *or* an.
Plus groove, Ian, etc.

Ū'VI-US

pl: Jú'pi-tẽr Plū'vi-us.
s: Vē-sū'vi-us.
Plus movie us.

UV'ŪR-LI

k(c̲): dē C̲ŏv'ẽr-lēy.
l: lŏv'ẽr-ly.
Plus hover, Lee, etc.
Plus shove her, Lee, etc.

Ū'ZȦ-B'L

f: c̦on-fūṣ'a̲-ble, dif-fūṣ'i-ble, fūṣ'i-ble, in-fūṣ'i-ble, trans-fūṣ'i-ble.
k(c̲): ex-c̲ūṣ'a̲-ble, in-ex-c̲ùṣ'a̲-ble (-eks-).
l: löṣ'a̲-ble.
m: a̲-mūṣ'a̲-ble.
y: ūṣ'a̲-ble.
Plus choose a bull, etc.

Ū'ZI-ĂN

th: C̲är-thū'ṣi-ăn.
Cf. ū'zhun.

UZ'I-NES

b: buz'zi-ness.
f: fuz'zi-ness.
m: muz'zi-ness.
w: wuz'zi-ness.

VERSIFICATION SELF-TAUGHT

VERSIFICATION SELF-TAUGHT

PART I

THE FOUNDATIONS OF VERSIFICATION

LESSON I

PRELIMINARIES. VOCABULARY OF POETRY

The preliminary questionnaire is to permit a stock-taking of the potential poet's equipment, at the moment of starting. The value of this stock-taking is in direct proportion to the student's frankness and completeness. In each instance, it is better to answer too much than too little. Save this until you have finished the course, and answer each question afresh. Repeat this at each new stage in your poetic career. This will permit a periodical stock-taking of your poetic progress.

1. What first awoke your interest in writing poetry?...................................

2. Who are your favorite poets?...

3. What qualities do you prefer in poetry?...

4. Which of the following do you prefer, and why? Simple lyrics. Songs. Ballads and stories in verse. Sonnets and other formal verse. Free verse. Experimental types of verse. Light and humorous verse. Prose—and what sort?...

5. What is your chief object in taking this course?...................................

6. What do you see as the final end of your interest in versification?..............

7. What are your chief obstacles?...

8. What is it about verse you chiefly do not understand?.............................

9. What books on the subject have you read or studied? Any other study of the subject?..

....

....

....

Verse, Poetry and Prose

Study the definitions of these three, given in the fore part of the book, until you have absorbed them. Note that poetry is merely a subhead of verse; and that word-arrangements are verse or prose, depending on the presence of a tendency toward rhythm-repetition, or its absence.

Preparing the Manuscript

Paper. Use white sheets, 8½ by 11 inches.

Carbons. In submitting poems for criticism, submit them in duplicate, retaining a carbon. In submitting poems to editors, always retain a carbon.

Heading. In the upper left hand corner, type your name and address thus:

John Doe
2100 Huntsville Road
Abilene, Texas

The Poem. Center your poem in the page, with the same approximate distance above and below; and approximately the same margins to left and right. Single-spacing is usually better for poetry. Very short poems may be double-spaced.

Signature. Your title has been centered above the body of the poem. Your signature should be typed off to the right, so that it ends about where your average lines end.

Book Manuscripts. In submitting a book manuscript of verse, there should be a separate title page, dedication page, acknowledgment page, foreword (if any), table of contents. The name and address need appear only on the title page; nor should individual poems be signed.

Punctuation. As far as possible, master and use the accepted punctuation, indenting, etc.

The Vocabulary, Word Order and Idiom of Poetry

The most serious failing of most poets and versifiers appears in their choice of idiom and word-usage. Read and reread the section on Vocabulary, in the fore part of this volume. Absorb this one all-vital lesson:

Use the same words, word order and idioms that you use in prose. This is as important for metric verse as for accent verse and free verse.

It is as important for rhymed verse as for unrhymed (blank) verse. Metric feet and rhymes must come in as naturally as the words in this sentence, or in any well-spoken sentence you use.

Once you have written your poem, go over it line by line and word by word, and remove all unnatural words, phrases and word usages, even though this requires reslanting a line, a stanza, or the entire poem. Let the verses say precisely what you mean, with no word warped out of place by any conventions of versification. When you have made this true of all the verse and poetry you write, you have taken a long forward step toward mastery.

The natural living vocabulary is easiest in free verse; next easiest in accent verse; and most difficult of all to achieve in metric verse, especially when rhyme is added. The excellent craftsman faces all difficulties and overcomes them. There is always a way of reslanting your lines, to overcome any inversion or unnatural speech order or word usage.

Written Exercises. Often a poem comes in the form of rough notes, at times with certain lines completed or worked out. Unless this is entirely unnatural to you, let this be your first exercise:

1. Prepare a poem outline. It may be in several stages: as, 1st, the idea as it originally came to you; then, later developments. If you wish to carry this process through to the completed poem, all the better.

2. Keeping in mind all that has been said about poetic vocabulary, prepare two poems, preferably not more than 30 lines each. They may be far shorter. They may be poems already on hand, or poems written freshly.

3. Make all needed corrections, marking the correct forms in the left margin, and the reason for each change in the right margin.

LESSON II

THE KINDS OF POETRY. THE LYRIC

How Poems Come

Poetry and verse, almost invariably an expression in some form of the poet's desire, come primarily from that vast reservoir in each of us called the unconscious mind. Some call this inspiration. The part of the intellect in the process is to direct the upflow of the desire; and, after it is expressed, to criticize and perfect the product.

At times the whole poem forms itself within the mind, before the first word is written down. At times a couplet, a single line, perhaps

the last line or some line late in the poem, comes first. The wise procedure is to write it down as it comes, and if necessary readjust the lines afterward. At times only a mood comes, and the poem or verses may thereupon develop spontaneously, without the poet's knowing at any stage what the next line or the future development will be. The important thing is to let it flow unhindered by the intellect; and to jot down each part that comes immediately, to prevent its being lost forever.

Classifying Poems

Poems are classified primarily from the manner in which the desire is expressed: whether directly (lyric), in a description (descriptive), contained in a story (narrative), or with the character or characters speaking it (dramatic). Additional classifications, based chiefly upon the mood of the lines, are didactic (poems pointing a moral), light verse, humorous verse, etc.

Lyric Poetry

In lyric poetry, the poet expresses his desire directly: "I *want* something." Thus Chaucer addresses his empty purse,

> For which unto your mercy thus I cry:
> Be heavy again, or elles might I die!

Lyrics are classified as follows:

The Simple Lyric. In a simple lyric, the poet expresses his desires directly and briefly. A simple lyric, and indeed any of the types and subtypes of poetry, may be in free verse, accent verse, or metric verse, rhymed or unrhymed. It should be noted that the word *lyric* is also used in a very different sense, as any group of words set to music. It is thus usual to speak of the *lyric* of any song, whether this "lyric" falls under lyric, descriptive, narrative, dramatic or some other type of poetry.

The Song. The word *song* means music made by the voice; a poem set to music; or a poem suitable for musical setting. As a subhead of lyric poetry, it means an example of lyric verse set to music, or suitable to be set to music. Songs are usually divided into concert or classical songs, and popular songs. A song of any type stands most chance of success, if it conforms to the current popular song-pattern.

The Elegy. An elegy is a formal expression of the poet's grief at death, whether of an individual or in general. Here the division, according to subject-matter, is not logical; there are no similar divisions of poems dealing with birth, youth, manhood and womanhood, love, drinking, hunting, war, and so on.

The Pastoral. A pastoral is a poem dealing with the lives of shepherds; in which the characters are pictured as ideal shepherds; or sometimes, by extension, dealing with outdoor and country life. This division is as illogical as the elegy; since there are no similar groupings of poems dealing with hunting, farming, manufacturing, or any of the professions. The characters are often given such names as Corydon, Lycidas, Strephon, Phyllis, Amaryllis, Chloe. It is better to class descriptive poems dealing with outdoor and country life, without the use of the convention of the ideal shepherds, as descriptive poems.

The Ode. The ode is the longest and most dignified form of lyric verse. It may be (1) regular or Pindaric, each section containing a strophe and an antistrophe of identical stanza form, followed by a contrasting epode; (2) irregular or pseudo-Pindaric, with no correspondence between its parts; or (3) Lesbian or Horatian, a simpler form, with uniform stanzas. It should be upon a dignified theme, and not too brief; although light verse odes of course may take any theme.

The Chant. The chant is a modern revival of an ancient form, in which the poem is to be chanted—that is, recited musically, with liberal use of monotone, broken by occasional tunes. Vachel Lindsay is the chief modern exponent.

Descriptive Poetry

In pure descriptive poetry, the desire is not expressed, but is implied in the poet's description. The implication usually is that the poet describes something he likes and wants to continue or to come into existence; or the reverse. Many of the poems commonly classed as lyrics more properly come under this grouping.

Written Exercises

1. Write a simple lyric, of not more than twenty lines.

2. Write a song lyric for a concert or classical song. Do not forget to follow some accepted pattern, at least in the main outlines of your stanzas, or stanzas and chorus.

3. Write a song lyric for a popular song. This may consist of a chorus only, and should follow approximately some accepted pattern. In these two last exercises, let the words be as singable as possible.

4. Write an elegy, a pastoral poem, or a chant.

5. Write a brief descriptive poem, of not more than twenty lines.

6. Make all needed corrections, in this and all subsequent exercises. Mark the correct forms in the left margin, and the reasons for each change in the right margin. At first, it may be wisest to have your completed work, with corrections, looked over by some qualified master of versification. But your objective should be to perfect yourself as a critic of your own work.

LESSON III

SAME. NARRATIVE POETRY. MIXED POETRY

Narrative Poetry

In narrative poetry, the poet embodies his desire in a story, that is, a series of connected happenings. Narrative poetry ranges from the most trivial account of an unimportant happening, to the story of a world war or the whole history of a deity or some other important personage. It may involve conversation (typical of drama), description, and lyric passages; but the main emphasis must be upon the story that is being told. Narrative poems are classified as follows:

The Ballad. A ballad is verse telling a brief story, usually using the devices of the old English ballads, or some similar group of anonymous folk verse. It may be of book length, as is G. K. Chesterton's *Ballad of the White Horse;* it is usually far shorter.

The English Ballad Stanza. When rhyme and metric verse reached England from France, which in turn had derived it from Italy and Latin literature, the devices of old English poetry were three:

1. Four accents to the line.
2. At least two examples of alliteration in each line.
3. A cesura, or break, midway of the line.

Only the first of these was retained, with the addition of rhyme, in the first ballads; and these had couplet rhyming, that is, each pair of lines rhymed with each other:

> He came also still to his mother's bower,   1
> As dew in April that falls on the flower.   1
> > *Song of the Incantation (14th century).*

Refrains were added to this, at first of four accents each; then of three accents, to give the singer a breathing space, and allow a flourish on the accompanying instrument. This form survived, where other forms (such as three 4-accent lines rhyming together, followed by a four or 3-accent refrain) were discarded, as having too much rhyme. The pattern then was,

> She sat down below a thorn,   1
> *Fine flowers in the valley,*   2
> And there she had her sweet babe born,   1
> *And the green leaves they grow rarely.*   2
> > *Fine Flowers in the Valley.*

In the final pattern, the 4, 3, 4, 3 accents were all used to carry forward the story; and only the second and fourth lines were rhymed, since rhyme turned out to be an unpopular alien importation.

> The king sits in Dumferline town,   1
>   Drinking the blood-red wine.   2
>   "O where will I get a good sailor   3
>   To sail this ship of mine?"   2
>
> Sir Patrick Spens.

In this development, we have all the devices that proved of major importance in the development of stanzas in English poetry. In terms of popularity, these were: the couplet (rhymed 1, 1) and the quatrain rhymed alternately (1, 2, 1, 2). When later the normal line of English poetry became fixed as the 5-foot iambic line, we have all the elements that enter into the famous English stanzas, up to the Shakespearean sonnet.

The Metrical Romance. A narrative poem of considerable length, usually centered around some quest, and dealing with war, love, religion, or some combination of these.

Stories in Verse. Stories in verse follow the same general rules of stories in prose, and should as a minimum be as well told. The same applies to full book-length novels in verse. These still retain some popularity. As always, they may be in free, accent or metric verse, rhymed or unrhymed.

The Epic. An epic is a long narrative poem, dealing with heroic events, usually with supernatural guidance and participation in the action. The earliest epics were anonymous, or attributed to some mythical or partly mythical author. Later authored epics have not proved as popular as the earlier ones.

Mixed Poetry

Poems were created before they were classified; and the poets very properly as a rule refuse to fit their products under any of the subsequent classifications. Any single poem may partake of the nature of any two of the classifications, or of more, or even of all.

Thus a narrative poem may include description, dramatic conversation, lyric interludes, and comic relief. The same is true of extended lyrics, descriptive poems, and dramas. The element of didacticism, or pointing a moral, is at least implicit in all poems: for it is an essential part of a desire that the poet wants to do something, or continue something, or have somebody else or something else do or continue something. Far more often, the didacticism is uttered outright, even in poems otherwise lyric, descriptive, narrative, or dramatic.

Thus A. E. Housman's famous collection of poems, *The Shropshire Lad*, is usually called a volume of lyrics, and the author a lyric poet. Yet most of the poems are definitely didactic; several are dramatic; and almost all contain an admixture of the various elements.

The only time when it is important to write a pure lyric, a pure descriptive poem, a pure narrative poem, or a pure dramatic poem, is when participating in a contest, where one of these is stipulated.

Written Exercises

1. Write a ballad, using any one of the accepted English ballad stanzas. It should not exceed 32 lines in length.

2. Write a brief narrative poem, of not more than 20 lines.

3. Write a brief poem, containing a story, conversation, and description, not over 30 lines.

4. Write a brief poem, containing lyric or narrative elements, and also a moral—that is, the didactic element.

5. (Optional) At any stage of the course, the student may desire to try one of the longer forms—an ode, elegy, long pastoral poem, chant, narrative poem, one act drama, or full play. This should be done by degrees, and should be made as perfect as possible.

If any of the instructions or statements, such as the skeleton form for rhyme-schemes (1, 1 for couplets, 1, 2, 1, 2 for alternately rhymed quatrains) are not clear now, later lessons will clear them up.

LESSON IV

SAME, CONCLUDED. DRAMATIC POETRY

Dramatic Poetry

In dramatic poetry, the poet embodies his desire exclusively in the spoken words of one or more characters. From the time of Shakespeare onward, the prevailing pattern for poetic drama in English consisted of five acts, each act of one or more scenes, written in heroic blank verse—that is, unrhymed iambic pentameter. There were three main types of these dramas:

1. Tragedy, ending in the death of one or more of the principal characters.
2. Comedy, not ending in such death or deaths.
3. History, or chronicle play.

This strict classification is no longer followed, and the pattern of the modern drama is far looser, ranging from one act plays onward, using any preferred rhythmic pattern.

In drama, the author is allowed to speak only in the stage directions.

There is an increasing demand for verse drama, one act or longer, for stage or radio, especially when written in natural free or accent verse.

Short Dramatic Verse. A number of the old English ballads are properly to be classified as drama, since they consist exclusively of conversation—questions and answers, without even stage directions. *The Nut Brown Maid* is a good example, and so is *Edward, Edward.* A typical brief verse drama is *Death and the Maiden,* set to music by Franz Schubert:

> *The Maiden.* Pass onward, Oh! pass onward,
> Go, wild and bloodless man!
> I am still young. Away, then,
> And touch me not, I pray,
> O touch me not, I pray.
> *Death.*   Give me your hand, my fair and tender child,
> As friend I come, and not to chasten.
> Be of good cheer! I bring you rest,
> To sleep within my soft arms hasten!

Notice that the poet speaks only in the stage directions (here restricted to the mere names of the characters). This is an absolute requirement of drama, verse or prose. The mere use of conversation in a narrative, descriptive or lyric poem does not make the poem dramatic.

Dramatic Monolog or Dramatic Lyric. Robert Browning took the soliloquy, a device common to English drama, especially to express the thoughts of a character, and made it an art form all his own. He called it the dramatic lyric; it is more properly termed the dramatic monolog. In this, one character alone does all the speaking; and by his words reveals his character and at times the characters of others, while telling the story or description that makes up the poem. Excellent examples are Browning's *My Last Duchess* and *Andrea del Sarto;* or, in prose, Ring Lardner's *Haircut.* The same device is used throughout Edgar Lee Masters' *Spoon River Anthology,* where each poem presents a character speaking after death, and telling what led up to the death.

Didactic Poetry

Didactic poetry is defined as poetry "conveying instruction; teaching some moral lesson." The moral, of course, embodies the desire of the poet; it is what he wants the reader to learn.

Poetry appeals primarily to the emotions; and, in proportion as the emotional appeal is soft-pedalled, didactic poetry becomes poetry of low rank, or mere verse. An obvious example is Longfellow's familiar *A Psalm of Life.* There is far more emotional appeal in such widely different didactic verse as most of Walt Whitman's *Leaves of Grass,* A. E. Housman's *A Shropshire Lad,* Edward Fitzgerald's translation of *The Rubaiyat* (or, quatrains) of Omar Khayyam, and many poems that are wide favorites.

It is impossible to draw an absolute line of demarcation between didactic poetry and the other fields. In proportion as the emphasis is laid upon the instruction or the moral, it is proper to class a poem as didactic.

Light, Humorous and Miscellaneous Verse

Any of the above types of poetry, if written with a sufficiently light touch, or with humor, wit, or some similar slant, is also to be classed as light verse. It is thus proper to speak of a light verse ballad, a humorous ballad, a witty ballad, a dialect ballad, a humorous ode, a witty dramatic monolog, a dialect sonnet, etc. All of these collectively are called light verse.

Written Exercises

1. Write a brief dramatic poem, using two or more characters. It should not exceed 20 lines in length.
2. Write a dramatic monolog of not over 30 lines.
3. Write a didactic poem of not over 20 lines.
4. Write an example of light verse, not over 20 lines.

LESSON V

RHYTHM-REPETITION. ACCENT VERSE

Rhythm in Verse

Study and absorb the definition of rhythm given in the fore part of the book. The one thing that distinguishes verse from prose in English is that verse has a tendency toward regularity or uniformity in rhythm, caused by the repetition of accents in a line, or the repetition of some rhythmic pattern of accented and unaccented syllables; while prose has a tendency toward variety, instead of uniformity. The precise dividing line is largely subjective, and is individual with each poet and reader.

Classification of Verse by Rhythm

From the standpoint of rhythm, verse may be accent verse, metric verse, or free verse. There are many subclassifications of metric verse, that we will soon study. Of these three, accent verse is the most natural to English verse. Metric verse, an importation from France and Italy, is far more artificial. Free verse, in which English verse originated, had been abandoned before English literary history begins. Its revival is a return to the greatest naturalness of all.

Early Accent Verse in English

Accent verse is verse with a definite number of accents to each line (also called each verse), with no unaccented syllables, or as many as the poet wishes to use, placed wherever he wishes them placed. In accent scansion, many syllables normally given a major or minor accent receive only a minor accent, and are classed as unaccented syllables.

Old English verse, which grew out of Anglo-Saxon verse, had three conventions or requirements:

1. Four accents to each line.
2. A break, called a cesura or section, midway of each line.
3. At least two examples of alliteration to each line.

Alliteration means identity of the opening consonantal sounds of accented syllables. Typical lines showing these three requirements, with the accents marked and the alliterations italicized, are:

*W*id'sith made ut'terance, | his *w*ord'-hoard unlocked'.
> Widsith, c. 600 A. D.

What! We of *S*pear'-*D*anes' | in *s*pent' *d*ays'.
> Beowulf, c. 1000 A. D.

In a *s*um'mer *s*ea'son, | when *s*oft' was the *s*un'.
> *The Vision of Piers Plowman*, William Langland, c. 1350.

When this 4-accent verse was used in the old English ballads, the cesura and the alliteration were requirements no longer; although both survived intermittently, as ornaments of verse. In the following typical lines, it is valuable not only to count the marked accents, but to count the number of syllables to each foot, as an indication of how accent verse was used, and how it may still be used:

It was' upon a Scer'ethursday that our lord' arose'.
> *Judas*, 13th century.

He came' also still'e, there his moth'er was'.
> *Song of the Incantation*, 14th century.

For I want' for to go' to Wid'dicombe fair'.
> *Widdicombe Fair.*

He court'ed the king's daugh'ter of fair' England'.
> *Earl Brand.*

These four lines have the following number of syllables each: and the following number of syllables to each foot:

        Judas: 14: 2, 5, 5, 2.
        Incantation: 11: 2, 4, 3, 2.
        Widdicombe Fair: 11: 3, 3, 2, 3.
        Earl Brand: 11: 3, 4, 2, 2.

Here we have feet ranging from 2 to 5 syllables. A modern example of accent verse, *The Listeners*, by Walter de la Mare, in three-accent verse, has lines as complexly rhythmed as:

    Though ev- | ery word | he spake
Fell ech- | oing through the shad- | owiness of the still house.

This scansion would give us 2, 5, and 7 syllables to the three feet. Even if we used a more natural scansion,

      Fell echoing | through the shadowiness | of the still house,

we would still have 4, 6, and 4 syllables to the three feet.
Typical examples of accent verse from *Mother Goose* include:

      Hark, | hark, | the dogs | do bark,
        The beggars | are coming | to town . . . .
      Pease | porridge | hot . . . .
      Three | blind | mice . . . .
      Deedle deedle | dumpling | my son | John.

While 4-accent verse is most ancient and native in English poetry, examples of 3-accent verse are almost as numerous; and the line can be of any length, so long as it is not made too unwieldy.

Writing Accent Verse. In writing accent verse, the only pattern required is so many accents to the line. Having arrived at that, let your effort at first be to make the various feet as different from each other as possible—or you will end up with mere metric verse. Thus for 3-accent verse, starting with the pattern TUM, TUM, TUM, like three drumbeats, we might get:

      Spring! Spring! Spring!
      With the flash | of birds | in the tree-limbs,
      With soft | tints | of the rainbow
      On the buds | and the awakening | blossoms.
      No | more | snow,
      No chill, | but a balm | in the air,

and so on. Accent verse is especially fitted to popular song lyrics, as in—

No' | more pain',
No' | more strain',
Now' | I'm sane', but
I' | had rather be punch'-drunk.

I Wish I Were in Love Again.

It is the usual rhythm for chants:

O de Glo'- | ry Road'! | O de Glo'- | ry Road'!
I'm gonter drap' | my load' | upon de Glo'- | ry Road'!

The Glory Road, Clement Wood.

Fat | black bucks | in a wine- | barrel room . . . .
Beat | an empty bar- | rel with the han- | dle of a broom.

The Congo, Vachel Lindsay.

In these two and many other chants, feet of four and more syllables are common.

Never forget that metric verse may also be correctly regarded as accent verse clipped and padded into identical feet. Hence, while all metric verse can be regarded and scanned as accent verse (by ignoring the unaccented syllables), it is best to write accent verse with a far freer and more natural rhythm than metric verse ever attains. For purposes of classification, use the term metric verse for that subhead of accent verse in which the unaccented syllables fit a pattern, as well as the accented syllables; and limit the term accent verse only to the remainder of accent verse,—that is, verse whose unaccents are not regular enough to qualify it as metric verse.

So much space has been devoted to this, because it is one of the four major stumbling blocks to most versifiers: the others being the vocabulary, free verse, and consonance. Practice scanning popular songs and favorite poems, especially of the last thirty years, and notice how many of them are accent verse, and not metric verse. Mastery of accent verse is a definite step toward mastery of versification. Achieve this consciously. Try to determine whether Shakespeare's maturer work, and Robert Frost's 5-foot lines, were intended as accent verse, or as metric verse, which the poets made freer and freer until they arrived at accent verse unintentionally.

Written Exercises

1. Write an example of 4-accent verse, rhymed or unrhymed, not over 10 lines.
2. Divide it into feet, by vertical bars; and write along your margin the number of syllables to each foot in each line. This is one test to

see whether you have real spontaneous accent verse, or merely metric verse with variations.

3. Write an example of 3-accent verse, not over 20 lines long, in some gay mood; preferably lyric.

4. Write an example of 3-accent verse, not over 20 lines long, in a serious or sad mood; preferably narrative. The natural rhythm of this should differ noticeably from the rhythm of (3).

Note that there is nothing sacred in the line-lengths indicated. If your verse comes shorter or longer, it is important to write it out fully, and then stop; rather than cut it off abruptly, or lengthen it unnecessarily. The only time where a length-limit of verses is important is where this is announced as one of the conditions of a poetry contest.

LESSON VI

SAME. METRIC VERSE. THE IAMB. SCANSION

Meter in Verse

Meter, as commonly used, is the systematic arrangement of the accented and unaccented syllables in verse. These syllables are divided into metric feet, which derive their names from classical Greek and Latin feet. A convenient and useful classification of metric feet is:

Two-syllabled feet: iamb, trochee (also spondee and pyrrhic).
Three-syllabled feet: anapest, amphibrach, dactyl (also amphimacer, bacchius, antibacchius, molossus, etc.)

Turn to the definitions of these feet, in the fore part of the book, and absorb them.

Scansion, Natural and Pattern

Scansion, of prose or verse, is its division into rhythmical units, called feet; with markings to divide the feet, and appropriate marks to distinguish accented from unaccented syllables, long from short syllables, etc.

The first step in scansion is to mark your syllables (where accent is the determinant) either as accented or unaccented. The proper accenting of a word can be gathered from its use in natural speech. If you are uncertain, consult a dictionary. The dictionary, however, will not always be accurate, since it often omits natural minor accents. Thus three out of four dictionaries before me accent *taciturnity* thus:

tac-i-turn′i-ty (one has it: tac″i-turn′i-ty)

This might well be its accenting, in three-syllabled metric feet. But, since most metric feet in English are two-syllabled (iambic or trochaic), its usual accenting in English versification is:

tac″i-turn′i-ty″

that is, with minor accents on the 1st and 5th syllables, and major accent on the third syllable. This is true of tens of thousands of words in the dictionary.

Natural scansion is the scansion of words as they are naturally used in good conversation. The feet in natural scansion may at times have far more than three syllables; and may have quite a number of minor accents, as well as the one major one. Here is the natural scansion of the opening of a famous soliloquy from *Hamlet:*

To be | or not to be. | That | is the question.
Whether | 'tis nobler | in the mind | to suffer
The slings | and arrows | of outrageous | fortune.

(To anticipate, the pattern here calls for *five* accents; but naturally each line has only four.) The natural scansion of the opening of Joyce Kilmer's *Trees* is as follows:

I think | that I shall never | see
A poem | lovely | as a tree.

Here the pattern, to anticipate again, calls for *four* accents per line. Naturally each line has only three.

The first stage in scansion is to master natural scansion. Note that it includes feet of a single accent, with no unaccent; and feet of four or more syllables, with one major accent, and at times several minor accents.

Free verse and prose require only natural scansion. Accent verse is satisfied with the division and the marking of accents only, ignoring the unaccents and minor accents. Metric verse requires more.

Pattern scansion is the division into feet, dictated by a preconceived metrical pattern. For instance, the metrical pattern may call for a succession of iambs, or trochees, or any other foot; an alternation of feet, as, an iamb followed by an anapest; or a more complex pattern, as in Sapphics. In pattern scansion, words can be divided ruthlessly; and minor accents regarded as the major accent of a foot. Also, a foot may consist all of unaccents (pyrrhic, of two; tribrach, of three). In

metric scansion, the effort is to fit each foot to the pattern, if possible; if not, to make it a variation as near the original as possible. Thus the quotation from *Hamlet*, in pattern scansion (ta TUM, ta TUM, ta TUM, ta TUM, ta TUM, or 5-foot iambic) would be:

Tŏ bé, | ŏr nót | tŏ bé. | Thát ĭs | thĕ quéstiŏn.
Whéthĕr | 'tĭs nó'- | *blĕr ĭn* | thĕ mínd | tŏ súffĕr
Thĕ slíngs | ănd ár- | *rŏws ŏf* | ŏutrá- | geŏus fórtŭne.

Here each line has a permitted extra unaccent at its end. The foot "to be," 3rd in line 1, has a minor accent elevated to major accenting. The two italicized feet are pyrrhics, without any accent: ta ta.

The pattern scansion of the couplet from *Trees*, in 4-foot iambic, ta TUM, ta TUM, ta TUM, ta TUM, is as follows:

Ĭ thínk | thăt Í | shăll név- | ĕr sée
Ă pó- | ĕm lóve- | *lў̆ ăs* | ă trée.

The one pyrrhic, in the second line, is italicized. Comparing the natural and the pattern scansion in both cases, note how the natural feet consisting of one accent are combined into longer feet, to fit the pattern.

Here is the rule for writing the best metric verse:

> The poetry, as a rule, is natural and effective, in proportion as the natural scansion differs from the metric scansion.

The Iamb

The first 2-syllabled foot is the iamb: an unaccent followed by an accent (⌣ ′); ta TUM. This is the commonest foot in English. But far more words in English are natural trochees (TUM ta): lovely, going, given, etc. The iamb is arrived at by prefacing a trochaic word with a one-syllabled unaccented article, preposition, conjunction, etc: The love'-|ly, in go'-|ing, but giv'-|en, etc.

Masculine and Feminine Endings and Rhymes

A line ending on an accent is said to have a masculine ending. A one-syllabled rhyme is called a masculine rhyme. A line ending on one unaccent is called a feminine ending. A two-syllabled rhyme, accent, unaccent, is called a feminine rhyme (glowing, going).

It is always permissible to add one or even two unaccents at the end of an accented foot terminating a line; or to omit one or even two unaccents at the beginning of a line. A line with its last foot perfect

is called *acatalectic;* a verse lacking a syllable at the beginning, or terminating in an imperfect foot, is called *catalectic.*

Iambic Verse in English: Heroic Blank Verse; the Heroic Couplet

Iambic verse may have any number of feet to each line; and may be rhymed or unrhymed (that is, blank verse).

Trochees, spondees, or pyrrhics may be substituted for iambs. So may anapests or other 3-syllabled feet, the extra unaccent being called a grace-note. (These were called cyclic anapests, etc., in classic prosody.) Similar substitutions are allowed for any of the feet.

Heroic blank verse, the favorite meter of Shakespeare's plays, Milton's epics, and much later poetry, is unrhymed 5-foot iambic verse.

The heroic couplet is iambic 5-foot verse, rhymed couplet fashion (1, 1; 2, 2; 3, 3; etc.). This will be taken up further under couplet rhyming.

Written Exercises

1. Make a list of 10 words that are perfect iambs, such as: *alert, delight, defy,* etc.

2. Make a list of 10 iambs each formed of two words: as, *to go, by Rome, the girl.*

3. Write a 5-line poem in this pattern: 1 iamb, 2 iambs, 3, 4, and finally 5 iambs. Do not add extra syllables at the end.

4. Do the same thing, with each final syllable catalectic—that is, with an extra unaccent.

5. Write about 10 lines of heroic blank verse. Enclose by bars each foot that is a variation, and write its name in the margin, after marking its scansion above it.

6. Write about 20 lines, rhymed or unrhymed, of iambic verse, none of it in 5-foot lines. Divide off all variational feet, scan them, and name them in the margin.

LESSON VII

SAME. THE TROCHEE. OTHER TWO-SYLLABLED FEET

The Trochee

The other important 2-syllabled foot is the trochee: an accent followed by an unaccent (' ‿); TUM ta. This foot is thus the reverse of the iamb. In fact, iambs and trochees may be regarded as variations of the same rhythm—an endless alternation of accent and unaccent:

ta TUM ta TUM ta TUM ta TUM ta TUM ta TUM ta

If this rhythm commences with an unaccent (ta), we call it iambic; if with an accent (TUM), we call it trochaic.

These meters were interchangeable, even in classic scansion. Take the line:

> Round about the cauldron go.

If this came from a 4-foot iambic line, it would be scanned:

> Round | about | the caul- | dron go.

This would be called catalectic iambic verse—that is, verse lacking a syllable at the beginning. A pause could be regarded as taking the place of the missing unaccent. As a matter of fact, the line is from the witch incantation scene in *Macbeth*, written in trochees. Hence it is properly scanned:

> Round a- | bout the | cauldron | go.

It now becomes catalectic trochaic verse—that is, verse terminating in an imperfect foot. Thus, depending on the company it is in—that is, whether the verse is predominantly iambic or trochaic—this line fits perfectly into either classification. The iamb and the trochee are interchangeable.

Trochaic Verse in English

Like iambic and all the other metric feet, trochaic verse may have any number of feet to each line; and may be unrhymed or rhymed. As in the case of iambic verse, an iamb may be substituted anywhere for a trochee; and so may a spondee or a pyrrhic. So may a dactyl or any 3-syllabled foot, the extra syllable being regarded as a grace-note. Longfellow's *Hiawatha* is in 4-foot trochaic verse, with feminine endings: that is, each line is perfect (acatalectic):

> Should you | ask me, | whence these | stories,
> Whence these legends and traditions,
> With the odors of the forest,
> With the dew and damp of meadows.

Now remember the all-important generalization about metric verse:

> The poetry, as a rule, is natural and effective, in proportion as the natural scansion differs from the metric scansion.

Longfellow tends to be annoyingly monotonous and accurate in scansion. But consider the natural scansion of the last two lines quoted:

With the ŏdŏrs | ŏf thĕ fórĕst,
With the dĕw | ănd dámp | ŏf mĕadŏws.

Here we have only one true trochee; with an anapest and an amphi-brach in the second line, and, in the first, two feet of 4 syllables each. Thus even these two lines from accurate Longfellow depart widely from the metric pattern. And yet it is all as natural as spoken prose. Compare the natural scansion with the pattern scansion:

With thĕ | ŏdŏrs | ŏf thĕ fórĕst,
With thĕ | dĕw ănd | dámp ŏf | mĕadŏws.

In fact, since the pattern is trochaic, there are many who would scan this:

With thĕ | ŏdŏrs | ŏf thĕ | fórĕst.

The scansion first given, showing the use of the pyrrhics, is more accurate. A pyrrhic can always be substituted for an iamb or a trochee.

Other Two Syllabled Feet: The Spondee, The Pyrrhic

The spondee, (′ ′), TUM, TUM, consists of two accented syllables. Examples:

Bright star; dogs run; huge hill.

Certain 2-syllabled words, such as *watch-spring, tailspin, hand-carved*, etc., may be used as spondees, although they usually fit more accurately into iambs, or even trochees.

By classic prosody, the spondee took as long to pronounce as the usual 3-syllabled feet; and hence took longer than the iamb or the trochee. In spite of this, it was used to substitute for either 2-syllabled or 3-syllabled feet. In English, it may at any time take the place of an iamb, a trochee, or one of the three usual 3-syllabled feet. Repeated spondees slow down the movement of a line.

The pyrrhic (˘ ˘), ta ta, is a foot consisting of two unaccented syllables. It has no accent. In Lesson VI, we saw it twice used to replace an iamb, in the quotation from *Hamlet*. In the two lines last discussed from *Hiawatha* in this lesson, there are three uses of the pyrrhic, to replace a trochee.

Written Exercises

1. Make a list of 10 words that are perfect trochees, such as *Janet, yielding, rapture*.

2. Make a list of 10 trochees, each formed of two words: as, *aid him, win the, name and.*

3. Write a 5-line poem ̄in this pattern: 5 trochees, 4 trochees, 3, 2, and finally 1 trochee. Make each foot a full trochee: that is, ending with an unaccent—feminine endings.

4. Do the same thing, omitting the final unaccent of each line (that is, making each final syllable catalectic, that is, imperfect).

5. Write 10 to 20 lines in unrhymed trochaic 4-foot meter, the rhythm of Hiawatha. (Be sure these all have feminine endings.)

6. Read the opening of *Macbeth*, IV, i (the witches' cauldron scene), and note the additional strength given by the masculine endings. Write at least 10 lines in 4-foot trochaic lines, with masculine endings.

7. Write not more than 10 lines of trochaic verse, with at least one variation (iamb, spondee, pyrrhic, dactyl, etc.) in each line. Underscore the variations, each foot being enclosed within two vertical lines, and write their names in the margin.

LESSON VIII

SAME. THREE-SYLLABLED FEET: THE ANAPEST; THE AMPHIBRACH

Three-Syllabled Feet in English

Of all the metric feet, the iamb is most natural in English. For the language has approximately as many unaccented syllables as accented; and a majority of sentences start with an iamb—usually an unaccented article, preposition, or the like, followed by a word with some accent on its first syllable. Trochees also have the same number of unaccents and accents; but the emphatic opening on an accented syllable gives an abrupt and staccato effect, like a command or a cry for help. A succession of trochaic lines tend to become far more monotonous than an equal number of iambic lines. It is not by accident that all the popular lines and stanzas in English—heroic blank verse, the heroic couplet, ballad meter, the famous named stanzas, the Shakespearean sonnet—are iambic; or, in the case of the ballad, which started as accent verse, tend toward the iamb.

Three-syllabled feet are as unnatural in English as the iamb is comparatively natural. The reason is obvious: the fact that it is not natural, in English, to use two unaccents for every accent. To use them naturally is more difficult than writing natural iambs and trochees. It is best to recognize this in advance, and be prepared for the more typical traps for the unwary versifier, in attempting them.

Just as iambs and trochees are interchangeable, depending merely on whether the series of alternate accents and unaccents starts with the unaccent (iambic) or with the accent (trochaic), there are three 3-syllabled feet which are similarly interchangeable. That is, we may regard these three feet as parts of an endless rhythm proceeding:

ta ta TUM ta ta TUM ta ta TUM ta ta TUM ta ta TUM, etc.

All three feet use this rhythm; the difference lying in whether the foot starts with two unaccents; with one; or with an accent. The three feet are the anapest (ta ta TUM), the amphibrach (ta TUM ta), and the dactyl (TUM ta ta).

The Anapest

The anapest consists of two unaccents followed by an accent: ta ta TUM (˘ ˘ ′). It can be regarded as an iamb with an extra unaccent at the beginning. Typical words which constitute complete anapests are:

> apprehend, coincide, interfere, supersede.

It should be noted that these and many other anapests consist of a 2-syllabled prefix added to a one-syllabled root-stem. Anapestic phrases are far commoner:

> to the end, with delight, into Rome.

In writing anapests, remember that two unaccents must start each line, and must come between each pair of accents. Here is an example of anapests, to the pattern of 1, 2, 3 and 4 to the line:

> At the end
> Of the fight for the flag,
> Let the heavens resound with the crash
> Of the shattering roar of applauding delight.

Note how, in metric patterns, words can be broken ruthlessly, to fit the pattern scansion. For here these are anapestic feet:

> -ens resound; -tering roar; of applaud-; -ing delight.

We will postpone discussion of the traps for unwary users of 3-syllabled feet until we have considered the next two feet.

The Amphibrach

The amphibrach consists of an unaccent, an accent, and an unaccent: ta TUM ta (˘ ′ ˘). It can be regarded as an iamb with an

extra unaccent at the end; or as a trochee preceded by an unaccent. Typical words which constitute complete amphibrachs are:

Alaska, delighted, dramatic, O'Reilly, suspended.

A typical amphibrachic structure would be prefix, one-syllabled root stem, suffix (as, *de-light-ed*). Typical amphibrachic phrases are:

to end it, chastise her, for Launah, and loving.

The ta TUM opening makes this foot slightly more natural in English verse than either of the other two common 3-syllabled feet. Note that amphibrachs can be rhymed two ways, feminine or masculine:

A bird is at best when he's winging;
A poet is known by his singing.

These are complete (or acatalectic) amphibrachic lines. When the last unaccent is omitted,

O give me the night and a moon,
And you to respond to my tune.

the lines are said to be catalectic—that is, with defective last feet.

Written Exercises

1. Write 10 words constituting perfect anapests.
2. Write 10 phrases constituting perfect anapests.
3. Write 10 words constituting perfect amphibrachs.
4. Write 10 phrases constituting perfect amphibrachs.
5. Write not more than 12 lines of anapestic verse. Underscore all feet that are variations, enclosing each in a bar, and marking in the margin the name of the variation.
6. Write not more than 12 lines of amphibrachic verse, treating the variations the same way. Never forget that, if there are too many variations, the original character of your verse alters, until it may veer outside of your set pattern entirely.

LESSON IX

SAME. THE DACTYL. SNARES FOR THE UNWARY

The Dactyl

The dactyl consists of an accented syllable, followed by two unaccents: TUM ta ta (´ ˘ ˘). It can be regarded as a trochee with an unaccented syllable added at the end. Typical words which constitute complete dactyls are:

antonym, heavenly, merriment, rhapsody.

It should be noted that an anapest is often constituted of a one-syllabled word-root, followed by two unaccented suffixes, or by a 2-syllabled suffix without accent: *mer-ri-ment, ed-ible.* Dactylic phrases follow these patterns:

> fly to the, happy in, fall upon.

Since either one or both unaccented syllables may be omitted at the end of a dactylic line, there are three ways of rhyming dactyls:

1. On a triple rhyme—that is, complete or acatalectic dactyls:

> Dusk, when the fireflies are glimmering,
> Dusk, when the starlight is shimmering,
> Dusk, and the whispering rest of it—
> Day? We have found here the best of it!

2. On a double or feminine rhyme, this being composed of catalectic dactyls:

> Out of the Spring and its rapture
> It is not hard to recapture
> Youth, though for years it has fled us;
> —Love, and the highroads it led us!

3. On a single or masculine rhyme, this being also catalectic:

> Come when the year's at the flood,
> Leaping and surging of blood,
> Melody bright in the soul,
> Life reunited and whole!

There are other ways *not* to rhyme dactyls. We will come to them soon.

Blending 3-Syllable Feet

A pleasing effect may be obtained by a formal or informal intermingling of anapests, amphibrachs and dactyls. Here is an example, fairly formalized:

> By the flow | of the in- | land river,
>   Whence the fleets | of i | ron have fled,
> Where the blades of the grave-grass quiver,
>   Asleep are the ranks of the dead.

> Únder thĕ | sód aňd thĕ | déw,
> Wáiting thĕ | júdgmĕnt | dáy,
> Under the one, the Blue;
> Under the other, the Gray.

> *The Blue and the Gray*, Francis Miles Finch.

The opening anapestic movement rhymes lines 1 and 3 on amphibrachs; inserts an iamb inside line 2; and opens line 4 with an iamb. The dactylic movement of the second quatrain (four lines) has a trochee inside lines 6 and 7. The rhyming of the last quatrain is, of course, dactylic, type 3—omitting both unaccents.

Snares for the Unwary

There are five other 3-syllabled feet. Their names are unimportant, but their function as wreckers is important; so we may as well record their names:

Tribrach	3 unaccented syllables	⌄⌄⌄	into the
Molossus	3 accented syllables	´´´	great souls flame
Amphimacer	accent, unaccent, accent	´⌄´	Holy Ghost
Bacchius	unaccent, accent, accent	⌄´´	alert love
Antibacchius	accent, accent, unaccent	´´⌄	eyes blind for

A spondee may always be substituted for an anapest, amphibrach, or dactyl. A molossus may occasionally be introduced, to slow down the movement of the line. A tribrach is rarely effective—it divorces the accents too definitely, and lets the rhythm taper off too far. The last three, while quite common in 3-syllabled verse, almost always add a regrettable awkwardness to the rhythm. Thus these two lines from Samuel Woodworth's *The Old Oaken Bucket:*

> The orchard, the meadow, | thĕ dĕep tán- | gled wildwood,
> And évery | lóved spót whĭch | my infancy knew.

The first line quoted has a bacchius; the second, an antibacchius. However natural the wording may be, the rhythm has departed from the essence of well-wrought 3-syllabled verse.

Far worse is the use of these feet in rhyming dactylic verse. From Tennyson's *The Charge of the Light Brigade*, out of 24 similar instances we choose:

> Stórmĕd a* wĭth | shót aňd shéll,
> Bóldlȳ thĕy | róde aňd wéll.

Here we have a dactyl followed by an amphimacer; and single-rhymed on the last syllable only of the amphimacer—a shift of the meter midway of the line. This can be defended as a combination of two meters; it is not permissible dactylic rhyming. Even worse is such a couplet as:

Cánnŏn tŏ | right ŏf thĕm,
Cánnŏn tŏ | left ŏf thĕm.

Here we have no rhyme at all; for rhyme applies to the accented syllable, and *right* and *left* have no kinship with rhyme; while following each with the identities *of them* cannot provide rhyme.

If the natural flow of your 3-syllabled verse cannot avoid an occasional amphimacer, bacchius or antibacchius, at least make these as infrequent as possible, as well as inconspicuous and natural.

Variations in English Verse

Remembering that accent verse is natural to English, and that meter is an alien importation, it is not surprising that it is the practice of the better poets to vary their meters almost incredibly. Plays from Shakespeare can be dated by his increasing freedom in the use of variations in his iambic lines. The same applies to all the great masters. The end of the process, which they often reach, is either accent verse or, among the greater poets, free verse—as appears amply in Shakespeare's later plays.

Always let your natural scansion differ from your pattern scansion. The vitality of your verse is in proportion to this difference.

Pleasing effects can be obtained by alternating rhythms in a single line; alternating the rhythms of each couplet; or alternating stanzas as to their rhythms—for instance, a 3-syllabled stanza, followed by a 2-syllabled one. These combinations of meters can be made very effective, to express different moods.

Written Exercises

1. Write 10 words constituting perfect dactyls.
2. Write 10 phrases constituting perfect dactyls.
3. Write not more than 12 lines of dactylic verse, triple-rhymed.
4. The same, double-rhymed or single-rhymed.
5. The same, alternating any two of these types of rhymes.
6. Write not more than 20 lines, using one rhythm in the odd-numbered lines, and another in the even-numbered lines.
7. Write an example of iambic verse, as full of variations as the later plays of Shakespeare; or a typical Robert Frost narrative poem; or any of the plays of Maxwell Anderson.

LESSON X

FREE VERSE. LINE LENGTH. INDENTING

Free Verse

Free verse has no rhythmic convention whatever, beyond the requirement that its rhythm must tend toward regularity or uniformity. It must not have the measured thudding drumbeat of accent verse. It must not exhibit the precise alternation of accent and unaccent shown in metric verse. And, of course, its rhythm must not exhibit the tendency toward variety shown by prose.

It is convenient to bound it by these three negatives. It must never be:

1. Metric verse. Many of Walt Whitman's lyric passages in *Leaves of Grass* are definitely metric, as in the lyric *Joy, Shipmate, Joy!*

> Our life is closed—our life begins;
> The long, long anchorage we leave,
> The ship is clear at last—she leaps!
> She swiftly courses from the shore.

If your product, when scanned, fits into any of the metric patterns, it is not free verse.

2. Accent verse. Again, some of Whitman is definitely accent verse, as this 6-accent pattern. It is divided here into feet with one major accent each, or its equivalent:

> Beat! | beat! | drums!— | blow! | bugles! | blow!
> Through | the windows | through doors —| burst | like a ruth- | less force!

Much of his *Out of the Cradle Endlessly Rocking* illustrates this.

3. Prose. Don't write prose, no matter how chopped up into brief lines, and think that it is free verse. The chopping-up process may make it more emotionally effective; but it cannot alter its innate prose quality.

If the product falls outside of these three classifications, it is free verse. If it falls within any of the three classifications, it is conceivably well worth writing; but it is not free verse.

The requirements of free verse are the same as those of all verse, and not in any wise more difficult than any other verse. Moreover, it is frequently the most natural and inevitable form in which to write what you have to say.

At times only scansion can determine whether the product is free

verse, or one of the other rhythmic types. It makes little difference, if it is good poetry, verse, or prose.

Free verse can be rhymed, as it is occasionally, as in some of the verse of Ogden Nash. It is usually written without this alien ornamentation. It may of course have alliteration and many other sound-repetition ornaments. The matter of rhythm alone determines whether it is free verse or not.

Certain poets are apparently tone-deaf to any verse except free verse. I have had numerous pupils of whom this was true, as it is apparently true of Carl Sandburg, and was true in almost as great a degree of Walt Whitman, when the matter of real poetry was involved.

Free verse would be the easiest verse of all to write, except for the race's familiarity with the two later developments, accent verse and metric verse. If you are imbued with either or both of these, you may have difficulty at first in achieving real free verse. Self-discipline in letting an emotional poetic mood express itself with complete naturalness, with complete elimination of the later accent and metric patterns, can always achieve it.

It is wise to practice scanning the better examples of accepted free verse, Whitman, Sandburg, and so many of the moderns, and compare the result with the scansion of your own free verse. To many, it comes naturally; to many more, it requires the mental or subconscious avoidance of the devices of accent verse and meter.

On the whole, free verse is not so much in demand in the field of light verse as well-wrought verse of either of the other types.

Line-Length in Verse

In free verse, there are several preferred ways of determining line-length. The simplest method, followed by Walt Whitman and many more, is to end the line where there is a natural break in the meaning—either a period, or some less conclusive punctuation or natural stop in meaning. A smaller group of versifiers prefer to do the reverse of this, and end at some definitely unnatural point: thereby attracting more attention to their verse, an attention at times mingled with exasperation.

In accent verse, the line-length is usually determined by the pattern—so many accents to the line. In metric verse, it is either fixed by the pattern; or, if the number of feet varies from line to line, the line terminates usually according to one of the two methods suggested for free verse.

The classical Greek and Latin line was normally a hexameter, that is, six-feet; but it was invariably broken in the middle by a cesura. The "long line" of Anglo-Saxon and Old English verse consisted of

four accent feet, similarly broken by a cesura. For centuries, the
French norm was the Alexandrine, a 6-foot iambic line. In English
versification, the norm is the 5-foot iambic line; witness the plays and
sonnets of Shakespeare, the epics of Milton, the heroic couplets of
the age of Pope and Dryden. Many poets achieve a typical line-length:
as, the overlong lines of Walt Whitman, the long lines of Robinson
Jeffers, the abnormally short lines of Elinor Wylie.

Let your line-length aid in achieving your objective. In general,
unless you have a specific line-length pattern, it is wisest to end the
line where the meaning ends.

Indenting

No poem need be indented. It is always proper to omit this.

Indenting may be used at the beginning of each stanza, paragraph
or division of a long poem, precisely as it is used in prose. Where
characters speak in your poem, it may be used at the beginning of each
speech. It may be used, for symmetry, to center short lines:

> The time I've lost in wooing,
> In watching and pursuing
> The light that lies
> In women's eyes
> Has been my heart's undoing.

As ordinarily used, indenting is used to set off lines that rhyme
together. Thus, couplet rhyming should *never* be indented:

> Willie and three other brats
> Licked up all the Rough-on-Rats.
> Father said, when mother cried,
> "Never mind, they'll die outside."

It is as incorrect to indent any lines that do not rhyme together.
Here, since lines 1 and 2 rhyme together, they must commence together, with neither indented; and the same of lines 3 and 4.

Written Exercises

1. Write 4 to 20 lines of free verse, a lyric.
2. Write the same, preferably realistic and descriptive.
3. Write the same, either narrative with dramatic elements, such as
dialog; or a brief dramatic poem, either with different characters
speaking, or a dramatic monolog.

4. A brief example of couplet rhyming, properly indented.

5. A brief example of alternate rhyming, properly indented. (In alternate rhyming, line 1 rhymes with line 3, line 2 with line 4, etc.)

LESSON XI

SOUND-REPETITION AS ORNAMENT. RHYME

The Function of Rhyme

The essence of verse is its use of rhythm-repetition. Repetition is pleasing to the human ear; and very soon repetition of the other element of words—their sounds—began to be used, as an ornament of verse. This started, of course, with the repetition of complete words and groups of words. Then rhyme was invented, early in the Christian era, probably by priests of the Alexandrian church, to render their teachings more palatable. It spread through Italy and France to England, where it arrived just before 1400; and is now deeply embedded in the language.

Rhyme is the repetition of an identical accented vowel sound, together with all the consonantal and vowel sounds following; with a difference in the consonantal sounds immediately preceding.

Rhyme deals with *sound* only; spelling makes no difference. Thus *beat* and *great* do not rhyme; but these words, in spite of their differing spelling, do rhyme:

> beat, Crete, suite, elite, mete, greet, conceit, Lafitte, etc.

Single or Masculine Rhymes

One-syllabled rhymes are called single or masculine rhymes. Note that this rhyme may be of a one-syllabled word, or of the final accented syllable of a longer word:

> day, they, bouquet, Bordelais, assegai, etc.

Double or Feminine Rhymes

Two-syllabled rhymes are called double or feminine rhymes. Here the identical accented vowels must be the ones in the syllable preceding the last syllable; and all subsequent sounds must be identical.

> ended, blended, pretended, defended; also, men did.

Triple and Longer Rhymes

Three-syllabled or triple rhymes have the accented syllables third from the end of the word; with all following sounds identical.

> breakable, implacable, mistakable, etc.

These, and longer rhymes, are more suitable to light verse than to serious poetry. Note that the foot-count stops with the identical accented vowel. Thus, in 4-foot verse,

> Rhyme, when | in its | proper | place
> Lends both dignity and grace.
> It is | unmis- | takable
> If it's | not too | breakable,

the third and fourth lines are counted as having only 3 feet; and need to be lengthened, as:

> It is | always | unmis- | takable,
> If it doesn't prove too breakable.

As first given, the lines would be correct for 3-foot verse:

> Rhyme, when | in its | place,
> Lends im- | pressive | grace;
> It is | unmis- | takable
> If it's not too breakable.

Minor Accent Rhymes

It is very effective to break the regular flow of rhymes on the major accents, by rhyming a major accent with a minor accent; or even by rhyming two minor accents together. Examples are:

tree, memory; Spring, rallying; hit, counterfeit; dead, comforted; less, wantonness.

Misplaced Accent Rhymes

Since rhyme was an alien importation, its use at first in English, especially in the popular ballads, was loose and approximate, rather than precise. Another reason for rhymes with the accent misplaced was the popularity of French as the court language in England, coupled with the fact that accent is absent or negligible in French. Hence in the ballads we find rhyming pairs such as:

plan, woman; sea, Jamie; tree, weary; John, yeoman.

To make these rhyme, the accents in the second words must be misplaced, in each instance. This same device is occasionally used with great effectiveness today. From my collected poems, *The Glory Road*, I take these examples:

> Death gives no life to the ravished dead;
> But for this your soul has been appointed. . . .

The choiring angels—and the vast anguish
That tore her soul when she won her wish. . . .

You can't ketch God wid no fly-paper—
But my boy Jesus caught de Lord wid prayer! . . . . .

Sugar Plum,
You says yes, I buys a ring;
You 'n' me has a church wedding.

In reading misplaced accent rhymes aloud, it is clear that these natural trochaic endings (ap-|pointed, anguish, fly-|paper, wedding) must not be read as iambs; that would be too unnatural. In other words, the accent should not be taken away from the proper place, and placed elsewhere, giving us: an-guish', wed-ding'. Instead, they should be read almost like spondees, with an accent on each—the second accent being fainter.

Mosaic Rhymes: Of Words, or Parts of Words

One or more of the rhymes may consist of more than one word:

make it, break it; needed, she did; mitre, fight her.

This device appears sometimes in serious poetry. It is always at home in popular songs and light verse, and at times is used with great cleverness: as when Byron rhymes *intellectual* with *hen-pecked you all*, Ingoldsby, *furniture* and *burn it, you're;* and Gilbert uses such couplings as:

monotony, got any; cerebellum too, tell 'em too;
lot o' news, hypotenuse; din afore, Pinafore;
strategy, *sat* a gee; wary at, Commissariat.

Popular songs furnish such popular examples as:

found her, around her; enfold you, hold you;
dream awhile, scheme awhile; Japs do it, Lapps do it;
direct us, respect us; flat in, Manhattan; gloomy, to me;
heat in it, meat in it; with 'em, rhythm, etc.

In light verse, parts of words may be used similarly: classic examples being Lewis Carroll's *soup, two p-* (where the next line begins: -enny-worth) and Canning's rhyming *adieu* with *U-* (niversity of Gottingen) and *gru-* (the next line completing the *el* of *gruel*). Gilbert does this brilliantly in *Iolanthe:*

Peers shall team in Christendom,
And a duke's exalted station
Be obtainable by com-
Petitive examination.

Written Exercises

1. Write 12 lines of verse with single rhymes, using any arrangement of rhymes (that is, any rhyme pattern). Be sure that every line is rhymed, and rhymed correctly.

2. Write not over 12 lines with double rhymes.

3. Write not over 12 lines alternating triple rhymes with single or double rhymes.

4. Write not over 12 lines with at least 4 uses of minor accent rhyme.

5. The same, with at least four examples of mosaic rhyme.

LESSON XII

SAME. RHYME, CONCLUDED. MENTAL RHYMING DICTIONARY

Rhymes of Split Familiar Phrases

An excellent light verse device is to split a familiar phrase at an unexpected point, and rhyme it here. Thus "The early bird catches the worm" could be rhymed at *early*, or *bird*, or *catches*.

> To fling at *me*, "The early bird
> Catches the worm" is quite absurd.
> I'm certain, if the truth were told,
> That all he catches is a cold.

End Rhyme and Internal Rhyme

Rhymes used at the ends of lines are called end rhymes. Rhymes used within the line are called internal rhymes. And, of course, rhymes may be used at the beginning of the line, as well.

> Hold the dam! The flood is rising,
> Crashing, smashing levees down.
> Bold of heart, we're realizing
> It's a task to save the town!

Here *rising, realizing, down, town,* are end rhymes; *crashing* and *smashing*, internal rhymes; while *hold* and *bold* rhyme at the beginnings of their lines.

Incorrect Rhymes

Identities do not rhyme. None of the words in the following groups rhyme:

bay, bey, obey, disobey
bare, bear, forbear, Baer
lying, underlying, overlying
loyalty, reality, possibility, probability (as single rhymes); for all of
   these end on -ty.
astrologic, biologic, geologic, pathologic

This rhyming dictionary makes the mis-rhyming of identities difficult;
since the words are properly grouped for rhyming, with the one rule:

Use only one word from each group.

Eye Rhymes are words spelled alike, but whose differing sounds
prevent rhyme. Certain of these have long been acceptable in English
verse, due to the scarceness of certain rhyme sounds. Among these are:

earth, hearth; are, bare; forth, north; flow, allow; love, prove.

These do not rhyme, and are properly to be classed as consonances,
which we will reach later. Other permitted consonances or assonances
are:

heaven, given; was, grass; bliss, is.

A common erroneous miscoupling is:

real, ideal, with steal.

The first two are double rhymes—E′al; the second a single rhyme, EL.
   A trick used in light verse is to use words spelled alike, but pronounced differently—either rhymed incorrectly, or each with its proper
rhyming mate. Among such groups are:

enough, plough, through, although.

A test of the accuracy of your ear for pronunciation lies in a comparison of *north* and *forth*, which do not rhyme. If you have trouble in
sensing the difference between them, divide them thus:

gnaw does not rhyme with *foe.*
nor does not rhyme with *fore* or *four.*

If the vowels do not rhyme, the addition of an -r to each, and then
of a -th, cannot make them rhyme. For, in rhyme, the accented rhyming
vowels must be identical in sound.

Words with Differing Terminal Consonant Sounds cannot rhyme. This fault is far too common. Examples are:

> main, game; hate, shape; feed, sleet; blame, games;
> miss, kissed; singer, finger; silver, deliver.

Mispronunciation cannot excuse false rhymes. The following fail as rhymes for this reason:

> fork, talk; car, ma; morn, dawn; mourn, alone; pork, choke;
> lord, broad; charm, balm; stalking, corking, etc.;
> martin, parting; burden, herding; rind, mine; friend, men;
> hand, man; fete, met; Hades, spades; heinous, Venus.

Two Pairs of Rhymes cannot constitute an acceptable double rhyme. This fault is common in popular songs. Examples are:

> childhood, wildwood; Norfolk, war talk; long hill, strong will.

In most of these cases, we have two pairs of rhymes, at times a rhyme on the accented syllables, and also a sound-repetition on the unaccented syllables that would constitute another pair of rhymes, if accented.

Rhyme-Induced Rhymes

The chief fault in rhymed verse is inserting a rhyming word merely for the purpose of rhyming, and because of the presence in the verse of the word it is to rhyme with. Examples,

> We celebrate this merry Christmas,
> Although we are not on an *isthmus*.
>
> Do not speak only to embarrass,
> As Helen may have done to *Paris*.

Don't yank words in, merely to make a rhyme. Rhymed verse is good in proportion as its every word comes in as naturally and inevitably as do the words in good prose.

Undesirable Rhymes

There are certain rhymes that have been used so often that they should be avoided, unless used in an utterly fresh sense. Among these are:

> kiss, bliss; June, moon; love, dove; spring, wing.

Do not, as a rule, place close together words whose sounds are too similar. Quatrains with the following word-sounds would exhibit this fault:

> sleep, meet, deep, greet; shame, pain, maim, rain.

A Mental Rhyming Dictionary

Shortly before 1920, I invented a mental rhyming dictionary, to be used when a printed one is unavailable. Write down, having memorized them in advance, all the possible consonantal sounds in the language. Here is a convenient way:

Single Sounds	Double	Triple	Rare
Vowel (no consonant)			
B	BL, BR		BW
CH			
D	DR		DW
F	FL, FR		
G	GL, GR		GW
H	HW		
J			
K (C)	KL, KR, KW (QU)		
L			
M			
N			
P	PL, PR		PW
R			
S	SK (SC), SL, SM, SN, SP, ST, SW	SKR (SCR), SKW (SQU) SPL, SPR, STR	SV
SH	SHR		
T	TR, TW		
th (thin)	thR		
TH (this)			
V			VL
W			
Y			
Z			ZH, ZL

This gives 23 single sounds; 24 double sounds; 5 triple sounds; and 8 rare sounds, or 60 altogether. Now apply your sound to be rhymed to

this, and write out the rhymes that occur to you. Thus rhymes for *mate* would be found to include—I run down the list rapidly:

> ate, abate, date, fate, gate, hate, Kate, late, pate, rate, sate, tete-a-tete, wait (single sounds); freight, great, crate, plate, prate, skate, slate, state, trait (double sounds); straight (triple sounds). None of the rare sounds.

Be careful also to add next the minor accent rhymes, of the general type of:

> syndicate, conglomerate, abbreviate, indicate, intimate.

Then go ahead and use this specially prepared rhyming dictionary. The same can be done with 2-syllabled rhymes (as, for *backing*):

> hacking, jacking, lacking, packing, racking, sacking, tacking; blacking, clacking, cracking, quacking, slacking, smacking, stacking, tracking.

An omitted pair are found in *thwacking* (thW) and *whacking* (HW). The same thing can be done with triple or longer rhymes.

Written Exercises

1. Write from 8 to 20 lines of verse, using end rhyme and at least one example of internal rhyme to every two lines.

2. I shall not ask you to write any incorrect rhymes. If you find any in any of your poems, add the poem here, and correct the rhymes in the margin. Correcting rhymes may call for reslanting whole lines. Indicate how this is done, as well.

3. Find in your verse several examples of rhyme-induced rhymes; and correct them, even if this calls for entire reslanting of a stanza.

LESSON XIII

STANZA PATTERNS: COUPLETS

The Stanza

A stanza is one or more lines of verse, constituting a division of a poem or verse. A line is also called a *verse;* but, since verse also means the whole product of versification, the word *line* is clearer. A stanza corresponds, in versification, to a paragraph in prose; which may, of course, consist of one sentence, or many. A stanza may be indented, just as a prose paragraph is indented; or, more usually, divided from the other stanzas by a space.

A stanza is also, in popular speech, called a *verse*. In view of the various other meanings of *verse*, it is best to use *stanza*.

Any line or group of lines, which could constitute a stanza, also constitutes a complete poem or example of verse, when used alone.

Stanzas of One Line

A stanza of any length may be used formally, that is, as one of a number of similar units which constitute the poem, or which reappear regularly in it; or it may be used informally.

A rhymed alphabet, one line to each letter, and spaced stanza-wise, illustrates one type of formal one-line stanza, such as *Tom Thumb's Alphabet*, from *Mother Goose*:

> **A** was an Archer, and shot at a frog.

> **B** was a Butcher, and had a great dog.

> **C** was a Captain, all covered with lace, etc.

The fact that couplet rhyming (1, 1; 2, 2, etc.) is used to tie together each pair of one-line stanzas does not alter their nature. In *Judgment Day*, in my *Glory Road*, a formal one-line stanza introduces each successive section of the poem, of this general type:

> "Why did dey hang him, Mary?" . . . .
> "What did yo' boy do, Mary? . . . .
> "But why did dey hang him, Mary?"

A one-line stanza may be inserted informally at any place in a poem that the poet desires. It is sometimes used with great effectiveness as a last line, for contrast, or for summary.

Naturally, a one-line stanza cannot have end-rhyme within the stanza. It may have end-rhyme linking it to other stanzas (as in the rhymed alphabet referred to); and it may, of course, have internal rhyme.

One-Line Poems

If the poet wishes, he may embody his entire poem in one line. Walt Whitman did this repeatedly; and so did Sidney Lanier, in his *Poem Outlines;* as, for instance—

> Birth is but a folding of our wings.

Two-Line Stanzas; Couplets

A stanza of two lines is called a couplet. It was formerly called a distich. It may, of course, be free verse, accent verse, or metric verse; and it may be rhymed or unrhymed. This is true of stanzas of any length. An example of an unrhymed free verse couplet is:

> A young moon deserts the cloudy chase,
> And dreams in a garden of stars.
>
> *Day's End*, Gloria Goddard.

Elegiac Couplet

In classic prosody, an elegiac couplet consisted of a dactylic hexameter, followed by a so-called dactylic pentameter. Here is an example in English metric verse based on accent:

> In the hexameter rises the fountain's silvery column,
> In the pentameter aye falling in melody back.
>
> Translation from Schiller, Coleridge.

Couplet Rhyming

Where each pair of lines rhyme together, this is called couplet rhyming. Couplet rhyming may be used in couplet stanzas, in longer stanzas, or in verse that is stichic—that is, not divided into stanzas.

> Men like a girl with verve and grace, 1
> And do not mind a pretty face. 1

An example of couplet rhyming in longer stanzas is:

> Our principal exports, all labelled and packed, 1
> At the ends of the earth are delivered intact: 1
> Our soap or our salmon can travel in tins 2
> Between the two poles and as like as two pins; 2
> So that Lancashire merchants whenever they like 3
> Can water the beer of a man in Klondike 3
> Or poison the meat of a man in Bombay, 4
> And that is the meaning of Empire Day. 4
>
> *Songs of Education: Geography*, G. K. Chesterton.

The numbers to the right, indicating words which rhyme together, express the rhyme scheme—couplet rhyming, in this case.

Heroic Couplets

Iambic 5-foot lines, using couplet rhyming, are called heroic couplets. This was the favorite form of the ages of Dryden and Pope.

> Ill fares the land, to hastening ills a prey,   1
> Where wealth accumulates, and men decay.   1
>
> *The Deserted Village*, Oliver Goldsmith.

Miscellaneous

Couplets may be rhymed, but not by couplet rhyming. Here the rhyme-scheme links stanza to stanza:

> I once thought maps were things as fixed   1
> As stars, or faith, hope and charity.   2
>
> Each day, designs once so well known.   3
> Grow hopelessly tangled and intermixed.   1
>
> The maps I once thought fixed have grown   3
> As antiquated as B. C.   2
>
> *Maps*, Alan Dubois.

Couplets as complete poems are perennially popular, unrhymed or rhymed:

> Modern sex
> Is largely checks. . . .
>
> A husband, in the 19th Cent.,
> Was also called a permanent. . . .
>
> I wouldn't say that she is dumb;
> Her perfume always is *Pour l'Homme*. . . .
>
> Let her be fair, and not too bright,
> And with a green traffic light.
>
> *Solomon Says*, Alvin Winston.

Written Exercises

1. Write a poem, rhymed or unrhymed, of not more than 8 one-line stanzas.
2. Write at least two poems, of one line each.
3. Write not less than 8 lines of heroic couplets.
4. Write a poem of under 20 lines in couplet stanzas, couplet rhymed.
5. (Optional). Write a poem of not more than 16 lines, in couplets, and every line rhymed, but without couplet rhyming.

LESSON XIV

SAME. TERCETS OR TRIPLETS

Tercets or Triplets

Stanzas of three lines are called tercets or triplets. In early Wales and Ireland, they were called triads. The tercet has never become as common in English as the couplet or the quatrain. Like all the stanza lengths, it may be free verse, or metric verse, or formal accent verse:

> I have had playmates, I have had companions,
> In my days of childhood, in my joyful school-days;
> All, all are gone, the old familiar faces.
>
> *The Old Familiar Faces*, Charles Lamb.

In this formal use, the third line above is repeated unaltered as the third line of each tercet, which makes an effective use of the refrain. Again, tercets may be rhymed or unrhymed.

Rhyme in the Tercet

There are four possible end-rhyme schemes within the tercet: 1, 1, 1; 1, 1, 2; 1, 2, 1; 1, 2, 2. Here are typical examples:

> Little eyes of brown,   1
> In your dainty gown,   1
> Let us go to town!   1
>
> There are things to do,   2
> There are joys to woo,   2
> Waiting you and me.   3
>
> Joy and melody,   3
> Posies for your gown,   1
> Laughter light and free,   3
>
> Love, and ecstasy!   3
> Little eyes of brown,   1
> Let us go to town.   1
>
> *Invitation*, Carveth Wells.

Here the tercets, regarded independently, rhyme in the order given above. But, with the rhymes interlocked, note that the numbering changes. Starting with any of the four rhyme-schemes above, it is possible to interlock the successive tercets, by repeating rhyme-sounds from stanza to stanza.

Terza Rima

The most famous interlocking of tercet stanzas by rhyme occurs in a form called terza rima, using the third of the patterns given above (1, 2, 1). Here the rhyme scheme proceeds: 1, 2, 1; 2, 3, 2; 3, 4, 3; 4, 5, 4, etc. As it originated in Italy, terza rima was not divided into stanzas, while the end of the poem or canto (a long portion of a poem) was a couplet, using as its rhyme-sound the terminal sound of the central line of the preceding tercet: thus, if *n* be the last rhyme sound, n-1, n, n-1; n, n. Thus terza rima is a definite form of chain verse, the rhyming forming the link. Dante used it throughout his *Divina Commedia*. In English, it is usually written in 5-foot iambic lines.

Shelley's *Ode to the West Wind* uses terza rima, in 14-line units, broken up into tercets and the concluding couplet:

If I were a dead leaf thou mightest bear;	1
If I were a swift cloud to fly with thee;	2
A wave to pant beneath thy power, and share	1
The impulse of thy strength, only less free	2
Than thou, O uncontrollable! If even	3
I were as in my boyhood, and could be	2
The comrade of thy wanderings over heaven,	3
As then, when to outstrip thy skyey speed	4
Scarce seemed a vision—I would ne'er have striven	3
As thus with thee in prayer in my sore need.	4
O! lift me as a wave, a leaf, a cloud!	5
I fall upon the thorns of life! I bleed!	4
A heavy weight of hours has chained and bowed	5
One too like thee—tameless, and swift, and proud.	5

This 14-line form is sometimes used as a separate poem, usually without stanzaic division. It is at times called a terza rima sonnet.

Triplets as Complete Poems

Like all other stanzaic forms, triplets of any sort may be used as separate poems. These may veer from free verse:

> Youth is the happy hour
> When we are still young enough
> To choose our own mistakes.

to the most formal accent or metric verse.

Written Exercises

1. Write three tercets as complete poems, one in free verse; one in accent verse; one in any meter.

2. Write a poem, not more than 24 lines, in tercets. Either have it rhymed, or use one or more lines as a refrain, as Charles Lamb did in the example quoted.

3. Write a sonnet in terza rima.

LESSON XV

SAME. STANZAS OF FOUR LINES: THE QUATRAIN

The Quatrain

A stanza or poem of four lines is called a quatrain. This is the most popular stanza length in English versification. It may be unrhymed or rhymed; formal or informal; free verse, accent verse, or metric verse, with line-length and choice of meter as the poet desires.

An effective formal quatrain stanza in iambic blank verse is found in William Collins' *Ode to Evening:*

> Or, if chill blustering winds, or driving rain,
> Prevent my willing feet, be mine the hut
> That, from the mountain's side,
> Views wilds and swelling floods,
>
> And hamlets brown, and dim-discovered spires,
> And hears their simple bell, and marks o'er all
> Thy dewy fingers draw
> The gradual dusky veil.

The form here is two 5-foot iambic lines, followed by two 3-foot iambic lines; and all unrhymed. Any poet is always at liberty to invent his own forms, which may gain the stamp of popular approval and wide popularity and use.

Ballad Measure

The most famous of the English quatrain forms is ballad measure, which we have found to be 4, 3, 4, 3 feet in accent verse, rhymed 1, 2, 3, 2:

> In Ireland, far over the sea,   1
> There dwelleth a bonny king;   2
> And with him a young and comely knight,   3
> Men call him Sir Cauline.   2

> *Ballad of Sir Cauline,* Anonymous.

King and *Cauline* were intended to rhyme, however crudely the device was first used. As natural English accent verse suffered a long eclipse from metric verse, ballad measure tended to become iambic, even in the hands of Coleridge, who at least faintly sensed accent verse, and sometimes used it:

> Day after day, day after day,   1
> We stuck, nor breath nor motion;   2
> As idle as a painted ship   3
> Upon a painted ocean.   2
>
> *The Rime of the Ancient Mariner*, S. T. Coleridge.

Alternate Rhyming

Popular as a quatrain rhyme-scheme is alternate rhyming. When done in 5-foot iambic verse, this is called the *elegiac stanza:*

> Beneath those rugged elms, that yew-tree's shade,   1
> Where heaves the turf in many a moldering heap,   2
> Each in his narrow cell for ever laid,   1
> The rude forefathers of the hamlet sleep.   2
>
> *Elegy Written in a Country Churchyard*, Thomas Gray.

The alternately rhymed quatrain is far more common in four or even 3-foot lines, with added briskness and vivacity:

> Most children, in their early days,   1
> Will irritate their parents plenty;   2
> But this is trivial, to the ways,   1
> Their parents irk *them* when they're twenty.   2
>
> *Reversable*, Alfred Turner.

The In Memoriam Stanza

A 4-foot iambic quatrain rhymed 1, 2, 2, 1 was chosen by Tennyson for his *In Memoriam*, and this gives its name to this stanza:

> O, yet we trust that somehow good   1
> Will be the final goal of ill,   2
> To pangs of nature, sins of will,   2
> Defects of doubt, and taints of blood.   1

An entirely different effect is produced, when shorter or longer lines are used, or different meters, accent verse, etc. It would still be *In Memoriam* rhyming, but no longer the *In Memoriam* stanza.

The Rubáiyát Stanza

A 5-foot iambic quatrain, rhymed 1, 1, 2, 1, was chosen by Edward Fitzgerald for his rendition of the Rubáiyát (or quatrains) of Omar Khayyám; and this is called the Rubáiyát stanza.

And that inverted Bowl they call the Sky,	1
Whereunder crawling cooped we live and die,	1
Lift not your hands to *It* for help—for It	2
As impotently moves as you or I.	1

Possible Quatrain Rhyme-Schemes

With only two lines of the quatrain rhymed, and two unrhymed, there are six possible rhyme-schemes for the quatrain: 1, 2, 3, 2 (as in ballad measure); 1, 1, 2, 3; 1, 2, 2, 3; 1, 2, 3, 3, each containing an example of couplet rhyming; and 1, 2, 1, 3 and 1, 2, 3, 1.

With three lines of the quatrain rhymed together, and one line unrhymed, there are four possible rhyme-schemes: 1, 1, 1, 2 (found in some of the old ballads; often the 2 rhyme being repeated from stanza to stanza as a refrain); 1, 1, 2, 1 (as in the Rubáiyát stanza); 1, 2, 1, 1 and 1, 2, 2, 2.

With all four lines of the quatrain rhymed, there are four possible patterns: 1, 1, 1, 1; couplet rhyming, 1, 1, 2, 2, which is very popular; alternate rhyming, 1, 2, 1, 2; and the In Memoriam stanza, 1, 2, 2, 1.

Quatrains Common in Hymns

Three popular hymn quatrains are:

Long Meter: four 4-foot iambic lines.
Common Meter: four iambic lines, of 4, 3, 4, 3 feet. (The same as the developed ballad meter.)
Short Meter: four iambic lines, of 3, 3, 4, 3, feet.

Any rhyming is permitted in any of these, though Long Meter is commonly rhymed 1, 2, 3, 2. All of these may be used as doubled quatrains, or eight lines.

Quatrains as Complete Poems

Quatrains are exceedingly popular as individual poems. These may be free, accent or metric verse, of any meter; with lines of any desired length; unrhymed or rhymed. An example is:

> The golf links lie so near the mill
> That almost every day
> The laboring children can look out
> And see the men at play.
>
> Sarah N. Cleghorn.

You are now equipped with an understanding of the proper vocabulary, the word and idiom choice, the types, the rhythms, the device of rhyme, and the simpler stanza forms, of poetry and verse. This is far more than many accepted poets ever achieve. If you have absorbed the first fifteen lessons, you may regard yourself as graduated from the Foundations of Versification Course.

Written Exercises

1. Write three quatrains that are complete poems: one in free verse, one in accent verse, and one in rhymed metric verse, using any preferred rhyme-scheme.

2. Write at least one example of the In Memoriam and of the Rubáiyát stanzas.

3. Write a poem of not over 20 lines in ballad measure.

4. Write a poem, not over 20 lines, in alternately rhymed quatrains.

PART II

ADVANCED VERSIFICATION

LESSON I

STANZA PATTERNS OF FIVE AND SIX LINES

The Cinquain

A stanza or poem of five lines is called a cinquain. It was formerly called a quintain. As in all stanza lengths, it may be in accent, free or metric verse; of any meter or combination of meters; unrhymed, or with any rhyme scheme. The possible rhyme-schemes in stanzas longer than quatrains are left to each individual poet to work out for himself. And there may always be interlinking with subsequent stanzas, through rhyme-sound repetition. All these things are true of all stanzas.

One of the possible variations is used by Shelley in his *To a Skylark:*

All the earth and air	1
With thy voice is loud,	2
As, when night is bare,	1
From one lonely cloud	2
The moon rains out her beams, and heaven is overflowed.	2

The rhythm here is four 3-foot trochaic lines, followed by a 6-foot iambic line. A 6-foot iambic line, which still dominates French verse, is called an Alexandrine. It was often used in English versification to terminate a group of unrhymed or rhymed iambic 5-foot lines.

This same rhyme-scheme is followed in the simplest and most logical of all cinquain rhyme-schemes: a quatrain of 4- or 5-foot accent or iambic verse, alternately rhymed, followed by a fifth line rhyming on the *2* sound: 1, 2, 1, 2, 2.

It will repay the effort to study the rhyme-scheme of Poe's *To Helen,* which contains 3 cinquains. The number of feet differ from stanza to stanza: 4, 4, 4, 4, 3; 4, 4, 4, 3, 3; 4, 4, 4, 4, 2. Even more significant is the fact that the three rhyme-schemes differ: 1, 2, 1, 2, 2; 1, 2, 1, 2, 1; 1, 2, 2, 1, 2. The great masters never hesitate to alter the stanzaic

rhyme-scheme, when this will improve the effectiveness and naturalness of the product.

Cinquains as Complete Poems

Any form of five or more lines, which may be used for a stanza,
may also be used as a complete poem. One of the most famous of these
is Adelaide Crapsey's form, called simply the cinquain. It consists of
1, 2, 3, 4, and 1 iambic feet, usually unrhymed:

> The night
> Brings rest to all,
> And sleep, and easing dreams:
> To all but those who love. To these,
> High love.
>
> *Night*, Lois Lodge.

A more famous cinquain form is the limerick, which will be reached
later under Poem Patterns. The Japanese tanka, found under the
same heading, is also a cinquain, or longer.

The Sestet

Stanzas or poems of six lines are called sestets, or sextets. The
term is commonly used to apply to the concluding six lines of a sonnet.
It may be used in free verse, or in accent verse, as in Gloria Goddard's
We Walk Together:

> Gibraltar's steep unyielding ways,
> Or the stabbing beauty of plundered Greece;
> Tossed on a bleakly troubled sea,
> Or lulled by blue Sorrento's hills,
> Always our binary bright in the sky,
> Always we walk together.

The Venus and Adonis Stanza

The most logical development of the sestet, in English versification,
combines the alternately rhymed quatrain and the couplet, the latter
used terminally. In 5-foot iambics, this is the stanza used by Shakespeare in *Venus and Adonis:*

> Thus he that overrul'd I oversway'd,   1
> Leading him prisoner in a red-rose chain;   2
> Strong-temper'd steel his stronger strength obey'd, 1
> Yet was he servile to my coy disdain.   2
> O, be not proud, nor brag not of thy might   3
> For mastering her that foil'd the god of fight!   3

A far swifter movement is obtained by using this rhyme-scheme with 4-foot iambs, or, better still, with 4-foot accent verse. And, since the metric and other versification possibilities of each line are limited only by the poet's choice, the possible sestet patterns are practically unlimited.

Tail-Rhyme Stanzas

Here is a favorite stanza of Burns:

Wee, sleekit, cow-rin', tim'rous beastie, **1**
O what a panic's in thy breastie! **1**
Thou need na start awa sae hasty, **1**
   Wi' bickering brattle!   **2**
I wad be laith to rin and chase thee **1**
   Wi' murd'ring pattle!   **2**

This is predominantly iambic, with a rhythmic pattern of 4, 4, 4, 2, 4, 2 feet. The dominant feature of such stanzas is the presence of two or more short lines rhyming together, and serving as "tails" to the various parts of the stanza. Whittier's *The Last Leaf* uses this rhyme scheme, 1, 1, 2, 3, 3, 2, with the *1* and *3* lines 4-foot iambic, and the *2* lines 2-foot trochaic—another instance of tail-rhyme. For longer instances of tail-rhyme, see Michael Drayton's *Agincourt* (rhyme-scheme 1, 1, 1, 2, 3, 3, 3, 2), Tennyson's *The Lady of Shalott* and *The Charge of the Light Brigade*, etc.

Written Exercises

1. Write a poem of not over 20 lines in cinquains, using a uniform stanza scheme, as to rhyme and rhythm, throughout.

2. Write the same, varying the rhyme scheme in each stanza: and the rhythm scheme also, if this may be done with advantage.

3. Write an unrhymed cinquain in the Adelaide Crapsey pattern.

4. Write a rhymed cinquain in the same, using any desired rhyme scheme.

5. Write a free verse sestet as a complete poem.

6. Write at least one Venus and Adonis stanza.

7. Write a poem in tail-rhyme, the stanzas uniform but of any desired length.

LESSON II

SAME. STANZAS OF SEVEN LINES AND LONGER

The Septet
A stanza or poem of seven lines is called a septet. It has the same complete liberty as to rhythm, rhyme and line-length that other groups of lines have.

Rhyme Royal
The most famous septet is called Rhyme Royal, and consists of 5-foot iambic lines: a quatrain alternately rhyming; an added fifth line rhyming on the *2* sound; with a terminal couplet, couplet-rhymed. Chaucer used this in about 14,000 lines of his poetry; John Masefield revived it far later, for narrative verse. The pattern is:

What of these many glories will endure?   1
    Not life; it treads the dead-end path of death.   2
Not beauty; only while vision lasts is it sure,   1
    And it is tombed before the end of breath.   2
    But I have heard this word from Ashtoreth: 2
Love must endure. Its seed, its song, will never   3
Darken to night; its glory lives forever.   3

Hymn to Ashtoreth, Claire Clare.

The Canopus Stanza
The internal couplet tended to interrupt the flow of the narrative; the terminal couplet stopped it. In 1920 appeared a stanza, in *Canopus*, reprinted in my *The Glory Road*, which used the same number of rhymes, but eliminated both couplets. Gamaliel Bradford has called this the best stanza form for narrative verse ever invented in English:

Without a word they knew it. His face burning,   1
    "We can return." But they knew, at his word,   2
That there are paths that do not know returning,   1
    And as their downward-stumbling footsteps stirred   2
The stony steep, the roadway dust, the gray   3
    And morning hush, each rustle made or heard   2
Sang to them they had found the starrier way.   3

The Octave: Ottava Rima
In dealing with stanzas of eight and more lines, only those will be singled out for treatment that have earned an important place in Eng-

lish versification. Any poet can arrive at the others, by combining such units as the couplet, tercet, and quatrain, in any preferred rhythm and rhyme scheme.

Ottava rima is an Italian stanza, consisting of six 5-foot iambic lines rhymed alternately, terminated by a couplet of these lines with couplet rhyming.

Alas! how deeply painful is all payment!	1
Take lives, take wives, take aught except men's purses,	2
As Machiavel shows those in purple raiment,	1
Such is the shortest way to general curses.	2
They hate a murderer much less than a claimant	1
On that sweet ore which every body nurses.—	2
Kill a man's family, and he may brook it,	3
But keep your hands out of his breeches' pocket.	3

Don Juan, Lord Byron.

This is completely in the ancient English tradition: an alternately rhymed quatrain, two added lines in the same pattern, terminated by a rhymed couplet. Certain authorities, however, always pointed out that, as in the case of Rhyme Royal, the couplet seems "to put on the brakes with a jar"—James Russell Lowell's expressive phrase.

The Spenserian Stanza
This is sufficiently treated in the fore part of the book.

Refrains
Any of the stanza forms can have, substituted for any part of them, or added on at the end, a refrain, repeated from stanza to stanza without variation, or with minor or major modifications, so long as the element of repetition continues. This device appears effectively in *Maryland, My Maryland; Rock Me to Sleep, Mother;* Poe's *The Raven,* and especially in all songs with separate refrains or choruses.

Variations in Stanza Patterns
We have already seen how Poe varied his stanza pattern in *To Helen.* In such a poem as *The Raven,* he preserved his stanza form throughout. Many other of his greater poems change it, whenever in his opinion this increases the effectiveness of his presentation. Thus the four stanzas of *To One in Paradise* have these rhyme schemes:

1, 2, 1, 2, 3, 2; 1, 2, 1, 2, 1, 2, 1; 1, 2, 2, 1, 2, 1, 2; 1, 2, 1, 2, 1, 2.

The first and last stanzas are similar in construction and mood, and frame the two inner stanzas, which in turn are in approximately the same form and mood. My *Gwine to Hebb'n* elaborates this idea still

further. The first and final stanzas have this rhyme scheme: 1, 2, 3, 4; 1, 5, 3, 4. All except the 4th and 8th lines, in addition, have either central internal repetition or rhyme. This first pattern is followed by an 8-line stanza containing refrain, rhymed 1, 2, 1, 2, 1, 1, 1, 2, the lines rhymed on *2* being brief identical refrains. This pattern with refrain appears as the second and fourth stanzas. Midway of the poem comes still a third pattern, a sestet including refrain, rhymed 1, 2, 1, 1, 1, 2, the *2* lines being the refrain.

A further progression in the direction of free stanza variation is found in Wordsworth's *Ode on the Intimations of Immortality*, where the stanzas range from 8 to 39 lines; and the line-length from 2 to 5 iambic feet. All poems referred to should be read and studied. Still further variation would come from an intermingling of free, accent, and differently metered stanzas. These are most effective when they mirror the changing or contrasting moods of the poem.

Written Exercises

1. Write at least 3 stanzas of Rhyme Royal.

2. Write a poem of seven or more lines, using the Canopus stanza throughout.

3. Write at least one example of ottava rima.

4. Write at least one Spenserian stanza.

5. Write a poem embodying refrain inside your stanza form.

6. Start work upon a poem, not over 40 lines, using three separate stanza patterns, skilfully interwoven. Finish this before Lesson V is reached.

LESSON III

STANZAS IN THE ODE

The Odes of Keats

The eight stanzas of Keats' *To a Nightingale* follow this pattern:

Thou wast not born for death, immortal Bird!	1
No hungry generations tread thee down;	2
The voice I heard this passing night was heard	1
In ancient days by emperor and clown:	2
Perhaps the self-same song that found a path	3
Through the sad heart of Ruth, when, sick for home,	4
She stood in tears amid the alien corn;	5
The same that oft-times hath	3
Charm'd magic casements, opening on the foam	4
Of perilous seas, in faery lands forlorn.	5

The devices here repay enormous study. The rhyme-scheme is simple: an alternately rhymed iambic quatrain, five feet to the line; followed by a sestet using one of the accepted sestet rhyme-schemes for the Italian sonnet: 3, 4, 5, 3, 4, 5. But the omission of two expected feet in each 8th line is very effective. Barring three archaisms, the stanza is a splendid example of the sort of vocabulary to use—each word precise, specific, brief and pithy; and, best of all, evocative of overtones that are highly emotional. Consider the natural overtones to these words:

> death, immortal, bird, hungry, tread, night,
> ancient, emperor, song, sad heart, Ruth, home,
> tears, magic, foam, perilous seas.

It is no wonder that the three concluding lines here, with three lines from Coleridge's *Kubla Khan*,

> A savage place! as holy and enchanted
> As e'er beneath a waning moon was haunted
> By woman wailing for her demon lover.

were chosen by Kipling and others as the peaks of English poetry. In addition to the evocative quality of the words used, this also illustrates assonance (savage, enchanted); phonetic syzygy, as in waning. haunted; and alliteration in the last line.

On a Grecian Urn, by Keats, has as its normal stanza the same 10-line pattern, with, however, the 8th line filled out to a 5-foot iambic line, like the rest. But only the 3rd and 4th stanzas have the sestet rhyme-scheme given above: 3, 4, 5, 3, 4, 5. The patterns for the 1st, 2nd and 5th stanzas are: 3, 4, 5, 4, 3, 5; 3, 4, 5, 3, 5, 4; with a return to 3, 4, 5, 4, 3, 5 at the end. The three stanzas of *To Psyche* have respectively 22, 26, and 18 lines: the norm being 5-foot iambic, with lines ranging down to two feet, and with different rhyme schemes for each stanza. The three magnificent stanzas *To Autumn* have 11 lines each; starting with a quatrain rhymed 1, 2, 1, 2, in 5-foot iambics; followed by 7 lines, rhymed 3, 4, 5, 4, 3, 3, 5 in the first stanza, and 3, 4, 5, 3, 4, 4, 5 in the last two. *On Melancholy* returns to the 10-line stanza, opening with the inevitable alternately-rhymed 5-foot iambic quatrain, and with the first two sestets rhymed 3, 4, 5, 3, 4, 5 and the final one rhymed 3, 4, 5, 4, 3, 5. For these greater odes, then, the pattern of Keats is simple: in 5-foot iambic lines as a rule, the rhyme scheme opening on an alternately rhymed quatrain, followed by a sestet (or, in one case, a septet) on three rhyme sounds, always

opening 3, 4, 5; always closing on the *5* sound; and with variations on the final tercet or quatrain portion of this final sestet or septet.

Odic stanzas of far greater complexity could be invented. But the greater effectiveness comes from using the more familiar units, the iambic 4- or 5-foot line, the quatrain rhymed alternately, the couplet, and the naturalized 3, 4, 5, 3, 4, 5 sestet rhyme, including variations. This will be true, until another form becomes as familiar and pleasing in our versification.

Spacing Rhymes

As a rule, rhymes should not be placed too far apart. In the old ballads, where the rhyme-scheme was 1, 2, 3, 2, the two rhyming sounds occur only 7 feet apart. The same is true, when the quatrain is rhymed 1, 2, 1, 2. In the elegiac stanza, of a 5-foot iambic quatrain, the rhymes are 10 feet apart.

A ballad otherwise effective, as Sidney Lanier's *The Revenge of Hamish*, loses much of its effectiveness because of the overlong spacing of the rhymes, as in this example:

> And gazed hungrily o'er, and the blood from his back
>   drip-dripped in the brine,   1
> And a sea-hawk flung down a skeleton fish as he flew,   2
> And the mother stared white on the waste of blue,   2
> And the wind drove a cloud to seaward, and the sun
>   began to shine.   1

Here the rhyme-sound *blue* is only four feet, of 11 syllables, from its rhyming mate, *flew*. But *shine* is 16 feet, of 41 syllables, away from *brine*.

In light verse and even in serious poetry, there are devices by which suspense can be created by holding up a terminal rhyme. See the last stanza of the White Knight's song from Lewis Carroll's *Alice in Wonderland* as a case in point. Here 51 feet, of 101 syllables, separate *weight* from the terminal *gate;* yet this gives increased suspense, climax, and effectiveness. The usual rule is to have your rhyming mates fairly close to each other.

Symmetry in Poems

For all the merit in stanza-pattern variation, when used by a master, mere variation for variation's sake is almost always harmful. The tighter the pattern, the more disturbing minor variations can be. A poem in quatrains, with the odd-numbered lines having double or feminine rhymes, and the even-numbered lines having single or mas-

culine lines, can be spoiled entirely by letting the last stanza have double rhymes throughout. A poem in quatrains rhymed 1, 2, 1, 2 can be spoiled completely by having one stanza rhymed 1, 2, 2, 1, or even 1, 2, 3, 2. Unless, of course, the thing to be said is so powerful, that the variation in technique is not even noticed.

The same thing applies to varying the number of lines in stanzas of formal pattern; and especially to varying the lengths of lines from stanza to stanza. As, for instance, using (without good reason) a 4-foot or a 6-foot line in the middle of a 5-foot pattern, whether blank verse or rhymed. As a rule, symmetry is extremely important, in any sort of formal verse. The ear and the eye come to expect a certain pattern, and resent any unnecessary break in it. The effect may be as gruesome as a three-legged dog or a two-headed calf.

Written Exercises

1. Write an ode, of at least 30 lines, using some formal pattern, with variations such as Keats used, if these are desired. In view of the preferred informality of most modern poetry, the subject chosen may be light, and the product light verse, if desired.

LESSON IV

STANZA-PATTERN DEVELOPMENT. LIGHT VERSE. SONG LYRICS

Stanza-Pattern Development in English Verse

In review, consider the following development:
1. The ballad. 4-accent verse.
    a. Beginning in couplets, rhymed 1, 1.
    b. Couplet interrupted by refrains, rhymed 1, 2R, 1, 2R.
    c. Quatrain, rhymed 1, 2, 3, 2; at times, 1, 2, 1, 2.
2. Cinquain pattern, 4- or 5-foot iambics, rhymed 1, 2, 1, 2, 2.
3. Venus and Adonis stanza, rhymed 1, 2, 1, 2, 3, 3.
4. Rhyme Royal, rhymed 1, 2, 1, 2, 2, 3, 3.
5. Ottava Rima, rhymed 1, 2, 1, 2, 1, 2, 3, 3.
6. Spenserian stanza, rhymed 1, 2, 1, 2, 2, 3, 2, 3, 3 (last line an Alexandrine).
7. Keatsian ode (normal pattern), rhymed 1, 2, 1, 2, 3, 4, 5, 3, 4, 5.
8. Shakespearean sonnet, 1, 2, 1, 2; 3, 4, 3, 4; 5, 6, 5, 6; 7, 7.
A comparison of all these forms shows the simplicity of their con-

struction from such simple units as the rhymed couplet and the alternately rhymed quatrain.

Stanzas in Light Verse

In poetry, where the appeal is to the deeper emotions, it is clear that this cannot primarily come from the mere ornaments of verse, rhyme and so on. The important thing is what the poem has to say, not how it says it. Hence, as a rule, such ornaments as rhyming should be entirely unobtrusive; and, in reading aloud, the ornaments should never be loud-pedalled, but if anything should be treated so naturally that the listener may not even be aware of them, except as a faint addition to the pleasure. The tremendous emotional appeal of Negro spirituals, some of which have no rhyme at all, is a case in point. The more matured poetry of Shakespeare, and the poetry of Robert Frost and a few more, indicate the same thing.

In proportion as poetry emphasizes the ornaments, it tends to be lighter in mood. Thus double rhyme should be used at best only sparingly in serious poetry; and triple rhyme hardly ever. But when the progression has arrived at light verse, whose purpose emphasizes to please or amuse, the process is reversed. Since pleasure is given by the use of rhyme and other ornaments, increasingly by repeated, surprising and ridiculous rhymes, the rhyming should not only be exceptionally precise; it should be obtrusive and loud-pedalled. This brings us to such a masterpiece as W. S. Gilbert's finale to Act I in *Iolanthe*. Among the dozen brilliant stanza patterns are:

> Iolanthe (to Strephon) When tempests wreck thy bark
> And all is drear and dark,
> If thou shouldst need an Ark,
> I'll give thee one!
> Phyllis (to Tolloller) I heard the minx remark,
> She'd meet him after dark
> Inside St. James's Park,
> And give him one!

Then comes another pattern, using rhymes from a foreign language:

> Lord Mountararat: This gentleman is seen
> With a maid of seventeen,
> A-taking of his *dolce far niente;*
> And wonders he'd achieve,
> For he asks us to believe
> She's his mother—and he's nearly five-and-
> twenty!

Then comes a splendid use of accent verse:

Strephon : The lady of my love has caught me talking to another—
Peers:　　Oh, fie! Strephon is a rogue.
Strephon: I tell her very plainly that the lady is my mother—
Peers:　　Taradiddle, taradiddle, tol lol lay!
Strephon: She won't believe my statement, and declares we must be
　　　　　parted
　　　　　Because on a career of double-dealing I have started,
　　　　　Then gives her hand to one of these, and leaves me broken-
　　　　　hearted—
Peers:　　Taradiddle, taradiddle, tol lol lay!

From this 4-accent verse, the Lord Chancellor snaps into 1-foot anapests, with triple mosaic rhyme:

> Go away, madam;
> I should say, madam,
> You display, madam,
> 　Shocking taste.
> It is rude, madam,
> To intrude, madam,
> With your brood, madam,
> 　Brazen-faced.

He retorts to the Fairy Queen in her iambic pattern, structurally akin
to the limerick:

> A plague on this vagary,
> I'm in a nice quandary!
> 　Of hasty tone
> 　With dames unknown
> I ought to be more chary;
> It seems that she's a fairy
> From Andersen's library
> 　When I took her for
> 　The proprietor
> Of a Ladies' Seminary!

And so the tricky patterns go on, to the delicious climax. By all odds,
the poet who wishes to qualify for the heights in light verse must
become familiar with the best of Gilbert.

　The same is true of Guy Wetmore Carryl, an American whose
Fables for the Frivolous, *Mother Goose for Grown-Ups*, and *Grimm
Tales Made Gay*, have never been excelled for perfection of intricate
stanza construction and witty rhyming—and all done as naturally as

good prose speech. Other masters of light verse include, in differing moods, C. S. Calverley, F. P. Adams, Ted Robinson, Samuel Hoffenstein, Ogden Nash, and Dorothy Parker. The stanzaic forms of Phyllis McGinley also will repay study.

Song Lyrics

Lyrics to be set to music are ordinarily of two main groups, concert songs and popular songs. In writing either, the poet should familiarize himself with the preferred current patterns, and not depart too widely from these, if he wishes acceptance and popularity. Here the word-usage should always be natural. But triple mosaic rhymes are far more acceptable here than in serious poetry (as, best of it; rest of it; adoring you, imploring you, etc.). Moreover, in both types of songs (with the exception of comic patter songs), the words chosen should be those that are most singable: especially words using *m*, *n*, *l* or *r* for the rhyme sound, especially when coupled with long *ah*, long *O*, long *I*, long *A*, or short *ah*. If these are done, and some acceptable pattern is used, the success of the song will as a rule depend upon the wideness of its emotional appeal.

Written Exercises

1. Write 2 couplets in light verse.
2. Write at least one quatrain in light verse.
3. Write not more than 32 lines in light verse, with a stanza of the general complexity of one of the Gilbert stanzas quoted, this stanza being used throughout.
4. Write a concert song lyric. This may have a refrain, if desired.
5. Write a popular song lyric. This may consist only of an extended chorus (as in *South of the Border*, for instance).

LESSON V

CLASSICAL SCANSION. SAPPHICS

Classical Hexameters

The Greek and Roman classical hexameter was a far more complicated line than the English iambic pentameter. First of all, the syllables were long or short, not accented or unaccented. The rules for determining whether a syllable was long or short were complicated, and can best be learned from some textbook on classical scansion, or some authoritative article on it. Classical meters, based on the length

or duration of syllables, have never been effectively acclimatized in English verse.

The Greek dactylic hexameter, later used by the Romans, had six feet. Its first four must be either dactyls or spondees; the fifth must be a dactyl; the sixth must be a trochee or a spondee.

In English, such hexameters are most effectively written in accent verse: that is, accent dactyls, spondees and trochees replace the durational ones. This was the method used by Longfellow in his *Evangeline:*

This is the | forest pri- | meval, the | murmuring | pines and the | hemlocks.

It should be noted that the classic hexameter also has a break or cesura midway of the line, here indicated by the comma.

The Elegiac Couplet

The Greek elegiac couplet consisted of a dactylic hexameter, followed by a so-called pentameter. In this, the 1st and 2nd feet, and the 4th and 5th, were the same as the first two feet of the classic hexameter. The 3rd foot consisted of one long syllable; the 6th, of one long syllable or one short syllable. When written in English, this is usually written in accent feet.

Classic Hendecasyllabics

A hendecasyllabic is a line of 11 syllables. The classic hendecasyllabic was composed of a spondee, a dactyl, and three trochees. In accent verse in English, this would give:

′ ′ | ′ ⌣ ⌣ | ′ ⌣ | ′ ⌣ | ′ ⌣

Here is how Tennyson treated the hendecasyllabic in English:

O you | chorus of | indo- | lent re- | viewers,
Irresponsible, indolent reviewers,
Look, I come to the test, a tiny poem
All composed in a meter of Catullus.

Sapphics

Sapphics, named after Sappho of Lesbos, were quatrains with this pattern: three lines of equal length, 5 feet each: a trochee, a spondee or trochee, a dactyl, a trochee, a spondee or trochee (except that the third line required a trochee in its second foot, forbidding a spondee); followed by a briefer fourth line, of two feet: a dactyl and a trochee. Here is the pattern, in English accent verse:

$$\text{′}\smile \left| \begin{array}{c} \text{′ ′} \\ \text{or} \\ \text{′}\smile \end{array} \right| \text{′}\smile\smile \left| \text{′}\smile \right| \begin{array}{c} \text{′ ′} \\ \text{or} \\ \text{′}\smile \end{array}$$

$$\text{′}\smile \left| \begin{array}{c} \text{′ ′} \\ \text{or} \\ \text{′}\smile \end{array} \right| \text{′}\smile\smile \left| \text{′}\smile \right| \begin{array}{c} \text{′ ′} \\ \text{or} \\ \text{′}\smile \end{array}$$

$$\text{′}\smile \left| \text{′}\smile \right| \text{′}\smile\smile \left| \text{′}\smile \right| \begin{array}{c} \text{′ ′} \\ \text{or} \\ \text{′}\smile \end{array}$$

$$\text{′}\smile\smile \left| \text{′}\smile \right.$$

Here is a light verse of accent Sapphics in English, from George Canning's *The Friend of Humanity and the Needy Knife-Grinder:*

> Needy knife-grinder! Whither are you going?
> Rough is the road; your wheel is out of order—
> Bleak blows the blast;—your hat has got a hole in't.
>   So have your breeches. . . .
>
> I give you sixpence! I will see you damned first,—
> Wretch! whom no sense of wrongs can rouse to vengeance!
> Sordid, unfeeling, reprobate, degraded,
>   Spiritless outcast!

No matter how amusing this may be, only the 4th and 8th lines accurately fit the Sapphic pattern. Let this be regarded, then, technically, as a Horrible Example. If you wish to write Sapphics in English accent verse, at least follow the rigid pattern.

Written Exercises

1. Write not more than 12 lines in English accent hexameters, otherwise following the Greek model.

2. Write 12 or more lines of accent Sapphics, without rhyme.

3. Write 12 or more lines of accent Sapphics, using rhyme or consonance (which will be taken up next). Note that the rhymes must be 2-syllabled, either following the pattern of the trochee or of the spondee.

LESSON VI

SOUND REPETITION AS ORNAMENT

Repetition of Words and Groups of Words

Two major elements of a word are its rhythm and its sound. We have found that the required convention for verse and poetry in Eng-

lish is rhythmic repetition. Very early, sound repetition was added, as an ornament: although this is not necessary for poetry.

The first and most natural sound repetition to be used was the repetition of an entire word or of groups of words. This required far less ingenuity than repeating parts merely of a word or words. Such repetition is natural in prose, especially for emphasis:

> Help! Help! Help! . . . .

> Come on, boys! Come on! Hurry up and come on! . . .
> Give me liberty, or give me death! . . . .
> I love your face, I love your smile, I love your heart.

This device was carried over naturally into verse.

> I couldn't hear nobody pray, O Lord,
> Couldn't hear nobody pray.
> Away down yonder on-a my knees,
> And I couldn't hear nobody pray.
>
> > > Negro spiritual.

> Then I wish I was in Dixie, hooray, hooray!
> In Dixieland I'll take my stand
> To live and die in Dixie.
> Away, away, away down South in Dixie!
> Away, away, away down South in Dixie.
>
> > > *Dixie,*
> > > Dan Emmett.

Notice that this has no end-rhyme. There is internal rhyme (Dixieland, stand; hooray, away), but no end-rhyme. Yet the repeated repetition of words and groups of words give it at least the effectiveness of end-rhyme.

Many of the Negro spirituals depend on this as their sole ornament, with tremendous emotional effectiveness. One famous song consists merely of an embroidery of these lines, by repetition alone:

> Sometimes I feel like a motherless child,
> A long way from home;
> True believer, a long way from home.

> Sometimes I feel like an eagle in the air, etc.

Another elaborate one merely repeats this:

> Somebody's knocking at your door.
> O, sinner, why don't you answer?
> Knocks like Jesus.

Yet the effect of the multiple repetitions gives the impression of elaborate stanzaic construction, which in this case comes merely from repetition of words and groups of words.

This type of repetition is almost universal in all kinds of poetry, free, accent, metric, rhymed or unrhymed. The use of a group of words, whether meaningless or with meaning, as a refrain or chorus, is of course familiar to all of us.

For excellent uses of such repetition, read Vachel Lindsay's *The Congo*, G. K. Chesterton's *Lepanto*, or Poe's *The Bells*.

Alliteration: Repetition of Introductory Accented Consonants

The sounds in words are of two kinds, vowels and consonants. In certain localities—collectively, in the more northerly countries—the consonants are heard more clearly, and the words tend to be full of consonants, with the vowels subordinated. These countries gave rise to *alliteration*, or the repetition of introductory accented consonants, and to similar repetitions. This was a requirement of Anglo-Saxon and Old English verse, for instance. It is no longer a requirement, but it is still a popular ornament—alike in prose and poetry.

The language is full of alliterative couplings (time and tide, tried and true, bag and baggage, etc.), as well as of familiar alliterative likenesses (busy as a bee, red as a rose, dead as a doornail, etc). There are many words utilizing alliteration, of the general type of *topsy-turvy*, *shilly-shally*, etc.

Alliteration persisted, as a frequent ornament, in the early ballads; in *Mother Goose;* and in poetry since. Swinburne's constant over-use of it warns us not to carry it to excess; the result of this being to drown the sense under a flood of repeated sounds:

> Welling water's winsome word,
> Wind in warm wan weather.

A Child's Laughter, Algernon Charles Swinburne.

Repetition of Vowel Sounds: Assonance

In certain localities—collectively, in the more equatorial or subtropical countries—the vowels are heard more clearly, and the words tend to be full of vowels, with the consonants subordinated. Some of these countries gave rise to assonance:

the repetition of the last accented vowel (sometimes with all subsequent vowel sounds) in a word, with a difference in the consonantal sounds after them.

Assonance is sometimes called *vowel rhyme*. Dominant in Provençal, early French, Spanish and Portuguese poetry, it has never made itself at home in English verse.

It is common, however, in such popular types of verse as the early ballads; in verse written today by those not schooled in versification, who mistake it for rhyme; and similarly in many popular song lyrics. This calls for such couplings as the following—all accurate assonances, but not rhymes at all:

> mate, take, shape
> sleet, deep, meek
> line, time
> fishes, ditches
> Norwich, porridge
> eagle, needle
> Tucker, supper, butter

Written Exercises

1. Write a poem, not of the song lyric type, using repetition of words and groups of words. It should not exceed 20 lines.

2. Write the same, as a song lyric.

3. Write three brief examples of verse, of not more than 12 lines each, illustrating alliteration.

4. Write not more than 12 lines of verse, utilizing 2-syllabled assonance. George Eliot's *Song of Joan* in *The Spanish Gipsy* (beginning "Maiden crowned with glossy blackness"), might be read as the type of model to follow.

LESSON VII

SAME. CONSONANCE. MISCELLANEOUS

Consonance: Repetition of Terminal Consonant Sounds

Consonance is the repetition of all consonantal and vowel sounds following an accented vowel sound in a word, with a difference in the sound of the accented vowel preceding the repeated sound elements.

Consonance, called also off-rhyme, sour rhyme, and analyzed rhyme, originated naturally in a culture which heard most clearly the consonantal sounds, and paid less attention to the vowels. It is common in the old English ballads:

> back, lake; mass, grace; stone, in, son; fast, burst;
> man, groan, begone; hair, near; queen, mine; cradle,
> saddle; middle, girdle, etc.

It was used intermittently by the masters of English poetry down to the 20th century. It was first systematically used by Emily Dickinson, who apparently preferred it to rhyme. Of course, rhyme is very limiting, due to the limited accurate rhymes in the language; while consonance multiplies the possible terminal words by approximately ten times; as well as possessing a freshness that many rhymes have long ago lost. It is now commonly used by many accepted poets.

Thus *death* has no rhyming mates, except *breath, saith* (archaic), proper names like *Macbeth*, minor accent rhymes like *twentieth, Elizabeth*, and archaic verb forms like *answereth*. Consonance adds to this limited group the following:

> faith, wraith, etc.
> bath, path, wrath, etc.
> beneath, heath, teeth, etc.
> myth, with, pith, etc.
> growth, both, oath, etc.
> broth, cloth, Goth, etc.
> booth, ruth, truth, youth, etc.

There are also sound couplings such as *lithe, blithe, wreathe*, etc., with definite sound identities.

In my *Golden Willow*, entirely in consonance, the following groups of sounds are coupled:

> willow, shallow, hollow, mellow
> airy, very, starry, glory
> unceasing, lacing, hissing, caressing
> softer, after, left her, drift her
> meadow, shadow, credo, tornado

The increased naturalness of word-usage that consonance permits, plus the novelty and freshness of the coupled sounds, is very effective. Consonance may be used exclusively; intermingled formally with rhyme; or used intermittently with rhyme.

Finding Consonance in a Rhyming Dictionary

Once you have discovered how to find and use rhymes in the *Unabridged Rhyming Dictionary*, it is no more difficult to find consonance;

although the process requires a little more time. The rhymes are grouped under 19 vowel sounds. According to this, there are as a maximum 18 possible places to look for words in consonance with the chosen word. Thus, seeking words in consonance with *mate*, you would look up the following lists—the words grouped under:

AT, ĂT, ĒT, ET, ĪT, IT, ŌT, ÔT, OT, OIT, OUT, OOT, ŪT, UT

and you would then have all the possible words in consonance with *mate*. The same process would be used with two and three-syllabled words.

Devices Similar to Alliteration

The most obvious device similar to alliteration is to repeat unaccented consonants. An example:

> *T*o *t*ake the road *t*o yes*t*erday's *t*errain.

Here four out of the five t's are unaccented; yet the effect is pleasing.

A more remote device is to use sounds related, but not identical; as, any of the sounds in the following groupings:

> Dentals: t, d, th (as in *thin*), TH (as in *THis*)
> Labials: b, p. (*M* is sometimes added.)
> Gutturals or velars: g, k, ng.
> Labiodentals: f, v.
> Sibilants: s, z, sh, zh, ch, j.
> Nasals: m, n, ng, nk.
> Liquids: l, r.

For typical couplings such as these,

> *Th*e *d*aily *t*ormen*t* of un*truth*.

> Sonnet, Daniel

> *And m*ur*m*uri*ng* of i*nn*u*m*erable bees.

> Alfred Tennyson.

Sidney Lanier uses the term *phonetic syzygy*, the latter word, from the Greek, meaning sound-coupling. The English word is simpler.

The Creative Function of Rhyme

Rhyme, first of all, definitely limits the poet's word-usage. For, once a rhyming word has been arrived at, the lines that rhyme with it, instead of ending with any of the possible words in the language (for blank verse gives this freedom), must end with one of the limited group of words that rhyme with the word first chosen.

But the function of rhyme is not wholly negative and limiting. By a sort of paradox, it becomes also positive and inspiration-awakening. It is always a fault, if a word chosen as a rhyme dictates a rhyming mate which is irrelevant, second-rate, or not at all the appropriate word for the thing in mind. But, once the rhyming word is chosen, the need for selecting from the limited group spurs the creative poetic faculty to weigh and consider all possible uses of these words; and may evoke a poetic idea not before considered. Thus in my *The Path*, accent verse quatrains rhyming 1, 2, 3, 2, with alternate feminine and masculine line-endings, once I had written:

> I guess the little folk must use it,
> Whatever there is that lives in woods,

a consideration of the limited number of rhymes to *woods*, and what could be done with each of them, finally produced,

> Bowling the crimson partridge berries,
> Playing leapfrog on toadstool hoods,

which was distinctly better than any nebulous prior idea as to how to end the quatrain. A similar process always may take place, in proportion as the poetic image is not fixed and rigid within the poet's mind, but is fluidic and developing.

Written Exercises

1. Write not more than 16 lines of verse, using consonance throughout for every line, instead of rhyme.

2. Write a poem with some formal interweaving of consonance and rhyme.

3. Write a rhymed poem, not over 20 lines, with at least 3 examples of consonance. Let it also contain examples of phonetic syzygy within at least 4 lines.

LESSON VIII

THE TYPOGRAPHY OF POETRY. POEM PATTERNS

The Typography of Poetry

If you encountered the following:

> When I was one-and-twenty, I heard a wise man say, "Give crowns and pounds and guineas, but not your heart away. Give pearls away, and rubies, but keep your fancy free." But I was one-and-twenty, no use to talk to me.

you could not fail to recognize it as verse; and might hail it as poetry, as do so many who care for it and the rest of A. E. Housman's *A Shropshire Lad*. It does not make it any the more poetry to have it set in the typography usual to poetry:

> When I was one-and-twenty,
>   I heard a wise man say,
> "Give crowns and pounds and guineas,
>   But not your heart away.
> Give pearls away, and rubies,
>   But keep your fancy free."
> But I was one-and-twenty,
>   No use to talk to me.

This second form of typography, so common today, is no older than the beginning of the Christian era, or almost 1,950 years. Up to that time, all poetry, and this includes Sappho, Homer, the great Greek dramatists, and many of the Latin poets, had been written in the same typography as prose—that first given; with the same logical division into paragraphs, etc.

The second form, which developed out of the poet's work-sheets, on which he tested his individual lines for scansion, etc., has done much damage to poetry, coupled with the unnatural word choice and usage, whose origin we have already traced. The poet is at liberty to use either form, or any other form which best brings out the results he aims at. Today, this includes also minor variations, such as the omission of capital letters at the beginning of each line, while still using the second form; the omission of punctuation; excessively short lines (as A. A. Milne did in his volumes of light verse), excessively long lines, and so on.

The Poem Pattern as a Whole: Self-Criticism

Certain poems, that we will take up next, have their pattern rigidly or largely fixed in advance. These include the sonnet, the French forms, etc. In most poems, the individual poet determines his pattern, the number of stanzas, their construction, and the like.

There are two general types: those with a rigid formal pattern, or several of these, for the various stanzas; and those with no formal pattern, with stanzas of different lengths, etc. Many poems, having started with a certain stanza, use this undeviatingly throughout. Such are Poe's *The Raven, The Rubáiyát of Omar Khayyám, In Memoriam*, and thousands more.

Other poems take a chosen norm, and deviate from it slightly when need arises. Coleridge's *The Rime of the Ancient Mariner* and G. K. Chesterton's *The Ballad of the White Horse* are of this type. From these, the pattern veers toward increasing freedom through such poems as Wordsworth's most famous ode and Chesterton's *Lepanto*, to most of the poetry of Whitman, where there is no pattern except the poet's own changing pattern from stanza to stanza.

Once the poem has been written, the second vital function of the poet comes into play: self-criticism. Now for the first time it is time to call the critical brain into play, to answer questions of this type: Does the poem express what the poet desires to say? What is this word or message, and does it progress uniformly and with mounting climactic effect from start to finish? Has it the quality of growth, climax, the typical quality of a great sonata or symphony? Is it free from irrelevancies, detours, and distracting beauties, out of harmony with the whole?

This is the time when all faults should be rigorously eliminated, even if this requires the reslanting and rewriting of a part or even of the whole poem. This is the time when all weak passages, all tepid phrases, lines, or stanzas, should be stepped up to fit the mood of the whole. This is the time when all redundant and superfluous beauties, no matter how effective when considered alone, should be eliminated, if they fail to conduce to the effect desired of the poem as a whole.

The poet who lacks the power of self-criticism peters out fast. By wide reading and deep thinking as to the function of poetry, and of your poem, its intended effect, and whether or not it achieves this, equip yourself to be your most valuable critic.

Written Exercises

1. Write a poem of not more than 12 lines, and write it out in both the typography commonly used for poetry, and the typography more common to prose. Which do you like the better?

2. If you have one in your files, or can write one, add here a poem with an unnecessary section, which you mark in the margin "Out," to indicate it is to be removed from the poem.

3. Give a first draft of a poem which did not come perfectly; and indicate the needed rewriting, with such explanations in the margin as will aid in explaining your revisions.

LESSON IX

POEM PATTERNS AS A WHOLE: THE SHAKESPEAREAN SONNET

The Shakespearean Sonnet

A sonnet is a poem or stanza of fourteen iambic pentameter lines, with a rigidly prescribed rhyme-scheme. The two main varieties are the Shakespearean (or Elizabethan) and the Italian (or Petrarchan).

Recalling the two most popular units of stanzaic rhyme-scheme in English, the alternately rhymed quatrain, and the rhymed couplet, the structure of the Shakespearean sonnet is the essence of simplicity. It consists of three alternately rhymed quatrains, followed by a terminal rhyming couplet. Its pattern then is: 1, 2, 1, 2; 3, 4, 3, 4; 5, 6, 5, 6; 7, 7. The example given in the fore part of this volume indicates the structure.

For all that the sonnet is named after Shakespeare, the first Shakespearean sonnet appeared in England seven years before Shakespeare was born. In *Tottel's Miscellany* (1557), Surrey, who imported the sonnet from Italy with Wyatt, published the first sonnet following the pattern now called Shakespearean. In the same collection, Surrey had a sonnet rhymed 1, 2, 1, 2; 1, 2, 1, 2; 1, 2, 1, 2; 1, 1, which hews to the same pattern more strictly, since it is built entirely upon only two rhyme sounds. Edmund Spenser then began to write sonnets, with the same interweaving of rhyme from quatrain to quatrain that is seen in the Spenserian stanza named after him: 1, 2, 1, 2; 2, 3, 2, 3; 3, 4, 3, 4; 5, 5. This is the so-called *Spenserian sonnet*.

Neither the limitation that the poem must be restricted to only two rhymes, nor the compulsory interweaving of rhyme from quatrain to quatrain, is rooted in English customs of versification. Neither form achieved any of the popularity of the Shakespearean sonnet.

Writing the Shakespearean Sonnet

In writing the Shakespearean sonnet, and indeed any poem or example of light verse beyond brief length, all the principles of good writing, as true of prose as of verse, must come into play. There must be three definite parts, the opening; the main part of the poem; and the conclusion. The opening should possess two characteristics: some point of contact with the listener or reader, which will attract his attention at once; and enough strength to make it worth his while to listen or read further. The main part of the poem should embrace the points to be made, or the story to be told, building up always in an order of climax. The conclusion should be the climax or resolution, and should be stronger in dignity than any of the rest of the poem.

To put it another way, the two most memorable lines are usually the first line and the last line of a sonnet; and these cannot possess mediocrity or tepidity. They must be both memorable and worth remembering. In the actual creation of a sonnet, it is frequent that one of these lines comes first; and thereafter, of course, it dictates the development of the rhyming pattern. Unless at least one of these two lines is good enough to be retained in man's memory, for its essential truth or beauty, the sonnet will never be ranked among man's best.

The Shakespearean sonnet pattern, with its liberal natural rhyme-scheme and its absence of artificial stipulations as to development of the theme idea, above all must be written in the same easy natural flow of words that good prose has. A sonnet that has inversions, archaisms, stilted and warped word order, poeticized ellipses, and so on is foredoomed to extinction.

Consonance may, of course, be used instead of rhyme. Instead of the regular corseted beat of strict iambic verse, the poet is wise if he introduces at least as many metric variations as Shakespeare did: and these include trochees, spondees, pyrrhics, anapests, and other feet, instead of iambs, and even a succession of such feet. A graceful use of double rhyme instead of single is also found in his sonnets, and often is of great assistance.

For study, I recommend many of the outstanding sonnets by John Masefield, Arthur Davison Ficke, G. K. Chesterton, Edwin Arlington Robinson, Edna St. Vincent Millay, and my own *The Eagle Sonnets*. The sonnets in slang or in the colloquial vernacular by John V. A. Weaver also indicate a direction in which the form flows effectively.

Written Exercises

1. Choose your favorite sonnet by Shakespeare, or by any of the above, and scan it carefully. Copy it out, enclosing within bars all lines that show metric variation. Name these in the margin.

2. Write one or more Shakespearean sonnets, making your first and last lines as effective as possible.

3. Commence a sonnet sequence of at least three Shakespearean sonnets. Complete it before Lesson XII is reached.

LESSON X

SAME. THE SONNET, CONCLUDED

The Italian or Petrarchan Sonnet

Absorb carefully what has been written of the Italian sonnet, in the fore part of this volume. Especially master the fourfold division of the sonnet into two end-stopped quatrains, followed by two end-stopped tercets. The pattern then becomes:

1, 2, 2, 1; 1, 2, 2, 1; 3, 4, 5; 3, 4, 5; or, 3, 4, 3; 4, 3, 4.

It is always a violation of the strict Italian sonnet form to divide the ending, as to meaning, into three couplets—3, 4; 3, 4; 3, 4.

We have encountered the details of this rhyme-scheme before. 1, 2, 2, 1 is the In Memoriam stanza, as far as rhyming goes; 3, 4, 5, 3, 4, 5 is the pattern used to end the Keats odes; while 3, 4, 3, 4, 3, 4 appeared in ottava rima, and is in reality the alternately rhymed quatrain, tailed by two more lines on the same rhyme-scheme. But no unit of this rhyme-scheme has ever achieved the popularity of the units in the Shakespearean sonnet; and the strict stipulations as to four rhymes each on the first two rhyme-sounds, and the development of the idea in its fourfold division, are not native to English verse at all. There is great danger that the Italian sonnet may become too formalized to be natural, in English versification. The poet should always strive to make his product as natural as possible.

Writing the Italian Sonnet

When writing the Italian, Miltonic, or Wordsworthian sonnet, and even more emphatically when writing ballades, villanelles, rondeaux redoublé, chants royal, and other long fixed forms, you will do well to make use of a device I invented many years ago, which furnishes, even during the writing of the verse, an easy check on whether or not the strict rule against identities in rhyming is being followed. Before the actual writing begins, the pattern to be followed is indicated thus:

Rhyme Scheme	(1)	(2)	(3)	(4)
1				
2				
2				
1				
1				
2				
2				
1				
3				
4				
3				
4				
3				
4				

Obviously, the numbers in parenthesis refer to the sounds to be used in the rhyme-scheme, as applied. As each line is written, write down, in its appropriate column, the opening consonantal sound actually used. This will at any moment let you check, to make sure that no identity has crept in. Here is one of the deftest light verse Italian sonnets I have encountered, *Assignment*, by Stephen Schlitzer, illustrating how this method should be used, during the writing:

	Rhyme Scheme	(1)	(2)	(3)	(4)
The best authorities on verse agree	1	GR			
We must submerge our souls before we rise.	2		R		
Burn with emotion! Suffer! Sympathize!	2		th		
Become the comrades of mortality;	1	T			
Be one with robber, banker, refugee;	1	J			
Live! Live! Though life be but a pack of lies;	2		L		
Go down to hell, and up to Paradise	2		D		
In order to excel in poetry.	1	TR			
But I'll be damned before I go to pieces	3			P	
Merely to make a sonnet more complete,—	4				PL
Assault my neighbor's wife; destroy my nieces,	3			N	
Or starve myself in some forlorn retreat;	4				TR
Or let you break my heart with your caprices,	3			PR	
To give the world five more iambic feet!	4				F

Studying our rhyme-check system, we see that the rhyme-sounds on (1) are GR, T, J, and TR; on (2) R, th, L, and D; on (3), P, N, and PR; on (4) PL, TR, and F. No identities; rhyming perfect. The natural flow of every line demands the highest praise. I am very proud that this *Assignment* was written as an exercise in one of my poetry classes. It will end up in the best anthologies in the language.

If this rhyme-check system is valuable in all sonnet forms except the Shakespearean, it is indispensable in the ballade, the chant royal, and many other French forms.

Miltonic, Wordsworthian and Other Sonnets

The treatment of the Miltonic, Wordsworthian and other sonnets in the fore part of this volume is sufficient, and should be absorbed thoroughly.

Written Exercises

1. Write one strict Italian sonnet, on a serious or frivolous theme. Be sure to use the division into two end-stopped quatrains and two end-stopped tercets (even though sonnets in English do not always demand this strictness. Incidentally, end-stopped means that the meaning and the punctuation stop with the end of the quatrain or tercet, and are not carried over. This requires, for punctuation, a period, dash indicating complete break, colon, or at least a semi-colon; or, of course, an interrogation or exclamation point).

2. Write at least one Italian sonnet more loosely.

3. Write a Miltonic or Wordsworthian sonnet, stating which. On one of the three sonnets, add the rhyme-check scheme, showing the rhyme-scheme, and the application of it, as in the example given.

LESSON XI

THE LIMERICK. THE LITTLE WILLIE

The Limerick

The limerick, as Brander Matthews points out, is the only fixed form indigenous to the English language. *Mother Goose's Melodies*, first published in Boston in 1719, contained the three stages in its development:

1. With a nonsense line used as lines 1 and 5, such as "Hickory, dickory, dock," and so on.

2. With the rhyming sound in, and often the whole line 1, repeated in line 5:

> As I was going to Bonner,
> Upon my word of honor,
>   I met a pig
>   Without a wig,
> As I was going to Bonner.

This was the form chosen by Edward Lear, great reviver of the limerick, for his. Incidentally, he set his limericks up as quatrains, 3, 3, 4, 3 feet (predominantly anapestic), with internal rhyme in the third line:

> There was an Old Man of Cape Horn,
> Who wished he had never been born;
> So he sat on a Chair till he died of despair,
> That dolorous man of Cape Horn.

3. A new rhyming word used in the fifth line, as in this example from *Mother Goose:*

> There was an old soldier of Bister
> Went walking one day with his sister,
>   When a cow at one poke
>   Tossed her into an oak
> Before the old gentleman missed her.

This is the developed form regularly used today. The limerick writer who cannot discover a third rhyme on his (1) sound for the fifth line is properly regarded as a slacker.

By far the largest number of limericks is written with a geographical name terminating line 1: Nome, Alaska, Greenwich, Tring, Twickenham, Birmingham, and so on. The next largest group have a proper name used here: "a sculptor named Phidias," "a young lady named Bright," "a maiden named Maud," and so on. A third group has some phrase descriptive of a person: "A young man very fond of pajamas." The fourth and trickiest group have any sort of line that introduces the trick rhyming: "I'd rather have Fingers than Toes," " 'There's a train at 4:04,' said Miss Jenny"; and so on.

The fifth line, of course, is supposed to have some sort of trick ending, as a rule. It calls for real ingenuity to discover words that can make perfect rhymes out of such terminals as Calcutta, Australia, Vladivostock, Popocatapetl, and so on. Born limerick-writers possess this ingenuity. It can be coined into pieces of eight, when Limerick Last Line Contests, with large prizes, are the moment's rage.

Little Willies

Spontaneous stanzaic forms spring up into popularity overnight, and at times the boom dies as quickly. Such a form was this anonymous masterpiece, from a college magazine:

> Tobacco is a filthy weed—
> I like it.
> It satisfies no normal need—
> I like it.
> It makes you thin, it makes you lean,
> It takes the hair right off your bean,
> It's the worst darned stuff I've ever seen.
> I like it.

The contrast between the brief tail-rhyme refrain and the strong attack on Lady Nicotine adds greatly to the effectiveness. While this form died out after its sudden flare of popularity, the fame of the similarly engendered Little Willies increases and spreads.

Frances Palm has produced one of the most effective of the recent ones:

> Baby fell into a boiling pot.
> Mama ran crying from the spot.
> Papa said, "Now don't you cry,
> He'll make soft soap, if he's mixed with lye."

A true Little Willie is in quatrain form; with a tricky effective surprise last line; and is imbued with definite sadism, preferably toward some member of one's immediate family. It is an ideal way to work off conflicts harmlessly.

Written Exercises

1. For this, the least onerous of the lessons, write at least two good limericks. Since the limerick was early used as a religious and didactic verse form, even those who are not attuned to light verse can use the form to express their sentiments or emotions.

2. Write at least 3 Little Willies. If one of the three is excellent, you can congratulate yourself. Remember, a verse form is difficult in proportion as it is short.

LESSON XII

THE FRENCH AND OTHER FIXED FORMS

The Fixed Forms

The importance of spontaneous creation of poetic patterns, where the thing to be said dictates its own pattern, is made emphatic by the fact that, in general, in English, only successful light verse has been written in the fixed forms; never serious poetry. The poems that the race has taken to its heart, whether the populace as a whole or the limited group of poetry-worshippers, have not followed the multifarious fixed forms. The Shakespearean sonnet is perhaps the only emphatic exception, and it consists of three alternately rhymed quatrains, followed by a rhymed couplet. But there is an enduring popularity to many of the fixed forms, including the limerick, the Little Willie, and many others, in light verse.

The overall rules for the fixed forms are only two:

1. No identities, in place of rhyme. *The Unabridged Rhyming Dictionary* makes identity almost impossible.

2. The refrain must have meaning, and be an integral and natural part of the poem's progression.

Absorb the treatment of the forms, through the triolet-rondeau family, in the fore part of this volume.

Syllable-Count Verse

The tanka, the hokku, and all the forms that have sprung out of this and a syllable-count interpretation of Adelaide Crapsey's cinquain, eliminate the existing requirement for verse in our culture: the tendency toward repetition in rhythm. The result, based upon syllable count, is none of the varieties of verse we are familiar with: not free verse, accent verse nor metric verse. Its construction is so simple, that hundreds of variations have been built upon the idea, especially in the United States.

Miscellaneous Fixed Forms

The arrangement of the poems with fixed patterns starts with the simplest, and progresses to the more complex. Thus a kyrielle is an inevitable pattern in the verse of any language; it is merely a certain type of quatrain verse with an identical refrain line ending each stanza. With a pattern so simple, it is possible that real poetry could be poured into the mold. It lends itself also to effective light verse.

The pantoum, of Malayan origin, is intermittently popular in light verse. The one danger is that it be carried out to too great length.

The shaped whimsey, with an appeal transcending the rhythm, sound and meaning of words, since it uses them to sketch out a picture, has possibilities of wide popularity.

The Triolet-Rondeau Family

When we arrive at this group of poems, the value of the rhyme-check method, described under The Italian Sonnet, becomes increasingly evident. When you are writing formal verse, the first thing to do is to mark down the pattern, line by line; as, for a triolet:

```
1R
        2R
1
1R
1
            2
1R
        2R
```

On studying this pattern, it is clear that the two-line refrain (1R and 2R) must be arrived at first. Once we have this, fill it in, in the appropriate places (lines 1, 2, 4, 7, and 8). That leaves only three additional lines to be written, two on the *1* sound, one on the *2* sound. By listing the consonantal sounds already used, as they are used, a constant-check can be kept on the rhyming, to make sure that no identities are used.

Excellent light and occasional verse can be written in these forms. They are not so suitable to serious poetry, although there is an occasional exception to this.

Written Exercises

1. Write a tanka; a hokku.
2. Write a kyrielle, of not more than 20 lines.
3. Write one of the following: a quatern; a retourné; a pantoum; or any example of chain verse.
4. Write a shaped whimsey, or one of the themes-with-variation group.
5. Write either a villanelle, or one or more of the triolet-rondeau group.

Barring the tanka and hokku, this whole exercise is optional. If you are not interested in learning the fixed forms, substitute for these assignments a corresponding assignment in serious poetry or verse, in which you design your own patterns.

LESSON XIII

THE FIXED FORMS, CONCLUDED. THE BALLADE FAMILY

Writing the Ballade

After absorbing the treatment of the ballade family in the fore part of this volume, the following aspects should be considered.

1. The refrain is so important, that it should be decided upon first. Since this line appears four times in the poem, it must have power, dignity, a musical quality, and in addition should evoke strong emotional overtones. Consider the refrain of the most famous of all ballades, Villon's to the "ladies of old time,"

Mais où sont les neiges d'antan?

I know no translation that has caught anything resembling the rhythm of this, chiefly due to the difference in languages. The best known translation is:

Where are the snows of yesteryear?

This should be rejected at once, because of the artificial last word. Yet it is effective, especially when it is remembered that the refrain is to be repeated again and again. One of the extremely effective refrains is W. E. Henley's, from his *Ballade of Dead Actors:*

Into the night go one and all.

This has a melancholy finality that makes it one of the finest ballade refrains in English. In an utterly differing mood is this refrain from Austin Dobson:

This was the Pompadour's fan.

There is the sardonic chuckle in Chesterton's refrain,

I think I shall not hang myself today.

It is by the refrain most of all that a ballade is remembered. Be sure, then, that your refrain is worthy of the extended treatment.

2. The 8-line ballade requires 5 rhymes on the *3* sound (including the refrain); 6 on the *1* sound; and 14 on the *2* sound. Identities are wholly unacceptable. When we have a rhyme-scheme this complicated, the rhyme-check method described under the discussion of the Italian sonnet becomes essential, during the course of writing the

ballade. Moreover, you should make sure that there are at least 14 acceptable rhyming words on the sound you have tentatively chosen for this *2* sound. If there are not, you must of course change this sound, before you have gone too far.

3. No *sound* in the refrain may be changed in any way. It is therefore forbidden to alter "Where are the snows of yesteryear" to "Here are the snows of yesteryear," for your last refrain, for instance. But this prohibition applies to sounds only. The words, the spelling, the meaning may be altered, provided the sounds are unaltered. This permits puns and all sorts of plays on words. These are the essence of a good light verse rondeau refrain, for instance; and they have their place in the more extended ballade.

4. It is one of the astonishing things in the history of English versification that, when the great revival of the French forms took place in the 1890's, accent verse was chosen, instead of metric verse. For this revival took place among precise versifiers, experts in the use of meter; and their choice of the more natural medium is surprising. But this accent verse, as used, was not used with too great freedom. It is well, if you wish to write ballades, to saturate yourself with the best of those already written, in order to catch the mood.

All that has been said about the ballade applies to all of its forms, and multipliedly to the immense chant royal and the tricky sestina.

Written Exercises

1. After becoming familiar with good typical ballades (such as those in the collection of Gleeson White, or of Helen Louise Cohen), write from 5 to 10 lines which would make good refrains for ballades.

2. Write a ballade, using one of these. Use the rhyme-check system in the margin, indicating each consonantal sound used.

3. Write a ballade with double refrain; a chant royal; or a sestina, unrhymed or rhymed.

LESSON XIV

MISCELLANEOUS: TRANSLATION, PARODY, ETC.

Dialect Verse

In writing any dialect verse, Negro, Irish, Scotch, French-Canadian, or any other, there are several important considerations to remember. First of all, do not overuse the dialect. If you apply it to every word, the result will be unreadable and ununderstandable to the average

reader. Use only enough dialect to give the effect of the speech you wish to depict, letting the reader's imagination or voice add the rest. Second, never think that mere misspelling makes dialect. Thus, *cum* is not a dialect version of *come;* it is merely a phonetic spelling of it. Third, be sure that the words chosen, and especially the idioms, are suitable to the dialect chosen.

Parody

Parody, in verse, is an imitation of another example of verse, usually with intent to burlesque it. Parodies are of three types:

1. Word-rendering, the substitution of such words in the original pattern as will turn the original meaning into a trivial or frivolous one.

> EXAMPLE: rewriting the famous "To be or not to be" soliloquy from *Hamlet* as "To sneeze or not to sneeze."

2. Form-rendering, imitating the entire style of the author. This is most effective when you have chosen an author with marked mannerisms.

> EXAMPLE: Alvin Winston's parody of Kipling's *Recessional*, which appeared during the financial "recession" of 1936–37:

> God of our Incomes, known of old
>   As something, before '29,
> Beneath whose nodding we behold
>   Dividends fail and bonds decline,
>   Lord God of Costs, please let us get
>   Some income yet, some income yet!

In this type, as in all forms of parody, the effectiveness of course depends upon the closeness with which your parody follows the pattern, and indeed the very rhyming sounds and the important words of the original. Here "Lord God of Costs," as a substitute for "Lord God of Hosts," is excellent. It is almost comparable to the immortal Gellett Burgess—Burgess Johnson parody of Gray's "The short and simple annals of the poor," which they rendered as "The short and simple flannels of the poor."

3. Sense-rendering, utilizing both the author's style and his typical themes, carried out as he would have used them, but subtly exaggerated as to both style and theme.

> EXAMPLE: the selections from *The Jack-and-Jiliad* in my *The Complete Handbook for Poets*, especially the Edna St. Vincent Millay parody:

Up through the bushes, upon a foggy day,
Jack and Jill went climbing up the steepest way;
And Jack had a bucket, and Jill a spray of brier,
And the sun rose dripping, a bucketful of fire.

Up to the spring-edge—when Jack had a stumble,
And Jill, a-clutching wildly on his arm, began to tumble;
And Jack broke his cranium, and worse luck was Jill's,
And they gave all their money for the doctor bills.

On Translating Poetry

Poetry cannot be translated effectively; it must be recreated in the second language, to regain the emotional appeal it had in the first language. In making translations, it is well to consider the material Edward Fitzgerald had to work with, when he translated the *Rubáiyát* or quatrains of Omar Khayyám. These two lines, for instance,

> Hell is a spark from my useless worries,
> Paradise is a moment of time when I am tranquil,

reappear in his translation, which is really a recreation, as:

> Heav'n but the Vision of fulfilled Desire,
> And Hell the Shadow from a Soul on fire,
> Cast on the Darkness into which Ourselves,
> So late emerged from, shall so soon expire.

It is of course obvious that a translation must, on the negative side, possess no more faults than any other verse or poetry. It must hence be in every way as natural as prose. Moreover, the translator should weigh carefully the emotional overtones of each word used in the original poem, and seek to carry over that appeal into the second language, a process often requiring a shrewd use of the trial and error method. If the translation is to be faithful, the translator should seek to awaken in its readers the equivalent of the emotions that the original awoke in its readers. Any devices of poetry (rhyme, alliteration, etc.) that are as much at home in English as in the first language should be retained, if possible; any devices that jar the English ear, such as quantity meter and assonance, should not be used.

Arranging a Volume

Before arranging your volume of poetry, it is wise to examine half a dozen volumes by leading contemporary poets, perhaps those most similar to your own collection, to study their method of arrangement. Thereafter, present the material the way all writing should be pre-

sented: roughly, opening with a section which establishes contact with your readers, and at the same time possesses power and a fairly wide appeal; following this with the other sections, in mounting power and climactic order, until you close with the strongest section of all. Treat the whole volume as one long poem or message from yourself to your reader, and so arrange it that it has the maximum emotional appeal, from start to finish.

Typographically, prepare it precisely as a printed volume appears, omitting only the publisher's name. That is, include proper title page, dedication page, page of acknowledgments, table of contents, section heads, and index if needed. It is well to pattern yourself on the best contemporary models.

Written Exercises

1. Write a parody of some familiar poem, not over 30 lines long. Be sure to utilize the rhythm and rhyme patterns of the original.

2. (Optional) Parody some brief *Mother Goose* rhyme in the manner of half a dozen different poets, with whom you are familiar.

3. Translate a poem, not over 20 lines, from some foreign language into English. This may be a song lyric, if desired. Copy out, to accompany it, the original, in the foreign language; next give a literal prose translation of it, word for word; and, finally, your finished translation or recreation or:

4. If unable to translate from a foreign language, do the same thing with some English poem, not over 16 lines long. Give the poem first; then a restatement of it in prose; then your translation or recreation.

LESSON XV
MARKETING

Directly, or Through an Agent?

Not one poet in a thousand can successfully market through an agent. Reputable agents, as a rule, take only poets with a market waiting for them. Even at that, the returns for the agent are small. Moreover, marketing is extremely educational. If for any reason the poet is entirely unable to market his own verse, it may be necessary to pay an agent to do the marketing.

Make Your Whole Life a Sales Campaign for Your Poems

The position in society granted to an accepted poet or light verse writer is not a low one. To qualify for it, your poems must receive

publication, and become known. Magazine publication is excellent; book publication more enduring. If you can make your poems sell enough to support you, you are fortunate; it is far more probable that they will merely contribute to your income.

Regard it this way: writing your poems is half your job; marketing, the other half. Inscribe on the walls of your soul Robert Frost's great line,

> The trial by market everything must come to;

and make it your business to see that your poetry receives proper presentation and publication. It may well be that the fault is in the poetry; if that is so, improve it, until the faults are eliminated. If there are faults in your method of marketing, struggle constantly to rectify them.

All the principles of salesmanship, as applied to any other product, apply to your poetry. Earn the right to be called "the poet," by living up to the best in your poetry. This means that everything connected with you is a part of your lifelong sales campaign: your personality, your manners, your dress. Eccentricities are permitted; but make them aid in building up the picture of yourself that you want others to have. Of course, your home is important in your sales campaign too: here you may entertain editors, publishers, critics, other poets, possible patrons and rooters for your poetry; and they will insensibly judge your product in part by the factory from which it emanates. If you live in a garret, make it a memorable garret; if in a penthouse, let it bear the stamp of your poet's role, as well. Your husband or wife, your parents, children, friends and acquaintances, are all part of the picture too, and should click into place in your sales campaign.

Your speech, especially your skill in reading your poems aloud, can be made one of your best assets. Many poets receive more for reading their poems aloud, and talking on poetry, than from the mere sale of individual poems, or the royalties on volumes. There are also, of course, such mechanical rights as royalties from musical settings of your poems, and from their use on phonographs, radio, moving pictures and television. Perhaps, from mention of some of these aspects, the impossibility of doing the whole job of marketing through an agent becomes clearer.

How to Submit Poems

Become acquainted with your market, whether magazine or book, before offering your product to it. You would not try to sell potatoes to a potato grower; be as wise in submitting your poetry. Personal submission is always better than submission by mail, for it permits you to earn the editor's good will, and learn his especial needs, which

some other poem of yours may meet. There is no editorial office in the world that is locked against the right approach.

Next to personal submission, the right sort of letter always adds to your chances of sale or acceptance. The letter should be adapted to the poem, and most of all to the editor. It should never be too long. It should open with some point of contact; should say the thing that is the proper sales talk for the particular situation; and should end when you are through. Sometimes a mere—

> I trust that this poem is up your alley,

is enough. But the brief personal note is always better than the mere impersonal sending of a poem.

A stamped and addressed return envelope accompanying the manuscript is always an appreciated courtesy.

Create Your Own Markets

In discussion with the editor, or by correspondence, it is possible to suggest all sorts of poems or verse that he will buy. There is no magazine absolutely locked against poetry, if the proper approach is made, and the editor can be made to see that the poetry is appropriate. This applies to the *National Hog Cultivators' Monthly* no less than to *Poetry*. Build up your own list of poetry markets, those that pay and those that don't, and add to it constantly. It is wise to offer your poem first to the paying markets. It is often wise, if they all reject it, to give it publication in some non-paying magazine; for all this is part of your publicity campaign for future poems.

Especially consider planning and securing the acceptance of groups of poems, such as Love Through the Year (month by month); Great Statesmen (in verse); Famous Movie Stars (in verse), and so on and on.

Rejections

Rejections will far outnumber the acceptances. This, at least, is my experience. Try to learn from each one. Count yourself lucky when your rejection is more than a mere printed slip.

Acceptances

Each printed poem becomes in turn a salesman for you, good or bad. Learn from each acceptance; it indicates the editor's attitude toward you and your work, and the particular selection may be significant. It is wise usually to send along two or three poems, rather than one; so that the editorial teeth may gnash at one or more in rejection, while accepting at least one.

Know the whole magazine market for poetry; and create new markets for yourself in unexpected magazines. As to anthologies, those

that pay you for reprint rights are to be treasured first. Second, those where inclusion is a mark of honor, as any group of The Best Poems of the Year. Pay-as-You-Enter anthologies, especially when the payment is subtly disguised, are sucker traps.

Finally, try to secure publication of at least one worth-while volume of poetry or verse. First try the publishers who publish on their own financial responsibility. If this fails, never be too proud to pay for your own. Most poets have started so. But be sure that you are not being overcharged.

In Conclusion

Thirty years ago, I would have scoffed at all of this advice. Was I not one of the elect, a poet, who was sure to astound the world? I do not scoff at any of it today.

If you have absorbed the fifteen lessons of the Foundations of Versification Course, and these fifteen lessons in Advanced Versification, and have faithfully written the exercises, you may properly regard yourself as a graduate in each. May all the best luck in the world go with you. You'll need it. Let this autobiographical note go with your godspeed.